Handbook of Research on Swarm Intelligence in Engineering

Siddhartha Bhattacharyya
RCC Institute of Information Technology, India

Paramartha Dutta
Visva–Bharati University, India

A volume in the Advances in Computational
Intelligence and Robotics (ACIR) Book Series

ENGINEERING
SCIENCE REFERENCE

An Imprint of IGI Global

Managing Director:	Lindsay Johnston
Managing Editor:	Austin DeMarco
Director of Intellectual Property & Contracts:	Jan Travers
Acquisitions Editor:	Kayla Wolfe
Production Editor:	Christina Henning
Development Editor:	Caitlyn Martin
Typesetter:	Kaitlyn Kulp
Cover Design:	Jason Mull

Published in the United States of America by
Engineering Science Reference (an imprint of IGI Global)
701 E. Chocolate Avenue
Hershey PA, USA 17033
Tel: 717-533-8845
Fax: 717-533-8661
E-mail: cust@igi-global.com
Web site: http://www.igi-global.com

Library of Congress Cataloging-in-Publication Data

Handbook of research on swarm intelligence in engineering / Siddhartha Bhattacharyya and Paramartha Dutta, editors.
  pages cm
 Includes bibliographical references and index.
  ISBN 978-1-4666-8291-7 (hardcover) -- ISBN 978-1-4666-8292-4 (ebook) 1. Swarm intelligence. I. Bhattacharyya, Siddhartha, 1975- editor. II. Dutta, Paramartha, editor.
  Q337.3.H36 2015
  620.00285'63824--dc23
                          2015003786

This book is published in the IGI Global book series Advances in Computational Intelligence and Robotics (ACIR) (ISSN: 2327-0411; eISSN: 2327-042X)

British Cataloguing in Publication Data
A Cataloguing in Publication record for this book is available from the British Library.

For electronic access to this publication, please contact: eresources@igi-global.com.

Advances in Computational Intelligence and Robotics (ACIR) Book Series

ISSN: 2327-0411
EISSN: 2327-042X

MISSION

While intelligence is traditionally a term applied to humans and human cognition, technology has progressed in such a way to allow for the development of intelligent systems able to simulate many human traits. With this new era of simulated and artificial intelligence, much research is needed in order to continue to advance the field and also to evaluate the ethical and societal concerns of the existence of artificial life and machine learning.

The **Advances in Computational Intelligence and Robotics (ACIR) Book Series** encourages scholarly discourse on all topics pertaining to evolutionary computing, artificial life, computational intelligence, machine learning, and robotics. ACIR presents the latest research being conducted on diverse topics in intelligence technologies with the goal of advancing knowledge and applications in this rapidly evolving field.

COVERAGE

- Natural Language Processing
- Agent technologies
- Neural Networks
- Computer Vision
- Pattern recognition
- Brain Simulation
- Synthetic Emotions
- Cognitive Informatics
- Algorithmic Learning
- Computational intelligence

IGI Global is currently accepting manuscripts for publication within this series. To submit a proposal for a volume in this series, please contact our Acquisition Editors at Acquisitions@igi-global.com or visit: http://www.igi-global.com/publish/.

Titles in this Series

For a list of additional titles in this series, please visit: www.igi-global.com

Handbook of Research on Swarm Intelligence in Engineering
Siddhartha Bhattacharyya (RCC Institute of Information Technology, India) and Paramartha Dutta (Visva-Bharati University, India)
Engineering Science Reference • copyright 2015 • 568pp • H/C (ISBN: 9781466682917) • US $335.00 (our price)

Handbook of Research on Advancements in Robotics and Mechatronics
Maki K. Habib (The American University in Cairo, Egypt)
Engineering Science Reference • copyright 2015 • 993pp • H/C (ISBN: 9781466673878) • US $515.00 (our price)

Handbook of Research on Advanced Intelligent Control Engineering and Automation
Ahmad Taher Azar (Benha University, Egypt) and Sundarapandian Vaidyanathan (Vel Tech University, India)
Engineering Science Reference • copyright 2015 • 795pp • H/C (ISBN: 9781466672482) • US $335.00 (our price)

Handbook of Research on Artificial Intelligence Techniques and Algorithms
Pandian Vasant (Universiti Teknologi Petronas, Malaysia)
Information Science Reference • copyright 2015 • 873pp • H/C (ISBN: 9781466672581) • US $495.00 (our price)

Handbook of Research on Synthesizing Human Emotion in Intelligent Systems and Robotics
Jordi Vallverdú (Universitat Autònoma de Barcelona, Spain)
Information Science Reference • copyright 2015 • 469pp • H/C (ISBN: 9781466672789) • US $245.00 (our price)

Recent Advances in Ambient Intelligence and Context-Aware Computing
Kevin Curran (University of Ulster, UK)
Information Science Reference • copyright 2015 • 376pp • H/C (ISBN: 9781466672840) • US $225.00 (our price)

Recent Advances in Intelligent Technologies and Information Systems
Vijayan Sugumaran (Oakland University, USA & Sogang University, Seoul, Korea)
Information Science Reference • copyright 2015 • 309pp • H/C (ISBN: 9781466666399) • US $200.00 (our price)

Emerging Research on Swarm Intelligence and Algorithm Optimization
Yuhui Shi (Xi'an Jiaotong-Liverpool University, China)
Information Science Reference • copyright 2015 • 341pp • H/C (ISBN: 9781466663282) • US $225.00 (our price)

Face Recognition in Adverse Conditions
Maria De Marsico (Sapienza University of Rome, Italy) Michele Nappi (University of Salerno, Italy) and Massimo Tistarelli (University of Sassari, Italy)

www.igi-global.com

701 E. Chocolate Ave., Hershey, PA 17033
Order online at www.igi-global.com or call 717-533-8845 x100
To place a standing order for titles released in this series, contact: cust@igi-global.com
Mon-Fri 8:00 am - 5:00 pm (est) or fax 24 hours a day 717-533-8661

Dr. Siddhartha Bhattacharyya would like to dedicate this book to:
"My respected father Late Ajit Kumar Bhattacharyya, my respected mother Late Hashi Bhattacharyya, my brothers-in-law Tapan, Abani and Pinaki and all my students."

Dr. Paramartha Dutta would like to dedicate this book to:
"My respected father Late Arun Kanti Dutta and my respected mother Mrs. Bandana Dutta"

List of Contributors

Table of Contents

Section 2
Applications

Detailed Table of Contents

Section 1
Theoretical Foundations

Chapter 1
Sandip Dey, Camellia Institute of Technology, India
Siddhartha Bhattacharyya, RCC Institute of Information Technology, India
Ujjwal Maulik, Jadavpur University, India

In this chapter, an exhaustive survey of quantum behaved techniques on swarm intelligent is presented. The techniques have been categorized into different classes, and in conclusion, a comparison is made according to the benefits of the approaches taken for review. The above-mentioned techniques are classified based on the information they exploit, for instance, neural network related, meta-heuristic and evolutionary algorithm related, and other distinguished approaches are considered. Neural Network-Based Approaches exhibit a few brain-like activities, which are programmatically complicated, for instance, learning, optimization, etc. Meta-Heuristic Approaches update solution generation-wise for optimization, and the approaches differ based on the problem definition.

Chapter 2
J. Anuradha, VIT University, India
B. K. Tripathy, VIT University, India

The data used in the real world applications are uncertain and vague. Several models to handle such data efficiently have been put forth so far. It has been found that the individual models have some strong points and certain weak points. Efforts have been made to combine these models so that the hybrid models will cash upon the strong points of the constituent models. Dubois and Prade in 1990 combined rough set and fuzzy set together to develop two models of which rough fuzzy model is a popular one and is used in many fields to handle uncertainty-based data sets very well. Particle Swarm Optimization (PSO) further combined with the rough fuzzy model is expected to produce optimized solutions. Similarly, multi-label classification in the context of data mining deals with situations where an object or a set of objects can be assigned to multiple classes. In this chapter, the authors present a rough fuzzy PSO algorithm that performs classification of multi-label data sets, and through experimental analysis, its efficiency and superiority has been established.

Chapter 3

Debi Prasanna Acharjya, VIT University, India
Ahmed P. Kauser, VIT University, India

Currently, a huge amount of data is available across various domains including biological data. Classification of these data, clustering, and data analysis is tedious and has become popular in recent research. In particular, bio-inspired computing is the field that mends together mathematics, computer science, and biology to develop tools to store, scrutinize, and interpret the biological data. It is also used to solve real life problems like sequencing biological data, data clustering, and optimization. Swarm intelligence is an emerging field of biologically inspired artificial intelligence technique that is based on the behavioral models of social insects. This chapter provides an overview of swarm intelligence algorithms in solving bio-inspired computing problems. It is an attempt to explore the working nature, applications, and generative power of various bio-inspired computing algorithms. The main intent is to furnish a comprehensive study of swarm intelligence algorithms in the literature so as to inspire further research in the area of biologically inspired computing.

Chapter 4

Amartya Neogi, Dr. B. C. Roy Engineering College, India

In this chapter, the author expands the notion of computational intelligence using the behavior of cockroaches. An introduction to cockroach as swarm intelligence emerging research area and literature review of its growing concept is explained in the beginning. The chapter also covers the ideas of hybrid cockroach optimization system. Next, the author studies the applicability of cockroach swarm optimization. Thereafter, the author presents the details of theoretical algorithm and an experimental result of integration of robot to some cockroaches to make collective decisions. Then, the author proposes his algorithm for traversing the shortest distance of city warehouses. Then, a few comparative statistical results of the progress of the present work on cockroach intelligence are shown. Finally, conclusive remarks are given. At last, the author hopes that even researchers with little experience in swarm intelligence will be enabled to apply the proposed algorithm in their own application areas.

Chapter 5

Santosh Kumar, Indian Institute of Technology (Banaras Hindu University), India
Deepanwita Datta, Indian Institute of Technology (Banaras Hindu University), India
Sanjay Kumar Singh, Indian Institute of Technology (Banaras Hindu University), India

Swarm Intelligence (SI) and bio-inspired computation has gathered great attention in research in the last few years. Numerous SI-based optimization algorithms have gained huge popularity to solve the complex combinatorial optimization problems, non-linear design system optimization, and biometric features selection and optimization. These algorithms are inspired by nature. In biometrics, face recognition is a non-intrusive method, and facial characteristics are probably the most common biometric features to identify individuals and provide a competent level of security. This chapter presents a novel biometric feature selection algorithm based on swarm intelligence (i.e. Particle Swarm Optimization [PSO] and Bacterial Foraging Optimization Algorithm [BFOA] metaheuristics approaches). This chapter provides the stepping stone for future researchers to unveil how swarm intelligence algorithms can solve the complex optimization problems to improve the biometric identification accuracy. In addition, it can be utilized for many different areas of application.

Chapter 6

Liquefaction in soil is one of the other major problems in geotechnical earthquake engineering. This chapter adopts Minimax Probability Machine (MPM) for prediction of seismic liquefaction potential of soil based on Shear Wave Velocity (Vs) data. MPM has been used as a classification technique. Two models (MODEL I and MODEL II) have been adopted. In MODEL I, input variables are Cyclic Stress Ratio (CSR), and Vs MODEL II uses Peck Ground Acceleration (PGA) and Vs as input variables. The developed MPM has been compared with the Artificial Neural Network (ANN) and Support Vector Machine (SVM) models. The developed MPM is a robust tool for determination of liquefaction susceptibility of soil.

The practical Economic Dispatch (ED) problems have non-convex objective functions with complex constraints due to the effects of valve point loadings, multiple fuels, and prohibited zones. This leads to difficulty in finding the global optimal solution of the ED problems. This chapter proposes a new swarm-based Mean-Variance Mapping Optimization (MVMOS) for solving the non-convex ED. The proposed algorithm is a new population-based meta-heuristic optimization technique. Its special feature is a mapping function applied for the mutation. The proposed MVMOS is tested on several test systems and the comparisons of numerical obtained results between MVMOS and other optimization techniques are carried out. The comparisons show that the proposed method is more robust and provides better solution quality than most of the other methods. Therefore, the MVMOS is very favorable for solving non-convex ED problems.

Chapter 8

Significant researches are going on for high performance droplet routing in Digital Microfluidic Biochip (DMFB). This chapter elaborates an ant colony optimization based droplet routing technique for high performance design in DMFB. The method is divided into two phases. (1) In the first phase, two dedicated ants generated from each source of the droplets traverse the rectilinear path between the source-target pairs and deposit pheromone to construct rectangular bounding box. Initial bounding box helps in restricted ant movements in the next phase. (2) In the second phase, real routing path is generated. Detour and stalling phenomena are incurred to resolve routing conflict. The method has explored both single ant and multiple ant systems to address detours from the conflicting zone in search for the best possible route towards destination. The method has been simulated on several existing benchmarks and comparative results are quite encouraging.

Section 2
Applications

Chapter 9

Subhadip Chandra, Camellia Institute of Technology, India
Siddhartha Bhattacharyya, RCC Institute of Information Technology, India

This chapter is intended to propose a quantum inspired self-supervised image segmentation method by quantum-inspired particle swarm optimization algorithm and quantum-inspired ant colony optimization algorithm, based on optimized MUSIG (OptiMUSIG) activation function with a bidirectional self-organizing neural network architecture to segment multi-level grayscale images. The proposed quantum-inspired swarm optimization-based methods are applied on three standard grayscale images. The performances of the proposed methods are demonstrated in comparison with their conventional counterparts. Experimental results are reported in terms of fitness value, computational time, and class boundaries for both methods. It has been noticed that the quantum-inspired meta-heuristic method is superior in terms of computational time in comparison to its conventional counterpart.

Chapter 10

V. Santhi, VIT University, India
B. K. Tripathy, VIT University, India

The image quality enhancement process is considered as one of the basic requirement for high-level image processing techniques that demand good quality in images. High-level image processing techniques include feature extraction, morphological processing, pattern recognition, automation engineering, and many more. Many classical enhancement methods are available for enhancing the quality of images and they can be carried out either in spatial domain or in frequency domain. But in real time applications, the quality enhancement process carried out by classical approaches may not serve the purpose. It is required to combine the concept of computational intelligence with the classical approaches to meet the requirements of real-time applications. In recent days, Particle Swarm Optimization (PSO) technique is considered one of the new approaches in optimization techniques and it is used extensively in image processing and pattern recognition applications. In this chapter, image enhancement is considered an optimization problem, and different methods to solve it through PSO are discussed in detail.

Chapter 11

A class of self-organizing readily deployable network (MANET: Mobile Ad-hoc Network) has been developed to address applications such as distributed collaborative computing, disaster recovery, and digital battlefield. Some of these applications need collaboration software running in the network to help in their mission. Because of the inherent nature of MANET, collaborative software application deployment has not been easy. Researchers have focused on those challenges like minimizing power, computing and memory utilization, and routing. With advancement of high-end devices, power, computing, and memory is not much of a constraint now. Mobility is still a challenge and is a major inhibitor for researchers to think about software application deployment architecture on MANET. This chapter proposes a self-organized software deployment architecture by which any 3-tier application can be deployed in a MANET. After the application is deployed, this chapter also enhances the previously proposed adaptive movement influenced by swarm intelligent principles.

Chapter 12

In this chapter, Gravitational Search Algorithm (GSA) and Particle Swarm Optimization (PSO) technique were applied for intelligent allocation of energy to the Plug-in Hybrid Electric Vehicles (PHEVs). Considering constraints such as energy price, remaining battery capacity, and remaining charging time, they optimized the State-of-Charge (SoC), a key performance indicator in hybrid electric vehicle for the betterment of charging infrastructure. Simulation results obtained for maximizing the highly non-linear objective function evaluates the performance of both techniques in terms of global best fitness and computation time.

Chapter 13

This chapter introduces the methodology of particle swarm optimization algorithm usage as a tool for finding customer profiles based on a previously developed predictive model that predicts events like selection of some products or services with some probabilities. Particle swarm optimization algorithm is used as a tool that finds optimal values of input variables within developed predictive models as referent values for maximization value of probability that customers select/buy a product or service. Recognized results are used as a base for finding similar profiles between customers. The presented methodology has practical value for decision support in business, where information about customer profiles are valuable information for campaign planning and customer portfolio management.

Pixel classification among overlapping land cover regions in remote sensing imagery is a challenging task. Detection of uncertainty and vagueness are always key features for classifying mixed pixels. This chapter proposes an approach for pixel classification using hybrid approach of Fuzzy C-Means and Particle Swarm Optimization methods. This new unsupervised algorithm is able to identify clusters utilizing particle swarm optimization based on fuzzy membership values. This approach addresses overlapping regions in remote sensing images by uncertainties using fuzzy set membership values. PSO is a population-based stochastic optimization technique inspired from the social behavior of bird flocks. The authors demonstrate the algorithm for segmenting a LANDSAT image of Shanghai. The newly developed algorithm is compared with FCM and K-Means algorithms. The new algorithm-generated clustered regions are verified with the available ground truth knowledge. The validity and statistical analysis are performed to demonstrate the superior performance of the new algorithm with K-Means and FCM algorithms.

In this chapter, the Particle Swarm Optimization method is applied to four different structural configurations of a linear switched reluctance generator with tubular topology. The optimization process involves the search of the values for a defined set of geometric parameters that maximize the rate of change of the generator's inductance with the relative displacement of its mover part. The optimization algorithm is applied to each structural configuration in order to find the optimum geometry as well to identify the most suitable configuration for electric generation.

Mobile Ad hoc Network or MANET is a collection of heterogeneous mobile nodes and is infrastructure-less by choice or by default. MANET is prone to confront a lot of challenges in designing a proper Quality of Service (QoS) model where transmission reliability has an important contrtibution. This chapter proposes an optimised message transmission scheme inspired by Artificial Bee Colony Optimisation (ABCO) technique. In this proposed scheme, QoS parameters that have been taken into consideration are throughput, delay, packet loss, and bandwidth utilisation. Here, three agents, namely message selection agent, message forwarding agent, and QoS factor calculating agent, have been introduced to govern and optimise the whole message transmission scheme. Through this method, a significant improvement in QoS factor can be achieved in comparison with the existing schemes. QualNet simulator has been used to evaluate the proposed concept.

WSN consists of spatially dispersed and dedicated sensors for monitoring the physical conditions of the universe and organizing the collected data at a central location. WSN incorporates a gateway that provides wireless connectivity back to the wired world and distributed sensor nodes. Various applications have been proposed for WSN like Ecosystem and Seismic monitoring, where deployment of nodes in a suitable manner is of an immense concern. Currently, sensor nodes are mobile in nature and they are deployed at an accelerated pace. This chapter focuses on developing the mobile nodes in an apt technique to meet the needs of WSNs properly. It considers the swarm intelligence-based movement strategies with the assistance of local communications through which the randomly deployed sensors can arrange themselves to reach the optimal placement to meet the issues like lower cost, lower power consumption, simpler computation, and better sensing of the total area.

This chapter introduces a novel technique to evaluate composite power system reliability indices and their sensitivities with respect to the control parameters using a dynamically directed binary Particle Swarm Optimization (PSO) search method. A key point in using PSO in power system reliability evaluation lies in selecting the weighting factors associated with the objective function. In this context, the work presented here proposes a solution method to adjust such weighting factors in a dynamic fashion so that the swarm would always fly on the entire search space rather of being trapped to one corner of the search space. Further, a heuristic technique based on maximum capacity flow of the transmission lines is used in classifying the state space into failure, success, and unclassified subspaces. The failure states in the unclassified subspace can be discovered using binary PSO technique. The effectiveness of the proposed method has been demonstrated on the IEEE RTS.

To recognize different patterns, identification of local regions where the pattern classes differ significantly is an inherent ability of the human cognitive system. This inherent ability of human beings may be imitated in any pattern recognition system by incorporating the ability of locating the regions that contain the maximum discriminating information among the pattern classes. In this chapter, the concept of Genetic

Algorithm (GA) and Bacterial Foraging Optimization (BFO) are discussed to identify those regions having maximum discriminating information. The discussion includes the evaluation of the methods on the sample images of handwritten Bangla digit and Basic character, which is a subset of Bangla character set. Different methods of sub-image or local region creation such as random creation or based on the Center of Gravity (CG) of the foreground pixels are also discussed here. Longest run features, extracted from the generated local regions, are used as local feature in the present chapter. Based on these extracted local features, together with global features, the algorithms are applied to search for the optimal set of local regions. The obtained results are higher than that results obtained without optimization on the same data set.

Chapter 20

In this chapter, a Particle Swarm Optimization-Based Session Key Generation for wireless communication (PSOSKG) is proposed. This cryptographic technique is solely based on the behavior of the particle swarm. Here, particle and velocity vector are formed for generation of keystream by setting up the maximum dimension of each particle and velocity vector. Each particle position and probability value is evaluated. Probability value of each particle can be determined by dividing the position of a particular particle by its length. If probability value of a particle is less than minimum probability value then a velocity is applied to move each particle into a new position. After that, the probability value of the particle at the new position is calculated. A threshold value is selected to evaluate against the velocity level of each particle. The particle having the highest velocity more than predefined threshold value is selected as a keystream for encryption.

Preface

The field of computational intelligence has assumed importance of late thanks to the evolving soft computing and artificial intelligent methodologies, tools, and techniques for envisaging the essence of intelligence embedded in real life observations. As a consequence, scientists have been able to explain and understand real life processes and practices which previously often used to remain unexplored because of their underlying imprecision, uncertainties, and redundancies, owing to the unavailability of appropriate methods for describing the inexactness, incompleteness, and vagueness of information representation. This understanding has been made possible to a greater extent by the advent of the field of computational intelligence, which tries to explore and unearth the intelligence, otherwise insurmountable, embedded in the system under consideration. To be specific, imparting intelligence has become the thrust of various computational paradigms irrespective of the nature of application domains. In fact, it is at present very difficult, if not impossible, to identify an application, especially one that is computation intensive, but is devoid of the influence of "intelligence" in it. Though the primary need of computational intelligence stemmed from the different computational issues pertaining to image processing and pattern recognition, of late, scientists and researchers across different platforms and disciplines of engineering, science, medical, business, and financial applications have resorted to this paradigm for better research throughputs and end results. Thus, the use of this computational paradigm is no more limited to the fields of computing or computing related disciplines and the present scenario demands a wider perspective of the application of computational intelligence to virtually every sphere of human civilization that handles meaningful information. Keeping this broader spectrum of the application of computational intelligence across different platforms/disciplines in mind, this book is targeted to inculcate a knowledge base of various research initiatives involving swarm intelligence in different disciplines of engineering.

Swarm Intelligence has emerged as a new generation methodology belonging to the class of evolutionary computing. While evolutionary computation, essentially being biologically inspired, could prove itself as an effective paradigm primarily useful for the purpose of search and optimization, achieving the task of identifying an optimal solution out of a search space, typically vast and/or complex, through the process of evolution, very much similar in line of natural evolution process, is the spirit of functioning of an evolutionary technique. The underlying process of evolution is usually governed by some stochastic heuristic, applicable in a specific optimization context.

In swarm intelligence, searching out an optimal in a search space is characterized by the way a swarm moves towards its goal. A swarm consists of a number of particles, each of which is engaged in the search process while on the move and maintaining the best solution at any generation in the evolution in addition to the best reported by the entire swarm until that moment. The global best information gets updated whenever any particle in the swarm comes across a better alternative. By virtue of the information at the disposition of each and every particle in the swarm, exploration of the search space is done in a parallel and more time-efficient manner.

Swarm intelligence, by this time, could prove itself an effective optimization technique, being a new generation one, as has already been indicated, among the evolutionary computation family. Because of its inherent implementation simplicity and efficient exploration mechanism, it has been able to draw the attention of the research community to a large extent. There are a large number of applications in various walks of life.

The editors of the present volume were inspired to compile what the research community is thinking about swarm intelligence as a potential avenue of optimization in various contexts. As a result of their initiative, there are a number of interesting reports in the present scope.

The book would come to benefit several categories of students and researchers. At the student level, this book can serve as a treatise/reference book for the special papers at the masters level aimed at inspiring possibly future researchers. Newly inducted PhD aspirants would also find the contents of this book useful as far as their compulsory coursework is concerned.

At the researcher level, those interested in interdisciplinary research would also be benefited by the book. After all, the enriched interdisciplinary contents of the book would be a subject of interest to the faculties, existing research communities, and new research aspirants from diverse disciplines of the concerned departments of premier institutes across the globe. This is expected to bring different research backgrounds (due to its cross platform characteristics) close to one another to form effective research groups all over the world. Above all, availability of the book should be ensured to as many universities and research institutes as possible through whatever graceful means it may be.

In the first chapter, a comprehensive survey on swarm intelligence-based image analysis is provided. This is an effective foundation for researchers particularly engaged newly in the relevant field.

Chapter 2 reports a PSO coupled with rough fuzzy model. It has been found to be very effective and comparatively superior to other existing methods for multi-label data classification, especially useful in the context of data mining.

Bio-computation/bio-inspired computation engulfs a major effort. In the present scope of Chapter 3, the authors made a sincere effort to identify various challenges associated to this kind of computation. An impressive review in this respect, particularly application of swarm intelligence-based techniques for solving such problems, has been reported.

A new swarm approach based on the movement characteristic of cockroaches has been investigated in the fourth chapter. By presenting his algorithm, the author tries to establish the worth of this new technique supplemented by adequate numerical and statistical justification.

In the fifth chapter, the authors have attempted to address the effectiveness of swarm intelligence on an interesting application area of identifying optimum biometric features.

In Chapter 6, the applicability of Minimax Probability Machine (MPM) has been explored and effectively exploited for predicting important geotechnical features such as seismic liquefaction potential of soil. The authors justify the robustness and performance of the MPM approach in comparison to Artificial Neural Network (ANN) and Support Vector Machine (SVM)-based techniques in terms of two separate models.

The significance of swarm intelligence in optimization of economic applications has been reported in the seventh chapter. Mean Variance Mapping Optimization Scheme (MVMOS) has been established by comparing with other existing techniques, to be effective for Economic Dispatch (ED) problem of non-convex nature in specific.

Choice of efficient strategy for droplet routing in digital microfluidic biochip is particularly challenging in respect of performance. In course of Chapter 8, the authors applied Ant Colony Optimization for achieving this task. The reporting is quite convincing.

Chapter 9 has shown how effective a swarm-based optimization technique could be for achieving multi-level image segmentation. The authors have supplemented ingredients of quantum computation in their swarm approach to have come across impressive computational improvement.

Chapter 10 offers an informative platform where various image enhancement techniques have been considered. This chapter is devoted to explore as to how particle swarm-based optimization technique could be effectively applied for the purpose of image enhancement.

Chapter 11 proposes a self-organized software deployment architecture by which any three-tier application can be deployed in a swarm intelligent Mobile Ad-hoc Network to address applications such as distributed collaborative computing, disaster recovery, and digital battlefield.

Chapter 12 deals with an important present day application of electric engineering. Particle swarm technique has been applied for integration of large-scale penetration of Plug-in Hybrid Electric Vehicles. Reported results are quite encouraging.

An application component of Decision Support System has been taken up in the thirteenth chapter. Mining of prospective customers based on their profiles as a part of business strategy of selling suitable products to them has been framed in terms of a probabilistic framework and particle swarm technique has been used to achieve the most effective choice of purchasers.

Chapter 14 deals with an interesting application concerning infrared imagery where remote sensed landscape images acquisitioned from satellite need pixel classification. Such applications are prone to uncertainty and vagueness leading to pixel representation suffering from mixed interpretation. A hybridized solution involving fuzzy mathematical ingredients coupled with particle swarm technique has been offered here to mitigate this classification problem. The results reported are quite encouraging.

For maximization of the generator inductance change rate to ensure optimum geometric topology towards identifying the best structural configuration in a linear switched reluctance generation process, PSO has been effectively applied in Chapter 15.

Relevant QoS parameters in MANET such as throughput, delay, packet loss, bandwidth utilization, are considered to ensure optimized message transmission by using Artificial Bee Colony Optimization (ABCO)-based swarm intelligent techniques is reported in Chapter 16.

Identification of physical locations for deploying Wireless Sensor Nodes (WSN) appears crucial in most of the applications. Chapter 17 reports as to how relevant QoS parameters, such as cost, power usage, resulting computational overhead, effective sensing of the deployed area, are taken into consideration towards mitigating optimum node deployment strategy in WSN framework by using swarm intelligence.

The eighteenth chapter exploits swarm movement throughout the entire spectrum of search space so as to dynamically adjust the weight function associated to the fitness, especially useful in power system reliability evaluation.

The nineteenth chapter highlights how evolutionary optimization has been effectively applied to find out the maximum discrimination prevalent in the Bangla character, especially of handwritten type. Balanced exploitation of local features such as the Centre of Gravity (CG) of the foreground pixels and the longest run along with global feature counterparts gives rise to an efficient swarm intelligence mechanism for this purpose.

Swarm Intelligence has been used for session key generation for encryption in wireless communication in Chapter 20. The novelty is that the maximum dimension and velocity vector corresponding to every particle are determined. Subsequently, the probability value of every particle is obtained with respect to the previous position and updated position to ascertain the velocity of that particle, which in turn is used for the said purpose.

Last but not the least, the book is intended to bring a broad spectrum of application domains under the purview of swarm intelligence so that it is able to trigger further inspiration among various research communities to contribute in their respective fields of applications, thereby orienting these application fields towards intelligence.

Once the purpose, as stated above, is achieved, a larger number of research communities may be brought under one umbrella to share their ideas in a more structured manner. In that case, the present endeavor may be seen as the beginning of such an effort in bringing various research applications close to one another.

Siddhartha Bhattacharyya
RCC Institute of Information Technology, India

Paramartha Dutta
Visva-Bharati University, India

Section 1
Theoretical Foundations

Chapter 1
Quantum Behaved Swarm Intelligent Techniques for Image Analysis:
A Detailed Survey

Sandip Dey
Camellia Institute of Technology, India

Siddhartha Bhattacharyya
RCC Institute of Information Technology, India

Ujjwal Maulik
Jadavpur University, India

ABSTRACT

In this chapter, an exhaustive survey of quantum behaved techniques on swarm intelligent is presented. The techniques have been categorized into different classes, and in conclusion, a comparison is made according to the benefits of the approaches taken for review. The above-mentioned techniques are classified based on the information they exploit, for instance, neural network related, meta-heuristic and evolutionary algorithm related, and other distinguished approaches are considered. Neural Network-Based Approaches exhibit a few brain-like activities, which are programmatically complicated, for instance, learning, optimization, etc. Meta-Heuristic Approaches update solution generation-wise for optimization, and the approaches differ based on the problem definition.

INTRODUCTION

Image segmentation (Jahne, 1993; Jain, 1989) is a fundamental and significant technique in image processing. This technique is used to segregate an image into several non-overlapping consequential and homogeneous regions. The basic property of image segmentation is that each segmented region must share some common features of image, such as, texture, color or pixel intensity. Occasionally, the

DOI: 10.4018/978-1-4666-8291-7.ch001

analogous grouping is known as clusters. A basic *prior* knowledge or even a presupposition about the image may be very useful for successful classification. This knowledge may help ones to find the appropriate features for this classification. Mathematically, let an image (I) is separated into p number of homogeneous, non-overlapping sub-regions viz., $R_1, R_2, \ldots R_p$. Each pixel in image (I) must be allocated to only one R_k for $k = 1, 2, \ldots, p$. According to the rule of image segmentation, each R_k $(k = 1, 2, \ldots, p)$ must satisfy the following properties:

$$a) \, R_1 \cup R_2 \cup \ldots \cup R_p = I \tag{1}$$

$$b) \, R_i \cap R_j = \varnothing, i \neq j \tag{2}$$

$$c) \, i, j \in \{1, 2, \ldots, p\} \tag{3}$$

In many occasions, segmentation was proved to be a useful and significant stair in image analysis. A good segmentation can reduce the computational overhead for the subsequent phases in image analysis. Segmentation is very useful for detecting and extracting the specific features of object from both graphic and nonnumeric data set. Segmentation has been successfully employed in different fields of application, such as, pattern recognition, surveillance, machine learning, medical sciences, artificial intelligence, economics, defense remote sensing to name a few. Segmentation techniques are generally classified into two classes viz., feature space based and image domain based (Lucchese & Mitra, 2001). Thresholding acts as a popular tool in image segmentation (Hammouche et al., 2008). One popular example of the former technique may be histogram thresholding whereas, region growing and merging, splitting and merging, edge detection based techniques may be some popular examples for later category (Lucchese & Mitra, 2001). Based on the characteristics of image pixel in its neighboring areas like discontinuity and resemblance, some segmentation techniques have been presented in (Freixenet et al., 2002). A review in this literature has been presented in (Gonzalez & Woods, 2002). Later, Bhattacharyya presented a detailed survey on different image thresholding and segmentation techniques based on classical and non-classical approaches (Bhattacharyya, 2011a).

Optimization can be described as an underlying way of finding feasible solutions of defined problems of various domains. Mathematically, it is defined as maximization or minimization function, subject to a group of constraints (if any). Optimization tries to discover best results (most acceptable) under the given circumstances. Two types of optimization can be defined based on the number of objectives (criteria) to be optimized. These are single objective optimization and multi-objective optimization. For the former type, the number of objectives to be optimized is solely one whereas, for the later type, minimum two objectives are optimized simultaneously. In multi-objective optimization, the number of objectives may vary subject to the nature of problem. In general, the objectives of conflicting type are used as fitness functions in this category (Deb et al., 2002). In general, in multi-objective optimization, multiple solutions are to be found out in chorus and the acceptable solutions are considered among them based on the importance of the unidentified objectives (Nocedal, 1999; Rao, 1996).

Mathematically an optimization problem can be defined as follows:

$$Max / Min \; f_1(x), f_1(x), \dots f_m(x)$$

$$subject \; to \quad \begin{array}{l} h_1(x) \le 0, h_2(x) \le 0, \dots, h_n(x) \le 0 \\ x \in S \subset \mathbb{R} \end{array} \qquad (4)$$

As mentioned in equation (4), the optimization problem has $m \, (m \ge 1)$ number of objective functions and $n \; (n \ge 0)$ number of constraints. S denoted the search space where, $S = [x_{\min}, x_{\max}]$, and $x_{\max}$ represent user-defined minimum and maximum design variables. For single-objective optimization problem the value of m is exactly one whereas, for multi-objective optimization problem, $m > 1$. The solutions in multi-objective optimization is known as Pareto-optimal solutions. Since, there is a trade-off between the participating objectives in this case, there must be a compromize in one another for optimal solutions (Bandyopadhyay et al., 2007). In this literature, a number of researchers have proposed different Pareto-based techniques on various fields. Horn *et al.* (Horn et al., 1994) has proposed Niched-Pareto Genetic Algorithm (NPGA), a popular multi-objective optimization technique. Srinivas and Deb (Srinivas & Deb, 1994) have proposed a different multi-objective optimization technique on genetic algorithm called, Non-dominated Sorting Genetic Algorithm (NSGA), later an extended version of NSGA known as, Non-dominated Sorting Genetic Algorithm II (NSGA-II) have been proposed by Deb *et al* (Deb et al., 2002). The authors have used non-dominated sorting approach for better efficiency (Chong, 2001; Spall, 2003).

Schrödinger's equation is an important aspect for describing quantum computing (QC) (Han & Kim, 2002). Quantum mechanical system is known to be originator of the concept of quantum system. Feynman (Feynman, 1982) has first introduced an abstract model to show the usefulness of quantum system for certain computations. According to his perception, the proposed model can efficiently perform the basic tasks of quantum physics and can be used as a simulator. Later, Deutsch (Deutsch & Jozsa, 1992) has extended the conception done by Feynman (Feynman, 1982). The author explained that any physical process can be modeled using the quantum system. Of late, the features of quantum computing, for instance, entanglement, superposition, interference to name a few, have been used in classical algorithms to tender a speed-up and thus to accelerate their efficiency (Mcmohan, 2008). For this reason, quantum computers are far more capable in finding factor of large numbers (Shor, 1997) and in searching databases (Grover, 1998) compared to classical systems.

THRESHOLDING EVALUATION METRICS

Thus far, a number of researchers have proposed different thresholding methods. These methods have been widely used in various application areas. Sezin and Sankur (Sezgin & Sankur, 2004) first presented a detailed survey on different thresholding methods and categorized them into different classes. Later, another survey paper has been presented by Bhattacharyya (Bhattacharyya, 2011a) in another fashion. Sezin and Sankur (Sezgin & Sankur, 2004) grouped the thresholding methods into six classes. Each of these classes is described below in short.

1. **Histogram Shape-Based Methods:** In this category different property of histogram of image, like valleys, peaks or curvatures are considered to determine threshold value. An example may include Ramesh's method (Ramesh et al., 1995).
2. **Clustering-Based Methods:** Here, the input samples are grouped into foreground and background classes to compute the desired threshold value. A popular example of this category is Otsu's method (Otsu, 1979).
3. **Entropy-Based Methods:** Similar to the above method, the entropy of the background and foreground areas is calculated. One renowned example of this category is Kapur's method (Kapur et al., 1985).
4. **Object Attribute-Based Methods:** In this category, resemblance between the original image and its binary version is considered for evaluation. Different similarities for instance, fuzzy shape similarity and many others may be considered here. An example of this category may include Tsai's method (Tsai, 1995).
5. **Spatial Methods:** These methods employ the concept of probability distribution between the image pixels. One popular example of this category is Cheng's method (Cheng & Chen, 1999).
6. **Local Methods:** The methods in this category acclimatize the pixel values according to the local image features. A thresholding method proposed by Niblack (Niblack, 1986) is an example of this category.

To describe some popular thresholding method of different categories, let us consider the probability distribution between the pixels frequencies of input image (gray scale) as given by

$$f_j = \frac{n_j}{N}, j \in \left[0, 255\right] \tag{5}$$

and

$$P_T = \sum_{j=0}^{T} f_j \tag{6}$$

Here, n_j and f_j represent total number of pixels and frequency of j_{th} pixel intensity of the image where, $j \in \left[0, 255\right]$, N is the total image pixels in the image. A measure $\left(P_T\right)$ is introduced by computing sum of the probability distributions from 0 to the threshold value, T. A few renowned thresholding methods are described in the following section.

1. Wu's Method

This is a popular entropy based thresholding method proposed by Wu, Songde and Hanquing (Wu et al., 1998). In this method, the following probability distributions are considered to find the object and background classes of the input image. Let us consider the probability distributions as given by

$$A : p(j) = \frac{f_j}{P_T}, j \in [0, T]$$

$$B : p(j) = \frac{f_j}{P_T}, j \in [T+1, 255] \tag{7}$$

Here, f_j and P_T are calculated using equations (5) and (6), respectively. Apart from that, the entropies for foreground and background distributions are considered in this method. These two distributions are given by (Wu et al., 1998)

$$H_{br}(T) = -\sum_{j=0}^{T} f_j \log(f_j) \tag{8}$$

and

$$H_{fr}(T) = -\sum_{j=T+1}^{255} f_j \log(f_j) \tag{9}$$

where, $H_{fr}(T)$ and $H_{br}(T)$ are known as foreground and background class entropies. The optimum threshold value is determined by minimizing $W(T)$ as given by (Wu et al., 1998)

$$W(T) = \left| H_{br}(T) - H_{fr}(T) \right| \tag{10}$$

2. Renyi's Method

This is another popular entropy-based method (Sahoo, 1997; Sezgin, 2004). In this method, the probability distributions for object and background classes of the gray level images are used. For the sake of simplicity, let us consider the 256 probability distributions for 256 different pixel intensity values in the input image as given by $f_0, f_1, \ldots, f_{255}$. Besides that, two classes for object (D_1) and background (D_2) are computed from the above mentioned distributions as given by

$$D_1 : \frac{f_0}{p(D_1)}, \frac{f_1}{p(D_1)}, \ldots, \frac{f_T}{p(D_1)}$$

$$D_2 : \frac{f_{T+1}}{p(D_2)}, \frac{f_{T+2}}{p(D_2)}, \ldots, \frac{f_{255}}{p(D_2)}$$

where,

$$p(D_1) = \sum_{j=0}^{T} f_j, \, p(D_2) = \sum_{j=T+1}^{255} f_j \tag{11}$$

and

$$p(D_1) + p(D_2) = 1 \tag{12}$$

The foreground and background class entropies are considered as follows (Sahoo et al., 1997).

$$H_f^\rho = \frac{1}{1-\rho} \ln \left(\sum_{j=0}^{T} \left[\frac{p_j}{p(D_1)} \right]^\rho \right) \tag{13}$$

$$H_b^\rho = \frac{1}{1-\rho} \ln \left(\sum_{j=T+1}^{255} \left[\frac{p_j}{p(D_2)} \right]^\rho \right) \tag{14}$$

Here, ρ is a parameter and generally, $\rho \in [0,1)$. For optimization, $\{ H_f^\rho + H_b^\rho \}$ is minimized.

3. Yen's Method

Yen's method is another popular entropy-based method developed by Yen, Chang and Chang (Sezgin, 2004 ; Yen, 1995). In this method, similar concept has been adopted as Kapur's method (Kapur et al., 1985) for foreground and background probability distributions. Yen used the entropic correlation as given by (Yen et al., 1995)

$$Yn(T) = H_b^T(T) + H_f^T(T)$$

$$= -\log \left(\sum_{j=0}^{T} \left[\frac{f_j}{p(D_1)} \right]^2 \right) - \log \left(\sum_{j=T+1}^{255} \left[\frac{f_j}{p(D_2)} \right]^2 \right) \tag{15}$$

Here, $p(D_1)$ and $p(D_2)$ are computed using the equation (25). The optimum threshold value is determined by maximizing $Yn(T)$. Note that, Renyi's method is transformed to Yen's method when $\rho = 2$ (Sezgin, 2004 ; Johannsen, 1982) .

4. Johannsen's Method

Johannsen's Method is another popular thresholding method proposed by Johannsen and Bille (Johannsen & Bille, 1982) . The authors minimize $G(T)$ to find the optimal threshold value of gray scale image as given by

$$G(T) = G_b(T) + G_f(T)$$

$$= \log(P_T) + \frac{1}{P_T}\{F(p_T) + F(P_{T-1})\} + \log(1 - P_{T-1}) + \frac{1}{(1 - P_{T-1})}\{F(p_T) + F(1 - P_T)\} \qquad (16)$$

where, $F(b) = -b \log(b)$. The measures p_j and P_T are determined using the equations (5) and (6), respectively .

5. Silva's Method

Silva, Lins and Rocha (Silva & Rocha, 2006) presented a thresholding method called, Silva's method. In this method, firstly, the entropy between the gray level distributions and its binary version is derived using the following equation (Silva & Rocha, 2006)

$$U = \sum_{i=0}^{255} f_i \log_2(f_i) \qquad (17)$$

In its way, firstly, $\{f_0, f_1, \ldots, f_{255}\}$ *(priori probability distribution)* is derived using equation (5). Later, the threshold value T is found out using the posteriori probability distributions $\{P_T, 1 - P_T\}$ for $P_T \leq 0.5$. It is related with the entropy-based probability distribution as given below

$$U'(T) = g(P_T) \qquad (18)$$

where,

$$g(p) = -b \log_2(b) - (1 - b) \log_2(1 - b).$$

Again, the measure, P_T is derived using the equation (6).

Another measure called, loss factor (δ) is introduced here as follows:

$$\delta\left(U \middle/ \log(256)\right) = -\frac{3}{7}\left(U \middle/ \log(256)\right) + 0.8, \text{ if } U \middle/ \log(256) < 0.7$$

$$= \left(\frac{U}{\log(256)} \right) - 0.2 \text{, if } \frac{U}{\log(256)} \geq 0.7 \tag{19}$$

The optimum threshold is found out by minimizing $|F(T)|$ as given by

$$|F(T)| = \left| \frac{U'(T)}{\left(\frac{U}{\log(256)} \right)} - \delta \left(\frac{U}{\log(256)} \right) \right| \tag{20}$$

6. Linear Index of Fuzziness

Sometimes, Linear Index of Fuzziness can be used as thresholding method. Theoretically, the fuzzy measures can be described as a degree of measurement for which a gray level, h in the image can be fitted in the foreground image with its background image (Sezgin & Sankur, 2004) . Huang and Wang first presented the term called, index of fuzziness. They employed index of fuzziness after calculating the distance between the original image and its binary version (Huang, 1995; Tizhoosh, 2005). Linear Index of Fuzziness (χ_l) can be defined as follows:

$$\chi_l = \frac{2}{AB} \sum_{g=0}^{L-1} g(h) \times \min\{\mu_B(h), 1 - \mu_B(h)\} \tag{21}$$

where, A and B represent the length and the width of the image, respectively. The image comprises L gray levels where, $h \in [0, 1, ..., L]$, $\mu_Y(g)$ is called the membership function and $g(h)$ is the histogram of the data set (Huang & Wang, 1995). Minimization of χ_l gives the optimum threshold value of the given image (Huang, 1995 ; Tizhoosh, 2005).

7. Pun's Method

This is an entropy-based method proposed by Pun (Pun, 1980; Sezgin, 2004). In this proposed method, Pun has worked with g number of statistically independent symbol source ($g = 256$). To form the working formula, the following entropy (Pun, 1980).

$$H'(T) = -P_T \log[P_T] - [1 - P_T] \log[1 - P_T] \tag{22}$$

is divided by the source entropy as given by (Pun, 1980)

$$H(T) = H_{br}(T) + H_{fr}(T) \tag{23}$$

It gives,

$$\frac{H'(T)}{H(T)} \geq P(\gamma) = \gamma \frac{\log P_T}{\log(\max(p_0, p_1, \ldots, p_T))} + (1-\beta) \frac{\log(1-P_T)}{\log(\max(p_{T+1}, p_{T+2}, \ldots, p_g))} \tag{24}$$

where,

$$H_b(T) = \gamma H(T) \tag{25}$$

Now, $H_{br}(T)$ and $H_{fr}(T)$ are derived from the following formula (Pun, 1980)

$$H_{br}(T) = -\sum_{i=0}^{T} f_i \log(f_i) \tag{26}$$

and

$$H_{fr}(T) = -\sum_{i=T+1}^{g-1} f_i \log(f_i) \tag{27}$$

The optimum threshold in the given image is derived by getting a particular threshold value, T which is influenced by the equation (25) with the argument γ which maximizes $P(\gamma)$ in equation (24) (Pun, 1980).

8. Kapur's Method

Kapur, Sahoo and Wong first proposed an enropy-based method called, Kapur's Method (Kapur, 1985 ; Sezgin, 2004). The authors have considered two different signal sources, one is foreground image and other is background image, for finding optimal solutions (Kapur et al., 1985). The following are class distribution of object (O) and background (B) of the gray level image (Kapur et al., 1985)

$$O: p(i) = \frac{f_i}{P_T}, i \in [0, T] \tag{28}$$

and

$$B: p(i) = \frac{f_i}{P_T}, i \in [T+1, 255] \tag{29}$$

where, f_i and P_T are computed using equations (5) and (6), respectively. $H_{br}(T)$ and $H_{fr}(T)$ are two class entropies (for background and foreground image) are computed by using equations (26) and (27), respectively with $p(i) = f_i$ (Kapur et al., 1985). The optimum threshold value is determined by maximizing $H(T)$ using equation (23) (Kapur et al., 1985).

9. Brink's Method

In 1996, A. D. Brink and N. E. Pendock proposed a cross entropy-based thresholding method called, Brink's Method (Brink, 1996; Sezgin, 2004). They have used the original grayscale image as a prior distribution. The average of upper and lower intensity values of threshold is considered for computation. The means $\mu_f(T)$ and $\mu_b(T)$ (for background and foreground image, respectively) are computed as follows:

$$\mu_b(T) = \sum_{j=0}^{T} jf_j \text{ and } \mu_f(T) = \sum_{j=T+1}^{255} jf_j \tag{30}$$

where, f_j for $j \in [0, 255]$ is computed using equation (5) (Brink, 1996). For the sake of computation, two probability distribution functions called, *priori* probability distribution $p(z)$ and *posteriori* probability distribution $q(z)$ are introduced. The cross-entropy between these two distributions is given below (Brink & Pendock, 1996):

$$Z_C(q, p) = \int q(z) \log \frac{q(z)}{p(z)} dy \tag{31}$$

For discrete probability distribution, the equivalent cross-entropy can be depicted as (Brink & Pendock, 1996).

$$Z_C(q, p) = \sum_{z=1}^{N} q_z \log \frac{q_z}{p_z} \tag{32}$$

Subject to, $\sum_{z=1}^{N} p_z = \sum_{z=1}^{N} q_z (= 1)$ where, N is the number of discrete points. The non-symmetric equation (31) is transformed to its equivalent symmetry measure as follows (Brink, 1996).

$$Z_M(p, q) = Z_C(q, p) + Z_C(p, q)$$

$$= \sum_{z=1}^{N} q_z \log \frac{q_z}{p_z} + \sum_{z=1}^{N} p_z \log \frac{p_z}{q_z} \tag{33}$$

The equation (33) can be rewritten using the concept of means as given by (Brink & Pendock, 1996)

$$\sum_{k=0}^{Q} g_k = \left[\sum_{k=0}^{M} \mu_b(T) \right]_{g_k \le T} + \left[\sum_{k=0}^{M} \mu_f(T) \right]_{g_k > T} \tag{34}$$

where, Q is the number of pixels in image and $g_k \in [0, 255]$ is the corresponding pixel intensity value.

Afterward, histogram of gray level frequency is considered to reduce computational hazard. Hence, equation (34) may lead to following form (Brink & Pendock, 1996):

$$Z_C(T) = \sum_{k=0}^{T} f_k \mu_b(T) \log \frac{\mu_b(T)}{k} + \sum_{k=T+1}^{255} f_k \mu_f(T) \log \frac{\mu_f(T)}{k} \tag{35}$$

where, f_k represents the frequency of each gray level k.

Similarly, equation (33) is rewritten as (Brink & Pendock, 1996)

$$Z_M(T) = \sum_{k=0}^{T} f_k \left[\mu_b(T) \log \frac{\mu_b(T)}{k} + k \log \frac{k}{\mu_b(T)} \right] +$$
$$\sum_{k=T+1}^{255} f_k \left[\mu_f(T) \log \frac{\mu_f(T)}{k} + k \log \frac{k}{\mu_f(T)} \right] \tag{36}$$

The optimum threshold is determined by minimizing $Z_C(T)$ or $Z_M(T)$ as given above (Brink, 1996; Sezgin, 2004).

10. Correlation Coefficient

The correlation coefficient (ρ) is a popular measure for image segmentation. It refers to the degree of resemblance between the original images and its extracted version. It can be represented as

$$r = \frac{\frac{1}{n^2} \sum_{i=1}^{n} \sum_{j=1}^{n} \left(U_{ij} - \overline{U} \right) \left(W_{ij} - \overline{W} \right)}{\sqrt{\frac{1}{n^2} \sum_{i=1}^{n} \sum_{j=1}^{n} \left(U_{ij} - \overline{U} \right)^2} \sqrt{\frac{1}{n^2} \sum_{i=1}^{n} \sum_{j=1}^{n} \left(W_{ij} - \overline{W} \right)^2}} \tag{37}$$

where, $U_{ij}, 1 \le i, j \le n$ and $W_{ij}, 1 \le i, j \le n$ are the original image and its segmented version, respectively. $n \times n$ signifies the dimension of the selected image. $\overline{U}$ and $\overline{W}$ are the mean values of these two images respectively. The quality of segmentation depends on the value of ρ. Higher value of correlation coefficient always refers to a better quality of segmentation. Despite having some limitations, correlation coefficient has been successfully used in many segmentation problems.

SWARMS

Since the last few decades, one interesting diversion for a dedicated group of peoples became discovering various insects from different areas in the natural world. These peoples always try to discover new creatures and analyze their social behavior passionately. Different animals behave differently in the nature. For example, a group of birds congregates together to fly in the sky. A set of ants follow their self created rules and walk in a collective way to find the source of food. Fishes form a school while swimming (Shaw, 1962). The above group of examples can be named as swarm behavior. This has gradually become a subject of interest for different fields, such as biology, computer science and many others. In the recent years, a few scientists in the above mention fields studied elaborately and made experiments by producing a model on biological swarms. They tried to inspect the behaviors of the social animals using the model. Furthermore, number of researchers has been showing their profound interests on developing different algorithms using swarm behavior and produced various methods in the form of swarm intelligence. This has a direct impact in optimization. Some typical application areas of this kind may include military applications and transportation systems (Pachter & Chandler, 1998), telecommunicate systems (Bonabeau et al., 1999), and robotics (Arkin, 1998; Beni, 1989).

An elevated vision of a swarm advocates that the agents in swarm can be very effective and useful to achieve a few decisive deeds and attain some goal as well. The participating agents exercise simple confined rules to oversee their actions. The agents sometimes interact of the whole group to fulfill its objectives. The nature of the independent agent is that it does not trail commands from its leader (Flake, 1999). For instance, when a flock of birds gather for flying, they only regulate their movements in an organized manner. The birds in the neighboring areas remain very close and traverse in the dedicated path to avoid collisions between each other. One interesting feature is that no one among them can be considered as leader, all of them have equal participation in this movement. In reference to the above discussions, swarm intelligence can be described as combined astuteness of decentralized system that works with simple agents. This swarm intelligence is very useful in the systems that deal with artificial intelligence. A typical application of using swarm intelligence using cellular robotic systems was presented in (Beni &Wang, 1989).

PRINCIPLES OF SWARM INTELLIGENCE

In the context of general behaviors of swarm, the basic principles of swarm intelligence can be introduced as follows (Millonas, 1994):

1. **Principle of Proximity:** A swarm should be competent enough to deal with environmental behavioral responses that may be triggered by communications among various agents in swarm. The responses may vary according to the complexity of interactions among the agents.
2. **Principle of Quality:** A swarm should be intelligent enough and capable as well to deal with other different quality factors. That may include food and safety.
3. **Principle of Different Response:** A swarm should be able to face typical fluctuating situations from environment. Each agent in swarm should be capable to handle this situation efficiently.
4. **Principle of Solidity and Compliance:** In diverse situations, swarms should be very much efficient to acclimatize the fluctuations from environmental behavior devoid of hastily shifting modes.

OVERVIEW OF META-HEURISTIC ALGORITHMS

The term "meta-heuristic" can be described as an iterative search procedure which is generally used to explore the search space for optimal solutions. Meta-heuristic acts as a guide and it assist to find optimal solutions. In its process, it may sometimes apply additional intelligence or different learning strategies to avoid local trapping and thus it enhances its searching capability. At each iteration, it tries to find a single solution or a group of solutions according to the nature of optimization. The chosen heuristics may differ from each other ranging from low to high level procedures, or a simple to complex learning process. One of the interesting features of meta-heuristics is that these are not problem or domain specific, rather they can be applied into variety of problem areas. Apart from that, they can apply some previous knowledge of searching (that can be stored in memory) to its way in reaching optimality (Blum, Glover, 2003).

Meta-heuristics can be classified into following categories:

1. **Nature-Move vs. Non-Nature Move:** According to the origin of algorithm, meta-heuristics may be grouped into nature-moved or non-nature moved version. A few popular examples of the former category may include Genetic Algorithms and Ant Colony Optimization whereas; Tabu Search and Iterated Local Search are the examples of latter category. This type of classification could not become meaningful for some reasons. There may have some hybrid type of algorithms which cannot be classified into any category.

2. **Single Point Searching vs. Population-Based Searching:** It is based on the number of solutions that meta-heuristic can handle at a single time. The former category works as local searching-based meta-heuristic, which includes Tabu Search, Variable Neighborhood Search and many others. On the other hand, the algorithms in the second category perform searching simultaneously on a set of agents. Thus, population-based searching is more efficient than single point searching. Genetic Algorithms, Particle Swarm Optimization and Ant Colony Optimization are three population-based optimization techniques.

3. **Static vs. Dynamic Objective Function:** Meta-heuristics can also be classified in accordance with its usability. During searching, if the objective function does not change as specified in the problem demonstration, it is called static but if it needs to be modified during searching, it is dynamic. Some example of the latter type may include Guided Local Search (GLS) and many others.

4. **One vs. Various Neighborhood Structures:** Based on the type of neighborhood structure, meta-heuristics can be classified into single or various neighborhood structures. Most of the meta-heuristics are of the first category, there may have few examples of latter type also. One example of various neighborhood structures is Variable Neighborhood Search (VNS).

5. **With-Memory vs. Memory-Less Methods:** In this classification, the meta-heuristics may be classified based on search history. For the former one, the recent visited moves are stored in memory and the decision about the next step of visit in the search space is taken according to the data stored in memory. The memory-less method employs Markov process, where the next move solely depends on the current state for search process. Tabu search (TS) is an example of the latter category.

The overview of different swarm intelligence based algorithms is described in the following parts:

1. **Genetic Algorithm:** John Holland (Holland, 1975) a scientist from the University of Michigan first developed an evolutionary algorithm called, Genetic Algorithm (GA). GA uses the "mechanics" called natural biological evolution for its search process. This algorithm is basically follow population based approach for optimization, where population diversity is made using three genetic operators called, Selection, Recombination and Mutation in succession. In GA, each individual is called chromosome which is associated with a fitness function. The better fitness value indicates a good individual in the population. The steps of GA are illustrated through the following algorithm.
   a. Start.
   b. Initialization of population.
   c. Calculate fitness value of each individual in population.
   d. Repeat for a number of generations.
   e. Repeat for each individual in population.
   f. Select two individuals using a selection method (e.g. tournament selection).
   g. Apply recombination and mutation operator for population diversity.
   h. Calculate fitness value of each individual.
   i. Fill the population of chromosomes with better individuals.
   j. Go to step e.
   k. Go to step d.
   l. End.

2. **Ant Colony Optimization:** Ant Colony Optimization (ACO) is a popular population based meta-heuristic method proposed by Colorni, Dorigo and Maniezzo (Dorigo et al., 1996).The authors got inspiration to construct ACO from the day by day activities of real ants. Ants are always in search for food. For this reason, they always try to find the food source here and there from their nest. Trey deposit a hormone called, *pheromone* on their paths as the direction for the other ants to follow. More amount of *pheromone* concentration indicates more favorable path to traverse. The basic aim of constructing ACO is to find the shortest path for source of food from their nest. The following steps are followed while constructing the algorithm of Ant Colony Optimization:
   a. Start.
   b. Creation of pheromone matrix.
   c. Initialization of population.
   d. Compute fitness for each individual.
   e. Save the best solution for future use.
   f. Repeat for a number of generations
   g. Use pheromone matrix to determine population.
   h. Evaluate fitness using the given objective function.
   i. Compare this solution with the previous one to update the best solution.
   j. Update the pheromone matrix.
   k. Go to step f.
   l. End.

3. **Particle Swarm Optimization:** In the year of 1995, James Kennedy and Russell Eberhart (Kennedy & Eberhart, 1995) first developed a population based optimization technique called, Particle Swarm Optimization (PSO). PSO is stochastic in nature and the authors got inspiration of developing this robust optimization technique from the association of swarms and the intelligence they adopt during movement. In PSO, the individuals which form the population of swarm is called particle. The

concept is that each individual particle is act in multi-dimensional space, where the particle uses its own previous flying experience or they adopt the experience of other individuals for updating its position. Each particle, *j* stores its best position among different runs (*pbest$_j$*) and the best value in the swarm is stored in *gbest*. The basic algorithm of PSO is given here.

a. Start.
b. Initialization of population.
c. Repeat for a number of generations.
d. Repeat until all particle are visited.
e. Evaluate fitness for each particle's position.
f. Update *pbest*.
g. Go to step d.
h. Store the best of *pbest* as *gbest*.
i. Update the velocity and position for each individual.
j. Go to step c.
k. End.

4. **Differential Evaluation:** In 1996, Storn and Price (Storn & Price, 1995) introduced a population-based optimization technique called, Differential Evaluation (DE). DE is a stochastic, powerful evolutionary algorithm and can be successfully applied for solving different problems in various fields like engineering, communication, finance, statistics, and many others. Like GA, three different operators namely, mutation, recombination and selection are applied successively for population diversity. In DE, some control parameters like scaling factor, crossover rate are used. These parameters have a direct influence in speedy convergence in optimization. Hence, the parameters need to be tuned enough at beforehand to have a good result at less time period and with a very high efficiency. The algorithm of DE is given below.

a. Start.
b. Initialization of population.
c. Repeat for a number of generations.
d. Repeat until all individuals are visited.
e. Apply mutation operator in all individuals.
f. Apply recombination operator in all individuals.
g. Evaluate fitness for all individuals in population.
h. Apply selection for constructing the population for next generation.
i. Go to step d.
j. Go to step c.
k. End.

5. **Simulated Annealing:** Kirkpatrick *et al.* (Kirkpatrik et al., 1983) first introduced Simulated Annealing, a popular meta-heuristic technique in 1982. The source of motivation to develop this method was the physical annealing process. A very basic feature of material substance is that after heating with a high temperature, it being gradually cooled and form into a uniform formation. As compared to hill climbing, SA consents to downwards steps always. The working principle of SA is that the better moves in the search space are always honored and the worse moves are always ignored. The rules of thermodynamics are applied in SA to guarantee a better move. To date, many researchers have effectively applied SA in different fields as a faithful optimization tool. The algorithm of SA is mentioned below.

    a.   Start.

    b.   Generate an initial configuration, *P*.

    c.   Evaluate fitness of the vector individual and store the result as the best solution.

    d.   Introduce a initial temperature variable, *TI* and assign a very high value in *TI*.

    e.   Introduce another final temperature variable, *TH* and assign a very low value in *TH*.

    f.   Repeat until *TI< TH*.

    g.   Repeat for a number of generations.

    h.   Perturb the configuration. Let it produce *S*.

    i.   Evaluate fitness of *S*.

    j.   Set *D=* Fitness value of *S*- Fitness value of *P*.

    k.   If *D>0*.

    l.   Select *S* as the current configuration.

    m.   If *D<0*.

    n.   Select *S* as the current configuration if random $(0, 1)< e^{-D/TI}$.

    o.   Go to step g. Set $TI = TI \times \vartheta$, ϑ is a predefined reduction factor.

    p.   Go to step f.

    q.   End

6.   **Tabu Search:** Glover and Laguna first proposed a popular meta-heuristic method known as Tabu Search (TS) (Glover, 1989, 1990). Unlike the first four methods described above, TS acts on a single individual and explore search space to discover the optimal solutions. The best features of TS are that it is uncomplicated, flexible and very powerful. It is very common in TS that it sometimes get stuck into local optima and intelligence may need to be applied to make it free from this entrap. Apart from that the proper parameter tuning is sometimes proved to be very useful for getting a good optimized result. A few fundaments components of TS are listed below

    a.   Neighborhood.

    b.   Tabu.

    c.   Attributes.

    d.   Tabu list.

    e.   Aspiration criterion.

The algorithm of TS is given below.

a.   Start

b.   Generate an initial vector individual.

c.   Evaluate fitness of the vector individual and store the result as the best solution. Introduce a tabu memory: $T_m = \varnothing$.

d.   Repeat for a number of generations.

e.   Create a set of neighbors, *S* of the vector individual.

f.   Repeat for each element in *S*.

g.   If the element is not in the memory and has a better fitness value than the previous one then. Add the element in T_m and mark it as the best solution.

h.   Go to step g.

i.   Update tabu memory.

j.   Go to step e.

k.   End.

QUANTUM COMPUTING FUNDAMENTALS

The concept of Quantum Computing (QC) has been originated from the theory of quantum mechanics. A wave function $|\psi\rangle$ in Hilbert space is invoked for describing quantum machines. Theoretically, a Hilbert space comprises a set of basic states (Mcmohan, 2008; Bhattacharyya, 2011b). The following are the fundamental constituents of QC.

A brief description of them is presented in the subsequent subsections.

1. Qubit

For a two-state QC, quantum bit or in short qubit is considered as the repository where smallest unit of information can be stored. These two states are sometimes refers to state "0" and state "1" (Hey, 1999). Here, $|0\rangle$ and $|1\rangle$ are known as two-state column vectors which can be expressed as (Bhattacharyya, 2011b).

$$|0\rangle = \begin{bmatrix} 1 \\ 0 \end{bmatrix} \text{ and } |1\rangle = \begin{bmatrix} 0 \\ 1 \end{bmatrix} \tag{38}$$

The bracket notations $|.\rangle$ and $\langle.|$ have been introduced by Paul Dirac for qubit representation (Araujo et al., 2008). After the name of the inventor, the above notations are known as dirac symbol and very specifically, sometimes called *ket* and *bra*, *respectively*. One notation is complex conjugate transpose to each other.

2. Quantum Superposition

Quantum superposition is equivalent to the linear combination of participating vectors. Any qubit in QC may be represented either in "0" state or in "1" state or it can also be represented using linear combination (superposition) of the state vectors. The quantum superposition of a quantum system is represented by (Han & Kim, 2002).

$$|\psi\rangle = \alpha|0\rangle + \beta|1\rangle \tag{39}$$

where, α, β are complex numbers. $|\psi\rangle$ satisfies the normalized form of the qubit states as given by (Han & Kim, 2002).

$$|\alpha|^2 + |\beta|^2 = 1 \tag{40}$$

The probabilities to measure the states $|0\rangle$ and $|1\rangle$ are $|\alpha|^2$ and $|\beta|^2$, respectively (Han & Kim, 2002). Generally, the state space for a number of qubits can be described as follows (Araujo et al., 2008).

$$\underbrace{\left|0000\right\rangle}_{4\ qubits}, \underbrace{\left|0001\right\rangle}_{4\ qubits}, \underbrace{\left|0010\right\rangle}_{4\ qubits}, \cdots, \underbrace{\left|1111\right\rangle}_{4\ qubits}$$

Mathematically, the dot product of α and β is computed as (Araujo et al., 2008).

$$e = \alpha.\beta \tag{41}$$

and the angle between the qubit phase, ξ is measured as (Araujo et al., 2008)

$$\xi = \arctan\left(\frac{\beta}{\alpha}\right) \tag{42}$$

3. Quantum Gate

Quantum gate plays a significant role in quantum computing. Sometimes, quantum logic operations necessitate developing different quantum algorithms or quantum behaved algorithms (Bhattacharyya, 2011b). A quantum gate can be utilized to accelerate the convergence rate using the participating qubit states. The basic property of a quantum gate is that it is reversible. Suppose, a quantum gate is represented using a unitary operator, U. U must satisfy the following relations:

$$U^+ = U^{-1}, UU^+ = U^+U = I \text{ and } U = e^{iHt} \tag{43}$$

where, U is called the Hermitian unitary operator (Han, 2002).

A few distinctive examples of quantum gates are hadamard gate, rotation gate, NOT gate, controlled NOT gate to name a few. (Hey, 1999; Araujo, 2008). It is known that the Q-gates performing the transformation operation, preserves orthogonality of qubits.

4. Quantum Coherence and Decoherence

In conjunction with the quantum superposition, the theory of coherence and decoherence are invoked. Coherence is said to be subsisted between two waves until there is a stable phase relationship between the waves. Decoherence works just opposite to coherence. Decoherence occurs when the measured phase relationship is devastated or the quantum superposition between the states is destroyed. With reference to equation (39), the required probabilities for collapsing the quantum superposition to $\left|0\right\rangle$ and $\left|1\right\rangle$ are $\left|\alpha\right|^2$ and $\left|\beta\right|^2$, respectively (Han & Kim, 2002).

5. Quantum Measurement

Von Neumann measurement strategy is introduced for measuring the output state. According to this strategy, one basic state among the all fundamental participating states is selected as output. Firstly, the basis is selected at random and this must be ensured that the system must exist in it. As the basic states are in superposed form, quantum computing commences a probabilistic measurement strategy to transform the superposed state into the required single state.

An example of quantum inspired representation is presented below.

Qubit can be used as the basic unit to form Q-bit individual (Araujo, 2008; Han, 2003). A Q-bit individual can be formed using number of Q-bit strings as a set, as given below

$$s = \begin{bmatrix} \alpha_1 & \alpha_2 & \alpha_3 & \dots & \alpha_r \\ \beta_1 & \beta_2 & \beta_3 & \dots & \beta_r \end{bmatrix} \tag{44}$$

According to the equation (44), s comprises r number of qubits. Each α_j and β_j in s satisfies the equation (38) $\forall j = 1, 2, \dots, r$.

A typical example of Q-bit individual with four qubits $(r = 4)$ is given below:

$$t = \begin{bmatrix} \dfrac{1}{\sqrt{2}} & -\dfrac{1}{2} & -\dfrac{1}{\sqrt{2}} & \dfrac{\sqrt{3}}{2} \\ \dfrac{1}{\sqrt{2}} & \dfrac{\sqrt{3}}{2} & \dfrac{1}{\sqrt{2}} & -\dfrac{1}{2} \end{bmatrix} \tag{45}$$

The states corresponding to the equation (45) can be shown as

$$t = \left(\frac{\sqrt{3}}{8}\right)|0000\rangle - \left(\frac{1}{8}\right)|0001\rangle - \left(\frac{\sqrt{3}}{8}\right)|0010\rangle + \left(\frac{1}{8}\right)|0011\rangle - \left(\frac{3}{8}\right)|0100\rangle + \left(\frac{\sqrt{3}}{8}\right)|0101\rangle$$

$$+ \left(\frac{3}{8}\right)|0110\rangle - \left(\frac{\sqrt{3}}{8}\right)|0111\rangle + \left(\frac{\sqrt{3}}{8}\right)|1000\rangle - \left(\frac{1}{8}\right)|1001\rangle - \left(\frac{\sqrt{3}}{8}\right)|1010\rangle + \left(\frac{1}{8}\right)|1011\rangle$$

$$- \left(\frac{3}{8}\right)|1100\rangle + \left(\frac{\sqrt{3}}{8}\right)|1101\rangle + \left(\frac{3}{8}\right)|1110\rangle - \left(\frac{\sqrt{3}}{8}\right)|1111\rangle \tag{46}$$

Hence, 16 states of the Q-bit individual can be expressed as

$$\underbrace{|0000\rangle}_{4\ qubits}, \underbrace{|0001\rangle}_{4\ qubits}, \underbrace{|0010\rangle}_{4\ qubits}, \cdots, \underbrace{|1111\rangle}_{4\ qubits}$$

with probabilities $\dfrac{3}{64}, \dfrac{1}{64}, \dfrac{3}{64}, \dfrac{1}{64}, \dfrac{9}{64},$

$$\frac{3}{64}, \frac{9}{64}, \frac{3}{64}, \frac{3}{64}, \frac{1}{64}, \frac{3}{64}, \frac{1}{64}, \frac{9}{64}, \frac{3}{64}, \frac{9}{64}, \frac{3}{64},$$

respectively. (Han, 2002; Araujo, 2008). The engrossed readers may well refer to (Han, 2002) for other type of representations.

QUANTUM BASED ALGORITHMS

Quantum Computation has so far passes through advance theoretical studies by different researchers. A few of these studies has been performed by Feynman (Feynman, 1982) and later by Deutsch (Deutsch & Jozsa, 1992), and others. Feynman (Feynman, 1982), in his study, developed a structural framework to design quantum computer. Since the early 1980, after the anticipation of quantum mechanical system, the term, quantum computing has become to be very popular to the researchers of different fields (Benioff, 1982). This machine can be used efficiently in meticulous kind of problems (Grover, 1998).

1. **Neural Network Based Approaches:** Matsui *et al.* (Matsui et al., 2000) developed a Qubit Neuron Model which demonstrates quantum learning capabilities. This model has been used later by Kouda *et al.* (Kouda et al., 2004) on a quantum based multi-layer feed forward neural network in 2004. In the next year, Kouda *et al.* (Kouda et al., 2005) have used this model on non-linear controlling problems in addition to the effect of quantum mechanics (QM). Their experiments proved its learning efficacy of that model. Ezhov (Ezhov, 2001) proposed a variant of quantum model for neural network. The authors designed this model to solve various classification problems. Their proposed model can be defined as an addition to the model which was designed for quantum associative memory. Apart from that the model can utilizes Everett version of quantum mechanics. Few researchers have introduced quantum computation with different applications, for instance, parallel learning, quantum associative memory, and empirical analysis in artificial neural networks (ANN). Some works related to above discussions are presented in (Chrisley,1995; Kak,1995; Menneer, 1995; Behrman,1996). Menneer intensely discussed various applications of quantum theory in conjunction with artificial neural networks in her Ph. D. thesis. She showed that QUANNs are more proficient than ANN in reference to classification (Menneer & Narayanan, 1998). Ventura and Martinez presented another quantum version of associative memory and formed quantum associative memory. They have used the learning manner into quantum version (Ventura, 1998). Weigang also proposed a parallel Self-Organizing Map (SOM) and pointed out the learning manner in quantum computing atmosphere. The author also developed an Entanglement Neural Networks (ENN) using quantum teleportation (Weigang, 1998). Narayanan and Manneer (Narayanan, 2000) introduced a quantum-inspired neural network using the fundamental principles of quantum computing to represent the problem variables. Garis *et al.* (Garis et al., 2003) presented a work on quantum versus evolutionary systems where a distinguished approach was adopted. They used a quantum neural network to determine the fitness values of all individuals in population concurrently. Perus (Perus, 1997; Perus, 1998) used the idea of neuronal-pattern- restoration from memory, which can be described as a similar way as collapsing in wave function. Memory can be judged as a superposition of lots of stored patterns. With the effect of an exterior stimulus trigger, one of them can be put background to forward, or

vice-versa. He has used this concept to present a few motivating papers (Perus, 1997; Perus, 1998). Menneer and Narayanan (Menneer & Narayanan, 1995) used the numerous universes observation from theory of quantum computing to one-layer Artificial Neural Networks. Later, Lagaris *et al.* (Lagaris et al., 1997) proposed ANNs to solve Partial and Ordinary Differential Equations. The time involves for training is much fewer for classification tasks in Quantum Artificial Neural Networks (QUANNs) than in Classical Artificial Neural Networks (CLANNs). Hence, in this respect, the efficiency of QUANNs is better than CLANNs (Menneer & Narayanan, 2000). The reason behind it is that each module network learns only single pattern, which results quick learning of the training set in QUANNs (Menneer & Narayanan, 2000). This idea was also utilized by Perus (Perus & Dey, 2000) and the author presented a paper on Neural Networks as the basis for Quantum Associate Networks (Perus & Dey, 2000) Perus and Dey also presented another paper inspired by the same idea as in (Perus & Dey 2000). Hu (Hu) did his research about quantum computation using neural networks for image processing and pattern recognition and submitted his work in his PhD thesis.

2. **Meta-Heuristic Based Approaches:** A proper coupling between the basic quantum features and the fundamental properties of genetic algorithms has been explored to some extent by Rylander et al. (Rylander et al., 2001). They tried to investigate benefits and shortcomings of quantum approach to the popular evolutionary algorithm called, genetic algorithm, where qubits were the basic ingredients to form the population. Han and Kim (Han & Kim, 2002) proposed a quantum behaved evolutionary algorithm. They have used their proposed algorithm to solve knapsack problem. In addition to the basic quantum features, they have also applied quantum rotation gate for faster convergence. Later, the authors have presented another improved version of quantum inspired algorithm in (Han & Kim, 2004). The authors used a new strategy where the whole evolution stage was done into two dissimilar segments. Instead of using usual quantum gates, they have employed h-epsilon gate with a termination criterion. Zhang and Li (Zhang & Li, 2003) presented a quantum genetic algorithm. They applied a different strategy for optimality. Their proposed work is supposed to work better than the work as presented in (Han & Kim, 2002). Narayan and Moore (Narayan & Moore, 1996) used a modified scheme for quantum crossover to develop a quantum inspired genetic algorithm. Furthermore, a modified genetic algorithm using quantum probability representation was developed by Li and Zhuang (Li & Zhuang, 2002). In this algorithm, they have regulated the crossover and mutation processes to accomplish quantum representation (Li & Zhuang, 2002). Zhang *et al.* (Zhang et al., 2004) developed a popular quantum genetic algorithm and used their proposed work to solve certain kind of applications. Giraldi *et al.* (Giraldi et al., 2004) presented a survey on quantum behaved genetic algorithms, where the authors find few drawbacks of the existing algorithms, later they proposed a number of quantum inspired genetic algorithms for circuit design. Quantum computation has been used in few applications in different areas. Some of the typical examples may include quantum genetic algorithms used for feature selection (Zhang et al., 2004), quantum inspired algorithms for interval and fuzzy uncertainty, handling probabilistic (Martinez et al., 2003) to name a few. Some authors have combined quantum computation with genetic algorithms and developed applications where fitness functions were varied between genetic steps based on the number of outer time-dependent inputs. A few distinctive examples of this category are given in (Weinacht, 2002; Turinici, 2004). These papers include some schemes for quantum control processes. Here, genetic algorithms are employed for optimally shaped fields to force few preferred physical process (Weinacht, 2002; Turinici, 2004). In 2010, Bhattacharyya *et al.* proposed a quantum inspired genetic algorithm (QIGA) for bi-level image thresholding (Bhattacharyya, 2010). Later, Bhattacharyya and

Dey presented another version of QIGA where fuzzy objective function was used for gray level image thresholding (Bhattacharyya, 2011b). Another variant quantum inspired genetic algorithm was proposed in (Dey, 2013c) where a group of thresholding methods have been evaluated as the objective functions. Later, Dey *et al.* (Dey et al., 2014c) proposed a quantum behaved GA and a quantum behaved PSO for bi-level image thresholding. Thus far, different quantum behaved meta-heuristic algorithms have been developed for multi-level image thresholding. Some of them have been presented in (Dey, 2013b, 2014b). Another efficient quantum inspired meta-heuristic algorithms for multi-level image thresholding for colour images have been presented by Dey *et al.* (Dey, 2013a, 2014a). A different quantum based multi-objective particle swarm optimization and ant colony optimization for multi-level image thresholding, has been proposed by Dey *et al.* (Dey et al., 2014e). Dey *et al.* (Dey et al., 2014d) proposed an algorithm regarding quantum behaved automatic clustering technique for image thresholding to find optimal number of clusters.

3. **Other Distinguished Approaches:** Aytekin *et al.* (Aytekin et al., 2013) developed a quantum based automatic object extraction technique where quantum mechanical principles have been used as the basic constituents of the proposed technique. With reference to Artificial Intelligence (AI), some authors have developed many quantum behaved applications on AI. Some of them have been presented in (Hirsh, 1999; Hogg, 1999; Kak, 1999; Ventura, 1999). Hogg (Hogg, 1998) proposed a new framework for structured quantum search. In his proposed framework, he used Grovers algorithm (Grover, 1998) to associate the cost with the activities of quantum gate. Alfares and Esat investigated the usefulness of quantum algorithms in few distinctive engineering optimization problems (Alfares & Esat, 2003). The authors found that several problems may occur in certain algorithms when the characteristics of quantum computing are used. Though, these problems can be kept away by applying certain other algorithms. Later, Hogg (Hogg & Portnov, 2000) proposed extended version of his previous work called, quantum behaved technique on combinatorial optimization. Moore *et al.* (Moore et al., 1995) presented another framework for universal quantum-inspired techniques. Lukac and Perkowski (Lukac & Perkowski, 2002) applied a different approach where they have considered each individual in the population as quantum circuits and used the elements of population for the objective quantum circuit. Two popular quantum algorithm developed so far are Quantum Fourier Transform (QFT) (Shor, 1997), and the Grover Search Algorithm (Grover, 1998). Different problems can be efficiently solved using QFT, for instance, discrete logarithm, factoring and order finding and many others (Nielsen & Chuang, 2000). Another eminent algorithm called, BBHT algorithm (Boyer et al., 1998) (BBHT is short form of the name of authors') used Grover algorithm for its efficient implementation.

Evolution of Quantum Behaved Swarm Intelligent Techniques

Feynman (Feynman, 1982) and Deutsch (Deutsch & Jozsa, 1992) presented their theoretical studies on quantum computing. Rylander et al. (Rylander et al., 2001) used the popular genetic algorithm and basic features of quantum computing together to form a quantum based swarm intelligent technique. The authors tried to overcome the general shortcomings of basic evolutionary algorithms using quantum properties. Narayan and Moore (Narayan & Moore, 1996) presented a research work on quantum inspired genetic algorithm where the authors applied a modified idea for quantum crossover. In addition, Li and Zhuang (Li & Zhuang, 2002) presented a modified genetic algorithm where the authors have used quantum probability representation scheme. In 2002, Han and Kim (Han & Kim, 2002) developed a quantum inspired evolutionary algorithm to solve knapsack problem. Zhang and Li (Zhang & Li, 2003) developed another quantum inspired genetic algorithm where, the authors have applied dissimilar optimal strategies. Zhang *et al.* (Zhang et al., 2004) presented a quantum based genetic algorithm to solve some different kind of applications. Giraldi *et al.* (Giraldi et al., 2004) proposed several quanta behaved genetic algorithms for circuit design. Another quantum inspired algorithms are exemplified as quantum inspired algorithms for interval and fuzzy uncertainty, handling probabilistic (Martinez et al., 2003), quantum genetic algorithms for feature selection (Zhang et al., 2004). The basic quantum features and genetic algorithm have been combined in the form of algorithm by a group of authors where the fitness functions have been used in a different fashion. The fitness functions have been changed between genetic steps based on several outer time-dependent inputs. Few typical examples of this class have been presented in (Weinacht, 2002; Turinici, 2004). Bhattacharyya *et al.* developed a quantum inspired genetic algorithm (QIGA) for image thresholding (Bhattacharyya, 2010). This algorithm uses correlation coefficient as the fitness function to find optimized threshold values. Another quantum inspired genetic algorithm was introduced by Bhattacharyya and Dey. The authors used fuzzy objective function for gray level image thresholding (Bhattacharyya, 2011b). Later, a different version of quantum inspired genetic algorithm was proposed in (Dey et al., 2013c) where a number of thresholding methods have been used as objective functions. Dey *et al.* (Dey et al., 2014c) proposed a quantum inspired GA and a quantum inspired PSO for bi-level image thresholding. In the perspective of quantum inspired multi-level image thresholding, several algorithms have been presented in (Dey, 2013b,2014 b). Dey *et al.* developed two quantum inspired meta-heuristic algorithms for multi-level image thresholding for colour images (Dey, 2013a,2014 a).

Some sample results of Quantum Inspired Meta-heuristic Algorithms for Image Thresholding are shown in Table 1, Table 2, Table 3, Table 4, Table 5, Table 6 and Table 7. Few distinguished examples of sample figures of the above mentioned algorithms are presented in Figure 1, Figure 2, Figure 3, Figure 4 and Figure 5, respectively.

Comparison among the Different Techniques

Neural Network Based Approaches have some characteristics as described below.

1. This approach can be applied to solve several problems devoid of uncovering and describing the process of such problem solving.
2. The author is unaware about building necessary algorithms for the problem domain.
3. Also, the programs need not be developed separately.
4. The results from similar kind of problems are banked. The neural network is used to learn these results of the problems that were solved before. Thereafter, the other comparables problems are invoked to solve in this approach.
5. This approach can be adopted efficiently.
6. Neural networks can be appreciated as dedicated hardware systems. It is very common to use neural networks as software simulation. It uses learning, exploiting, and other procedure to solve. Some dedicated neural networks are available now a day, which can be utilized for parallel processing to have the faster solutions.
7. A group of behaviors used in this approach may include learning, feature extraction, optimization, categorization, association, noise immunity and generalization.
8. In some cases, it may be very harder for neural nets to be trained.

Table 1. The optimum threshold value (θ) and fitness value (σ) (Bhattacharyya, 2010)

Sl. No.	Lena		Peppers	
	θ	σ	θ	σ
1	119	0.832016	132	0.851033
2	119	0.832016	131	0.851015
3	118	0.831948	132	0.851033
4	119	0.832016	132	0.851033
5	116	0.831401	132	0.851033
6	117	0.831752	131	0.851015
7	119	0.832016	134	0.850795
8	118	0.831948	132	0.851033
9	119	0.832016	127	0.849943
10	119	0.832016	132	0.851033

Table 2. Comparative performance analysis of QIGA and GA (Bhattacharyya, 2011b)

Image	QIGA			GA		
	v_c	N	T	v_c	N	T
Lena	0.722982	40	2554.4	0.722982	3500	6559.0
Peppers	0.675204	43	2666.4	0.675204	3500	6384.0

Meta-Heuristic Based Approaches draw the following characteristics as described below.

1. Meta- heuristics are generation-based approach. In every generation, they explore the search space for better solution.
2. As compared to other approaches, these can reach relatively speedy towards awfully good solutions.
3. These approaches are efficiently applied for large intricate problems.
4. Stuck into local optima is most common problem. Meta-heuristics can be used successfully to overcome these sorts of situations.
5. Unlike neural network based approaches, some intelligent can be applied in this kind of problems to have quicker convergence and better results.
6. Meta-heuristics are very common and popular in solving combinatorial optimization problems.
7. This approach does not guarantee to have always the best feasible solution of a given problem.

Other Distinguished Approaches have the following characteristics.

Table 3. Optimum results of QIGA, GA (Holland, 1975; Reeves, 1993), QIPSO and PSO (Kennedy & Eberhart, 1995) for three gray scale images Lena, Peppers and Woman using coefficient (Dey et al., 2014 c)

	Lena						Peppers					
TN	QIGA			GA								
	θ_{op}	v_{op}	T	θ_{op}	v_{op}	T	θ_{op}	v_{op}	t	θ_{op}	v_{op}	t
1	*119*	0.830751	343	*119*	0.830751	*4652*	131	0.850624	*343*	131	0.850624	*4448*
$\sigma(v)$	0			0.025			0			0.012		
$\sigma(t)$	4.32			29.30			3.84			25.24		
TN	QIPSO			PSO			QIPSO			PSO		
	θ_{op}	v_{op}	T	θ_{op}	v_{op}	T	θ_{op}	v_{op}	t	θ_{op}	v_{op}	t
1	*119*	0.830751	325	*119*	0.830751	*3342*	131	0.850624	*330*	131	0.850624	*3124*
$\sigma(v)$	0			0.006			0			0.001		
$\sigma(t)$	3.67			27.20			3.73			28.38		
	Woman											
TN	QIGA			GA								
	θ_{op}	v_{op}	T	θ_{op}	v_{op}	T						
1	*123*	0.856899	342	*123*	0.856899	*4685*						
$\sigma(v)$	0			0.016								
$\sigma(t)$	3.91			26.34								
TN	QIPSO			PSO								
	θ_{op}	v_{op}	T	θ_{op}	v_{op}	T						
1	*123*	0.856899	328	*123*	0.856899	*3063*						
$\sigma(\nu)$	0			0.002								
$\sigma(t)$	3.97			26.38								

Table 4. Best results of QIGA, QIPSO, QIDE, QIACO, QISA and QITS for Multi-level Thresholding for Lena (Dey et al., 2014 b)

	Lena								
K	QIGA			QIPSO			QIDE		
	θ	U_{best}	t	θ	U_{best}	t	θ	U_{best}	t
2	118	1424.30	4.48	118	1424.30	0.02	118	1424.30	4.12
3	99,157	1763.29	10.47	99,157	1763.29	2.13	99,157	1763.29	10.39
4	84,127,169	1913.75	17.12	84,126,169	1913.79	3.32	83,125,168	1913.74	2.70
5	80,116,146,180	1970.44	23.10	79,115,146,180	1970.47	4.46	79,115,146,180	1970.47	21.20
K	QIACO			QISA			QITS		
	θ	U_{best}	t	θ	U_{best}	t	θ	U_{best}	t
2	118	1424.30	4.41	118	1424.30	6.30	118	1424.30	6.18
3	99,157	1763.29	13.07	99,157	1763.29	15.50	99,157	1763.29	16.41
4	84,127,169	1913.75	18.38	85,125,170	1912.85	45.19	84,128,168	1913.14	42.00
5	80,116,145,180	1970.31	23.24	81,118,147,179	1969.87	56.14	81,120,147,182	1968.91	53.29

Table 5. Best result of QITSMLTCI and TS for multi-level thresholding for Tulips(Dey et al., 2014a)

	Tulips		
	QITSMLTCI		
D	$\left(\theta_r\right)\left(\theta_b\right)\left(\theta_g\right)$	γ_B	t
2	(139) (125) (116)	10909.76	01.14
4	(56,124,195) (69,120,175) (61,116,181)	12792.40	13.22
6	(38,63,105,154,210) (57,97,130,163,203) (47,85,120,154,199)	13119.14	16.41
	TS		
D	$\left(\theta_r\right)\left(\theta_b\right)\left(\theta_g\right)$	γ_B	t
2	(139) (125) (116)	10909.76	01.35
4	(57,122,199) (70,121,172) (62,113,176)	12791.73	22.12
6	(48,68,108,173,211) (61,95,130,164,200) (49,79,119,159,204)	13116.47	35.42

To review different quantum based techniques, a strategy is followed. The neural network based techniques are grouped into one category. Some techniques uses meta-heuristic based approaches. They are classified into second class. The remaining techniques are grouped into third category. In this group, different techniques are fitted in. For instance, artificial intelligence, a soft computing based approach,

Table 6. Best result of QITSMLTCI and TS for multi-level thresholding for Barche (Dey et al., 2014a)

Barche			
QITSMLTCI			
D	$\left(\theta_r\right)\left(\theta_b\right)\left(\theta_g\right)$	γ_B	t
2	(106) (99) (92)	5949.75	01.03
4	(74,127,169) (54,105,150) (47,91,134)	7258.03	11.14
6	(64,107,142,164,187) (46,81,122,151,179) (46,78,104,133,152)	7472.60	15.19
TS			
D	$\left(\theta_r\right)\left(\theta_b\right)\left(\theta_g\right)$	γ_B	t
2	(106) (99) (92)	5949.75	01.15
4	(74,127,169) (55,110,150) (44,92,133)	7257.34	25.14
6	(61,106,141,172,193) (43,86,128,154,184) (42,77,101,131,153)	7470.81	37.20

Table 7. Five representative favorable results of the test images for QIAGA and CAGA (Dey et al., 2014 d)

QIAGA											
Lena			Peppers			Barbara			Jet		
SN	nc	CS(nc)	SN	nc	CS(nc)	SN	nc	CS(nc)	SN	nc	CS(nc)
1	9	0.2552	1	7	0.2368	1	8	0.3188	1	8	0.2244
2	8	0.2695	2	7	0.3760	2	9	0.3444	2	8	0.3055
3	7	0.2697	3	8	0.3488	3	9	0.3510	3	6	0.3140
4	8	0.3533	4	8	0.3857	4	6	0.4667	4	9	0.3330
5	7	0.3657	5	7	0.4547	5	6	0.4742	5	7	0.4403
CAGA											
Lena			Peppers			Barbara			Jet		
SN	nc	CS(nc)	SN	nc	CS(nc)	SN	nc	CS(nc)	SN	nc	CS(nc)
1	9	0.2413	1	9	0.3222	1	9	0.2516	1	7	0.3440
2	8	0.2812	2	7	0.4101	2	8	0.2703	2	8	0.3525
3	9	0.3495	3	7	0.4330	3	7	0.3842	3	10	0.4005
4	8	0.3978	4	8	0.4966	4	9	0.4496	4	6	0.5042
5	9	0.4133	5	7	0.5498	5	7	0.5019	5	8	0.5162

has been used to build a number of quantum inspired technique. The performance varies according to the approaches it adapt for constructing such quantum based techniques.

Figure 1. (a) Thresholded image for Lena for θ =118 (b) Thresholded image for Peppers for θ =132 (Bhattacharyya, 2010)

Figure 2. (a) Thresholded image for Lena for θ =128 (b) Thresholded image for Peppers for θ =128 (Dey et al., 2014 c)

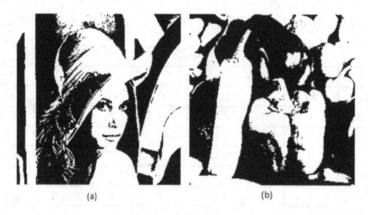

Figure 3. (a) Thresholded image of Lena for θ_op =119 (b) Thresholded image for Peppers for θ_op =131 (c) Thresholded image for Woman for θ_op =123 after using correlation coefficient (Dey et al., 2014b)

Figure 4. (a) Original image; for K = 2, 3, 4, 5, (b)-(e), for Lena, after using QIPSO for multi-level thresholding (Dey et al., 2014a)

Figure 5. Test image after thresholding for D = 2, 4, 6 in (a), (c), (e) for Tulips and, (b), (d), (f) for Barche, respectively, after exercising QITSMLTCI for multi-level thresholding

CONCLUSION

In this chapter, a detailed survey of different quantum behaved techniques is presented. The techniques proposed by a number of researchers are grouped into different category according to the approaches used. The techniques belonging to the first category, uses the properties of quantum computing on neural networks. Popular meta-heuristic algorithms like, genetic algorithms, particle swarm optimization, simulated annealing, tabu search are coupled with the features of quantum computing to form different quantum behaved techniques. This type of algorithms is categorized in to the second category and finally, the rest techniques are suitable for third group. The review finds the benefits and deficiencies of the technique belonging to the different categories.

REFERENCES

Alfares, F., & Esat, I. I. (2003). Quantum algorithms; how useful for engineering problems. In *Proc. of the Seventh World Conference on Integrated Design and Process Technology*. Austin, TX: Academic Press.

Araujo, T., Nedjah, N., & Mourelle, L. (2008). Quantum-inspired evolutionary state assignment for synchronous finite state machines. *Journal of Universal Computer Science, 14*(15), 2532–2548.

Arkin, R. (1998). *Behavior-based robotics*. Cambridge, MA: MIT Press.

Aytekin, C., Kiranyaz, S., & Gabbouj, M. (2013). Quantum mechanics in computer vision: Automatic object extraction. In *Proc. ICIP 2013* (pp. 2489–2493). Academic Press. doi:10.1109/ICIP.2013.6738513

Bandyopadhyay, S., Maulik, U., & Mukhopadhyay, A. (2007). Multiobjective genetic clustering for pixel classification in remote sensing imagery. *IEEE Transactions on Geoscience and Remote Sensing, 45*(5), 1506–1511. doi:10.1109/TGRS.2007.892604

Behrman, E. C., Niemel, J., Steck, J. E., & Skinner, S. R. (1996). A quantum dot neural network. *IEEE Transactions on Neural Networks*.

Beni, G., & Wang, J. (1989). Swarm intelligence in cellular robotic systems. In *Proceeding of NATO Advanced Workshop on Robots and Biological System*. Academic Press.

Benioff, P. (1982). Quantum mechanical models of turing machines that dissipate no energy. *Physical Review Letters, 48*(23), 1581–1585. doi:10.1103/PhysRevLett.48.1581

Bhattacharyya, S. (2011a). A brief survey of color image preprocessing and segmentation techniques. *Journal of Pattern Recognition Research, 1*(1), 120–129. doi:10.13176/11.191

Bhattacharyya, S., & Dey, S. (2011b). An efficient quantum inspired genetic algorithm (QIGA) with a chaotic map model based interference and fuzzy objective function for gray level image thresholding. In *Proceedings of International Conference on Computational Intelligence and Communication Networks (CICN 2011)*. Academic Press. doi:10.1109/CICN.2011.24

Bhattacharyya, S., Dutta, P., Chakraborty, S., Chakraborty, R., & Dey, S. (2010). Determination of optimal threshold of a gray-level image using a quantum inspired genetic algorithm with interference based on a random map model. In *Proceedings of 2010 IEEE International Conference on Computational Intelligence and Computing Research (ICCIC 2010)*. IEEE. doi:10.1109/ICCIC.2010.5705806

Blum, C. & Roli, A. (n.d.). *Metaheuristic in combinatorial optimization: Overview and conceptual comparison*. IRIDIA: Technical Report, 2001-13.

Bonabeau, E., Dorigo, M., & Theraulaz, G. (1999). *Swarm intelligence: From natural to artificial systems*. Oxford Univ. Press.

Boyer, M., Brassard, G., Høyer, P., & Tapp, A. (1998). Tight bounds on quantum searching. *Fortschritte der Physik, 4*(5), 493–505. doi:10.1002/(SICI)1521-3978(199806)46:4/5<493::AID-PROP493>3.0.CO;2-P

Brink, A. D., & Pendock, N. E. (1996). Minimum cross entropy threshold selection. *Pattern Recognition, 29*(1), 179–188. doi:10.1016/0031-3203(95)00066-6

Cheng, H. D., & Chen, Y. H. (1999). Fuzzy partition of two-dimensional histogram and its application to thresholding. *Pattern Recognition*, *32*(5), 825–843. doi:10.1016/S0031-3203(98)00080-6

Chong, E. K. P., & Zak, S. (2001). *An H., introduction to optimization* (2nd ed.). New York: John Wiley & Sons.

Chrisley, R. (1995). Quantum learning. In *Proceedings of the International Symposium, Saariselka*. Lapland, Finland: Finnish Association of Artificial Intelligence.

De Garis, H., Gaur, A., & Sriram, R. (2003). Quantum versus evolutionary systems: Total versus sampled search. In *Proceedings of 5th. Int. Conf. on Evolvable Systems (ICES)*. Academic Press.

Deb, K., Pratap, A., Agarwal, S., & Meyarivan, T. (2002). A fast and elitist multiobjective genetic algorithm: Nsga-II. *IEEE Transactions on Evolutionary Computation*, *6*(2), 182–197. doi:10.1109/4235.996017

Deutsch, D., & Jozsa, R. (1992). Rapid solution of problems by quantum computation. *Royal Society of London Proceedings Series*, *439*(1907), 553–558.

Dey, S., Bhattacharyya, S., & Maulik, U. (2013a). Quantum inspired meta-heuristic algorithms for multi-level thresholding for true colour images. In *Proceedings of IEEE Indicon 2013*. IEEE.

Dey, S., Bhattacharyya, S., & Maulik, U. (2013c). Chaotic map model based interference employed in quantum inspired genetic algorithm to determine the optimum gray level image thresholding. *Global Trends in Intelligent Computing Research and Development*, 68-110.

Dey, S., Bhattacharyya, S., & Maulik, U. (2014a). New quantum inspired tabu search for multi-level colour image thresholding. In *Proceedings of 8th International Conference on Computing for Sustainable Global Development (INDIACom-2014)*. Academic Press.

Dey, S., Bhattacharyya, S., & Maulik, U. (2014c). Quantum inspired genetic algorithm and particle swarm optimization using chaotic map model based interference for gray level image thresholding. *Swarm and Evolutionary Computation*, *15*, 38–57. doi:10.1016/j.swevo.2013.11.002

Dey, S., Bhattacharyya, S., & Maulik, U. (2014d). Quantum inspired automatic clustering for multi-level image thresholding. In *Proceedings of International Conference on Computational Intelligence and Communication Networks (ICCICN 2014)*. Academic Press.

Dey, S., Bhattacharyya, S., & Maulik, U. (2014e). Quantum behaved multi-objective PSO and ACO optimization for multi-level thresholding. In *Proceedings of International Conference on Computational Intelligence and Communication Networks (ICCICN 2014)*. Academic Press.

Dey, S., Saha, I., Maulik, U., & Bhattacharyya, S. (2013b). New quantum inspired meta-heuristic methods for multi-level thresholding. In *Proceedings of 2013 International Conference on Advances in Computing, Communications and Informatics (ICACCI)*. Academic Press.

Dey, S., Saha, I., Maulik, U., & Bhattacharyya, S. (2014b). Multi-level thresholding using quantum inspired meta-heuristics. *Knowledge-Based Systems*, *67*, 373–400. doi:10.1016/j.knosys.2014.04.006

Dorigo, M., Maniezzo, V., & Colorni, A. (1996). The ant system: Optimization by a colony of cooperating agents. *IEEE Transactions on Systems, Man, and Cybernetics. Part B, Cybernetics, 26*(1), 29–41. doi:10.1109/3477.484436 PMID:18263004

Ezhov, A. A. (2001). Pattern recognition with quantum neural networks. In Proceedings of Advances in Pattern Recognition ICAPR 2001. Springer Berlin Heidelberg.

Feynman, R. (1982). Simulating physics with computers. *International Journal of Theoretical Physics, 21*(6-7), 467–488. doi:10.1007/BF02650179

Flake, G. (1999). *The computational beauty of nature*. Cambridge, MA: MIT Press.

Freixenet, J., Muñoz, X., & Raba, D. (2002). Yet another survey on image segmentation: Region and boundary information integration. In *Proceedings of the 7th European Conference on Computer Vision (ECCV '02)*. Academic Press. doi:10.1007/3-540-47977-5_27

Giraldi, G. A., Portugal, R., & Thess, R. N. (2004). *Genetic algorithms and quantum computation*. Available: http://www.arxiv.org/pdf/cs.NE/0403003

Glover, F. (1989). Tabu search, part I. *ORSA Journal on Computing, 1*, 190–206.

Glover, F. (1990). Tabu search, part II. *ORSA Journal on Computing, 2*(1), 4–32. doi:10.1287/ijoc.2.1.4

Glover, F. & Kochenberger. (2003). *Handbook on metaheuristics*. Kluwer Academic Publishers.

Gonzalez, R. C., & Woods, R. E. (2002). *Digital image processing*. Prentice Hall.

Grover, L. K. (1998). Quantum computers can search rapidly by using almost any transformation. *Physical Review Letters, 80*(19), 4329–4332. doi:10.1103/PhysRevLett.80.4329

Hammouche, K., Diaf, M., & Siarry, P. (2008). A multilevel automatic thresholding method based on a genetic algorithm for a fast image segmentation. *Computer Vision and Image Understanding, 109*(2), 163–175. doi:10.1016/j.cviu.2007.09.001

Han, K. H., & Kim, J. H. (2002). Quantum-inspired evolutionary algorithm for a class combinational optimization. *IEEE Transactions on Evolutionary Computation, 6*(6), 580–593. doi:10.1109/TEVC.2002.804320

Han, K. H., & Kim, J. H. (2004). Quantum-inspired evolutionary algorithms with a new termination criterion, h-epsilon gate, and twophase scheme. *IEEE Transactions on Evolutionary Computation, 8*(2), 156–169. doi:10.1109/TEVC.2004.823467

Hey, T. (1999). Quantum computing: An introduction. Computing & Control Engineering, 10, 105–112.

Hirsh, H. (1999). A quantum leap for AI. *IEEE Intelligent Systems*, 9.

Hogg, T. (1998). Highly structured searches with quantum computers. *Physical Review Letters, 80*(11), 2473–2476. doi:10.1103/PhysRevLett.80.2473

Hogg, T. (1999). Quantum Search Heuristics. *IEEE Intelligent Systems*, 12–14.

Hogg, T., & Portnov, D. A. (2000). Quantum optimization. *Information Sciences, 128*(3-4), 181–197. doi:10.1016/S0020-0255(00)00052-9

Holland, J. H. (1975). *Adaptation in natural and artificial systems*. Ann Arbor, MI: Univ. Michigan Press.

Horn, J., Nafpliotis, N., & Nafpliotis, D. E. (1994). A niched pareto genetic algorithm for multiobjective optimization. In *Proc. of the First IEEE Conference on Evolutionary Computation, IEEE World Congress on Computational Intelligence*. IEEE.

Hu, Z. Z. (n.d.). *Quantum computation via neural networks applied to image processing and pattern recognition*. (PhD thesis). University of Western Sydney, Sydney, Australia.

Huang, L., & Wang, G. M. (1995). Image thresholding by minimizing the measures of fuzziness. *Pattern Recognition, 28*(1), 41–51. doi:10.1016/0031-3203(94)E0043-K

Jahne, B. (1993). *Digital image processing* (2nd ed.). New York: Springer-Verlag. doi:10.1007/978-3-662-21817-4

Jain, K. (1989). *Fundamentals of digital image processing*. Upper Saddle River, NJ: Prentice-Hall.

Johannsen, G., & Bille, J. (1982). A threshold selection method using information measures. *ICPR, 82*, 140–143.

Kak, S. (1995). Quantum neural computing. *Advances in Imaging and Electron Physics, 94*, 259–313. doi:10.1016/S1076-5670(08)70147-2

Kak, S. (1999). Quantum computing and AI. *IEEE Intelligent Systems*, 9–11.

Kapur, J. N., Sahoo, P. K., & Wong, A. K. C. (1985). A new method for gray-level picture thresholding using the entropy of the histogram. *Graphical Models and Image Processing, 29*(3), 273–285. doi:10.1016/0734-189X(85)90125-2

Kennedy, K., & Eberhart, R. (1995). Particle swarm optimization. In *Proc. of IEEE International Conference on Neural Networks (ICNN95)*. IEEE.

Kirkpatrik, S., Gelatt, C. D., & Vecchi, M. P. (1983). Optimization by simulated annealing. *Science, 220*(4598), 671–680. doi:10.1126/science.220.4598.671 PMID:17813860

Kouda, N., Matsui, N., & Nishimura, H. (2004). A multilayered feedforward network based on qubit neuron model. *Systems and Computers in Japan, 35*(13), 43–51. doi:10.1002/scj.10342

Kouda, N., Matsui, N., Nishimura, H., & Peper, F. (2005). An examination of qubit neural network in controlling an inverted pendulum. *Neural Processing Letters, 22*(3), 277–290. doi:10.1007/s11063-005-8337-2

Lagaris, I. E., Likas, A., & Fotiadis, D. I. (1997). Artificial neural network methods in quantum mechanics. *Computer Physics Communications, 104*(1-3), 1–14. doi:10.1016/S0010-4655(97)00054-4

Li, B., & Zhuang, Z. Q. (2002). Genetic algorithm based-on the quantum probability representation. *Lecture Notes in Computer Science, 2412*, 500–505.

Lucchese, L., & Mitra, S. K. (2001). Color image segmentation: A state-of-art survey. *Proceedings of the Indian National Science Academy, 67-A*, 207–221.

Lukac, M., & Perkowski, M. (2002). Evolving quantum circuits using genetic algorithm. In *Proceedings of the NASA/DOD Conference on Evolvable Hardware*. IEEE.

Martinez, M., Longpre, L., Kreinovich, V., Starks, S. A., & Nguyen, H. T. (2003). Fast quantum algorithms for handling probabilistic, interval, and fuzzy uncertainty. In *Proceedings of Fuzzy Information Processing Society, 2003. NAFIPS 2003.22nd International Conference of the North American* (pp. 395–400). Academic Press.

Matsui, N., Takai, M., & Nishimura, H. (2000). A network model based on qubit-like neuron corresponding to quantum circuit. *The Institute of Electronics Information and Communications in Japan (Part III: Fundamental Electronic Science), 83*(10), 67–73.

Mcmohan, D. (2008). *Quantum computing explained*. Hoboken, NJ: John Wiley & Sons, Inc.

Menneer, T. (1998). *Quantum artificial neural networks*. (Ph. D. thesis). The University of Exeter, Exeter, UK.

Menneer, T., & Narayanan, A. (1995). *Quantum-inspired neural networks, technical report R329*. Exeter, UK: Department of Computer Science, University of Exeter.

Menneer, T., & Narayanan, A. (2000). Quantum artificial neural networks vs classical artificial neural networks: Experiments in simulation. In *Proceedings of the IEEE Fourth International Conference on Computational Intelligence and Neuroscience* (pp. 757-759). IEEE.

Moore, M. P., & Narayanan, A. (1995). *Quantum-inspired computing*. Exeter, UK: Department of Computer Science, Old Library, University of Exeter.

Narayanan, A., & Manneer, T. (2000). Quantum artificial neural network architectures and components. *Information Sciences, 128*(3-4), 231–255. doi:10.1016/S0020-0255(00)00055-4

Narayanan, A., & Moore, M. (1996). Quantum inspired genetic algorithm. In *Proc. of the IEEE Conference on Evolutionary Computation (ICEC'96)* (pp. 61–66). IEEE. doi:10.1109/ICEC.1996.542334

Niblack, W. (1986). *An introduction to image processing*. Englewood Cliffs, NJ: Prentice-Hall.

Nielsen, M. A., & Chuang, I. L. (2000). *Quantum computation and quantum information*. Cambridge, UK: Cambridge Univ. Press.

Nocedal, J., & Wright, S. J. (1999). Numerical optimization. Springer.

Otsu, N. (1979). A threshold selection method from gray level histograms. *IEEE Transactions on Systems, Man, and Cybernetics, SMC-9*, 62–66.

Pachter, M., & Chandler, P. (1998). Challenges of autonomous control. *IEEE Control Systems Magazine, 18*(4), 92–97. doi:10.1109/37.710883

Perus, M. (1997). Mind: Neural computing plus quantum consciousness. In Mind versus computer. IOS Press.

Perus, M. (1998). Common mathematical foundations of neural and quantum informatics. *Zeitschrift für Angewandte Mathematik und Mechanik, 78*(1), 23–26.

Perus, M. (2000). Neural networks as a basis for quantum associate networks. *Neural Network World, 10*(6), 1001–1013.

Perus, M., & Dey, S. K. (2000). Quantum system can realize content addressable associative memory. *Applied Mathematics Letters, 13*(8), 31–36. doi:10.1016/S0893-9659(00)00092-6

Pun, T. (1980). A new method for gray-level picture threshold using the entropy of the histogram. *Signal Processing, 2*(3), 223–237. doi:10.1016/0165-1684(80)90020-1

Ramesh, N., Yoo, J. H., & Sethi, I. K. (1995). Thresholding based on histogram approximation. *IEE Proceedings. Vision Image and Signal Processing, 142*(5), 271–279. doi:10.1049/ip-vis:19952007

Rao, S. S. (1996). *Engineering optimization - Theory and practice*. New York: John Wiley & Sons.

Reeves, C. R. (1993). Using genetic algorithms with small populations. In *Proc. of the Fifth International Conference on Genetic Algorithms*. Morgan Kaufmann.

Rylander, B., Soule, T., Foster, J., & Alves-Foss, J. (2001). Quantum evolutionary programming. In *Proceedings of the Genetic and Evolutionary Computation Conference (GECCO-2001)*. Morgan Kaufmann.

Sahoo, P., Wilkins, C., & Yeager, J. (1997). Threshold selection using Renyi's entropy. *Pattern Recognition, 30*(1), 71–84. doi:10.1016/S0031-3203(96)00065-9

Sezgin, M., & Sankur, B. (2004). Survey over image thresholding techniques and quantitative performance evaluation. *Journal of Electronic Imaging, 13*(1), 146–165. doi:10.1117/1.1631315

Shaw, E. (1962). The schooling of fishes. *Scientific American, 206*(6), 128–138. doi:10.1038/scientificamerican0662-128 PMID:14458553

Shor, P. W. (1997). Polynomial-time algorithms for prime factorization and discrete logarithms on a quantum computer. *SIAM Journal on Computing, 26*(5), 1484–1509. doi:10.1137/S0097539795293172

Silva, J., Lins, R., & Rocha, V., Jr. (2006). Binarizing and filtering historical documents with back-to-front interference. In *Proceedings of SAC ACM Symposium on Applied Computing*. New York: ACM Press.

Spall, J. C. (2003). *Introduction to stochastic search and optimization, estimation, simulation and control*. Wiley. doi:10.1002/0471722138

Srinivas, N., & Deb, K. (1994). Multiobjective optimization using nondominated sorting in genetic algorithms. *Evolutionary Computation Journal, 2*(3), 221–248. doi:10.1162/evco.1994.2.3.221

Storn, R., & Price, K. (1995). *Differential evolution-a simple and efficient heuristic for global optimization over continuous spaces*. Technical Report TR-95-012. ICSI.

Tizhoosh, H. (2005). Image thresholding using type II fuzzy sets. *Pattern Recognition, 38*(12), 2363–2372. doi:10.1016/j.patcog.2005.02.014

Tsai, D. M. (1995). A fast thresholding selection procedure for multimodal and unimodal histograms. *Pattern Recognition Letters, 16*(6), 653–666. doi:10.1016/0167-8655(95)80011-H

Turinici, G., Le Bris, C., & Rabitz, H. (2004). Efficient algorithms for the laboratory discovery of optimal quantum controls. *Physical Review E: Statistical, Nonlinear, and Soft Matter Physics*, *40*(016704). PMID:15324201

Ventura, D. (1999). Quantum computational intelligence: Answers and questions. *IEEE Intelligent Systems*, 14–16.

Ventura, D., & Martinez, T. (1997). An artificial neuron with quantum mechanical properties. In *Proc. Intl. Conf. Artificial Neural Networks and Genetic Algorithms* (pp. 482–485). Academic Press.

Ventura, D., & Martinez, T. (1998). Quantum associative memory. *IEEE Transactions on Neural Networks*.

Weigang, L. (1998). *A study of parallel self-organizing map*. Retrieved from http://xxx.lanl.gov/quant-ph/9808025

Weinacht, T. C., & Bucksbaum, P. H. (2002). Using feedback for coherent control of quantum systems. *Journal of Optics B*, R35–R52.

Wu, L. U., Songde, M. A., & Hanqing, L. U. (1998). An effective entropic thresholding for ultrasonic imaging. In *Proceedings of ICPR'98: Intl. Conf. Patt. Recog.* (pp. 1522–1524). Academic Press.

Yen, J., Chang, F., & Chang, S. (1995). A new criterion for automatic multilevel thresholding. *IEEE Transactions on Image Processing*, *4*(3), 370–378. doi:10.1109/83.366472 PMID:18289986

Zhang, G., Hu, L., & Jin, W. (2004). Resemblance coefficient and a quantum genetic algorithm for feature selection. Lecture Notes in Computer Science, 3245, 155–168.

Zhang, G. X., Li, W. D. J. N., & Hu, L. Z. (2004). A novel quantum genetic algorithm and its application. *Tien Tzu Hsueh Pao*, *32*(3), 476–479.

Zhang, W. J. G., & Li, N. (2003). An improved quantum genetic algorithm and its application. *Lecture Notes in Artificial Intelligence*, *2639*, 449–452.

ADDITIONAL READING

Araujo, T., Nedjah, N., & Mourelle, L. (2008). Quantum-Inspired Evolutionary State Assignment for Synchronous Finite State Machines. *Journal of Universal Computer Science*, *14*(15), 2532–2548.

Aytekin, C., Kiranyaz, S., & Gabbouj, M. (2013). Quantum Mechanics in Computer Vision: Automatic Object Extraction, *Proc. ICIP 2013*, 2489–2493. doi:10.1109/ICIP.2013.6738513

Bandyopadhyay, S., Maulik, U., & Mukhopadhyay, A. (2007). Multiobjective Genetic Clustering for Pixel Classification in Remote Sensing Imagery. *IEEE Transactions on Geoscience and Remote Sensing*, *45*(5), 1506–1511. doi:10.1109/TGRS.2007.892604

Bhattacharyya, S., & Dey, S. (2011a). An Efficient Quantum Inspired Genetic Algorithm (QIGA) with a Chaotic Map Model Based Interference and Fuzzy Objective Function for Gray Level Image Thresholding" in *Proceedings of International Conference on Computational Intelligence and Communication Networks (CICN 2011), 121-125, Gwalior, India.* doi:10.1109/CICN.2011.24

Bhattacharyya, S., Dutta, P., Chakraborty, S., Chakraborty, R., & Dey, S. (2010). Determination of Optimal Threshold of a Gray-level Image Using a Quantum Inspired Genetic Algorithm with Interference Based on a Random Map *Model, in Proceedings of 2010 IEEE International Conference on Computational Intelligence and Computing Research (ICCIC 2010), 422-425, Coimbatore, India.* doi:10.1109/ICCIC.2010.5705806

Chrisley, R. (1995). Quantum learning, (eds. P. Pylkknen and P. Pylkk) New directions in cognitive science, *Proceedings of the international symposium, Saariselka*, Lapland, Finland, Helsinki. Finnish Association of Artificial Intelligence, 77–89.

Dey, S., Bhattacharyya, S., & Maulik, U. (2013a). Quantum Inspired Meta-heuristic Algorithms for Multi-level Thresholding for True Colour Images *in Proceedings of IEEE Indicon 2013, Mumbai, India, 12/2013.*

Dey, S., Bhattacharyya, S. & Maulik, U. (2013c). eds. B. K. Tripathy and D. P. Acharjya) Chaotic Map Model based Interference Employed in Quantum Inspired Genetic Algorithm to Determine the Optimum Gray Level Image Thresholding, *Global Trends in Intelligent Computing Research and Development*, 68-110.

Dey, S., Bhattacharyya, S., & Maulik, U. (2014a). New Quantum Inspired Tabu Search for Multi-level Colour Image Thresholding, *in Proceedings of 8th International Conference On Computing for Sustainable Global Development (INDIACom-2014), BVICAM, New Delhi*, 311–316.

Dey, S., Bhattacharyya, S., & Maulik, U. (2014c). Quantum inspired genetic algorithm and particle swarm optimization using chaotic map model based interference for gray level image thresholding. *Swarm and Evolutionary Computation, 15*, 38–57. doi:10.1016/j.swevo.2013.11.002

Dey, S., Saha, I., Maulik, U., & Bhattacharyya, S. (2013b). New Quantum Inspired Meta-heuristic Methods for Multi-level Thresholding, *in Proceedings of 2013 International Conference on Advances in Computing, Communications and Informatics (ICACCI), 1236-1240, 22-25 Aug., Mysore, 08/2013.*

Dey, S., Saha, I., Maulik, U., & Bhattacharyya, S. (2014b). Multi-level Thresholding using Quantum Inspired Meta-heuristics. *Knowledge-Based Systems, 67*, 373–400. doi:10.1016/j.knosys.2014.04.006

Huang, L., & Wang, G. M. (1995). Image thresholding by minimizing the measures of fuzziness. *Pattern Recognition, 28*(1), 41–51. doi:10.1016/0031-3203(94)E0043-K

Jahne, B. (1993). *Digital Image Processing* (2nd ed.). New York: Springer-Verlag. doi:10.1007/978-3-662-21817-4

Jain, K. (1989). *Fundamentals of Digital Image Processing*. Upper Saddle River, NJ: Prentice-Hall.

Menneer, T., & Narayanan, A. (2000). Quantum artificial neural networks vs classical artificial neural networks: Experiments in simulation, *in Proceedings of the IEEE Fourth International Conference on Computational Intelligence and Neuroscience, Atlantic City, NJ, 757-759.*

Millonas, M. (1994). *Swarms, Phase Transitions, and Collective Intelligence.* Reading: Addison-Wesley Publishing Company.

Moore, M. P., & Narayanan, A. (1995). *Quantum-Inspired Computing* (p. 344). Exeter, UK: Department of Computer Science, Old Library, University of Exeter.

Narayanan, A., & Manneer, T. (2000). Quantum artificial neural network architectures and components. *Information Sciences, 128*(3-4), 231–255. doi:10.1016/S0020-0255(00)00055-4

Niblack, W. (1986). *An Introduction to Image Processing* (pp. 115–116). Englewood Cliffs, NJ: Prentice-Hall.

Nielsen, M. A., & Chuang, I. L. (2000). *Quantum computation and quantum information.* Cambridge: Cambridge Univ. Press.

Reeves, C. R. (1993). Using Genetic Algorithms with Small Populations, *Proc. of the Fifth International Conference on Genetic Algorithms, Morgan Kaufman, San Mateo, CA, 92-99.*

Rylander, B., Soule, T., Foster, J., & Alves-Foss, J. (2001). Quantum evolutionary programming, *in Proceedings of the Genetic and Evolutionary Computation Conference (GECCO-2001), Morgan Kaufmann,* 1005–1011.

Sahoo, P., Wilkins, C., & Yeager, J. (1997). Threshold selection using Renyi's entropy,''. *Pattern Recognition, 30*(1), 71–84. doi:10.1016/S0031-3203(96)00065-9

Sezgin, M., & Sankur, B. (2004). Survey over image thresholding techniques and quantitative performance evaluation. *Journal of Electronic Imaging, 13*(1), 146–165. doi:10.1117/1.1631315

Silva, J., Lins, R., & Rocha, V., Jr. (2006). Binarizing and Filtering Historical Documents with Back-to-Front Interference. *Proceedings of SAC. ACM Symposium on Applied Computing. Dijon. France. New York: ACM Press,* 853–858.

Ventura, D. (1999). Quantum Computational intelligence: Answers and Questions. *IEEE Intelligent Systems,* 14–16.

Wu, L. U., Songde, M. A. & Hanqing, L. U. (1998). An effective entropic thresholding for ultrasonic imaging. *ICPR'98: Intl. Conf. Patt. Recog.,* 1522–1524.

Yen, J., Chang, F., & Chang, S. (1995). A new criterion for automatic multilevel thresholding, *Proceedings of 1995. IEEE Transactions on Image Processing, 4*(3), 370–378. doi:10.1109/83.366472 PMID:18289986

Zhang, G. X., Li, W. D. J. N., & Hu, L. Z. (2004). A novel quantum genetic algorithm and its application. *Tien Tzu Hsueh Pao, 32*(3), 476–479.

Zhang, W. J. G., & Li, N. (2003). An improved quantum genetic algorithm and its application. *Lecture Notes in Artificial Intelligence, 2639,* 449–452.

KEY TERMS AND DEFINITIONS

Genetic Algorithm: It can be defined as heuristic search procedure that works on the principles of biological evolution.

Image Thresholding: It is a popular tool of image segmentation used to distinguish objects from its background in any gray level image.

Meta-Heuristic Algorithms: It is basically as an iterative search process used to explore the search space to find optimal solutions.

Multi-Objective Optimization: It is the method to optimize variable objective functions simultaneously.

Optimization: It is an underlying method to find feasible solutions of defined problems of different domains.

Quantum Computing: It uses quantum-mechanical properties of quantum computer like entanglement, superposition etc. for performing operations of required data.

Thresholding Methods: These are useful segmentation tools used for image thresholding.

Chapter 2
An Uncertainty–Based Model for Optimized Multi–Label Classification

J. Anuradha
VIT University, India

B. K. Tripathy
VIT University, India

ABSTRACT

The data used in the real world applications are uncertain and vague. Several models to handle such data efficiently have been put forth so far. It has been found that the individual models have some strong points and certain weak points. Efforts have been made to combine these models so that the hybrid models will cash upon the strong points of the constituent models. Dubois and Prade in 1990 combined rough set and fuzzy set together to develop two models of which rough fuzzy model is a popular one and is used in many fields to handle uncertainty-based data sets very well. Particle Swarm Optimization (PSO) further combined with the rough fuzzy model is expected to produce optimized solutions. Similarly, multi-label classification in the context of data mining deals with situations where an object or a set of objects can be assigned to multiple classes. In this chapter, the authors present a rough fuzzy PSO algorithm that performs classification of multi-label data sets, and through experimental analysis, its efficiency and superiority has been established.

INTRODUCTION

In the past few years, although information retrieval has become easier, retrieving relevant information from the repository has become a challenge as the data available in the repositories grow exponentially. Retrieval of meaningful and appropriate data is crucial for qualitative decision making. This can be achieved by an efficient knowledge discovery or data mining tool. Classification, clustering and feature selection are some of the popular mechanisms those help in analyzing data to identify hidden patterns. Classification is a supervised technique that classifies the pattern based on the sample data using standard algorithms.

DOI: 10.4018/978-1-4666-8291-7.ch002

Classification problem will become complex when there exist high possible combination of patterns. Rule generation by tree or other induction techniques face the difficulty in generating unambiguous optimized rule from the complex, vague data. Clustering is a popular unsupervised learning technique that partitions data into clusters of data having similar characteristics. The challenging job of clustering is that, the sharp identification of the dissimilarity and the degree of similarity that helps to classify the data into different groups. The dynamic and adaptable nature of algorithms is important for formation of good clustering. Feature selection is the problem of filtering out the essential data and discarding the irrelevant information from the given inputs. This is an important preprocessing step that the performance of knowledge discovery can be enhanced or reduced. The self-adaptability nature of evolutionary algorithm handles these problems in a simple and easy way to produce the best solution from a large data.

Modern optimization techniques have aroused great interest among the scientific and technical community in a wide variety of fields recently, because of their ability to solve problems with a non-linear and non-convex dependence of design parameters. Several new optimization techniques have emerged in the past two decades that mimic biological evolution, or the way biological entities communicate in nature. The most representative algorithms include Genetic Algorithms (GA), Particle Swarm Optimization (PSO) and the method of Differential Evolution (DE).

By analogy with natural selection and evolution, in classical GA the set of parameters to be optimized (genes) defines an individual or potential solution X (chromosome) and a set of individuals makes up the population, which is evolved by means of the selection, crossover and mutation genetic operators. The optimization process used by the GA follows the next steps. The genetic algorithm generates individuals (amplitude excitations and phase perturbations of the antenna elements). The individuals are encoded in a vector of real numbers, that represents the amplitudes, and a vector of real numbers restrained on the range $(0, 2\pi)$, that represents the phase perturbations of the antenna elements.

One of the main drawbacks of GA is their lack of memory, which limits the search and convergence ability of the algorithms. In GA, the concept of memory relies on elitism, but there is no stronger operator to propagate accurate solutions in a faster way. However, the PSO algorithm emerges as a powerful stochastic optimization method inspired by the social behavior of organisms such as bird flocking or fish schooling, in which individuals have memory and cooperate to move towards a region containing the global or a near optimal solution. PSO like any other evolutionary algorithm is an optimization technique that performs randomized search in the solution space for an optimal solution by updating generations.

Particle Swarm Optimization (PSO) like any other evolutionary algorithm it is an optimization technique that performs randomized search in the solution space for an optimal solution by updating generations. PSO has less number of computations compared to Genetic Algorithm (GA), as it does not have operations like cross over and mutation. PSO has a swarm of particles, where swarm represents a set of solutions (solution space) and a particle represents a potential solution. It was developed by Kennedy and Eberhart (Kennedy et al, 1995) in 1995. This model was developed based on the behavior of flock of birds flying coherently with a competition that leads to a flight with uniform speed and direction influenced by its positions, velocity and their previous state. PSO has swarm of particles searching for the solution in the solution space. Each particle keeps track of its coordinates in the problem space which are associated with the best solution (fitness) it has achieved so far. This value is called *pbest*. Another "best" value that is tracked by the particle swarm optimizer is the best value, obtained so far by any particle in the neighbors of the particle. This location is called l*best*. When a particle takes all the population as its topological neighbors, the best value is a global best and is called *gbest*. Different topologies of particles are used in the search space out of those, the most popular are

Figure 1. Different Topologies used in PSO

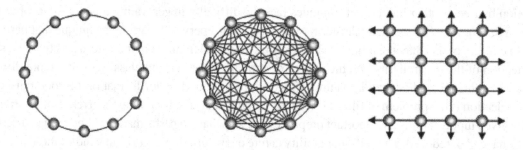

1.   Ring (lbest) topology.
2.   Global (gbest) topology.
3.   Von- Neumann topology.

The particle swarm optimization concept consists of, at each time step, changing the velocity of (accelerating) each particle toward its *pbest* and *lbest* locations (local version of PSO). Acceleration is weighted by a random term, with separate random numbers being generated for acceleration toward *pbest* and *lbest* locations.

Each particle is associated with position x(t) and velocity v(t) (updated after every iteration) evaluated by using (2) and (1) respectively that mutually affects the other particle in the swarm. The parameters *gbest* and *pbest* determines the global best and local best solution respectively. The pbest associated with each particle represents its best solution. The gbest is the overall best solution of the particle in the swarm adjusted basing upon the performance of the swarm and its outcome (fitness value).

Velocity updation

$$v(t+1) = w \times v(t) + c_1 \times \mathrm{r1} \times (pbest(t) - x(t)) + c_2 \times \mathrm{r2} \times (gbest(t) - x(t)) \tag{1}$$

Position updation

$$x(t+1) = x(t) + v(t+1) \tag{2}$$

Here, w is an inertia weight and c_1 and c_2 are acceleration constants, r1 and r2 are random values.

STANDARD PSO ALGORITHM

Step 1: Initialize max iteration, constants c_1, c_2 and swarm size. Particles in swarm are initialized randomly where each particle represents in the candidate solution.
Step 2: For each particle p_i in the swarms do step 3.
Step 3: Calculate fitness value (fv_i) of the particle p_i.
Step 4: If the fv_i is better than the best fitness value (pbest) in history then Set pbest = p_i
Step 5: Choose the particle with the best fitness value of all the particles as the gbest

Step 6: For each particle p_i in swarm s do step 7 and 8

Step 7: Calculate particle velocity v_i by (1)

Step 8: Update particle position x_i by (2)

Step 9: Repeat the step 3 to 8 until the maximum number of iterations or there are no more changes in the gbest value of a particle.

PSO is more advantages over other optimization techniques such as Genetic Algorithm (GA), Ant Colony Optimization (ACO) and Bee Colony Optimization because of the following reasons.

- Easy to implement and has very less parameters compared to other techniques.
- Has less number of operations compared to GA which has more computations with operations such as selection, cross over and mutation.
- Each particle finds its best performance by comparing its earlier performances, also fixes the best performance by comparing its neighborhood particles. It has efficient memory capability.
- The particles are guided by the most successful particle to improve it in attaining the global optima. Thus it maintains the diversity of the swarm where as in GA, the worst solutions are discarded there by eliminating the possibility of good generation from its offsprings.

PARAMETER SELECTION IN PSO

Several variants of PSO are available that focuses and improves the convergence, getting trapped in local optima, accuracy of result. PSO algorithm depends on many parameters such as constants c_1, c_2 and inertia weight w. A wrong initialization of the parameter may mislead the particle search. Inertia weights have a high impact in searching the optimal solution in solution space which controls the exploration and exploitation of searching.

The balance between the local and the global search is attained through inertia weight. By choosing a larger value of inertia weight, a global search is performed while a smaller value leads to local search. It is adjusted dynamically to change the search ability according to the requirement. Inertia weight in velocity updation is used in many ways such as fixed weight, random value between [0, 1], linearly decreasing, non-linearly decreasing and exponent decreasing values.

The exponent decrease in inertia weight can be computed as (3)

$$w = (w_{ini} - w_{end} - d_1) \exp\left(\frac{1}{1 + d_2 t / t_{max}}\right) \tag{3}$$

where, w_{ini} and w_{end} represents the actual initial weight and the maximum weight, t_{max} and t represents the maximum iteration and t^{th} iteration, d_1 and d_2 are the values used to control the inertia weight between w_{ini} and w_{end}.

In the linear decrease value of inertia weight, the PSO starts exploring with the ability of global search and gradually the value is reduced to perform local search. It improves the performance (Shi et al, 2001). Nonlinear weight updation model are complex and are suitable for problems of dynamic in nature. Nonlinear function of inertia weight value follows the change in environment that has the ability to have dynamic balance between the local and the global search. Nonlinear updation of inertia value can be computed as in (4)

$$w = w_{end} + (w_{end} - w_{start}) \times \left(\left(1 - t / t_{\max} \right)^{k_1} \right)^{k_2}$$

(4)

where, w_{end} and w_{start} are the final and the initial weights, k_1 and k_2 are the constants whose values are greater than1.

To define the change in inertia weight in the adaptive model, it needs two inputs viz., current best performance evaluation and the current inertia weight. The normalized best performance is computed using triangular fuzzy membership function having *low, medium and high*. Based on these values, the inertia weights are calculated and shown to perform well on different objective functions. The normalized current best performance (NCBPE) is calculated by using (5), where CBPE represents current best performance.

$$NCBPE = (CBPE - CBPE_{min})/ (CBPE_{max} - CBPE_{min})$$

(5)

Other various inertia weight updation formulas (Bansal et al, 2011) are listed in Table 1.. Bansal et al has performed an experimental analysis using this inertia weight and the performance are measured using various objective functions such as sphere, Griewank, Rosenbrock, Rastrigin, Ackley.

The evaluation result reveals that the best average error is obtained when Chaotic inertia weight is used. Choosing the constant inertia weight in PSO algorithm gives the best average number of iteration among the tabulated weights. Minimum error is obtained when constant or linear decreasing inertia weight is used. Similarly the worst performance on average error, average number of iteration and minimum error are produced when chaotic random inertia weight, constant inertia weight and chaotic random inertia weight or global local best inertia weights are chosen respectively.

ADAPTIVE PSO

Standard PSO algorithm does not perform well on a dynamic environment. The algorithm needs some change in strategies that adapts the swarm to recognize and perform according to the change in environment. Some of the adaptable factors in PSO are the number of particles which are again randomized, combination of previous strategies, resetting certain particle. Small population PSO(SPPSO) uses less number of particles in swarm of about five or less. This particle set is replaced (regenerated) in every N iterations except the *gbest*. The performance of SPPSO improves on dynamic problems (Valle et al, 2011).

PSO also has the complaint of premature convergence. Adaptive PSO algorithms can overcome the above problem. In standard PSO r_1 and r_2 are the random values used in the velocity updation formula. Dynamic adaption PSO introduced in (Yang et al, 2007) has modified the velocity updation formula where the randomness in velocity updating formula is reduced. The algorithm also introduces two other factors namely evaluation speed factor and aggregation degree factor (Yang et al, 2007). The r_1 and r_2 value is modified based on the number of particles and the number of iteration and it holds for updating inertia weight also. Evaluation speed factor can be calculated by (6). For computation, it takes into

Table 1. Different inertia weights

Sr. No.	Name of Inertia Weight	Formula of Inertia Weight
1.	Constant Inertia Weight	$w=c$ $c=0.7$(*Considered* for Experiments)
2.	Adaptive Inertia Weight	$$w_i(t+1) = w(0) + (w(n_t) - w(o)) \frac{e^{m_i(t)-1}}{e^{m_i(t)+1}}$$ $$m_i(t) = \frac{gbest - current}{gbest + current}$$
3.	Oscillating Inertia Weight	$$w(t) = \frac{w_{max} + w_{min}}{2} + \frac{w_{max} - w_{min}}{2} \cos\left(\frac{2\pi t}{T}\right)$$ $$T = \frac{2S_1}{3 + 2k}$$
4.	Random Inertia Weight	$$w = 0.5 + \frac{Rand()}{2}$$
5.	Chaotic Inertia Weight	$z=4 \times z \times (1-z)$ $$w = (w_1 - w_2) \times \frac{MAXiter - iter}{MAXiter} + w_2 \times z$$
6.	Chaotic Random Inertia Weight	$z=4 \times z \times (1-z)$ $w=0.5 \times rand() + 0.5 \times z$
7.	Global-Local Best Inertia Weight	$$Inertia \text{ weight } w_i = 1.1 - \frac{gbest_i}{pbest_i}$$
8.	Simulated Annealing Inertia Weight	$$w_k = w_{min} + (w_{max} - w_{min}) \times \lambda^{(k-1)}$$ λ-0.95
9.	Sigmoid Increasing Inertia Weight	$$w_k = \frac{(w_{start} - w_{end})}{(1 + e^{u*(k-n*gen)})} + w_{end}$$ $$u = 10^{(\log(gen)-2)}$$
10.	Sigmoid Decreasing Inertia Weight	$$w_k = \frac{(w_{start} - w_{end})}{(1 + e^{-u*(k-n*gen)})} + w_{end}$$ $$u = 10^{(\log(gen)-2)}$$
11.	Linear Decreasing Inertia Weight	$$w_k = w_{max} - \frac{w_{max} - w_{min}}{iter_{max}} \times k$$
12.	Logarithm Decreasing Inertia Weight	$$w = w_{max} + (w_{min} - w_{max}) \log_{10}(a + \frac{10t}{T_{max}})$$

continued on following page

Table 1. Continued

Sr. No.	Name of Inertia Weight	Formula of Inertia Weight
13.	Exponent Decreasing Inertia Weight	$w = (w_{max} - w_{min} - d_1)\exp(\dfrac{1}{1 + \dfrac{d_2 t}{t_{max}}})$
14.	Natural Exponent Inertia Weight Strategy (e1 - PSO)	$w(t) = w_{min} + (w_{max} - w_{min}).e^{-[\frac{t}{\left[\frac{MAXITER}{10}\right]}]}$
15.	Natural Exponent Inertia Weight Strategy (e2 - PSO)	$w(t) = w_{min} + (w_{max} - w_{min}).e^{-[\frac{t}{\left[\frac{MAXITER}{4}\right]}]^2}$

account of the run history of each particle that reflects its evaluation speed. The value of h should be between 0 and 1. Smaller the value implies faster in speed.

$$h_i^t = \left| \frac{\min(F(pbest_i^{t-1}), F(pbest_i^t))}{\max(F(pbest_i^{t-1}), F(pbest_i^t))} \right| \tag{6}$$

$F(pbest_i^t)$ is the fitness function of the pbest$_i^t$

Aggregation degree is computed by (7) where $\overline{F_t}$ is the mean fitness of the particles in the tth iteration.

$$s = \left| \frac{\min(F_{tbest}, \overline{F_t})}{\max(F_{tbest}, \overline{F_t})} \right| \tag{7}$$

h and s are the typical characteristics of the PSO algorithm that exhibit the search ability. Using the parameters evaluation speed and aggregation degree, inertia weight is adjusted.

$$w = f(h_i^t, s) \tag{8}$$

This helps the algorithm to move faster in the search space and to come out of the local optima (Yang et al, 2007). In order to improve the performance in jumping out of the local optima and to prevent the similarity of the swarm inertia weight computing formula is enhanced as in (9).

$$w = w_{ini} - \alpha(1 - h_i^t) + \beta s \tag{9}$$

when the s parameter value increases, the inertia weight should also increase proportionately. The value of α and β takes the value between [0, 1].

In order to avoid stuck in local optima, mutation operation is introduced (Wang et al, 2007). The gbest particle is put under mutation by (10) and compared against its original value; whichever is best is considered for further evaluation.

$$\text{gbest }(i) = \text{gbest }(i) + w(i) * N(x_{min,}\ x_{max}) \tag{10}$$

where N is the distributed function with scaled parameter $t = 1$. $N(x_{min,}\ x_{max})$ is the random number between x_{min} and x_{max}. The value of $w(i)$ is the average velocity of the particle in the population. Performance of PSO is sensitive to noisy data and hence the performance detoriates. In the presence of noisy data, the object function value is disturbed, therefore it could not differentiate between good and bad solution. If the algorithm fails to select the true neighborhood solution, discards the good solution then the accuracy of the algorithm fails. Performing resampling of the swarms reduce the problem of sensitivity to noisy data. The resampling leads to re-evaluating the solution many times. The performance measure is carried out by taking the mean over the evaluations using objective function. The particles in this model have less effect due to deception, blindness and disorientation. The experimental result reveals that, this algorithm performs better than other algorithms.

The acceleration coefficient c_1 and c_2 are adjusted adaptively that improves the performance of efficiency and accuracy. Compute the difference between the *gbest* value of the previous and the current iteration. If the difference is a larger value, then the c_1 value is enlarged that extends the search region with global search ability at the same time c_2 value should be reduced to a smaller value so that premature convergence can be avoided. Increase in difference value reveals that the particles converge to an optimal point. To speed up the process of convergence c_1 is set to smaller value and c_2 is set to bigger value. In order to decide what value to be set for c_1 and c_2 and when is derived from the fuzzy rules.

Rule 1: If df is Small, then c_1 is Big and c_2 is Small.
Rule 2: If df is Medium, then c_1 is Medium and c_2 is Medium.
Rule 3: If df is Big, then c_1 is Small and c_2 is Big.

df is the difference between the *gbest* of the previous and the current iteration and its value are fuzzified using triangular membership function (small, medium, big).

Another way of adaptability in PSO is adjusting the population size based on the value of diversity of the population. A ladder function is proposed by De Bao and Chun Xia that can increase or reduce the population size of the swarm based on the value of diversity. Initially maximum generations (*maxgen*) are assigned which is divided into R periodic each having same generations T. The Figure 2 shows the variable population with respect to generations.

N_{max}, N_{min} and N_{av} are the population sizes of maximum, minimum and average respectively. The maximum number of population is constant and it is fixed initially. N_{min} is the minimum value of population that is unbounded and evolves after some ladder (generation). T is the period of every ladder.

maxgen $= T \times R$

Figure 2. Variable population of Ladder PSO

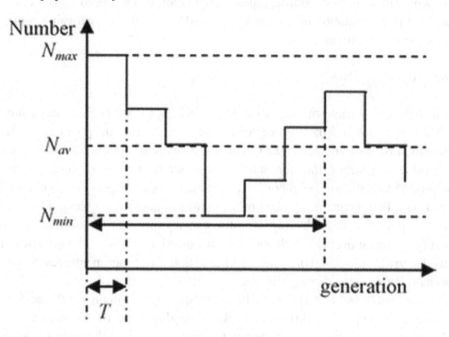

The ladder PSO (Bao et al, 2009) algorithm works in five steps given below:

Step 1: Initialize population in maximum number randomly.
Step 2: Update particles according to operator of original PSO in each ladder.
Step 3: Calculating scores of particles and ranking particles according to the scores which they derived.
Step 4: Evaluate the diversity in the terminal time of each T period.
Step 5: Adding or decreasing particles according to the diversity which derived in Step 4.

PSEUDO CODE OF LADDER PSO

```
Begin
Initialize the parameters
Initialize the population size
For iteration = 1: (maxgen/T)
    For generation = 1: T
        For i= 1: population size
        If f(x_i) < f(x_pbest) then x_pbest = x_i
        P_gbest = min(p=neighbors)
    For d  = 1: Dimension
    Compute the velocity by (1.1)
    Update the position by (1.2)
    If v_id(t+1) > v_max then v_id(t+1) = v_max
    else if  v_id (t+1) < - v_max then v_id (t+1) = - v_max
```

```
    end
    if x_id (t+1) > x_max  then x_id (t+1) = x_max
    else if x_id (t+1) < x_min  then x_id (t+1) = x_min
    end
    end // end of for
    end // end of for
Apply q tournament method to calculate scores of particles
Rank population according to scores
Calculate the diversity values
Perform adding or decreasing the particle
End
End
```

The diversity function can be calculated by (11)

$$\mathrm{div(T)} = \left[\frac{1}{\pi} \left(a \tan\left(\overline{AH}\right) + \frac{\pi}{2} \right) \right] \frac{E_t}{\log(N)} \qquad (11)$$

If the particles in the population are similar then $E_t = 0$ and if it is totally dissimilar then, $E_t = \log(N)$, where N is the population size. The diversity function can have the value in [0, 1].

Discrete Binary PSO (DBPSO)

Kennedy and Eberhart introduced binary PSO in 1997. The particles in the swarm are represented in binary form that indicates the presence or absence of a particle in the search space. The velocity of particle having good potential is set to 1 and is set to 0 for other particles. Here transformation functions like sigmoid function is applied to the velocity computed using (12). This method could compress the value to lie in the range [0, 1].

Velocity updation:

$$f(v(t+1)) = \frac{1}{1 + e^{-v(t+1)}} \qquad (12)$$

Particle updation:

$$x(t+1) = \begin{cases} 1, & if \quad rand < f(v(t+1)); \\ 0, & Otherwise. \end{cases}$$

where, f(v(t+1)) is a sigmoidal function that determines the velocity of the particle at t+1 state and *rand* is the random number.

The particles with position value 1 will be involved in the next generation of exploration. The conventional PSO algorithm has the drawback of premature convergence. Some particles become inactive when it is similar to the gbest and will lose their velocity. In further generations this particle will become inactive and their role in global and local search becomes very less causing prematurity. This drawback was overcome by Immune Binary PSO (IBPSO) where the particles were given vaccination i.e. modifying the bits based on prior knowledge. Immune selection of the particle is performed to avoid earlier convergence. It works in two steps namely immune test and probability selection based on the antibody concentration. Immune test is based on the fitness value and can be computed using (13)

$$D(x_i) = \frac{1}{\sum\limits_{j=1}^{N}\left|f_i - f_j\right|}, i = 1, 2, ..., N \tag{13}$$

The probability selection based on antibody concentration is given in (14)

$$P(x_i) = \frac{\sum\limits_{j=1}^{N}\left|f_i - f_j\right|}{\sum\limits_{i=1}^{N}\sum\limits_{j=1}^{N}\left|f_i - f_j\right|}, i = 1, 2, ...N \tag{14}$$

where f_i is the fitness value of the ith particle.

Probability Based Discrete PSO (PBPSO) is a variant of Binary PSO. Here, the positions of the particle is calculated based on probability using (15)

$$P_{ij} = \frac{X_{ij} - X_{min}}{X_{max} - X_{min}} \tag{15}$$

PBPSO preserves both the velocity as well as position update rule of PSO algorithm. Instead of velocity (V) the particle position (X) is considered as a pseudo probability to determine the actual probability $p \in [0, 1]$ for actual state of a bit for each component of the solution vector in binary space. Modified Discrete PSO (MDPSO) is another variant of PSO introduced by (Parsopoulos et al, 2008). The particle position updation formula is completely reframed as given in (16) and there are no acceleration constants and inertia weights. The velocity value lies in the interval [0, 1]. α is the predefined static probability, which is usually fixed as 0.5.

$$x_i(t+1) = \begin{cases} x_i(t), & \text{if } 0 \le V \le \alpha; \\ p_i(t), & \text{if } \alpha \le V \le \frac{1}{2}(1+\alpha); \\ g_i(t), & \text{if } \frac{1}{2}(1+\alpha) \le V \le 1. \end{cases} \tag{16}$$

Probability Based Discrete PSO is constantly avoids local optimal solution and reaches to the optimal solution in less number of function evaluations.

DISTRIBUTED PSO

In Particle Swarm Evolver (PSE) model, more than one swarm are defined with the set of particles and the number of swarms can be fixed or adaptive. These swarms work independently. The swarm having the best gbest value across the swarms will be selected as the final solution. A hybrid model PSE with PSO and GA has a set of swarms defined as shown in Figure 3.

Each swarms of PSO explore (achieving global minimum and adaptability) and exploit (achieving stability) independently. Hybrid of GA with PSO will enhance the performance of PSO. Each particl in the swarm is chosen as chromosomes for computing GA operation.

Procedure of PSO – GA

Step 1: Perform P number of iterations for each PSO.
Step 2: Choose the best PSOs based on their x_{gbest} as parents.
Step 3: Perform cross over by randomly mixing their particles.
Step 4: Perform mutation by replacing a random particle in.
Step 5: PSO with a completely random particle.
Step 6: Repeat the process for the convergence.

Figure 3. A hybrid model of PSE using PSO – GA method

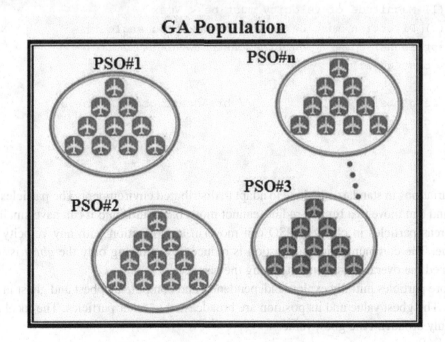

The Crossover probability and Mutation probability value can be chosen by experience or by literature (such as 0.95, 0.01 respectively).

The particles work in a distributed manner by computing its own velocity and position, updating its own personal best *pbest* and its own best personal location. Each particles best measurement is then broadcasted to other particles to find the global best particle. The computation of position and velocity are done locally and the global updation alone are broadcasted which reduce the communication and also improves the scalability of the algorithm (Hereford et al, 2006),

Pseudo Code of Distributed PSO (DPSO)

```
pbest = -1; gbest = -1;
Initialize pbest and gbest
While (target not found or time not expired)
        Make measurement and update, if necessary
        meas = make_measurement();
if (meas > pbest)            // Update pbest,  if true
    Up_pbest();                    // Update pbest value and location
            if (meas > gbest)        // Update gbest, if true
            Set gflag;               // Set a flag
            Up_gbest();              // Update gbest value and location
            end
        end
Move();                  // Move bot based on PSO update equation
        // For simulation, constrain bot movement
        // Two conditions:
        // (1) Magnitude of velocity must be < Vmax
        // (2) Direction must be within in max turn angle
If (new gbest found)         // broadcast new gbest value
        Broadcast(gbest);
end
 If (gbest is global gbest)          // broadcast gbest location
        Broadcast(gbest_location);
end
End while
```

Several variations in standard are done to adapt to distributed environment. The particles movement is restricted and can move to a limited radius, cannot move backwards and it can have small maximum velocity whereas particles in classical PSO can move in any direction with any velocity within the bounded value. The communication congestion is reduced by allowing only the *gbest* is broadcasted after determined the overall best solution among the particles.

One or more particles initially explore independently and compute its pbest and gbest in a specified time interval. The gbest value and its position are broadcasted to other particles. The local particles in swarm will only broadcast the gbest value

In case of multiple swarms, there is more than one swarm and they explore independently. These swarms have attraction and repulsive nature. The particles in the particular swarm are attracted by the gbest and the local best position. Similarly, the particles across the swarms are repulsive by the gbest of all the other swarms. The repulsive natures of the particles in swarms are defined by modifying the classical velocity updation formula.

$$V(t) = V_{PSO}(t) + C3*rand()*f(Xforeign\text{-}gbest(t-1), X(t-1); Xgbest(t-1))$$

$V_{PSO}(t)$ is the velocity of the particle computed using (1). $X_{gbest}(t-1)$ is the position of the global best of the current swarm and $X_{foreign\text{-}gbest}(t-1)$ is the position of the global best of the other considered swarm. The function f always ignores $X_{gbest}(t-1)$ and repulses the particle by pushing it in the opposite direction of $X_{foreign\text{-}gbest}(t-1)$ except in case the repulsor is between the particle and the global best of the current swarm. In this case, f is the function that accelerates the particle towards $X_{gbest}(t-1)$. The function f is:

```
if (X(t-1) < X_foreign-gbest(t-1)) and (X_foreign-gbest(t-1)< X_gbest(t-1)) or
   (X_gbest(t-1)< X_foreign-gbest(t-1)<  X(t -1)) then
       return -Φ (X(t-1),  X_foreign-gbest(t-1))
else
       return Φ(X(t-1), X_foreign-gbest(t-1))
where,
       Φ(X(t-1), X_foreign-gbest(t-1)) = sig(dis)*(1- |dis/ (U-L)|)
```

Where, dis=$X(t-1) - X_{foreign\text{-}gbest}(t-1)$, *sig* indicates the sign function and U and L are the upper and lower bound of the interval respectively. The symbol Φ is equal to the sign of the difference of its arguments multiplied by 1 minus the normalized distance of its arguments. In other words, the repulsive factor increases with the proximity to the repulsor and we obtain a value that does not depend on the space dimension.

FEATURE SELECTION

Feature selection (FS) aims at selecting relevant features from a larger set of features in a classification problem in a way that optimizes the classification performance (Dash et al 1997). The irrelevant features do not affect the decision taken in data analysis and the redundant features will not add more information to the target class. Eliminating such irrelevant and redundant features will reduce the dimensionality of the data and hence improves accuracy and reduces time complexity. Feature Selection algorithms can be broadly classified into two types namely Filter approach and Wrapper approach. Filter approach, selects the best feature subset by eliminating redundant and irrelevant features based on data property before performing classification. In wrapper approach, learning algorithms are applied to select the subset of most relevant features (Vipual et al, 2012). Filter approach is less expensive than wrapper approach.

PSO feature selection is performed in different ways by using binary PSO, continuous PSO, Multiple PSO, adaptive PSO etc., A binary PSO has the particles in the swarm that are represented in binary form which indicates the presence or absence of a particle in the search space. The velocity of particle having good potential is set to 1 and 0 for other particles as shown in (17)

$$x(t+1) = \begin{cases} 1, & if \quad rand < \quad f(v(t+1)); \\ 0, & Otherwise. \end{cases} \tag{17}$$

Adaptive PSO are implemented in different ways and updation of particle or weight is based on the best movement of particle in previous iteration towards the global result. Based on the better movement of the particle in previous iteration, the inertia weight is set to high and in converse, it is set low when the particle is not good enough. w^i_{min} and w^i_{max} represent the lower and upper limit of the particle in exploration space where as w_i represents the inertia weight (Rezazadeh et al, 2011).

$$W^i_{min} = \frac{rank_i}{swarm_{size}} * W_{max}$$

$$W_i = W^i_{min} + (W_{max} - W^i_{min}) * (\frac{number\ of\ improved\ in\ swarm_i}{swarm_{size}}) \tag{18}$$

FS has been implemented by many evolutionary algorithms like the Genetic Algorithms (GAs) and Particle Swarm Optimization (PSO). A comparative analysis of the algorithms on multimodal problem generator reveals that PSO fares much better than GA (Kennedy et al, 1998). An Improved Feature Selection (IFS) (Huang et al, 2008) is introduced which uses Multi Swarm PSO (MSPSO) to dynamically execute Support Vector Machines (SVM) for FS. Recently, much work has been done on a multi-objective approach for FS in classification using PSO, referred to as MOPSO (MOPSO) (Xue et al, 2013). This approach uses two-level Pareto front FS algorithms (Abido et al, 2007)(Knowles et al 2000) namely non-dominated sorting PSO (NSPSO) and CMDPSO which uses the concepts of crowding, mutation and dominance and its pseudocode is:

```
Begin
      Initialize swarm
      Initialize leaders in an external archive
      Quality(leaders)
      g = 0
While g < gmax
      For each particle
            Select leader
            Update Position (Flight)
            Mutation
            Evaluation
            Update pbest
      End For
      Update leaders in the external archive
      Quality(leaders)
      g++
End While
```

```
        Report results in the external archive
End.
```

Leaders are the particles that have moved to a good position and will guide the flight (positions) of other particles. Evaluation gives the fitness value of the particle and pbest is the local best particles. Leaders are selected by finding the particles best position globally which can guide other particles.

CLASSIFICATION

Data mining is the process of discovering knowledge from large data. It unifies the research in the field of statistics, machine learning, AI and Database systems. Data classification is mostly carried out using supervised learning technique where the class label of the instance in knows previously. Hence, a hybrid of machine learning methods and PSO will produce the best result compared to conventional classification algorithms (Sousa, 2004). In literature, PSO is used to find the optimal positions of the class centroids, to determine the optimal weights in Neural Network, generate optimal number of rules etc,. Improved Michigan PSO (IMPSO) classification has an adaptive inertia factor that has the flexibility to control the search space. It maintains a balance between local and global search thus improving accuracy. Further it is extended to select the best half particle going into the next generation.

Lale Ozbakır et al.,(Ozbakır et al, 2010) proposed a novel approach for exploring comprehensible classification rule from trained neural network with Particle Swarm Optimizer (PSO). PSO with time varying inertia weight explores best value to optimize ANN output function. PSO based classification rule mining algorithm aims at finding small set of rules from the training data set. PSO is applied to extract or select the minimal best set of rules based on the classification accuracy as fitness value. This approach provides better results compared to other algorithms (Wang et al, 2007). PSO is used as an optimizer used to extract the best classified results from any classification algorithm. The Figure 4 shows the PSO – SVM classification flowchart.

The particles in the solution space are explored and the best particles at local and global level are selected based on the classification accuracy. The flowchart in Figure 4 uses SVM classifier for finding the fitness value of the particle. SVM classifier can be replaced by any classifier like Neural Network, Bayesian etc., Fuzzy classification algorithm using FIS models are used to set the cognitive factors c_1 and c_2. This improves the diversity and convergence of PSO exploration in obtaining optimized results. Figure 5 show the optimal fuzzy classification in PSO with dynamic and adaptive parameters.

The most popular algorithm that is used to train the Artificial Neural network is Back propagation algorithm. In literature, training neural network using PSO algorithm for weight adjustment has proven to be superior to BPN. Evolutionary computing in ANN is mostly used for fixing weights, network architecture and learning algorithms. Compared to GA PSO has less number of operations and the representation of particles is also simpler. The fitness function of the algorithm varies depends on the problem or application. In classification problem, a measure to find classification accuracy might be the fitness function. The following section gives the classification problem on ANN with PSO using benchmark data set iris.

PSO algorithm is applied to classify the input patterns using ANN. The performance of ANN is measure using classification accuracy, which determines the fitness value. Based on this value by PSO algorithm, the position of the particle and its velocity are adjusted. The convergence point of the algo-

Figure 4. Optimized classification using SVM and PSO

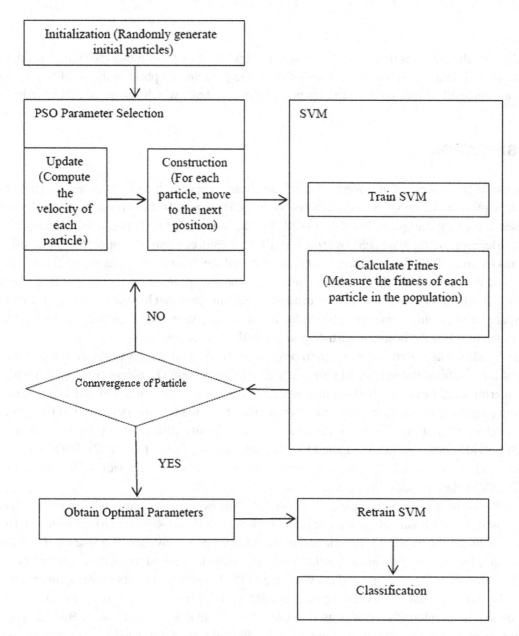

Figure 5. Fuzzy classification using PSO

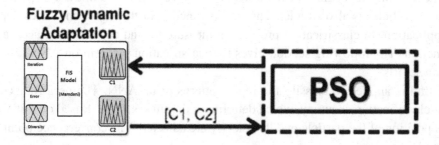

Table 2. Classification for iris dataset

Data Set Iris	Neural Network Model (MLP – PSO)
Records: 150	Training: 105 (70%) Testing: 45 (30%) (or cross validation methods)
Attributes: 4	Input nodes: 4, hidden layer:1 Nodes in hidden layer: 6
Class label: 3	Nodes in Output layer: 3
	Synaptic links between input and hidden layer: 4*6 = 24 Synaptic links between hidden layer and output layer: 6*3 = 18 Total links: 42
	Fitness value: percentage of misclassification
	Particles: group of weights (initially fixed randomly)

rithm is when there is no change in the fitness value/ particle value. There are only few parameters in PSO to be adjusted. In order to get better results number of hidden layer and its nodes, range of weights has to be chosen carefully.

Multi objective PSO (MOPSO) is a special class of optimization problem that has several objectives which are competing or incommensurable whose objective function has to be minimized simultaneously. An optimization tool to such problem will improve the solution. Pareto based scheme is one such solution for multi objective problem. All objective functions of each particle are evaluated simultaneously and based on the principle of Pareto optimality; the non dominated best position is selected as leader to guide the particles (Parsopoulos et al, 2008). Multi objective PSO can be handled in two ways. First method, particles explore on each objective function separately and determination of best solution is like single objective function. The main challenge in these algorithms is the manipulation of information from each objective function in order to guide the particle to the Pareto optimal solution. Second method, all objective functions of each particles are evaluated simultaneously and based on the principle of Pareto optimality, the non dominated best position is selected as leader to guide the particles. There may be many non dominated solutions that are equally good, the most challenging job is that, selection of one best particle as leader (Parsopoulos et al, 2008).

Multi Objective PSO Procedure

1. Initialize swarm, velocities and best positions
2. Initialize external archive (initially empty)
3. While (stopping criterion not satisfied) Do
4. for each particle
   4.1 Select a member of the external archive (if needed)
   4.2 Update velocity and position
   4.3 Evaluate new position
   4.4 Update best position and external archive
5. End For
6. End While

Multi objective PSO in associative rule mining has set multiple objectives like confidence, comprehensibility, and interestingness. Exploring on this multi objective using the Pareto optimality in PSO technique is to extract the best associative rules. The position of the particle is updated based on the dominance of the particle (Beiranvand et al, 2014).

CLUSTERING

Clustering, which has attained a major focus of research under unsupervised learning is being applied in various fields not limited to data mining, pattern recognition, statistics, machine learning, image processing, medical diagnosis and digital signal processing.

A cluster is a set of data objects having similar characteristics, which are different from other such sets. The aim of clustering is to identify the similarity of patterns in a given data set and classify the objects depending upon this similarity into various clusters. The Hard C means (k-means) was widely used which generates prototypes resulting in a crisp partition of a data set (Mc Queen, 1967). Most of the real world data are not crisp in nature but rather vague and imprecise. One of the earliest models of handling such type of data sets is the notion of fuzzy sets introduced by Zadeh (1965). The algorithm using fuzzy techniques to classify uncertain and vague data sets, which extends the hard c-means algorithm is called the Fuzzy c-means (FCM) algorithm and it generates overlapping clusters (Bezdek, 1981). It derives capability to handle vagueness in data through membership of objects in various clusters as defined in (19).

$$\mu_{ik} = \frac{1}{\sum_{j=1}^{c} \left(\frac{d_{ik}}{d_{jk}} \right)^{\frac{2}{m-1}}} \tag{19}$$

Hybrid clustering model of Fuzzy PSO generates optimized cluster centroids resulting in well compact and separated cluster. The fuzzy PSO model generates an optimal best partition and its procedure is given below.

The Procedure for Fuzzy PSO

Step 1: Initialize the parameters such as number of clusters c, initial position of the particle, initial velocity, inertia weight w, constants c1,c2, threshold value ε for stopping criteria.

Step 2: calculate membership value $\mu_{ik}^{(t)}$ using (19) for all particles (i=1,2,..., c and k = 1,2,..., n) and update centroid value using (20).

$$c_j = \frac{\sum_{i=1}^{N} \mu_{ij}^{m} x_i}{\sum_{i=1}^{N} \mu_{ij}^{m}} \tag{20}$$

Step 3: For each Particle, calculate the fitness value by using fuzzy objective function given in equation (21).

$$J_m = \sum_{i=1}^{N} \sum_{j=1}^{c} \mu_{ij}^m \left\| x_i - c_j \right\|^2 \tag{21}$$

Step 4: Update the global best and the local best.

Step 5: Update the velocity v_i and position p_i of the particle.

Step 6: Compare the gbest values, if their difference is less than the ε then stop; otherwise iterate t by going to step 3.

The centroids are chosen as a particle in the swarm. By finding membership the particle values are adjusted, similarly the position of the particle is also adjusted based on the *pbest* and *gbest* which guides the flight of swarm in reaching the optimal solution.

Another model, which can handle uncertain, vague and incomplete data is the Rough set introduced by Pawlak (1982). Rough set theory is used in the process of rule extraction, reasoning and pattern matching. Clusters formed by fuzzy and rough models have chances of getting stuck in local optima, introducing PSO to such models perform global exploration and hence drifts the solution to global optima. Multi-objective Immunized Particle Swarm Optimization is a hybrid evolutionary algorithm with Immunized PSO. The algorithm uses Pareto optimal approach for unsupervised problems that automatically evolves the cluster centers and simultaneously optimizing one or more objective functions. Optimizing the objective function is based on the Pareto optimality using non dominant solution or dominant objective function as represented in (22) and (23). K means clustering gives the initial clusters which are then guided by IPSO for optimized result using Pareto scheme. Let z_1 and z_2 are the clustering solutions that belongs to Z with objective functions $f_i(z_1)$ and $f_i(z_2)$ respectively, then the dominant solution of multi objective problem can be defined as (22).

$$f_i(z_1) \le f_i(z_2), \quad \forall i, i = 1, 2, \dots M$$

and

$$\exists j : f_j(z_1) < f_j(z_2), \quad j \in 1, 2 \dots M \tag{22}$$

Whereas, if none of the solutions dominates then it is a non dominant solution given by (23)

$$p^* := \{ z \in Z : \neg \exists z' \in Z : z' < Z \} \tag{23}$$

The Pareto front is the image of this set in the objective space and is represented by

$$fp* := \{ [f_1(z), f_2(z), \dots f_M(z)] : z \in p^* \} \tag{24}$$

Most common cluster validity indices used to measure the performance of a clustering algorithm using inter and intra cluster distances are Davies Bouldin (DB) index and Dunn (D) index given by (Bezdek, 1988) is used for validating the formation of the clusters. DB is a ratio of average dispersion of objects within cluster to separation between clusters and is shown in (25). Cluster separation is measured by $d(X_k, X_l)$ given in (26) where X_k and X_l partition of cluster k and cluster ℓ respectively. Scattering of objects within a cluster is measured by $S_{rf}(x_k)$ given in (25). D index is used to measure the clusters that are compact and separated. The expressions for the DB and the D index for rough Fuzzy clustering are given in (27) and (28) (Mitra et al., 2010).

The average distance between objects within the cluster X_k is given below.

$$S_{rf}(X_i) = \begin{cases} w_{low} \dfrac{\sum_{x_k \in \underline{A}X_i} \mu_{ik}^m \left\| x_k - v_i \right\|^2}{\sum_{x_k \in \underline{A}X_i} \mu_{ik}^m} + w_{up} \dfrac{\sum_{x_k \in (\overline{A}X_i - \underline{A}X_i)} \mu_{ik}^m \left\| x_k - v_i \right\|^2}{\sum_{x_k \in (\overline{A}X_i - \underline{A}X_i)} \mu_{ik}^m}, & \text{if } \underline{A}X_i \neq \varphi \wedge \overline{A}X_i - \underline{A}X_i \neq \varphi \\[4ex] \dfrac{\sum_{x_k \in (\overline{A}X_i - \underline{A}X_i)} \mu_{ik}^m \left\| x_k - v_i \right\|^2}{\sum_{x_k \in (\overline{A}X_i - \underline{A}X_i)} \mu_{ik}^m}, & \text{if } \underline{A}X_i = \varphi \wedge \overline{A}X_i - \underline{A}X_i \neq \varphi \\[4ex] \dfrac{\sum_{x_k \in \underline{A}X_i} \mu_{ik}^m \left\| x_k - v_i \right\|^2}{\sum_{x_k \in \underline{A}X_i} \mu_{ik}^m}, & \text{otherwise} \end{cases}$$

(25)

Here, u_{ik} represent the membership of the object k in the ith cluster and the value of m is 1. Between clusters separation is computed by the following equation.

$$d(X_k, X_l) = \frac{\sum_{i,j} \left\| x_i - x_j \right\|}{\left| c_k \right| \left| c_l \right|}$$

(26)

Here $x_1, x_2, \ldots, x_n$ is the set of objects in the cluster partition X_k and X_l. Here, x_i and x_j represent the cluster objects and c and c_l represent the kth and l^{th} clusters respectively.

The DB index minimizes intra cluster distance and maximizes inter cluster distance and is given by

$$DB_{rf} = \frac{1}{c} \sum_{i=1}^{c} \max_{j \neq i} \left\{ \frac{S_{rf}(X_i) + S_{rf}(X_j)}{d(X_i, X_j)} \right\}$$

(27)

The compactness and separation of clusters are measured by

$$D_{rf} = \min_{j} \left\{ \min_{i \neq j} \left\{ \frac{d(X_i, X_j)}{\max_k S_{rf}(X_k)} \right\} \right\} \quad (28)$$

Here, i, j and k represent the cluster numbers. The denominator of DB_{rf} is same as the numerator of D_{rf}. An optimal partition is obtained by maximizing the inter cluster separation while minimizing the intra cluster distance.

MULTI LABEL CLASSIFICATION

Real world classification problems are of multi label in nature. A pattern may belong to more than one class. In recent years, much focus is made in development of algorithms to handle multi label classification and label ranking. Problems like classification of text, video, images, emotions, music and functional genome belongs to more than one category (Zhang, 2007). Conventional classification algorithms are not capable of handling these datasets. The traditional data mining algorithms of single-label classification, also known as multi-class classification, associates an instance x with a single label l from a previously known finite set of labels L. A single-label dataset D is composed of n tuples $(x_1, l_1), (x_2, l_2), \cdots, (x_n, l_n)$. The multi-label classification task associates a subset of labels $S \subseteq L$ with each instance. A multi-label dataset D is therefore composed of n examples $(x_1, S_1), (x_2, S_2), \cdots, (x_n, S_n)$.

These problems can be handled two ways. The first method is transformation method that is independent of algorithm as they convert the problem into a single label classification for which a wide group of learning algorithms exists. The second method handles with specific features that extend the conventional algorithms like SVM, NN, nearest neighborhood, ensemble methods and many others. Mulan, Meka are open source machine learning tool for handling multi label data sets.

A DYNAMIC CLUSTERING ALGORITHM FOR MULTI LABEL CLASSIFICATION

Soft computing techniques like Rough set and Fuzzy set are proven to perform well on Data mining and pattern Recognition. Hybridization of the above techniques has been found successful in literature. The proposed algorithm uses rough fuzzy c means for clustering and PSO for finding the best prototype that gives better partition. The particles in swarm are the cluster prototypes that partition the patterns. Here, rough fuzzy C-means (RFCM) algorithm is used for generating clusters. This model constructs the lower approximation $\underline{A}X_i$ and the boundary region ($\overline{A}X_i - \underline{A}X_i$) of each cluster based on the membership value μ_{ik} of the objects x_k with respect to cluster c_i. The centroid value is updated basing upon the membership values of the objects in lower approximation and boundary region using equation in step 7. The cluster partitioning of the particle is evaluated by DB and D indices which gives the fitness value of the particle. The fitness value of the particle is compared against its history to identify its best solution and it is *pbest* the local best solution. The particle with the best fitness value in swarm is *gbest* the global best solution. The velocity of each particle is updated using (1) and the position of the particle is updated using (2). The above procedure is iterated until convergence i.e. there is no more change in the particle position and their gbest value. In order to generate dynamic clusters, a new centroid is chosen by steps 13 to 15. An objects in boundary region is chosen to be a new centroid such that it is far away from the existing clusters and has many objects closer to it (measured through Euclidean distance).

Proposed Algorithm – ML - RFPSO

Step 1: Initialize the parameter P (population size), c_1, c_2 (constants), w (inertia weight) and maximum number of iteration.

Step 2: Create a swarm with P particles and initialize X (particle position), *pbest* (for each particle), and velocity V (for each particle) and *gbest* for the swarm.

Step 3: Assign initial means v_i for initial number of the c clusters.

Step 4: Compute μ_{ik} by (4.1) for c clusters and N data objects.

Step 5: Assign each data object (patterns) x_k to the lower approximation $\underline{A}X_i$ or boundary region $\underline{A}X_i - \overline{A}X_i, \overline{A}X_j - \underline{A}X_j$ of cluster pairs X_i and X_j by computing the difference in its membership μ_{ik}-μ_{jk} to cluster centroid pairs v_i and v_j.

Step 6: Let μ_{ik} be first maximum and μ_{jk} be the next maximum.

If μ_{ik}-μ_{jk} is less than θ (threshold value), then

$x_k \in \overline{A}X_i - \underline{A}X_i$ and $x_k \in \overline{A}X_j - \underline{A}X_j$ and x_k cannot be a member of lower approximation of any cluster.

else

$x_k \in \underline{A}X_i$ such that membership μ_{ik} is maximum over the c clusters.

Step 7: Compute the new mean for each cluster X_i, by

$$
v_i = \begin{cases}
w_{low} \dfrac{\sum\limits_{x_k \in \underline{A}X_i} \mu_{ik}^m x_k}{\sum\limits_{x_k \in \underline{A}X_i} \mu_{ik}^m} + w_{up} \dfrac{\sum\limits_{x_k \in (AX_i - \underline{A}X_i)} \mu_{ik}^m x_k}{\sum\limits_{x_k \in (AX_i - \underline{A}X_i)} \mu_{ik}^m}, & \text{if } \underline{A}X_i \neq \phi \wedge \overline{A}X_i - \underline{A}X_i \neq \phi \\[4ex]
\dfrac{\sum\limits_{x_k \in (AX_i - \underline{A}X_i)} \mu_{ik}^m x_k}{\sum\limits_{x_k \in (AX_i - \underline{A}X_i)} \mu_{ik}^m}, & \text{if } \underline{A}X_i = \phi \wedge \overline{A}X_i - \underline{A}X_i \neq \phi \\[4ex]
\dfrac{\sum\limits_{x_k \in \underline{A}X_i} \mu_{ik}^m x_k}{\sum\limits_{x_k \in \underline{A}X_i} \mu_{ik}^m}, & \text{otherwise}
\end{cases}
$$

Step 8: Compute the fitness value fv_i for each particle using DB and D ratio by (26) and (27) respectively.
Step 9: Calculate the *pbest* for each particle

if $(pbest < fv_i)$ then set $pbest = \mathrm{p}_i$

Step 10: Calculate the *gbest* of the swarm

if $(gbest < fv_i)$ then set *gbest* to fv_i and its corresponding particle i.

Step 11: Update the velocity matrix for each particle by (1).
Step 12: Update the position matrix for each particle by (2).
Step 13: Perform union of all upper approximation $\bigcup_{i=0}^{c} (\overline{AX}_i - \underline{AX}_i)$.
Step 14: Find the object o_k having maximum number of objects close to it (using Euclidean distance) and it is far away from the centroid v_i (greater than the threshold) of c clusters.
Step 15: Add o_k to centroids $\{v\}$ and increment the c (number of clusters).
Step 16: Repeat steps (2) – (15) until convergence i.e., there are no more new assignments in the clusters or no change in gbest value.
Step 17: Perform union of objects in lower boundary. These objects are used for classification based on KNN as they are definitely classifiable.
Step 18: Compute distance between test instance and to the set of objects obtained through step 16.
Step 19: Select the first k minimum objects based on distance.
Step 20: For each class label $l \in L$ in test case perform f(l = 1) and f(l = 0) in KNN using
$$f(l) = \sum_{o_k \in N(x_i)} e^{-d(t_i, o_k)} \mu_{o_k}.$$
Step 21: If f(l =1) $\geq$ f(l =0) then predicted class label is 1 else predicted class label is 0.
Step 22: Repeat the steps 17 to 21 for each test instances.

In centroid calculation by step 7, w_{low} and w_{up} represent the weights attached to the objects in the lower approximation and the boundary region during the clustering process such that their sum is equal to 1. The parameter w_{low} is taken to have values lying in (0.5, 1). The Clustering process is influenced by these parameters as they represent the relative importance to the lower approximations and the boundary regions. Each cluster formed by RFPSO algorithm has a pair of lower and boundary region by step 5 and 6 of algorithm and the objects in boundary region are intersecting. The objects in the lower approximation are definitely classifiable as belonging to a cluster whereas objects in boundary region are uncertain. The PSO procedure in this algorithm ensures that the clusters formed are optimal since PSO explores on the set of prototypes to identify the best prototype of the clusters.

Multi label classification is performed from the objects in definitely classifiable partitions i.e. lower approximation. The algorithm generates the best k nearest instances for the test data object from the objects in all lower approximation of clusters. Here, the objects in lower approximation are alone considered for prediction as they are certainly classifiable. Using distance measure, k nearest neighboring objects is selected. By (29) (Lin et al, 2010), the function counts the objects in KNN that are close to the test data object for each label in label set. The label having highest value is considered as the predicted class label.

$$f(l_i = b) = \sum_{o_k \in N(x_i)} e^{-d(t_i, o_k)} \mu_{o_k} \tag{29}$$

Here, b is the value of class label l having value 1 or 0, t_i is the test instance and o_k is the object belongs to KNN ($N(x_i)$) and μ_{o_k} is the membership of the object belonging to the cluster. Membership value of the object in lower approximation is 1 as they are certainly classifiable. Therefore the equation (29) can be rewritten as (30).

$$f(l_i = b) = \sum_{o_k \in N(x_i)} e^{-d(t_i, o_k)} \tag{30}$$

Evaluation Metrics

The measures used for binary or multi class classification are not suitable for problems of multi label in nature. Finding accuracy of the algorithm is more difficult than the conventional classification algorithms as we need to consider multiple labels. Below are the five metrics given for evaluating the accuracy of multi label classifier. Consider the test set $S = \{(x_1, y_1), (x_2, y_2), \ldots (x_n, y_n)\}$, where $x_1, x_2, \ldots x_n$ are the instances with class labels $\ell = \{y_1, y_2, \ldots y_n\}$ respectively. The measures like hamming loss, one error, coverage, ranking loss and average precision are given below.

Hamming Loss

Hamming Loss evaluates the number of misclassified instances. It is determined by counting the number of false predictions that is false negative and false positive and is given in equation (19). Smaller the hloss value, the more accurate the classification is. When $\text{hloss}_C(h) = 0$ the classification is perfect.

$$\text{hloss}_C(h) = \frac{1}{n} \sum_{i=1}^{n} \frac{1}{Q} \left| h(x_i) \Delta Y_i \right| \tag{31}$$

Here, Δ is the symmetric difference between the two sets. Q is number of class label, $h(x_i)$ is the multi label classifier with label set, indicating the confidence of y to be proper label of x_i.

One Error

It evaluates how many times the top ranked label is not in the set of proper labels of the instance. If the one-error$_C$(f) is smaller, the performance is better, that is one-error$_C$(f) = 0, the classification is perfect.

$$\text{one-error}_C(f) = \frac{1}{n} \sum_{i=1}^{n} \left\| \left[\arg\max_{y \in l} f(x_i, y) \right] \notin y_i \right\| \tag{32}$$

where, n is number of patterns, the function f $(\cdot, \cdot)$ is the ranking quality of different labels for each instance. Function f(x_i,y) gives the rank of y derived from h(x_i, y).

Coverage

It evaluates how far we need, on the average, to go down the list of labels in order to cover all proper labels of the instance. Smaller the value of coverage$_c$(f), better the performance.

$$\text{Coverage}_c(f) = \frac{1}{n} \sum_{i=1}^{n} \max_{y \in l_i} rank_f(x_i, y) - 1 \tag{33}$$

Ranking Loss

It evaluates the average fraction of labels that are reversely ordered for the instances. When rloss$_c$(f) is smaller, the performance is good. If rloss$_c$(f) = 0, the classification is perfect.

$$\text{rloss}_c(f) = \frac{1}{n} \sum_{i=1}^{n} \frac{1}{|l_i||\overline{l_i}|} \left| \{(y_1, y_2) | f(x_i, y_1) \leq f(x_i, y_2), (y_1, y_2) \in l_i \times \overline{l_i}\} \right| \tag{34}$$

where, l_i is the label set and $\overline{l_i}$ is the complement of label set.

Average Precision

It evaluates the average fraction of proper labels ranked above a particular label $y \in l_i$. The classification is good if it has higher value. When avgprec$_c$(f) = 1, then the performance is the best.

$$\text{Avgprec}_c(f) = \frac{1}{n} \sum_{i=1}^{n} \frac{1}{|l_i|} \times \sum_{y \in l_i} \frac{\left| \{y' | rank_f(x_i, y') \leq rank_f(x_i, y), y' \in l_i\} \right|}{rank_f(x_i, y)} \tag{35}$$

Accuracy

Accuracy measures the symmetric closeness of Y_i to Z_i, where Y_i is the predicted class label and Z_i is the actual label.

$$\text{Accuracy} = \frac{1}{n} \sum_{i=1}^{n} \frac{|Y_i \cap Z_i|}{|Y_i \cup Z_i|} \tag{36}$$

where, N is the number of patterns

Precision

Precision evaluates the percentage of true positive from all the positive classified examples by the classification model.

$$\text{Precision} = \frac{1}{n}\sum_{i=1}^{n}\frac{\left|Y_i \cap Z_i\right|}{\left|Z_i\right|} \tag{37}$$

Recall

Recall is the percentage of examples classified as positive by a classification model that are true positive.

$$\text{Recall} = \frac{1}{n}\sum_{i=1}^{n}\frac{\left|Y_i \cap Z_i\right|}{\left|Y_i\right|} \tag{38}$$

F-Measure

F-Measure is a combination of Precision and Recall. It is the harmonic average of the two metrics and it is used as an aggregated performance score.

$$\text{F-Measure} = \frac{1}{n}\sum_{i=1}^{n}\frac{2\left|Y_i \cap Z_i\right|}{\left|Z_i\right| + \left|Y_i\right|} \tag{39}$$

Micro Averaging

Consider a binary evaluation measure $F(t_p, t_n, f_p, f_n)$ that is calculated based on the number of true positives (t_p), true negatives (t_n), false positives (f_p) and false negatives (f_n). Micro-averaged precision (Mic-P) represents the ratio of examples correctly classified as ℓ (t_p) and incorrectly (f_p) classified as ℓ. Micro-averaged recall (Mic-R) represents the ratio of examples correctly classified as ℓ, and all examples actually pertaining to the class ℓ (f_n). Micro-averaged F-measure (Micro-F1) represents a harmonic mean of Micro-Precision and Micro-Recall.

$$\text{Micro-F1} = \frac{2(Mic - P) \times (Mic - R)}{(Mic - P + Mic - R)}$$

where,

$$\text{Mic–P} = \frac{\sum_{i=1}^{|L|} tp_i}{\sum_{i=1}^{|L|}(tp_i + fp_i)}, \quad \text{Mic-R} = \frac{\sum_{i=1}^{|L|} tp_i}{\sum_{i=1}^{|L|}(tp_i + fn_i)},$$

|L| is the number of label set.

Results of ML-RFPSO

Different multi label data sets considered for validation of our results is given in Table 3. These are the standard data sets considered in literature for evaluation multi label sets. Table 4 shows the performance of ML - RFPSO on the data set listed in Table 3. From the table, it is obvious that the performance of ML - RFPSO is good, as it has produced less value on one error and ranking loss. Similarly it generates reasonable performance on average precision. Further to show the superiority of the results, the proposed algorithm is compared against some existing algorithms in this line and the results are summarized in Table 5, 6 and 7.

On seeing the results of ML – RFPSO, accuracy and average precision is good and also generates low one error and hamming loss. In order to study the superiority of the proposed algorithm, a comparative analysis is performed. Some of the popular adoption algorithms like MLKNN, BPMLL, BOOSTEX-TER, ADTBOOST.MH and RANK SVM are considered for verification and validation of the results. The evaluation metrics like one error, coverage, ranking loss and Average precision are evaluated on various data set and algorithms and are summarized in Tables 5, 6, and 7. The ↓ indicates that for an ideal result, the value should be low. Similarly, the ↑ indicates that the value should be high for the good performance of an algorithm.

The performance is measure based on the label predication capability of an algorithm evaluated through various metrics explained in the previous section. The best results are indicated by bold letters

Table 3. Multi label data sets

Data Set	Instances	Attributes	Class Labels	Training Instances	Test Instances
ADHD	200	15	3	140	60
Emotions	593	72	6	391	202
Yeast	2417	103	14	1500	917
scene	2407	300	6	1211	1196

Table 4. Performance of ML – RFPSO

	ADHD	Scene	Emotions	Yeast
Accuracy↑	0.935926	0.889517	0.7646062	0.763814
Hamming Loss↓	0.054074	0.113483	0.283938	0.232186
Recall↑	0.925	0.575978	0.5716421	0.530675
Specificity	0.938571	0.956482	0.804718	0.862631
Precision↑	0.871852	0.757786	0.558941	0.626708
Micro –F1↑	0.887615	0.652044	0.5437657	0.571554
Fbeta	0.854662	0.70876	0.540734	0.606312
One Error↓	0.036337	0.021267	0.1091531	0.124228
Coverage↓	1.7743778	4.231404	3.123762	9.670389
Ranking Loss↓	0.054356	0.04805	0.1293075	0.220878
Avg. Precision↑	0.896314	0.83685	0.837164	0.698905

Table 5. Comparison of different algorithms on Emotion data set

	ML - RFPSO	ML-KNN	BPMLL	BOOS TEXTER	ADT BOOST.MH	RANK SVM
Hamming loss↓	0.283938	**0.262**	0.433	0.302	0.321	0.387
One Error↓	**0.1091531**	0.386	0.668	0.356	0.4245	0.5027
Coverage↓	3.123762	**2.327**	3.159	3.635	3.072	3.8792
Ranking Loss↓	**0.1293075**	0.320	0.4792	0.363	NA	0.3682
Avg. Precision↑	**0.837164**	0.708	0.542	0.6589	0.627	0.6035

Table 6. Comparison of different algorithms on yeast data set

	ML - RFPSO	MLKNN	BPMLL	BOOS TEXTER	ADT BOOST.MH	RANK SVM
Hamming loss↓	0.232186	**0.194**	0.322	0.22	0.207	0.207
One Error↓	**0.124228**	0.234	0.805	0.278	0.244	0.243
Coverage↓	9.670389	6.301	**2.523**	6.55	6.39	7.09
Ranking Loss↓	0.220878	0.167	0.2631	**0.186**	NA	0.195
Avg. Precision↑	0.698905	**0.762**	0.428	0.737	0.744	0.749

Table 7. Comparison of different algorithms on scene data set

	ML - RFPSO	ML-KNN	BPMLL	BOOS TEXTER	ADT BOOST. MH	RANK SVM
Hamming loss↓	**0.113483**	0.169	0.267	0.179	0.193	0.253
One Error↓	**0.021267**	0.3	0.466	0.311	0.375	0.491
Coverage↓	4.231404	**0.939**	5.447	0.939	1.102	1.382
Ranking Loss↓	**0.04805**	0.168	0.1547	0.168	NA	0.278
Avg. Precision↑	**0.83685**	0.803	0.629	0.798	0.755	0.682

in the table. The results summarized in table reveals that the performance of ML – RCM is good on many measures. Form the results on Yeast data set, we cannot conclude the superiority of the algorithm as each of the algorithm shows the best result on some measure. MLKNN is shows better performance than ML-RFPSO on its average precision and hamming loss while the proposed algorithm shows good result on one error. But one can draw conclusion from other data set as it is visible and evident from tables 5 and 7. From these tables it is visible and evident that the performance of ML-RFPSO is superior to other exiting algorithms. The results of proposed ML- RFPSO algorithm on Scene and Emotion data set has many ideal results on the metrics and is comparably good to other adoption methods.

The superiority of ML – RFPSO can be visualized from the graph shown in Figures 6 to 9. The performance of MLKNN is close by ML-RFPSO on some cases or better on particular case. MLKNN and ML - RFPSO are competitive adoption algorithms. ML – RCM is a centroid based method, where as MLKNN is statistical based method and both of them as its own merits and demerits. In general, by experimental analysis both are competitive at time superior to other.

Figure 6. Comparison of hamming loss values for various data sets

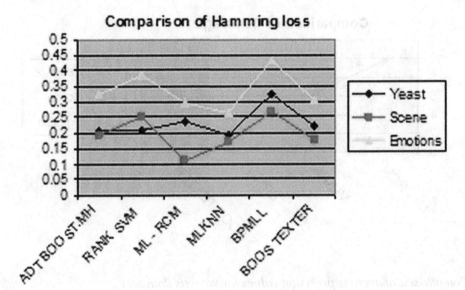

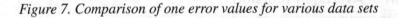

Figure 7. Comparison of one error values for various data sets

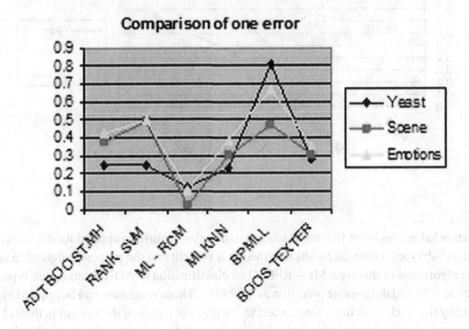

CONCLUSION AND FUTURE WORK

PSO is proven to a simple yet successful tool for enhancing the results obtained from any data mining algorithm. It is a flexible tool that can be easily hybridized with any other technique. In recent years, they are prominent in solving complex problems like multi objective and multi label classification problems. Here we propose an uncertainty based PSO algorithm to classify multi label data set.

Figure 8. Comparison of coverage values for various data sets

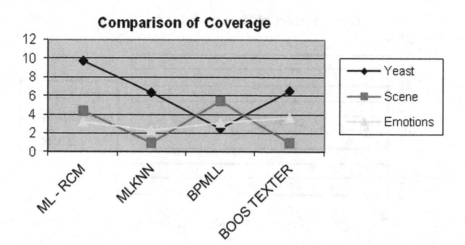

Figure 9. Comparison of average precision values for various data sets

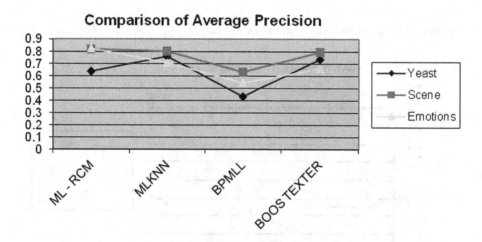

To our knowledge, this is the first multi label classification algorithm applied for decision making of ADHD and its sub types. From the results obtained, it is evident that the proposed algorithm is competitive to other algorithms of this type. ML – RFPSO on classification of ADHD and its sub types provides the accuracy as 92% and the average precision as 0.895021. These results are can be applied in academic environment by the teachers as the screening test to identify the nature of the student in their class, based on which special attention can be provided. The accuracy of the algorithm can be further improved by hybridizing the clustering algorithm with possibilistic approach or fuzzy techniques. This algorithm can be further studied to data with multiple decision classes on Learning Disability (LD) dataset where each category of LD is influencing the other types.

REFERENCES

Abido, M. A. (2007). *Two-level of non-dominated solutions approach to multiobjective particle swarm optimization*. ACM.

Bansal, J. C., Singh, P. K., Saraswat, M., Verma, A., Singh, J. S., & Abraham, A. (2011), Inertia weight strategies in particle swarm optimization. In *Proceedings of Third World Congress on Nature and Biologically Inspired Computing*. IEEE. doi:10.1109/NaBIC.2011.6089659

Beiranvand, V., Kashani, M. M., & Bakar, A. (2014). Multi objective PSO algorithm for mining numerical association rule without priori discretization. *Expert Systems with Applications, 41*(9), 4259–4273. doi:10.1016/j.eswa.2013.12.043

Bezdek, J. C. (1981). *Pattern recognition with fuzzy objective function algorithm*. New York: Plenum. doi:10.1007/978-1-4757-0450-1

Bezdek, J. C., & Pal, N. R. (1988). Some new indexes for cluster validity. *IEEE Transactions on Systems, Man, and Cybernetics. Part B, Cybernetics, 28*(3), 301–315. doi:10.1109/3477.678624 PMID:18255949

Chuang, L. Y., Chang, H. W., Tu, C. J., & Yang, C. H. (2008). Improved binary PSO for feature selection using gene expression data. *Computational Biology and Chemistry, 32*(1), 29–38. doi:10.1016/j.compbiolchem.2007.09.005 PMID:18023261

Dash, M., & Liu, H. (1997). Feature selection for classification. *Intelligent Data Analysis, 1*(4), 131–156. doi:10.1016/S1088-467X(97)00008-5

De Bao, C., & Chun Xia, Z. (2009). Particle swarm optimization with adaptive population size and its application. *Applied Soft Computing, 9*(1), 39–48. doi:10.1016/j.asoc.2008.03.001

Dubois, D., & Prade, H. (1990). Rough fuzzy sets and fuzzy rough sets. *International Journal of General Systems, 17*(2-3), 191–209. doi:10.1080/03081079008935107

Hereford, J. M. (2006). A distributed particle swarm optimization algorithm for swarm robotic applications. In *Proceedings of the IEEE Congress on Evolutionary Computation* (pp. 1678 -1685). IEEE. doi:10.1109/CEC.2006.1688510

Huang, C. J., & Dun, J. F. (2008). A distributed PSO-SVM hybrid system with feature selection and parameter optimization. *Applied Soft Computing, 8*(4), 1381–1391. doi:10.1016/j.asoc.2007.10.007

Imran, M., Hashim, R., & Khalid, N. E. A. (2013). An overview of particle swarm optimization variants. *Procedia Engineering, 53*, 491–496. doi:10.1016/j.proeng.2013.02.063

Kennedy, J., & Eberhart, R. (1995). Particle swarm optimization. *IEEE International Conference on Neural Networks, 4*, 1942-1948.

Kennedy, J., & Eberhart, R. C. (1997). A discrete binary version of the particle swarm algorithm. In *Proceedings of 1997 IEEE International Conference on Systems, Man, and Cybernetics, Computational Cybernetics and Simulation* (vol. 5, pp. 4104–4108). IEEE. doi:10.1109/ICSMC.1997.637339

Kennedy, J., & Spears, W. (1998). Matching algorithms to problems: an experimental test of the particle swarm and some genetic algorithms on the multimodal problem generator. In *Proceedings of IEEE Congress on Evolutionary Computation* (CEC'98) (pp. 78-83). IEEE. doi:10.1109/ICEC.1998.699326

Knowles, J. D., & Corne, D. W. (2000). Approximating the non-dominated front using the pareto archived evolution strategy. *Evolutionary Computation, 8*(2), 149-172.

Lingras, P., & West, C. (2004). Interval set clustering of web users with rough k-means. *Journal of Intelligent Information Systems, 23*(1), 5–16. doi:10.1023/B:JIIS.0000029668.88665.1a

McQueen, J. (1967). Some methods for classification and analysis of multivariate observations. In *Proc. Fifth Berkeley Symp. Math. Statistics and Probability* (pp. 281-297). Academic Press.

O¨zbakar, L., & Delice, Y. (2010). Exploring comprehensible classification rules from trained neural networks integrated with a time-varying binary particle swarm optimizer. *Engineering Applications of Artificial Intelligence.* doi:10.1016/j.engappai.2010.11.008

Parsopoulos, K. E., & Vrahatis, M. N. (2008). *Multi-objective particles swarm optimization approaches.* IGI Global Publishers.

Pawlak, Z. (1982). Rough set. *International Journal of Information and Computer Science*, 341 - 356.

Pawlak, Z. (1991). Rough Sets, theoretical aspects of reasoning about data. Kluwer Academic Publishers.

Rezazadeh, I., Meybodi, M. R., & Naebi, A. (2011). Adaptive particle swarm optimization algorithm for dynamic environments. In Proceedings of ICSI (LNCS), (vol. 6728, pp. 120 – 129). Berlin: Springer.

Shi, Y., & Eberhart, R. C. (2001). Fuzzy adaptive particle swarm optimization. In *Proceedings of the IEEE Congress on Evolutionary Computation.* Seoul, South Korea. IEEE.

Sousa, T., Silva, A., & Neves, A. (2004). Particle swarm based data mining algorithms for classification tasks. *Parallel Computing, 30*(5-6), 767–783. doi:10.1016/j.parco.2003.12.015

Valle, Y. D., Venayagamoorthy, G. K., Mohagheghi, S., Hernandez, J. C., & Harley, R. G. (2008). Particle swarm optimization: Basic concepts, variants and applications in power systems. *IEEE Transactions on Evolutionary Computation, 12*(2), 171–195. doi:10.1109/TEVC.2007.896686

Vanneschi, L., Codecasa, D., & Mauri, G. (2011). A comparative study of four parallel and distributed PSO methods. *New Generation Computing, 29*(2), 129–161. doi:10.1007/s00354-010-0102-z

Wang, H. (2007). A hybrid particle swarm optimization with Cauchy mutation. In *Proceedings of IEEE Swarm Intelligence Symposium* (pp. 356 – 360). IEEE.

Wang, Z., Sun, X., & Zhang, D. (2007). A PSO – based classification rule mining algorithm. *Advanced Intelligent Computing Theories and Applications, LNCS, 4682*, 377–384.

Xiao, L. L. (2010). A particle swarm optimization and immune theory based algorithm for structure learning of Bayesian networks. *International Journal of Database Theory and Applications, 3*(2), 61–69.

Xue, B., Zhang, M., & Browne, M. N. (2013). Particle swarm optimization for feature selection in classification: A multi-objective approach. *IEEE Transactions on Cybernetics, 43*(6).

Yang, X. M., Yuan, J. S., Yuan, J. Y., & Mao, H. (2007). A modified particle swarm optimizer with dynamic adaptation. *Applied Mathematics and Computation, 189*(2), 1205–1213. doi:10.1016/j.amc.2006.12.045

Zadeh, L. A. (1965). Fuzzy sets. *Information and Control, 8*(3), 338–353. doi:10.1016/S0019-9958(65)90241-X

Zhang, L. M., & Zhou, Z. H. (2007). ML-KNN: A lazy learning approach to multi - label learning. *Pattern Recognition, 40*(7), 2038–2048. doi:10.1016/j.patcog.2006.12.019

KEY TERMS AND DEFINITIONS

Artificial Neuron Network: A network modeled by using artificial neurons in parallel to biological neurons to mimic the human brain.

Classification: It is a process similar to clustering except that it comes under supervised learning in contrast to clustering, which comes under unsupervised learning approach.

Clustering: A process to divide a set of data into groups called clusters, where the elements inside a group have higher similarity to each other than the similarity between elements of different groups.

Feature: These are attributes in a data table.

Fuzzy Set: A set in which the belongingness of elements to the set are given by membership functions providing values lying between 0 and 1.

Genetic Algorithm: These are the search and optimization algorithms which are capable of searching large solution spaces to find the optimal solutions using the methods of natural selection.

Optimization: It is a process of finding the optimal (maximum or minimum) value of a function called the objective function subject to certain constraints.

Rough Set: A set in which the uncertainty is captured in the boundary region. It is approximated by a pair of crisp sets called the lower and upper approximation of the set.

Chapter 3
Swarm Intelligence in Solving Bio–Inspired Computing Problems:
Reviews, Perspectives, and Challenges

Debi Prasanna Acharjya
VIT University, India

Ahmed P. Kauser
VIT University, India

ABSTRACT

Currently, a huge amount of data is available across various domains including biological data. Classification of these data, clustering, and data analysis is tedious and has become popular in recent research. In particular, bio-inspired computing is the field that mends together mathematics, computer science, and biology to develop tools to store, scrutinize, and interpret the biological data. It is also used to solve real life problems like sequencing biological data, data clustering, and optimization. Swarm intelligence is an emerging field of biologically inspired artificial intelligence technique that is based on the behavioral models of social insects. This chapter provides an overview of swarm intelligence algorithms in solving bio-inspired computing problems. It is an attempt to explore the working nature, applications, and generative power of various bio-inspired computing algorithms. The main intent is to furnish a comprehensive study of swarm intelligence algorithms in the literature so as to inspire further research in the area of biologically inspired computing.

INTRODUCTION

Research and development in the area of Bio inspired computing using swarm intelligence has a deep impact and emphasize on various field of engineering and technology such as healthcare, decision support system, gene expression and microarray classification, etc. Bio inspired computing is an interdisciplinary area which combines bioinformatics, computational biology and computational intelligence.

DOI: 10.4018/978-1-4666-8291-7.ch003

Bioinformatics is a shorten form of 'biological informatics' defined as the application of analytical and computational tools to capture and interpret the biological data. A major activity in bioinformatics is to develop software tools, databases and visualization methods to generate useful biological knowledge. Major research efforts in the field include creating data bases and visualization methods for sequence analysis, gene finding, genome annotation, protein structure alignment analysis and prediction and prediction of gene expression. Though the creation of database is easy, but the classification, clustering and prediction are challenging. A major activity in Bio inspired computing is to design innovative systems like various aerodynamic parts of aircrafts, Artificial intelligent robots, realistic creatures, tele surgery robots and medical diagnosis robots. Major research efforts in the field include algorithm development that could extract metaphor from biological system.

Computational biology on the other hand is the application of computer science, mathematics, and statistics to the problems in biology. A major activity in computational biology signifies the development of algorithms, mathematical models, and methods for statistical inference to understand biology. Major research efforts in the field include identification of disease-causing genes, reconstruction of the evolutionary histories of species, and the unlocking of the complex regulatory codes that turn genes on and off. Computational Intelligence is a glowing recognized prototype with recent systems having many of the characteristics of bio inspired computers. In addition, it is capable of executing an assortment of tasks that are intricate to do using conventional methods. It is a methodology involving adaptive mechanism from nature and an ability to learn that facilitate intelligent behaviour in multifarious and varying environments, such that the system is supposed to possess one or more features of reason, such as generalization, discovery, association and abstraction. In order to achieve these characteristics, these methodologies uses intelligent techniques such as rough set (Pawlak, 1982, 1991), fuzzy set (Zadeh, 1965), neural networks (McCulloch & Pitts, 1943), evolutionary computation and swarm intelligence (Beni & Wang, 1989). Latest development aim to incorporate components to take advantage of harmonizing features and to develop systems that acts together leading to hybrid and abstraction architecture such as rough fuzzy, rough set and swarm intelligence, fuzzy- rough with swarm intelligence, particle swarm optimization, ant colony optimization and K-means etc (Niknam & Amiri, 2010; Tripathy, Acharjya & Cynthya, 2011; Wang, Yang, Teng, Xia & Richard, 2007; Ahmed, Mehdi & Adil, 2013; Ganesh, Aruldoss, Renukadevi & Devaraj, 2012). Swarm intelligence (SI) is artificial intelligence, based on the collective behaviour of decentralized, self-organized systems. It is a scientific theory that discusses complex and sophisticate behaviours of social creature groups like ant colonies, honey bees, and bird flocks. The expression was introduced by Beni & Wang (1989) in the context of cellular robotic systems.

The objective of this book chapter is to highlight the swarm intelligence and bio inspired computing research communities the astonishing applications of swarm intelligence in bio inspired computing. Hence this chapter discusses some inspiring examples to illustrate how swarm intelligence techniques can be applied to solve bio inspired computing problems. Innovative ideas will be stimulated and shared through the fusion of diverse techniques and applications. The motivational examples include. swarm intelligence in healthcare; swarm intelligence in medical decision support system; swarm intelligence in gene expression and swarm intelligence in microarray classification. The chapter is structured as follows. The chapter starts with a general introduction to bio-inspired computing followed by preliminary ideas and fundamental concepts of bio inspired computing. This will be further followed by relevant soft computing and swarm intelligence algorithms that are used in bio-inspired computing. In succession, various applications of these algorithms in real life situations are presented. Further, few open ended research problems are presented in the context of bio-inspired computing that can be solved by using swarm intelligence techniques. Finally, the chapter will be concluded with a conclusion.

INFORMATION SYSTEM

The most fundamental objective of information retrieval and data mining is to learn the knowledge for classification. But, one may not face a simply classification while dealing real world problems. Ordering of objects is one such problem. Before classification and clustering using rough computing, one must know about an information system. An information system contains a finite set of objects typically represented by their values on a finite set of attributes. Such information system may be conveniently described in a tabular form in which each row represents an object whereas each column represents an attribute. Each cell of the information system contains an attribute value.

An information system is a table that provides a convenient way to describe a finite set of objects called the universe by a finite set of attributes thereby representing all available information and knowledge. The attribute sets along with the objects in an information system consists of the set of condition attributes and decision attributes. This is otherwise known as decision table (Pawlak, 1991). Let us denote the information system as $I = (U, A, V, f)$, where $U = \{x_1, x_2, \cdots, x_n\}$ is a finite non-empty set of objects called the universe and $A = \{a_1, a_2, \cdots, a_m\}$ is a non-empty finite set of attributes. For every $a \in A$, V_a is the set of values that attribute a may take. Also $V = \bigcup_{a \in A} V_a$. In addition, for every $a \in A$, $f_a : U \to V_a$ is the information function. Further, $C, D \subset A$ are two subsets of attributes that are called condition (C) and decision (D) attributes, respectively. In such cases, the information system is called as decision table or decision system.

For example, a sample decision system is presented in Table 1 in which $U = \{x_1, x_2, x_3, x_4, x_5, x_6\}$ represents a nonempty finite set of objects; and $C = \{a_1, a_2, a_3\} = \{\text{Humidity, Windy, Cloudy}\}$ be a finite set of condition attributes whereas $D = \{\text{Weather}\}$ be the decision attribute. In particular, object x_1 is characterized in the table by the attribute value set (humidity, high), (windy, less), (cloudy, full) and (weather, mild) which form the information about the object. The decision system presented in Table 1 is a qualitative system, where all the attribute values are discrete and categorical (qualitative).

In the information system shown in Table 2, $U = \{x_1, x_2, x_3, x_4, x_5\}$ represents a set of patients and $A = \{\text{Temperature, Blood Pressure, Cholesterol}\}$ represents a finite set of attributes. This information system is a quantitative system, since all the attribute values are non categorical (Acharjya & Geetha, 2014). An information system which contains both qualitative and quantitative attribute values is termed as hybrid information system.

Indiscernibility Relation

Universe can be considered as a large collection of objects. Each object is associated with some information (data, knowledge) within it. In order to find knowledge about the universe, it is essential to process these attribute values. Therefore, sufficient amount of information to uniquely identify, classify these

Table 1. Qualitative information system

Objects	Humidity (a_1)	Windy (a_2)	Cloudy (a_3)	Weather (D)
x_1	High	Less	Full	Mild
x_2	High	Yes	Full	Hot
x_3	Normal	Yes	No	Hot
x_4	High	Yes	Full	Mild
x_5	Low	Yes	Full	Cool
x_6	High	No	Normal	Hot

Table 2. Quantitative information system

Object	Temperature (F)	Blood Pressure	Cholesterol
x_1	98.7	112	180
x_2	102.3	143	184
x_3	99	125	197
x_4	98.9	106	193
x_5	100.3	134	205

objects into equivalence classes is required to acquire knowledge about the universe. It is carried out based on indiscernibility relation among these objects. It indicates that objects of a class cannot discern from one another based on available set of attributes of the objects (Pawlak, 1982; Tripathy, Acharjya & Cynthya, 2011). The indiscernibility relation generated in this way is the mathematical basis of rough set theory. Any set of all indiscernible objects is called an elementary concept, and form a basic granule (atom) of knowledge about the universe. Any union of the elementary sets is referred to be either crisp (precise) set or rough (imprecise) set. Let $P \subseteq C$ and x_i, $x_j \in U$. Then we say x_i and x_j are indiscernible by the set of attributes P in C if and only if the following (3) holds.

$$f(x_i, a) = f(x_j, a), \qquad \forall \quad a \in C \tag{1}$$

For example, given the decision table in Table 1, indiscernibility relations can be appreciated as bellows.

$$U \, / \, (C = a_1) = \{\{x_1, x_2, x_4, x_6\}, \{x_3\}, \{x_5\}\}$$

$$U \, / \, (C = a_2) = \{\{x_1\}, \{x_2, x_3, x_4, x_5\}, \{x_6\}\}$$

$$U \, / \, (C = a_3) = \{\{x_1\}, \{x_2, x_4\}, \{x_3\}, \{x_5\}, \{x_6\}\}$$

$$U \, / \, (C = \{a_1, a_2, a_3\}) = \{\{x_1\}, \{x_2, x_4\}, \{x_3\}, \{x_5\}, \{x_6\}\}$$

From the above analysis, it is clear that an indiscernibility relation is an equivalence relation that partitions the set of cases into equivalence classes. Each class contains a set of indiscernible objects for the given set of condition attributes C. The graphical illustration is shown in the following Figure 1.

FOUNDATIONS OF ROUGH COMPUTING

In real world, invent of computers, communication technologies, and database systems have created a new space for knowledge extraction. Therefore, data handling and data processing, knowledge discovery is of prime importance in recent years. Knowledge discovery in database is a growing field in computer science to solve many real world problems. It consists of several steps such as selection, preprocessing, transformation, data mining and evaluation. Data mining, data handling and processing is of prime importance in recent years. In the hierarchy of data processing, data is the root which transforms into information and further refined to avail it in the form of knowledge. Rough set of Z. Pawlak (1982, 1991) is a mathematical approach for various purposes such as feature selection, feature extraction, attributes reduction and extraction of decision rules in data. The main advantage is that, it does not need any preliminary or additional information about the data. Therefore, it classifies imprecise, uncertain or incomplete information expressed in terms of data. In general, it helps in knowledge discovery methods using partition properties and the discernibility matrix. Moreover, the importance of rough sets leads to artificial intelligence and swarm intelligence in the area of decision analysis.

The rough set philosophy was developed based on the assumption that with every object of the universe of discourse, we associate some information (data, knowledge). Objects characterized by same information are indiscernible in view of the available information about them. The indiscernibility relation obtained in this way is the mathematical foundation of rough set theory. In this section we give some definitions and notations as developed by Z. Pawlak (1982), which shall be referred in the rest of the paper.

Let U be a finite nonempty set called the universe. Suppose $R \subseteq U \times U$ is an equivalence relation on U. The set of all objects of the universe under consideration for particular discussion is considered as a universal set. So, there is a need to classify objects of the universe based on the indiscernibility relation (equivalence relation) among them. The equivalence relation R partitions the set U into disjoint subsets. Elements of same equivalence class are said to be indistinguishable. Equivalence classes induced by R are called elementary concepts. Every union of elementary concepts is called a definable set. The

Figure 1. Partitions of the information system determined by the three conditions attributes

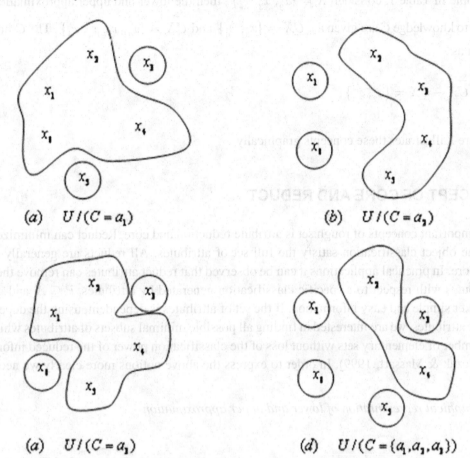

$(a) \quad U/(C = a_1)$

$(b) \quad U/(C = a_2)$

$(a) \quad U/(C = a_3)$

$(d) \quad U/(C = \{a_1, a_2, a_3\})$

empty set is considered to be a definable set, thus all the definable sets form a Boolean algebra and (U, R) is called an approximation space. Given a target set X, we can characterize X by a pair of lower and upper approximations. We associate two subsets $\underline{R}X$ and $\overline{R}X$ called the R–lower and R–upper approximations of X respectively and are given by

$$\underline{R}X = \bigcup\{Y \in U / R : Y \subseteq X\} \tag{2}$$

and

$$\overline{R}X = \bigcup\{Y \in U / R : Y \cap X \neq \phi\} \tag{3}$$

The R–boundary of X, $BN_R(X)$ is given by $BN_R(X) = \overline{R}X - \underline{R}X$. We say X is rough with respect to R if and only if $\overline{R}X \neq \underline{R}X$, equivalently $BN_R(X) \neq \phi$. X is said to be R–definable if and only if $\overline{R}X = \underline{R}X$ or $BN_R(X) = \phi$. So, a set is rough with respect to R if and only if it is not R–definable.

For example in Table 1, consider $X = \{x_2, x_3, x_6\}$, then the lower and upper approximations of X with respect to knowledge C are given as. $\underline{C}X = \{x_3, x_6\}$ and $\overline{C}X = \{x_2, x_3, x_4, x_6\}$. The C-boundary of X is given as

$$BN_C(X) = \overline{C}X - \underline{C}X = \{x_2, x_4\}.$$

The Figure 2 illustrates these concepts graphically.

THE CONCEPT OF CORE AND REDUCT

One of the important concepts of rough set is attribute reduction and core. Reduct can minimize subset and make the object classification satisfy the full set of attributes. All reducts are generally used in computing core. In practical applications it can be observed that reduct attributes can remove the superfluous attributes with respect to a specific classification generated by attributes $P \subseteq A$ and give the decision maker simple and easy information. If the set of attributes is dependent, using the dependency properties of attributes, we are interested in finding all possible minimal subsets of attributes which have the same number of elementary sets without loss of the classification power of the reduced information system (Walczak & Massart, 1999). In order to express the above notions more clearly we need some

Figure 2. Graphical representation of lower and upper approximation

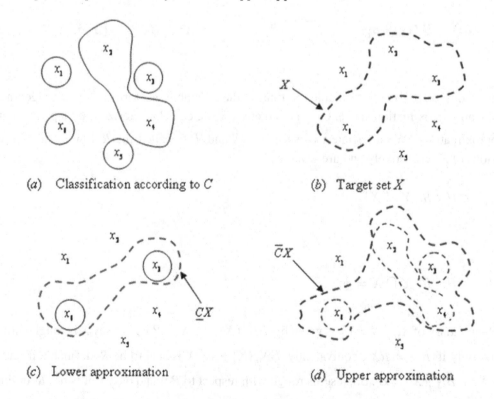

auxiliary notations. Let $P \subseteq A$ and $a \in P$. We say that the attribute a is dispensable in P if the following condition equation (4) holds; otherwise a is indispensable in P.

$$U \, / \, P = U \, / \, (P - \{a\}) \tag{4}$$

Set P is independent if all its attributes are indispensable. Reduct P' of P is a subset of attributes P such that the equivalence class induced by the reduced attribute set P' are the same as the equivalence class structure induced by the attribute set P. i.e., $U \, / \, P = U \, / \, P'$. The core of the attribute set P is the set of all indispensable attributes of P. The important property connecting the notion of core and reducts is defined in equation (5), where Red(P) is the set off all reducts of P.

$$\text{Core} \, (P) = \bigcap \text{Red}(P) \tag{5}$$

The core can be interpreted as the most characteristic part of knowledge, which cannot be eliminated when reducing the knowledge. To illustrate these, consider the information system as in Table 1.

1. First of all compute the indiscernibility relations for the combination of attributes. Therefore, we get.

$$U \, / \, (a_1, a_2) = \{\{x_1\}, \{x_2, x_4\}, \{x_3\}, \{x_5\}, \{x_6\}\}$$

$$U \, / \, (a_2, a_3) = \{\{x_1\}, \{x_2, x_4, x_5\}, \{x_3\}, \{x_6\}\}$$

$$U \, / \, (a_1, a_3) = \{\{x_1, x_2, x_4\}, \{x_3\}, \{x_5\}, \{x_6\}\}$$

2. Search for the indispensable attributes. From the above analysis it is clear that $U \, / \, (a_1, a_2) = U \, / \, (a_1, a_2, a_3)$. Therefore, the attribute a_3 is dispensable. Also, $U \, / \, (a_2, a_3) \neq U \, / \, (a_1, a_2, a_3)$ and hence the attribute a_1 is indispensable. Similarly, $U \, / \, (a_1, a_3) \neq U \, / \, (a_1, a_2, a_3)$ and hence a_2 is indispensable.

3. On considering single attributes, we have $U \, / \, (a_1, a_2) \neq U \, / \, (a_1)$ and $U \, / \, (a_1, a_2) \neq U \, / \, (a_2)$. Therefore, the only reduct is given as Red $(C) = \{a_1, a_2\}$.

4. Finally, the core is defined as Core $(C) = \{a_1, a_2\}$.

For this simple example, the attributes needed to represent the information system are $\{a_1, a_2\} =$ {humidity, windy} and they are the only feature in the reduct subsets. However it is observed that, in an information system C may have many reducts.

OVERVIEW OF SWARM INTELLIGENCE MODELS

The collective behaviour of decentralized, self-organized systems, natural or artificial is known as swarm intelligence. The concept was employed in artificial intelligence and was introduced by Beni and Wang (1989). It consists of a population of simple agents that interact locally with one another and with their environment. But, there is no centralized control structure dictating how individual agents should behave. The interaction could be local and to a certain degree random. In addition, interactions between such agents lead to the emergence of global behaviour, unknown to the individual agents. The basic inspiration comes from nature with special reference to biological systems. However, the definition of swarm intelligence is still not clear. In principle, it should be a multi-agent system that has self-organized behaviour and that shows some intelligent behaviour. Various natural systems of swarm intelligence include ant colonies, bird flocking, animal herding and fish schooling. In the following sections, we present a brief overview of recent trends in swarm intelligence models like particle swarm optimization, ant colony optimization and artificial bee colony. The general framework for nature inspired computing (Hazem & Glasgow, 2012) is depicted in the following Figure 3.

Swarm Intelligence Advantages and Limitations

The general framework of swarm intelligence models is discussed in the previous section. The models have certain advantages and limitations. A list of advantages and limitations are briefly discussed in this section.

Advantages:

1. Swarm intelligence is very simple to implement and helps in designing complex systems.
2. The adoptability helps in self organization and auto configuration.
3. Swarm intelligence does not require a centralized control, pre processing, and classification.

Figure 3. General framework for nature inspired computing

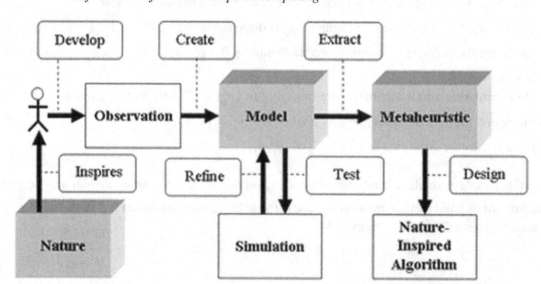

4.   Swarm intelligence will respond to dynamic and rapid environments.
5.   With the help of swarm intelligence, designing and implementing Meta heuristics algorithms becomes easier.
6.   These algorithms are scalable since the control mechanisms are not dependent of swarm size.
7.   Swarm intelligence algorithms have no single point of failure and the fault tolerance capability of swarm intelligence systems is remarkably high.

Limitations:

1.   Swarm intelligence algorithms are not suitable for time critical applications like nuclear reactors because Swarm Intelligence is not pre defined or pre-processed.
2.   These algorithms of swarm intelligence do not have a centralized control that may result in stagnation.
3.   The limitation mentioned above can be reduced by hybridizing various swarm intelligence techniques to fine tune the parameters that may solve the stagnation problem.

Ant Colony Optimization

Ant colony optimization is a class of optimization algorithms modeled on the actions of an ant colony. It is a population-based metaheuristic algorithm that can be used to find approximate solutions to difficult combinatorial optimization problems. The basic principle of ant colony optimization is simulation of ability of ants to find the shortest path between their nest and food source. Ants are capable of finding the shortest path between their nest and food source, without any visible, central and active coordination mechanism. In general, ants drop a pheromone, a chemical from their body, on the path which leads them for the various decisions. The path optimization between nest and food is achieved by ant colonies by exploiting the pheromone quantity dropped by the ants. The path selection of the ants is done on the basis of the pheromone concentration deposited on various paths. With high concentration of pheromone value the path is getting selected based on probability. The indirect pheromone based communication is known as stigmergy. There is a natural evaporation of the pheromone, which favors the shorter path than the larger one. The following Figure 4 depicts how ants are finding the shortest route to collect food.

Ant colony optimization technique is a probabilistic technique generally used for problems that deal with finding better paths through graphs. In this technique, simulation agents (artificial ants) locate optimal solutions by moving through a parameter space representing all possible solutions. This computing technique is developed based on the behaviour of natural ants which lay down pheromones while exploring their environment to resources. In similar to natural ants, the simulated agents record their positions and the quality of their solutions. This helps in later simulation iterations more ants locate better solutions (Dorigo & Thomas, 2004). The basic flow of ant colony optimization (Dorigo & Thomas, 2004) is presented in Algorithm 1.

The basic flow chart of ant colony optimization algorithm is presented in the following Figure 5.

Applications of Ant Colony Optimization

The significant study of ant colony algorithms has contributed in abundance to the set of swarm intelligent algorithms. Clustering is used as a data processing technique in many different areas, including

Figure 4. Ant colony optimization principles

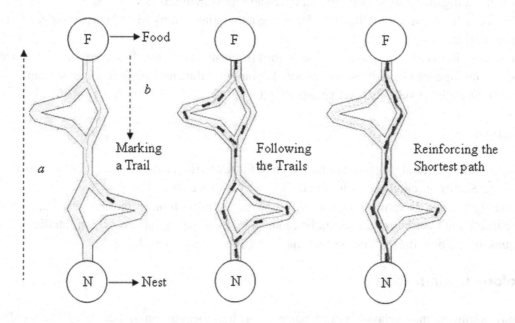

Algorithm 1.

1.   Represent the solution space by a construction graph.
2.   Set ant colony optimization parameters and initialize pheromone trails.
3.   Generate simulation agent (ant) solutions from each simulation agents walk on the construction graph mediated by pheromone trails.
4.   Update pheromone intensities.
5.   Go to step 3, and repeat the process until convergence or termination conditions are met.

artificial intelligence, bioinformatics, data mining, image analysis and segmentation, machine learning, information retrieval, medicine, pattern recognition, spatial database analysis and statistics. Ant-based clustering is a biologically inspired data clustering technique falls under the category of bio inspired computing. Mohamed Jafar & Sivakumar (2010) provides an overview of ant based clustering algorithms. The significant studies that were published in the recent years are textual document clustering, knowledge discovery in DNA, biomedical data processing, data clustering, classification and gene expression.

Chandra Mohan & Baskaran (2012) provides an overview about the ant colony optimization based research and implementation on several engineering domains like traveling salesman problem, scheduling, structural and concrete engineering, digital image processing, electrical engineering, clustering and routing algorithm. Major research efforts and applications in ant colony optimization include water resources systems analysis, traffic signal timings, image segmentation, electrical distribution system optimization and image processing (Mohamed & Sivakumar, 2010; Chandra Mohan & Baskaran, 2012). The following Figure 6 depicts the numerous applications of ant colony across various fields.

Figure 5. Flow chart of ant colony optimization algorithm

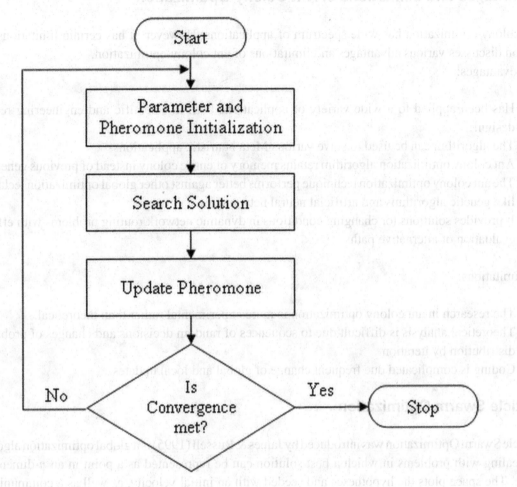

Figure 6. Various applications of ant colony optimization

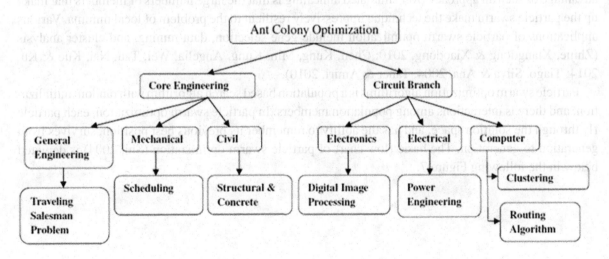

Advantages and Limitations of Ant Colony Optimization

Ant colony optimization has wide spectrum of applications. However, it has certain limitations. This section discusses various advantages and limitations of ant colony optimization.

Advantages:

1. Has been applied to a wide variety of applications both in scientific and engineering research design.
2. The algorithm can be used to solve various Meta heuristic applications.
3. Ant colony optimization algorithm retains memory of entire colony instead of previous generation.
4. The ant colony optimization technique performs better against other global optimization techniques like genetic algorithms and artificial neural network.
5. It provides solutions for changing conditions in dynamic network routing problems with effective evaluation of alternative paths.

Limitations:

1. The research in ant colony optimization is more experimental rather than theoretical.
2. Theoretical analysis is difficult due to sequences of random decisions and changes of probability distribution by iteration.
3. Coding is complicated due frequent change of global and local updates.

Particle Swarm Optimization

Particle Swarm Optimization was introduced by James & Russell (1995) is a global optimization algorithm for dealing with problems in which a best solution can be represented as a point in an n-dimensional space. The space plots the hypotheses and seeded with an initial velocity, as well as a communication channel between the particles. Particles then move through the solution space, and are evaluated according to some fitness criterion after each time quantum. In due course of time, particles are accelerated towards those particles within their communication grouping which have better fitness values. The main advantage of such an approach over simulated annealing is that the large numbers of members that make up the particle swarm make the technique impressively resilient to the problem of local minima. Various applications of particle swarm optimization include gene selection, data mining, and cluster analysis (Zhijie, Xiangdong & Xiaodong, 2010; Chen, Kung, Min, Kung, Angelia, Wei, Tzu, Nai, Kuo & Ku, 2014; Tiago, Silva & Ana, 2004; Taher & Amiri, 2010).

Particle swarm optimization algorithms is a population based search algorithm with random initialization, and there is interactions among population members. In particle swarm optimization, each particle fly through the solution space, and has the ability to remember its previous best position, survives from generation to generation. The basic flow chart of particle swarm optimization (Shi, 2004) is depicted below in the following Figure 7.

Algorithm 2.

1.   Initialize a population of particles with random positions and velocities on *D* dimensions in the problem space.

2.   For each particle, evaluate the desired optimization fitness function in *D* variables.

3.   Compare particle's fitness evaluation with its *pbest*. If current value is better than *pbest*, then set *pbest* equal to the current value, and P_i equals to the current location X_i in *D*-dimensional space.

4.   Identify the particle in the neighborhood with the best success so far, and assign its index to the variable *g*.

5.   Change the velocity and position of the particle by using the following equations:

$$v_{id} = v_{id} + c_1 \, rand \, () \, (p_{id} - x_{id}) + c_2 \, Rand() \, (p_{gd} - x_{gd})$$

(6)

$$x_{id} = x_{id} + v_{id}$$

(7)

where c_1 and c_2 are positive constants, and *rand* () and *Rand* () are two random functions in the range [0, 1]; $X_i = (x_{i1}, x_{i2}, x_{i3}, \cdots, x_{id})$ represents the ith particle; $P_i = (p_{i1}, p_{i2}, p_{i3}, \cdots, p_{id})$ represents the best previous position (the position giving the best fitness value) of the ith particle; the symbol *g* represents the index of the best particle among all the particles in the population; $V_i = (v_{i1}, v_{i2}, v_{i3}, \cdots, v_{id})$ represents the rate of the position change (velocity) for the particle i.

6.   Loop to step 2, until a criterion is met, usually a sufficiently good fitness or a maximum number of iterations.

Applications of Particle Swarm Optimization

Particle swarm optimization applications includes gene selection, data mining, cluster analysis. Clustering analysis is a popular data analysis, data mining and knowledge acquisition technique generally used in engineering and biological research. The main purpose of clustering is to form groups of similar and dissimilar objects in separate classes based on the values of their attributes. It is observed that, swarm-based algorithms furnish fruitful results compared to conventional clustering techniques. Niknam & Amiri (2010) introduced a novel algorithm using particle swarm optimization for nonlinear partitioned clustering problem using fuzzy adaptive particle swarm optimization, ant colony optimization and k-means algorithms. It is found that the hybridization of particle swarm optimization, ant colony optimization and k-means algorithms provides better cluster partition.

Figure 7. Basic flow chart of particle swarm optimization

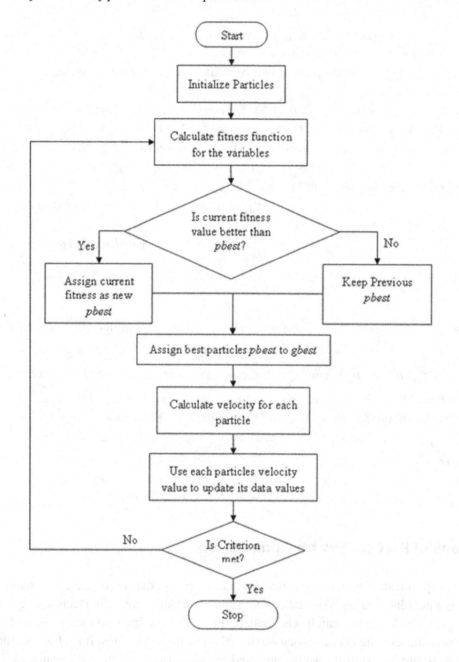

Advantages and Limitations of Particle Swarm Optimization

The applications of particle swarm optimization spreads from science and engineering research to biological research. However, it has certain limitations. This section discusses various advantages and limitations of particle swarm optimization algorithm.

Advantages:

1.   The main advantage is particle swarm optimization can be applied to both scientific and engineering research and biological research.
2.   These algorithms are used to solve nonlinear optimization problems.
3.   The algorithm can easily be implemented since the global search of the algorithm is efficient.
4.   The algorithm runs faster since the dependency on the initial solution is smaller.
5.   Parameter selection and parameter tuning are easily done since the issues are already available in literature.
6.   It is easy to calculate and very simple.
7.   Such algorithms have no overlapping and mutation. The implementation of such algorithms is easy since the velocity, position and memory are easily calculated.

Limitations:

1.   The major limitation of this algorithm is that, it does not work out the problems of non-coordinate system, such as the solution to the energy field and moving rules of the particles in the energy field.
2.   It does not work out the problems of scattered data.

Artificial Bee Colony

Artificial bee colony algorithm proposed by Karabago (2008) is a meta-heuristic algorithm for solving optimizing numerical problem (Karaboga & Akay, 2009; Karaboga & Celal, 2011; Karaboga & Basturk, 2008). The fundamental concept behind the algorithm is that it simulates the foraging behaviour of honey bees. The algorithm has three phases such as employed bee, onlooker bee and scout bee. In the first two phases, bees exploit the sources by local searches in the neighborhood of the solutions selected. The employed bee phase follows deterministic selection whereas the probabilistic selection is followed in the onlooker bee phase. In scout bee phase, solutions that are not beneficial anymore for search progress are abandoned and new solutions are inserted instead of them to explore new regions in the search space. It is observed that, the algorithm has a well-balanced exploration and exploitation ability. The basic flow of artificial bee colony (Karaboga & Celal, 2011) is presented below.

Algorithm 3.

```
1.        Initialize Population
2.        repeat
3.                  Place the employed bees on their food sources
4.                  Place the onlooker bees on the food sources depending on their
nectar amounts
5.                  Send the scouts to the search area for discovering new food
sources
6.                  Memorize the best food source found so far
7.        until requirements are met
```

Figure 8. Basic flow chart of Artificial Bee Colony

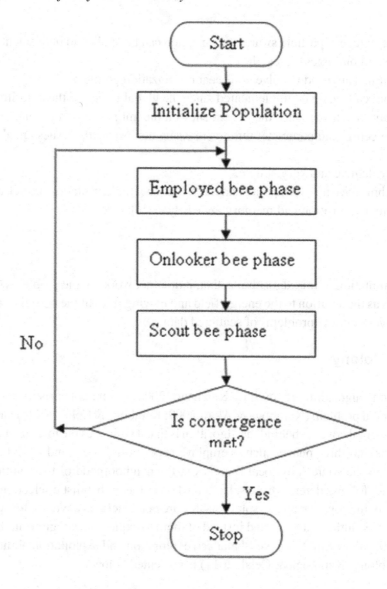

The basic flow chart of artificial bee colony optimization is depicted below in the following Figure 8.

Applications of Artificial Bee Colony Optimization

The main application of artificial bee colony is clustering analysis. Dervis Karaboga & Celal Ozturk (2011) used artificial bee colony for data clustering on benchmarking problems and found that the performance of artificial bee colony is better as compared to other classification techniques. In addition, artificial bee colony can successfully be applied to several engineering domain problems like Travelling Salesman Problem, scheduling, routing protocol, solving puzzles and optimization.

Advantages and Limitations of Artificial Bee Colony

The section list out the main advantages and limitations of artificial bee colony though it is widely used in clustering analysis and engineering research problems.

Advantages:

1. The algorithm has strength in both local and global searches.
2. It can be widely implemented in several optimization problems.

Limitations:

1. Parameter tuning is very difficult in artificial bee colony since it has more number of parameters to be tuned.
2. Probabilistic approach is used in the local search that may provide wrong results. Similarly, the algorithm produces wrong results if the parameters are not fine tuned.

SWARM INTELLIGENCE IN MICROARRAY CLASSIFICATION

Microarray basically consists of hefty number of gene sequences under multiple conditions and across collection of related samples. Microarray may be used in an extensive variety of fields, including biotechnology, disease diagnosis and computers. Microarray data classification is a supervised leaning task that predicts the diagnostic category of a sample from its expression array phenotype. Knowledge gained through classification of microarray gene expression data is increasingly important as they are useful for phenotype classification of diseases (Kumar, Albert, Renukadevi & Devaraj, 2012). High dimensionality of microarray data sets is a vital issue to be considered while designing classifiers. It is a challenging task to choose relevant genes involved in different types of diseases. The most significant area of microarray technology is the data clustering analysis. Recent advances in microarray technology allow scientists to measure the expression levels of thousands of genes simultaneously in biological organisms and have made it possible to create databases that contain useful information of genomic, diagnostic, and prognostic for researchers. Microarray based disease classification system takes labeled gene expression data samples and generates a classifier model that classifies new data samples into different predefined diseases. The major limitation is that, the developed algorithm should be systematically analyzed to select relevant genes from high dimensional data. In general, particle swarm optimization is used to select the best and infectious genes from microarray data. The following Figure 9 depicts the best gene selection using particle swarm optimization.

From the above figure it is clear that, microarray has emerged as a powerful tool to analyze thousands of genes which furnish insights of the functioning of cells. The major difficulty in microarray is to find the availability of sample in large number of genes. In addition, these data is highly redundant, noisy and informative. Rough set techniques are generally employed in microarray data to find the redundancies whereas particle swarm optimization algorithm facilitates identification of informative genes among thousands of genes. Recently developed swarm intelligence approaches for microarray includes fuzzy-genetic swarm algorithm (Kumar, Albert, Renukadevi & Devaraj, 2012), bat inspired classification

Figure 9. Microarray data for best gene selection using particle swarm optimization

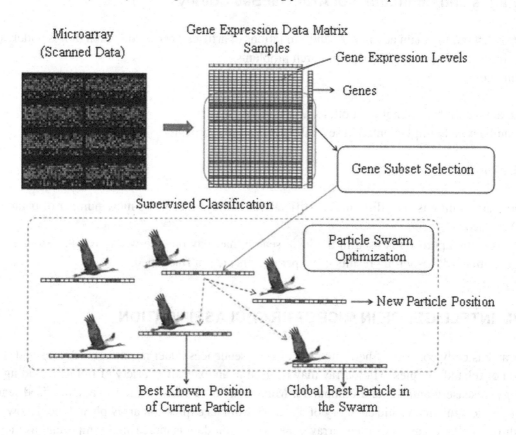

(Mishra, Shaw & Mishra, 2012), binary particle swarm optimization- combat genetic algorithm (Li, Cheng, Jung & Cheng, 2012).

SWARM INTELLIGENCE IN GENE EXPRESSION

The classification of gene expression data samples involves feature selection and classifier design. Feature selection is the process of choosing a subset of features from the original feature set with the help of pre-processing tool to solve classification problems and it is considered as NP-hard problems. The challenge in classifier design is to extract the proper information from the training samples and to allocate the samples contained in the previously defined diagnostic classes by measurements of expression of the selected genes. Choosing the correct category of the selected genes is again a complicated task. In general, swarm intelligence based algorithms are used to solve such problems.

Gene expression data are expected to be of significant help in the development of efficient disease diagnoses and classification platforms. In order to select a small subset of informative genes from the data for disease classification, recently, many researchers are analyzing gene expression data using various computational intelligence techniques. However, due to the small number of samples compared to the hefty number of irrelevant and noisy genes, many of the computational methods face difficulty to select the small subset. On the contrary, swarm intelligence based techniques select the small subset of informative genes that is relevant for the disease classification. Recently, several gene selection methods based on particle swarm optimization have been proposed to select informative genes from gene expression data (Saberi, Sigeru, Deris & Yoshioka, 2011). The following Figure 10 depicts the gene regulatory network from gene expression profiling data where swarm intelligence techniques can be applied to get better results (Lee & Wen, 2009). In the Figure 10, PPI refers to protein–protein interactions and TFBS refers to transcription factor binding sites.

Feature selection is a process of selecting a subset of features from original data set. The intention is to provide a reduced set of the input features while preserving the important discriminatory information. Particle swarm optimization are used to find the important features in the data set whereas rough set is used to identify core and reduct based on dependency of attributes. Recently developed swarm intelligence approaches for gene expressions includes Modified Binary Particle Swarm Optimization (Saberi, Sigeru, Deris & Yoshioka, 2011), Ant, Intelligent Dynamic Swarm and Rough Set (Changseok, Wei, Yuk & Sin, 2010), Rough Set and ant colony optimization (Yumin, Miao & Wang, 2010), Rough Set and particle swarm optimization (Wang, Jie, Xiaolong, Xia & Jensen, 2007), and Rough Set artificial bee colony (Yurong, Lixin, Xie & Wang, 2012).

SWARM INTELLIGENCE IN HEALTHCARE

In the previous section, we have discussed gene expression technologies are used to predict the diagnosis and treatment of a disease. A major challenge facing healthcare organization is to provide of quality

Figure 10. Inferring gene regulatory network from gene expression profiling data

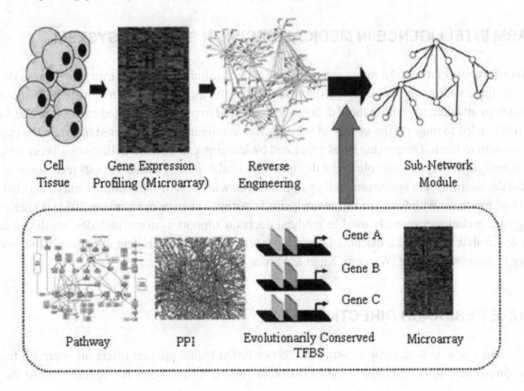

services at affordable cost. Quality service implies diagnosing patients correctly and administrating treatments that are effective. The cost of clinical tests should also be minimized. They can achieve these results by employing appropriate intelligent decision support system. A method to predict a critical condition of a patient, affect to a specific disease, at an early stage in absence of clinician is the need of the hour. Swarm intelligence has emerged as a solution for this problem. Particle swarm optimization-based fuzzy expert system for the diagnosis of disease is used to this context. However, such methods are not applicable to all diseases. On the other hand, intuitionistic fuzzy sets are used to determine the symptoms of diseases, formulation of medical knowledge and diagnosis on the basis of composition of intuitionistic fuzzy relations. In addition, swarm intelligence techniques such as ant colony optimization and particle swarm optimization have been hybridized with rough set theory to furnish fruitful results in healthcare.

Machine learning techniques provide support and solution for knowledge discovery in many areas of health care such as disease diagnosis, patient monitoring and hospital management. Expecting the outcome of a disease is one of the most interesting and tedious tasks in health care industry. Medical datasets are often classified by a large number of diseases and finding the exact attribute for a disease is a tedious task for physicians. Ant colony optimization is generally used to discover the rules from the medical dataset and in turn provide the classification of disease. Ant colony optimization is applicable to healthcare since it retains memory of entire colony instead of previous generation only. But, medical dataset usually contains uncertainties and missing values. To extract maximum out of the available data, rough set is generally used without a strong a priori reasoning about the data. Recently developed swarm intelligence approaches for healthcare include cancer biomarkers discovery using a swarm intelligence (Emmanuel, Mario &Victor, 2010), Intuitionistic Fuzzy Sets (Supriya, Ranjit & Roy, 2001), Rough Set-bee colony optimization (Suguna & Thanushkodi, 2010) and Hybrid Metaheuristic Algorithm (Uma & Kirubakaran, 2012).

SWARM INTELLIGENCE IN MEDICAL DECISION SUPPORT SYSTEM

Enormous amount of medical data are generated and added to clinical databases everyday. Classifying and analyzing these voluminous of biological data to extract useful information is a tedious task. Discovery of relationships and patterns within these data has the potential to provide new medical knowledge. On the contrary, it helps to improve the quality of service. The intelligence is considered based on the capacity of the system to learn. Diagnosing rules generated by learning can be used in diagnosis processes. Machine intelligence plays a vital role in the design of medical expert systems. Various techniques used in medical decision support system ant colony optimization with genetic algorithm (Uma & Kirubakaran, 2012) and rough set with formal concept analysis (Tripathy, Acharjya & Cynthya, 2011). Other swarm intelligence techniques recently used in medical decision support systems includes intelligent agents (Uma & Kirubakaran, 2012), machine learning Algorithms (Prasad, Krishna & Sagar, 2011), and Ant Colony Optimization (Baig, Waseem, Khan & Fariha, 2011).

FUTURE RESEARCH DIRECTIONS

The challenge now is to develop swarm intelligence based technique that offers an approach to solve bio- inspired computing problems. Amalgamation of various technologies has become one of the most promising tasks in bio-inspired computing research. In addition, some authors discussed hybridization of rough set with swarm intelligence. But, rough set has generalized to many extent such as rough fuzzy set, fuzzy rough set, intuitionistic fuzzy rough set, rough set on fuzzy approximation space, rough set on intuitionistic fuzzy approximation space, rough set with formal concept analysis, rough set on two universal sets, multigranular rough set to name a few. From the perspective and features of computational intelligence, swarm intelligence can be hybridized to any of the techniques mentioned above. This has not discussed by authors. This provides ample scope of research in bio-inspired computing.

CONCLUSION

Swarm intelligence has increasingly gained attention in bio-inspired computing research to classify the high dimensional data generated from biological systems. Various swarm intelligence methods available to solve bio-inspired computing problems are particle swarm optimization, ant colony optimization, and artificial bee colony optimization. In addition, there are methods which hybridize rough set with above mentioned optimization techniques to get better result. Rough set theory is an extensive tool that have been applied in the biological domain to discover the data dependencies, feature selection, pattern selection, decision support system and classification of sample data. Most of the current literature on rough set based tools in bio-inspired computing focuses on classification and reduction issues. However, it is observed that, the scope of rough set theory is not utilized at most. This chapter discusses various swarm intelligence methods available for bio-inspired computing and its application to gene expression, microarray classification, swarm intelligence in healthcare, and intelligent decision support system for disease diagnosis. From the survey, it is evident that the swarm intelligence approach offers a promising way of solving a number of bio-inspired computing problems. It is also observed that swarm intelligence by itself or in combination with other computational intelligence technologies works remarkably well in many bioinformatics problems.

REFERENCES

Acharjya, D. P., & Geetha Mary, A. (2014). Privacy preservation in information system. In Advances in secure computing, internet services, and applications (pp. 49-72). IGI Global.

Ahmed, T. S., Mehdi, G. D., & Adil, S. (2013). Data missing solution using rough set theory & swarm intelligence. *International Journal of Advanced Computer Science & Information Technology*, 2(3), 1–16.

Baig, A. R., Waseem, S., Khan, S., & Fariha, A. (2011). ACO based discovery of comprehensible and accurate rules from medical datasets. *International Journal of Innovative Computing, Information, & Control*, 7(11), 6147–6159.

Beni, G., & Wang, J. (1989). Swarm intelligence. In *Proceedings Seventh Annual Meeting of the Robotics Society of Japan* (pp. 425-428). RSJ Press.

Chandra Mohan, B., & Baskaran, R. (2012). A survey: Ant colony optimization based recent research & implementation on several engineering domain. *Expert Systems with Applications*, 39(4), 4618–4627. doi:10.1016/j.eswa.2011.09.076

Changseok, B., Wei, C. Y., Yuk, Y. C., & Sin, L. L. (2010). Feature selection with intelligent dynamic swarm & rough set. *Expert Systems with Applications, 37*(10), 7026–7032. doi:10.1016/j.eswa.2010.03.016

Chen, K. H., Kung, J. W., Min, L. T., Kung, M. W., Angelia, M. A., Wei, C. C., & Ku, S. C. et al. (2014). Gene selection for cancer identification - a decision tree model empowered by particle swarm optimization algorithm. *BMC Bioinformatics, 15*(49), 15–49. PMID:24555567

Dorigo, M., & Thomas, S. (2004). *Ant colony optimization.* The MIT Press. doi:10.1007/b99492

Emmanuel, M., Mario, M. A., & Victor, T. (2010). Compact cancer biomarkers discovery using a swarm intelligence feature selection algorithm. *Computational Biology and Chemistry, 34*(4), 244–250. doi:10.1016/j.compbiolchem.2010.08.003 PMID:20888301

Ganesh, P. K., Aruldoss, A. V. T., Renukadevi, P., & Devaraj, D. (2012). Design of fuzzy expert system for microarray data classification using a novel genetic swarm algorithm. *Expert Systems with Applications, 39*(2), 1811–1821. doi:10.1016/j.eswa.2011.08.069

Hazem, A., & Glasgow, J. (2012). *Swarm intelligence: Concepts, models & applications.* Technical Report. Queen's University.

James, K., & Russell, E. (1995). Particle swarm optimization. In *Proceedings of IEEE International Conference on Neural Networks (pp.* 1942-1948). IEEE.

Karaboga, D., & Bahriye Akay, B. (2009). A comparative study of artificial bee colony algorithm. *Applied Mathematics and Computation, 214*(1), 108–132. doi:10.1016/j.amc.2009.03.090

Karaboga, D., & Basturk, B. (2008). On the performance of artificial bee colony (ABC) algorithm. *Applied Soft Computing, 8*(1), 687–697. doi:10.1016/j.asoc.2007.05.007

Karaboga, D., & Celal, O. (2011). A novel clustering approach: Artificial Bee Colony (ABC) algorithm. *Applied Soft Computing, 11*(1), 652–657. doi:10.1016/j.asoc.2009.12.025

Lee, W. P., & Wen, S. T. (2009). Computational methods for discovering gene networks from expression data. *Briefings in Bioinformatics, 10*(4), 408–423. PMID:19505889

Li, Y. C., Cheng, H. Y., Jung, C. L., & Cheng, H. Y. (2012). A hybrid BPSO-CGA approach for gene selection & classification of microarray data. *Journal of Computational Biology, 19*(1), 68–82. doi:10.1089/cmb.2010.0064 PMID:21210743

McCulloc, W. S., & Pitts, W. (1943). A logical calculus of the ideas immanent in nervous activity. *The Bulletin of Mathematical Biophysics, 5*(4), 115–133. doi:10.1007/BF02478259

Mishra, S., Shaw, K., & Mishra, D. (2012). A new meta-heuristic bat inspired classification approach for microarray data. *Procedia Technology, 4*, 802–806. doi:10.1016/j.protcy.2012.05.131

Mohamed, J. O. A., & Sivakumar, R. (2010). Ant-based clustering algorithms: A brief survey. *International Journal of Computer Theory & Engineering, 2*(5), 787–796.

Niknam, T., & Amiri, B. (2010). An efficient hybrid approach based on PSO, ACO & k-means for cluster analysis. *Applied Soft Computing, 10*(1), 183–197. doi:10.1016/j.asoc.2009.07.001

Pawlak, Z. (1982). Rough sets. *International Journal of Computer & Information Sciences*, *11*(5), 341–356. doi:10.1007/BF01001956

Pawlak, Z. (1991). *Rough sets-Theoretical aspects of reasoning about data*. Kluwer Academic Publishers.

Prasad, B. D. C. N., Krishna, P. P. E. S. N., & Sagar, Y. (2011). An approach to develop expert systems in medical diagnosis using machine learning algorithms (ASTHMA) and a performance study. *International Journal on Soft Computing*, *2*(1), 26–33. doi:10.5121/ijsc.2011.2103

Saberi, M. M., Sigeru, O., Deris, S., & Yoshioka, M. (2011). Modified binary particle swarm optimization for selecting the small subset of informative genes from gene expression data. *IEEE Transactions on Information Technology in Biomedicine*, *15*(6), 813–822. doi:10.1109/TITB.2011.2167756 PMID:21914573

Suguna, N., & Thanushkodi, K. (2010). A novel rough set reduct algorithm for medical domain based on bee colony optimization. *Journal of Computing*, *2*(6), 49–54.

Supriya, K. D., Ranjit, B., & Roy, A. R. (2001). An application of intuitionistic fuzzy sets in medical diagnosis. *Fuzzy Sets and Systems*, *117*(2), 209–213. doi:10.1016/S0165-0114(98)00235-8

Tiago, S., Silva, A., & Ana, N. (2004). Particle swarm based data mining algorithms for classification tasks. *Parallel Computing*, *30*(5/6), 767–783.

Tripathy, B. K., Acharjya, D. P., & Cynthya, V. (2011). A framework for intelligent medical diagnosis using rough set with formal concept analysis. *International Journal of Artificial Intelligence & Applications*, *2*(2), 45–66. doi:10.5121/ijaia.2011.2204

Uma, S. M., & Kirubakaran, E. (2012). Intelligent heart diseases prediction system using a new hybrid metaheuristic algorithm. *International Journal of Engineering Research & Technology*, *1*(8), 1–7.

Walczak, B., & Massart, D. L. (1999). Rough set theory. *Chemometrics and Intelligent Laboratory Systems*, *47*(1), 1–16. doi:10.1016/S0169-7439(98)00200-7

Wang, X., Yang, J., Teng, X., Xia, W., & Richard, J. (2007). Feature selection based on rough sets & particle swarm optimization. *Pattern Recognition Letters*, *28*(4), 459–471. doi:10.1016/j.patrec.2006.09.003

Yuhui, S. (2004). Particle swarm optimization. IEEE Neural Networks Society, 8-14.

Yumin, C., Miao, D., & Wang, R. (2010). A rough set approach to feature selection based on ant colony optimization. *Pattern Recognition Letters*, *31*(3), 226–233. doi:10.1016/j.patrec.2009.10.013

Yurong, H., Lixin, D., Xie, D., & Wang, S. (2012). A novel discrete artificial bee colony algorithm for rough set based feature selection. *International Journal of Advancements in Computing Technology*, *4*(6), 295–305. doi:10.4156/ijact.vol4.issue6.34

Zadeh, L. A. (1965). Fuzzy sets. *Information and Control*, *8*(3), 338–353. doi:10.1016/S0019-9958(65)90241-X

Zhijie, L., Xiangdong, L., & Xiaodong, D. (2010). Comparative research on particle swarm optimization & genetic algorithm. *Computer and Information Science*, *3*(1), 120–127.

KEY TERMS AND DEFINITIONS

Classification: Objects that are indiscernible based on their attribute values are belongs to same class and we call it as classification.

Clustering: Grouping of objects according to some pre-defined criteria based on some algorithm techniques is known as clustering.

Evolutionary Algorithms: Systems made by writing an algorithm that generate a random set of solutions for the given problem which can be optimized by iteration.

Global Optimization: An algorithm that deals with problems in which a best solution can be represented as a point in an *n*-dimensional space.

Indiscernibility: Objects for which attribute values are exactly same are termed as indiscernible.

Information Systems: A dataset which provides information about objects and its attributes in a given context is called as information system.

Rough Set: A model, proposed by Pawlak to capture imprecision in data through boundary approach.

Swarm Intelligence: The behavioural models of social insects such as ant colonies, honey bees, firefly, and bird flocks are termed as swarm intelligence.

Chapter 4
Studies of Computational Intelligence Based on the Behaviour of Cockroaches

Amartya Neogi
Dr. B. C. Roy Engineering College, India

ABSTRACT

In this chapter, the author expands the notion of computational intelligence using the behavior of cockroaches. An introduction to cockroach as swarm intelligence emerging research area and literature review of its growing concept is explained in the beginning. The chapter also covers the ideas of hybrid cockroach optimization system. Next, the author studies the applicability of cockroach swarm optimization. Thereafter, the author presents the details of theoretical algorithm and an experimental result of integration of robot to some cockroaches to make collective decisions. Then, the author proposes his algorithm for traversing the shortest distance of city warehouses. Then, a few comparative statistical results of the progress of the present work on cockroach intelligence are shown. Finally, conclusive remarks are given. At last, the author hopes that even researchers with little experience in swarm intelligence will be enabled to apply the proposed algorithm in their own application areas.

1. INTRODUCTION

Swarm intelligence (SI) as an emerging research area, has attracted many researchers' attention since the concept was proposed in 1980s. It has now become an interdisciplinary frontier and focus of many disciplines including artificial intelligence, economics, sociology, biology, etc. It has been observed a long time ago that some species survive in the cruel nature taking the advantage of the power of swarms, rather than the wisdom of individuals. The individuals in such swarm are not highly intelligent, yet they complete the complex tasks through cooperation and division of labour and show high intelligence as a whole swarm which is highly self-organized and self-adaptive.

The growing complication of real life problems has encouraged computer scientists to investigate for proficient problem-solving techniques. The behavior of ants, termites, bird's fishes, bees slime,

DOI: 10.4018/978-1-4666-8291-7.ch004

moulds, and other creatures have enthused swarm intelligence investigators to create new optimization algorithms. Decentralized control and self-organization for those creatures are extraordinary features of swarm-based systems. Such decentralized consensus building behaviors are observed in a variety of social organisms, including ants (Pratt et al. 2002), honeybees (Britton et al., 2002) and cockroaches (Ame et al. 2006) and have inspired much research on the development of self-organized task allocation strategies for multi-robot systems.

During the past decade, a number of new computational intelligence (CI) algorithms have been proposed. Unfortunately, they spread in a number of unrelated publishing directions which may hamper the use of such published resources. Those provide the author with motivation to analyze the existing research for categorizing and synthesizing it in a meaningful manner. The mission of this chapter is really important since those algorithms are going to be a new revolution in computer science. The author hopes that it will stimulate the readers to make novel contributions or to even start a new paradigm based on nature phenomena.

Swarm intelligence is a soft bionic of the nature swarms, i.e. it simulates the social structures and interactions of the swarm rather than the structure of an individual in traditional artificial intelligence. The individuals can be regarded as agents with simple and single abilities. Some of them have the ability to evolve themselves when dealing with certain problems to make better compatibility (Wang et al. 2005). A swarm intelligence system usually consists of a group of simple individuals autonomously controlled by a plain set of rules and local interactions. These individuals are not necessarily unwise, but are relatively simple compared to the global intelligence achieved through the system. Some intelligent behaviors never observed in a single individual will soon emerge when several individuals begin cooperate or compete. The swarm can complete the tasks that a complex individual can do while having high robustness and flexibility and low cost. Swarm intelligence takes the full advantage of the swarm without the need of centralized control and global model, and provides a great solution for large-scale sophisticated problems.

The idea computational intelligence may come from observing the behavior of creatures. Ant colony Optimization (ACO) was presented by studying the behavior of ants, and Particle Swarm Optimization (PSO) was presented by of examining the movements of flocking gulls. Through inspecting the behavior of the cockroach, Cockroach Swarm Optimization (CSO) is proposed in this chapter. Cockroach optimization is a new development under SI paradigm; cockroach optimization algorithms are inspired by collective cockroach social behavior. The artificial structure can be viewed as the model for modeling the common behavior of cockroaches. CSO somehow belongs to the swarm intelligence.

A cockroach is an invertebrate walking animal in the phylum of arthropods. It has six legs, and each leg is composed of multiple segments: coxa, trochanter, femur, tibia and tarsus (foot). The upper leg segments generally point upwards and the lower segments downwards. The legs project out from the trunk like a salamander. They are oriented around its trunk in a way that the two front legs point forwards while the four rear legs typically point backwards to maintain stability in walking. Such orientation can be beneficial in climbing over an obstacle; i.e., a cockroach can easily move its front legs forward to reach the top of an obstacle while the rear legs power its motion by raising its trunk up and pushing it forward. As a result, it can climb over the obstacle (Wei et al. 2004). Moreover, front legs are also used to detect stimulus coming from the front while rear legs perceive stimulus from the back.

Cockroaches can move and run swiftly and smoothly no matter what terrains to transverse. Their movement smoothness, flexible self-control, and regulation ability have aroused researchers' deep interests to seek the secret of the movement. Cockroach's control over its agile movement far exceeds high speed computer control in terms of response time and control functions. Scientists have failed to find satisfactory explanation about cockroach's supreme performance and control ability in adverse conditions. It is foreseen that overcoming this difficulty will be an important breakthrough for many correlative subjects, lead to the emergence of new research methods, and promote the development of intelligent robot technology to the benefit of humankind.

Cockroaches tend to aggregate in dark places. Cockroaches perform group choice that is a form of self-organized collective decision. It emerges form the local interactions between individuals. Both machines and insects are capable, independently of each other, to perform such collective decision.

Each individual can be in two states, moving or stopped. A stopped cockroach (alone or in an aggregate) could start moving either spontaneously or after collision with a moving larva. While moving, a cockroach could encounter other stopped or moving larvae.

Now, decisions must be made in everyday life. It can be especially hard if the individuals live in the group, as it is the case in many insects. In order to achieve their goals such as finding resources they must cooperate to increase individual success. One example of such social animals is cockroaches.

The interesting questions are: (i) how do they make the decision and (ii) how do they cope with the crowding effect. Another approach was used by Ame et al. (2006) who designed the behavioral model describing how cockroaches optimize group size and then tested it experimentally. Cockroaches perform group choice that is a form of self-organized collective decision. It emerges from the local interactions between individuals.

1. Cockroaches search for the darkest location in the search space and the fitness value is directly proportional to the level of darkness (find darkness phase).
2. Cockroaches socialize with nearby cockroaches (find friend phase).
3. Cockroaches periodically become hungry and leave the friendship to search for food (find food phase).

The overall work plan of the proposed chapter is as follows:

1. An introduction to fundamentals of cockroach swarm intelligence in literature review section in detail.
2. State the fundamental differences between real cockroach and artificial cockroach
3. Introduction to some hybrid CSO system.
4. Outline of current research applications in CSO.
5. Details of theoretical cockroach swarm optimization algorithm and an interesting experimental result of integration of robot to some cockroaches to take collective decision making.
6. Frame the proposed algorithm for cockroach swarm optimization for travelling salesman problem (city warehouse traversing).
7. Critical discussion of the proposed algorithm.
8. Limitations of cockroach swarm optimization at present.
9. Comparative statistical results of the progress of the present work on cockroach intelligence.
10. Conclusion of the proposed chapter.

Why the author has selected the cockroach swarm optimization as an inspiration for the proposed study? Because,

- In nature, the cockroach has a lot of advantages. It can move rapidly over unstructured terrain and it can even climb vertical walls using its sticky pads, claws and spines. A robot that could perform these tasks would be very useful for numerous exploration, defense and humanitarian missions,

- Real-world optimization problems are often very challenging to solve, and many applications have to deal with NP-hard problems. To solve such problems, optimization tools have to be used, though there is no guarantee that the optimal solution can be obtained. In fact, for NP problems, there are no efficient algorithms at all. As a result, many problems have to be solved by trial and errors using various optimization techniques. In addition, new algorithms like CSO have to be developed to see if they can cope with these challenging optimization problems,

- The idea of computational intelligence may come from observing the behavior of creatures. How to describe behavior by projecting creatures' motions to formulas, without questions, becomes an extremely important phase,

- A cockroach has an exceptional ability to navigate freely in all-weather conditions. In addition to its visual navigation, it has a powerful detection system built into its legs and feelers to detect its contact states with the environment. These sensing and navigation abilities are important for biologically inspired robot which needs to execute demanding tasks in difficult situations, such as search and rescue, homeland security, logistics in natural disaster, etc.,

- Some hard problems like travelling sales person, chess playing, intelligent human computer interaction, natural language understanding, robotics, business and planning cannot justify by conventional method. Hence the non-conventional process like natural science is always inspiring direction for solving the technical problems. There are many fields of application like Process optimization, Telecommunication, Entertainment; etc. that can be solved affordably by using the analogy of natural science theme.

2. BACKGROUND

2.1 Literature Review

The cockroach *Blattella germanica* forms mixed clusters of males and females with generation overlap in its natural environment. During daytime, cockroaches rest in a common shelter often located in cracks or crevices and forage mainly at night. *Blattella germanica* is a relevant biological model to examine whether organisms characterized by simple social organization and the absence of any sophisticated means of communication can form and use incident scent trails. Experimental evidence suggests that cockroaches have the ability to use chemical trails. Indeed, previous studies had shown that a pre-applied solution of fecal extracts on the substrate could induce trail-following in cockroaches (Miller and Koehler, (2000); Miller et al. (2000)). However, navigation in *Blattella germanica* relied also on multiple sensory channels, implying the use of idiothetic cues or learned visual landmarks (Durier and Rivault, 1999; Durier and Rivault, 2000; Rivault and Durier, 2004). During outward trips, the exploratory behaviors of cockroaches were affected by the presence of novel objects introduced in their familiar home range (Durier and Rivault, 2002) and they could build a representation of rewarding events to locate food sources during foraging trips (Durier and Rivault, 2000).

Garnier et al. (2005) tried to reproduce the aggregation behavior observed in cockroaches using Alice micro-robots (Caprari et al. 2002). The aggregation process for the robots was directly inspired by a biological model of displacement and aggregation developed from experiments with first instar larvae of the German cockroach Blattella Germania (Jeanson et al. 2005). Although each robot has only limited perception and communication abilities, with a small set of simple behavioral rules, the results showed that the group of robots was able to select collectively an aggregation site among two identical or different shelters.

Another self-organizing aggregation behavior happened in cockroach larvae. Jeanson et al. 2005 investigated their behaviors at both individual and collective levels at different densities in a homogeneous medium. Jeanson et al. (2005), modeled the larvae's observed behaviors which depended on the presence of nearby larvae. Their model showed that using only local information could lead the whole group into clusters. They tried to prove that cockroaches perform the global aggregation from local interactions. To do this they measured the important system parameters from the experiments with cockroach larvae like probability of stopping in an aggregate or probability of starting to move. A numerical model of behaviors of cockroaches was created from those measurements and tried to be validated by numerical simulations. Although their numerical model revealed a quantitative disagreement with real experiments, they claimed that it also offered strong evidence that aggregation could be explained in terms of local interactions between individuals.

Even simple aggregation behaviors, like aggregation of cockroaches, has influenced swarm robotics (Garnier et al. 2005[a]). Also in the field of swarm robotics, foraging for energy is a topic of interest in recent years. For honeybee colonies, nectar is a source (and also a storage form) of energy, thus it was thought that the insights they got by studying the economic gains and costs of honeybee foraging would be useful also in the domain of swarm intelligence and swarm robotics. The aggregation behavior of cockroaches has been the source of inspiration for a site selection mechanism with robots (Garnier et al. 2009).

R.D. Beer et al. (1990[a]); R.D. Beer et al. (1990[b]) simulated the artificial insect inspired by a cockroach, and developed a neural model for behavior and locomotion controls observed in the natural insect. The simulation model was integrated with the antennas and mouth containing tactile and chemical sensors to perceive information from the environment; that is, it performs by wandering, edge following, seeking food and feeding food.

While biologists have been developing models and simulations of animal behavior, roboticists have been searching for the means to distribute the control tasks faced by autonomous machines, and make their performance more reliable. The fusion of these disciplines was inevitable. In an experiment aimed toward both the AI community and biologists, Beer developed a computer simulation of an artificial cockroach R.D. Beer et al. (1990[a]); R.D. Beer et al. (1990[b]). His control scheme used a model of living neurons as a building block for simple behaviors. Despite the simplicity of its components, the simulated insect could coordinate six legs for walking, avoid obstacles, and search for food in its virtual world.

Studies have shown that cockroaches not only have distaste for the light, but they also enjoyed the company of friends. Jeanson et al. 2005, determined, through experiment, that cockroach larvae exhibit a complex collective behavior that ultimately results in the formation of aggregates- in other words, cockroaches like to hang out with friends. Ame et al. 2006, further studied the social behavior of cockroaches by guiding groups of cockroaches with cockroach-like robots. Interestingly, that experiment showed that the individual decisions of cockroaches modulate the collective behavior of the entire group, which supported the hypothesis that collective behavior is aggregated from simple decentralized behavior. This experiment also accentuated the hypothesis that cockroaches prefer to be in groups, as well as in the dark. Garnier et al. (2005[a]) were able to mimic the behavior of cockroaches with a group of cockroach-like robots, each programmed with a simple set of behaviors. Garnier, et al. (2005[a]) showed that the collective behavior of cockroaches could be simulated by groups of robots, each programmed with a simple set of behaviors based on the findings in (Jeanson et al. 2005).

The aggregation process cited above was directly inspired by a biological model of displacement and aggregation developed from experiments with first instar larvae of the german cockroach Blattella germanica (Jeanson et al. 2003; Jeanson et al. 2005). This model was built by quantifying individual behaviors of cockroaches that was their displacement interactions among individuals and with the environment in a homogeneous circular arena (11 cm diameter). Each of these individual behaviors was described in a probabilistic way: researchers measured experimentally the probability distribution for a given behavior to happen. This analysis showed that cockroaches display a correlated random walk (constant rate to change direction and forward oriented distribution of turning angles) in the center of the arena (Jeanson, et al. 2003). When reaching the periphery of the arena, cockroaches display a wall following behavior (also called thigmotactic behavior) with a constant rate to leave the edge and came back into the central part of the arena (Jeanson et al. 2003). In addition, cockroaches could stop at any moment, stay motionless for some time and then move again. Analysis showed that the stopping rate for an individual increases with the number of stopped cockroaches in the direct neighborhood (i.e. within the range of antenna contact). On the contrary, the rate to leave an aggregate decreases with this number Jeanson et al. 2005. Thus, this dual positive feedback leads to the quick and strong formation of aggregates. A more detailed description of the model can be found in (Jeanson et al. 2003; Jeanson et al. 2005).

Jeanson et al. (2005) studied aggregation strategies in cockroaches. A self-organized model of the aggregation behavior of cockroaches in a bounded circular arena was developed by (Jeanson et al. 2005) and Garnier et al. (2005[a]). The authors used an approach which was similar to microscopic modelling developed by (Martinoli et.al 2003; Martinoli et.al. 2004) and Jeanson et al. 2005. They first defined a self-organized model for the behaviors of the cockroaches and measured the important transition probabilities between behaviors along with the average time spent on each behavior by real cockroaches. They compared the results obtained from the developed numerical model with the real experiments' results and claimed that their model better approximates real data than most of the previous global level models which showed that the cockroaches might behave based on local interaction rules.

2.2 Differences between Real Cockroach and Artificial Cockroach

From the above literature the differences between real cockroach and artificial cockroach is shown in Table 1 as follows:

2.3 Introduction to Hybrid Cockroach Based System

2.3.1 The Fuzzy Cockroach System

A Cockroach-based fuzzy knowledge bases fusion architecture integrating various fuzzy rule sets and fuzzy sets is proposed. In order to keep the rationality among fuzzy rule sets and fuzzy sets, the author estimate and integrate multiple fuzzy knowledge bases simultaneously. The proposed architecture is shown in Figure 1. The architecture mainly includes the cockroach optimization-based fuzzy knowledge encoding and cockroach optimization-based fuzzy knowledge optimization. One fuzzy knowledge base contains particular fuzzy rule sets and fuzzy sets for some specific goal. This dissertation is devoted

Table 1. Differences between real cockroach and artificial cockroach

Criteria	Real Cockroach	Artificial Cockroach
Pheromone Depositing Behavior	Pheromone is deposited both ways while ants are moving (i.e. on their forward and return ways).	Pheromone is often deposited only on the return way after a candidate solution is constructed and evaluated.
Pheromone Updating Amount	The pheromone trail on a path is updated, in some cockroach species, with a pheromone amount that depends on the quantity and quality of the food	Once a cockroach has constructed a path, the pheromone trail of that path is updated on its return way with an amount that is inversely proportional to the path length stored in its memory.
Memory Capabilities	Real cockroach has no memory capabilities.	Artificial cockroaches store the paths they walked onto in their memory to be used in retracing the return path. They also use its length in determining the quantity of pheromone to deposit on their return way.
Return Path Mechanism	Real cockroach use the pheromone deposited on their forward path to retrace their return way when they head back to their nest	Since no pheromone is deposited on the forward path, artificial cockroaches use the stored paths from their memory to retrace their return way.
Pheromone Evaporation Behavior	Pheromone evaporates too slowly making it less significant for the convergence.	Pheromone evaporates exponentially making it more significant for the convergence.
Ecological Constraints	Exist, such as predation or competition with other species and the colony's level of protection.	Ecological constraints do not exist in the artificial/virtual world.

to the fusion of multiple fuzzy knowledge bases. Fuzzy sets describe the linguistic variables, linguistic values, and membership functions. Fuzzy rule sets describe the linguistic-based If-Then rules. Fuzzy rule sets and fuzzy sets of a knowledge base will be encoded to a cockroach. One cockroach stands for a solution for a given problem. Therefore, the overall fuzzy knowledge bases will form the initial cockroach optimization population. After encoding expected knowledge bases, the cockroach optimization-based fuzzy knowledge fusion will search the optimal cockroach from the fuzzy knowledge bases population by means of the best fitness value. Finally one optimal fuzzy knowledge base is produced by this series of cockroach optimization-based fusion.

Cockroaches face many decision-making problems while searching for the best solution. The following are cockroaches' choice dilemmas:

- What is the next solution component to be added to the partial solution?
- Should the partial solution be abandoned or not?
- Should the same partial solution be expanded without recruiting the nest mates?

The majority of the choice models are based on random utility modeling concept. These approaches are highly rational. They are based on assumptions that decision-makers possess perfect information processing capabilities and always behave in a rational way (trying to maximize utilities). In order to offer alternative modeling approach, researchers started to use less normative theories. According to this idea in the chosen model, that assumption can be considered that cockroaches are using fuzzy logic.

Artificial cockroaches use approximate reasoning and rules of fuzzy logic in their communication and acting. During the jth stage cockroaches fly/walk from the hive and choose say 'B' solutions from the set of partial solutions S_i at stage st_j (forward pass).

Figure 1. Cockroach optimization based fuzzy-knowledge fusion architecture

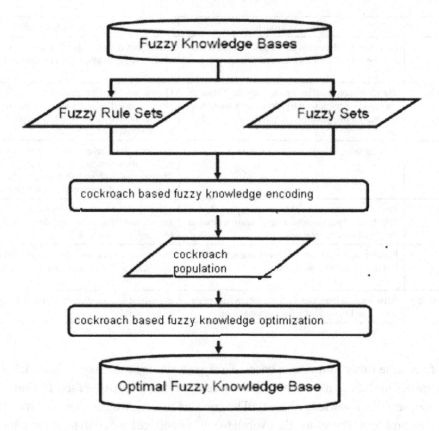

When adding the solution component to the current partial solution during the forward pass, specific cockroach perceives specific solution component as "less attractive", "attractive" or "very attractive". The author also assume that an artificial cockroach can perceive a specific attributes as "short", "medium" or "long" etc.

Figure 2. Fuzzy set describing distance

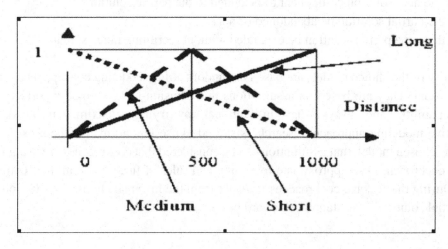

2.3.2 The Genetic Cockroach System

Cockroaches live in nearly all habitats and survive for more than 300 million years. In this concept, an integration of cockroaches competitive swarm behavior with advanced evolutionary operations may be thought of. The concept of cockroach genetic algorithm may possess strong snatching-food ability to rush forward to a target and high migration ability to escape from local minimum. Integration of the artificial-cockroach behaviors with biological evolution may promote the exploration and exploitation of algorithms. Cockroaches are able to jump away to numbers-of-meters distance. Driving-out-induced jumping and harsh-environment-induced escaping will significantly enhance the exploration ability. Therefore, this hybrid concept may be able to prevent premature convergence.

3. APPLICATIONS OF COCKROACH SWARM INTELLIGENCE

Swarm robotics can be useful for military application as well. (Pettinaro et al. 2002) proposed a self-reconfigurable robot system for foraging, searching and rescuing, which has the ability to cope with occasional failure. Military experts believe that the bionic aero vehicles inspired from swarm intelligence technology will become applicable in a few years. It can be foreseen that machine bees or cockroaches with reconnaissance equipment and bombs will possibly show up in future war.

Bionic cockroach robots can be applied broadly to earthquake relief, riot, search and rescue, and space exploration in rugged and unstructured natural terrain. Cockroach's quick reflection and dodge mechanism can be applied to aeroplane collision avoidance. To bring bio-robots a step closer to real applications, novel locomotion mechanism, multi-sensor information processing and fusion, and intelligent control must be thoroughly investigated to emulate cockroach's moving rapidity, flexibility and stability. Cockroach limb is intriguing, and has calculation function and local intelligence. Intensive research is required to mimic the mechanism configuration and physiological characteristics of insect limb.

3.1 Multi-Sensing in Bionic Cockroach Robot

A cockroach has an exceptional ability to navigate freely in all-weather conditions. In addition to its visual navigation, it has a powerful detection system built into its legs and feelers to detect its contact states with the environment. These sensing and navigation abilities are important for biologically inspired robot which needs to execute demanding tasks in difficult situations, such as search and rescue, homeland security, logistics in natural disaster, etc.

Multi-sensor information fusion technology is the key to realize intelligent motion control of cockroach robot. To ensure the fidelity of time-dependent sensor information, the information processing has to be carried out in real time. In face of a large amount of information including visual images, the real-time processing becomes very difficult. Cockroach has visual, tactile, taste, smell sense function, etc. For practicality, only visual and tactile sensors are considered at this stage. The vision system mainly utilizes infrared imaging sensors, and the tactile sensing system is built upon optical fibre sensors.

Collective behavior based on self-organization has been shown in group-living animals from insects to vertebrates. These findings have stimulated engineers to investigate approaches for the coordination of autonomous multirobot systems based on self-organization. In this experimental study, the author will show collective decision-making by mixed groups of cockroaches and socially integrated autonomous robots, leading to shared shelter selection. Individuals, natural or artificial, are perceived as equivalent, and the collective decision emerges from nonlinear feedbacks based on local interactions. Even when in the minority, robots can modulate the collective decision-making process and produce a global pattern not observed in their absence. These results demonstrate the possibility of using intelligent autonomous devices to study and control self-organized behavioral patterns in group-living animals.

Inspired by obstacle avoidance and the escape behavior of scorpions and cockroaches, such behavior is implemented in the walking machines as a negative tropism

Special applications:

- Distributing system of interacting autonomous agents' performance enhancement.
- Process optimization and robustness.
- Self organized control and cooperation in decentralized environment division of process and distributed task allocation.

3.2 Exploitation of Collective Behavior of Animal Societies

A possible development of swarm intelligence is the controlled exploitation of the collective behavior of animal societies. No example is available in this area of swarm intelligence although some promising research is currently in progress: For example, in the Leurre project, small insect-like robots are used as lures to influence the behavior of a group of cockroaches. The technology developed within this project could be applied to various domains including agriculture and cattle breeding.

The study of cockroaches, locusts, and caterpillars is inspiring new frontiers in advanced robotics. New research delves deep into the neurological functioning of the cockroach, giving engineers the information they need to design more compact, versatile and efficient robots -- for both earthbound missions and those in outer space.

Prof. Amir Ayali of Tel Aviv University's Department of Zoology, 2011, said that the study of cockroaches had already inspired advanced robotics. Robots have long been based on these six-legged houseguests, whose nervous system is relatively straightforward and easy to study. But until now, walking machines based on the cockroach's movement have been influenced by outside observations and mainly imitate the insect's appearance, not its internal mechanics. He and his fellow researchers were delving deeper into the neurological functioning of the cockroach. This, he said, would give engineers the information they need to design robots with a more compact build and greater efficiency in terms of energy, time, robustness and rigidity. Such superior robotics could be even used to explore new terrain in outer space. A cockroach is supported by at least three legs at all times during movement, which provides great stability. "Not only do cockroaches arguably exhibit one of the most stable ways to walk, called a tripod gate," he explains, "but they move equally quickly on every kind of terrain. Their speed and stability is almost too good to be true." In their lab, Prof. Ayali and his fellow researchers were conducting a number of tests to uncover the mysteries of the cockroach's nervous system, studying how sensory feedback from one leg is translated to the coordination of all the other legs. Their analysis of the contribution of each leg was shared with collaborating scientists at Princeton University, who used the information to construct models and simulations of insect locomotion.

When the biological model of aggregation behavior is restricted to certain zones in the environment (for instance by natural preferences for dark places as in cockroaches (Rust et al. 1995) the group of *mini-robots Alice* preferentially aggregate in only one of these zones, i.e. they collectively choose a single "resting" site. The results of their experiments were also used to calibrate a computer simulation of robots Alice that would allow extending the exploration of this collective decision model in further studies.

Construction Industry (Su, 2012) uses various kinds of materials. To set suitable statistical sampling acceptance plans greatly impacts construction qualities. In statistical sampling acceptance plans, methods of attribute acceptance sampling plans were widely applicable. However, to identify suitable attribute acceptance sampling plans under settings of acceptance probabilities is the key to ensure construction qualities.

This research used a swarm intelligent algorithm, namely Roach Infestation Optimization (RIO), to calculate parameters of the attribute acceptance sampling plans including the numbers of samples, acceptances, and rejections under predefined risks of producers and customers. The resultant plans simultaneously aimed at two objectives, i.e. minimizing the total number of samples and the discrepancy among predefined risks and calculated risks. This research provided optimal results of single, double, and triple sampling acceptance plans. Various resultant plans were provided for project managers to face different needs and gave higher profits.

In order to *optimize disassembly sequence for waste or malfunctioning* products, (Ying et al. 2011), a product disassembly hybrid graph model was established, which described the connection and precedence relationships between the product parts. The disassembly condition was deduced based on the hybrid graph model. Then, all the feasible disassembly sequences were obtained through the geometry inference method. The target function was constituted and the cockroach swarm optimization algorithm which suited the disassembly sequence planning was constructed. Further, by inputting some disassembly sequences and other controlling parameters, the optimal valid disassembly sequence could be obtained based on the cockroach swarm optimization. Finally, a case study was given to illustrate the validity of the proposed method and proved that the cockroach swarm optimization was superior to the particle swarm optimization

In this paper, an improved cockroach swarm optimization, called cockroach swarm optimization with expansion gird (CSO-EG), (Wanhui et al.2012) was presented and applied to motion planning of autonomous mobile robot. In CSO-EG, the expansion gird method was used to model workspace. By computing the weight factor, the Euclidean distance from each candidate to the destination cell and the pheromone strength of each candidate cell were used as the heuristic information together. For increasing the variety of path, a random choosing cell strategy was introduced. The simulation experiments demonstrated that the CSO-EG algorithm could quickly get the optimal or near-optimal path in a workspace populated with obstacles.

The article Yang et al. (2012) introduced algorithm thinking of cockroach swarm optimization (CSO). An improved CSO was presented and *applied to continuous optimization* problem. That paper analyzed performances of the improved CSO. The experiment results showed that CSO could get a relative fast convergence solution in small population size.

Cockroach swarm optimization (CSO) is modified and applied to solve the vehicle routing problem (VRP) (Zhaohui et al. 2011). The mapping from [−1,1] to the routing set was constructed as the encode method, and VRP was solved by taking advantage of CSO for continuous function. Compare with particle swarm optimization (PSO) the experimental results on vehicle routing problem without time window and with time windows showed that CSO could improve success rate of searching best route and was a feasible and effective method for vehicle routing problem.

For solving function optimization problems, a new continuous cockroach swarm optimization (CCSO) Cheng, et al.[b], was put forward in that paper. Some biological characteristics of cockroach had been simulated, such as gregarious colony, non-fixing nest, and disorderly crawling path and so on. The algorithm had truck throwing food in solution space. The cockroaches could crawl to the food and search for optimal solutions. Logistic chaotic map was used in nest distribution and throwing food. The experimental results showed that CCSO was superior to API and PPBO in solving precision, convergent rates and optimization rate.

Cockroach Swarm Optimization (CSO) presented in this paper, was an optimization algorithm inspired by the behaviors of *cockroach swarm foraging*. The cockroach belongs to Insecta Blattodea, likes warm, dark and moist places, and has the habits, such as omnivorous, swarming, chasing, dispersing, and ruthless. Its swarming and chasing habits reflect cockroaches can communicate with each other effectively. Cockroach could feel the change of surroundings because of its sensitive antennae. The dispersing habit refers to cockroaches could quickly disperse to the surroundings while the environment had a sudden change, this could reduce the harm from predators which might improve the survival rate (Chen et al. 2010). The ruthless habit was defined as while food shortage there would occur the bigger eat the smaller, the stronger eat the weaker. It was these habits that could be used as a model for function optimization algorithm.

4. THEORETICAL STUDY COCKROACH SWARM OPTIMIZATION AND AN EXPERIMENTAL RESULTS OF INTEGRATION OF ROBOT TO COCKROACH FOR COLLECTIVE DECISION MAKING

4.1 Study of Cockroach Swarm Optimization

CSO is constructed mainly through imitating the chase-swarming behavior of cockroach individuals, to search the global optimum. But if only carrying out this behavior, the CSO may fall into local optimum, while dispersing behavior may keep individuals diversity, at the same time, to imitate ruthless behavior can improve the results.

Cockroach swarm optimization algorithm (CSOA) was proposed in (Chen and Tang 2010; Chen, 2011), Cheng et al. (2010). The main concept of CSOA is that located in the *D-dimensional* search space R^D, there is a swarm of cockroaches which contains N cockroach individuals. The ith individual denotes a D-dimensional vector $X(i) = (x_{i1}, x_{i2}, ..., x_{iD})$ *for (i=1, 2, ..., N)*, the location of each individual is a potential solution to the targeted problem. $X(i)$ denotes the current location of the ith cockroach individual, $X'(i)$ denotes the new location, *visual* denotes the visual distance of cockroach, $P(i)$ denotes the optimal individual within the visual scope of $X(i)$, P_g denotes the global optimal individual, *step* is a fixed parameter, N is the population size, D is the space dimension. The model of CSOA consists of three behaviors, namely, chase-swarming, dispersing and ruthless which are explained as below:

- **Chase-Swarm Behavior:** Each individual cockroach $X(i)$ will run after (within its visual range) a cockroach $P(i)$ which carries the local optimum. Chase-swarm characteristics allow for automatic swarming since any cockroach will roughly chase after the local optimum in its visual field. This behavior is modeled in below equation as:

$$X'(i) = \begin{cases} X(i) + step.rand.\big[P(i) - X(i)\big] & \text{if } X(i) \neq P(i) \\ X(i) + step.rand.\big[P(g) - X(i)\big] & \text{if } X(i) = P(i) \end{cases}, \tag{1}$$

where,

$$P(i) = \text{Opt}_j \{X(j), \|X(i)-X(j)\| \leq \text{visual}, i=1, 2,..,N \text{ and } j=1,2,.., N\}, \tag{2}$$

$$P_g = \text{Opt}_i \{X(i), i=1, 2,..,N\} \tag{3}$$

denotes the global optimum individual cockroach, step represent a fixed value, rand stands for random number within the interval [0,1].

- **Dispersing Behavior:** The dispersing behavior causes random searching since at any point, a cockroach can move in a random direction. During a certain time interval, each individual cockroach will be randomly dispersed for the purpose of keeping the diversity of the current swarm. This behavior is modeled through Equation (4),

$$X'(i) = X(i) + \text{rand }(1,D), \ i=1,2,...,N, \tag{4}$$

where, *rand(1, D)* is a *D-dimensional* random vector which falls within a certain interval.

- **Ruthless Behavior:** The ruthless behavior is when a stronger cockroach consumes a weaker one. At a certain time interval, the cockroach which carries the current best value substitute another cockroach in a randomly selection manner. This behavior is modeled through the Equation (5) as:

$X(k) = P_g$ (5), where k is a random integer within the interval of [1,N].

Built of these three behaviors, the working procedure of the CSOA algorithm can be classified into following steps:

Step I: Setting parameters and initializing population. Set the value of parameters *step, N, D*; generate a cockroach population $X(i) = (x_{i1}, x_{i2}, ..., x_{iD})$ *for (i=1, 2, ..., N)* within feasible region randomly.

Step II: Search *P(i)* and P_g by *equation (2) & (3)*.

Step III: Performing chase-swarming by the equation *(1)*. $X(i) \leftarrow X'(i)$ and update Pg.

Step IV: To carry out dispersing behavior by the equation (4). If the new position $X'(i)$ superior than the original location *X(i)*, then, $X(i) \leftarrow X'(i)$, otherwise, return to the original location *X(i)*. Update P_g.

Step V: To carry out ruthless behavior by the *equation (5)*.

Step VI: Checking stopping criterion. If yes, generate output; otherwise go back to Step II.

4.1.1 Performance and Complexity Analysis

CSO algorithm can be illustrated by *2-D* model (see Figure 3). The chase-swarming behavior lead to the fact that $X(i)$ always approach to $P(i)$. Similarly, $P(i)$ approach to P_g. But chase-swarming may lead to all individuals gather around a position, fail to get global optimum and get an accurate result. While dispersing behavior may keep individuals diversity, which can improve the ability of avoiding fall into local optimum. Ruthless behavior can enhance the ability of local searching. The latter two behaviors not only can help CSO escape from local optimum, but also improve the accuracy. Its convergence will be illustrated in Section by the results of solving benchmark Problems. Its time complexity is a polynomial of *N*, that is $O(C.N^2)$, where C represents a constant.

The algorithm is mostly concerned with the spatial location of each cockroach instead of temporal location. It also generates groups of cockroaches which move towards the local optimum individual. That local optimum however, is a moving target and will move to an alternative local optimum or to a global optimum. Offer a novel optimization strategy based on cockroach behavior. This optimization relies more on convergence to a calculated local and global optimum rather than finding an optimized solution from random behavior.

4.1.2 Modified Cockroach Swarm Optimization

Chen presented a modified cockroach swarm optimization (MCSO), Chen (2001) with the introduction of inertia weight to chase swarming component of original CSO as shown below. Other models remain as in original CSO.

- **Chase-Swarming Behavior:**

$$x_{(i)} = \begin{cases} w.xi + step.rand[P(i) - X(i)], & if \ X(i) \neq P(i) \\ w.xi + step.rand[Pg - X(i)], & if \ X(i) = P(i) \end{cases}, \tag{6}$$

where, w is an inertia weight which is a constant.

Figure 3. 2-D path of a cockroach consisting of the X(i) chase P(i) yielding the new position X'(i)

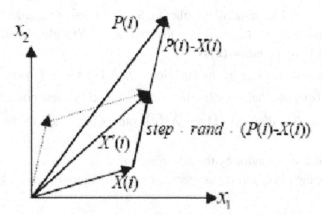

MCSO is extended with additional component called hunger behavior.

- **Hunger Behavior:** At interval of time, when cockroach is hungry, it migrates from its comfortable shelter and friends company to look for food (Havens et al. 2008, Williams et al. 2007). Hunger behavior was modelled using Partial Differential Equation (PDE) migration techniques. Cockroach migrates from its shelter to any available food source x_{food} within the search space. A threshold hunger is defined, when cockroach is hungry and threshold hunger is reached; it migrates to food source. Hunger behavior prevents local optimum and enhances diversity of population.

The PDE migration method is described by Kerckhove (2012) as:

$$\frac{\partial u}{\partial t} = -c \frac{\partial u}{\partial x},$$

(7)

with u (0; x) = u_0(x)

Parameter c is the migration controlling speed.

u[t; x] = u_0[-ct + x]

In u_0 (x-ct); u_0 (x) displaces *ct*.

u_0 (x-ct) satisfies migration equation at any initial population distribution u_0(x).

Hunger behavior is modelled as:

if (hunger == t_{hunger})

$x_i = x_i + (x_i - c) + x_{food}$,

(8)

where x_i denotes cockroach position, $(x_i -c)$ denotes cockroach migration from its present position, c is a constant which controls migration speed, x_{food} denotes food location, t_{hunger} denotes hunger threshold and hunger is a random number [0,1].

4.1.3 Improved Cockroach Swarm Optimization (ICSO) Models

- **Chase-Swarming Behavior:**

$$x_{(i)} = \begin{cases} w.xi + step.rand[P(i) - X(i)], & if \ X(i) \neq P(i) \\ w.xi + step.rand[Pg - X(i)], & if \ X(i) = P(i) \end{cases},$$

(9)

where, *w* is an inertia weight which is a constant, step is a fixed value, rand is a random number within [0,1], *P(i)* is the personal best position, P_g is the global best position.

$$P(i)=Opt_j \{x_j, \ | \ x_i\text{-}x_j \ | \leq visual\}, \tag{10}$$

where, perception distance visual is a constant.

j = 1; 2; …,N, i = 1; 2,…N.

$$P_g = Opt_i \{x_i\} \tag{11}$$

- **Hunger Behavior:**

if (hunger == t$_{hunger}$)

$$x_i = x_i + (x_i\text{ -}c) + x_{food}; \tag{12}$$

where x_i denotes cockroach position, $(x_i\text{-}c)$ denotes cockroach migration from its present position, c is a constant which controls migration speed, x_{food} denotes food location, t_{hunger} denotes hunger threshold and hunger is a random number within [0,1].

- **Dispersion Behavior**

$$x_i = x_i + rand(1,D); \ i = 1; \ 2,….,N, \tag{13}$$

where, *rand(1,D)* is a *D-dimensional* random vector that can be set within a certain range.

- **Ruthless Behavior**

$$x_k = P_g , \tag{14}$$

where, *k* is a random integer within [1,N], P_g is the global best position.

The algorithm for ICSO is illustrated in Algorithm 2 and its computational steps given as:

1. Initialise cockroach swarm with uniform distributed random numbers and set all parameters with values.
2. Find *P(i)* and P_g using *equation (10) and (11)*.
3. Perform chase-swarming using *equation (9)*.
4. Perform hunger behavior using *equation (12)*.
5. Perform dispersion behavior using *equation (13)*.
6. Perform ruthless behavior using *equation (14)*.
7. Repeat the loop until stopping criteria is reached.

Stochastic constriction is used in the paper of ZhaoHui et al. (2010) to improve the performance of original cockroach swarm optimization algorithm (CSO) Hui et al. (2010). A stochastic constriction cockroach swarm optimization (SCCSO) algorithm was presented. The constriction factor controls cockroach movement and prevents swarm explosion; cockroach was able to exploit local neighborhood and explore the search space.

Algorithm 2. An improved cockroach swarm optimization algorithm

```
INPUT: Fitness function: f(x); x∈R^D
set parameters and generate an initial population of cockroach
set P_g = x_1
for i = 2 to N do
    if f(x_i) < f(Pg) then
    Pg = x_i
    end if
end for
for t = 1 to T_max do
    for i = 1 to N do
        for j = 1 to N do
            if abs(x_i -x_j) < visual; f(x_j) < f(x_i) then
                P_i = x_i
            end if
        end for
        if P(i) ==x(i) then
            x_i = w.x_i + step.rand:(Pg-x_i)
        else
            x_i = w.x_i + step.rand:(P_i-x_i)
        end if
        if f(x_i) < f(P_g) then
            Pg = x_i
        end if
    end for
    if (Hunger == t_hunger) then
        x_i^n = x_i + (x_i-c) + x_fd
        hunger_i = 0
        Increment hunger_i counters
    end if
    for i = 1 to N do
        x_i = x_i + rand (1,D)
        if f(x_i) < f(P_g) then
            P_g = x_i
        end if
    end for
    k = rand_int ([1,N])
    x_k = P_g;
end for
Check Termination Condition
```

The performance of SCCSO was investigated and compared with that of original CSO, modified cockroach swarm optimization (MSCO) (Chen 2001) and LSRS (Grosan et al. 2009) on high dimension problems for finding the global optimal. LSRS was considered for performance comparison with the proposed algorithm because it has been proved for high dimension in literature (Ali et al. 2005).

The selected benchmarks are multi-modal and multi-dimensional problems which are considered as very hard global optimization problems. The global optimization problems of the form: minimize f(x) subject to $x \in \Omega$, where x is a continuous variable vector with domain $\Omega \subset \mathfrak{R}^D$ and $f(x) : \Omega \to \mathfrak{R}$ is a continuous real-valued function. Between the upper and lower limits of each dimension is Ω described. x^* represents global solution while $f(x^*)$ represents the corresponding function fitness value (Ali et al. 2005).

The effects of stochastic constriction factor on cockroach swarm optimization (CSO) algorithm improve its accuracy; and the algorithm solves multidimensional benchmark problems.

4.1.4 Stochastic Constriction Cockroach Swarm Optimization

Constriction factor was introduced by (Clerc and Kennedy 2002) to prevent swarm explosion in particle swarm optimization (PSO); PSO is one of the existing and popular SI algorithms. They proposed a constriction as:

$$\chi = \frac{2}{|2 - \varphi - \sqrt{\varphi^2 - 4\varphi}|},$$ (15)

where, $\varphi = c_1 + c_2$, $\varphi > 4.0$, c_1 is the recognition factor and c_2 is the social factor.

Shi described χ as a constant which is approximately $0:729$, φ is commonly set to 4.1 (Shi 2004). An algorithm with constriction constant 0.729 is equivalent to algorithm of inertia weight 0.729 with $c_1 = c_2 = 1:49445$, Shi (2004). Constriction PSO was experimentally com- pared with inertia weight PSO (Eberhart et al. 2000, Yan et al. 2012); constriction PSO performs better than inertia weight PSO.

Similarly, a constriction factor is considered in this paper to control cockroach movement during swarming process for avoidance of swarm explosion. The author uses a stochastic constriction factor (SCF) instead of a constant constriction. SCF allows generation of different values as constriction factor in each iteration. SCF helps to maintain the stability of swarm enhances local and global search and improves the speed and convergence of the algorithm. The algorithm utilized little CPU time in seconds to solve multidimensional problems and obtains optimal results.

The chase -swarming behavior, equation(1) of CSO (Hui et al. 2010) was modified in this paper with the introduction of SCF ξ. ξ randomly takes values between zero and one in each iteration. ξ controls entire cockroach movement, not only cockroach position as with inertia weight w of CSO in ZhaoHui (2011). Chase-swarming equation now becomes:

$$xi = \begin{cases} \xi(xi + step.rand.(Pi - xi)), & \text{if } xi \neq Pi \\ \xi(xi + step.rand.(Pg - xi)), & \text{if } xi = Pi \end{cases}$$ (16)

Algorithm 3. Stochastic constriction cockroach swarm optimization algorithm

```
INPUT: Fitness function: f(x), x∈R^D
set parameters and generate an initial population of cockroach
set P_g = x_1
for i = 2 to N do
    if f(x_i) < f(P_g) then
        P_g = x_i
    end if
end for
for t = 1 to T_max do
    for i = 1to N do
        for j = 1to N do
            if abs(x_i-x_j) < visual; f(x_j) < f(x_i) then
                Pi = x_i
            end if
        end for
        if (P_i ==x_i) then
            x_i = ξ (xi + step.rand.(Pg -xi_))
        else
            xi = ξ (xi + step.rand.(Pi _xi)_)
        end if
        if f(xi) < f(Pg) then
            Pg _ xi
        end if
    end for
    for i = 1 to N do
        xi _ xi + rand (1,D)
        if f(xi) < f(Pg) then
            Pg _ xi
        end if
    end for
    k = randin_t((1,N])
    xk _ Pg;
end for
Check termination condition
```

The *algorithmic steps for SCCSO* are illustrated in Algorithm 3 and its computational steps given as:

1. Initialize cockroach swarm with uniform distributed random numbers and set all parameters with values.
2. Find P_i and P_g using *equation (10) and (11)*.
3. Exhibit chase-swarming using *equation (16)*.

4.   Exhibit dispersion behavior using *equation (13)*.
5.   Exhibit ruthless behavior using *equation (14)*.
6.   Repeat the loop until stopping criteria is reached.

4.2 Integration of Robots into Groups of Cockroaches to Take Decision

Autonomous robots, perceived as congeners and acting as interactive decoys, are interesting research tools. By their ability to respond and adapt to animal behavior, they open possibilities to study individual and social animal behaviors. Here a description describe an experimental study that makes a step toward building such mixed societies of artificial and natural agents, using real and robotic cockroaches is demonstrated.

Their experimental setup consisted of a circular arena endowed with two shelters (Figure 4). In the presence of two identical shelters, each large enough to host the entire group, all the cockroaches choose collectively to rest under one of the shelters (Jeanson, 2005; Ame et al. 2006). When one shelter is darker than the other, cockroaches select the darker shelter by amplifying their individual preference through inter individual interactions. This self-organized choice does not require leadership, reference to the final pattern, or explicit comparison between the shelters. This mechanism leads to shelter selection and optimal group formation Ame et al. 2006.

A mathematical model in quantitative agreement with the experiments was developed by Ame et al. 2006, considering the following experimental facts: (i) Individuals explore their environment randomly

Figure 4. Experimental setup showing the cockroaches (Periplaneta americana) and the robots. Two shelters (150 mm) made of plastic disks covered by red film filters are suspended (30 mm) above the floor of a circular arena (diameter 1 m). The darkness under the shelter is controlled by the number of layers of red film. Cockroaches aggregate under the shelters.

and thus encounter sites randomly; (ii) they rest in sites according to their quality, in this case determined mainly by darkness; and (iii) they are influenced by the presence of conspecifics through social amplification of resting time, all individuals being considered equal. This model also forms the core behavioral module of the robots, enabling them to respond stochastically to social stimuli according to *Equations 17 to 18* (below). The robots are designed to discriminate (i) cockroaches from other robots, these two types of agents being considered here as conspecifics; (ii) shelters from the rest of the arena and shelter darkness; and (iii) the wall around the circular arena and other obstacles (supporting science online). The model was used as a quantitative explanation as well as overall guidance for the design of the robot.

The model described mixed groups where robots and cockroaches exhibit similar behavior. The differential equations giving the time evolution of the number of individuals in the shelters and outside are,

$$dx_i/dt = R_i x_e - Q_i x_i \quad i=1,2 \tag{17}$$

$$dr_i/dt = R_{ri} r_e - Q_{ri} r_i \quad i=1,2 \tag{18}$$

$$C = x_e + x_1 + x_2$$
$$M = r_e + r_1 + r_2$$

Variables x_i and r_i represent the numbers of cockroaches and robots present in shelter i, respectively, and x_e and r_e the numbers outside the shelters. Parameters C and M correspond respectively to the total numbers of cockroaches and robots. The functions R and Q, giving respectively the rate per individual of entering or quitting shelters, are

$$R_i = \mu_i \{1 - [(x_i + \omega r_i)/S_i]\} \tag{19}$$

$$R_{ri} = \mu_{ri} \{1 - [(x_i + \omega r_i)/S_i]\} \tag{20}$$

$$Q_i = \theta_i / \{1 + \rho[(x_i + \beta r_i)/S_i]^n\} \tag{21}$$

$$Q_{ri} = \theta_{ri} / \{1 + \rho_r[(\gamma x_i + \delta r_i)/S_i]^{nr}\} \tag{22}$$

Each cockroach outside shelters has a rate R_i of entering shelter *i (R = 1/mean exploring time)*; the equivalent rate for robots is R_{ri}. Because these functions *(Equations 19 and 20)* take into account a crowding effect, they decrease with the ratio between the number of individuals present in shelter i and its carrying capacity S_i. The carrying capacity corresponds to the maximum number of cockroaches that can be hosted in shelter *i*. In *Equations 19 and 20,* parameter w represents the surface of one robot expressed as a multiple of the surface of one insect. The term μ_i represents the maximal kinetic constant of entering the shelter for insects; μ_{ri} is the equivalent term for robots. Each cockroach in shelter *i* has a rate Q_i of leaving it to start exploring *(Q = 1/mean resting time)*; the equivalent rate for robots is Q_{ri}. The parameter θ_i is the maximal rate of leaving a shelter for cockroaches (θ_{ri} for robots); the parameters

ρ and n take into account the influence of the cockroaches' conspecifics (ρ_r and n_r for robots). When both shelters are identical, the parameters characterizing them are equal: $S_1 = S_2$; $\mu_1 = \mu_2$; $\mu_{r1} = \mu_{r2}$; $\theta_1 = \theta_2$; $\theta_{r1} = \theta_{r2}$. When one shelter is darker than the other, then $\theta_1 \neq \theta_2$; $\theta_{r1} \neq \theta_{r2}$.

Parameters γ, β, and δ correspond respectively to the influence of insects on robots, of robots on insects, and of robots on robots. The greater they are, the greater the mutual influences. The influence of insects on insects is imposed by biology and is not modulated in our experiments. However, parameters γ, δ, and β could be modulated by changing the hardware and/or software of the robots. As in insect societies, the inter attraction between cockroaches is chemotactile and is mainly based on a blend of hydrocarbons coating their body (Wyatt 2003; Said et al. (2005^a); Said et al. (2005^b); Caprari et al. 2005). The robots are coated with this blend, and the higher the pheromone concentration, the higher the value of β.

Acceptance of robots within a cockroach group is related to the ability of robots to bear the correct chemical signal and to behave appropriately. Chemical analyses and behavioral tests were performed to identify the main molecules constituting the odor that carries cockroach identity (supporting online). This odor was then collected from male cockroaches and calibrated to a known concentration used to condition filter papers dressing the robots. The concentration on the filter paper (per cm^2) was the same as that on one cockroach. Therefore, natural and artificial agents were equally attractive to one another. Tests with encounters between robots and cockroaches showed that cockroaches were lured to, and interacted with, chemically dressed robots. Comparisons with unmarked robots showed the importance of this chemical message (supporting online).

Pheromone luring was used here to allow acceptance of the robot in the group and not to attract the insects to a specific shelter. As robots become members of the group, they can take part in and influence dynamically the collective decision-making process. Not only do these robots explore their environment autonomously, but they are also able to tune their resting time in relation to the presence of cockroaches, as cockroaches do (Jeanson et al. 2005, Ame et al. 2006). In turn, the insects are influenced by the presence of robots, closing the loop of interaction between animals and machines. The shelter selection emerges from the social interactions between natural and artificial individuals. The first set of experiments showed the sharing of the collective decision-making for shelter selection in mixed cockroach-robot groups. The robots were programmed to select dark shelters as cockroaches do. Interactions between robots and cockroaches led to the selection of a common shelter (Figure 5). Given the choice between two identical dark shelters, both types of groups chose to rest under one of the shelters and behaved as a whole, irrespective of their natural or human-made origin. In most trials, both cockroach groups and mixed groups selected one of the shelters. In 28 of 30 trials (93%), mixed groups presented a clear choice for one of the shelters, and 75% of cockroaches and 85% of robots aggregated under the same shelter. Comparisons of these results with computer simulations of the model confirmed that the choice corresponds to the coexisting stable states of a nonlinear system (Figure 5, A and C). The second set of experiments was designed to show the control of the collective choice by mixed groups when shelters differed in attractiveness- in this case, darkness (Figure 6). Cockroaches prefer to aggregate under the darker shelter (brown bars in Figure 6A). This selection process is explained by the same model as above, with a bias induced by the darkness level of the shelters ($\theta_1 \neq \theta_2$, $\theta_{r1} \neq \theta_{r2}$; Figure 6C). When cockroach groups selected one of the shelters (22 of 30 trials), the darker shelter was selected in 73% of the cases and the lighter one in only 27% of the cases (Figure 6A). As in the first set of experiments with two identical dark shelters, these proportions correspond to the coexistence of multiple stable states in a nonlinear system.

In the case of mixed groups (yellow bars in Figure 6A), the robots were programmed to prefer the lighter shelter, contrary to the cockroaches. This effect was obtained by keeping the same behavioral

Figure 5. Shared collective choice between two identical shelters. (A and B) Experimental results for 30 trials. (A and C) Experimental results for 30 trials. Groups of 16 cockroaches (brown bars) selected one of the two shelters. Mixed groups of 12 cockroaches and four robots (yellow bars) presented the same distribution, demonstrating that the mixed groups made the same collective decision as cockroaches alone. The probability of selecting one of the shelters is about 0.5, in accordance with a dynamics leading to stable multiple states (Jeanson et al. 2005, Ame et al. 2006).

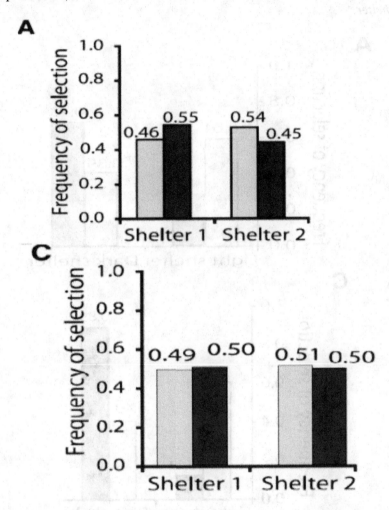

model and swapping the parameters controlling the robot response to darkness with respect to those measured for cockroaches. Given the choice between a dark and a light shelter, robots were able to induce a change of the global pattern by inverting the collective shelter preference. Under these conditions, the shelter less preferred by the cockroaches (i.e., the lighter one) was selected by mixed groups in 61% of the trials, versus only 27% of the trials done without robots. Despite the individual preference of robots for lighter shelters, they were socially driven by the cockroaches into the darker shelter in 39% of the trials (Figure 6A). At the technical level, author introduced lures able to perceive animal response and able to respond to it. The robots were designed to interact and to collaborate autonomously both with the animals and with one another. This work could be extended to vertebrates, taking into account sound, visual cues, and social organization. Possible ways to identify individual behavioral algorithms could

Figure 6. Controlled collective choice between dark and light shelters. (A and C) Experimental results (A) Groups of cockroaches without robots (brown bars) selected the dark shelter in 73% and the light shelter in 27% of the trials. Mixed groups with robots programmed to prefer the light shelter (yellow bars) selected it in 61% of the trials. The robots induced a change of the collective choice by modulating the nonlinear collective mechanism. Nonetheless, the dark shelter was still selected in 39% of the trials because the robots also socially responded to the cockroaches. In all selections, robots and cockroaches shared the same shelter.

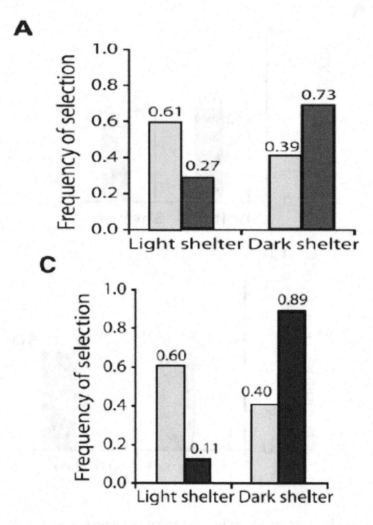

be to replace some animals within a group by robots or other artificial devices and to compare collective responses in "mixed" and "natural" groups (Michelsen et al. 1992; Patricelli et al. 2002; Schutter et al. 2001; Ishii et al. 2004). They could also be used to test hypotheses about the origin of cooperation among group members.

The above observation further revealed intricate social behavior in cockroaches with a novel experiment. These studies showed that cockroaches could be persuaded to aggregate under the lighter of two dark discs by cockroach-like robots. In essence, they determined that cockroaches prefer to optimize the number of friends and the darkness of the shelter simultaneously. It was also developed a simple behavior model for the cockroaches that was able to accurately predict how they aggregate under shelters. This model relied on two rates - R the rate of entering a shelter, and Q the rate of quitting a shelter. These rates were defined by the capacity of the shelter and the number of individuals (and robots) in the shelter.

4.2.1 Summary

- Cockroaches perform group choice that is a form of self-organized collective decision. It emerges form the local interactions between individuals.
- Both machines and insects are capable, independently of each other, to perform such collective decision.
- The robots are accepted by the cockroaches groups and actively take part in the collective choice.
- Most of the time, they gather with the cockroaches under the same shelter.
- When the robots are programmed to have an opposite preference compared to insects, they are able to induce a change in the global pattern by reversing the collective shelter preference.
- The mixed group of robots and insects gather in the less preferred shelter by the insects.
- The above experimental results demonstrate the existence of shared and controlled collective choice between machines and animals.

5. PROPOSED ALGORITHM FOR TRAVERSING SHORTEST DISTANCE CITY WAREHOUSE USING COCKROACH SWARM OPTIMIZATION

The city warehouse shortest distance problem is a TSP problem and is chosen for several reasons:

It is a shortest path problem to which the ant colony metaphor is easily adapted. It is a very difficult (NP-hard) problem. It has been studied a lot (it is considered to be "the benchmark problem" in combinatorial optimization and therefore many sets of test problems are available, as well as many algorithms with which to run comparisons. It is a didactic problem: it is very easy to understand and explanations of the algorithm behavior are not obscured by too many technicalities.

Travelling salesman problem (TSP) is about finding the most optimal path in terms of cost or distance while visiting a given set of cities. It is required that each city must be visited only once and the trip should end at the starting city, making the trip round. The aspect of determining a Hamiltonian tour associated with minimum cost makes TSP one of the discrete optimization problems and classified as NP-hard.

Application of TSP is in areas such as logistics, transportation and semiconductor industries. Collection of parcels and delivery in logistics companies, uncovering an optimized scan chains route in integrated chips testing, are some of the potential applications of TSP. Proficient way out for such areas will guarantee that the tasks are carried out efficiently and thus boost the productivity. As TSP is significant in many industries, it is so far being studied by researchers from various disciplines and it remains as an important test bed for many newly developed algorithms.

In this section, the author proposes a new cockroach swarm optimization (CSO) algorithm for city warehouse travelling salesman problem (CWTSP) problem. In CSO, a series of biological behavior of cockroach are simulated such as grouping living and searching food, moving-nest, and individual equal and so on. For cockroaches crawl and search the optimal solution in the solution space, it is assumed that the solution which has been searched as the food can split up some new food around solution's position.

By simulating cockroach's behavior of searching food, the author propose a cockroach swarm optimization. The CSO possesses simple formula and fully utilizes cockroach swarm's equality and swarm intelligence. To find better solution around the local optimal solution, the author uses the food- splitting strategy, which enhances the local search capability. Moving-nest make CSO possesses strong global search.

5.1 The Step of Cockroach Crawling

To apply CSO to CWTSP, define the step of cockroach crawling as *Step(x,y)*. In CWTSP, *Step (x,y)* represents that x- city warehouse interchange its place with y-city warehouse in a solution. Supposing that the solution is [1,2,3,4, 5], the processing of *Step(2,4)* is shown in Figure 7.

In fact, the author regard [1,2,3,4,5] as a position or coordinate of 6- dimensional space, then a cockroach crawls from A [1,2,3,4,5] to B [4,3,5,1,2] can be shown in Figure 8.

Figure 7. The step of cockroach's crawling

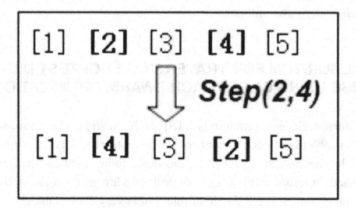

Figure 8. The road of cockroach's crawling

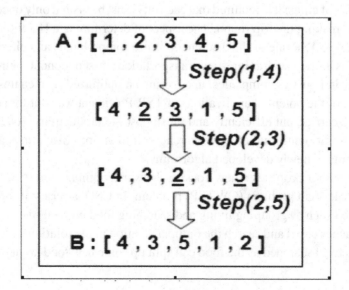

The road of cockroach crawling from A to B is defined in *formula (23)*:

$$Road\ (B, A) = B - A = Step(1,4) ++ Step(2,3) ++ Step(2,5) \tag{23}$$

5.2 The Strategy of Food Splitting

Supposing that in CWTSP the number of warehouse is D and m cockroaches form a swarm, look on the whole solution of TSP as *D-dimensional space* and each cockroach, foods, nest of cockroach are looked as a point in the D-dimensional space, and the *i*-th cockroach represents a D-dimensional vector $c_i=(c_{i1}, c_2... c_{iD})$. It means that each cockroach is a potential global optimum of the function $f(x)$ over a given domain D. Here $f(x)$ is used for evaluating the cockroach, using the cockroach's positional coordinates as input values. The output value is often named fitness value, and according to the fitness value, the cockroach is updated to move towards the better area by the corresponding operators till the best point is found. In fact, look on all foods and cockroaches as D-dimensional vector. The spot optimal is defined as *SOE* (Spot Optimal Eatables). To search better solution around the local optimal solution, the author introduces a food-splitting strategy. It can be shown in Figure 9.

In Figure 9, the $N*Rstep\ (r_x, r_y)$ represents the distance from *SOE* to its splitting foods. N is a positive integer, it is defined its value according to the need. If in TSP the city number is D (D-TSP), r_x and r_y are the stochastic number selected from a uniform distribution in $[1,D]$. So $Rstep()$ represents the one step distance of cockroach crawling and $N*Rstep\ (r_x, r_y)$ is N step distance in stochastic direction. $N*Rstep$ (r_x, r_y) and the strategy of food splitting can be defined by following formula:

$$SOE + N * Rstep(r_x, r_y)\ (r_x, r_y) \in [1, D];\ r_x \neq r_y \tag{24}$$

Figure 9. Food-splitting

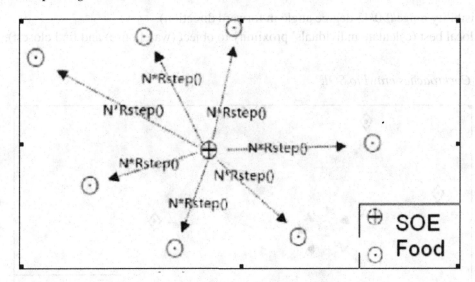

5.3 Moving-Nest

In CSO the distance is abstract and difference from real worlds. It can be measured and recorded by the amount of *Step()* which cockroach crawls. As a result an interesting result is obtained that in D-CWTSP the farthest distance between any two solutions is *D Step()*. In other word, the maximum quantity of steps which is needed by *formula (25)* is *D*. To increase the diversity of solutions, in every searching all cockroaches start to crawl from a new nest (stochastic solution) to the *SOE* or a food, and in this process CSO will evaluate the fitness value after every step of cockroach moving, and record the solution better than *SOE*. Symbol *c* represents cockroach's vector and symbol *f* represents food's vector. The process of cockroach crawling to food and *SOE* can be showed by following formula:

$$f_i - c_j = Road(c_j, f_i)$$

$$SOE - c_j = Road(c_j, SOE) \qquad , \qquad (25)$$

$c_i(i = 1..m)$ is the $i - th$ cockroach, f_j $(j = 1...n)$ is the $j - th$ eatable.

This process can be show in Figure 10.

5.4 Procedure of CSO Optimizing CWTSP

When CSO algorithm is used to optimize the TSP problem, firstly, all the cockroaches are initialized with the random solutions, and then take the formulas for evolution until the terminal rule coming. The whole procedure of CSO optimizing the TSP problem can be described as follows:

5.4.1. Pseudocode

- Set visibility range (90/45 degree angle in forward direction).
- Find local best (calculate individuals' proximity to object (warehouse) and find closest).

Figure 10. Cockroaches crawl to SOE

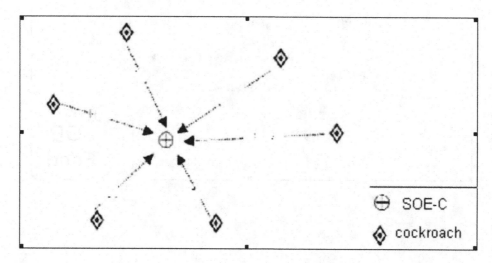

- Move randomly towards local best.
- Local best reaches target, marks it and moves to next target.
- If clustered, individuals interact and increases probability of dispersion (from 0.1 to 0.5).
- Values to be optimized.

5.4.2. Flow chart of the proposed CWTSP

The flowchart of CWTSP using CSO is depicted in *Figure 11*. The parameters of the proposed model are as follows:

N_i: Neighbors (Ni) of cockroach i,
p_i: Personal best solution (p_i),
l_i: Group best solution (l_i),
x_i: Cockroach location (x_i),
$hunger_i$: Update hunger of ith cockroach,
t_{hunger}: Hunger threshold/interval,
P_k: Is the darkest known location for the individual cockroach,
a_i: The velocity of the cockroach,
b_i: Private thinking of the cockroach agent,
w: Inertia weight component,
C: probability of cockroach as a tailer,
c: Is a constant which controls migration speed,
x_{food}: Denotes food location,
$(x_i - c)$: Denotes cockroach migration from its present position,
t_{max}: Is maximum iteration,
A1, A2, A3: Are group parameters,
C_0: Is cockroach parameters,
N_a: Is number of cockroach agents.

5.4.3. Mathematical Algorithm

Step 1: Initialize the swarm and parameters of CSO; the population size is set as m; the eatable size is set as n and choose the optimal eatable as SOE, int i, j; the maximum iteration will be set by the user; The probability of mutation is set (w = 0.5); The probability of cockroach as a tailer (C) is about 60%.

Step 2: Generate cockroach location (x_i) randomly and $hunger_i = rand\{0, t_{hunger}-1\}$. Each x_i in the population represents a candidate solution to the CWTSP.

$$x_i = x_i + (x_i - c) + x_{food}; \tag{26}$$

Step 3: Evaluate each cockroach-subset (x_i) using Backpropagation Neural Network (BPNN).

Step 4: Update the individual solution $F(x_i)$. Individual solution $F(x_i)$ is calculated according to the prediction rate (validation-set RMSE) of the evolved subset of (x_i). The values of the BPNN inputs are feature-subsets. One output of BPNN is used to determine shortest distance of city warehouse.

Figure 11. Flowchart of proposed CWTSP using CSO

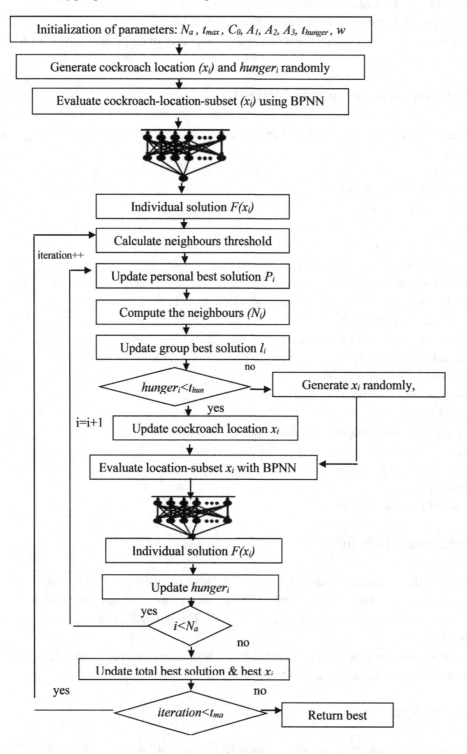

Step 5: Calculate neighbor's threshold value (d_g):

$$M = [M_{ik}] = \frac{\| F(x_i) - F(x_k) \|}{2},$$ (27)

d_g =median$\{M_{jk} \in M : 1 \leq j < k \leq N_a\}$

Repeat Steps 6.1 to 6.8 for those x_i with partial solutions. Steps 6.1 to 6.8 are as follows:

for $i = 1$ *to* N do

Step 6.1: Updating personal best solution (p_i) for the individual cockroach agent:

$$pi = \begin{cases} pi = xi \ if \ F(xi) < F(pi) \\ pi, \quad otherwise \end{cases},$$ (28)

Step 6.2: Compute the neighbors (N_i) of cockroach i as

For k = 1 to N_a

$$N_i \begin{cases} Ni = Ni + 1 \ if \ k : 1 \leq k \leq Na, \ (k \neq i) \ AND \ Mik < dg \\ Ni, \quad otherwise \end{cases},$$ (29)

Step 6.3: Update the darkest local location or group best solution (l_i) according to:

For r=1 to N_i

$$l_i \begin{cases} li = ljr = \arg\min k\{F(Pk)\}, k = \{i, jr\} \ if \ rand[0,1] < Amin\{Ni, 3\} \\ li, \quad otherwise \end{cases},$$ (30)

where, $\{i, j\}$ are the indices of the two socializing cockroaches and P_k is the darkest known location for the individual cockroach agent personal best.

Step 6.4: Update cockroach location (x_i):

$$x_i \begin{cases} xi = C0 \oplus CR(C0 \oplus CR(w \oplus MT(xi), pi), li) \ if \ hungeri < thunger \\ xi, = random \quad otherwise \end{cases},$$ (31)

The update x_i consists of three components: The first component is $a_i = w \oplus MT(x_i)$, which represents the velocity of the cockroach. *MT* represents the mutation operator with the mutation probability of *w*. In other words, a uniform random number rand [0, 1] is generated. If rand [0,1] is less than w then single insert move mutation operator is applied. The second component is $b_i = C_0 \oplus CR(a_i, p_i)$, which is the cognition part of the cockroach agent representing the private thinking of the cockroach agent itself. *CR* represents the crossover operator between a_i and p_i with the probability of *Co*. Two points crossover (point1 and point2) are selected randomly, where point1<point2, point1>1 and point2<*m*. The third component is $x_i = C_0 \oplus CR(b_i, l_i)$, which is the social part of the cockroach agent representing the collaboration among the group. CR represents the crossover operator between b_i and l_i with the probability of C_0.

Step 6.5: Evaluate each subset of (x_i) using BPNN.

Step 6.6: Strategy for food splitting: Update the individual solution F(x_i) based on validation-set RMSE of BPNN.

Step 6.7: Update hunger$_i$:

$$hunger_i = hunger_i + rand[0,1] * t_{hunger} , \tag{32}$$

Step 6.8: Update iteration-best solution T^{IB}.

$$T^{IB} = \arg \max q(F(x_i)) , \tag{33}$$

where, function q(.) gives the quality of the solution.

Step 7: Update the total best solution T^{TB} by the current iteration-best solution T^{IB} using:

$$T^{TB} \begin{cases} T^{TB} & if \ q(T^{TB}) \geq q(T^{IB}) \\ T^{IB} & otherwise \end{cases} , \tag{34}$$

Step 8: Update best x_i subset.

Step 9: Stopping criterion: The algorithm stops with the total-best solution T^{TB} and best subset of (x_i). The search will terminate if the global iteration has been reached.

5.4.4 Non-Mathematical Algorithm

Shown in Algorithm 4.

6. DISCUSSION

Regarding the role of performance factors (like robustness, reliability, flexibility, stopping criteria etc.) of proposed algorithm the author is depicting his critical viewpoint in the following paragraph. As the

Algorithm 4. Non-Mathematical Algorithm

Step 1: Initialize the swarm and parameters of CSO; the population size is set as m; the food size is set as n and chooses the optimal food as SOE.

Step 2: All of the cockroaches crawl to foods

```
for(i=1;i<=n; i++)
  for(j=1;i<=m; j++)
{
{
evaluate the solution which is generated when the cockroach crawl to eatable.
if (solution is better than SOE)
{
update SOE with the solution
}
}
The cockroaches are set a new solution (new nest)
}
```

Step 3: All of the cockroaches crawl to SOE

```
for(i=1;i<=n;i++)
{
{
evaluate the solution which is generated when cockroach crawl to SOE.
if(solution is better than SOE)
{
update SOE with the solution;
}
}
The cockroach is set a new solution (new nest)
}
```

Step 4: If the terminal rule is satisfied, stop the iteration and output the results, otherwise go to step2.

proposed algorithm is yet to be implemented, it is up to the research scholar who may find the performance readings based on author's viewpoint. Before starting discussion on the important performance factors following points should be kept in mind by the readers/researchers.

1. Population size (number of cockroaches) should not be taken more than 50. It is advisable to take initial population as 10 and then increment it by 10.
2. Maximum iteration may be varying from 1000 to 2500.
3. Dimension of the problem may be chosen as 06/07 and then increment it up to 30.
4. The mutation operator may be taken as 0.2-0.3.
5. The speed, accuracy, robustness, stability, and searching capabilities of the algorithm may be tested with renowned benchmark test functions like *Rosenbrock, Ackley Griewank, Rastrigin* etc. available in the literature.

6. All the problems are composed of continuous variables and have different degree of complexity and multi-modality. The set of test functions include unimodal and multimodal functions which are scalable (the problem size can be varied as per the user's choice).

The author's critical viewpoint is as follows:

- **Inertia Weight:** The inertia weight, w controls the momentum of the cockroach by weighing the contribution of the previous velocity-basically controlling how much memory of the previous cockroach direction will influence the new velocity.

The value of w extremely important to ensure convergent behavior, and to optimally tradeoff exploration and exploitation. For $w \geq 1$, velocities increase over time, accelerating towards the maximum velocity (assuming the velocity clamping is used), and the swarm diverges. Cockroaches fail to change direction in order to move back towards promising areas. For $w < 1$, cockroaches decelerate until their velocities reach zero (depending on the values of the acceleration coefficients). Large values for w facilitate exploration, with increased diversity. However, too small values eliminate the exploration ability of the swarm. Little momentum is then preserved from the previous time step, which enables quick changes in direction. The smaller w, the more do the cognitive and social components control position updates.

- **Stopping Criteria:** The stopping condition should not cause the CWTSP using CSO to prematurely converge, since sub-optimal solutions will be obtained. The stopping condition should protect against oversampling of the fitness. If a stopping condition requires frequent calculation of the fitness function, computational complexity of the search process can be significantly increased.
  - *Terminate when a maximum number of iterations, has been exceeded:* It is obvious to realize that if this maximum number of iterations is too small, termination may be before a good solution has been found. The criterion is used in conjunction with convergence criteria to force termination if the algorithm fails to converge.
  - *Terminate when no improvement is observed over a number of iterations:* If the average change in cockroach positions is small, the swarm can be considered to have converged. Alternatively, if the average cockroach velocity over a number of iterations is approximately zero, only small position updates are made, and the search can be terminated. The search can also be terminated if there is no significant improvement over a number of iterations.
- **Constriction Coefficient:** It is very similar to the inertia weight to balance the exploration-exploitation trade-off, where the velocities are constricted by a constant χ referred by constriction coefficient. Both approaches have the objective of balancing exploration and exploitation, and in doing so of improving convergence time and the quality of solutions found. Low values of w and χ results in exploitation with little exploration, while large values result in exploration with difficulties in refining solutions.
- **Population Size:** It is the number of cockroaches in the swarm, i.e. the more cockroaches in the swarm, the larger the initial diversity of the swarm- provided that a good uniform initialization scheme is used to initialize the cockroaches. A large swarm allows larger parts of the search space to be covered per iteration. However, having more population size increases the per iteration computational complexity and degrades to a parallel random search. It is also the case that more cockroaches may lead to fewer iteration to reach a good solution, compared to smaller population

size. A smooth search space will need fewer cockroaches that a rough surface to locate optimal solutions.

- **Neighborhood Size:** The neighborhood size defines the extent of social interaction within the swarm. The smaller the neighborhoods, the less interaction occurs. While smaller neighborhoods are slower in convergence, they have more reliable convergence to optimal solutions. To get the advantages of small and large neighborhood sizes, start the search with small neighborhoods and increase the number of Iterations.

- **Number of Iterations:** It is problem-dependent. Too little iteration may terminate the search prematurely. A too large number of iterations have a consequence of unnecessary added computational complexity.

- **Accuracy:** It is represented by the global optimum position. If prior knowledge about the optimum solution is available, then the quality of solution can be expressed as the error of the global best position.

- **Reliability:** When the performance of algorithms with random initial conditions is evaluated, it is done over a sufficiently large number of simulations. Reliability refers to the percentage of simulations that reached a specified accuracy (fitness value or error). The reliability of a cockroach swarm can be defined as

$$reliability \ (S(t), \varepsilon) = \frac{n\varepsilon}{N} \times 100, \tag{35}$$

where, ε is specified accuracy level, N is the total number of simulations, and $n\varepsilon$ is the number of simulations that converged to the specified accuracy. The larger the value of reliability, the more simulations converged to the specified accuracy level, and the more reliable the swarm is.

- **Robustness:** the smaller the variance of a performance criterion over a number of simulations, the more robust or stable the cockroach swarms. The robustness of a swarm can be expressed as the range,

$$robustness \ (S(t)) = [\bar{\theta} - \sigma\theta, \bar{\theta} + \sigma\theta], \tag{36}$$

where, $\bar{\theta}$ is the average of the performance criterion over a number of simulations, and $\sigma\theta$ is the variance in the performance criterion. The smaller the value of $\sigma\theta$, the smaller the range of performance values to which the simulations converge and hence the more stable the cockroach swarm.

- **Efficiency:** The efficiency of the cockroach swarm is expressed as the number of iterations, or number of maximum iterations to find a solution with a specified accuracy, ε. Cockroach swarm efficiency expresses the relative time to reach a desired solution.

- **Diversity:** Diversity is a very important aspect in population-based optimization algorithm like cockroach swarm optimization. Large diversity directly implies that a large area of the search space can be explored. Diversity can be calculated as:

$$diversity\ (S(t)) = \frac{1}{ns}\sum_{i=1}^{ns}\sqrt{\sum_{j=1}^{nx}(x_{ij}(t)-\bar{x}_j(t))^2}\ , \qquad\qquad (37)$$

where, $\bar{x}_f(t)$ is the average of the j-th dimension over all cockroaches, i.e.

$$\bar{x}_j(t) = \frac{\sum_{i=1}^{ns}x_{ij}(t)}{ns}\ , \qquad\qquad (38)$$

Again, swarm diversity is

$$diversity\ (S(t)) = \frac{1}{diameter\ (S(t))}\frac{1}{ns}\sum_{i=1}^{ns}\sqrt{\sum_{j=1}^{nx}(x_{ij}(t)-\bar{x}_j(t))^2}\ , \qquad\qquad (39)$$

where, diameter *(S(t))* is the diameter of the swarm, i.e. the distance between the two furthest apart cockroaches.

The diversity formulation in *Equation (39)* is independent of the swarm size $n_s = |S|$, the dimensionality, n_x of the search space and the search range in each dimension.

- **Flexibility:** One of the most important features of social insects like cockroach is that they can solve these problems in a very flexible and robust way. Flexibility allows adaptation to changing environments, while robustness endows the cockroach group with the ability to function even though some individuals may fail to perform their tasks. Stigmergy is often associated with flexibility: when the environment changes because of an external perturbation, the cockroaches respond *appropriately* to that perturbation, as if it were a modification of the environment caused by the group's activities. In other words, the group can *collectively* respond to the perturbation with individuals exhibiting the same behavior. When it comes to artificial cockroach/agents, this type of flexibility is priceless, i.e. it means that the agents can respond to a perturbation without being reprogrammed to deal with that particular perturbation.

- **Feasibility:** Cockroach updates routing tables of nodes viewing their node of origin as a destination node. In fact, while moving, a cockroach collects information about the path it traversed and which connects its source node with its current node: the cockroach can therefore modify only the entries of the routing tables that influence the routing of them and calls that have the insect's source node as destination.

- **Convenience:** It means stagnation of cockroaches, where they constrain the search too much, leading to a premature convergence *(stagnation)* of the algorithm. The total number of cockroach *m,* assumed constant over time, is an important parameter. Too many cockroaches would quickly reinforce suboptimal trails and lead to early convergence to bad solutions, whereas too few cockroaches would not produce desired results.

7. LIMITATIONS OF COCKROACH SWARM OPTIMIZATION ALGORITHM FOR CITY WAREHOUSE TRAVERSING PROBLEM

- **Limitations of Cockroach Swarm Optimization:** Even if it were true that current robots or computers *had* attained insect-level intelligence, this wouldn't indicate that human-level artificial intelligence is attainable. The number of neurons in an insect brain is about 10,000 and in a human cerebrum about 30,000,000,000. But if one put together 3,000,000 cockroaches (this seems to be the A.I. idea behind "swarms"), a large cockroach colony can be collected, not human-level intelligence. If anybody somehow managed to graft together 3,000,000 natural or artificial cockroach brains, the results certainly wouldn't be anything like a human brain, and it is unlikely that it would be any more "intelligent" than the cockroach colony would be. Other species have brains as large as or larger than humans, and none of them display human-level intelligence — natural language, conceptualization, or the ability to reason abstractly. The notion that human- level intelligence is an "emergent property" of brains (or other systems) of a certain size or complexity is nothing but hopeful speculation.
- *When clustering high dimensional datasets*, the CWTSP using CSO clustering algorithm is notoriously slow because its computation cost is exponential increased with the size of the dataset dimension. Dimensionality reduction techniques offer solutions that both improve the computation time, and yield reasonably accurate clustering results in high dimensional data analysis.

8. FUTURE PROSPECT

The combination of ants, bees, and cockroach swarming behavior offers a dynamic search and rescue team behavior that has not been previously implemented. While multiple sources indicates improvements in search and rescue responses using swarming patterns, successful usage of robots during *recent disaster situations* have yet to be significant. Though the effectiveness of robots in these situations can be a function of numerous variables, one of these variables could be inter-robot behavior. Rather than using individual species-inspired swarming algorithms, the author believes that using a combination of existing swarming algorithms can improve the search and rescue response as compared to the algorithms implemented individually. The author further predicts that the inclusion of cockroach swarm optimization will allow for automatic clustering around these target areas and streamline exploration and movement between different target areas. This behavior could be used in those situations to have clustering around rubble sites and danger zones but also have a steady progression between areas. The cockroach algorithm provides natural clustering around points if interest such as disaster locations for locations where individuals are likely to be trapped. The points of interest can also be moving targets allowing a robot team to find, congregate and explore a target site, and then naturally move on to a new site.

On the other hand, new studies have also shown the existence of collective memory in animal groups. The presence of such memory establishes that the previous history of the group structure influences the collective behavior exhibited in future stages. According to such principle, it is possible to model complex collective behaviors by using simple individual rules and configuring a general memory.

A possible development of swarm intelligence is the controlled exploitation of the collective behavior of animal societies. No example is available in this area of swarm intelligence although some promising research is currently in progress: For example, in the **Leurre** project, small insect-like robots are used as lures to influence the behavior of a group of cockroaches. The technology developed within this project could be applied to various domains including agriculture and cattle breeding.

Swarm intelligence may become a valuable tool for optimizing the operations of various business. Whether similar gains will be made in helping companies better organize themselves and develop more effective strategies remain to be seen. At the very least, though, the field provides a fresh new framework for solving such problems, and it questions the wisdom of certain assumptions regarding the need for employee supervision through command-and-control management. In future some companies could build their entire business from the ground up using the principles of swarm intelligence, integrating the approach throughout their operations, organizations and strategy. The result: the ultimate self-organizing enterprise that could adapt quickly- and instinctively to fast changing market.

The chapter demonstrated the use of insects (i.e. cockroach) showing swarming behaviour in various optimization techniques. There are some animals which have potential for swarming behaviour but they are yet to be discovered for real time implementation. The algorithm based on Rats, Bats and Dolphins are primarily studied but experimental studies are not carried out further. Some of the ongoing research is swarming behaviour of elephant can be discovered. Behaviour of sheep and African dogs are also under study and shown some promising behaviour. Such undiscovered behaviour can be implemented by taking some standard benchmark first and then it can be implemented on real time data collection.

Other future trends:

- **Complex, Real-World Applications:** More and more studies have focused on real-world applications such as highly nonlinear design problems in engineering and industry. These applications tend to be complex with diverse and stringent constraints, and thus the problems can typically be multimodal.

- **Data Intensive Applications:** The data volumes are increasing dramatically, driven by the information technology and social networks. Thus, data intensive data mining techniques tend to combine with bio-inspired algorithms such as cockroach swarm optimization, cuckoo search etc to carry out fault detection and filtering as well as image processing.

- **Computationally Expensive Methods:** Even with the best optimization algorithms, the computational costs are usually caused by the high expense of evaluating objective functions, often in terms of external finite element or finite volume solvers, as those in aerospace and electromagnetic engineering. Therefore, approximate methods to save computational costs in function evaluations are needed.

- **Novel Applications:** Sometimes, the existing methods and also new algorithms can be applied to study very new problems. Such novel applications can help to solve interesting and real- world problems. For example, bio-inspired algorithms like cockroach swarm optimization algorithm may be combined with traditional approaches to carry out classifications, feature selection and even combinatorial optimization such as the travelling salesman problem.

- **Theoretical Analysis:** Despite the rapid developments in applications, theoretical analysis still lacks behind. Any theoretical analysis will help to gain insight into the working mechanisms of bio-inspired algorithms, and certainly results concerning stability and convergence are useful. However, many algorithms still remain to be analyzed by mathematical tools. Future research efforts should focus more on the theoretical analysis.

- **Large Scale Problems:** The applications swarm optimization is diverse; however, the vast majority of the application papers have dealt with small or moderate scale problems. The number of design variables is typically less than a hundred. As real-world applications are large scale with thousands or even millions of design variables, researchers should address complex large-scale problems to test the scalability of optimization algorithms and to produce truly useful results.

- **True Intelligence in Algorithms:** As the significant developments expand in bio-inspired computation, some researchers may refer to some algorithms as 'intelligent algorithm'. However, care should be taken when interpreting the meaning. Despite the names, algorithms are not truly intelligent at the moment. Some algorithms with fine-tuned performance and integration with expert systems may seem to show some low-level, basic intelligence, but they are far from truly intelligent. In fact, truly intelligent algorithms are yet to be developed.

9. COMPARATIVE STATISTICAL RESULTS OF THE PROGRESS OF THE WORK ON COCKROACH

Figure 12 shows the distribution of the swarm algorithms covered here. It is clearly observed that PSO was the most frequently found algorithm, representing a quarter of all papers analyzed. The ABC algorithm was the second one, representing 13% of the total.

Finally, regarding the application, Figure 13 shows the main classes of problems to which the swarm optimization algorithms were applied. Scheduling problems are the most frequently found, closely followed by the KP.

Figure 12. Algorithms distribution

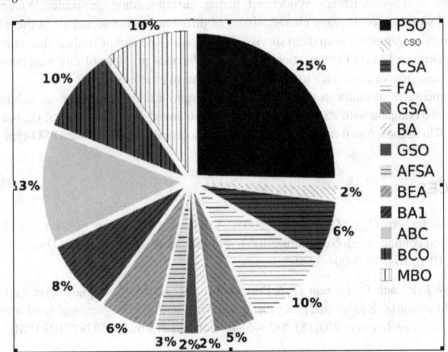

Figure 13. Applications of the swarm algorithms

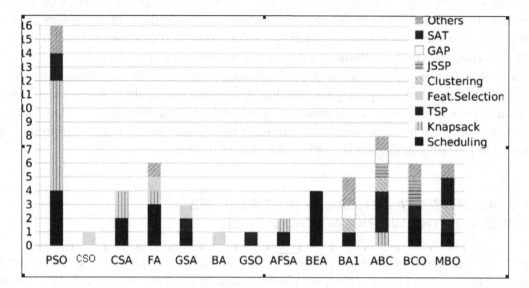

10. CONCLUSION

In the conclusive remarks the author suggested that the Swarm Intelligence and its optimization techniques have lot to do in the future. The previous work has shown that the SI optimization algorithms and methods have immense potential to solve many problems which are dynamic in nature as well as having convex and non-convex characteristics. The reviewed literature suggest implementation of cockroach swarm optimization as well as to study the social behavior of other undiscovered animals sheep, desert bighorn, Elephants, pigs, wild horses, Rhinos, Wildebeest, llamas, Giraffes, Antelope species, Whales in future.

The natural world conceals many characteristics of different creatures, and all of them have some unique behaviors or features to keep them survive. In this paper, the author studied and proposed a new algorithm, Cockroach Swarm Optimization for shortest distance problem of city warehouse, through modeling the behaviors of cockroach to solve the optimization problems.

The experimental results indicate that CSO can better improve the performance on finding the global best solutions. To compare with PSO-type algorithms, CSO avoids the prolix limits, i.e. the maximum velocities, in all iterations. And it can locate the global best solution much faster than PSO-type algorithm.

REFERENCES

Ali, M., Khompatraporn, C., & Zabinsky, Z. (2005). A numerical evaluation of several stochastic algorithm on selected continuous global optimization test problems. *Journal of Global Optimization, 31*(4), 635–672. doi:10.1007/s10898-004-9972-2

Ame, J., Halloy, J., Rivault, C., Detrain, C., & Deneubourg, J. L. (2006). Collegial decision making based on social amplification leads to optimal group formation. *Proceedings of the National Academy of Sciences of the United States of America, 103*(15), 5835–5840. doi:10.1073/pnas.0507877103 PMID:16581903

American Friends of Tel Aviv Univ. (2011, February). Roaches inspire robotics: Researchers use common cockroach to fine-tune robots of the future. *Science Daily,* p. 7.

Beer, R. (1990). Intelligence as adaptive behavior: An experiment in computational neuroethology. Academic Press.

Beer, R., Chiel, H., & Sterling, L. (1990). A biological perspective on autonomous agent design. *Robotics and Autonomous Systems, 6*(1-2), 169–186. doi:10.1016/S0921-8890(05)80034-X

Britton, N. F., Franks, N. R., Pratt, S. C., & Seeley, T. D. (2002). Deciding on a new home: How do honeybees agree? *Proceedings. Biological Sciences, 269*(1498), 1383–1388. doi:10.1098/rspb.2002.2001 PMID:12079662

Caprari, G., Colot, A., Siegwart, R., Halloy, J., & Deneubourg, J. L. (2005). Animal and robot mixed societies - Building cooperation between microrobots and cockroaches. *IEEE Robotics & Automation Magazine, 12*(2), 58–65. doi:10.1109/MRA.2005.1458325

Caprari, G., Estier, T., & Siegwart, R. (2002). Fascination of down scaling - Alice the sugar cube robot. *Journal of Micro-Mechatronics, 1*(3), 177–189.

Chen, Z. (2011). A modified cockroach swarm optimization. *Advances in Engineering Software, 32*(1), 49–60.

Chen, Z., & Tang, H. (2010). Cockroach swarm optimization. In *Proceedings of IEEE 2nd International Conference on Computer Engineering and Technology* (ICCET) (pp. 652–655). IEEE.

Cheng, L., Xu, Y.-H., Zhang, H.-B., Qian, Z.-L., & Feng, G. (2010). New bionics optimization algorithm: Food truck-cockroach swarm optimization algorithm. *Computer Engineering, 36,* 208–209.

Cheng, L., Zhu, D. C., Wang, Z. B., Qian, Z. L., & Pan, Y. (n.d.). *The research in CSO of continuous optimization problem.* Department of Computer Science and Engineering, Huaian College of Information Technology.

Cheng, L., Yang, Y., Qian, Z. L., Han, R., & Pan, Y. (n.d.). *Continuous cockroach swarm optimization with logistic chaotic map for solving function optimization problems.* Department of Computer Science and Engineering, Huaian College of Information Technology.

Clerc, M., & Kennedy, J. (2002). The particle swarm explosion, stability, and convergence in a multidimensional complex space. *IEEE Transactions on Evolutionary Computation, 6*(1), 58–73. doi:10.1109/4235.985692

Dawei, L., Zhaohui, C., & Binyan, Z. (2005). Particle swarm optimization algorithm with chaos and its performance testing. In *Proceedings of the Second International Conference on Impulsive Dynamical Systems and Applications* (pp. 1330-1335). Academic Press.

Durier, V., & Rivault, C. (1999). Path integration in cockroach larvae. *Blattella germanica* (L.) (Insect: Dictyoptera): direction and distance estimation. *Animal Learning & Behavior, 27*(1), 108–118. doi:10.3758/BF03199436

Durier, V., & Rivault, C. (2000). Learning and foraging efficiency in German cockroaches. *Blattella germanica* (L.) (Insecta: Dictyoptera). *Animal Cognition, 3*(3), 139–145. doi:10.1007/s100710000065

Durier, V., & Rivault, C. (2002). Influence of a novel object in the home range of the cockroach. *Blattella germanica. Medical and Veterinary Entomology, 16*(2), 121–125. doi:10.1046/j.1365-2915.2002.00348.x PMID:12109704

Eberhart, R., & Shi, Y. (2000). Comparing inertia weights and constriction factors in particle swarm optimization. In *Proceedings of the Congress on Evolutionary Computing* (pp. 84-89). Academic Press.

Garnier, S., Gautrais, J., Asadpour, M., Jost, C., & Theraulaz, G. (2009). Self-organized aggregation triggers collective decision making in a group of cockroach-like robots. *Adaptive Behavior, 17*(2), 109–133. doi:10.1177/1059712309103430

Garnier, S., Jost, C., Jeanson, R., Gautrais, J., Asadpour, M., Caprari, G., & Theraulaz, G. (2005a). Collective decision-making by a group of cockroach-like robots. In *Proceedings of Swarm Intelligence Symposium, SIS 2005* (pp. 233–240). Academic Press. doi:10.1109/SIS.2005.1501627

Garnier, S., Jost, C., Jeanson, R., Gautrais, J., Asadpour, M., Caprari, G., & Theraulaz, G. (2005b). Aggregation behaviour as a source of collective decision in a group of cockroach-like-robots. In *Advances in Artificial Life: 8th European Conference, ECAL 2005* (LNAI), (*Vol 3630*, pp. 169-178). Springer. doi:10.1007/11553090_18

Grosan, C., & Abraham, A. (2009). A novel global optimization technique for high dimensional functions. *International Journal of Intelligent Systems, 24*(4), 421–440. doi:10.1002/int.20343

Havens, T., Spain, C., Salmon, N., & Keller, J. (2008). Roach infestation optimization. In *Proceedings of IEEE Swarm Intelligence Symposium*. IEEE.

Ishii, H., Aoki, T., Nakasuji, M., Miwa, H., & Takanishi, A. (2004). *2004 IEEE international conference on robotics and automation*. IEEE.

Jeanson, R., Blanco, S., Fournier, R., Deneubourg, J. L., Fourcassi'e, V., & Theraulaz, G. (2003). A model of animal movements in a bounded space. *Journal of Theoretical Biology, 225*(4), 443–451. doi:10.1016/S0022-5193(03)00277-7 PMID:14615202

Jeanson, R., Rivault, C., Deneubourg, J. L., Blanco, S., Fournier, R., Jost, C., & Th'eraulaz, G. (2005). Self-organized aggregation in cockroaches. *Animal Behaviour, 69*(1), 169–180. doi:10.1016/j.anbehav.2004.02.009

Jeanson, R., Rivault, C., Deneubourg, J.-L., Blanco, S., Fournier, R., Jost, C., & Theraulaz, G. (2005). Self-organized aggregation in cockroaches. *Animal Behaviour, 69*(1), 169–180. doi:10.1016/j.anbehav.2004.02.009

Kerckhove, M. (2012). From population dynamics to partial differential equations. *The Mathematica Journal, 14*.

Martinoli, A., & Easton, K. (2003). Modeling swarm robotic systems. In *Proc. of the Eight Int. Syrup. on Experimental Robotics ISER-02*. Sant'Angelo d'Ischia, Italy: Springer. doi:10.1007/3-540-36268-1_26

Martinoli, A., Easton, K., & Agassounon, W. (2004). Modeling swarm robotic systems: A case study in collaborative distributed manipulation. Int. Journal of Robotics Research, 23(4), 415-436.

Michelsen, A., Andersen, B. B., Storm, J., Kirchner, W. H., & Lindauer, M. (1992). How honeybees perceive communication dances, studied by means of a mechanical model. *Behavioral Ecology and Sociobiology, 30*(3-4), 143–150. doi:10.1007/BF00166696

Miller, D. M., & Koehler, P. G. (2000). Trail-following behavior in the German cockroach (Dictyoptera: Blattellidae). *Journal of Economic Entomology, 93*(4), 1241–1246. doi:10.1603/0022-0493-93.4.1241 PMID:10985037

Miller, D. M., Koehler, P. G., & Nation, J. L. (2000). Use of fecal extract trails to enhance trap catch in German cockroach (Dictyoptera: Blattellidae) monitoring stations. *Journal of Economic Entomology, 93*(3), 865–870. doi:10.1603/0022-0493-93.3.865 PMID:10902343

Patricelli, G. L., Uy, J. A., Walsh, G., & Borgia, G. (2002). Male displays adjusted to female's response. *Nature, 415*(6869), 279–280. doi:10.1038/415279a PMID:11796996

Pettinaro, G. C., Kwee, I. W., Gambardella, L. M., Mondada, F., Floreano, D., Nolfi, S., ... (2002). Swarm robotics: A different approach to service robotics. In *Proceedings of the 33rd International Symposium on Robotics 2002*. Academic Press.

Pratt, S., Mallon, E. B., Sumpter, D. J. T., & Franks, N. R. (2002). Quorum sensing, recruitment, and collective decision-making during colony emigration by the ant leptothorax albipennis. *Behavioral Ecology and Sociobiology, 52*(2), 117–127. doi:10.1007/s00265-002-0487-x

Rivault, C., & Durier, V. (2004). Homing in German cockroaches, Blattella germanica (L.) (Insecta: Dictyoptera): multi-channelled orientation cues. *Ethology, 110*(10), 761–777. doi:10.1111/j.1439-0310.2004.01018.x

Rust, M. K., Owens, J. M., & Reierson, D. A. (1995). *Understanding and controlling the German cockroach*. Oxford, UK: Oxford University Press.

Saïd, I., Costagliola, G., Leoncini, I., & Rivault, C. (2005). Cuticular hydrocarbon profiles and aggregation in four Periplaneta species (Insecta: Dictyoptera). *Journal of Insect Physiology, 51*(9), 995–1003. doi:10.1016/j.jinsphys.2005.04.017 PMID:15950236

Saïd, I., Gaertner, C., Renou, M., & Rivault, C. (2005). Perception of cuticular hydrocarbons by the olfactory organs in Periplaneta americana (L.) (Insecta: Dictyoptera). *Journal of Insect Physiology, 51*(12), 1384–1389. doi:10.1016/j.jinsphys.2005.09.001 PMID:16226272

Schutter, G. D., Theraulaz, G., & Deneubourg, J. L. (2001). Article. *Annals of Mathematics and Artificial Intelligence, 31*, 223. doi:10.1023/A:1016638723526

Shi, Y. (2004). Particle swarm optimization. *IEEE Neural Networks Society*, 8-13.

Shi Y.Y., Liu Z.F., Zhang, H.C., & Hu, U. D. (2011). Product disassembly sequence planning based on cockroach swarm optimization. *Journal of Hefei University of Technology (Natural Science), 11*.

Su, M. H. (2012). *Roach infestation optimization for attribute acceptance sampling plan in construction industry.* Department of Construction Engineering, Master's Thesis.

Wang M, Zhu Y.L. (2005). A survey of swarm intelligence. *Comput Eng, 31*(22), 194e6.

Wanhui, L. (2012). *A new cockroach swarm optimization for motion planning of mobile robot.* Applied Mechanics and Materials.

Wei, T. E., Quinn, R. D., & Ritzmann, R. E. (2004). A CLAWAR that benefits from abstracted cockroach locomotion principles (M. Armada, Ed.). Academic Press.

Williams, J. B., Louis, M., Christine, R., & Nalepal, A. (2007). *Cockroaches ecology, behaviour and natural history* Johns Hopkins University Press.

Wyatt, D. (2003). *Pheromones and animal behaviour.* Cambridge, UK: Cambridge Univ. Press. doi:10.1017/CBO9780511615061

Yan, C., Guo, B., & Wu, X. (2012). Empirical study of the inertia weight particle swarm optimization with constrained factor. *International Journal of Soft Computing and Software Engineering, 2*(2).

ZhaoHui, C., & Haiyan, T. (2010). Cockroach swarm optimization. In *Proceedings of Computer Engineering and Technology (ICCET).* IEEE.

ZhaoHui, C. (2011). A modified cockroach swarm optimization. Elsevier Ltd.

Zhaohui, C., & Haiyan, T. (2011). Cockroach swarm optimization for vehicle routing problems. *Energy Procedia, 13*, 30–35.

ADDITIONAL READING

Eric, B., Guy, T., & Macro, D. (1999, September). *Swarm Intelligence: From Natural to Artificial Systems.* Santa Fe Institute Studies in the Sciences of Complexity.

Fernández, D. V., Francisco, H. P., & José, I. L. (2012). *Parallel Architectures and Bioinspired Algorithms, Series: Studies in Computational Intelligence* (Vol. 415). Springer. doi:10.1007/978-3-642-28789-3

Fisher, L., (2009, December). *The Perfect Swarm: The Science of Complexity in Everyday Life.*

Lewis, A., Mostaghim, S., & Randall, M. (2009). *Biologically-Inspired Optimisation Methods Parallel Algorithms. Systems and Applications, Series: Studies in Computational Intelligence* (Vol. 210). Springer. doi:10.1007/978-3-642-01262-4

Lim, C. P., & Dehuri, S. (2010). *Innovations in Swarm Intelligence. Series: Studies in Computational Intelligence* (Vol. 248). Springer.

Miller, P., (2010, August). *The Smart Swarm: How Understanding Flocks, Schools, and Colonies Can Make Us Better at Communicating, Decision Making, and Getting Things Done.*

Shangce, G. (2012, March). *Bio-Inspired Computational Algorithms and Their Applications.* InTech.

Stephan, Olariu., & Albert, Y. Z. (2005, September). *Handbook of Bioinspired Algorithms and Applications.* (CRC Computer and Information Science Series) Chapman & Hall.

Xin, S.Y., Zhihua, C., Renbin, X., Amir, H. G., & Mehmet, K., (2013, May). *Swarm Intelligence and Bio-Inspired Computation Theory and Applications.* Elsevier.

KEY TERMS AND DEFINITIONS

Cockroach Swarm Optimization: It is an optimization algorithm inspired by the behaviors of cockroach swarm foraging. CSO is constructed mainly through imitating the chase-swarming behavior of cockroach individuals, to search the global optimum.

Dispersing Behavior: A biological dispersal refers to both the movement of individuals (animals, plants: fungi, bacteria, etc.) from their birth site to their breeding site, as well as the movement from one breeding site to another. Dispersal is also used to describe the movement of propagules such as seeds and spores.

Hunger Behavior: Hunger is a sensation experienced when one feels the physiological need to eat food. In contrast, satiety is the absence of hunger; it is the sensation of feeling full. Appetite is another sensation experienced with eating; it is the desire to eat food. There are several theories about how the feeling of hunger arises.

Hybrid Cockroach System: Used to study the neuromechanical control architecture in running cockroaches and improve the performance of legged robots using fuzzy logic, evolutionary algorithm etc.

Shortest Distance City Warehouse: Approximation Algorithms for the k-center Problem: An experimental/ informally, given a set of cities, with intercity distances specified, one has to pick k cities ... so as to minimize the maximum distance of any city from its closest warehouse.

Swarm Intelligence: Swarm intelligence (SI) is the collective behavior of decentralized, self-organized systems, natural or artificial. The concept is employed in work on artificial *intelligence*. The expression was introduced by Gerardo Beni and Jing Wang in 1989, in the context of cellular robotic systems. Examples in natural systems of SI include ant colonies, bird flocking, animal herding, bacterial growth and fish schooling. It is based on the collective behavior of decentralized, self-organized systems.

Traveling Salesman Problem: Given a list of cities and the distances between each pair of cities, what is the shortest possible route that visits each city exactly once and returns to the origin city? It is an NP-hard problem in combinatorial optimization, important in operations research and theoretical computer science. The TSP has several applications even in its purest formulation, such as planning, logistics, and the manufacture of microchips. Slightly modified, it appears as a sub-problem in many areas, such as DNA sequencing. In these applications, the concept *city* represents, for example, customers, soldering points, or DNA fragments, and the concept *distance* represents travelling times or cost, or a similarity measure between DNA fragments. In many applications, additional constraints such as limited resources or time windows may be imposed.

APPENDIX

External Links

Cockroaches Offer Inspiration for Running Robots

The sight of a cockroach scurrying for cover may be nauseating, but the insect is also a biological and engineering marvel, and is providing researchers at Oregon State University with what they call "bioinspiration" in a quest to build the world's first legged robot that is capable of running effortlessly over rough terrain... If successful, Schmitt said, running robots could serve valuable roles in difficult jobs, such as military operations, law enforcement or space exploration. Related technology might also be applied to improve the function of prosthetic limbs for amputees, or serve other needs. (http://www. sciencedaily.com/releases/2009/12/091228163304.htm)

Roaches Inspire Robotics: Researchers Use Common Cockroach to Fine-Tune Robots of the Future

He and his fellow researchers are delving deeper into the neurological functioning of the cockroach. This, he says, will give engineers the information they need to design robots with a more compact build and greater efficiency in terms of energy, time, robustness and rigidity. Such superior robotics can be even used to explore new terrain in outer space. (http://www.sciencedaily.com/releases/2011/02/110207101022.htm)

Lessons from Cockroaches Could Inform Robotics

Running cockroaches start to recover from being shoved sideways before their dawdling nervous system kicks in to tell their legs what to do, researchers have found. These new insights on how biological systems stabilize could one day help engineers design steadier robots and improve doctors' understanding of human gait abnormalities. (http://www.ns.umich.edu/new/multimedia/videos/21233-lessons-from-cockroaches-could-inform-robotics)

Cockroaches and Running Robots

While the average human being probably doesn't find the sight of a cockroach dashing through the kitchen at 1 a.m. anything short of disgusting, researchers at Oregon State think it's inspiring. They are using the creature, a biological and engineering marvel, as "bioinspiration" for the world's first legged robot that can run over rugged terrain.... Schmitt thinks that the running robots could serve a valuable role in military operations, law enforcement or space exploration, and the technology could also be used to improve prosthetic limbs. (http://www.psmag.com/science-environment/cockroaches-and-running-robots-6983/)

Researchers Use the Common Cockroach to Fine-Tune Robots of the Future

Prof. Amir Ayali of Tel Aviv University's Department of Zoology says the study of cockroaches has already inspired advanced robotics. Robots have long been based on these six-legged houseguests, whose nervous system is relatively straightforward and easy to study. But until now, walking machines based on the cockroach's movement have been influenced by outside observations and mainly imitate the insect's appearance, not its internal mechanics. He and his fellow researchers are delving deeper into the neurological functioning of the cockroach. This, he says, will give engineers the information they need to design robots with a more compact build and greater efficiency in terms of energy, time, robustness and rigidity. Such superior robotics can be even used to explore new terrain in outer space. (http://www.physorg.com/news/2011-02-common-cockroach-fine-tune-robots-future.html)

An Army of Robotic Insects

Cockroaches are not the only insects that have captured the scientific imagination. Projects that highlight both the flight of the locust and the crawling of the soft-bodied caterpillar are also underway. Locusts are amazing flyers, Prof. Ayali notes. Scientists are studying both their aerodynamic build and their energy metabolism for long-distance flights. Recordings of their nervous systems and simultaneous video tracking to observe the movement of their wings during flight can be expected to lead to better technology for miniscule flying robots. As for caterpillars, engineers are trying to recreate in soft-bodied robots what they call the creatures' "endless degrees of freedom of movement." "Caterpillars are not confined by a stiff structure — they have no rigid skeletons," says Prof. Ayali. "This is exactly what makes them unique." (http://www.physorg.com/news/2011-02-common-cockroach-fine-tune-robots-future.html)

Roboroaches: Students Prepare to Control Roaches with Remote-Control Brains

By looking at what electrical impulses can do in a cockroach brain, co-founder Greg Gage hopes he can show the next generation of neuroscientists what the brain is made of before they ever get to college. "You could argue that there are slight differences between the neurons in cockroaches and in humans," he told AOL News. "But they are really similar: They both encode information the same way, and they both look the same way. So you can learn a lot about human physiology from studying these simple creatures." (http://www.aolnews.com/2011/03/15/roboroaches-students-prepare-to-control-roaches-with-remote-con/)

Stealth Behavior Allows Cockroaches to Seemingly Vanish

Aside from helping scientists understand animal (cockroach) locomotion, these findings will go into making better robots. (http://www.sciencedaily.com/releases/2012/06/120606193851.htm)

If Only a Robot Could Be More Like a Cockroach

He believes the research could help lead to better robots to search collapsed mines and buildings, to pilot drones, and for space exploration, where signals from Earth to a far off planet takes minutes, hours or longer. So, to make a robot that can turn, back up, climb over or burrow under and obstacle without the guidance of a far off rescue worker using computer controls, what could be better than mimicking an insect's comparatively simple brain? Easier said than done. To get these first recordings of neural activity, Research Assistant Allan Pollack spent more than a year perfecting techniques to perform brain surgery in an area the size of the head of a pin. (http://www.eurekalert.org/pub_releases/2010-05/cwru-ioa050510.php)

Cyborg Cockroaches Could Power Own Electric 'Brains'

Engineers have been attempting to gain control of insects' bodies for some time, to act as discreet spies or to take advantage of their advanced sense of smell to detect chemicals or explosives. (http://www. newscientist.com/article/mg20126884.200-cyborg-cockroaches-could-power-own-electric-brains.html)

Journals Related to Swarm Intelligence

1. *Swarm Intelligence,* Springer, link.springer.com/journal/11721
2. *Swarm and Evolutionary Computation*, Elsevier.
3. International Journal of Swarm Intelligence, InderScience pub, www.inderscience.com/ijsi
4. *International Journal of Swarm Intelligence Research,* www.igi-global.com/journal/journal-swarm-intelligence-research/1149
5. *International Journal of Swarm Intelligence and Evolutionary Computation*, ResearchGate, www.researchgate.net/journal/2090-4.
6. *Evolutionary Intelligence*, Springer, 2008-Present.
7. *Journal of Artificial Evolution and Applications*, Hindawi, 2008-2010.
8. *Evolutionary Computation*, MIT Press, 1993-Present, Quarterly (spring, summer, fall, winter).
9. *IEEE Transactions on Evolutionary Computation*, IEEE Press, 1997-Present.
10. *International Journal of Applied Evolutionary Computation*, IGI Global, 2010-Present.
11. *Computational Optimization and Applications*, Springer, 1992-Present.

Chapter 5
Swarm Intelligence for Biometric Feature Optimization

Santosh Kumar
Indian Institute of Technology (Banaras Hindu University), India

Deepanwita Datta
Indian Institute of Technology (Banaras Hindu University), India

Sanjay Kumar Singh
Indian Institute of Technology (Banaras Hindu University), India

ABSTRACT

Swarm Intelligence (SI) and bio-inspired computation has gathered great attention in research in the last few years. Numerous SI-based optimization algorithms have gained huge popularity to solve the complex combinatorial optimization problems, non-linear design system optimization, and biometric features selection and optimization. These algorithms are inspired by nature. In biometrics, face recognition is a non-intrusive method, and facial characteristics are probably the most common biometric features to identify individuals and provide a competent level of security. This chapter presents a novel biometric feature selection algorithm based on swarm intelligence (i.e. Particle Swarm Optimization [PSO] and Bacterial Foraging Optimization Algorithm [BFOA] metaheuristics approaches). This chapter provides the stepping stone for future researchers to unveil how swarm intelligence algorithms can solve the complex optimization problems to improve the biometric identification accuracy. In addition, it can be utilized for many different areas of application.

1. INTRODUCTION

Generally hard or complex optimization problems are defined as problems cannot be solved to optimality or to any guaranteed bound by any deterministic (exact) approach within a 'reasonable amount of time. These problems can be divided into numerous categories depending on whether they are continuous or discrete domain, constrained or unconstrained, mono or multi-objective function based static or dynamic. In order to find satisfactory solutions for these problems, swarm intelligence (SI) algorithm or

DOI: 10.4018/978-1-4666-8291-7.ch005

bio-inspired metaheuristics approaches play important role to get optimal solution of problems. Swarm Intelligence (SI) is an innovative distributed intelligent paradigm for solving the hard or complex optimization problems that takes motivation from the collective behavior of a group of social insect colonies, Ant Colony Optimization (ACO), fish schooling and other animal societies. SI systems are typically consists of a population of individual or simple agents (an entity capable of performing/executing certain operations) interacting locally with one another and with their environment. The entities of such system with very limited (optimal solution of certain individual populations) individual capability can jointly or cooperatively perform many complex tasks necessary for their survival. Although, normally in SI system has no centralized control structure and power dictating how individual agents should behave local interactions between such agents often lead to the emergence of global and self-organized behavior (Boussaïda, 2013).

A metaheuristics approach is an algorithm designed to solve approximately a wide range of hard optimization problems without having to deeply adapt to each problem. Indeed, the Greek prefix ''Meta'', present in the name, is used to indicate that these algorithms are ''higher level'' heuristics, in contrast with problem-specific heuristics. Metaheuristics are generally applied to a problem for which there is no satisfactory problem-specific algorithm to solve them. They are widely used to solve complex problems in industry and services, in areas ranging from finance to production management and engineering. Almost all metaheuristics approaches share the following characteristics:

- They are nature-inspired (based on some principles from physics, biology or ethology) and they make use of stochastic components (involving random variables).
- They do not use the gradient or Hessian matrix of the objective function.

They have several parameters that need to be fitted to the problem at hand bio-inspired computation and swarm intelligence based algorithms have attracted significant attention in recent years for solving the complex and combinatorial optimization problems of data clustering, feature selection and maximization of matching scores for authentication of human in biometrics (Tan & Bhanu, 2006) computer vision, data mining and machine learning based algorithms.

Motivated from the natural and social behavioral phenomena, bio-inspired computation algorithms have significant research area during the recent years from both multidisciplinary research and the scientific research purpose. In the last thirty years, a great interest has been devoted to bio-inspired metaheuristics and it has encouraged and provides successful algorithms and computational simulated tools for dealing with complex and optimization problems (Karakuzu, 2009).

These approaches are motivated from natural processes generally start with an initial set of variables and then evolve to obtain the global minimum or maximum of the objective function and it has been an escalating interest in algorithms motivated by the behaviors of natural phenomena which are incorporated by many scientists and researchers to solve hard optimization problems. Hard problems cannot be solved to optimality, or to any guaranteed bound by any exact (deterministic) method within a 'reasonable'' time limit (Rajabioun, 2011), (Chih & Huang, 2011), (Baojiang & Shiyonga, 2007), (Dorig, Maniezzo, & Colorni, 1996), (Farmer & Packard, 1986), (Kima, Abrahamb, & Choa 2007), (Kirkpatrick, Gelatt, & Vecchi 1983), (Tang et al., 1996). It is computational problems such as optimization of objective functions (Du & Li 2008); (Yao, Liu, & Lin, 1999) pattern recognition (Yi et al., 2008), (Tan & Bhanu, 2006) control objectives (Chih &Huang, 2011), (Karakuzu, 2008), (Kim, Maruta & Sugie, 2008), image processing (Cordon, Santamarı, & Damas, 2006) (Yang, 2009) and filter modeling (Kalinlia & Karaboga, 2005); (Lin, Chang, & Hsieh, 2008).

There are different approaches have been implemented by researches so far, for example Genetic algorithm (GAs) (Tang et.al, 1996) is the most well-known and mostly used evolutionary computation technique and it was developed in the early 1970s at the University of Michigan by John Holland and his students, whose research interests were devoted to the study of adaptive systems (Holland, 1975).

The basic genetic algorithm is very general and it can be implemented differently according to the problems: Representation of solution (chromosomes), selection strategy, type of crossover (the recombination operator) and mutation operators. The fixed-length binary string is the most common representation of the chromosomes applied in GAs and a simple bit manipulation operation allow the implementation of crossover and mutation operations. Emphasis is mainly concentrated on crossover as the main variation operator that combines multiple (generally two) individuals that have been selected together by exchanging some of their parts. An exogenous parameter $p_c \in [0.6, 1.0]$ (crossover rate) indicates the probability per individual to undergo crossover. After evaluating the fitness value of each individual in the selection pool, Individuals for producing offspring are selected using a selection strategy.

A few of the popular selection schemes are mainly roulette-wheel selection, tournament selection and ranking selection, etc. After crossover operation, individuals are subjected to mutation process. Mutation initiates some randomness into the search space to prevent the optimization process from getting trapped into local optima. Naturally, the mutation rate is applied with less than 1% probability but the appropriate value of the mutation rate for a given optimization problem is an open issue in research. Simulated Annealing (Kirkpatrick, Gelatto, & Vecchi, 1983) is inspired by the annealing technique used by the different metallurgists to get a ''well ordered'' solid state of minimal energy (while avoiding the ''meta-stable'' structures, characteristic of the local minima of energy).

Ant Colony optimization (ACO) algorithm is a metaheuristics technique to solve problems that has been motivated by the ants' social behaviors in finding shortest paths. Real ants walk randomly until they find food and return to their nest while depositing pheromone on the ground in order to mark their preferred path to attract other ants to follow (Jackson, 2006) (Goss et al., 1989) (Dorigo, Maniezzo, & Colorni, 1996).

Particle Swarm Optimization (PSO) was introduced by James Kennedy and Russell Eberhart as a global optimization technique in 1995. It uses the metaphor of the flocking behavior of birds to solve optimization problems (Kennedy & Eberhart, 1995). It is similar to a genetic algorithm (GA) in the system is initialized with a population of random solutions. It is unlike a GA, however, in that each potential solution is also assigned a randomized velocity and the potential solutions of a problem known particles. This particle flown through the problem space, each particle keeps track of its coordinates in the problem space which are associated with the best solution or fitness it has achieved so and fitness value is also stored. This value is called pbest. Another "best" value is tracked by the global version of the particle swarm optimizer is the overall best value and its location, obtained so far by any particle in the population. This location is known as gbest. The particle swarm optimization concept consists of at each time step changing the velocity (accelerating) of each particle toward its pbest and gbest locations. Particle acceleration is weighted by a random term with separate random numbers being generated for acceleration toward pbest and gbest locations.

Bacterial foraging optimization algorithm (BFOA) has been widely accepted as a global optimization algorithm of current interest for optimization and control. BFOA is inspired by the social foraging behavior of Escherichia coli. BFOA has already drawn the attention of researchers because of its efficiency in solving real-world optimization problems arising in several application domains.

Firefly algorithm is a population based metaheuristic algorithm. It has become an increasingly important popular tool of Swarm Intelligence that has been applied in almost all research area so of optimization, as well as science and engineering practice. Fireflies have their flashing light. There are two fundamental functions of flashing light of firefly: (1) to attract mating partners and (2) to warn potential predators. But the flashing lights comply with more physical rules. On the one hand, the light intensity of source (I) decrease as the distance (r) increases according to the term. This phenomenon inspired (Yang, 2010) to develop the firefly algorithm (Tarasewich & McMullen, 2002), (Senthilnath, Omkar, & Mani, 2011) (Yang, 2010) (Boussaïd, Lepagnot, & Siarry, 2013).

Bat-inspired algorithm is a metaheuristics optimization algorithm. It was invented by Xin-She Yang in 2010 (Yang, 2011) (Tripathi, Bandyopadhyay, & Pal, 2007) and it is based on the echolocation behavior of microbats with varying pulse rates of emission and loudness and honey bee algorithm (Karaboga, 2005). Such algorithms are progressively analyzed, deployed and powered by different researchers in many different research fields (Baojiang & Shiyonga, 2007), (Rajabioun, 2011), (Ellabib, Calamai, & Basir, 2007) (Hamzaçebi, 2008), (Lozano, Herrera, & Cano, 2008) (Yang, 2011), (Tripathi, Bandyo-padhyay, & Pal, 2007).

These algorithms are used to solve different optimization problems. However, there is no specific algorithm or direct algorithms to achieve the best solution for all optimization problems. Numerous algorithms give a better solution for some particular problems than others. Hence, searching for new heuristic optimization algorithms is an open problem (Karaboga, 2005) and it requires a lot of exploration of new metaheuristic algorithms for solving of hard problems.

Recently, one of the metaheuristic approaches has been developed for solving the hard or complex optimization and data clustering problem which is NP-hard problem known as Black Hole (BH) metaheuristic approach (Hatamlou, 2013). BH algorithm is inspired by the black hole phenomenon. Black Hole algorithm (BH) starts with an initial population of candidate solutions to an optimization problem and an objective function that is calculated for them similar to other population-based algorithms.

Ant Colony Optimization (ACO) is a nature inspired metaheuristics algorithm to find the solution of hard or complex optimization problems. ACO method was proposed by Marco Dorigo and colleagues. Ant colonies and more generally insect societies are distributed systems that in spite of the simplicity of their individuals present a highly structured social organization.

The main motivation of ACO algorithmic approach studies the models which are derive from the real ant behavior and uses these models as source of inspiration for the design of novel algorithm for solution of optimization and distributed control problem in our society. Ant colonies behavior and their communication, ACO takes inspiration from the foraging behavior of real ants. In fact, an important insight of early research on ant's behavior was that most of the communication among individuals or between individuals and the environmental is based on the use of chemicals produced by the ants. These chemicals are called pheromones. This is a different from what happen in human and in other higher species whose most important senses are visual or acoustic. The behavior of ant colonies has motivated different kind of ant algorithms depending upon several aspects of theses behavior.

In ACO, foraging, division of labor, brood shorting and their co-operation in the transport facilities from source food to the destination (nest). In all above activities, ants co-ordinates their activities via stigmergy, a form of indirect communication mediated by modification of the environment. Ants initially diversify or explore the area surrounding their nest for searching their food by performing a randomized walk. Along their path between food source and destination, ants deposit a chemical pheromone trail on the ground in order to identify some shortest path that should provide guidance other ants to the food source (Dorigo & Blum, 2005). After some time, the shortest path between the destination and the food source demonstrates a higher concentration of pheromone traits on path and therefore, this process attracts more ants. In ACO, double bridge experiments with two branches of equal length (r = 1), when a trail starts, there is no phermonace on the two branches. Hence, the ants do not have preferences and they select with the same probability any of two branches. Due to random fluctuation in concentration of pheromone trails, a few more ants will chose one branch over other. Because ant deposits pheromone while random walk, a large number of ant on a branch results in the larger amount of pheromone on that branch. This will provide ants converge to one path, is known as autocatalytic or positive feedback process. Artificial ant colonies exploited this characteristic of real ant colonies to build solutions to an optimization problem and exchange information (probability of short and long path phermonace trails updating and minimum cost paths) on their quality through a communication scheme that is reminiscent of the one adopted by real ants (Dorig et al., 2006).

2. BIOMETRIC SYSTEM

Biometric system is a pattern recognition based system. It acquires biometric data from an individual, extracts a salient feature set from the data, compares feature set against the feature set(s) stored in the database and executes an action based on the result of the comparison (Jain, Flynn, & Ross, 2008). Establishing one's identity has become complicated in a vastly interconnected cloud network. The need of a consistent cloud security based technique has increased in the wake of heightened concerns about security. Biometrics is the science of establishing the identity of an individual based on their physical, chemical and behavioral traits. Nowadays numerous biometric methods are used and deployed for authentication which means the process of ensuring correct identification of the user including three categories bellow:

- Something users know, e.g. Password, PIN.
- Something users have, e.g. ATM, Smart cards.
- Something users are, e.g. Fingertips, the iris.

2.1. Biometric Characteristics

Biometrics offers a natural and reliable solution to certain aspects of identity management by utilizing fully automated or semi-automated schemes to recognize individuals (Human or Animal) based on their inherent physical and/or behavioral characteristics (Figure 1). With the help of physiological and behavioral characteristics currently used for automatic identification include fingerprints, iris, voice, retina, hand, ear, handwriting, keystroke, and finger shape (Figure 2). However, this is only a partial list as new measures (such as ear gait, shape, optical skin reflectance, head resonance and body odor) are being produced all of the time. Due to the broad range of characteristics used in identification or verification, the imaging requirements for the technology vary greatly. Here always one question arises: Which biometric characteristic is best? The ideal biometric characteristic has five qualities: robustness, distinctiveness, availability, accessibility and acceptability are discussed below (Pun & Moon, 2004):

Figure 1. Biometric characteristic (1) Physiological Characteristics (2) Behavioral Characteristics

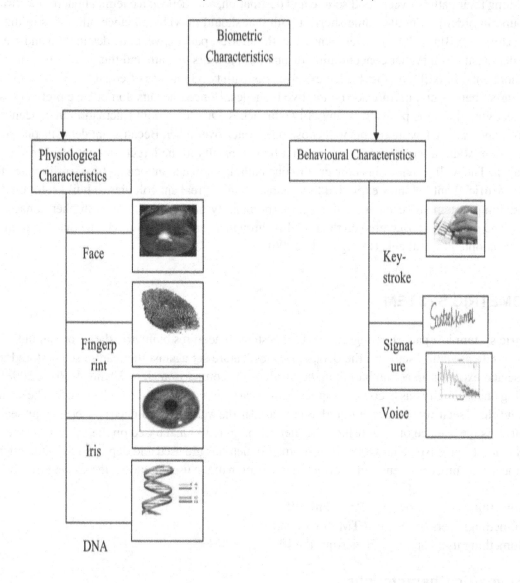

- **Robustness:** By "robust", we mean unchanging on an individual over time.
- **Distinctive:** By "distinctive", we mean showing great variation over the population.
- **Available:** By "available", we mean that the entire population should ideally have these measuring multiples.
- **Accessible:** By "accessible", we mean easy to image using electronic sensors.
- **Acceptable:** By "acceptable", we mean that people do not object to having this measurement taken from them.

Several different aspects of human physiology, chemistry or behaviour characteristics can be used for biometric authentication. The selection of a particular biometric for use in a specific application involves a weighting of several factors. Biometric traits are classified as follows:

Figure 2. General biometric system

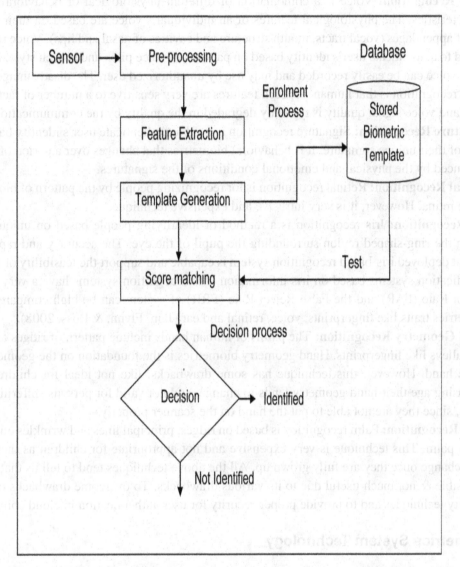

2.2. Different Biometrics Techniques

- **Fingerprint Recognition:** Fingerprint is a pattern of ridges and valleys on the surear of the fingertip whose formation is determined during the first seven month fetal development. It has been empirically determined that the fingerprints of same twins are different. Fingerprint recognition refers to the automated method of verifying a match between two human fingerprints. The dryness of fingers, soiled fingers can affect the system and it can show error. One problem with large scale fingerprint recognition systems is that they require a huge amount of computation resources. Finally, fingerprints of small fraction of population may be unstable for automatic identification because of genetic factors aging; occupational reason like manual works may have large number of cuts and bruises on their fingerprints that keep changing (Jain & ross, 2008) (Wayman, 2000) (Jantz, 1997).

- **Voice Recognition:** Voice is a combination of different physiological or behavioral biometric characteristics. The physiological features of an individual's voice are based on their shape and size of appendages (vocal tracts, mouth structure and cavities of nasal and lips). Voice recognition is used to authenticate user's identity based on patterns of voice pitch and speech style. However a user's voice can be easily recorded and may use by unauthorized user. The disadvantages of voice based recognition is that human's speech features are very sensitive to a number of factor such as noise and voice signal quality is typically degraded in the quality by the communication channel.
- **Signature Recognition:** Signature recognition is used to authenticate user's identity based on the traits of their unique signature. It is behavioral biometrics that changes over a period of time. It is influenced by the physical and emotional conditions of the signatures.
- **Retinal Recognition:** Retinal recognition is for recognizing people by the pattern of blood vessels on the retina. However, it is very intrusive and expensive technique.
- **Iris Recognition:** Iris recognition is a method of identifying people based on unique patterns within the ring-shaped region surrounding the pupil of the eye. The accuracy and rapidity of at present deployed iris-based recognition system is capable and support the feasibility of large scale identification systems based on iris information. Iris recognition systems have a very low False Accept Rate (FAR) and the False Reject Rate (FRR) of system can be high compared to other biometrics traits like fingerprints, voice, retinal and ear (Jain, Flynn, & Ross, 2008).
- **Hand Geometry Recognition:** The palms of human hands include pattern of ridges and numerous valleys like fingerprints. Hand geometry biometrics is the foundation on the geometric shape of the hand. However, this technique has some drawbacks, like not ideal for children as with increasing age their hand geometry tends to change, and not valid for persons suffering from arthritis, since they are not able to put the hand on the scanner properly.
- **Palm Recognition:** Palm recognition is based on ridges, principal lines and wrinkles on the surear of the palm. This technique is very expensive and not appropriate for children as there lines of palm change once they are fully grown up. All the above techniques tend to tell us that none of it is feasible & not much useful due to its various drawbacks. To overcome drawbacks of all these security techniques and to provide proper security for user authentication in cloud computing.

2.3. Biometrics System Technology

Biometric technologies are automated methods of verifying or recognizing the identity of a living person based on a physiological or behavioral characteristic (Al-Aqrabi, Liu, & Xu, 2012) (Vu, Pham, &Truong, 2012). There are two key words in this definition: "automated" and "person". The word "automated" differentiates biometrics from the larger field of groups of people (Jackson, 2010) or to probabilistically link persons to groups, but biometrics is interested only in recognizing people as individuals. All of the measures used contain both physiological and behavioral components, both of which can vary widely or be quite similar across a population of individual's human identification science. A generic biometric system demonstrated as having five modules as follows in Figure 2.

1. **Sensor as Acquisition Module:** In biometric system a suitable biometric reader or scanner is required to capture the raw biometric data of individuals. For example, fingerprint images, an optical fingerprint (minutiae points) sensor can be used to capture the friction, ridge shape and size of individual fingerprint.

2. **Pre-Processing Module:** The related biometrics preprocessing technologies, including: noise removing from capture image, edge sharpening, image restoration, image segmentation, pattern extraction and dis-classification etc. Some preprocessing steps before feature extraction are noise filtering (for example with Gaussian windows (Jain Flynn, & Ross, 2008) and re-sampling. Resampling is carried out in some systems in order to obtain a shape-based representation consisting of equidistant points. Other systems avoid the resampling step as some discriminative speed characteristics are lost in the process.

3. **Feature Extraction Module:** In biometric system basic elements in pattern recognition system, and some introduction of pattern recognition systems on biometrics such as fingerprint, palmprint, hand, ear, iris, and ear, as well as dental, DNA and retina recognition. In quality assessment and feature extraction, it determines the quality and suitability of biometric data acquired by the sensor in assessed. The obtained data is subjected to a signal enhancement algorithm in order to improve its quality. In order to facilitate matching or comparison of the raw digital representation is usually further processed by feature extractor to generate a compact but expressive representation called feature set. For example the position and orientation of minutiae points in a fingerprint image would be computed in feature extraction module.

4. **Matching Process Module:** The features extracted in the previous stage have to be compared against those stored in the database (template database) in order to establish the identity of the input biometric characteristics. In simplest form, matching involves the generation of a match score by comparing the feature sets pertaining to two images. The match score indicates the similarity between two images.

5. **Decision Process Module:** In the decision stage, the match score(s) generated in the matching module are used to make a final decision. In the identification mode of operation, the output is a list of potential matching identities sorted in terms of their match score.

2.4. Biometric System Process

Depending on the application context, biometrics system may operate either in the verification or identification mode.

-   **Verification Process:** In the verification mode, where the subject (people) claims an identity, the input image is compared against that of the claimed identity via their respective feature sets in order to validate the claim. It is used for positive recognition where the main objective is to prevent multiple subjects from using the same identity.

-   **Identification Process:** In the identification mode, where the subject (people/object) does not claim an identity, the input ear image is compared against a set of labeled (it is used to indicate that the identity of the images in the database is known) ear images in a database in order to determine the best match and, therefore, its identity. Identification is a critical component in the negative recognition application where the system establishes whether the person is who she denies to be. The main scope of the negative recognition is to prevent a single person from using the multiple identities.

3. FACE AS BIOMETRIC SYSTEM

Face recognition non–intrusive, invasive, inexpensive and most biometric identifier based methodology and facial attributes are probably the most common biometric feature used by humans to recognize one other. In order that a facial recognition system works well in practice as follows:

1. **Face Detection:** It should automatically detect whether a face is present in the in acquired image.
2. **Face Location:** To locate the face if there is in the used face database.
3. **Recognition of Face:** To recognize the face from a general viewpoint from any posture/profile.

Biometrics is automated methods of recognizing a person based on a physiological or behavioral characteristic. The different features that are measured are face, fingerprints, hand shape, calligraphy, iris, retinal, vein, and voice. Face recognition has a number of strengths to recommend it over other biometric modalities in certain circumstances. Face recognition as a biometric derives a number of advantages from being the primary biometric that humans use to recognize one another. It is well-accepted and easily understood by people, and it is easy for a human operator to arbitrate machine decisions in fact face images are often used as a human-verifiable backup to automated fingerprint recognition systems (see Figure 3).

Face recognition has the advantage ubiquity and of being universal over other major biometrics, in that everyone has a face and everyone readily displays the face (Whereas, for instance, fingerprints are captured with much more difficulty and a significant proportion of the population has fingerprints that cannot be captured with quality sufficient for recognition.) With some configuration and co-ordination of one or more cameras, it is easy to acquire face images without active participation of the subject. Such passive identification might be desirable for customization of user services and consumer devices, whether that be opening a house door as the owner walks up to it, or adjusting mirrors and car seats to the drivers presets when sitting down in their car.

1. **Acquisition Module:** It is the module where the face image under consideration is presented to the system. It can request an image from several different environments: The face image can be an image file that is located on a disk or it can be captured by a frame grabber or can be scanned from paper with the help of a scanner.
2. **Preprocessing Process:** This is done to enhance the images to improve the recognition performance of the system:
    a. **Image Normalization:** It is done to change the acquired image size to a default size say, 128×128 on which the system can operate.
    b. **Histogram Equalization:** For images that are too dark or too light, it modifies the dynamic range and improves the contrast of the image so that facial features become more apparent.
    c. **Median Filtering:** For noisy images especially obtained from a camera or from a frame grabber, median filtering can clean the image without much loss of information.
    d. **Background Removal:** In order to deal primarily with facial information itself, face background can be removed. This is important for face recognition systems where entire information contained in the image is used. It is obvious that, for background removal, the preprocessing module should be capable of determining the face outline.

Figure 3. Outline of typical face recognition

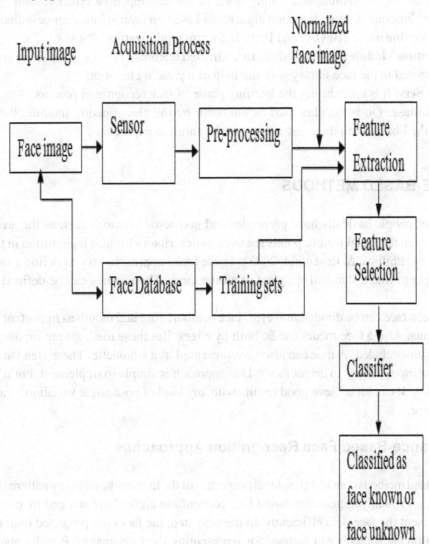

e. **Translational and Rotational Normalizations:** In some cases, it is possible that in the face image of subject the head is somehow shifted or rotated (pose problem). The head plays a major role in the determination of facial features. The pre- processing module determines and normalizes the shifts and rotations in the head position.

f. **Illumination Normalization:** Face images taken under different illuminations can degrade recognition performance especially for face recognition systems based on the principal component analysis in which Entire face information is used for recognition.

3. **Feature Extraction:** This module finds the key features in the face that will be used in classification. It is responsible for composing a feature vector that is well enough to represent the image.

4. **Feature Selection:** The feature selection seeks for the optimal set of d features out of m features obtained from feature extraction module. Several methods have been previously used to perform

feature selection on training and testing data. In the developed face recognition system I have utilized evolutionary feature selection algorithms based on swarm intelligence called the Bacteria Foraging Optimization (BFOA) and Particle Swarm Optimization (PSO).

5. **Classification Module:** In this module, the extracted features of the face image are compared with the ones stored in the face library with the help of a pattern classifier.
6. **Training Sets:** It is used during the learning phase of face recognition process.
7. **Face Database:** On being classified as unknown by the classification module, the face can be added to the library with their feature vectors for future comparisons.

4. FEATURE-BASED METHODS

Facial feature of people basically have properties and geometric relations such as the areas, distances and angles between the facial feature points are used as descriptors for face recognition in this approach (Zhao, Chellappa, Phillips, & Rosenfeld, 2003). These facial approaches try to define a face as a function and attempts to find a standard template of all the faces. The features can be defined independent of each other.

For example, a face can be divided into eyes, face contour, nose and mouth as important discriminant feature key points. Also a face model can be built by edges. But these methods are limited to faces that are frontal and un-occluded. A face can also be represented as a silhouette. These standard patterns are compared to the input images to detect faces. This approach is simple to implement, but it's inadequate for face detection. It cannot achieve good results with any kind of pose angle variation, scale difference and shape change.

4.1. Appearance-Based Face Recognition Approaches

Appearance-based methods consider the global properties of the face image intensity pattern (Kaur, Jakhar, & Singh, 2011). Typically appearance-based face recognition algorithms proceed by computing basis vectors to represent the face data efficiently. In the next step, the faces are projected onto these vectors and the projection coefficients can be used for representing the face images. Popular algorithms such as Principal Component Analysis (PCA), Local Descriminat Analysis (LDA) Independent Component Analysis (ICA), LFA, Correlation Filters, manifolds and tensor faces are based on the appearance of the face. Holistic approaches to face recognition have trouble dealing with pose variations. In general, appearance-based methods rely on techniques from statistical analysis and machine learning to find the relevant characteristics of face images. For feature extraction purpose in this book chapter, appearance-based methods like Principle Component Analysis (PCA), Linear Discriminant Analysis (LDA), Discrete Cosine Transform (DCT) and Discrete Wavelet Transform (DWT) have been used. They are described in detail in the next subsection.

4.1.1. Principal Component Analysis (PCA)

PCA is an orthogonal linear transformation that transforms the data to a new coordinate system such that greatest variance by any projection of the data comes to lie on the first coordinate; the second greatest variance comes up in the second coordinate, and so on. The basic working principal of PCA is illustrated as follows. Eigenfaces also known as Principal Components Analysis (PCA) find the minimum mean squared error linear subspace that maps from the original N dimensional data space into an M-dimensional feature space. By doing this, Eigenfaces (where typically M << N) achieve dimensionality reduction by using the M eigenvectors of the covariance matrix corresponding to the largest eigenvalues. The resulting basis vectors are obtained by finding the optimal basis vectors that maximize the total variance of the projected data (i.e. the set of basis vectors that best describe the data) (Turk & Pentland, 1991).

Usually the mean x is extracted from the data, so that PCA is equivalent to Karhunen-Loeve Transform (KLT). So, let Xnxm be the data matrix where $x_1, ..., x_m$ are the image vectors (vector columns) and n is the number of pixels per image. The KLT basis is obtained by solving the Eigen value problem (Kirby & Sirovich, 1990) as follows:

Let

$$X = \{X_1, X_2, X_3, X_4, \cdots X_m\}$$

be a random vector with observations $X_i \in R^d$

1.   Compute the mean μ

$$\mu = \frac{1}{n} \sum_{i=1}^{m} X_i$$

2.   Compute the Covariance Matrix S

$$S = \frac{1}{n} \sum_{i=1}^{m} (X_i - \mu)(X_i - \mu)^{T_i}$$

3.   Compute the eigenvalues λ_i and the eigenvectors of S

$$Sv_i = \lambda_i v_i, i = 1, 2 .... m$$

Order the eigenvectors descending by their eigenvalues. The k principal components are the eigenvectors corresponding to the k largest eigen values. The k principal components of the observed vector k are then given by:

$$y = w^T(x - \mu)$$

where $W = (v_1, v_2 .... v_k)$

4.   The reconstruction from the PCA basis is given by:

$$X = Wy + \mu$$

$$W = (v_1, v_2 \ldots \ldots v_k)$$

5. The Eigen faces method then performs face recognition by:
   a. Projecting all training samples into PCA subspace.
   b. Projecting the query image into the PCA subspace.
   c. Finding the nearest neighbor between the projected training images and the projected query image.

Still there's one problem left to solve. Imagine we are given 400 images sized 100 X 100 pixel. The pca solves the Covariance matrix, $S=XX^T$ where $size(x)=100\times400$ in our example. It would end up with 10000 X 10000 matrixes, roughly 0.8 GB. Solving this problem is not feasible. Therefore we will need to apply a trick. From your linear algebra lessons you know that an M X N matrix with M > N can only have (N–1) non-zero eigenvalues. Therefore, it's possible to take the eigen-value decomposition of size N X N instead:

$$X^T X v_i = \lambda_i v_i$$

and get the original eigenvectors of $S=XX^T$ with a left multiplication of the data matrix:

$$XX^T (Xv_i) = \lambda(Xv_i)$$

The resulting eigenvectors are orthogonal; to get ortho-normal eigenvectors they need to be normalized to unit length. It can see how the grayscale values are distributed within the specific Eigen faces (see Figure 4).

4.1.2. Linear Discriminant Analysis (LDA)

Linear Discriminant Analysis (LDA) is a supervised learning based classification approach which is widely used to find linear combinations of features while preserving class separability. Unlike PCA, LDA tries to model the differences between classes. Classic LDA is designed to take into account only two classes. Specifically, it requires data points for different classes to be far from each other, while point from the same class is close. Consequently, LDA obtains differenced projection vectors for each class. Suppose we have m samples $x_1, \ldots, x_m$ belonging to c classes; each class has mk elements. It can assume that the mean has been extracted from the samples, a sin PCA. The ratio of between-class scatter to the within-class scatter is calculated which the optimizing criterion in LDA is:

Let X be a random vector with samples drawn from c classes

$$X = \{X_1, X_1, \ldots \ldots X_c\}$$

$$X = \{X_1, X_1, \ldots \ldots X_i\}$$

Figure 4. Eigenfaces of few images of database

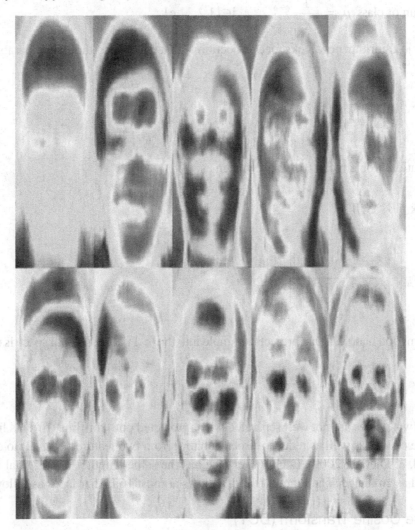

The scatter matrices S_B and S_w are calculated as:

$$S_B = \sum_{i=1}^{c} (\mu_i - \mu)(\mu_{i-\mu})^T$$

$$S_w = \sum_{i=1}^{c} \sum_{x_i \in X_j = 1}^{c} (\mathbf{x}_j - \mu_i)(\mathbf{x}_j - \mu_i)^T$$

where μ is the total mean

$$\mu = \frac{1}{N} \sum_{i=1}^{n} X_i, \text{ where } i \in (1,2,3\ldots n)$$

and μ_i is the mean of class $\mu_i = \dfrac{1}{\left\|X_i\right\|} \sum_{x_{j \in X_i}}^{n} x_j$ $i \in \{1,2,\dots,c\}$

Fisher's classic algorithm now looks for a projection W that maximizes the class reparability criterion:

$$W_{opt} = \arg\max_w \frac{\left\|W^T S_B W\right\|}{\left\|W^T S_w W\right\|}$$

The optimization problem can then be rewritten as:

$$W_{pca} = \arg\max_w \left|W^T S_T W\right|$$

$$W_{fld} = \arg\max_w \frac{\left\|W^T W_{pca}^T S_B W_{pca} W\right\|}{\left\|W^T W_{pca}^T S_w W_{pca} W\right\|}$$

The transformation matrix W that projects a sample into the (c-1)-dimensional space is then given by:

$$W = W_{fld}^T W_{pca}^T$$

In Figure 5, two classes are not well separated when projected onto this line (b) This line succeeded in separating the classes as well as reduces dimensionality from two features (x1, x2) to only a value y (Chelali, Djerad, & Djeradi, 2009). Each Fisher face has the same length as an original image, thus it can be displayed as an image. The Figures 6 and 7 shows at most 16 Fisher faces as follows:

4.1.3. Discrete Cosine Transform (DCT)

Discrete Cosine Transform (DCT) has emerged as a popular transformation technique which is widely used in signal and image processing field due to its strong and well known "energy compaction" property: The most of information of signal tends to be concentrated in a few low-frequency components of the DCT. The exploitation of these DCT techniques for feature extraction in face recognition system has been described by several research groups (Samra et al., 2003), (Yankun & Chongqing, 2004), (Matos, Batista, & Poel, 2008), (Poel, Van, & Zhu, 2006), (Pan & Bolouri, 1999), (Hafed & Levine, 2001). DCT transforms a sequence of data points in terms of a sum of cosine functions oscillating at different frequencies based on energy compaction properties. DCT was found to be an effective method that yields high recognition rates with low computational complexity. DCT exploits inter-pixel redundancies to render excellent de-correlation for most natural images. After de-correlation each transform coefficient can be encoded independently without losing compression efficiency. The DCT helps separate the image into parts (or spectral sub-bands) of differing importance (with respect to the image's visual quality). Therefore, it can be used to transform images, compacting and allow an effective dimensionality reduction. They have been widely used for data compression. The DCT is based on the Fourier Discrete Trans-

Figure 5. Projection of two classes onto line

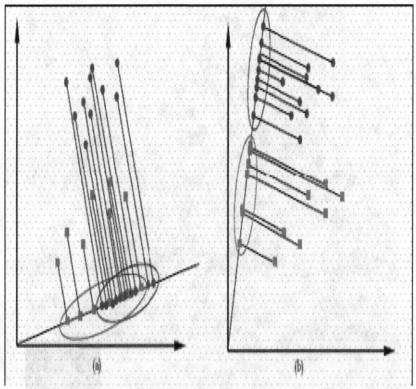

form (FDT), however, using only real numbers. When a DCT is performed over an image, the energy is compacted in the upper-left corner. Suppose an M × N image, where each image corresponds to a 2-D matrix, DCT coefficients are calculated as follows (Schwerin & Paliwal, 2008):

Let f(x, y) is M × N (2 D) image given as input. DCT coefficient of 2-D matrix of given input image is calculated. 2-D matrix can be truncated can be truncated retaining the upper-left area, which has the most information reducing the dimensionality of the problem. The output of given image is shown in Figure 8.

$$f(u,v) = \frac{1}{\sqrt{MN}} \alpha(u) \times \alpha(v) \sum_{x=0}^{M-1} \sum_{y=0}^{N-1}) \times F(x,y)$$

where $F(x,y) = f(x,y) \times \cos(\frac{(2x+1)\mu\Pi}{2M}) \times \cos(\frac{(2y+1)\mu\Pi}{2N})$ and u=1,2,..............M and v =1,......................N.

α(w) = 1 if w=0

$\sqrt{2}$ Otherwise

Figure 6. Few sample images of Fisherfaces of face database

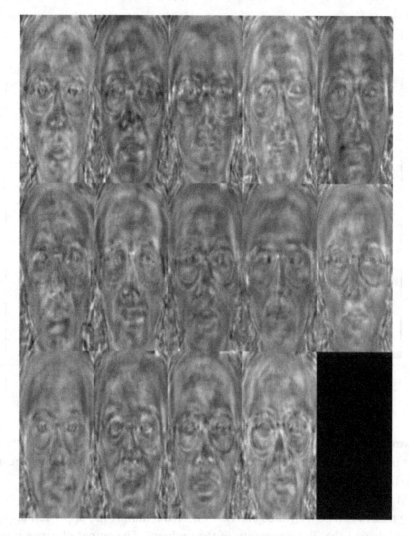

5. FEATURE SELECTION (FS)

Feature selection (FS) is a global optimization problem in machine learning which reduces the number of features and removes irrelevant noisy, redundant data from given database. Although feature selection is primarily performed to select relevant and informative features it can have other motivations including:

- General data reduction from high dimension to lower dimension, to limit storage requirements and increase algorithm speed.
- Feature set reduction, to save resources in the next round of data collection or during utilization.
- Performance improvement, to gain in predictive accuracy.
- Data understanding, to gain knowledge about the process that generated the data or simply visualize the data

Figure 7. Matching of faces based on Fisherfaces from Yale face database

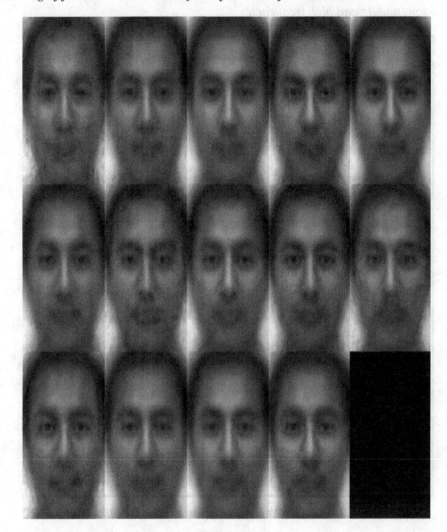

In feature extraction phase of proposed face recognition system, all the feature approaches exploited the top N principal components or most discriminative feature values or components of face database (or transform coefficients).These methods are used directly for dimension reduction into lower order. However, there may be some useful information in lower order principal components leading to a significant contribution in improving the recognition rate. This is known as curse of dimensionality.

Feature selection thus becomes an important step affecting the performance of a pattern recognition system. In this book chapter, search methods based on swarm intelligence algorithms are developed to select the appropriate principal components or transform coefficients from the set of extracted feature vectors. Feature selection approaches are Bacterial Foraging Optimization (BFO) and Particle Swarm Optimization (PSO) which is used to select more discriminative feature values from is given dataset. There are given as follows in section 5.1.

Figure 8. (a) A typical face image (b) its DCT transformed image and (c) typical division of the DCT coefficients into low, middle and high frequencies

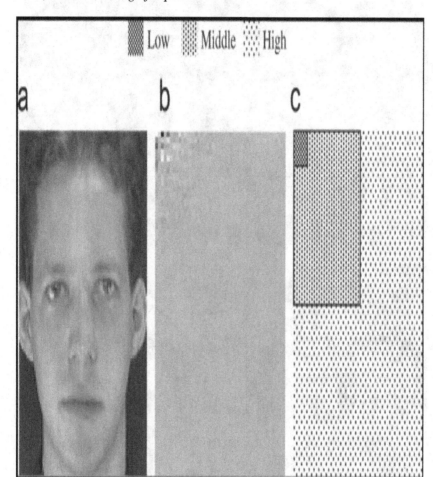

5.1. Bacterial Foraging Optimization(BFO)

BFO is based on foraging strategy of bacteria Escherichia coli. After many generations, bacteria with poor foraging strategies are eliminated while; the individuals with good foraging strategy survive signifying survival of the fittest. The whole process can be divided into three sections, namely chemotaxis, reproduction and elimination and dispersal (Passino, 2002).

• **Chemotaxis:** Chemotaxis is the process in which bacteria direct their movements according to certain chemical s in their environment. This is important for bacteria to findfood by climbing up nutrient hills and at the same time avoids noxious substances. The sensors they use are receptor proteins which are very sensitive and possess high gain. That is a small change in the concentration of nutrients can cause a significant change in behavior (Liu & Passino, 2002). Suppose that we want to find the minimum of J (θ), where $\theta \in R^D$ is the position of a bacterium in D-dimension al space and the cost function J (θ) is an attractant- repellant profile (where nutrients and noxious substances are located). Then J (h) ≤ 0 represents a nutrient rich environment J(θ) =0 represents neutral medium and J(h)>0 represents noxious substances.

- $\circ$ Let $\theta^i \in h(i,j,l)$ represent i^{th} bacterium at j^{th} chemotactic, k^{th} reproductive and l^{th} elimination-dispersal step.
- $\circ$ The position of the bacterium at the $(j+1)^{th}$ chemotactic step is calculated in terms of the position in the previous chemotactic step and the step size C (i) (termedas run length unit) applied in a random direction $\theta(i): \theta^i(j+1,k,l) = \theta^i(j,k,l) + C(i) \times \phi(i)$.
- $\circ$ Where $\phi(i)$ is the unit random direction to discrete tumble and it is given by $\phi(i) = \dfrac{\Delta(i)}{\sqrt{\Delta^T(i)\Delta(i)}}$ where $\Delta(i) \in R^D$ is a randomly generate d vector with elements within the interval [-1, +1].
- $\circ$ The cost of each position is determined by the following equation:

$$J(i,j,k,l) = J(i,j,k,l) + J_{cc}(\theta, \theta^i(j,k,l)) \qquad (1)$$

It can be noticed that equation (1) the cost of a determined position J(i, j, k, l) is also affected by the attractive and repulsive forces existing among the bacteria of the population given by Jcc. If the cost at the location of the ith bacterium at $(j + 1^{th})$ chemotactic step denoted by J(i, j + 1, k, l) is better (lower) than at the position $\theta^i(j,k,l)$ at the jth step, then the bacterium will take another chemotactic step of size C(i) in this same direction, up to a maximum number of permissible steps called Ns.

- **Swarming:** Swarming is a general type of motility that is promoted by flagella and allows bacteria to move rapidly over and between surfaces and through viscous environments. Under certain conditions, cells of chemota ctic strains of E. coli excrete an attractant, aggregate in response to gradients of that attractant and form patterns of varying cell density. Central to this self-organization into swarm rings is chemotaxis. The cell-to-cell signaling in E. coli swarm may be represented by the following equation (2):

$$j_{cc}(\theta, \theta^i(j,k,l)) = \sum_{i=1}^{s}\left[-d_{attrac\tan t}\exp\left(-w_{attrac\tan t}\sum_{m=1}^{D}\theta_m - \theta^i_m\right)^2\right]$$
$$+\sum_{i=1}^{s}\left[-h_{repellant}\exp\left(-w_{repellant}\sum_{m=1}^{D}\theta_m - \theta^i_m\right)^2\right] \qquad (2)$$

where h = $[h_1, h_2, \ldots, h_D]^T$ is a point in the D-dimensional search space, Jcc(h,h_i (j,k, l)) is the objective function value that is to be added to the actual objective function and dattractant, wattractant, hrepellant, wrepellant are the coefficients which determine the depth and width of the attractant and the height and width of the repellant. These four parameters are to be chosen judiciously for a given problem, him is the mth dimension of the position of the ith bacterium hi in the population of the S bacteria.

- **Reproduction:** The least healthy bacteria eventually die while each of the healthier bacteria (those yielding lower value of the objective function) asexually split into two bacteria, which are then placed in the same location. This keeps the swarm size constant.

- **Elimination and Dispersal:** Gradual or sudden changes in the local environment where a bacterium population lives may occur due to various reasons e.g. a significant local rise of temperature may kill a group of bacteria that are currently in a region with a high concentration of nutrient gradients. Events can take place in such a fashion that all the bacteria in a region are killed or a group is dispersed into a new location. To simulate this phenomenon in BFOA some bacteria are liquidated at random with a very small probability while the new replacements are randomly initialized over the search space.

In Das, Biswas Dasgupta, & Abraham, (2009), the authors discussed some variations on the original BFOA algorithm and hybridizations of BFOA with other optimization techniques. They also provided an account of most of the significant applications of BFOA. However, experimentation with complex optimization problems reveal that the original BFOA algorithm possesses a poor converge nice behavior compared to other nature-inspired algorithms, like GAs and PSO and its performance also heavily decreases with the growth of the search space dimensionality.

Listing 1. Pseudo code of BFO Algorithm

```
1.          Initialize parameters D, S, Nc, Nₛ, Nᵣₑ, Nₑ𝒹, Pₑ𝒹, C(i)(i=1,. . ., S)
and θⁱ where i∈(i,2,3…S).
2.          while terminating condition is not reached do
3.          /* Elimination dispersal loop *\
4.          for i=1----Nᵣₑ𝒹    do
5.          /* reproduction loop *\
6.          for k=1……Nre Do
7.          /* Chemotaxis loop *\
8.          for j=1……Nc do
9.          for each bacterium i=1…….S do
10.         compute fitness function
```

11.
$$J(i,j,k,l) = J(i,j,k,l) + \mathrm{J}_{cc}(\theta,\theta^i(j,k,l))$$

(3)

```
12.         Jₗₐₛₜ=J (I, j, k, l)
13.         Tumble= generate a random vector Δ(i)∈Rᴰ
14.         move: Compute the position of the bacterium
```
$\theta^i(\mathrm{j}+1,\mathrm{k},\mathrm{l}) = \theta^i(\mathrm{j},\mathrm{k},\mathrm{l}) + \mathrm{C}(\mathrm{i}) \times \phi(\mathrm{i})$ at j+1th characteristics step.
```
15.         compute fitness function
```
$$J(i,j,k,l) = J(i,j,k,l) + \mathrm{J}_{cc}(\theta,\theta^i(j,k,l)) \tag{4}$$
```
16.         swim: m=0
17.         while M< Nₛ       do
18.         M=M+1
19.         if j(I, j+1, k, l) <Jₗₐₛₜ
20.         then
21.         Jₗₐₛₜ =J(I, j+1, k, l)
```

continued on following page

Listing 1. Continued

22.   move: Compute the position of bacterium $\theta^i(j+1,k,l)$ at J+1th chemo-tactic step using following step

23. $\theta^i(j+1,k,l) = \theta^i(j,k,l) + C(i) \times \phi(i)$

24.   Compute fitness function

25. $J(i,j,k,l) = J(i,j,k,l) + J_{cc}(\theta, \theta^i(j,k,l))$ (5)

26.   else

27.   M=Ns

28.   end

29.   end

30.   end

31.   end

32.   /* Re-production Process */

33.   for

34.   i=1,2……S do

35. $j_{Health^{(i)}} = \sum_{j=1}^{N_C+1} J(i,j,k,l)$

36.   end

37.   sort bacterium in order to ascending $J_{Health^{(i)}}$ (highest cost means low health)

38.   end

39.   (The least healthy bacterium dies and the other heathier bacteria splt each into two bacteria which are placed in same location)

40.   end

41.   elimination-dispersal

42.   for i=1…..Sdo

43.   eliminate and disperse the ith bacterium with probability Ped

44.   end

45.   end

5.2. Particle Swarm Optimization (PSO)

Particle Swarm Optimization (PSO) was initially proposed by James Kennedy and Russell Eberhart approach in 1995 which maintains a group of candidate solutions known as particles (Kennedy & Eberhart, 2001). It is nature inspired algorithms and uses the metaphor of the flocking behavior of birds (Abbass, 2001), (Abraham, Grosan, & Ramos, 2006) fish schooling, ant colony and bee hives to solve optimization problems. The ability of PSO a global stochastic optimization technique is to solve many complex search problems efficiently and accurately has made it an interesting research area. Many autonomous particles are stochastically generated in the problem search space in particle swarm intelligence and each particle presents a candidate solution to a problem and is demonstrated by a velocity, location in the search space of problem it has a memory to preserve the its previous best position which helps it in remembering and provide best result to the problem.

5.2.1. Neighborhood Selection Strategies in PSO

In PSO, swarm of N particles autonomous particles or entities is flying around in a hyper-dimensional (D-dimensional) search space. In addition, every swarm particle has numerous sort of topology (set or rules) which is useful to describe the interconnections among the particles. With each particle being attracted towards the best solution found by the particles neighborhood and the best solution found by the particle. The set of particles to which a particle j is topologically connected j neighborhood particle.

In PSO, two basic topologies for neighbor selection have been used to identify some other particle to influence the individual. These topologies are: (1) global best (gbest) and (2) local best (lbest). In global best (gbest), the best neighbor in the entire initialized total population influence the target particle. On the other hand, local best (lbest) considers small number of swarm population and particles exchange information locally according to partial knowledge of the solution in space. In basic PSO the initialization phase, the positions and velocities of all individuals are randomly initialized. The position of each particle refers to a solution to a problem. Then the position moving process of a particle in the solution space related to a solution search process. The state of the position I is demonstrated by its current position, where D stands for the number of variable encountered in the optimization problem. The particle position i is updated during the evolutionary process.

The state of the position I is demonstrated by its current position $X_i = \left[x_{i1}, x_{i2}, \cdots x_{iD} \right]$ where D stands for the number of variable encountered in the optimization problem. The particle position i is updated during the evolutionary process.

$$v_{id}(t+1) = w \times v_{id}(t) + c_1 \times r_{id}(t) \times \left[p_{Bestid} - x_{id} \right] + c2 \times r2d(t) \times \left[g_{bestid} - x_{id} \right] \qquad (6)$$

$$x_{id}(t+1) = x_{id}(t) + v_{id}(t+1) \qquad (7)$$

where x_{id} represents the dth dimension of the next current position of the particle i and v_{id} demonstrates the dth variable of the next and current velocity of the particle. p_{Bestid} shows the dth variable of the personal historical best position founded by particle I up to now. g_{bestid} is variable of global best position founded by the overall particle so far c_1 and c_2 are the acceleration parameters which are commonly 2.0. r_{1d} and r_{2d} are two random numbers drawn for uniform distribution are (0, 1) and w is inertia weight which is used to set up the balance between the ability of global and local search feature of the particle swarm optimization. In PSO, the particle behavior is demonstrated by the velocity and position update according to equation (6) and (7) and the weight component of (1) models the tendency of the particle to continue in the same direction as before and second component of (1) is referred to as the particle "memory" and self–knowledge or remembrance. It represents the self learning behavior of the particle. The third component in (1) is referred to as co-operation "social knowledge", "group knowledge" which reflects the social learning behavior of the particle. Equation (7) indicates the position of the particle in the solution space will be changed in the local of its current position and next velocity. After received each update, we check out the position and velocity of each particle to guarantee them being within predefine certain range of value. In order to keep the particles from flying out of the problem space, (Kennedy & Eberhart, 1948) defined a clamping scheme to limit the velocity of each particle v_{id} therefore, that each component of is kept within the range [-Vmax, +Vmax].

The parameter choice for Vmax required some care since it appeared to influence the balance between exploration and exploitation characteristics of metaheuristic. As has been noted in (Angeline, 1998), the Vmax particle swarm succeeds at finding optimal regions of the search space, but has no feature that enables it to converge on optima. If the particle position and velocity are exceeded the range, they are modified as follow:

$$v_{id} = \min(v_d^{\max}, \max(v_d^{\min}, v_{id})$$

$$x_{id} = p_{Best} \tag{8}$$

where $v_d^{\max}, v_d^{\min}$ maximum and minimum are values of the dth variable of the velocity respectively and p_{Best} is the mean of the dth variable of the personal historical best position of all particles calculated by equation (8).

An Inertia weight w is a proportional agent that is related with the speed of last time and the formula for the change of the speed is given in equation (9). When w is bigger, bigger the PSO search ability

Listing 2. Pseudo code of Particle Swarm Optimization (PSO)

```
1.          Initialize the population of particle (N) with random position and
velocity in given (D- dimension) search space.
2.          while terminating condition is not reached
3.          do
4.              for each particle i=1 to N Do
5.              adapt velocity of the particle of the particle using
```

$$6. \qquad v_{id}(t+1) = w \times v_{id}(t) + c_1 \times r_{id}(t) \times \left[p_{Bestid} - x_{id}\right] + c_2 \times r2_d(t) \times \left[g_{bestid} - x_{id}\right]$$

(9)

```
7.              update the position of the particle using
```

$$8. \qquad x_{id}(t+1) = x_{id}(t) + v_{id}(t+1)$$

```
9.              evaluate the fitness f(x_i)
```

$$10. \qquad f(x_i) < f(p_i)$$

```
11.                 p ← x_i
12.             end
```

$$13. \qquad \text{If } f(x_i) < f(p_g) \text{ then}$$

```
14.                 p
                     g ← x_i
15.             end
16.         for end
```

for the whole while w is smaller, search ability is smaller and when ω =1, so at the later period of the several generations of PSO, there is a lack of the searching ability for the partial. Experimental results demonstrate that particle swarm optimization has the biggest speed of convergence when $w \in [0.8, 1.2]$. While experimenting, ω is confined from 0.9 to 0.4 according to the linear decrease, which makes PSO search for the bigger space at the beginning and locate the position quickly where there is the most optimist solution.

Rather than applying inertia to the velocity memory, Clerc and Kennedy applied a constriction factor χ. The velocity update scheme proposed by Clerc and it can be expressed for the dth dimension of ith particle as by follows:

$$v_{id}(t+1) = \chi(v_{id}(t) + c_1(p_{id}(t) - x_{id}(t) + c_2 p_2(p_{gd}(t) - x_{id}(t))))$$

$$\chi = \frac{2}{\varphi - 2 + \sqrt{\varphi^2 - 4\phi}}$$

where $\varphi = \varphi_1 + \varphi_2 > 4$, this is known as hybrid cooperative PSO approach which improves the convergence rate of standard PSO.

In Figure 9, initially, the particles are scattered randomly in the search space. As they search for the optimum value, the particles balance the objectives of following the value gradient and random exploration. Over time they begin to congregate in the general area of the optimum value. Finally, the particles converge to the optimum value of a given hard or complex problem.

5.2.2. Major PSO Variants

Standard PSO exhibits some deficiencies including suffering from being premature and inefficient in solving complex multimodal optimization problem. On method to strengthen, the capacity of PSO is to dynamically adapt its parameters when the particle evaluating process. In addition a fuzzy adaptive mechanism was used to the value of w. (Kinnedy & Eberhart, 2001) recommendation that the proper value for acceleration parameter w is set to linearly decease over linearly.

- **Advantages and Disadvantages of PSO:** PSO is a population and intelligence based metaheuristics algorithm. PSO s have no overlapping and mutation calculation and search can be carried out by speed of the particle, deriving the development of the several generations, only the most PSO can transmit information on to the other particle and speed of the searching is very fast. Position and velocity of particle calculation in PSO is very simple compared with the other swarm intelligence method.

It occupies the biggest optimization ability and it can be completed easily. One of the drawbacks of the "*standard PSO*" is premature convergence and trapping in local optima of the problem. A great effort has been deployed to provide PSO convergence results through the stability analysis of the trajectories (Clerc & Kennedy, 2002), (Ozcan & Mohan, 1999) (Vandenbergh & Engelbrecht, 2006).

Figure 9. Example of a particle swarm optimization swarms progression in two-dimensions

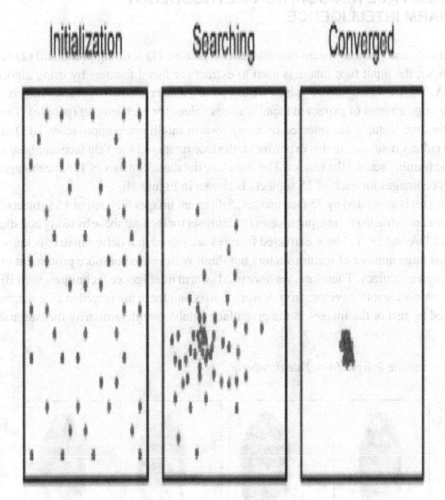

These studies were aimed at understanding theoretically how PSO algorithm works and why under certain conditions it might fail to find a good solution. Considerable research has been also conducted into further refinement of the original formulation of PSO in both continuous and discrete problem spaces and areas such as dynamic environment, parallel implementation and multi-objective Optimization (Reyes & Coello, 2006). Modified versions of PSO based on diversity, mutation, crossover and efficient initialization using different distribution. A large number of hybrid variants have been proposed, such as (Valdez, Melin, & Castillo, 2011a, 2011b). In 2008, Poli categorized a large number of publications dealing with PSO applications stored in the IEEE Xplore database. Therefore many papers related with the applications of PSO have been presented in the literature and several survey papers regarding these studies can be found in(Kennedy & Eberhart, 2001), (Clerc, 2006) (Poli, Kennedy,& Blackwell, 2007), (Banks, Vincent, & Anyakoha, 2008) (Thangaraj, Pant, Abraham, & Bouvry, 2011), (Castillo & Melin, 2012).

6. PROPOSED FACE RECOGNITION METHODOLOGY USING SWARM INTELLIGENCE

The proposed face recognition system consists of two phases: (1) training phase and (2) testing phase. In training phase, the input face image is used to extract the facial features by using algorithms DCT, PCA and LDA. The extracted feature values are stored in a matrix, known as feature matrix. This matrix represents the huge amount of extracted facial features values for each subject (people). The unique and most discriminative features are selected by using swarm intelligence approaches BFO and PSO and stored in face gallery database. In this experiment, the face images of the Yale face database are exploited to generate the training set and the test set. The Yale face database consists of 165 face images as subject, 11 different face images for each of 15 subjects is shown in Figure 10.

The training set is generated by 75 face images, 5 different images for each of 15 subjects. In proposed system, features are extracted from input images (training set) of face database by using holistic approaches such as PCA, LDA and DCT. These extracted features are stored in a define matrix is known as feature matrix. It holds huge number of feature vectors but these vectors are not more prominent to identifying the face with better accuracy. Therefore, we have used swarm intelligence techniques such BFO and PSO to select discriminant features vectors from feature matrix and these are stored in face database. The test set is generated by rest of the images in the given face database with similarity measurement of match

Figure 10. Few sample images from Yale database

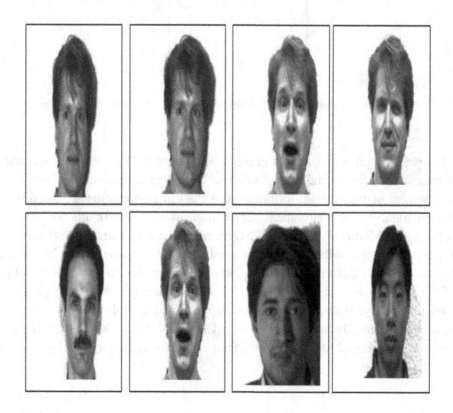

score of selected prominent features of test set. The schematic description of proposed face recognition system by swarm intelligence (SI) is shown in Figure 11. In this experiment, two different methods are followed and a comparison of the two is made. They are described in the subsection below:

6.1. BFO-Based Feature Selection Algorithm

In proposed face recognition system, PCA is used on the face images of database to obtain the optimal bases before LDA. Then generate the eigenvectors as the feature vector set (which will be input to the BFO) through LDA. Feature selection applies the BFO algorithm on the feature vector sets and pick up the position of bacteria B with max (Jhealth) value. This position represents the best feature subset of the features defined in feature extraction step.

Figure 11. Proposed face recognition using swarm intelligence approach

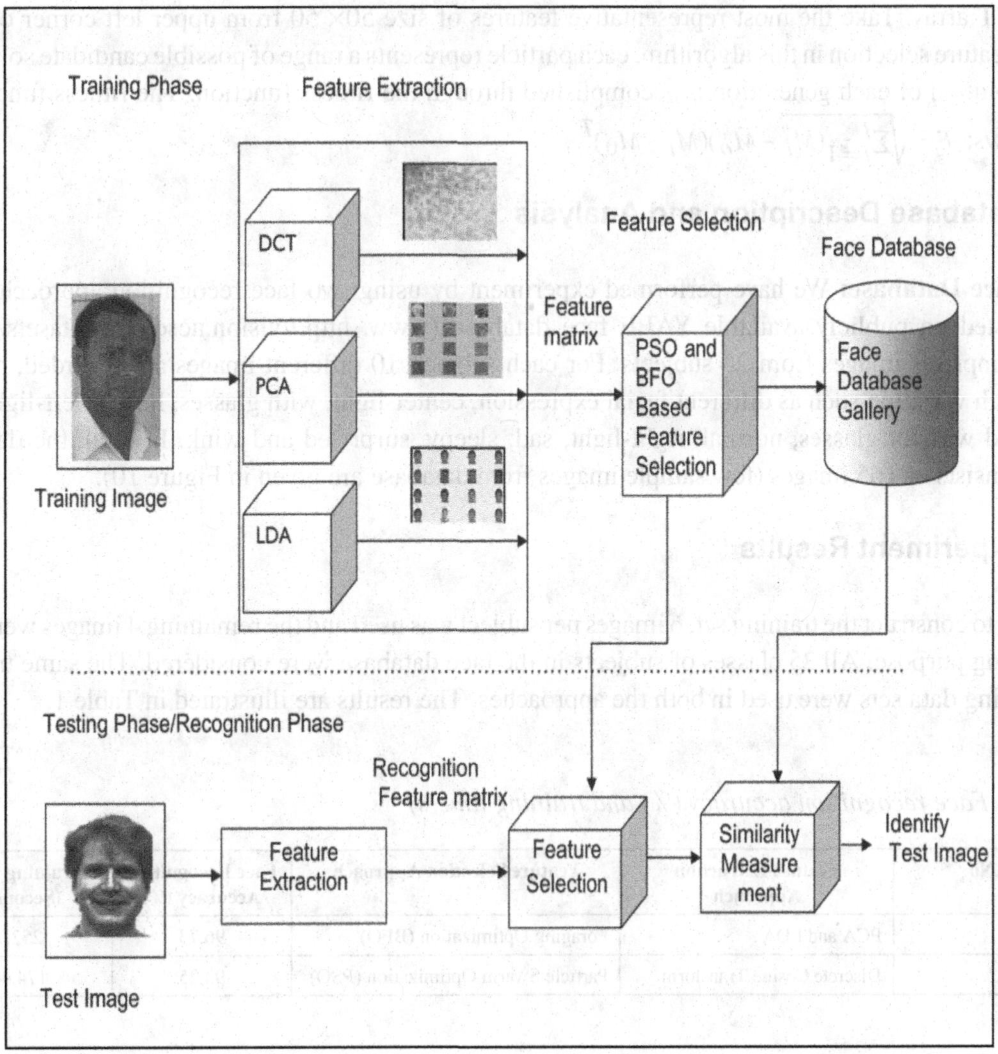

Classification: Calculate the difference between the feature subset (obtained through feature selection) of each image of facial gallery and the test image with the help of Euclidean Distance defined below. The index of the image which has the smallest distance with the image under test is considered to be the required index. For an N-dimensional space, the Euclidean distance between two any points, p_i and q_i is given by:

$$D = \sum_{i=1}^{n} sqrt(p_i - q_i)^2$$

where p_i and q_i are the co-ordinate values of p and q in given n space dimension.

6.2. PSO-Based Feature Selection Algorithm

The feature extraction obtained by applying Discrete Cosine Transformation (DCT) to image and stored into DCT array. Take the most representative features of size 50× 50 from upper left corner of DCT array. Feature selection in this algorithm, each particle represents a range of possible candidate solutions. The evolution of each generation is accomplished through the fitness function. The fitness function is as follows: $F = \sqrt{\sum_{i=1}^{l} (M_i - M_O)(M_i - M_0)^T}$

6.3. Database Description and Analysis

- **Face Database:** We have performed experiment by using two face recognition approaches and tested on publicly available YALE face database (www. http://vision.ucsd.edu/datasetsAll). It comprises images from 25 subjects. For each subject, 10 different images are recorded, one for each variation such as different facial expression, center-light, with glasses, happy, left-light with and without glasses, normal, right-light, sad, sleepy, surprised and wink. In total, the database consists of 165 images (few sample images from database are given in Figure 10).

6.4. Experiment Results

In order to construct the training set, 6 images per subject was used and the remaining 4 images were used for testing purpose. All 25 classes of subjects in the face database were considered. The same training and testing data sets were used in both the approaches. The results are illustrated in Table 1.

Table 1. Face recognition accuracy (%) and training time(s)

S.No	Feature Extraction Approach	Feature Selection Approach	Face Recognition Accuracy (%)	Training Time (Seconds)
1.	PCA and LDA	Foraging Optimization (BFO)	96.73	252.7
2.	Discrete Cosine Transform	Particle Swarm Optimization (PSO)	93.25	174.46

6.5. Comparative Analysis

On comparing BFO-based approach with PSO-based approach for feature selection approach, it is illustrated that the average face recognition rate of BFO is better than that of PSO-based feature selection method. Also, on analysis it is demonstrated that number features required by BFO are less than that required for recognition using PSO (Table 1). However, in terms of computational time for training and testing process, PSO-based selection algorithm takes less training time than the BFO-based selection algorithm. Hence, BFO is computationally expensive than PSO. Therefore, the effectiveness of BFO in finding the optimal feature subset compared to PSO compensates its computational inefficiency.

7. CONCLUSION AND FUTURE DIRECTION

In this book chapter, a novel BFO-based feature selection algorithm for face recognition (FR) is proposed and the algorithm is applied to feature vectors extracted by using Discrete Cosine Transform (DCT). The appearance based algorithm such as PCA and LDA yields face recognition accuracy of 96.73% which is better than Discrete Cosine Transform (DCT) using Particle Swarm Optimization (PSO) as feature selection method. The algorithm is exploited to search the feature space for the optimal feature subset. Evolution is driven by a fitness function defined in terms of class separation. The classifier performance and the length of selected feature vector were considered for performance evaluation using the Yale face database. Experimental results show the superiority of the BFO-based feature selection algorithm in generating excellent recognition accuracy with the minimal set of selected features. It founds out that the underlying bacterial foraging principle and the PSO swarm optimization can be integrated into evolutionary computational algorithms to provide a better search strategy for finding optimal feature vectors for face recognition. This proposed system, in comparison to other object recognition systems so far is more advantageous and result-oriented because it cannot work on presumptions, it is unique and provides fast and contactless authentication. In future, swarm intelligence algorithms can provide to improve the face recognition accuracy by applying the different feature extraction techniques. It can improve the user identification process using face recognition system vastly. Finally, it demonstrated that the two swarm optimization methods namely bacterial foraging optimization (BFO) and particle swarm optimization (PSO) may be useful for the design and development of robust face recognition system by selecting the prominent feature from given database.

REFERENCES

Abbass, H. A. (2001). MBO: Marriage in honey bees optimization-A haplometrosis polygynous swarming approach. In *Proceedings of IEEE Congress on Evolutionary Computation* (pp. 207-214). IEEE. doi:10.1109/CEC.2001.934391

Aickelin, U., Bentley, P., Cayzer, S., Kim, J., & McLeod, J. (2003). Danger theory: The link between AIS and IDS? In *Artificial immune systems* (pp. 147–155). Springer Berlin Heidelberg. doi:10.1007/978-3-540-45192-1_15

Angeline, P. J. (1998). Evolutionary optimization versus particle swarm optimization: Philosophy and performance differences. In *Evolutionary programming VII* (pp. 601–610). Springer Berlin Heidelberg. doi:10.1007/BFb0040811

Blackwell, T. (2007). Particle swarm optimization in dynamic environments. In *Evolutionary computation in dynamic and uncertain environments* (pp. 29–49). Springer Berlin Heidelberg. doi:10.1007/978-3-540-49774-5_2

Banks, A., Vincent, J., & Anyakoha, C. (2007). A review of particle swarm optimization. Part I: Background and development. *Natural Computing*, *6*(4), 467–484. doi:10.1007/s11047-007-9049-5

Banks, A., Vincent, J., & Anyakoha, C. (2008). A review of particle swarm optimization. Part II: Hybridisation, combinatorial, multicriteria and constrained optimization, and indicative applications. *Natural Computing*, *7*(1), 109–124. doi:10.1007/s11047-007-9050-z

Boussaïd, I., Lepagnot, J., & Siarry, P. (2013). A survey on optimization metaheuristics. *Information Sciences*, *237*, 82–117. doi:10.1016/j.ins.2013.02.041

Beielstein, T., Parsopoulos, K. E., & Vrahatis, M. N. (2002). Tuning PSO parameters through sensitivity analysis. Technical Report, Reihe Computational Intelligence CI124/02. Department of Computer Science, University of Dortmund Universität Dortmund.

Boussaïd, I., Lepagnot, J., & Siarry, P. (2013). A survey on optimization metaheuristics. *Information Sciences*, *237*, 82–117. doi:10.1016/j.ins.2013.02.041

Castillo, O., & Melin, P. (2012). Optimization of type-2 fuzzy systems based on bio-inspired methods: A concise review. *Information Sciences Elsevier*, *205*, 1–19. doi:10.1016/j.ins.2012.04.003

Clerc, M., & Kennedy, J. (2002). The particle swarm-explosion, stability, and convergence in a multidimensional complex space. *IEEE Transactions on Evolutionary Computation*, *6*(1), 58–73. doi:10.1109/4235.985692

Clerc, M. (2006). *Particle swarm optimization*. London, UK: ISTE. doi:10.1002/9780470612163

El Dor, A., Clerc, M., & Siarry, P. (2012). Hybridization of differential evolution and particle swarm optimization in a new algorithm: DEPSO-2S. In *Swarm and evolutionary computation* (pp. 57–65). Springer Berlin Heidelberg. doi:10.1007/978-3-642-29353-5_7

Dorigo, M., Maniezzo, V., & Colorni, A. (1996). Ant system: Optimization by a colony of cooperating agents. *IEEE Transactions on Systems, Man, and Cybernetics. Part B, Cybernetics*, *26*(1), 29–41. doi:10.1109/3477.484436 PMID:18263004

Eberhart, R. C., & Shi, Y. (2000). Comparing inertia weights and constriction factors in particle swarm optimization. In *Proceedings of the 2000 Congress on Evolutionary Computation* (pp. 84-88). Academic Press. doi:10.1109/CEC.2000.870279

Er, M. J., Chen, W., & Wu, S. (2005). High-speed face recognition based on discrete cosine transform and RBF neural networks. *IEEE Transactions on Neural Networks*, *16*(3), 679–691. doi:10.1109/TNN.2005.844909 PMID:15940995

Grosan, C., Abraham, A., & Chis, M. (2006). *Swarm intelligence in data mining*. Springer Berlin Heidelberg. doi:10.1007/978-3-540-34956-3_1

Heppner, F., & Grenander, U. (1990). *A stochastic nonlinear model for coordinated bird flocks. American Association for the Advancement of Science*. AAAS.

Hatamlou, A. (2013). Black hole: A new heuristic optimization approach for data clustering. *Information Sciences, 222*, 175–184. doi:10.1016/j.ins.2012.08.023

Hafed, Z. M., & Levine, M. D. (2001). Face recognition using discrete cosine transform. *International Journal of Computer Vision, 43*(3), 167–188. doi:10.1023/A:1011183429707

Idoumghar, L., Melkemi, M., Schott, R., & Aouad, M. I. (2011). Hybrid PSO-SA type algorithms for multimodal function optimization and reducing energy consumption in embedded systems. *Applied Computational Intelligence and Soft Computing, 3*.

Jain, A. K., Pankanti, S., Prabhakar, S., Hong, L., & Ross, A. (2004, August). Biometrics: A grand challenge. In *Proceedings of the 17th IEEE International Conference on Pattern Recognition* (vol. 2, pp. 935-942). IEEE.

Jain, A. K., Flynn, P., & Ross, A. A. (2008). Handbook of biometrics. Springer Publication.

Jantz, R. L. (1987). Anthropological dermatoglyphic research. *Annual Review of Anthropology, 16*(1), 161–177. doi:10.1146/annurev.an.16.100187.001113

Jakhar, R., Kaur, N., & Singh, R. (2011). Face recognition using bacteria foraging optimization-based selected features. *International Journal of Advanced Computer Science and Applications, 1*(3). doi:10.14569/SpecialIssue.2011.010317

Zhao, W., Chellappa, R., Phillips, P. J., & Rosenfeld, A. (2003). Face recognition: A literature survey. *ACM Computing Surveys, 35*(4), 399–458. doi:10.1145/954339.954342

Kennedy, J., Kennedy, J. F., & Eberhart, R. C. (2001). *Swarm intelligence*. Morgan Kaufmann.

Kennedy, J. (2010). Particle swarm optimization. In Encyclopedia of machine learning (pp. 760-766). Springer US.

Kennedy, J., & Eberhart, R. (1997). Discrete binary version of the particle swarm algorithm. In *Proceedings of the IEEE International Conference on Systems, Man and Cybernetics* (vol. 5, pp. 4104–4108). IEEE. doi:10.1109/ICSMC.1997.637339

Moon, Y. S. (2004). Recent advances in ear biometrics. In *Proceedings of the 6th IEEE International Conference on Automatic Ear and Gesture Recognition* (pp. 164–169). IEEE.

Kirkpatrick, S. (1984). Optimization by simulated annealing: Quantitative studies. *Journal of Statistical Physics, 34*(5-6), 975–986. doi:10.1007/BF01009452

Kirby, M., & Sirovich, L. (1990). Application of the Karhunen-Loeve procedure for the characterization of human faces. *IEEE Transactions on Pattern Analysis and Machine Intelligence, 12*(1), 103–108. doi:10.1109/34.41390

Kennedy, J. (2010). Particle swarm optimization. In Encyclopedia of machine learning (pp. 760-766). Springer US.

Kennedy, J., & Eberhart, R. (1995). Particle swarm optimization. In *Proceedings of IEEE International Conference on Neural Networks* (vol. 4, pp. 1942–1948). IEEE. doi:10.1109/ICNN.1995.488968

Matos, F. M., Batista, L. V., & Poel, J. (2008). Face recognition using OCT coefficients selection. In *Proceedings of the ACM Symposium on Applied Computing* (pp. 1753-1757). ACM.

Ozcan, E., & Mohan, C. K. (1999). Particle swarm optimization: surfing the waves. In *Proceedings of the 1999 IEEE Congress on Evolutionary Computation (CEC 99)*. IEEE. doi:10.1109/CEC.1999.785510

Passino, K. M. (2002). Biomimicry of bacterial foraging for distributed optimization and control. *IEEE Control Systems Magazine, 22*(3), 52–67. doi:10.1109/MCS.2002.1004010

Pant, M., Thangaraj, R., & Abraham, A. (2009). Particle swarm optimization: Performance tuning and empirical analysis. Foundations of Computational Intelligence, 3, 101-128.

Podilchuk, C., & Zhang, X. (1996). Face recognition using OCT-based feature vectors. In *Proceedings of IEEE International Conference on Acoustics, Speech and Signal Processing* (vol. 4, pp. 2144-2147). IEEE.

Yu, M., Yan, G., & Zhu, Q. W. (2006, August). New face recognition method based on dwt/dct combined feature selection. In *Proceedings of IEEE International Conference on Machine Learning and Cybernetics* (pp. 3233-3236). IEEE. doi:10.1109/ICMLC.2006.258432

Samra, A. S., El Taweel Gad Allah, S., & Ibrahim, R. M. (2003). Face recognition using wavelet transform, fast Fourier transform and discrete cosine transform. In *Proceedings of IEEE 46th Midwest Symposium on Circuits and Systems* (vol. 1, pp. 272-275). IEEE.

Turk, M. A., & Pentland, A. P. (1991). Face recognition using eigenfaces. In *Proceedings IEEE Computer Society Conference on Computer Vision and Pattern Recognition (CVPR, 91)* (pp. 586-591). IEEE.

Vision. (n.d.). Retrieved from http://vision.ucsd.edu/datasetsAll

KEY TERMS AND DEFINITIONS

Biometric Profile: Information used to represent an individual or group in an information system.

Biometric System: It is a pattern recognition based system. It acquires biometric data from an individual, extracts a salient feature set from the data, compares feature set against the feature set(s) stored in the database, and executes an action based on the result of the comparison.

Biometric Traits: Class of phenotypic characteristics (e.g., face or stripe pattern) used as source for constructing a biometric profile.

Biometrics: Biometrics means "life measurement" but the term is usually associated with the use of unique physiological characteristics to identify an individual.

Ear Recognition: It is non –intrusive methodology and attributes are probably the most common biometric feature used by humans to recognize one other.

Identification Process: In identification mode, where the subject (people/object) does not claim an identity, the input ear image is compared against a set of labeled (it is used to indicate that the identity of the images in the database is known) ear images in a database in order to determine the best match and, therefore, its identity.

Principal Component Analysis: It is unsupervised dimension reduction approach for large database size. It is used to find the eigen values for face recognition.

Verification Process: One to One matching process. Biometrics can also be used to verify a person's identity. For example, one can grant physical access to a secure area in a building by using finger scans or can grant access to a bank account at an ATM by using retinal scan.

Chapter 6
Minimax Probability Machine:
A New Tool for Modeling Seismic Liquefaction Data

Pijush Samui
VIT University, India

Hariharan Rajadurai
VIT University, India

Yıldırım Huseyin Dalkiliç
Erzincan University, Turkey

J. Jagan
VIT University, India

ABSTRACT

Liquefaction in soil is one of the other major problems in geotechnical earthquake engineering. This chapter adopts Minimax Probability Machine (MPM) for prediction of seismic liquefaction potential of soil based on Shear Wave Velocity (Vs) data. MPM has been used as a classification technique. Two models (MODEL I and MODEL II) have been adopted. In MODEL I, input variables are Cyclic Stress Ratio (CSR), and Vs MODEL II uses Peck Ground Acceleration (PGA) and Vs as input variables. The developed MPM has been compared with the Artificial Neural Network (ANN) and Support Vector Machine (SVM) models. The developed MPM is a robust tool for determination of liquefaction susceptibility of soil.

INTRODUCTION

Liquefaction of soil during earthquake is a major concern for the stability of civil engineering structure. Liquefaction is a phenomenon whereby a granular material transforms from a solid state to a liquefied state as a consequence of increase in pore water pressure. The effective stress of the soil therefore reduces causing loss of bearing capacity. Liquefaction of saturated sandy soils during the past earthquakes has resulted in building settlement and/or severe tilting, sand blows, lateral spreading, ground cracks, landslides, dam and high embankment failures and many other hazards. So, the determination of liquefaction susceptibility of soil is an important task in civil engineering. Liquefaction of soil depends on the following parameters:

DOI: 10.4018/978-1-4666-8291-7.ch006

- Intensity of earthquake and its duration,
- Location of ground water table,
- Soil type,
- Soil relative density,
- Particle size gradation,
- Particle shape,
- Depositional environment of soil,
- Soil drainage conditions,
- Confining pressures,
- Aging and cementation of the soil deposits,
- Historical environment of the soil deposit,
- Building/additional loads on the soil deposit.

Civil engineers use different methods for determination of liquefaction susceptibility of soil (Seed & Idriss, 1971; Dobry et al., 1981; Seed et al., 1983; Seed & Idriss, 1982; Seed et al., 1985; Robertson & Campanella, 1983; Skempton, 1986; Seed & de-Alba, 1986; Stokoe et al., 1988a; Ambraseys, 1988; Tokimatsu & Uchida, 1990; Stark & Olson, 1995; Arango, 1996; Andrus & Stokoe, 1997; Youd & Noble, 1997a; Olsen, 1997; Robertson & Wride, 1998; Andrus & Stokoe, 2000; Moss et al., 2006). Liquefaction potential is evaluated by comparing equivalent measure of earthquake loading and liquefaction resistance. Earthquake loading characterization is generally done by using cyclic shear stress. By normalizing the cyclic shear stress amplitude by initial effective overburden stress, a cyclic stress ratio (CSR) is defined. CSR represents the level of cyclic loading induced at different depths in a soil profile, which corresponds to a specific earthquake. The resistance is mostly characterized based on field observation and potential for liquefaction is classified by comparing CSR with the liquefaction resistance, cyclic resistance ratio (CRR) [Factor of safety (FS) $= \dfrac{\text{CRR}}{\text{CSR}}$]. There are different methods available for determination of liquefaction potential based on standard penetration test (SPT) (Seed & Idriss, 1967, 1971; Seed et al., 1983; Seed et al., 1984; Youd et al., 2001). These methods proposed boundary lines that separate field conditions causing liquefaction from conditions not causing liquefaction in sandy soils. Using this method, the CSR induced by the earthquake at any point in the ground is estimated as (Seed & Idriss, 1971).

$$CSR = \frac{\tau_{av}}{\sigma'_v} = 0.65 \left(\frac{a_{max}}{g} \right) \left(\frac{\sigma_v}{\sigma'_v} \right) r_d \tag{1}$$

where τ_{av} = average equivalent uniform cyclic shear stress caused by the earthquake and is assumed to be 0.65 of the maximum induced stress; a_{max} = peak horizontal ground surface acceleration; g = acceleration of gravity; σ'_v = initial vertical effective stress at the depth in question; σ_v = total overburden stress at the same depth and r_d = shear stress reduction coefficient to adjust for the flexibility of the soil profile and it has been estimated from the chart by Seed and Idriss (1971). The value of CSR is corrected to an earthquake magnitude of 7.5, using the magnitude correction (C_m) proposed by Seed et al. (1985). Seed et al. (1985) proposed a standard blow count N_{60}. N_{60} has determined from the following relation:

$$N_{60} = N.(ER/60\%) \tag{2}$$

where ER= percent of the theoretical free-fall energy; and N= SPT, N value corresponding to the ER. The value of N_{60} is corrected to an effective stress of 100 kPa. $(N_1)_{60}$ is obtained by using the following relation:

$$(N_1)_{60} = C_N \times N_{60} \tag{3}$$

where C_N is the effective stress correction factor and is calculated from the following relation:

$$C_N = \frac{2.2}{(1.2 + \sigma'_v/P_a)} \tag{4}$$

where, P_a = 1atm of pressure in the same units used for σ'_v

Factor of safety (FS) against liquefaction for any earthquake is given by the following relation:

$$FS = \left(CRR_{7.5, \sigma=1, \alpha=0} K_\sigma K_\alpha / CSR \right) MSF \tag{5}$$

where CSR= calculated cyclic stress ratio by using the Equation (1); K_σ is the overburden correction factor and K_α is static shear stress correction factor. MSF is the magnitude scaling factor and it is calculated by using different formula (Seed & Idriss, 1982; Ambraseys, 1988; Arango, 1996; Andrus & Stokoe, 1997; Youd & Noble, 1997a).

Although the above SPT-based method remains an important tool for evaluating liquefaction resistance, it has some drawbacks, primarily due to the variable nature of the SPT (Robertson & Campanella, 1985; Skempton, 1986).

The first cone penetration test (CPT)-based method for liquefaction evaluation was developed by Robertson and Campanella (1985). This method has been revised and updated by many researchers (Seed & de-Alba, 1986; Stark & Olson, 1995; Olsen, 1997; Robertson & Wride, 1998; Moss et al., 2006). In this method, normalization of tip resistance (q_{c1N}) is done by using the following relations:

$$q_{c1N} = C_Q \left(q_c/P_a \right) \tag{6}$$

where

$$C_Q = \left(P_a/\sigma'_v \right)^n \tag{7}$$

where C_Q = normalizing factor for cone penetration resistance; P_a = 1atm of pressure in the same units used for σ'_v; n = exponent that varies from 0.5 to 1, depending on the grain characteristics of the soil

(Olsen, 1997) and q_c = field cone penetration resistance measured at the tip. In this method, FS against liquefaction for any earthquake is calculated by Equation (5).

The engineering practitioners commonly use the above two penetration based methods (SPT and CPT) for assessment of liquefaction potential. On the other hand, shear wave velocity (V_s) may offer engineers a third tool that is lower cost and provides more physically meaningful measurements. The advantages of using V_s for evaluating liquefaction potential have been described by many researchers (Dobry et al., 1981; Seed et al., 1983; Stokoe et al., 1988a; Tokimatsu & Uchida, 1990). Based on V_s, Andrus et al (1999) and Andrus and Stokoe (2000) have evaluated liquefaction potential for different sites.

The most comprehensive study of the application of field-based V_s measurements to seismic-lique-faction assessments has been presented by Andrus and Stokoe (2000). According to Andrus and Stokoe (2000), CRR has been calculated from the following formula:

$$CRR = 0.03 \left(\frac{V_s}{100} \right)^2 + 0.9 \left(\frac{1}{V_{slc} - V_{sl}} - \frac{1}{V_{slc}} \right) \qquad (8)$$

where

$$V_{sl} = V_s \left(\frac{P_a}{\sigma'_v} \right)^{0.25} \qquad (9)$$

V_{sl} =overburden-stress corrected shear wave velocity;

P_a = atmospheric pressure approximated by 100kPa; and σ'_v = initial vertical effective stress in kPa.

For sands and gravels

V_{slc} =220 m/sec, fine content (FC) $\leq 5\%$

=210 m/sec, FC$\approx$20%

=200 m/sec, FC$\geq$35%

In this method, FS against liquefaction for any earthquake is calculated by Equation (5).

Recently, Boulanger and Idriss (2004) have recommended guidelines for estimation of the CSR and the CRR for fine grained soils like silts and clays. They have defined the terms "sand-like" and "clay-like" to describe fine-grained soils whose stress-strain during monotonic and cyclic undrained shear loading is fundamentally similar to that of sands and clays, respectively. The term "liquefaction" is used to describe the onset of high excess pore water pressures and large shear strains during undrained cyclic loading of sand-like soils, while the term "cyclic failure" is used to describe the corresponding of clay-like soils.

The stress-strain of a sand specimen that develops liquefaction can look quite similar, in some cases, to that of a soft clay specimen that develops cyclic failure. Fine-grained soils transition from sand-like to clay-like behaviour occurs at plasticity indices (PI) between about 3 and 8, with the transition point appearing to be slightly lower for ML-CL soils than for ML soils. For practical purposes, it has been recommended by Boulanger and Idriss (2004) that fine grained soils be categorized as sand-like (i.e., susceptible to liquefaction) if they have a PI < 7 and clay-like (i.e., susceptible to cyclic failure, not liquefaction) if they have a PI ≥ 7. This criterion may be adjusted on a site-specific basis if justified by the results of detailed in situ and laboratory testing.

Every model has their own advantages and disadvantages. Juang et al. (2000a, 2002) proposed mapping function to determine the probability liquefaction (P_L). Cetin (2000) and Cetin et al. (2004) proposed probabilistic models for assessing liquefaction triggering based on SPT data. Moss (2003) and Moss et al. (2005) employed the approach developed by Cetin (2000) to analyze a large database of CPT. Goh (1994, 1996, 2002) suggested the use of artificial neural network(ANN) based approach for assessing the liquefaction potential from actual N, q_c and V_s data. Juang et al., (2000b) used ANN to determine the limit state for liquefaction triggering. Kurup and Dudani, (2001) applied ANN to determine liquefaction potential based on CPT data. ANN has been used by many researchers for modeling of sesismic liquefaction data (Goh, 1994b; 1996a; Agrawal et al., 1997; Ali and Najjar, 1998; Najjar and Ali, 1998; Ural and Saka, 1998; Juang and Chen, 1999; Goh, 2002; Javadi et al., 2006; Young-Su and Byung-Tak, 2006; Goh and Goh, 2007). Kurup and Garg (2005) used ART based networks to evaluate liquefaction potential.

This article examines the capability of Minimax Probability Machine (MPM) for prediction of liquefaction susceptibility of soil based on shear wave velocity (V_s). MPM is developed by Lanckriet et al. (2002). It is constructed in probabilistic framework. It has been used to solve different problems in engineering and science (Yang et al., 2010; Zhou et al., 2013; Shen et al., 2013; Yoshiyama and Sakurai, 2014). This article adopts MPM as a classification technique. This study uses the database collected from the work of Andrus and Stokoe (1997). The dataset represented 88 sites that liquefied and 98 sites that did not liquefy. Two models (MODEL I and MODEL II) have been developed. In MODEL I, input variables are V_s and Cyclic Stress Ratio (CSR). Peak Ground Acceleration (PGA) and V_s have been used as input variables for MODEL II. The developed MPM have been compared with the ANN and Support Vector Machine (SVM) models.

DETAILS OF MPM

This section describes MPM as a classification tool. In MPM, it is assumed that the positive definite covariance matrices exist in each of the two classes. The main aim of MPM is to determine the following hyperplane that separates the two classes of points.

$$a^T z = b, \ a, z \in R^n \text{ and } b \in r \tag{10}$$

where z is a random vector, R^n is n-dimensional vector space, r is one dimensional vector space, a and b are constants.

The main formulation of MPM is given below:

$$\max_{\alpha,b,a\neq 0} \alpha \text{ subjected to} \quad \begin{array}{l} \inf P_r\left\{a^T x \geq b\right\} \geq \alpha \\ \inf P_r\left\{a^T y \leq b\right\} \geq \alpha \end{array} \tag{11}$$

where α is the lower bound of the accuracy for the classification of future data points.

The above optimization problem is solved by Lagrangian Multiplier. So, the above optimization problem (2)

$$\max_{k,a} k \text{ subjected to} \quad \begin{array}{l} -b + a^T x \geq k\sqrt{a^T \Sigma_a a} \\ b - a^T y \geq k\sqrt{a^T \Sigma_y a} \end{array} \tag{12}$$

By eliminating k, the optimization problem (3) is written in the following way

$$\min \sqrt{a^T \Sigma_y a} + \lambda\sqrt{a^T \Sigma_x a}$$

Subjected to $a^T (\overline{x} - \overline{y}) = 1$ \hfill (13)

The optimization problem (4) is solved by convex programming technique.

In carrying out the formulation of MPM, the data has been divided into two sub-sets such as

1. A training dataset: In this study, 130 out of the 186 data (70%) are considered for training.
2. A testing dataset: In this study, the remaining 56 data (30%) is considered for testing.

The datasets are normalized between 0 and 1. The following formula has been adopted for normalization.

$$d_{normalized} = \frac{\left(d - d_{min}\right)}{\left(d_{max} - d_{min}\right)} \tag{14}$$

where d=any data (input or output), d_{min}= minimum value of the entire dataset, d_{max}= maximum value of the entire dataset, and $d_{normalized}$=normalized value of the data. Radial basis function has been used as kernel function. Figure 1 shows the flow chart of MPM for prediction of liquefaction susceptibility of soil.

Table 1 shows the statistical parameters of the dataset.

The program of MPM has been constructed by using MATLAB.

RESULTS AND DISCUSSION

The design value of width (σ) of radial basis function has been determined by trial and error approach. The performance of training dataset is expressed in percentage and is determined as the ratio of number of data predicted accurately by the MPM to the total number of data in the training set. The obtained

Figure 1. Flow chart of the MPM

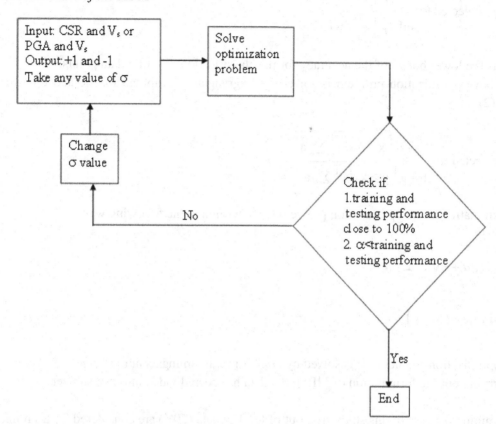

Table 1. Statistical parameters of the dataset

Variable	Mean	Standard Deviation	Kurtosis	Skewness
CSR	0.19	0.10	3.43	0.78
V_s (m/sec)	142.83	31.30	5.04	1.02
PGA	0.22	0.12	2.83	0.68

weight parameters are utilized to validate the results in the testing dataset. The performance of testing dataset is expressed in percentage and is determined as the ratio of number of data predicted accurately by the MPM to the total number of data in the testing set. Figure 2 shows the adopted data division gives the best performance.

Figure 3 shows the variation of performance of testing dataset with σ values for MODEL I.

The developed MPM gives best testing performance at $\sigma = 0.9$. For MODEL I, training performance is 99.23% and testing performance is 98.21%. The value of α is 96%. So, the value of α is lower than the training and testing performances. Therefore, the validity of α has been checked. Table 2 and 3 shows the performance of training and testing datasets respectively.

Figure 4 and 5 depicts the plot between CSR and V_s for training and testing dataset respectively.

Figure 2. Effect of data division on testing performance (%)

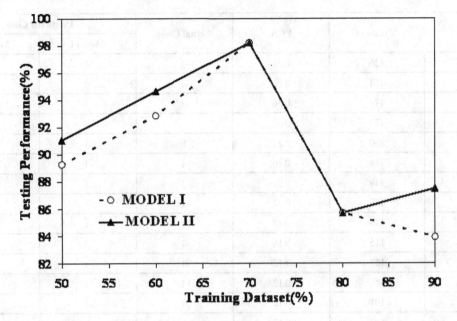

Figure 3. Effect of σ on testing performance (%)

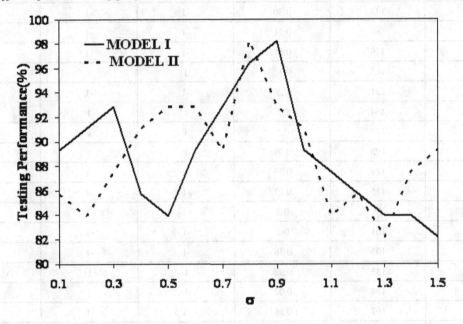

For MODEL II, the developed MPM gives best testing performance at σ=0.8 as shown in Figure 1. So, the design value of σ is 0.8. For MODEL II, training performance is 98.46% and testing performance is 98.21%. The value of α is 97% for MODEL II. Therefore, the validity of α has been checked for MODEL II. Figure 6 and 7 illustrates the plot between PGA and V_s for training and testing dataset respectively.

Table 2. Performance of training dataset

CSR	V_s (m/sec)	PGA	Actual Class	Predicted Class	
				Model I	Model II
0.3	136	0.36	-1	-1	-1
0.29	154	0.36	-1	-1	-1
0.29	173	0.36	-1	-1	-1
0.24	177	0.32	1	1	1
0.24	200	0.32	1	-1	1
0.14	118	0.16	-1	-1	-1
0.22	149	0.32	-1	-1	-1
0.22	158	0.32	-1	-1	-1
0.13	147	0.12	-1	-1	-1
0.16	115	0.16	-1	-1	-1
0.12	122	0.12	-1	-1	-1
0.14	98	0.12	-1	-1	1
0.14	101	0.12	-1	-1	-1
0.13	143	0.12	1	1	1
0.13	127	0.13	1	1	1
0.26	131	0.36	-1	-1	-1
0.18	90	0.21	-1	-1	-1
0.45	126	0.51	-1	-1	-1
0.09	105	0.12	1	1	1
0.41	131	0.5	-1	-1	-1
0.4	164	0.5	1	1	1
0.4	173	0.5	1	1	1
0.08	195	0.08	1	1	1
0.26	127	0.27	-1	-1	-1
0.27	115	0.27	-1	-1	-1
0.18	90	0.2	-1	-1	-1
0.23	101	0.3	-1	-1	-1
0.29	105	0.36	-1	-1	-1
0.02	133	0.02	1	1	1
0.02	164	0.02	1	1	-1
0.28	107	0.36	-1	-1	-1
0.29	94	0.36	-1	-1	-1
0.28	109	0.36	-1	-1	-1
0.29	122	0.36	-1	-1	-1
0.26	128	0.36	-1	-1	-1
0.27	107	0.36	-1	-1	-1
0.26	122	0.36	-1	-1	-1

continued on following page

Table 2. Continued

CSR	V$_s$(m/sec)	PGA	Actual Class	Predicted Class	
				Model I	Model II
0.29	154	0.36	-1	-1	-1
0.23	105	0.3	-1	1	-1
0.26	106	0.29	-1	-1	-1
0.13	143	0.16	-1	-1	-1
0.42	274	0.46	1	1	1
0.07	155	0.06	1	1	1
0.12	152	0.16	-1	-1	-1
0.33	133	0.22	1	1	1
0.33	127	0.22	1	1	1
0.27	146	0.18	1	1	1
0.27	133	0.18	1	1	1
0.27	130	0.18	1	1	1
0.06	146	0.04	1	1	1
0.06	127	0.04	1	1	1
0.06	130	0.04	1	1	1
0.27	133	0.18	1	1	1
0.27	127	0.18	1	1	1
0.08	146	0.05	1	1	1
0.08	133	0.05	1	1	1
0.08	130	0.05	1	1	1
0.24	146	0.16	1	1	1
0.24	127	0.16	1	1	-1
0.33	146	0.22	1	1	1
0.12	127	0.12	1	1	1
0.12	124	0.12	1	1	1
0.1	90	0.11	1	1	1
0.05	126	0.06	1	1	1
0.19	105	0.24	1	1	1
0.02	131	0.03	1	-1	1
0.02	164	0.03	1	1	1
0.02	173	0.03	1	1	1
0.19	124	0.2	1	1	1
0.2	115	0.2	1	1	1
0.17	126	0.19	1	1	1
0.15	101	0.2	1	1	1
0.15	131	0.18	1	1	1

continued on following page

Table 2. Continued

CSR	V$_s$(m/sec)	PGA	Actual Class	Predicted Class	
				Model I	Model II
0.15	133	0.18	1	1	1
0.15	173	0.18	1	1	1
0.37	126	0.42	-1	-1	-1
0.15	157	0.14	-1	-1	-1
0.15	131	0.14	-1	-1	-1
0.15	148	0.14	-1	-1	-1
0.15	137	0.14	-1	-1	-1
0.15	146	0.14	-1	-1	-1
0.15	178	0.14	1	1	1
0.15	154	0.14	-1	-1	-1
0.12	143	0.15	-1	-1	-1
0.13	135	0.16	-1	-1	-1
0.12	117	0.16	-1	-1	-1
0.12	121	0.16	-1	-1	-1
0.12	138	0.16	-1	-1	-1
0.12	145	0.16	1	1	1
0.12	133	0.16	1	1	1
0.21	146	0.24	-1	-1	-1
0.22	148	0.24	-1	-1	-1
0.21	179	0.24	-1	-1	-1
0.57	157	0.24	-1	-1	-1
0.21	145	0.24	-1	-1	1
0.21	176	0.24	-1	-1	-1
0.41	206	0.46	1	1	1
0.2	204	0.27	1	1	1
0.2	116	0.27	-1	-1	-1
0.19	125	0.27	-1	-1	-1
0.12	120	0.15	-1	-1	-1
0.12	105	0.15	-1	-1	-1
0.12	220	0.15	1	1	1
0.16	136	0.19	1	1	1
0.16	161	0.19	1	1	1
0.16	173	0.19	1	1	1
0.11	195	0.15	1	1	1
0.11	200	0.15	1	1	1
0.11	131	0.15	1	1	1
0.11	149	0.15	1	1	1

continued on following page

Table 2. Continued

CSR	V_s(m/sec)	PGA	Actual Class	Predicted Class	
				Model I	Model II
0.11	168	0.15	1	1	1
0.24	143	0.25	-1	-1	-1
0.33	126	0.42	1	1	1
0.2	97	0.27	-1	-1	-1
0.11	158	0.15	1	1	1
0.21	116	0.25	-1	-1	-1
0.2	130	0.25	-1	-1	-1
0.26	209	0.25	-1	-1	-1
0.22	150	0.25	-1	-1	-1
0.12	120	0.15	1	1	1
0.19	127	0.2	1	1	1
0.43	197	0.5	-1	-1	-1
0.32	149	0.48	1	1	1
0.15	135	0.2	-1	-1	-1
0.33	145	0.42	-1	-1	-1
0.28	134	0.36	-1	-1	-1
0.31	135	0.42	1	1	1
0.44	174	0.5	-1	-1	-1
0.14	163	0.15	-1	-1	-1
0.16	154	0.19	1	1	1
0.49	176	0.5	-1	-1	-1
0.46	153	0.5	-1	-1	-1
0.47	183	0.5	-1	-1	-1
0.49	181	0.5	-1	-1	-1

Table 3. Performance of testing dataset

CSR	V_s(m/sec)	PGA	Actual Class	Predicted Class	
				Model I	Model II
0.29	161	0.36	-1	-1	-1
0.24	195	0.32	1	1	1
0.22	131	0.32	-1	-1	-1
0.22	168	0.32	-1	-1	-1
0.24	199	0.32	1	1	1
0.13	103	0.12	-1	-1	1
0.11	163	0.16	1	1	1
0.1	101	0.12	1	1	1

continued on following page

Table 3. Continued

CSR	V_s (m/sec)	PGA	Actual Class	Predicted Class	
				Model I	Model II
0.41	133	0.5	-1	-1	-1
0.09	155	0.08	1	1	1
0.26	124	0.27	-1	1	-1
0.05	126	0.06	1	1	1
0.02	131	0.02	1	1	1
0.02	173	0.02	1	1	1
0.28	102	0.36	-1	-1	-1
0.13	124	0.13	1	1	1
0.26	122	0.3	-1	-1	-1
0.23	105	0.29	-1	-1	-1
0.17	271	0.23	1	1	1
0.24	130	0.16	1	1	1
0.33	130	0.22	1	-1	1
0.06	127	0.18	1	1	1
0.06	133	0.04	1	1	1
0.27	146	0.18	1	1	1
0.27	130	0.18	1	1	1
0.08	127	0.05	1	1	-1
0.24	133	0.16	1	1	1
0.07	150	0.1	1	1	1
0.1	101	0.13	1	1	1
0.02	133	0.03	1	1	1
0.1	90	0.2	1	1	1
0.19	105	0.21	1	1	1
0.02	164	0.18	1	1	1
0.15	157	0.14	-1	1	-1
0.15	136	0.14	-1	-1	-1
0.15	152	0.14	-1	-1	-1
0.2	212	0.27	1	1	1
0.06	195	0.06	1	1	1
0.12	148	0.16	1	1	1
0.21	134	0.24	-1	-1	-1
0.21	145	0.24	-1	-1	-1
0.21	142	0.24	-1	-1	-1
0.2	193	0.27	1	1	-1
0.12	115	0.12	1	1	1
0.11	153	0.15	-1	-1	-1

continued on following page

Table 3. Continued

CSR	V_s (m/sec)	PGA	Actual Class	Predicted Class	
				Model I	Model II
0.15	130	0.14	-1	-1	-1
0.11	177	0.15	1	1	1
0.11	199	0.15	1	1	1
0.44	116	0.42	-1	-1	-1
0.13	115	0.13	1	1	1
0.36	158	0.42	1	1	1
0.22	162	0.25	-1	-1	-1
0.22	171	0.25	-1	-1	1
0.16	79	0.19	-1	-1	-1
0.21	144	0.19	-1	-1	-1
0.1	179	0.12	1	1	1
0.46	210	0.5	-1	-1	-1

Figure 4. Plot between CSR and V_s for MODEL I using training dataset

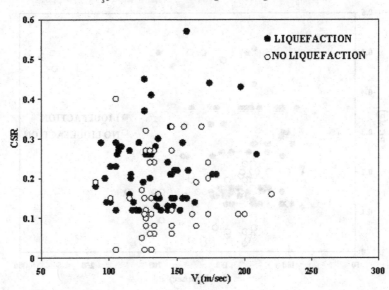

The performance of training and testing have been shown in Table 2 and Table 3 respectively. The performance of MODEL I and MODEL II is almost same.The developed MPM has been compared with the ANN and SVM models (Samui, 2008). Table 4 shows the comparison.

It is clear from Table 4 that the developed MPM outperforms the ANN and SVM models. The developed ANN and SVM have no control over future prediction. However, the developed MPM has control over future prediction. ANN uses many tuning parameters such number of hidden layers, epochs, transfer function, number of neurons in the hidden layer, etc. There are two tuning parameters in the

Figure 5. Plot between CSR and V_s for MODEL I using testing dataset

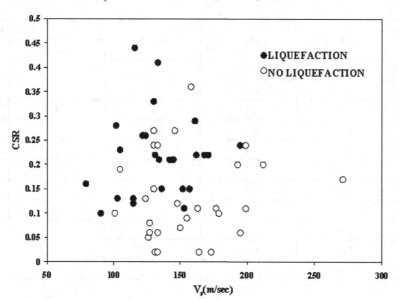

Figure 6. Plot between PGA and Vs for MODEL II using training dataset

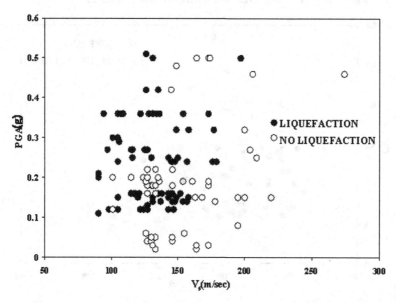

Table 4. Comparison between ANN, MPM and SVM models

Input Variables	ANN [Training Performance (%)]	SVM [Training Performance (%)]	ANN [Testing Performance (%)]	SVM [Testing Performance (%)]	MPM [Training Performance (%)]	MPM [Testing Performance (%)]
CSR, V_s	96	97	87	94	99.23	98.21
PGA, V_s	83	84	76	82	98.46	98.21

Figure 7. Plot between PGA and Vs for MODEL II using testing dataset for BP model

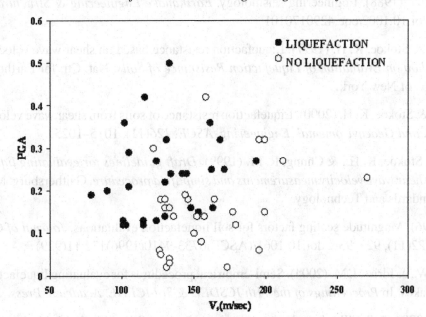

SVM model. MPM uses only one tuning parameter. The performance of training and testing datasets are almost same. So, there is no overtraining in the MPM. Therefore, the developed MPM has good generalization capability.

CONCLUSION

This article uses MPM for prediction of liquefaction susceptibility of soil based on V_s. The details methodology of MPM has been described. The performance of two developed MPM models (MODEL I and MODEL II) are encouraging. It shows good generalization capability. The developed MPM outperforms the ANN and SVM models. The developed MPM can be used as a quick tool for determination of liquefaction susceptibility of soil. This article shows that MPM can predict liquefaction susceptibility of soil based on only two parameters (V_s and PGA). In summary, it can be concluded that the developed MPM can be used to model different problems in engineering.

REFERENCES

Agrawal, G., Chameau, J. A., & Bourdeau, P. L. (1997). Assessing the liquefaction susceptibility at a site based on information from penetration testing. In N. Kartam, I. Flood, & J. H. Garrett (Eds.), Artificial neural networks for civil engineers: fundamentals and applications (pp. 185–214). New York: Academic Press.

Ali, H. E., & Najjar, Y. M. (1998). Neuronet-based approach for assessing liquefaction potential of soils. *Transportation Research Record, 1633*(, 1633), 3–8. doi:10.3141/1633-01

Ambraseys, N. N. (1988). Engineering seismology. *Earthquake Engineering & Structural Dynamics*, *17*(1), 1–105. doi:10.1002/eqe.4290170101

Andrus, R. D., & Stokoe, K. H. (1997). Liquefaction resistance based on shear wave velocity. In *Proc., NCEER Workshop on Evaluation of Liquefaction Resistance of Soils*. Nat. Ctr. for Earthquake Engrg. Res., State Univ. of New York.

Andrus, R. D., & Stokoe, K. H. (2000). Liquefaction resistance of soils from shear wave velocity. *Journal of Geotechnial. and Geoenviromental. Engineering, ASCE, 126*(11), 1015–1025.

Andrus, R. D., Stokoe, K. H., & Chung, R. M. (1999). *Draft guidelines for evaluating liquefaction resistance using shear wave velocity measurements and simplified procedure*. Gaithersburg, MD: National Institute of Standards and Technology.

Arango, I. (1996). Magnitude scaling factors for soil liquefaction evaluations. *Journal of Geotechnical Engineering, 122*(11), 929–936. doi:10.1061/(ASCE)0733-9410(1996)122:11(929)

Boulanger, R. W., & Idriss, I. M. (2004). Semi-empirical procedures for evaluating liquefaction potential during earthquakes. In *Proceedings of the 11th ICSDEE & 3rd ICEGE. Academic Press*.

Cetin, K. O. (2000). *Reliability-based assessment of seismic soil liquefaction initiation hazard*. (PhD dissertation). University of California, Berkeley, CA.

Cetin, K. O., Seed, R. B., Der Kiureghian, A., Tokimatsu, K., Harder, L. F. Jr, Kayen, R. E., & Moss, R. E. S. (2004). Standard penetration test-based probabilistic and deterministic assessment of seismic soil liquefaction potential. *Journal of Geotechnical and Geoenvironmental Engineering, 130*(12), 1314–1340. doi:10.1061/(ASCE)1090-0241(2004)130:12(1314)

Dobry, R., Stokoe, K. H., Ladd, R. S., & Youd, T. L. (1981). Liquefaction susceptibility from S-wave velocity. In *Proc., ASCE Nat. Convention, In Situ Tests to Evaluate Liquefaction Susceptibility*. New York: ASCE.

Goh, A. T. C. (1994). Seismic liquefaction potential assessed by neural networks. *Journal of Geotechnical Engineering, 120*(9), 1467–1480. doi:10.1061/(ASCE)0733-9410(1994)120:9(1467)

Goh, A. T. C. (1994b). Seismic liquefaction potential assessed by neural network. *Journal of Geotechnical and Geoenvironmental Engineering, 120*(9), 1467–1480. doi:10.1061/(ASCE)0733-9410(1994)120:9(1467)

Goh, A. T. C. (1996). Neural-network modeling of CPT seismic liquefaction data. *Journal of Geotechnical Engineering, 122*(1), 70–73. doi:10.1061/(ASCE)0733-9410(1996)122:1(70)

Goh, A. T. C. (1996a). Neural-network modeling of CPT seismic liquefaction data. *Journal of Geotechnical Engineering, 122*(1), 70–73. doi:10.1061/(ASCE)0733-9410(1996)122:1(70)

Goh, A. T. C. (2002). Probabilistic neural network for evaluating seismic liquefaction potential. *Canadian Geotechnical Journal, 39*(1), 219–232. doi:10.1139/t01-073

Goh, A. T. C. (2002). Probabilistic neural network for evaluating seismic liquefaction potential. *Canadian Geotechnical Journal, 39*(1), 219–232. doi:10.1139/t01-073

Goh, A. T. C., & Goh, S. H. (2007). Support vector machines: Their use in geotechnical engineering as illustrated using seismic liquefaction data. *Computers and Geotechnics, 34*(5), 410–421. doi:10.1016/j.compgeo.2007.06.001

Javadi, A. A., Rezania, M., & Mousavi Nezhad, M. (2006). Evaluation of liquefaction induced lateral displacements using genetic programming. *Computers and Geotechnics, 33*(4-5), 222–233. doi:10.1016/j.compgeo.2006.05.001

Juang, C. H., & Chen, C. J. (1999). CPT-based liquefaction evaluation using artificial neural networks. *Computer-Aided Civil and Infrastructure Engineering, 14*(3), 221–229. doi:10.1111/0885-9507.00143

Juang, C. H., Chen, C. J., Rosowsky, D. V., & Tang, W. H. (2000b). CPT-based liquefaction analysis, Part 2: Reliability for design. *Geotechnique, 50*(5), 593–599. doi:10.1680/geot.2000.50.5.593

Juang, C. H., Chen, C. J., Tang, W. H., & Rosowsky, D. V. (2000a). CPT-based liquefaction analysis. Part 1. Determination of limit state function. *Geotechnique, 50*(5), 583–592. doi:10.1680/geot.2000.50.5.583

Juang, C. H., Yuan, H., Lee, D. H., & Ku, C. S. (2002). Assessing CPT-based methods for liquefaction evaluation with emphasis on the cases from the Chi-Chi, Taiwan, earthquake. *Soil Dynamics and Earthquake Engineering, 22*(3), 241–258. doi:10.1016/S0267-7261(02)00013-1

Kurup, P. U., & Dudani, N. K. (2001). CPT evaluation of liquefaction potential using neural networks. In *Proceedings of the Fourth International Conference on Recent Advances in Geotechnical Earthquake Engineering and Soil Dynamics*. Academic Press.

Kurup, P. U., & Garg, A. (2005). *Evaluation of liquefaction potential using ART based neural networks*. Paper presented at the Transportation Research Record, 84th Transportation Research Board Annual Meeting, Washington, DC.

Lanckriet, G., El Ghaoui, L., Bhattacharyya, C., & Jordan, M. (2002). A robust minimax approach to classification. *Journal of Machine Learning Research, 3*, 555–582.

Moss, R. E. S. (2003). *CPT-based probabilistic assessment of seismic soil liquefaction initiation*. (PhD dissertation). Univ. of California, Berkeley, CA.

Moss, R. E. S., Seed, R. B., Kayen, R. E., Stewart, J. P., Kiureghian, A., & Cetin, K. O. (2006). CPT-based probablistic and deterministic assesment of in situ seismic soil liquefaction potential. *Journal of Geotechnical and Geoenviromental Engineering, ASCE, 132*(8), 1032–1051. doi:10.1061/(ASCE)1090-0241(2006)132:8(1032)

Moss, R. E. S., Seed, R. B., Kayen, R. E., Stewart, J. P., & Tokimatsu, K. (2005). Probabilistic liquefaction triggering based on the cone penetration test. In E. M. Rathje (Ed.), Geotechnical special publication: Vol. 133. *CD Rome ASCE*. Reston, VA.

Olsen, R. S. (1997). Cyclic liquefaction based on the cone penetrometer test. In *Proc., NCEER Workshop on Evaluation of Liquefaction Resistance of Soils*. National Center for Earthquake Engineering Research.

Robertson, P. K., & Campanella, R. G. (1983). Interpretation of cone penetration tests. Part I: Sand. *Canadian Geotechnical Journal, 20*(4), 718–733. doi:10.1139/t83-078

Robertson, P. K., & Campanella, R. G. (1985). Liquefaction potential of sand using the CPT. *Journal of Geotechnical Engineering, 111*(3), 384–403. doi:10.1061/(ASCE)0733-9410(1985)111:3(384)

Robertson, P. K., & Wride, C. E. (1998). Cyclic liquefaction and its evaluation based on the SPT and CPT. In YoudT. L.IdrissI. M., (Eds.), *Proc. of the 1998 NCEER Workshop on Evaluation of liquefaction Resistance of Soils*. NCEER.

Seed, H. B., & De Alba, P. (1986). *Use of SPT and CPT tests for evaluating the liquefaction resistance of sands, Use of in situ tests in geotechnical engineering*. ASCE.

Seed, H. B., & Idriss, I. M. (1967). Analysis of soil liquefaction: Niigata earthquake. *J. Soil Mech. and Foun. Div, ASCE, 93*(3), 83–108.

Seed, H. B., & Idriss, I. M. (1971). Simplified procedure for evaluating soil liquefaction potential. *Journal of the Soil Mechanics and Foundations Division, 97*(9), 1249–1273.

Seed, H. B., & Idriss, I. M. (1982). *Ground motions and soil liquefaction during earthquakes*. Oakland, CA: Earthquake Engineering Research Institute Monograph.

Seed, H. B., Idriss, I. M., & Arango, I. (1983). Evaluation of liquefaction potential using field performance data. *Journal of the Geotechnical Engineering Division, 109*(3), 458–482. doi:10.1061/(ASCE)0733-9410(1983)109:3(458)

Seed, H. B., Tokimatsu, K., Harder, L. F., & Chung, R. (1985). Influence of SPT procedures in soil liquefaction resistance evaluation. *Journal of Geotechnical Engineering, 111*(12), 861–878.

Seed, H. B., Tokimatsu, K., Harder, L. F., & Chung, R. M. (1984). Influence of SPT procedures in soil liquefaction resistance evaluation, Earthquake Engrg. Res. Ctr., Univ. of California, Berkeley, California. Rep. No. UCB/EERC-84/15.

Shen, C., Wang, P., Paisitkriangkrai, S., & Van Den Hengel, A. (2013). Training effective node classifiers for cascade classification. *International Journal of Computer Vision, 103*(3), 326–347. doi:10.1007/s11263-013-0608-1

Skempton, A. W. (1986). Standard penetration test procedures and the effects in sands of overburden pressure, relative density, particle size, aging and overconsolidation. *Geotechnique, 36*(3), 425–447. doi:10.1680/geot.1986.36.3.425

Stark, T. D., & Olson, S. M. (1995). Liquefaction resistance using CPT and field case histories. *Journal of Geotechnical Engineering, 121*(12), 856–869. doi:10.1061/(ASCE)0733-9410(1995)121:12(856)

Stokoe, K. H., Nazarian, S., Rix, G. J., Sanchez Salinero, I., Sheu, J. C., & Mok, Y. J. (1988a). In situ seismic testing of hard-to-sample soils by surface wave method: Earthquake engineering and soil dynamics II—Recent advances in ground-motion evaluation. Geotechnical Special Publication, ASCE, 20, 264–289.

Tokimatsu, K., & Uchida, A. (1990). Correlation between liquefaction resistance and shear wave velocity. *Soil and Foundation, 30*(2), 33–42. doi:10.3208/sandf1972.30.2_33

Ural, D. N., & Saka, H. (1998). Liquefaction assessment by neural networks. *Electronic Journal of Geotechnical Engineering*. Retrieved from http://geotech.civen.okstate.edu/ejge/ppr9803/index.html

Yang, L., Wang, L., Sun, Y., & Zhang, R. (2010). Simultaneous feature selection and classification via minimax probability machine. *International Journal of Computational Intelligence Systems*, *3*(6), 754–760. doi:10.1080/18756891.2010.9727738

Yoshiyama, K., & Sakurai, A. (2014). Laplacian minimax probability machine. *Pattern Recognition Letters*, *37*(1), 192–200. doi:10.1016/j.patrec.2013.01.004

Youd, T. L., Idriss, I. M., Andrus, R. D., Arango, I., Castro, G., Christian, J. T., Dobry, R., ….Stokoe, K. H. (2001). Liquefaction resistance of soils: summary report from the 1996 NCEER and 1998 NCEER/NSF workshops on evaluation of liquefaction resistance of soils. *Journal of Geotechnical and Geoeniromental Engineering, ASCE, 127*(10), 817-833.

Youd, T. L., & Noble, S. K. (1997a). Magnitude scaling factors. In *Proc., NCEER Workshop on Evaluation of Liquefaction Resistance of Soils*. Nat. Ctr. for Earthquake Engrg. Res., State Univ. of Buffalo.

Young Su, K., & Byung-Tak, K. (2006). Use of artificial neural networks in the prediction of liquefaction resistance of sands. *Journal of Geotechnical and Geoenvironmental Engineering, 132*(11), 1502–1504. doi:10.1061/(ASCE)1090-0241(2006)132:11(1502)

Zhou, Z., Wang, Z., & Sun, X. (2013). Face recognition based on optimal kernel minimax probability machine. *Journal of Theoretical and Applied Information Technology, 48*(3), 1645–1651.

ADDITIONAL READING

Andrews, D. C. A., & Martin, G. R. (2000). Criteria for Liquefaction of Silty Soils. *Proceedings of 12th World Conference on Earthquake Engineering*, Auckland, New Zealand.

Andrus, R. D. (1994). *In situ characterization of gravelly soils that liquefied in the 1983 Borah Peak Earthquake*. Ph.D. Dissertation, University of Texas, Austin.

Arulanandan, K., & Symbico, J. (1993). Post-Liquefaction Settlement of Sands. Predictive Soil Mechanics: *Proceedings of the Wroth Memorial Symposium* (pp. 94110). London: Thomas Telford.

Bańka, S., & Jaroszewski, K. (2007). Artificial neural networks in diagnostic system for purifying fumes installation. *Computer Assisted Mechanics and Engineering Sciences, 14*(4), 531–541.

Bardet, J. P., Mace, N., Tobita, T., & Hu, J. (1999a). Large-Scale Modeling of Liquefaction-Induced Ground Deformation Part I: A Four-Parameter MLR Model. *Proceedings of the Seventh U.S.-Japan Workshop on Earthquake Resistant Design of Lifeline Facilities and Countermeasures Against Soil Liquefaction*. Mid-America Center for Earthquake Engineering Research, Buffalo, NY: Technical Report No. MCEER-99-0019.

Bardet, J. P., Mace, N., Tobita, T., & Hu, J. (1999b). Large-Scale Modeling of Liquefaction-Induced Ground Deformation Part II: MLR Model Applications and Probabilistic Model. *Proceedings of the Seventh U.S.-Japan Workshop on Earthquake Resistant Design of Lifeline Facilities and Countermeasures Against Soil Liquefaction*. Mid-America Center for Earthquake Engineering Research, Buffalo, NY: Technical Report No. MCEER-99-0019.

Barrios, D., Manrique, D., Plaza, M. R., & Ríos, J. (2001). An algebraic model for generating and adapting neural networks by means of optimization methods. *Annals of Mathematics and Artificial Intelligence, 33*(1), 93–111. doi:10.1023/A:1012337000887

Bartlett, S. F., & Youd, T. L. (1992). Empirical Analysis of Horizontal Ground Displacement Generated by Liquefaction-Induced Lateral Spread. National Center for Earthquake Engineering Research, Buffalo, NY: Technical Report No. NCEER-920021.

Bartlett, S. F., & Youd, T. L. (1995). Empirical Prediction of liquefaction-Induced Lateral Spread. *Journal of Geotechnical Engineering, 121*(4), 316–329. doi:10.1061/(ASCE)0733-9410(1995)121:4(316)

Beaty, M. H. (2001). *A Synthesized Approach for Estimating Liquefaction-Induced Displacements of Geotechnical Structures*. Ph. D. Thesis, University of British Columbia, Vancouver, Canada.

Beaty, M. H., & Byrne, P. M. (1998). An Effective Stress Model for Predicting Liquefaction Behaviour of Sand. *Proceedings of a Specialty Conference on Geotechnical Earthquake Engineering and Soil Dynamics III* (pp. 766-777). Geotechnical Special Publication No. 75.

Boulanger, R. W., & Seed, R. B. (1995). Liquefaction of Sand Under Bi-directional Monotonic and Cyclic Loading. *Journal of Geotechnical Engineering, 121*(12), 870–878. doi:10.1061/(ASCE)0733-9410(1995)121:12(870)

Bray, J. D., Sancio, R. B., Durgunoglu, H. T., Onalp, A., Seed, R. B., Stewart, J. P., & Emrem, C. et al. (2001). Ground Failure in Adapazari, Turkey. *Proceedings of Earthquake Geotechnical Engineering Satellite Conference of the XVth International Conference on Soil Mechanics & Geotechnical Engineering*, Istanbul, Turkey.

Bray, J. D., & Stewart, J. P. (2000). Damage Patterns and Foundation performance in Adapazari. In Youd, T. L., Bardet, J. P., & Bray, J. D. (Eds.), 1999 Reconnaissance Report, Earthquake Spectra, Supplement A (Vol. 16, pp. 163-189). Kocaeli, Turkey. doi:10.1193/1.1586152

Cao, L. F., Teh, C. I., & Chang, M. F. (2001). Undrained Cavity Expansion in Modified Cam Clay I: Theoretical Analysis. *Geotechnique, 51*(4), 323–334. doi:10.1680/geot.2001.51.4.323

Cetin, K. O., Der Kiureghian, A., & Seed, R. B. (2002). Probabilistic Models for the Initiation of Seismic Soil Liquefaction. *Structural Safety, 24*(1), 67–82. doi:10.1016/S0167-4730(02)00036-X

Cetin, K. O., & Seed, R. B. (2000). Earthquake-Induced Nonlinear Shear Mass Participation Factor (rd). *Geotechnical Engineering Research Report No. UCB/GT2000/08*, University of California, Berkeley.

Cetin, K. O., & Seed, R. B. (2001). Nonlinear Shear Mass Participation Factor (Rd) For Cyclic Shear Stress Ratio Evaluation. *Research Report No. UCB/GT-2000/08, University of California*, Berkeley.

Chang, W. S., Bray, J. D., Gookin, W. B., & Riemer, M. F. (1997). Seismic Response Of Deep Stiff Soil Deposits in the Los Angeles, California Area During The 1994 Northridge, Earthquake. *Geotechnical Research Report No. UCB/GT/9701*, University of California, Berkeley.

Chen, Z. G., & Li, D. Y. (2007). Intrusion detection based on kernel fisher discriminant analysis and minimax probability machine classifier. *Journal of the University of Electronic Science and Technology of China, 36*(6), 1192–1194.

Chen, Z. G., & Wang, S. (2008). Minimax probability machine with genetic feature optimized for intrusion detection. *Information Technology Journal, 7*(1), 185–189. doi:10.3923/itj.2008.185.189

Chen, Z. Y., & Zhao, G. F. (2002). Application of artificial neural networks to the prediction of ultimate shear strength of high strength concrete columns reinforced with concrete filled steel tube. *Engineering Mechanics, 19*(6), 1–5.

Cheng, Q. H., & Liu, Z. X. (2006). Chaotic load series forecasting based on MPMR. *Proceedings of the 2006 International Conference on Machine Learning and Cybernetics* (Vol. 2006, pp. 2868-2871). doi:10.1109/ICMLC.2006.259071

Dang, T. D., & Nguyen, H. N. (2009). Multi-class minimax probability machine. *KSE 2009 - The 1st International Conference on Knowledge and Systems Engineering* (pp. 150-153).

Dias, F. M., Antunes, A., & Mota, A. M. (2004). Artificial neural networks: A review of commercial hardware. *Engineering Applications of Artificial Intelligence, 17*(8), 945–952. doi:10.1016/j.engappai.2004.08.011

Evans, M. D. (1987). *Undrained Cyclic Triaxial Testing of Gravels: The Effect of Membrane Compliance.* Ph.D. Thesis, University of California, Berkeley.

Finn, W. D. L. (1998). Seismic Safety of Embankment Dams Development in Research and Practice 1988-1998. *Proceedings of a Specialty Conference on Geotechnical Earthquake Engineering and Soil Dynamics III* (pp. 812-853). Geotechnical Special Publication No. 75.

Finn, W. D. L., Ledbetter, R. H., & Beratan, L. L. (1986). Seismic Soil-Structure Interaction: Analysis and Centrifuge Model Studies. *Nuclear Engineering and Design, 94*(1), 53–66. doi:10.1016/0029-5493(86)90153-6

Finn, W. D. L., Ledbetter, R. H., & Wu, G. (1994). Liquefaction in Silty Soils: Design and Analysis. Ground Failures under Seismic Conditions. *Geotechnical Special Publication ASCE, 44*, 51–76.

France, J. W., Adams, T., Wilson, J., & Gillette, D. (2000). Soil Dynamics and Liquefaction. *Geotechnical Special Publication ASCE, 107.*

Georgy, M. E., & Barsoum, S. H. (2005). Artificial neural networks model for parametric estimating of construction project costs. *Journal of Engineering and Applied Sciences (Asian Research Publishing Network), 52*(6), 1050–1066.

Geyskens, P., Der Kiureghian, A., & Monteiro, P. (1993), Bayesian Updating of Model Parameters. *Structural Engineering Mechanics and Materials Report No. UCB/SEMM-93/06*, University of California, Berkeley.

Hamada, M., O'Rourke, T. D., & Yoshida, N. (1994). Liquefaction-Induced Large Ground Displacement. *Performance of Ground and Soil Structures during Earthquakes: Proceedings Thirteenth International Conference on Soil Mechanics and Foundation Engineering* (pp. 93-108). Japanese Society of Soil Mechanics and Foundation Engineering, Tokyo

Harder, L. F., Jr. (1977). *Liquefaction of Sand under Irregular Loading Conditions.* M.S. Thesis, University of California, Davis.

Harder, L. F., Jr. (1988). *Use of Penetration Tests to Determine the Cyclic Loading Resistance of Gravelly Soils During Earthquake Shaking.* Ph.D. Thesis, University of California, Berkeley.

Harder, L. F. Jr. (1997). Application of the Becker Penetration Test for Evaluating the Liquefaction Potential of Gravelly Soils. *Proc., NCEER Workshop on Evaluation of Liquefaction Resistance of Soils, NCEER-97-0022.*

Harder, L. F. Jr, & Boulanger, R. (1997). Application of Ks and Ka Correction Factors. *Proc., NCEER Workshop on Evaluation of Liquefaction Resistance of Soils, NCEER-970022.*

Hausmann, M. R. (1990). *Engineering Principals of Ground Modification.* McGraw Hill.

Hooshmand, R., & Joorabian, M. (2005). Application of artificial neural networks in controlling voltage and reactive power. *Scientia Iranica, 12*(1), 99–108.

Huang, K., Yang, H., King, I., & Lyu, M. R. (2006). Imbalanced learning with a biased minimax probability machine. *IEEE Transactions on Systems, Man, and Cybernetics. Part B, Cybernetics, 36*(4), 913–923. doi:10.1109/TSMCB.2006.870610 PMID:16903374

Huang, K., Yang, H., King, I., & Lyu, M. R. (2006). Maximizing sensitivity in medical diagnosis using biased minimax probability machine. *IEEE Transactions on Bio-Medical Engineering, 53*(5), 821–831. doi:10.1109/TBME.2006.872819 PMID:16686404

Ince, H., & Trafalis, T. B. (2006). Kernel methods for short-term portfolio management. *Expert Systems with Applications, 30*(3), 535–542. doi:10.1016/j.eswa.2005.10.008

Ishihara, K. (1985). Stability of Natural Deposits During Earthquakes. *Proceedings 11th International Conference on Soil Mechanics and Foundation Engineering* (Vol. 1, pp. 321-376), San Francisco.

Ishihara, K. (1993). Liquefaction and Flow Failure During Earthquakes: Thirty-Third Rankine Lecture. *Geotechnique, 43*(3), 351–415. doi:10.1680/geot.1993.43.3.351

Ishimara, K., & Yoshimine, M. (1992). Evaluation of Settlements in Sand Deposits Followiing Liquefaction during Earthquakes. *Soil and Foundation, 32*(1), 173–188. doi:10.3208/sandf1972.32.173

Jong, H. L., & Seed, R. B. (1988). *A Critical Investigation of Factors Affecting Seismic Pore Pressure Generation and Post-Liquefaction Flow Behavior of Saturated Soils.* Geotechnical Engineering Research Report No. SU/GT/88-01, Stanford University.

Juang, C. H., Yuan, H., Lee, D. H., & Lin, P. S. (2003). Simplified Cone Penetration Test-based Method for Evaluating Liquefaction Resistance of Soils. *Journal of Geotechnical and Geoenvironmental Engineering, 129*(1), 66–80. doi:10.1061/(ASCE)1090-0241(2003)129:1(66)

Koizumi, Y. (1966). Change in Density of Sand Subsoil caused by the Niigata Earthquake. *Soil and Foundation, 8*(2), 38–44. doi:10.3208/sandf1960.6.2_38

Kong, Y., Liu, X. W., & Zhang, S. (2009). Minimax Probability Machine Regression for wireless traffic short term forecasting. *Proceedings 1st UK-India International Workshop on Cognitive Wireless Systems, UKIWCWS.* doi:10.1109/UKIWCWS.2009.5749407

Kumar, R., Jain, S., Kumari, B., & Kumar, M. (2014). Protein sub-nuclear localization prediction using SVM and Pfam domain information. *PLoS ONE*, *9*(6), e98345. doi:10.1371/journal.pone.0098345 PMID:24897370

Kwok, J. T., Tsang, I. W. H., & Zurada, J. M. (2007). A class of single-class minimax probability machines for novelty detection. *IEEE Transactions on Neural Networks*, *18*(3), 778–785. doi:10.1109/TNN.2007.891191 PMID:17526343

Lee, H. T., Wang, M., Maev, R., & Maeva, E. (2003). A study on using scanning acoustic microscopy and neural network techniques to evaluate the quality of resistance spot welding. *International Journal of Advanced Manufacturing Technology*, *22*(9-10), 727–732. doi:10.1007/s00170-003-1599-9

Lee, S. M., Kim, D. S., & Park, J. S. (2007). A hybrid approach for real-time network intrusion detection systems. *Proceedings - 2007 International Conference on Computational Intelligence and Security, CIS* (pp. 712-715). doi:10.1109/CIS.2007.10

Liao, S. S. C., & Lum, K. Y. (1998). Statistical Analysis and Application of the Magnitude Scaling Factor in Liquefaction Analysis. *Geotechnical Earthquake Engineering and Soil Dynamics III*, *1*, 410–421.

Liao, S. S. C., Veneziano, D., & Whitman, R. V. (1988). Regression Models for Evaluating Liquefaction Probability. *Journal of Geotechnical Engineering*, *114*(4), 389–409. doi:10.1061/(ASCE)0733-9410(1988)114:4(389)

Liu, H. B., & Xiong, S. W. (2008). A kind of fast fuzzy support vector machines. *Journal of System Simulation*, *20*(24), 6664–6667.

Liu, Z., Xie, X., & Zhang, D. (2006). Predict chaotic time series using minimax probability machine regression. *Information Technology Journal*, *5*(3), 529–533. doi:10.3923/itj.2006.529.533

Maksoud, T. M. A., Atia, M. R., & Koura, M. M. (2003). Applications of artificial intelligence to grinding operations via neural networks. *Mining Science and Technology*, *7*(3), 361–387.

Mat Raffei, A. F., Asmuni, H., Hassan, R., & Othman, R. M. (2014). Fusing the line intensity profile and support vector machine for removing reflections in frontal RGB color eye images. *Information Sciences*, *276*, 104–122. doi:10.1016/j.ins.2014.02.049

Meiling, Y., Kunshi, Z., & Lianshou, L. (2005). Application of artificial neural network to the identification of quark and gluon jets. *International Journal of Modern Physics A*, *20*(32), 7603–7611. doi:10.1142/S0217751X05024365

Mitchell, J. K., Baxter, C. D. P., & Munson, T. C. (1995). Performance of Improved Ground during Earthquakes. Soil Improvement for Earthquake Hazard Mitigation, ASCE, 1-36.

Mu, X., & Zhou, Y. (2009). A novel Gaussian kernel function for minimax probability machine.

NCEER. (1997). *Proceedings of the NCEER Workshop on Evaluation of Liquefaction Resistance of Soils*. In Youd, T. L., & Idriss, I. M. (Eds.), Technical Report No. NCEER-970022.

Ng, J. K. C., Zhong, Y., & Yang, S. (2007). A comparative study of Minimax Probability Machine-based approaches for face recognition. *Pattern Recognition Letters, 28*(15), 1995–2002. doi:10.1016/j.patrec.2007.05.021

Nourani, V., Mogaddam, A. A., & Nadiri, A. O. (2008). An ANN-based model for spatiotemporal groundwater level forecasting. *Hydrological Processes, 22*(26), 5054–5066. doi:10.1002/hyp.7129

Ohsaki, Y. (1966). Niigata Earthquakes, 1964, Building Damage and Soil Conditions. *Soil and Foundation, 6*(2), 14–37. doi:10.3208/sandf1960.6.2_14

Olmi, R., Pelosi, G., Riminesi, C., & Tedesco, M. (2002). A neural network approach to real-time dielectric characterization of materials. *Microwave and Optical Technology Letters, 35*(6), 463–465. doi:10.1002/mop.10639

Pellaco, L., Costamagna, P., De Giorgi, A., Greco, A., Magistri, L., Moser, G., & Trucco, A. (2014, May 22). Fault diagnosis in fuel cell systems using quantitative models and support vector machines. *Electronics Letters, 50*(11), 824–826. doi:10.1049/el.2014.0565

Peng, X., & King, I. (2007). Large scale imbalanced classification with biased minimax probability machine. *IEEE International Conference on Neural Networks - Conference Proceedings* (pp. 1685-1690). doi:10.1109/IJCNN.2007.4371211

Peng, X., & King, I. (2009). A biased minimax probability machine-based scheme for relevance feedback in image retrieval. *Neurocomputing, 72*(7-9), 2046–2051. doi:10.1016/j.neucom.2008.11.020

Peng, X., Xu, D., & Shen, J. (2014). A twin projection support vector machine for data regression. *Neurocomputing, 138*, 131–141. doi:10.1016/j.neucom.2014.02.028

Poulos, S. J., Castro, G., & France, J. W. (1985). Liquefaction Evaluation Procedure. *Journal of Geotechnical Engineering, 111*(6), 772–792. doi:10.1061/(ASCE)0733-9410(1985)111:6(772)

Proceedings of the 2009 WRI Global Congress on Intelligent Systems (pp. 491-494).

Rauch, A. F., & Martin, J. R., II. (2001). Prediction the Maximum and Distribution of Displacements on Liquefaction-Induced Lateral Spreads. *Proceedings: Fourth International Conference on Recent Advances in Geotechnical Earthquake Engineering and Soil Dynamics*, San Diego, California.

Riemer, M. F. (1992). *The Effects of Testing Conditions on the Constitutive Behavior of Loose, Saturated Sands under Monotonic Loading.* Ph.D. Thesis, University of California, Berkeley.

Riemer, M. F., Seed, R. B., & Sadek, S. (1993). *The SRS/RFT Soil Evaluation Testing Program.* Geotechnical Report No. UCB/GT-93/01, University of California, Berkeley.

Robertson, P. K., & Wride, C. E. (1998). Evaluating Cyclic Liquefaction Potential Using The Cone Penetration Test. *Canadian Geotechnical Journal, 35*(3), 442–459. doi:10.1139/t98-017

Sancio, R. B., Bray, J. D., Riemer, M. F., & Durgunoglu, H. T. (2003). An Assessment of the Liquefaction Susceptibility of Adapazari Silt. *Proceedings Paper 172, Pacific Conference on Earthquake Engineering*, New Zealand.

Seed, H. B., & Idriss, I. M. (1982). *Ground motion and soil liquefaction during earthquakes. Monograph.* Oakland, California: Earthquake Engineering Research Institute.

Seed, H. B., Tokimatsu, K., Harder, L. F., & Chung, R. M. (1984). The Influence of SPT Procedures in Soil Liquefaction Resistance Evaluations. *Earthquake Engineering Research Center Report No. UCB/ EERC-84/15*, University of California, Berkeley.

Seed, H. B., Tokimatsu, K., Harder, L. F., & Chung, R. M. (1985). Influence of SPT Procedures in soil liquefaction resistance evaluations. *Journal of Geotechnical Engineering, 111*(12), 1425–1445. doi:10.1061/(ASCE)0733-9410(1985)111:12(1425)

Seed, R. B., Cetin, K. O., Der Kiureghian, A., Tokimatsu, K., Harder, L. F. Jr, Kayen, R. E., & Moss, R. E. S. (2002). SPT-Based Probabilistic and Deterministic Assessment of Seismic Soil Liquefaction Potential. *Journal of Geotechnical and Geoenvironmental Engineering.*

Seed, R. B., Cetin, K. O., Moss, R. E. S., Kammerer, A. M., Wu, J., Pestana, J. M., & Riemer, M. F. (2001). Recent Advances in Soil Liquefaction Engineering and Seismic Site Response Evaluation. *4th Int. Conf. Recent Advances in Geotechnical Earthquake Engineering and Soil Dynamics*, San Diego, California.

Seed, R. B., & Harder, L. F. (1990). SPT-Based Analysis of Cyclic Pore Pressure Generation And Undrained Residual Strength. *H. B. Seed Memorial Symposium* (Vol. 2, pp. 351-376). BiTech Publishing, Ltd., Berkeley, California.

Shan, Z. C., Lin, C. S., & Xiang, Q. (2008). Chaos prediction of wave hydrodynamic pressure signals based on local support vectors machine. *Journal of System Simulation, 20*(23), 6470–6472.

Shibata, T., & Teparaksa, W. (1988). Evaluation of Liquefaction Potentials of Soils using Cone Penetration Tests. *Soil and Foundation, 28*(2), 49–60. doi:10.3208/sandf1972.28.2_49

Srivastava, S., Srivastava, K., Sharma, R. S., & Raj, K. H. (2004). Modelling of hot closed die forging of an automotive piston with ANN for intelligent manufacturing. *Journal of Scientific and Industrial Research, 63*(12), 997–1005.

Sun, J., Bai, Y., Luo, J., & Dang, J. (2009). Modelling of a chaotic time series using a modified minimax probability machine regression. *The Chinese Journal of Physiology, 47*(4), 491–501.

Sun, J. C. (2007). Prediction of chaotic time series based on modified minimax probability machine regression. *Chinese Physics, 16*(11), 3262–3270. doi:10.1088/1009-1963/16/11/020

Sun, X., Li, L., & Wang, Z. (2010). Using manifold learning and minimax probability machine for face recognition. *Proceedings 2nd International Conference on Modeling, Simulation, and Visualization Methods* (pp. 229-232). doi:10.1109/WMSVM.2010.46

Takeda, A., & Kanamori, T. (2014). Using financial risk measures for analyzing generalization performance of machine learning models. *Neural Networks, 57*, 29–38. doi:10.1016/j.neunet.2014.05.006 PMID:24914491

Tandon, V., & El Mounayri, H. (2001). A novel artificial neural networks force model for end milling. *International Journal of Advanced Manufacturing Technology, 18*(10), 693–700. doi:10.1007/s001700170011

Tian, Y., Zhang, Q., & Ping, Y. (2014). Large-scale linear nonparallel support vector machine solver. *Neurocomputing, 38*, 114–119. doi:10.1016/j.neucom.2014.02.032 PMID:24317341

Toprak, S., Holzer, T. L., Bennett, M. J., & Tinsley, J. C. (1999). CPT and SPT-based Probabilistic Assessment of Liquefaction Potential. *Proceedings of Seventh U.S.-Japan Workshop on Earthquake Resistant Design of Lifeline Facilities and Countermeasures Against Liquefaction.*

Torija, A. J., Ruiz, D. P., & Ramos Ridao, T. F. (2014). A tool for urban soundscape evaluation applying Support Vector Machines for developing a soundscape classification model. *The Science of the Total Environment, 482-483*(1), 440–451. doi:10.1016/j.scitotenv.2013.07.108 PMID:24007752

Trafalis, T. B., Santosa, B., & Richman, M. B. (2006). Learning networks for tornado detection. *International Journal of General Systems, 35*(1), 93–107. doi:10.1080/03081070500502850

Tu, L., & Zhang, S. (2009). Study on VOC classification approach based on MPM. *Chinese Society of Agricultural Machiner, 40*(3), 184–188.

Wang, D. C., Wang, C. X., Zhu, T. Y., & Qin, J. (2010). Support vector machines based algorithm for the disastrous weather forecast. *Journal of Wuhan University of Technology, 32*(24), 121–124.

Wang, F., Yao, X., & Han, J. (2007). Minimax Probability Machine multialgorithmic fusion for iris recognition. *Information Technology Journal, 6*(7), 1043–1049. doi:10.3923/itj.2007.1043.1049

Wang, F., Yao, X., & Han, J. (2008). Improving iris recognition performance via multi-instance fusion at the score level. *Chinese Optics Letters, 6*(11), 824–826. doi:10.3788/COL20080611.0824

Wang, J., Wang, S. T., Deng, Z. H., & Qi, Y. S. (2010). Image thresholding based on minimax probability criterion. *Pattern Recognition and Artificial Intelligence, 23*(6), 880–884.

Wang, W. (1979). *Some Findings in Soil Liquefaction.* Beijing: Research Report, Water Conservancy and Hydroelectric Power Scientiific Research Institute.

Wang, X., Wong, B. S., & Tan, C. (2010). Recognition of welding defects in radiographic images by using support vector machine classifier. *Research Journal of Applied Sciences. Engineering and Technology, 2*(3), 295–301.

Wang, Y., & Han, J. (2006). Study on iris image classification approach based on minimax probability machine. *Journal of Xi'an Jiaotong University, 40*(6), 651–654.

Wyczółkowski, R., & Wysoglad, B. (2007). An optimization of heuristic model of water supply network. *Computer Assisted Mechanics and Engineering Sciences, 14*(4), 767–776.

Xiao, G., Jiang, Y., Song, G., & Jiang, J. (2010). Support-vector-machine tree-based domain knowledge learning toward automated sports video classification. *Optical Engineering (Redondo Beach, Calif.), 49*(12).

Xu, Z., King, I., & Lyu, M. R. (2007). Feature selection based on minimum error minimax probability machine. *International Journal of Pattern Recognition and Artificial Intelligence, 21*(8), 1279–1292. doi:10.1142/S0218001407005958

Yang, L., & Ju, R. (2014). A DC programming approach for feature selection in the Minimax Probability Machine. *International Journal of Computational Intelligence Systems, 7*(1), 12–24. doi:10.1080/187 56891.2013.864471

Ye, Q., Ye, N., & Yin, T. (2014). Enhanced multi-weight vector projection support vector machine. *Pattern Recognition Letters, 42*(1), 91–100. doi:10.1016/j.patrec.2014.02.006

Youd, T. L., Idriss, I. M., Andrus, R. D., Arango, I., Castro, G., Christian, J. T., & Dobry, R..... Stokoe, K. H. (1997). *Summary Paper, Proc., NCEER Workshop on Evaluation of Liquefaction Resistance of Soils,* NCEER97-0022.

Youd, T. L., Idriss, I. M., & Ronald Andrus, D., Ignacio Arango, Gonzalo Castro, John Christian, T., Richardo Dobry,....Kenneth Stokoe II, H. (2001). Liquefaction Resistance of Soils. Summary Report from the 1996 NCEER and 1998 NCEER/NSF Workshops on Evaluation of Liquefaction Resistance of Soils. *Journal of Geotechnical and Geoenvironmental Engineering, 124*(10).

Youd, T. L., & Noble, S. K. (1997). Liquefaction Criteria Based on Statistical and Probabilistic Analyses. *Proceedings of the NCEER Workshop on Evaluation of Liquefaction Resistance of Soils* (pp. 201-205).

Zhang, S. W., Hao, L. Y., & Zhang, T. H. (2014). Prediction of protein-protein interaction with pairwise kernel support vector machine. *International Journal of Molecular Sciences, 15*(2), 3220–3233. doi:10.3390/ijms15023220 PMID:24566145

Zhenguo, C., Hongde, R., & Xingjing, D. (2008). Minimax probability machine classifier with feature extraction by kernel pca for intrusion detection. *International Conference on Wireless Communications, Networking and Mobile Computing,* WiCOM 2008.

Zhou, Y., Wang, R., & Xia, K. (2011). Nonlinear prediction of fast fading channel based on minimax probability machine. *Proceedings of the 2011 6th IEEE Conference on Industrial Electronics and Applications, ICIEA 2011*(451-454). Beijing, China. doi:10.1109/ICIEA.2011.5975626

KEY TERMS AND DEFINITIONS

Artificial Neural Network: Artificial Neural Networks are the modeling technique which was inspired from the central nervous system, capable of machine learning and pattern recognition.

Classification: It is defined as the action of categorizing something.

Earthquake: An earthquake is the sudden shaking of earth's crust which leads to the great destruction in life and property.

Liquefaction: Liquefaction is the phenomenon in which the strength and the stiffness of the soil get reduced.

Minimax Probability Machine: It is defined as the process of building the classifiers by minimizing the maximum probability of misclassification.

Prediction: Prediction is defined as the action of forecasting something earlier.

Shear Wave Velocity: The velocity (ν) of a shear wave is equal to the square root of the ratio of shear modulus (G), to density (ρ) of the medium, $v = \sqrt{G/\rho}$.

Support Vector Machine: Support Vector Machines are supervised learning machine techniques that analyze data either for the prediction or classification purposes.

Chapter 7
Swarm–Based Mean–Variance Mapping Optimization (MVMO^S) for Solving Non–Convex Economic Dispatch Problems

Truong Hoang Khoa
Universiti Teknologi Petronas, Malaysia

Balbir Singh Mahinder Singh
Universiti Teknologi Petronas, Malaysia

Pandian M. Vasant
Universiti Teknologi Petronas, Malaysia

Vo Ngoc Dieu
HCMC University of Technology, Vietnam

ABSTRACT

The practical Economic Dispatch (ED) problems have non-convex objective functions with complex constraints due to the effects of valve point loadings, multiple fuels, and prohibited zones. This leads to difficulty in finding the global optimal solution of the ED problems. This chapter proposes a new swarm-based Mean-Variance Mapping Optimization (MVMO^S) for solving the non-convex ED. The proposed algorithm is a new population-based meta-heuristic optimization technique. Its special feature is a mapping function applied for the mutation. The proposed MVMO^S is tested on several test systems and the comparisons of numerical obtained results between MVMO^S and other optimization techniques are carried out. The comparisons show that the proposed method is more robust and provides better solution quality than most of the other methods. Therefore, the MVMO^S is very favorable for solving non-convex ED problems.

INTRODUCTION

The economic dispatch (ED) is one of essential optimization problems in power system operation. Its objective is to allocate the real power output of the thermal generating units at minimum fuel production cost while satisfying all units and system contraints (Xia & Elaiw, 2010).

Traditionally, the cost function objective of the ED problem is the quadratic function approximations and this problem is solved by using mathematical programming methods such as lambda iteration method, Newton's method, gradient search, dynamic programming (Wollenberg & Wood, 1996), linear

DOI: 10.4018/978-1-4666-8291-7.ch007

programming (Parikh & Chattopadhyay, 1996), non-linear programming (Nanda, Hari, & Kothari, 1994), quadratic programming (Fan & Zhang, 1998), and Maclaurin series-based Lagrangian (MSL) method (Hemamalini & Simon, 2009). Among of them, the linear programming methods have fast computation time with reliable solution. However, they suffers the main disadvantage associated with the piecewise linear cost approximation. The non-linear programming methods suffer problems in convergence and algorithm complexity. The Newton-based algorithms have difficulty in handling a large number of inequality constraints (Al-Sumait, Al-Othman, & Sykulski, 2007). MSL method can directly deal with the non-convex ED problem by using the Maclaurin expansion of non-convex terms in the objective function. Although this method can quickly find a solution for the problem, the obtained solution quality is not high, especially for the large-scale systems. In general, the conventional methods are not capable for solving non-convex ED problems (Dieu, Schegner, & Ongsakul, 2013).

The quadratic function is not exactly representing the practical ED problem which can contain non-convex and nonlinear objective and constraints. The effects of valve point loadings, multiple fuels, or prohibited operating zones can cause the input-output curve of thermal generators more complicated. For this reason, the practical ED problem should be formulated as non-convex objective function. More advanced methods based on artificial intelligence have been previously developed to deal with ED problems such as Hopfield neural network (HNN) (Lee, Sode-Yome, & Park, 1998; P Vasant, Ganesan, Elamvazuthi, et al., 2012), evolutionary programming (EP) (Sinha, Chakrabarti, & Chattopadhyay, 2003), differential evolution (DE) (Noman & Iba, 2008), genetic algorithm (GA) (Chiang, 2005), ant colony optimization (ACO) (Pothiya, Ngamroo, & Kongprawechnon, 2010), artificial immune system (AIS) (Panigrahi, Yadav, Agrawal, & Tiwari, 2007), biogeography-based optimisation (BBO) (Padmanabhan, Sivakumar, Jasper, & Victoire, 2011), particle swarm optimization (PSO) (Ganesan, Vasant, & Elamvazuthy, 2012; Mahor, Prasad, & Rangnekar, 2009; P Vasant, Ganesan, & Elamvazuthi, 2012), and artificial bee colony (ABC) algorithm (Le, Vo, & Vasant). Among of these methods, the HNN method based on the minimisation of its energy function can be only applied to the convex optimization problems. This method can be easily implemented on large-scale systems but it suffers long computational time and local optimum solution (Dieu, Schegner, et al., 2013). The GA method is critically dependent on the fitness function and sensitive to the mutation and crossover rates, the encoding scheme of its bits, and the gradient of the search space curve leading toward solutions. The EP method may prove to be very effective in solving nonlinear ED problems without any restrictions on the shape of the cost curves. However, a solution by EP method may get trapped in a suboptimal state for large-scale problems. In general, these methods also involve a large number of iterations and their optimal solutions are susceptible to the related control parameters (J.-B. Park, Lee, Shin, & Lee, 2005). The DE method is a population-based stochastic parallel search technique which has the advantages such as simple and compact structure, few control parameters, and high convergence characteristic. However, there is no guaranty for this method to always get optimal solution. Moreover, the DE method suffers slow computation when dealing with large-scale problems. Recently, PSO is the most popular method applied for solving the ED problems. It can be applied to global optimization problems with non-convex or non-smooth objective functions. Although this method can provide high-quality solutions with short computational time and stable convergence property (Eberhart & Shi, 1998), it seems to be susceptible to the tuning of some weights or parameters. The PSO method is continuously improved for dealing with large-scale and complex problems in power systems. Although these artificial intelligence methods do not always guarantee to find the best global optimal solution in finite computational time, they can find near global optimal solution for non-convex optimization problems.

Besides the single mentioned methods, hybrid methods have been also developed for solving the non-convex ED problems such as combination of evolutionary programming with sequential quadratic programming (EP-SQP) (Attaviriyanupap, Kita, Tanaka, & Hasegawa, 2002), integration particle swarm optimization with sequential quadratic programming (PSO-SQP) (Victoire & Jeyakumar, 2004), hybrid technique integrating the uniform design with the genetic algorithm (UHGA) (He, Wang, & Mao, 2008), self-tuning hybrid differential evolution (self-tuning HDE) (Wang, Chiou, & Liu, 2007), and fuzzy adaptive particle swarm optimization algorithm with Nelder–Mead simplex search (FAPSO-NM) (Niknam, 2010), hybrid genetic algorithm, pattern search and sequential quadratic programming (GA-PS-SQP) (Alsumait, Sykulski, & Al-Othman, 2010). These hybrid methods become powerful search methods for obtaining higher solution quality due to using the advantages of each element method to improve their search ability for the complex problems. Nevertheless, they may be slower and more complicated than the element methods because of combination of several operations.

The methods mentioned above are the meta-heuristic search methods which are based on a population for searching an optimal solution for the problems (Pandian Vasant & Global, 2013). They are so-called "population-based stochastic optimization techniques". Mean-variance mapping optimization (MVMO) is a novel optimization algorithm which has been conceived and developed by István Erlich in 2010 (I. Erlich, Venayagamoorthy, & Worawat, 2010). This algorithm also falls into the category of the so-called "population-based stochastic optimization techniques". Recently, the extensions of MVMO has been developed which named swarm based mean-variance mapping optimization (MVMO^S) (Rueda & Erlich, 2013a). Unlike the single particle MVMO, the search process of MVMO^S is started with a set of particles. In addition, two parameters of MVMO including the scaling factor and variable increment parameters have been extended to enhance the mapping. Hence, the ability for global search of MVMO^S is found to be more powerful than the original version.

In this book chapter, MVMO^S is proposed as a novel optimization technique for solving the non-convex economic dispatch problems including valve point loading effects, multiple fuels and prohibited operating zone.

BACKGROUND

Economic Dispatch

The demand for electricity has grown due to the rapid economic development and gradual increase in the world's population. At the same time, the price of fossil fuels is highly volatile due to facing depletion. Coal, oil and natural gas are the popular choices for thermal generating units. These fuels represents irreplaceable natural resources and conservation is used as a way to increase energy efficiency. Hence, the economical operations of the electrical power systems become more importance. The problem of economic allocation of generating units has been concerned by engineers since early 1920's (Happ, 1977). In addition, the issues of saving fuel cost is taken into account as well. The process of allocating an amount of real power output of thermal generating units to meet the required power load demand at the minimum fuel cost is called as economic dispatch (ED). The ED problem was investigated by the digital computer in 1954 and is being used to date (Happ, 1977). Over the past decades, there have been a lot of various methods have been used for solving ED problems. In general, there are three main categories including methods based on mathematical programming (classical calculus -based techniques), methods based on artificial intelligence and hybrid methods. The pratical generation problems are considered such as valve point loadings, multiple fuels, or prohibited zones make the ED become the non-convex problems which is more diffcult to be solved. The non-convex optimization problem is still a challenge for solution methods. Hence, there is always a need for developing new techniques for solving non-convex problems, especially for large-scale systems.

Mean-Variance Mapping Optimization

Mean-variance mapping optimization (MVMO) is a novel optimization algorithm which has been developed by István Erlich in 2010 (I. Erlich et al., 2010). This algorithm falls into the category of the so-called "population-based stochastic optimization technique". The similarities between MVMO and the other known stochastic algorithms are in three evolutionary operators including selection, mutation and crossover. The key feature of MVMO is a special mapping function which applied for mutating the offspring based on mean-variance of the n-best dynamic population saved in an archive.

So far MVMO has been successfully applied for solving different power system optimization problems such as:

- The optimal reactive power dispatch problem (Nakawiro, Erlich, & Rueda, 2011).
- The optimal of reactive sources in wind farm (I Erlich, Nakawiro, & Martinez, 2011).
- The optimal transmission expansion planning (Pringles & Rueda, 2012).
- The identification of Gaussian mixture models (Gonzalez-Longatt, Rueda, Erlich, Bogdanov, & Villa, 2012).
- The identification of dynamic equivalents (Cepeda, Rueda, & Erlich, 2012).

The extensions of MVMO which named swarm based mean-variance mapping optimization (MVMO[S]) (Rueda & Erlich, 2013a), has been developed to enhance the global search ability of MVMO. MVMO[S] has also been successfully applied in some power system optimization problems as:

- Optimal dispatch of reactive power sources (Rueda & Erlich, 2013b).
- Short-term transmission expansion planning (Rueda Torres & Erlich, 2013).

PROBLEM FORMULATION

The purpose of the ED problem is to minimize the total cost of the fuel used in thermal generating units of a system while satisfying various constraints including system and unit operating constraints. The non-convex ED problems are considered as follows (Dieu, Schegner, et al., 2013):

- ED problem with valve point effects.
- ED problem with multiple fuels.
- ED problem with both valve point effects and multiple fuels.
- ED problem with prohibited operating zones.

The objective function of the ED problem is represented as:

$$\text{Minimize } F_T = \sum_{i=1}^{N} F_i(P_i) \; i = 1, 2, \ldots, N$$

Generally, the total fuel cost of a thermal generating unit is considered as a quadratic function as (Wollenberg & Wood, 1996):

$$F_i(P_i) = a_i + b_i P_i + c_i P_i^2 \tag{2}$$

ED Problem with Valve Point Effects (VPE)

In this study, the valve point effects are considered as practical operation of generators. The VPE causes the fuel cost function highly nonlinear with multiple local optimum where the fuel cost function is described as the superposition of sinusoidal functions and quadratic functions. The model of ED problem with VPE is given as equation (3) (Sinha et al., 2003):

$$F_i(P_i) = a_i + b_i P_i + c_i P_i^2 + \left| e_i \times \sin(f_i \times (P_{i,\min} - P_i)) \right| \tag{3}$$

There are two constraints involved in ED problems that must be satisfied throughout the optimization process as follows:

Real Power Balance Equation: The total active power output of generating units must be equal to total active load demand plus power loss:

$$\sum_{i=1}^{N} P_i = P_D + P_L \tag{4}$$

The power loss P_L can be approximately calculated by Kron's formula (Wollenberg & Wood, 1996):

$$P_L = \sum_{i=1}^{N} \sum_{j=1}^{N} P_i B_{ij} P_j + \sum_{i=1}^{N} B_{0i} P_i + B_{00} \tag{5}$$

Generator Capacity Limits: The active power output of generating units should be within between their upper and lower bounds by:

$$P_{i,\min} \leq P_i \leq P_{i,\max} \tag{6}$$

ED Problem with Multiple Fuels (MF)

The ED problem with MF has piecewise quadratic cost functions which is a non-convex and complicated optimization problem since it contains the discontinuous values at each boundary, forming multiple local optimal. The fuel cost function of unit i with MF is represented by (Lee et al., 1998):

$$F_i(P_i) = \begin{cases} a_{i1} + b_{i1}P_i + c_{i1}P_i^2, \text{fuel 1}, \ P_{i,\min} \leq P_i \leq P_{i1} \\ a_{i2} + b_{i2}P_i + c_{i2}P_i^2, \ \text{fuel 2}, \ P_{i1} < P_i \leq P_{i2} \\ \dots \\ a_{ij} + b_{ij}P_i + c_{ij}P_i^2, \ \text{fuel } j, \ P_{ij-1} < P_i \leq P_{i,\max} \end{cases} \tag{7}$$

The objective of the ED problem with MF is to minimize the total cost (1) where the fuel cost function for each generator is given in (7) subject to the real power balance constraint (4) and generator capacity limits (6).

ED Problem with VPE and MF

The thermal generating units can be supplied with multiple fuel sources and their boilers have also valve points for controlling their power outputs. The solution of the practical ED problem is more accurate when the cost curve includes both VPE and MF. The fuel cost function of each generating unit is represented as follows (Chiang, 2005):

$$F_i(P_i) = \begin{cases} a_{i1} + b_{i1}P_i + c_{i1}P_i^2 + \left| e_{i1}.\sin(f_{i1}.(P_{i1}^{\min} - P_{i1})) \right|, \text{for fuel 1}, P_i^{\min} \leq P_i \leq P_{i1} \\ a_{i2} + b_{i2}P_i + c_{i2}P_i^2 + \left| e_{i2}.\sin(f_{i2}.(P_{i2}^{\min} - P_{i2})) \right|, \text{for fuel 2}, P_{i1} \leq P_i \leq P_{i2} \\ \vdots \\ a_{ik} + b_{ik}P_i + c_{ik}P_i^2 + \left| e_{ik}.\sin(f_{ik}.(P_{ik}^{\min} - P_{ik})) \right|, \text{for fuel } k, P_{ik-1} \leq P_i \leq P_i^{\max} \end{cases} \tag{8}$$

The objective of the ED problem with MF is to minimize the total cost (1) where the fuel cost function for each generator is given in (8) subject to the real power balance constraint (4) and generator capacity limits (6).

ED Problem with Prohibited Operating Zones (POZ)

Prohibited Operating Zones

Because of the prohibited operating zones, the whole operating region of a generating unit will be broken into several isolated feasible sub-regions and their feasible operating points should be located at one of the sub-regions as follows (Dieu, Schegner, et al., 2013):

$$P_i \in \begin{cases} P_{i,\min} \leq P_i \leq P_{i1}^l \\ P_{ik-1}^u \leq P_i \leq P_{ik}^l, \ k = 2, ..., n_i \ \ ; \ \forall i \ \in \Omega \\ P_{in_i}^u \leq P_i \leq P_{i,\max} \end{cases} \tag{9}$$

Equation (9) indicates that if unit i has n_i POZ, it will have $(n_i + 1)$ feasible disjoint operating regions which will form a non-convex set.

The fuel cost curve has discontinuous characteristics which will include additional constraints on the unit operating range.

Ramp Rate Constraints

The increased or decreased power output of a unit from its initial operating point to the next one should not exceed its ramp up and down rate limits. The ramp rate constraints are determined by:

$$P_i - P_{i0} \leq UR_i, \text{ if generation increases} \tag{10}$$

$$P_{i0} - P_i \leq DR_i, \text{ if generation decreases} \tag{11}$$

For the units with no POZ, its fuel cost function can be a quadratic function (2) or a quadratic function with VPE (3). The equality and inequality constraints for this problem include the real power balance constraint (4), generator capacity limits (6).

MEAN-VARIANCE MAPPING OPTIMIZATION

Original Mean - Variance Mapping Optimization (MVMO)

The similarities between MVMO and the other known stochastic algorithms lie in three evolutionary operators those are selection, mutation and crossover. The key feature of MVMO is a special mapping function which applied for mutating the offspring based on mean-variance of the solutions stored in the archive. The flowchart of MVMO are shown in Figure 1.

The mean $\overline{x}_i$ and variance v_i are calculated as follows (I. Erlich et al., 2010):

$$\overline{x}_i = \frac{1}{n} \sum_{j=1}^{n} x_i(j) \tag{12}$$

$$v_i = \frac{1}{n} \sum_{j=1}^{n} (x_i(j) - \overline{x}_i)^2 \tag{13}$$

Figure 1. MVMO flowchart

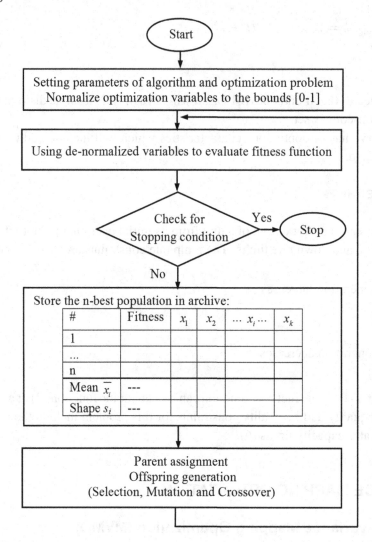

where $j = 1,2,..., n$ (n is population size).

The transformation of x_i^* to x_i via mapping function is depicted as Figure 2. The transformation mapping function, h, is calculated by the mean $\bar{x}$ and shape variables s_{i1} and s_{i2} as follows (I. Erlich et al., 2010):

$$h(\bar{x}_i, s_{i1}, s_{i2}, x) = \bar{x}_i.(1 - e^{-x.s_{i1}}) + (1 - \bar{x}_i).e^{-(1-x).s_{i2}} \tag{14}$$

where,

$$s_i = -\ln(v_i).f_s \tag{15}$$

Figure 2. Variable mapping

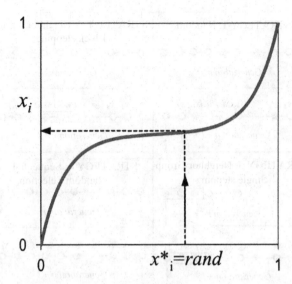

The scaling factor f_s is a MVMO parameter which allows for controlling the search process during iteration. s_i is the shape variable.

All variables are initialized within the limit range [0,1]. The output of mapping function is always inside [0,1] . However, the function evaluation is carried out always in the original scales.

MVMO is a single-agent search algorithm because it uses a single parent-offspring in each iteration. Therefore, the number of fitness evaluations is identical to the number of iterations.

Among k variables of the optimization problem, m variables are selected for mutation operation. There are four strategies for selecting the variables as illustrated in Figure 3:

Strategy 1: Selecting variables randomly.
Strategy 2: Selection of neighbor group: moving the group of variables forward in multiple steps.
Strategy 3: Selection of neighbor group: moving the group of variables forward in single steps.
Strategy 4: Sequential selection of the first variable and the selection of the rest randomly (or) and random selection for the rest.

Extention of MVMO – Swarmed Based Mean-Variance Mapping Optimization (MVMO^S)

The MVMO-algorithm is extended with two important parameters including *variable f_s factor* and *variable increment Δd* , and start the search with a set of particles.

Variable f$_s$ Factor

In (15), the factor f_s allows the modification of the shape factor calculated from the variance. The extension of f_s factor is for the need of exploring the search global space at the beginning whereas, at the end of the iterations, the focus should be on the exploitation. It is determined by (Rueda & Erlich, 2013a):

Figure 3. Strategies of variable selection (m=3)

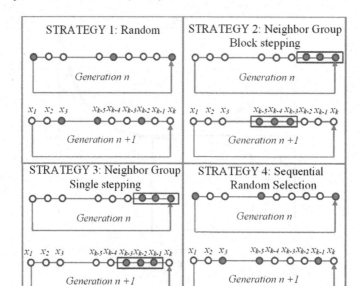

$$f_s = f_s^* \cdot \left(1 + rand()\right) \tag{16}$$

where,

$$f_s^* = f_{s\_ini}^* + \left(\frac{i}{i_{final}}\right)^2 \left(f_{s\_final}^* - f_{s\_ini}^*\right) \tag{17}$$

rand () is a random number with the bounds [0, 1].

In (17), the variable i represents the iteration number, $f_{s\_ini}^*$ is the initial and $f_{s\_final}^*$ is final values of f_s^*.

For the more the better search ability, the initial and final values of f_s^* it is recommended that $f_{s\_ini}^* < 1$ and $f_{s\_final}^* > 1$. The suggested range of initial values of f_s^* is from 0.9 to 1.0 and for final values of f_s^* is from 1.0 to 3.0 .When $f_{s\_final}^* = f_{s\_ini}^* = 1$, the option for controlling the f_s factor is not used.

Variable Increment Δd

The extension of variable increment Δd is used for the asymmetric characteristic of the mapping function. The factor Δd is used in the MVMO algorithm as presented in (18) (Rueda & Erlich, 2013a):

At the start of the algorithm, the initial values of d_i (typically between 1-5) are set for all variables. At every iteration, if $s_i > d_i$, d_i will be multiplied by Δd leads to increased d_i. In case $s_i < d_i$, the current d_i is divided by Δd which is always greater than 1.0 resulting in reduced value of d_i. Therefore, d_i will always oscillate around the current shape factor s_i. Furthermore, Δd is randomly varied around the value $(1 + \Delta d_0)$ with the amplitude of Δd_0 adjusted in accordance to (19), where Δd_0 can be allowed to decrease from 0.4 to 0.01.

$$\Delta d_0 = \Delta d_0^{ini} + \left(\frac{i}{i_{final}}\right)^2 \left(\Delta d_0^{final} - \Delta d_0^{ini}\right) \tag{19}$$

Swarm Variant of MVMO

The search process of the MVMO^S is started with a set of particles where each has its own memory defined in terms of the corresponding archive and mapping function. Initially, each particle performs m steps independently to collect a set of reliable individual solutions. Then, the particles start to communicate and to exchange information.

It is not worth to follow particles which are very close to each other since this would entail redundancy. To avoid closeness between particles (i.e. redundancy), the normalized distance of each particle's local best solution $x^{lbest,i}$ to the global best x^{gbest} is calculated by: (Rueda & Erlich, 2013a)

$$D_i = \sqrt{\frac{1}{n} \sum_{k=1}^{n} (x_k^{gbest} - x_k^{lbest,i})^2} \tag{20}$$

where, n denotes the number of optimization variables.

The i-th particle is discarded from the optimization process if the distance D_i is less than a certain user defined threshold D_{min}.

Algorithm 1. (18)

```
s_i1 = s_i2 = s_i
if s_i > 0 then
Δd = (1 + Δd_0) + 2 . Δd_0 (rand() - 0.5)
    if s_i > d_i
        d_i = d_i . Δd
    else
        d_i = d_i / Δd
    end if
    if rand() ≥ 0.5 then
        s_i1 = s_i  ;   s_i2 = d_i
        else
        s_i1 = d_i  ;   s_i2 = s_i
        end if
end if
```

A zero threshold means that all particles are considered throughout the whole process whereas a unit threshold will result in dropping all particles except the global best. In this case after $(m^*n_p + n_p)$ fitness evaluations only one particle, the gbest, remains. Intermediate threshold values entail better adaptation to any optimization problem.

After an independent evaluation, if the particle is further considered, the global best solution guides the search by assigning x^{gbest}, instead of $x^{lbest,i}$, as parent for every particle's offspring. The remaining steps are identical with those of the classical MVMO. A subset of dimensions in the parent vector is directly inherited whereas the remaining dimensions are selected and mutated based on local statistics (mean and variance) of the particle via mapping function.

The flowchart of MVMO^S is depicted in Figure 4, where i and k are the function evaluation and particle counters, respectively; m and n_p are for maximum number of independent runs and total number of particles, respectively.

IMPLEMENTATION OF MVMO^S TO NONCONVEX ED PROBLEMS

Calculation of Power Output for Slack Unit

To guarantee that the equality constraint (4) is always satisfied, a slack generating unit is randomly selected from N generating units and therefore its power output will be dependent on the power outputs of remaining N-1 generating units in the system. The method for calculation of power output for the slack unit is given in (Kuo, 2008). The power output of the slack unit is as follows:

$$P_s = P_D + P_L - \sum_{\substack{i=1 \\ i \neq s}}^{N} P_i \tag{21}$$

where s is a random unit selected from N units

The transmission power loss in (5) is rewritten by considering P_S as an unknown variable

$$P_L = B_{ss}P_s^2 + \left(2\sum_{\substack{i=1 \\ i \neq s}}^{N} B_{si}P_i + B_{0s} \right) P_s + \sum_{\substack{i=1 \\ i \neq s}}^{N}\sum_{\substack{i=1 \\ i \neq s}}^{N} P_i B_{ij} P_j + \sum_{\substack{i=1 \\ i \neq s}}^{N} B_{0i}P_i + B_{00} \tag{22}$$

Substituting (22) into (21), a quadratic equation is obtained as follows:

$$A \times P_S^2 + B \times P_S + C = 0 \tag{23}$$

where A, B and C are given by:

$$A = B_{ss} \tag{24}$$

Figure 4. MVMO^S flowchart

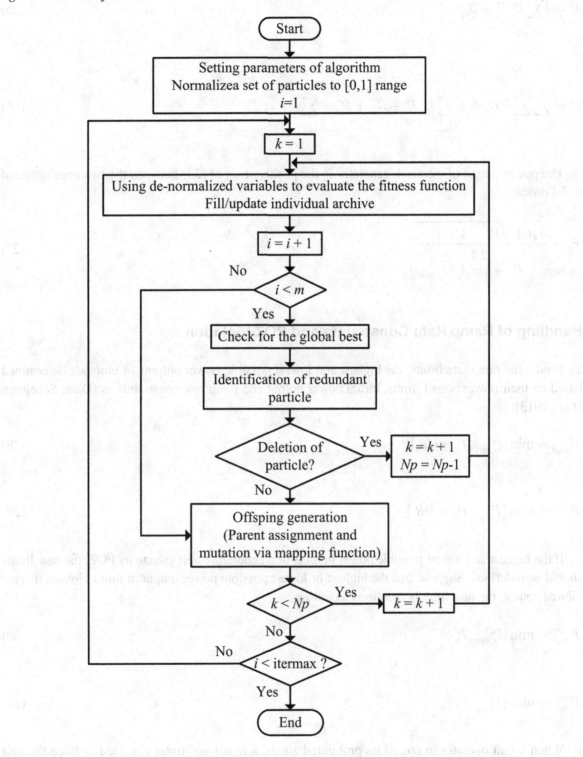

$$B = 2\sum_{\substack{i=1 \\ i \neq s}}^{N} B_{si} P_i + B_{0s} - 1 \tag{25}$$

$$C = \sum_{\substack{i=1 \\ i \neq s}}^{N} \sum_{\substack{i=1 \\ i \neq s}}^{N} P_i B_{ij} P_j + \sum_{\substack{i=1 \\ i \neq s}}^{N} B_{0i} P_i + B_{00} + P_D - \sum_{\substack{i=1 \\ i \neq s}}^{N} P_i \tag{26}$$

The power output of the slack generator is the positive root of (23) between the two ones obtained as follows:

$$P_s = \frac{-B \pm \sqrt{B^2 - 4 \times A \times C}}{2A} \tag{27}$$
$$\text{where} \quad B^2 - 4 \times A \times C \geq 0$$

Handling of Ramp Rate Constraints and POZ Violation

To handle the ramp rate limits, the highest and lowest possible power outputs of units are determined based on their power output limits, initial power output and ramp rate constraints as (Dieu, Schegner, et al., 2013):

$$P_{i,\text{high}} = \min\{P_{i,\max}, P_{i0} + UR_i\} \tag{28}$$

$$P_{i,\text{low}} = \max\{P_{i,\min}, P_{i0} - DR_i\} \tag{29}$$

If the highest and lowest possible power outputs of a generating unit violate its POZ, the new limits should be redefined. Suppose that the highest or lowest possible power output of unit i violates its prohibited zone k, the new limit is redefined as follows:

$$P_{i,\text{high}}^{\text{new}} = \min\{P_{i,\text{high}}, P_{ik}^l\} \tag{30}$$

$$P_{i,\text{low}}^{\text{new}} = \max\{P_{i,\text{low}}, P_{ik}^u\} \tag{31}$$

When a unit operates in one of its prohibited zones, a repairing strategy is used to force the unit either to move toward the lower bound or upper bound of that zone. For making a decision based on the operating point of a unit located in one of its prohibited zones, the middle point of each prohibited zone $P_{ik}{}^m$ is firstly determined by:

$$P_{ik}^m = \frac{P_{ik}^l + P_{ik}^u}{2} \tag{32}$$

This middle point divides a prohibited zone in two sub-zones, the left and right prohibited sub-zones with respect to the point. Therefore, the operating point P_i of unit i violating its prohibited zone k will be adjusted by:

$$P_i^{new} = \begin{cases} P_{ik}^l & \text{if } P_i \leq P_{ik}^m \\ P_{ik}^u & \text{if } P_i > P_{ik}^m \end{cases} \tag{33}$$

The initial solution should be also checked for POZ violation. If the violation is found, the repairing strategy is used to move the operating point to a feasible region. The fitness function FT_d to be minimized corresponding to each particle for the considered problem is calculated:

$$FT_d = \sum_{i=1}^N F_i(x_{id}) + K_s \times \left(P_{sd} - P_s^{\lim} \right)^2 \tag{34}$$

where K_s is the penalty factor for the slack unit, P_{sd} is the power output of the slack unit, and the power limits for the slack unit $P_s{}^{lim}$ are determined based on its calculated output as follows:

$$P_s^{\lim} = \begin{cases} P_{s,high} & \text{if } P_{sd} > P_{s,high} \\ P_{s,low} & \text{if } P_{sd} < P_{s,low} \\ P_{sd} & \text{otherwise} \end{cases} \tag{35}$$

where $P_{s,high}$ and $P_{s,low}$ are the highest and lowest possible power outputs of the slack unit.

Implementation of MVMO^S

The steps of procedure of MVMO^S for the non-convex ED problem are described as follows:

Step 1: Setting the parameters for MVMO^S including $iter_{max}$, n_var, n_par, $mode$, d_i, Δd_0^{ini}, Δd_0^{final}, archive zize, $f_{s\_ini}^*$, $f_{s\_final}^*$, n_randomly, n_randomly_min, indep.runs(m), D_{min}

Set $i = 1$, i donates the function evaluation

Step 2: Normalize initial variables to the range [0,1] (i.e. swarm of particles).

x_normalized = rand(n_par,n_var)

Step 3: Set $k = 1$, k donates particle counters.

Step 4: De-normalized variables, Check for POZ violation and repair, Using De-normalized variables to evaluate fitness function FT_d, store f_{best} and x_{best} in archive.

Step 5: Increase $i = i+1$. If $i < m$ (independent steps), go to Step 6. Otherwise, go to Step 7.

Step 6: Check the particles for the global best, collect a set of reliable individual solutions. The i-th particle is discarded from the optimization process if the distance D_i is less than a certain user defined threshold D_{min}.

Step 7: Create offspring generation through three evolutionary operators: selection, mutation and crossover.

Step 8: If $k < n_p$, increase $k = k+1$ and go to step 4. Otherwise, go to step 9.

Step 9: Check termination criteria. If stoping criteria is satisfied, stop. Otherwise, go to step 3.

De-normalization of optimization variables. The output of mapping function is always inside [0,1]. However, the function evaluation is carried out always in the original scales. The de-normalization of optimization variables is carried by using (36):

$$P_i = P_{i,min} + \text{Scaling} \cdot \text{x\_normalized}(i,:) \tag{36}$$

where,

$$\text{Scaling} = P_{i,max} - P_{i,min}$$

2. **Termination Criteria:** The algorithm of the proposed MVMO^S is terminated when the maximum number of iterations $iter_{max}$ is reached.

NUMERICAL RESULTS

The proposed MVMO^S has been applied to the non-convex ED problems with valve point effects, multiple fuel options and prohibited operating zones. Different systems corresponding to the formulated problems are used for tested. For each case, the algorithm of MVMO^S is executed for 50 independent trials on a Intel Core i5-3470 CPU 3.2 GHz PC with 4GB of RAM. The implematation of the proposed MVMO^S is coded in Matlab R2013a platform.

Selection of Parameters

The parameters of MVMO^S include $iter_{max}$, n_var, n_par, $mode$, d_i, Δd_0^{ini}, Δd_0^{final}, archive zize, $f_{s\_ini}^*$, $f_{s\_final}^*$, n_randomly, indep.runs(m), D_{min}. Since different parameters of the proposed method have effects on the performance of MVMO^S. Hence, it is important to determine an optimal set of parameters of the proposed methods for dealing with ED problems. For each problem, the selection of parameters is carried out by varying only one parameter at a time and fixing the others. The parameter is first fixed at the low value and then increased. Multiple runs are carried out to choose the suitable set of parameters. The typical parameters are selected as follows:

- $iter_{max}$: Maximum number of iterations depend on the dimension of problems. The maximum number of iterations is selected in the range from 6000 to 70000 iterations
- n_var: Number of variable (generators), dimension of problems.
- n_par: Number of particles is varied from 5, 10, 20, 30, 40 and 50, respectively. The number of particles is chosen by experiments for each case.
- *mode*: There are four variable selection strategy for offspring creation . Afer all simulations, strategy 4 (*mode* = 4) is suporior to the other strategy.
- Δd_0^{ini}, Δd_0^{final} : The range of Δd_0 in (14) is [0.01 – 0.4]. By experiments, Δd_0^{ini} and Δd_0^{final} is set to 0.4 and 0.02, respectively for all cases.
- , $f_{s\_final}^*$: The range of values of $f_{s\_ini}^*$ is from 0.9 to 1.0 and for values of $f_{s\_final}^*$ is from 1.0 to 3.0. For all cases, $f_{s\_ini}^*$ is set to 0.95 in the range [0.9, 1.0] and $f_{s\_final}^*$ is set to 3 in the range 3 in the range [1.0, 3.0].
- $indep.runs(m)$: The maximum number of independent runs can be selected in the range from 400 to 2000.
- D_{min} is set to 0 for all cases.

System with Valve Point Effects

The test system has 13 units with vavle point effects is from (Sinha et al., 2003). The power load demand of this system is 1800MW and 2500MW. The transmission power loss is neglected in this case. The obtained results by the MVMO^S corresponding to the two load demand are shown in Table 1 including power outputs, minimum total costs, average total costs, maximum total costs, standard deviations, and computational times.

The parameters for MVMO^S are as follows for all the cases of load demands 1800MW and 2520 MW: $iter_{max}$ = 70000, n_var (generators) = 13, n_p = 20, *archive size* = 5, *mode* =4, indep.runs (m) = 2000, $n\_randomly$ = 5, $n\_randomly\_min$ = 4, $f_{s\_ini}^*$ = 0.95, $f_{s\_final}^*$ = 3, d_i =1, Δd_0^{ini} = 0.4, Δd_0^{final} = 0.02, D_{min} = 0.

In Table 2, the optimal solutions and CPU times of proposed MVMO^S are compared with those of other optimization methods for two load demands 1800MW and 2520MW. For computational time, it may not be directly comparable among the methods because these mothods were run and coded on different computers and programming languages. However, a CPU time comparison is used to show the efficiency of the compared methods. For the case of load demands 1800MW, the minimum total cost by MVMO^S is less than CEP, FEP, MFEP, IEEP (Sinha et al., 2003), PSO, EP-SQP, PSO-SQP (Victoire & Jeyakumar, 2004), HDE (Wang et al., 2007), and CGA-MU (Chiang, 2005), and close to UHGA (He et al., 2008), Self-tuning HDE (Wang et al., 2007), GA-PS-SQP (Alsumait et al., 2010) and NIPSO (Dieu, Schegner, & Ongsakul, 2011). The computational time of MVMO^S is faster than CEP, FEP, MFEP, IEEP, PSO, and EP-SQP, slower than UHGA, CGA-MU, HDE, Self-tuning HDE, GA-PS-SQP, and NIPSO, and close to PSO-SQP. For the case of load demands 2520MW, the minimum total cost by MVMO^S is less than GA, SA, GA-SA, EP-SQP, PSO-SQP (Victoire & Jeyakumar, 2004), UHGA (He et al., 2008),

Table 1. Obtained results for 13-unit system with valve point effects for load demands 1800 MW and 2520 MW by MVMO^S

Unit	Power Outputs P_i (MW)	
1	628.3192	628.3452
2	149.1500	299.1906
3	223.3430	299.1924
4	109.8517	159.7318
5	109.8444	159.7299
6	60.0000	159.7328
7	109.7613	159.7314
8	109.8649	159.7320
9	109.8655	159.7077
10	40.0000	77.3682
11	40.0000	77.3731
12	55.0000	92.3625
13	55.0000	87.8023
Total power (MW)	1800.0000	2520.0000
Min Cost ($/h)	17964.0235	24170.0137
Average Cost ($/h)	18016.0155	24193.4933
Max Cost ($/h)	18086.5929	24226.8256
Standard deviation($/h)	27.1568	23.6363
Average CPU time (s)	33.86	34.32

ESO (Pereira-Neto, Unsihuay, & Saavedra, 2005), and SA-PSO (Kuo, 2008), and close to NIPSO (Dieu et al., 2011). The computational time of MVMO^S is slower than ESO and NIPSO. The PSO, EP-SQP and PSO-SQP was executed on a Pentium II 500 MHz PC. The HDE and self-tuning HDE was run on a Pentium 1.5 GHz with 768 MB of RAM.The computational time for ESO, UHGA, CGA-MU and NIPSO were from a Pentium IV PC, Pentium IV 2.99 GHz PC, Pentium III - 700 PC, 2.1GHz PC with 2GB of RAM, respectively. There is no computer processor reported for CEP, FEP, MFEP and IEEP and no computational time for the other methods.

10-Unit System with Multiple Fuels

The data of the test system including 10 thermal generating units with multiple fuel options is from (Lee et al., 1998). The system load demand for this case are adjusted from 2400MW to 2700 MW gradually neglecting transmission power loss. The solutions obtained by MVMO^S for different system load demands are shown in Table 3 including power outputs, minimum total costs, average total costs, maximum total costs, standard deviations, and computational times.

The parameters for MVMO^S for all different system load demands are as follows: $iter_{max} = 6000$, n_var (generators) $= 10$, $n_p = 5$, *archive size* $= 5$, *mode* $=4$, indep.runs (*m*) $= 400$, $n\_randomly = 4$, $n\_randomly\_min = 3$, $f^*_{s\_ini} = 0.95$, $f^*_{s\_final} = 3$, $d_i = 1$, $\Delta d^{ini}_0 = 0.4$, $\Delta d^{final}_0 = 0.02$, $D_{min} = 0$.

A comparison of the best total costs and CPU times of the MVMO^S and the other optimizaion methods is summarized as in Table 4. For this test system, the best total costs of the MVMO^S are less than those from HNN (J. Park, Kim, Eom, & Lee, 1993), IEP (Y.-M. Park, Won, & Park, 1998) and SQPSO (Niu, Zhou, Zhang, & Deng, 2012) for the load demand of 2400 MW, IEP and SQPSO for the load demand of 2500 MW and 2600MW, HNN, IEP, AHNN (Lee et al., 1998) and SQPSO for the load demand of 2700 MW, and close to those from the other methods for the remaining cases. The computational times of the MVMO^S are slower than the other methods. The CPU times for the HNN, AHNN, SQPSO, ALHN (Dieu, Ongsakul, & Polprasert, 2013), and PGPSO (Dieu, Schegner, et al., 2013) methods were from a IBM PC-386, Compaq 90, Intel Core2 Duo 1.66 GHz, 2.1 GHz, and 2.1 GHz – 2 GB RAM PC. There is no CPU time reported for the IEP, MPSO (J.-B. Park et al., 2005) and AIS (Panigrahi et al., 2007) method. It has indicated that the MVMO^S can obtain the good solutions due to its powerful global search ability.

Large-Scale Systems with Multiple Fuels

Based on the basic 10-unit system, the large-scale systems are created by duplicating the basic 10-unit system with the load demand of 2700 MW adjusted to the system size proportionally. The large-scale systems consist of 30, 60 and 100 units neglecting transmission power loss. The results obtained by the

Table 2. Comparison of best total cost and CPU times for 13 unit system with valve point effects

Method	1800MW		2520MW	
	Cost ($/h)	CPU(s)	Cost ($/h)	CPU(s)
GA	-	-	24398.23	-
SA	-	-	24970.91	-
GA-SA	-	-	24275.71	-
CEP	18048.21	293.41	-	-
FEP	18018.00	166.43	-	-
MFEP	18028.09	315.98	-	-
IFEP	17994.07	156.81	-	-
PSO	18030.72	77.37	-	-
EP-SQP	17991.03	121.93	24266.44	-
PSO-SQP	17969.93	33.97	24261.05	-
UHGA	17964.81	15.33	24172.25	-
ESO	-	-	24177.78	1.0
SA-PSO	-	-	24171.40	-
HDE	17975.73	1.65	-	-
CGA-MU	17975.34	21.91	-	-
Self-tuning HDE	17963.89	1.41	-	-
GA-PS-SQP	17964.25	11.06	-	-
NIPSO	17963.84	0.861	24169.92	0.772
MVMO^S	17964.02	33.86	24170.01	34.32

Table 3. Obtained results for 10-unit system with multiple fuels for load demands 2400MW, 2500MW, 2600MW and 2700 MW by MVMO^S

Load Demand Unit	2,400 MW		2,500 MW		2,600 MW		2,700 MW	
	F_i	P_i (MW)	F_i	P_i (MW)	F_i	P_i (MW)	F_i	P_i (MW)
1	1	189.7424	2	206.5188	2	216.5442	2	218.2478
2	1	202.3415	1	206.4574	1	210.9059	1	211.6610
3	1	253.9030	1	265.7394	1	278.5431	1	280.7316
4	3	233.0465	3	235.9532	3	239.0966	3	239.6318
5	1	241.8386	1	258.0185	1	275.5196	1	278.4992
6	3	233.0446	3	235.9529	3	239.0970	3	239.6312
7	1	253.2765	1	268.8685	1	285.7198	1	288.5798
8	3	233.0451	3	235.9532	3	239.0968	3	239.6309
9	1	320.3798	1	331.4869	1	343.4939	3	428.4873
10	1	239.3819	1	255.0512	1	271.9831	1	274.8994
Total Power (MW)		2400.000		2500.000		2600.000		2700.000
Min total cost ($/h)		481.7226		526.2388		574.3808		623.8092
Average total cost ($/h)		481.7226		526.2388		574.4025		623.8092
Max total cost ($/h)		481.7226		526.2388		574.7413		623.8092
Standard deviation ($/h)		0.0		0.0		0.0865		0.0
Average CPU (s)		3.77		3.78		3.79		3.80

proposed MVMO^S for these systems including minimum total costs, average total costs, maximum total costs, standard deviations, and computational times are given in Table 5.

The parameters for MVMO^S for all different system are as follows:, $n_p = 5$, *archive size* = 5, *mode* = 4, indep.runs (m) = 800, $n\_randomly = 15$, $n\_randomly\_min = 10$, $f^*_{s\_ini} = 0.95$, $f^*_{s\_final} = 3$, $d_i = 1$, $\Delta d_0^{ini} = 0.4$, $\Delta d_0^{final} = 0.02$, $D_{min} = 0$. The maximum number of iterations are set to 30000, 40000 and 50000 for 30-unit, 60-unit and 100-unit, respectively. The number of variable (generators) are set to 30, 60, 100 for 30-unit, 60-unit and 100-unit systems, respectively.

Table 6 shows the comparison of the average total costs and CPU times of the MVMO^S and CGA, IGA-AMUM (Chiang & Su, 2005) and ALHN (Dieu, Ongsakul, et al., 2013). The average total costs obtained by MVMO^S are less than CGA and IGA-AMUM and ALHN for all systems. The CPU times of MVMO^S are faster than CGA and IGA-AMUM and slower than ALHN. The computational times for CGA and IGA-AMUM were from a PIII-700 PC and the computational times for ALHN were from a 2.1 GHz - 2 GB RAM PC. Test results shows that MVMO^S can provide very good solutions for non-convex ED with multiple fuels for large-scale systems.

10-Unit System with Both Valve Point Effects and Multiple Fuels

The data of 10-unit test with VPE and MF is given in (Chiang, 2005). This system supplies to power load demand of 2700 MW with transmission power loss neglected. The result obtained by the proposed

Table 4. Comparison of best total cost and CPU times for 10 unit system with multiple fuels

Method	2400 MW		2500 MW	
	Cost ($/h)	CPU (s)	Cost ($/h)	CPU (s)
HNN	487.87	~60	526.13	~60
IEP	481.779	-	526.304	-
AHNN	481.72	~4	526.230	~4
SQPSO	481.732	0.339	526.245	0.35
MPSO	481.723	-	526.239	-
AIS	481.723	-	526.240	-
ALHN	481.723	0.042	526.239	0.043
PGPSO	481.723	0.228	526.239	0.228
MVMO^s	481.723	3.77	526.239	3.78
Method	2600 MW		2700 MW	
	Cost ($/h)	CPU (s)	Cost ($/h)	CPU (s)
HNN	574.26	~60	626.12	~60
IEP	574.473	-	623.851	-
AHNN	574.37	~4	626.24	~4
SQPSO	574.387	0.3484	623.832	0.324
MPSO	574.381	-	623.809	-
AIS	574.381	-	623.809	-
ALHN	574.381	0.047	623.809	0.057
PGPSO	574.381	0.225	623.810	0.233
MVMO^s	574.381	3.79	623.809	3.80

Table 5. Results for large-scale systems with MF

No. of Units	30	60	100
Min total cost ($/h)	1871.4275	3742.8550	6238.0920
Average total cost ($/h)	1871.4586	3744.3140	6245.2738
Max total cost ($/h)	1872.9712	3754.0725	6261.5361
Standard deviation ($/h)	0.2183	3.1227	6.2007
Average CPU time (s)	27.07	51.76	99.61

MVMO^s including power outputs, minimum total cost, average total cost, maximum total cost, standard deviation, and computational time for this system are shown in Table 7.

The parameters for MVMO^s for this case are as follows: $iter_{max} = 20000$, n_var (generators) $= 10$, $n_p = 5$, $archive\ size = 4$, $mode = 4$, indep.runs $(m) = 400$, $n\_randomly = 4$, $n\_randomly\_min = 3$, $f^*_{s\_ini} = 0.95$, $f^*_{s\_final} = 3$, $d_i = 1$, $\Delta d_0^{ini} = 0.4$, $\Delta d_0^{final} = 0.02$, $D_{min} = 0$.

Table 6. Comparison of average total cost and CPU times for large-scale systems with MF

Method	No. of Units	Cost ($)	CPU Time (s)
CGA	30	1873.691	263.64
	60	3748.761	517.88
	100	6251.469	573.70
IGA-AMUM	30	1872.047	80.47
	60	3744.722	157.19
	100	6242.787	275.67
ALHN	30	1881.746	0.253
	60	3765.186	0.354
	100	6247.822	0.404
MVMO^S	30	1871.4586	27.07
	60	3744.3140	51.76
	100	6245.2738	97.61

The best total cost and computational time obtained by MVMO^S are compared to other methods including CGA_MU, IGA_MU (Chiang, 2005), DE, RGA, PSO (Manoharan, Kannan, Baskar, & Iruthayarajan, 2008), PSO-LRS, NPSO, NPSO-LRS (Selvakumar & Thanushkodi, 2007), SQPSO (Niu et al., 2012), PSO-TVIW, PSO-TVAC, SOH-PSO (Luong, Vasant, Dieu, Khoa, & Khanh), and PGPSO (Dieu, Schegner, et al., 2013), which are shown in Table 8. The best total cost obtained by MVMO^S for this system is less than the methods in Table 8. The computatitonal time of MVMO^S is less than CGA_MU, and slower than the other methods. The computational times for the CGA_MU and IGA_MU methods were from a PIII-700 PC, the computational times for the PSO-LRS, NPSO, and NPSO-LRS methods were from a Pentium IV 1.5 GHz - 128 MB RAM, the computational times for the DE, RGA, and PSO method were from a Pentium IV 1.8 GHz - 1 GB RAM PC, the computational times for PSO-TVIW, PSO-TVAC and SOH-PSO were from a Dell Studio Laptop Core (TM) 2 Duo CPU T6400@ 2.0 GHz - 4G RAM, and the computational times for SQPSO and PGPSO were from Intel Core2 Duo 1.66 GHz and 2.1 GHz - 2 GB RAM PC, respectively. Test result shows that the MVMO^S can obtain better result than many other methods for non-convex ED problem with valve point effects and multiple fuels.

Large-Scale Systems with Both Valve Point Effects and Multiple Fuels

The test systems consist of 10, 20, 40, 80 and 160 units units neglecting transmission power loss. The large-scale systems are created by duplicating the basic 10-unit system with the load demand of 2700 MW adjusted to the system size proportionally. The results obtained by the proposed MVMO^S for these systems including minimum total costs, average total costs, maximum total costs, standard deviations, and computational times are given in Table 9.

The parameters for MVMO^S for all different system are as follows:, $n_p = 5$, *archive size* = 5, *mode* = 4, indep.runs $(m) = 800$, $f^*_{s\_ini} = 0.95$, $f^*_{s\_final} = 3$, $d_i = 1$, $\Delta d_0^{ini} = 0.4$, $\Delta d_0^{final} = 0.02$, $D_{min} = 0$.

The maximum number of iterations are set to 30000, 40000, 50000 and 70000 for 20-unit, 40-unit, 80-unit and 100-unit, respectively. The number of variable (generators) are set to 20, 40, 80 and 160 for

Table 7. Obtained results for 10-unit system with VPE and MF for load demands 2700 MW by MVMO^S

Unit	Fuel F_i	P_i (MW)
1	2	218.1050
2	1	210.9169
3	1	280.6571
4	3	239.9551
5	1	279.9208
6	3	239.3922
7	1	287.7207
8	3	239.0145
9	3	428.4452
10	1	275.8725
Total Power (MW)	2700.000	
Min total cost ($/h)	623.8297	
Average total cost ($/h)	623.8604	
Max total cost ($/h)	623.9148	
Standard deviation ($/h)	0.0187	
Average CPU time (s)	12.30	

20-unit, 40-unit, 80-unit and 160-unit systems, respectively. *n_randomly* is set to 10 and *n_randomly_min* is set to 5 for 20-unit and 40-unit systems, respectively. *n_randomly* is set to 20 and *n_randomly_min* is set to 10 for 80-unit and 160-unit systems, respectively.

In Table 10, The comparison of the average total costs and CPU times between the proposed MVMO^S and the CGA_MU, IGA_MU (Chiang, 2005) and PGPSO (Dieu, Schegner, et al., 2013) is carried out. In all cases, the MVMO^S obtained the average total costs less than CGA_MU, IGA_MU and PGPSO, especially for the large-scale systems. The computational times of the MVMO^S are faster than CGA_MU, and slower than IGA_MU and PGPSO. The CGA_MU and IGA_MU methods were run on a PIII - 700 PC. The CPU time for the PGPSO methods was from a 2.1 GHz - 2 GB RAM PC.

System with Prohobited Operating Zones

The test system includes 15 thermal generating units, considering ramp rate constraints and system transmission power loss. The power load demand for this case is 2630MW. The results obtained by the proposed MVMO^S are given in Table 11 including power outputs, power loss, minimum total cost, average total cost, maximum total cost, standard deviation, and computational time.

The parameters for MVMO^S for this system are as follows: $iter_{max} = 20000$, *n_var* (generators) = 10, $n_p = 5$, *archive size* = 5, *mode* =4, indep.runs (*m*) = 400, *n_randomly* = 5, *n_randomly_min* = 4, $f_{s\_ini}^* = 0.95$, $f_{s\_final}^* = 3$, $d_i = 1$, $\Delta d_0^{ini} = 0.4$, $\Delta d_0^{final} = 0.02$, $D_{min} = 0$.

In Table 12, the best total cost, CPU time and power loss obtained by the MVMO^S are compared to other methods including AIS (Panigrahi et al., 2007), GA, PSO (Gaing, 2003), SOH-PSO (Chaturvedi, Pandit, & Srivastava, 2008), SA-PSO (Kuo, 2008), PGPSO (Dieu, Schegner, et al., 2013) and PSO-MSAF

Table 8. Comparison of best total cost and CPU time for 10-unit system with VPE and MF

Method	Best Cost ($/h)	CPU Time (s)
CGA_MU	624.7193	26.64
IGA_MU	624.5178	7.32
DE	624.5146	2.8236
RGA	624.5081	4.1340
PSO	624.5074	3.3852
PSO-LRS	624.2297	1.81
NPSO	624.1624	0.76
NPSO-LRS	624.1273	1.60
SQPSO	623.8476	0.324
PSO-TVIW	623.8444	3.92
PGPSO	623.8431	1.494
PSO-TVAC	623.8399	3.95
SOH-PSO	623.8362	3.8
MVMO^S	623.8297	12.30

Table 9. Results for large-scale systems with VPE and MF

No. of Units	20	40	80	160
Min total cost ($/h)	1247.6806	2495.4162	4991.2018	9982.9736
Average total cost ($/h)	1247.7349	2496.5806	4994.1996	9992.3135
Max total cost ($/h)	1247.8100	2506.8681	5002.8486	10014.5567
Standard deviation ($/h)	0.0330	2.9753	4.004	7.3995
Average CPU time (s)	23.30	44.25	86.07	206.93

(Subbaraj, Rengaraj, Salivahanan, & Senthilkumar, 2010). The best total cost and power loss obtained by MVMO^S are less than these methods. The computational time of MVMO^S is close to PSO-MSAF and slower than the other methods.The GA and PSO, SOH_PSO, PGPSO, and PSO-MSAF methods were run on a Pentium III 550 - 256 MB RAM, Pentium IV 2.8 GHz - 512 MB RAM, 2.1 GHz - 2 GB RAM PC and Pentium IV 2.60 GHz - 512 MB RAM, respectively. There is no computational time reported for the AIS and SA-PSO methods. The comparison has shown that the MVMO^S can provide better solution quality than many other methods for the non-convex ED with prohibited operating zones.

DISCUSSION

In this study, the proposed algorithm is run 50 independent trials. The mean cost, max cost, average cost and standard deviation obtained by the proposed method to evaluate the robustness characteristic of the proposed method for ED problems. As observed from Table 1, 3, 5, 7, 9 and Table 11, the power

Table 10. Comparison of average total cost and CPU times for large-scale systems with VPE & MF

Method	No. of Units	Total cost ($)	CPU time (s)
CGA_MU	20	1,249.3893	80.48
	40	2,500.9220	157.39
	80	5,008.1426	309.41
	160	10,143.7263	621.30
IGA_MU	20	1,249.1179	21.64
	40	2,499.8243	43.71
	80	5,003.8832	85.67
	160	10,042.4742	174.62
PGPSO	20	1,248.9623	4.078
	40	2,499.6127	18.645
	80	5,003.0250	43.191
	160	10,032.4883	91.570
MVMO^s	20	1247.7349	23.30
	40	2496.5806	44.25
	80	4994.1996	86.07
	160	9992.3135	206.93

Table 11. Obtained results for 15-unit system with POZ for load demands 2630 MW by MVMO^S

Unit	P_i (MW)	Unit	P_i (MW)
1	455.0008	9	58.0121
2	380.0000	10	152.4384
3	130.0000	11	80.0000
4	130.0000	12	79.9950
5	170.0000	13	25.0000
6	460.0000	14	17.1708
7	430.0000	15	15.000
8	74.9777		
Power loss (MW)		27.5948	
Total power (MW)		2657.5948	
Min total cost ($/h)		32673.2084	
Average total cost ($/h)		32680.6140	
Max total cost ($/h)		32693.6578	
Standard deviation ($/h)		5.2590	
Average CPU time (s)		19.06	

output obtained by MVMO^S always satisfy all the constraints after 50 independent trials and the difference between the maximum and minimum costs obtained the proposed MVMO^S is small. Table 13 shows the ratio between the standard deviation and the minimum cost for all systems. The ratio between the standard deviation and the minimum cost is less than 0.151%. It clearly shows that the performance the proposed MVMO^S is very robust. In addition, the comparison of the total cost obtained by MVMO^S and many other methods from Table 2, 4, 6, 8 and Table 10 shows that the MVMO^S can obtained better total costs than many other methods. Consequently, the MVMO^S can obtain near global solution with high probability, especially for large-scale system. However, the computation time is relatively high for large-scale systems. Similar to the original MVMO, the number of iterations in MVMO^S is equivalent to the number of offspring fitness evaluations which is usually time consuming in practical applications. Besides the powerful global search ability, the proposed MVMO^S is also easy to be implemented for ED problem. Unlike other swarm-based optimization techniques, MVMO^S does not strictly require many particles. In this study, number of particles is set to 5 for all cases except the system with valve point effects where number of particles is set to 20.

FUTURE RESEARCH DIRECTIONS

Since the advantages and disadvantages of the MVMO^S are discussed in discussion section, the future research directions will be considered as follows:

- Improve, modify the mean-variance mapping optimization algorithm to achieve good solution quality and fast computational time.
- Combine the mean-variance mapping optimization algorithm with one of another optimization techniques such as particle swarm optimization, augmented lagrange hopfield network, genetic algorithm, fuzzy logic, etc... to obtain better solution quality and short computation time as well.
- The mean-variance mapping optimization will be applied for solving hydrothermal economic dispatch with cascaded hydro plants.
- The mean-variance mapping optimization will be also applied for solving emission constrained economic dispatch.

Table 12. Comparison of best total cost and CPU times for systems with POZ

Method	Power Loss (MW)	Total Power (MW)	Best Cost ($/h)	CPU Time (s)
AIS	32.4075	2662.04	32854.00	-
GA	38.2782	2668.40	33113.00	4.95
PSO	32.4306	2662.40	32858.00	2.74
SOH-PSO	32.2800	2662.29	32751.00	0.0936
SA-PSO	30.9080	2660.90	32708.00	10.37
PGPSO	30.6644	2660.66	32705.75	1.632
PSO-MSAF	30.4900	2660.49	32713.09	19.15
MVMO^S	27.5948	2657.5948	32673.20	19.06

Table 13. The ratio between the standard deviation and the minimum cost for all systems

System	System with VPE		System with MF				System with VPE & MF	System with POZ
	1800 MW	2520 MW	2400MW	2500MW	2600MW	2700MW		
Ratio(%)	0.151	0.098	0	0	0.015	0	0.003	0.016
System	Large-scale systems with MF			Large-scale systems with VPE & MF				
	30-unit	60-unit	100-unit	20-unit	40-unit	80-unit	160-unit	
Ratio(%)	0.012	0.083	0.099	0.0026	0.119	0.080	0.074	

CONCLUSION

In this chapter, the proposed MVMO^S has been efficiently applied for solving the non-convex ED problems. By powerful global search ability and starting search process with set of particles, the MVMO^S can provide global solution to non-convex ED problems. The proposed method has been tested on different systems with non-convex generator's characteristics including valve point effects, multiple fuels, and prohibited operating zones .The numerical results show that the MVMO^S exhibits a robust performance and also provides the near optimal solutions for all test systems, expecially for lagre-scale system. The proposed method has merits as follows: easy implementation, good solutions, robustness of algorithm and applicable to large-scale system. Therefore, the proposed MVMO^S could be favorable for solving the non-convex ED problems.

ACKNOWLEDGMENT

This research work is sponsored by Graduate Assistant Scheme of Universiti Teknologi Petronas.

REFERENCES

Al-Sumait, J., Al-Othman, A., & Sykulski, J. (2007). Application of pattern search method to power system valve-point economic load dispatch. *International Journal of Electrical Power & Energy Systems*, 29(10), 720–730. doi:10.1016/j.ijepes.2007.06.016

Alsumait, J., Sykulski, J., & Al-Othman, A. (2010). A hybrid GA–PS–SQP method to solve power system valve-point economic dispatch problems. *Applied Energy*, 87(5), 1773–1781. doi:10.1016/j.apenergy.2009.10.007

Attaviriyanupap, P., Kita, H., Tanaka, E., & Hasegawa, J. (2002). A hybrid EP and SQP for dynamic economic dispatch with nonsmooth fuel cost function. *IEEE Transactions on Power Systems*, 17(2), 411–416. doi:10.1109/TPWRS.2002.1007911

Cepeda, J. C., Rueda, J. L., & Erlich, I. (2012). Identification of dynamic equivalents based on heuristic optimization for smart grid applications. In *Proceedings of Evolutionary Computation (CEC), 2012 IEEE Congress* (pp. 1-8). IEEE. doi:10.1109/CEC.2012.6256493

Chaturvedi, K. T., Pandit, M., & Srivastava, L. (2008). Self-organizing hierarchical particle swarm optimization for nonconvex economic dispatch. *IEEE Transactions on Power Systems*, *23*(3), 1079–1087. doi:10.1109/TPWRS.2008.926455

Chiang, C.-L. (2005). Improved genetic algorithm for power economic dispatch of units with valve-point effects and multiple fuels. *IEEE Transactions on Power Systems*, *20*(4), 1690–1699. doi:10.1109/TPWRS.2005.857924

Chiang, C.-L., & Su, C.-T. (2005). Adaptive-improved genetic algorithm for the economic dispatch of units with multiple fuel options. *Cybernetics and Systems: An Internationl Journal*, *36*(7), 687–704. doi:10.1080/01969720591008788

Dieu, V. N., Ongsakul, W., & Polprasert, J. (2013). The augmented Lagrange Hopfield network for economic dispatch with multiple fuel options. *Mathematical and Computer Modelling*, *57*(1), 30–39. doi:10.1016/j.mcm.2011.03.041

Dieu, V. N., Schegner, P., & Ongsakul, W. (2011). A newly improved particle swarm optimization for economic dispatch with valve point loading effects. In *Proceedings of Power and Energy Society General Meeting, 2011 IEEE* (pp. 1-8). IEEE. doi:10.1109/PES.2011.6039332

Dieu, V. N., Schegner, P., & Ongsakul, W. (2013). *Pseudo-gradient based particle swarm optimization method for nonconvex economic dispatch*. Springer.

Eberhart, R. C., & Shi, Y. (1998). Comparison between genetic algorithms and particle swarm optimization. In *Evolutionary programming VII* (pp. 611–616). Springer Berlin Heidelberg. doi:10.1007/BFb0040812

Erlich, I., Nakawiro, W., & Martinez, M. (2011, July). Optimal dispatch of reactive sources in wind farms. In *Proceedings of Power and Energy Society General Meeting, 2011 IEEE* (pp. 1-7). IEEE. doi:10.1109/PES.2011.6039534

Erlich, I., Venayagamoorthy, G. K., & Worawat, N. (2010, July). A mean-variance optimization algorithm. In *Proceedings of Evolutionary Computation (CEC), 2010 IEEE Congress* (pp. 1-6). IEEE. doi:10.1109/CEC.2010.5586027

Fan, J.-Y., & Zhang, L. (1998). Real-time economic dispatch with line flow and emission constraints using quadratic programming. *IEEE Transactions on Power Systems*, *13*(2), 320–325. doi:10.1109/59.667345

Gaing, Z.-L. (2003). Particle swarm optimization to solving the economic dispatch considering the generator constraints. *IEEE Transactions on Power Systems*, *18*(3), 1187–1195. doi:10.1109/TPWRS.2003.814889

Ganesan, T., Vasant, P., & Elamvazuthy, I. (2012). A hybrid PSO approach for solving non-convex optimization problems. *Archives of Control Sciences*, *22*(1), 87–105. doi:10.2478/v10170-011-0014-2

Gonzalez-Longatt, F. M., Rueda, J. L., Erlich, I., Bogdanov, D., & Villa, W. (2012, October). Identification of Gaussian mixture model using mean variance mapping optimization: Venezuelan case. In *Proceedings of Innovative Smart Grid Technologies (ISGT Europe), 2012 3rd IEEE PES International Conference and Exhibition* (pp. 1-6). IEEE.

Happ, H. (1977). Optimal power dispatch: A comprehensive survey. *IEEE Transactions on Power Apparatus and Systems*, *96*(3), 841–854. doi:10.1109/T-PAS.1977.32397

He, D, Wang, F, & Mao, Z. (2008). Hybrid genetic algorithm for economic dispatch with valve-point effect. *Electric Power Systems Research*, 78(4), 626–633. doi:10.1016/j.epsr.2007.05.008

Hemamalini, S., & Simon, S. (2009). Maclaurin series-based Lagrangian method for economic dispatch with valve-point effect. *Generation, Transmission & Distribution, IET, 3*(9), 859–871. doi:10.1049/iet-gtd.2008.0499

Kuo, C.-C. (2008). A novel coding scheme for practical economic dispatch by modified particle swarm approach. *IEEE Transactions on Power Systems, 23*(4), 1825–1835. doi:10.1109/TPWRS.2008.2002297

Le Dinh, L., Vo Ngoc, D., & Vasant, P. (2013). Artificial bee colony algorithm for solving optimal power flow problem. *The Scientific World Journal*, 2013. PMID:24470790

Lee, K. Y., Sode-Yome, A., & Park, J. H. (1998). Adaptive Hopfield neural networks for economic load dispatch. *IEEE Transactions on Power Systems, 13*(2), 519–526. doi:10.1109/59.667377

Luong, L. D., Vasant, P., Dieu, V. N., Khoa, T. H., & Khanh, D. V. (2013). Self-organizing hierarchical particle swarm optimization for large-scale economic dispatch with multiple fuels considering valve-point effects. In *Proceedings of the 7th Global Conference on Power Control and Optimization (PCO'2013)*. Academic Press.

Mahor, A., Prasad, V., & Rangnekar, S. (2009). Economic dispatch using particle swarm optimization: A review. *Renewable & Sustainable Energy Reviews, 13*(8), 2134–2141. doi:10.1016/j.rser.2009.03.007

Manoharan, P., Kannan, P., Baskar, S., & Iruthayarajan, M. (2008). Penalty parameter-less constraint handling scheme based evolutionary algorithm solutions to economic dispatch. *IET Generation, Transmission & Distribution, 2*(4), 478–490. doi:10.1049/iet-gtd:20070423

Nakawiro, W., Erlich, I., & Rueda, J. L. (2011, July). A novel optimization algorithm for optimal reactive power dispatch: A comparative study. In *Proceedings of Electric Utility Deregulation and Restructuring and Power Technologies (DRPT), 2011 4th International Conference* (pp. 1555-1561). IEEE. doi:10.1109/DRPT.2011.5994144

Nanda, J., Hari, L., & Kothari, M. (1994). Economic emission load dispatch with line flow constraints using a classical technique. *IEE Proceedings. Generation, Transmission and Distribution, 141*(1), 1–10. doi:10.1049/ip-gtd:19949770

Niknam, T. (2010). A new fuzzy adaptive hybrid particle swarm optimization algorithm for non-linear, non-smooth and non-convex economic dispatch problem. *Applied Energy, 87*(1), 327–339. doi:10.1016/j.apenergy.2009.05.016

Niu, Q., Zhou, Z., Zhang, H.-Y., & Deng, J. (2012). An improved quantum-behaved particle swarm optimization method for economic dispatch problems with multiple fuel options and valve-points effects. *Energies, 5*(9), 3655–3673. doi:10.3390/en5093655

Noman, N., & Iba, H. (2008). Differential evolution for economic load dispatch problems. *Electric Power Systems Research, 78*(8), 1322–1331. doi:10.1016/j.epsr.2007.11.007

Padmanabhan, B., Sivakumar, R., Jasper, J., & Victoire, T. A. A. (2011). Bacterial foraging approach to economic load dispatch problem with non convex cost function. In *Swarm, evolutionary, and memetic computing* (pp. 577–584). Springer.

Panigrahi, B., Yadav, S. R., Agrawal, S., & Tiwari, M. (2007). A clonal algorithm to solve economic load dispatch. *Electric Power Systems Research, 77*(10), 1381–1389. doi:10.1016/j.epsr.2006.10.007

Parikh, J., & Chattopadhyay, D. (1996). A multi-area linear programming approach for analysis of economic operation of the Indian power system. *IEEE Transactions on Power Systems, 11*(1), 52–58. doi:10.1109/59.485985

Park, J., Kim, Y., Eom, I., & Lee, K. (1993). Economic load dispatch for piecewise quadratic cost function using Hopfield neural network. *IEEE Transactions on Power Systems, 8*(3), 1030–1038. doi:10.1109/59.260897

Park, J.-B., Lee, K.-S., Shin, J.-R., & Lee, K. Y. (2005). A particle swarm optimization for economic dispatch with nonsmooth cost functions. *IEEE Transactions on Power Systems, 20*(1), 34–42. doi:10.1109/TPWRS.2004.831275

Park, Y.-M., Won, J.-R., & Park, J.-B. (1998). A new approach to economic load dispatch based on improved evolutionary programming. *Engineering Intelligent Systems for Electrical Engineering and Communications, 6*(2), 103–110.

Pereira-Neto, A., Unsihuay, C., & Saavedra, O. (2005). Efficient evolutionary strategy optimisation procedure to solve the nonconvex economic dispatch problem with generator constraints. *IEE Proceedings. Generation, Transmission and Distribution, 152*(5), 653–660. doi:10.1049/ip-gtd:20045287

Pothiya, S., Ngamroo, I., & Kongprawechnon, W. (2010). Ant colony optimisation for economic dispatch problem with non-smooth cost functions. *International Journal of Electrical Power & Energy Systems, 32*(5), 478–487. doi:10.1016/j.ijepes.2009.09.016

Pringles, R. M., & Rueda, J. L. (2012, September). Optimal transmission expansion planning using mean-variance mapping optimization. In Proceedings of Transmission and Distribution: Latin America Conference and Exposition (T&D-LA), 2012 Sixth IEEE/PES (pp. 1-8). IEEE. doi:10.1109/TDC-LA.2012.6319132

Rueda, J. L., & Erlich, I. (2013, April). Evaluation of the mean-variance mapping optimization for solving multimodal problems. In *Proceedings of Swarm Intelligence (SIS), 2013 IEEE Symposium* (pp. 7-14). IEEE. doi:10.1109/SIS.2013.6615153

Rueda, J. L., & Erlich, I. (2013, April). Optimal dispatch of reactive power sources by using MVMO s optimization. In *Proceedings of Computational Intelligence Applications in Smart Grid (CIASG), 2013 IEEE Symposium* (pp. 29-36). IEEE. doi:10.1109/CIASG.2013.6611495

Rueda Torres, L. J., & Erlich, I. (2013). Short-term transmission expansion planning by using swarm mean-variance mapping optimization In *Proceedings of the 17th International Conference on Intelligent Systems Application to Power Systems*. Academic Press.

Selvakumar, A. I., & Thanushkodi, K. (2007). A new particle swarm optimization solution to nonconvex economic dispatch problems. *IEEE Transactions on Power Systems, 22*(1), 42–51. doi:10.1109/TPWRS.2006.889132

Sinha, N., Chakrabarti, R., & Chattopadhyay, P. (2003). Evolutionary programming techniques for economic load dispatch. *IEEE Transactions on Evolutionary Computation, 7*(1), 83–94. doi:10.1109/TEVC.2002.806788

Subbaraj, P., Rengaraj, R., Salivahanan, S., & Senthilkumar, T. (2010). Parallel particle swarm optimization with modified stochastic acceleration factors for solving large scale economic dispatch problem. *International Journal of Electrical Power & Energy Systems, 32*(9), 1014–1023. doi:10.1016/j.ijepes.2010.02.003

Vasant, P., Ganesan, T., & Elamvazuthi, I. (2012, January). An improved PSO approach for solving non-convex optimization problems. In *Proceedings of ICT and Knowledge Engineering (ICT & Knowledge Engineering), 2011 9th International Conference* (pp. 80-87). IEEE. doi:10.1109/ICTKE.2012.6152418

Vasant, P., Ganesan, T., Elamvazuthi, I., Barsoum, N., & Faiman, D. (2012, November). Solving deterministic non-linear programming problem using Hopfield artificial neural network and genetic programming techniques. In *AIP Conference Proceedings-American Institute of Physics* (*Vol. 1499*, No. 1, p. 311). Academic Press. doi:10.1063/1.4769007

Vasant, P., & Global, I. (2013). *Meta-heuristics optimization algorithms in engineering, business, economics, and finance.* Information Science Reference. doi:10.4018/978-1-4666-2086-5

Victoire, T., & Jeyakumar, A. E. (2004). Hybrid PSO–SQP for economic dispatch with valve-point effect. *Electric Power Systems Research, 71*(1), 51–59. doi:10.1016/j.epsr.2003.12.017

Wang, S.-K., Chiou, J.-P., & Liu, C. (2007). Non-smooth/non-convex economic dispatch by a novel hybrid differential evolution algorithm. *Generation, Transmission & Distribution, IET, 1*(5), 793–803. doi:10.1049/iet-gtd:20070183

Wollenberg, B., & Wood, A. (1996). Power generation, operation and control. John Wiley & Sons.

Xia, X., & Elaiw, A. (2010). Optimal dynamic economic dispatch of generation: A review. *Electric Power Systems Research, 80*(8), 975–986. doi:10.1016/j.epsr.2009.12.012

ADDITIONAL READING

Bhattacharya, A., & Chattopadhyay, P. K. (2010). Solving complex economic load dispatch problems using biogeography-based optimization. *Expert Systems with Applications, 37*(5), 3605–3615. doi:10.1016/j.eswa.2009.10.031

Cai, J., Ma, X., Li, L., & Haipeng, P. (2007). Chaotic particle swarm optimization for economic dispatch considering the generator constraints. *Energy Conversion and Management, 48*(2), 645–653. doi:10.1016/j.enconman.2006.05.020

Chakravarty, P., & Venayagamoorthy, G. K. (2011). *Development of optimal controllers for a DFIG based wind farm in a smart grid under variable wind speed conditions.* Paper presented at the Electric Machines & Drives Conference (IEMDC), 2011 IEEE International. doi:10.1109/IEMDC.2011.5994901

Chaturvedi, K. T., Pandit, M., & Srivastava, L. (2009). Particle swarm optimization with time varying acceleration coefficients for non-convex economic power dispatch. *International Journal of Electrical Power & Energy Systems, 31*(6), 249–257. doi:10.1016/j.ijepes.2009.01.010

Chen, C.-L. (2007). Non-convex economic dispatch: A direct search approach. *Energy Conversion and Management, 48*(1), 219–225. doi:10.1016/j.enconman.2006.04.010

Coelho, L. S., & Lee, C.-S. (2008). Solving economic load dispatch problems in power systems using chaotic and Gaussian particle swarm optimization approaches. *International Journal of Electrical Power & Energy Systems, 30*(5), 297–307. doi:10.1016/j.ijepes.2007.08.001

Dieu, V. N., & Ongsakul, W. (2009). Enhanced augmented Lagrange Hopfield network for constrained economic dispatch with prohibited operating zones. *Engineering Intelligent Systems, 17*(1), 19.

Dieu, V. N., & Schegner, P. (2012). Real power dispatch on large scale power systems by augmented lagrange hopfield network. *International Journal of Energy Optimization and Engineering, 1*(1), 19–38. doi:10.4018/ijeoe.2012010102

Dieu, V. N., & Schegner, P. (2013). Augmented Lagrange Hopfield network initialized by quadratic programming for economic dispatch with piecewise quadratic cost functions and prohibited zones. *Applied Soft Computing, 13*(1), 292–301. doi:10.1016/j.asoc.2012.08.026

Duman, S., Güvenç, U., & Yörükeren, N. (2010). Gravitational Search Algorithm for Economic Dispatch with Valve-Point Effects. *International Review of Electrical Engineering, 5*(6).

Elamvazuthi, I., Ganesan, T., & Vasant, P. (2011, December). A comparative study of HNN and Hybrid HNN-PSO techniques in the optimization of distributed generation (DG) power systems. In *Advanced Computer Science and Information System (ICACSIS), 2011 International Conference* (pp. 195-200). IEEE.

Elamvazuthi, I., Vasant, P., & Ganesan, T. (2013). *Hybrid Optimization Techniques for Optimization in a Fuzzy Environment Handbook of Optimization* (pp. 1025–1046). Springer.

Erlich, I., Shewarega, F., Feltes, C., Koch, F., & Fortmann, J. (2012, July). Determination of dynamic wind farm equivalents using heuristic optimization. In *Power and Energy Society General Meeting, 2012 IEEE* (pp. 1-8). IEEE. doi:10.1109/PESGM.2012.6345508

Fink, L. H., Kwatny, H. G., & McDonald, J. P. (1969). Economic dispatch of generation via valve-point loading. *IEEE Transactions on Power Apparatus and Systems, PAS-88*(6), 805–811. doi:10.1109/TPAS.1969.292396

Ganesan, T., Elamvazuthi, I., Ku Shaari, K. Z., & Vasant, P. (2013). Swarm intelligence and gravitational search algorithm for multi-objective optimization of synthesis gas production. *Applied Energy, 103*, 368–374. doi:10.1016/j.apenergy.2012.09.059

Ganesan, T., Vasant, P., & Elamvazuthi, I. (2013). Hybrid neuro-swarm optimization approach for design of distributed generation power systems. *Neural Computing & Applications*, *23*(1), 105–117. doi:10.1007/s00521-012-0976-4

Hemamalini, S., & Simon, S. P. (2010). Artificial bee colony algorithm for economic load dispatch problem with non-smooth cost functions. *Electric Power Components and Systems*, *38*(7), 786–803. doi:10.1080/15325000903489710

Holtschneider, T., & Erlich, I. (2013, April). Optimization of electricity pricing considering neural network based model of consumers' demand response. In *Computational Intelligence Applications In Smart Grid (CIASG), 2013 IEEE Symposium* (pp. 154-160). IEEE.

Hooshmand, R.-A., Parastegari, M., & Morshed, M. J. (2012). Emission, reserve and economic load dispatch problem with non-smooth and non-convex cost functions using the hybrid bacterial foraging-Nelder–Mead algorithm. *Applied Energy*, *89*(1), 443–453. doi:10.1016/j.apenergy.2011.08.010

Lee, F. N., & Breipohl, A. M. (1993). Reserve constrained economic dispatch with prohibited operating zones. *IEEE Transactions on Power Systems*, *8*(1), 246–254. doi:10.1109/59.221233

Lee, J.-C., Lin, W.-M., Liao, G.-C., & Tsao, T.-P. (2011). Quantum genetic algorithm for dynamic economic dispatch with valve-point effects and including wind power system. *International Journal of Electrical Power & Energy Systems*, *33*(2), 189–197. doi:10.1016/j.ijepes.2010.08.014

Liao, G.-C. (2011). A novel evolutionary algorithm for dynamic economic dispatch with energy saving and emission reduction in power system integrated wind power. *Energy*, *36*(2), 1018–1029. doi:10.1016/j.energy.2010.12.006

Liao, X., Zhou, J., Zhang, R., & Zhang, Y. (2012). An adaptive artificial bee colony algorithm for long-term economic dispatch in cascaded hydropower systems. *International Journal of Electrical Power & Energy Systems*, *43*(1), 1340–1345. doi:10.1016/j.ijepes.2012.04.009

Lin, C., & Viviani, G. (1984). Hierarchical economic dispatch for piecewise quadratic cost functions. *IEEE Transactions on*(6) *Power Apparatus and Systems*, 1170-1175.

Orero, S. O., & Irving, M. R. (1996, November). Economic dispatch of generators with prohibited operating zones: a genetic algorithm approach. In *Generation, Transmission and Distribution, IEE Proceedings-* (Vol. 143, No. 6, pp. 529-534). IET. doi:10.1049/ip-gtd:19960626

Park, J.-B., Jeong, Y.-W., Shin, J.-R., & Lee, K. Y. (2010). An improved particle swarm optimization for nonconvex economic dispatch problems. *IEEE Transactions on Power Systems*, *25*(1), 156–166. doi:10.1109/TPWRS.2009.2030293

Pothiya, S., Ngamroo, I., & Kongprawechnon, W. (2008). Application of multiple tabu search algorithm to solve dynamic economic dispatch considering generator constraints. *Energy Conversion and Management*, *49*(4), 506–516. doi:10.1016/j.enconman.2007.08.012

Pothiya, S., Ngamroo, I., & Kongprawechnon, W. (2010). Ant colony optimisation for economic dispatch problem with non-smooth cost functions. *International Journal of Electrical Power & Energy Systems*, *32*(5), 478–487. doi:10.1016/j.ijepes.2009.09.016

Roy, R., & Ghoshal, S. (2008). A novel crazy swarm optimized economic load dispatch for various types of cost functions. *International Journal of Electrical Power & Energy Systems*, *30*(4), 242–253. doi:10.1016/j.ijepes.2007.07.007

Rueda, J. L., Cepeda, J. C., & Erlich, I. (2012, July). Estimation of location and coordinated tuning of PSS based on mean-variance mapping optimization. In *Power and Energy Society General Meeting, 2012 IEEE* (pp. 1-8). IEEE. doi:10.1109/PESGM.2012.6345025

Safari, A., & Shayeghi, H. (2011). Iteration particle swarm optimization procedure for economic load dispatch with generator constraints. *Expert Systems with Applications*, *38*(5), 6043–6048. doi:10.1016/j.eswa.2010.11.015

Subbaraj, P., Rengaraj, R., & Salivahanan, S. (2011). Enhancement of Self-adaptive real-coded genetic algorithm using Taguchi method for Economic dispatch problem. *Applied Soft Computing*, *11*(1), 83–92. doi:10.1016/j.asoc.2009.10.019

Vasant, P. (2010). Hybrid simulated annealing and genetic algorithms for industrial production management problems. *International Journal of Computational Methods*, *7*(02), 279–297. doi:10.1142/S0219876210002209

Vasant, P. (2013). Hybrid mesh adaptive direct search genetic algorithms and line search approaches for fuzzy optimization problems in production planning. In *Handbook of Optimization* (pp. 779–799). Springer Berlin Heidelberg. doi:10.1007/978-3-642-30504-7_30

Vasant, P. (2013a). Hybrid Linear Search, Genetic Algorithms, and Simulated Annealing for Fuzzy Non-Linear Industrial Production Planning Problems. *Meta-heuristics Optimization Algorithms in Engineering, Business, Economics, and Finance*, 87.

Vasant, P., & Barsoum, N. (2009). Hybrid genetic algorithms and line search method for industrial production planning with non-linear fitness function. *Engineering Applications of Artificial Intelligence*, *22*(4), 767–777. doi:10.1016/j.engappai.2009.03.010

Vo, D. N., Schegner, P., & Ongsakul, W. (2013). Cuckoo search algorithm for non-convex economic dispatch. *IET Generation. Transmission & Distribution*, *7*(6), 645–654. doi:10.1049/iet-gtd.2012.0142

Yang, X.-S., Sadat Hosseini, S. S., & Gandomi, A. H. (2012). Firefly algorithm for solving non-convex economic dispatch problems with valve loading effect. *Applied Soft Computing*, *12*(3), 1180–1186. doi:10.1016/j.asoc.2011.09.017

Yaşar, C., & Özyön, S. (2011). A new hybrid approach for nonconvex economic dispatch problem with valve-point effect. *Energy*, *36*(10), 5838–5845. doi:10.1016/j.energy.2011.08.041

Zare, K., Haque, M. T., & Davoodi, E. (2012). Solving non-convex economic dispatch problem with valve point effects using modified group search optimizer method. *Electric Power Systems Research*, *84*(1), 83–89. doi:10.1016/j.epsr.2011.10.004

Zhisheng, Z. (2010). Quantum-behaved particle swarm optimization algorithm for economic load dispatch of power system. *Expert Systems with Applications*, *37*(2), 1800–1803. doi:10.1016/j.eswa.2009.07.042

APPENDIX

Table 14. Unit data for 30-unit system with valve point effects

Unit	a_i ($/h)	b_i ($/h)	c_i ($/h)	e_i ($/h)	f_i ($/h)	P_{imin} (MW)	P_{imax} (MW)
1	0.00028	8.1	550	300	0.035	0	680
2	0.00056	8.1	309	200	0.042	0	360
3	0.00056	8.1	307	150	0.042	0	360
4	0.00324	7.74	240	150	0.063	60	180
5	0.00324	7.74	240	150	0.063	60	180
6	0.00324	7.74	240	150	0.063	60	180
7	0.00324	7.74	240	150	0.063	60	180
8	0.00324	7.74	240	150	0.063	60	180
9	0.00324	7.74	240	150	0.063	60	180
10	0.00284	8.6	126	100	0.084	40	120
11	0.00284	8.6	126	100	0.084	40	120
12	0.00284	8.6	126	100	0.084	55	120
13	0.00284	8.6	126	100	0.084	55	120

Table 15. Unit data for 10-unit system with multiple fuels

Unit	Fuel type	a_{ij} ($/h)	b_{ij} ($/MWh)	c_{ij} ($/MW^{2}h)	P_{ijmin} (MW)	P_{ijmax} (MW)
1	1	26.97	-0.3975	0.002176	100	196
	2	21.13	-0.3059	0.001861	196	250
2	2	1.865	-0.03988	0.001138	50	114
	3	13.65	-0.198	0.00162	114	157
	1	118.4	-1.269	0.004194	157	230
3	1	39.79	-0.3116	0.001457	200	332
	3	-2.876	0.03389	0.000804	332	388
	2	-59.14	0.4864	1.18E-05	388	500
4	1	1.983	-0.03114	0.001049	99	138
	2	52.85	-0.6348	0.002758	138	200
	3	266.8	-2.338	0.005935	200	265
5	1	13.92	-0.08733	0.001066	190	338
	2	99.76	-0.5206	0.001597	338	407
	3	-53.99	0.4462	0.00015	407	490
6	2	1.983	-0.03114	0.001049	85	138
	1	52.85	-0.6348	0.002758	138	200
	3	266.8	-2.338	0.005935	200	265

Table 15. Continued

Unit	Fuel type	a_{ij} ($/h)	b_{ij} ($/MWh)	c_{ij} ($/MW²h)	P_{ijmin} (MW)	P_{ijmax} (MW)
7	1	18.93	-0.1325	0.001107	200	331
	2	43.77	-0.2267	0.001165	331	391
	3	-43.35	0.3559	0.000245	391	500
8	1	1.983	-0.03114	0.001049	99	138
	2	52.85	-0.6348	0.002758	138	200
	3	266.8	-2.338	0.005935	200	265
9	3	14.23	-0.01817	0.000612	130	213
	1	88.53	-0.5675	0.001554	213	370
	3	14.23	-0.01817	0.000612	370	440
10	1	13.97	-0.09938	0.001102	200	362
	3	46.71	-0.2024	0.001137	362	407
	2	-61.13	0.5084	4.16E-05	407	490

Table 16. Unit data for 10-unit system with valve point effects and multiple fuels

Unit	Fuel Type	a_{ij} ($/h)	b_{ij} ($/MWh)	c_{ij} ($/MW²h)	e_{ij} ($/h)	f_{ij} (1/MW)	P_{ijmin} (MW)	P_{ijmax} (MW)
1	1	26.97	-0.3975	0.002176	0.02697	-3.975	100	196
	2	21.13	-0.3059	0.001861	0.02113	-3.059	196	250
2	2	1.865	-0.03988	0.001138	0.001865	-0.3988	50	114
	3	13.65	-0.198	0.00162	0.01365	-1.98	114	157
	1	118.4	-1.269	0.004194	0.1184	-12.69	157	230
3	1	39.79	-0.3116	0.001457	0.03979	-3.116	200	332
	3	-2.876	0.03389	0.000804	-0.00288	0.3389	332	388
	2	-59.14	0.4864	1.18E-05	-0.05914	4.864	388	500
4	1	1.983	-0.03114	0.001049	0.001983	-0.3114	99	138
	2	52.85	-0.6348	0.002758	0.05285	-6.348	138	200
	3	266.8	-2.338	0.005935	0.2668	-23.38	200	265
5	1	13.92	-0.08733	0.001066	0.01392	-0.8733	190	338
	2	99.76	-0.5206	0.001597	0.09976	-5.206	338	407
	3	-53.99	0.4462	0.00015	-0.05399	4.462	407	490
6	2	1.983	-0.03114	0.001049	0.001983	-0.3114	85	138
	1	52.85	-0.6348	0.002758	0.05285	-6.348	138	200
	3	266.8	-2.338	0.005935	0.2668	-23.38	200	265
7	1	18.93	-0.1325	0.001107	0.01893	-1.325	200	331
	2	43.77	-0.2267	0.001165	0.04377	-2.267	331	391
	3	-43.35	0.3559	0.000245	-0.04335	3.559	391	500
8	1	1.983	-0.03114	0.001049	0.001983	-0.3114	99	138

Table 16. Continued

Unit	Fuel Type	a_{ij} ($/h)	b_{ij} ($/MWh)	c_{ij} ($/MW²h)	e_{ij} ($/h)	f_{ij} (1/MW)	P_{ijmin} (MW)	P_{ijmax} (MW)
	2	52.85	-0.6348	0.002758	0.05285	-6.348	138	200
	3	266.8	-2.338	0.005935	0.2668	-23.38	200	265
9	3	14.23	-0.01817	0.000612	0.01423	-0.1817	130	213
	1	88.53	-0.5675	0.001554	0.08853	-5.675	213	370
	3	14.23	-0.01817	0.000612	0.01423	-0.1817	370	440
10	1	13.97	-0.09938	0.001102	0.01397	-0.9938	200	362
	3	46.71	-0.2024	0.001137	0.04671	-2.024	362	407
	2	-61.13	0.5084	4.16E-05	-0.06113	5.084	407	490

Table 17. Unit data for 15-unit system with prohibited zones

Unit	a_i ($/h)	b_i ($/MWh)	c_i ($/MW²h)	P_{imin} (MW)	P_{imax} (MW)	S_{imax} (MW)	UR_i (MW)	DR_i (MW)	P_{i0} (MW)
1	671	10.1	0.000299	150	455	50	80	120	400
2	574	10.2	0.000183	150	455	0	80	120	300
3	374	8.8	0.001126	20	130	30	130	130	105
4	374	8.8	0.001126	20	130	30	130	130	100
5	461	10.4	0.000205	150	470	0	80	120	90
6	630	10.1	0.000301	135	460	0	80	120	400
7	548	9.8	0.000364	135	465	50	80	120	350
8	227	11.2	0.000338	60	300	50	65	100	95
9	173	11.2	0.000807	25	162	30	60	100	105
10	175	10.7	0.001203	25	160	30	60	100	110
11	186	10.2	0.003586	20	80	20	80	80	60
12	230	9.9	0.005513	20	80	0	80	80	40
13	225	13.1	0.000371	25	85	20	80	80	30
14	309	12.1	0.001929	15	55	40	55	55	20
15	323	12.4	0.004447	15	55	40	55	55	20

Table 18. Prohibited zones for 15-unit system

Unit	Prohibited Zone 1	Prohibited Zone 2	Prohibited Zone 3
2	[185 225]	[305 335]	[420 450]
5	[180 200]	[305 335]	[390 420]
6	[230 255]	[365 395]	[430 455]
12	[30 40]	[55 65]	

Key Terms and Definitions

Economic Dispatch: Economic dispatch is one of the power management tools that is used to determine real power output of thermal generating units to meet the active load demand. The ED results in minimum fuel generation cost, minimum transmission power losses while satisfying all units, as well as system constraints.

Mean-Variance Mapping Optimization: Mean-variance mapping optimization (MVMO) is a new population based meta-heuristic optimization algorithm which has been developed and introduced by István Erlich in 2010. This algorithm possesses conceptual similarities to other known heuristic algorithms in three evolutionary operators including selection, mutation and crossover. However, the special feature of MVMO is the mapping function applied for the mutation based on the mean and variance of n-best population saved in an archive. The searching space of the algorithm is always restricted inside [0,1] range, however, the fitness function is calculated in the original boundaries. MVMO is a single agent search algorithm because it utilizes only a single parent in the offspring generation at each iteration.

Meta-Heuristic: Meta-heuristic and heuristic refer to experience-based techniques to find a solution to an optimization problem. Meta-heuristic is a higher-level procedure than heuristic. Many meta-heuristics implement some form of stochastic optimization. Hence, the solution is found dependent on generating the set of random variables. Meta-heuristic is classified into two forms: population based optimization and trajectory based optimization. Meta-heuristics can often achieve better solutions with shorter computational time than iterative methods, or simple heuristics by searching over a large set of feasible solutions. For this reason, they are useful approaches for optimization problems. A meta-heuristic will be successful on a given optimization problem if it can balance between the exploration and the exploitation.

Multiple Fuel Options: Many thermal generating units of the electric power system can be supplied with multi fuel sources such as coal, natural gas and oil require that their fuel cost functions may be segmented as piecewise quadratic cost functions, where each of which reflects the effects of different fuel types. Figure 5 describes the fuel cost curve of each generators with multiple fuels.

Figure 5. Fuel cost curve of units with multiple fuels

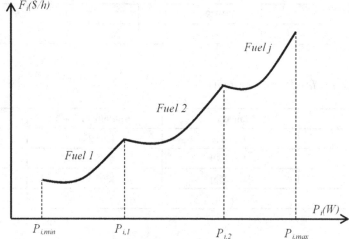

Non-Convex Optimization: A non-convex optimization is a complex problem with multiple local solution, which is difficult to find global optimal solution. In order to deal with this problem, the most used techniques are meta-heuristic algorithm.

Prohibited Operating Zones: The thermal generating unit must avoid operating in the prohibited zones where causes undue vibration of the turbine shaft. It might bring damage to the shaft and bearings. The cost curve of generator with prohibited operating zones is divided into disjointed convex sub-regions as described in Figure 6.

Swarm Based Mean-Variance Mapping Optimization: Swarm based mean-variance mapping optimization (MVMO^S) is an extension of the original version MVMO. The difference between MVMO and MVMO^S is the initial search process with particles. MVMO starts the search with single particle while MVMO^S starts the search with a set of particles. At the beginning of the optimization process of MVMO^S, a set of reliable individual solutions is selected within independent steps of each particle. After that, the particles start to communicate and to exchange information. MVMO is extended two parameters including the scaling factor and variable increment parameter to enhance the mapping. Therefore, the search global ability of MVMO^S is strengthened.

Valve Point Effects: Valve point effects is a natural characteristic of a thermal turbine. The turbine of generating unit has many admission steam valves. The opening of these steam valves increase the throttling losses rapidly, leading to rise the incremental heat rate suddenly. The valve point effects produces a rippling effect on the input-output curve. The ripples like in Figure 7.

Figure 6. Fuel cost curve of units with prohibited zones

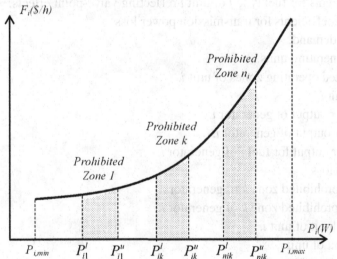

Figure 7. Fuel cost curve of units with valve-point effects

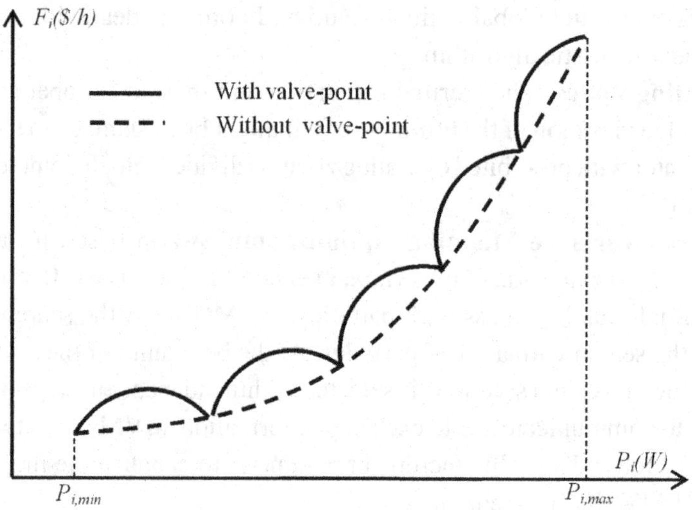

Nomenclature

a_i, b_i, c_i: Fuel cost coefficients of unit i.

e_i, f_i: Fuel cost coefficients of unit i reflecting valve-point effects.

a_{ij}, b_{ij}, c_{ij}: Fuel cost coefficients for fuel type j of unit i.

e_{ij}, f_{ij}: Fuel cost coefficients for fuel type j of unit i reflecting valve-point effects.

B_{ij}, B_{0i}, B_{00}: B-matrix coefficients for transmission power loss.

P_D: Total system load demand.

N: Total number of generating units.

n_i: Number of prohibited operating zones of unit i.

P_i: Power output of unit i.

$P_{i,max}$: Maximum power output of generator i.

$P_{i,min}$: Minimum power output of generator i.

$P_{ij,min}$: Minimum power output for fuel j of generator i.

P_L: Total transmission loss.

P_{ik}^l: Lower bound for prohibited zone k of generator i.

P_{ik}^u: Upper bound for prohibited zone k of generator i.

DR_i: Ramp down rate limit of unit i.

UR_i: Ramp up rate limit of unit i.

$iter_{max}$: Maximum number of iterations.

n_var: Number of variable (generators).

n_par: Number of particles.

Mode: Variable selection strategy for offspring creation.

archive zize: n-best individuals to be stored in the table.

d_i: Initial smoothing factor.

Δd_0^{ini}: Initial smoothing factor increment.

$\Delta d_0^{\text{final}}$: Final smoothing factor increment.

$f_{s\_\text{ini}}^*$: Initial shape scaling factor.

$f_{s\_\text{final}}^*$: Final shape scaling factor.

D_{min}: Minimum distance threshold to the global best solution.

n_randomly: Initial number of variables selected for mutation.

indep.runs: m steps independently to collect a set of reliable individual solutions.

Chapter 8
Advanced Strategy for Droplet Routing in Digital Microfluidic Biochips Using ACO

Indrajit Pan
RCC Institute of Information Technology, India

Tuhina Samanta
Indian Institute of Engineering Science and Technology, India

ABSTRACT

Significant researches are going on for high performance droplet routing in Digital Microfluidic Biochip (DMFB). This chapter elaborates an ant colony optimization based droplet routing technique for high performance design in DMFB. The method is divided into two phases. (1) In the first phase, two dedicated ants generated from each source of the droplets traverse the rectilinear path between the source-target pairs and deposit pheromone to construct rectangular bounding box. Initial bounding box helps in restricted ant movements in the next phase. (2) In the second phase, real routing path is generated. Detour and stalling phenomena are incurred to resolve routing conflict. The method has explored both single ant and multiple ant systems to address detours from the conflicting zone in search for the best possible route towards destination. The method has been simulated on several existing benchmarks and comparative results are quite encouraging.

INTRODUCTION

Digital microfluidic biochip (DMFB) revolutionizes the medical diagnosis process rendering multiple tasks executed on a single chip. Microfluidic based biochips are presently aiding different pathological experimentations and many biochemical laboratory procedures due to their advantages of automation, cost diminution, portability, and competence (Pamula, Srinivasan & Fair, 2004). Growing trends of demand and need for incorporation of multiple-functionality makes the design process complex and costly for digital microfluidic biochip. It has laid a scope for optimization in computer aided design and test before on-chip fabrication. In present days it is a thriving field for researchers and they are exploring

DOI: 10.4018/978-1-4666-8291-7.ch008

Figure 1. Schematic Layout of DMFB

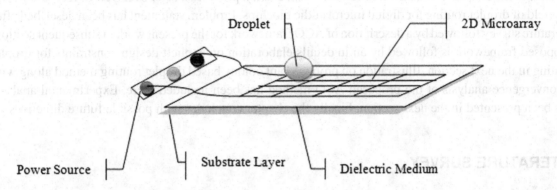

different design aspects to deliver a fully customized biochip (Fair, Su & Chakrabarty, 2006). Digital microfluidic biochip is a small test cites which comprises an array of electrodes sandwiched between two parallel plates. The droplets are manipulated (stored, transported, mixed or reacted) over the electrodes by changing the voltage of two adjacent electrodes and droplets are transported from one electrode to the next by electro-wetting on dielectric (EWOD) technique (Pamula et al., 2004) (Figure 1). Droplet routing is one of the fundamental issues in design of DMFB and major variants in this field are direct addressing mode, cross-referencing mode and pin-constrained droplet routing and design (Chakrabarty, 2010). Mostly, geometry level synthesis of biochip design involves droplet routing, and all the problems are formulated as complex optimization problems, which are NP hard in nature (Su, Ozev & Chakrabarty, 2004; De Micheli, 1994).

Researchers and CAD developers propose several models to solve those optimization problems. Mostly explored field is integer linear program (ILP) solver. ILP solver is a deterministic process which can provide solutions even for hard bioassay protocols. Meta heuristic search procedures are modern in their nature and are merely deployed in the field of biochip design automation. Some works exploring meta-heuristic techniques, named tabu search (TS) and simulated annealing (SA), are found in (Paul, Elena & Madsen, 2009; Xiao & Young, 2010) respectively. Droplet routing in digital microfluidic biochip can be modeled as a combinatorial optimization (CO) problem, and aim of this work is to solve the CO problem using a Meta heuristic strategy named ant colony optimization (ACO). ACO is basically a probabilistic model that uses stochastic search procedure to generate solution (Chun, Huang & Hao, 2009).

In this chapter a new ACO paradigm has been proposed to address droplet routing problem in DMFB. The droplet routing problem is a constrained optimization problem, where constraints are governed by the input bioassay protocol and resource utilization (mainly electrode usage and droplet routing completion time) constraints. The proposed method is divided into phases. Given a search space, (1) in the first phase, a restricted movement zone for the ants are constructed by computing rectangular bounding box between the source target pairs of all the droplets. (2) Next, an adaptive local search technique is employed by the real ants to mark the routing paths for all the droplets. Pheromone deposited by the real ants on their way towards target contains the information of elapsed routing time and remaining Manhattan distance (rectilinear distance) from the target location. Consecutive ants use those pre-deposited pheromone during search for their routing path towards the predefined target location with the shortest route and in turn optimizes the resource utilization. Basic objective in this optimization process is to minimize electrode utilization and routing completion time for all the droplets.

Rest of the chapter is organized as follows. Next section provides a brief overview of recent works in the field of droplet routing for digital microfluidic biochips. Problem statement has been described after literature survey followed by a description of ACO framework for the present work in subsequent section. Proposed framework is followed by an in details elaboration on explicit design constraints for droplet routing in the next section. Illustration on proposed ant colony based droplet routing method along with a convergence analysis of the proposed ACO method has been included there. Experimental analysis has been presented in the next section. Finally the chapter concludes with possible future directives.

LITERATURE SURVEY

Pathological analysis is a prime application for microfluidic based lab-on-a-chip systems. Conventional microfluidic devices were made up on the basis of continuous-flow in microchannels and those devices were very less flexible in terms of reconfigurability and scalability (Pamula et al., 2004). Those devices were not very suitable to deal with real physiological samples. In (Pamula et al., 2004) authors have addressed this issue through a newly proposed fully integrated and reconfigurable droplet-based paradigm for lab on a chip (LOC). These digital microfluidic based devices are claimed to be efficient for clinical diagnostics of human physiological fluids. The microdroplets, which act as solution-phase reaction chambers, are manipulated using the electrowetting effect. These digital droplet based devices were claimed to be reliable and repeatable in high-speed operations of microdroplets like human whole blood, serum, plasma, saliva, etc. These varieties of fluids were tested to be at par with electrowetting operability on chip and it was tested that they could hold their physiological properties without unintended degenerations. In (Pamula et al., 2004), authors have also demonstrated a colorimetric enzymatic glucose assay on serum, plasma, urine, and saliva to establish interoperability of several bioassays on real physiological samples in their proposed system. In their observations, these test results were very much at par with the reference method. Only failure was observed by them in the analysis of urine due to interference by uric acid. Thus the authors of (Pamula et al., 2004) have proposed a lab-on-a-chip architecture in conjunction with previously developed digital microfluidic components for integrated and automated analysis of multiple analytes on a monolithic device. This type of devices are familiar with sample injection, on-chip reservoirs, droplet formation structures, fluidic pathways, mixing areas and optical detection sites, on the same substrate. A pipelined operation of two glucose assays has been also discussed on a prototype digital microfluidic lab-on-chip to establish the proof-of-concept.

In order to address scalability issues of droplet-based "digital" biochips towards concurrent assays and for next-generation system-on-chip (SOC) designs that are expected to include fluidic components; in (Su & Chakrabarty, 2004), authors have proposed a system design methodology that can be potentially applied for classical architectural-level synthesis techniques to the design of digital microfluidics-based biochips. Here the authors have discussed an optimal scheduling strategy based on integer linear programming. As the scheduling problems are NP-complete in nature, the authors have also developed two heuristic techniques that scale well for large problem instances. A clinical diagnostic procedure, namely multiplexed in-vitro diagnostics on human physiological fluids has been demonstrated to evaluate the proposed method.

A review in (Erickson, 2005) provides a detailed discussion on various tools, techniques and different applications of numerical simulation for integrated microfluidic devices. It comprises in depth analysis on fundamental microfluidic operations likes dispensing, mixing, splitting etc towards numerical processing for global integration of systems. Along with these discussions, the author has also addressed important areas of microscale transportation, such as thermal analysis and chemical reactivity and specificity. An overview of the advantages and disadvantages of common numerical techniques with the existing numerical tools have been discussed to identify interoperability for microscale transport analysis. As a part of this review, it was observed that, increasing complexity of microfluidic devices leads to impracticality of experimental validation for newly proposed model. This emerged as a need for microfluidic simulator to validate any new proposition.

In (Fair et al., 2006) authors focused on a scalable, dynamically reconfigurable architecture in contrast to continuous-flow systems that rely on permanently etched microchannels, micropumps, and microvalves. The replaced model is based on a group of unit cells, serving as a microfluidics array which can suitably accommodate reconfiguration to change their functionality during the concurrent execution of a set of bioassays. Applications of these devices encompass clinical diagnosis, DNA sequencing, molecular biology and many more. This leads to increasing design complexity and system integration challenges. This article presents an overview of an integrated system level design methodology which can potentially address key issues in the synthesis, testing and reconfiguration of digital microfluidic biochips. Different actuation mechanisms and associated design automation challenges and inclinations are also discussed. The authors have suggested a top-down design-automation approach with an expectation to ease out troubles of manual optimization of bioassays, time-consuming hardware design, and costly testing and maintenance procedures. The proposed top down design challenges were expected to facilitate the integration of fluidic components with a microelectronic component in next-generation systems-on-chips (SOCs).

In (Griffith et al., 2006) a computational approach for designing a digital microfluidic system has been introduced. They have proposed a coordination technique for droplet motion using planar array of electrodes for biochemical analysis based on electrowetting or Dielectrophoresis. Authors have attempted to suggest a technique for rapid simulation and control of digital microfluidic system following the close proximity in array layout design and droplet routing strategies. In this paper, the effects of changes in the basic array-layout design, droplet-routing control techniques, and droplet spacing on system performance are characterized. Authors have considered microfluidic arrays with hardware limited row-column addressing and a polynomial-time algorithm for coordinating droplet movement under such hardware limitations. Some critical dilution control requirements were simulated and tested through the proposed method.

In (Fair et al., 2007) possible efforts to develop various LoC applications using electrowetting-based digital microfluidics have been discussed considering the advantages of portability, sample and reagent volume reduction, faster analysis, increased automation, low power consumption, compatibility with mass manufacturing and high throughput of digital microfluidic devices.

The author of (Floriano, 2007) has edited sixteen chapters which include thoughts and proposals of leading scientists on precise microchip-based assays for a variety of applications. The articles present state of the art progresses in the microelectronics arena, the resultant miniaturization of component device features to nanometer size particles, and the ensuing growth in the development and use of microchip-based techniques in leading laboratories around the world. Considering the tough challenges of microelectronics, some very promising advancement has been proposed to translate into products such as sensors and devices that use nanometer-sized building blocks for real-world applications. The contributors to this volume are part of growing interdisciplinary efforts among pioneers in microelectronics, nanoscience, and health.

The work in (Fouillet et al., 2008) deals with microfluidic studies for lab-on-a-chip development. In the first part of the article, authors have proposed a microsystem which is tailor made for biologists to integrate complex protocols. Bottom-up architecture was used for chip design to develop and validate elementary fluidic design and those were assembled after validation. This approach has been claimed to accelerate development and industrialization while minimizing the effort in designing and simplifying chip-fluidic programming. This claim was demonstrated by performing on chip serial dilutions of 2.8-folds, four times. The second part of this paper concerns the development of new innovative fluidic functions in order to extend EWOD-actuated digital fluidics' capabilities. Finally, work is shown concerning the coupling of EWOD actuation and magnetic fields for magnetic bead manipulation

Point of care testing is emerging as a key factor in improving the clinical outcome in health care management. Characteristics of a point of care device are rapid results, integrated sample preparation and processing, small sample volumes, portability, multifunctionality and low cost (Sista et al., 2008). In (Sista et al., 2008) digital microfluidic platform has been introduced as a point of care testing. Authors have demonstrated the performance of magnetic bead-based immunoassays (cardiac troponin I) on a digital microfluidic cartridge in less than 8 minutes using whole blood samples. The same microfluidic cartridge was further used in a 40-cycle real-time polymerase chain reaction within 12 minutes by shuttling a droplet between two thermal zones. Capability of the same cartridge was adjudged to perform sample preparation for bacterial infectious disease pathogen and for human genomic DNA using magnetic beads. It was ratified that the modularity and scalability afforded by digital microfluidics, multifunctional testing capability, such as combinations within and between immunoassays, DNA amplification, and enzymatic assays, can be brought to the point of care at a relatively low cost because a single chip can be configured in software for different assays required along the path of care.

In (Paul et al., 2009) a Tabu Search metaheuristic for the synthesis of digital microfluidic biochips has been discussed. This can determine allocation, resource binding, scheduling and placement for a given biochemical application and a biochip architecture. Authors have also considered the reallocation and movement of modules during operations for the improvement of completion time of the biochemical application. The proposed heuristic has been evaluated using three real-life case studies and ten synthetic benchmarks.

Two different tutorials (Chakrabarty, 2010 and Chakrabarty, 2010) on this domain, provide an overview of droplet-based microfluidic biochips. Computer aided design (CAD) tools have been described for the automated synthesis and optimization of biochips from bioassay protocols. These CAD techniques allow biochip users to concentrate on the development of nanoscale bioassays, leaving chip optimization and implementation details to design-automation tools. Advancements in fluidic-operation scheduling, module placement, droplet routing, pin-constrained chip design, and testing are also addressed.

Authors of (Chakrabarty et al., 2010) have discussed about the droplet-based "digital" microfluidic technology platform and emerging applications. The physical principles underlying droplet actuation have been also taken under consideration. Finally, the paper presents some computer aided design tools for simulation, synthesis and chip optimization. These tools mainly target modeling and simulation, scheduling, module placement, droplet routing, pin-constrained chip design, and testing.

In (Hwang et al, 2006), prospect of microfluidics towards sensor systems for high-throughput biochemical analysis has been addressed. Main focus of this paper remained on the droplet routing problem, which is a key issue in biochip physical design automation. A systematic droplet routing method was proposed which can be integrated with biochip synthesis. The proposed approach claimed to minimize the number of cells used for droplet routing, while satisfying constraints imposed by throughput considerations and fluidic properties. A real-life biochemical application has been used to evaluate the proposed method

In (Yang et al., 2007) authors have addressed the critical droplet routing problem for biochip synthesis. It is critical because unlike traditional VLSI routing problems, in addition to routing path selection, the biochip routing problem needs to address the issue of scheduling droplets under the practical constraints imposed by the fluidic property and the timing restriction of the synthesis result. In this paper, authors have first discussed a network flow based routing algorithm which is capable to route a set of non-interfering nets concurrently for the droplet routing problem on biochips. Proposed method is a two-stage technique, which involves a global routing followed by detailed routing. In global routing a set of non-interfering nets are identified and then the network-flow approach is taken to generate optimal global-routing paths for the nets. In detailed routing, first a polynomial-time algorithm manages simultaneous routing and scheduling through the global-routing paths with a negotiation-based routing scheme.

Authors of (Yang et al, 2008) have attempted to solve the droplet routing problem under a scalable cross-referencing biochip paradigm, which uses row/column addressing scheme to activate electrodes. The main challenge of this type of biochips is the electrode interference which prevents simultaneous movement of multiple droplets. Authors initially addressed the optimal solution of droplet routing problem with basic integer linear programming (ILP) formulation. However considering the complexity of the problem a progressive ILP scheme has been suggested to determine the locations of droplets at each time step. Experimental results demonstrate the efficiency and effectiveness of progressive ILP scheme on a set of practical bio assays.

In (Cho & Pan, 2008), a high-performance droplet router for a digital microfluidic biochip has been introduced. This is mainly bypassibility and concession based mechanism. This algorithm first routes a droplet with higher bypassibility which is less likely to block the movement of the others. In case of deadlock among multiple droplets, this algorithm resolves it by backing off some droplets for concession. The final compaction step further enhances timing as well as fault tolerance by tuning each droplet movement greedily. The experimental results on hard benchmarks show that the algorithm achieves over 35 x and 20 x better routability with comparable timing and fault tolerance than existent method.

(Xu & Chakrabarty, 2008) presents a droplet-manipulation method based on a cross-referencing based addressing method that uses row and column based addressing to access electrodes. Authors have mapped the bioassays on a cross referencing mode chip and formulated it as a clique-partitioning problem. Basic objective was to inculcate simultaneous movement of a large number of droplets on a microfluidic array. Concurrency is enhanced through the use of an efficient scheduling algorithm that determines the order in which groups of droplets are moved. The proposed design-automation method facilitates high-throughput applications on a pin-constrained biochip, and it is evaluated using random synthetic benchmarks and a set of multiplexed bioassays.

In (Huang & Ho, 2009), authors propose a fast routability and performance driven droplet router for DMFBs. The method comprises a global moving vector analysis for constructing preferred routing tracks to minimize the number of used unit cells followed by an entropy-based calculation to determine the routing order of droplets for better routability and finally a routing compaction technique by dynamic programming to minimize the latest arrival time of droplets. Experimental results show that the algorithm achieves 100% routing completion for all test cases on three Benchmark Suites which was not achieved by other methods so far. In addition to routability, the algorithm performed better in runtime, qualitatively reduced the latest arrival time and reduced the used unit cells.

(Rahaman et al., 2010) deal with a challenging problem related to the design of DMFB. Specifically the design problem considered is related to high performance droplet routing, where each droplet has single source location and single target location. The objectives are (1) minimizing the number of electrodes used in the DMFB, and (2) minimizing the total routing time of all the droplets or arrival time of a droplet that is the last to arrive at its target(latest arrival time). Authors have proposed a simple algorithm for concurrent path allocation to multiple droplets, based on the Soukup's routing algorithm, together with the use of stalling, and possible detouring of droplets in cases of contentions.

Authors of (Rahaman et al., 2010) have addressed the same droplet routing issues in digital microfluidic biochips through classical shortest-path algorithm. The method was further extended for three pin nets where droplets emerge from two different source locations and converge to a single target location. This classical shortest path based technique is robust enough to manage detour and stalling scenarios in case of deadlock among concurrent droplet routing paths. Experimental analysis of this technique show promising results on standard benchmarks.

In (Xu & Chakrabarty, 2008), authors have devised a cross router to address droplet routing challenges in cross referenced mode biochip. The researches on cross referencing mode biochip can enhance the potentiality of pin constrained chip design. An approach conceded towards the design of cheaper and lighter biochips to facilitate hybrid device integration. DMFB that uses cross-referencing technology to drive droplets movements scales down the number of control pins on chip, which not only brings down the manufacturing cost but also allows large-scale chip design. However, the cross-referencing scheme that imposes different voltage on rows and columns to activate the cells, might cause severe electrode interference, and hence greatly decreases the degree of parallelism of droplet routing. This paper proposes a new method that solves the droplet routing problem on cross-referencing biochip directly. Experimental results on public benchmarks demonstrate the effectiveness and efficiency of the method in comparison with the existent work on this problem.

Transportation and manipulation of different droplets can results in the contamination problem caused by liquid residue of different biomolecules. In (Huang et al., 2009), authors propose a contamination aware droplet routing algorithm for digital microfluidic biochips. In order to reduce the routing complexities and the numbers of used cells, first preferred routing tracks are constructed by analyzing the global moving vector of droplets to guide the droplet routing. A k-shortest path routing technique is applied to minimize the contaminated spots among various sub problems, this is followed by a minimum cost circulation technique for optimized wash droplet scheduling to clean the contaminated spots. Furthermore, a look-ahead prediction technique is used to determine the contaminations between successive sub problems. After that, the MCC-based algorithm is used to circulate wash droplet for removing contamination within any specific sub problem and consecutive sub problems. Minimum cost circulation effectively reduces execution time and the used cells. The method was applied on standard benchmark suite to analyze its efficacy.

Authors in (Zhao & Chakrabarty, 2010) have proposed a wash-operation synchronization method to manipulate wash droplets to clean the residue that is left behind by sample and reagent droplets. They have also synchronized the wash-droplet routing with sample/reagent droplet-routing steps by controlling the arrival order of droplets at cross-contamination sites. The proposed method minimizes droplet-routing time without cross-contamination, and it is especially effective for tight chip-area constraints. A real-life application is used for evaluation.

(Lin & Chang, 2011) presents a design automation flow that considers the cross-contamination problems on pin-constrained biochips. The factors that make the problems harder on pin-constrained biochips are explored. To cope with these cross contaminations, this paper proposes an early crossing minimization algorithm during placement and systematic wash droplet scheduling and routing that require only one extra control pin and zero assay completion time overhead for practical bioassays. Experimental results show the effectiveness and scalability of these algorithms for practical bioassays.

Multiplexing several assays on the same digital microfluidic biochip often leads to undesirable mixing of the residue left by one assay with the droplets of the subsequent assay. Hence, cleaning the droplet pathways of such a biochip by wash droplets between successive assays is required. However a wash droplet has a finite capacity of cleaning. This demands efficient use and circulation of wash droplets so that the method can effectively serve the purposed within an acceptable time limit. (Rahaman et al., 2011) formulates the wash droplet allocation and scheduling problem in terms of graph Eulerization and Capacitated Chinese Postman Problem. Thereby the authors have proposed an efficient solution to that formulation along with some simulated validations.

In (Zhao & Chakrabarty, 2012), a droplet-routing method has been proposed that can avoid cross-contamination in the optimization of droplet flow paths. The proposed approach targets disjoint droplet routes and minimize the number of cells used for droplet routing. Authors have also attempted to minimize the number of wash operations that must be used between successive routing steps to share unit cells in the microfluidic array. Two real-life biochemical applications are used to evaluate the proposed droplet-routing methods.

In (Roy et al., 2013), authors have proposed an intelligent route path exploration technique that attempts to bypass the cross contamination spots depending on the fluidic constraints employed during routing. The path is further refined using intelligent detour by identifying zones of friction between two adjacent route paths. This optimizes the overall route time by reducing the overall time for stalling while routing. The technique found to be efficient in simulations for overall as well as average route time and major reduction in the number of crossovers.

A design automation method for pin-constrained lab-on-chip system has been proposed in (Hwang et al., 2006) This method can manipulate nanoliter volumes of discrete droplets on a microfluidic array. This method minimally assigns adequate number of control pins to address droplet transportation on lab-on-chip system. This reduces design complexity and product cost.

Independent control of electrodes using a large number of input pins is not feasible for low-cost disposable biochips that are envisaged for wide range of applications. Authors of (Xu and Chakrabarty, 2006) assumed that a more promising design strategy might be the division of microfluidic array into smaller partitions and use a small number of electrodes to control the electrodes in each partition. Authors have proposed a partitioning algorithm based on the concept of "droplet trace", which is extracted from the scheduling and droplet routing results produced by a synthesis tool. An efficient pin assignment method, referred to as the "Connect-5 algorithm", is combined with the array partitioning technique based on droplet traces. The array partitioning and pin assignment methods have been evaluated using a set of multiplexed bioassays.

A broadcast-addressing-based design technique for pin-constrained multi-functional biochips has been presented in (Xu and Chakrabarty, 2008). This method provides high throughput for bioassays and it eases the number of control pins by identifying and connecting control pins with "compatible" actuation sequences. This technique was simulated on a multifunctional chip designed to execute a set of multiplexed bioassays, the polymerase chain reaction, and a protein dilution assay.

In (Lin & Chang, 2009), a comprehensive pin-constrained biochip design flow has been discussed that addresses the pin-count issue at all design stages. This method consists of three major stages comprising of pin-count aware stage assignment that partitions the reactions in the given bioassay into execution stages followed by pin-count aware device assignment that determines a specific device used for each reaction and finally, a guided placement, routing, and pin assignment that utilize the pin-count saving properties from the stage and device assignments to optimize the assay time and pin-count. In this technique, both for the stage and device assignments, basic integer linear programming formulations and effective solution-space reduction schemes has been proposed to minimize the assay time and pin-count. Experimental simulation has established the efficiency of this method and a 55-57% pin-count reduction over the existing literature.

Authors have proposed a droplet routing algorithm for pin constrained digital microfluidic biochip which is capable to integrate pin-count reduction with droplet routing stage in (Huang & Ho, 2011), The algorithm shows its competence of minimizing the number of control pins, the number of used cells, and the droplet routing time. The method first adopts a basic integer linear programming (ILP) formulation for optimal solution of the droplet routing problem for pin constrained digital microfluidic biochips with simultaneous multiobjective optimization. Considering the complexity of ILP formulation, authors have also proposed a two-stage technique of global routing followed by incremental ILP based routing to reduce the solution space. Further runtime minimization of the method has been incurred through deterministic ILP formulations that casts the original routing optimization problem into a decision problem, and solve it by a binary solution search method. The binary solution search operates in logarithmic order of time complexity. Extensive simulation of the method establishes the robustness of the proposed technique.

In (Zhao & Chakrabarty, 2011) another integer linear programming (ILP) based optimization method has been discussed to solve the droplet-routing and the pin-mapping design problems concurrently. This co-optimization method optimizes routing pathways and generates a single pin-assignment schedule, and attempts to minimize the number of control pins. This method claimed to be provides a realistic and feasible pin assignment schedule for any bioassay. The effectiveness of the proposed co-optimization method is demonstrated for a commercial biochip that is used to perform n-plex immunoassays, as well as an experimental chip for multiplexed in-vitro diagnostics.

In (Zhao & Chakrabarty, 2011), a modified broadcast addressing based design technique for pin-constrained multifunctional biochips has been discussed. This proposed method claimed to generate high throughput for bioassays and it reduces the number of control pins by identifying "compatible" actuation sequences. Author also described two scheduling methods to map fluidic operations on the pin-constrained design, in order to minimize the completion time while avoiding pin-actuation conflicts. The proposed methods are evaluated using multifunctional chips designed to execute a set of multiplexed bioassays, the polymerase chain reaction, and a protein dilution assay.

A design method to generate an application independent pin assignment configuration with a minimum number of control pins is presented in (Luo & Chakrabarty, 2013). Layouts of a commercial biochip and laboratory prototypes has been used as case studies to evaluate the proposed design method for determining a suitable pin assignment configuration. In comparison with previous pin assignment algorithms, the proposed method found to reduce the number of control pins and facilitate the "general-purpose" use of digital microfluidic biochips for a wide range of applications.

Authors have proposed a heuristic algorithm to simultaneously perform droplet routing and electrode actuation in (Mukherjee et al., 2012). This proposed method is capable of performing droplet routing with minimal electrode usages in optimized routing completion time along with minimal number of control pin assignment on the routing path for successful droplet transportation. This proposed method is a co-optimization technique that finds the possible shortest path between the source and the target pair for a droplet and assigns control pins in an optimal manner to actuate the routing path. Intersection regions for multiple droplets are also assigned with pins in an efficient manner to avoid unnecessary mixing between several droplets. The proposed method is tested on various benchmarks and random test sets, and experimental results are quite encouraging.

In (Chatterjee et al., 2013) a multi-objective optimization algorithm has been proposed which simultaneously minimizes several resources during bioassay operations in a digital microfluidic biochip. Authors have designed a progressive droplet routing as a constrained multi-objective optimization problem to address three objective functions as electrode usages, latest arrival time, and control pin allocation. A composite objective function is constructed by a weighted sum of the first two objective functions. This composite function is minimized pertaining to an upper bound on the third objective function, control pin allocation. A fractional constant weight factor (λ) is chosen to confer upon the necessary weight parameters on the two factors involved in the composite objective function for accurate optimization procedure.

An optimal pin-count design scheme for digital microfluidic biochips has been cited in (Dinh et al., 2014). The method integrates a very simple combinational logic circuit within the original chip. This proposed scheme can provide high throughput for bioassays with an information theoretic minimum number of control pins. Furthermore, to cope with the rapid growth of the chip's scale, authors also proposed a scalable and efficient heuristics. Through experiments, authors have demonstrated that the proposed scheme can obtain much fewer number of control pins compared with the previous state-of-the-art works.

Another pin-count minimization technique for cross-referencing DMFB has been presented in (Yeung et al., 2014) This algorithm can simultaneously optimize routing and control pin assignment. Experiments show that the proposed scheme can reduce pin-count by 23% to 32% with minimal effect on routing time.

Electrowetting-on-dielectric (EWOD) is a popular technology for operations on pin-constrained digital microfluidic biochips (PDMFB). However operational reliability is a major concern for EWOD chips because change in actuation voltage or over charging can directly affect the execution of bioassays (Yeh et al., 2014). The trapped charge problem is the major factor in degradation of chip reliability, and this problem is induced by excessive applied voltage. In PDMFB, signal merging is an inevitable consequence and that can result in trapped charges due to unawareness of the applied voltage. Apart from this, another concern is the wire routing required for accomplishing electrical connections, this increases the design complexity of pin-constrained EWOD chips (Yeh et al., 2014). However, previous research has failed to address the problems of excessive applied voltage and wire routing.

A network-flow-based algorithm for reliability-driven pin-constrained EWOD chips is presented in (Yeh et al., 2014). The proposed algorithm not only minimizes the reliability problem induced by signal merging, but also prevents the operational failure caused by inappropriate addressing results. The proposed algorithm also provides a comprehensive routing solution for EWOD chip-level designs.

An application-independent design method for pin-assignment configuration with a minimum number of control pins has been cited in (Luo & Chakrabarty, 2014). Layouts of commercial biochips and laboratory prototypes are used as case studies to evaluate the proposed design method for determining a suitable pin-assignment configuration. Compared with previous pin-assignment algorithms, the proposed method can reduce the number of control pins and facilitate the general-purpose use of digital microfluidic biochips for a wider range of applications.

In (Roy et al., 2014), authors have proposed a new technique for interconnection wire routing for the control electrodes operating at identical time sequence. They have defined a double layer dual wire system running in parallel along two separate planes in mutually perpendicular directions. Authors have further proposed an algorithm to develop a feasible wire plan for a given layout with an aim to optimize the overall number of pin count. Multiphasing on same pin has been proposed to resolve the issue of wire planning in cases of cross contamination at any particular site.

A problem/ situation independent pin assignment methodology has been proposed in (Yeung & Yang, 2014), which uses only $\sqrt{2}(\sqrt{m} + \sqrt{n})$ number of pins. The resulting DMFB are still fully reconfigurable. They have developed a droplet router specifically for cross-referencing DMFB with shared control pins. Reduction on pin count ranges from 50% to 67%.

PROBLEM FORMULATION

Droplet routing is a fundamental task in physical modeling of DMFB, where resource binding and scheduling is performed. Droplet routing is similar to VLSI net routing with predefined source and destination locations equivalent to the pins of a net belonging to each droplet. During routing, the droplets pay heed to the static blockages present on chip, or the blocked region brings forth by the routing constraints. Droplet routing obeys some fluidic constraints to maintain desired functionality of the chip (Rahaman et al., 2010). Normally the droplets move either horizontally (row-wise) or vertically (column-wise). No diagonal movement is allowed to prevent unwanted mixing of different fluidic samples. In a particular time instance there can be multiple nets on DMFB in quest of their targets. Owing to this scenario, there are the possibilities of two different droplets to arrive side by side at the same time. Hence it can unintentionally merge with the other. Droplet routing algorithm has to be devised in such a manner so that no two droplets arrive at adjacent electrodes at the same time instance. The adjacency margins have to be maintained properly from the aspect of row (horizontal), column (vertical) and diagonals to protect two different droplets from unwanted mixing. These constraints are more elaborately discussed in Section 5. Finally, routing completion time need to be optimized and checked for droplet routing to assure successful completion of the task. Always there is an upper bound of time, within which a particular net should be routed. This time constraint should strictly be maintained. During droplet routing phase, two major routing aspects are emphasized for every type of net; (i) one is minimization of total electrode usage, and (ii) minimizing the routing completion time or latest arrival time among all nets.

Droplet routing problem can be viewed as a combinatorial optimization problem, where all or some of the constraints are optimized simultaneously. Concurrent movement of droplets over the chip area efficiently uses the resources and makes the operations fast. In this chapter, ant colony optimization (ACO) heuristic is explored. ACO is a modern day's Meta heuristic approach for solving hard combinatorial optimization problems (Dorigo & Blum, 2004; Dorigo & Stutzle, 2006). The inspiring source of ACO is the pheromone trail laying and following behavior of real ants, which use deposited pheromone as a communication medium.

Framework for ACO Algorithm

ACO algorithm is a stochastic search procedure that generates solution from a pheromone model tackled from a combinatorial optimization problem (Dorigo et al., 2004, 2006). Given a problem model P (S, C, f) consisting of

- A finite search space S.
- A set of constraints C.
- An objective function f to be optimized.

ACO tries to optimize a constrained objective function f or an unconstrained objective function f. In unconstrained problem formulation C is an empty set. The decision variables are assigned on the basis of local search method by the real ants propagating over the search space. In the proposed problem framework, a constrained objective function f is optimized as follows,

Given a search space over a two dimensional biochip area, and the droplet routing constraints, major objective is to minimize electrode usages, and latest arrival time for all the droplets. This proposed method is mainly divided in to two phases.

1. In the first phase, two different ants are respectively propagated in horizontal (row-wise) and in vertical (column-wise) direction from a specific source to mark out the bounded box for that Source (S_i) - Target (T_i) pair.
2. In the second phase different static and fluidic constraints associated with droplet routing in DMFB are solved and complete the routing procedure with optimal objective function generation.

In these two above mentioned stages propagation of ant is directed by a pheromone updating /deposition function. At any k^{th} time stamp the pheromone deposition function is represented by the following equation:

$$T_{ij} \leftarrow \sum_{k=1}^{m} (1 - \Phi) t_{ij} + \Delta T_{ij}^{k} \tag{1}$$

where ant is moving from i^{th} electrode to j^{th} electrode and,

- $[(1 - \Phi) t_{ij}]$ represents net carry forward pheromone from $(k - 1)^{th}$ to k^{th} time stamp and Φ is pheromone evaporation rate, and t_{ij} counts the time elapsed till the present location.
- ΔT_{ij}^{k} is the newly deposited pheromone for k^{th} time stamp, which will be added with the carry forwarded amount from $(k - 1)^{th}$ time.

For multiple droplets traversing through the same path, τ_{ij} is updated with,

$$T_{ij}^{m} \leftarrow T_{ij} + \sum_{k=1}^{m} (1 - \Phi) t_{ij} + \Delta T_{ij}^{k} \tag{2}$$

where, τ^m_{ij} is the total amount of pheromone deposited on the jth electrode, it is being visited by m number of ants, with m = 1, 2, ... The convergence property of this method can be established if the above sum of pheromone is found to be bounded within a finite range. Detail analysis of pheromone evaporation rate and convergence is described in later section.

DESIGN CONSTRAINTS FOR DROPLET ROUTING

Source and Sink Requirement

The droplet routing path from a source location to a target location is considered as a net. In a net N_i, initially a droplet resides on the source electrode (x^s, y^s), at time t = 0, where (x^s, y^s) is the coordinate location of the source electrode on a two dimensional plane. After successful completion of droplet routing, each net ends at the target location, where (x^t, y^t) is the coordinate location of the destination electrode on a two dimensional plane.

Fluidic Constraints

Concurrent droplet movement is essential to optimize droplet movement and their accessibility at the target cells, hence to optimize area and throughput. In order to avoid any unwanted mixing during concurrent transportation of droplets, fluidic constraints need to be maintained. Let d_i at (x^t_i, y^t_i) and d_j at (x^t_j, y^t_j) denote two independent droplets at time t. Then, the following constraints, generally called Fluidic Constraint, should be satisfied for any t during routing:

- **Static Constraint:** $|x^t_i - x^t_j| \geq 2$ or $|y^t_i - y^t_j| \geq 2$
- **Dynamic Constraint:** $|x^{t+1}_i - x^t_j| \geq 2$ or $|y^{t+1}_i - y^t_j| \geq 2$ or $|x^t_i - x^{t+1}_j| \geq 2$ or $|y^t_i - y^{t+1}_j| \geq 2$

To satisfy the fluidic constrains, a zone called critical zone is specified around a droplet position. At any instance of time t, critical zone of a moving droplet is the region of eight electrodes surrounding the droplet. An example critical zone formation is shown in Figure 2. Let at a time instance t_1 a droplet S_1 is present on the electrode A. The electrodes under critical zone are those marked by the gray color in Figure 2. No other droplet can enter that critical region at time stamp t_1, to avoid unnecessary mixing. As the droplet S_1 moves to the next electrode position in the next time stamp $t_1 + 1$, previous critical zone is updated with the present critical zone.

Electrode Activation

Droplet transportation is managed over the two dimensional chip through proper activation of electrodes. The activation sequences are aimed to maintain horizontal and vertical movement of droplets without any diagonal transportation as discussed elaborately in (Fair et al., 2006). During electrode hop of a particular droplet from one electrode to its horizontal/ vertical adjacent one, destination cell is activated, while deactivating the precedent cell. All the diagonal and non-diagonal adjacent cells of the active cell are kept deactivated to keep the droplet in its position. An explanatory representation of electrode activation is shown in Figure 3. In figure 3 (a), with respect to the location of droplet S_1, horizontal and

Figure 2. Critical zone for a droplet on DMFB

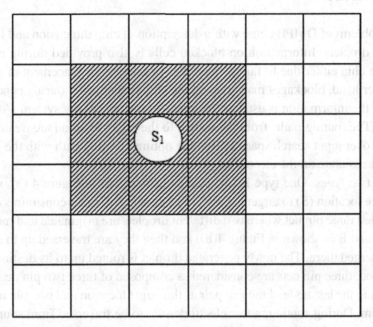

vertically adjacent electrode cells (marked with right up diagonal bars) are attainable for S_1 where as diagonally adjacent electrode cells (marked with horizontal bars) are restricted for movements as per the rules of droplet routing in DMFB. In figure 3 (b) a possible movement of the droplet, S_1 has been depicted. This change of electrode location can be attained through proper actuation of destined electrode by applying activation voltage.

Figure 3. (a) Electrode actuation constraint (b) Droplet movement

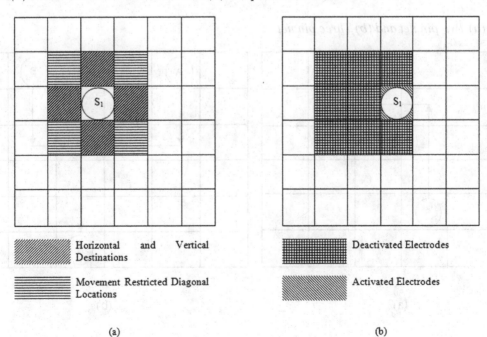

(a)

(b)

PROPOSED METHOD

All the standard problems of DMFB come with a description of chip dimension and location of source-target pairs for the droplets. Information on blocked cells is also provided during routing. The static blocks occur on the chip either due to failed electrodes or may be for placement of on chip waste reservoirs. On the other hand, blockages may arise on the chip dynamically during concurrent movement of the droplets. All the information is used as the inputs to the ant colony system (ACS) to resume the movement of ants. The routing paths from the source to the target location are treated as nets, and the real ants propagate over input search space to find the optimal routing path with the gathered information of deposited pheromone on the electrodes.

The nets are of two types. One type is two pin net as depicted in Figure 4 (a), where a droplet is routed from a source location (S) to target location (T) following all other constraints of droplet routing. Another type is called three pin net where two different droplets are originated and routed from two different locations (A and B as shown in Figure 4(b)) and then they are traversed up to a common mixing location (M) and merged there. The newly generated droplet is routed up to its destined location (T). In this proposed method, three pin nets are considered as composed of three two pin nets as, A → M, B → M, and M → T having the last node of the end pair as the target location and two-pin net routing method is used to route them. During routing, a few electrodes are to be traversed from source location to the target location in minimum required time and by using least number of electrodes.

A formal high level description of the proposed method is shown in Algorithm 1. The whole task is divided in to two parts. At first the bounded box for every net between their source and target coordinates are marked. The function ConstructBoundedBox() is used to accomplish the task (Algorithm 2). In this method, two different ants are propagated from source location of every net. One ant starts moving in the horizontal direction and another move in vertical direction towards the respective target of the source of initiation. Here the ants' movement is only guided by the fact of minimization of tour cost between source and target pair. The bounded box is generated by computing rectilinear distance between the

Figure 4. (a) Two pin net and (b) Three pin net

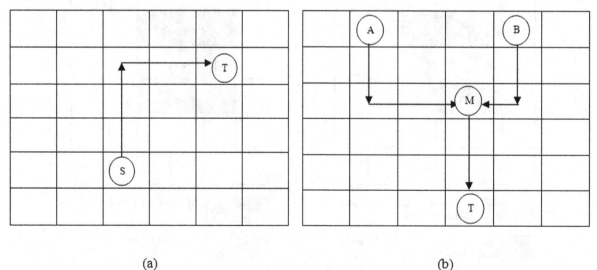

(a)   (b)

Algorithm 1. Top level ACO framework for droplet routing

```
Input: ACO problem BA = (S, C, f), S = two dimensional array of electrodes,
Number of nets(n), C = Fluidic constraints, f = objective function
Output: f = {Electrode usages, Routing completion time}
index (n) = 1; Initialize pheromone (r), Initialize MST = 0;
begin
        ConstructBoundedBox(n);
        for i = 1 to n do
            RouteOnNets(n, blk);
        end
end
```

Algorithm 2. ConstructBoundedBox(): Procedure for constructing bounding box

```
Initialize MST = 0, tempMST  = ∞, xˢ [], yˢ[], xᵗ [], yᵗ [] ;
for i = 1 to n do
    xˢ, yˢ ← Source  coordinates;  xᵗ, yᵗ ← Target coordinates;
    tᴴ ← xˢ+ + towards xᵗ ;      tⱽ ← yˢ+ + towards yᵗ;
    MST ← Compute Manhattan Distance;
    if (MST > tempᴹˢᵀ) then
                tᴴ ← tⱽ ;
                tⱽ← tᴴ ;
end
tempᴹˢᵀ ← MST ;
end
```

electrode pairs in each step. All other static and dynamic fluidic constraints of droplet routing are not considered in this phase.

In the next operation, routing of nets is performed following all the constraints of droplet routing. The method named RouteOnNet() is described in Algorithm 3 that performs net routing. Here, simultaneously ants are initiated from all the source locations of the nets. These ants' routing is guided by the boundary of bounded box marked by the method ConstructBoundedBox(). At every time instant, each ant propagates to a new location and deposits some pheromone on that new location. Pheromone deposition is guided by Equation 1. When an ant is moving from the ith electrode to the jth electrode, $(1 - \phi) \times t_{ij}$ represents net carry forward pheromone from $(k-1)^{th}$ to k^{th} time stamp and ϕ is pheromone evaporation rate. $\Delta \tau_{ij}^{k}$ is the newly deposited pheromone for k^{th} timestamp, which will be added with the carry forwarded pheromone from $(k-1)^{th}$ timestamp. Any newly generated move / location by an ant is selected based on three major factors:

1. New location chosen should be block free. If this is found to be a blocked location then substitutive measures are to be taken, as discussed later.

2. Next they are checked for different static and dynamic routing constraints. If a fluidic conflict is found between respective new locations of two droplets, then stalling of one droplet is performed and passes on the other one. Stalling of a droplet is prioritized based on the distance of the present location of the droplets from their target locations. High priority is assigned to the droplets with larger number of remaining electrodes towards target than that of the other droplet to be traversed to reach the target, and the droplet with high priority is allowed to move first by stalling the other one.

3. When none of the conflicting droplets is taken to the new location, this routing conflict is resolved by calling detour operation.

4. Resource utilization and routing completion time is minimized by repeated use of same electrode, and finding the shortest path for routing towards target location abided by all the routing constraints.

Figure 5 (a) shows a condition of stalling. Here Droplet from S_1 is targeted towards D_1 and from S_2 another droplet is going to D_2. However the dotted square zone is a conflicting area where one droplet (S_1) may be stalled and another (S_2) will pass by. Once the droplet (S_2) passing the conflicting area goes out of critical zone, the stalled droplet will proceed. Another situation may arise (Figure 5(b)) where source and target of one droplet will fall in the path of another droplet. In such cases none of the conflicting droplets may be able to move on to new location. Here stalling may not solve out the deadlock. Then detour of one droplet is performed through a new alternative path. As in figure 5 (b), for one droplet (from S_2) it may not be possible to follow its shortest path along the dotted line due to conflict. So it has taken a new path to reach its destination D_2. These are the deadlock conditions. In this proposed method

Algorithm 3. RouteOnNets (n, (x, y), blk): Procedure for routing on different nets

```
tempMST = ∞;
while (n ≠ NULL) do
            lx ← xs; ly ← ys; m ← selected movement; (*Consider Bounded Box*)
                    while (MST ≠ NULL) do
                        m ← new movement(m´); (lx, ly) ← (lx´, ly´);
                                            (*Update position coordinates*)
                        if ((lx´, ly´) within blk) then
                                ManageBlock();
                        else
                                CheckConstraint(n, (lx´, ly´), τ);
                        if (success) then
                                tempMST ← Remaining Manhattan Distance;
(*Update tempMST*)
                                    tij ← Time elapsed; (*Update routing time*)
                                    τi ← {tij + Δτi, tempMST} (*Update Pheromone*);
                        end
                end
        end
    end
```

stalling and detour has been tackled by ManageBlock() operation by generating real ant movement as per the required condition.

The proposed method is illustrated in Figure 6 and Figure 7. A 6×6 dimensional microarray of electrodes accomplishing thirty six electrodes is shown in Figure 6(a). Figure 6(a) shows different electrode addresses starting from (1, 1) to (6, 6). The microarray has seven blocked electrodes in the locations of (2, 3), (2, 4), (3, 3), (3, 4), (5, 2), (5, 3) and (5, 4). Initial bounding box creation for every source-target pair net is shown in Figure 6(c).

Now the second phase of the proposed method, which manages the concurrent routing of all nets, is being explained in Figure 7 through its sub components from Figure 7 (a) to Figure 7 (f). In Figure 7 (a) depicts the status of three different droplets at time, t = 0. Each ant from every source starts propagating towards their respective target at this, t = 0. The direction of ant's movement from its source is guided by the bounded box and location of its target.

Figure 5. (a) Stalling and (b) Detour

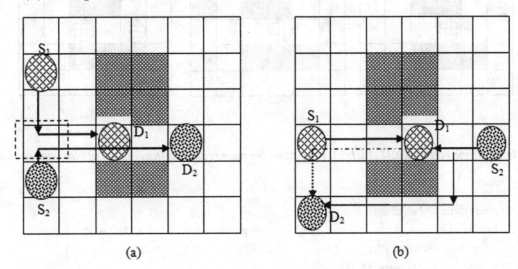

Figure 6. (a) 6×6 Array of electrodes (b) Initial droplet positions (c) Bounding box

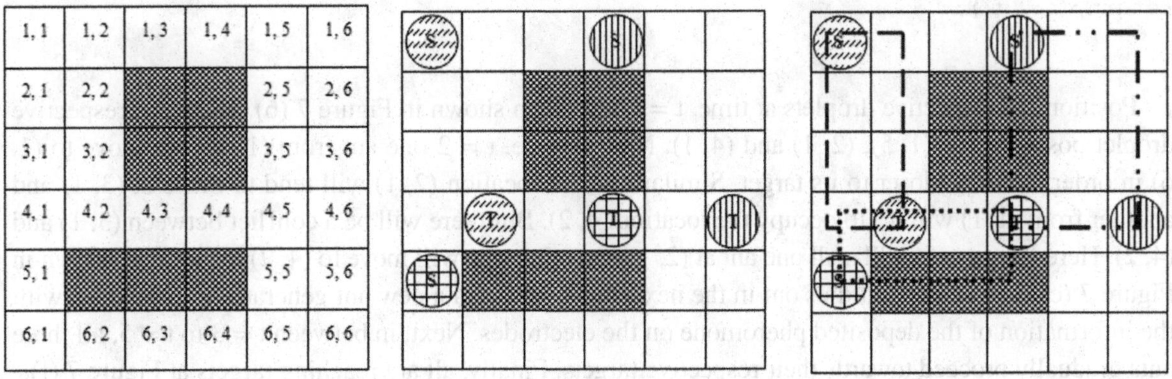

Figure 7. Droplet routing example (a) t = 0 (b) t = 1 (c) t = 2 (d) t = 3 (e) t = 4 (f) t = 5

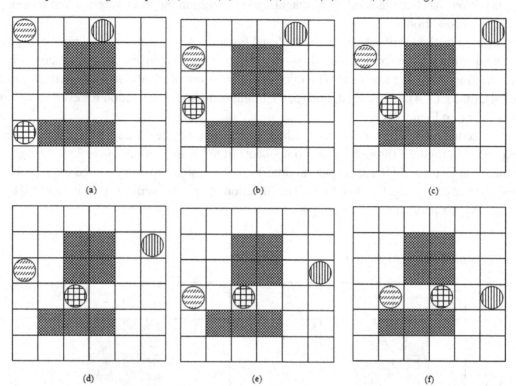

Algorithm 4. ManageBlock(n, (l_x, l_y), blk): Procedure for managing routing conflict of blockage avoidance

```
temp^MST = ∞
while (target not reached) do
        Generate new move m¹ and m² in opposite directions to each other;
        t¹ = RouteOnNet (n[], (l_x, l_y), blk);
(*time to route to the next location*)
        t² = RouteOnNet (n[], (l_x, l_y), blk);
end
return (t¹, t²);
```

Positions of respective droplets at time, t =1 have been shown in Figure 7 (b) where the respective droplet positions are (1, 5), (2, 1) and (4, 1). Now at time, t = 2 one ant from (1, 5) will move to (1, 6) in order to come closer to its target. Similarly ant at location (2, 1) will tend to move at (3, 1) and another from (4, 1) will try to occupy the location (4, 2). But there will be a conflict between (3, 1) and (4, 2). Here the process will stall one ant at (2, 1) and other one will move to (4, 2) location as shown in Figure 7 (c). The stalled ant dies out in the next time cycle, and a new ant generates to propagate with the information of the deposited pheromone on the electrodes. Next, in between t = 3 to t = 5, all three ants gradually proceed towards their respective targets. Finally, all are reaching targets at Figure 7 (f).

Single Ant System

In single ant system, whenever conflict generates for any pair of ants dedicated to route for two droplets movements, one of the propagating ants stops there, which may be granted as died out. A new ant initiates its journey towards the target either of the free move-ahead directions by considering the conflicting or blocked region as a local maximum. The new ant's movement is guided by RouteOnNet() method and its pheromone information gets updated accordingly. Once this ant terminates at its target, the residual pheromone along the path between source and target is regarded as a routing solution. The ultimate pheromone trail at the target location gives an account of routing completion time.

Multiple Ant System

In Multiple ant system, if there is any routing conflict or presence of any blockage on the path of a propagating ant, then present ant dies out and two ants generate from the conflicted/ blocked location and propagate in the orthogonally opposite directions of the antecedent ant's movement. Any backward propagation of ant is not allowed. Partial solution generated up to conflicted/ blocked location is considered as local maxima. Both the newly generated ants proceed toward the target and which meets the target first is regarded as a best solution between the target and the local maxima. Finally the residual pheromone trail is observed as a complete solution between source and target and the final pheromone value on termination gives us an idea of time requirement for routing completion.

Electrode Usages

In every source target pair, the minimum number of electrodes to be traversed by a droplet is represented by the Manhattan distance (rectilinear distance) between the source and the target electrode. Count on electrodes on which pheromone is deposited in the first phase of the algorithm gives a lower bound in electrode usages for routing.

Total electrode usage is counted by tracing pheromone trail between the source-target routes after an ant reaches the target successfully. Multiple electrode count for all the routes are canceled by detecting previously deposited pheromone on the path. To reduce the number of electrode usage, checking is done at all iterations of ant propagation, to find electrode with maximum pheromone deposition using Equation (1) and (2), and Manhattan distance calculation from the present location. Choice is made for electrodes with higher pheromone value, as more ants pass through these electrodes.

PHEROMONE EVAPORATION RATE AND ACO CONVERGENCE ANALYSIS

In the first phase of proposed method, when the bounded box is being marked, the evaporation rate Φ is 1 and it remains constant. No k term will come for summing up in equation (1). Only $\Delta\tau_{ij}$ amount of pheromone is deposited at k = 1. The amount of pheromone deposition is same for all electrodes in every (Si − Ti) pair. Here pheromone has not any significant role to play in ants' movement and decision procedure in order to mark bounding box. Hence ants' propagation to create the bounding box (the first phase of this algorithm) converges within a finite time.

In the second phase of proposed method the static and fluidic conflicts are judged at every time stamp between multiple nets. Accordingly the previously traced electrodes along the boundary of the bounded box are deposited with pheromone. In a normal principle of ANTNET (Dorigo et al., 2006) pheromone is densely deposited in a farthest location of target and it is merely deposited at closer locations of target. Following to this principle, in this method for a $(S_i - T_i)$ pair the newly deposited pheromone at each kth time stamp $\Delta\tau_{ij}^k$ can be expressed in terms of remaining Manhattan distance (R_m) of the target electrode.

$$\Delta T_{ij}^k = R_m \tag{3}$$

In (Dorigo et al., 2006), it has been cited that finding an optimal solution in an ANTNET method is also depended on the amount of pheromone evaporation. Otherwise the solution will converge in a suboptimal solution, where goodness factor of the solution will be less. Authors have suggested that the evaporation at any location of an ANTNET should be inversely proportional of the target distance.

Evaporation Rate

In proposed method, target distance is always measured in terms of required number of electrodes hop from a specific location. This measure is guided by remaining Manhattan estimate of target. Hence, this is assumed that at initial state, remaining Manhattan of a target location for a net is R_m, then computation of MAX (R_m) among all nets can be done. This MAX (R_m) is the maximum of Manhattan distance (R_{MAX}) among all the source-target pairs. In this proposed method, pheromone evaporation is assumed to be governed by $(1 - \Phi)$. Evaporation rate Φ is guided by the routing completion time to assure nominal evaporation at the onset of routing and maximum evaporation when a droplet reaches its target. Hence, the evaporation Φ at any electrode will be represented as,

$$\Phi \propto R_m^{-1} \tag{4}$$

$$\Phi_{MIN} = k \times R_{MAX}^{-1} \cong R_{MAX}^{-1} \tag{5}$$

Assuming Inequality constant k = 1, evaporation rate Φ can be minimum when a droplet reaches its target location maximizing the factor $(1 - \Phi_{MIN})$. Φ_{MIN} is a very small value and $<< 1$ at the completion of routing. So at the completion of routing, deposited pheromone τ_{ij} can be expressed as,

$$T_{ij} \leftarrow \sum_{k=1}^{m} (1 - R_{MAX}^{-1}) t_{ij}^k + R_m \tag{6}$$

where, t_{ij} is the routing time counted for moving from the ith to the jth electrode. At the end of droplet routing, remaining Manhattan value R_m in the Equation (5) is zero, and first term in the summation is,

$$T_{ij} \leftarrow \sum_{k=1}^{m} T_{ij}^{k} \tag{7}$$

Hence, after completion of ith droplet routing, pheromone value is counted as,

$$T_{i} \leftarrow T_{ij} + \sum_{k=1}^{m} T_{ij}^{k} \tag{8}$$

where, m is the number of hops required to reach the target location, and τ_{i} contains information of routing completion time only.

If, $m \rightarrow \infty$, then $R_{MAX} \rightarrow \infty$

Which is a contradicting statement as R_{MAX} is predefined static constant value.

Also $m \rightarrow \infty$ with $\Phi_{MIN} \rightarrow 0$

(By maximizing the evaporation rate)

Hence no carry forward pheromone will be there for guided routing of the ants. Hence, m is a finite integer value leading to a static pheromone deposition τ_{ij}. Equation (8) represents a finite value, guided by the total time count on a fixed integer value m.

The above analysis considers only single ant propagation from the source S_i to the target T_i. Convergence time for the searching phenomena by propagation of multiple ants is discussed next.

Convergence Time Analysis for Multiple Ant Propagation

Single ant succeeds in reaching the target location when there is no routing conflict, and routing convergence is governed by the Maximum Manhattan distance R_{MAX}, where $m = R_{MAX}$ in Equation (5) and (6). The convergence time is considered as t0 for single ant system. Multiple ant propagation is conceived during any routing conflict and routing around blockages on the search space. Multiple ants are generated for the following three cases.

- **Detour:** Given a set of n input droplet locations, each routing path may face at most n routing conflicts and detour is incurred next. Each detour generates maximum two ants to explore the local search space in orthogonally opposite direction, increasing the convergence time by $O(2 \times n)$.
- **Stalling:** When an ant faces stalling due to routing conflict, the present ant dies out generating a new ant from the same location. Hence iteration time is incremented to $O(n)$, assuming worst case scenario of stalling for all the routing paths.
- **Obstacle:** Θ numbers of obstacles deliberately generate $2 \times \theta$ ants for traversing around the obstacle regions, heading in opposite directions. Therefore routing time is incremented to $O(2 \times \theta)$.

If all the three cases are counted in convergence time analysis, total computation time is increased to $t_n = t_0 + t_{iter} = t_0 + O(2 \times n) + O(n) + O(2 \times \theta) \approx t_0 + O(n) + O(\theta)$.

Hence, upper bound of convergence time is dependent on the input set of droplets n and the obstacles θ. For increased iteration due to routing conflict, pheromone deposition rate and time to reach the target formulae in Equation (6) and (8) changes to

$$T_{ij} \leftarrow \sum_{k=1}^{\Re} (1 - R_{MAX}^{-1}) t_{ij}^k + R_m \tag{9}$$

and

$$\tau_i \leftarrow \tau_{ij} + \sum_{k=1}^{\Re} \tau_{ij}^k \tag{10}$$

However the summation terms in Equation (9) and Equation (10) can be proved to be finite integer values. Initial search space for ant propagation is bounded by creating a rectangular bounding box. During routing conflict, n number of ants can generate on average n/2 routing conflict locations. The maximum hop count R is bounded by the predefined search space, array size of the chip, and upper bound on routing conflict. Hence, in this proposed algorithm $R < \infty$ is true for all i values, leading to bounded values of Equation (9) and Equation (10).

EXPERIMENTAL RESULTS

Proposed droplet routing algorithm is implemented in C on a PC running on Intel chip with 2 GB RAM and 2.5 GHz clock speed in Linux platform. The in-vitro benchmarks and some of the hard test sets (Cho et al., 2008; Xiao & Young, 2010) also used in the simulation of proposed single ant and multi ant algorithm. It has been observed that the method is capable of serving both the two-pin and three-pin nets. Details of benchmarks are presented in Table 1.

In Table 2, comparative test results are shown between single and multiple ants based droplet routing algorithm on standard benchmarks. For in-vitro and protein test cases average value of all the sub-problems are cited in the table. In single ant system (SAS), a single new ant generates from any conflict region to traverse towards the destination cell. Multi ant system (MAS) avails at least two new ants generating from a routing conflict zone. Hence total ant count in MAS is greater than that in SAS system. However, performance study in terms of resource utilization shows improvement in results for MAS. MAS are capable of collating more information on carry-forward pheromone, because of their multiplicity and helps in reaching close towards optimal solution than in case of SAS. A comparative graphical analysis between single and multi ant system has been given in Figure 8. Figure 8(a) shows ant count for each instance, and Figure 8(b) shows CPU execution time for SAS and MAS. MAS take greater execution time than that in SAS, ensuing more multiplicative property.

Figure 9 (a) and 9(b) manifests the fact that optimization procedure is improved in droplet routing for MAS. However the CPU usage of single ant system is better than multiple ant system, because in later

Table 1. Benchmark details

Benchmark	Dimension	Blockage	# Nets
in-vitro 1	16×16	77	20
in-vitro 2	14×14	51	23
protein_1	21×21	84	30
protein_2	13×13	48	26
test 12 _12	12×12	11	48
test 16 _16	16×16	39	96
test 24 _24	24×24	119	144
test 32 _32	32×32	269	192

Table 2. Comparative results between single ant and multiple ant based droplet routing algorithm

Benchmark	Single Ant System				Multiple Ant System			
	Ant #	Latest Arrival Time	Total Electrodes	CPU Exec. (Secs.)	Ant #	Latest Arrival Time	Total Electrodes	CPU Exec. (Secs.)
in-vitro 1	20	29	80	0.187	38	17	52	0.195
in-vitro 2	23	30	72	0.187	37	16	47	0.197
protein_1	30	45	123	0.19	60	22	88	0.24
protein_2	26	33	70	0.186	40	13	53	0.192
test 12_12	48	51	28	0.21	54	20	28	0.272
test 16_16	96	118	52	0.21	140	26	44	0.275
test 24_24	144	246	88	0.21	348	40	74	0.291
test 32_32	192	317	113	0.23	409	56	98	0.313

Figure 8. Single Ant System (SAS) and Multi Ant System (MAS) performance for different benchmarks ((a) total number of ants (b) CPU execution time (sec)

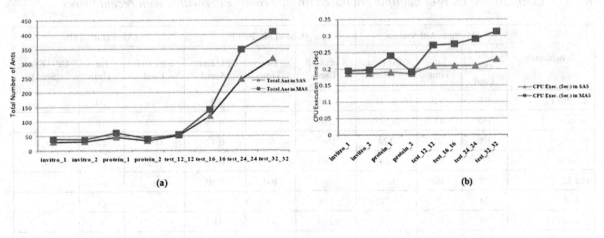

case computation time increases because of increase in iteration. Comparative study among the results of proposed multiple ant system with the results of algorithms used in Cho et al., 2008 and Xiao et al., 2010 has been shown in Table 3.

Experimental results of multiple ant system cite much faster routing completion time for both in-vitro and hard test sets. The proposed method drastically reduces total electrode usage compared to other previously proposed works for the in-vitro benchmark suits. Even the results show improvement in CPU execution over (Cho et al., 2008). They run their experiments on an Intel 2.6 GHz 32-bit Linux machine with 4GB RAM. Notable improvement in CPU time is achieved in the proposed method as it restricts the search space and number of iterations for ACO within a boundary. One disadvantage in the iterative approach is that, for multi ant system, routing completion time exceeds the values presented in (Xiao et al., 2010). Multiple ants generated from any region require more time to complete their tour through multiple paths to reach target, which results in comparatively higher routing completion time. However, electrode usages are improving in MAS algorithm by optimizing the cost function, by choosing the best suited routing path from pheromone deposition information of multiple ants.

Figure 9. Performance of droplet routing algorithm for Single Ant System (SAS) and Multi Ant System (MAS) (a) comparison of latest arrival time (b) comparison of electrode usage

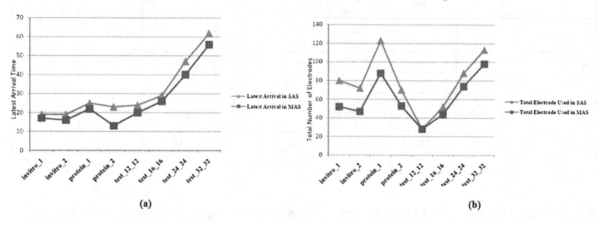

(a)　　　　　　　　　　　　　　　　(b)

Table 3. Comparative study of multiple ant based droplet routing algorithm with recent works

Benchmark	Multiple Ant System			(Cho et al., 2008)			(Xiao et al., 2010)		
	Unit Cell Used	La. Time	CPU Exec. (Secs.)	Unit Cell Used	La. Time	CPU Exec. (Secs.)	Unit Cell Used	La. Time	CPU Exec. (Secs.)
in-vitro 1	200	52	0.195	258	-	0.06	246	20	-
in-vitro 2	182	47	0.197	246	-	0.14	250	19	-
protein_1	309	88	0.24	1688	-	0.47	1164	20	-
protein_2	177	53	0.192	963	-	0.32	952	20	-
test 12_12	28	20	0.272	67	100	0.10	-	-	-
test 16_16	44	26	0.275	118	78	0.39	-	-	-
test 24_24	78	40	0.291	249	47	0.67	-	-	-
test 32_32	98	56	0.313	394	68	1.52	-	-	-

FUTURE RESEARCH DIRECTIONS

In this chapter, droplet routing for direct-addressing mode digital microfluidic biochip has been addressed. The work can also be extended for cross-referencing mode biochip design with more resource optimization. This meta-heuristic based co-optimization approach can also be used for further stringent requirement of pin-constrained biochip design. Cross referencing and pin constrained design of digital microfluidic biochips is receiving major attention in recent time to enhance the chip performance. Same meta-heuristic approach can also be extended for simultaneous and weighted optimization of various performance parameters of droplet routing like pin count, number of electrode usages and routing completion time. The work can be further extended for cross contamination avoidance and wash droplet scheduling for residue removal.

CONCLUSION

Meta-heuristic search strategies are modern methods to solve combinatorial optimization problems. In this chapter, ant colony optimization (ACO) based search technique has been explored to solve droplet routing problem in digital microfluidic biochip. To the best of or knowledge, ACO is not explored till date in the field of design automation for digital microfluidic biochip. A guided ACO search technique has been proposed to find solution to constrained droplet routing problem. Pheromone deposition and evaporation rate, and convergence analysis of this proposed algorithm in the multiple ant system is also done to check for validation and success of the proposed strategy. Experimental results are compared with two recent works and the proposed ACO based approach prevails in almost all the cases.

REFERENCES

Chakrabarty, K. (2010). Digital microfluidic biochips: A vision for functional diversity and more than Moore. In *Proceedings of 23rd International Conference on VLSI Design* (pp. 452 – 457). Academic Press. doi:10.1109/VLSI.Design.2010.33

Chakrabarty, K. (2010). Design automation and test solutions for digital microfluidic biochips. *IEEE Transactions on Computer-Aided Design of Integrated Circuits and Systems, 57*, 4–17.

Chakrabarty, K., Fair, R., & Zeng, J. (2010). Design tools for digital microfluidic biochips: Towards functional diversification and more than Moore. *IEEE Transactions on Computer-Aided Design of Integrated Circuits and Systems, 29*(7), 1001–1017. doi:10.1109/TCAD.2010.2049153

Chatterjee, S., Rahaman, H., & Samanta, T. (2013), Multi-objective optimization algorithm for efficient pin-constrained droplet routing technique in digital microfluidic biochip. In *Proceedings of 14th International Symposium on Quality Electronic Design* (ISQED) (pp. 252 – 256). Santa Clara, CA: Academic Press. doi:10.1109/ISQED.2013.6523618

Cho, M., & Pan, D. (2008). A high-performance droplet routing algorithm for digital microfluidic biochips. *IEEE Transactions on Computer-Aided Design of Integrated Circuits and Systems, 27*(10), 1714–1724. doi:10.1109/TCAD.2008.2003282

De Micheli, G. (1994). *Synthesis and optimization of digital circuits*. McGraw-Hill.

Dinh, T. A., Yamashita, S., & Ho, T. Y. (2014). A logic integrated optimal pin-count design for digital microfluidic biochips. In Proceedings of Design, Automation and Test in Europe Conference and Exhibition (DATE). Academic Press.

Dorigo, M., & Blum, C. (2004). *Ant colony optimization theory: A survey*. PHI.

Dorigo, M., & Stutzle, T. (2006). *Ant colony optimization*. PHI.

Erickson, D. (2005). Towards numerical prototyping of labs-on-chip: Modeling for integrated microfluidic devices. *Journal of Microfluidics and Nanofluidics*, *4*, 159–165.

Fair, R. B., Khlystov, A., Tailor, T. D., Ivanov, V., Evans, R. D., Srinivasan, V., & Zhou, J. et al. (2007). Chemical and biological applications of digital-microfluidic devices. *IEEE Design & Test of Computers*, *24*(1), 10–24. doi:10.1109/MDT.2007.8

Fair, R. B., Su, F., & Chakrabarty, K. (2006). Microfluidics-based biochips: Technology issues, implementation platforms and design automation challenges. *IEEE Transactions on Computer-Aided Design of Integrated Circuits and Systems*, *25*(2), 265–277.

Floriano, P. N. (2007). *Microchip-based assay systems methods and applications*. Totowa, NJ: Humana Press. doi:10.1007/978-1-59745-426-1

Fouillet, Y., Jary, D., Chabrol, C., Claustre, P., & Peponnet, C. (2008). Digital microfluidic design and optimization of classic and new fluidic functions for lab on a chip systems. *Journal of Mircofluidics and Nanofluidics*, *4*(3), 159–165. doi:10.1007/s10404-007-0164-5

Griffith, E. J., Akella, S., & Goldberg, M. K. (2006). Performance characterization of a reconfigurable planar-array digital microfluidic system. *IEEE Transactions on Computer-Aided Design of Integrated Circuits and Systems*, *25*(2), 345–357. doi:10.1109/TCAD.2005.859515

Huang, T. W., & Ho, T. Y. (2009). A fast routability and performance driven droplet routing algorithm for digital microfluidic biochips. In *Proceeding of IEEE International Conference on Computer Design* (pp. 445 – 450). IEEE. doi:10.1109/ICCD.2009.5413119

Huang, T. W., & Ho, T. Y. (2011). A two-stage integer linear programming-based droplet routing algorithm for pin-constrained digital microfluidic biochips. *IEEE Transactions on Computer-Aided Design of Integrated Circuits and Systems*, *30*(2), 215–228. doi:10.1109/TCAD.2010.2097190

Huang, T. W., Lin, C. H., & Ho, T. Y. (2009). A contamination aware droplet routing for digital microfluidic biochips. In *Proceedings of IEEE/ ACM International Conference on Computer Aided Design* (pp. 151 – 156). IEEE/ACM.

Hwang, W. L., Su, F., & Chakrabarty, K. (2006). Droplet routing in the synthesis of digital microfluidic biochips. In *Proceedings of Design Automation and Test in Europe (DATE) Conference* (pp. 323 – 328). Academic Press.

Hwang, W. L., Su, F., & Chakrabarty, K. (2006). Automated design of pin constrained digital microfluidic arrays for lab-on-a-chip applications. In *Proceedings of Design Automation and Test in Europe (DATE) Conference* (pp. 925 – 930). Academic Press. doi:10.1145/1146909.1147144

Lin, C. C. Y., & Chang, Y. W. (2009). ILP based pin-count aware design methodology for microfluidic biochips. In *Proceedings of ACM Design Automation Conference* (pp. 258 – 263). San Francisco, CA: ACM. doi:10.1145/1629911.1629982

Lin, C. C. Y., & Chang, Y. W. (2011). Cross-contamination aware design methodology for pin-constrained digital microfluidic biochips. *IEEE Transactions on Computer-Aided Design of Integrated Circuits and Systems*, *30*(6), 817–828. doi:10.1109/TCAD.2011.2108010

Lin, C. H., Huang, T. W., & Ho, T. Y. (2010). A contamination aware droplet routing algorithm for the synthesis of digital microfluidic biochips. *IEEE Transaction on Computer Aided Design of Integrated Circuits and Systems*, 1682 – 1695.

Luo, Y., & Chakrabarty, K. (2012). Design of pin constrained general – Purpose digital microfluidic biochips. In *Proceeding of 49th Design Automation Conference* (pp. 18 – 25). Academic Press.

Luo, Y., & Chakrabarty, K. (2013). Design of pin-constrained general-purpose digital microfluidic biochips. *IEEE Transactions on Computer-Aided Design of Integrated Circuits and Systems*, *32*(9), 1307–1320. doi:10.1109/TCAD.2013.2260192

Mukherjee, R., Rahaman, H., Banerjee, I., Samanta, T., & Dasgupta, P. (2012). A heuristic method for co-optimization of pin assignment and droplet routing in digital microfluidic biochip. In *Proceedings of IEEE International Conference on VLSI Design* (pp. 227 -232). IEEE. doi:10.1109/VLSID.2012.75

Pamula, V., Srinivasan, V., & Fair, R. (2004). An integrated digital microfluidic lab- on-a-chip for clinical diagnostics on human physiological fluids. *Journal of Lab Chip*, *4*, 310–315. PMID:15269796

Paul, P., Elena, M., & Madsen, J. (2009). Tabu search-based synthesis of dynamically reconfigurable digital microfluidic biochips. In *Proceedings of IEEE/ACM Int. Conf. Computer Architecture and Synthesis for Embedded Systems Conference* (pp. 195 – 203). IEEE/ACM.

Rahaman, H., Chakrabarty, K., Bhattacharya, B. B., Mitra, D., & Ghoshal, S. (2011). On residue removal in digital microfluidic biochips. In *ACM Proceedings of 21st Symposium on Great Lakes Symposium on VLSI* (pp. 391 – 394). ACM.

Rahaman, H., Roy, P., & Dasgupta, P. (2010). A novel droplet routing algorithm for digital microfluidic biochips. *ACM Online Proceedings of 20th Symposium on Great Lakes Symposium on VLSI* (pp. 441-446). ACM.

Rahaman, H., Singha, K., Samanta, T., & Dasgupta, P. (2010). Method of droplet routing in digital microfluidic biochip. In *Proceedings of IEEE/ASME International Conference on Mechatronics and Embedded Systems and Applications* (pp. 251-256). IEEE.

Roy, P., Bhattacharya, S., Bhattacharyay, R., Imam, F. J., Rahaman, H., & Dasgupta, P. (2014). A novel wire planning technique for optimum pin utilization in digital microfluidic biochips. In *Proceedings of 13th International Conference on Embedded Systems VLSI Design* (pp. 510 – 515). Mumbai, India: Academic Press. doi:10.1109/VLSID.2014.95

Roy, P., Howladar, P., Bhattacharjee, R., Rahaman, H., & Dasgupta, P. (2013). A new cross contamination aware routing method with intelligent path exploration in digital microfluidic biochips. In *Proceedings of 8th International Conference on Design & Technology of Integrated Systems in Nanoscale Era (DTIS)* (pp. 50 – 55). Academic Press. doi:10.1109/DTIS.2013.6527777

Sista, R., Hua, Z., Thwar, P., Sudarsan, A., Srinivasan, V., Eckhardt, A., & Pamula, V. et al. (2008). Development of a digital microfluidic platform for point of care testing. *Lab on a Chip*, 8(12), 2091–2104. doi:10.1039/b814922d PMID:19023472

Su, F., & Chakrabarty, K. (2004). Architectural-level synthesis of digital microfluidics-based biochips. In *Proceedings of IEEE International Conference on Computer-Aided Design* (pp. 223 – 228). San Jose, CA: IEEE.

Su, F., Ozev, S., & Chakrabarty, K. (2004). Test planning and test resource optimization for droplet-based microfluidic systems. In *Proceedings of Europe Test Symposium* (pp. 72 -77). Academic Press.

Wu, C.-G., Han, H., & Zhi-Feng, H. (2009). A pheromone-rate-based analysis on the convergence time of ACO algorithm. *IEEE Transactions on Systems, Man, and Cybernetics. Part B, Cybernetics*, 39(4), 910–923. doi:10.1109/TSMCB.2009.2012867 PMID:19380276

Xiao, Z., & Young, E. F. Y. (2010). Cross router: A droplet router for cross-referencing digital microfluidic biochips. In *Proceedings of 15th Asia and South Pacific Design Automation Conference (ASP-DAC)* (pp. 269 – 274). Academic Press. doi:10.1109/ASPDAC.2010.5419884

Xiao, Z., & Young, E. F. Y. (2010). Droplet-routing-aware module placement for cross-referencing biochips. In *Proceedings of International Symposium on Physical Design* (pp. 193 – 199). Academic Press. doi:10.1145/1735023.1735067

Xu, T., & Chakrabarty, K. (2006). Droplet-trace based array partitioning and a pin assignment algorithm for the automated design of digital microfluidic biochips. In *Proceedings of 4th IEEE Conference on CODES + ISSS 2006* (pp. 112 – 117). IEEE.

Xu, T., & Chakrabarty, K. (2008). A droplet manipulation method for achieving high throughput in cross referencing based digital microfluidic biochips. *IEEE Transaction on Computer Aided Design of Integrated Circuits and Systems*, 27(11), 1905–1917. doi:10.1109/TCAD.2008.2006086

Xu, T., & Chakrabarty, K. (2008). Integrated droplet routing and defect tolerance in the synthesis of digital microfluidic biochips. *ACM Journal on Emerging Technologies in Computing Systems*, 4(3), 11.1 – 11.24

Xu, T., & Chakrabarty, K. (2008). Broadcast electrode-addressing for pin-constrained multi-functional digital microfluidic biochips. In *Proceedings of Design Automation Conference* (pp. 173 – 178). Academic Press. doi:10.1145/1391469.1391514

Yang, C. L., Yuh, P. H., & Chang, Y. W. (2007). Bioroute: A network-flow based routing algorithm for digital microfluidic biochips. In *Proceedings of IEEE/ACM Int. Conf. on Computer-Aided Design* (pp. 752 – 757). IEEE/ACM.

Yang, C. L., Yuh, P. H., Sapatnekar, S., & Chang, Y. W. (2008). A progressive ilp based routing algorithm for cross-referencing biochips. In *Proceedings of Design Automation Conference* (pp. 284 – 289). Academic Press.

Yeh, S., Chang, J., Huang, T., Yu, S., & Ho, T. (2014). Voltage-aware chip-level design for reliability-driven pin-constrained EWOD chips. *IEEE Transactions on Computer-Aided Design of Integrated Circuits and Systems*, *33*(9), 1302–1315. doi:10.1109/TCAD.2014.2331340

Yeung, J. H. C., & Young, E. F. Y. (2014). General purpose cross-referencing microfluidic biochip with reduced pin-count. In *Proceedings of 19th Asia and South Pacific Design Automation Conference (ASP-DAC)* (pp. 238 – 243). Singapore: Academic Press. doi:10.1109/ASPDAC.2014.6742896

Yeung, J. H. C., Young, E. F. Y., & Choy, C. S. (2014). Reducing pin count on cross-referencing digital microfluidic biochip. In *Proceedings of IEEE International Symposium on Circuits and Systems (ISCAS)* (pp. 790 – 793). Melbourne, Australia: IEEE. doi:10.1109/ISCAS.2014.6865254

Zhao, Y., & Chakrabarty, K. (2010). Synchronization of washing operations with droplet routing for cross-contamination avoidance in digital microfluidic biochips. In *Proceedings of IEEE/ACM Design Automation Conference* (pp. 635 – 640). IEEE/ACM. doi:10.1145/1837274.1837437

Zhao, Y., & Chakrabarty, K. (2011). Co-optimization of droplet routing and pin assignment in disposable digital microfluidic biochips. In *Proceedings of ACM/IEEE International Symposium on Physical Design* (pp. 69 – 76). ACM/IEEE. doi:10.1145/1960397.1960413

Zhao, Y., & Chakrabarty, K. (2012). Cross contamination avoidance for droplet routing in digital microfluidic biochips. *IEEE Transactions on Computer-Aided Design of Integrated Circuits and Systems*, *31*(6), 817–830. doi:10.1109/TCAD.2012.2183369

Zhao, Y., Xu, T., & Chakrabarty, K. (2011). Broadcast electrode-addressing and scheduling methods for pin-constrained digital microfluidic biochips. *IEEE Transactions on Computer-Aided Design of Integrated Circuits and Systems*, *30*(7), 986–999. doi:10.1109/TCAD.2011.2116250

ADDITIONAL READING

Adamson, A. W. (1990). *Physical chemistry of surfaces* (5th ed.). New York: Wiley.

Antropov L. (2001), *Theoretical electrochemistry*, Honululu: University Press of the Pacific

Arzpeyma, A., Bhaseen, S., Dolatabadi, A., & Adams, P. W. (2008). A coupled electro-hydrodynamic numerical modeling of droplet actuation by electrowetting. *Journal of Colloids and Surfaces A: Physicochem Engineering Aspects*, *323*(1-3), 28–35. doi:10.1016/j.colsurfa.2007.12.025

Berthier, J., & Silberzan, P. (2005). *Microfluidics for Biotechnology*. Artech House.

Blake, T. D. (2006). The physics of moving wetting lines. *Journal of Colloid Interface*, *299*(1), 1–13. doi:10.1016/j.jcis.2006.03.051 PMID:16631781

Blake, T. D., Clarke, A., & Stattersfield, E. H. (2000). An investigation of electrostatic assist dynamic contact wetting. *Langmuir*, *16*(6), 2928–2935. doi:10.1021/la990973g

Bohringer, K. F. (2006). Modeling and controlling parallel tasks in droplet-based microfluidic systems. *IEEE Transactions on Computer-Aided Design of Integrated Circuits and Systems*, *25*(2), 334–344. doi:10.1109/TCAD.2005.855958

Chakrabarty, K., & Su, F. (2006). *Digital Microfluidic Biochips: Synthesis, Testing, and Reconfiguration Techniques*. Boca Raton, FL: CRC Press. doi:10.1201/9781420008302

Cho, S. K., Fan, S. K., Moon, H., & Kim, C. J. (2002), Towards digital microfluidic circuits: Creating, transporting cutting and merging liquid droplets by electrowetting-based actuation, *Proceedings of MEMS*, 32 - 35

Decamps, C., & De Coninck, J. (2000). Dynamics of continuous spreading under electrowetting conditions. *Langmuir*, *16*(26), 10150–10153. doi:10.1021/la000590e

Motamed, Z. K., Kadem, L., & Dolatabadi, A. (2010). Effects of dynamic contact angle on numerical modeling of electrowetting in parallel plate microchannels. *Journal of Microfluidics and Nanofluidics*, *8*(1), 47–56. doi:10.1007/s10404-009-0460-3

Mugele, F., & Baret, J. (2005). Electrowetting from basics to applications. *Journal of Physics*, *17*, 705–774.

Pan, I., Chatterjee, S., & Samanta, T. (2012), Droplet routing and wash droplet scheduling algorithm to remove cross-contamination in digital microfluidic biochip, *Proeedings of 12th IEEE International Conference on Intelligent Systems Design and Applications*, 155 – 160, Kochi, India

Pan, I., & Samanta, T. (2013), Efficient droplet router for digital microfluidic biochip using particle swarm optimizer, *Proceedings of SPIE International Conference on Communication and Electronics System Design*, 87601Z-1 – 87601Z-10, Jaipur, India doi:10.1117/12.2012352

Pan, I., & Samanta, T. (2014), Weighted optimization of various parameters for droplet routing in digital microfluidic biochips, *Proceedings of International Symposium on Intelligent Informatics/ Advances in Intelligent Systems and Computing, Springer Series*, 235, 131 - 139 doi:10.1007/978-3-319-01778-5_14

Pan, I., & Samanta, T. (2014). A droplet clustering and residue removal technique for cross contamination avoidance in digital microfluidic biochip, *International Journal of Computer Information Systems and Industrial Management Applications. MIR Labs Journal*, *6*, 171–183.

Pollack, M. G., Shenderov, A. D., & Fair, R. B. (2002). Electrowetting based actuation of droplets for integrated microfluidic. *Journal of Lab on Chip*, *2*(2), 96–101. doi:10.1039/b110474h PMID:15100841

Ren, H., Fair, R. B., Pollack, M. G., & Shaughnessy, E. J. (2002). Dynamics of electrowetting droplet transport. *Journal of Sensors and Actuators*, *87*(1), 201–206. doi:10.1016/S0925-4005(02)00223-X

Song J., Evans H., Lin R. Y., Hsu B. Y. & Fair R. B. (2009), A scaling model for electrowetting-on-dielectric microfluidic actuators, *Journal of Microfluidics and Nanofluidics*, 75 – 89

Su, F., & Chakrabarty, K. (2005), Unified high-level synthesis and module placement for defect-tolerant microfluidic biochips, *Proceedings of IEEE Design Automation Conference*, 13 – 17, San Jose, CA doi:10.1145/1065579.1065797

Van Mourik, S., Veldman, A. E. P., & Dreyer, M. E. (2005). Simulation of capillary flow with a dynamic contact angle. *Journal of Microgravity Science and Technology*, *17*(3), 87–93. doi:10.1007/BF02872093

Wang, K. L., & Jones, T. B. (2005). Electrowetting dynamics of microfluidic actuation. *Langmuir*, *21*(9), 4211–4217. doi:10.1021/la0468702 PMID:15835997

Xu, T., Chakrabarty, K., & Pamula, V. K. (2010). Defect-tolerant design and optimization of a digital microfluidic biochip for protein crystallization. *IEEE Transactions on Computer-Aided Design of Integrated Circuits and Systems*, *29*(4), 552–565. doi:10.1109/TCAD.2010.2042888

Yang, C. L., Yuh, P. H., Sapatnekar, S., & Chang, Y. W. (2008), A Progressive ILP based routing algorithm for cross-referencing biochips, *Proceedings of Design Automation Conference*, 284 - 289

Zhao, Y., & Chakrabarty, K. (2009), Cross-contamination avoidance for droplet routing in digital microfluidic biochips, *Proceedings of IEEE/ACM Design Automation and Test in Europe*, 1290 – 1295, California

Zisman, W. A., & Fowkes, F. (1964). *Contact Angle, Wettability and Adhesion* (pp. 1–51). ACS. doi:10.1021/ba-1964-0043.ch001

KEY TERMS AND DEFINITIONS

Bioassay Protocol: Several pathological operations are transfigured in to biochip operations. In order to accomplish this, information on sample operations is structured in a sequence compatible for on chip operations. This sequence is known as bioassay protocol. Normally biochemists provide the master input regarding the pathological operations which are then codified in the form of bioassay protocol.

Biochip Operations: There are three basic operations in biochip. Those are dispensing, routing and detection. Apart from these some important operations are mixing, splitting and garbage collection.

Continuous Fluid Flow Based Biochip: This is called first generation biochip. Fluids were circulated by external mechanical micro pumps by combination of capillary forces and electro kinetic mechanisms. This generation couldn't support multiple droplet operations and was less effective.

Cross Contamination: Performance optimization of digital microfluidic biochip often require reuse of same electrodes by different test fluids at different time interval. In such cases, succeeding fluid may get contaminated through the residue left by its preceding fluid. This type of contamination is familiar as cross contamination and this often causes in erroneous results at the detector.

Cross Referencing Biochip: It is row – column or two dimensional array addressing scheme for the electrodes of digital microfluidic biochip. Total number of addressing pin required is remarkably less in compare to direct addressing scheme but operations are complex and require extra caution to avoid unwanted mixing.

Dielectrophoresis: Dielectrophoresis (DEP) is a phenomenon in which a force is exerted on a dielectric particle when it is subjected to a non-uniform electric field. This force does not require the particle to be charged. All particles exhibit dielectrophoretic activity in the presence of electric fields. However, the strength of the force depends strongly on the medium and particles' electrical properties, on the particles' shape and size, as well as on the frequency of the electric field.

Digital Microfluidic Biochip (DMFB): This second generation biochip or which is the modern technology. Fluidic operations are manipulated by electrowetting mechanisms or dielectrophoresis. They are capable of multiple operations at same time instance.

Direct Addressing Mode Biochip: Individual electrodes are controlled via separately designated pins. Number of address pins required are same as number of electrodes. It is easy to operate but design is heavy and complex due to huge pin requirement.

Droplet Routing: Test droplets are open transported from a specified location to another location as per the bioassay protocol. Transmission of droplets over the biochip is known as droplet routing.

Electrowetting: The electrowetting effect has been defined as the change in solid-electrolyte contact angle due to an applied potential difference between the solid and the electrolyte. The phenomenon of electrowetting can be understood in terms of the forces that result from the applied electric field.

Source Reservoir: Reservoir associated or connected externally to some of the electrodes of biochip and it contains samples of fluids and chemicals required to carry out designated tests. Fluids and chemical droplets are dispensed from these source reservoirs at the beginning of operations.

Three Pin Net: In some of the digital microfluidic biochip operations two different test droplets coming from two different source electrodes are merged at a designated electrode and then the merged droplet is routed to a specific target electrode. These types of operational requirements come with the details of two different source locations along with a target location. They are known as three pin net.

Two Pin Net: In some of the digital microfluidic biochip operations droplets are dispensed at a specific location (known as source location) and then they are routed towards a designated terminal location (known as target location). These types of operational requirements come with the information of source location and corresponding target location. They are known as two pin net.

Wash Droplet: Mainly water droplets are strategically routed in between two consecutive uses of any electrode to minimize the risk of cross contamination. This type of droplet is familiar as wash droplet.

Waste Reservoir: A few reservoirs are associated with the biochip for collection of post operative samples and residues. These post operative samples are called waste and the reservoir is called waste reservoir.

Section 2
Applications

Chapter 9
Quantum Inspired Swarm Optimization for Multi–Level Image Segmentation Using BDSONN Architecture

Subhadip Chandra
Camellia Institute of Technology, India

Siddhartha Bhattacharyya
RCC Institute of Information Technology, India

ABSTRACT

This chapter is intended to propose a quantum inspired self-supervised image segmentation method by quantum-inspired particle swarm optimization algorithm and quantum-inspired ant colony optimization algorithm, based on optimized MUSIG (OptiMUSIG) activation function with a bidirectional self-organizing neural network architecture to segment multi-level grayscale images. The proposed quantum-inspired swarm optimization-based methods are applied on three standard grayscale images. The performances of the proposed methods are demonstrated in comparison with their conventional counterparts. Experimental results are reported in terms of fitness value, computational time, and class boundaries for both methods. It has been noticed that the quantum-inspired meta-heuristic method is superior in terms of computational time in comparison to its conventional counterpart.

INTRODUCTION

Image segmentation is one of the most important challenges encountered in the field of image processing (Gonzalez & Woods, 2002), which is crucial for image understanding and analysis to interpret its contents. The objective of image segmentation is to extract meaningful non-overlapping homogeneous regions from an image. The process of image segmentation is executed based on the principle that each of the pixels in a region is similar to other with respect to some characteristics such as intensity, texture

DOI: 10.4018/978-1-4666-8291-7.ch009

or color. Segmentation can be carried out by several classical techniques, viz. histogram based, edge based, region based split/ merge techniques (Ho & Lee, 2001). Histogram based approaches are those in which pixels are classified using the histogram of the images according to their color intensity. Pixels representing marked intensity shifts are extracted and then linked into contours that represent object boundaries are offered in edge based approaches. These approaches offer low computational cost but on the other hand pose serious difficulties in setting the appropriate thresholds and producing continuous one-pixel-wide contours (Sahoo, 1988; Helterbrand, 1996). Region based approaches aim to detect regions satisfying a certain homogeneity criterion. This class includes region growing (Adams, 1994; Chang, 1994; Hojjatoleslami, 1998) and pyramidal methods (Rezaee, Van der Zwet, Lelieveldt, van der Geest, & Reiber, 2000) which are powerfull but may lead to an over segmentation. Split/merge approaches aim to overcome the problem of over segmentation by means of a two phase process. The first phase subdivides the original image into primitive homogeneous regions. The second one tries to get a better segmentation by merging neighboring regions which are judged similar enough (Chun, 1996; Bhandarkar, 1999).

The objects in an image usually have a strong correlation with the regions of the segmented image. The resulted segmented image is labeled in such a way that facilitates the description of the original image so that it can be interpreted by the system that handles the image. To determine which are the features that can lead to successful classification, *a priori* knowledge or/and presumption about the image are generally needed. Most of the image segmentation algorithm yield segmentation of different objects with respect to the image background.

Here both methods are capable to perform multilevel image segmentation of gray scale images. The soft computing approaches applied in this direction either resorts to a deterministic analysis of homogeneous intensity values of images or to an application of heuristic search and optimization techniques, though these techniques suffer from several degrees of random time complexity.

Swarm intelligence (Englebrecht, 2002), which takes inspiration from the social behavior of insects and other animals, is a relatively new computational approach to solve problems. In a PSO system, particles fly around in a multidimensional search space. During flight, each particle adjusts its position according to its own experience, and the experience of its neighboring particles, making use of the best position encountered by itself and its neighbors.

In particular, ants have inspired a number of techniques collectively known as ant colony optimization (Dorigo & Stutzle, 2005). Ant colony based algorithms are bio-mimetic evolutionary algorithms. These algorithms have parallel positive feedback mechanisms having advantages of parallelism, robustness and easy combination with other methods. The discreteness of parallelism of the ant colony based algorithms makes them potential candidates for digital image analysis and hence can be applied to image processing.

Quantum computing is a new field in computer science, which has emerged to offer a speed-up of the classical algorithms by inducing physical phenomena like interference, superposition, entanglement etc. (McMohan, 2008). The time complexity of quantum computing has been reduced, due to the utilization of parallelism present in *qubits* (quantum bits), the building blocks of quantum computer. The various approaches towards this direction can be classified as quantum algorithms and quantum inspired algorithms. There are so many features present in quantum computing like linear superposition, coherence and decoherence operators, interference, rotation gates entanglement etc. In this chapter we propose a quantum inspired ant colony optimization based optimized multilevel sigmoidal (OptiMUSIG) activation function to generate multiple class boundaries for multilevel image segmentation. This approach is targeted to increase time efficiency with respect to the conventional ant colony optimization based optimized multiple class boundaries for multilevel image segmentation.

In this chapter, the optimized class boundaries needed to segment gray-level images into different, are generated by Ant Colony Optimization (ACO) and proposed Quantum Inspired ACO (QIACO). The resultant optimized class boundaries are used to generate an optimized multilevel sigmoidal (Opti-MUSIG) activation function for effecting multilevel image segmentation using BDSONN architecture. Application of the proposed approach is depicted using three standard gray scale images, viz. the Lena, the Baboon and The Cameraman images. Results of multilevel segmentation using the proposed QIACO method shows a better result over its conventional algorithm with respect to time efficiency as well as fitness value.

The chapter is organized as follows. A brief review of image segmentation techniques is discussed in the section titled IMAGE SEGMENTATION. In the next section the optimized multilevel sigmoidal activation function is discussed with the Bi-directional Self-organizing neural network (BDSONN) architecture proposed by Bhattacharyya, Dutta, & Maulik, (2006). Of late, MUSIG (Bhattacharyya *et al.*, 2008) and OptiMUSIG (De, Bhattacharyya, & Dutta, 2008) is discussed in the following section. PARTICLE SWARM OPTIMIZATION and ANT COLONY OPTIMIZATION techniques are discussed later. Quantum computing is introduced in the next section titled FUNDAMENTALS OF QUANTUM COMPUTING. Then the proposed algorithm of quantum inspired particle swarm optimization and ant colony optimization based multilevel image segmentation described in the section PROPOSED ALGO-RITHM. EXPERIMENTAL RESULTS illustrates the comparative results of multilevel image segmenta-tion on three real life images for the quantum inspired and conventional algorithms and CONCLUSIONS draw a line of conclusion to the chapter with the further direction of research.

IMAGE SEGMENTATION

Image segmentation is a fundamental process for understanding and analyzing various image informa-tion. Segmentation subdivides an image into multiple regions or objects based on shape, color, posi-tion, intensity or homogeneity of image regions. In a segmented image, non-overlapping regions are homogeneous in nature and the union of any two regions is heterogeneous. Image segmentation can be carried out by various techniques which are mostly based on the discontinuity and homogeneous inten-sity levels. Image segmentation is useful in the fields of feature extraction, object recognition, satellite image processing, medical image processing and so many.

Texture and non-texture regions based image can be segmented by local spectral histograms and graph partitioning methods (Liu, & Wang, 2006). Histogram thresholding is one of the examples of feature space based segmentation techniques, Split and merge, region growing and merging, edge detection based methods are few instances of image domain based segmentation techniques (Lucchese & Mitra, 2001). A group of researchers classified the segmentation method on the basis of the pixels of the images in relation to their local neighborhoods (Freixenet, Munoz & Raba, 2002).

Thresholding technique (Gonzalez & Woods, 2002), is an important image segmentation tech-nique, which considers the pixel value of an image, such as gray level or color level or texture. In this technique, it is presumed that the adjacent pixel values lying within a certain range belong to the same class (Gonzalez & Woods, 2002). The determination of the threshold value of the examined image is the trickiest part of this approach. The pixels whose intensity values exceed the threshold value are assigned in one segment and the remaining to the other. Otsu's (Otsu, 1979) thresholding method, one of the oldest methods, has been employed to analyze the maximum seperability of classes. The goodness of the threshold value has been determined by the methods that include evaluating the heterogeneity of both classes and the homogeneity of every class. Vandenbroucke, Macaire, & Postaire (2003) presented a color image segmentation method by pixel classification in a hybrid color space which is adjusted to analyze the image. A hybrid color image segmentation technique based on histogram thresholding and fuzzy c-means algorithm is proposed by Tan & Isa (2011). The histogram thresholding technique cannot be efficiently employed for blurred images or for multiple image component segmentation as this technique overlooks all the spatial relationship information of the image except the pixel intensity.

An image segmentation method referred to as the first watershed then normalized cut method, based on watershed and graph theory was proposed by Yang, Guo, Zhao, & Xiao, (2007). Shi & Malik (2000) treated the problem of image segmentation as graph partitioning problem. They presented graph theoretic framework based algorithm to partition a grey scale image into brightness and texture based regions. The proposed normalized cut is used as quantitative metric for the segmentation.

Since real-life images exhibit a valid amount of uncertainty, fuzzy set theory has been resorted to image segmentation. The most popular method based on membership values of different classes is fuzzy c-means (FCM) clustering algorithm (Bejdek, 1981). It is a very efficient technique in clustering multidimensional feature spaces. Each data point belongs to a cluster to a degree specified by a membership grade. The FCM algorithm partitions a collection of n pixels $X_i, i = 1, \ldots, n$ into c-fuzzy groups, and finds a cluster centre in each group such that a cost function of dissimilarity measure is minimized. However, the FCM algorithm does not fully utilize the spatial information and it only works well on noise free images. A modified version of the objective function for the standard FCM algorithm to allow the labels in the immediate neighborhood of a pixel to influence its labeling was proposed by Ahmed, Yamany, Mohamed, Farag & Moriarty (2002). The modified FCM algorithm improved the results of conventional FCM method on noisy images. A geometrically guided FCM algorithm is introduced by Noordam, Van den Broek, & Buydens (2000), based on a semi-supervised FCM technique for multivariate image segmentation. In this method, the local neighborhood of each pixel is applied to determine geometrical condition information of each pixel before clustering.

Segmentation and clustering of image data followed by the extraction of specified regions can also be accomplished by neural networks due to the inherent advantages of adaptation and graceful degradation. Kohonen (1989) proposed self-organizing feature map (SOFM), which is a competitive neural network used for data clustering. Jiang & Zhou (2004) used SOFM method for image segmentation. The pixels of an image are grouped with several SOFM neural networks and the final segmentation is obtained by grouping the clusters thus obtained. This method also has been used in medical image segmentation through identification of regions of interest (Chang, 2007; Reddick, 1997). Bhattacharyya, Dutta, Maulik, & Nandi (2007) represents how the multilevel activation functions works for true color image segmentation, using a self-supervised parallel self-organizing neural network (PSONN).

PRINCIPLES OF MULTILEVEL IMAGE SEGMENTATION USING BDSONN ARCHITECTURE

The primary objective of object extraction from a noisy background is the segmentation of an image scene into foreground regions corresponding to different localized homogeneous object regions and background regions corresponding to non-object regions. The BDSONN (Bhattacharyya *et al.*, 2006, 2007, 2011) architecture is a three-layer network structure assisted by bi-directional propagation of network states for self-supervised organization of input information. This network architecture comprises an input layer for accepting real world inputs and two competing self-organizing network layers viz. an intermediate and an output layer. The number of neurons in each of the network layers corresponds to the number of pixels in the input image. The first layer of the network accepts fuzzy membership values of the constituent pixels from the input image scene. This fuzzy input information is propagated to the other network layers for further processing. Consequently the network layers resemble fuzzy layers of neurons, guided by the fuzzy membership information. The neurons in each layer of the network are connected to each other within the same layer following a cellular network structure. The strengths of these intra-layer interconnections are fixed and full and equal to 1. Though each neuron in a particular layer of the network is connected to the corresponding neuron and to its second order neighbors of the previous layer following a neighborhood-based topology through forward path inter-layer interconnections. As well, the output layer neurons are similarly connected to the intermediate layer neurons via the backward path inter-layer interconnection paths. The strengths of these inter-layer interconnections between the input layer and the intermediate layer, the intermediate layer and the output layer and between the output layer and the intermediate layer neurons are decided by the relative measures of the membership values at the individual neurons of the different layers. Figure 1 shows a schematic of the BDSONN architecture using fully connected network layers and second order neighborhood based inter-layer interconnections.

The input layer of the network architecture acts as a switching layer of network inputs. This layer accepts the fuzzy membership values of the input image information and switches them to the intermediate layer for further processing. The fuzzy cardinality values corresponding to the different neighborhood fuzzy subsets in the input layer are accumulated at the central candidate neurons of the different fuzzy neighborhoods through the intra-layer interconnections. These fuzzy cardinality values are reflective of the neighborhood fuzzy subset context information and indicate the membership distribution within a neighborhood. These values are used for defining the context sensitive thresholding information necessary for the characteristic transfer function of the processing neurons.

The inter-layer interconnections serve twofold purposes. The connections between the corresponding neurons in the different layers of the network are meant for the propagation of the context sensitive thresholding information from the neurons of one layer to those of the other layer.

The second order inter-layer interconnections between the candidate neurons of one layer and the second order neighbors of the corresponding neuron in the other layer are meant for propagating the network states from one layer to the other. The strengths of these second order inter-layer interconnections are decided from the relative measures of the membership values at the constituent neurons. If μ_j is the membership value at the j th candidate neuron at one layer and μ_{ij} is the membership value at the i th second order neighbor of the j th candidate neuron in the same layer, then the inter-layer interconnection strength, $w_{ijj'}$, between the corresponding other layer j' th candidate neuron, and the i th second order neighbor of the other layer is decided by the fuzzy complement operator given as follows.

Figure 1. BDSONN architecture

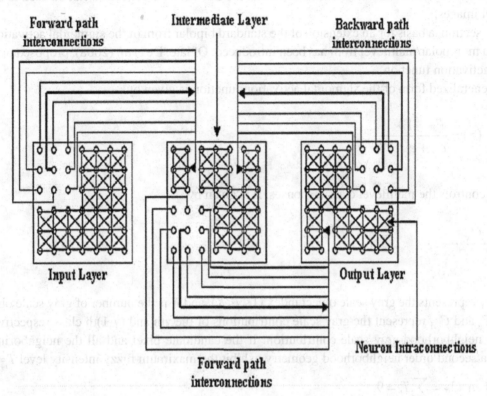

$$w_{ijj'} = \overline{\mu_i - \mu_{ij}} \tag{1}$$

Thus the interconnection strength is a function of the fuzzy membership values at the neurons in a particular network layer. These types of neighborhood based inter-layer interconnections exist between the input layer and the intermediate layer, the intermediate layer and the output layer in the forward direction and between the output layer and the intermediate layer in the backward direction. Interested readers may refer to Bhattacharyya *et al.*, (2006) for details of the architecture and operation of the BDSONN architecture.

MUSIG AND OPTIMUSIG ACTIVATION FUNCTION

Multilevel Sigmoidal (MUSIG) Activation Function

The BDSONN (Bhattacharyaa *et al.*, 2007) architecture is efficient in extracting objects from binary noisy images. It is characterized by the standard bi-level sigmoidal activation function. Multilevel extension can be induced in the architecture by effecting a functional modification. Such a modification brought by resorting to a multilevel version of the standard sigmoidal activation function. This function would be able to generate multilevel outputs pertaining to the multiple grey levels in the multilevel image.

The advantages by such a modified scheme are that the BDSONN architecture can be used to segment multilevel images.

In this section, a basis for an extension of the standard bipolar from of the sigmoidal activation function into a multipolar/multilevel from has been introduced. Of late, De *et al.* (2008), proposed optimized MUSIG activation function.

The generalized form of the sigmoidal activation function is given by

$$y = f_{GSIG}(x) = \frac{1}{\alpha_\gamma + e^{-\lambda(x-\theta)}},$$
(2)

where α_γ controls the multilevel class responses. It is given by

$$\alpha_\gamma = \frac{C_N}{C_\gamma - C_{\gamma-1}}.$$
(3)

Here, γ represents the grey scale object index ($1 \leq \gamma < K$), and K is the number of gray scale objects or classes. C_γ and $C_{\gamma-1}$ represent the gray scale contributions of the γth and (γ-1)th class respectively and C_N is the neighborhood gray scale contribution. If the candidate pixel and all the neighboring eight pixels in a second order neighborhood geometry exhibit the maximum fuzzy intensity level $T_i=1$, $i=1$, 2, ... 9, then $C_N = \sum_{i=1}^{9} T_i = 9$

If $\alpha_\gamma = 1$, then the generalized sigmoidal activation function reduces to the characteristics standard bi-level sigmoidal activation function given as

$$y = f_{SIG}(x) = \frac{1}{\alpha_\gamma + e^{-\lambda(x-\theta)}}.$$
(4)

The λ parameter in the expression, decides the steepness of the function. The θ parameter is a fixed threshold value. The functional response of the standard bi-level sigmoidal activation function is limited to the normal range of [0, 1], i.e. the function exhibits bipolar responses. It can only generate bright or dark responses.

Equation (2) suggests different subnormal functional responses, $y_{s_{\alpha_\gamma}}$ ($0 \leq y_{s_{\alpha_\gamma}} \leq 1$) which can be obtained by tailoring the α_γ parameter suitably. A superposition of such different responses forms the multilevel activation function. This function is capable to generate multipolar responses. From the generalized sigmoidal activation function the multilevel form can be generated as

$$f(x; \alpha_\gamma, c_\gamma) \leftarrow f(x; \alpha_\gamma, c_\gamma) + (\gamma - 1)f(\gamma c_\gamma), \ (\gamma - 1)c_{\gamma-1} \leq x < \gamma c_\gamma,$$
(5)

where

$$f(x; \alpha_\gamma, c_\gamma) = \frac{1}{\alpha_\gamma + e^{-\lambda[x - (\gamma - 1)c_{\gamma - 1} - \theta]}} \qquad (6)$$

The closed form of the MUSIG function is given by

$$f_{MUSIG}(x) = \sum_{\gamma = 1}^{K} f(x + (\gamma - 1)c_{\gamma - 1}), (\gamma - 1)c_{\gamma - 1} \leq x < \gamma c_\gamma \qquad (7)$$

Substituting equation (6), one gets

$$f_{MUSIG}(x; \alpha_\gamma, c_\gamma) = \sum_{\gamma = 1}^{K - 1} \frac{1}{\alpha_\gamma + e^{-\lambda[x - (\gamma - 1)c_{\gamma - 1} - \theta]}} \qquad (8)$$

If c_γ is assumed to be equal for all the classes, then several identical subnormal responses, $y_{S_{\alpha\gamma}}$, are obtained over the gray scale gamut. The resultant MUSIG activation function thus comprises several identical subnormal transition lobes. Otherwise, equation (8) yields different subnormal transition lobes with response of varying shapes and ranges. The different subnormal lobes derived from different α_γ parameters are compounded to ensure continuity of the resultant MUSIG function. Moreover, it is evident from equation (7) that there are $(K-1)$ many α parameters.

However, by assuming the homogeneity of the underlying image information, the class boundaries used by the MUSIG activation function are selected heuristically from the gray scale histogram of the input images. Since real life images are heterogeneous in nature, so the class boundaries would differ from one image to another. For that reason, the optimized class boundaries derived from the image context would faithfully incorporate the intensity distribution of the images. Using optimized class boundaries, an optimized form of the MUSIG activation function can be represented as (De *et al.*, 2008, 2010),

$$f_{OptiMUSIG} = \sum_{\gamma = 1}^{K - 1} \frac{1}{\alpha_{\gamma_{opt}} + e^{-\lambda[x - (\gamma - 1)c_{\gamma_{opt}} - \theta]}}, \qquad (9)$$

where $c_{\gamma_{opt}}$ are the optimized gray scale contributions corresponding to optimized class boundaries. $\alpha_{\gamma_{opt}}$ are the respective optimized class responses. These parameters can be suitably derived by the proper optimization of the segmentation of input images.

PARTICLE SWARM OPTIMIZATION

Particle swarm optimization (PSO) is a population-based stochastic optimization algorithm based on the metaphor of social interaction and communication such as bird flocking and fish schooling. In order to gain a deep insight into the mechanism of PSO, many theoretical analyses have been done on the algorithm.

As for the algorithm itself, Van den Bergh (2002), proved that the canonical PSO is not a global search algorithm, even not a local one, according to the convergence criteria provided by Solis & Wets (1981).

In addition to the theoretical analyses mentioned above, there has been a considerable amount of work done in developing the original version of PSO, through empirical simulations. Shi & Eberhart (1998), introduced the concept of inertia weight to the original PSO, in order to balance the local and global search during the optimization process.

Overview of PSO

PSO introduced by Kennedy & Eberhart (1995) simulates the behaviors of bird flocking. In PSO, the solutions to the problem are represented as particles in the search space. PSO is initialized with a group of random particles (solutions) and then searches for optimum value by updating particles in successive generations. In each iteration, all the particles are updated by following two best values. The first one is the best solution (fitness) it has achieved so far. This value is called "pbest". Another "best" value that is tracked by the particle swarm optimizer is the best value, obtained so far by any particle in the population. This best value is a global best and called "gbest".

Particle Swarm has two primary operations: Velocity update and Position update. During each generation each particle is accelerated toward the particles previous best position and the global best position. At each iteration, a new velocity value for each particle is calculated based on its current velocity, the distance from its previous best position, and the distance from the global best position. The new velocity value is then used to calculate the next position of the particle in the search space. This process is then iterated a set number of times or until a minimum error is achieved.

After finding the two best values, the particle updates its velocity and positions with the following formulae

$$v[t+1] = v[t] + c1 \times rand1 \times (pbest[t] - present[t]) + c2 \times rand2 \times (gbest[t] - present[t]) \qquad (10)$$

where v[] is the particle velocity, present[] is the current particle. pbest[] and gbest[] are local best and global best position of particles. rand () is a random number between (0,1). c1 and c2 are learning factors. Usually $c1 = c2 = 2$.

The outline of basic Particle Swarm Optimizer is as follows

1. Initialize the population.
2. Evaluate fitness of the individual particle (update pbest).
3. Keep track of the individual's highest fitness (gbest).
4. Modify velocities based on pbest and gbest.
5. Update the particle position.
6. Terminate if the condition is met.
7. Go to step 2.

ANT COLONY OPTIMIZATION

Swarm intelligence approach in solving complicated optimization problems is relatively new. The major advantage of this approach is that system of simple communicating agents is capable of solving complex problems (Fogel, 1997, 2006). The social insects' behavior such as finding the best food source, building of optimal nest structure, brooding, protecting the larva, guarding, etc., show intelligent behavior on the swarm level (Englebrecht, 2002). A swarm behavior is not determined just by the behavior of individuals, but the interactions among individuals play a vital role in shaping the swarm behavior (Englebrecht, 2002). Computational modeling of swarms' behavior is found to be useful in various application domains like function optimization (Tsutsui, 2004a, 2004b), finding optimal routes (Dorigo & Gambardella, 1997), scheduling (Dorigo & Stutzle, 2005), image and data analysis (Wang, 2005) to name a few. Different applications originated from the study of different swarms like ant colonies and bird flocks (Englebrecht, 2002).The ant colony optimization algorithm (ACO) is a probabilistic computational search technique useful for finding the based possible path in search graphs. The first algorithm was proposed by Dorigo (1992) which was aimed, at searching for an optimal path in a graph based on the behaviors exhibited by ants while searching for food outside of their colony.

Overview of ACO

Ants generally start searching in their quest for food randomly through all possible paths that lead to food. Once they find their food they return to their colony leaving behind pheromone trails. If the following ants make the path, they do not hover randomly; instead follow the trail to find food.

Ant Colony Optimization (ACO) is a paradigm for designing meta heuristic algorithms for combinatorial optimization problems. The essential feature of ACO algorithms is the combination of *a priori* information about the structure of a promising solution with a posteriori information about the structure of previously obtained good solutions. Metaheuristic algorithms are algorithms which, in order to escape from local optima, drive some basic heuristic: either a constructive heuristic starting from a null solution and adding elements to build a good complete one, or a local search heuristic starting from a complete solution and iteratively modifying some of its elements in order to achieve a better one. The metaheuristic part permits the low level heuristic to obtain solutions better than those it could have achieved alone, even if iterated.

ACO algorithms are designed to emulate ants' behavior of laying pheromone on the ground while moving from one position to another for solving optimization problems. Pheromone is a type of chemical emitted by an organism to communicate between members of the same species. Pheromone which is responsible for clumping or grouping behavior in a species and brings individuals into closer proximity is known as aggregation pheromone. Thus, aggregation pheromone causes individuals to aggregate around good positions which in turn produce more pheromone to attract individuals of the same species.

The pheromone trail starts to evaporate with time, thereby reducing its attractive strength. The more time it takes for an ant to travel down the path and return back, the more time the pheromones have to evaporate. By comparison, a short path gets marched over faster, and thus the pheromone density remains high as it is laid on the path as fast as it can evaporate. The pheromone evaporation prevents the convergence of the algorithm to a local optimum. In absence of any evaporation of pheromone the following ants would be attracted to the traversed paths by the leading ant, thereby leading to a constrained solution space.

This procedure adopted by the real world ants is adapted in implementing the ant colony optimization algorithm, which always leads to the shortest one (Goss, 1989; Deneubourg, 1990) between two unequal length paths. This self-organized system adopted by ants, referred to as "stigmergy", is characterized by both a positive feedback resulting out of the deposit of pheromone for attracting other ants and a negative one resulting out of the dissipation of the pheromone due to evaporation. A pseudo code for the ACO algorithm is listed below.

```
Do
    Generate_Trialsolutions()
    Update_Pheromone()
    Search_Paths()
Loop while (not_termination)
```

The generation of the trial solutions in the ACO algorithm by the **Generate_Trialsolutions()** procedure associates the selection of subsequence node in the search space. This procedure is referred to as edge selection. An ant will switch from one node to another (from i node to j node) with probability

$$P_{ij} = \frac{\psi_{ij}^{\gamma}(t)\kappa_{ij}^{\delta}(t)}{\sum \psi_{ij}^{\gamma}(t)\kappa_{ij}^{\delta}(t)} \tag{11}$$

where, $\psi_{ij}(t)$ is the amount of pheromone on edge (i,j) at time t, $\kappa_{ij}(t)$ is the acceptability of edge (i, j) at time t, γ and δ control the influence of parameters κ_{ij} and ψ_{ij} respectively.

The **Update_Pheromone()** process on a given edge (i, j), would yield the amount of pheromone at the next instant of time $(t + 1)$. It is determined by

$$\psi_{ij}(t+1) = (1 - \varepsilon)\psi_{ij}(t) + \Delta\psi_{ij} \tag{12}$$

where, $\Psi_{ij}(t+1)$ is the amount of pheromone on that edge at time $(t + 1)$, ε is the rate of pheromone evaporation and $\Delta\Psi_{ij}$ is the amount of deposited pheromone. For the kth ant travelling on edge (i, j), $\Delta\psi_{ij}^{k} = \frac{1}{C}$, where C is the cost/length of the kth ant's path. For all other ants, $\Delta\psi_{ij}^{k} = 0$.

FUNDAMENTALS OF QUANTUM COMPUTING

Quantum Computing (QC) can be described by exploiting the principle of the theory of quantum physics (Mcmohan, 2008). A wave function

$$|\psi\rangle = \sum_{j} c_j = 1 \tag{13}$$

where, $|\psi\rangle$ is referred as the linear superposition of the basis states, c_j are complex numbers that follow the unitary condition given by

$$\sum_j c_j = 1 \tag{14}$$

In the Dirac bracket notation, the ket $|\bullet\rangle$ is analogous to a column vector while the bra $\langle\bullet|$ is analogous to the complex conjugate transpose of the ket.

The smallest unit of information stored in a two-state quantum system is referred as quantum bit or *qubit* (McMohan, 2008). A *qubit* may be either in the "1" state or in the "0" state or in any other state which results out of a superposition of these states.

Coherence and decoherence are wave theoretic concepts, which are interrelated to linear superposition. In the theory of wave function, coherence is exhibited between two waves as long as a constant phase relationship exists between them. In quantum system, coherence is manifested as a linear superposition of its constituent basis states of the wave function $|\psi\rangle$ like wave theory. Coherence gets ruined if the phase relationship ceases to exist or the linear superposition of the basis states is destroyed. This results in decoherence. The coefficients c_i are called probability amplitudes, and $|c_i|^2$ give the probability of $|\psi\rangle$ collapsing into state $|\phi_i\rangle$ if it decoheres. In such an eventually, the wave function $|\psi\rangle$ must collapse to exactly one of the basis states. This is referred to as the unitary condition and expressed as equation (13).

Interference is a familiar wave phenomenon, where waves in phase interfere constructively and those out of phase interfere destructively. At the quantum level, interference also applies to the probability waves of quantum mechanics. Boyarsky & Gora (2010) represents a deterministic model for quantum interference (Talbi, 2007; Chandra, 2013) based on the probability density function of the wave function ψ. They applied nonlinear deterministic point transformation τ_i, $i=1,2$ on a quantum system of two wave functions, $|\psi_i\rangle$, $i=1,2$. These transformations (τ_i) were chosen such that the probability density functions corresponding to these transformations equals the observed density matrix, $\rho_i = |\psi_i\rangle\langle\psi_i|$, $i=1,2$ (McMohan, 2008).

Another interesting feature of quantum system is entanglement, which is used to exhibit correlations between different qubits (Vedral, Plenio, Rippin & Knight, 1997). This feature is also described by the density matrix of a quantum state (McMohan, 2008).

QUANTUM INSPIRED PARTICLE SWARM OPTIMIZATION

In terms of classical mechanics, a particle is depicted by its position vector xi and velocity vector v_i, which determine the trajectory of the particle. The particle moves along a determined path, but this is not the case in quantum mechanics. In world of quantum physics, the term *trajectory* is meaningless as it is not possible to determine position vector as well as velocity vector simultaneously due to uncertainty principle. In this chapter, Quantum Inspired Particle Swarm Optimization technique combines the conception of conventional PSO and quantum computing. *Qubits* and quantum inspired rotation gate (QR gate) are used to characterize particles' behavior and update their velocity towards an improved solution.

QUANTUM INSPIRED ANT COLONY OPTIMIZATION

Quantum Inspired Ant Colony Optimization (QIACO) is a new optimization technique which combines the concept of quantum computing and classical ACO. In QIACO, *qubits* and quantum inspired rotation gate (QR gate) are used to represent ants of various ant colonies and update ants' position by a probabilistic process. Here QR gate is used as an update operator of QIACO to drive the individual ant towards a better solution.

There are various techniques for unsupervised subjective measures to determine the segmentation efficiency (Zhang, 1996). In this chapter the proposed algorithm and the classical one have been evaluated using correlation coefficient as fitness value (V).

The standard measure of correlation coefficient (ρ) (Bhattacharyya, 2008) can be used to assess the quality of achieved segmentation. It is given by

$$\rho = \frac{(1/n^2)\sum_{i=1}^{n}\sum_{j=1}^{n}(I_{ij}-\overline{I})(S_{ij}-\overline{S})}{\sqrt{(1/n^2)\sum_{i=1}^{n}\sum_{j=1}^{n}(I_{ij}-\overline{I})^2}\sqrt{(1/n^2)\sum_{i=1}^{n}\sum_{j=1}^{n}(S_{ij}-\overline{S})^2}} \tag{15}$$

where, I_{ij}, $1\leq i,j\leq n$ and S_{ij}, $1\leq i,j\leq n$ are the original and segmented images respectively, each of dimensions $n \times n$. $\overline{I}$ and $\overline{S}$ are their respective mean intensity values. A larger value of ρ implies better quality of segmentation.

The convergence speed of QIPSO and QIACO are dependent on the rotation angle. An appropriate angle is very helpful to accelerate the speed of convergence as well as improve the searching ability of the algorithm. Many studies are interested in the research of the rotation angles and the update strategies (Zhang, 2011). Fixed rotation angles in lookup table are proposed in by Han & Kim (2000); a H_{ε} gate is employed in (Han & kim, 2004) to avoid premature convergence; the adjustments of the rotation angles which decrease gradually with the iterations are introduced in (Zhang, 2006; Zhang, 2007). In the processing of evolution, the update operation of QR-gate is only guided by the current best individual who has the maximum fitness but not always has a reasonable structure of the solution, and each update step is performed on a full *n*-dimensional vector. This leads to the possibility of some components of the *n*-dimensional vector having been moved closer to the best solution, while others have actually been moved away from the best solution (Van den Bergh & Engelbrecht, 2004). This kind of holistic information exchange may cause the sharp decline of the search ability with the increase of the dimension. So it still can potentially get trapped in suboptimal locations in search space. In order to solve the above problems and improve the performance of the classical swarm based multilevel image segmentation, an improved QIPSO and QIACO with adaptive rotation angle based multilevel gray scale image segmentation are proposed in this chapter. The experimental results show that the convergence speed, accuracy, and stability of the proposed algorithms are superior to traditional counterpart.

Since the *qubit* representation can achieve a linear superposition of states given its probabilistic approach, it is conductive to population diversity. A *qubit* is the basic computing unit in a QIACO and is defined as a column vector: $(\alpha\beta)^T$ (a *qubit* is often represented as $|\psi\rangle = \alpha|0\rangle + \beta|1\rangle$ in quantum mechanical ket-notation), where the numbers of α and β satisfy the normalization condition $|\alpha|^2+|\beta|^2=1$. The values of $|\alpha|^2$ and $|\beta|^2$ denote the probabilities that the *qubit* will be found in the states of "0" and "1" respectively. By a process of probabilistic observation, each *qubit* can be rendered into one binary bit. A multi-*qubit* system can be extended naturally.

However, QIPSO and QIACO both used quantum-inspired rotation gate (QR-gate) to update the state of *qubits* only. The QR gate is represented as follows:

$$U(\Delta\theta_i) = \begin{pmatrix} \cos(\Delta\theta_i) & -\sin(\Delta\theta_i) \\ \sin(\Delta\theta_i) & \cos(\Delta\theta_i) \end{pmatrix} \qquad (16)$$

The QR-gate is a unitary operation which is used to change the phase of the *qubit* and does not change the length of the *qubit*. The QR gate is employed to update the state of a *qubit* as follows:

$$\begin{pmatrix} \alpha_i' \\ \beta_i' \end{pmatrix} = U(\Delta\theta_i)\begin{pmatrix} \alpha_i \\ \beta_i \end{pmatrix} = \begin{pmatrix} \cos(\Delta\theta_i) & -\sin(\Delta\theta_i) \\ \sin(\Delta\theta_i) & \cos(\Delta\theta_i) \end{pmatrix} \qquad (17)$$

where (α_i, β_i) and (α_i', β_i') are the ith *qubits* of the particle or pheromone before and after the updating, respectively. $\Delta\theta_i$ represents the rotation angle of each *qubit* whose value can be adjusted by some strategies.

Adjustment Strategy of the QR-Gate

In QIPSO and QIACO, the evolution of the individual is guided by the current best individual and adjusted by the QR-gate, so that the individual approximates and converges to the global optimal solution ultimately. A QR-gate is used to change the state of the direction and speed of the individual in case of QIPSO. In QIACO, QR-gate is used to change the state of the quantum pheromone assimilation to evolve the individual. In the processing of evolution, the choice of the quantum rotation angles is very important, and a suitable choice of the rotation angles can help improving the search ability of the algorithm. Different design of the quantum rotation angle is suitable for different problem. Although the designs of the quantum rotation angle are different, the core idea of the designs is the same—to make the current individual evolve to a higher fitness solution.

Considering the feature of the problem and the relation between the current individual and the current best individual, an adaptive rotation angle is proposed in this study, and the rotation angle is defined as follows:

$$\Delta\theta_i = \tan^{-1}\frac{\beta_i}{\alpha_i} \qquad (18)$$

In Quantum Inspired Ant Colony Optimization (QIACO) for multilevel image segmentation, a population P having X number initial strings are produced by randomly selecting pixel intensities. Each string in P is of length $l = \sqrt{M \times N}$, where M and N represents the width and height of an image. A real random number (0, 1) is generated and assigned to each pixel encoded in P by exploring the concept of *qubits*. Then followed by a quantum interference to produce p' and P'', respectively. In this algorithm, number of threshold are fixed it instigates the participating ants to get the best search path at each iteration. A pheromone matrix ρ_j is produced for each ant j at the very beginning the elements of trial pheromone matrix are randomly generated real numbers between (0, 1). For each individual j in P'' if $P''(j) > q_0$, where q_0 is the *priori* defined number between (0, 1), the maximum pheromone assimilation is presumed as threshold value for the gray levels, i.e., $P''(ij) = \arg\max \rho_{ij}$; otherwise, $P''(ij) = rand(0, 1)$. At the end of each generation the pheromone matrix is updated using $\rho_{ij} = t \rho_{ij} + (1-t)b$ where i and j represent the particular string and its corresponding position. b is the best string of different generations and t is said to be the persistence of trials, $t \in [0, 1]$. QIACO is executed for n number of generations K is the number of class boundaries, X represents the size of the population. The proposed QIACO is illustrated in algorithm 2.

Proposed QIPSO Methodology

The time complexity analysis of the proposed QIPSO is describe below.

1. To build the particle matrix, ρ, QIPSO required $O(X \times l)$ time.
2. For the generation of initial strings needs $O(X \times l)$ time.
3. Similarly, QIPSO requires $O(X \times l)$ for the assignment of real numbers in each pixel encoded in the population strings.
4. The required time for performing the quantum interference in QIPSO is $O(X \times l)$.
5. The time needed to generate QR gate is $O(X \times l)$.
6. The time taken by QIPSO for the computation of fitness value is $O(X \times K)$.
7. The time needed to update velocity matrix is $O(X \times l)$.
8. For a predefined number of iterations, the time required for execution of QIACO is $O(X \times l \times n)$, where n represents the number of iterations.

Therefore, it can be concluded that for the proposed QIPSO for multilevel image segmentation, the overall time complexity is $O(X \times l \times n)$.

Proposed QIACO Methodology

The time complexity analysis of the proposed QIACO is describe below.

1. To build the pheromone matrix, ρ, QIACO required $O(X \times l)$ time.
2. For the generation of initial strings needs $O(X \times l)$ time.
3. Similarly, QIACO requires $O(X \times l)$ for the assignment of real numbers in each pixel encoded in the population strings.
4. The required time for performing the quantum interference in QIACO is $O(X \times l)$.

Algorithm 1. Quantum Inspired Particle Swarm Optimization for multilevel image segmentation

```
Input: Number of iterations: n
Size of swarm: X
Persistence of trials: t
Priori defind number: q₀
Output:  Optimal class boundaries K
```

1: Create the particle matrix, ρ

2: Select pixel values randomly to produce X number of initial strings, P, where length of each string is $l = \sqrt{M \times N}$, where M and N represents the width and height of an image.

3: Using the notion of *qubits* to assign real value between (0,1) to each pixel encoded in P. Let it creates P'.

4: **if 1st iteration**

P' undergoes an quantum interference to produce P''.

5:        Locating 8 class boundaries as pixel values from the string P. It should satisfy corresponding value in $P'' > rand$ (0,1). Let it produce $p*$.

6:        Evaluate the fitness of each string in $P*$.

7:        Record the best string *pbest* from $P*$.

9: **for** a predefined number of iterations ($n>1$) **do**

10:          Apply QR gate

11:          P' undergoes an quantum interference to produce P''.

12:          Segment the image using P''.

13:          Evaluate the fitness of each string in $P*$.

14:          Record the global best string in *gbest*

15:          **if** *pbest > gbest* then

16:            *gbest = pbest*

17:          **end if**

18:          Update velocity matrix

19:          Update position

20: **end for**

21: Class boundaries $K=T_B$ are reported

22: Generate OptiMUSIG activation function

23: Applying OptiMUSIG on BDSONN architecture

5. The time needed to generate P' is $O(X \times l)$.
6. The time taken by QIACO for the computation of fitness value is $O(X \times K)$.
7. The time needed to generate P'' is $O(X \times l)$.
8. The quantum rotation gate is updated at each generation with time $O((X \times l)$.
9. The pheromone matrix is updating at each generation requires $O(l)$.

10. For a predefined number of iterations, the time required for execution of QIACO is $O(X \times l \times n)$, where n represents the number of iterations.

Therefore, it can be concluded that for the proposed QIACO for multilevel image segmentation, the overall time complexity is $O(X \times l \times n)$.

EXPERIMENTAL RESULTS

The application of the proposed methods to find out the optimized class boundaries (K) of gray level images has been represented. Three real life gray scale images (Lena, Baboon and Cameraman) with dimensions 128×128 are tested here for ACO and QIACO. The dynamic intensity range is [0, 255],[0, 215] and [0, 254] for the images Lena, Baboon and Cameraman, respectively. The initial string sizes for the conventional PSO & ACO and QIPSO & QIACO based optimization techniques are taken to be 10 and 50, respectively.

Table 1 lists all the fitness values (V) and corresponding required time (T) (in seconds) to obtain the desired output of Lena with 500 and 1000 iterations applied for both the processes PSO & QIPSO. Similarly, Table 2 lists all the fitness values (V) and corresponding required time (T) (in seconds) to obtain the desired output of Lena with 500 and 1000 iterations applied for both the processes ACO & QIACO. Similarly, Table 3 and Table 4 represent all the fitness values (V) and corresponding required time to execute the image of Baboon with 500 and 1000 iterations respectively. Like above, Table 5 and Table 6 represent all the fitness value and required computational time using the image of Cameraman with 500 and 1000 iterations respectively. Within the above mentioned Tables the best fitness values in each set of run is depicted by bold and italic face.

Table 7 and 8 shows corresponding class boundaries (K) for the PSO & QIPSO and ACO and QIACO based multilevel segmented images of Lena with 500 iterations respectively. Table 9 and 10 shows corresponding class boundaries (K) for the PSO & QIPSO and ACO and QIACO based multilevel segmented images of Lena with 1000 iterations respectively. Similarly Table 11 and 12 represents corresponding class boundaries (K) for the PSO & QIPSO and ACO and QIACO based multilevel segmented images of Baboon with 500 and iterations respectively. Table 13 and 14 represents corresponding class boundaries (K) for the PSO & QIPSO and ACO and QIACO based multilevel segmented images of Baboon with 1000 and iterations respectively. As previous, Table 15 and 16 lists corresponding class boundaries (K) for the QIACO and ACO based multilevel segmented images of Cameraman with 500 iterations respectively. Similarly, Table 17 and 18 lists corresponding class boundaries (K) for the QIACO and ACO based multilevel segmented images of Cameraman with 1000 iterations respectively.

Figure 2 represents the flow of the proposed QIPSO. In the initial stage particle matrix is generated. After that, by selecting pixel values randomly, produce X number of initial strings, P, where length of each string is $l = \sqrt{M \times N}$, where M and N represents the width and height of an image. Then applying fuzzification on the initial string to convert the real values in *qubit* notion. Check whether it is the first iteration or not. If yes, perform quantum interference on the swarms. Of late, segmentation has been done using those interfered swarms. Calculate the fitness value of each segmented image using the fitness function and find out the best particle and store the corresponding string as *pbest*. From the next iteration, apply QR gate on the particles. Apply quantum interference on the modified particles. Segment

Algorithm 2. Quantum Inspired Ant Colony Optimization for multilevel image segmentation

Input: Number of iterations: n

Size of population: X

Persistence of trials: t

Priori defind number: q_0

Output: Optimal class boundaries K

1: Create the pheromone matrix, ρ

2: Select pixel values randomly to produce X number of initial strings, P, where length of each string is

$l = \sqrt{M \times N}$, where M and N represents the width and height of an image.

3: Using the notion of *qubits* to assign real value between $(0,1)$ to each pixel encoded in P. Let it creates P'.

4: P' undergoes an quantum interference to produce P''.

5: Locating 8 class boundaries as pixel values from the string P. It should satisfy corresponding value in $P'' >$ *rand* $(0,1)$. Let it produce $p*$.

6: Evaluate the fitness of each string in $P*$.

7: Record the best string b from $P*$.

8: Repeat step (5) to generate P''.

9: **for** a predefined number of iterations (n) **do**

10:　　　　**for** all $i \in P''$ **do**

11:　　　　　　**for** all j^{th} position in i **do**

12:　　　　　　　　**if** $(rand\ (0,1) > q_0)$ **then**

13:　　　　　　　　　　$P''_{ij} = \arg \max \rho_{ij}$

14:　　　　　　　　**else**

15:　　　　　　　　　　$P''_{ij} = rand\ (0,1)$

16:　　　　　　　　**end if**

17:　　　　　　**end for**

18:　　　　**end for**

19:　　　　Compute the fitness of P''

20:　　　　The best string c from $P**$ is recorded.

21:　　　　Compute the fitness of b and c.

22:　　　　Update the string with best string along of its corresponding class boundaries in T_B from $P**$.

23:　　　　Record the best string of step (22) in b and its corresponding class boundaries $T_B \in P**$.

24:　　　　**for** all $i \in P''$ **do**

25:　　　　　　**for** all j^{th} position in i **do**

26:　　　　　　　　Update ρ_{ij} using QR gate

27:　　　　　　**end for**

28:　　　　**end for**

29: **end for**

30: Class boundaries $K = T_B$ are reported

31: Generate OptiMUSIG activation function

32: Applying OptiMUSIG on BDSONN architecture

Table 1. Comparative performance analysis of PSO and QIPSO for Lena with 500 & 1000 iterations

SL. NO.	Number of Iterations 500				Number of Iterations 1000				
	QIPSO		PSO		QIPSO		PSO		
	FITNESS VALUE*(V)*	*(T)*	FITNESS VALUE*(V)*	*(T)*	FITNESS VALUE*(V)*	*(T)*	FITNESS VALUE*(V)*	*(T)*	
1	0.99057444	127	*0.99078564*	716	0.99023265	251	0.99022325	1433	
2	0.99018725	126	0.98943267	702	0.99035698	254	0.99003727	1378	
3	0.98998627	125	0.98988765	692	0.99023569	255	0.98923894	1359	
4	0.99032143	127	0.99024262	623	0.99113569	256	0.99025698	1244	
5	0.99073241	127	0.98974888	708	0.98989561	251	0.98109545	1403	
6	0.98981432	127	0.98957342	649	0.99023258	252	0.99028945	1444	
7	0.99014210	125	0.98887999	705	0.99056974	256	0.98921006	1366	
8	0.99081143	124	0.99022222	695	0.99032356	252	0.99028955	1212	
9	*0.99099288*	128	0.98965678	679	0.99079845	251	*0.99056894*	1265	
10	0.99072756	126	0.99039025	672	*0.99189562*	251	0.98985648	1412	

Table 2. Comparative performance analysis of ACO and QIACO for Lena with 500 & 1000 iterations

SL. NO.	Number of Iterations 500				Number of Iterations 1000				
	QIACO		ACO		QIACO		ACO		
	FITNESS VALUE*(V)*	*(T)*	FITNESS VALUE*(V)*	*(T)*	FITNESS VALUE*(V)*	*(T)*	FITNESS VALUE*(V)*	*(T)*	
1	0.99047234	128	*0.99085462*	715	0.99036218	255	0.99025745	1422	
2	0.99009925	128	0.98953378	701	0.99007020	255	0.99003727	1356	
3	0.98986927	127	0.9898414	698	0.99022928	255	0.98999640	1367	
4	0.99032256	128	0.99023181	622	0.99112836	254	0.99048826	1246	
5	0.99074171	128	0.98974903	703	0.98980557	255	0.98108108	1408	
6	0.98990600	128	0.98967067	640	0.99043322	256	0.99027708	1413	
7	0.99012500	127	0.98867802	705	0.99017188	254	0.98971001	1379	
8	0.99080641	128	0.99021194	699	0.99039731	255	0.99022766	1291	
9	*0.990981882*	129	0.98968324	676	0.99077597	255	*0.99048891*	1243	
10	0.99072925	128	0.99035962	678	*0.99116374*	255	0.98982899	1402	

image using these particles and compute corresponding fitness values. Store the global best as *gbest*. After that update the velocity matrix and particle position respectively. At the end of the terminating condition a set of optimal class boundaries are reported. Optimized multi level sigmoidal (OptiMUSIG) activation function is generated. By applying this activation function on BDSONN architecture, multi-level segmented image is obtained as output.

Figure 3 represents the flow of the proposed QIACO. In the initial phase, Pheromone matrix is created. After that, by selecting pixel values randomly, produce X number of initial strings, P, where length of each string is $l = \sqrt{M \times N}$, where M and N represents the width and height of an image. Then ap-

Table 3. Comparative performance analysis of PSO and QIPSO for Baboon with 500 & 1000 iterations

SL. NO.	Number of Iterations 500				Number of Iterations 1000			
	QIPSO		PSO		QIPSO		PSO	
	FITNESS VALUE(V)	(T)	FITNESS VALUE(V)	(T)	FITNESS VALUE(V)	(T)	FITNESS VALUE(V)	(T)
1	0.98992356	131	*0.97856256*	721	0.97819412	261	0.97645800	1460
2	0.99009854	133	0.97445698	722	0.97717125	261	0.97612358	1260
3	0.99035645	131	0.9741258	699	*0.97989546*	252	0.97745871	1441
4	*0.99089542*	141	0.97362883	656	0.97682389	251	0.97602597	1445
5	0.97709890	137	0.97284598	649	0.97723984	261	0.97354698	1446
6	0.97854569	132	0.97545821	729	0.97845987	260	0.97732304	1450
7	0.97844569	131	0.97484698	728	0.97825234	260	*0.97754811*	1456
8	0.97898500	132	0.97542567	727	0.97824259	261	0.97540024	1423
9	0.97791245	137	0.97688954	729	0.97794698	261	0.97738856	1458
10	0.97799561	132	0.97671232	725	0.97752231	290	0.97674658	1478

Table 4. Comparative performance analysis of ACO and QIACO for Baboon with 500 & 1000 iterations

SL. NO.	Number of Iterations 500				Number of Iterations 1000			
	QIACO		ACO		QIACO		ACO	
	FITNESS VALUE(V)	(T)	FITNESS VALUE(V)	(T)	FITNESS VALUE(V)	(T)	FITNESS VALUE(V)	(T)
1	0.98991084	133	*0.97827974*	729	0.97819412	265	0.97639190	1459
2	0.99003493	132	0.97444530	727	0.97717125	264	0.97688118	1277
3	0.99036939	139	0.97468930	698	*0.97958430*	255	0.97747801	1440
4	*0.9907578*	140	0.97362883	650	0.97687497	254	0.97656747	1442
5	0.97709310	136	0.97285517	644	0.97740078	263	0.97355730	1442
6	0.97859263	133	0.97594825	725	0.97884024	264	0.97730476	1439
7	0.97840780	130	0.97486869	725	0.97829368	264	*0.97798161*	1431
8	0.97834004	138	0.97547663	725	0.97824191	264	0.97541414	1427
9	0.97794625	142	0.97687756	725	0.97796653	269	0.97735407	1422
10	0.97794401	140	0.97673301	724	0.9775838	292	0.97674970	1425

plying fuzzification on the initial string to convert the real values in *qubit* notion. Then quantum interference has been applied on these *qubits*. Locating 8 class boundaries as pixel values from the string *P*. It should satisfy corresponding value in *P''>rand* (0,1). Let it produce segmented images with class boundaries. After that, find out the fitness value of each segmented image with the fitness function. The best fitness value with its respective class boundaries is stored for further use. Then the pheromone matrix is updated using QR gate for the exploration of the search space. The above steps from quantum interference are repeated until the end condition appears. Then a set of optimal class boundaries is ob-

Table 5. Comparative performance analysis of PSO and QIPSO for Cameraman with 500 & 1000 iterations

| SL. NO. | Number of Iterations 500 | | | | Number of Iterations 1000 | | | | |
| | QIPSO | | PSO | | QIPSO | | PSO | | |
	FITNESS VALUE(V)	(T)	FITNESS VALUE(V)	(T)	FITNESS VALUE(V)	(T)	FITNESS VALUE(V)	(T)	
1	0.99195241	127	0.99112548	648	0.99225487	241	0.99202154	1435	
2	0.99230020	122	0.99074569	729	0.99261254	252	0.99112487	1444	
3	0.99240999	126	0.99190423	723	0.99265612	249	0.99212547	1462	
4	0.99202385	121	0.99141287	730	0.99272315	247	0.99251254	1425	
5	0.99203587	129	0.99160215	729	0.99224598	252	0.99233265	1435	
6	0.99242569	121	*0.99212587*	731	0.99251254	253	0.99222600	1465	
7	0.99230211	122	0.99177845	732	0.99270056	252	*0.99275487*	1415	
8	*0.99268972*	123	0.99182548	726	*0.99325487*	248	0.99221569	1459	
9	0.99235678	121	0.99112345	729	0.99274568	244	0.99106000	1445	
10	0.99240021	121	0.99184587	728	0.99221254	249	0.99174658	142	

Table 6. Comparative performance analysis of ACO and QIACO for Cameraman with 500 & 1000 iterations

| SL. NO. | Number of Iterations 500 | | | | Number of Iterations 1000 | | | | |
| | QIACO | | ACO | | QIACO | | ACO | | |
	FITNESS VALUE(V)	(T)	FITNESS VALUE(V)	(T)	FITNESS VALUE(V)	(T)	FITNESS VALUE(V)	(T)	
1	0.99196484	128	0.99193827	649	0.99246712	248	0.99241973	1425	
2	0.99238970	126	0.99079510	729	0.99261933	251	0.99198215	1420	
3	0.99240999	125	0.99190423	725	0.99265612	247	0.99255930	1420	
4	0.99218661	127	0.99141761	729	0.99270816	249	0.99256723	1421	
5	0.99224775	127	0.99168262	726	0.99224762	255	0.99233464	1417	
6	0.99250116	129	*0.99218040*	728	0.99255311	250	0.99222651	1413	
7	0.99233238	127	0.99170074	726	0.99270012	250	*0.99263575*	1418	
8	*0.99258542*	125	0.99189751	725	*0.99280127*	249	0.99227766	1422	
9	0.99231848	124	0.99114938	725	0.99273675	249	0.99106163	1421	
10	0.99244438	124	0.99188131	728	0.99222255	248	0.99175517	1425	

tained. Of late, optimized multi level sigmoidal (OptiMUSIG) activation function is generated. By applying this activation function on BDSONN architecture, multilevel segmented image is obtained as output.

Figure 4 shows conventional PSO based multilevel segmented images of Lena (a to j) and (k to t) with 500 and 1000 iterations respectively. Figure 5 shows QIPSO based multilevel segmented images of Lena (a to j) and (k to t) with 500 and 1000 iterations respectively. Figure 6 and 7 show multilevel segmented images of Lena, based on classical ACO and quantum inspired ACO with 500 iterations (for (a to j)) and 1000 iterations (for (k to t)) (for 6 and 7 both) respectively.

Table 7. Optimized class boundaries of PSO and QIPSO for image Lena with 500 iterations

SL. NO.	CLASS BOUNDARIES OF QIPSO								CLASS BOUNDARIES OF PSO							
	K_1	K_2	K_3	K_4	K_5	K_6	K_7	K_8	K_1	K_2	K_3	K_4	K_5	K_6	K_7	K_8
1	0	30	62	91	121	151	196	255	0	34	64	105	133	158	189	255
2	0	31	57	91	118	156	182	255	0	29	59	89	115	155	196	255
3	0	25	63	87	129	159	199	255	0	21	52	99	128	156	192	255
4	0	34	61	92	126	152	185	255	0	26	56	95	129	158	184	255
5	0	26	60	92	116	154	193	255	0	45	65	91	126	152	185	255
6	0	42	64	99	135	150	191	255	0	33	58	89	124	157	189	255
7	0	41	64	87	134	156	181	255	0	25	66	92	127	159	183	255
8	0	30	55	84	123	159	198	255	0	39	61	99	129	153	187	255
9	0	47	71	99	122	152	183	255	0	34	66	98	135	159	185	255
10	0	30	69	97	131	154	188	255	0	36	76	93	129	160	199	255

Table 9. Optimized class boundaries of PSO and QIPSO for image Lena with 1000 iterations

SL. NO.	CLASS BOUNDARIES OF QIPSO								CLASS BOUNDARIES OF PSO							
	K_1	K_2	K_3	K_4	K_5	K_6	K_7	K_8	K_1	K_2	K_3	K_4	K_5	K_6	K_7	K_8
1	0	33	60	112	136	155	182	255	0	43	66	106	124	156	181	255
2	0	48	76	121	136	166	199	255	0	35	64	99	123	156	208	255
3	0	37	62	89	125	155	198	255	0	19	66	95	127	166	189	255
4	0	39	56	99	124	156	188	255	0	35	65	94	118	152	191	255
5	0	35	65	113	125	156	198	255	0	36	66	96	126	155	195	255
6	0	25	53	99	128	156	186	255	0	26	62	93	121	159	196	255
7	0	25	66	114	125	156	185	255	0	47	62	96	125	141	198	255
8	0	34	63	94	139	158	198	255	0	49	66	96	126	156	178	255
9	0	29	56	99	125	148	183	255	0	46	76	101	122	152	191	255
10	0	38	66	115	138	165	185	255	0	32	66	97	129	157	195	255

Table 10. Optimized class boundaries of ACO and QIACO for image Lena with 1000 iterations

SL. NO.	CLASS BOUNDARIES OF QIACO								CLASS BOUNDARIES OF ACO							
	K_1	K_2	K_3	K_4	K_5	K_6	K_7	K_8	K_1	K_2	K_3	K_4	K_5	K_6	K_7	K_8
1	0	31	62	100	133	159	184	255	0	46	66	101	124	154	188	255
2	0	42	75	102	130	164	194	255	0	39	64	94	123	152	201	255
3	0	33	66	89	120	158	198	255	0	19	62	96	127	162	185	255
4	0	31	59	95	124	156	188	255	0	38	66	96	118	151	190	255
5	0	39	60	103	129	155	192	255	0	37	60	96	127	158	193	255
6	0	23	59	98	128	153	182	255	0	27	67	95	127	155	192	255
7	0	23	63	104	126	154	187	255	0	44	63	96	127	149	191	255
8	0	30	60	98	130	156	196	255	0	41	64	95	125	151	178	255
9	0	29	58	92	125	149	188	255	0	44	73	101	126	154	194	255
10	0	34	62	105	132	163	186	255	0	30	64	97	128	157	193	255

Table 11. Optimized class boundaries of PSO and QIPSO for image Baboon with 500 iterations

SL. NO.	CLASS BOUNDARIES OF QIPSO								CLASS BOUNDARIES OF PSO							
	K_1	K_2	K_3	K_4	K_5	K_6	K_7	K_8	K_1	K_2	K_3	K_4	K_5	K_6	K_7	K_8
1	0	61	96	105	129	146	172	215	0	22	75	97	123	152	185	215
2	0	76	115	126	126	154	174	215	0	35	66	115	133	156	181	215
3	0	56	85	115	136	146	175	215	0	41	65	92	112	145	192	215
4	0	56	97	126	141	159	187	215	0	46	62	98	137	151	195	215
5	0	65	82	101	136	152	171	215	0	65	99	106	126	156	175	215
6	0	54	96	115	131	157	175	215	0	78	91	126	132	155	186	215
7	0	62	71	98	126	145	161	215	0	66	93	115	125	141	168	215
8	0	46	83	117	122	144	165	215	0	68	81	102	128	156	179	215
9	0	76	92	118	139	156	178	215	0	76	98	126	145	162	176	215
10	0	61	96	103	128	141	178	215	0	75	92	125	144	155	170	215

Table 12. Optimized class boundaries of ACO and QIACO for image Baboon with500 iterations

SL. NO.	CLASS BOUNDARIES OF QIACO								CLASS BOUNDARIES OF ACO							
	K_1	K_2	K_3	K_4	K_5	K_6	K_7	K_8	K_1	K_2	K_3	K_4	K_5	K_6	K_7	K_8
1	0	67	90	109	123	148	173	215	0	27	70	97	120	150	185	215
2	0	72	105	116	129	155	178	215	0	35	63	105	135	155	187	215
3	0	51	83	110	134	149	170	215	0	41	64	91	119	149	191	215
4	0	56	97	120	140	159	187	215	0	41	65	93	131	157	191	215
5	0	63	86	107	138	159	174	215	0	64	95	107	128	153	177	215
6	0	54	92	117	136	159	175	215	0	71	99	120	134	155	181	215
7	0	64	74	99	124	143	168	215	0	66	92	112	124	144	167	215
8	0	49	82	107	126	147	167	215	0	64	88	109	128	156	176	215
9	0	72	91	108	132	155	175	215	0	75	99	124	141	161	178	215
10	0	68	92	113	124	144	176	215	0	74	96	121	141	154	178	215

Similarly Figure 8 shows conventional PSO based multilevel segmented images of Lena (a to j) and (k to t) with 500 and 1000 iterations respectively. Figure 9 shows QIPSO based multilevel segmented images of Lena (a to j) and (k to t) with 500 and 1000 iterations respectively. Figure 10 and 11 show multilevel segmented images of Lena, based on classical ACO and quantum inspired ACO with 500 iterations (for (a to j)) and 1000 iterations (for (k to t)) respectively.

As previous, Figure 12 shows conventional PSO based multilevel segmented images of Lena (a to j) and (k to t) with 500 and 1000 iterations respectively. Figure 13 shows QIPSO based multilevel segmented images of Lena (a to j) and (k to t) with 500 and 1000 iterations respectively. Figure 14 and 15 show multilevel segmented images of Lena, based on classical ACO and quantum inspired ACO with 500 iterations (for (a to j)) and 1000 iterations (for (k to t)) respectively. Figure 16 shows the graphical comparison among the best fitness values (*V*) of all set of runs.

Table 13. Optimized class boundaries of PSO and QIPSO for image Baboon with 1000 iterations

SL. NO.	CLASS BOUNDARIES OF QIPSO								CLASS BOUNDARIES OF PSO							
	K_1	K_2	K_3	K_4	K_5	K_6	K_7	K_8	K_1	K_2	K_3	K_4	K_5	K_6	K_7	K_8
1	0	75	81	105	125	145	166	215	0	76	108	126	136	156	178	215
2	0	58	85	115	129	145	174	215	0	56	93	104	122	142	161	215
3	0	71	91	114	138	155	172	215	0	75	106	119	139	156	185	215
4	0	60	82	118	132	151	165	215	0	66	106	115	138	142	170	215
5	0	75	89	114	146	165	176	215	0	69	95	118	124	156	176	215
6	0	66	93	115	135	144	162	215	0	75	99	121	139	155	178	215
7	0	68	96	118	136	155	185	215	0	66	88	115	125	152	179	215
8	0	61	92	124	145	161	176	215	0	69	81	102	122	146	172	215
9	0	61	89	105	139	151	175	215	0	66	96	113	136	154	187	215
10	0	65	96	118	145	156	179	215	0	52	88	116	139	155	189	215

Table 14. Optimized class boundaries of ACO and QIACO for image Baboon with 1000 iterations

SL. NO.	CLASS BOUNDARIES OF QIACO								CLASS BOUNDARIES OF ACO							
	K_1	K_2	K_3	K_4	K_5	K_6	K_7	K_8	K_1	K_2	K_3	K_4	K_5	K_6	K_7	K_8
1	0	71	87	104	128	149	167	215	0	74	101	124	137	153	178	215
2	0	59	87	112	125	145	176	215	0	59	91	106	123	143	167	215
3	0	72	98	119	137	152	172	215	0	72	102	114	131	153	180	215
4	0	60	87	111	132	152	167	215	0	67	100	116	136	147	170	215
5	0	73	98	117	143	164	170	215	0	65	94	119	129	152	177	215
6	0	61	90	114	132	147	165	215	0	71	97	120	132	150	173	215
7	0	68	97	117	136	153	183	215	0	62	84	111	129	151	170	215
8	0	68	90	121	144	161	175	215	0	64	88	106	125	144	174	215
9	0	66	84	107	131	151	173	215	0	66	94	114	135	154	182	215
10	0	68	98	117	140	159	172	215	0	57	89	113	130	158	180	215

Table 15. Optimized class boundaries of PSO and QIPSO for image Cameraman with 500 iterations

SL. NO.	CLASS BOUNDARIES OF QIPSO								CLASS BOUNDARIES OF PSO							
	K_1	K_2	K_3	K_4	K_5	K_6	K_7	K_8	K_1	K_2	K_3	K_4	K_5	K_6	K_7	K_8
1	0	31	86	115	122	155	170	254	0	52	110	125	145	167	170	254
2	0	41	62	112	122	151	172	254	0	42	74	101	131	151	175	254
3	0	25	71	111	135	161	174	254	0	48	86	100	125	154	174	254
4	0	46	72	113	132	162	180	254	0	45	61	95	127	155	170	254
5	0	39	62	114	131	160	174	254	0	53	97	109	144	160	177	254
6	0	32	75	104	121	152	164	254	0	36	72	118	130	154	176	254
7	0	41	82	101	122	142	160	254	0	52	87	106	141	155	174	254
8	0	42	81	112	132	164	185	254	0	34	79	108	135	150	171	254
9	0	46	74	125	131	161	180	254	0	42	81	119	120	154	178	254
10	0	31	75	115	134	162	175	254	0	40	85	111	145	165	177	254

Table 16. Optimized class boundaries of ACO and QIACO for image Cameraman with 500 iterations

SL. NO.	CLASS BOUNDARIES OF QIACO								CLASS BOUNDARIES OF ACO							
	K_1	K_2	K_3	K_4	K_5	K_6	K_7	K_8	K_1	K_2	K_3	K_4	K_5	K_6	K_7	K_8
1	0	33	83	113	128	150	172	254	0	50	100	126	149	164	174	254
2	0	40	68	111	126	159	176	254	0	44	76	106	130	157	177	254
3	0	29	75	113	139	160	173	254	0	49	84	105	126	154	176	254
4	0	42	77	115	134	163	188	254	0	41	60	97	124	156	172	254
5	0	32	62	114	136	161	176	254	0	53	95	119	149	163	175	254
6	0	35	74	104	126	152	168	254	0	32	72	108	132	157	175	254
7	0	45	88	102	125	149	169	254	0	54	87	116	140	157	175	254
8	0	48	82	117	136	165	185	254	0	35	79	118	136	159	175	254
9	0	46	75	121	131	160	181	254	0	48	84	109	122	151	171	254
10	0	33	75	118	136	165	178	254	0	49	80	121	146	162	175	254

Table 17. Optimized class boundaries of PSO and QIPSO for image Cameraman with 1000 iterations

SL. NO.	CLASS BOUNDARIES OF QIPSO								CLASS BOUNDARIES OF PSO							
	K_1	K_2	K_3	K_4	K_5	K_6	K_7	K_8	K_1	K_2	K_3	K_4	K_5	K_6	K_7	K_8
1	0	55	82	114	135	155	175	254	0	45	82	115	131	165	170	254
2	0	42	96	115	148	165	179	254	0	46	86	128	145	166	188	254
3	0	46	95	121	140	158	178	254	0	38	75	115	145	169	187	254
4	0	39	81	115	145	169	185	254	0	55	76	114	149	158	170	254
5	0	34	74	100	130	155	188	254	0	58	96	116	147	167	178	254
6	0	40	70	124	145	154	179	254	0	42	85	118	136	166	184	254
7	0	45	85	116	144	164	177	254	0	42	90	115	139	155	175	254
8	0	44	96	118	146	154	178	254	0	43	84	128	146	154	178	254
9	0	36	64	81	112	148	165	254	0	46	75	115	134	156	176	254
10	0	40	65	118	124	147	168	254	0	35	78	119	135	150	175	254

Table 18. Optimized class boundaries of ACO and QIACO for image Cameraman with 1000 iterations

SL. NO.	CLASS BOUNDARIES OF QIACO								CLASS BOUNDARIES OF ACO							
	K_1	K_2	K_3	K_4	K_5	K_6	K_7	K_8	K_1	K_2	K_3	K_4	K_5	K_6	K_7	K_8
1	0	53	85	114	130	159	172	254	0	44	85	118	130	161	177	254
2	0	46	95	114	141	163	175	254	0	42	89	121	143	163	180	254
3	0	46	93	120	142	159	179	254	0	38	78	113	140	163	180	254
4	0	39	81	116	143	163	180	254	0	50	77	117	142	159	177	254
5	0	39	78	108	131	156	181	254	0	55	93	117	142	161	173	254
6	0	40	74	120	141	157	176	254	0	49	81	114	136	161	181	254
7	0	49	80	119	143	160	177	254	0	45	92	116	135	156	173	254
8	0	43	96	119	140	159	173	254	0	44	84	120	140	159	179	254
9	0	35	63	80	117	147	168	254	0	46	76	113	134	156	176	254
10	0	43	65	108	125	148	168	254	0	32	71	115	135	155	175	254

Figure 2. Flow chart of QIPSO based multilevel image segmentation

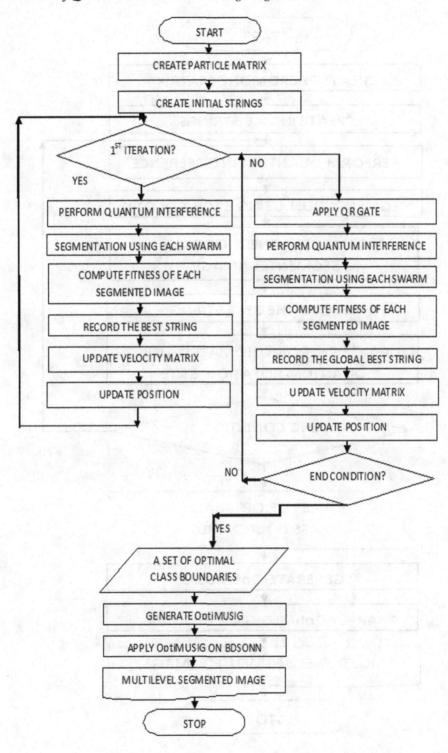

Figure 3. Flow chart of QIACO based multilevel image segmentation

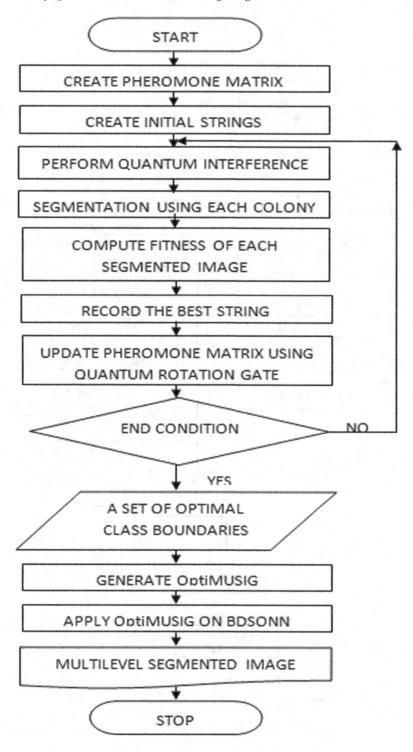

CONCLUSION

The classical OptiMUSIG activation function which is an optimized version of conventional MUSIG activation function is preferable for multilevel image segmentation. Two new algorithms inspired by particle swarm optimization and ant colony optimization method as well as quantum computing to resolve the problem of time efficiency of conventional OptiMUSIG proposed in this chapter. From the results obtained, it is evident that the Quantum Inspired Optimization based OptiMUSIG is much more efficient as far as execution time is concerned. Methods however, remain to be investigated to apply the proposed method for the segmentation of color images. The authors are engaged in this direction.

Figure 4. Output of PSO based multilevel image segmentation with 500 iterations (a – j) and with 1000 iterations (k – t) for LENA

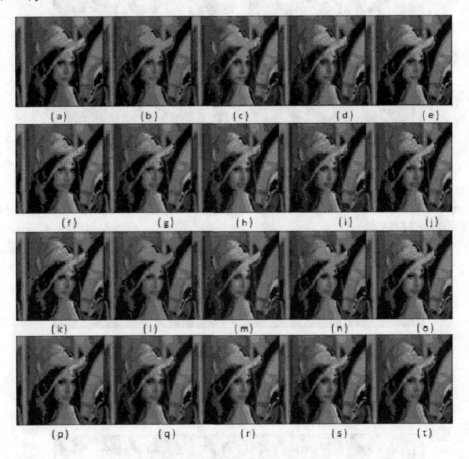

Figure 5. Output of QIPSO based multilevel image segmentation with 500 iterations (a − j) and with 1000 iterations (k − t) for LENA

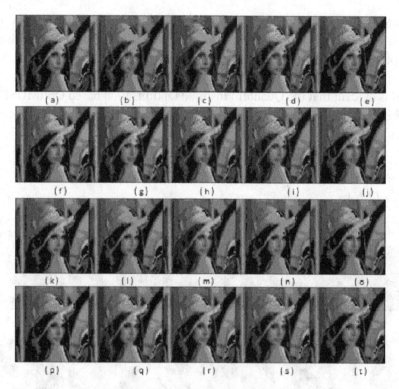

Figure 6. Output of ACO based multilevel image segmentation with 500 iterations (a − j) and with 1000 iterations (k − t) for LENA

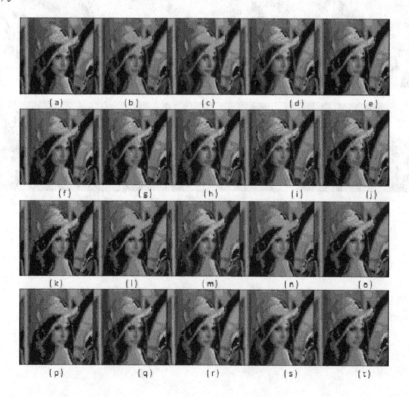

Figure 7. Output of QIACO based multilevel image segmentation with 500 iterations (a – j) and with 1000 iterations (k – t) for LENA

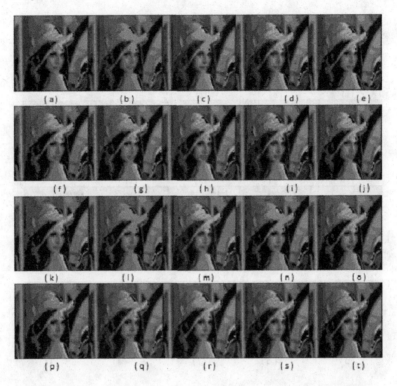

Figure 8. Output of PSO based multilevel image segmentation with 500 iterations (a – j) and with 1000 iterations (k – t) for BABOON

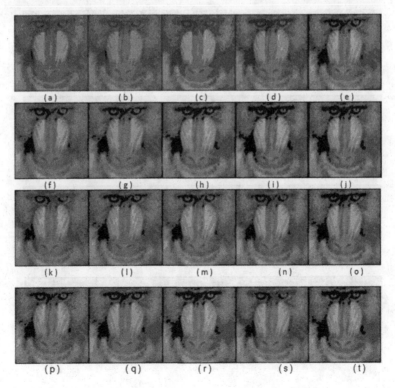

Figure 9. Output of QIPSO based multilevel image segmentation with 500 iterations (a – j) and with 1000 iterations (k – t) for BABOON

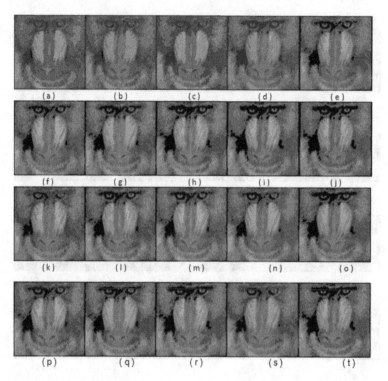

Figure 10. Output of ACO based multilevel image segmentation with 500 iterations (a – j) and with 1000 iterations (k – t) for BABOON

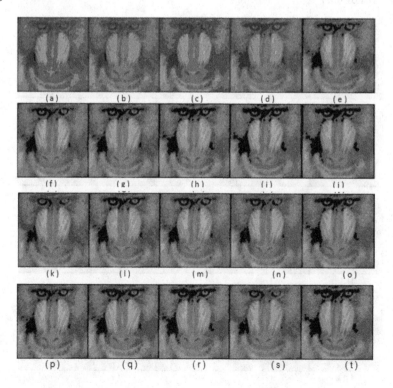

Figure 11. Output of QIACO based multilevel image segmentation with 500 iterations (a – j) and with 1000 iterations (k – t) for BABOON

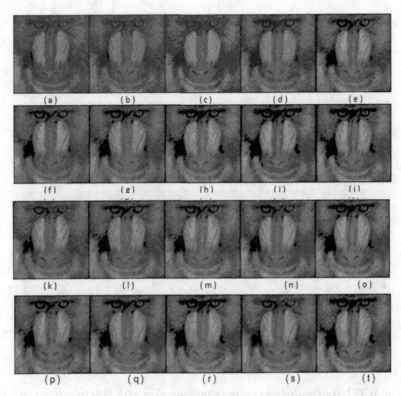

Figure 12. Output of PSO based multilevel image segmentation with 500 iterations (a – j) and with 1000 iterations (k – t) for CAMERAMAN

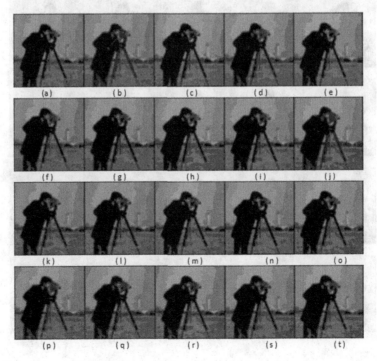

Figure 13. Output of QIPSO based multilevel image segmentation with 500 iterations (a – j) and with 1000 iterations (k – t) for CAMERAMAN

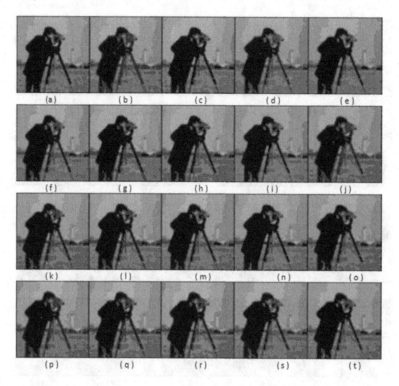

Figure 14. Output of ACO based multilevel image segmentation with 500 iterations (a – j) and with 1000 iterations (k – t) for CAMERAMAN

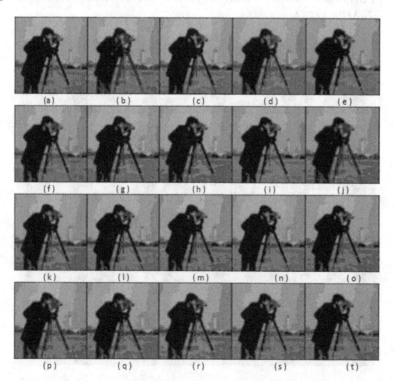

Figure 15. Output of QIACO based multilevel image segmentation with 500 iterations (a − j) and with 1000 iterations (k − t) for CAMERAMAN

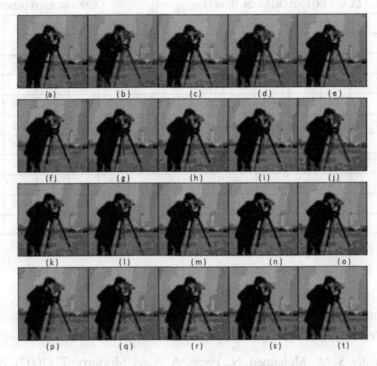

Figure 16. Comparison chart with all the images with 500 & 1000 iterations with their best fitness

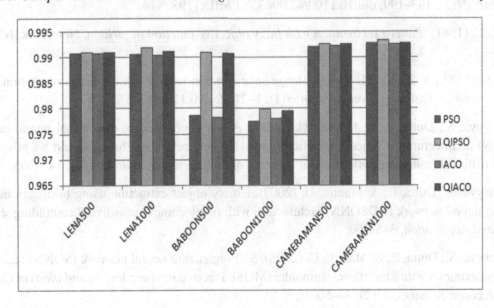

Table 8. Optimized class boundaries of ACO and QIACO for image Lena with 500 iterations

SL. NO.	CLASS BOUNDARIES OF QIACO								CLASS BOUNDARIES OF ACO							
	K_1	K_2	K_3	K_4	K_5	K_6	K_7	K_8	K_1	K_2	K_3	K_4	K_5	K_6	K_7	K_8
1	0	32	64	90	120	150	196	255	0	36	67	100	131	155	187	255
2	0	34	59	101	119	157	183	255	0	29	59	86	117	154	196	255
3	0	23	65	89	128	159	194	255	0	21	54	98	12	155	194	255
4	0	35	63	90	127	151	181	255	0	25	55	91	129	156	184	255
5	0	28	63	92	114	156	193	255	0	41	67	97	125	159	186	255
6	0	42	64	102	135	152	190	255	0	31	52	87	124	153	188	255
7	0	44	66	88	134	155	187	255	0	20	63	97	124	150	189	255
8	0	32	59	86	120	156	199	255	0	36	60	90	126	158	187	255
9	0	49	75	100	124	155	185	255	0	39	64	92	127	158	185	255
10	0	32	67	99	130	154	191	255	0	35	71	97	12	161	192	255

REFERENCES

Adams, R., & Bischof, L. (1994). Seeded region growing. *IEEE Transactions on Pattern Analysis and Machine Intelligence*, *16*(6), 641–647. doi:10.1109/34.295913

Ahmed, M. N., Yamany, S. M., Mohamed, N., Farag, A. A., & Moriarty, T. (2002). A modified fuzzy c-means algorithm for bias field estimation and segmentation of MRI data. *IEEE Transactions on Medical Imaging*, *21*(3), 193–199. doi:10.1109/42.996338 PMID:11989844

Bejdek, J. C. (1981). *Pattern recognition with fuzzy objective function algorithm*. New York, NY: Plenum Press.

Bhandarkar, S. M., & Zhang, H. (1999). Image segmentation using evolutionary computation. *IEEE Transactions on Evolutionary Computation*, *3*(1), 1–21. doi:10.1109/4235.752917

Bhattacharyya, S., Dutta, P., & Maulik, U. (2006). A self supervised bi-directional neural network (BDSONN) architecture for object extraction guided by beta activation function and adaptive fuzzy context sensitive thresholding. *International Journal of Intelligent Technology*, *1*(4), 345–365.

Bhattacharyya, S., Dutta, P., & Maulik, U. (2007). Binary object extraction using bi-directional self-organizing neural network (BDSONN) architecture with fuzzy context sensitive thresholding. *Pattern Analysis and Application*, 345-360.

Bhattacharyya, S., Dutta, P., & Maulik, U. (2008). Self organizing neural network (SONN) based gray scale object extractor with a multilevel sigmoidal (MUSIG) activation function. *Foundations of Computing and Decision Sciences, 33*(2), 46–50.

Bhattacharyya, S., Dutta, P., & Maulik, U. (2011). Multilevel image segmentation with adaptive image context based thresholding. *Applied Soft Computing, 11*(1), 946–962. doi:10.1016/j.asoc.2010.01.015

Bhattacharyya, S., Dutta, P., Maulik, U., & Nandi, P. K. (2007). Multilevel activation functions for true color image segmentation using self – organizing neural network (PSONN) architecture: A comparative study. *International Journal on Computer Sciences, 29*(1), 9-21.

Boyarsky, A., & Gora, P. (2010). A random map model for quantum interference. *Communications in Nonlinear Science and Numerical Simulation, 15*(8), 1974–1979. doi:10.1016/j.cnsns.2009.08.018

Chandra, S., Bhattacharyya, S., & Chakraborty, S. (2013). A quantum inspired time efficient OptiMUSIG activation function for multilevel image segmentation. In *Proceedings of India Conference (INDICON), 2013 Annual IEEE*. IEEE.

Chang, P. L., & Teng, W. G. (2007). Exploiting the self- organizing map for meical image segmentation. In *Proceedings of Twentieth IEEE International Symposium on Computer – Based Medical Systems 20*. IEEE.

Chang, Y. L., & Li, X. (1994). Adaptive image region-growing. *IEEE Transactions on Image Processing, 3*(6), 868–872. doi:10.1109/83.336259 PMID:18296257

Chun, D. N., & Yang, H. S. (1996). Robust image segmentation using genetic algorithm with a fuzzy measure. *Pattern Recognition, 29*(7), 1195–1211. doi:10.1016/0031-3203(95)00148-4

De, S., Bhattacharyya, S., & Dutta, P. (2008). OptiMUSIG: An optimized gray level image segmentor. [IEEE.]. *Proceedings of ADCOM, 2008*, 78–87.

De, S., Bhattacharyya, S., & Dutta, P. (2010). Efficient grey-level image segmentation using an optimized MUSIG (OptiMUSIG) activation function. *International Journal of Parallel, Emergent and Distributed Systems*, 1-39.

Deneubourg, J. L., Aron, S., & Pasteels, J. M. (1990). The self- organizing exploratory pattern of the Argentine ant. *Journal of Insect Behavior, 3*(159). doi:10.1007/BF01417909

Dorigo, M. (1992). *Optimization, learning and natural algorithms*. (Doctoral dissertation). Politechnico di Milano, Milano, Italy.

Dorigo, M., & Gambardella, L. M. (1997). Ant colony system: A cooperative learning approach to the travelling salesman problem. *IEEE Transactions on Evolutionary Computation, 1*(1), 53–66. doi:10.1109/4235.585892

Dorigo, M., & Stutzle, T. (2005). *Ant colony optimization*. New Delhi: Prentice Hall of India Private Limited.

Englebrecht, A. P. (2002). *Computational intelligence: An introduction*. New York: John Wiley and sons.

Fogel, D. B. (1997). The advantage of evolutionary computation. World Scientific Press.

Fogel, D. B. (2006). Evolutionary computation: Toward a new philosophy of machine intelligence. Wiley- IEEE Press.

Freixenet, J., Munoz, X., & Raba, D. (2002). Yet another survey on image segmentation: Region and boundary information integration. In *Proceedings of the 7th European Conference on Computer Vision (ECCV'02)* (vol. 2352, pp. 408-422). Berlin: Springer.

Gonzalez, R. C., & Woods, R. E. (2002). *Digital image processing*. Englewood Cliffs, NJ: Prentice-Hall.

Goss, S., Aron, S., Deneubourg, J. L., & Pasteels, J. M. (1989). The self-organized exploratory pattern of the Argentine ant. *Naturwissenschaften*, *76*(12), 579–581. doi:10.1007/BF00462870

Han, K. H., & Kim, J. H. (2000). Genetic quantum algorithm and its application to combinatorial optimization problem. In *Proceedings of the Congress on Evolutionary Computation* (vol. 2, pp. 1354-1360). Academic Press.

Han, K. H., & Kim, J. H. (2004). Quantum inspired evolutionary algorithms with a new termination criterion, He gate, and two- phase scheme. *IEEE Transactions on Evolutionary Computation*, *8*(2), 156–169. doi:10.1109/TEVC.2004.823467

Helterbrand, J. D. (1996). One-pixel-wide closed boundary identification. *IEEE Transactions on Image Processing*, *5*(5), 780–783. doi:10.1109/83.499916 PMID:18285168

Ho, S. Y., & Lee, K. Z. (2001). An efficient evolutionary image segmentation algorithm. In *Proceedings of IEEE Congress on Evolutionary Computation* (pp. 1327-1334). IEEE.

Hojjatoleslami, S. A., & Kittler, J. (1998). Region growing: A new approach. *IEEE Transactions on Image Processing*, *7*(7), 1079–1084. doi:10.1109/83.701170 PMID:18276325

Jiang, Y., & Zhou, Z. (2004). SOM ensemble- based image segmentation. *Neural Processing Letters*, *20*(3), 171–178. doi:10.1007/s11063-004-2022-8

Kennedy, J., & Eberhart, R. (1995). Particle swarm optimization. In *Proc. IEEE International Conference on Neural Networks* (pp. 1942 – 1948). IEEE. doi:10.1109/ICNN.1995.488968

Kohonen, T. (1989). *Self- organization and associative memory*. Berlin, Germany: Springer- Verlag.

Liu, X., & Wang, D. (2006). Image and texture segmentation using local spectra histograms. *IEEE Transactions on Image Processing*, *15*(10), 3066–3077. doi:10.1109/TIP.2006.877511 PMID:17022270

Lucchese, L., & Mitra, S. K. (2001). Color image segmentation: A state- of- art survey. *Proceedings of the Indian National Sciencee Academy*, *67-A*, 207–221.

McMahon, D. (2008). Quantum computing explained. Hoboken, NJ: John Wiley & Sons, Inc.

Noordam, J. C., Van den Broek, W. H. A. M., & Buydens, L. M. C. (2000). Geometrically guided fuzzy *C*-means clustering for multivariate image segmentation. In *Proc. Int. Conf. Pattern Recogn* (vol. 1, pp. 462-465). Academic Press.

Otsu, N. (1979). A threshold selection method from gray level Histograms. *IEEE Transactions Systems. Man and Cybernetics, 9*(1), 62-66. doi: .1979.431007610.1109/TSMC

Reddick, W. E., Glass, J. O., Cook, E. N., Elkin, T. D., & Deaton, R. J. (1997). Automated segmentation and classification of multispectral magnetic resonance images of brain using artificial neural networks. *IEEE Transactions on Medical Imaging*, *16*(6), 911–918. doi:10.1109/42.650887 PMID:9533591

Rezaee, M. R., Van der Zwet, P. M. J., Lelieveldt, B. P. E., van der Geest, R. J., & Reiber, J. H. C. (2000). A multiresolution image segmentation technique based on pyramidal segmentation and fuzzy clustering. *IEEE Tans. On Image Processing*, *9*(7), 1238–1248. doi:10.1109/83.847836 PMID:18262961

Sahoo, P. K., Soltani, S., & Wong, A. K. C. (1988). A survey of thresholding technique. *CVGIP*, *41*, 233–260.

Shi, J., & Malik, J. (2000). Normalized cuts and image segmentation. *IEEE Transactions on Pattern Analysis and Machine Intelligence*, *22*(8), 888–905. doi:10.1109/34.868688

Shi, Y., & Eberhart, R. C. (1998). A modified particle swarm optimizer. In *Proc. IEEE International Conference on Evolutionary Computation*. IEEE Press.

Solis, F. J., & Wets, R. J.-B. (1981). Wets, minimization by random search techniques. *Mathematics of Operations Research*, *6*(1), 19–30. doi:10.1287/moor.6.1.19

Talbi, H., Batouche, M., & Draa, A. (2007). A quantum-inspired evolutionary algorithm for multiobjective image segmentation. *International Journal of Mathematics*, *1*(2), 109–114.

Tan, K. S., & Isa, N. A. M. (2011). Color image segmentation using histogram thresholding fuzzy C-means hybrid approach. *Pattern Recognition*, *44*(1), 1–15. doi:10.1016/j.patcog.2010.07.013

Tsutsui, S. (2004a). Ant colony optimization for continuous domains with aggregation pheromones metaphore. In *Proc. 5th Internat. Conf. on Recent Advances in Soft Computing (RASC'04)* (pp. 207-212). Academic Press.

Tsutsui, S., & Ghosh, A. (2004b). An extension of ant colony optimization for function optimization. In *Proc. 5th Asia Pasific Conference on Simulated evolution and Learning (SEAL04)*. Academic Press.

Van den Bergh, F. (2002). *An analysis of particle swarm optimizers*. (Doctoral dissertation). Univ. Pretoria, Pretoria, South Africa.

Van den Bergh, F., & Engelbrecht, A. P. (2004). A cooperative approach to participate swam optimization. *IEEE Transactions on Evolutionary Computation*, *8*(3), 225–239. doi:10.1109/TEVC.2004.826069

Vandenbroucke, N., Macaire, L., & Postaire, J. G. (2003). Color image segmentation by pixel classification in an adapted hybrid color space: Application to soccer image analysis. *Computer Vision and Image Understanding*, *90*(2), 190–216. doi:10.1016/S1077-3142(03)00025-0

Vedral, V., Plenio, M. B., Rippin, M. A., & Knight, P. L. (1997). Quantifying entanglement. *Physical Review Letters*, *78*(12), 2275–2279. doi:10.1103/PhysRevLett.78.2275

Wang, S. (2005). Classification with incomplete survey data: A Hopfield neural network approach. *Computers and Operations Research (Elsevier)*, *32*(10), 2583–2594. doi:10.1016/j.cor.2004.03.018

Yang, W., Guo, L., Zhao, T., & Xiao, G. (2007). Improving watersheds image segmentation method with graph theory. In *Proceedings of 2nd IEEE Conference on Industrial electronics and Applications* (pp. 2550-2553). IEEE.

Zhang, G. (2011). Quantum inspired evolutionary algorithm: A survey and empirical study. *Journal of Heuristics*, *17*(3), 303–351. doi:10.1007/s10732-010-9136-0

Zhang, G. X., Li, N., Jin, W. D., & Hu, L. Z. (2006). Novel quantum genetic algorithm and its application. *Frontiers of Electrical and Electronic Engineering in China, 1*(1), 31–36. doi:10.1007/s11460-005-0014-8

Zhang, G. X., & Rong, H. (2007). Improved quantum-inspired genetic algorithm based time-frequency analysis of radar emitter signals. In *Rough sets and knowledge technology.* Springer.

Zhang, Y. (1996). A survey on evaluation methods for image segmentation. *Pattern Recognition, 8*(2), 1335–1346. doi:10.1016/0031-3203(95)00169-7

ADDITIONAL READING

Bhandarkar, S. M., & Zhang, H. (1999). Image segmentation using evolutionary computation. *IEEE Transactions on Evolutionary Computation, 3*(1), 1–21. doi:10.1109/4235.752917

Bhattacharyya, S., Dutta, P., & Maulik, U. (2006). A self supervised bi-directional neural network (BDSONN) architecture for object extraction guided by beta activation function and adaptive fuzzy context sensitive thresholding. *International Journal of Intelligent Technology., 1*(4), 345–365.

Bhattacharyya, S., Dutta, P., Maulik, U., & Nandi, P. K. (2007). Multilevel activation functions for true color image segmentation using self – organizing neural network (PSONN) architecture: A comparative stusy. *International journal on Computer Sciences,* 291), 09-21. ISSN 1306-4428.

Boyarsky, A., & Gora, P. (2010). A random map model for quantum interference. *Communications in Nonlinear Science and Numerical Simulation, 15*(8), 1974–1979. doi:10.1016/j.cnsns.2009.08.018

Chang, P. L., & Teng, W. G. (2007). Exploiting the self- organizing map for meical image segmentation, *Twentieth IEEE International Symposium on Computer – Based Medical Systems 20*(220)June, 281-288.

De, S., Bhattacharyya, S. & Dutta, P. (2010). Efficient grey-level image segmentation using an optimized MUSIG (OptiMUSIG) activation function, *International Journal of Parallel, Emergent and Distributed Systems.* iFirst article, 1-39.

Dorigo, M. (1992). *Optimization, Learning and Natural Algorithms.* (Doctoral dissertation). Politechnico di Milano, Italie.

Dorigo, M., & Gambardella, L. M. (1997). Ant colony system: A cooperative learning approach to the travelling salesman problem. *IEEE Transactions on Evolutionary Computation, 1*(1), 53–66. doi:10.1109/4235.585892

Dorigo, M., & Stutzle, T. (2005). *Ant Colony Optimization.* New Delhi: Prentice Hall of India Private Limited.

Fogel, D. B. (2006). Evolutionary computation: Toward a New Philosophy of Machine Intelligence. – Wiley- IEEE Press, 61-84.

Gonzalez, R. C., & Woods, R. E. (2002). *Digital Image Processing, NJ.* Englewood Cliffs: Prentice-Hall.

Goss, S., Aron, S., Deneubourg, J. L., & Pasteels, J. M. (1989). The self-organized exploratory pattern of the Argentine ant. *Naturwissenschaften, 76*(12), 579–581. doi:10.1007/BF00462870

Han, K. H., & Kim, J. H. (2004). Quantum inspired evolutionary algorithms with a new termination criterion, He gate, and two- phase scheme. *IEEE Transactions on Evolutionary Computation, 8*(2), 156–169. doi:10.1109/TEVC.2004.823467

Kennedy, J., & Eberhart, R. (1995). "Particle Swarm Optimization" *Proc. IEEE International Conference on Neural Networks (Perth, Australia), IEEE Service Center, Piscataway, NJ*, 1942 - 1948 doi:10.1109/ICNN.1995.488968

Kohonen, T. (1989). *Self- organization and Associative Memory*. Berlin, Germany: Springer- Verlag.

Liu, X., & Wang, D. (2006). Image and texture segmentation using local spectra histograms. *IEEE Transactions on Image Processing, 15*(10), 3066–3077. doi:10.1109/TIP.2006.877511 PMID:17022270

McMahon, D. (2008). Quantum computing explained, Hoboken, New Jesey: John Wiley & Sons, Inc.

Noordam, J. C., Van den Broek, W. H. A. M., & Buydens, L. M. C. (2000). Geometrically guided fuzzy C-means clustering for multivariate image segmentation, *Proc. Int. Conf. Pattern Recogn, 1*, 462-465.

Otsu, N. (1979). A threshold selection method from gray level Histograms. *IEEE Transactions Systems. Man and Cybernetics, SMC, 9*(1), 62-66. Doi: . 1979.4310076.10.1109/TSMC

Sahoo, P. K., Soltani, S., & Wong, A. K. C. (1988). A survey of Thresholding technique. *CVGIP, 41*, 233–260.

Shi, J., & Malik, J. (2000). Normalized cuts and image segmentation. *IEEE Transactions on Pattern Analysis and Machine Intelligence, 22*(8), 888–905. doi:10.1109/34.868688

Shi, Y., Eberhart, & R.C. (1998) "A modified particle swarm optimizer," Proc. *IEEE International Conference on Evolutionary Computation, IEEE Press, Piscataway, NJ*, 69–73.

Tsutsui, S. (2004a). Ant colony optimization for continuous domains with aggregation pheromones metaphore. *In: Proc. 5th Internat. Conf. on Recent Advances in Soft Computing (RASC'04), United Kingdom*, 207-212.

Wang, S. (2005). Classification with incomplete survey data: A Hopfield neural network approach. *Computers and Operations Research (Elsevier), 32*(10), 2583–2594. doi:10.1016/j.cor.2004.03.018

Zhang, G. (2011). Quantum inspired evolutionary algorithm: A survey and empirical study. *Journal of Heuristics, 17*(3), 303–351. doi:10.1007/s10732-010-9136-0

Zhang, Y. (1996). A survey on evaluation methods for image segmentation. *Pattern Recognition, 8*(2), 1335–1346. doi:10.1016/0031-3203(95)00169-7

KEY TERMS AND DEFINITIONS

Ant Colony Optimization: Ant colony optimization (ACO) is a population-based metaheuristic that can be used to find approximate solutions to difficult optimization problems. In ACO, a set of software agents called artificial ants search for good solutions to a given optimization problem.

BDSONN: This architecture is a three-layer network structure assisted by bi-directional propagation of network states for self-supervised organization of input information.

Image Segmentation: It is the process of partitioning a digital image into multiple segments on the basis of their similarities.

Optimization: Optimization is the process of finding the greatest or least value of a function for some constraint, which must be true regardless of the solution. In other words, optimization finds the most suitable value for a function within a given domain.

Particle Swarm Optimization: It is a computational method that optimizes a problem by iteratively trying to improve a candidate solution with regard to a given measure of quality.

Quantum Computing: Quantum computing is the area of study focused on developing computer technology based on the principles of quantum theory, which explains the nature and behavior of energy and matter on the quantum level.

Swarm Intelligence: Swarm intelligence is the collective behavior of decentralized, self-organized systems, natural or artificial.

Chapter 10
Image Enhancement Techniques Using Particle Swarm Optimization Technique

V. Santhi
VIT University, India

B. K. Tripathy
VIT University, India

ABSTRACT

The image quality enhancement process is considered as one of the basic requirement for high-level image processing techniques that demand good quality in images. High-level image processing techniques include feature extraction, morphological processing, pattern recognition, automation engineering, and many more. Many classical enhancement methods are available for enhancing the quality of images and they can be carried out either in spatial domain or in frequency domain. But in real time applications, the quality enhancement process carried out by classical approaches may not serve the purpose. It is required to combine the concept of computational intelligence with the classical approaches to meet the requirements of real-time applications. In recent days, Particle Swarm Optimization (PSO) technique is considered one of the new approaches in optimization techniques and it is used extensively in image processing and pattern recognition applications. In this chapter, image enhancement is considered an optimization problem, and different methods to solve it through PSO are discussed in detail.

INTRODUCTION

In real life scenario, huge amount of data available in the form of images and its quality need to be enhanced for making it ready to apply high level image processing techniques like pattern recognition, feature extraction, analysis and any other automation engineering applications. In general, process of improving the quality of images is called image enhancement and it is considered as one of the important preprocessing techniques for high level processing of images. The enhancement can be performed by hardware devices through software algorithms but this chapter deals with various software techniques

DOI: 10.4018/978-1-4666-8291-7.ch010

in particular. Gorai and Ghosh (2009) outlined in their work, that in image enhancement process images are transferred from one level to another level through the process of intensity transformation or filtering approaches to improve the perception of information for human viewers, or to provide better input for other automated engineering applications.

In general image enhancement processes include histogram equalization, intensity transformation, smoothing, sharpening, contrast adjustment, frequency domain filtering and pseudo coloring as explained by Gonzales and Woods (1987). Majority of the image enhancement work usually manipulates the image histogram by some transformation function to obtain the required contrast enhancement. Consequently, this operation also delivers the maximum information contained in the image. In detail, the histogram transformation is considered as one of the fundamental processes for contrast enhancement of gray level images, which facilitates the subsequent higher level operations such as detection and identification. Histogram processing could be carried out either by local processing or by global processing. In linear contrast stretching, the gray value of input image is mapped to the complete range of gray values in the output image. Similarly in Pseudo coloring gray values are mapped to color values artificially to highlight and enhance the important regions in images. Generalizing gray scale image enhancement to color image enhancement is not a trivial task. Several factors, such as selection of a color model, characteristics of the human visual system, and color contrast sensitivity, must be considered for color image enhancement. Color images could be separated into the chromaticity and intensity components. The intensity components are also called luminance components. The quality of color images could be increased by applying any of the image enhancement techniques on luminance part of color images.

Some of the image/signal processing applications include iris recognition, fruit quality grading, face detection, object recognition, image segmentation, synthetic aperture radar image processing, image classification, image fusion and many more. Recently various areas of automation engineering find its use and contribution of image processing techniques and it includes medical imaging, people identification proposed by Xiaodong and Zhong (2006), indoor security surveillance elaborated by Xiang and Yan (2007) and crowd monitoring in outdoor environments proposed by Dorigo and Stützle (2004) etc. Many classical enhancement methods exist but it does meet the requirements of automation engineering.

In recent years, it has been proved that it is possible to identify and exploit the underlying principles of computational intelligence for solving scientific, engineering and industrial problems. Thus it is required to incorporate the computational intelligence as a part of it. Evolutionary algorithms have been previously used to perform image enhancement. Gorai and Ghosh (2009)'s have stated that the enhancement process could have been be carried out through genetic programming (GA) by adapting various techniques so as to fit the demands of the human interpreter. But based on literature review, among many optimization techniques, particle swarm optimization (PSO) proposed by Eberhard et al. (2001) and ant colony optimization techniques proposed by Dorigo and Stützle (2004) are considered as two important techniques. Both methods have found a strongly increasing number of applications in diverse fields, including image and signal processing research fields. In this chapter, image enhancement process through PSO technique is focused. In comparison to GA, PSO does not require selection, crossover and mutation operations. Moreover PSO takes less time to converge to better optima. The resulted gray-level enhanced images by PSO are found to be better compared with other automatic image contrast enhancement techniques. Both objective and subjective evaluations are performed on the resulted image which says about the goodness of PSO as stated in Gorai and Ghosh (2009)'s work.

In this chapter, various image quality enhancement techniques using PSO and its comparative analysis are presented. The rest of the chapter is organized as follows: In the subsequent sections the basics of image enhancement process, Particle Swarm Optimization (PSO) technique and applications of Particle Swarm Optimization technique (PSO) are presented in detail. Finally the chapter is ending with conclusion.

BACKGROUND

Image quality enhancement is considered as an important process as it plays a vital role in many real time applications. For example, in medical applications to extract hidden features from dark regions image enhancement process is applied. Similarly for remote sensing applications certain features can be extracted from satellite images after enhancing its quality. In addition to these above said applications image enhancement process could be extended to many real time applications. The basics of image enhancement process and particle swarm optimization techniques are presented in the subsequent sections.

Image Enhancement Process

Image enhancement process is considered as low level image processing technique in which the enhancement function take images as input, process it and produces images as output. It is also considered as one of the important processing techniques for enhancing the quality of images which are to be used as input for other automated image processing techniques as stated in Xiang and Yan (2007)'s work. The pictorial representation of image enhancement process is shown in Figure 1. In order to perform enhancement task, a transformation function is required which will take the intensity value of each pixel from the input image and generate a new intensity value for the corresponding pixel to produce the enhanced output image as outlined in Gorai and Ghosh (2009)'s work.

In general, quality enhancement processes can be carried out either in spatial domain or in frequency domain. In spatial domain it is carried out through intensity transformations, unsharp masking and filtering approaches. Image processing based on spatial domain directly operate upon image gray level, divided into point operation and spatial filtering. Point operation includes gray-scale correction, grayscale transformation and histogram equalization, in order to make image even, to enlarge dynamic range or to expand contrast. Spatial filtering can be cut into image smoothing and image sharpening. Image smoothing generally is used to eliminate image noise, but easily cause the edges fuzzy. Algorithms

Figure 1. General block diagram for image enhancement in both spatial domain and frequency domain

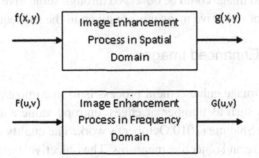

include average filtering and median filtering. The purpose of image sharpening is to highlight the edges to facilitate object recognition. Common algorithms consist of Gradient operator, high pass filter, mask matching method, statistical difference method.

The algorithm based on frequency domain, a correction for transformation coefficients in the image transform domain, is an indirect enhancement algorithm. Frequency smoothing filtering is commonly used in frequency domain filtering, including frequency sharpening filtering and homomorphic filtering. In general masking or filtering approaches are carried out either through convolution or through correlation process which is explained by Gonzales and Woods (1987). The process of enhancing image quality in spatial domain is carried out using (1) and (2).

A gray-level image is represented as a two dimensional function $f(x,y)$ where $f(.)$ represents intensity value of a pixel at coordinate location x_i, y_j, where i, j assume values from 0 to (M-1), where M represents number of rows and columns. The intensity values of gray scale image range from 0 to L-1, where L represents number of gray shades. The value of

$$g(x,y)=T[f(x,y)] \tag{1}$$

$$g(x,y)=f(x,y)*h(x,y) \tag{2}$$

In Eq.1, T represents intensity transformation function, $f(x,y)$ represents an input image and $g(x,y)$ represents enhanced output image. Similarly, in (2) $h(x,y)$ represents filter transfer function and * represents either convolution or correlation operation in spatial domain.

The process of enhancing image quality in frequency domain is carried out using (3), in which $F(u,v)$ represents image in frequency domain and $H(u,v)$ represents filter transfer function and * represents either convolution or correlation function. If convolution is carried out in spatial domain then multiplication is performed in frequency domain and vice versa.

$$G(u,v)=F(u,v)*H(u.v) \tag{3}$$

Qinqing et al. (2011, June)'s outlined that, Pseudo-color enhancement is the technology which, in accordance with the linear or non-linear mapping functions, transforms each gray level in a black and white image into a different color matching a point of the color space and then a color image come out. It makes it easier to identify details of an original image and to identify the target. The methods of color enhancement mainly include density segmentation method, the spatial gray level - color transformation, frequency pseudo-color enhancement.

The quality of the enhanced image could be observed through subjective and objective measures. The expressions which are used for objective measures are given in the subsequent sections.

Evaluation of Quality of Enhanced Images

The objective of PSO based image enhancement process is to maximize the fitness function which is achieved through parameters such as number of edges, entropy value and overall intensity values as stated in Venkatalakshmi and Shalinie (2010,October)'s work. The quality of the enhanced image could be measured through subjective and objective measures. The objective measures are considered as valuable metrics it could be carried out without human interventions. Many objective measures are available to evaluate the quality of enhanced images which include finding number of edges and calculating the entropy value, mean square error and so on.

Entropy

Entropy value reveals the average information content of given image, if the intensity values are distributed uniformly then the measured entropy value would be more.

A mathematical expression used to measure the information is the entropy given in (4).

$$H = -\sum_{i=1}^{n} p_i \log_2 p_i \tag{4}$$

The reduction in the information content is not desirable as the available gray-levels are not efficiently used. But through enhancement process it information content could be increased.

Mean Square Error

Root Mean square error (MSE) is a statistical measure which reveals the quality of enhanced images. The MSE calculates the error between the original and enhanced images. The obtained value of MSE decides the quality of the enhanced images. The mathematical expression to calculate mean square error is shown in (5).

$$MSE = \frac{1}{mn} \sum_{i=1}^{m} \sum_{j=1}^{n} (f(i,j) - f'(i,j))^2 \tag{5}$$

where $f(i,j)$ represents the original image, $f'(i,j)$ represents the enhanced image and mn represents the size of images

Peak Signal to Noise Ratio (PSNR)

The peak signal to noise ratio is a statistical measure of the ratio between the original image and the modified or distorted image in decibels. The root mean square error (RMSE) between original image and enhanced images are calculated using the Eq. 6 which in turn used to calculate peak signal to noise ratio as shown in Eq. 7.

$$RMSE = \sqrt{\frac{1}{mn} \sum_{i=1}^{m} \sum_{j=1}^{n} (f(i,j) - f'(i,j))^2} \tag{6}$$

$$PSNR = 20 \log \left(\frac{255^2}{RMSE} \right) \tag{7}$$

where $f(i,j)$ represents the original image, $f'(i,j)$ represents the enhanced image and mn represents the size of images

Particle Swarm Optimization (PSO) Technique

Particle Swarm Optimization technique found many applications in various fields. It is predominantly used in signal processing applications, for examples, for the design of filters, vector quantization, image processing, image compression, image segmentation, image enhancement, classification of EEG data by a neural network removal of periodic noise, and monitoring of sensors. The original basic version of PSO algorithms have been improved (called improved PSO) to achieve early convergence in solving dynamic optimization problems. In the subsequent sections, the basic of PSO technique is presented elaborately.

PSO is an evolutionary based computational algorithm and it is proposed by Kennedy and Eberhart (1995). PSO was developed in 1995 by Dr. James Kennedy, a social psychologist, and Dr. Russell Eberhart. It could be implemented and has proven both very effective and quick when applied to a diverse set of optimization problems. In Daniel and Martin (2008)'s paper it is stated that, swarm intelligence deals with the behavior of natural or artificial swarms. Examples of artificial swarms include groups of robots, intelligent mobile devices that can communicate with each other, or virtual swarms in the form of a computer program. Swarms are systems that consist of many individuals or particles that are organized and coordinated through the principles of decentralized control, indirect communication, and self-organization.

Initial intent was to simulate the behavior of unpredictable choreography of a bird flock and it was modified to incorporate nearest neighbor velocity matching, eliminate ancillary variables and incorporate multidimensional search and acceleration by distance as outlined in Eberhart and Shi (2001).

Kennedy and Eberhart (1995) stated that Particle swarm optimization has roots in two main component methodologies namely flock of bird, school of fish, and swarming theory in particular. It is also related to evolutionary computation, and has ties to both Genetic Algorithms (GAs) and Evolutionary Programming (EP).

The concept of swarm intelligence is the investigation of different types of emergent collective behaviors in swarms. The member of the swarm is called a particle and it can interact with each other particle in addition to its social neighborhoods. As outlined in Engelbrecht (2005)'s work and Janson et al. (2008)'s work, the social neighborhoods of all particles in swarm form a PSOs social network. Thus PSO simulates the behavior of birds or swarms. PSO initializes a group of random particles (random solutions), and then obtain the optimal solution through iterations. In each iteration, each particle updates itself by tracking the two optimum values: the first is the optimal solution found by the particle itself and it is called best (personal Best), the other is the best current solution sought out by the whole population called best (global Best). When finding these two optimal values, the particles update their own speeds and arrive at new locations.

In general in social networks of PSO, each particle is moved by two elastic forces, one force move the particle to the fittest location and it is updated in each iteration. For particle i, its velocity vector v_i is updated with some magnitude and other force make the particle to move to the best location with some magnitude. In PSO the velocity and position are represented as a vector as per formula shown in Eq. 4. which is explained in Engelbrecht (2007)'s work.

$$v_i(t+1) = wv_i(t) + c_1r_1(y_i(t) - x_i(t)) + c_2r_2(y_g(t) - x_i(t)) \tag{8}$$

x_i, implies the current position of the particle, y_i denote the personal best position and y_g denote the global best position found by particle i. The parameter w controls the influence of the previous velocity vector, once the velocities of all particles have been updated, the particles move with their new velocity to their new positions according to the formula given in Eq. 8.

$$x_i(t+1) = x_i(t) + v_i(t) \tag{9}$$

After all particles have been moved to their new position, the function is evaluated in new positions and the corresponding personal best positions and the global best position are updated. Typical termination criteria for PSO algorithms have been executed until a maximum number of iterations it undergoes or the global best position has not been changed for a certain number of iterations, or a function value has been found which is better than a required threshold value. Daniel and Martin (2008), listed advantages of using Particle Swarm Optimization technique in their work and listed below.

Advantages

- PSO uses only the functions values at the positions of the particles to guide the search and therefore is very suitable for dealing with non-differentiable objective functions.
- PSO is a population-based and random influenced search method and therefore a PSO algorithm is not so likely to become trapped in a local minimum.
- PSO can control the balance between the global and local exploration of the search space and therefore can be used successfully for different types of objective functions.
- PSO does not use complex operations and therefore can be implemented easily and efficiently.

One of the reasons for popularity of PSO technique is that it is very simple in nature and easy to implement as there are very few parameters need to be adjusted. In recent days, PSO technique is widely applied to optimization function, neural network training, fuzzy system control and other applications of genetic algorithms as presented by Qinqing et al. (2011, June). Thus Particle Swarm Optimization technique can be used across a wide range of applications, as well as for specific applications focused on a specific requirement as stated in Eberhart et al. (2001)'s work. In the subsequent sections, the application of Particle Swarm Optimization technique for image enhancement is presented in detail.

APPLICATIONS OF PARTICLE SWARM OPTIMIZATION (PSO) TECHNIQUE IN IMAGE ENHANCEMENT PROCESSES

Image enhancement processes are carried out so far using classical approaches but it does not served the purpose of providing high quality images for applications such as automation engineering. In order to attain the desired quality in the output images, computational intelligent technique is combined with classical approaches. In particular, one of the optimization techniques called PSO technique is exploited to enhance the quality of images. It is proved that the implementation of PSO algorithm is very simple and possible through any programming language. In this section, various image enhancement techniques using PSO based approaches are presented.

Image Enhancement through Gamma Correction and Intensity Preservation

Kwok et al. (2006) have proposed image enhancement technique through contrast adjustment using PSO. There are two contradicting objectives to be met in this proposal including i) the preservation of mean image intensity and ii) the maximization of information content in the image. This observation naturally matches the structure of the PSO technique. Hence the standard algorithm is modified to incorporate the optimization of a multiple goals leading to the multi-objective particle swarm optimization (MPSO). In this proposal image quality is enhanced through contrast adjustment with the preservation of mean image intensity of the original image. Gamma correction method is used to preserve the mean intensity of the enhanced image.

But as per results in Table 1, the traditional gamma correction method has not preserved mean intensity value but it has been achieved through a modified multi-objective particle swarm optimization algorithm.

Proposed Gamma correction method preserves image mean intensity and increases average information content as shown in the table. The average information content is measured through the parameter entropy. The original image needs quality enhancement is shown in Figure 2. The enhanced image through various methods is shown in Figure 3. In Figure 3, (a) shows enhanced image through continuous contrast enhancement (b) shows bi level continuous contrast enhancement, (c) shows enhance image through Gamma corrected contrast enhancement (d) shows image enhancement through multi-objective particle swarm optimization.

Gray–Level Image Enhancement

PSO based algorithm has produced better results than conventional methods such as histogram equalization and contrast stretching. The most important property of PSO is that, it can produce better result with proper tuning of parameters and it is exploited in this work for enhancing the image quality. In Gorai and Ghosh (2009)'s proposal, image enhancement process is carried out by considering both local and global information of an images. This proposed function uses four parameters namely a, b, c and k to produce optimal result to the objective function. These four parameters consider values empirically in the base function but are fine-tuned through PSO till optimum result is obtained. In Figure 4 the original image and enhanced images through various approaches are shown. In Figure 4, (a) represents the original image (b) represents the enhanced image through linear contrast stretching (c) represents enhanced im-

Table 1. Summary of results using cameraman image

Approach Used	Mean Intensity	Information Content
Continuous Contrast Enhancement	116.17	6.88
Bi-level Continuous Contrast Enhancement	127.49	6.63
Gamma correction	119.48	7.99
Multi-objective PSO	116.34	7.98

Figure 2. Cameraman image – original

Figure 3. Enhanced images (a) Continuous contrast enhancement (b) Bi-level continues contrast enhancement (c) Gamma corrected contrast enhancement (d) MPSO optimized contrast enhancement

age through histogram equalization (d) represents enhanced image through Genetic algorithm and (e) represents enhanced image through PSO based approach.

Parameter used in PSO equation is called the inertia weight. The process starts with maximum inertia value and gradually reduces it to minimum. Therefore initially inertia component is big and explore larger area in the solution space, but gradually inertia component becomes small and exploit better solutions in the solution space. Inertia value is calculated as given in (10).

$$W^T = W_{max} - \frac{W_{max} - W_{min}}{t_{max}} \times t \qquad (10)$$

Figure 4. (a) Original image (b) Linear contrast stretching (c) Histogram equalization (d) GA based enhancement, and (e) Proposed PSO based method

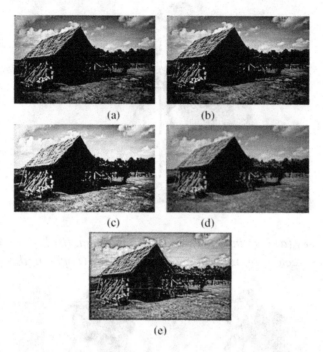

Parameters, and are positive acceleration constants, given a random number in [0, 2]. These parameters are fixed for each particle throughout its life. This proposal shows better results compare to conventional methods.

To evaluate the quality of an enhanced image, Gorai and Ghosh (2009)'s formed an objective function by combining three performance measures, namely entropy value, sum of edge intensities and number of edgels (edge pixels). It is observed that compared to the original image good contrast and enhanced image has more number of edgels and have a higher intensity of the edges. In addition to these parameters the third parameter entropy value of the image is also included in forming objective function. Entropy value reveals the information content in the image. If the distribution of the intensities is uniform, then the histogram of the image is equalized and the entropy of the image would be more. The objective function considered in Gorai and Ghosh (2009)'s work is given below.

$$F(I_e) = \log(\log(E(I_s))) \times \frac{n\_edgels(I_s)}{M \times N} \times H(I_e) \tag{11}$$

Gorai and Ghosh (2009)'s have proposed a PSO based automatic image enhancement technique for gray level images. Authors have compared the results of proposed technique with some other image enhancement techniques, like linear contrast stretching, histogram equalization and genetic algorithm based image enhancement. Authors have proved that proposed method have given better results compared to other techniques mentioned above. In PSO, the most important property is that, it can produce better result with proper tuning of parameters and it is exploited in this work.

Customized Image Enhancement Algorithm

In this proposal Venkatalakshmi and Shalinie (2010, October) have customized PSO in order to maximize an objective fitness criterion and to improve the contrast, details present in the image. In general, new solutions are created using two operators in PSO which are g-best and p-best. However, customized PSO does not use p-best instead particles update themselves with the g-best alone, hence called customized PSO. The objectives of customized PSO are to maximize the number of pixels in the edges, increase the overall intensity of the edges, and increase the measure of the entropy which produces uniform distribution in histogram and hence quality of an image also increases. The adaptive parameters which are defined in local enhancement technique are derived from images. It uses an objective fitness criterion that is proportional to the number of edges in the image and to a clumping factor of the intensity transformation curve. It is proved that the customized PSO produced better results than PSO and it is shown in Table 2. In Figure 5 both original image and enhanced image using PSO based approaches are shown.

In Table 2 the number of edges obtained using Sobel edge detector is shown. It is observed that using customized PSO the details present are increased to greater extent. The comparative results of PSO with customized PSO and ordinary edge detector are shown in Table 2. It is clear from Table 2 that the Customized PSO based method achieves the best detail content in the enhanced images when compared with the number of edges in the enhanced image using PSO and both are greater than the number of edges in the original image. This ensures that the proposed PSO method yields better quality of solution and reveal the superior properties of customized PSO. Thus the proposed PSO method yields high quality solutions with better computation efficiency. It can be shown from Figure 5, that the brightness and contrast of the enhanced image using customized PSO and PSO appear visibly and is more than the brightness and contrast of the original images. Also, it can be shown clearly, that the brightness of the enhanced images using customized PSO is better than the brightness of the enhanced images using PSO.

Table 2. The number of edges obtained using Sobel edge detector

Image	Original	PSO	Customized PSO
Cameraman	2485	2674	2884

Figure 5. (a) Original image (b) Equalized image

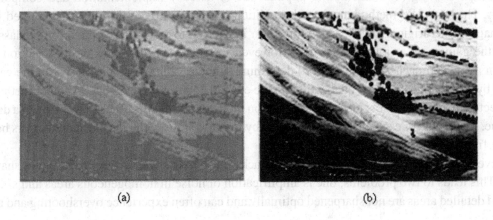

(a) (b)

Improved Image Enhancement Technique

In Qinqing et al. (2011, June)'s proposal image enhancement is carried out through the concept of simulated annealing in PSO to formulate improved PSO algorithm. Simulated Annealing (SA), originally proposed by the Kirpatrick et al, can be used to solve combinatorial optimization problems, or NP complete problem. In this method the system jump from local minimum and it continues to search for global minimum. If system not jumps out from local minimum, the local minimum will be the final results by the iterative search method. Simulated annealing PSO algorithm takes particle swarm optimization algorithm as the main body and introduces simulated annealing mechanism. Simulated annealing PSO provides better ability to get over the local minimum points and also improve the convergence speed and accuracy. The primary process involves generation of the initial population randomly, then updates the individual and global extreme of each particle and then updates the position and velocity of each particle by PSO algorithm. Proposed simulated annealing PSO algorithm provides better results than classical image enhancement methods.

Hue-Preserving Color Image Enhancement Using PSO

Gorai and Ghosh (2011) have proposed color image enhancement using PSO. In this proposal enhancement process is carried out in intensity domain using a parameterized transformation function in which the parameters are optimized using PSO. To maximize the fitness function parameters considered edges and entropy values. Scaling factor α is calculated from the enhanced intensity image and enhanced color image is formed by scaling. If any pixel faces gamut problem during scaling, then it is corrected by considering HIS color space. The enhanced color images by PSO are found to be better compared to other automatic color image enhancement techniques. The algorithm is tested on several color images and results are compared with two other popular color image enhancement techniques like hue-preserving color image enhancement without gamut problem (HPCIE) and a genetic algorithm based approach to color image enhancement (GACIE). Visual analysis, detail and background variance of the resultant images are reported. It has been found that the proposed method produces better results compared to other two methods.

A Modified Unsharp Masking

The Unsharp Masking (UM) method is popular due to its easy implementation and computational simplicity. The basic UM method involves the addition of a proportion of the high-pass filtered version of the image to the original image. This proportion is referred to as the UM's gain. In the classic UM method, the gain is set as a constant value. However, there are no guidelines on its selection. There have been a few approaches that attempt to determine suitable values for gain. Based on the gains are obtained by applying histogram equalization on the edge histogram of the image. Another method uses edge detectors to classify pixels into classes based on their edge strengths. Each class is given a different gain value. The gains for each class were obtained by minimization of the mean squared errors between ideal and filtered images.

However, the classic method has some drawbacks due to all areas of the image being sharpened equally. This leads to two problems; one is amplification of noise in homogeneous areas and second is, edges and detailed areas are not sharpened optimally and can often experience overshooting and ringing artifacts. There have been several approaches that attempt to overcome the shortcomings by modifying or furthering the basic method. Several modified UM methods employ the use of nonlinear filters in place of the linear high-pass filter. Mai et al. (2011)'s have proposed modified Unsharp Mask that can be applied both globally and locally. The proposed method focuses on optimization of the gain. However, it also optimizes a second parameter, the Laplacian coefficient. The proposed method addresses the shortcomings of the classic UM through optimization of its parameters by PSO technique. In Figure 6 the original image is shown in (a) and enhanced image using PSO technique is shown in (b).

The proposed method optimizes the parameters based on the maximization of information content, which is measured by entropy. The linear equation for the Unsharp Masking method is given by (12).

$$g(x,y)=f(x,y)+\lambda H\{g(x,y)\} \tag{12}$$

Here $f(x,y)$ represents input image, $g(x,y)$ represents enhanced output image and parameter λ controls the quality of $g(x,y)$. The high-pass component of the UM equation, H is created using the Laplacian operator shown in (13).

$$\nabla^2 = \frac{\partial^2}{\partial x^2} + \frac{\partial^2}{\partial y^2} \tag{13}$$

The parameter entropy is used to quantify the information content of an image and it is calculated using (4). The unit of entropy H is bits.

The algorithm proposed by Mai et al. (2011) optimizes the Unsharp Mask's parameters using Particle Swarm Optimization and proved that it is very easy to implement. The results showed that the proposed method outperforms the classic UM method; it is able to increase the information content to a greater degree. The proposed method was also found to be more effective when applied by a simple local method in comparison to the global method

Figure 6. (a) Original bridge color image (b) Proposed method using PSO

(a)　　　　　　　　　　(b)

Hybrid Approach to Enhance Low Resolution Images

Masra et al. (2012)'s proposed a novel hybrid approach based on discrete wavelet transform (DWT) and particle swarm optimization (PSO). Proposed method is developed in both spatial and frequency domain. In order to remove low frequency content from the images, it is transformed into frequency domain. DWT is used to decompose the input low resolution image into different sub bands. Each of the interpolated high frequency sub band (LH, HL, HH) is then summed up with the interpolated output image of the frequency domain. Reduction of low frequencies from the input image is carried out in frequency domain. In order to achieve high resolution image, the estimated high frequency sub bands of the intermediate stage and the interpolated low resolution input image have been combined by using inverse DWT. To generate a better high resolution image particle swarm optimization (PSO) technique has been used. The original and enhanced images are shown in Figure 7(a) and Figure 7(b) respectively.

Thus, Masra et al. (2012)'s have proposed a hybrid novel method to enhance low resolution images of different categories. It basically merges the frequency domain and nature inspired optimization algorithm to produce optimum results. The particle swarm optimization (PSO) technique is combined with discrete wavelet transform, to result in desired output. The efficiency of proposed method is not only proved from visual enhancement but also through measures.

OTHER APPLICATIONS OF PSO IN IMAGE PROCESSING

Particle swarm optimization technique is not only used for enhancing the quality of images but also used in other applications such as auto focusing for RF tomography, diagnosing medical images, noise removal in SAR images, image filtering, image restoration and face recognition. In the subsequent sections applications of particle swarm optimization techniques in other applications are presented.

Autofocusing for RF Tomography

As outlined in Parker and Norgard (2008, May)'s work RF tomography uses a geometrically diverse network of sensors to collect scattering data from a scene of interest. By utilizing multiple look angles,

Figure 7. (a) Original image (b) Enhanced image using proposed method using PSO

high resolution images can be formed. Indeed, such images can be created even when ultra-narrow band waveforms are employed. As the spectrum of the modern battlefield becomes increasingly cluttered, these potentially narrowband imaging techniques will become ever more valuable. RF tomography can also be applied to foliage, building, and ground penetration applications, making it a highly relevant tool in the emerging landscape of urban warfare and unconventional threats.

RF tomography offers the potential for producing high resolution images with limited spectrum availability. It also offers a framework for coherently combining data from geometrically diverse sensors. However, in order to produce high-quality images from these sensor constellations, autofocusing must be applied to correct uncertainties in the sensor positions.

Parker and Norgard (2008, May) have proposed a new technique for autofocussing RF tomography. High resolution images of targets are captured with narrow band waveforms through RF tomography which employs geometric diversity. In order to properly capitalize on this spatial diversity, precise knowledge of the sensor positions is required to sub-wavelength accuracy. An auto focusing approach is proposed to compensate uncertainties exists through PSO. By selecting several focusing targets throughout the image, this optimization was able to produce sharpened, high-quality results for the entire scene without the numerical expense of repeatedly re-computing the entire image. Results from both simulated and measured data verified the utility of the proposed algorithm.

Diagnosis of Brain Tumor

Magnetic resonance imaging (MRI) is a noninvasive medical test that helps physicians to diagnose and treat patients' medical problems. MR imaging uses a powerful magnetic field, radio frequency pulses and a computer to produce detailed pictures of organs, soft tissues, bones and body structures unlike ionizing radiation (X-rays). MRI provides detailed pictures of brain and nerve tissues in multiple planes without obstruction by overlying bones. Brain MRI is the procedure of choice for most brain disorders. It provides clear images of the brainstem and posterior brain, which are difficult to view on a CT scan. In general, Magnetic Resonance Imaging (MRI) is one of the best technologies currently being used for diagnosing brain tumor. In order to make automatic detection of brain tumor with high accuracy an intelligent system need to be added with conventional segmentation process. In general, Fuzzy C Means clustering algorithm, Genetic Algorithm (GA), and Particle Swarm Optimization (PSO) techniques are used to automate the medical system for diagnosis. PSO technique is computationally very efficient optimization technique and it is exploited in Gopal and Karnan (2010, December)'s work for brain tumor image segmentation. The proposed method is relatively simple, reliable, and efficient. PSO gives best classification accuracy and average error rate. The Average classification error of PSO is 0.059% and the accuracy is 92.8% and tumor detection is 98.87%.

According to Gopal and Karnan (2010, December)'s work, many techniques are existing to classify and identifying tumor including hierarchical self-organizing Map with Fuzzy C-Means, Genetic Algorithm with Fuzzy C-Means and Ant Colony Optimization with Fuzzy C-Means. Authors have proposed algorithm by combining both PSO and Fuzzy C means techniques and compared its performance analysis with exiting techniques. In Figure 8, the tumor segmented pixel is shown.

Gopal and Karnan (2010, December)'s have concluded that the proposed approach average classification error using GA is 0.078% and average accuracy using GA is 89.6%. PSO gives best classification accuracy and average error rate. The Average classification error of PSO is 0.059% and the accuracy is

Figure 8. Tumor segmented pixel

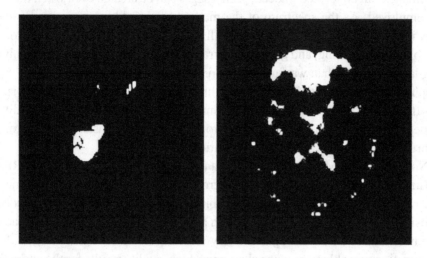

92.8% and tumor detection is 98.87%. The average classification error could be reduced by increasing the number of samples. Authors have proved that the results obtained have provided that for brain tumor segmentation, PSO based algorithm has performed well.

Speckle Reduction from SAR Images

In recent days, researchers have shown much attention on analysis and processing synthetic aperture radar (SAR) images for real time applications. However, all SAR images inherently affected with noise called speckle noise and some SAR images often exhibit low contrast, in such case interpretation of the image is very difficult. In order to extract features or to analyze images it is mandatory to remove the speckle noise. Thus, the removal of the speckle and the enhancement of the edge-features and the contrast of SAR images are very critical in SAR image processing. In general noise could be removed using any of the classical approaches but to get best results computational intelligence could be added as a part. Based on the literature survey, the speckle noise reduction is carried out in transform domain predominantly.

An adaptive method for speckle noise reduction from Synthetic Aperture Radar (SAR) images is proposed in Li et al (2010)'s work. In order to remove speckle noise mirror-extended curvelet transform and the improved particle swarm optimization (PSO) algorithm is used. In this work, an improved gain function, which integrates the speckle reduction with the feature enhancement, is introduced to non-linearly shrink and stretch the curvelet coefficients. The behavior of PSO algorithm is employed as a global search strategy for the best de-speckled and enhanced image. In order to increase the convergence speed and avoid the premature convergence, two further improvements, a new learning scheme and a mutation operator for the classical PSO algorithm are presented. Experimental results demonstrate that the proposed method can efficiently reduce the speckle and enhance the edge features and the contrast of SAR images. The obtained results are shown in Figure 9.

A new learning scheme and a mutation operator for the classic PSO algorithm are introduced to speed up its convergence and avoid the premature convergence. Experimental results on the real SAR images indicate that the proposed adaptive method outperforms UWT-based and FDCT-based non-adaptive methods.

Figure 9. Speckle reduction from SAR images

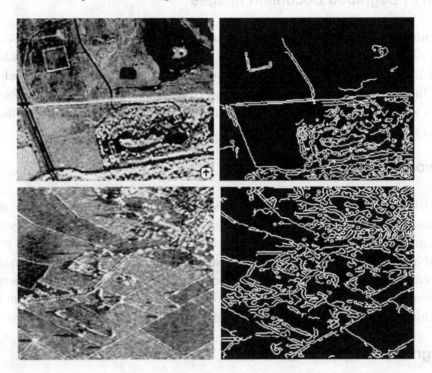

Signal De-Convolution

In this work, a new approach for the signal de-convolution process is used for enhancement of neutron radiography projections. The original signal is recovered from noise through signal de-convolution. Signal de-convolution is an ill-posed inverse problem, so regularization techniques are used to smooth solutions by imposing constraints in the objective function. This paper proposes a new approach based on a synergy of two swarm intelligence algorithms: particle swarm optimization (PSO) and bacterial foraging optimization (BFO). Here, new approach is employed through the prior knowledge of degradation phenomenon.

Design of Image Filter

Fuzzy Logic and particle swarm optimization technique based approach is proposed to design a new filter. The proposed filter effectively judges the input pixel vector for its corruption using PSO to optimize the noise detectors to enhance the noise detection performance. Subsequently, in order to enhance the restoration performance of proposed filter, the color ratio of spot's region in the restored image is employed to determine the spot's color. Also, the pixel vectors with different color ratios in the spot region are detected. Finally, the vector median filter is utilized to restore the corrupted pixels. Experimental results demonstrate that the proposed image filter outperforms the existing other well-known filters in restoration performance. And the system can be widely applied in microarray image processing.

Restoration of Degraded Document Images

Historical document images need to be restored as it carries immense value in terms of culture, history and economics. These documents are digitized and restoration process is applied. In order to preserve the content of historical degraded document computational intelligence based approach is employed with bilateral. In this paper, a novel approach is proposed to enhance ancient historical documents. Both the approaches are then tested visually and quantitatively to show the effectiveness of the approach as outlined in Quraishi et al. (2013, March)'s work.

Video Networks Planning Optimization

In this paper, issues of deploying a camera network in a complex environment with obstacles are examined. A camera network is composed of a distributed collection of cameras, each of which has sensing and communicating capabilities. To deploy such camera network, a kinetics based particle swarm optimization (PSO) approach is presented. By introducing a kinetics constraint factor to standard PSO, the fields are covered such that each camera is repelled by both other cameras and obstacles, thereby forcing the network to spread throughout the monitored area. The coverage enhancement is fulfilled by finding an optimal orientation for each camera, guided by PSO optimizer.

Face Recognition

Face Recognition (FR) under varying lighting conditions is a very challenging problem. Babu et al. (2014) have proposed a novel approach for enhancing the performance of a FR system, employing a unique combination of Active Illumination Equalization (AIE), Image Sharpening (IS), Standard Deviation Filtering (SDF), Mirror Image Superposition (MIS) and Binary Particle Swarm Optimization (BPSO). AIE is used for removal of non-uniform illumination and MIS is used to neutralize pose variance. Discrete Wavelet Transform (DWT) and Discrete Cosine Transform (DCT) are used for efficient feature extraction and BPSO-based feature selection algorithm is used to search the feature space for the optimal feature subset. Experimental results, obtained by applying the proposed algorithm on Color FERET, Pointing Head Pose and Extended Yale B face data bases; show that the proposed system outperforms other FR systems

CONCLUSION

In this chapter, image enhancement process is considered as the optimization problem and many approaches are presented using PSO. In general, the objective of image enhancement is achieved by maximizing the number edges, increase the overall intensity of the edges, and increase the measure of the entropy, increasing the contrast and so on. In order to carry out all these processes optimization technique PSO is exploited. The various approaches using PSO for image enhancement is presented in this chapter which would be helpful for research community. The chapter is concluded with other applications of PSO. The simplicity of PSO technique is exploited in this paper. The enhanced results shown in various papers proved the efficiency of PSO based enhanced techniques.

REFERENCES

Babu, S. H., Shreyas, H. R., Manikantan, K., & Ramachandran, S. (2014, January). Face recognition using active illumination equalization and mirror image superposition as pre-processing techniques. In *Proceedings of Signal and Image Processing (ICSIP), 2014 Fifth International Conference on* (pp. 96-101). IEEE. doi:10.1109/ICSIP.2014.21

Dorigo, M., & Stützle, T. (2004). *Ant colony optimization*. Cambridge, MA: MIT Press. doi:10.1007/b99492

Eberhart, R. C., & Kennedy, J. (1995, October). A new optimizer using particle swarm theory. In *Proceedings of the Sixth International Symposium on Micro Machine and Human Science* (*Vol. 1*, pp. 39-43). Academic Press. doi:10.1109/MHS.1995.494215

Eberhart, R. C., & Shi, Y. (2001). Particle swarm optimization: developments, applications and resources. In *Evolutionary Computation, 2001: Proceedings of the 2001 Congress on* (*Vol. 1*, pp. 81-86). IEEE. doi:10.1109/CEC.2001.934374

Engelbrecht, A. P. (2005). *Fundamentals of computational swarm intelligence* (Vol. 1). Chichester, UK: Wiley.

Engelbrecht, A. P. (2007). *Computational intelligence: An introduction*. John Wiley & Sons. doi:10.1002/9780470512517

Gonzalez, R. C. (2009). *Digital image processing*. Pearson Education India.

Gonzalez, R. C., & Woods, R. E. (1987). Digital image fundamentals. *Digital Image Processing*, 52-54.

Gopal, N. N., & Karnan, M. (2010, December). Diagnose brain tumor through MRI using image processing clustering algorithms such as fuzzy C means along with intelligent optimization techniques. In *Proceedings of Computational Intelligence and Computing Research (ICCIC), 2010 IEEE International Conference on* (pp. 1-4). IEEE. doi:10.1109/ICCIC.2010.5705890

Gorai, A., & Ghosh, A. (2009, December). Gray-level image enhancement by particle swarm optimization. In *Proceedings of Nature & Biologically Inspired Computing, 2009: NaBIC 2009. World Congress on* (pp. 72-77). IEEE. doi:10.1109/NABIC.2009.5393603

Gorai, A., & Ghosh, A. (2011, September). Hue-preserving color image enhancement using particle swarm optimization. In Proceedings of Recent Advances in Intelligent Computational Systems (RAICS), 2011 IEEE (pp. 563-568). IEEE. doi:10.1109/RAICS.2011.6069375

Janson, S., Merkle, D., & Middendorf, M. (2008). Molecular docking with multi-objective particle swarm optimization. *Applied Soft Computing*, 8(1), 666–675. doi:10.1016/j.asoc.2007.05.005

Kwok, N. M., Ha, Q. P., Liu, D. K., & Fang, G. (2006, October). Intensity-preserving contrast enhancement for gray-level images using multi-objective particle swarm optimization. In *Proceedings of Automation Science and Engineering, 2006: CASE'06. IEEE International Conference on* (pp. 21-26). IEEE. doi:10.1109/COASE.2006.326849

Li, Y., Gong, H., Feng, D., & Zhang, Y. (2011). An adaptive method of speckle reduction and feature enhancement for SAR images based on curvelet transform and particle swarm optimization. *IEEE Transactions on Geoscience and Remote Sensing, 49*(8), 3105–3116.

Li, Y., Gong, H., & Wang, Q. (2010, August). Adaptive enhancement with speckle reduction for SAR images using mirror-extended curvelet and PSO. In *Proceedings of Pattern Recognition (ICPR), 2010 20th International Conference on* (pp. 4520-4523). IEEE. doi:10.1109/ICPR.2010.1098

Lin, W. C., Hsu, S. C., & Cheng, A. C. (2014, June). Mass detection in digital mammograms system based on PSO algorithm. In *Proceedings of Computer, Consumer and Control (IS3C), 2014 International Symposium on* (pp. 662-668). IEEE. doi:10.1109/IS3C.2014.178

Mai, C. L. D. A., Nguyen, M. T. T., & Kwok, N. M. (2011, October). A modified unsharp masking method using particle swarm optimization. In *Proceedings of Image and Signal Processing (CISP), 2011 4th International Congress on* (Vol. 2, pp. 646-650). IEEE. doi:10.1109/CISP.2011.6100322

Masra, S. M. W., Pang, P. K., Muhammad, M. S., & Kipli, K. (2012, December). Application of particle swarm optimization in histogram equalization for image enhancement. In *Proceedings of Humanities, Science and Engineering (CHUSER), 2012 IEEE Colloquium on* (pp. 294-299). IEEE. doi:10.1109/CHUSER.2012.6504327

Parker, J. T., & Norgard, J. (2008, May). Autofocusing for RF tomography using particle swarm optimization. In *Proceedings of Radar Conference, 2008: RADAR'08* (pp. 1-6). IEEE. doi:10.1109/RADAR.2008.4721018

Qinqing, G., Guangping, Z., Dexin, C., & Ketai, H. (2011, June). Image enhancement technique based on improved PSO algorithm. In *Proceedings of Industrial Electronics and Applications (ICIEA), 2011 6th IEEE Conference on* (pp. 234-238). IEEE. doi:10.1109/ICIEA.2011.5975586

Quraishi, M. I., De, M., Dhal, K. G., Mondal, S., & Das, G. (2013, March). A novel hybrid approach to restore historical degraded documents. In *Proceedings of Intelligent Systems and Signal Processing (ISSP), 2013 International Conference on* (pp. 185-189). IEEE. doi:10.1109/ISSP.2013.6526899

Venkatalakshmi, K., & Shalinie, S. M. (2010, October). A customized particle swarm optimization algorithm for image enhancement. In *Proceedings of Communication Control and Computing Technologies (ICCCCT), 2010 IEEE International Conference on* (pp. 603-607). IEEE. doi:10.1109/ICCCCT.2010.5670768

Xiang, Z., & Yan, Z. (2007). Algorithm based on local variance to enhance contrast of fog-degraded image. *Journal of Computer Applications, 2*, 80.

Zhong, T. X. L. (2006). Compare and analysis of enhancement methods of sonar image. *Ship Electronic Engineering, 2*, 045.

KEY TERMS AND DEFINITIONS

Entropy: Average information content of image denoted by H.

Filtering: The process of removing unwanted component present in the signal through the elimination of certain frequency components.

Histogram Equalization: Processing distributing intensity values uniformly throughout the image.

Image Enhancement: The process of increasing the quality of an image through intensity transformations and filtering approaches.

Image Restoration: Process of reconstructing an image from the degraded image with the knowledge of degradation process.

Intensity Transformation: Process of mapping each intensity value of an input image into the corresponding output intensity value through mathematical expression.

Spatial Filtering: Process of moving a mask over an image and performing convolution or correlation.

Chapter 11
A Self–Organized Software Deployment Architecture for a Swarm Intelligent MANET

Soumya Sankar Basu
IBM India Private Limited, India

ABSTRACT

A class of self-organizing readily deployable network (MANET: Mobile Ad-hoc Network) has been developed to address applications such as distributed collaborative computing, disaster recovery, and digital battlefield. Some of these applications need collaboration software running in the network to help in their mission. Because of the inherent nature of MANET, collaborative software application deployment has not been easy. Researchers have focused on those challenges like minimizing power, computing and memory utilization, and routing. With advancement of high-end devices, power, computing, and memory is not much of a constraint now. Mobility is still a challenge and is a major inhibitor for researchers to think about software application deployment architecture on MANET. This chapter proposes a self-organized software deployment architecture by which any 3-tier application can be deployed in a MANET. After the application is deployed, this chapter also enhances the previously proposed adaptive movement influenced by swarm intelligent principles.

INTRODUCTION

Wireless network allows users to access information and services electronically, regardless of their geographic position. Demands for user mobility and portable computing, lead to the development of a class of self-organizing, readily deployable network architecture known as MANET. It operates without any fixed pre-installed communication infrastructure. Ad-hoc networks have found great interest in applications such as distributed collaborative computing, disaster recovery and digital battlefield.

A group of nodes form MANET to achieve a common goal and that is nothing but swarming as it can easily be compared with an aggregation of similar animals cruising in same direction. Collaboration software can help in these goals. Initial challenges in MANET like mobility, memory, computation power did not allow researchers to think about application software deployment over MANET.

DOI: 10.4018/978-1-4666-8291-7.ch011

With technology advancement a MANET can now be formed of high end heterogeneous type of devices where power, computing and memory is not much of a constraint.

Communication between two arbitrary nodes in an ad-hoc network requires routing over wireless multi hop paths. The nodes taking part in a route being mobile cause frequent link failure. Thus mobility of nodes presents the most challenging issue for communication within the network. In our prior work we proposed adaptive movement algorithms (Basu & Chaudhuri, 2003; Basu & Chaudhuri, 2004) to stabilize network connectivity.

Swarm Intelligence (SI) is the collective behavior of decentralized, self-organized systems, natural or artificial (Zhang, Agarwal, Bhatnagar, Balochian, & Yan 2013). SI systems are typically made up of elements interacting locally with each other and by that influencing the environment. These are inspired by nature especially biological systems. Natural examples of SI are ant colonies, bird flocking, animal herding, bacterial growth, fish schooling etc.

Research in SI started in the late 1980s (Zhang, Agarwal, Bhatnagar, Balochian, & Yan 2013). Apart from the applications to conventional optimization problems, SI can also be applied in to a variety of fields in fundamental research, engineering, industries, and social sciences such as library materials acquisition, communications, medical dataset classification, dynamic control, heating system planning, moving objects tracking, and prediction.

Swarm intelligence has several powerful properties desirable in many network systems. . A key element of future design paradigms is emergent intelligence – simple local interactions of autonomous swarm members, with simple primitives, giving rise to complex and intelligent global behaviour. Swarm intelligence has found its interest in MANET also.

In this chapter I propose self-organized software deployment architecture using which a three tier collaborative software application can be deployed. I also enhance our previously proposed adaptive movement scheme using Swarm Intelligence principles. To the best of my knowledge no proposal has been made on how to deploy a multitier application over an ad-hoc network.

In the current scheme the network selects a node as application server and another node as database server dynamically based on some predefined preconfigured network performance characteristics e.g. number of one hop neighbors, strength of neighbors, node willingness etc. If the application software is not much memory hungry both application server and database can be hosted in a single node.

After an application server and database server is identified, a three tier application can easily be deployed in a self organized manner. Usually a three tier application needs a web application server to host the application and a database server to have the database. Clients connect to the application server through HTTP/HTTPs (w3C).

The application server can host any collaborative application as per the network's need. The scheme will also outline the backup and recovery mechanism for application server and/or database server so that the network can self-restore itself in case there is a failure in the application server and database server and continue using the collaborative software.

All nodes can access the software through HTTP protocol either using a browser or programmatically. To secure the on air communication HTTPS can also be implemented. The scheme also proposes an authentication mechanism for the nodes by which individual nodes can have their own login in the deployed application, and application can implement user based access mechanism for various application functionalities.

With the help of the Application Server, I propose to enhance our earlier recommended adaptive algorithms by leveraging three fundamental rules of Swarm Intelligence namely collision avoidance between neighbors, matching the velocity of neighbors and staying near the neighbors. Following this scheme the network behaves like a wireless LAN.

The network being like a LAN, the mobility will not change the neighbourhood of the nodes. As a result, the deployed software application will work without a glitch even if the network is on the move.

The next section discusses background of this proposal and why this is required. Proposed scheme is described in subsequent section followed by example of the scheme. The chapter ends with a conclusion and future research directions.

BACKGROUND

In recent years MANET have received considerable amount of attention in both commercial and military applications due to it's striking properties of building a network on the fly and not requiring a preplanned infrastructure. Some challenges MANET has faced are limited wireless transmission range, hidden terminal problem, loss of packets due to transmission errors, mobility induced route changes and battery constraints.

Nowadays devices are equipped with powerful CPUs, large hard disk drives and good sound and imaging capabilities, forming a network with those overcome things like battery constraints.

MANET's are formed when a group of people want to carry out a common mission. Collaborative software can help them in their mission. Node mobility did not allow application deployment over MANET.

Communication between nodes in a MANET requires routing over multi hop wireless paths. The key difficulty arises because without a fixed infrastructure these paths consist of links whose end points are likely to move independent of each other. As a result, node mobility causes the frequent failure and activation of links, leading to increased network congestion while routing reacts to this change.

Initial focus of the researchers was to find stable route that can adapt with network mobility. The effectiveness of a routing algorithm depends on the timeliness and the detail of the topology information available to the nodes. A crucial algorithm design objective in order to achieve routing responsiveness and efficiency is the minimization of reaction to mobility.

Existing schemes for routing can broadly be classified into four categories, flooding, proactive routing, reactive routing and dynamic cluster based routing (Gerla, Pei & Lee, 1999).

Flooding does not require any knowledge of the network topology. In this kind of scenario, each node has a unique sequence number. To send a message packet a sender node broadcasts the packet to its neighbors. Each receiving node first compares the sequence number of the packet with its own sequence number; if greater than it has not sent the packet so broadcasts to all its neighbors else the packet is discarded. Flooding is completed when destination node receives the packet.

Flooding has got several advantages. It is simple to implement. In networks with high topology changes and small data packets, it is more efficient in discovering and maintaining routes than any other protocol. It could be more reliable in delivering the packets, as there is a possibility that a node receives the packet through multiple paths.

However there are some major disadvantages of flooding. Packets might be delivered to too many nodes that do not necessarily need the packet. Collision might happen in the destination so it may not actually receive the packet. It uses broadcasting that is not too reliable to delivery of data especially in IEEE 802.11.

Under light traffic conditions flooding can be reasonably robust, however it generates significant amount of traffic in large networks. At times it is difficult to achieve flooding reliably when the topology is highly dynamic.

Proactive routing protocols attempt to maintain consistent and up-to-date routing information from each node to every other node in the network. Each node maintains one or more tables to store the routing information. All nodes update these tables to maintain a consistent view of the network.

As and when the network topology changes, the nodes propagate update messages throughout the network. Different routing protocol varies in the method by which the topology change information is distributed across the network and the number of necessary routing related tables.

A proactive routing protocol is also known as Table Driven Protocol. There are several proactive routing protocols.

Destination-Sequenced Distance-Vector (DSDV) is one of the early protocols of this kind (Perkins & Bhagwat, 1994). It is based on the classical Bellman-Ford routing algorithm. The major improvement introduced is freedom from loop in routing table.

In DSDV each node maintain routing table with all available destinations, the number of hops to reach the destination and the sequence number assigned by the destination. The sequence number is used to differentiate stale routes from the new ones and hence avoid the formation of loops.

The route labeled with the highest sequence number is used as the latest. If two routes have the same sequence number then the shortest route is used. Based on past history nodes estimate the settling time of routes.

Route updates can be both time driven and event driven. Updates are sent in two ways a full dump or an incremental update. Full dump includes the full routing table where as the incremental update contains the changes since the last update is sent.

In Wireless Routing Protocol (WRP) (Murthy & Aceves, 1996) each node maintains a distance table, a routing table, a Link-Cost table and a message retransmission list.

The distance table stores the distance of each destination nodes via each neighbour. The routing table contains the distance to each node, the predecessor and the successor on this path and a tag to identify if the entry is a simple path a loop or invalid.

The link cost table contains cost of link to each neighbour and the number of timeouts since an error free message was received from that neighbour. Message retransmission list contains information to let a node know which of its neighbour has not acknowledged the update message. Nodes exchange routing tables using update messages periodically as well as on link change.

Global State routing (GSR) (Chen & Gerla, 1998) takes the idea of Link state and applies the same to DSDV. Each node here maintains a Neighbour table, a Topology table (Link State), a Next hop table and a Distance table.

Fisheye State routing (FSR) (Iwata, Chiang, Pei, Gerla, & Chen, 1999), is an improvement over GSR. Unlike GSR in FSR the update message contains information of closer nodes only.

Proactive approach increases network traffic in highly dynamic networks. It does not scale well to large, highly dynamic network, although it can ensure high quality routes in a static topology.

Reactive protocols take a lazy on demand approach. This type of routing creates a route only when it is necessary. When a node requires a route to a destination it initiates a route discovery process. Process is completed once a route is found or all possible route permutations are evaluated. Once a route has been established it is maintained until the route is valid and it is required.

Ad hoc On-demand Distance Vector Routing (AODV) (Perkins & Royer, 1999) is a reactive version of DSDV. To find a route the source broadcasts a route request packet. Neighbors in turn broadcast the packet to their neighbors till it reaches the destination or an intermediate node that has recent route information.

A node discards a route request packet it has already seen. The route request packet uses sequence numbers to ensure loop freeness. While forwarding a route request a node records the node fro which the first copy of the request came. This information is used for sending route replies. As the route reply packet traverses back to the source, the nodes along the path enter the forward route into their tables.

Dynamic Source Routing Protocol (DSRP) (Johnson & Maltz, 1999) is similar to AODV except it maintains a route cache.

For highly dynamic mobile multi hop networks, The Temporally Ordered Routing Algorithm (TORA) (Park & Corson, 1997) is proposed. It finds multiple routes from a source node to a destination node. Control messages are localized to a very small set of nodes near the occurrence of any topological change.

In Associativity Based Routing (ABR) (Toh, 1996) a new metric is introduced as the degree of association stability. All nodes generate periodic beacon to signify its existence. Each time a beacon is received from a node the associativity tables are updated accordingly. Route is selected based on the associativity states of nodes and so is likely to be long lived.

For reactive routing, frequent route finding is a significant overhead for highly dynamic networks. The main downside of reactive approach compared to proactive routing is significant delay at route setup time and the large volume of control traffic required supporting route query mechanism.

In dynamic cluster based routing, the network is organized dynamically into partitions known as clusters with the objective of maintaining relatively stable effective topology. The membership of each cluster changes over time to address node mobility and is decided by the clustering strategy defined by individual algorithm. Complete routing information is maintained for intra cluster nodes. Inter cluster routing is achieved by hiding the topology details within a cluster.

Cluster Based Routing Protocol (CBRP) (Jiang, Li, & Tay, 1999) divides the network into multiple clusters, each of them having a cluster head. When a new node comes up it enters the undecided state, starts a timer and broadcasts beacon. On receiving the beacon cluster head responds immediately. After receiving the response the undecided node becomes a member. If the undecided node times out, it makes itself a cluster head. Cluster heads are changed as infrequently as possible.

In Hierarchical State Routing (HSR) (Iwata, Chiang, Pei, Gerla, & Chen, 1999) the network is partitioned into clusters and a cluster head elected as CBRP. Furthermore the cluster heads organize themselves into clusters and so on. Thus a hierarchy is formed.

Zone based Hierarchical Link State routing protocol (ZHLS) (Ng & Lu, 1999) divides the network into non-overlapping zones. There is no zone head. It defines two levels of topologies, node level and zone level. A node level topology tells how nodes of a zone are connected to each other physically. A virtual link between two zones exists if at least one node of a zone is physically connected to some node of the other zone. Zone level topology tells how zones are connected together.

Cluster head Gateway Switch Routing (CGSR) (Chiang, 1997) uses DSDV as basis. The mobile nodes are aggregated into clusters and a cluster head is elected. All nodes in the communication range of the cluster head belong to its cluster. A gateway node is a node that is in the communication range of two or more cluster heads. Routing happens through these gateways.

Several other clustering algorithms are also proposed. Each algorithm relies either on a proactive or reactive approach and the clustering strategies vary.

Swarm Intelligence also found it's interest in solving routing challenges in MANET. Swarm Intelligence can be classified as a set of methods to solve dynamic optimization problems. It typically uses collaborative agents called ants. Ant inspired routing algorithms were developed and tested for both fixed and wireless network with superior results (Heissenbüttel & Braun, 2003; DiCaro, & Dorigo, 1998; Bonabeau, Henaux, Guerin, Snyers, Kuntz, & Theraulaz, 1998; Schoonderwoerd, Holland, & Bruten, 1997; White & Pagurek, 1998).

All swarm intelligence based routing solutions in MANET follows a general principle (Stojmenovic, 2005). The ants deposit a certain amount of material called pheromone on the ground while traversing a path. A reason behind this technique is that the more ants follow a particular trail, the more attractive is that for other ants. In this way the ants dynamically found a path on the fly, using the explained notion to communicate indirectly amongst themselves.

In case of routing, pheromone amounts are considered for each possible destination. Ant chooses a trail depending on the amount of pheromone deposited on the ground. Each ant compares the amounts of trails on each link towards the destination node. The more the concentration of pheromone in a particular trail,, the higher the probability of the trail being selected by an ant. The ant reinforces the selected trail with its own pheromone.

The concentration of the pheromone on these links evaporates with time at a certain rate. If pheromone decays too quickly then good solutions will loose their appeal before exploitation. On the other hand if pheromone decays too slowly then bad solutions will remain as viable options in the system.

As in the cases in the above mentioned routing algorithms, for swarm intelligence based routing also each node in the MANET maintains a routing table to help determining the route. The neighbours of the node are stored as rows and, all of the other nodes in the network as columns.

There are few swarm intelligent (ant-based) routing algorithms developed for wired networks. The most well known of these are AntNet (DiCaro & Dorigo, 1998) and Ant-Based Control (ABC) (Schoonderwoerd, Holland & Bruten, 1997).

The basic concept behind both AntNet and ABC is similar – they use ants as investigation agents (Stojmenovic, 2005). These ants are used for traversing the network node to node and updating routing related parameters. A routing table is built based on the probability distribution functions derived from the trip times of the routes discovered by the ants.

However the approaches used in AntNet and ABC are different. In AntNet, there are two kinds of ants, forward and backward ants. On the other hand in ABC there is only one kind of ant. The other difference between the two is in the routing table updating. In ABC the probabilities of the routing tables are updated when an ant visit the nodes, while in AntNet the probabilities are updated only when the backward ant visits a node.

Swarm intelligence based routings in MANET can be classified into three types (Stojmenovic, 2005) Path Based Ant Routing, Flooding Based Ant routing, and Position Based Ant Routing.

Path Based Ant Routing does not use the geographic positions of nodes, and follow the well known traditional definition of an ant that travels through the network, creating a path, possibly travels back to its source, and eventually disappears. There are three main protocols in this category, Accelerated Ants Routing (Matsuo & Mori, 2001), Source Update Routing (Islam, Thulasiraman, & Thulasiram, 2003) and Random Walk Based Route Discovery(Roth, & Wicker 2003).

Accelerated Ants Routing (Matsuo & Mori, 2001) described the first ant based routing scheme for MANET. It is a straightforward adaptation of a well known scheme for communication networks, with two additions (Stojmenovic, 2005). They followed the Ants-Routing method (Subramaniam, Druschel, & Chen, 1997) and added a 'no return' rule which does not allow ants to select the neighbour where the message came from.

They also added an 'N step backward exploration rule'. This is identical to the all column update scheme proposed by Guerin (Guerin, 1997). It is applied when an ant moves backward (and consequently routing entries toward the destination are updated).

Performance evaluation showed that the Accelerated Ants Routing algorithm achieves good acceleration for routing table's convergence with respect to the Ants-Routing method, even if network topology was dynamically changed (Stojmenovic, 2005).

Source Update Routing (Islam, Thulasiraman & Thulasiram, 2003) proposed an ant colony optimization (ACO) algorithm, called source update, for all-pair routing in ad hoc networks. 'All pair' routing means that routing tables are created at each node, for all source-destination pairs, in the form of a matrix.

In this algorithm each ant memorizes the whole path to its destination and uses it to return back to the source. While the ant is searching for the destination, the routing table updates are performed to form a trail that leads back to the source.

The algorithm is claimed to be scalable, but apparently this is with respect to the number of processors on a parallel computer, not the number of nodes in an ad hoc network (Stojmenovic, 2005).

Random Walk Based Route Discovery (Roth, & Wicker 2003) presented the scheme called 'Termite' which expands on the ABC algorithm (RSchoonderwoerd, Holland & Bruten, 1997). In the Termite protocol, data traffic follows the largest pheromone trails, if any exist on any link.

If there are no pheromone trails on any link, a route request is performed by a certain number of ants. Each ant performs a random walk over the network. In the random walk, ants and packets uniformly randomly choose their next hop, except for the link they arrived on. Once an ant reaches a node containing pheromone to the requested destination, a route reply packet is returned to the requestor. All routing decisions in Termite are random.

There are two major Flooding Based Ant routing proposed. AntAODV (Marwaha, Tham & Srinivasan, 2002, Marwaha ; Tham, & Srinivasan, 2002) and ARA (Gunes, Sorges, & Bouazizi, 2002) . There are couple of others flooding bases proposal PERA (Baras, & Mehta, 2003) and ANSI (Rajagopalan, Jaikaeo, & Shen, 2003).

AntAODV (Marwaha, Tham, & Srinivasan, 2002; Marwaha, Tham, & Srinivasan, 2002) is a hybrid approach using AODV (Perkins & Royer, 1999) and reactive Ant Based exploration.

From a source to destination if there is a fresh route, the source uses that. Otherwise the source keeps the messages in buffer until an ant arrives with a route to the destination. Each ant follows a blind flooding approach in finding a route. Only difference of this with AODV AODV (Perkins & Royer, 1999) is there is no route discovery process here, it relies on ants for the same.

ARA (Gunes, Sorges, & Bouazizi, 2002) presents a detailed routing scheme including route discovery and maintenance mechanisms. Route discovery is achieved by flooding forward ants to the destination while establishing reverse links to the source. This approach uses ants only for building routes initially and hence is a completely reactive algorithm.

Routes are maintained primarily by data packets flowing through the network. In case of a failure, an attempt is made to send the packet over an alternate link. Otherwise, it is returned to the previous hop for similar processing. A new route discovery is launched if the packet is eventually returned to the source.

PERA (Probabilistic Emergent Routing Algorithm) (Baras, & Mehta, 2003) encompassed two ant-based routing schemes for ad hoc networks. One scheme only uses one-to-one communications where a message sent by one node is only processed at one neighbouring node, while the other utilizes the inherent broadcast one-to-all nature of wireless networks where a message sent by one node is received by all its neighbours.

ANSI (Ad hoc Networking with Swarm Intelligence) (Rajagopalan, Jaikaeo, & Shen, 2003) proposed route discovery and maintenance as a combination of proactive and reactive activities. Proactive ants are broadcast periodically to maintain routes in a local area. Whenever other routes are required, a forward reactive ant is broadcast.

There are primarily two proposals in Position Based Ant Routing. Proactive, Zone Grouping, Logical Link Based Routing (Heissenbüttel & Braun, 2003) and Ant-Based Location Updates (Camara, & Loureiro, 2001).

Proactive, Zone Grouping, Logical Link Based Routing (Heissenbüttel & Braun, 2003) describes a proactive position and ant based routing algorithm for large mobile ad hoc networks. The plane is divided into geographical areas with all nodes within the same area belonging to the same logical router. All the nodes within a logical router share and use the same routing tables.

In Ant-Based Location Updates (Camara, & Loureiro, 2001) the authors proposed a protocol that employs ants only to collect and distribute information about node's locations in an adhoc network. Routing tables contain information about previous and current locations and timestamps of each node. When a host receives an ant it compares the routing table present in the ant packet with its routing table and updates the entries having older information.

The major focus of the above-mentioned routing algorithms is to find a relatively stable route and reduce control message overhead. Each of these schemes has constant route maintenance overhead. Also none of these schemes guarantee the constant network connectivity during the movement, as a result of which message packets might have to be broadcast more than once. In the worst case some node may become disconnected from the rest of the network.

To address this, previously we suggested a development of an adaptive topology management scheme for MANET (Basu, & Chaudhuri, 2003; Basu, & Chaudhuri, 2004). We intended to maintain the topology through message communication and hence reduce the concept of dynamic routing.

To deal with this, we have initially proposed an algorithm for coordinated self adaptive movement scheme (Basu, & Chaudhuri, 2003) of mobile nodes to maintain the neighborhood topology by message communication.

Before starting movement, mobile nodes elect a node as the movement coordinator. Movement coordinator is responsible for maintaining the network connectivity. Nodes move in such a fashion that their distance from the coordinator does not increase a predefined maximum value. The predefined value in turn ensures the network connectivity.

Each node sends a periodic hello message to the coordinator. On arrival of hello messages, coordinator can keep track of which node tends to move out of the predefined maximum value and takes necessary action. Coordinator can issue start or stop signal to the nodes. This approach defines some control traffic but results removal of routing overhead and by virtue of the restricted movement, the neighborhood for each node is maintained throughout.

The above-mentioned approach works well, but virtually the network becomes a star connection keeping the coordinator at the center. Also the span of the network turns out to be very small.

In this scheme we did not intend to use a Global Positioning System (GPS) for the adaptive movement. That increased the algorithm intricacy. Making an allowance for the large availability and affordability of GPS receiver we have considered that each node in the network is enabled with a GPS receiver.

The GPS free scheme (Basu, & Chaudhuri, 2004) defines some movement control messages but as the neighbourhood is continuously maintained, routing overhead is removed. This scheme is an adaptive topology management scheme for MANET.

The network decides a leader before starting movement. The leader maintains a network distance matrix with it. Every node, broadcast their position information obtained from the GPS, to the leader in a predefined periodic interval. By analyzing the positions, the leader apprehends the neighbourhood breakage possibilities and instructs the nodes to control their movement.

With these adaptive movement algorithms for mobile nodes, the neighborhood topology is maintained. The nodes remain connected throughout their movement by introducing some movement control message and the network behave as mobile wireless LAN.

Both the schemes have few shortcomings. They depend too much upon a leader or coordinator and the leader or coordinator selection mechanism is trivial. The scheme is too much dependent on one node but there is no failover method in case of failure. Finally the scheme does not talk about message communication mechanism between coordinator/leader and the nodes. How to secure the communication is also open ended there.

In the current scheme I propose to overcome these. Firstly following a three-tier-architecture (Techpedia) I propose to select an Application Server and Database server within the network. The Application Server can host any collaborative software application needed for the network.

The scheme will also propose a failover mechanism of Application Server. Along with hosting the software application, it additionally will replace the need of coordinator or leader as proposed in our earlier adaptive movement schemes MANET (Basu, & Chaudhuri, 2003; Basu, & Chaudhuri, 2004) and will enhance the adaptive movement schemes using swarm intelligent principles to keep the network connected. In this enhancement I have used some philosophies of Swarm Intelligence without proposing usage of any agents like ant.

To reiterate, in three-tier-architecture, there are primarily three physically distinct elements as shown in the following picture (figure 1). Data tier stores the data, typically in a Database. Data tier is physically realized as a Database Server. Application tier hosts the software application logic. It is typically realized by an Application Server. End users interact with the software through Presentation tier. It is usually realized by a browser running in a computer or smartphone currently. There can be other means also to realize Presentation tier.

Presentation tier interacts with Application server usually following HTTP or HTTPs protocol. Application tier interacts with Data tier to access or store application data whenever required.

In MANET, the presentation tier will reside in individual nodes as a native application or web application or hybrid application.

To the best of my knowledge no such scheme is proposed before. Following section will describe my proposed scheme in detail.

Figure 1.

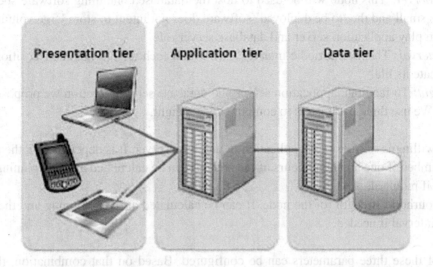

PROPOSED SCHEME

In this scheme I propose self-organized application deployment architecture over MANET and a swarm intelligent movement pattern following which the neighbourhood of each node will be maintained throughout the movement and the network will be a stable one in terms of connectivity.

In the scheme the network selects a node as application server and another node as database server dynamically based on some predefined preconfigured network performance characteristics. The application server can host any application as per the network's need. If the network feels a single node can serve as both application server and database.

This section is subdivided into seven subsections. a) Definitions, b) Assumptions, c) Control Messages, d) Application and Database Server Selection, e) Communication Mechanism, f) Swarm Intelligent Movement Scheme and g) Backup and Recovery Mechanism.

Definitions subsection defines key terminologies used in the scheme. Assumptions subsection outlines the basic assumptions behind the scheme. The Control Messages subsection defines the messages to be transmitted between the nodes in order to select the application and database server.

Application and Database Server Selection discusses the proposed selection scheme. Communication Mechanism describes the way of communication between the nodes and the application server, and the communication between Database Servers.

Swarm Intelligent Movement Scheme discusses our proposed movement scheme to maintain neighbourhood topology. The final subsection discusses about the recovery mechanism of the network in case a Database Server or Application Server opting out from the role.

Definitions

Application Server: Application server is the most important node within the network. It hosts the collaborative software and controls the movement of nodes in a swarm intelligent way once the network is in move.

Database Server: This node will be used to host the database containing software specific data. If the network is small and the 'to be deployed' software does not intent to store large volume of data the same node can play application server and database server role.

Beacon Interval: This is a periodic interval after which each node sends their position to required nodes to indicate its life.

Node Weight: To facilitate application server and database server selection we propose to compute node weight. We use three parameters to compute node weight.

- Node's willingness to serve as application or database server. It is dependent on the node.
- Total number of one hop neighbours of the node. It can be calculated at the beginning and may be updated if required.
- 'Neighbourhood strength' of the node. It can be calculated at the beginning and then updated at regular interval if needed.

Weights of these three parameters can be configured. Based on that combination, the weight of individual node can be calculated.

These three are just indicative parameters. Network may want to use any other set of parameters also.

Willingness: This parameter indicates whether a node wants to take responsibility of being the application server or database server. It is a Boolean value.

Hop Strength: This indicates the strength of a hop between two nodes. We have four predefined values (0.25, 0.5, 0.75 and 1) depending on the distance between two nodes to compute hop strength.

If D is taken as the neighbourhood distance:

- Strength of one hop is 0.25 when 0.75D < (distance) <= D.
- Strength is 0.5 when 0.5D < (distance) <= 0.75D.
- Strength is 0.75 when 0.25D < (distance) <= 0.5D.
- Strength is 1 When 0 < (distance) <= 0.25D.

In case of two hop neighbours the hop strength is taken as the minimum between the two one hop neighbour strengths. For example if node n1 is connected to node n2 via node n4, hop strength between n1 and n2 will be taken as minimum {hop strength (n1,n4), hop strength (n4,n2)}

Neighbour Score: Neighbour score for a particular node is calculated as summation of its hop strengths.

- One hop neighbour score = [1 * (number of one hop neighbours with strength 1) + 0.75 * (number of one hop neighbours with strength 0.75) + 0.5 * (number of one hop neighbours with strength 0.5) + 0.25 * (number of one hop neighbours with strength 0.25)].
- Two hop neighbour score = [1 * (number of two hop neighbours with strength 1) + 0.75 * (number of two hop neighbours with strength 0.75) + 0.5 * (number of two hop neighbours with strength 0.5) + 0.25 * (number of two hop neighbours with strength 0.25)].

Neighbourhood Strength: Neighbourhood strength of a node is calculated based on neighbour scores.
Neighbourhood Strength = one hop neighbour score + two hop neighbour score

Assumptions

The network needs to stick to the following assumptions in order to follow the proposed scheme.

1. Free space propagation model, where the received signal strength solely depends on its distance from the transmitter. Any message packet sent in a single hop from a source node to a destination node is lost in transit only if the destination node moves out of the communication range with which the message is sent from the source node.
2. Each node is identified with a unique identification number.
3. In alignment with two key principles of swarm intelligence namely matching the velocity of neighbors and staying near the neighbors; nodes have a predefined maximum and minimum velocity.
4. Network is connected i.e. there is a path between any two nodes.
5. Half of the actual communication range is taken as the allowable neighbourhood distance, in order to keep provision for the communication to be continued between the nodes trying to go apart.
6. Initially every node treats all other nodes at a distance less than the neighbourhood distance as its neighbours.
7. All nodes have a GPS unit that gives approximate three-dimensional position (longitude, latitude and altitude), velocity and accurate time in Universal Time Coordinate (UTC) format. (The algorithm assumes a planar movement so altitude information is not used).
8. Location information is as received from GPS is assumed correct. GPS receiver information comes in longitude, latitude. Transformation of longitude/latitude to linear distance is dependent on the geographical area. Each node has got the conversion information of the operation area.
9. For all relative coordinate calculation purpose y-axis is taken as parallel to the direction of movement and the movement direction is taken as the negative direction.
10. For rotations, clockwise direction is taken as the positive direction to be consistent with navigators, scouts, pilots, soldiers and other GPS and compass users. Although in traditional geometry the convention is to take anticlockwise direction as positive.
11. Nodes willing to take up application server or database server responsibility have the necessary software installed.
12. Each node is aware of the destination and route towards it.

Control Messages

The scheme uses different kinds of control messages namely a) Position message b) Neighbourhood message c) Election message d) Propose Application Server message e) Application Server Declaration message and f) Database Server Declaration message

Message header of each kind of control message contains the destination node identifier, sender node identifier, and the route (if available). Any node receiving any message reads the header information first. If the message is not for the recipient it forwards the packet according to the route information (either present in the header or within the node). In case of broadcast message, header does not contain any destination information.

Position message is sent by each individual node and contains the position information obtained through the GPS receiver in its possession. Neighbourhood, Election, Propose Application Server, Application Server Declaration and Database Server Declaration messages are sent by individual nodes and are used in the Application and Database server selection.

On broadcast of Election message, selection process starts. Neighbourhood message contains all neighbours ids and their hop strengths. Propose Application Server message contains two node ids of the nodes having maximum node weights.

Application and Database Server Selection

One application server and a back up application server is selected before the network starts its movement and communicated to all nodes in the network. Both the application servers identify their database server internally and that is transparent to other nodes.

Depending on data volume application server may decide not to have a separate database server and host the database itself.

The selection is initiated initially by the node having the least identification number and subsequently by the application server if needed.

During the selection process if multiple nodes have same weight, the node with smaller identification number is selected.

The algorithm is as follows

1. Initiator node of the network broadcasts Election message.
2. At network startup each node broadcasts its position message otherwise go to step 6.
3. Each node calculates the distance of the nodes from which it receives position message. If the distance is less than or equal to allowable neighbourhood distance the node identifies those nodes as neighbours.
4. Each node send Neighbourhood message to all its neighbours.
5. After receiving Neighbourhood message from all neighbours each node calculates their Neighbourhood Strength.
6. Each node calculates their Node Weight and sends to all its neighbours.
7. Each node identifies two nodes with the highest Node Weights and forms Propose Application Server message.
8. Each node sends the Propose Application Server message to its neighbours and keeps the information and the timestamp of sending the message.
9. On receiving Propose Application Server message, each node compares with its own copy of the information.
10. If the received message has more updated information, it updates the information and timestamp and sends the information to its neighbours.
11. Else the node ignores the information.
12. Repeat step 10 until all the nodes have the same copy of Propose Application Server message.
13. After a predefined timeout period, if an eligible application server node does not get any other Propose Application Server message from its neighbours, declares itself as an application server through Application Server Declaration message.
14. The next eligible node is identified as backup application server. Application server keeps the information about backup.

15. Both the application server and backup application server identifies the node with the highest Node Weight among their one hop neighbours as database servers.
16. Both the application servers communicate their decisions to the identified node through Database Server Declaration message.
17. Application server intimates the backup application server about its database server and vice versa.

Communication Mechanism

Once the Application Server is identified all nodes can connect to that through HTTP/HTTPs. Each node can communicate with it through HTTP/HTTPs. By this nodes and Application server can have a two way communication.

For safety purpose we propose the Application server to have an authentication mechanism for each node. Each node will have a user id and password, using which they can login. From that Application Server can identify the node and can show a node its relevant information only.

Application Server can thus provide any instruction to the nodes. This way all communication between Application Server and the nodes are secure and confidential.

Nodes can communicate through the application or else they have a choice of using any regular routing algorithm to talk. As the network will behave like LAN, there will not be any extra overhead for routing.

Identified database servers will run periodic database replication to make sure both the database is in synch. This will help in case one database server needs to opt out for some reason.

Swarm Intelligent Movement

After the Application Server is identified and each node is aware about the same the network starts moving. During the movement each individual node sends position message to the Application Server after each beacon interval. The beacon interval is calculated as in Lemma1 (Basu, & Chaudhuri, 2004) below.

Application Server uses this information to direct each node's movement in a swarm intelligent way. Our scheme applies three fundamental principles of swarm intelligence a) collision avoidance between neighbors, b) matching the velocity of neighbors and c) staying near the neighbors.

We define a node as a neighbour of another node only if they are within half of the actual communication range. This ensures neighbours are staying near. Also the network assumes each node to have a velocity in between a predefined maximum and minimum. This indirectly makes sure that the velocities of neighbours are matched.

The Application Server maintains the position of each node and the movement instruction given to that node (if any) in last two consecutive intervals in the database. The movement model is as follows:

After receiving position message from all nodes the Application Server

- Identifies every pair of nodes for which the distance has exceeded the neighbourhood distance.
- Identifies every pair of nodes for which the distance is less than 15% of neighbourhood distance.
- Spots the nodes whose movement direction is deviated from the normal direction.
- Identifies the nodes to be asked to change direction so as to get them back in actual movement direction.

Analyzing the aforementioned nodes Application Server decides the actions as follows and creates the action of nodes accordingly. Nodes can login in their page and get the instruction.

- For each pair of nodes identified in 1 above, Application Server calculates the relative coordinates of the nodes considering itself as the origin. According to the convention of y-axis determination as stated in the assumptions the Application Server can spot which node has moved ahead. Application Server decides to stop the node ahead so that the node behind can make up the distance.

- For each pair of nodes identified in 2 above, Application Server calculates the relative coordinates of the nodes considering itself as the origin. According to the convention of y-axis determination as stated in the assumptions the Application Server can spot which node is chasing a node ahead. Application Server decides to stop that node to avoid collision between neighbours.

- For the nodes identified in 3 above, Application Server identifies the change in movement direction and deviation angle. Even if the node changes direction in between beacon interval, Application Server finds out it from the previous interval. Application Server had the previous position of the node and gets the current position. From these two positions Application Server finds out whether it has moved in the right movement direction. If not, Application Server calculates the deviation of the nodes movement from the actual direction of movement. The Application Server also calculates the average speed of the node during the last beacon interval. After calculating the deviation Application Server decides to change their movement direction as in Lemma2 (Basu, & Chaudhuri, 2004) below and asks them to move with the calculated average speed during the last beacon interval.

- Application Server decides for the node identified in 4 also as in Lemma2 (Basu, & Chaudhuri, 2004) below. The instruction speed is same as the speed instructed to the node during the previous rotation instruction.

- For other type of nodes Application Server asks them to move on its pleasure with their preferred velocity.

Two kinds of conflicts might occur in the above-mentioned decision scheme. Application Server resolves these conflicts as follows:

- At any instance it might happen that a particular node is moved ahead from a neighbour and deviated from the desired movement direction. In this case direction change gets priority and the node is not stopped. Lemma3 (Basu, & Chaudhuri, 2004) below establishes that even if the node ahead is moving it won't move out of communication range.

- Also at any instance a node might be ahead of a neighbour and was asked to change direction in the previous beacon interval. In this case the node is asked to stop. When Application Server asks it to move again it is asked to change direction as in Lemma2 (Basu, & Chaudhuri, 2004) below.

Lemma1: Beacon interval should be taken as $D/4V - 2T_p$ D being the neighbourhood distance, V the predefined maximum velocity and T_p being the maximum message propagation time.

Proof: The beacon interval is calculated primarily as a function of the neighbourhood distance. Keeping in mind the worst scenario, at a particular instance two neighbours can be at neighbourhood distance, and can be moving in the opposite direction. Assuming both the nodes are moving with the predefined maximum velocity, two nodes will reach the point of breakage from each other after D/2V period where D is the neighbourhood distance and V being the predefined maximum velocity.

To allow the leader to have the revival time the leader should have another beacon time in hand before actual breakage may occur. Thus the beacon interval should be taken as D/4V. To make the interval more realistic, control message propagation time should also be taken into consideration.

Maximum time required to propagate control message would be twice the time for the leader to send a packet to the furthest node (node at the maximum number of hops) once for the position information to reach the leader and the next is for the decision to reach the node. The processing time within the leader is considered to be negligible compared to other times.

Consequently T_p being the maximum propagation time, the beacon interval should be taken as D/4V - $2T_p$

Lemma2: For a node that changed direction from its original line of movement, has to reverse its direction by (2 * deviation angle) for the next beacon interval and reverse its direction again by the original deviation angle in the subsequent beacon interval, to come back to the original line again.

Proof: Let (x, y) be the position of the node at an instance from when it changed the direction. Let Θ be the deviation angle, and Φ be the angle by which its movement direction is reversed to bring it back to its actual line of movement. 'l' is taken as the linear distance traveled by the node in a beacon interval.

Now two cases may arise. We will determine Φ and show that in both the following two cases $\Phi = 2* \Theta$ which proves the first part of the lemma.

Case 1 Θ is in positive direction: Figure 2 explains the movement.

The position of the node after the next beacon interval would be $(x + l*\cos (90- \Theta), y + l*\sin (90- \Theta))$ = $(x + l*\sin \Theta, y + l*\cos \Theta) = (x_1, y_1)$ say. If (x_2, y_2) be the position of the node after the next interval after applying Φ in the reverse direction of Θ, x_2 would be equal to $x_1 - l* \cos (180 - (\Phi + 90 - \Theta))$ and y_2 would be equal to $y1 + l* \sin (180 - (\Phi + 90 - \Theta))$

As the Y-axis is taken as parallel to the movement direction, if the node has to come back to its original line of movement x2 should be equal to x.

Figure 2.

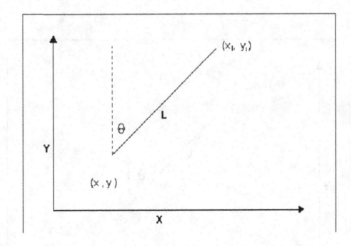

Now $x_2 = x$

$\Rightarrow x_1 - l^* \cos(180 - (\Phi + 90 - \Theta)) = x$

$\Rightarrow x + l^* \sin\Theta + l^* \cos(90 - \Theta + \Phi) = x$

$\Rightarrow l^* \sin\Theta - l^* \sin(\Phi - \Theta) = 0$

$\Rightarrow \sin(\Phi - \Theta) = \sin\Theta$

$\Rightarrow \Phi - \Theta = \Theta$

$\Rightarrow \Phi = 2^* \Theta$

Case 2 Θ is in negative direction: Figure 3 shows the situation.

As in case 1 in this case x_1 would be equal to x - l*sin Θ and x_2 would be equal to x_1 + l*cos (90+ Θ- Φ).

Here $x_2 = x$

$\Rightarrow x_1 + l^* \cos(90 + \Theta - \Phi) = x$

$\Rightarrow x - l^* \sin\Theta - l^* \sin(\Theta - \Phi) = x$

$\Rightarrow l^* \sin(\Phi - \Theta) = l^* \sin\Theta$

$\Rightarrow \Phi - \Theta = \Theta$

$\Rightarrow \Phi = 2^* \Theta$

Figure 3.

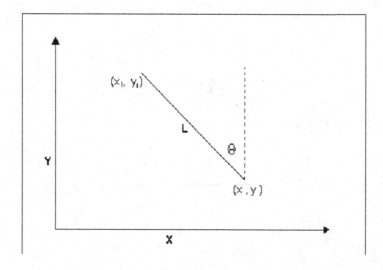

Now for the node to continue in the line of movement has to change its direction by Θ in opposite direction of Φ.

Lemma3: Between a pair of nodes, if the same node has changed direction and moved ahead, the leader can first address the direction change of the node ahead instead of stopping it and still assure that the node ahead will not move out of communication range.

Proof: Let (x, y) and (h, k) be the positions of two nodes when the distance between them was just the neighbourhood distance.

If 'L' be the neighbourhood distance then $L^2 = (h-x)^2 + (k-y)^2$. According to the definition of neighbourhood distance the communication range D of the nodes are $2*L$.

Let us assume that the second node has changed direction and moved ahead after next beacon interval. Let Θ be the deviation angle of the second node, l_1 & l_2 be the linear distances traveled by the nodes respectively in a beacon interval. The deviation of the second node is taken in the positive direction.

After the first beacon interval, when the second node has changed direction as well as moved ahead the position of the nodes would be $(x, y+l_1)$ and $(h + l_2*\sin \Theta, k + l_2*\cos \Theta)$ respectively.

The direction change of the second node is handled as in lemma 2. After next beacon interval the positions would be $(x, y+2*l_1)$ and $(h, k+2* l_2*\cos \Theta)$. If S be the distance between the two nodes at this instance

$$S^2 = (h-x)^2 + (k+2* l_2*\cos \Theta - y - 2*l_1)^2$$

To prove the proposition we need to prove $S <= 2*L \Rightarrow S^2 <= 4*L^2$

Now $S^2 = (h-x)^2 + (k+2* l_2*\cos \Theta - y - 2*l_1)^2$. The term $(h-x)^2$ is definitely less than or equal to $4*(h-x)^2$. Thus the scope of the proof is reduced to $(k+2* l_2*\cos \Theta - y - 2*l_1)^2 <= 4*(k-y)^2$

For $(k+2* l_2*\cos \Theta - y - 2*l_1)^2$ to be less than or equal to $4*(k-y)^2$, $2* l_2*\cos \Theta - 2*l_1$ needs to be less than or equal to $(k-y)$. As boundary case we would assume the maximum value of $\cos \Theta$ and the expression $2* l_2*\cos \Theta - 2*l_1$ would reduce to $2* l_2 - 2*l_1$.

As in lemma 1 the beacon interval is $D/4V - 2T_P$. So maximum value of l_1 or l_2 is less than D/4 and consequently $2* l_2 - 2*l_1$ is less than $D/2 = L$.

Maximum value of $(k-y)$ is equal to L. Hence $2* l_2*\cos \Theta - 2*l_1$ is definitely less than $(k-y)$.

Thus even if the node ahead moves, it won't go out of the communication range. In a similar fashion it can be proved when Θ is taken in the negative direction.

Backup and Recovery of Application and Database Servers

During the network movement it may so happen that Application or Database Server may need to opt out from this responsibility. Our scheme proposes a backup and recovery mechanism to handle the same.

When Application Server and Database Server are identified we propose to identify two sets. One is the primary and the other is the backup. In between primary and backup Database Servers a periodic data replication is scheduled so that both the Database Server has same copy of data.

Three scenarios may happen, a) Primary Application Server and Database Server wants to opt out from their responsibilities, b) Primary Application Server wants to opt out from their responsibilities and c) Primary Database Server wants to opt out from its responsibility.

For scenario a, b we propose the following steps.

1. All nodes are requested to stop.
2. Primary Application Server sends Propose Application Server message to the Backup Application Server.
3. Backup Application Server becomes Primary and send Application Server Declaration message to all nodes.
4. Each node updates their Application Server information.
5. Primary Application Server initiates an Application and Database Server selection.
6. After the end of the Application and Database Server selection algorithm Primary Application Server gets two candidates for backup. It picks up the first one as backup.
7. The backup Application Server selects its Database Server if needed, else itself plays the role.
8. After the backup Database Server is identified the replications starts between primary and backup Database Servers.
9. Primary Application Server asks the network to move keeping in mind the last instruction given by the erstwhile Application Server before all the nodes were stopped for the recovery.

For scenario c the following steps are proposed.

1. Primary Application Server considers the Backup Database server as database for time being.
2. It then identifies the next eligible node from its one hop neighbours without hampering the network movement.
3. After identification Primary Application Server informs the same to temporary Database Server.
4. Periodic data replication is setup.
5. After first replication Primary Application Server makes the newly identified Database Server as primary and the temporary one is retreated as Backup Database server.

EXAMPLE

This section provides an example on how to select the Application Server and Database Server and then how the neighbourhood of each node remains intact following the proposed Swarm Intelligent movement scheme.

This section has three subsections, a) Network Definition, b) Application Server Identification and c) Movement.

Network Definition subsection describes the example network. Application Server identification shows the neighbourhood table and identifies the Application Server node. The example being a relatively small network, Application Server and Database Server role will be played by the same node.

Movement subsection will show the movement of the network for 1 hour. It will show the observation of the Application Server after each beacon interval and it's decision about node. This subsection shows that the neighbourhood is intact after one hour of movement. As a result any deployed collaborative software application in the network will work seamlessly even if the network moves.

Network Definition

The example is shown with a sample network consisting of 12 nodes. Nodes are named as Node1 to Node12. The communication range is taken as 10 km. Thus the neighbourhood distance is 5 km. The maximum and minimum velocity is assumed as 60 km/hr and 20 km/hr respectively. The beacon interval is taken as 10 minutes.

In the beginning nodes are assigned velocities and positions randomly. Table 1 shows the neighbourhood table. One node pair is appearing once in the table.

Application Server Identification

As this is a small network of only twelve nodes there will not be a separate Database Server. Application Server can play both the roles of Application Server and Database Server.

Table 2 depicts the neighbourhood summary and the Node Weights. Node1 and Node12 are not willing to take additional responsibilities.

Node8 is selected as the primary Application Server and Node6 is the backup.

Movement

Table 3 shows the movements snap of each node in 10 minutes interval for one hour.

The following chart (Figure 4) depicts the distance between all pair of neighbours initially and after one hour of movement and shows that the neighbourhood is maintained for each pair. Numbers in the x axis denote each pair, and they are in the order as mentioned in the neighbourhood table described above in the network definition.

It clearly depicts the fact that no neighbourhood is broken after one hour of movement.

Table 1.

Node	Neighbours
Node1	Node2, Node6, Node8, Node11, Node12
Node2	Node6, Node11, Node12
Node3	Node4, Node8, Node11
Node4	Node5, Node6, Node8, Node9, Node11
Node5	Node6, Node7, Node8, Node9, Node10, Node12
Node6	Node7, Node8, Node10, Node11, Node12
Node7	Node8, Node9, Node10, Node12
Node8	Node9, Node10, Node11, Node12
Node9	Node10
Node10	Node12
Node11	Node12

Table 2.

Node	Number of 1 Hop Neighbours	Number of 1 Hop Neighbours with Strength 1	Number of 1 Hop Neighbours with Strength 0.75	Number of 2 Hop Neighbours with Strength 1	Number of 2 Hop Neighbours with Strength 0.75	Node Weight
Node1	5	3	2	2	1	0
Node2	4	2	2	1	2	10
Node3	3	1	2	2	2	9
Node4	5	4	1	2	0	11.75
Node5	7	5	2	1	2	16
Node6	9	6	3	1	0	18.25
Node7	6	5	1	2	2	15.25
Node8	10	6	4	0	1	19.75
Node9	5	2	3	3	1	13
Node10	5	4	1	2	3	14
Node11	7	5	2	1	3	16.75
Node12	8	5	3	2	1	0

Table 3.

Interval	Application Server's Observation	Decision
1	Node4 has a deviation angle of 45 degree in the negative direction and the average speed during the last beacon interval was 20 km/hr. Node12 has a deviation angle of 30 degree in the positive direction and the average speed during the last beacon interval was 34 km/hr. For the following node pairs the distance is greater than the neighbourhood distance. The position observations are also as follows: Node4, node5. Node5 is ahead. Node4, node6. Node6 is ahead. Node4, node8. Node8 is ahead. Node4, node9. Node9 is ahead. Node4, node11. Node11 is ahead. Node4, node3. Node3 is ahead. Node12, node2. Node2 is ahead. Node12, node1. Node1 is ahead. Node12, node11. Node11 is ahead.	Node4 is asked to rotate 90 degree in positive direction with a speed of 20 km/hr Node12 is asked to rotate 60 degree in negative direction with a speed of 34 km/hr Node5, Node6, node8, Node9, Node11, Node3, Node2 and Node1 are asked to stop.
2	For the following node pairs the distance is greater than the neighbourhood distance. The position observations are also as follows: Node6, node10. Node10 is ahead. Node5, node10. Node10 is ahead. Node5, node12. Node12 is ahead. Node5, node4. Node5 is ahead. Node4, node6. Node6 is ahead. Node4, node8. Node8 is ahead. Node4, node9. Node9 is ahead. Node4, node11. Node11 is ahead. Node12, node10. Node10 is ahead. Node9, node10. Node10 is ahead. Node8, node10. Node10 is ahead.	Node4 is asked to rotate 45 degree in negative direction. Node10, Node5, Node12, Node6, Node8, Node9 and Node11 are asked to stop. Node3, Node2 and Node1 are free to move.

continued on following page

Table 3. Continued

Interval	Application Server's Observation	Decision
3	For the following node pairs the distance is greater than the neighbourhood distance. The position observations are also as follows: Node6, node7. Node7 is ahead. Node6, node10. Node10 is ahead. Node5, node7. Node7 is ahead. Node5, node10. Node10 is ahead. Node5, node12. Node12 is ahead. Node4, node9. Node4 is ahead. Node3, node8. Node3 is ahead. Node3, node11. Node3 is ahead. Node2, node6. Node2 is ahead. Node2, node11. Node2 is ahead. Node2, node12. Node2 is ahead. Node1, node2. Node2 is ahead. Node1, node6. Node1 is ahead. Node1, node8. Node1 is ahead. Node1, node11. Node1 is ahead. Node1, node12. Node1 is ahead. Node10, node12. Node10 is ahead. Node9, node10. Node10 is ahead. Node8, node10. Node10 is ahead. Node7, node8. Node7 is ahead. Node7, node9. Node7 is ahead. Node7, node12. Node7 is ahead.	Node7, Node10, Node4, Node3, Node12, Node2 and Node1 are asked to stop. Node5, Node6, Node8, Node9 and Node11 are free to move.
4	For the following node pairs the distance is greater than the neighbourhood distance. The position observations are also as follows: Node6, node7. Node7 is ahead. Node6, node2. Node2 is ahead. Node11, node2. Node2 is ahead. Node2, node12. Node2 is ahead. Node1, node2. Node2 is ahead. Node1, node12. Node1 is ahead. Node10, node12. Node10 is ahead. Node8, node9. Node8 is ahead. Node9, node7. Node7 is ahead. Node12, node7. Node7 is ahead.	Node7, Node2, Node1, Node10 and Node8 are asked to stop. Node12 is asked to rotate 30 degree in positive direction. Node4 and Node3 are free to move.
5	For the following node pairs the distance is greater than the neighbourhood distance. The position observations are also as follows: Node6, node10. Node6 is ahead. Node5, node8. Node5 is ahead. Node5, node9. Node5 is ahead. Node5, node10. Node5 is ahead. Node5, node12. Node5 is ahead. Node5, node4. Node5 is ahead. Node3, node8. Node3 is ahead. Node1, node20. Node1 is ahead.	Node6, Node5, Node3 and Node1 are asked to stop. Node7, Node2, Node10 and Node8 receive are free to move.
6	For the following node pairs the distance is greater than the neighbourhood distance. The position observations are also as follows: Node6, node7. Node7 is ahead. Node6, node2. Node2 is ahead. Node1, node2. Node2 is ahead. Node1, node8. Node8 is ahead. Node1, node11. Node11 is ahead. Node1, node12. Node12 is ahead. Node10, node12. Node12 is ahead.	Node7, Node2, Node8, Node11 and Node12 are asked to stop. Node6, Node5, Node3 and Node1 are free to move

Figure 4.

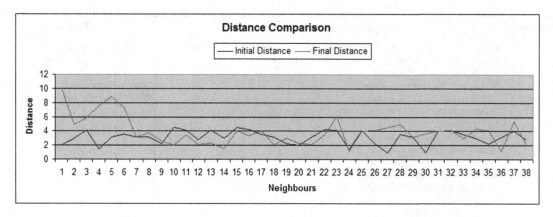

FUTURE RESEARCH DIRECTIONS

Applications on MANET demands usage of collaborative software. Due to several reasons it was not possible in MANET. In this chapter I proposed on how to deploy collaborative application software on a MANET. Future research can be in three directions.

Firstly the movement algorithm works in a start-stop paradigm to help the network to be connected throughout. Though the fact that the network remains connected have several advantages like possibility of deploying application, removing routing overhead, start-stop paradigm makes the network slower in today's movement age. Future enhancements can work towards improving the start-stop mechanism so that any node does not stop much.

Secondly the scheme does not handle possibility of a node opting out from the network. In an ad-hoc network this can be a common scenario. Further enhancements can take care of this scenario.

Last but not the least the approach presented in this chapter will not only help deploying an application in MANET, it will also help integration of ad-hoc networks where by more than one network can use same application but secure their data using the security mechanism built in the application. This can be a possible future work.

Further enhancements can have a cloud (Software As A Service model) by which multiple ad-hoc networks can access the same application and the Application Server gets some revenue out of the same.

CONCLUSION

Advancement of ubiquitous computing encouraged the development of a self organizing readily deployable infrastructure less ad-hoc network known as MANET. It has found great interest in applications such as distributed collaborative computing, disaster recovery and digital battlefield.

Collaborative computing often needs collaborative software. It was not possible to install a software in MANET due to various reasons like power constraint, memory constraint and node mobility. Improvement of devices at affordable cost overcomes power and memory constraint.

In this chapter I propose on how to deploy three-tier application software on a MANET. In order to do that, we need an Application Server and a Database Server. We proposed a mechanism on how we can select those. Along with hosting the application, the Application Server is also responsible to control network movement using Swarm Intelligence principles (collision avoidance between neighbors, matching the velocity of neighbors and staying near the neighbors).

Following the movement pattern neighbourhhod is maintained for all nodes and even if the nodes are mobile, it behaves like a wireless LAN. As a result all nodes are always connected to the Application Server through some route and software can easily be deployed in the Application Server.

We have shown our movement scheme in an example.

DEDICATION

This Chapter is dedicated to my daughter Srisa Basu.

REFERENCES

W3C Specifications. (n.d.). Retrieved from http://www.w3.org/protocols/

Baras, J. S. & Mehta, H. (2003). A probabilistic emergent routing algorithm for mobile ad hoc networks. In *Proc. WiOpt*. Sophia-Antipolis, France: Academic Press.

Basu, S. S., & Chaudhuri, A. (2003). Self-adaptive topology management for mobile ad-hoc network. *Journal of the Institution of Engineers (India)*, *84*, 7–13.

Basu, S. S., & Chaudhuri, A. (2004). "Self adaptive MANET: A centralized approach" – Foundations of computing and decision sciences. *Institute of Computing Science Poznan University of Technology, Poland*, *29*(4), 271–286.

Bonabeau, E., Henaux, F., Guerin, S., Snyers, D., Kuntz, P., & Theraulaz, G. (1998). Routing in telecommunication networks with 'smart' ant-like agents. In *Proc. 2nd Int. Workshop on Intelligent Agents for Telecommunication Applications*. Paris, France: Academic Press. doi:10.1007/BFb0053944

Camara, D., & Loureiro, A. (2001). GPS/ant-like routing algorithm in ad hoc networks. Telecommunication Systems, 18, 85-100.

Chen, T. W., & Gerla, M. (1998). Global state routing: A New routing scheme for ad-hoc wireless networks. In *Proc. IEEE ICC'98*. IEEE. Retrieved from http://www.ics.uci.edu/~atm/adhoc/paper-collection/gerla-gsr-icc98.pdf

Chiang, C. C. (1997). Routing in clustered multihop, mobile wireless networks with fading channel. In *Proc. IEEE SICON'97* (pp. 192-211). IEEE.

DiCaro, G., & Dorigo, M. (1998). AntNet: Distributed stigmergetic control for communication networks. *Journal of Artificial Intelligence Research*, *9*, 317–365.

Gerla, M., Pei, G., & Lee, S. J. (1999). *Wireless, mobile ad-hoc network routing*. Paper presented at IEEE/ACM FOCUS'99, New Brunswick, NJ. Retrieved from www.cs.ucla.edu/NRL/wireless/PAPER/focus99.pdf

Guerin, S. (1997). *Optimisation multi-agents en environment dynamique: Application au routage dans les reseaux de telecommunications.* (DEA Dissertation). University of Rennes I, France.

Gunes, M., Sorges, U., & Bouazizi, I. (2002). ARA - The ant colony based routing algorithm for manets. In *Proc. ICPP Workshop on Ad Hoc Networks IWAHN* (pp. 79-85). Academic Press. doi:10.1109/ICPPW.2002.1039715

Heissenbüttel, M., & Braun, T. (2003). Ants-based routing in large scale mobile ad-hoc networks. In *Proceedings of Kommunikation in Verteilten Systemen KiVS03.* Leipzig, Germany: Academic Press.

Islam, M. T., Thulasiraman, P., & Thulasiram, R. K. (April 2003). A parallel ant colony optimization algorithm for all-pair routing in MANETs. In *Proc. IEEE Int. Parallel and Distributed Processing Symposium IPDPS.* Nice, France: IEEE. doi:10.1109/IPDPS.2003.1213470

Iwata, A., Chiang, C. C., Pei, G., Gerla, M., & Chen, T. W. (1999). Scalable routing strategies for ad hoc wireless networks. IEEE Journal on Selected Areas in Communications. Retrieved from http://www.cs.ucla.edu/nrl/wireless/paper/jsac99.ps.gz

Jiang, M., Li, J., & Tay, Y. C. (1999). Cluster based routing protocol. IETF Draft. Retrieved from http://www.ietf.org/internet-drafts/draft-ietf-manet-cbrp-spec-01.txt

Johnson, D. B., & Maltz, A. (1999). The dynamic source routing protocol for mobile ad hoc networks. IETF Draft. Retrieved from http://www.ietf.org/internet-drafts/draft-ietf-manet-dsr-03.txt

Marwaha, S., & Tham, C. K. (2002). A novel routing protocol using mobile agents and reactive route discovery for ad hoc wireless networks. In *Proc. IEEE ICON. IEEE.* doi:10.1109/ICON.2002.1033329

Marwaha, S., Tham, C. K., & Srinivasan, D. (2002). Mobile agent based routing protocol for mobile ad hoc networks. In *Proc. IEEE GLOBECOM. IEEE.* doi:10.1109/GLOCOM.2002.1188062

Matsuo, H., & Mori, K. (2001). Accelerated ants routing in dynamic networks. In *Proceedings of 2nd Int. Conf. Software Engineering, Artificial Intelligence, Networking & Parallel Distributed Computing.* Nagoya, Japan: Academic Press.

Murthy, S., & Garcia-Luna-Aceves, J. J. (1996). *An efficient routing protocol for wireless networks. ACM Mobile Networks and Applications Journal.*

Park, V. D., & Corson, M. S. (1997). *A highly adaptive distributed routing algorithm for mobile wireless networks.* IEEE Infocom. doi:10.1109/INFCOM.1997.631180

Perkins, C., & Royer, E. M. (1999). Ad hoc on demand distance vector routing. In *Proceedings of the 2nd IEEE Workshop on Mobile Computing Systems and Applications* (pp. 90-100). IEEE. Retrieved from www.beta.ece.ucsb.edu/~eroyer/txt/aodv.ps

Perkins, C. E., & Bhagwat, P. (1994). *Highly dynamic destination-sequenced distance-vector routing (DSDV) for mobile computers.* Comp. Comm. Rev. doi:10.1145/190314.190336

Rajagopalan, S., Jaikaeo, C. & Shen, C.C. (2003). *Unicast routing for mobile ad hoc networks with swarm intelligence* (Technical Report #2003-07). University of Delaware.

Roth, M., & Wicker, S. (2003). Termite: Emergent ad-hoc networking. In *Proceedings of the 2nd Mediterranean Workshop on Ad-Hoc Net- works* (Med-Hoc-Net'2003). Mahdia, Tunisia: Academic Press.

Schoonderwoerd, R., Holland, O. E., & Bruten, J. L. (1997). Ant-like agents for load balancing in telecommunication networks. In *Proc. First ACM Int. Conf. on Autonomous Agents* (pp. 209-216). ACM. doi:10.1145/267658.267718

Stojmenovic, M. (2005). Swarm intelligence for routing in ad hoc wireless networks. In Security and routing in wireless networks (pp. 167-188). Nova Science Publishers.

Subramaniam, D., Druschel, P., & Chen, J. (1997). Ants and reinforcement learning: A case study in routing in dynamic networks. In *Proc. IEEE MILCOM*. Atlantic City, NJ: IEEE.

Techpedia Three Tier Architecture. (n.d.). Retrieved from http://www.techopedia.com/definition/24649/three-tier-architecture

Toh, C. K. (1996). A novel distributed routing protocol to support Ad hoc mobile computing. In *Proc. 1996 IEEE 15th Annual Int'l. Phoenix Conf* (pp. 480–486). Comp. and Comm. Retrieved from http://www.ics.uci.edu/~atm/adhoc/paper-collection/toh-distributed-routing-ipccc96.pdf

White, T., & Pagurek, B. (1998). Towards multi-swarm problem solving in networks. In *Proc. Third Int. Conf. Multi-Agent Systems ICMAS* (pp. 333-340). ICMAS. doi:10.1109/ICMAS.1998.699217

Zhang, Y., Agarwal, P., Bhatnagar, V., Balochian, S., & Yan, J. (2013). Swarm intelligence and its applications. *The Scientific World Journal*. doi:10.1155/2013/528069

KEY TERMS AND DEFINITIONS

3-Tier Architecture: A 3-tier architecture is an n tier architecture addressing proper separation of concern. Presentation tier hosts the user interfaces, middle tier hosts the application business logic and the data tier hosts the application database.

Adaptive Movement: Adaptive movement is the adjustable movement of the mobile nodes in a network according to the situations.

MANET: MANET or Mobile Ad Hoc Network is a temporary self-configuring, infrastructure-less network of mobile heterogeneous devices connected with wireless links.

Software Deployment Architecture: Software deployment architecture describes the structure of the physical systems on which the different components of an application software is installed. It also describes the connectivity between the physical systems.

Software Deployment: Software deployment deals with where and how different components of an application software is installed.

Swarm Intelligence: Swarm intelligence is the collective behavior of decentralized, self-organized natural or artificial systems.

Topology Management: Topology management is managing and / or organizing the physical arrangement of the mobile nodes in a network.

Wireless LAN: Wireless LAN or Wireless Local Area Network refers to a LAN where the nodes are connected through wireless links.

Chapter 12
Swarm Intelligence–Based Optimization for PHEV Charging Stations

Imran Rahman
Universiti Teknologi Petronas, Malaysia

Balbir Singh Mahinder Singh
Universiti Teknologi Petronas, Malaysia

Pandian Vasant
Universiti Teknologi Petronas, Malaysia

M. Abdullah-Al-Wadud
King Saud University, Saudi Arabia

ABSTRACT

In this chapter, Gravitational Search Algorithm (GSA) and Particle Swarm Optimization (PSO) technique were applied for intelligent allocation of energy to the Plug-in Hybrid Electric Vehicles (PHEVs). Considering constraints such as energy price, remaining battery capacity, and remaining charging time, they optimized the State-of-Charge (SoC), a key performance indicator in hybrid electric vehicle for the betterment of charging infrastructure. Simulation results obtained for maximizing the highly non-linear objective function evaluates the performance of both techniques in terms of global best fitness and computation time.

INTRODUCTION

Recent researches on green technologies for transportation sector are gaining popularity among the research communities from different areas. In this wake, Plug-in hybrid electric vehicles (PHEVs) have great future because of their charge storage system and charging facilities from traditional grid system. Several researchers have proved that a great amount of reductions in greenhouse gas emissions and the increasing dependence on oil could be accomplished by electrification of transport sector (Caramanis & Foster, 2009). Future transportation sector will depend much on the advancement of this emerging field of vehicle optimization. Indeed, the adoption of hybrid electric vehicles (HEVs) has brought significant market success over the past decade. Vehicles can be classified into three groups: internal combustion engine vehicles (ICEV), hybrid electric vehicles (HEV) and all- electric vehicles (AEV) (Tie & Tan, 2013). Plug-in hybrid electric vehicles (PHEVs) which is very recently introduced promise to boost up the

DOI: 10.4018/978-1-4666-8291-7.ch012

overall fuel efficiency by holding a higher capacity battery system, which can be directly charged from conventional power grid system, that helps the vehicles to operate continuously in "all-electric-range" (AER). All-electric vehicles or AEVs is a kind of transport which use electric power as only sources to run the system. Plug-in hybrid electric vehicles with a connection to the smart grid can own all of these strategies. Hence, the widely extended adoption of PHEVs might play a significant role in the alternative energy integration into traditional grid systems (Lund & Kempton, 2008). There is a need of efficient mechanisms and algorithms for smart grid technologies in order to solve highly diverse problems like energy management, cost reduction, efficient charging station etc. with different objectives and system constraints (Hota, Juvvanapudi, & Bajpai, 2014).

According to a statistics of Electric Power Research Institute (EPRI), about 62% of the entire United States (US) vehicle will comprise of PHEVs within the year 2050 (Soares et al., 2013). Moreover, there is an increasing demand to implement this technology on the electric grid system. Large numbers of PHEVs have the capability to make threats to the stability of the power system. For example, in order to avoid disturbance when several thousand PHEVs are introduced into the system over a small period of time, the load on the power grid will need to be managed very carefully. One of the main targets is to facilitate the proper communication between the power grid and the PHEV. For the maximization of customer contentment and minimization of burdens on the grid, a complicated control appliance will need to be addressed in order to govern multiple battery loads from a numbers of PHEVs properly (Su & Chow, 2012a). The total demand pattern will also have an important impact on the electricity production due to differences in the needs of the PHEVs parked in the deck at certain time (Su & Chow, 2011). Proper management can ensure strain minimization of the grid and enhance the transmission and generation of electric power supply. The control of PHEV charging depending on the locations can be classified into two groups; household charging and public charging. The proposed optimization focuses on the public charging station for plug-in vehicles because most of PHEV charging is expected to take place in public charging location (Su & Chow, 2012). Wide penetration of PHEVs in the market depends on a well-organized charging infrastructure. The power demand from this new load will put extra stress on the traditional power grid (Morrow, Karner, & Francfort, 2008). As a result, a good number of PHEV charging stations with suitable facilities are essential to be built for recharging electric vehicles, for this some strategies have been proposed by the researchers (Mayfield, Jul. 2012). Charging stations are needed to be built at workplaces, markets/shopping malls and home. Boyle (2007) proposed the necessity of building new smart charging station with effective communication among utilities along with sub-station control infrastructure in view of grid stability and proper energy utilization. Furthermore, sizeable energy storage, cost minimization; Quality of Services (QoS) and intelligent charging station for optimal power are underway (Hess et al., 2012). In this wake, numerous techniques and methods were proposed for deployment of PHEV charging stations (Z. Li, Sahinoglu, Tao, & Teo, 2010).

One of the main targets is to facilitate the proper interaction between the power grid and the PHEV. For the maximization of customer satisfaction and minimization of burdens on the grid, a complicated control mechanism will need to be addressed in order to govern multiple battery loads from a numbers of PHEVs appropriately (Su & Chow, 2012b). Charging infrastructures are essential in order to facilitate the large-scale penetration of PHEVs. Different computational intelligence-based methods have been used by some researchers for charging station optimization of PHEV. Most of them applied traditional methods which are needed to be improved furthermore.

Swarm intelligence came from the mimic of the living colony such as ant, bird, and fish in nature, which shows unparalleled excellence in swarm than in single in food seeking or nest building. Drawing inspiration from this, researches design many algorithms simulating colony living, such as ant colony algorithm, particle swarm optimization algorithm, artificial bee colony algorithm, and gravitational search algorithm, which shows excellent performance in dealing with complex optimization problems (Jia-zhao, C., Yu-xiang, Z., & Yin-sheng, L., 2012). The intrinsic characteristics of all the population-based meta-heuristic algorithms like Particle swarm optimization (PSO) and Gravitational search algorithm (GSA) are to maintain a good compromise between exploration and exploitation in order to solve the complex optimization problems (Rashedi, E., Nezamabadi-Pour, 2009).

PSO is based on two fundamental disciplines: social science and computer science. In addition, PSO uses the swarm intelligence concept, which is the property of a system, whereby the collective behaviors of unsophisticated agents that are interacting locally with their environment create coherent global functional patterns. PSO algorithm has been successfully used for solving many problems related to power systems (Venayagamoorthy, G. K., Mohagheghi,2008) such as voltage security, optimal power flow, power system operation and planning, dynamic security, power quality, unit commitment, reactive power control, capacitor placement and optimizing controller parameters.

Moreover, GSA is based on the law of gravity and mass interactions where the searcher agents are a collection of masses which interact with each other based on the Newtonian gravity and the laws of motion (Rashedi, E., Nezamabadi-Pour, 2009). This method has also been used by the researchers for post-outage bus voltage magnitude calculations, solving economic dispatch with valve-point effects, optimal sizing and suitable placement for distributed generation (DG) in distribution system, Solving thermal unit commitment (UC) problem and finding out optimal solution for optimal power flow (OPF) problem in a power system (N. M., Puteh, M., & Mahmood, M. R., 2013).

The performance of PHEV depends upon proper utilization of electric power which is solely affected by the battery state-of-charge (SoC). In Plug-in hybrid electric vehicles (PHEVs), a key parameter is the state-of-charge (SoC) of the battery as it is a measure of the amount of electrical energy stored in it. It is analogous to fuel gauge on a conventional internal combustion (IC) car (Chiasson, J., & Vairamohan, B., 2005). State-of-charge determination becomes an increasingly vital issue in all the areas that include a battery. Previous operation policies made use of voltage limits only to guard the battery against deep discharge and overcharge. Currently, battery operation is changing to what could rather be called battery management than simply protection. For this improved battery control, the battery SoC is a key factor indeed (Piller, Perrin, & Jossen, 2001).

A charging station is one way that the operator of an electrical power grid can adapt energy production to energy consumption, both of which can vary randomly over time. Basically, PHEVs in a charging station are charged during times when production exceeds consumption and are discharged at times when consumption exceeds production (S. Li, Bao, Fu, & Zheng, 2014). It is expected that mostly recharging will occur at home even if there is a sufficient public charging station network. It does not necessarily mean that there is no or lower need of public charging stations because many residences do not have adequate facilities for recharging EVs (Ul-Haq, Buccella, Cecati, & Khalid, 2013). There is a need of in-depth study on maximization of average SoC in order to facilitate intelligent energy allocation for PHEVs in a charging station.

The purpose of this chapter is to optimize state-of-charge with respect to total cost, charging time, present SoC. Two swarm intelligence-based methods, Particle swarm optimization (PSO) and Gravitational search algorithm (GSA) were applied for solving the optimization problem.

BACKGROUND

The vehicular network recently accounts for around 25% of CO_2 emissions and over 55% of oil consumption around the world. Carbon dioxide is the primary greenhouse gas emitted through human activities like combustion of fossil fuels (coal, natural gas, and oil) for energy and transportation. Several researchers have proved that a great amount of reductions in greenhouse gas emissions and the increasing dependence on oil could be accomplished by electrification of transport sector (Holtz-Eakin & Selden, 1995). Charging of PHEV/EV influences many parameters such as power rating, time of charging and location, cost, charging equipment, and effect on the power grid. Issues like charging time, distribution, standardization of demand policies for charging stations and proper regulatory procedures are needed to be addressed for the successful deployment of Electric vehicle charging station (Z. Li et al., 2010).

Most of the electric vehicles charging generally occur at charging area in one's house where the vehicle can be connected to a garage outlet for Slow charging (Level-1). Level-2 charging is normally known as the primary technique for battery charging for both public and private utilities and needs an outlet of 240V. Future technologies focus on primary; fast charging and can be executed in most cases (Anegawa, 2009; Botsford & Szczepanek, 2009; Rawson & Kateley, 1999). Usually for Level-1 and 2 charging uses single-phase systems. Level-3(DC fast charging) is made for commercial and public applications and would operate just like a normal filling station. Off-board three-phase solutions are applied to Level-3 chargers and high power. Level-2 or 3 chargers installed in parking lots, shopping centers, hotels, theaters, restaurants, etc. are expected to use by the general public stations (Aggeler, Canales, Coccia, Butcher, & Apeldoorn, 2010).

Opportunity Charging (Level-1 Charging)

The slowest of all available methods is Level-1 charging. In the United States, Level-1 charging uses a standard 120V/15A single-phase outlet which is grounded, such as NEMA 5-15R. The connection may use a standard J1772 connector into the electric vehicle ac port. No additional infrastructure is required for home or business sites. At night, low off-peak rates for charging are likely to be available. The total cost of a residential Level-1 charging infrastructure has been estimated around $500 - $880 (De Sousa, Silvestre, & Bouchez, 2010; Morrow, Karner, & Francfort, 2008).

Primary Charging (Level-2 Charging)

Level-2 charging is the basic method for dedicated public and private facilities. At present, Level-2 equipment performs charging through 208V or 240V (at up to 80A, 19.2 kW). It may require dedicated equipment and a connection installation for home or public charging (Rawson & Kateley, 1999), although vehicles such as the Tesla have the power electronics on board. Most homes have 240 V service available, and Level-2 devices can charge a typical EV battery overnight. Owners seem likely to prefer Level-2 technology owing to its faster charging time and standardized vehicle-to-charger connection. A separate billing meter is typical. The cost of residential Level-2 infrastructure installation is around $2,150. For example, the Tesla Roadster charging system has imposed additional cost of $3,000 (Motors, 2009).

Fast Charging (Level-3 Charging)

Level-3 (DC fast charging) can be installed in highways and urban refueling points which is similar to petrol stations. It generally operates with a 480 V or higher three phase circuit and needs an off-board charger to provide regulated ac-dc conversion. Level-3 charging is very rear in the residential premises. Standards for dc plugs and hardware are in progress. CHAdeMO-a Japanese protocol is gaining world-wide recognition (Yilmaz & Krein, 2012). Installation cost is a vital issue. Level-3 charging infrastructure costs between $30,000 and $160,000 have been reported. An efficient energy management system is proposed (Dusmez, Cook, & Khaligh, 2011) which notably reduce total time of PHEVs charging in fast charging infrastructure by the use of additional super capacitors and flywheel. The simulations for two batteries between 10kWh and 15kWh show that the charging time on average is 15 min to charge from a minimum SOC 20% to maximum 95% in the latest configuration. Finally, Figure 1 summarizes the charging methods.

Charging Infrastructures

Maintenance of the charging infrastructures is another cost factor (Brown, Mikulin, Rhazi, Seel, & Zimring, 2010). There are increasing numbers of literatures on various aspects of the EV charging allocation strategies which includes the maintenance and scheduling of various chargers (Caramanis & Foster, 2009; Gan, Topcu, & Low, 2011; Kefayati & Caramanis, 2010; Ma, Callaway, & Hiskens, 2010; Pang, Dutta, Kim, Kezunovic, & Damnjanovic, 2010; Sojoudi & Low, 2011). Most of the works focus specially on residential charging schemes. Kulshrestha, Wang, Chow, and Lukic (2009) conducted studies based on simulation in energy management strategy (EMS) for PHEV/EV charging at parking areas where meta-heuristic algorithms for the purpose of efficient scheduling are applied. The electric vehicle charging for public garages is also considered (Su & Chow, 2011) where the objective is to maximize the throughput of service whereas the total cost of energy is not considered in the optimization. Subramanian et al. (2012) suggested a scheduling optimization using a combination of alternative energy and energy from the traditional grid.

The next section provides an overview of the charging infrastructure requirements for PHEVs/EVs in single-family household, multi-family household and commercial situations.

Figure 1. Charging infrastructure for PHEVs

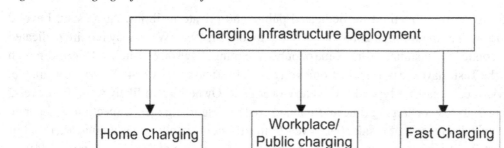

These scenarios include the following:

- Household garage charging.
- Apartment complex charging.
- Commercial complex charging.
- Charging from renewable energy sources.

Household Garage Charging

In order to install electric vehicle charging supply in a household garage, dedicated branch circuit from an existing house distribution panel to a convenience outlet or to a EVSE (Electric Vehicle Supply Equipment) is necessary (Morrow et al., 2008).

Apartment Complex Charging

Installation of the EV/PHEV charging supply in an apartment complex typically consists of installing new dedicated branch circuits from the central meter distribution panel to either a convenience outlet or to an EVSE (Morrow et al., 2008).

Commercial Complex Charging

Installation of the electric vehicle charging supply in a commercial complex parking lot typically consists of installing new dedicated branch circuits from the central meter distribution panel to an EVSE for Level-2 charging. Large parking lots provide an opportunity to control a fleet of PHEVs in an intelligent manner.

Effective use of PHEVs in parking areas to prevent the transmission lines getting overloaded and to act as shock observers when the wind power changes drastically is explored by Venayagamoorthy and Mitra (2011). A fuzzy logic controller was proposed (Mitra & Venayagamoorthy, 2010) which takes the total state of charge of a parking lot, instantaneous demand and wind power generated as inputs and gives control signals for charging/discharging of the PHEVs. Simulations on a12 bus system model show that when PHEVs charge and discharge according to the control signal, overloading of the transmission lines during high wind speeds can be prevented and the wind power supply fluctuations to the grid can be minimized.

Charging from Renewable Energy Sources

The ability of PHEVs/EVs to assist the integration of renewable energy sources into the existing power grid is potentially the most transformative impact on the electricity system. Deployment of large-scale photovoltaic (PV) charging equipment in a parking lot is explained by Neumann, Schär, and Baumgartner (2012). PV parking lot charging and different business models to charge PHEVs/EVs with solar energy are also studied by Letendre (2009). Economics and environmental impacts of PV based workplace charging station has also been discussed (Birnie, 2009; Tulpule, Marano, Yurkovich, & Rizzoni, 2013). The analysis shows the technical feasibility of a PV powered workplace parking lot with benefits to the owner of the vehicle as compared to facilities of household charging. Authors conclude that the owner will get the return of establishment and maintenance cost and profit within the lifespan of the photovoltaic panels. According to Birnie (2009), introducing a solar collector into a parking shade would result in a much more rapid pay-back-period, encouraging widespread installation of solar capacity. Zhang, Tezuka, Ishihara, and Mclellan (2012) explained smart control strategies for the integration of both EVs and PV together with the present electricity systems. Co-benefits of introducing large penetration of PHEVs and photovoltaic mechanisms have been analyzed by Denholm, Kuss, and Margolis (2013). The study came to a conclusion that PV has the capability of acting like a potential source of mid-day generation capacity for PHEVs as well as provide a dispatch able load during low demand periods (generally in the spring season). For this wake, a 2.1 kW PV charging station combined with the utility at Santa Monica is explained (Ingersoll & Perkins, 1996). Zhu, Yu, Ning, and Tang (2012) presented optimal charging control policy using stochastic semi-Markov decision (SMDP) process and later average reward was calculated using vehicle admission probability.

Smart grid has brought new opportunities and challenges for the development of electric vehicle Infrastructure facilities like charging station systems and parking lots. Recent advancement in renewable energy sector opens the option for a green infrastructure system which will minimize the burden of PHEVs in tradition grid-dependent charging stations.

Energy allocation to PHEV charging station is subjected to various constraints such as charging time, SoC and price which will be highlighted in the problem formulation section. Different constraints make the entire search space limited to a particular suitable region. So, powerful optimization algorithms should be implemented in order to achieve high quality solutions with a stable convergence rate.

MAIN FOCUS OF THE CHAPTER

Problem Statement

One of the important constraints for accurate charging is State-of-Charge (SoC). Charging algorithm can precisely be managed by the precise state of charge evaluation (Shafiei & Williamson, 2010). An approximate graph of a typical Lithium-ion cell voltage versus SoC is shown in Figure 2 indicates that the slope of the curve below 20% and above 90% is high enough to result in a significant voltage difference to be depended on by measurement circuits and charge balancing control. There is a need of in-depth study on maximization of average SoC in order to facilitate intelligent energy allocation for PHEVs in a charging station.

The idea behind smart charging is to charge the vehicle when it is most favourable, which could be when electricity price, demand is lowest, when there is excess capacity (Su & Chow, 2012a). When a vehicle is plugged in into a smart charging station a request for energy demand is sent to Substation Control Center (SCC), which decides based on the available energy from utility and either accepts the request or reject it. Performance of this kind of load management is measured in terms of delay, delivery ration and jitter. As a matter of fact EVs may be charged at any time of a day depending on requirement to top their batteries even during peak demand hours. Increasing load on the grid during peak hours may require extra power generation through any source which may increase the cost and greenhouse gases emission (Ul-Haq, Buccella, Cecati, & Khalid, 2013).

Suppose, there is a charging station with the capacity of total power P. Total N numbers of PHEVs need to be served in a day (24 hours). The proposed system should allow PHEVs to leave the charging

Figure 2. Li-ion cell voltage vs. State-of-Charge

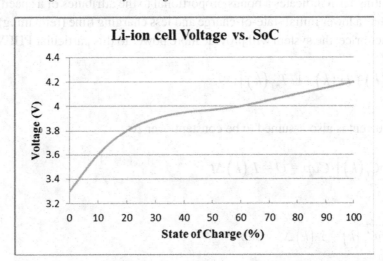

station before their expected leaving time for making the system more effective. It is worth to mention that, each PHEV is regarded to be plugged-in to the charging station once. The main aim is to allocate power intelligently for each PHEV coming to the charging station. The State-of-Charge is the main parameter which needs to be maximized in order to allocate power efficiently. For this, the objective function considered in this chapter is the maximization of average SoC and thus allocate energy for PHEVs at the next time step. The constraints considered are: charging time, present SoC and price of the energy (Su & Chow, 2012b).

The objective function is defined as:

$$\text{üüü } J\left(k\right) \quad \sum_i w_i\left(k\right) SoC_i\left(k+\right) \tag{1}$$

$$w_i\left(k\right) = f\left(C_{r,i}\left(k\right),\ T_{r,i}\left(k\right), D_i\left(k\right)\right) \tag{2}$$

$$\text{üüüü}\left(\ \right) = \left(1-\quad _i\left(\ \right)\right)\cdot\ _i \tag{3}$$

where $C_{r,i}(k)$ is the battery capacity (remaining) needed to be filled for i no. of PHEV at time step k; C_i is the battery capacity (rated) of the i no. of PHEV; remaining time for charging a particular PHEV at time step k is expressed as $T_{r,i}(k)$; the price difference between the real-time energy price and the price that a specific customer at the i no. of PHEV charger is willing to pay at time step k is presented by $D_i(k)$; $w_i(k)$ is the charging weighting term of the i no. of PHEV at time step k (a function of charging time, present SoC and price of the energy); $SoC_i(k+1)$ is the state of charge of the i no. of PHEV at time step $k+1$.

Here, the weighting term indicates a bonus proportional to the attributes of a specific PHEV. For example, if a PHEV has a lower initial state-of-charge and less charging time (remaining), but the driver is eager to pay a higher price, the system will provide more power to this particular PHEV battery charger:

$$w_i(k) \alpha \left[Cap_{r,i}(k) + D_i(k) + 1/T_{r,i}(k) \right] \tag{4}$$

The charging current is also assumed to be constant over Δt.

$$\left[SoC_i(k+1) - SoC_i(k) \right] \cdot Cap_i = Q_i = I_i(k) \Delta t \tag{5}$$

$$SoC_i(k+1) = SoC_i(k) + I_i(k) \Delta t / Cap_i \tag{6}$$

where the sample time Δt is defined by the charging station operators, and $I_i(k)$ is the charging current over Δt.

The battery model is regarded as a capacitor circuit, where C_i is the capacitance of battery (Farad). The model is defined as

$$C_i \cdot \frac{dV_i}{dt} = I_i \tag{7}$$

Therefore, over a small time interval, one can assume the change of voltage to be linear,

$$C_i \cdot \left[V_i(k+1) - V_i(k) \right] / \Delta t = I_i \tag{8}$$

$$\text{(9)}$$

As the decision variable used here is the allocated power to the PHEVs, by replacing $I_i(k)$ with $P_i(k)$ the objective function finally becomes:

$$J(k) = \sum w_i \cdot \left[SoC_i(k) + \frac{2P_i(k)\Delta t}{0.5 C_i \cdot \left[\sqrt{\frac{2P_i(k)\Delta t}{C_i} + V^2_i(k)} + V_i(k) \right]} \right] \tag{10}$$

Possible real-world constraints could include the charging rate (i.e., slow, medium, and fast), the time that the PHEV is connected to the grid, the desired departure state-of-charge, the maximum electricity price that a user is willing to pay, certain battery requirements etc. Furthermore, the available communication bandwidth could limit sampling time, which would have effects on the processing ability of the vehicle.

Power obtained from the utility ($P_{utility}$) and the maximum power ($P_{i,max}$) absorbed by a specific PHEV are the primary energy constraints being considered in this chapter. The overall charging efficiency of a particular charging station is described by η. From the system point of view, charging efficiency is supposed to be constant at any given time step. Maximum battery SoC limit for the i no. of PHEV is $SoC_{i,max}$. When SoC_i reaches the values close to $SoC_{i,max}$, the i no. of battery charger shifts to a standby mode. The state of charge ramp rate is confined within limits by the constraint ΔSoC_{max}. The overall control system is changed the state when i) system utility data updates; ii) a new PHEV is plugged-in; iii) time period Δt has periodically passed.

Table 1 shows all the objective function parameters that were tuned for performing the optimization. There are total three (03) kinds of parameter: fixed, variables and constraints. Total charging time is fixed to 20 minutes and charging station efficiency assumed to be 0.9. The values are retrieved from various literatures (Hota, Juvvanapudi, & Bajpai, 2014; Su, 2012; Wencong & Mo-Yuen, 2011). Moreover, State-of-Charge is in the range of 0.2 to 0.8 (Chang, 2013).

Table 1. Parameter settings of the objective function

Parameter	Values
Fixed Parameters	Maximum power, $P_{i,max}$ = 6.7 kWh
	Charging station efficiency, η = 0.9
	Total charging time, Δt = 20 Minute
	Power allocation to each PHEV: 30 W
Variables	$0.2 \leq$ State-of-Charge (SoC) ≤ 0.8
	Waiting time ≤ 30 Minutes (1800 Seconds)
	16 kWh $\leq$ Battery Capacity (C_i) ≤ 40 kWh
Constraints	$$\sum_i P_i(k) \leq P_{utility}(k) \times \eta$$
	$$0 \leq P_i(k) \leq P_{i,max}(k)$$
	$$0 \leq \ddot{u}\ddot{u}\ddot{u}_i(\ ) \leq \quad_{i,max}$$
	$$0 \leq SoC_i(k+1) - SoC_i(k) \leq \Delta SoC_{max}$$

PROPOSED METHODS

Particle Swarm Optimization

PSO is an evolutionary computation technique which is proposed by Eberhart and Yuhui (2001). The PSO is inspired from social behavior of bird flocking. It uses a number of particles (candidate solutions) which fly around in the search space to find best solution. Meanwhile, they all look at the best particle (best solution) in their paths. In other words, particles consider their own best solutions as well as the best solution has found so far.

A PSO system begins with a primary initial population of random individuals, signifies solutions of problem, to which are allocated random velocities. Each particle in PSO should consider the current position, the current velocity, the distance to *pbest*, and the distance to *gbest* to modify its position. PSO is an iterative stochastic optimization method. It simulates the behavior of flocks of birds or schools of fish. In PSO, each solution is a "bird" (or, more generally, a "particle") in the search space. All of the particles have (1) fitness values (which are evaluated by the fitness function to be optimized) and (2) velocities (which direct the flying of the particles). The particles fly through the search space by following the current optimum particles. At each iteration, each of the particles is updated by following the individual and group bests. Gradually, the particles tend toward the global "near-optima" region.

PSO was mathematically modeled as followed as:

$$V_i^{t+1} = wv_i^t + c_1. \; rand \; .\left(pbest_i - x_i^t\right) + c_2.rand.\left(gbest - x_i^t\right) \tag{11}$$

$$x_i^{t+1} = x_i^t + V_i^{t+1} \tag{12}$$

where v_i^t is the velocity of particle i at iteration, w is a weighting function usually used as follows

$$\omega = \omega_{max} - \frac{w_{max} - \omega_{min}}{Itre_{max}} \; Itre \tag{13}$$

Appropriate values for ω_{min} and ω_{max} are 0.4 and 0.9. Appropriate value ranges for c_1 and c_2 are 1 to 2, but 2 is most appropriate in many cases. rand is a random number between 0 and 1, x_i^t is the current position of particle i at iteration t, $pbest_i$ is the *pbest* of agent i at iteration t and *gbest* is the best solution so far. The parameter settings for PSO are demonstrated in Table 2. Total size of the swarm is 100 and PSO inertia is taken as 0.9. PSO is also fairly immune to the size and non-linear nature of the objective function being considered. The algorithm does not converge with less iterations, while more iterations increase computation complexity, so the maximum iterations are 100. Moreover, from the previous literature experiences, maximum 100 iterations are suitable for the PSO-based optimization.

The main advantage of PSO is its simplicity, while being capable of delivering accurate results consistently. It is fast and also very flexible, being applicable to a wide range of problems, with limited computational requirements (Eberhart & Yuhui, 2001). For these reasons, the present work focuses on

Table 2. PSO parameter settings

Parameters	Values
Size of the swarm	100
Maximum no. of steps	100
PSO parameter,c1	1.4
PSO parameter,c2	1.4
PSO inertia (w)	0.9
Maximum iteration	100
Number of runs	50

meta-heuristics optimization approaches, namely PSO applied in order to optimize the State-of-Charge for Charging Plug-in Hybrid Electric Vehicles.

Figure 3 shows the Structural diagram for PSO algorithm. The system initially has a population of random selective solutions. Each potential solution is called a particle. Each particle is given a random velocity and is flown through the problem space. The particles have memory and each particle keeps track of its previous best position (called the *pbest*) and its corresponding fitness. There exist a number of *pbest* for the respective particles in the swarm and the particle with greatest fitness is called the global best (*gbest*) of the swarm. The basic concept of the PSO technique lies in accelerating each particle towards its *pbest* and *gbest* locations, with a random weighted acceleration at each time step (Ganesan, Vasant, & Elamvazuthy, 2012).

Gravitational Search Algorithm

GSA is an optimization method which has been introduced by Rashedi et al. in the year of 2009. In GSA, the specifications of each mass (or agent) are total four, which is mass (inertial), position, mass (active gravitational) and mass (passive gravitational). The position of the mass presents a solution of a particular problem, and masses (gravitational and inertial) are obtained by using a fitness function. GSA can be considered as a collection of agents (candidate solutions), whose masses are proportional to their value of fitness function. During generations, all masses attract each other by the gravity forces between them. A heavier mass has the bigger attraction force. Therefore the heavier masses which are probably close to the global optimum attract the other masses proportional to their distances.

Law of Gravity: The law states that particles attract each other and the force of gravitation between two particles is directly proportional to the product of their masses and inversely proportional to the distance between them.

Law of Motion: The law states that the present velocity of any mass is the summation of the fraction of its previous velocity and the velocity variance. Variation in the velocity or acceleration of any mass is equal to the force acted on the system divided by inertia mass.

The gravitational force is expressed as follows:

$$F_{ij}^d(t) = G(t) \frac{M_{pi}(t) \times M_{aj}(t)}{R_{ij}(t) + \varepsilon} \left(x_j^d(t) - x_i^d(t) \right) \tag{14}$$

Figure 3. Structural diagram of Particle Swarm Optimization

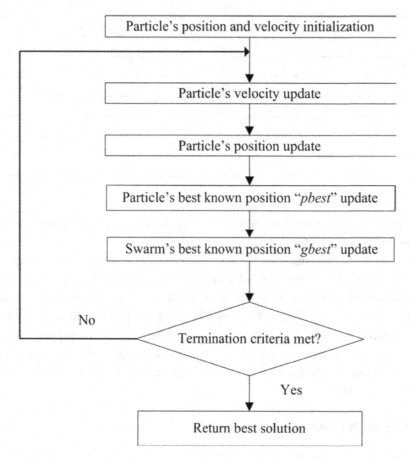

where M_{aj} is the active gravitational mass related to agent j, M_{pi} is the passive gravitational mass related to agent i, G(t) is gravitational constant at time t, ε is a small constant and $R_{ij}(t)$ is the Euclidian distance between two agents i and j. The G(t) is calculated as-

$$G(t) = G_0 \times \exp(-\alpha.iter / \max iter) \tag{15}$$

where α and G_0 are descending coefficient and primary value respectively, current iteration and maximum number of iterations are expressed as iter and maxiter. In a problem space with the dimension d, the overall force acting on agent i is estimated as following equation:

$$F_i^d(t) = \sum_{j=1, j \neq i}^{N} rand_j F_{ij}^d(t) \tag{16}$$

where $rand_j$ is a random number with interval [0, 1]. From law of motion we know that, an agent's acceleration is directly proportional to the resultant force and inverse of its mass, so the acceleration of all agents should be calculated as follow:

$$ac_i^d\left(t\right) = \frac{F_i^d\left(t\right)}{M_{ii}\left(t\right)} \tag{17}$$

where t a specific is time and M_{ii} is the mass of the object i. The velocity and position of agents are calculated as follow:

$$vel_i^d\left(t+1\right) = rand_i.vel_i^d\left(t\right) + ac_i^d\left(t\right) \tag{18}$$

$$x_i^d\left(t+1\right) = x_i^d\left(t\right) + vel_i^d\left(t+1\right) \tag{19}$$

where $rand_i$ is a random number with interval [0, 1].

Gravitational and inertia masses are simply calculated by the fitness evaluation. A heavier mass means a more efficient agent. This means that better agents have higher attractions and walk more slowly. Assuming the equality of the gravitational and inertia mass, the values of masses are calculated using the map of fitness. We update the gravitational and inertial masses by the following equations:

$$M_{ai} = M_{pi} = M_{ii} = M_i, i = 1, 2, \ldots, N \tag{20}$$

In Gravitational search algorithm, all agents are initialized first with random values. Each of the agents is a candidate solution. After initialization, velocities for all agents are defined using (18). Moreover, the gravitational constant, overall forces, and accelerations are determined by equations (15), (16) and (17) respectively. The positions of agents are calculated using (19). At the end, GSA will be terminated by meeting the stopping criterion of maximum 100 iterations. The parameter settings for GSA are demonstrated in Table 3. The GSA parameters were selected: Primary parameter, $G_0 = 100$, Acceleration coefficient, $\alpha = 20$ and No. of mass agents=100. Since each agent could observe the performance of the others, the gravitational force is an information-transferring tool.

Table 3. GSA parameter settings

Parameters	Values
Primary parameter, G_0	100
No. of mass agents, n	100
Acceleration coefficient, α	20
Constant parameter	.01
Power of 'R'	1
Maximum iteration	100
Number of runs	50

The Algorithm Outline

The outline of gravitational search algorithm is given in Algorithm 1.

Moreover, the step involves in optimization using GSA is shown Figure 4. Here, we assume that the gravitational and the inertia masses are the same. However, for some applications different values for them can be used. A bigger inertia mass provides a slower motion of agents in the search space and hence a more precise search. Conversely, a bigger gravitational mass causes a higher attraction of agents. This permits a considerable convergence (Rashedi, Nezamabadi-Pour, & Saryazdi, 2009). When an algorithm finds an optimal solution to a given problem, one of the important factors is speed and rate of convergence to the optimal solution. For heuristics, the additional consideration of how close the heuristic solution comes to optimally is generally the primary concern of the researcher(Barr, Golden, Kelly, Resende, & Stewart Jr, 1995). In GSA, the stable convergence and better exploitation rate ensures good quality solution, which is expressed in terms of best fitness function.

Solutions and Recommendations

The PSO and GSA algorithm were applied to find out global best fitness of the objective function. All the simulations were run on a Core™ i5-3470M CPU@ 3.20 GHz processor, 4.00 GB RAM and MATLAB R2013a.

Figure 5 shows the convergence behavior of GSA. The result derived in this chapter reveals that each object of the standard GSA converges to a stable point. Here, the assumption was that the gravitational and inertia masses are the same. However, for some applications different values for them can be used.

Algorithm 1.

```
1.          Initialization of  total N mass agents randomly
2.          Computation of  G(t), Fitness (Best and Worst)
3.          For each of the agent I, evaluate:
    3.1.                 Fitness_i
    3.2.                 Mass_i
    3.3.        Force of Mass_i
    3.4.        Acceleration of Mass_i
    3.5.         Mass_i velocity update
    3.6.        New position of Agent_i
                If (Probability_i>Threshold)
                                {
                If
        Then return Best Fitness solution so far
        Else
                Modification of solution
                                }
4.       Failed to meet stopping criteria,
         Go To Step 2, Else Stop
```

Figure 4. Structural diagram of Gravitational Search Algorithm

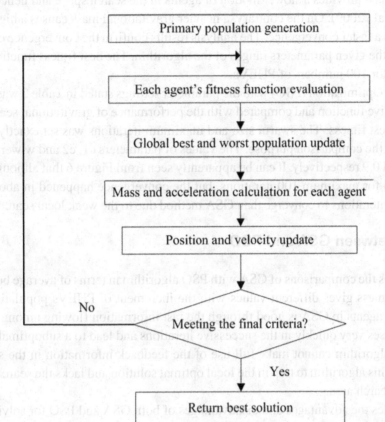

Figure 5. Iteration vs. fitness value, J (k) for GSA [100 PHEVs]

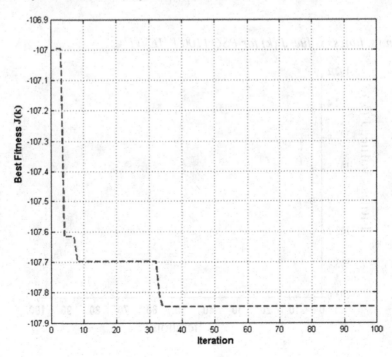

A heavier inertia mass provides a slower motion of agents in the search space and hence a more precise search (Rashedi et al., 2009). On the contrary, a heavier gravitational mass causes a higher attraction of agents. This allows a faster convergence. The analysis results confirm the convergence characteristics of GSA according to the given parameters ranges of the algorithm. The best fitness function convergences after 35 iterations for 100 numbers of PHEVs.

Particle Swarm Optimization (PSO) with the parameter settings stated in Table 2 was also performed for the same objective function and compared with the performance of gravitational search algorithm in terms of average best fitness. The swarm size and maximum iterations was set exactly same to that of GSA technique for the comparison purpose. The values of parameters c1, c2 and w were set as standard values, 1.4, 1.4 and 0.9 respectively. It can be apparently seen from Figure 6 that although the algorithm has been set to run for maximum 100 iterations, but the convergence happened in about 10 iterations. So, PSO takes less iterations to converge than GSA method due to the weak local search ability of GSA.

Comparison between GSA and PSO

Table 4 summarizes the comparisons of GSA with PSO algorithm in terms of average best fitness. Here, the average best fitness gives different values with the increment of PHEVs population. The convergence rate of mass agents in GSA is good through the fast information flowing among mass agents, so its diversity decreases very quickly in the successive iterations and lead to a suboptimal solution. In the case of PSO, the algorithm cannot make full use of the feedback information in the system. There is also possibility of this algorithm to trap in the local optimal solution and lacks the searching capabilities within the whole search area.

Table 5 illustrates the advantages and disadvantages of both GSA and PSO for solving different optimization problems. Energy scheduling at a PHEV charging station is subjected to different constraints that limit the search space to a certain feasible region. PSO can easily handle the constraints separately, eliminating the need for additional parameters (Su & Chow, 2012a). PSO method is good for multi-

Figure 6. Iteration vs. fitness value, J (k) for PSO [100 PHEVs]

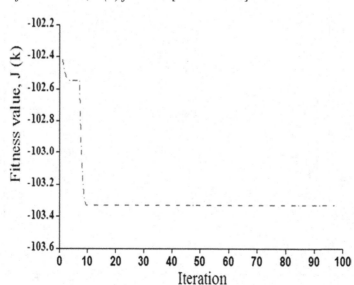

Table 4. Average best fitness comparison between GSA and PSO

Average Best Fitness for	PSO	GSA
50 PHEVs	142.839	158.8289
100 PHEVs	171.102	182.3097
500 PHEVs	150.869	152.36437
1000 PHEVs	156.802	161.52349

Table 5. Advantages and disadvantages of PSO and GSA

Optimization Method	Advantages	Disadvantages
PSO	Less parameters tuning Easy constraint Good for multi-objective optimization	Low quality solution Needs memory to update velocity Slow convergence rate
GSA	High quality solution Good convergence rate Local exploitation capability	Needs more Computational time More parameters tuning

objective optimization while GSA takes slightly more computational time with parameters tuning. The performance of both algorithms varies with the applications and different objective functions.

The average best fitness of both algorithms are represented with respect to number of vehicles (PHEVs) in Figure 7. From the figure it is clear that, Gravitational Search Algorithm (GSA) outperforms Particle Swarm Optimization (PSO) in terms of Average best fitness. Here, the average best fitness gives different values with the increment of PHEVs population. The rate of convergence of mass agents in GSA is good through the fast information flowing among mass agents, so its diversity decreases very quickly

Figure 7. Average best fitness vs. no. of PHEVs

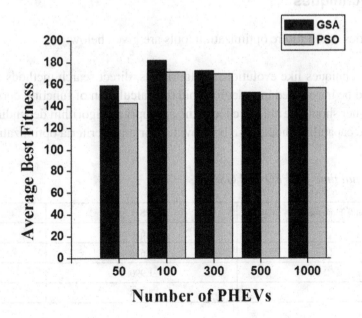

in the successive iterations and lead to a suboptimal solution. Starting from 50 numbers of PHEVs up to 1000 PHEVs, GSA shows better fitness value than PSO.

Table 6 shows the computational time requirement for PSO and GSA method. As the number of PHEVs increased from 100 to 500 and then 1000, PSO technique shows better result than standard GSA method in terms of computational time.

Stability

Here, the average best fitness gives different values with the increment of PHEVs population. The rate of convergence of mass agents in GSA is good through the fast information flowing among mass agents, so its stability decreases very quickly in the successive iterations and lead to a suboptimal solution.

Robustness

The similar numeric patterns of Average best fitness shows the robustness of GSA method. This method resists change without adapting its initial stable configuration for different cases (no. of PHEVs) which proves GSA as a robust algorithm.

So, it can be concluded that, PSO obtains better result in terms of computational time while GSA performs well for achieving the best fitness values compared to PSO.

FUTURE RESEARCH DIRECTIONS

This paragraph summarizes the review results and suggests future directions of optimization techniques and procedures. The specific research field is relatively new and possible future perspectives have to be emphasized, so that new techniques can be realized.

Optimization Techniques

Possible characteristics of the future optimization tools are given below:

- Optimization techniques like evolutionary algorithms, direct search methods and other heuristic methods should be introduced in order to avoid the calculation of function derivatives. The experienced researcher should be able to choose the appropriate algorithm depending on the problem. Multi-objective capability should also be provided for multi-criteria optimization problems.

Table 6. Computational time for PSO and GSA

Computational Time (sec.)	PSO	GSA
50 PHEVs	1.650	2.721
100 PHEVs	1.686	4.439
500 PHEVs	1.990	18.165
1000 PHEVs	2.398	36.275

- The future optimization tools should be capable of performing parallel processing evaluations on the same computer by using modern multi-core processor technology or to distribute the calculations to a cluster of computers. Such ability will substantially improve the simulation runtime.
- Advanced controlling mechanisms are necessary for allocating sufficient energy to a particular charging station in order to facilitate large-scale PHEV penetration in upcoming years.
- The future optimization tools should have the capability of stable convergence and thus provides good solution to the desired objective functions.
- Exploration and exploitation of the search space is essential in order to get desired solution within acceptable computation time.
- Finally, optimization of charging station needs proper selection of available resources as well as efficient available technique implementation.

Demand Side Management

Demand Side Management (DSM) is defined by Department of Energy (DOE) [69] as "Changes in electric usage by end-use customers from their normal consumption patterns in response to changes in the price of electricity over time, or incentive payments designed to induce lower electricity use at times of high wholesale market prices or when system reliability is jeopardized." Therefore, the demand side management programs should be incorporated into the existing Intelligent Energy Management System (iEMS) model in order to avoid voltage sag and blackout and to maximize the financial benefits. In addition, this under-utilized capacity could effectively power a national fleet of PHEVs with little need to increase the energy delivery capacity of the existing grid infrastructure (Gerkensmeyer, Kintner-Meyer, & DeSteese, 2010).

Trade-Off between Cost and Performance

Considering the effects of cost and performance on the marketability of PHEVs, the objective function is defined to minimize drivetrain cost and driving performance requirements are selected as constraints to ensure that the vehicle performance is not sacrificed during the optimization. The battery is the key component within an electric vehicle (EV) which determines its overall capital cost and performance. Therefore, the task of determining the cost effectiveness of EVs is predominantly one of identifying the future trajectory of battery cost and performance. To meet power requirements: batteries have lower discharge power at low SoC and lower charge power at high SoC. To reduce safety risks, limiting the maximum SoC avoids overcharge situations.

CONCLUSION

Researchers are trying to design efficient controller for charging station and several literatures on optimization-based methods were published in this wake. These vehicles will help the government in its role of promoting energy security and environmental protection, when successfully marketed to consumers. Efforts are also to be taken for provision of affordable and accessible infrastructure for recharging. Hence, thrust in research and development on the aforementioned design considerations and technological challenges coupled with government support in terms of incentives to the automobile owners and to the manufacturers will go a long way in accelerating the deployment of large-scale PHEVs. In the future, more objective functions (such as minimizing the overall charging time, etc.) should be considered in order to satisfy both client interests and the requirements of the power grid. However, conflicts can arise when multiple objective functions are applied. The easiest solution to this problem involves combining all of the objectives into a single function. In this case, the weights assigned to each can be fixed or dynamically changed during the optimization process.

In this chapter, Particle swarm optimization (PSO) and Gravitational search algorithm (GSA)-based optimization were performed in order to optimally allocate power to each of the PHEVs entering into the charging station. A sophisticated controller will need to be designed in order to allocate power to PHEVs appropriately. For this wake, the applied algorithm is a step towards real-life implementation of such controller for PHEV charging stations. Here, four (04) different numbers of PHEVs were considered for MATLAB Simulation and then obtained results were compared with PSO in terms of average best fitness and computational time. The success of the electrification of transportation sector solely depends on charging infrastructure. Only proper charging control and infrastructure management can assure the larger penetration of PHEVs. The researchers should try to develop efficient control mechanism for charging infrastructure in order to facilitate upcoming PHEVs in highways. In future, more vehicles should be considered for intelligent power allocation strategy as well as hybrid versions of PSO and GSA should be applied to ensure higher fitness value and low computational time.

ACKNOWLEDGMENT

The authors would like to thank Universiti Teknologi PETRONAS (UTP) for supporting the research under UTP Graduate Assistantship (GA) scheme.

REFERENCES

Aggeler, D., Canales, F., Coccia, A., Butcher, N., & Apeldoorn, O. (2010). Ultra-fast DC-charge infrastructures for EV-mobility and future smart grids. In Proceedings of Innovative Smart Grid Technologies Conference Europe (ISGT Europe). Gothenburg, Sweden: IEEE. doi:10.1109/ISGTEUROPE.2010.5638899

Anegawa, T. (2009). *Desirable characteristics of public quick charger*. Retrieved December, 1, 2011 from www.chademo.com

Association of Bay Area Governments. (2010). *Bay area electrified vehicle charging infrastructure: Options for accelerating consumer*. Bay Area, CA: Renewable and Appropriate Energy Laboratory.

Barr, R. S., Golden, B. L., Kelly, J. P., Resende, M. G., & Stewart, W. R. Jr. (1995). Designing and reporting on computational experiments with heuristic methods. *Journal of Heuristics*, *1*(1), 9–32. doi:10.1007/BF02430363

Birnie, D. P. III. (2009). Solar-to-vehicle (S2V) systems for powering commuters of the future. *Journal of Power Sources*, *186*(2), 539–542. doi:10.1016/j.jpowsour.2008.09.118

Botsford, C., & Szczepanek, A. (2009). Fast charging vs. slow charging: Pros and cons for the new age of electric vehicles. In *Proceedings of International Battery Hybrid Fuel Cell Electric Vehicle Symposium*. Stavanger, Norway: World Electric Vehicle Association.

Boyle, G. (Ed.). (2007). *Renewable electricity and the grid: the challenge of variability*. Earthscan.

Caramanis, M., & Foster, J. M. (2009, December). Management of electric vehicle charging to mitigate renewable generation intermittency and distribution network congestion. In *Proceedings of the 48th IEEE Conference on Decision and Control*. Shanghai: IEEE. doi:10.1109/CDC.2009.5399955

Chang, W. Y. (2013). The state of charge estimating methods for battery: A review. *ISRN Applied Mathematics*, 2013.

Chiasson, J., & Vairamohan, B. (2005). Estimating the state of charge of a battery. *IEEE Transactions on Control Systems Technology*, 13(3), 465–470. doi:10.1109/TCST.2004.839571

De Sousa, L., Silvestre, B., & Bouchez, B. (2010). A combined multiphase electric drive and fast battery charger for electric vehicles. In *Proceedings of Vehicle Power and Propulsion Conference (VPPC)*. Lille, France: IEEE. doi:10.1109/VPPC.2010.5729057

del Valle, Y., Venayagamoorthy, G. K., Mohagheghi, S., Hernandez, J.-C., & Harley, R. G. (2008). Particle swarm optimization: Basic concepts, variants and applications in power systems. *IEEE Transactions on Evolutionary Computation*, 12(2), 171–195. doi:10.1109/TEVC.2007.896686

Denholm, P., Kuss, M., & Margolis, R. M. (2013). Co-benefits of large scale plug-in hybrid electric vehicle and solar PV deployment. *Journal of Power Sources*, 236, 350–356. doi:10.1016/j.jpowsour.2012.10.007

Dubey, H. M., Pandit, M., Panigrahi, B. K., & Udgir, M. (2013). Economic load dispatch by hybrid swarm intelligence based gravitational search algorithm. *International Journal of Intelligent Systems and Applications*, 5(8), 21–32. doi:10.5815/ijisa.2013.08.03

Dusmez, S., Cook, A., & Khaligh, A. (2011). Comprehensive analysis of high quality power converters for level 3 off-board chargers. In *Proceedings of Vehicle Power and Propulsion Conference (VPPC)*. Chicago: IEEE doi:10.1109/VPPC.2011.6043096

Eberhart, R. C., & Shi, Y. (2001). Particle swarm optimization: Developments, applications and resources. In *Proceedings of the 2001 Congress on Evolutionary Computation*. Seoul, South Korea: IEEE. doi:10.1109/CEC.2001.934374

Gan, L., Topcu, U., & Low, S. (2011). Optimal decentralized protocol for electric vehicle charging. In *Proceedings of Decision and Control and European Control Conference (CDC-ECC)*. IEEE. doi:10.1109/CDC.2011.6161220

Ganesan, T., Vasant, P., & Elamvazuthy, I. (2012). A hybrid PSO approach for solving non-convex optimization problems. *Archives of Control Sciences*, 22(1), 87–105. doi:10.2478/v10170-011-0014-2

Gerkensmeyer, C., Kintner-Meyer, M. C., & DeSteese, J. G. (2010). *Technical challenges of plug-in hybrid electric vehicles and impacts to the US power system: Distribution system analysis*. United States Department of Energy. doi:10.2172/974954

Hess, A., Malandrino, F., Reinhardt, M. B., Casetti, C., Hummel, K. A., & Barceló-Ordinas, J. M. (2012). Optimal deployment of charging stations for electric vehicular networks. In *Proceedings of the First Workshop on Urban Networking*. Nice, France: ACM. doi:10.1145/2413236.2413238

Holtz-Eakin, D., & Selden, T. M. (1995). Stoking the fires? CO_2 emissions and economic growth. *Journal of Public Economics*, *57*(1), 85–101. doi:10.1016/0047-2727(94)01449-X

Hota, A. R., Juvvanapudi, M., & Bajpai, P. (2014). Issues and solution approaches in PHEV integration to the smart grid. *Renewable & Sustainable Energy Reviews*, *30*(0), 217–229. doi:10.1016/j.rser.2013.10.008

Ingersoll, J. G., & Perkins, C. A. (1996). The 2.1 kW photovoltaic electric vehicle charging station in the city of Santa Monica, California. In *Proceedings of Twenty Fifth IEEE Photovoltaic Specialists Conference*. Washington, DC: IEEE. doi:10.1109/PVSC.1996.564423

Jia-zhao, C., Yu-xiang, Z., & Yin-sheng, L. (2012). A unified frame of swarm intelligence optimization algorithm. *Knowledge Discovery and Data Mining*, *135*, 745–751. doi:10.1007/978-3-642-27708-5_103

Kefayati, M., & Caramanis, C. (2010). Efficient energy delivery management for PHEVs. In *Proceedings of First IEEE International Conference on Smart Grid Communications (SmartGridComm)*. Gaithersburg, MD: IEEE. doi:10.1109/SMARTGRID.2010.5621990

Kulshrestha, P., Wang, L., Chow, M. Y., & Lukic, S. (2009). Intelligent energy management system simulator for PHEVs at municipal parking deck in a smart grid environment. In Proceedings of Power & Energy Society General Meeting. Alberta, Canada: IEEE. doi:10.1109/PES.2009.5275688

Letendre, S. (2009). Solar electricity as a fuel for light vehicles. In *Proceedings of the 2006 American Solar Energy Society Annual Conference*. Boulder, CO: ASES.

Li, Z., Sahinoglu, Z., Tao, Z., & Teo, K. H. (2010, September). Electric vehicles network with nomadic portable charging stations. In Proceedings of Vehicular Technology Conference Fall. Ottawa, Canada: IEEE. doi:10.1109/VETECF.2010.5594437

Lund, H., & Kempton, W. (2008). Integration of renewable energy into the transport and electricity sectors through V2G. *Energy Policy*, *36*(9), 3578–3587. doi:10.1016/j.enpol.2008.06.007

Ma, Z., Callaway, D., & Hiskens, I. (2010). Decentralized charging control for large populations of plug-in electric vehicles. In *Proceedings of 49th IEEE Conference on Decision and Control (CDC)*. Yokohama: IEEE. doi:10.1109/CDC.2010.5717547

Mayfield, D. (2012). *Site design for electric vehicle charging stations, NREL*. US Department of Energy.

Mitra, P., & Venayagamoorthy, G. K. (2010). Intelligent coordinated control of a wind farm and distributed smartparks. In *Proceedings of Industry Applications Society Annual Meeting (IAS)*. Houston, TX: IEEE. doi:10.1109/IAS.2010.5615930

Morrow, K., Karner, D., & Francfort, J. (2008). *Plug-in hybrid electric vehicle charging infrastructure review*. US Department of Energy-Vehicle Technologies Program.

Motors, T. (2009). Tesla roadster spec sheet 2009. *USA Today*. Retrieved from www.usatoday.com

Neumann, H. M., Schär, D., & Baumgartner, F. (2012). The potential of photovoltaic carports to cover the energy demand of road passenger transport. *Progress in Photovoltaics: Research and Applications*, *20*(6), 639–649.

Pang, C., Dutta, P., Kim, S., Kezunovic, M., & Damnjanovic, I. (2010). PHEVs as dynamically configurable dispersed energy storage for V2B uses in the smart grid. In *IET Conference Proceedings*. Cyprus: IEEE. doi:10.1049/cp.2010.0903

Piller, S., Perrin, M., & Jossen, A. (2001). Methods for state-of-charge determination and their applications. *Journal of Power Sources*, *96*(1), 113–120. doi:10.1016/S0378-7753(01)00560-2

Rashedi, E., Nezamabadi-Pour, H., & Saryazdi, S. (2009). GSA: A gravitational search algorithm. *Information Sciences*, *179*(13), 2232–2248. doi:10.1016/j.ins.2009.03.004

Rawson, M., & Kateley, S. (1999). *Electric vehicle charging equipment design and health and safety codes* (No. 1999-01-2941). SAE Technical Paper.

Sabri, N. M., Puteh, M., & Mahmood, M. R. (2013). A review of gravitational search algorithm. *Int. J. Advance. Soft Comput. Appl*, *5*(3), 1–39.

Shafiei, A., & Williamson, S. S. (2010). Plug-in hybrid electric vehicle charging: Current issues and future challenges. In *Proceedings of Vehicle Power and Propulsion Conference (VPPC)*. Lille, France: IEEE. doi:10.1109/VPPC.2010.5729134

Soares, J., Sousa, T., Morais, H., Vale, Z., Canizes, B., & Silva, A. (2013). Application-specific modified particle swarm optimization for energy resource scheduling considering vehicle-to-grid. *Applied Soft Computing*, *13*(11), 4264–4280. doi:10.1016/j.asoc.2013.07.003

Sojoudi, S., & Low, S. H. (2011). Optimal charging of plug-in hybrid electric vehicles in smart grids. In *Proceedings of Power and Energy Society General Meeting*. San Diego, CA: IEEE. doi:10.1109/PES.2011.6039236

Su, W., & Chow, M. Y. (2010). An intelligent energy management system for PHEVs considering demand response. In *Proceedings of FREEDM Annual Conference*. NC State University.

Su, W., & Chow, M. Y. (2011). Performance evaluation of a PHEV parking station using particle swarm optimization. In *Proceedings of Power and Energy Society General Meeting*. San Diego, CA: IEEE. doi:10.1109/PES.2011.6038937

Su, W., & Chow, M.-Y. (2012a). Performance evaluation of an EDA-based large-scale plug-in hybrid electric vehicle charging algorithm. *IEEE Transactions on Smart Grid*, *3*(1), 308–315. doi:10.1109/TSG.2011.2151888

Su, W., & Chow, M.-Y. (2012b). Computational intelligence-based energy management for a large-scale PHEV/PEV enabled municipal parking deck. *Applied Energy*, *96*, 171–182. doi:10.1016/j.apenergy.2011.11.088

Subramanian, A., Garcia, M., Dominguez-Garcia, A., Callaway, D., Poolla, K., & Varaiya, P. (2012). Real-time scheduling of deferrable electric loads. In *Proceedings of American Control Conference (ACC)*. Montreal, Canada: IEEE. doi:10.1109/ACC.2012.6315670

Tan, W. S., Hassan, M. Y., Rahman, H. A., Abdullah, M. P., & Hussin, F. (2013). Multi-distributed generation planning using hybrid particle swarm optimisation-gravitational search algorithm including voltage rise issue. *IET Generation, Transmission, & Distribution, 7*(9), 929–942. doi:10.1049/iet-gtd.2013.0050

Tie, S. F., & Tan, C. W. (2013). A review of energy sources and energy management system in electric vehicles. *Renewable & Sustainable Energy Reviews, 20*, 82–102. doi:10.1016/j.rser.2012.11.077

Tulpule, P. J., Marano, V., Yurkovich, S., & Rizzoni, G. (2013). Economic and environmental impacts of a PV powered workplace parking garage charging station. *Applied Energy, 108*, 323–332. doi:10.1016/j.apenergy.2013.02.068

Ul-Haq, A., Buccella, C., Cecati, C., & Khalid, H. A. (2013). Smart charging infrastructure for electric vehicles. In *Proceedings of International Conference on Clean Electrical Power (ICCEP)*. Alghero: IEEE. doi:10.1109/ICCEP.2013.6586984

Vasant, P., Ganesan, T., & Elamvazuthi, I. (2012). An improved PSO approach for solving non-convex optimization problems. In *Proceedings of Engineering 9th International Conference on ICT and Knowledge*. Bangkok: IEEE. doi:10.1109/ICTKE.2012.6152418

Venayagamoorthy, G. K., & Mitra, P. (2011). SmartPark shock absorbers for wind farms. *IEEE Transactions on Energy Conversion, 26*(3), 990–992. doi:10.1109/TEC.2011.2159549

Yilmaz, M., & Krein, P. T. (2012). Review of charging power levels and infrastructure for plug-in electric and hybrid vehicles. In *Proceedings of Electric Vehicle Conference (IEVC)*. Greenville, SC: IEEE. doi:10.1109/IEVC.2012.6183208

Zhang, Q., Tezuka, T., Ishihara, K. N., & Mclellan, B. C. (2012). Integration of PV power into future low-carbon smart electricity systems with EV and HP in Kansai Area, Japan. *Renewable Energy, 44*, 99–108. doi:10.1016/j.renene.2012.01.003

Zhu, L., Yu, F. R., Ning, B., & Tang, T. (2012). Optimal charging control for electric vehicles in smart micro grids with renewable energy sources. In *Proceedings of Vehicular Technology Conference (VTC)*. Yokohama: IEEE.

ADDITIONAL READING

Arumuggam, K., & Singh, B. S. M. (2013). Optimization of hybrid solar and wind power generation. *Journal of Applied Sciences, 13*(6), 869–875. doi:10.3923/jas.2013.869.875

Axsen, J., & Kurani, K. S. (2013). Hybrid, plug-in hybrid, or electric—What do car buyers want? *Energy Policy, 61*, 532–543. doi:10.1016/j.enpol.2013.05.122

Bauer, P., Zhou, Y., Doppler, J., & Stembridge, N. (2010, June). Charging of electric vehicles and impact on the grid. In MECHATRONIKA, 13th International Symposium, Teplice (pp. 121-127).

Bayram, I. S., Michailidis, G., Devetsikiotis, M., Granelli, F., & Bhattacharya, S. (2012). *Smart Vehicles in the Smart Grid: Challenges, Trends, and Application to the Design of Charging Stations Control and Optimization Methods for Electric Smart Grids* (pp. 133–145). Springer. doi:10.1007/978-1-4614-1605-0_6

Boschert, S. (20 Talatahari, S., Khalili, E., & Alavizadeh, S. (2013). Accelerated particle swarm for optimum design of frame structures. Mathematical Problems in Engineering, 2013. 06). Plug-in hybrids: The cars that will recharge America: New Society Publishers.

Boulanger, A. G., Chu, A. C., Maxx, S., & Waltz, D. L. (2011). Vehicle electrification: Status and issues. *Proceedings of the IEEE*, *99*(6), 1116–1138. doi:10.1109/JPROC.2011.2112750

Ceylan, O., Ozdemir, A., & Dag, H. (2012). Branch Outage Simulation Based Contingency Screening by Gravitational Search Algorithm. *International Review of Electrical Engineering*, *7*(1).

Chan, C. C. (2002). The state of the art of electric and hybrid vehicles. *Proceedings of the IEEE*, *90*(2), 247–275. doi:10.1109/5.989873

Contestabile, M., Offer, G. J., Slade, R., Jaeger, F., & Thoennes, M. (2011). Battery electric vehicles, hydrogen fuel cells and biofuels. Which will be the winner? *Energy & Environmental Science*, *4*(10), 3754–3772. doi:10.1039/c1ee01804c

Di Silvestre, M. L., Sanseverino, E. R., Zizzo, G., & Graditi, G. (2013). An optimization approach for efficient management of EV parking lots with batteries recharging facilities. *Journal of Ambient Intelligence and Humanized Computing*, *4*(6), 641–649. doi:10.1007/s12652-013-0174-y

Duman, S., Güvenç, U., Sönmez, Y., & Yörükeren, N. (2012). Optimal power flow using gravitational search algorithm. *Energy Conversion and Management*, *59*, 86–95. doi:10.1016/j.enconman.2012.02.024

Duman, S., Güvenç, U., & Yörükeren, N. (2010). Gravitational search algorithm for economic dispatch with valve-point effects. *International Review of Electrical Engineering*, *5*(6), 2890–2895.

Ehsani, M., Gao, Y., & Emadi, A. (2009). *Modern electric, hybrid electric, and fuel cell vehicles: fundamentals, theory, and design*. CRC press.

Eiben, A. E., & Smit, S. K. (2011). Parameter tuning for configuring and analyzing evolutionary algorithms. *Swarm and Evolutionary Computation*, *1*(1), 19–31. doi:10.1016/j.swevo.2011.02.001

Elgammal, A., & Sharaf, A. (2012). Self-regulating particle swarm optimised controller for (photovoltaic-fuel cell) battery charging of hybrid electric vehicles. *Electrical Systems in Transportation, IET*, *2*(2), 77–89. doi:10.1049/iet-est.2011.0021

Fazelpour, F., Vafaeipour, M., Rahbari, O., & Rosen, M. A. (2014). Intelligent optimization to integrate a plug-in hybrid electric vehicle smart parking lot with renewable energy resources and enhance grid characteristics. *Energy Conversion and Management*, *77*, 250–261. doi:10.1016/j.enconman.2013.09.006

Ganesan, T., Elamvazuthi, I., Ku Shaari, K. Z., & Vasant, P. (2013). Swarm intelligence and gravitational search algorithm for multi-objective optimization of synthesis gas production. *Applied Energy*, *103*(0), 368–374. doi:10.1016/j.apenergy.2012.09.059

Ganesan, T., Vasant, P., & Elamvazuthi, I. (2013). Hybrid neuro-swarm optimization approach for design of distributed generation power systems. *Neural Computing & Applications*, *23*(1), 105–117. doi:10.1007/s00521-012-0976-4

Ganesan, T., Vasant, P., & Elamvazuthi, I. (2014). Hopfield neural networks approach for design optimization of hybrid power systems with multiple renewable energy sources in a fuzzy environment. *Journal of Intelligent and Fuzzy Systems*, *26*(5), 2143–2154.

Hamadicharef, B. (2011). Bibliometric analysis of particle swarm optimization (PSO) research 2000-2010. In Artificial Intelligence and Computational Intelligence (pp. 404-411). Springer Berlin Heidelberg.

Hannan, M. A., Azidin, F. A., & Mohamed, A. (2014). Hybrid electric vehicles and their challenges: A review. *Renewable & Sustainable Energy Reviews*, *29*(0), 135–150. doi:10.1016/j.rser.2013.08.097

Hendtlass, T. (2007, September). Fitness estimation and the particle swarm optimisation algorithm. In Evolutionary Computation, 2007. CEC 2007. IEEE Congress on (pp. 4266-4272). IEEE. doi:10.1109/CEC.2007.4425028

Inoa, E., Guo, F., Wang, J., & Choi, W. (2011, May). A full study of a PHEV charging facility based on global optimization and real-time simulation. In Power Electronics and ECCE Asia (ICPE & ECCE), 2011 IEEE 8th International Conference on (pp. 565-570). IEEE. doi:10.1109/ICPE.2011.5944611

Jiang, S., Ji, Z., & Shen, Y. (2014). A novel hybrid particle swarm optimization and gravitational search algorithm for solving economic emission load dispatch problems with various practical constraints. *International Journal of Electrical Power & Energy Systems*, *55*, 628–644. doi:10.1016/j.ijepes.2013.10.006

Karbowski, D., Rousseau, A., Pagerit, S., & Sharer, P. (2006, October). Plug-in vehicle control strategy: from global optimization to real time application. In *22nd Electric Vehicle Symposium, EVS22*, Yokohama, Japan.

Khajehzadeh, M., Taha, M. R., El-Shafie, A., & Eslami, M. (2012). A modified gravitational search algorithm for slope stability analysis. *Engineering Applications of Artificial Intelligence*, *25*(8), 1589–1597. doi:10.1016/j.engappai.2012.01.011

Krause, J., Cordeiro, J., Parpinelli, R. S., & Lopes, H. S. (2013). A survey of swarm algorithms applied to discrete optimization problems. Swarm Intelligence and Bio-inspired Computation: Theory and Applications. Elsevier Science & Technology Books, 169-191.

Martens, D., Baesens, B., & Fawcett, T. (2011). Editorial survey: Swarm intelligence for data mining. *Machine Learning*, *82*(1), 1–42. doi:10.1007/s10994-010-5216-5

Mirjalili, S., Mohd Hashim, S. Z., & Moradian Sardroudi, H. (2012). Training feedforward neural networks using hybrid particle swarm optimization and gravitational search algorithm. *Applied Mathematics and Computation*, *218*(22), 11125–11137. doi:10.1016/j.amc.2012.04.069

Mohamed, A. Z., Lee, S. H., Hsu, H. Y., & Nath, N. (2012). A faster path planner using accelerated particle swarm optimization. *Artificial Life and Robotics*, *17*(2), 233–240. doi:10.1007/s10015-012-0051-3

Mullan, J., Harries, D., Bräunl, T., & Whitely, S. (2012). The technical, economic and commercial viability of the vehicle-to-grid concept. *Energy Policy*, *48*(0), 394–406. doi:10.1016/j.enpol.2012.05.042

Mwasilu, F., Justo, J. J., Kim, E.-K., Do, T. D., & Jung, J.-W. (2014). Electric vehicles and smart grid interaction: A review on vehicle to grid and renewable energy sources integration. *Renewable & Sustainable Energy Reviews*, *34*(0), 501–516. doi:10.1016/j.rser.2014.03.031

Pan, F., Bent, R., Berscheid, A., & Izraelevitz, D. (2010, October). Locating PHEV exchange stations in V2G. In Smart Grid Communications (SmartGridComm), 2010 First IEEE International Conference on (pp. 173-178). IEEE.

Panigrahi, B. K., Shi, Y., & Lim, M. H. (2011). *Handbook of Swarm Intelligence*. Berlin: Springer. doi:10.1007/978-3-642-17390-5

Preetham, G., & Shireen, W. (2012, January). Photovoltaic charging station for Plug-In Hybrid Electric Vehicles in a smart grid environment. In Innovative Smart Grid Technologies (ISGT), 2012 IEEE PES (pp. 1-8). IEEE. doi:10.1109/ISGT.2012.6175589

Quinn, C., Zimmerle, D., & Bradley, T. H. (2010). The effect of communication architecture on the availability, reliability, and economics of plug-in hybrid electric vehicle-to-grid ancillary services. *Journal of Power Sources*, *195*(5), 1500–1509. doi:10.1016/j.jpowsour.2009.08.075

Sadrnia, A., Nezamabadi-Pour, H., Nikbakht, M., & Ismail, N. (2013). A Gravitational Search Algorithm Approach for Optimizing Closed-Loop Logistics Network. In P. Vasant (Ed.), *Meta-Heuristics Optimization Algorithms in Engineering, Business, Economics, and Finance* (pp. 616–638). Hershey, PA: Information Science Reference. doi:10.4018/978-1-4666-2086-5.ch020

Sandy Thomas, C. (2009). Transportation options in a carbon-constrained world: Hybrids, plug-in hybrids, biofuels, fuel cell electric vehicles, and battery electric vehicles. *International Journal of Hydrogen Energy*, *34*(23), 9279–9296. doi:10.1016/j.ijhydene.2009.09.058

Sarafrazi, S., Nezamabadi-Pour, H., & Saryazdi, S. (2011). Disruption: A new operator in gravitational search algorithm. *Scientia Iranica*, *18*(3), 539–548. doi:10.1016/j.scient.2011.04.003

Singh, J. D. (2012). Nonconvex Economic Load Dispatch Problem with Dynamic Constraint through Gravitational Search Algorithm. *Artificial Intelligent Systems and Machine Learning*, *4*(8), 494–501.

Tate, E. D., Harpster, M. O., & Savagian, P. J. (2008). The electrification of the automobile: from conventional hybrid, to plug-in hybrids, to extended-range electric vehicles (No. 2008-01-0458). SAE Technical Paper.

Tong, S. J., Same, A., Kootstra, M. A., & Park, J. W. (2013). Off-grid photovoltaic vehicle charge using second life lithium batteries: An experimental and numerical investigation. *Applied Energy*, *104*, 740–750. doi:10.1016/j.apenergy.2012.11.046

Tulpule, P., Marano, V., & Rizzoni, G. (2009, June). Effects of different PHEV control strategies on vehicle performance. In *American Control Conference (ACC)*, Montreal, Canada: IEEE. doi:10.1109/ACC.2009.5160595

Vasant, P., Ganesan, T., & Elamvazuthi, I. (2012, January). An improved PSO approach for solving nonconvex optimization problems. In ICT and Knowledge Engineering (ICT & Knowledge Engineering), 2011 9th International Conference on (pp. 80-87). IEEE. doi:10.1109/ICTKE.2012.6152418

Vasant, P. M. (2013). *Handbook of Research on Novel Soft Computing Intelligent Algorithms: Theory and Practical Applications*. IGI Global.

Waraich, R. A., Galus, M. D., Dobler, C., Balmer, M., Andersson, G., & Axhausen, K. W. (2013). Plug-in hybrid electric vehicles and smart grids: Investigations based on a microsimulation. *Transportation Research Part C, Emerging Technologies*, *28*, 74–86. doi:10.1016/j.trc.2012.10.011

Wirasingha, S. G., Schofield, N., & Emadi, A. (2008, September). Plug-in hybrid electric vehicle developments in the US: Trends, barriers, and economic feasibility. In *Vehicle Power and Propulsion Conference*, 2008. IEEE (pp. 1-8). IEEE. doi:10.1109/VPPC.2008.4677702

Wu, J., Wang, J., Li, K., Zhou, H., Lv, Q., Shang, L., & Sun, Y. (2013). Large-Scale Energy Storage System Design and Optimization for Emerging Electric-Drive Vehicles. Computer-Aided Design of Integrated Circuits and Systems. *IEEE Transactions on*, *32*(3), 325–338.

Yang, J., He, L., & Fu, S. (2014). An improved PSO-based charging strategy of electric vehicles in electrical distribution grid. *Applied Energy*, *128*(0), 82–92. doi:10.1016/j.apenergy.2014.04.047

Zeng, J. C., & Cui, Z. H. (2004). A Guaranteed Global Convergence Particle Swarm Optimizer. *Journal of Computer Research and Development, 8,* 1333-1338.

Zhang, L., Brown, T., & Samuelsen, S. (2013). Evaluation of charging infrastructure requirements and operating costs for plug-in electric vehicles. *Journal of Power Sources*, *240*, 515–524. doi:10.1016/j.jpowsour.2013.04.048

Zhou, F. Q., Lian, Z. W., Wang, X. L., Yang, X. H., & Xu, Y. S. (2010). Discussion on operation mode to the electric vehicle charging station. *Power System Protection and Control*, *38*(21), 63–67.

KEY TERMS AND DEFINITIONS

All Electric Range: All electric range is a mode of electric vehicle when it is only run by charged batteries in order to reduce the overall fuel consumption. Calculation of all electric range varies according to the designs of the hybrid electric vehicles. The "all electric range" (AER) test quantifies the electric-only miles possible with the battery for a particular configuration and vehicle class. Calculating AER is made more complicated because of variations in PHEV design. A vehicle like the Fisker Karma that utilizes a serial hybrid design has a clear AER. Similarly a vehicle like the Chevy Volt which disengages the internal combustion engine (ICE) from the drive train while in electric mode has a clear AER, however blended mode PHEVs which utilize the ICE and electric motor in conjunction do not have a clear AER because they utilize gasoline and grid provided electricity at the same time.

Charging Station: Charging station is an important component for the healthy growth of the electric vehicle industry. Charging station refers to an infrastructure similar to petrol station (for conventional vehicle) that provides electric energy for the charging of plug-in hybrid electric vehicles (PHEVs). Many charging stations are on-street facilities provided by electric utility companies, mobile charging stations have been recently introduced. From the grid standpoint, a charging station is one way that the operator of an electrical power grid can adapt energy production to energy consumption, both of which can vary randomly over time. Basically, EVs in a charging station are charged during times when production exceeds consumption and are discharged at times when consumption exceeds production. In this way, electricity production need is not drastically scaled up and down to meet momentary consumption, which would increase efficiency and lower the cost of energy production and facilitate the use of intermittent energy sources, such as photovoltaic and wind.

Energy Security: The interest in energy security is based on the notion that an uninterrupted supply of energy is critical for the functioning of an economy. However, an exact definition of energy security is hard to give as it has different meanings to different people at different moments in time. It has traditionally been associated with the securing of access to oil supplies and with impending fossil fuel depletion. With an increase in natural gas use, security concerns also arose for natural gas, widening the concept to cover other fuels. Because oil is nowadays a globally traded commodity, physical shortages show up in the price of oil on the world market, in the form of a long-term increase and of short-term fluctuations.

Gravitational Search Algorithm: Gravitational Search Algorithm (GSA) is a heuristic optimization algorithm which has been gaining much interest among the scientific community recently. GSA is a nature inspired algorithm based on the Newton's famous law of gravity and the law of motion. GSA is classified under population-based method and is reported to be more instinctive. In GSA, the agent has four parameters which are position, inertial mass, active gravitational mass, and passive gravitational mass. GSA is a memory-less algorithm. However, it works efficiently like the algorithms with memory.

Particle Swarm Optimization: Particle Swarm Optimization (PSO) algorithm was introduced by Kennedy and Eberhart in 1995, which is a heuristic global optimization method and a member of swarm intelligence family. PSO is a computational intelligence-based technique that is not largely affected by the size and nonlinearity of the problem, and can converge to the optimal solution in many problems where most analytical methods fail to converge.

Plug-In Hybrid Electric Vehicles: Plug-in Hybrid Electric Vehicles (PHEVs) are being made with relatively large sized batteries that can be charged during off-peak hours, and permit the vehicle owner to use exclusively electric made for 30 – 60 miles of driving as well as switching into traditional gasoline for longer trips. PHEVs offer customers the opportunity for fuel at gasoline-equivalent prices of less than $1.00 per gallon. For a given size battery bank, the range of a PHEV can be prolonged significantly before batteries need recharging by turning on the engine or fuel cell whenever the vehicle power demand exceeds some threshold.

Smart Charging: Smart charging refers to the intelligent control of electric vehicle charging by the assigned authority. Smart charging can be both direct and indirect depending upon the user demand and available infrastructure. The main concept of smart charging lies in the charging of vehicle when the price and demand are lowest as well as excess amount of available capacity. Charging itself is simple, once connected to the station charging takes place automatically. The system offers different options for customizing and personalizing charging, including the length of each charge. The control center managing the grid oversees the entire network as well as each individual charge, which enables users to check the operating status of charging stations and any eventual maintenance requirements. The control center also keeps track of each vehicles consumption.

Smart Grid: Smart grid is an intelligent bi-directional electrical power system. It ensures most advanced and efficient communication network between suppliers and consumers of electricity. Unlike traditional power grid, smart grid offers better system sustainability and network security. The "smart grid" includes advanced utility Supervisory Control and Data Acquisition (SCADA) systems that can keep track of thousands of data points of loads and resources, smart meters that can communicate to the utility SCADA center, and smart appliances that can respond instantaneously to economic or reliability imperatives. The smart grid will make use of technologies, such as state estimation that improve fault detection and allow self-healing of the network without the intervention of technicians. This will ensure more reliable supply of electricity, and reduced vulnerability to natural disasters or attack. Next-generation transmission and distribution infrastructure will be better able to handle possible bi-direction energy flows, allowing for distributed generation such as from photovoltaic panels on building roofs, but also the use of fuel cells, charging to/from the batteries of electric cars, wind turbines, pumped hydroelectric power, and other sources.

State-of-Charge: State-of-Charge (SoC) of a PHEV battery is expressed as the ratio of its capacity of current ($Q(t)$) to the nominal capacity (Q_n). The nominal capacity is known by the vehicle manufacturer and shows the maximum amount of charge that can be stored in the battery. SoC estimation is a fundamental challenge for battery use. The SoC of a battery, which is used to describe its remaining capacity, is a very important parameter for a control strategy. The SoC can be defined as follows: $SoC = Q(t) / Q_n$. Recently, with the development of artificial intelligence, various new adaptive systems for SOC estimation have been developed .The new developed methods include back propagation (BP) neural network, radial basis function (RBF) neural network, fuzzy logic methods, support vector machine, fuzzy neural network, and Kalman filter. The adaptive systems are self-designing ones that can be automatically adjusted in changing systems. As batteries have been affected by many chemical factors and have nonlinear SOC, adaptive systems offer good solution for SOC estimation.

Vehicle-to-Grid: Vehicle-to-grid (V2G) systems represent a means by which power capacity in parked vehicles can be used to generate electricity for the grid. In vehicle-to-grid (V2G) concept, an electric vehicle acts both as a load and power source in smart grid environment. A V2G-capable vehicle offers reactive power support, active power regulation, tracking of variable renewable energy sources, load balancing, and current harmonic filtering. These technologies can enable ancillary services, such as voltage and frequency control and spinning reserve. Success of the V2G concept depends on standardization of requirements and infrastructure decisions, battery technology, and efficient and smart scheduling of limited fast-charge infrastructure. The benefits of V2G technologies can only be realized if a combination of infrastructure, including regulation, metering and wiring in buildings, electric-drive vehicles, and fuel production and distribution systems are all available.

APPENDIX: NOMENCLATURE

PHEVs: Plug-in hybrid electric vehicles.

EPRI: Electric power research institute.

V2G: Vehicle-to-grid.

SoC: State-of-charge.

ICEV: Internal combustion engine vehicles.

AEVs: All-electric vehicles.

HEVs: Hybrid electric vehicles.

AER: All-electric-range.

$\mathbf{I}_i(\mathbf{k})$: Charging current over Δt.

$\mathbf{V}_i(\mathbf{k})$: Charging voltage over Δt.

$\mathbf{C}_{r,i}(\mathbf{k})$: Remaining battery capacity required to be filled for i-th PHEV at time step k.

$\mathbf{C}_i$: Rated battery capacity of the i-th PHEV (Farad).

$\mathbf{T}_{r,i}(\mathbf{k})$: Remaining time for charging the i-th PHEV at time step k.

$\mathbf{D}_i(\mathbf{k})$: Price difference.

$\mathbf{w}_i(\mathbf{k})$: Charging weighting term of the i-th PHEV at time step.

$\mathbf{SoC}_i(\mathbf{k}+1)$: State-of-charge of the i-th PHEV at time step $k+1$.

$\mathbf{SoC}_{i,max}$: User-defined maximum battery SoC limit for the i-th PHEV.

$\mathbf{J(k)}$: Objective function.

$\mathbf{P}_{utility}$: Power available from the utility.

$\mathbf{P}_{i,max}$: Maximum power that can be absorbed by a specific PHEV.

η: Overall charging efficiency of the charging station.

Δt: Total charging time.

PSO: Particle swarm optimization.

GSA: Gravitational search algorithm.

$\mathbf{M}_{aj}$: Active gravitational mass related to agent j.

$\mathbf{M}_{pi}$: Passive gravitational mass related to agent i.

$\mathbf{R}_{ij}(t)$: Euclidian distance between two agents i and j.

$\mathbf{M}_{ii}$: Mass of the object i.

rand_i: Random number with interval $[0, 1]$.

pbest: Best value achieved by the individual.

gbest: Best value of the group.

$\mathbf{x}_i^t$: Current position of particle i at iteration t.

EMS: Energy management strategy.

EVSE: Electric vehicle supply equipment.

DG: Distributed generation.

DSM: Demand side management.

SMDP: Stochastic semi-Markov decision.

Chapter 13

Particle Swarm Optimization Algorithm as a Tool for Profiling from Predictive Data Mining Models

Goran Klepac
Raiffeisenbank Austria Zagreb, Croatia

ABSTRACT

This chapter introduces the methodology of particle swarm optimization algorithm usage as a tool for finding customer profiles based on a previously developed predictive model that predicts events like selection of some products or services with some probabilities. Particle swarm optimization algorithm is used as a tool that finds optimal values of input variables within developed predictive models as referent values for maximization value of probability that customers select/buy a product or service. Recognized results are used as a base for finding similar profiles between customers. The presented methodology has practical value for decision support in business, where information about customer profiles are valuable information for campaign planning and customer portfolio management.

INTRODUCTION

This chapter will present novel methodology of particle swarm optimization algorithm usage as a tool for finding customer profiles based on previously developed predictive models which predicts events like selection of some products or services with some probabilities.

It means that particle swarm optimization algorithm will be used as a tool which should find optimal values of input variables within developed predictive models as referent values for maximization value of probability that customer will select/ buy some product or service.

Basic idea is holistic process which includes development of multinomial predictive models (predictive models with more than two states which represents probability for selecting/buying product /services), and usage of this model developed on historical data sample for finding typical customer/buyer based on evaluated values of input variables by using particle swarm optimization algorithm.

DOI: 10.4018/978-1-4666-8291-7.ch013

This problem is not so expressed in case of predictive models with binomial outputs, which represents probability of buying some product or service.

Even in situation when those predictive models are not solved with linear models (like neural networks, SVM, Bayesian networks), and linear dependencies are not so obvious, regarding binominal output, profiles could easily been recognized, thanks to attribute relevance analysis which is relatively simple and unambiguous.

Task about profiling customers based on selecting/buying product /services in situation when predictive model are used for probability of N possible states calculation, became hard task which demands lot of manual work with doubtful results.

Contrary to situation with binomial states of output variable in predictive model, attribute relevance analysis for multinomial output, regarding overlapping in impact zones, and combinatory expansion could not provide clear information for setting input variable values for determination buying preferences represented as values for buying or not, one of the many product/services.

For retailers, web shops, and other industries it is challenging task, which can be solved by using particle swarm optimization algorithm in combination with existing predictive model.

In that case, for each observed product/service, aim variable within predictive model should reach criteria of maximum probability of selecting/buying product /services by using particle swarm optimization algorithm. Final result will give optimal values of input variables for each product /services which could be behavior characteristics, or socio demographic characteristics and from which model are developed based on attribute relevance analysis.

Result of those analytical approach are characteristic points in multidimensional spaces which can be used for case base reasoning, or clustering by distance measure usage as well as for profiling.

Other benefits, which proposed method provides is answers on questions like:

- Does typical buyer of product/service "A" is most similar to buyer of product/service "F" or most similar to buyer of product/service "G"?
- Buyers of which products are similar to each other?
- If buyer "A" bought product "X", regarding its similarity, which next product should be offered to him?

This methodology could be applied on predictive models based on multinomial logistic regression, Bayesian networks, neural networks, support vector machines, and other types of predictive models.

Main advantage of proposed solution is automatic determination of profiles based on selecting/buying product /services in situation where single model makes prediction for numerous product /services.

Beside advantages of proposed methodology, consumption about similar behavior in neighborhood of recognized points within input variables demands additional checks.

Consumption about similar behavior in neighborhood of recognized points could be, or not be the case. It depends on empirical customer behavior, and it demands additional tests during implementation of proposed methodology. This test can also be interesting for determination of optimal distances in recognized points within input variables.

Practical value of presented method is also visible in situation after predictive model calibration and repeating analytical procedure based on particle swarm optimization, for new characteristic point values calculation in multidimensional spaces.

These results can be valuable for transitional profiling of the buyers, and understanding trends about profile characteristics migration within own portfolio.

Taking in account nature of particle swarm optimization which are not exact (precise), for this purpose it is important to define thresholds regarding new calculations which determine significant shifts in profile transitions regarding preference of buying some product /service.

BACKGROUND

There are numerous case studies dedicated to predictive modeling in business, and usage of data mining techniques for building predictive models for purposes like churn detection, next best offer, fraud detection (Larose, 2005; Klepac, 2010;Klepac, 2014, Klepac, 2015).

In case of predictive modeling, particle swarm optimization (PSO) algorithm is mostly used as an algorithm for learning optimization in neural networks (Clerck, 2013; Kurbatsky, 2014, Russel, 2001).

Particle swarm optimization algorithm are used in many areas, mostly for solving problems in domain of optimization (Adhikari, 2013 ;Anagnostopoulos, 2012; Babahajyani 2014 ; El-Shorbagy, 2013).

In literature particle swarm optimization algorithm is not recognized as a methodology that can directly contribute on customer profiling. Mostly it is used as tool for neural networks optimization which could be used as a tool for profiling or for clustering purposes (Devi, 2014; Konstantinos, 2010; Xing, 2014).

Particle swarm optimization algorithm has great potential for solving problems which are not only primary focused on optimization (Singh, 2010; Tosun, 2014; Yosuf, 2010).

Problems in domain of business could be used by adoption and inventive usage of PSO algorithm (Olson, 2011; Rajesh 2013; Xing, 2014a).

Besides optimization for neural networks in domain of business, PSO are also used as learning optimization tool in domain of engineering, environmental science, social science (Clerk, 2013; Olson, 2011, Russel, 2001).

Neural networks and particle swarm optimization algorithm could be also used in area of time series forecasting (Adhikari, 2013). This approach is the same as in the situation where particle swarm optimization algorithm has been used as a as tool for learning optimization for neural networks on non temporal data . Main differences are related to nature of temporal data and their characteristics which demands different approach in building predictive models by using neural networks.

Different types of neural network algorithms (Alexander, 1995), demands different approaches in usage of soft computing techniques (Devi, 2014) along with neural networks. It means that e.g. in the situation where particle swarm optimization algorithm has been used as a as tool for learning optimization for neural network, regarding fact do we try to optimize learning for error back propagation model or for self organizing maps it demands different approaches in particle swarm optimization algorithm usage.

Evolutionary algorithms, as well as particle swarm optimization algorithm could be applied on various business areas (Arora, 2013; Nguyen, 2010; Taleizadeh, 2013).

One of the application area could be customer relationship management systems.

Usage of data mining techniques in customer relationship management systems, are mostly concentrated on finding typical profile of churner, buyer or subscriber (Giudici, 2003; Giudici, 2009). Neural networks, plays significant role in predictive modeling as well as for profiling. Taking in consider anatomy of neural networks, and final output after modeling with neural network it is obvious that profiling in case of multinomial output from the model is not an easy task (Larose, 2005).

Profiling could be interpreted as diversification task. In case when predictive model exists, it could be used as a base for diversification.

Particle swarm optimization algorithm has potential for diversification tasks (Cheng, 2013 ; Kress, 2010; Konstantinos, 2010). This idea leads us to ideas presented in this chapter, where particle swarm optimization algorithm became tool for diversification (profiling) based on predictive model constructed by neural network usage.

Evolutionary approach, which is one of the particle swarm optimization algorithm characteristics, gives opportunity for finding optimal solution regarding aimed profiles. This approach saves time and human work on *manual* profiling, and speed up profiling process .

From the other side, it could give a perspective on changes in customer profile characteristic through time, in case when it is appropriate used as a part of more complex system for profile analysis.

Customer relationship management paradigm demands fast information about customers. It includes information about changes in buying preferences, which implies changes in customer profiles. In situation when company operates with numerous items, or group of items, it is unrealistic to make customer profiling without some sophisticated tool like it will be presented in this chapter.

Presented methodology gives opportunity to companies for faster reaction, and faster revelation in customer profile changes. Customer profile changes, implies market changes and that has an influence on changes in market strategies. Most important feature of presented methodology is ability to recognize important areas and customer characteristics where changes became significant in comparison with previous period. Particle swarm optimization algorithm as a profiling tool usage, in combination with predictive models has additional advantage. Each predictive model calibration, which should be done periodically, could potentially have an influence on customer profiles. Profiles after predictive model calibration could be extracted by particle swarm optimization algorithm usage. This could be the base for strategic business decisions, regarding observed market trends.

In presented solution PSO algorithm has more active role in customer profiling, based on developed predictive model.

IMPORTANCE OF CUSTOMER PROFILING

Customer Profiling Purpose

Customer profiling, is one of the most important thing in customer relationship management. Campaign planning, new product development, cross selling activities, up selling activities and other activities in relation with customer portfolio management are closely related with customer profiles.

It is unrealistic to expect that whole customer portfolio has same profile characteristics. Profile characteristics vary by product usage, product group usage and regarding time component, because, as time goes by, same customer group can change their attitudes and preferences. Profile monitoring and customer profile recognition is key factor of successful customer relationship management.

For companies which have low number of products and services in selling assortments, customer profiling is easier task in comparison to companies with high number of products and services in selling assortments.

Even in situation where a company has narrow set of product and services in selling assortments, profiling is non trivial task. Profiling is not (should not be) concentrated on socio demographic characteristics only . Profiling should take also in consideration customer behavioral characteristics. Customer behavioral characteristics are not obvious and recognizable as socio demographic variables. Even socio demographic characteristics could be represented with set of standard variables like age, gender, region etc., and if company wants to base profiles on this variables (which is not recommended) profiling is not trivial task. It should be done taking in consider aim variable which represents usage of some product or group of products. Taking in consider customer behavioral characteristic as a part of profiling makes profiling more complicated. First problem in situation when companies decide to include behavioral characteristics as profiling elements is relevant behavioral characteristics recognition, significant for profiling. Behavioral characteristics are more powerful determinants for profiling, than socio demographic characteristics. Problem with them is in fact, that it is not easy to recognize key behavioral characteristics which will show typical customer profile.

Extracting Behavioral Characteristic for Profiling

For behavioral characteristic recognition useful auxiliary tool is hypothesis consideration. Hypothesis deliberation leads us to understanding, and discovering causalities of some observed problem. We recommend that analytical process should not be only pure pattern extraction from disposable data sources. It should be supervised and supported by business experts, which can express their opinions about causalities, which can be proved or disproved on analytical way.

In that case, some incorrect consumption, which has an influence on business decisions by decision makers, could be challenged and rejected.

It is possible to skip this stage, but it is recommended, because on that way company has opportunity for better understanding causalities of observed problem.

For example, if company as aim has up selling, it could be solved by making predictive models which also contains patterns / profiles of buyers of targeted products. After this stage experts also can generate hypothesis based on revealed patterns, about causalities as well as in first phase, before making predictive models.

While using hypotheses, common question is which hypothesis is true or most probable. Analyst will choose most probable answer using intuition and then will look for hypothesis confirmation using available data. By using hypotheses, analyst must be aware of wider perspective, avoiding to be focused only on one hypothesis and always looking for approval and alternatives.

This approach, gives opportunity to experts to express their expert knowledge about key profiling factors. Most important thing, if we are observing this methodology through prism of predictive model development and attribute relevance analysis, that each hypothesis generated by expert will be approved or rejected on analytical way.

Attribute relevance analysis is key process in model development. It assures right variable selection and avoids model building with irrelevant attributes, which can cause with unpredictable outputs. Beside mentioned function, attribute relevance analysis has important role in understanding of key factors in relation with customer relationship management. It does not mean that this stage in modeling will provide all the answers important for customer understanding, but it for sure raises right questions and opens horizons in customer understanding for specific portfolio.

Sometimes important relation and patterns could be found in attribute relevance analysis stage.

Often customer needs are not so obvious, but combination of several reveled relations could be good direction for getting idea where is the root of the problem. Developed predictive model could have high predictive power, but it does not mean that company fully understands reasons why some product is more popular for one customer segment, and other customer segment does not like it. Unfortunately, further investigation about these trends often stops, after predictive model has been done, and it is mistake, because, company in that case only has probability calculator for buying some product without deeper understanding what is actually going on. By using predictive models as probability calculator it is possible to recognize who will buy some product, but without deeper understanding of causes it is impossible to make good strategy for further selling activities. That is the reason why predictive model development should not be only aim of customer relationship modeling projects.

Extracted relations and knowledge about influences on some event, like willingness for buying some product or service became powerful tool for strategic business planning in marketing.

It can be used for making effective commercials which targeted customer's specific motivators and fits with behavioral characteristics recognized through attribute relevance analysis.

Business Decisions Based on Recognized Profiles

Customer willingness for buying some product or service can vary through time. Reason for that can be in seasonal factors, or in attitude changes which can be caused by customer lifetime cycle. Predictive models in process of calibration can recognize those relations, but it is most important that business side is aware of those facts, and to use it for strategic business planning.

Example for that could be situation with buyers with small kids. In certain period of time they could be oriented on buying items for small children. After some time, they change their habits, because same children has different needs regarding needed items, and company should recognize this shift.

Additional problem is that all buyers do not have children at same age, and they changes preferences and needs in different period of time.

From this point it is possible that this coherent segment after specific point starts to divide on sub segments with different needs which can be visible from profile characteristics.

A predictive model which calculates probability of buying for many products, are too complex as a tool for profiling, because there is to many combinatory states for precise profiling. Hypothetically, it could be used for this purpose, but it is not convenient for practical business purposes.

For successful periodic profiling based on complex predictive model automatic procedure should be used. There is no prescribed methodology or method for that purpose. This chapter will represent novel methodology which includes existence of developed predictive model. Predictive model could be based on different data mining models like neural networks (which will be represented in this chapter), Bayesian network, logistic regression, linear regression, decision trees etc.

Analyst knows basic relations based on attribute relevance analysis, but regarding combinatory explosion caused with variety of outputs in output variable, it is very hard, or almost impossible to make precise profiling in that conditions.

Solution is to use evolutionary approach, in our case particle swarm optimization algorithm to make profiling. That approach gives us opportunity for automatic profile detection. It could speed up profiling process and also gives an opportunity for profile comparison. It also could be use as a part of a tool for monitoring profile changes.

Segment migration could be recognized trough profile migration, and that could be signal for changes in company policy regarding company strategy. Presented methodology could be also used as a part of early warning system

Early warning systems, for example can be much more effective based on presented methodology if it uses presented methodology as a part of it.

That approach can result with extended framework for early warning system, which can be extended regarding specifics of some company and business area. Changes in profiles which prepare to buy some product or group of products for sure belongs in early warning system area.

PARTICLE SWARM OPTIMISATION ALGORITHM AND PROFILING FROM PREDICTIVE MODELS

Relation between Predictive Modeling and Profiling

Final result of predictive modeling should not be predictive model as only aim of that process. Predictive modeling should be also concentrated on understanding reasons and causes of events, which is object of predictive modeling. In case of predictive modeling for recommendation systems, next best offer, buying preferences it is important to understand profiles and characteristics, which has highest odds for selection of specific items. In general, a predictive model contains determined number of variables, and profiles are determined with their values. It means that referent profile, in light of predictive model is determined with final number of variables, which contains specific values, or scales within variables.

Understanding of those relations and values, leads us in deeper understanding of client preferences, which could be base for further hypothesis generation concentrated on deeper understanding and further analytics of customer behavior and preferences.

Predictive model development at final stage provides tool for probability calculation, but development phase should reveal main characteristic of portfolio structure, basic information about important variables that has greatest influence on customer decisions.

Data cleaning, data preprocessing, factor analysis, attribute relevance analysis, makes significant contribution to this aim.

Predictive model complexity increases with number of input variables, as well as number of states in output variable. Greater impact on complexity has increasing number of states in output variable.

In other words, it is great challenge to recognize typical profile of customer which prefers buying, or usage product of service *e.g.*"A" in situation where we use predictive model which has function to predict probability of buying, for n product (where n >2).

Complexity from other side rises with higher number of predictors, because they cause numerous potential combinations regarding state from output variable.

During developing phase in case of models with output variables with two possible states, it is easier to determine profiles for two different states. First reason lays in fact that measures for attribute relevance analysis like Information Value and Weight of evidence gives clear picture of zones, which has higher impact on observed binary states.

When number of states in output variable from predictive model is greater than two, complexity rises, and in stage of model development common task for understanding profiles is recognition of attributes which has greatest impact on aim variables with multiple states.

It could be on help for general picture about impact on preferences, but it is not sufficient for typical profile recognition for specific product or service. Often in that case, users try to find out manually typical profile, by varying values of predictors for each state in output variable within model.

It is time consuming and imprecise process, and in case of numerous states in output variable few of the output states are usually covered on this way.

Profiling is important, because it introduces new dimension in predictive modeling, which is on help for decision support process. Knowing typical user profiles for certain product or service means adequate marketing strategy for those product or services. It leads us to the fact that based on that knowledge company could design campaigns for existing and future customers.

Finding right customer characteristics leads us to recognition of motivators and reasons for buying some specific product or service.

From the other hand, market is dynamic environment, and as predictive models should be calibrated, typical profiles for products and services should be calibrated as well in line with model calibration.

It is nontrivial task, taking in consider all difficulties connected with profiling from predictive models in situation especially where number of states in output variable from predictive model is greater than two.

Attribute Relevance Analysis and Profiling

Robust and stable predictive models have few attributes incorporated into model. It could be 6-12 of most predictive attributes.

Initial data sample could contain more than hundreds of potential predictors. Some of them could be socio demographic values assigned to each customer, and other has behavioral characteristics defined by experts and extracted from existing transactional data as derived variables.

Attribute relevance analysis has two important functions:

- Recognition of most important variables which has greatest impact on target variable.
- Understanding relations and logic between most important predictor and target variable, and understanding relations and logic between most important predictors from target variable perspective.

Both functions are in line with customer profile recognition, especially in situation when we are developing predictive model for probability calculation product or services buying.

Attribute relevance analysis besides importance measuring, evaluates attribute characteristics. Attribute characteristics evaluation includes measuring attribute values impact on target variables. It helps on understanding relations and logic between most important predictor and target variable, and understanding relations and logic between most important predictors from target variable perspective.

After attribute relevance analysis stage, analyst has initial picture about profiles, which includes behavioral characteristics as well.

From perspective of predictive modeling there are two basic types of predictive models important from profiling point:

- Predictive models with binomial target variable.
- Predictive models with multinomial target variable.

In case of predictive models with binomial target variable common approach for attribute relevance analysis is usage of Weight of Evidence and Information Value calculation by using following formulas:

$$WoE = \ln\left(\frac{Dnb}{Db}\right)$$

$$IV = \sum_{i=1}^{n} (Dnb_i - Db_i) * \ln\left(\frac{Dnb_i}{Db_i}\right)$$

Weight of evidence is calculated as a natural logarithm of ratio between distributions of e.g. non-buyers (D_{nb}) and e.g. buyers (D_b) in distribution spans. Information value is calculated as sum of differences between distribution of non-buyers and buyers in distribution spans and product of corresponding weight of evidence.

Advantage in this situation is clear diversification regarding two output states, presented through Weight of Evidence measure, as it is shown in *Figure 1*.

Let assume, that graph on *figure 1* represents Weight of evidence measure result for variable *District*. All customers, which lives in districts with positive Weight of evidence value, prefer to buy product (aim variable is constructed as buying product X = Yes or buying product X = No).

All customers which lives in districts with negative Weight of evidence value, do not buy product X. After attribute relevance analysis and recognition of most predictive variables, analyst has relatively clear picture about customers, which prefer to by product X.

It is still manual work, but it is not impossible to recognize typical profile "buyer of product X" by maximizing probability for buying product "X" through predictive model. Attribute relevance analysis done by Weight of evidence gives pretty good starting point for doing this.

In situation with multinomial target variable it is much more complicated and almost impossible even manually to make typical profiles like : "buyer of product A", "buyer of product B", … "buyer of product N".

In case of predictive models with multinomial target variable common approach for attribute relevance analysis is usage of e.g. information gain calculation.

Figure 1. Illustration weight of evidence result

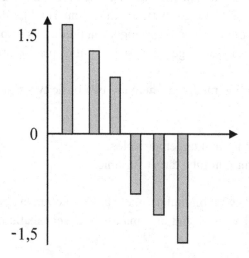

Information gain can be calculated by following formula (Han, 2006):

$$Info(D) = -\sum_{i=1}^{n} p_i \log_2(p_i)$$

where p_i is probability that an arbitrary tuple in D belongs to class C_i (Han, 2006). This measure is recommended for usage in situation where output variable has more than two states for prediction. There are many measures which can be used for this purpose. *Info gain* is presented as one possible solution for attribute relevance analysis in situation when we are operating with more than two states in output variable.

Figure 2 shows hypothetic example of information gain calculation for three classes.

As it is visible from *figure 2*, we do not have clear cuts in impact zones, it is overlapped. It complicates profiling and it is hard, or even impossible to make profiling like in is presented in situation with binary output.

As it is also visible from the figure 2, different output classes for the same predictor, in the same zones could have significant influences for several output classes. Also, those zones (bins) could be different for different output classes, with different info gain values through observed zones.

Information gain is valuable measure for attribute relevance analysis and for finding appropriate predictors, which will be base for predictive model.

In both situation aim is to maximize probability for buying specific product, in case when we try to recognize typical profile. Manually it is relatively easy task in situation with binary output from predictive model.

In situation when predictive model has more than two output states and 6-12 predictors, efficient profiling became hard task.

Let assume that we have business problem where company developed predictive model with more than two output states. Output states represent probability for buying specific product or service. Predictive model contains ten variables as predictors. Taking in consider fact that predictive model contains in output variable several states, and taking in consider expected situation like it is visible from figure 2, overlapping for different predictors for different output states is expected.

This situation is main reason beside many output states in aim variable, for difficulties in profiling based on predictive models.

This is the main reason of difficulties for finding clear cut in predictors regarding profiling, and for finding clear distinction between profiles which are related to specific value of output state.

Using Particle Swarm Optimization Algorithm as Automatic Profiling Tool from Predictive Models

Profiling by using particle swarm optimization algorithm could be done for each predictive model based on different methods (neural networks, support vector machines, Bayesian networks). As an illustration we will present situation when predictive model is based on error back propagation neural network model.

Important step after attribute relevance analysis and before modeling is continuous variables normalization. For each input variable, normalization is crucial factor.

Figure 2. Illustration of info gain calculation

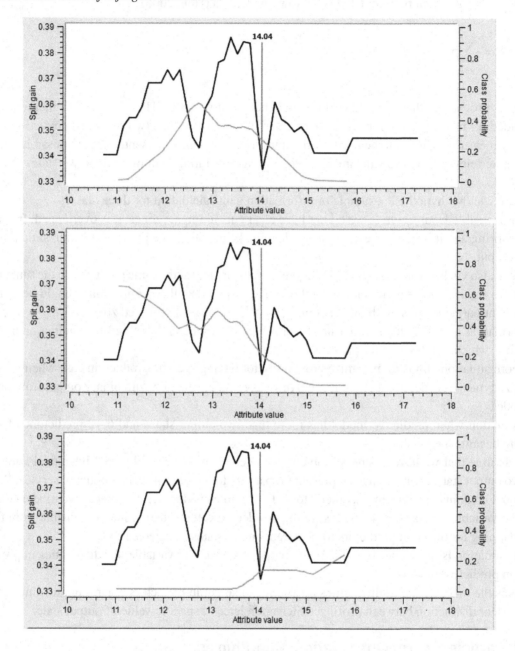

Normalization is important step in modeling. Normalization transforms each predictor values on same scale. Scale can vary, but it is common procedure for using scale between zero and one.

Normalization has function for giving opportunity to all predictors to contribute to model predictive power. Without normalization there are few potential problems which we can expect regarding different scale of predictors.

First problem is connected with higher influence of variables which contains bigger numbers. It is especially visible in situation where we are using values without normalization for k- means clustering purposes. Let suppose that variables, which we are taking in consideration for k-mean clustering are: gender, age, yearly income, number of buying in shop …

Regarding nature of k-mean clustering and nature of distance functions, variables with higher scale (values) will have strongest influence on final output. At the end, in some extreme situation it can result with output where k-mean clustering results are based on one variable, by neglecting other variables.

In mentioned situation where we operate with variables: gender, age, yearly income, number of buying in shop, it is easy to assume that yearly income could became more influencing variable. As a result clustering without normalization would be based on this variable, with weak, or almost no influence of other variables. To avoiding this situation, normalization as a step is very important.

Presented arguments are in high correlation with models like k-means clustering, but it also has significant influence on other models like neural networks.

That leads us to the second problem, which is in line with nature of models like neural networks, or logistic regression. Expected outputs from those models are between zero and one. Neural networks, regarding their anatomy and construction operates (prefer to operate) with input values between zero and one. Regarding that facts, preferred normalization should be done in way that all input variables are in range from zero to one.

Analyst should make additional analysis regarding missing values within predictors, how to declare it, does it have some special meaning, and should it be part of the model. For example, if we have missing values in customer phone number value; it can be interpreted on different ways, depending on problem for which we are developing predictive model.

Let suppose that company has 60% of missing values in variable phone number. If it is data sample which contains customers which bought some product, and after e-mail campaign for some additional product, they left phone number for contact because, they want to buy additional product. Empty field means that customer is not interested for buying additional product.

Different situation could be if 60% of missing values in variable phone number represents data sample of loan users. Paying debt preferences could be in correlation with willingness to provide phone number to bank. Data preparation before normalization process depends on data interpretation, and it is in service for achieving as much as possible better predictive power of the model.

Suppose that continuous variable has a minimum value min (y) and a maximum value max(y), than formula for min max transformation is:

$$y_i' = \frac{y_i - \min\big(y\big)}{\max\big(y\big) - \min\big(y\big)} * (\max(y') - \min(y')) + \min\big(y'\big)$$

where Y_i' is the transformed value of continuous variable Y for case i. In case of normalization for modeling with error back propagation neural network and sigmoid function as activation function usage, recommendation is that normalization should be done with min(y') = 0 and max(y') =1.

After neural network training on empirical data (development sample), neural network calculates probability of buying specific j-th product or service. P_j represents probability that customer with characteristic from Y_1' ..Y_n' will buy j-th product or service, where *j*>0.

Figure 3 shows neural network model for calculation probability of buying j-th product for customers with characteristic from Y_1' .. Y_n'.

Figure 3. Neural network model for calculation probability of buying j-th product

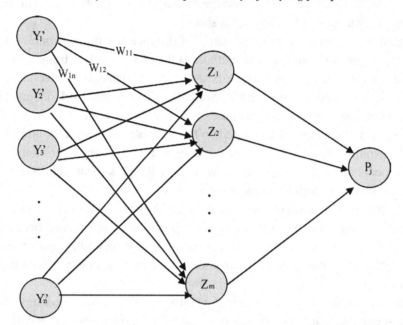

Output Z_k are linear combinationbs of input variables Y'_I weighted by W_{ik} expressed by formula:

$$Z_{k=}\sum_{i=1}^{n}Y'_i w_{ik}$$

Output from neuron Z_k are calculated by using sigmoid function:

$$Output\left(Z_k\right)=\frac{1}{1+e^{-Z_k}}$$

Error back propagation model has main two stages in model training. First stage is concentrated on output calculation regarding empirical input. Second stage is concentrated on error calculation between empirical result and calculated result as well as error back propagation and correction to each existing neuron.

Process stops when termination criteria has meet, it can be satisfactory value of overall error, or number of defined epochs.

For discovering client profile which has highest preference of buying j-th product, it is necessary to find such combination of Y'_1 to Y'_n values which gives maximum value of P_j.

Maximum value of P_j for j-th product, in model should not always be 1.

Manual approach which includes *trial and error* approach could easily be interpreted as manual evolutional process, similar to algorithms based on evolutional principles. This process is time consuming, too costly, imprecise and with uncertain outcome.

In situation when we have numerous products which is included in model (huge number of *j*) it is almost impossible to finish this task manually with satisfactory results.

From the other hand, taking in consider all problems regarding overlapping values from information gain calculation with respect to aim variable, it is nontrivial task, and for solution we propose usage of particle swarm optimization algorithm.

Usage of particle swarm optimization algorithm in combination with neural networks is not new idea.

Main difference in common usage of particle swarm optimization algorithm in combination with neural networks and proposed usage in fact that particle swarm optimization algorithm are mostly used as a tool for learning optimization in neural network.

Proposed approach use trained neural network in combination with particle swarm optimization algorithm for finding optimal customer profile, which are inclined for buying specific product or service.

This approach results in improvement of fast profiling in situation when we would like to determine profiles from complex predictive models with many predictors and many outputs from the aim variable. This leads to the fact that same methodology could be used periodically for monitoring changes in customer profiles. From perspective of decision support system it is valuable information.

Particle swarm optimization for this purpose could be used as:

$$v = v_c + c_1 r_1 \left(pbest - Y_i' \right) + c_2 r_2 \left(gbest - Y_i' \right)$$

$$Y_i' = Y_i' + v$$

where:

- Y_i' is i-th particle in swarm. It is input value from neural network initially generated randomly or by random selection from empirical data. We generate swarm of size N randomly using uniform distribution. Values of particle are in range (0,1), which represents normalized value into neural network.
- **gbest** is best solution of swarm.
- **pbest** is best solution for particular particle.
- c_1, c_2 is acceleration factors range (0,4).
- r_1, r_2 is random value range (0,1), factor which stops quick converging.
- **v** is velocity.
- v_c is current velocity.

Number of particles is determined with number of input variables into the predictive model.

Basic algorithm for each j-th product where criteria is maximization of P_j using predictive model (neural network in presented case) using Y_1' to Y_n' as particles and swarm of size N is:

1. For each j-th product.
2. Initialize swarm of size N and randomly assign initial values of particles from Y1' to Yn' in range (0,1).
3. Evaluate fitness (for each particle).

4.   Calculate pbest, gbest and v.
5.   Calculate new position for each particle.
6.   Go to 3 until reaching stopping criteria (stopping criteria could be convergence, predefined number of iteration or decreasing fitness trend).

As a final result after stopping condition is satisfied, profiles (values of Y_1' to Y_n') should be appointed for each product (*j-th* product).

Values of Y_1' to Y_n' for *j-th* product shows typical customer profile which prefer to chose *j-th* product with maximized P_j value which represents probability for buying *j-th* product or service.

Particle swarm optimization algorithm, presented on that way became powerful tool for automatic profile detection based on created predictive model. Evolutionary approach, integrated within particle swarm optimization algorithm speed up process of finding profiles which best fits to specific state into output variable.

This approach gives opportunity to companies for making periodic, frequent profiling in service of profile monitoring and strategic marketing planning.

These methodologies are convenient for early detection for changes in market trends. That could be the base for new product development, or base for cross selling, and up selling activities.

Other advantage of proposed methodology could be in recognition of dominant behavioral characteristics. If some behavioral characteristic for buying some specific product or many of them became dominant in comparison with previous period, and if their influence rise, it means that it should be seriously observed as significant factor in further selling activities.

Let suppose that using shopping coupons which buyers can take from specific magazine, is in great correlation with increasing number of buying some specific product. If previously, that characteristic was not so evident, or significant, that can lead us to few hypotheses (conclusions).

One of than can be that this magazine within its content motivate readers for buying those product, directly or indirectly.

Another one can be that readers are targeted market for that product and that they prefer to by that product.

Company can generate many hypotheses, and it can be triggers and motivators for additional ideas for selling strategies. Each hypothesis should be tested, and after hypothesis confirmation, marketing department can make strategy for further selling activities which should result with higher income for the company.

As it is visible from presented example, automatic profiling beside automatic profile detection purpose has additional service. It is base for generating hypothesis which should serve as milestones for better strategic planning, as well as an early warning market signals strongly related to specific product, or group of product which company sells.

It is obvious, that presented methodology, has multipurpose usability for strategic marketing planning.

Beside recognized profiles using PSO algorithm, in situation when output variable has many states, interesting information could be found, about similarity between generated profiles based on input values for each correspondent output value, which represents willingness for buying specific product or service.

It could be extracted by using Euclidian distances by formula:

$$D(o,i) = \sqrt{\left(Y'_{o,1} - Y'_{i,1}\right)^2 + \left(Y'_{o,2} - Y'_{i,2}\right)^2 + \ldots + \left(Y'_{o,n} - Y'_{i,n}\right)^2}$$

where:

- **D(o,i)** is distance between observed profile and tested profile (observed profile ($Y'_{o,n}$) is profile for which we would like to find most similar one, and tested profiles ($Y'_{i,n}$) are remain profiles).
- $Y'_{o,n}$ are input values from observed profile calculated with PSO algorithm, for which we are searching nearest profile in list of candidates for comparison, determined with PSO algorithm.
- $Y'_{i,n}$ are input values from predictive models calculated with PSO algorithm which makes list of candidates for comparison as nearest profile, calculated with PSO algorithm.

This information about similarity could be used for cross selling purposes in situation where significant similarity between two profiles which represents willingness for buying specific product or service exists. It implies that two similar characteristic profiles has propensity for buying two or more different products or services.

Proposed methodology could be base for new clustering approach. These clustering methods are concentrated on similarity of product or service usage/buying.

Such recognized patterns can discover interesting relationships between customers segments. Company can discover that for example, buyers of product "A" are similar to buyers of product "B" and "C". Difference can be e.g. in minor behavior characteristic like part of the day preferred for buying activities.

This detail can be used for planning marketing activities, or for generating hypothesis which can be usable for testing. Confirmed hypothesis, company can use for further marketing activities.

Additional advantage of calculating distances is periodical observing changes in distances which can show changes in characteristics between recognized segments. This approach can be usable for trend monitoring, as well as a part of the early warning system.

Distances can be calculated partially, in way that algorithm takes in account only socio demographics data, or behavioral data only. Also, analyst can take in account only targeted set of variables, for which exist special reason for observing, with neglecting other variables.

During the time, distance between two or more segments can remain the same, or distance can be higher or lower. If it remains the same, it means that there are no changes between segment characteristics.

If distance became greater, it implies that segments regarding their characteristic became more different, and it is possible that in the future it loose most of their mutual characteristics.

If calculated distance during period of time became lower, it implies that segments regarding their characteristic became more similar, and it is possible that in the future it has more and more mutual characteristics.

It is the opportunity for the company for potential cross selling, if we are talking about different type of products.

Strategy, regarding distance calculation can be focusing on characteristics which are main factors for segments discrimination. This approach gives an opportunity for monitoring unstable characteristics and their trends.

From the other hand, stable characteristics which are mainly mutual characteristics for several segments, should also be monitored. Reason for that is an early recognition factor which shows early trend of changes in some group characteristic.

It could not be determined in advance, which approach should be used in general. It depends on company position on the market, number of recognized segments, number of predictors which consists predictive models, and other factors.

As it is recommended that profiling process should be automated, distance calculation based on proposed methodology should also be automated. Automatic solution should be in line with previously recognized business needs. It includes decisions about variables which will be in focus for distance calculations. It also includes observation and recognition of stable and unstable characteristics within profiles, as well as analytical output design.

Preliminary Results Based on Empirical Data

Described methodology has been applied on empirical data of one Croatian retailer. In his assortment he has more than 10 000 products which he sales through shopping malls.

It is unrealistic and inconvenient to make predictive model for each product.

Strategy was to make predictive models on product group level. Products groups have been made on products, which were recognized as strategic products for this company.

Fourteen groups of product were created.

Criteria for recognition buyer X as a buyer of product in product group was buying product/products in product group in at least 80% cases when he or she visited mall in last year. If buyer satisfied this condition, his/hers profile characteristics has been assigned for buying defined group of products.

It was possible to assign same profile characteristics to different group of products. It was base for predictive mode learning sample construction.

Based on that, learning sample has been divided on development sample and test sample on 80:20 ratio. Neural network model has been developed, and it was base for applying particle swarm optimization algorithm.

Developed model of neural network had 12 input variables, and that determine number of particles in individual case.

Initial swarm was constructed with 7 members, for each of fourteen groups.

Stopping criteria for PSO algorithm was achieving fitness of any particle within swarm greater or equal than 0.82 (on scale from 0..1 which represents probability for buying observed product), or keeping similar (5% changes) or repeating fitness (recognized repeating patterns similar to e.g.: 0.5, 0.6, 0.5, 0.6, 0.5) on swarm in last 200 epoch with fitness within swarm less than 0.80.

In case of meeting criteria where any particle within swarm are greater or equal than 0.80, algorithm has remembered values and tries to achieve better results until convergence.

Final profiling results by using PSO algorithm are shown in *Table 1*.

Success rate for profiling was 71.42% (10 successfully recognized profiles of 14). From *table 1* it is evident that successfully recognized profiles have lower number of epochs. One of the reasons was that successfully recognized profiles met stopping criteria earlier. In case of unsuccessful profiling number of epoch are longer. Reason for that is observing 200 epochs in which fitness changes are within 5% or recognition of repeating patterns above fitness value of 0.82.

Table 1. Profiling result

Group Number	Best Fitness (0..1)	Number of Epochs in PSO	Successful Profiling
1.	0.21	1431	No
2.	0.73	1527	No
3.	0.84	893	Yes
4.	0.91	784	Yes
5.	0.92	754	Yes
6.	0.88	801	Yes
7.	0.85	384	Yes
8.	0.54	1566	No
9.	0.33	1721	No
10.	0.87	932	Yes
11.	0.86	1016	Yes
12.	0.89	1155	Yes
13.	0.92	711	Yes
14.	0.87	802	Yes

It is interesting that significant numbers of recognized profiles was in strong correlation with eating habits. Vegetarians, customers who prefer mostly to buy dairy products and customers which mostly buys meet were recognized by particle swarm optimization algorithm in low number of epochs.

It leads us to conclusion that they have distinctive profiles. Detailed analysis on profile characteristics confirms that conclusion.

Other profiles were not so distinctive and were recognized by particle swarm optimization algorithm in higher number of epochs.

For several type of products swarm optimization algorithm was unable to find appropriate solution.

Recognized profiles give a good hint about typical profile of buyer vegetarian product, or typical buyer of dairy products, as well as for customers which mostly buys meet.

There were some behavioral patterns, as well as socio demographics characteristics which shows great discriminative power regarding eating habits.

Other recognized profiles were not so distinctive, because they have more similar mutual characteristics and it became evident after detailed analysis on profile characteristics for those segments.

With successfully recognized profiles similarity has been calculated. Similarity definition was that two profiles are similar if they have differences less than 15%. Reason for that was avoiding situation where two profiles are declared as similar because other are much more different from observed one and difference between them are e.g. 60%. From business perspective it is not similar profiles from perspective of decision-making.

Result of similarity calculation is shown in *Table 2*.

Further analysis shows that similar profiles are different in average with 2-3 variables of 12. Variables *age* and *number of buying in last 3 months* as predictors in predictive model mostly caused differences. From business perspective it implies profile characteristics which are creditable for profile differentiation which makes differentiation for buying two different product /group of products.

Table 2. Similar profiles

Profile Based on Group Number	Similar to Profile Based on Group Number
2	10
4	13
7	12

Similarity was mostly case in situation where profiles were not so distinctive and were recognized by particle swarm optimization algorithm in higher number of epochs.

Similarity was mostly the case in situation with profiles which buys similar products like specific kind of tools (construction tools, gardening tools, house maintenance tools …) .

For example, main difference between construction tools, gardening tools, house maintenance tools buyers were in preferred period where buyers buys tools.

Buyers mostly buy house maintenance tools during weekend in the morning. Buyers mostly buy gardening tools in the second part of the week, and construction tools buyers mostly buy during whole week, but not during the weekend.

This variable can give us a hint about customers' behavior characteristics regarding buying habits.

Hypothesis is that house maintenance tool buyers use those tools during weekends for making small works on houses.

Hypothesis is that gardening tools buyers, plan to spend weekend on garden, and they are buying gardening tools the second part of the week as a preparation for those activities.

Hypothesis is that construction tools buyers buys those tools for business purposes, and that is the reason why they buy it during whole week, but not during the weekend.

From reveled result, it is visible power of presented methodology, which first recognize profiles from predictive models, and in the next step it opens many optional ways for making deeper analysis and for applying additional methods, like distance functions in service of deeper understanding of client portfolio.

It leads us to possibility for creating queries, based on recognized profiles like: *"Find all profiles similar to profile A, and which is not similar to profile B"* or: *"Find all profiles similar to profile A or C, and which has more than two factors similar with profile B"*.

Same methodology could be useful also for detecting trend changes in profiling, like it was situation with observed case study.

After initial analyze, same analyze has been done several times each quarter in one year.

It shows that some dominant buyer characteristics have been changed.

Few profile variables (buyer characteristics for specific product) changed expected value through time, as well as variables itself.

It was base for changing tactical plans regarding future campaigns.

FUTURE RESEARCH DIRECTIONS

Presented methodology is based on using neural network model with PSO algorithm for profiling. As it was stipulated, same methodology could be applied on any type of trained predictive model. Most similar situation regarding model type if we are talking about neural networks are predictive models based on other type of neural networks not only error back propagation model like Hopfield model, or radial basis function. Similar situation regarding methodology as well could be with support vector machines, multinomial regression, and decision trees.

Subject of future research could be aimed on usage of presented methodology with predictive models based on Bayesian networks. Reason for that is in their complexity based on links between chance nodes. It means that predictive models based on Bayesian networks demands different approach in situation when we would like to use it in combination with PSO algorithm for profiling.

Other problem is related to fact that evidence means certain event, which implies potential usage of binary states as outputs from chance nodes within Bayesian network. It leads us to on binary PSO usage and adoption, except in situation when we do not have intention to set all chance nodes as a certain events. It depend on potential solution, but for sure it demands additional research and conclusions for finding optimal approach for usage Bayesian networks with PSO algorithm for customer profiling purposes.

Other interesting topic is clustering and usage of e.g. *K-means clustering* on profiles recognized by PSO algorithm usage based on predictive model.

Clustering could recognize similar profiles and consolidate similar profiles together. At the end it could imply revelation that customers which buys product groups *A,B,C,D* are similar to customers which buys product groups *E,F,G,H*.

Additionally, decision trees could be used for finding common denominator within clusters, as well as common differences between clusters. All those information are valuable from perspective of business decision-making.

DISCUSSION

Predictive model developing should not be only aim in cases when company develops predictive models for churn detection, best next offer, up sell, cross sell and similar models. Developing process should be way for understanding relations, and key driven factors for appearance which we are modeling. It is much easier to achieve in situation where we have binary output in aim variable, and it became complicated in situations with models which have more than two states in aim variable.

Predictive models should not be only used as a probabilistic calculator, because in that case business background remains unknown and unhidden. Understanding of business background is crucial factor for strategic management. Knowledge about typical users of some specific product is base for strategic business activities. If for example, typical buyer of black beer with specific flavor, meets matching criteria of age between 20-30 years, lives in specific regions, shows increasing trend for buying those product from June till October, visits stores in average once a week, drives mostly red cars, it is significant information for making business strategy regarding marketing activities.

Typical buyer of black beer with specific flavor could change its habits or characteristics during period of time. It could be changed in way that typical buyer of black beer with specific flavor, meets matching criteria of age between 30-35 years, lives in specific regions, shows increasing trend for buying those product from May till August, visits stores in average once a month.

Changing in characteristics could be caused by time component because same buyers became older, and we have loyal buyers because they did not give up to by same product. Changing in habits connected with increasing buying trends from May till August instead June till October could imply changing in factors like preferred period of holidays.

Profile changes demands changes in marketing strategies and marketing planning.

Significant profile transformation demands greater changes in marketing strategies.

This hypothetic example illustrates strong connection between analytics and strategic business thinking.

Portfolio management demands continuous portfolio monitoring, and in situation where company operates with numerous products on market, which are covered with some predictive models which calculates probability for buying, or next best offer, it is impossible to operate or monitoring portfolio without systematic approach.

Presented model is appropriate solution in this case, and it can be used as well as element for more complex systems. Particle swarm optimization algorithm in combination with built predictive model (based on e.g. neural network) is a solid base for automation of profiling processes.

Periodical processing on available data with particle swarm optimization algorithm in combination with built predictive model should result with derived typical profiles, and what is more important with migration trends (differences) of some characteristic within profiles.

Those results observed during period of time could give pretty clear picture about changes in customers/buyers profiles, and could be trigger for further market activities, as well as generator of new ideas for product development.

As it was seen from presented empirical results, there is no guarantee that proposed model will be successful for generating typical profiles for all the products covered with predictive model. However, empirical results show that it is efficient for most of the modalities of output variable. It implies that proposed methodology could be efficient for intended purpose.

Additional advantage which proposed model offers is ability to calculate similarity between profiles. It is useful functionality in situation where companies try to find "profile clusters". Profile clustering is useful in situation where company try to optimize market activities and to save costs regarding marketing budget. On the other side, it could be generator for new ideas for new product development.

For example, if a buyer of black beer with specific flavor has similar profile like chips buyers, and garden equipment buyers, it could be good starting point for cross selling activities, or good starting point for new product development.

Generic profile calculation has additional advantage in combination with functions for distance calculation. In combination, that methodology could give an answer on questions, which is the main similarity between garden equipment buyer and buyers which prefer to buy construction material.

Also, same methodology can give the answers on questions like, which is the main differences between buyer of black beer with specific flavor, and buyer of beer without flavors.

Regarding nature of market, which can change their characteristics during period of time, same methodology can provide information about profile migration, which could be presented with profile migration maps for specific products or group of products. Also, it can give an answer does profiles for several targeted products became more diversified or became more similar during period of time.

That information is valuable source for portfolio management, as well as for market trends recognition.

It is important to have in mind, that a good predictive model mostly contains behavioral variables which holds the model, and has great influence on predictive power. That fact, leads us to conclusion that proposed methodology could be good tool for recognition and differentiation based on behavioral characteristics. Behavioral characteristics, like for example, buying habits, preferred buying time, buying frequency, store visiting, could be valuable source for good profiling. Changes in those characteristics could imply different buying patterns or preferences. Taking in account all factors which makes differentiation between typical consumers of specific products, supported with presented methodology based on particle swarm optimization algorithm, in combination with built predictive model, outputs can provide valuable information for understanding customer behavior.

It is not hard to assume benefits of applying additional data mining methods like Self Organizing Maps and decision trees. In case where we have generated profiles based on particle swarm optimization algorithm, in combination with built predictive model, Self Organizing Maps could be used for customer profile clustering. Clustered profiles, which contain behavioral characteristics processed with decision trees, could give insight about key driven factors about main differences in recognized buyer's segments.

Generally speaking, it leads us to conclusion that company instead of single profile monitoring, could also monitor profile groups. Also, same as for single profiles, periodical processing on profile group level during period of time could give pretty clear picture about changes in customers/buyers profiles on recognized group level, and could be trigger for further market activities, as well as generator of new ideas for product development and cross selling.

CONCLUSION

Particle swarm optimization algorithm is mostly used as a learning optimization tool for neural networks. It implies changing on weights for achieving optimal fitness.

Chapter represents different approach, in which PSO are used as tool for changing input values of developed predictive model with intention to find optimal customer profile which are willingness to buy specific product.

It is nontrivial task especially in situation when predictive model calculates probability for numerous product / group of products by using numerous input variables.

In that case, PSO algorithm is useful for fast profiling, when numerous combination exists, and when it is time consuming to make profiles manually with uncertain results.

Additional advantage is profile similarity calculation based on given results.

Predictive models based on neural networks are not the only option on which PSO algorithm could be applied for customer profiling. It could be applied on predictive models based on support vector machines, multinomial regression, decision trees, decision trees and Bayesian networks.

Presented methodology has practical value for decision support in business, where information about customer profiles which prefers to buy some product or group products are valuable information for campaign planning.

Also, described methodology could be used frequently (e.g. on quarterly basis) for determination about changes in customer profiles, which implies changes in customer behavior or preferences during certain period of time. This information is valuable source for changes in marketing strategy and in situation when it is automatic process with PSO algorithm, it could be semi-automated process, which is not time consuming.

It is important to keep in mind that presented methodology does not guarantee that it is able to find profiles for each defined product / group of product. As it is seen on results based from empirical data it is not surprising that for some defined product / group of product it is not possible to find reliable customer profile. It depends on data itself, as well as on type of predictive model.

Situation in which for the most of the product / group of product adequate profiles are recognized with certain threshold is acceptable.

REFERENCES

Adhikari, R., & Agrawal, R. K. (2013). Hybridization of artificial neural network and particle swarm optimization methods for time series forecasting. *International Journal of Applied Evolutionary Computation*, *4*(3), 75–90. doi:10.4018/jaec.2013070107

Afify, A. (2013). Intelligent computation for manufacturing. In Z. Li & A. Al-Ahmari (Eds.), *Formal methods in manufacturing systems: Recent advances* (pp. 211–246). Hershey, PA: Engineering Science Reference; doi:10.4018/978-1-4666-4034-4.ch009

Aleksander, I., & Morton, H. (1995). *An introduction to neural computing*. International Thompson Computer Press.

Anagnostopoulos, C., & Hadjiefthymiades, S. (2012). Swarm intelligence in autonomic computing: The particle swarm optimization case. In P. Cong-Vinh (Ed.), *Formal and practical aspects of autonomic computing and networking: Specification, development, and verification* (pp. 97–117). Hershey, PA: Information Science Reference; doi:10.4018/978-1-60960-845-3.ch004

Arora, V., & Ravi, V. (2013). Data mining using advanced ant colony optimization algorithm and application to bankruptcy prediction. *International Journal of Information Systems and Social Change*, *4*(3), 33–56. doi:10.4018/jissc.2013070103

Babahajyani, P., Habibi, F., & Bevrani, H. (2014). An on-line PSO-based fuzzy logic tuning approach: Microgrid frequency control case study. In P. Vasant (Ed.), *Handbook of research on novel soft computing intelligent algorithms: Theory and practical applications* (pp. 589–616). Hershey, PA: Information Science Reference; doi:10.4018/978-1-4666-4450-2.ch020

Cheng, S., Shi, Y., & Qin, Q. (2013). A study of normalized population diversity in particle swarm optimization. *International Journal of Swarm Intelligence Research*, *4*(1), 1–34. doi:10.4018/jsir.2013010101

Clerck, M. (2013). *Particle swarm optimization*. London: Iste.

Devi, V. S. (2014). Learning using soft computing techniques. In B. Tripathy & D. Acharjya (Eds.), *Global trends in intelligent computing research and development* (pp. 51–67). Hershey, PA: Information Science Reference; doi:10.4018/978-1-4666-4936-1.ch003

El-Shorbagy. (2013). *Numerical optimization & swarm intelligence for optimization: Trust region algorithm & particle swarm optimization*. Lap Lambert Academic Publishing.

Giudici, P. (2003). *Applied data mining: Statistical methods for business and industry*. John Wiley &Sons Inc.

Giudici, P., & Figini, S. (2009). *Applied data mining for business and industry*. Wiley. doi:10.1002/9780470745830

Han, J., & Kamber, M. (2006). *Data mining: Concepts and techniques*. Morgan Kaufmann.

Klepac, G. (2010). Preparing for new competition in the retail industry. In A. Syvajarvi & J. Stenvall (Eds.), *Data mining in public and private sectors: Organizational and government applications* (pp. 245–266). Hershey, PA: Information Science Reference; doi:10.4018/978-1-60566-906-9.ch013

Klepac, G. (2014). Data mining models as a tool for churn reduction and custom product development in telecommunication industries. In P. Vasant (Ed.), *Handbook of research on novel soft computing intelligent algorithms: Theory and practical applications* (pp. 511–537). Hershey, PA: Information Science Reference; doi:10.4018/978-1-4666-4450-2.ch017

Klepac, G., Kopal, R., & Mršić, L. (2015). *Developing churn models using data mining techniques and social network analysis*. Hershey, PA: IGI Global; doi:10.4018/978-1-4666-6288-9.ch001

Konstantinos, E. P., & Michael, N. V. (2010). Applications in machine learning. In K. Parsopoulos & M. Vrahatis (Eds.), *Particle swarm optimization and intelligence: Advances and applications* (pp. 149–167). Hershey, PA: Information Science Reference; doi:10.4018/978-1-61520-666-7.ch006

Konstantinos, E. P., & Michael, N. V. (2010). Established and recently proposed variants of particle swarm optimization. In K. Parsopoulos & M. Vrahatis (Eds.), *Particle swarm optimization and intelligence: Advances and applications* (pp. 88–132). Hershey, PA: Information Science Reference; doi:10.4018/978-1-61520-666-7.ch004

Kress, M., Mostaghim, S., & Seese, D. (2010). Intelligent business process execution using particle swarm optimization. In Information resources management: Concepts, methodologies, tools and applications (pp. 797-815). Hershey, PA: Information Science Reference. doi:10.4018/978-1-60566-705-8.ch003

Kurbatsky, V., Sidorov, D., Tomin, N., & Spiryaev, V. (2014). Optimal training of artificial neural networks to forecast power system state variables. *International Journal of Energy Optimization and Engineering*, *3*(1), 65–82. doi:10.4018/ijeoe.2014010104

Larose, D. T. (2005). *Discovering knowledge in data: An introduction to data mining*. John Wiley &Sons Inc. doi:10.1002/0471687545

Nguyen, S., & Kachitvichyanukul, V. (2010). Movement strategies for multi-objective particle swarm optimization. *International Journal of Applied Metaheuristic Computing*, *1*(3), 59–79. doi:10.4018/jamc.2010070105

Olson, E. A. (2011). *Particle swarm optimization: Theory, techniques and applications*. Nova Science Pub Inc.

Rajesh, R., Pugazhendhi, S., & Ganesh, K. (2013). Genetic algorithm and particle swarm optimization for solving balanced allocation problem of third party logistics providers. In J. Wang (Ed.), *Management innovations for intelligent supply chains* (pp. 184–203). Hershey, PA: Business Science Reference; doi:10.4018/978-1-4666-2461-0.ch010

Russel, C. E., Yuhui, S., & Kennedy, J. (2001). *Swarm intelligence*. Morgan Kaufmann.

Singh, S., & Singh, J. N. (2012). *Application of particle swarm optimization: In the field of image processing*. Lap Lambert Academic Publishing.

Taleizadeh, A. A., & Cárdenas-Barrón, L. E. (2013). Metaheuristic algorithms for supply chain management problems. In Supply chain management: Concepts, methodologies, tools, and applications (pp. 1814-1837). Hershey, PA: Business Science Reference. doi:10.4018/978-1-4666-2625-6.ch106

Tosun, Ö. (2014). Artificial bee colony algorithm. In J. Wang (Ed.), *Encyclopedia of business analytics and optimization* (pp. 179–192). Hershey, PA: Business Science Reference; doi:10.4018/978-1-4666-5202-6.ch018

Xing, B., & Gao, W. (2014). Post-disassembly part-machine clustering using artificial neural networks and ant colony systems. In *Computational intelligence in remanufacturing* (pp. 135–150). Hershey, PA: Information Science Reference; doi:10.4018/978-1-4666-4908-8.ch008

Xing, B., & Gao, W. (2014a). Overview of computational intelligence. In *Computational intelligence in remanufacturing* (pp. 18–36). Hershey, PA: Information Science Reference; doi:10.4018/978-1-4666-4908-8.ch002

Yosuf, M. S. (2010). *Nonlinear predictive control using particle swarm optimization: Application to power systems*. Heidelberg, Germany: VDM Verlag Dr. Müller.

ADDITIONAL READING

Abbasimehr, H., Tarokh, M. J., & Setak, M. (2011). Determination of Algorithms Making Balance Between Accuracy and Comprehensibility in Churn Prediction Setting. *International Journal of Information Retrieval Research*, *1*(2), 39–54. doi:10.4018/IJIRR.2011040103

Agosta, L. (2000). *The Essential Guide to Data Warehousing*. Upper Saddle River, N.J.: Prentice Hall.

Aleksander, I., & Morton, H. (1995). *An introduction to neural computing*. NY: International Thompson Computer Press.

Alippi, C. (2003). A Perturbation Size-Independent Analysis of Robustness in Neural Networks by Randomized Algorithms. In M. Mohammadian, R. Sarker, & X. Yao (Eds.), *Computational Intelligence in Control* (pp. 22–40). Hershey, PA: Idea Group Publishing; doi:10.4018/978-1-59140-037-0.ch002

Almeida, F., & Santos, M. (2014). A Conceptual Framework for Big Data Analysis. In I. Portela & F. Almeida (Eds.), *Organizational, Legal, and Technological Dimensions of Information System Administration* (pp. 199–223). Hershey, PA: Information Science Reference; doi:10.4018/978-1-4666-4526-4.ch011

Bakshi, K. (2014). Technologies for Big Data. In W. Hu & N. Kaabouch (Eds.), *Big Data Management, Technologies, and Applications* (pp. 1–22). Hershey, PA: Information Science Reference; doi:10.4018/978-1-4666-4699-5.ch001

Bang, J., Dholakia, N., Hamel, L., & Shin, S. (2009). Customer Relationship Management and Knowledge Discovery in Database. In J. Erickson (Ed.), *Database Technologies: Concepts, Methodologies, Tools, and Applications* (pp. 1778–1786). Hershey, PA: Information Science Reference; doi:10.4018/978-1-60566-058-5.ch107

Berry, J. A. Michaell, Linoff G., (1997) Data mining techniques for marketing sales and customer support. NY: John Wiley &Sons Inc.

Chen, D., & Mohler, R. R. (2010). Intelligent Control and Optimal Operation of Complex Electric Power Systems Using Hierarchical Neural Networks. In G. Rigatos (Ed.), *Intelligent Industrial Systems: Modeling, Automation and Adaptive Behavior* (pp. 291–320). Hershey, PA: Information Science Reference; doi:10.4018/978-1-61520-849-4.ch011

Dieu, V. N., & Ongsakul, W. (2012). Hopfield Lagrange Network for Economic Load Dispatch. In P. Vasant, N. Barsoum, & J. Webb (Eds.), *Innovation in Power, Control, and Optimization: Emerging Energy Technologies* (pp. 57–94). Hershey, PA: Engineering Science Reference; doi:10.4018/978-1-61350-138-2.ch002

Dresner, H. (2008). *Performance management revolution*. NY: John Wiley &Sons Inc.

Elamvazuthi, I., Vasant, P., & Ganesan, T. (2012). Integration of Fuzzy Logic Techniques into DSS for Profitability Quantification in a Manufacturing Environment. In M. Khan & A. Ansari (Eds.), *Handbook of Research on Industrial Informatics and Manufacturing Intelligence: Innovations and Solutions* (pp. 171–192). Hershey, PA: Information Science Reference; doi:10.4018/978-1-4666-0294-6.ch007

Feng, J., Xu, L., & Ramamurthy, B. (2009). Overlay Construction in Mobile Peer-to-Peer Networks. In B. Seet (Ed.), *Mobile Peer-to-Peer Computing for Next Generation Distributed Environments: Advancing Conceptual and Algorithmic Applications* (pp. 51–67). Hershey, PA: Information Science Reference; doi:10.4018/978-1-60566-715-7.ch003

Garrido, P., & Lemahieu, W. (2008). Collective Intelligence. In G. Putnik & M. Cruz-Cunha (Eds.), *Encyclopedia of Networked and Virtual Organizations* (pp. 280–287). Hershey, PA: Information Science Reference; doi:10.4018/978-1-59904-885-7.ch037

Gavrilova, M. L., & Monwar, M. (2013). Chaotic Neural Networks and Multi-Modal Biometrics. In *Multimodal Biometrics and Intelligent Image Processing for Security Systems* (pp. 130–146). Hershey, PA: Information Science Reference; doi:10.4018/978-1-4666-3646-0.ch009

Hemalatha, M. (2012). A Predictive Modeling of Retail Satisfaction: A Data Mining Approach to Retail Service Industry. In P. Ordóñez de Pablos & M. Lytras (Eds.), *Knowledge Management and Drivers of Innovation in Services Industries* (pp. 175–189). Hershey, PA: Information Science Reference; doi:10.4018/978-1-4666-0948-8.ch014

Hussain, A., & Liatsis, P. (2009). A Novel Recurrent Polynomial Neural Network for Financial Time Series Prediction. In M. Zhang (Ed.), *Artificial Higher Order Neural Networks for Economics and Business* (pp. 190–211). Hershey, PA: Information Science Reference; doi:10.4018/978-1-59904-897-0.ch009

Janecek, A., & Tan, Y. (2011). Swarm Intelligence for Non-Negative Matrix Factorization. [IJSIR]. *International Journal of Swarm Intelligence Research*, 2(4), 12–34. doi:10.4018/jsir.2011100102

Kawamura, H., & Suzuki, K. (2011). Pheromone-style Communication for Swarm Intelligence. In S. Chen, Y. Kambayashi, & H. Sato (Eds.), *Multi-Agent Applications with Evolutionary Computation and Biologically Inspired Technologies: Intelligent Techniques for Ubiquity and Optimization* (pp. 294–307). Hershey, PA: Medical Information Science Reference; doi:10.4018/978-1-60566-898-7.ch016

Kazienko, P., & Ruta, D. (2011). The Impact of Customer Churn on Social Value Dynamics. In I. Management Association (Ed.), *Virtual Communities: Concepts, Methodologies, Tools and Applications* (pp. 2086-2096). Hershey, PA: Information Science Reference. doi:10.4018/978-1-60960-100-3.ch613

Kim, M., Park, M., & Park, J. (2009). When Customer Satisfaction Isn't Good Enough: The Role of Switching Incentives and Barriers Affecting Customer Behavior in Korean Mobile Communications Services. In I. Lee (Ed.), *Handbook of Research on Telecommunications Planning and Management for Business* (pp. 351–363). Hershey, PA: Information Science Reference; doi:10.4018/978-1-60566-194-0.ch022

Kolomvatsos, K., & Hadjiefthymiades, S. (2012). On the Use of Fuzzy Logic in Electronic Marketplaces. In V. Mago & N. Bhatia (Eds.), *Cross-Disciplinary Applications of Artificial Intelligence and Pattern Recognition: Advancing Technologies* (pp. 609–632). Hershey, PA: Information Science Reference; doi:10.4018/978-1-61350-429-1.ch030

Lee, K., & Paik, T. (2006). A Neural Network Approach to Cost Minimizatin in a Production Scheduling Setting. In J. Rabuñal & J. Dorado (Eds.), *Artificial Neural Networks in Real-Life Applications* (pp. 297–313). Hershey, PA: Idea Group Publishing; doi:10.4018/978-1-59140-902-1.ch014

Lin, D., & Liao, G. (2010). Computational Intelligence Clustering for Dynamic Video Watermarking. In L. Wang & T. Hong (Eds.), *Intelligent Soft Computation and Evolving Data Mining: Integrating Advanced Technologies* (pp. 298–318). Hershey, PA: Information Science Reference; doi:10.4018/978-1-61520-757-2.ch014

Malhotra, R. (2014). SIDE: A Decision Support System Using a Combination of Swarm Intelligence and Data Envelopment Analysis. [IJSDS]. *International Journal of Strategic Decision Sciences*, 5(1), 39–58. doi:10.4018/ijsds.2014010103

Michaell, B. J. A., & Gordon, L. (2000). *Mastering data mining*. NY: John Wiley &Sons Inc.

Michaell, B. J. A., & Gordon, L. (2003). *Mining the web*. NY: John Wiley &Sons Inc.

Moein, S. (2014). Optimization Algorithms. In *Medical Diagnosis Using Artificial Neural Networks* (pp. 182–199). Hershey, PA: Medical Information Science Reference; doi:10.4018/978-1-4666-6146-2.ch013

Pacini, E., Mateos, C., & Garino, C. G. (2013). Schedulers Based on Ant Colony Optimization for Parameter Sweep Experiments in Distributed Environments. In S. Bhattacharyya & P. Dutta (Eds.), *Handbook of Research on Computational Intelligence for Engineering, Science, and Business* (pp. 410–448). Hershey, PA: Information Science Reference; doi:10.4018/978-1-4666-2518-1.ch016

Qi, J., Li, Y., Li, C., & Zhang, Y. (2009). Telecommunication Customer Detainment Management. In I. Lee (Ed.), *Handbook of Research on Telecommunications Planning and Management for Business* (pp. 379–399). Hershey, PA: Information Science Reference; doi:10.4018/978-1-60566-194-0.ch024

Sharkey, A. J., & Sharkey, N. (2006). The Application of Swarm Intelligence to Collective Robots. In J. Fulcher (Ed.), *Advances in Applied Artificial Intelligence* (pp. 157–185). Hershey, PA: Idea Group Publishing; doi:10.4018/978-1-59140-827-7.ch006

Shen, Y., Li, Y., Wu, L., Liu, S., & Wen, Q. (2014). Big Data Overview. In Y. Shen, Y. Li, L. Wu, S. Liu, & Q. Wen (Eds.), *Enabling the New Era of Cloud Computing: Data Security, Transfer, and Management* (pp. 156–184). Hershey, PA: Information Science Reference; doi:10.4018/978-1-4666-4801-2.ch008

Shi, Y. (2012). *Innovations and Developments of Swarm Intelligence Applications* (pp. 1–398). Hershey, PA: IGI Global; doi:10.4018/978-1-4666-1592-2

Sirkeci, I., & Mannix, R. (2010). Segmentation Challenges Posed by 'Transnationals' in Mobile Marketing. In K. Pousttchi & D. Wiedemann (Eds.), *Handbook of Research on Mobile Marketing Management* (pp. 94–114). Hershey, PA: Business Science Reference; doi:10.4018/978-1-60566-074-5.ch006

Weiss, G. (2009). Data Mining in the Telecommunications Industry. In J. Wang (Ed.), *Encyclopedia of Data Warehousing and Mining* (2nd ed., pp. 486–491). Hershey, PA: Information Science Reference; doi:10.4018/978-1-60566-010-3.ch076

Werro, N., & Stormer, H. (2012). A Fuzzy Logic Approach for the Assessment of Online Customers. In A. Meier & L. Donzé (Eds.), *Fuzzy Methods for Customer Relationship Management and Marketing: Applications and Classifications* (pp. 252–270). Hershey, PA: Business Science Reference; doi:10.4018/978-1-4666-0095-9.ch011

Willis, R., Serenko, A., & Turel, O. (2007). Contractual Obligations between Mobile Service Providers and Users. In D. Taniar (Ed.), *Encyclopedia of Mobile Computing and Commerce* (pp. 143–148). Hershey, PA: Information Science Reference; doi:10.4018/978-1-59904-002-8.ch025

Willis, R., Serenko, A., & Turel, O. (2009). Contractual Obligations Between Mobile Service Providers and Users. In D. Taniar (Ed.), *Mobile Computing: Concepts, Methodologies, Tools, and Applications* (pp. 1929–1936). Hershey, PA: Information Science Reference; doi:10.4018/978-1-60566-054-7.ch155

Xing, B., & Gao, W. (2014). Overview of Computational Intelligence. In *Computational Intelligence in Remanufacturing* (pp. 18–36). Hershey, PA: Information Science Reference; doi:10.4018/978-1-4666-4908-8.ch002

Yusoff, N., Sporea, I., & Grüning, A. (2012). Neural Networks in Cognitive Science: An Introduction. In P. Lio & D. Verma (Eds.), *Biologically Inspired Networking and Sensing: Algorithms and Architectures* (pp. 58–83). Hershey, PA: Medical Information Science Reference; doi:10.4018/978-1-61350-092-7.ch004

KEY TERMS AND DEFINITIONS

Bayesian Network: Probabilistic graphical model based on conditional probabilities, which contains connected conditional probability tables within chance nodes.

Data Mining: Discipline which reveals useful patterns from huge amount of data.

Decision Tree: Decision support method that uses a tree-like graph with algorithm for partitioning.

Neural Network: Mathematical modelinspired on human neural systemwhich has ability to learn from data.

Predictive Model: Model, mostly based on data mining methodology and historical data which has purpose to predict some event.

PSO: Particle swarm optimization – algorithm based on evolutionary principle and swarm.

Support Vector Machine: Supervised learning models for classification and regression.

Chapter 14
Remote Sensing Image Classification Using Fuzzy–PSO Hybrid Approach

Anasua Sarkar
Government College of Engineering and Leather Technology, India

Rajib Das
Jadavpur University, India

ABSTRACT

Pixel classification among overlapping land cover regions in remote sensing imagery is a challenging task. Detection of uncertainty and vagueness are always key features for classifying mixed pixels. This chapter proposes an approach for pixel classification using hybrid approach of Fuzzy C-Means and Particle Swarm Optimization methods. This new unsupervised algorithm is able to identify clusters utilizing particle swarm optimization based on fuzzy membership values. This approach addresses overlapping regions in remote sensing images by uncertainties using fuzzy set membership values. PSO is a population-based stochastic optimization technique inspired from the social behavior of bird flocks. The authors demonstrate the algorithm for segmenting a LANDSAT image of Shanghai. The newly developed algorithm is compared with FCM and K-Means algorithms. The new algorithm-generated clustered regions are verified with the available ground truth knowledge. The validity and statistical analysis are performed to demonstrate the superior performance of the new algorithm with K-Means and FCM algorithms.

INTRODUCTION

Remote sensing is defined as the art and science of obtaining information about an object without being in direct physical contact with the object by Cogalton and Green in 1999 (Cogalton, 1999). Several methods exist for classifying pixels into known classes (for example, an urban area or turbid water) in remote sensing images. Mathematically, a remote sensing image can be defined as a set,

DOI: 10.4018/978-1-4666-8291-7.ch014

$$\mathcal{P} = \left\{ p_{ijk} | 1 \le i \le r, 1 \le j \le s, 1 \le k \le n \right\} \tag{1}$$

of $r \times s \times n$ information units for pixels, where $p_{ij} \in \left\{ p_{ij1}, p_{ij2}, \ldots p_{ijk} \right\}$ is the set of spectral band values for n bands associated with the pixel of coordinate *(i,j)*. In order to find homogeneous regions in the image we model this image by fuzzy sets, that considers both the spatial image objects and the imprecision attached to them.

Let us denote the space on which the remote sensing image is defined by $\mathcal{P}$ (usually $\mathbb{R}^n$ or $\mathbb{Z}^n$). We denote the points of $\mathcal{P}$ (pixels or voxels) as the spatial variables x, y. Let $d_p(x, y)$ denotes the spatial distance between two pixels $\left\{ x, y \right\} \epsilon \mathcal{P}$. In several earlier works on remote sensing, d_p is taken as the Euclidean distance on $\mathcal{P}$ (Maulik, 2012)(Bandyopadhyay, 2005).

A crisp object $\mathcal{C}$ in the remote sensing image is a subset of $\mathcal{P}$, $\mathcal{C} \subseteq \mathcal{P}$. Henceforth, a fuzzy object is defined as a fuzzy subset $\mathcal{F}$ of $\mathcal{P}$, $\mathcal{F} \subseteq \mathcal{P}$. This fuzzy object $\mathcal{F}$ is defined bi-univoquely by its membership function, μ. $\mu_{\mathcal{F}}(x) \epsilon (0, 1]$ is known as the membership function, which represents the membership degree of the point x to the fuzzy set $\mathcal{F}$. When the value of $\mu_{\mathcal{F}}(x)$ is closer to *1*, the degree of membership of *x* in $\mathcal{F}$ will be higher. Such a representation allows for a direct mapping of mixed pixels in overlapping land cover regions in remote sensing images. Let $\mathcal{F}$ denotes the set of all fuzzy sets defined on $\mathcal{P}$. For any two pixels x, y, we denote by $d_{\mathcal{F}}(x, y)$ as their distance in fuzzy perspective. The definition of a new method utilizing the particle swarm movements over fuzzy membership matrix is the scope of this chapter.

Clustering is one unsupervised classification method based on maximum intra-class similarity and minimum inter-class similarity. Other already proposed clustering, which can be applied for pixel classification in remote sensing imagery are - self-organizing map (SOM) (Spang, 2003), K-Means clustering (Tavazoie, 2001)(Hoon, 2004), simulated annealing (Lukashin, 1999), graph theoretic approach (Xu, 1999), fuzzy c-means clustering (Dembele, 2003) and scattered object clustering (de Souto, 2008). Several other methods like clustering based on symmetry (Maulik, 2009)(Sarkar, 2009)(Sarkar1, 2009) (Bandyopadhyay, 2005), supervised multi-objective learning approach (Maulik, 2012), also may be applicable efficiently for detection of arbitrary shaped land cover regions in remote sensing imagery problem.

The membership functions of both rough sets and fuzzy sets also enable efficient handling of overlapping partitions. Therefore, recently rough set theory is being used for clustering (Bandyopadhyay, 2008) (Cordasco, 2007)(Gonzalez, 1992)(Dembele, 2003)(Qin, 2003). Lingras (Xu, 1999)(Dembele, 2003) (Qin, 2003) used rough set theory to develop interval representation of clusters. This model is useful when the clusters do not necessarily have crisp boundaries.

Fuzzy set theory is a methodology to illustrate how to handle uncertainty and imprecise information in a difficult condition. The fuzzy models are normally used in land coverage detection of remote sensing image, pattern recognition and image processing (Bandyopadhyay, 2005)(Dave, 1989). Applying the concepts of fuzzy membership function (Wang, 1997)(Pappis, 1993), fuzzy clustering (Huang, 2008), fuzzy-rule based systems (Bardossy, 2002), fuzzy entropy (De Luca, 1972) and fuzzy integrals (Kumar, 1997) in algorithms, the remote sensing image identification becomes more feasible.

In the literature, earlier distances proposed comparing fuzzy membership functions do not include spatial information and therefore were not used in remote sensing (Chen, 1995) (Jain, 1995). The belongingness and non-belongingness of one pixel to one cluster can be utilized to detect as the approximated using Entropy theory on fuzzy sets. Luca and Termini (De Luca, 1972) defines a fuzzy entropy pseudo metric as an objective function for convergence in their algorithm. However, their metric fails to satisfy the separability condition (Bloch, 1999). In decision problems, the entropy functions have been combined with membership comparison approach earlier (Coppia, 2005)(Yager, 1992)(Bouchon-Meunier, 1993). (Bhandari, 1992) introduces one method on fuzzy divergence, mimicking Kulback's approach. However, this distance does not satisfy triangular inequality.

Following these works, we propose a new distance measure introducing Shannon's entropy in fuzzy membership comparisons for classifying pixels among overlapping land cover regions. We demonstrate the performance of the new distance metric in pixel classification of a chosen LANDSAT remote sensing image of Shanghai. The quantitative evaluation over three existing validity indices indicates the satisfactory performance of our new ENTROpy based FUZZY algorithm (FPSO) to detect imprecise clusters. We compare our obtained solutions with those of K-Means and FCM algorithms to verify with the ground truth knowledge. The statistical tests also demonstrate the significance of our new FPSO algorithm over K-Means and FCM algorithms.

BACKGROUND

Fuzzy C-Means Algorithm

Clustering is an unsupervised pattern classification method based on maximum intra-class similarity and minimum inter-class similarity. In a well-known partitional clustering approach, named fuzzy clustering, points may belong to more than one cluster. Therefore, for each point in a cluster, one set of membership levels is associated. This set of levels indicates the amount of association between the point and each of the clusters. One of the most widely used fuzzy clustering algorithms is the Fuzzy C Means algorithm. Fuzzy set theory was introduced in 1965 by Zadeh (Zadeh, 1965) as a mean to model the vagueness and ambiguity in complex systems. Fuzzy set theory handles the concept of partial membership to a set, with real valued membership degrees ranging from 0 to 1.

Introduced by Ruspini (Ruspini, 1970) and improved by Dune and Bezdek (Dunn, 1974) (Bezdek, 1981), the Fuzzy Cmeans (FCM) algorithm partitions a finite dataset $X = \{x_1, x_2, ..., x_N\}$ into a collection of K fuzzy clusters, satisfying criterions (Reddi, 1984). Let m be the exponential weight of membership degree, $m \in (1, \infty]$. The objective function $W_{m\mu}$ of FCM is defined as,

$$W_m(U,C) = \sum_{i=1}^{N}\sum_{j=1}^{K}\left(\mu_{ij}\right)^m\left(d_{ij}\right)^2 \tag{2}$$

where μ_{ij} is the membership degree of point x_i to centroid c_j and d_{ij} is the distance between x_i and c_j. Let $U_j = \left(\mu_{1j}, \mu_{2j}, ..., \mu_{Kj}\right)^T$. Then $U = \left(U_1, U_2, ..., U_N\right)$ is the membership degree matrix and $C = \{c_1, c_2, ..., c_K\}$ is the set of cluster centroids. W_m indicates the compactness and uniformity degree of clusters. Generally, a smaller W_m reflects a more compact cluster set.

The algorithm of FCM is an iteration process mathematically described as follows,

1. Initialize *m, M* and initial cluster centroid set $C^{(0)}$. Set the iteration terminating threshold ε to a small positive value and iteration time q to zero. Calculate $U^{(0)}$ according to $C^{(0)}$ with the following equation,

$$\mu_{ij} = \frac{1}{\sum_{k=1}^{K} \left(\dfrac{d_{ij}}{d_{ik}} \right)^{\frac{2}{(m-1)}}} \tag{3}$$

where $\displaystyle\sum_{j \in O_k , \ k=1,\dots,K} \mu_{ij} = 1$. If $d_{ij} = 0$, then $\mu_{ij} = 1$ and sets $\mu_{ik, k \neq j} = 0$ for membership of this pixel to other clusters.

2. Update $c^{(q+1)}$ according to $U^{(q)}$ with the following equation,

$$c_j = \frac{\sum_{i=1}^{N} \left(\mu_{ij} \right)^m x_i}{\sum_{i=1}^{N} \left(\mu_{ij} \right)^m} \tag{4}$$

3. Calculate $U^{(q+1)}$ according to $c^{(q+1)}$.
4. Compare $U^{(q+1)}$ with $U^{(q)}$. If $\left\| U^{(q+1)} - U^{(q)} \right\| \leq \varepsilon$, stop iteration. Otherwise, go to step 2.

PSO Algorithm

PSO is a population-based algorithm that uses a population of individuals to probe the best position in the search space. In PSO, the individual is called a particle, which moves stochastically in the direction of its own best previous position and the whole swarm's best previous position. Suppose that the size of the swarm is *N* and the search space is *M* dimensional, then the position of the *i*th particle is presented as $X_i = \{x_{i1}, x_{i2}, \dots, x_{iM}\}$. The velocity of this particle is presented as $V_i = \{v_{i1}, v_{i2}, \dots, v_{iM}\}$. The best previous position of this particle is denoted as $P_i = \{p_{i1}, p_{i2}, \dots, p_{iM}\}$. Consequently, the best previous position discovered by the whole swarm is denoted as $P_S = \{p_{S1}, p_{S2}, \dots, p_{SM}\}$. Let the maximum number of iteration be *T* and *t* be the present iteration. The unit time is denoted by $\Delta\tau$. Then the position of a particle and its velocity are changed following the constraints shown below (Gonzalez, 1992), (Lukashin, 1999)(Xu, 1999),

$$v_{im}^{t+1} = \omega^t * v_{im}^t + \frac{rand(\ )*c_1*\left(p_{im} - x_{im}^t\right)}{\Delta\tau} + \frac{rand(\ )*c_2*\left(p_{Sm} - x_{im}^t\right)}{\Delta\tau} \tag{5}$$

$$x_{im}^{t+1} = x_{im}^{t} + v_{im}^{t} * \Delta \tau \qquad\qquad (6)$$

$$\omega^{t} = \omega_{max} - \frac{t*\left(\omega_{max} - \omega_{min}\right)}{T} \qquad\qquad (7)$$

where $1 \leq t \leq T$, $1 \leq m \leq M$, and *rand()* generates the random number with uniform distribution $U(0,1)$. c_1 and c_2 are acceleration coefficients. ω is the inertia weight, with ω_{max} and ω_{min} as it's the maximum and minimum values respectively.

For the initial matrix,

$$X = \begin{bmatrix} x_{11} & x_{12} & x_{1M} \\ x_{21} & x_{22} & x_{2M} \\ x_{n1} & x_{n2} & x_{NM} \end{bmatrix},$$

the equation to generate particle value is,

$$x_{initial} = x_{im} = x_{min} + \left(x_{max} - x_{min}\right)* rand\left(\ \right), \ \forall m = \left\{1,...,M\right\} , n = \left\{1,...,N\right\}. \qquad (8)$$

Then the boundary constraints for x_{im}^{t+1} and v_{im}^{t+1} are as follows,

$$x_{im}^{t+1} = \begin{cases} x_{im}^{t+1}, & x_{min} \leq x_{im}^{t+1} \leq x_{max} \\ x_{initial}, & x_{im}^{t+1} > x_{max} \\ x_{initial}, & x_{im}^{t+1} < x_{min} \end{cases} \qquad\qquad (9)$$

$$v_{im}^{t+1} = \begin{cases} v_{im}^{t+1}, & -v_{max} \leq v_{im}^{t+1} \leq v_{max} \\ v_{max}, & v_{im}^{t+1} > v_{max} \\ -v_{max}, & v_{im}^{t+1} < -v_{max} \end{cases} \qquad\qquad (10)$$

where $\left\{v_{max}, v_{min}\right\}$ and $\left\{x_{max}, x_{min}\right\}$ are respectively maximum and minimum values for v and x, respectively.

RELATED WORKS

There is a canopy of existing works using Fuzzy set theory and PSO based approaches on the problem of multi-spectral image segmentation on remote sensing images.

(Dixon, 2008) experiments SVM method to the Landsat Thematic Mapper (TM) image classification, comparing the results with the maximum likelihood classifier (MLC), the neural network classifier and the decision tree classifier. They show SVM classifier obtain higher classification accuracy than those of the other classifiers (Dixon, 2008). Mountraki and Im make their experiments using several methods for analysis of airborne- and satellite-derived imagery which are proposed and assessed (Mountrakis, 2011).

Foody works on the SVM algorithm to classify the airborne image, which shows that SVM method often provide a higher accuracy than those existing stat-of-the-art classification methods (Foody, 2004) for multiclass image segmentation problem. Chiang and Hao implement an SVM-based fuzzy inference system which exhibits reliable performance using fuzzy rule based modeling (Chiang, 2004). Further, Melgani and Bruzzone experiment on the problem of the classification of hyper spectral remote sensing images by support vector machines (SVMs) in their relevant work (Melgani, 2004). Zhang et al. (Zhang, 2012) experiment with Fuzzy topology integrated Support Vector Machine approach on remote sensing image classification problem. They find the significant boundary and the interior parts of the classification using the fuzzy topology space. They demonstrate that their FTSVM method achieves higher classification accuracy than standard SVM and other classification methods (Zhang, 2012).

In SVM classification, the accuracy depends on whether the training data is sufficient to provide a representative description of each class or not. In general, the higher number of training pixels, the higher the classification accuracy. However, due to low image resolution, complexity of ground substances, diversity of disturbance, etc., many mixed pixels exist in a remotely sensed image (Zhang, 2012).

The SVM-FAHP method (Liu, 2012) divides 3PL provider selection into two stages. SVM is used in the first stage to classify all the enterprises for further election. Then fuzzy AHP is utilized to estimate the superior enterprises from those were selected in the first stage. In comparison with the classical methods, this model based on SVM-FAHP (Liu, 2012) improves the selection efficiency by reducing the computational cost during decision-making process and also decreases the cost of information collection simultaneously. The FAHP model uses the uncertainty problem very efficiently. The example study shows that the SVMFAHP model is feasible and effective.

SVMs are particularly useful in the remote sensing field for their ability to generate outputs even with limited training samples. This is a frequent necessary restriction for remote sensing problems. However, SVM faces the parameter assignment problem which can significantly affect obtained results. The classification algorithm SVM is a supervised approach with several advantageous features. This algorithm supports self-malleability with speedy learning and limited needs on training samples. Therefore SVM has been proved to be very methodology in pattern recognition field on processing of data acquired through remote sensing devices. Several earlier researches on both real world data and simulated datasets have shown that SVMs exhibit superiority over most of the state-of-the-art algorithms.

Zhibin Liu, Haifen Yang and Shaomei Yang (Liu, 2009) experiment to solve the shortcomings of traditional linear SCDA assessment methods. They propose an improved support vector machine (SVM) method combined with the multistage dynamic fuzzy decision. The algorithm takes as input the multistage fuzzy decision rules outputs as the sampling data. Then this algorithm uses the SVM algorithm to begin evaluation using those training points. This technique not only utilizes the advantages of multilayer SVM classifier, but also overcomes the problem of finding out the high grade training sample data.

This model utilizes the principle of structural risk minimization and therefore upgrades the accuracy and generalization ability of SVM much more. It utilizes the method of less learning over the problem of more learning, with an overall optimum solution. A very good feature of SVMs is that only the support vectors are of importance during training. This method also is superior to the neural network approach, as that method only provides partial optimal solution.

Yan Li, Li Yan, and Jin Liu (Li, 2009) divide the categories in remote sensing classification based on two views, basic thought and novel categorization algorithms. According to their survey, the approaches for remote sensing classification has been changed from per-pixel multispectral-based approaches to multiscale object-based approaches. The new category of the categorization algorithms comprises of the support vector machine (SVM), fuzzy Clustering (FCM) algorithm, evolutionary algorithm (EA), as well as implementation with Artificial Neural Networks (ANNs). This redirection leads to the development of several new hybrid remote sensing image classification methods in the past years. The research works are combinations of the multi scale object-based approaches with existing categorization algorithms like, SVM, fuzzy clustering algorithm, EA, ANNs.

In the past decades, several experiments with remote sensing devices generate several multisource datasets. Therefore the scientific challenge comes to be how to use these multisource imagery, like data in formats of multispectral, hyper spectral, radar, LIDAR, optical infrared sensors. The requirement becomes to efficiently utilize all these data in remote sensing applications to improve the classification accuracy.

Qiu Zhen Ge, Zhang Chun Ling, Li. Qiong, Xin Xian Hui and Guo Zhang (Ge, 2008) in their work, project the image categorization problem as an image texture learning problem. They view a remote sensing image as a collection of regions, each obtained from the output classes after image segmentation. These approaches provide efficient segment classes through a chosen metric distance function. Therefore, the segmentation problem becomes convertible to the regular categorization algorithm.

Sparse SVM (Ge, 2008) method has been developed to radically decrease the regions that are needed to classify in the remote sensing images. The chosen regions by a sparse SVM algorithm are utilized in the next phases as the target concepts in the traditional diverse density approaches. Therefore, the SVM classification method becomes to be very reliable in remote sensing image analysis problems. Several works show that the SVM approaches combined with Fuzzy improvements can produce superior results than the Nearest Neighbour (NN) approaches in the category of the supervised classifications.

Surveying several approaches over recent works in hyper dimensional feature space reveals the potentialities of SVM classifiers. Three significant useful properties of different SVM approaches in remote sensing image classification problems are shown below.

1. SVMs are more efficient than other conventional nonparametric classifiers like RBF neural networks and the K-NN classifier. The SVM approaches provide more categorization accurateness in terms of validity indices, requires computational times, and utilizes a trend of constancy to parameter setting.

2. Several research works reveal that SVMs are more effective than the traditional pattern recognition approaches, which incorporates a combination of existing feature extraction/selection methods and a conventional classifier.

To search existing works on remote sensing applications, the study on several existing clustering algorithms is needed. The most common applied algorithms in field of remote sensing image classifications are, hierarchical clustering algorithm, k-means algorithm, expectation maximization clustering algorithm and self-organizing maps (SOM) algorithm. Different factors need to be considered while comparing these algorithms, like number of clusters, size of dataset, type of dataset and type of software used to generate input dataset.

The hybrid FSVM (Fuzzy-SVM) method has been used to enhance the SVM in reducing the effect of outliers and noises (fuzziness) in data points. This method is very efficient in remote sensing applications, in which data points do not have any modeled characteristics (Chinag, 2004). Combing the advantages of traditional SVM framework and the fuzzy basis function inference system, Chiang and Hao (Chiang, 2004) propose an SVM-based fuzzy inference system on remote sensing imagery. The method exhibit a reliable performance in for classification and prediction of remote sensing images. Consequently, Tsujinishi and Abe (Tsujinishi, 2003) solve unclassifiable regions for multiclass problems in remote sensing images. They utilize fuzzy LSSVMs to resolve this problem.

Fuzzy topology is an enhanced form of ordinary topology by introducing the concept of membership value in a fuzzy set using fuzzy logic theory. The combined method of Fuzzy based SVM, named FSVM uses Fuzzy topology. The FSVM algorithm imposes a fuzzy membership to each input point which may belong to multiple classes on the decision surface. By using different types of fuzzy membership definitions, they apply FSVM to solve different kinds of problems.

This enhances the effectiveness of SVM even in fuzzy domain (Warrender, 1999). In spite of the efficiency of the SVM approach, this method still has some classification limits for its theory. For each class, the SVM usually treats all training points of this class uniformly following the theory of SVM. In many real-world problems, the consequences of choosing the training points affect the classification outputs. It is frequently that some specific training points are more important than others in the classification problem of remote sensing images. Therefore to choose more important training points becomes very important.

Foody and Mathur (Foody, 2004b) showed that only a quarter of the original training samples acquired from SPOT HRV satellite imagery was sufficient to produce an equally high accuracy for a two-crop classifier. Mantero et al. (Mantero, 2005) estimated probability density of thematic classes using an SVM. The SVMbasedapproachusedarecursiveproceduretogeneratepriorprobability estimates for known and unknown classes by adapting the Bayesian minimum-error decision rule. The approach was tested using synthetic data and two optical sensor data (i.e., Daedalus ATM and Landsat TM) and confirmed method effectiveness, especially when the availability of ground reference data was limited.

Bruzzone et al. (Bruzzone, 2006) implement the Transductive inference learning theory . They incorporate this method into an SVM for remote sensing classification. Their SVM-based method defines the separating hyperplanes according to their algorithm that integrates the unlabeled samples together with the training samples. Their experiments demonstrate that the proposed method is effective, for a set of ill-posed remote sensing classification problems with limited training samples.

Foody and Mathur (Foody, 2006) propose a method with on mixed pixel training samples over conventional pure pixel samples, for an SVM classifier. The analysis of a three-wave band multispectral SPOT HRV image showed the benefits of mixed pixel sampling on a crop type classification task. Foody et al. (Foody, 2006) evaluate 4 different dataset reduction approaches for a one-class problem (cotton class vs. other classes) using SVMs. They work on LISS-III data and found that significant data reduction is feasible ($\sim$90%) with minimal information loss. Sahoo et al. (Sahoo, 2007) incorporate localized, highly sensitive transformations to capture subtle changes in hyperspectral signatures. They compare the outputs of so called S-transform method with those of the classifiers without S-transform method. The results come satisfactory. The implemented algorithm is on an SVM which exhibits additional robustness for small data samples in a geological classification.

Blanzieri and Melgani (Blanzieri, 2008) investigate a local k-nearest neighbor (k-NN) adaptation method to formulate localized variants of SVM approaches. Their results exhibit encouraging improvements, specifically with the integration of non-linear kernel functions. Tuia and Camps Valls (Tuia, 2009) experiment the issue of kernel pre-determination by developing a regularization method to identify the kernel structure from the analysis of unlabeled samples. Camps-Valls et al. (Camps-Valls, 2010) experiment with an improved version of their method to assess kernel independence in various image types using the Hilbert–Schmidt independence criterion.

Marconcini et al. (Marconcini, 2009) develop an algorithm with the incorporation of spatial information through composite kernels. Their approach find satisfactory improvements howeover with an additional computation cost. Camps-Valls et al. (Camps-Valls, 2008) experiment in another work to develop a method using composite kernels for multi-temporal classification of remote sensing data from multiple sources. This method has been tested using both synthetic and real optical Landsat TM data. They demonstrate that the cross-information composite kernel was the best in general, but a simple summation kernel also exhibit similar improved performance. They work with composite kernels in their earlier work (Camps-Valls, 2006c).

Chi et al. (Chi, 2008) develop a method, named primal SVM. This algorithm is capable of classify landcovers using areas with notably small amount of training examples. Their method experiment to replace the regularization-based earlier approaches using SVMs. The primal SVM vector development makes it possible to optimize directly on the primal representation, and therefore limits the number of samples in their approach. They evaluate their work on Hyperion imagery of the Okavango Delta (in Botswana) for vegetation classification. Primal SVM exhibits competitive accuracy results in comparison with the state-of-art alternative algorithms trained on larger datasets.

Gómez-Chova et al. (Gómez-Chova, 2008) incorporate an addition of a regularization term on the geometry of both labeled and unlabeled samples on SVM. The variation is based on graph Laplacian, leading to a Laplacian SVM variant. Their semisupervised classification approach offers new direction when compared with traditional SVMs with more efficient results. It shows its superiority in cases especially with small training datasets and for complex problems. Castillo et al. (Castillo, 2008) develop a modified version of SVM algorithm, namely bootstrapped SVM. The training method adapted in this bootstrapped SVM is to training pool. An incorrectly classified training sample in a training step is removed from the training pool. It is re-assigned to a correct label and re-introduced into proper class of the training set in the next training cycles. Their result shows the ability to capture data variability even in a highly biased binary dataset. With only 0.05% of the total number of training pixels it can show to achieve about the same accuracy level as the standard SVM.

An interesting SVM adaptation was proposed by Wang (Wang, 1997), where the space between support vectors is considered to provide a soft classification in addition to the traditional hard classification.

Demir and Erturk (Demir, 2009) offer an improved algorithm over hyperspectral SVM classifiers by incorporating border training samples in a two-step classification process.

Similarly, Song et al. (Song, 2005) experiment with an SVM adaptation for Landsat-based vegetation monitoring. Their SVMs parameter are set using an integration of one and two class SVM sequential classification steps. Further, Mathur and Foody (Foody, 2008) experiment with the methods for efficient reduction of field data. They conclude that for cropland segmentation mapping classification, the good results can be obtained with one third of the original dataset assuming t be training points in SVM methods. In their experiment, at the 24m ground pixel resolution acquired by the LISS-III sensor, their reduced dataset yield a small 1.34% accuracy with a loss at 90.66%.

Integration of a genetic algorithm (GA) and SVM for remote sensing classification has been experimented with a limited availability of training samples by Ghoggali et al. (Ghoggali, 2009) in their remote sensing works. The experimental results exhibit an ability to improve classification accuracy with a small training sample size. However, the computational load becomes heavy primarily due to the slow GA convergence. Ghoggali and Melgani (Ghoggali, 2008) combined genetic training into SVM classification in order to incorporate land cover transition rules in multi temporal classification. The results show an improved performance.

Bruzzone and Persello (Bruzzone, 2009) develop a new context-sensitive semi-supervised SVM classification model, which they successfully use on chosen dataset when some of training data are not reliable. Their model explores the contextual information of the neighboring pixels of each training sample and improves the unreliable training data. They experiment their algorithm using Ikonos and Landsat TM data and compare their obtained results with those based on some of the most popular classification algorithms like the standard SVM, a progressive semi-supervised SVM, maximum likelihood (ML) and k-nearest neighbor (k-NN) algorithm. Their implemented SVM algorithm is superior to the other classification models in terms of robustness and effectiveness, particularly when non-fully reliable training samples are used.

Huang and Zhang (Huang, 2010) experiment with a multi-SVM method using traditional vector stacking techniques on high resolution urban mapping. Gomez-Chova et al. (Gomez-Chova, 2010) implement a method to increase classification reliability and accuracy by combining labeled and unlabeled pixels using clustering and the mean map kernel methods. They experiment their approach to classify clouds using En visat's Medium Resolution Imaging Spectrometer (MERIS) data. Their experiment reveals that their method is specifically particularly successful when sample selection bias (i.e., training and test data follow different distributions) exists. Selecting an optimum SVM method for remote sensing classification is a very challenging task now a days. Foody and Mathur (Foody, 2004a) implement a single multiclass SVM classification method while typical multiclass SVMs are based mainly on the use of multiple binary analyses. They evaluate the results of their approach with other classification methods, like discriminant analysis (DA), decision trees (DT), and neural networks (NN). They also exhibit the SVM-based method is superior to the other methods with different sizes of training samples.

Bazi and Melgani (2006) experiment on a most appropriate feature subspace and model selection based on a genetic optimization model. They use three feature selection methods including steepest ascent, recursive feature elimination technique, and the radius margin bound minimization method. They make constrain with two criteria - the simple support vector count and the radius margin bound. They use those two criteria to identify an optimum SVM-based classification method for hyperspectral remote sensing image classification problem. The genetically optimized SVM using the support vector count as a criterion demonstrate the best performance for both simulated and real-world AVIRIS hyperspectral data.

Mathur and Foody (Foody, 2008) experiment with the performance of SVMs in non-binary classification tasks. Their results show their implemented one shot SVM classifier is superior to the binary-based multiple classifiers in terms of obtained accuracy but also in initial parameterization.

SVMs have also been used for feature selection. Pal (Pal, 2006) implement methods for feature selection based on SVMs. Showing the advantage of exhaustive search approaches for real world problems, the scientists puts importance on the use of a non-exhaustive search procedure in selecting features with high discriminating power from large search spaces. SVM-based methods combined with GA are comparatively better than the random forest feature selection method, in land cover classification problems with hyperspectral data. Earlier works also exhibit their small benefits. Zhang and Ma (Zhang, 2009) work on the issue of feature selection in SVM approaches. They implement a modified recursive SVM approach to classify hyperspectral AVIRIS data. The reduced dimensionality demonstrates slightly better results, however their method has higher computational demands compared with others.

On the same subject Archibald and Fann (Archibald, 2007) propose an hybrid integration of feature selection within the SVM classification approach. They obtain efficient accuracy while significantly reducing the computational load. Some studies show the improvements on the performance of SVM-based classification through algorithms and/or data fusion. Zhang et al. (Zhang, 2006) define a pixel shape index approach describing the contextual information of nearby pixels. They evaluate its efficiency over land cover classification using Quick Bird data based on SVMs. In their work, the pixel shape indices are combined with transformed spectral bands using methods like principal component analysis (PCA) or independent component analysis (ICA). They show that integration of spectral and shape features as well as the transformed spectral components in an SVM produce improved classification accuracy.

MEMBERSHIP BASED FUZZY PSO ALGORITHM

The new FPSO algorithm consists of two phases – initial FCM clustering of the chosen remote sensing image to generate Fuzzy membership matrix U and finally using that membership, the membership based PSO method to generate optimal pixel allocations for overlapping regions, as shown in Figure 1.

Initial random assignment put N pixels in K clusters for initializing FCM algorithm, as described in previous subsection. Then we obtain the initial cluster centroids $C^{(0)}$. The iteration terminating threshold value ϵ is set to 1E-05. We initialize the membership degree matrix U from the initial random allocations in FCM algorithm. Then we repeat the centroid updation method iteratively and compute the membership degree matrix $U^{(q)}$ for each of the q iterations. The iterations converge and stop, when the difference between the membership degree matrix in previous and current iterations, becomes less than the iteration-terminating threshold ϵ.

After the first phase of FCM algorithm, we obtain the membership matrix to generate the initial pixel positions in M $(= K)$ number of fuzzy classes to denote overlapping regions for our hybrid membership based PSO approach. The value $x_{intial} = U$ has been set and V_{intial} for our PSO approach is computed within the constraints $\left\{-v_{max}, v_{max}\right\} = \left\{0, 1\right\}$ using Rastrigrin function. The Rastrigrin function is shown below –

$$f\left(x_i\right) = \sum x_i^2 - 10 * \cos\left(2 * \pi * x_i\right) + 10 ,$$ (11)

$$x_{min} = \left[0, 0, \ldots, 0\right],$$ (12)

$$f_{x_{min}} = 0 .$$ (13)

Figure 1. The flowchart of FPSO algorithm for remote sensing classification

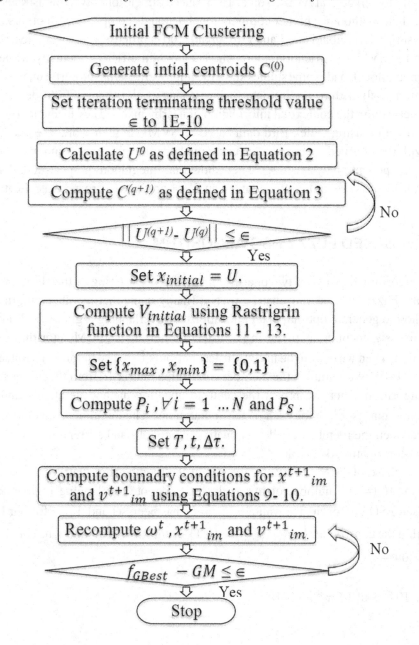

Similarly, $\left\{x_{max}, x_{min}\right\} = \left\{0,1\right\}$. Using these new constraints, we generate new membership degree matrix $U_{SE} = x_m^{t+1}$ and reassign the pixels to the clusters with maximum membership values. The cluster centroids are updated again and the iteration continues, until the convergence occurs with a difference between the old best particle in current population f_{GBest} and Global Minimum GM to be smaller than the terminating threshold $\in$. The validity indices are computed lastly over final PSO-optimized solutions.

APPLICATION OF FPSO ALGORITHM IN PIXEL CLASSIFICATION OF REMOTE SENSING IMAGERY

Experimental Framework

The new FPSO algorithm is implemented using MATLAB 2010 on MacBook dual-core processor. To compare well-known K-Means and FCM methods are also executed. Dunn (Dunn, 1973), Davies-Bouldin (DB) (Davies, 1979) and Silhouette (Rousseeuw, 1987) validity indices evaluate the effectiveness of FPSO over K-Means and FCM quantitatively. The efficiency of FPSO is also verified visually from the clustered images considering ground truth information of land cover areas.

Validity Indices

The fitness of a solution indicates the degree of goodness of the solution of the proposed algorithm (Young, 2001). In this article, three validity indices values, namely Davies-Bouldin (DB), Dunn and Silhouette indices, are used to determine the performance of the new hybrid algorithm. The validity indices are now described below.

1. **Davies – Bouldin Index (DB):** The Davies–Bouldin index (DB) (Davies, 1979) is a metric for evaluating clustering algorithms. This is an internal evaluation validity index. The best clustering solutions essentially minimizes the Davies Bouldin Index.

2. **Dunn Index:** The Dunn index (DI) (Dunn, 1973) is another metric for evaluating clustering algorithms. This is an internal validity index. For one allocation of clusters, a higher Dunn index indicates better clustering. Let C_i be a cluster of vectors. if there are M clusters, then the Dunn Index for the set is defined as,

$$DI_M = \min_{1 \le i \le M} \left\{ \min_{1 \le j \le m, j \ne i} \left\{ \frac{\delta\left(C_i, C_j\right)}{\max_{1 \le k \le M} \Delta_k} \right\} \right\} \tag{14}$$

3. **Silhouette Index s(C):** Let a denotes the average distance of a point from other points of same cluster and b denotes the minimum of the average distances of that point from the points in other clusters. Then the Silhouette Width (s) is defined as follows,

$$s = (b - a) / \max\{a, b\} \tag{15}$$

Silhouette Index s(C) (Rousseeuw, 1987) is the average Silhouette Width of all points, which reflects the compactness and separation of clusters. The value of s(C) varies from −1 to 1. For appropriate clustering s(C) should be high (Rousseeuw, 1987) .

PERFORMANCE ANALYSIS

The chosen LANDSAT image of Sanghai (Small, 2006) is available in seven bands viz. green, red and near infrared bands in the multispectral mode with distribution of the pixels in the feature space as shown in Figure 2. We have chosen red, green, blue and near infrared bands for our executions due to limitation of processor capacity. Figure 2 shows the original LANDAST image of Sanghai with histogram equalization with 7 classes, turbid water (TW), pond water (PW), concrete (Concr.), vegetation (Veg), habitation (Hab), open space (OS), and roads (including bridges)(B/R).

The river Huangpu cuts through the image, with one distinct black patch of water body on left bank near bottom-left corner of the image in Figure 2. In its upper right side of the river, a very thin line shows Su zhou river. There are two black patches in the upper-middle right bank of the river shown as a circle in Figure 2. Another canal is shown as another thin line stretching from the right bank of the river in the middle part of the image. In the lower right corner of the image, there exists another thin line indicating a canal. Figure 3 shows the scatter plot of pixel distribution for original Shanghai image.

The segmented Sanghai LANDAST images obtained by K-Means and FCM algorithms respectively are shown in Figures 4 and 6 for (K = 7). Figure 5 shows the scatter plot of cluster 1 and cluster 2 pixels as obtained in the solution of FCM algorithm. In Figure 4, K-Means algorithm fails to classify the two water bodies on the right bank of the river in upper-middle part of the image. FCM clustering solutions in Figure 6 also fails to detect this region as TW or PW class. However, new FPSO algorithm is able to separate these patches with proper indication of water bodies in Figure 7. The thin Su Zhou on the upper right side of the river is also misclassified by K-Means with Concrete and OS classes. FCM algorithm succeeds to detect this canal, but fails to classify the canal on left bank of river in lower middle part of image. However, our new FPSO algorithm is able to separate all three canals and the river into TW class in Figure 7. These indicate that FPSO algorithm detects the overlapping arbitrary shaped regions significantly with better efficiency than K-Means and FCM algorithms.

Figure 2. Original image of Shanghai

Figure 3. Scatter plot of original Shanghai image

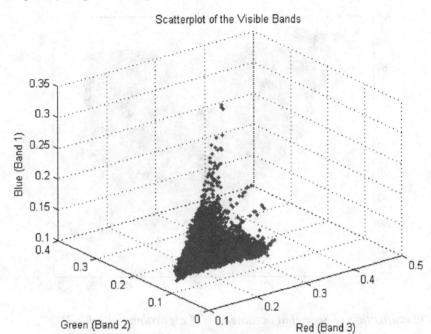

Figure 4. Pixel classification of Shanghai obtained by K-Means algorithm (with K=7)

The clustering results have been evaluated objectively by measuring validity measures Davies-Bouldin (DB), Dunn and Silhouette index, as defined in (Dunn, 1973)(Davies, 1979) and (Rousseeuw, 1987) respectively, for K-Means, FCM and FPSO algorithms on the Shanghai remote sensing image in Table 1. It can be noticed that, FPSO produces best final value for minimized DB index as 0.5569, while K-

Figure 5. FCM Cluster 1 and 2 plots

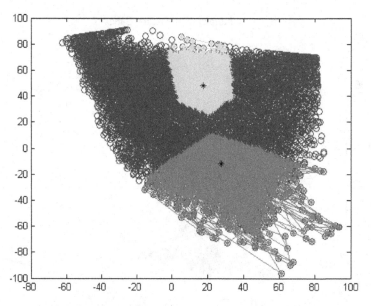

Figure 6. Pixel classification of Shanghai obtained FCM algorithm (with K=7)

Means obtains a DB value of 0.8376 and FCM obtains 0.7202. The maximizing Silhouette index values on Shanghai image for K-Means, FCM and FPSO are respectively 0.3404, 0.3331 and 0.5471. Similarly the Dunn index produced by FPSO algorithm (maximizing Dunn) is 3.0562, but K-Means and FCM algorithms provide a slightly smaller Dunn value of 1.2468 and 1.1624 respectively.

These results imply that FPSO optimizes DB, Dunn and Silhouette indices more than both K-Means and FCM. Hence, it is evident that FPSO is comparable in goodness of solutions to K-Means and FCM algorithms and even FPSO sometimes outperform to obtain superior fuzzy clustering results.

Figure 7. Pixel classification of Shanghai obtained by FPSO algorithm (with K=7)

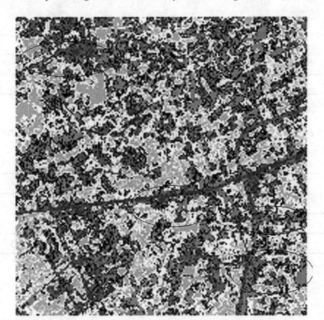

Table 1. Validity indices values of the classified remote sensing image provided by K-means, FCM and FPSO algorithms

Index	Shanghai Image		
	K-Means	*FCM*	*FPSO*
Davies-Bouldin index	0.8376	0.7202	0.5569
Silhouette index	0.3404	0.3331	0.5471
Dunn index	1.2468	1.1624	3.0596

TEST FOR STATISTICAL SIGNIFICANCE

A non-parametric statistical significance test called Wilcoxon's rank sum for independent samples has been conducted at 5% significance level (Hollander, 1999). Two groups have been created with the performance scores, Silhouette index values produced by 10 consecutive runs of K-Means, FCM and FPSO algorithms on the chosen remote sensing Image. From the medians of each group on the dataset in Table 2, it is observed that FPSO provides better median values than K-Means and FCM algorithms.

Table 3 shows the P-values and H-values produced by Wilcoxon's rank sum test for comparison of two groups, FPSO-K-Means and FPSO-FCM. All the P-values reported in the table are less than 0.005 (5% significance level). For the chosen remote sensing Image on Shanghai, comparative P-value of rank sum test between FPSO and K-Means is very small 5.31E-5, indicating the performance metrics produced by FPSO to be statistically significant and not occurred by chance. Similar results are obtained for other group with FCM algorithm also. Hence, all results establish the significant superiority of FPSO over K-Means and FCM algorithms.

Table 2. Median values of performance parameter Silhouette index over 10 consecutive runs on different algorithms

Data	Algorithms		
	K-Means	*FCM*	*FPSO*
Shanghai Image	0.3416	0.3331	0.5471

Table 3. P-values produced by rank sum while comparing FPSO with K-Means and FPSO with FCM respectively

Algorithm	Comparison with FPSO	
	H	*P-value*
K-Means	1	5.31E-5
FCM	1	4.73E-5

DISCUSSION

Fuzzy clustering algorithms can efficiently model fuzzy unsupervised patterns efficiently. One of the most popular fuzzy clustering algorithms is Fuzzy C-Means (FCM) algorithm. The FCM algorithm is based on an iterative optimization of a defined fuzzy objective function. However, the main drawback of the FCM algorithm is that the results are highly sensitive to the selection of initial cluster centers and it might converge to the Local optima.

In order to solve this problem, one approach is to use the swarm based optimization methods like PSO. However, the main problem of FCM is hidden in the nature of remote sensing data. The information on classes in remote sensing images are usually overlapped in spatial and spectral domain. However, by changing the characteristics of classifiers r combining some of them, one can solve these problems, and can produce better results.

One of the recent approaches is to use the kernel based methods with the clustering algorithms. In different recent works the clustering techniques are a hybrid of the FCM and the kernel algorithms. Kernel function can transform the input data space into a new higher (possibly infinite) dimensional space through some nonlinear mapping. In this hyperspace, the complex nonlinear problems lied in the original space can more likely be linearly represented and therefore can be solved efficiently in the transformed space. This follows the well-known Cover's theorem.

In recent years, some clustering techniques for remotely sensed image data has been proposed based on the above mentioned two methods. In one approach, after the preprocessing of data, the FCM clustering algorithm is optimized by a particle swarm algorithm (PSO-FCM). It then utilizes on the problem of for the wetland extraction. In other approaches to enhance superiority, a kernel-based fuzzy C-means clustering is used for clustering and recognition of multispectral remote sensing images.

However, due to high dimensionality of hyperspectral data, the above mentioned problems are intensified. In the other words, for optimization and nonlinear complex remote sensing problems, the number of local optima and nonlinear complexity are increased with higher dimensions of data. Consequently, we need to modify the classifier to handle these issues, to obtain more accurate results as expectable. This can be done by using our proposed aforementioned FPSO algorithm.

FUTURE RESEARCH WORKS

As a scope of future research, the time-efficiency of FPSO algorithm may be improved further by mapping it to the master-slave paradigm. Moreover, incorporation of spatial information in the feature vector as this is found to be effective in pixel classification, in lieu of intensity values at different spectral bands in FPSO method, constitutes an important direction for farther research.

CONCLUSION

Conventional hard classification methods fail to map land covers properly to the ground information. This problem can be overcome by mapping land cover regions to the fuzzy sets. Fuzzy approach seems natural in order to capture the overlapping regions in the image. Moreover, the PSO method can obtain optimal fuzzy membership values with efficient search stability without using any exhaustive search. Therefore, the contribution of this article lies in efficient detection of overlapping land cover regions in the remote sensing image by implementing a new hybrid Fuzzy membership based particle swarm optimization method, named FPSO clustering algorithm. The primary contributions are – to define one new velocity space in the domain of Fuzzy membership values, which will iterate the positions of the image pixels to allocate it to one fuzzy set of a particular land cover region with highest membership value.

The efficiency of the new FPSO algorithm is demonstrated over one chosen LANDSAT remote sensing image on Shanghai. Superiority of new FPSO clustering algorithm over the widely used K-Means and FCM algorithms is established quantitatively over three validity indices. The verification with ground truth information also shows significant efficiency of new FPSO algorithm over other two existing methods. Statistical tests also establish the statistical significance of FPSO over K-Means and FCM algorithms.

REFERENCES

Andermann, C., & Gloaguen, R. (2009). Estimation of erosion in tectonically active orogenies. Example from the Bhotekoshi catchment, Himalaya (Nepal). *International Journal of Remote Sensing*, *30*(12), 3075–3096. doi:10.1080/01431160802558733

Archibald, R., & Fann, G. (2007). Feature selection and classification of hyperspectral images with support vector machines. *IEEE Geoscience and Remote Sensing Letters*, *4*(4), 674–677. doi:10.1109/LGRS.2007.905116

Bandyopadhyay, S. (2005). Satellite image classification using genetically guided fuzzy clustering with spatial information. *International Journal of Remote Sensing*, *26*(3), 579–593. doi:10.1080/01431160512331316432

Bandyopadhyay, S., Maulik, U., & Wang, J. T. L. (2007). Analysis of biological data, a soft computing approach. In engineering and biology informatics (3rd ed.). World Scientific Publishing Co.

Bandyopadhyay, S., Mitra, R., Maulik, U., & Zhang, M. Q. (2010). Development of the human cancer microRNA network. *Silence*, *1*(1), 6. doi:10.1186/1758-907X-1-6 PMID:20226080

Bandyopadhyay, S., & Pal, S. K. (2001). Pixel classification using variable string genetic algorithms with chromosome differentiation. *IEEE Transactions on Geoscience and Remote Sensing, 39*(2), 303–308. doi:10.1109/36.905238

Barakat, N., & Bradley, A. P. (2010). Rule extraction from support vector machines, a review. *Neurocomputing, 74*(1-3), 178–190. doi:10.1016/j.neucom.2010.02.016

Bárdossy, A., & Samaniego, L. (2002). Fuzzy rule-based classification of remotely sensed imagery. *IEEE Transactions on Geoscience and Remote Sensing, 40*(2), 362–374. doi:10.1109/36.992798

Bazi, Y., & Melgani, F. (2006). Toward an optimal SVM classification system for hyperspectral remote sensing images. *IEEE Transactions on Geoscience and Remote Sensing, 44*(11), 3374–3385. doi:10.1109/TGRS.2006.880628

Bazi, Y., & Melgani, F. (2007). Semisupervised PSO-SVM regression for biophysical parameterestimation. *IEEE Transactions on Geoscience and Remote Sensing, 45*(6), 1887–1895. doi:10.1109/TGRS.2007.895845

Bentley, J. L. (1990). K-d trees for semi dynamic point sets. In *Proceedings of the 6th Annual 362 Symposium on Computational Geometry* (SCG 90). ACM-SIGACT ACM-SIGGRAPH.

Bezdek, J. C. (1981). *Pattern recognition with fuzzy objective function algorithms*. New York: Plenum Press. doi:10.1007/978-1-4757-0450-1

Bezdek, J. C. (1981). *Pattern recognition with fuzzy objective function algorithms*. New York: Plenum. doi:10.1007/978-1-4757-0450-1

Bhandari, D., Pal, N. R., & Majumder, D. D. (1992). Fuzzy divergence, probability measure of fuzzy events and image thresholding. *Pattern Recognition Letters, 13*(12), 857–867. doi:10.1016/0167-8655(92)90085-E

Blanzieri, E., & Melgani, F. (2008). Nearest neighbor classification of remote sensing images with the maximal margin principle. *IEEE Transactions on Geoscience and Remote Sensing, 46*(6), 1804–1811. doi:10.1109/TGRS.2008.916090

Bloch, I. (1999). On fuzzy distances and their use in image processing under imprecision. *Pattern Recognition, 32*(11), 1873–1895. doi:10.1016/S0031-3203(99)00011-4

Bouchon-Meunier, B., & Yager, R. R. (1993). Entropy of similarity relations in questionnaires and decision trees. In *Proceedings of Second IEEE International Conference on Fuzzy Systems* (pp. 1225-1230). IEEE. doi:10.1109/FUZZY.1993.327567

Bovolo, F., Bruzzone, L., & Marconcini, M. (2008). A novel approach to unsupervised change detection based on a semisupervised SVM and a similarity measure. *IEEE Transactions on Geoscience and Remote Sensing, 46*(7), 2070–2082. doi:10.1109/TGRS.2008.916643

Boyd, D. S., Sanchez-Hernandez, C., & Foody, G. M. (2006). Mapping a specific class for priority habitats monitoring from satellite sensor data. *International Journal of Remote Sensing, 27*(13), 2631–2644. doi:10.1080/01431160600554348

Brenning, A. (2009). Benchmarking classifiers to optimally integrate terrain analysis and multispectral remote sensing in automatic rock glacier detection. *Remote Sensing of Environment, 113*(1), 239–247. doi:10.1016/j.rse.2008.09.005

Brown, M., Gunn, S. R., & Lewis, H. G. (1999). Support vector machines for optimal classification and spectral unmixing. *Ecological Modelling, 120*(2–3), 167–179. doi:10.1016/S0304-3800(99)00100-3

Brown, M., Lewis, H. G., & Gunn, S. R. (2000). Linear spectral mixture models and support vector machines for remote sensing. *IEEE Transactions on Geoscience and Remote Sensing, 38*(5), 2346–2360. doi:10.1109/36.868891

Bruzzone, L., Chi, M., & Marconcini, M. (2006). A novel transductive SVM for semisupervised classification of remote-sensing images. *IEEE Transactions on Geoscience and Remote Sensing, 44*(11), 3363–3373. doi:10.1109/TGRS.2006.877950

Bruzzone, L., & Melgani, F. (2005). Robust multiple estimator systems for the analysis of biophysical parameters from remotely sensed data. *IEEE Transactions on Geoscience and Remote Sensing, 43*(1), 159–174. doi:10.1109/TGRS.2004.839818

Bruzzone, L., & Persello, C. (2009). A novel context-sensitive semisupervised SVM classifier robust to mislabeled training samples. *IEEE Transactions on Geoscience and Remote Sensing, 47*(7), 2142–2154. doi:10.1109/TGRS.2008.2011983

Burges, C. J. C. (1998). A tutorial on support vector machines for pattern recognition. *Data Mining and Knowledge Discovery, 2*(2), 121–127. doi:10.1023/A:1009715923555

Burges, C. J. C. (1998). A tutorial on support vector machines for pattern recognition. *Data Mining and Knowledge Discovery, 2*(2), 121–167. doi:10.1023/A:1009715923555

Camps-Valls, G., Bruzzone, L., Rojo-Alvarez, J. L., & Melgani, F. (2006b). Robust support vector regression for biophysical variable estimation from remotely sensed images. *IEEE Geoscience and Remote Sensing Letters, 3*(3), 339–343. doi:10.1109/LGRS.2006.871748

Camps-Valls, G., Gomez-Chova, L., Calpe-Maravilla, J., Martin-Guerrero, J. D., Soria-Olivas, E., Alonso-Chorda, L., & Moreno, J. (2004). Robust support vector method for hyperspectral data classification and knowledge discovery. *IEEE Transactions on Geoscience and Remote Sensing, 42*(7), 1530–1542. doi:10.1109/TGRS.2004.827262

Camps-Valls, G., Gomez-Chova, L., Munoz-Mari, J., Rojo-Alvarez, J. L., & Martinez-Ramon, M. (2008). Kernel-based framework for multitemporal and multisource remote sensing data classification and change detection. *IEEE Transactions on Geoscience and Remote Sensing, 46*(6), 1822–1835. doi:10.1109/TGRS.2008.916201

Camps-Valls, G., Gómez-Chova, L., Muñoz-Marí, J., Vila-Francés, J., Amorós-López, J., & Calpe-Maravilla, J. (2006a). Retrieval of oceanic chlorophyll concentration with relevance vector machines. *Remote Sensing of Environment, 105*(1), 23–33. doi:10.1016/j.rse.2006.06.004

Camps-Valls, G., Gomez-Chova, L., Munoz-Mari, J., Vila-Frances, J., & Calpe-Maravilla, J. (2006c). Composite kernels for hyperspectral image classification. *IEEE Geoscience and Remote Sensing Letters*, *3*(1), 93–97. doi:10.1109/LGRS.2005.857031

Camps-Valls, G., Mooij, J., & Scholkopf, B. (2010). Remote sensing feature selection by kernel dependence measures. *IEEE Geoscience and Remote Sensing Letters*, *7*(3), 587–591. doi:10.1109/LGRS.2010.2041896

Candade, N. (2004) Multispectral classification of Landsat images, a comparison of support vector machine and neural network classifiers. In *ASPRS Annual Conference Proceedings*. Denver, CO: Academic Press.

Cao, X., Chen, J., Imura, H., & Higashi, O. (2009b). A SVM-based method to extract urban areas from DMSP–OLS and SPOT VGT data. *Remote Sensing of Environment*, *113*(10), 2205–2209. doi:10.1016/j.rse.2009.06.001

Cao, X., Chen, J., Matsushita, B., Imura, H., & Wang, L. (2009a). An automatic method for burn scar mapping using support vector machines. *International Journal of Remote Sensing*, *30*(3), 577–594. doi:10.1080/01431160802220219

Carrão, H., Gonçalves, P., & Caetano, M. (2008). Contribution of multispectral and multitemporal information from MODIS images to land cover classification. *Remote Sensing of Environment*, *112*(3), 986–997. doi:10.1016/j.rse.2007.07.002

Castillo, C., Chollett, I., & Klein, E. (2008). Enhanced duckweed detection using bootstrapped SVM classification on medium resolution RGB MODIS imagery. *International Journal of Remote Sensing*, *29*(19), 5595–5604. doi:10.1080/01431160801961375

Chen, H., & Ho, P. (2008). Statistical pattern recognition in remote sensing. *Pattern Recognition*, *41*(9), 2731–2741. doi:10.1016/j.patcog.2008.04.013

Chen, J., Wang, C., & Wang, R. (2008a). Combining support vector machines with a pairwise decision tree. *IEEE Geoscience and Remote Sensing Letters*, *5*(3), 409–413. doi:10.1109/LGRS.2008.916834

Chen, J., Wang, C., & Wang, R. (2009). Using stacked generalization to combine SVMs in magnitude and shape feature spaces for classification of hyperspectral data. *IEEE Transactions on Geoscience and Remote Sensing*, *47*(7), 2193–2205. doi:10.1109/TGRS.2008.2010491

Chen, S. M., Yeh, M. S., & Hsio, P. Y. (1995). A comparison of similarity measures of fuzzy values. *Fuzzy Sets and Systems*, *72*(1), 79–89. doi:10.1016/0165-0114(94)00284-E

Chi, M., Feng, R., & Bruzzone, L. (2008). Classification of hyperspectral remote-sensing data with primal SVM for small-sized training dataset problem. *Advances in Space Research*, *41*(11), 1793–1799. doi:10.1016/j.asr.2008.02.012

Chiang, J. H., & Hao, P. Y. (2004). Support vector learning mechanism for fuzzy rule based modeling: A new approach. *IEEE Transactions on Fuzzy Systems*, *12*(1), 1–12. doi:10.1109/TFUZZ.2003.817839

Chiang, J. H., & Hao, P. Y. (2004). Support vector learning mechanism for fuzzy rule-based modeling: A new approach. *IEEE Transactions on Fuzzy Systems*, *12*(1), 1–12. doi:10.1109/TFUZZ.2003.817839

Clevers, J. G. P. W., van der Heijden, G. W. A. M., Verzakov, S., & Schaepman, M. E. (2007). Estimating grassland biomass using SVM band shaving of hyperspectral. *Data Photogrammetric Engineering & Remote Sensing, 73*(10), 1141–1148. doi:10.14358/PERS.73.10.1141

Cogalton, R. G., & Green, K. (1999). *Assessing the accuracy of remote sensed data, principles and practices*. London: Lewis Publishers.

Coppia, R., & D'Urso, P. (2005). Fuzzy unsupervised classification of multivariate time trajectories with the Shannon entropy regularization. *Computational Statistics & Data Analysis, 50*(6), 1452–1477. doi:10.1016/j.csda.2005.01.008

Cordasco, G., Scara, V., & Rosenberg, A. L. (2007). Bounded-collision memory-mapping schemes for data structures with applications to parallel memories. *IEEE Transactions on Parallel and Distributed Systems, 18*(7), 973–982. doi:10.1109/TPDS.2007.1024

Cordasco, G., Scarano, V., & Rosenberg, A. L. (2007). Bounded-collision memory-mapping schemes for data structures with applications to parallel memories. *IEEE Transactions on Parallel and Distributed Systems, 18*(7), 973–982. doi:10.1109/TPDS.2007.1024

Cortes, C., & Vapnik, V. (1995). Support-vector networks. *Machine Learning, 20*(3), 273–297. doi:10.1007/BF00994018

Dalponte, M., Bruzzone, L., & Gianelle, D. (2008). Fusion of hyperspectral and LIDAR remote sensing data for classification of complex forest areas. *IEEE Transactions on Geoscience and Remote Sensing, 46*(5), 1416–1427. doi:10.1109/TGRS.2008.916480

Dalponte, M., Bruzzone, L., Vescovo, L., & Gianelle, D. (2009). The role of spectral resolution and classifier complexity in the analysis of hyperspectral images of forest areas. *Remote Sensing of Environment, 113*(11), 2345–2355. doi:10.1016/j.rse.2009.06.013

Dash, J., Mathur, A., Foody, G. M., Curran, P. J., Chipman, J. W., & Lilles, T. M. (2007). Landcover classification using multi-temporal MERIS vegetation indices. *International Journal of Remote Sensing, 28*(6), 1137–1159. doi:10.1080/01431160600784259

Dave, R. N. (1989). Use of the adaptive fuzzy clustering algorithm to detect lines in digital images. *Intell. Robots Comput. Vision VIII, 1192*, 600–611.

Davies, D. L., & Bouldin, D. W. (1979). A cluster separation measure. *IEEE Transactions on Pattern Analysis and Machine Intelligence, 1*(2), 224–227.

de Hoon, M. J. L., Imoto, S., Nolan, J., & Miyano, S. (2004). Open source clustering software. *Bioinformatics (Oxford, England), 20*(9), 1453–1454. doi:10.1093/bioinformatics/bth078 PMID:14871861

De Luca, A., & Termini, S. (1972). A definition of non-probabilistic entropy in the setting of fuzzy set theory. *Information and Control, 20*(4), 301–312. doi:10.1016/S0019-9958(72)90199-4

de Souto, M. C. P., Soares, R.G.F., de Araujo, D.S.A., Costa, I.G., Ludermir, T.B., & Schliep, A. (2008). Ranking and selecting clustering algorithms using a meta-learning approach. In *Proc. of IEEE International Joint Conference on Neural Networks*. IEEE Computer Society.

de Souto, M. C. P., Costa, I. G., & Araujo, D. S. A., Ludermir, T. B., & Schliep, A. (2008). Clustering cancer gene expression data, a comparative study. *BMC Bioinformatics*, *9*(497). PMID:19038021

Dembele, D., & Kastner, P. (2003). Fuzzy c-means method for clustering microarray data. *Bioinformatics (Oxford, England)*, *19*(8), 973–980. doi:10.1093/bioinformatics/btg119 PMID:12761060

Demir, B., & Ertürk, S. (2007). Hyperspectral image classification using relevance vector machines. *IEEE Geoscience and Remote Sensing Letters*, *4*(4), 586–590. doi:10.1109/LGRS.2007.903069

Demir, B., & Erturk, S. (2009). Clustering-based extraction of border training patterns for accurate SVM classification of hyperspectral images. *IEEE Geoscience and Remote Sensing Letters*, *6*(4), 840–844. doi:10.1109/LGRS.2009.2026656

Dixon, B., & Canade, M. (2008). Multispectral land use classification using neural networks and support vector machines: One or the other, or both? *International Journal of Remote Sensing*, *29*(4), 1185–1206. doi:10.1080/01431160701294661

Dixon, B., & Candade, N. (2008). Multispectral land use classification using neural networks and support vector machines, one or the other, or both? *International Journal of Remote Sensing*, *29*(4), 1185–1206. doi:10.1080/01431160701294661

Duda, R. O., Hart, P. E., & Stork, D. G. (1981). *Pattern classification and scene analysis*. New York: Wiley.

Dunn, J. C. (1973). A fuzzy relative of the ISODATA process and its use in detecting compact well-separated clusters. *Journal of Cybernetics*, *3*(3), 32–57. doi:10.1080/01969727308546046

Dunn, J. C. (1974). A fuzzy relative of the ISODATA process and its use in detecting compact, well separated clusters. *Cybernetics*, *3*, 95–104.

Durbha, S. S., King, R. L., & Younan, N. H. (2007). Support vector machines regression for retrieval of leaf are a index from multi angle imaging spectroradiometer. *Remote Sensing of Environment*, *107*(1–2), 348–361. doi:10.1016/j.rse.2006.09.031

Eisen, M., Spellman, P., Brown, P., & Botstein, D. (1998). Cluster analysis and display of genome-wide expression patterns. *Proceedings of the National Academy of Sciences of the United States of America*, *95*(25), 14863–14868. doi:10.1073/pnas.95.25.14863 PMID:9843981

Esch, T., Himmler, V., Schorcht, G., Thiel, M., Wehrmann, T., Bachofer, F., & Dech, S. et al. (2009). Large-area assessment to f im pervious surface based on integrated analysis of single-date Landsat-7 images and geospatial vector data. *Remote Sensing of Environment*, *113*(8), 1678–1690. doi:10.1016/j.rse.2009.03.012

Everman, W. J., Medline, C. R., Jr, R. D. D., Bauman, T. T., & Biehl, L. (2008). The effect of postmergence herbicides on the spectral reflectance of corn. *Weed Technology*, *22*(3), 514–522. doi:10.1614/WT-07-021.1

Fauvel, M., Benediktsson, J. A., Chanussot, J., & Sveinsson, J. R. (2008). Spectral and spatial classification of hyper spectral data using SVMs and morphological profiles. *IEEE Transactions on Geoscience and Remote Sensing*, *46*(11), 3804–3814. doi:10.1109/TGRS.2008.922034

Fauvel, M., Chanussot, J., & Benediktsson, J. A. (2009). Kernel principal component analysis for the classification of hyperspectral remote sensing data over urban areas. *EURASIP Journal on Advances in Signal Processing*.

Filippi, A. M., & Archibald, R. (2009). Support vector machine-based end member extraction. *IEEE Transactions on Geoscience and Remote Sensing, 47*(3), 771–791. doi:10.1109/TGRS.2008.2004708

Foody, G. M. (2008). RVM-based multi-class classification of remotely sensed data. *International Journal of Remote Sensing, 29*(6), 1817–1823. doi:10.1080/01431160701822115

Foody, G. M., & Mathur, A. (2004). A relative evaluation of multiclass image classification by support vector machines. *IEEE Transactions on Geoscience and Remote Sensing, 42*(6), 1335–1343. doi:10.1109/TGRS.2004.827257

Foody, G. M., & Mathur, A. (2004a). A relative evaluation of multiclass image classification by support vector machines. *IEEE Transactions on Geoscience and Remote Sensing, 42*(6), 1335–1343. doi:10.1109/TGRS.2004.827257

Foody, G. M., & Mathur, A. (2004b). Toward intelligent training of supervised image classifications, directing training data acquisition for SVM classification. *Remote Sensing of Environment, 93*(1–2), 107–117. doi:10.1016/j.rse.2004.06.017

Foody, G. M., & Mathur, A. (2006). The use of small training sets containing mixed pixels for accurate hard image classification, training on mixed spectral responses for classification by a SVM. *Remote Sensing of Environment, 103*(2), 179–189. doi:10.1016/j.rse.2006.04.001

Foody, G. M., Mathur, A., Sanchez-Hernandez, C., & Boyd, D. S. (2006a). Training set size requirements for the classification of a specific class. *Remote Sensing of Environment, 104*(1), 1–14. doi:10.1016/j.rse.2006.03.004

Gath, I., & Geva, A. (1989). Unsupervised optimal fuzzy clustering. *IEEE Transactions on Pattern Analysis and Machine Intelligence, 11*(11), 773–781. doi:10.1109/34.192473

Gautam, R. S., Singh, D., Mittal, A., & Sajin, P. (2008). Application of SVM on satellite images to detect hotspots in Jharia coal field region of India. *Advances in Space Research, 41*(11), 1784–1792. doi:10.1016/j.asr.2007.05.011

Gawrys, M., & Sienkiewicz, J. (1994). RSL–The rough set library version 2.0 (ICS Research Report 27/94). Warsaw, Poland: Institute of Computer Science. W. U. of T.

Ge, Q. Z., Ling, Z. C., Qiong, L., Hui, X. X. & Zhang, G. (2008). *High efficient classification on remote sensing images based on SVM*. The International Archives of the Photogrammetry, Remote Sensing and Spatial Information Sciences.

Geman, S., Bienenstock, E., & Doursat, R. (1992). Neural networks and the bias/variance dilemma. *Neural Computation, 4*(1), 1–58. doi:10.1162/neco.1992.4.1.1

Ghoggali, N., & Melgani, F. (2008). Genetic SVM approach to semisupervised multi temporal classification. *IEEE Geoscience and Remote Sensing Letters, 5*(2), 212–216. doi:10.1109/LGRS.2008.915600

Ghoggali, N., Melgani, F., & Bazi, Y. (2009). A multiobjective genetic SVM approach for classification problems with limited training samples. *IEEE Transactions on Geoscience and Remote Sensing*, *47*(6), 1707–1718. doi:10.1109/TGRS.2008.2007128

Ghorai, S., Mukherjee, A., Sengupta, S., & Dutta, P. K. (2011). Cancer classification from gene expression data by NPPC ensemble. *IEEE/ACM Transactions on Computational Biology and Bioinformatics*, *8*(3), 659–671. doi:10.1109/TCBB.2010.36 PMID:20479504

Giraud-Carrier, C., Vilalta, R., & Brazdil, P. (2004). Introduction to the special issue on meta-learning. *Machine Learning*, *54*(3), 187–193. doi:10.1023/B:MACH.0000015878.60765.42

Glaab, E., Garibaldi, J., & Krasnogor, N. (2009). ArrayMining: A modular web-application for microarray analysis combining ensemble and consensus methods with cross-study normalization. *BMC Bioinformatics*, *10*(1), 358. doi:10.1186/1471-2105-10-358 PMID:19863798

Gomez-Chova, L., Camps-Valls, G., Bruzzone, L., & Calpe-Maravilla, J. (2010). Meanmap kernel methods for semisupervised cloud classification. *IEEE Transactions on Geoscience and Remote Sensing*, *48*(1), 207–220. doi:10.1109/TGRS.2009.2026425

Gómez-Chova, L., Camps-Valls, G., Muñoz-Marí, J., & Calpe, J. (2008). Semisupervised image classification with Laplacian support vector machines. *IEEE Geoscience and Remote Sensing Letters*, *5*(3), 336–340. doi:10.1109/LGRS.2008.916070

Gong, T., Xuan, J., Chen, L., Riggins, R. B., Li, H., Hoffman, E. P., & Wang, Y. et al. (2011). Motif-guided sparse decomposition of gene expression data for regulatory module identification. *BMC Bioinformatics*, *12*(82), 16. PMID:21426557

Gonzalez, R. C., & Woods, R. E. (1992). *Digital image processing*. Addison-Wesley.

Hollander, M., & Wolfe, D. (1999). *Nonparametric statistical methods* (2nd ed.). Wiley.

Hollander, M., & Wolfe, D. (1999). *Nonparametric statistical methods* (2nd ed.). Wiley.

Huang, X., & Zhang, L. (2010). Comparison of vector stacking, multi-SVMs fuzzy output, and multi-SVMs voting methods for multiscale VHR urban mapping. *IEEE Geoscience and Remote Sensing Letters*, *7*(2), 261–265. doi:10.1109/LGRS.2009.2032563

Hung, C. C., Liu, W., & Kuo, B. C. (2008). A new adaptive fuzzy clustering algorithm for remotely sensed images. In *Proceedings of Geoscience and Remote Sensing Symposium*. IEEE.

Jacobs, M. A., Barker, P. B., Bluemke, D. A., Maranto, C., Arnold, C., Herskovits, E. H., & Bhujwalla, Z. (2003). Benign and malignant breast lesions, diagnosis with multiparametric mr imaging. *Radiology*, *229*(1), 225–232. doi:10.1148/radiol.2291020333 PMID:14519877

Jain, A. K., & Dubes, R. C. (1988). *Algorithms for clustering data*. Englewood Cliffs, NJ: Prentice-Hall.

Jain, R., Murthy, S. N. J., & Chen, P. L. J. (1995). Similarity measures for image databases. In *Proceedings of IEEE International Conference on Fuzzy Systems* (pp. 1247-1254). IEEE.

Kennedy, J. (2000). Stereotyping, improving particle swarm performance with cluster analysis. In *Proceedings of the 2000 Congress on Evolutionary Computing* (vol. 2, pp. 1507 – 1512). Academic Press. doi:10.1109/CEC.2000.870832

Kumar, A. S., Basu, S. K., & Majumdar, K. L. (1997). Robust classification of multispectral data using multiple neural networks and fuzzy integral. *IEEE Transactions on Geoscience and Remote Sensing, 35*(3), 787–790.

Kwang, M. S., & Weng, H. S. (2002). Multiple ant-colony optimization for network routing. In *Proceedings of the First International Symposium on Cyber Worlds* (pp. 277—281). Academic Press.

Lahti, L., Schäfer, M., Klein, H.-U., Bicciato, S., & Dugas, M. (2012). Cancer gene prioritization by integrative analysis of mRNA expression and DNA copy number data, a comparative review. *Briefings in Bioinformatics*. PMID:22441573

Li, Y., & Liu, J. (2009). Remote sensing image classification development in the past decade. In *Proceedings of SPIE* (pp. 338-343). Academic Press.

Lin, C. F., & Wang, S. D. (2002). Fuzzy support vector machines. *IEEE Transactions on Neural Networks, 13*(2), 464–471. doi:10.1109/72.991432 PMID:18244447

Liu, G., Chen, J., & Zhong, J. (2012). An integrated SVM and fuzzy AHP approach for selecting third party logistics providers. *Electrotechnical Review*.

Liu, X. P., Li, X., Yeh, A. G. O., He, J. Q., & Tao, J. (2007). Discovery of transition rules for geographical cellular automata by using ant colony optimization. *Science in China Series D-Earth Sciences, 50*(10), 1578–1588. doi:10.1007/s11430-007-0083-z

Liu, Z., Yang, H., & Yang, S. (2009). Integration of multi-layer SVM classifier and multistage dynamic fuzzy judgment and its application in SCDA measurement. *Journal of Computers, 4*(11). doi:10.4304/jcp.4.11.1139-1144

Lukashin, A., & Futchs, R. (1999). Analysis of temporal gene expression profiles, clustering by simulated annealing and determining optimal number of clusters. *Nature Genetics, 22*(3), 281–285. doi:10.1038/10343 PMID:10391217

Machado, T. R., & Lopes, H. S. (2005). A hybrid particle swarm optimization model for the traveling salesman problem. In *Proceedings of the International Conference in Coimbra* (pp. 255—258). Academic Press. doi:10.1007/3-211-27389-1_61

Mackay, A., & Weigelt, B. Grigoriadis, A., Kreike, B., Natrajan, R., A'Hern, R., ... Reis-Filho, J. S. (2011). Microarray-based class discovery for molecular classification of breast cancer, analysis of interobserver agreement. *JNCI Journal of the National Cancer Institute, 103*(8), 662-673.

Man, Y., & Gath, I. (1994). Detection and separation of ring-shaped clusters using fuzzy clustering. *IEEE Transactions on Pattern Analysis and Machine Intelligence, 16*(8), 855–861. doi:10.1109/34.308484

Mantero, P., Gabriele, M., & Serpico, S. B. (2005). Partially supervised classification of remote sensing images through SVM-based probability density estimation. *IEEE Transactions on Geoscience and Remote Sensing, 43*(3), 559–570. doi:10.1109/TGRS.2004.842022

Marconcini, M., Camps-Valls, G., & Bruzzone, L. (2009). A composite semisupervised SVM for classification of hyperspectral images. *IEEE Geoscience and Remote Sensing Letters*, 6(2), 234–238. doi:10.1109/LGRS.2008.2009324

Maulik, U., & Bandyopadhyay, S. (2001). Nonparametric genetic clustering, comparison of validity indices. *IEEE Transactions on Systems, Man and Cybernetics. Part C, Applications and Reviews*, 31(1), 120–125. doi:10.1109/5326.923275

Maulik, U., & Bandyopadhyay, S. (2002). Performance evaluation of some clustering algorithms and validity indices. *IEEE Transactions on Pattern Analysis and Machine Intelligence*, 24(12), 1650–1654. doi:10.1109/TPAMI.2002.1114856

Maulik, U., & Bandyopadhyay, S. (2003). Fuzzy partitioning using areal-coded variable-length genetic algorithm for pixel classification. *IEEE Transactions on Geoscience and Remote Sensing*, 41(5), 1075–1081. doi:10.1109/TGRS.2003.810924

Maulik, U., Mukhopadhyay, A., & Bandyopadhyay, S. (2009). Combining pareto-optimal clusters using supervised learning for identifying co-expressed genes. *BMC Bioinformatics*, 10(1), 27. doi:10.1186/1471-2105-10-27 PMID:19154590

Maulik, U., & Sarkar, A. (2010). Evolutionary rough parallel multi-objective optimization algorithm. *Fundamenta Informaticae*, 99(1), 13–27.

Maulik, U., & Sarkar, A. (2012). Efficient parallel algorithm for pixel classification in remote sensing imagery. *GeoInformatica*, 16(2), 391–407. doi:10.1007/s10707-011-0136-5

Melgani, F., & Bruzzone, L. (2004). Classification of hyperspectral remote sensing images with support vector machines. *IEEE Transactions on Geoscience and Remote Sensing*, 42(8), 1778–1790. doi:10.1109/TGRS.2004.831865

Melgani, F., & Bruzzone, L. (2004). Classification of hyper spectral remote sensing images with support vector machines. *IEEE Transactions on Geosciences and Remote Sensing*, 42(8).

Mountrakis, G., Im, J., & Ogole, C. (2011). Support vector machines in remote sensing, A Review. *ISPRS Journal of Photogrammetry and Remote Sensing*, 66(3), 247–259. doi:10.1016/j.isprsjprs.2010.11.001

Mountrakis, G., Im, J., & Ogole, C. (2011). Support vector machines in remote sensing, A Review. *ISPRS Journal of Photogrammetry and Remote Sensing*, 66(2), 247–259. doi:10.1016/j.isprsjprs.2010.11.001

Nishida, N., Nagahara, M., Sato, T., Mimori, K., Sudo, T., Tanaka, F., & Mori, M. et al. (2012). Human cancer biology, microarray analysis of colorectal cancer stromal tissue reveals upregulation of two oncogenic microRNA clusters. *Clinical Cancer Research*, 1078.

Oleszkiewicz, J., Xiao, L., & Liu, Y. (2006). Effectively utilizing global cluster memory for large data-intensive parallel programs. *IEEE Transactions on Parallel and Distributed Systems*, 17(1), 66–77. doi:10.1109/TPDS.2006.10

Oleszkiewicz, J., Xiao, L., & Liu, Y. (2006). Effectively utilizing global cluster memory for large data-intensive parallel programs. *IEEE Transactions on Parallel and Distributed Systems*, 17(1), 66–77. doi:10.1109/TPDS.2006.10

Omran, M. (2005). *Particle swarm optimization methods for pattern recognition and image processing.* (Dissertation for the Doctoral Degree). University of Pretoria, Pretoria, South Africa.

Pacheco, P. (1997). *Parallel programming with MPI.* Morgan Kaufmann.

Pal, M. (2006). Support vector machine-based feature selection for land cover classification, a case study with DAIS hyperspectral data. *International Journal of Remote Sensing, 27*(14), 2877–2894. doi:10.1080/01431160500242515

Pappis, C. P., & Karacapilidis, N. I. (1993). A comparative assessment of measures of similarity of fuzzy values. *Fuzzy Sets and Systems, 56*(2), 171–174. doi:10.1016/0165-0114(93)90141-4

Pawlak, Z. (1982). Rough sets. *International Journal of Computer and Information, 11*(5), 341–356. doi:10.1007/BF01001956

Pawlak, Z. (1991). *Rough sets: Theoretical aspects of reasoning about data.* Kluwer Academic Publishers.

Qin, J., Lewis, D., & Noble, W. (2003). Kernel hierarchical gene clustering from microarray gene expression data. *Bioinformatics (Oxford, England), 19*(16), 2097–2104. doi:10.1093/bioinformatics/btg288 PMID:14594715

Reddi, S. S., Rudin, S. F., & Keshavan, H. R. (1984). An optimal multiple threshold scheme for image segmentation. *IEEE–SMC, 14*, 611–665.

Rousseeuw, P. (1987). Silhouettes, a graphical aid to the interpretation and validation of cluster analysis. *Journal of Computational and Applied Mathematics, 20*, 53–65. doi:10.1016/0377-0427(87)90125-7

Rousseeuw, P. J. (1987). Silhouettes, a graphical aid to the interpretation and validation of cluster analysis. *Computational & Applied Mathematics, 20*, 53–65. doi:10.1016/0377-0427(87)90125-7

Ruspini, E. (1970). Numerical methods for fuzzy clustering. *Information Sciences, 2*(3), 319–350. doi:10.1016/S0020-0255(70)80056-1

Sahoo, B. C., Oommen, T., Misra, D., & Newby, G. (2007). Using the one-dimensional s-transform as a discrimination tool in classification of hyperspectral images. *Canadian Journal of Remote Sensing, 33*(6), 551–560. doi:10.5589/m07-057

Salazar, R., Roepman, P., Capella, G., Moreno, V., Simon, I., Dreezen, C., ... Tollenaar, R. (2012). Gene expression signature to improve prognosis prediction of stage II and III colorectal cancer. *Journal of Clinical Oncology, 29*(1), 17-24.

Sarkar, A., & Maulik, U. (2009a). Parallel point symmetry based clustering for gene microarray data. In *Proceedings of Seventh International Conference on Advances in Pattern Recognition-2009* (ICAPR, 2009). Kolkata, India: IEEE Computer Society.

Sarkar, A., & Maulik, U. (2009b). Parallel clustering technique using modified symmetry based distance. In *Proceedings of 1st International Conference on Computer, Communication, Control and Information Technology* (C3IT 2009). MacMillan Publishers India Ltd.

Sarkar, A., & Maulik, U. (2013). Cancer gene expression data analysis using rough based symmetrical clustering. In Handbook of research on computational intelligence for engineering, science, and business. Hershey, PA: IGI Global.

Small, C. (2006). Urban landsat, cities from space. Palisades, NY: NASA Socioeconomic Data and Applications Center (SEDAC).

Smith, A. M. S., Wooster, M. J., Powell, A. K., & Usher, D. (2002). Texture based feature extraction, application to burn scar detection in earth observation satellite sensor imagery. *International Journal of Remote Sensing*, *23*(8), 1733–1739. doi:10.1080/01431160110106104

Song, X., Cherian, G., & Fan, G. (2005). Aν-insensitive SVM approach for compliance monitoring of the conservation reserve program. *IEEE Geoscience and Remote Sensing Letters*, *2*(2), 99–103. doi:10.1109/LGRS.2005.846007

Spang, R. (2003). Diagnostic signatures from microarrays, a bioinformatics concept for personalized medicine. *BIOSILICO*, *1*(2), 64–68. doi:10.1016/S1478-5382(03)02329-1

Stathakis, D., & Vasilakos, A. (2006). Comparison of computational intelligence based classification techniques for remotely sensed optical image classification. *IEEE Transactions on Geoscience and Remote Sensing*, *44*(8), 2305–2318. doi:10.1109/TGRS.2006.872903

Su, M.-C., & Chou, C.-H. (2001). A modified version of the k-means algorithm with a distance based on cluster symmetry. *IEEE Transactions on Pattern Analysis and Machine Intelligence*, *23*(6), 674–680. doi:10.1109/34.927466

Su, M. C., Chou, C. H., & Hsieh, C. C. (2005). Fuzzy c-means algorithm with a point symmetry distance. *International Journal of Fuzzy Systems*, *7*(4), 175–181.

Tavazoie, S., Hughes, J., Campbell, M., Cho, R., & Church, G. (2001). Systematic determination of genetic network architecture. *Bioinformatics (Oxford, England)*, *17*, 405–414. PMID:11331234

Ting, T. O., Rao, M. V. C., Loo, C. K., & Ngu, S. S. (2003). Solving unit commitment problem using hybrid particle swarm optimization. *Journal of Heuristics*, *9*(6), 507–520. doi:10.1023/B:HEUR.0000012449.84567.1a

Tsujinishi, D., & Abe, S. (2003). Fuzzy least squares support vector machines for multiclass problems. *Neural Networks*, *16*(5/6), 785–792. doi:10.1016/S0893-6080(03)00110-2 PMID:12850035

Tuia, D., & Camps-Valls, G. (2009). Semisupervised remote sensing image classification with cluster kernels. *IEEE Geoscience and Remote Sensing Letters*, *6*(2), 224–228. doi:10.1109/LGRS.2008.2010275

Tusher, V. G., Tibshirani, R., & Chu, G. (1940). Significance analysis of microarrays applied to the ionizing radiation response. *Proceedings of the National Academy of Sciences of the United States of America*, *98*(9), 5116–5121. doi:10.1073/pnas.091062498 PMID:11309499

Tyson, J. J., Baumann, W. T., Chen, C., Verdugo, A., Tavassoly, I., Wang, Y., & Clarke, R. et al. (2012). Dynamic models of estrogen signaling and cell fate in breast cancer cells. *Nature Reviews. Cancer*, *11*(7), 523–532. doi:10.1038/nrc3081 PMID:21677677

Vapnik, V. (1982). Estimation of dependences based on empirical data (2nd ed.). Springer Verlag.

Wang, F. (1990). Fuzzy supervised classification of remote sensing images. *IEEE Transactions on Geoscience and Remote Sensing, 28*(2), 194–201. doi:10.1109/36.46698

Wang, W. J. (1997). New similarity measures on fuzzy sets and on elements. *Fuzzy Sets and Systems, 85*(3), 305–309. doi:10.1016/0165-0114(95)00365-7

Warrender, C., & Forrest, S. (1999). Detecting intrusions using system calls, alternative data models. In *Proceedings of the IEEE Computer Society Symposium on Research in Security and Privacy*. IEEE. doi:10.1109/SECPRI.1999.766910

Xie, X. L., & Beni, G. (1991). A validity measure for fuzzy clustering. *IEEE Transactions on Pattern Analysis and Machine Intelligence, 13*(8), 841–847. doi:10.1109/34.85677

Xu, Y., Olman, V., & Xu, D. (1999). Clustering gene expression data using a graph theoretic approach, an application of minimum spanning trees. *Bioinformatics (Oxford, England), 17*, 309–318. PMID:12016051

Yager, R. Y. (1992). Entropy measures under similarity relations. *International Journal of General Systems, 20*(4), 341–358. doi:10.1080/03081079208945039

Young, K. Y. (2001). Validating clustering for gene expression data. *Bioinformatics (Oxford, England), 17*(4), 309–318. doi:10.1093/bioinformatics/17.4.309 PMID:11301299

Yu, G., Li, H., Ha, S., Shih, I.-M., Clarke, R., Hoffman, E. P., & Wang, Y. et al. (2011). PUGSVM, a caBIGtm analytical tool for multiclass gene selection and predictive classification. *Bioinformatics (Oxford, England), 27*(5), 736–738. doi:10.1093/bioinformatics/btq721 PMID:21186245

Zadeh, L. A. (1965). Fuzzy sets. *Information and Control, 8*(3), 338–353. doi:10.1016/S0019-9958(65)90241-X

Zhang, H., Shi, W., & Liu, K. (2012). Fuzzy-topology integrated support vector machine for remotely sensed image classification. *IEEE Transactions on Geoscience and Remote Sensing, 50*(3), 850–862. doi:10.1109/TGRS.2011.2163518

Zhang, H., Shi, W. & Liu, K. (2012). Fuzzy-topology integrated support vector machine for remotely sensed image classification. *IEEE Transactions on Geosciences and Remote Sensing, 50*(3).

Zhang, L., Huang, X., Huang, B., & Li, P. (2006). A pixel shape index coupled with spectral information for classification of high spatial resolution remotely sensed imagery. *IEEE Transactions on Geoscience and Remote Sensing, 44*(10), 2950–2961. doi:10.1109/TGRS.2006.876704

Zhang, R., & Ma, J. (2009). _ Feature selection for hyperspectral data based on recursive support vector machines. *International Journal of Remote Sensing, 30*(14), 3669–3677. doi:10.1080/01431160802609718

Zhu, G., & Blumberg, D. G. (2002). Classification using ASTER data and SVM algorithms: The case study of Beer Sheva, Israel. *Remote Sensing of Environment, 80*(2), 233–240. doi:10.1016/S0034-4257(01)00305-4

ADDITIONAL READING

Bandyopadhyay, S., Mukhopadhyay, A., & Maulik, U. (2007). An improved algorithm for clustering gene expression data. *Bioinformatics*, *23*(21), 2859–2865. doi:10.1093/bioinformatics/btm418 PMID:17720981

Bandyopadhyay, S., & Saha, S. (2007a). GAPS, A clustering method using a new point symmetry-based distance measure. *Pattern Recognition*, *10*(12), 3430–3451. doi:10.1016/j.patcog.2007.03.026

Bandyopadhyay, S., & Saha, S. (2008). A point symmetry based clustering technique for automatic evolution of clusters. *IEEE Transactions on Knowledge and Data Engineering*, *20*(11), 1–17. doi:10.1109/TKDE.2008.79

Chen, L., Pan, Y., & Hua, X. (2004). Scalable and efficient parallel algorithms for euclidean distance transform on the LARPBS model. *IEEE Transactions on Parallel and Distributed Systems*, *15*(11), 975–982. doi:10.1109/TPDS.2004.71

Chen, Y. L., & Hu, H. L. (2006). An overlapping cluster algorithm to provide non-exhaustive clustering. *European Journal of Operational Research*, *173*(3), 762–780. doi:10.1016/j.ejor.2005.06.056

Cho, R. J., Campbell, M. J., Winzeler, E. A., Steinmetz, L., Conway, A., Wodicka, L., & Davis, R. W. et al. (1998). A genome-wide transcriptional analysis of the mitotic cell cycle. *Molecular Cell*, *2*(1), 65–73. doi:10.1016/S1097-2765(00)80114-8 PMID:9702192

Chu, S. (1998). The transcriptional program of sporulation in budding yeast. *Science*, *202*(5389), 699–705. doi:10.1126/science.282.5389.699 PMID:9784122

DeRisi, J., Iyer, V., & Brown, P. (1997). Exploring the metabolic and genetic control of gene expression on a genome scale. *Science*, *282*, 257–264. PMID:9381177

Dhilon, I., Marcotte, E., & Roshan, U. (2003). Diametrical clustering for identifying anticorrelated gene clusters. *Bioinformatics (Oxford, England)*, *19*(13), 1612–1619. doi:10.1093/bioinformatics/btg209 PMID:12967956

Hollander, M., & Wolfe, D. (1999). *Nonparametric statistical methods* (2nd ed.). USA: Wiley.

Horn, D., & Axel, L. (2003). Novel clustering algorithm for microarray expression data in a truncated svd space. *Bioinformatics (Oxford, England)*, *19*(9), 1110–1115. doi:10.1093/bioinformatics/btg053 PMID:12801871

Hvidsten, T. R., Laegreid, A., & Komorowski, J. (2003). Learning rule-based models of biological process from gene expression time profiles using gene ontology. *Bioinformatics (Oxford, England)*, *19*(9), 1116–1123. doi:10.1093/bioinformatics/btg047 PMID:12801872

Iyer, V. R. (1999). The transcriptional program in the response of human fibroblasts serum. *Science*, *283*(5398), 83–87. doi:10.1126/science.283.5398.83 PMID:9872747

Jiang, K., Thorsen, O., Peters, A. E., Smith, B. E., & Sosa, C. P. (2008). An efficient parallel implementation of the hidden markov methods for genomic sequence-search on a massively parallel system. *IEEE Transactions on Parallel and Distributed Systems*, *19*(1), 15–23. doi:10.1109/TPDS.2007.70712

Kalyanaraman, A., Aluru, S., Brendel, V., & Kothari, S. (2003). Space and time efficient parallel algorithms and software for EST clustering. *IEEE Transactions on Parallel and Distributed Systems*, *14*(12), 1209–1221. doi:10.1109/TPDS.2003.1255634

Kanungo, T., Mount, D., Netanyahu, N., Piatko, C., Silverman, R., & Wu, A. (2002). An efficient k-means clustering algorithm, analysis and implementation. *IEEE Transactions on Pattern Analysis and Machine Intelligence*, *24*(7), 881–892. doi:10.1109/TPAMI.2002.1017616

Kim, S. Y. (2001). Effect of data normalization on fuzzy clustering of DNA microarray data. *BMC Bioinformatics*, *17*, 309–318. PMID:16533412

Liu, W., & Schmidt, B. (2006). Parallel pattern-based systems for computational biology, A case study. *IEEE Transactions on Parallel and Distributed Systems*, *17*(8), 750–763. doi:10.1109/TPDS.2006.109

Rajasekaran, S. (2005). Efficient parallel hierarchical clustering algorithms. *IEEE Transactions on Parallel and Distributed Systems*, *16*(6), 497–502. doi:10.1109/TPDS.2005.72

Rajko, S., & Aluru, S. (2004). Space and time optimal parallel sequence alignments. *IEEE Transactions on Parallel and Distributed Systems*, *15*(12), 1070–1081. doi:10.1109/TPDS.2004.86

Shahrour, F. A. (2004). FatiGO, a web tool for finding significant associations to gene ontology terms with groups of genes. *Bioinformatics (Oxford, England)*, *20*(4), 578–580. doi:10.1093/bioinformatics/btg455 PMID:14990455

Sharan, R., Maron-Katz, A., & Shamir, R. (2003). CLICK and EXPANDER, a system for clustering and visualizing gene expression data. *Bioinformatics (Oxford, England)*, *19*(14), 1787–1799. doi:10.1093/bioinformatics/btg232 PMID:14512350

The Gene Ontology Consortium. (2000). Gene ontology, tool for the unification biology. *Nature Genetics*, *25*, 25–29. PMID:10802651

Tou, J. T., & Gonzalez, R. C. (1974). *Pattern recognition principles*. Reading, MA: Addison-Wesley.

Wen, X., Fuhrman, S., Michaels, G. S., Carr, D. B., Smith, S., Barker, J. L., & Somogyi, R. (1998). Large-scale temporal gene expression mapping of central nervous system development. *Proceedings of the National Academy of Sciences of the United States of America*, *95*(1), 334–339. doi:10.1073/pnas.95.1.334 PMID:9419376

KEY TERMS AND DEFINITIONS

Clustering: Assigning similar elements to one group, which increases intra-cluster similarity and decreases inter-cluster similarity.

Fuzzy Set: Set of elements with membership values between 0 and 1 for each of the clusters to which it belongs according to fuzzy set theory by Zadeh.

K-Means Algorithm: Clustering algorithm to classify n elements in k clusters, which iteratively computes the cluster centroids as the means of all elements in one cluster.

Pixel Classification: Pixel Classification method classifies all pixels in a remote sensing image into classes.

PSO Algorithm: Particle Swam Optimization is a population-based algorithm that uses a population of individuals to probe the best position in the search space.

Remote Sensing: Remote Sensing is a method to interpret geospatial data exploring features, objects, and classes on Earth's land surface.

Validity Index: Index to estimate compactness of the clusters, leading to properly identified distinguishable clusters.

Chapter 15
Particle Swarm Optimization Method to Design a Linear Tubular Switched Reluctance Generator

Rui P. G. Mendes
Universidade da Beira Interior, Portugal

Maria do Rosário Alves Calado
Universidade da Beira Interior, Portugal

Sílvio José Mariano
Universidade da Beira Interior, Portugal

ABSTRACT

In this chapter, the Particle Swarm Optimization method is applied to four different structural configurations of a linear switched reluctance generator with tubular topology. The optimization process involves the search of the values for a defined set of geometric parameters that maximize the rate of change of the generator's inductance with the relative displacement of its mover part. The optimization algorithm is applied to each structural configuration in order to find the optimum geometry as well to identify the most suitable configuration for electric generation.

INTRODUCTION

The generation capabilities of a switched reluctance machines depends on the velocity of its movable part and on the rate of change of the machine's inductance with its relative displacement. The first factor relies on the nature of the external force that drives the generator and, consequently, imposes the operation velocity. The second factor relies on the geometric configuration of the machine which can be controlled, during the project, in order to maximize its generation capabilities. For this reason it becomes mandatory to choose the best dimensional parameters a value that regulates the generator geometry.

DOI: 10.4018/978-1-4666-8291-7.ch015

However, when the number of variables is huge, it becomes unpractical to perform the design procedure to all possible values combination. So, to avoid this exhaustive process, optimization methods are applied to reduce the search of the optimum variable values. In general, electric machine optimization is characterized by non-linear problems with objective functions dependent on large set of variables. For functions with more than 3 variables is impossible to map its evolution with the respective variables and thus, to identify the location of its maximum (or minimum) values. For these reasons, is discarded the application of exact methods that implies a continuum evaluation of the objective function gradient because they can be trapped in local maximum (or minimum) and because they need to perform additional function evaluations which, in these problems, are the most time and resource consuming steps. An alternative approach to exact methods, are the global optimization ones which are based in deterministic or stochastic procedures to perform the values search. In deterministic methods, a direct search of values is conducted according to the function evolution. The search through stochastic methods is supported through decisions based on random and/or probabilistic parameters. The latter methods are, usually, based on behavior and evolution of living beings communities.

Some of these methods are widely used in the design optimization of electric machines. In (Yao & Ionel, 2011) a comparison is made between the differential evolution (DE) an response surface (RS) optimization algorithms applied to permanent magnet synchronous motor. The application of genetic algorithm (GA) in the design optimization of permanent motors can be found in (Bianchi & Bolognani, 1998; Jolly, Jabbar, & Liu, 2005) and in (L. Moreau, Zaim, & Machmoum, 2012; Naayagi & Kamaraj, 2005; Owatchaiphong & Fuengwarodsakul, 2009) for the design optimization of rotary switched reluctance machines. A design optimization procedure that involves differential evolution algorithm and a finite element method (FEM) software is presented in (Wen, Zarko, & Lipo, 2006) for the optimization of a permanent magnet machine and in (Kurfurst, Duron, Skalka, Janda, & Ondrusek, 2011) the self-organizing migrating algorithm (SOMA) is applied to the optimization of the same type of electric machine. A non-classical stochastic method, elitist non-dominated sorting genetic algorithm version II, is proposed in (M. Balaji & Kamaraj, 2012c) and is applied to optimize the pole shape of a switched reluctance generator. In (Ziyan, Dianhai, & Chang-Seop, 2013) an optimal design of a switched reluctance motor is proposed using a multi-objective worst-case scenario algorithm based on FEM simulations and Kriging.

Other stochastic method that is commonly used for this type of optimization problems is the Particle Swarm Optimization (PSO) method that simulates the behavior of populations (like a flock of birds) in the search for food. In (Van der Geest, Polinder, Ferreira, & Zeilstra, 2012) the particle swarm algorithm is coupled with a FEM software to perform the design optimization of different permanent magnet machines. A design optimization of a transverse flux linear motor using particle swarm optimization method is presented in (H. M. Hasanien, 2011) and in (Wen et al., 2006) the same optimization method is applied to a permanent magnet motor. Also, for the optimization design of a permanent magnet machines, a multimodal function optimization based on the particle swarm method is proposed by (Jang-Ho et al., 2006) and in (Arkadan, ElBsat, & Mneimneh, 2009) this optimization algorithm is applied to a synchronous reluctance motor drive. In (Wang, Chen, Cai, & Xin, 2013) the particle swarm optimization algorithm is combined with the differential evolution algorithm for the optimization of a tubular permanent magnet synchronous generator and a multiobjective particle swarm approach is applied by (dos Santos Coelho, Barbosa, & Lebensztajn, 2010) to the design of a brushless DC wheel motor. A modified particle swarm optimization method is used in (G. Chen, Guo, & Huang, 2007) for the parameter identification of an induction motor.

The application of the Particle Swarm Optimization algorithm has also been proposed for the design of switched reluctance machines. In (Phuangmalai, Konghirun, & Chayopitak, 2012) the particle swarm algorithm is used in the optimal design of a 4/2 rotary switched reluctance motor and in (Balaji, M. and V. Kamaraj, 2011b; Jie, Hexu, Lin, Yan, & Yi, 2011) to the same type of motor but with a 8/6 pole configuration. The work of (Xiao & Ye, 2009) presents an improved particle swarm optimization combined with a back propagation neural network algorithm for the modeling of a switched reluctance generator. In (Qianwen, Yukun, & Ji, 2011) least squared support vector machine inductance model is proposed for a bearingless switched reluctance motor and optimized with particle swarm optimization algorithm and in (Akar, Fleming, & Edrington, 2012) the particle swarm optimization method is applied to the torque control strategy for switched reluctance machines.

The particle swarm optimization method will be used in this work to optimize the geometry of different structural configurations of a linear switched reluctance generator with tubular topology.

BACKGROUND

The Linear Switched Reluctance Generator

The switched reluctance machine is a device characterized for the absence of permanent magnets in its configuration, for a simple construction with low manufacturing costs, high reliability and strong fault tolerance capability when compared to other types of electric machines (Brady, O'Loughlin, Massey, Griffiths, & Villegas, 2012; Hao, Xing, & Hui, 2009). The switched reluctance machine is constituted by a static part (stator) and a movable one, where the electric phase windings are, usually, housed in static one. The movable part (rotor for a rotary type machine or translator in the case of a linear type one) is free of permanent magnets, excitation windings or other source of magnetic field which leads to a low inertia machine which enables a very fast actuation response. Due to the presence of salient poles in both parts, this type of machine is classified as a doubly salient machine (Arifin, Al-Bahadly, & Mukhopadhyay, 2012).

The switched reluctance machine can operate as actuator (motor) or generator where the same structure configuration and power electronic converter is used for these two modes of operation. The latter are only distinguee in the used control strategy, where different commutation periods are applied to the electronic switches of the power converter (T.J.E. Miller, 2001). As actuator, the machine develops a linear force due to the susceptibility of its movable part to occupy, the positions of minimum reluctance which is a phenomenon verified in magnetic circuits that tends to restructure themself in order to achieve a minimum reluctance configuration, when subjected to a magnetic field. This is accomplished by, sequentially, energizing and de-energizing the electric phases during the relative motion correspondent to a positive slope of the machine's inductance. As generator, the electric phases are excited establishing a magnetic flux whose intensity is decreased when the translator, driven by an external force, is forced to occupy the positions of maximum reluctance. The idealized electromagnetic characteristics correspondent to the maximum and minimum reluctance of the switched reluctance machine are defined by the relative positions of the translator (movable part) in respect to stator (stationary part) as illustrated in Figure 1. The maximum value of the machine's inductance (L_{max}) and its minimum value (L_{min}) corresponds, respectively, to the value of minimum and maximum reluctance of the magnetic circuit associated to each electric phase of the machine.

*Figure 1. Inductance variation as function of translator position
(Adapted from (Krishnan, 2001)).*

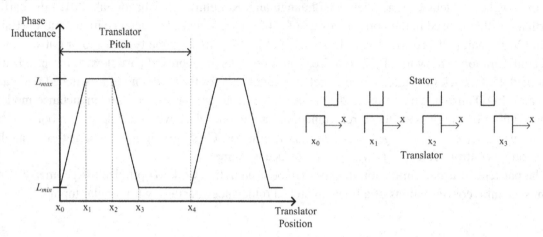

In the generator mode of operation, in opposition of the decreasing magnetic flux linked by a given electric phase, an electromotive force is developed in the phase windings terminals providing electric energy generation when connected to an electric load. This type of machines are characterized for operating within a large range of magnetic flux densities achieving, for some relative positions and electric current values, the saturation of the ferromagnetic core. For this reason, the switched reluctance machine presents high non-linear electromagnetic characteristics, which are evident in the magnetization profiles of the machine. The majority of the literature available for this type of electric machine is directed to rotary machines where its design procedure for switched reluctance machines is detailed in (Krishnan, 2001). The design of rotary generators can be found in (L. Moreau, Machmoum, & Zaim, 2006; Mueller, 2005; Xue, Cheng, Bao, & Leung, 2011; Xue, Cheng, Bao, Leung, & Cheung, 2012) for the application in wind energy conversion systems.

Referring to the project for these type of electric machines, a detailed design procedure has been proposed by (Boldea, 2010, 2013) for linear switched reluctance actuators with tubular and flat topologies, where the motoring mode was assessed. Another procedure, for linear actuators with flat topology, can be found in (Lobo, Hong Sun, & Krishnan, 2008). According to linear switched reluctance machines operating in generator mode, some devices with flat topology have been proposed and analysed as linear generators for direct drive conversion systems in (Brady et al., 2012; H. Chen, Wang, Gu, & Lu, 2010; Hao, Xing, & Hui, 2009; Pan, Yu, Cheung, & Guang-zhong, 2011; Sun, Cheung, Zhao, Lu, & Shi, 2011) and with tubular topology in (Mendes, Calado, Mariano, & Cabrita, 2011). However, with the exception of the direction of the forces applied to the generator, the working principles of the rotary switched reluctance machines are totally applied to the linear ones (Boldea, 2010). Since the geometry of the linear switched reluctance is derived from its rotary counterpart, both topologies share the same electromagnetic phenomenon aside from its motion and force directions.

The control of the switched reluctance generator must be applied to an electronic power converter which is responsible to conduct the electromechanical energy conversion of the machine. In Figure 2 is illustrated the schematics of a classical electronic power converter used for a three-phase switched reluctance machine. This power converter configuration can be used for both linear and rotary machine topologies operating in motor and/or generator modes. Other power converter topologies for this type of

Figure 2. Classic electronic power converter for a switched reluctance machine
(Adapted from (Takahashi, Goto, Nakamura, Watanabe, & Ichinokura, 2006)).

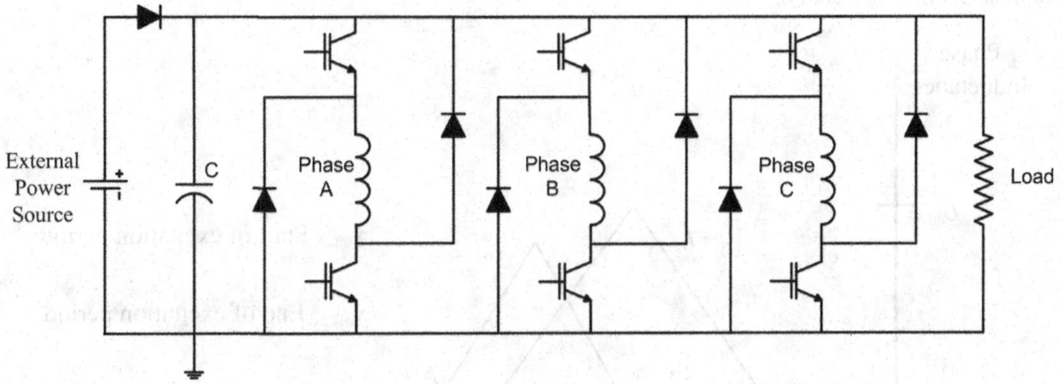

electric machines can been found in (Barnes & Pollock, 1998; Fleury et al., 2008; Jin-Woo Ahn, 2010; Miller, 1985).

Due to the absence of permanent magnets or other magnetic field source in the translator, an initial excitation field must be provided by an external electric power source in order to establish a magnetic field linked by the windings electric phase which will be responsible for the electromechanical energy conversion in the generator. In each energy conversion cycle, part of the electric generated energy will be stored in the converter capacitor and the remaining will be supplied to the electric load. The stored electric energy will be used for the magnetic field excitation in the consequent energy conversion cycle. Thus, the energy provided by the external power source will only be needed at the first stage of operation of the switched reluctance generator. For the same machine geometry, the physical processes adjacent to the mechanical energy conversion are equal to all electric phases, where the same current and voltage values are verified if the commutation periods are maintained.

As already referred, the operation of the switched reluctance machine, as actuator (motor) or generator, depends on the used control strategy. For generation mode of operation, the conventional control stragedy classifies each energy conversion cycle with two distinct periods of commutation, the excitation period and the generation period (Fleury, dos Santos e Silva, Domingos, & De Andrade, 2007; Hao & Gu, 2010; Mademlis & Kioskeridis, 2005; Radun, 1994; Takahashi et al., 2006). According to this conventional control strategy, the idealized (linear) inductance, electric current and linked magnetic flux evolution, in respect to the translator position, are shown in Figure 3.

The excitation period is characterized for the establishment of the magnetic field which stores the energy supplied by the capacitor. This period is initiated when the electronic switches are closed at x_{on}, as illustrated in Figure 4 (scheme a)). With the switches closed, an electric current rises in the respective electric phase windings developing a linked magnetic flux. During this period, the free-wheeling diodes are reverse biased blocking the flow of electric current through them. The electric energy supplied to the phase windings is stored, in the machine air gap, as magnetic potential energy. The excitation period end when the electronic switches are opened.

After this instant, the generation period is initiated. The translator is forced to move in the direction of decreasing inductance leading to a magnetic flux reduction due to the increasing reluctance of the machine. In opposition to the magnetic flux reduction, and electromotive force is developed at the phase windings terminals in order to maintain the electric current and, consequently, the linked magnetic flux.

Figure 3. Typical waveforms for the switched reluctance generator phase inductance (L_p), phase current (i_p), and linked magnetic flux (λ_p)
(Adapted from (T.J.E. Miller, 2001)).

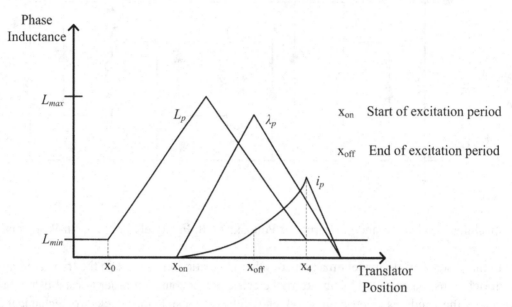

Figure 4. Electric phase current flow during a) excitation period and b) generation period
(Adapted from (Takahashi et al., 2006)).

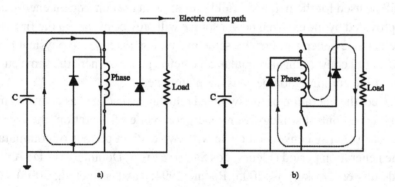

The generated electric current continues to flow through the free-wheeling diodes that are now forward biased as schematized in Figure 4 (scheme b)). The electric current is then supplied to the electric load and the capacitor. In this commutation period is verified the conversion of the stored magnetic energy and the input mechanical energy into electric energy supplied to the converter. The commutation instants shall be carefully specified in order to obtain more energy during the generation period than the one supplied during the excitation period. The generation period ends when the phase current is extinguished.

According to (T.J.E. Miller, 2001), the electric phase current may adopt different waveforms according to the absolute value of the developed electromotive force. Three possible waveforms are shown in Figure 5.

The current waveform in Figure 5 (current waveform a)) is obtained when the developed electromotive force is superior to the capacitor voltage (excitation voltage). In Figure 5 (current waveform b))

Figure 5. Idealized electric phase current waveforms for a switched reluctance generator (Adapted from (T.J.E. Miller, 2001)).

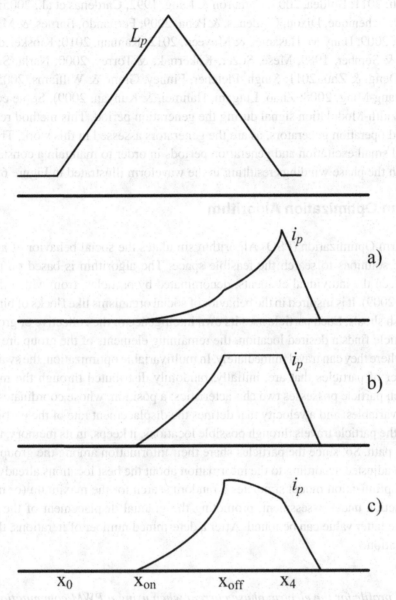

the corresponding waveform is verified when the electromotive voltage equals the absolute value of the capacitor voltage. When the absolute value of electromotive force is below the excitation voltage, the current assumes the wave form illustrated in Figure 5 (current waveform c)).

The commutation periods in open loop control are, usually, determined in function of the translator's position which involves the application of fixed commutation instants. However, when the latter parameters assume fixed values, the output voltage and current of the converter may become unstable and the generated energy can be lesser than the excitation energy, which is undesirable. For this reason, rises the need to apply closed loop control strategies that define the commutation periods in function of the required characteristics energy conversion system. Closed loop control strategies for switched reluctance generators can be found in the following published works: (Asadi, Ehsani, & Fahimi, 2006; Baiming & Emadi, 2011; Boldea, 2003; Cameron & Lang, 1992; Cardenas et al., 2005; Chang, Cheng, Lu, & Liaw, 2010; Echenique, Dixon, Cardenas, & Pena, 2009; Fernando, Barnes, & Marjanovic, 2011; Hao, Xing, & Gu, 2009; Hany M. Hasanien & Muyeen, 2012; Kannan, 2010; Kioskeridis & Mademlis, 2006; MacMinn & Sember, 1989; Mese, Sozer, Kokernak, & Torrey, 2000; Narla, Sozer, & Husain, 2012; Peng, Yi, Deng, & Zhu, 2011; Singh, Fletcher, Finney, Grant, & Williams, 2005; Torrey, 2002; Yuan-Chih & Chang-Ming, 2008; Zhao, Lingzhi, Hanmei, & Kunyan, 2009). Some control strategies applies a Pulse-Width-Modulation signal during the generation period. This method reveals to be suitable for low speed operation generators, as are the generators assessed in this work. The latter strategy comprises several small excitation and generation periods in order to maintain a constant value for the electric current on the phase windings resulting in the waveform illustrated in Figure 6.

Particle Swarm Optimization Algorithm

The Particle Swarm Optimization (PSO) Algorithm simulates the social behavior of a population that explores possible solutions to search the feasible space. The algorithm is based on the exchange of information between the individual elements, denominated by particles, from which the population is constituted (Rao, 2009). It is inspired in the behavior of social organisms like flocks of birds, bee swarms, ant colonies or fish shoals. Each particle uses its own intelligence or the collective or group intelligence. Every time a particle finds a desired location, the remaining elements of the group are informed about that location, to where they can travel immediately. In multivariable optimization, the swarm is composed by a fixed number of particles that are, initially, randomly distributed through the multidimensional search space. Each particle possesses two characteristics: a position, whose coordinates corresponds to the optimization variables, and a velocity that defines the displacement rate of the particles through the search space. As the particle travels through possible locations, it keeps, in its memory, the best position found thought its path. So, since the particles share their information among the group, their positions and velocities are adjusted according to the information about the best locations already discovered. To summarize, this optimization model simulates a random search for the maximum (or minimum) value the objective function under assessment, promoting the gradual displacement of the particles to the position where the latter value can be found. After a determined number of iterations, the particles will collide at this location.

Figure 6. Typical profile for the electric phase current when using a PWM commutation strategy (Adapted from (T.J.E. Miller, 2001)).

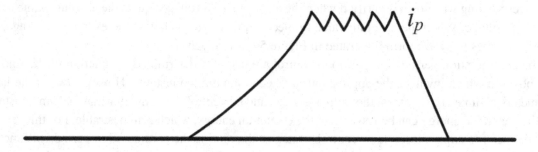

The computational implementation of the Particle Swarm Optimization algorithm is based on the instructions indicated in (Rao, 2009). Other types of formulation, topologies, parameter selection, particle position and further details about this algorithm can be found in (Clerc, 2010; Del Valle, Venayagamoorthy, Mohagheghi, Hernandez, & Harley, 2008; Xianjun, Zhifeng, Jincai, & CaiXia, 2010).

The succeeding enumerated PSO procedures are applied to the following type of optimization problems:

$$\min imize\ f(X)\ subject\ to: X_l \leq X \leq X_u$$

where, X_l and X_u are, respectively, the lower and upper boundaries of X, the vector that contains de optimization variables. For this type of problems, the PSO is implemented accordingly to the following instructions:

1. Establish the N particles number that will define the swarm size.
2. Generate, randomly, the initial population X by creating the vectors $X_1, X_2,...X_N$ inside the boundaries defined by X_l and X_u. For each position i and iteration k, the position of one particle defined by X_i^k, $X^0 = \left(X_1^0, X_1^0,..., X_N^0\right)$, that corresponds to the iteration $k=0$.
3. Define the velocity of all particles as *zero*. Initially, all particles should have null velocity. Establish the number of iterations as $k=1$.
4. In each k iteration:
   a. Find the best value of X_i^k, $P_{best,i}$, that corresponds to minimum value of the objective function $\left(f\left[X_i^k\right]\right)$, found to the present iteration by the particle i. Find the value of X_i^k, G_{best}, that corresponds to the minimum value of the function objective, found in all previous interations by the N particles.
   b. Determine the velocity of the particle i in each k iteration by:

$$V_i^k = V_i^{k-1} + c_1 r_1 \left[P_{best,i} - X_i^{k-1}\right] + c_2 r_2 \left[G_{best} - X_i^{k-1}\right]; i = 1, 2,..., N \tag{1}$$

where c_1 and c_2 are, respectively, the individual and group learning rates and r_1 and r_2 are random numbers generated through a uniform distribution between 0 and 1. The parameters c_1 and c_2 defines the influence of the best individual position and best group position in the direction of the displacement of particle i through the search space.

   c. Determine the position of particle i in iteration k:

$$X_i^k = X_i^{k-1} + V_i^k; i = 1, 2,..., N \tag{2}$$

And evaluate the value of the objective function for each position

$$\left(f\left[X_1^0\right], f\left[X_2^0\right],..., f\left[X_N^0\right]\right).$$

5.   Check the convergence of the current solution. If the convergence criteria are not verified, the step 4 procedure is repeated, the iteration number is updated to $k+1$ and new values of $P_{best,i}$ and G_{best} are calculated. The iterative process is continued until the convergence criteria are met.

To avoid situations where the particles are subjected to great oscillations at local minimum positions, an inertial parameter θ is defined in order to reduce the particle's velocity as the iterative process evolves. With this inertial parameter, the velocity for each particle i given by the expression (1), is rewritten as:

$$V_i^k = \theta V_i^{k-1} + c_1 r_1 \left[P_{best,i} - X_i^{k-1} \right] + c_2 r_2 \left[G_{best} - X_i^{k-1} \right]; \quad i = 1, 2, ..., N \tag{3}$$

The inertial parameter θ, given in function of the current iteration k, is given by:

$$\theta(k) = \theta_{max} - \left(\frac{\theta_{max} - \theta_{min}}{k_{max}} \right) k \tag{4}$$

where θ_{max} is defined as 0.9, θ_{min} as 0.4 and k_{max}, the maximum number of iterations, is initially established.

During the search for a global minimum value, the efficiency of the PSO algorithm is strongly dependent on the initial position of the N particles. If the latter are not, convenient distributed at the beginning of the optimization process, they can all be retained in a local minimum, and, for this reason, never find the global one, as pretended. However, when the optimization problem has more than 3 variables, is impractical to visualize the particles position so they can be uniformly distributed throughout the search space and thus, to increase the probabilities to find a global minimum. In, (Richards & Ventura, 2004) is suggested the application of the Centroidal Voronoi Tessalations algorithm which consists in the division of the search space into regions with similar dimensions. With these defined regions, the respective centroids are used as initially particle positions since they are equally distanced. With this procedure, a more uniform distribution is achieved for the initial particle's positions. In order to accomplish the same principle in this work, will be applied the *k-means* method to divide N points into z clusters, whose centroids are equally distanced. Thus, starting from a random distribution of N particles, and dividing the search space into $z=N$ clusters, are obtained N centroids uniformly distributed. The *k-means* algorithm will be applied through a function available in the software *Matlab*. To conclude the optimization algorithm procedure, the stop criteria shall be defined. The execution of the iterative process will end when the iteration number reaches a maximum value initially established. However, the maximum number of iterations may be insufficient to guarantee convergence of all particles in the optimal position found during the process or may be to large leading to an exceeding number of iterations after an optimal solution is found and, consequently, leading to an unnecessary dispended time and computational resources. In order to avoid this situation a convergence criteria shall be defined to end the optimization process when its evolution is no longer relevant. In (Zielinski & Laur, 2007), are defined several mechanisms to end the iterative process of the Particle Swarm Optimization algorithm. Two of the referred mechanisms will be applied to the optimization problem assessed in this work. So, it will be assumed that convergence have been achieved when the following criteria are verified:

1. The absolute value of the difference between the maximum and minimum values of the objective function verified for all the particles in the current iteration is less than a specified tolerance (tol_f):

$$\left| \max\left(f\left[P_{best} \right] \right) - \min\left(f\left[P_{best} \right] \right) \right| < tol_f \tag{5}$$

2. The maximum distance verified between the 15% particles of the total population with the best objective function values is less than a specified tolerance (tol_x).

The application of these criteria is applied to the vector with the best particle individual positions instead of the current calculated position, because the latter is subjected to greater value oscillations around the local minimum

OPTIMIZATION PROBLEM

The present problem of optimization is meant to find the values correspondent to determined geometrical parameters that maximize the electric generation capabilities of each structural model of the switched reluctance generator under assessment. To quantify the potential of each structural model as electric generator, the electromotive force that each model can develop at the electric phase windings will be taken into account. According to (Mademlis & Kioskeridis, 2005), the referred electromotive force is given by the following relation:

$$e = v \frac{dL}{dx} \tag{6}$$

As expressed in (6), the electromotive force (e) is proportional to the translator (movable part of the generator) velocity (v) and to the rate of change of the machine's inductance with its position $\left(\frac{dL}{dx} \right)$.

Since the translator velocity does not depend on the structure of the generator but, instead, on the nature of the external force that drives it, the potential of each structural model may be evaluated through the rate of change of the machine's inductance with its position because, the inductance is an electromagnetic characteristic that depends on the structural configuration of the electric generator. For different relative positions of the translator, in respect to the stator (stationary part of the generator), the generator will assume distinct configurations with particular values of inductance. Thus, each structural configuration will present inductance values between a maximum and a minimum values. Then, as greater is the difference between the value of inductance in the alignment position (L_a) and the inductance value in the unaligned position (L_u), greater will be the electromotive force developed at the terminals of each electric phase of the generator for a given velocity of the translator. Likewise, the lesser is the distance (Δx), that the translator must travel between these two alignment conditions, greater will be the developed electromotive force. However, these type o machines are characterized for non-linear magnetic characteristics, especially for high electric currents. Due to the complexity in accounting the rate of change of the inductance with the translator position in non-linear operating conditions, it will be assumed an ideal case of operation for the characterization of the generation potential subjacent to each structural model during the optimization process. This idealization implies a linear assessment of the electromagnetic characteristics of the electric machine. So, the generation capabilities for each generator configuration will be accounted through the factor (Q) which represents the linear rate of change of the inductance with the position of the translator between the aligned and unaligned positions:

$$Q = \frac{L_a - L_u}{\Delta x}$$
(7)

The factor Q, given by expression (7), is the objective function for each model whose value should be maximized by the variation of a given set of dimensional parameters that define the geometry of the respective structural model.

Therefore, for each geometric configuration under assessment, the following optimization problem is defined:

$$\text{find } X = \left\{ \begin{array}{c} x_1 \\ x_2 \\ \vdots \\ x_n \end{array} \right\} \text{ that maximize } Q(X),$$

$$\text{subject to: } X_l \leq X \leq X_u$$
(8)

where X is a n-dimensional vector correspondent to the n variable parameters involved in the optimization process. The vectors X_l and X_u, define, respectively, the lower and upper boundaries of the feasible search space for the n variable parameters. Although the objective function Q is the same for the 4 models that will be optimized, the dimension of the variable vector is different.

Objective Function

The objective function Q defined in (7) is a non-linear function that implies the utilization of a numerical model of the generator to perform a Finite Element Analysis (FEM) in order to calculate the value of its inductance. For this reason, the function Q is not defined for a analytic expression but rather for sequence of instructions that comprises a set of functions defined in *Matlab* and the software *MagNet 7.4.1* from *Infolytica* that allows the design of the generator under assessment and the respective magneto-static analysis by the Finite Element Method to calculate the inductance value for a given geometry and relative position of the translator. For this reason, the objective function is defined by a block of commands that provides the value of Q as output according to the vector of variables as input, as schematized in Figure 7.

The objective function Q is composed by three sub-functions, as schematized in Figure 8.

The function *ModelData* receives the vector with the variables correspondent to the optimization problem and provides all the necessary geometrical parameters for the design of the numerical model. This latter process is carried by the function *ModelDraw* that creates a two dimensional draw of the structural model under assessment. With model drawn, the magneto-static analysis is performed with

Figure 7. Objective function data flow

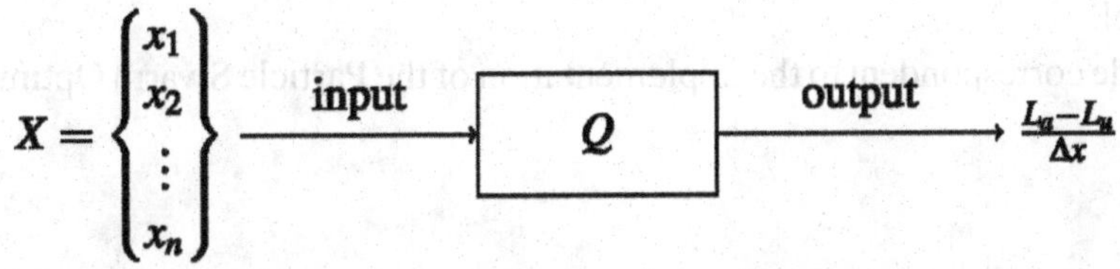

$$X = \begin{Bmatrix} x_1 \\ x_2 \\ \vdots \\ x_n \end{Bmatrix} \xrightarrow{\text{input}} \boxed{Q} \xrightarrow{\text{output}} \frac{L_a - L_u}{\Delta x}$$

Figure 8. Calculation sequence of function Q

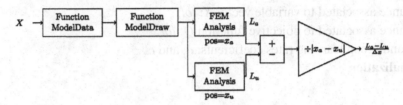

the translator in the aligned position (x_a) where the respective inductance value (L_a) is obtained. The same procedure is executed for the unaligned position (x_u) and the corresponding value of inductance (L_u) is calculated. With the inductance values for the two referred alignment conditions, the value of Q is determined.

Optimization Process

In the optimization process will be used the Particle Swarm Algorithm described in this chapter. To a proper implementation of this algorithm, it is necessary to define other procedures for the computation and treatment of the data involved in the optimization process as to perform the initial distribution of the particles and to check if their positions do not violate the boundaries defined to the variables. In the first case, an uniformly distribution of the particles in the feasible search space is defined by the imposed vector boundaries. For that, the function *kmeans,* available in the software *Matlab*, is used to provide an equally spaced population of particles throughout the search space from an initial randomly distributed one. The latter, to which the *k-means* algorithm is applied is composed with two particles whose positions corresponds to the lower and upper boundary positions, namely, to X_l and X_u, respectively. The remaining positions are randomly generated between the defined boundaries. Every time a new position vector is calculated for a particle, is necessary to check the validity of its position coordinates (variables), i.e., if their values fall inside the feasible zone. During the optimization process, this procedure is performed by a function defined as *checkBound* that verifies and corrects the several coordinates (variables) of each particle according to the following conditions:

$$X_i(j) < X_l(j) \Rightarrow X_i(j) = X_l(j)$$
$$X_i(j) > X_u(j) \Rightarrow X_i(j) = X_u(j)$$
for:

$$i = 1, 2, ..., N \text{ particles}$$
$$j = 1, 2, ..., m \text{ variables}$$

$$(9)$$

Before each boundary check, the vectors X_l and X_u may be updated in function of the geometric relations of each model.

The pseudo-code correspondent to the implementation of the Particle Swarm Optimization algorithm is described next:

Input Data

Number of variables: m

Number of variables: N

Maximum number of iterations: k_{max}

Error tolerance associated to variable vector X: tol_X

Error tolerance associated to objective function Q: tol_f

Individual and group learning rates coeficients: c_1 and c_2

Population Initialization

$X_1 = X_l$

$X_2 = X_u$

for $i \leftarrow 3$ to N do

    for $j \leftarrow 1$ to m do

$$X_i^0(j) \leftarrow X_l + r(X_u - X_l)$$

    end for

end for

$X^0 = kmeans(X^0)$

$X^0 = checkBound(X^0)$

for $i \leftarrow 1$ to N do

$$f_i^0(j) \leftarrow -Q(X_i^0)$$

end for

$P_{best} \leftarrow X^0$

$f_{P_{best}} \leftarrow f^0$

$f_{G_{best}} \leftarrow f^0$

$f_{G_{best}} \leftarrow \min(f^0)$

$i_G \leftarrow$ index correspondent to the minimum value of f

$G_{best} \leftarrow X_{i_G}^0$

Iterative Optimization Process

$k \leftarrow 0$

while $k \leq k_{max}$ do

    $k \leftarrow k + 1$

$$\theta \leftarrow 0.9 - \left(\frac{0.9 - 0.4}{k_{max}}\right)k$$

    for all $i \leftarrow 1$ to N do

$$V_i^k = V_i^{k-1} + c_1 r_1 \left[P_{best,i} - X_i^{k-1}\right] + c_2 r_2 \left[G_{best} - X_i^{k-1}\right]$$

$$X_i^k = X_i^{k-1} + V_i^k$$

end for

$$e_f \leftarrow \left| \max\left(f_{P_{best}} \right) - \min\left(f_{P_{best}} \right) \right|$$

$e_X \leftarrow$ value of the maximum distance verified between the number of particles correspondent to 15% of the population with the lesser values of $f_{P_{best}}$

if $e_f \leq tol_f$ and $e_X \leq tol_X$ then

Stop the iteration process

end if

end while

The parameters r, r_1 and r_2 are random numbers between 0 and 1 generated by the software *Matlab*, during the execution of the respective instructions.

DESCRIPTION OF THE STRUCTURAL MODELS

The optimization of 4 structural models of a linear switched reluctance generator with tubular topology is performed. Each model is constituted by 3 electric phases but, with distinct geometric configurations. The optimization algorithm to be implemented is meant to find the optimum values for determined parameters, assumed as optimization variables, which will define the geometry of each structural model. The geometry is ruled by several dimensional parameters that are dependent from the optimization variables with exception from the number of turns (N_t) in each electric coil, the electric conductor wire diameter (d_{wire}) and the relation between the length of the translator and the length of the stator (N_{size}) that will be held constant for all the structural models.

Model A

This structural configuration is characterized by two coils per phase connected in series. The schematic drawing of this configuration is illustrated in Figure 9. In this illustration, the model cross-sectional profile is shown as well the geometric parameters used for the design of the respective numerical model.

The variables involved in the optimization process of model A are listed in Table 1.

Table 1. Optimization variables used for model A

Variable	Parameter	Variable	Parameter
x_1	g	x_8	Di_s
x_2	n_p	x_9	n_s
x_3	h_{p+}	x_{10}	h_{s+}
x_4	b_p	x_{11}	b_s
x_5	l_p	x_{12}	l_s
x_6	t_p	x_{13}	t_s
x_7	a_p	x_{14}	a_s

Figure 9. Schematic drawing and respective parameters of model A

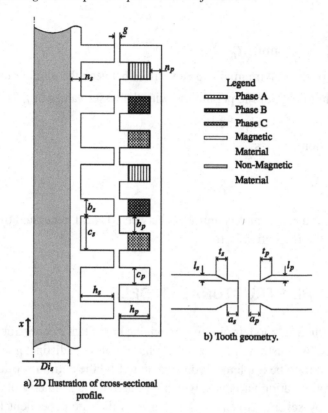

a) 2D Ilustration of cross-sectional profile.

b) Tooth geometry.

Attending to the parameters indicated in Table 2, l_{coil} is referred to thr width of the cross-section of each coil of conducting wire.

The parameter l_{coil} is calculated by the following expression:

Table 2. Geometrical parameters for model A

Parameter		Value	Parameter		Value
G_1	g	x_1	G_{11}	a_p	x_7
G_2	N_t	86	G_{12}	Di_s	x_8
G_3	d_{wire}	4 mm	G_{13}	n_s	x_9
G_4	N_{size}	2	G_{14}	h_s	$x_{10}+x_{13}+x_{14}$
G_5	n_p	x_2	G_{15}	b_s	x_{11}
G_6	h_p	$l_{coil}+2\ mm+x_3+x_6+x_7$	G_{16}	c_s	$1.5(G_7+G_8)-G_{15}$
G_7	b_p	x_4	G_{17}	l_s	x_{12}
G_8	c_p	G_7	G_{18}	t_s	x_{13}
G_9	l_p	x_5	G_{19}	a_s	x_{14}
G_{10}	t_p	x_6			

$$l_{coil} = \frac{A_{coil}}{h_{coil}} \tag{10}$$

where A_{coil} and h_{coil} are, respectively, the area and height of the cross-section of each coil and are given by:

$$A_{coil} = N_t \frac{\pi d_{wire}^2}{4}$$

$$h_{coil} = c_p - 2 \ mm$$

The displacement (Δx) between the alignment and nonalignment positions is calculated by:

$$\Delta x = \frac{1}{2}\left(b_s + c_s\right)$$

In order to the numerical model to be properly designed, the following conditions must be verified:

$$b_s \leq b_p \tag{11}$$

$$l_p \leq \frac{b_p}{2} - 1 \ mm \tag{12}$$

$$l_s \leq \frac{b_s}{2} - 1 \ mm \tag{13}$$

With the optimization variables identified and their relations with the dimensional parameters that rule the model geometry defined, it remains to establish the boundary values that will delineate the feasible search space. The boundary values for each variable are indicated in Table 3.

In order to respect the conditions imposed in the expressions (11-13), the upper boundaries of the variables x_5, x_6 and x_{11} are updated before their respective validity check. The purpose of the values indicated in Table 3 are only, for the referred variables, to define the first feasible search space to generate the initial population. So, at each iteration, the upper boundary values for x_5, x_6 and x_{11} are updated as indicated next:

$$x_{u_{11}} \leftarrow x_4$$

Table 3. Boundary values for the optimization variables used in model A

Variable	Lower Boundary	Upper Boundary
x_1	1	5
x_2	20	30
x_3	0	20
x_4	25	35
x_5	0	12
x_6	1	12
x_7	0	12
x_8	55	70
x_9	20	30
x_{10}	40	70
x_{11}	25	35
x_{12}	0	12
x_{13}	1	12
x_{14}	0	12

$$x_{u_5} \leftarrow \frac{x_4}{2} - 1$$

$$x_{u_6} \leftarrow \frac{x_{11}}{2} - 1$$

Model B

This model is characterized for independent magnetic circuits which are separated by rings made of a paramagnetic material. As in model A, in this structural configuration are used 2 coils of conducting wire per phase. In Figure 10 is illustrated the schematic drawing of the cross-sectional profile of this model, as well the geometry of the respective teeth. In the same illustration, are indicated the geometrical parameters used for the elaboration of the numerical model of this structural configuration.

In Table 4 are shown the optimization variables associated with model B.

The dimensional parameters that define its geometry are presented in Table 5 as well the respective relations with the optimization variables.

The parameter l_{Coil} is calculated through expression (10). The displacement (Δx) between the alignment and nonalignment positions is calculated by:

$$\Delta x = \frac{1}{2}\left(b_s + c_s\right)$$

Figure 10. Schematic drawing and respective parameters of model B

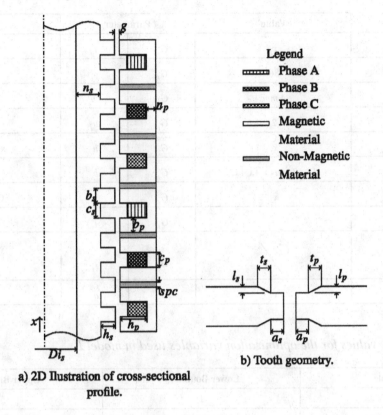

a) 2D Illustration of cross-sectional profile.

b) Tooth geometry.

Table 4. Optimization variables used for model B

Variable	Parameter	Variable	Parameter
x_1	g	x_8	Di_s
x_2	n_p	x_9	n_s
x_3	h_{p+}	x_{10}	h_{s+}
x_4	b_p	x_{11}	b_s
x_5	l_p	x_{12}	l_s
x_6	t_p	x_{13}	t_s
x_7	a_p	x_{14}	a_s

For model B, the conditions (11-13) must be respected. For this model, the feasible search space is defined by the boundaries presented in Table 6.

As defined to model A, the upper boundary values of model B associated to the variables x_5, x_6 and x_{11} will be updated before every validity check, in order to respect the conditions defined in (11-13). Thus, in every iteration, the upper boundary values for x_5, x_6 and x_{11}, will be updated as follows:

$$x_{u_{11}} \leftarrow x_4$$

Table 5. Geometrical parameters for model B

Parameter		Value	Parameter		Value
G_1	g	x_1	G_{11}	t_p	x_6
G_2	N_t	86	G_{12}	a_p	x_7
G_3	d_{wire}	4 mm	G_{13}	Di_s	x_8
G_4	N_{size}	2	G_{14}	n_s	x_9
G_5	n_p	x_2	G_{15}	h_s	$x_{10}+x_{13}+x_{14}$
G_6	h_p	$l_{coil}+2\ mm+x_3+x_6+x_7$	G_{16}	b_s	x_{11}
G_7	b_p	x_4	G_{17}	c_s	$G_7+G_8-G_{16}$
G_8	c_p	G_7	G_{18}	l_s	x_{12}
G_9	spc	$G_7 / 3$	G_{19}	t_s	x_{13}
G_{10}	l_p	x_5	G_{20}	a_s	x_{14}

Table 6. Boundary values for the optimization variables used in model B

Variable	Lower Boundary	Upper Boundary
x_1	1	5
x_2	20	30
x_3	0	20
x_4	25	35
x_5	0	12
x_6	1	12
x_7	0	12
x_8	55	70
x_9	20	30
x_{10}	40	70
x_{11}	25	35
x_{12}	0	12
x_{13}	1	12
x_{14}	0	12

$$x_{u_5} \leftarrow \frac{x_4}{2} - 1$$

$$x_{u_6} \leftarrow \frac{x_{11}}{2} - 1$$

Model C

This model comprises two teeth per magnetic pole instead of just one. In the same way as model B, this structural configuration is composed by independent magnetic paths for each electric phase that are separated by elements made of a paramagnetic material. In this model, only one coil of conducting wire is applied per phase. The cross-sectional profile for model C, its geometry and respective dimensional parameters are illustrated in Figure 11.

The optimization variables associated to this model are disposed in Table 7.

The dimensional parameters used to design the numerical model of this generator configuration are listed in Table 8 along with their respective relations with the optimization variables.

The parameter l_{coil} is calculated in the same as for models A and B, with expression (10). The displacement (Δx) between the alignment and nonalignment is also given by:

$$\Delta x = \frac{1}{2}\left(b_s + c_s\right)$$

In addition to the conditions (11-13), another on is imposed for this model:

$$b_{p2} \leq 2b_p + c_p \tag{14}$$

Figure 11. Schematic drawing and respective parameters of model C

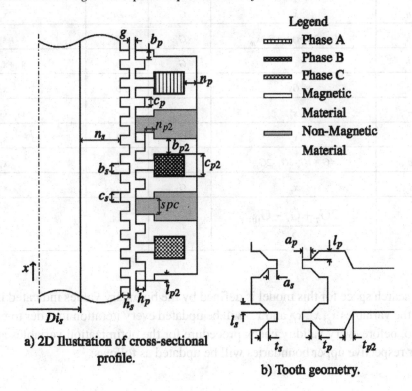

a) 2D Ilustration of cross-sectional profile.

b) Tooth geometry.

Table 7. Optimization variables used for model C

Variable	Parameter	Variable	Parameter
x_1	g	x_{10}	a_p
x_2	n_p	x_{11}	Di_s
x_3	h_{p+}	x_{12}	n_s
x_4	b_p	x_{13}	h_{s+}
x_5	n_{p2}	x_{14}	b_s
x_6	b_{p2}	x_{15}	l_s
x_7	t_{p2}	x_{16}	t_s
x_8	l_p	x_{17}	a_s
x_9	t_p		

Table 8. Geometrical parameters for model C

Parameter		Value	Parameter		Value
G_1	g	x_1	G_{14}	spc	$G_{21} + G_{22} - \dfrac{G_7}{3}$
G_2	N_t	86	G_{15}	l_p	x_8
G_3	d_{wire}	4 mm	G_{16}	t_p	x_9
G_4	N_{size}	2	G_{17}	a_p	x_{10}
G_5	n_p	x_2	G_{18}	Di_s	x_{11}
G_6	h_p	$l_{coil}+2\ mm+x_3+x_9+x_{10}$	G_{19}	n_s	x_{12}
G_7	b_p	x_4	G_{20}	h_s	$x_{13}+x_{16}+x_{17}$
G_8	c_p	G_7	G_{21}	b_s	x_{14}
G_9	n_{p2}	x_5	G_{22}	c_s	$G_7+G_8-G_{21}$
G_{10}	b_{p2}	x_6	G_{23}	l_s	x_{15}
G_{11}	c_{p2}	$4G_7+3G_8-2G_{13}-2G_{10}$	G_{24}	t_s	x_{16}
G_{12}	t_{p2}	x_7	G_{25}	a_s	x_{17}
G_{13}	l_{p2}	$\dfrac{2G_7+G_8-G_{10}}{2}$			

The feasible search space for this model is defined by the boundary values indicated in Table 9. The upper limits for the variables x_6, x_8, x_{14} and x_{15} will be updated every iteration in order to fulfil the conditions (11-14). So, before every validity check procedure for the optimization variables associated with this model, their respective upper boundaries will be updated as follows:

Table 9. Boundary values for the optimization variables used in model C

Variable	Lower Boundary	Upper Boundary
x_1	1	5
x_2	20	30
x_3	0	20
x_4	8	25
x_5	25	35
x_6	10	60
x_7	0	15
x_8	0	12
x_9	1	12
x_{10}	0	12
x_{11}	55	70
x_{12}	20	30
x_{13}	0	30
x_{14}	8	20
x_{15}	0	12
x_{16}	1	12
x_{17}	0	12

$$x_{u_{14}} \leftarrow x_4$$

$$x_{u_6} \leftarrow 3x_4$$

$$x_{u_8} \leftarrow \frac{x_4}{2} - 1$$

$$x_{u_{15}} \leftarrow \frac{x_{14}}{2} - 1$$

Model D

In this model, the stator geometry is very similar to the geometry presented for the same part in model A. However, the translator configuration is totally different. It have not a salient profile, as in all the previous models presented, and is composed, mostly, for a paramagnetic material in which are embedded segments of a material with high magnetic permeability. In Figure 12 is shown the cross-sectional profile of the model D as well the geometry for the tooth and magnetic segments.

For this model are assumed the optimization variables presented in Table 10.

Figure 12. Schematic drawing and respective parameters of model D

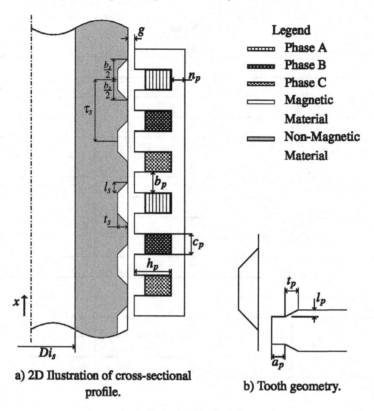

a) 2D Ilustration of cross-sectional profile.

b) Tooth geometry.

Table 10. Optimization variables used for model D

Variable	Parameter	Variable	Parameter
x_1	g	x_7	a_p
x_2	n_p	x_8	Di_s
x_3	h_{p+}	x_9	b_s
x_4	b_p	x_{10}	l_s
x_5	l_p	x_{11}	t_s
$x6$	t_p		

To each optimization variable corresponds a dimensional parameter, as well as their relations with the variables. Those parameters are shown in Table 11.

As for all the previous models, l_{coil} is calculated by expression (10). The displacement (Δx) between the alignment and nonalignment is also given by:

$$\Delta x = \frac{3}{4}\left(b_p + c_p\right)$$

Table 11. Geometrical parameters for model D

Parameter		Value	Parameter		Value
G_1	g	x_1	G_9	lp	$x5$
G_2	N_t	86	G_{10}	t_p	x_6
G_3	d_{wire}	4 mm	G_{11}	a_p	x_7
G_4	N_{size}	2	G_{12}	Di_s	x_8
G_5	n_p	x_2	G_{13}	bs	x_9
G_6	h_p	$l_{coil}+2\ mm+x_3+x_6+x_7$	G_{14}	l_s	x_{10}
G_7	b_p	x_4	G_{15}	t_s	x_{11}
G_8	c_p		G_7		

The conditions indicated in expressions (12) and (13) must be respected in order to achieve a valid geometry for this model. Further, the parameter b_s shall be within the limits imposed by the following condition:

$$1.1c_p \leq b_s \leq 1.9b_p + c_p \qquad (15)$$

The boundaries that define the feasible search space are listed in Table 12.

Given the restrictions imposed for the variables x_5, x_6 and x_9, the respective boundary values will be updated, every iteration, as follows:

$$x_{l_9} \leftarrow 1.1x_4$$

$$x_{u_9} \leftarrow 2.9x_4$$

Table 12. Boundary values for the optimization variables used in model D

Variable	Lower Boundary	Upper Boundary
x_1	1	5
x_2	20	30
x_3	0	20
x_4	25	35
x_5	0	12
x_6	1	12
x_7	0	12
x_8	70	100
x_9	10	40
x_{10}	0	15
x_{11}	1	40

$$x_{u_5} \leftarrow \frac{x_4}{2} - 1$$

$$x_{u_6} \leftarrow \frac{x_9}{2} - 1$$

RESULTS

Attending to the formulated optimization problem and the structural models with tubular topology defined for a linear switched reluctance generator, computations were performed with goal to find the optimal values for the geometrical parameters that could minimize the objective function $-Q$, given by expression (7). The values search was supported by the Particle Swarm Optimization algorithm. The optimization process was applied to each structural model. Ahead, are presented the values for each optimization variable that have resulted from the optimization procedure. In Table 13 are shown the initial parameters defined for the optimization process applied to each structural model.

In the following tables are presented the initial populations generated from which the iterative process was initiated. Table 14 corresponds to the model A, Table 15 corresponds to the model B, Table 16 corresponds to the model C and Table 17 corresponds to the model D.

The results of the optimization process applied to each model under assessment are listed in Table 18. The respective optimum values can be observed in Table 19 as well their corresponding objective function value. The evolution, with the number of iterations, of the errors associated to the objective function (e_f) and to the variable vector (e_x), is represented in Figure 13 and Figure 14, respectively.

Regarding the obtained results, it can be verified that model B was classified with the highest value for function Q (5.98), in comparison with the optimal values found for each model. The worst value of Q was obtained for model A, with a value of 1.73. The optimization process for this latter model was characterized, in respect to model B, with a lesser number iterations needed to achieve convergence while having, both models, the same number of variables. For model C, was verified the most extensive optimization process since more iterations were needed to converge to an optimal solution. This is a justifiable situation because model C has the largest number of variables involved in the optimization process. Assessing the optimal values obtained for the optimization variables, it was verified that, in most

Table 13. Initial data

Model		A	B	C	D
Number of Variables	m	14	14	17	11
Number of Particles	N	20	20	20	20
Maximum Number of Iterations	k_{max}	200	200	400	200
Error Tolerance for X	tol_X	5×10^{-2}			
Error Tolerance for Function Q	tol_f	5×10^{-4}			
Learning Rates Coefficients	c_1	0.75			
	c_2	2.25			

Table 14. Initial population for model A

Particle	Variables													
	x_1	x_2	x_3	x_4	x_5	x_6	x_7	x_8	x_9	x_{10}	x_{11}	x_{12}	x_{13}	x_{14}
1	4.7	22.9	15.1	32.5	4.6	7.2	0.9	55.8	25.3	63.4	32.5	1.6	7.3	5.6
2	4.4	26.2	7	30.1	4.8	1.8	2.9	56.8	21.8	47.2	29.2	0.6	10.9	11.3
3	4.6	29.8	8.8	26.1	3.1	5.5	7.1	58.9	26	61.3	26.1	1.4	4.3	3.8
4	3	25.1	16.4	32.9	7.7	5.2	9.7	63	23.5	68.2	32.9	6.6	7.8	7
5	5	30	20	35	12	12	12	70	30	70	35	12	12	12
6	3	24.9	6.8	34	4.4	2.2	9.4	60.8	22.4	52.1	26	1.6	11.4	11.5
7	3.3	20.6	4.7	28.5	9.9	1.2	0.5	57.5	26.5	62	28.5	5.4	7	3.6
8	4.8	23.4	11.7	27.2	9	3.8	6.1	65.5	28.9	68.8	27.2	1.7	2.6	3.1
9	4.1	28	3.7	29.9	5.3	8.1	8.5	66.3	22.8	60.4	29.9	2	2.3	6
10	4.3	29.1	2.5	34.1	7.6	2.1	3.3	63.2	29.6	68.9	26.6	11.6	11.5	5.8
11	1	20	0	25	0	1	0	55	20	40	25	0	1	0
12	4.2	21.4	8.4	34.2	9.5	11.6	7.9	55.5	28.5	68	31.8	9.1	9.2	4.7
13	2.7	25.1	1.7	27.6	9.6	1.3	11.1	66	24.9	57.4	27.4	5.5	11.6	6.6
14	3.6	21.7	14.1	25.3	3.3	1.5	1.2	67.4	26.9	49.5	25.3	0.4	5.8	4.6
15	4	21.9	13.7	26.8	4.4	7.9	9.4	56.2	29.3	63.3	26.8	5.2	5.9	3.7
16	1.8	23	9.4	27.3	10.1	3.1	2.7	57.6	22.3	53.1	27.3	11.1	5.7	2.2
17	1.3	24	5.2	33	5.2	11	2.2	59	21.5	44.1	33	7	7	1.7
18	1	23.4	3.2	32.9	3.7	6.8	2	64	22.6	59.6	31.9	9	6	1
19	1.9	29.1	3	33.3	6.5	12	0.9	61.6	21.1	68.9	25	9.3	10	10.4
20	4.4	22.5	16.3	27.4	11.2	4.8	2.4	58.8	26.2	54.2	27.4	10	7.4	6.6

cases, the values are coincident with the respective boundaries imposed while only a reduced number of variables achieved an optimum value between the lower and upper limits.

Evaluating the errors e_f, associated to the objective function displayed in Figure 12, it can be verified for the 4 models an abrupt rate of change with the first iterations while having a more gradual evolution as the iterative process progresses.

Regarding the error e_x, associated with the variable vector, it can be verified that it assumes a null value before the error e_f falls below the specified tolerance. This happens because the particles correspondent to 15% of the population with best values collapses at the same position much before the objective function value reach the convergence criteria. The evolution of e_x, with number of iterations also shows an initial abrupt reduction which is attenuated as the number of iterations increases. As shown in Figure 14, the optimization process of model D is characterized for a superior number of particles position oscillations while the remaining models presents a more stable position error evolution, as the optimization process evolves. However, its function error evolution remains stable during this particle's position oscillations. This is an indication that, for model D, the function gradient value may be small near the obtained optimal solution and thus different parameter values can be chosen for similar optimal machine characteristics.

Table 15. Initial population for model B

Particle	Variables													
	x_1	x_2	x_3	x_4	x_5	x_6	x_7	x_8	x_9	x_{10}	x_{11}	x_{12}	x_{13}	x_{14}
1	4.7	22.9	15.1	32.5	4.6	7.2	0.9	55.8	25.3	63.4	32.5	1.6	7.3	5.6
2	4.4	26.2	7	30.1	4.8	1.8	2.9	56.8	21.8	47.2	29.2	0.6	10.9	11.3
3	4.6	29.8	8.8	26.1	3.1	5.5	7.1	58.9	26	61.3	26.1	1.4	4.3	3.8
4	3	25.1	16.4	32.9	7.7	5.2	9.7	63	23.5	68.2	32.9	6.6	7.8	7
5	5	30	20	35	12	12	12	70	30	70	35	12	12	12
6	3	24.9	6.8	34	4.4	2.2	9.4	60.8	22.4	52.1	26	1.6	11.4	11.5
7	3.3	20.6	4.7	28.5	9.9	1.2	0.5	57.5	26.5	62	28.5	5.4	7	3.6
8	4.8	23.4	11.7	27.2	9	3.8	6.1	65.5	28.9	68.8	27.2	1.7	2.6	3.1
9	4.1	28	3.7	29.9	5.3	8.1	8.5	66.3	22.8	60.4	29.9	2	2.3	6
10	4.3	29.1	2.5	34.1	7.6	2.1	3.3	63.2	29.6	68.9	26.6	11.6	11.5	5.8
11	1	20	0	25	0	1	0	55	20	40	25	0	1	0
12	4.2	21.4	8.4	34.2	9.5	11.6	7.9	55.5	28.5	68	31.8	9.1	9.2	4.7
13	2.7	25.1	1.7	27.6	9.6	1.3	11.1	66	24.9	57.4	27.4	5.5	11.6	6.6
14	3.6	21.7	14.1	25.3	3.3	1.5	1.2	67.4	26.9	49.5	25.3	0.4	5.8	4.6
15	4	21.9	13.7	26.8	4.4	7.9	9.4	56.2	29.3	63.3	26.8	5.2	5.9	3.7
16	1.8	23	9.4	27.3	10.1	3.1	2.7	57.6	22.3	53.1	27.3	11.1	5.7	2.2
17	1.3	24	5.2	33	5.2	11	2.2	59	21.5	44.1	33	7	7	1.7
18	1	23.4	3.2	32.9	3.7	6.8	2	64	22.6	59.6	31.9	9	6	1
19	1.9	29.1	3	33.3	6.5	12	0.9	61.6	21.1	68.9	25	9.3	10	10.4
20	4.4	22.5	16.3	27.4	11.2	4.8	2.4	58.8	26.2	54.2	27.4	10	7.4	6.6

According to the error e_f obtained for models B and C, it can be verified that it takes more iterations to get close to the specified tolerance value, in comparison to the function error evolution for models A and D. Since the position error e_x for models B and C has a faster approximation to the respective specified tolerance, it can be deduced that for the latter models, the function value possess a larger gradient near the optimal solution.

CONCLUSION

The Particle Swarm Optimization Algorithm was used to perform the search for the optimum values of a defined set of geometrical parameters that could maximize the generation capabilities of a linear switched reluctance generator with tubular topology. The generation capabilities were quantified by the rate of change of the generator's inductance with the translator position. For that, a function Q was defined to represent the latter electromagnetic entity, assuming an ideal case of operation where the generator would be characterized by linear magnetic characteristics. The optimization algorithm was applied to 4 structural models with different configurations with the aim to predict which could be the best structure to be adopted for the assumed type of generator. For each considered model, were defined the variables

Table 16. Initial population for model C

Particle	Variables								
	x_1	x_2	x_3	x_4	x_5	x_6	x_7	x_8	x_9
1	4.9	26.2	0.9	9.9	29.6	27.5	8.2	2	6
2	1	20	0	8	25	10	0	0	1
3	3.3	22.5	4.5	9	25.1	27.1	14.9	0.4	11
4	4.2	22.3	3	20	32	37.4	14.4	5.6	10.4
5	3.3	25	5.3	17.9	28.3	39.1	2.3	4.2	1.8
6	5	30	20	20	35	60	15	9	12
7	1.7	26.7	2	16.4	28.2	18.6	11.9	1.4	9
8	3.6	25.3	0.3	8.5	30	12	6.2	3.1	1.8
9	1.2	24.7	12.5	13.6	32.9	40.7	11.3	5.8	1.2
10	4	23.9	8.3	14.3	28.1	42.9	4.2	6.1	3.9
11	2	24.8	1	13.8	32.1	15.8	3.2	2.9	8.5
12	3	29.6	15.2	9.8	25	29.5	13.3	3.9	8.8
13	4	26.7	10.5	9	31.9	27	1.3	3.5	7.3
14	4.3	27.4	12.5	19.7	30.4	10.9	14.7	8.9	5.4
15	1.1	24.4	5.9	19.4	27.2	58.1	1.8	5.3	1.1
16	3	26.9	15.6	14.9	31.2	40.6	10	1.7	5.2
17	4.5	26.1	4.7	12.9	29.5	38.8	13.4	5.4	1.3
18	1	27.3	11.7	20	27.4	53.6	7.6	7.8	5.7
19	1.9	25.1	11	16.1	34	48.4	10	7.1	11.2
20	3.9	24.7	8.2	9.7	33.9	25	11.2	0.8	8.9
	x_{10}	x_{11}	x_{12}	x_{13}	x_{14}	x_{15}	x_{16}	x_{17}	
1	8.4	66.5	22.2	1.8	9.9	4	5.9	9	
2	0	55	20	0	8	0	1	0	
3	8.1	61.4	23	27.4	9	1	4.7	6.3	
4	10.5	57.8	22.9	3.1	9.3	3.6	1.6	4.7	
5	3.3	58.9	21.2	12	12.7	5.4	10.1	0.6	
6	12	70	30	30	20	9	12	12	
7	5.5	55.7	29.9	28.3	16.4	7.2	10.7	7.3	
8	7.9	63.3	27.1	23.8	8.5	3.2	3.3	1.7	
9	5.8	56.6	28.1	3.8	10.2	0.9	2.2	3.1	
10	0.3	63	28.9	1	14.3	5.8	9.3	10	
11	9.8	58.7	23.8	0.1	9.5	3.8	10.6	10	
12	2.1	60	21.2	17.1	8	3	6.1	8.1	
13	4.4	64.7	28.3	3.3	9	3.5	9.5	6.2	
14	4.3	69.1	22.5	10.6	18.6	7.4	1.7	1.2	
15	8.1	60.9	21.3	18.4	16.2	6.8	4.9	7.8	
16	5.7	56	26.4	11.5	14.2	6.1	11.5	3	
17	6.6	60.7	23.8	20.6	10.7	4.3	10.3	4.6	
18	2.2	58.5	28.5	21.1	16	2.9	9.4	6.7	
19	5.7	60	25.5	18	15.2	4.8	4.5	9.7	
20	3.6	68.5	23.1	21.7	9.7	3.9	11.6	4.5	

Table 17. Initial population for model D

Particle	Variables										
	x_1	x_2	x_3	x_4	x_5	x_6	x_7	x_8	x_9	x_{10}	x_{11}
1	3.7	24.2	2.6	32	2.1	1.1	5.1	97.2	35.2	11.1	33
2	4.2	22.2	5.3	28.2	7.5	1.1	10	79.2	31.1	8.1	3.4
3	1.7	28.1	17.3	27.9	7	6.3	10.4	79.4	30.7	5.8	21
4	2.9	27.5	13	26.2	1	8	11.5	90.5	28.8	7.2	39.3
5	1.8	22.7	4.8	33.6	9	4.5	6.1	93.5	37	11.8	9.1
6	3.2	22	5.5	25.8	2.2	2.6	4.2	80.9	28.4	8.7	22
7	1.5	23.6	10.1	30.1	10.3	1.5	8.4	94.1	33.1	12.9	17
8	2	21.1	12.5	34.3	2.2	7.9	1.9	91.6	37.7	8.1	9.9
9	4.3	28.1	19.8	33.2	11.1	7.8	7.4	75.1	36.5	8.8	8.8
10	1	20	0	25	0	1	0	70	27.5	0	1
11	5	30	20	35	12	12	12	100	40	15	40
12	1.8	25.4	10.4	25.4	8.6	6.6	2.7	88.8	28	7.6	15.2
13	3.2	25.9	0.6	31.3	7.1	1.7	2.1	72.9	34.4	7.8	6.4
14	1.4	21.2	8	34.3	9.9	2.5	5.1	95.6	37.8	14.5	5.8
15	2.1	24.8	8.1	30.8	8.5	9.8	10.3	76.5	36.9	8.2	37.7
16	3.3	28.8	18.3	32.3	10.3	9.8	3.3	88.9	35.6	2.1	2.3
17	4.8	25.8	5.2	26.3	6.2	4.6	5.9	89.6	28.9	10.7	23.4
18	2.9	25.2	11.3	31.8	3.6	8.1	3.7	93.2	35	7.7	21.9
19	3.6	20.5	9.4	27.5	9.5	9.2	11.3	87.8	30.2	2	20
20	4.2	22.9	19.1	25.8	9	2.1	4.1	79.6	28.4	7.4	23.9

Table 18. Optimization process results

Model	A	B	C	D
Number of Evaluations of Function Q	1440	2760	5740	3360
Number of Iterations	71	137	286	182
e_f	2.35×10^{-4}	4.36×10^{-4}	4.49×10^{-4}	2.74×10^{-4}
e_x	0	0	0	0
Time Elapsed (min)	304	681	1189	757

involved in the optimization process as well their relation with the necessary dimensional parameters for the design of the respective structure. For each variable were specified the boundary values within which, their values could be searched during the optimization process. The objective function, classified as non-linear, was defined as a group of sub-functions related to different stages of calculations procedures that comprises the variable input data conditioning, the calculation of the associated dimensional parameters, the design of the numerical model of the generator and the respective magneto-static analysis through the finite element method. The optimization variables values were always rounded to one decimal place

Table 19. Optimal values

Model	A	B	C	D
x_1	1	1	1	1
x_2	20	30	30	30
x_3	0	0	20	0
x_4	25	25	20	25
x_5	0	2	35	0
x_6	1	12	60	1
x_7	2	0	15	0
x_8	70	70	1.2	100
x_9	30	30	12	72.5
x_{10}	40	70	2.9	18.1
x_{11}	25	25	70	30.4
x_{12}	0	2.1	30	-
x_{13}	1	12	30	-
x_{14}	0	12	20	-
x_{15}	-	-	1.2	-
x_{16}	-	-	12	-
x_{17}	-	-	12	-
Q	1.73	5.98	4.93	3.19

Figure 13. Evolution of the error, associated to the objective function, with the number of iterations

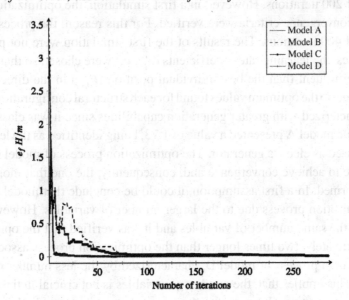

Figure 14. Evolution of the error, associated to the vector of variables, with the number of iterations

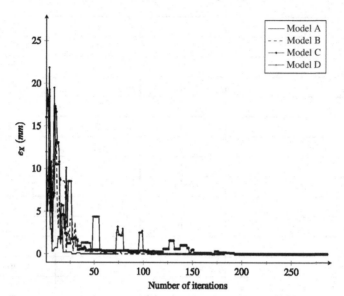

in order to avoid geometric irregularities during the design of the numerical model and also because, more numeric precision would be impractical for the physical implementation of the generator.

In every optimization processes, were assumed a population of 20 particles. To try to achieve an uniformly distribution for the population, the *kmeans* algorithm, provided by a function available in the software *Matlab*, was applied to an initial swarm of randomly spaced particles. The optimization process was executed for the 4 structural models under assessment. For each model optimization, was established maximum number of 200 iterations. However, in a first simulation, the optimization process for model C ended before the convergence criteria were verified. For this reason, the process was repeated for a maximum number of 400 iterations. The results of the first simulation were not presented. For all the optimization processes, the learning rates coefficients (c_1 e c_2) were chosen so that the best group position (G_{best}) was more influent than the best individual position (P_{best}) in the direction of each particle displacement. In respect to the optimum values found for each structural configuration, it can be concluded that model B is characterized with greater generation capabilities since it was classified with the larger value of Q (5.98) while model A presented a value of 1.73, being identified as the less suitable structural configuration to be used as electric generator. The optimization process of model C was the most time consuming procedure to achieve convergence and, consequently, the one that more objective function evaluations has performed. In a first assumption, it could be conclude that model C was characterized for the longest optimization process due to the larger number of variables. However, models A and B were simulated with the same number of variables and it was verified that the optimization process of model B was, approximately, two times longer than the optimization process associated with model A. Besides, the optimization process of model D, characterized by the less number of variables, was the second longest one. This implies that, the number of variables is not crucial in the duration that the applied algorithm takes to converge. In respect to the convergence criteria applied, it was verified that the maximum distance between the number of particles correspondent to 15% of the population with the best positions assumed the value zero much before the difference between the maximum and minimum value of the objective function drop below the specified tolerance. So, it can be concluded that, unless the maximum distance is evaluated to a greater portion of the total population, this convergence criteria associated with the variable vector is irrelevant.

ACKNOWLEDGMENT

R.P.G. Mendes gives his special thanks to the Fundação para a Ciência e a Tecnologia (FCT) for the Ph.D. grant (SFRH/BD/ 91626 / 2012).

REFERENCES

Ahn, J.-W., Liang, J., & Lee, D.-H. (2010). Classification and analysis of switched reluctance converters. *Journal of Electrical Engineering & Technology, 5*(4), 571–579. doi:10.5370/JEET.2010.5.4.571

Akar, F., Fleming, F., & Edrington, C. S. (2012). *A computationally intelligent maximum torque per ampere control strategy for switched reluctance machines.* Paper presented at the Electric Vehicle Conference (IEVC).

Arifin, A., Al-Bahadly, I., & Mukhopadhyay, S. C. (2012). State of the art of switched reluctance generator. *Energy and Power Engineering, 4*(6), 447–458. doi:10.4236/epe.2012.46059

Arkadan, A. A., ElBsat, M. N., & Mneimneh, M. A. (2009). Particle swarm design optimization of ALA rotor SynRM for traction applications. *IEEE Transactions on Magnetics, 45*(3), 956–959. doi:10.1109/TMAG.2009.2012482

Asadi, P., Ehsani, M., & Fahimi, B. (2006). *Design and control characterization of switched reluctance generator for maximum output power.* Paper presented at the Applied Power Electronics Conference and Exposition.

Baiming, S., & Emadi, A. (2011). *A digital control for switched reluctance generators.* Paper presented at the Mechatronics (ICM).

Balaji, M., & Kamaraj, V. (2011). Particle swarm optimization approach for optimal design of switched reluctance machine. *American Journal of Applied Sciences, 8*(4), 374–381. doi:10.3844/ajassp.2011.374.381

Balaji, M., & Kamaraj, V. (2012). Evolutionary computation based multi-objective pole shape optimization of switched reluctance machine. *International Journal of Electrical Power & Energy Systems, 43*(1), 63–69. doi:10.1016/j.ijepes.2012.05.011

Barnes, M., & Pollock, C. (1998). Power electronic converters for switched reluctance drives. *Power Electronics. IEEE Transactions on, 13*(6), 1100–1111. doi:10.1109/63.728337

Bianchi, N., & Bolognani, S. (1998). Design optimisation of electric motors by genetic algorithms. *IEEE Proceedings of Electric Power Applications, 145*(5), 475-483. doi:10.1049/ip-epa:19982166

Boldea, I. (2003). *Control of electric generators: A review.* Paper presented at the Industrial Electronics Society.

Boldea, I. (2010). *Variable speed generators*. Taylor & Francis.

Boldea, I. (2013). *Linear electric machines, drives, and MAGLEVs handbook*. Taylor & Francis. doi:10.1201/b13756

Brady, G., O'Loughlin, C., Massey, J., Griffiths, D., & Villegas, C. (2012). *Design and test of a linear switched reluctance generator for use in wave-energy applications* Paper presented at the 4th International Conference on Ocean Energy.

Cameron, D. E., & Lang, J. H. (1992). *The control of high-speed variable-reluctance generators in electric power systems*. Paper presented at the Applied Power Electronics Conference and Exposition.

Cardenas, R., Pena, R., Perez, M., Clare, J., Asher, G., & Wheeler, P. (2005). Control of a switched reluctance generator for variable-speed wind energy applications. *IEEE Transactions on Energy Conversion*, *20*(4), 781–791. doi:10.1109/TEC.2005.853733

Chang, Y. C., Cheng, C. H., Lu, L. Y., & Liaw, C. M. (2010). *An experimental switched-reluctance generator based distributed power system*. Paper presented at the Electrical Machines (ICEM).

Chen, G., Guo, W., & Huang, K. (2007). *On line parameter identification of an induction motor using improved particle swarm optimization*. Paper presented at the Control Conference.

Chen, H., Wang, X., Gu, J. J., & Lu, S. (2010). *Design of bilateral switched reluctance linear generator*. Paper presented at the Electric Power and Energy Conference (EPEC). doi:10.1109/EPEC.2010.5697236

Clerc, M. (2010). *Particle swarm optimization*. Wiley.

Del Valle, Y., Venayagamoorthy, G. K., Mohagheghi, S., Hernandez, J. C., & Harley, R. G. (2008). Particle swarm optimization: Basic concepts, variants and applications in power systems. *IEEE Transactions on Evolutionary Computation*, *12*(2), 171–195. doi:10.1109/TEVC.2007.896686

dos Santos Coelho, L., Barbosa, L. Z., & Lebensztajn, L. (2010). Multiobjective particle swarm approach for the design of a brushless DC wheel motor. *IEEE Transactions on Magnetics*, *46*(8), 2994–2997. doi:10.1109/TMAG.2010.2044145

Echenique, E., Dixon, J., Cardenas, R., & Pena, R. (2009). Sensorless control for a switched reluctance wind generator, based on current slopes and neural networks. *IEEE Transactions on Industrial Electronics*, *56*(3), 817–825. doi:10.1109/TIE.2008.2005940

Fernando, W. U. N., Barnes, M., & Marjanovic, O. (2011). *Excitation control and voltage regulation of switched reluctance generators above base speed operation*. Paper presented at the Vehicle Power and Propulsion Conference (VPPC).

Fleury, A., dos Santos e Silva, F., Domingos, J. L., & De Andrade, D. A. (2007). *A switched reluctance generator behavior under different conditions*. Paper presented at the Industrial Electronics.

Fleury, A., Andrade, D., Oliveira, E. S. L., Fleury-Neto, G. A., Oliveira, T. F., Dias, R. J., & Silveira, A. W. F. V. (2008). *Study on an alternative converter performance for switched reluctance generator*. Paper presented at the Industrial Electronics.

Hao, C., & Gu, J. J. (2010). Implementation of the three-phase switched reluctance machine system for motors and generators. *IEEE/ASME Transactions on Mechatronics, 15*(3), 421-432. doi: 10.1109/TMECH.2009.2027901

Hao, C., Xing, W., & Gu, J. J. (2009). *Sliding mode control of switched reluctance linear generator system*. Paper presented at the Networking, Sensing and Control.

Hao, C., Xing, W., & Hui, Z. (2009). *Electromagnetic design of switched reluctance linear machine*. Paper presented at the Power Electronics and Motion Control Conference.

Hasanien, H. M. (2011). Particle swarm design optimization of transverse flux linear motor for weight reduction and improvement of thrust force. *IEEE Transactions on Industrial Electronics, 58*(9), 4048–4056. doi:10.1109/TIE.2010.2100338

Hasanien, H. M., & Muyeen, S. M. (2012). Speed control of grid-connected switched reluctance generator driven by variable speed wind turbine using adaptive neural network controller. *Electric Power Systems Research, 84*(1), 206–213. doi:10.1016/j.epsr.2011.11.019

Jang-Ho, S., Chang-Hwan, I., Chang-Geun, H., Jae-Kwang, K., Hyun-Kyo, J., & Cheol-Gyun, L. (2006). Multimodal function optimization based on particle swarm optimization. *IEEE Transactions on Magnetics, 42*(4), 1095–1098. doi:10.1109/TMAG.2006.871568

Jie, G., Hexu, S., Lin, H., Yan, D., & Yi, Z. (2011). *Optimization design of switched reluctance motor based on particle swarm optimization*. Paper presented at the Electrical Machines and Systems (ICEMS).

Jolly, L., Jabbar, M. A., & Liu, Q. H. (2005). Design optimization of permanent magnet motors using response surface methodology and genetic algorithms. *IEEE Transactions on Magnetics, 41*(10), 3928–3930. doi:10.1109/TMAG.2005.854966

Kannan, S., & Suthapadmanabhan, K. (2010). Closed loop control of excitation parameters for high speed switched reluctance generator using MATLAB/SIMULINK. *International Journal on Electrical Engineering and Informatics, 2*(3), 232-243.

Kioskeridis, I., & Mademlis, C. (2006). Optimal efficiency control of switched reluctance generators. *IEEE Transactions on Power Electronics, 21*(4), 1062–1072. doi:10.1109/TPEL.2006.876827

Krishnan, R. (2001). *Switched reluctance motor drives: Modeling, simulation, analysis, design, and applications*. Taylor & Francis. doi:10.1201/9781420041644

Kurfurst, J., Duron, J., Skalka, M., Janda, M., & Ondrusek, C. (2011). *Magnet shape optimization of brushless machine by self-organizing migrating algorithm*. Paper presented at the Power Engineering, Energy and Electrical Drives (POWERENG).

Lobo, N. S., Hong Sun, L., & Krishnan, R. (2008). Comparison of linear switched reluctance machines for vertical propulsion application: Analysis, design, and experimental correlation. *IEEE Transactions on Industry Applications, 44*(4), 1134-1142. doi: 10.1109/TIA.2008.926294

MacMinn, S. R., & Sember, J. W. (1989). *Control of a switched-reluctance aircraft engine starter-generator over a very wide speed range*. Paper presented at the Energy Conversion Engineering Conference.

Mademlis, C., & Kioskeridis, I. (2005). Optimizing performance in current-controlled switched reluctance generators. *IEEE Transactions on Energy Conversion, 20*(3), 556–565. doi:10.1109/TEC.2005.852960

Mendes, R. P. G., Calado, M. R. A., Mariano, S. J. P. S., & Cabrita, C. M. P. (2011). *Design of a tubular switched reluctance linear generator for wave energy conversion based on ocean wave parameters.* Paper presented at the Electrical Machines and Power Electronics and 2011 Electromotion Joint Conference (ACEMP).

Mese, E., Sozer, Y., Kokernak, J. M., & Torrey, D. A. (2000). *Optimal excitation of a high speed switched reluctance generator.* Paper presented at the Applied Power Electronics Conference and Exposition.

Miller, T. J. E. (1985). Converter volt-ampere requirements of the switched reluctance motor drive. *IEEE Transactions on Industry Applications, IA-21*(5), 1136–1144. doi:10.1109/TIA.1985.349516

Miller, T. J. E. (2001). *Electronic control of switched reluctance machines.* Newnes.

Moreau, L., Machmoum, M., & Zaim, M. E. (2006). Design of low-speed slotted switched reluctance machine for wind energy applications. *Electric Power Components and Systems, 34*(10), 1139–1156. doi:10.1080/15325000600630376

Moreau, L., Zaim, M. E., & Machmoum, M. (2012). *Electromagnetic design optimization of a low speed slotted switched reluctance machine using genetic algorithm.* Paper presented at the Electrical Machines (ICEM).

Mueller, M. A. (2005). *Design and performance of a 20 kW, 100 rpm, switched reluctance generator for a direct drive wind energy converter.* Paper presented at the Electric Machines and Drives.

Naayagi, R. T., & Kamaraj, V. (2005). *A comparative study of shape optimization of SRM using genetic algorithm and simulated annealing.* Paper presented at the INDICON.

Narla, S., Sozer, Y., & Husain, I. (2012). Switched reluctance generator controls for optimal power generation and battery charging. *IEEE Transactions on Industry Applications, 48*(5), 1452–1459. doi:10.1109/TIA.2012.2209850

Owatchaiphong, S., & Fuengwarodsakul, N. H. (2009). *Multi-objective based optimization for switched reluctance machines using fuzzy and genetic algorithms.* Paper presented at the Power Electronics and Drive Systems.

Pan, J. F. Yu., Z., Cheung, N. C., & Guang-zhong, C. (2011). *Design and optimization for the linear switched reluctance generator.* Paper presented at the Power Electronics Systems and Applications (PESA).

Peng, H. Y., Ling, Z., Deng, W., & Zhu, J. (2011). *Increasing output power of switched reluctance generator with three-level power converter.* Paper presented at the Power and Energy Engineering Conference (APPEEC).

Phuangmalai, W., Konghirun, M., & Chayopitak, N. (2012). *A design study of 4/2 switched reluctance motor using particle swarm optimization.* Paper presented at the Electrical Engineering/Electronics, Computer, Telecommunications and Information Technology (ECTI-CON).

Qianwen, X., Yukun, S., & Ji, X. (2011). *Modeling inductance for bearingless switched reluctance motor based on PSO-LSSVM*. Paper presented at the Control and Decision Conference (CCDC).

Radun, A. (1994). *Generating with the switched reluctance motor*. Paper presented at the Applied Power Electronics Conference and Exposition.

Rao, S. S. (2009). *Engineering optimization: Theory and practice*. Wiley. doi:10.1002/9780470549124

Richards, M., & Ventura, D. (2004). Choosing a starting configuration for particle swarm optimization. In *Proceedings of 2004 IEEE International Joint Conference on Neural Networks* (pp. 2309-2312). IEEE.

Singh, N. K., Fletcher, J. E., Finney, S. J., Grant, D. M., & Williams, B. W. (2005). *Evaluation of sparse PWM converter for switched reluctance generator*. Paper presented at the Power Electronics and Drives Systems.

Sun, Z. G., Cheung, N. C., Zhao, S. W., Lu, Y., & Shi, Z. H. (2011). *Design and simulation of a linear switched reluctance generator for wave energy conversion*. Paper presented at the Power Electronics Systems and Applications (PESA).

Takahashi, A., Goto, H., Nakamura, K., Watanabe, T., & Ichinokura, O. (2006). Characteristics of 8/6 switched reluctance generator excited by suppression resistor converter. *IEEE Transactions on Magnetics*, *42*(10), 3458–3460. doi:10.1109/TMAG.2006.880388

Torrey, D. A. (2002). Switched reluctance generators and their control. *IEEE Transactions on Industrial Electronics*, *49*(1), 3–14. doi:10.1109/41.982243

Van der Geest, M., Polinder, H., Ferreira, J. A., & Zeilstra, D. (2012). *Optimization and comparison of electrical machines using particle swarm optimization*. Paper presented at the Electrical Machines (ICEM).

Wang, G. H., Chen, J., Cai, T., & Xin, B. (2013). Decomposition-based multi-objective differential evolution particle swarm optimization for the design of a tubular permanent magnet linear synchronous motor. *Engineering Optimization*, *45*(9), 1107–1127. doi:10.1080/0305215X.2012.720682

Wen, O., Zarko, D., & Lipo, T. A. (2006). *Permanent magnet machine design practice and optimization*. Paper presented at the Industry Applications Conference.

Xianjun, S., Zhifeng, C., Jincai, Y. & CaiXia, C. (2010). *Particle swarm optimization with dynamic adaptive inertia weight*. Paper presented at the Challenges in Environmental Science and Computer Engineering (CESCE).

Xiao, W. P., & Ye, J. W. (2009). *Improved PSO-BPNN algorithm for SRG modeling*. Academic Press.

Xue, X. D., Cheng, K. W. E., Bao, Y. J., & Leung, J. (2011). *Design consideration of c-core switched reluctance generators for wind energy*. Paper presented at the Power Electronics Systems and Applications (PESA).

Xue, X. D., Cheng, K. W. E., Bao, Y. J., Leung, P. L., & Cheung, N. (2012). Switched reluctance generators with hybrid magnetic paths for wind power generation. *IEEE Transactions on Magnetics*, *48*(11), 3863–3866. doi:10.1109/TMAG.2012.2202094

Yao, D. & Ionel, D. M. (2011). *A review of recent developments in electrical machine design optimization methods with a permanent magnet synchronous motor benchmark study.* Paper presented at the Energy Conversion Congress and Exposition (ECCE).

Yuan-Chih, C., & Chang-Ming, L. (2008). On the design of power circuit and control scheme for switched reluctance generator. *IEEE Transactions on Power Electronics, 23*(1), 445–454. doi:10.1109/TPEL.2007.911872

Zhao, H., Lingzhi, Y., Hanmei, P., & Kunyan, Z. (2009). *Research and control of SRG for variable-speed wind energy applications.* Paper presented at the Power Electronics and Motion Control Conference.

Zielinski, K., & Laur, R. (2007). Stopping criteria for a constrained single-objective particle swarm optimization algorithm. *Informatica, 31*, 51–59.

Ziyan, R., Dianhai, Z., & Chang-Seop, K. (2013). *Multi-objective worst-case scenario robust optimal design of switched reluctance motor incorporated with FEM and Kriging.* Paper presented at the Electrical Machines and Systems (ICEMS).

KEY TERMS AND DEFINITIONS

Aligned Position: In salient pole machines, corresponds to the relative position between the static and movable parts where the magnetic field stored energy is minimum.

Geometry Optimization: Aims to find the best values for a given geometric parameters in order to achieve the best generation performance of the electric machine.

Optimization Boundaries: Defines the values validity range for the values that the optimization variables may adopt.

Quality Factor: Quantifies the generation capabilities for a switched reluctance generator assuming a linear evaluation of its electromagnetic characteristics. It is defined by the rate of change of the generator's inductance with the relative displacement of its movable part.

Stator: Stationary part of a linear electric machine.

Translator: Movable part of a linear electric machine.

Unaligned Position: In salient pole machines, corresponds to the relative position between the static and movable parts where the magnetic field stored energy is maximum.

Chapter 16
Derivation and Simulation of an Efficient QoS Scheme in MANET through Optimised Messaging Based on ABCO Using QualNet

Abhijit Das
RCC Institute of Information Technology, India

Atal Chaudhuri
Jadavpur University, India

ABSTRACT

Mobile Ad hoc Network or MANET is a collection of heterogeneous mobile nodes and is infrastructure-less by choice or by default. MANET is prone to confront a lot of challenges in designing a proper Quality of Service (QoS) model where transmission reliability has an important contrtibution. This chapter proposes an optimised message transmission scheme inspired by Artificial Bee Colony Optimisation (ABCO) technique. In this proposed scheme, QoS parameters that have been taken into consideration are throughput, delay, packet loss, and bandwidth utilisation. Here, three agents, namely message selection agent, message forwarding agent, and QoS factor calculating agent, have been introduced to govern and optimise the whole message transmission scheme. Through this method, a significant improvement in QoS factor can be achieved in comparison with the existing schemes. QualNet simulator has been used to evaluate the proposed concept.

1. INTRODUCTION

Studying the evolution of any area of science and technology will not only stimulate our natural curiosity, but also gives us a deeper understanding of the main achievements in that area, making us aware of the existing trends and helps us to evaluate the prospects of specific developments. Computer networks, which is the broader area of our study, emerged relatively recently in the late 1960s. They have inherited many

DOI: 10.4018/978-1-4666-8291-7.ch016

useful properties from their predecessors, that is – older and more widely adopted telephone networks. This is not surprising since both computer and telephones are universal instrument of communications.

However, Computer Networks have brought something new into the world of communication – namely, the practically inexhaustible store of information accumulated by human civilization during the several thousand years of its existence. This repository of information is continuing to grow at a steadily increasing rate; which became self-evident in the mid – 1990s, when the rapid growth of the Internet clearly demonstrated that free and anonymous access to information and instant, written communications were highly valued by most individuals.

Below is a brief chronological account of the history of the aforesaid evolution:

- In the late 1950s, early networks of communicating computers included the military radar system Semi-Automatic Ground Environment (SAGE).
- In 1960, the commercial airline reservation system semi-automatic business research environment (SABRE) went online with two connected mainframes.
- In 1962, J.C.R. Licklider developed a working group he called the "Intergalactic Computer Network", a precursor to the ARPANET, at the Advanced Research Projects Agency (ARPA).
- In 1964, researchers at Dartmouth developed the Dartmouth Time Sharing System for distributed users of large computer systems. The same year, at Massachusetts Institute of Technology, a research group supported by General Electric and Bell Labs used a computer to route and manage telephone connections.
- Throughout the 1960s, Leonard Kleinrock, Paul Baran, and Donald Davies independently developed network systems that used packets to transfer information between computers over a network.
- In 1965, Thomas Marill and Lawrence G. Roberts created the first wide area network (WAN). This was an immediate precursor to the ARPANET.
- Also in 1965, the first widely used telephone switch that implemented true computer control was introduced by Western Electric.
- In 1969, the University of California at Los Angeles, the Stanford Research Institute, the University of California at Santa Barbara, and the University of Utah were connected as the beginning of the ARPANET network using 50 Kbit/s circuits.
- In 1972, commercial services using X.25 were deployed, and later used as an underlying infrastructure for expanding TCP/IP networks.
- In 1973, Robert Metcalfe wrote a formal memo at Xerox PARC describing Ethernet, a networking system that was based on the Aloha network, developed in the 1960s by Norman Abramson and colleagues at the University of Hawaii. In July 1976, Robert Metcalfe and David Boggs published their paper "Ethernet: Distributed Packet Switching for Local Computer Networks and collaborated on several patents received in 1977 and 1978. In 1979, Robert Metcalfe pursued making Ethernet an open standard.
- In 1976, John Murphy of Datapoint Corporation created ARCNET, a token-passing network first used to share storage devices.
- In 1995, the transmission speed capacity for Ethernet was increased from 10 Mbit/s to 100 Mbit/s. By 1998, Ethernet supported transmission speeds of a Gigabit. The ability of Ethernet to scale easily (such as quickly adapting to support new fibre optic cable speeds) is a contributing factor to its continued use today.

At present we are in a constant improvement in communication technologies. The user demand which is to be connected anytime and anywhere to both the wealth of information accessible through the Internet and other users and communities has also dramatically increased in recent times. All these things have inspired the pervasive deployment of wireless and wired networked systems. These systems are characterized by the fact of being large or very large and highly heterogeneous devices, communication technologies, protocols, and services. The very dynamic nature of the system is due to continual changes in topology, traffic patterns, and number of active users and services. Intelligent and autonomic management, control, and service provisioning in these complex networks, and in the future networks resulting from their integration and evolution, require the definition of novel protocols and techniques for all the architectural components of the network.

The benefits of wireless networks are both short and long-term including:

- **Convenience:** All notebook computers and many mobile phones today come equipped with the WiFi technology required to connect directly to a wireless LAN. One can securely access his network resources from any location within the coverage area. A coverage area is typically the facility provided by the network and can be stretched to include more than one building.
- **Mobility:** We can communicate while roaming. Employees can stay connected to the network even when they are not at their desks. People in meetings can access documents and applications. Salespeople can check the network for important details from any location.
- **Productivity:** Access to information and to the key applications helps us get the job done and encourages collaboration. Visitors can have secure guest access to the Internet and their business and / or personal data.
- **Ease of Setup:** When we do not have to run physical cables through a location, installation can be quick and cost-effective. Wireless LANs also make it easier to bring network connectivity to hard-to-reach locations, such as a warehouse or factory floor or an underground parking area.
- **Scalability:** As our business operations grow, we may need to quickly expand our network. Wireless networks can typically expand with existing equipment, while a wired network might require an additional wiring.
- **Security:** Controlling and managing access to a wireless network is important to its success. Advances in WiFi technology provide robust security protections so our data is easily available to only the people we allow access.
- **Cost:** It can cost less to operate a wireless LAN, which eliminates or reduces wiring costs during office moves, reconfigurations, or expansions.

One of its newer kinds is Mobile ad hoc network or MANET [1], which is a collection of mobile nodes or hosts that communicate among themselves via multi-hop in an infrastructure-less environment. MANET started with the aim to have the ability to establish a network among willing nodes without the assistance from any network infrastructure. This ability seemed to be very promising in situations like disaster or war (where the infrastructure is damaged or not available) or in areas where building the infrastructure is not possible (on the sea) or situations where an ad hoc network is more suitable than an infrastructure network (during campus recruitment of any company to any institute or similar kind of professional activities). Although there is a growing need for better QoS than best effort, QoS provisioning in MANET is a challenging task. Mobile Ad hoc network is a very complex distributed network where nodes are free to move and hence topology of the network is dynamic. Movement of the nodes does not only change the topology of the network but also causes traffic load condition to change dynamically. Moreover a node acts as a source or destination node in one traffic and the same node may act as an intermediate router between source and destination node in another traffic. Furthermore wireless characteristics of links pose additional challenge in MANET. Dynamic link capacity, bandwidth, mobile device limitations like battery power and processing power need to be considered for any system concerning QoS in MANET. Again, no QoS provisioning should not put much load on the nodes and should not increase the volume of information to be maintained to support its operation, due to the power limitation of the nodes in this kind of network.

Quality of Service (QoS) [2] means that the network should provide some kind of guarantee or assurance about the level or grade of service provided to an application. QoS refers to satisfying certain requirements of a connection, in terms of a set of constraints. Due to the mobility, limited resource, less security, dynamic topology, infrastructure less and wireless nature, it is complicated to sustain real-time applications with appropriate QoS. But at the same time, QoS is of enormous importance in MANETs since it can improve performance and allow critical information to flow even under difficult conditions.

In this chapter we focus on the message transmission component, which is at the very core of the functioning of every network since it implements the strategies used by network nodes to discover and use paths to forward data/information from sources to destinations. Here we propose an effective design of a very simple QoS system inspired from the swarm intelligence algorithms, which does not put much processing load on the nodes and reduce the state information to maintain the transmission reliability and thus is very lightweight by nature.

The fact that insect societies, and, more in general, nature, has served as a major source of inspiration for the design of novel network algorithms can be understood by noticing that these biological systems are characterized by the presence of a set of distributed, autonomous, minimalist units, that through local interactions self-organize to produce system-level behaviours which show life-long adaptivity to changes and perturbations in the external environment. Moreover, these systems are usually resilient to minor internal failures and losses of units, and scale quite well by virtue of their modular and fully distributed design. All these characteristics, both in terms of system organization and resulting properties, meet most of the necessary and desired properties of various protocols for ad hoc networks. More recently, also bees' colonies are attracting a growing interest. Behaviours observed in colonies of bees have influenced the large majority of various recent literatures.

In this chapter we have proposed an optimised algorithm inspired by artificial bee colony optimisation to design an efficient quality of service scheme for mobile ad hoc network through reliable messaging. The remaining content of the chapter is organized as follows:

- Section 2 briefly introduces ad hoc network generalities and challenges.
- Section 3 says about quality of service in MANET.
- Section 4 discusses on swarm intelligence in general.
- Section 5 specifies artificial bee colony optimisation with its details and then gives our algorithm.
- Section 6 shows the simulation results.
- Section 7 finally concludes our chapter with some open questions for the readers.
- Section 8 gives the references.

2. GENERALITIES AND CHALLENGES IN AD HOC NETWORK

Mobile Ad hoc Network or MANET operates in the lack of any supporting infrastructure. Hence, they offer quick, prompt and easy network deployment and are ideally suitable for situations where either there is no supporting structure available or to deploy one, is not feasible. The idea of mobile ad hoc in the form of packet radio networks first emerged in the early 1970s when they were first implemented to conduct a feasibility report about the performance of radio devices in providing communication in a battle field environment [3].

Mobile nodes or hosts in MANET themselves play an important role in establishing communication amongst various nodes in the network. These mobile nodes are free to move around and get organized in an arbitrary fashion. Each node is free to roam about while already being in communication with others. The path between each pair of the mobile nodes may have multiple links, and the nodes may also be heterogeneous. Hence, this organization allows an association of various links to be a part of a single network. In situations, where networks are constructed and destructed in an ad hoc manner, mobile ad hoc networking is an excellent choice.

2.1 Applications of Ad Hoc Network

Ad hoc networks are used in many applications [4]. Some of them are as follows.

- **Military Communication Environment:** Since battle field communication systems need some exceptional characteristics, such as high reliability, high invulnerability, flexibility, and deployment, etc., ad hoc network fairly meets with this very specific communication requirement for possessing the characteristics of self-organization and mobility of nodes respectively, which makes it the primary choice in digital battle field.

- **Urgent Communication Environment:** In case of visitation of some provident events, namely earthquakes, floods, fires or some other external disasters, the network communication environment even with very good infrastructures often could not work well. Since ad hoc networks could quickly provide urgent communications in special environment, it is very significant for the purpose of instantaneous rescue and relief works.

- **Temporary Communication Environment:** In commercial conferences, celebrations and exhibition occasions, people often tend to use ad hoc network techniques to organize some mobile terminals, namely laptops, pocket PCs, and PDAs, as a wireless and mobile, self-organized network, in order to exchange information. This could avoid wiring and deploying of the network routing devices to establish a temporary communicative environment.

- **Mobile Communication Environment:** Ad hoc networks can be used to provide some mobile vehicles with the facility of wireless communication. Recent study concentrates on the ways of adopting the ad hoc network techniques for freeway system so as to implement the autonomous wireless communication amongst automatic driven vehicles.

- **Collaborative Work:** For some business environments, the need for collaborative computing might be more important outside office environments than inside and where people do need to have outside meetings to cooperate and exchange information on a given project.

- **Commercial Sector:** Ad hoc can be used in emergency/rescue operations for disaster relief efforts, e.g. in fire, flood, or earthquake. Emergency rescue operations must take place where non-existing or damaged communications infrastructure and rapid deployment of a communication network is needed.

2.2 Data Communication in Ad Hoc Network

As mobile ad hoc network is very much application centric, data communication plays a very important role in its execution. In the existing wireless technology, routing support for mobile nodes is presently being understood as Mobile IP technology. Mobile IP is used to support mobile host roaming, where a mobile host connects to the network through various means other than its fixed-address domain space. On the other hand, the aim of a mobile ad hoc network is to advance mobility into the chain of autonomous wireless domains, where a set of nodes themselves establishes the network routing structure in an ad hoc manner.

Therefore the mobile nodes in MANET are equipped with wireless transmitters and receivers. Designing routing protocols for MANET has taken approaches similar to routing protocols used for conventional wired networks. Most of these protocols are based on table-driven [5, 6] or on-demand [7, 8] routing techniques.

The main task of any routing protocol is to aid communication within the network. The primary objective of a routing protocol is to establish correct routing between a source and a destination node to deliver messages in a timely fashion. In a mobile ad hoc network environment, it may be necessary for one mobile node to assist other nodes in forwarding a packet to its destination. In a mobile ad hoc network, to establish an active connection, the end node as well as the intermediate nodes can be mobile.

2.3 Routing in Ad Hoc Network

Routing protocols of mobile ad hoc network begs different approaches from existing Internet protocols, since most of the existing Internet protocols were designed to support routing in a network with fixed infrastructure. Routing is the process of exchanging information from one station to the other stations of the network. In the sphere of academics as well as industrial perspective, many people have shared their views by writing quite a few papers proposing their own routing solutions for MANET. Proposed solutions can be classified into six types: proactive or table-driven, reactive or on-demand, hierarchical, power-aware, geographical, and multicast protocols.

2.3.1 Table-Driven Protocols

Table-driven protocols are one of the oldest ways for facilitating routing in MANET. These protocols maintain consistent overview of the network. Each node uses routing tables to store the location information of other nodes in the network. This information is used to transfer data among various nodes of the network.

To ensure the relevance of the routing tables, these protocols adopt various mechanisms. One of the adopted methods is broadcasting "hello" – a special message containing address information, at fixed time intervals. On receiving this message, each node updates its routing tables with the most recent location information of other participating nodes. Destination Sequence Distance Vector routing protocol

(DSDV), Wireless Routing Protocol (WRP) and Cluster-head Gateway Switch Routing (CGSR) are some of the popular table-driven routing protocols for MANET.

Table-driven protocols might not be considered as an effective routing solution for mobile ad hoc network. Presence of high mobility, large routing tables and low scalability, all of these result in consumption of high bandwidth and battery life of the nodes. Moreover, continuous updates could create unnecessary network overhead in addition to the reduction of the battery life of the participating nodes maintaining network status all the time.

2.3.2 On-Demand Routing Protocols

Another category in the family of routing protocols for mobile ad hoc network is on-demand routing protocols. With on-demand protocols, if a source node requires a route to the destination for which it does not have route information, it initiates a route discovery process which goes from one node to the other until it reaches the destination or an intermediate node has a route to the destination.

It is the responsibility of the route request receiver node to reply back to the source node about the possible route to the destination. The source node uses this route for data transmission to the destination node. Some of the better known on-demand protocols are Ad hoc On-demand Distance Vector routing (AODV), Dynamic Source Routing (DSR) and Temporary Ordered Routing Algorithm (TORA). For all the above protocols, too many query packets not only could lead us toward a bottleneck, but would also consume a good amount of available bandwidth.

These protocols differ on storing the previously known route information and on how they use the established route data. Again, in a network with many participating nodes we may suffer with the same sort of problems which we have seen in table-driven protocols.

2.3.3 Hybrid or Mixed Routing Protocols

A hybrid routing protocol is developed by combining the salient features of table driven and on demand routing protocols. It uses the route discovery mechanism of reactive protocol and the table maintenance mechanism of proactive protocol so as to avoid latency and overhead problems in the network. Hybrid protocol is suitable for large networks where large number of nodes is present. In this protocol, large network is divided into set of zones where routing inside the zone is performed using proactive approach and that outside the zone is done using reactive approach. There are various popular hybrid routing protocols for MANET like Zone Routing Protocol (ZRP), Sharp Hybrid Adaptive routing Protocol (SHARP) etc.

Based on the method of delivery of data packets from the source to destination, classification of MANET routing protocols could be done as follows:

2.3.4 Unicast Routing Protocols

These are the routing protocols that consider sending information packets to a single destination from a single source.

2.3.5 Multicast Routing Protocols

Multicast is the delivery of information to a group of destinations simultaneously, using the most efficient strategy to deliver the messages over each link of the network only once, creating copies only when the links to the destinations split. Multicast routing protocols for MANET use both multicast and unicast for data transmission.

Multicast routing protocols for MANET can again be classified into two categories: Tree-based multicast protocol and Mesh-based multicast protocol. Mesh-based routing protocols use several routes to reach a destination while the tree-based protocols maintain only one path.

2.4 Challenges in Ad Hoc Network

Establishing a network on a commercial and experimental basis are two different scenarios. Present ad hoc systems lie in between these two situations. Low bandwidth with limited power poses a number of different operational requirements to these networks. In MANET, routine control functions such as routing, security, quality of service, etc. have specific requirements too [9, 10].

As used in fixed wireless networks, current Internet protocols are not sufficient enough to meet the operational requirements of ad hoc networks. This new art of network formation has got a lot of potential benefits and may even be able to change the whole art of wireless communication. Lack of efficient strategies to handle various network controls is one of the main challenges of MANET. However, in light of ongoing efforts and the growing interest in mobile ad hoc network, we are not very far from seeing revolutionary changes in the domain of wireless communication.

Continuing our discussion on challenges in MANET, the next section describes some of the major drawbacks of ad hoc networks:

- **Distributed Network:** As MANET is a distributed wireless network without any fixed infrastructure, the nodes in the network suffer from lack of centralized control and have to be self-sufficient for all the network related issues.
- **Dynamic Topology:** In MANET, the nodes are mobile and hence the network is self-organizing. Because of this, the topology of the network keeps changing over time. Consequently, the routing protocols designed for such networks and other network control issues must also be adaptive to the topology changes.
- **Power Awareness:** Since the nodes in an ad hoc network typically run on battery energy and are deployed in hostile terrains, they have stringent power requirements. This implies that the underlying protocols must be designed keeping in mind the conservation of battery life.
- **Addressing Scheme:** The network topology keeps changing dynamically and hence the addressing scheme used is quite significant. A dynamic network topology demands a ubiquitous addressing scheme, which avoids any duplicate addresses.
- **Network Size:** Heavy multimedia and commercial applications require large bandwidth and also the delay involved in the underlying protocols places a strict upper bound on the size of the network.
- **Security:** Security in an ad hoc network is extremely important in scenarios such as a battlefield. The five goals of security – availability, confidentiality, integrity, authenticity and non-repudiation – are difficult to be achieved at its maximum level in MANET, mainly because every node in the

network participates equally in message communication, and also node may join and / or depart at any time.

- **Reliability:** Reliability is another big issue due to the mobility induced packet losses, absence of infrastructure, limited wireless transmission range, broadcast nature and inherent transmission errors of the wireless medium.

2.5 Connection Stability in Wireless Ad Hoc Networks

Connection stability plays a very important role in the successful deployment of any network. It may be regarded as one of the most important aspects, since without connection, you don't have a network. Overall efficiency of any communication network is measured in terms of many different factors; connection stability is one of them. If a network technology offers a secure routing mechanism along with stable connection among the various participants, then we might be right to term this network a reliable one. One the other hand, missing of any of these factors could lead toward an unstable network environment.

Each wireless device in a wireless ad hoc network functions as a router, forwarding data packets for all participating devices in the network. As there is no pre-specified mechanism of handling clients' requests, there is a very high probability of getting poor connection services in wireless ad hoc networks. Moreover, connection or topology changes are quite common in these networks. Establishing effective strategies for various network controls is one of the fundamental requirements of a wireless ad hoc network.

The wireless ad hoc network is a vulnerable technology. It has potential to replace present fixed wireless network systems and is widely be regarded as one of the crucial technologies in the deployment of forth generation wireless systems. Having stable and secure connections among various wireless devices is one of the key aspects of a wireless communication network; not having enough strategies makes it difficult to accomplish this task in a wireless ad hoc network.

In order to have a successful technology both for the vendor and for the supplier, we have to take into account different technical aspects of wireless ad hoc networks, without which, we may not be able to come out with a technology that can cope with the communication needs of today's world.

3. QUALITY OF SERVICES IN MANET

QoS in wireless communication has been an intense interest area for the last two decades and has been growing continuously. At present, many different types of wireless networks are in operation, adopting different techniques and various strategies for routine network control. It might be right to expect different levels of quality of service from each type of wireless communication network.

Quality of services for a network is measured in terms of guaranteed amount of data which a network transfers from one place to another in a given time slot. In this section, we have focused on quality of service issues in MANET, where supporting suitable quality of service for the delivery of real-time communications such as audio and video poses a number of different technical challenges.

A mobile ad hoc network is an autonomous system of mobile nodes connected by wireless links forming a short, live, on-the-fly network. Nodes in MANET generally operate on low power battery devices. These nodes can function both as hosts and as routers. As a host, nodes function as a source and as a destination in the network. On the other hand, as a router, nodes act as intermediate bridges between the source and the destination giving store-and-forward services to all the neighboring nodes in the network.

In a mobile ad hoc network, nodes are free to move randomly and can organize themselves in arbitrary fashions, resulting in frequent and unpredictable changes in the network topology.

The size of the ad hoc network is directly related to the quality of service of the network. If the size of the mobile ad hoc network is large, it might make the problem of network control extremely difficult. Communication in MANET between two participating nodes can be seen as a complex end-to-end channel that changes routes with time.

In a mobile ad hoc network, a number of different routes with various levels of node capacity and power may be available for a source to transmit data to the destination. As a result, not all routes are capable of providing the same level of quality of service that can meet the requirements of mobile users. Moreover, even if the selected route between a source and the destination meets the user requirements, the network error characteristics are expected to vary with time due to the dynamic nature of MANET.

MANET is expected to play an important role in the deployment of future wireless communication systems. Therefore, it is extremely important that these networks should be able to provide efficient quality of service that can meet the vendor requirements. To provide efficient quality of service in MANET, there is a solid need to establish new architectures and services for routine network controls.

These new standards must be able to cope with the typical environment of MANET, especially changes between two communicating mobile nodes. New protocols need to be developed; these protocols must be capable of differentiating between the various service requirements of mobile users and be able to response to the topology changes in the network. All these issues must be addressed in order to provide standard quality of service for MANET.

In case of achieving Quality of Service of MANETs the characteristics of an adhoc network cause several challenges in the stipulation of QoS [11, 12, 13]. Some of these challenges are as follows:

- Limitations of the Wireless Network:
  - Packet loss due to transmission errors.
  - Variable capacity links.
  - Frequent disconnections/partitions.
  - Limited communication bandwidth.
  - Broadcast nature of the communications.
  - Limitations Imposed by Mobility.
  - Volatile network topology makes the algorithm much more complex.
  - Lack of mobility awareness by system.
- Limitations of the Mobile Computer:
  - Limited power resources (battery life).
  - Limited capacities.
- Limited physical security.

3.1 From Insect Societies to Network Protocols

Two specific classes of insect societies have inspired a relatively large volume of work in the specific domain of network routing: ant and bee colonies. More specifically, the ability of ant colonies to discover shortest paths between their nest and sources of food using a pheromone laying-following mechanism has been reverse-engineered and put to work in the general optimization framework of the Ant Colony Optimization (ACO) metaheuristic [14]. To date, ACO is a state-of-the-art metaheuristic for many problems in the domains of combinatorial optimization and network routing. More recently, the communication and recruitment strategies adopted for effective foraging within a beehive have inspired the development of some novel algorithms for routing problems.

In the following sections we discuss separately the general principles behind the swarm-inspired approaches to various problems.

4. SWARM INTELLIGENCE

A swarm is a large number of homogenous, simple agents interacting locally among themselves, and their environment, with no central control to allow a global interesting behaviour to emerge. Swarm-based algorithms have recently emerged as a family of nature-inspired, population-based algorithms that are capable of producing low cost, fast, and robust solutions to several complex problems [15]. Swarm Intelligence (SI) can therefore be defined as a relatively new branch of Artificial Intelligence that is used to model the collective behaviour of social swarms in nature, such as ant colonies, honey bees, and bird flocks. Although these agents (insects or swarm individuals) are relatively unsophisticated with limited capabilities on their own, they are interacting together with certain behavioural patterns to cooperatively achieve tasks necessary for their survival. The social interactions among swarm individuals can be either direct or indirect. Examples of direct interaction are through visual or audio contact, such as the waggle dance of honey bees. Indirect interaction occurs when one individual changes the environment and the other individuals respond to the new environment, such as the pheromone trails of ants that they deposit on their way to search for food sources. This indirect type of interaction is referred to as stigmergy, which essentially means communication through the environment.

In the past decades, biologists and natural scientists have been studying the behaviours of social insects because of the amazing efficiency of these natural swarm systems. In the late-80s, computer scientists proposed the scientific insights of these natural swarm systems to the field of Artificial Intelligence. In 1989, the expression "Swarm Intelligence" was first introduced by G. Beni and J. Wang in the global optimization framework as a set of algorithms for controlling robotic swarm. In 1991, Ant Colony Optimization (ACO) [16, 17, 18] was introduced by M. Dorigo and colleagues as a novel nature-inspired metaheuristic for the solution of hard combinatorial optimization (CO) problems. In 1995, particle swarm optimization was introduced by J. Kennedy et al. [19, 20], and was first intended for simulating the bird flocking social behaviour. By the late-90s, these two most popular swarm intelligence algorithms started to go beyond a pure scientific interest and to enter the realm of real-world applications. It is perhaps worth mentioning here that a number of years later, exactly in 2005, Artificial Bee Colony Algorithm was proposed by D. Karabago as a new member of the family of swarm intelligence algorithms [21, 22].

Since the computational modeling of swarms was proposed, there has been a steady increase in the number of research papers reporting the successful application of Swarm Intelligence algorithms in several optimization tasks and research problems. Swarm Intelligence principles have been successfully applied in a variety of problem domains [15] including function optimization problems, finding optimal routes, scheduling, structural optimization, and image and data analysis. Computational modeling of swarms has been further applied to a wide-range of diverse domains, including machine learning, bioinformatics and medical informatics, dynamical systems and operations research; they have been even applied in finance and business.

4.1 General Principles

To model the broad behaviours arisen from a swarm, we introduce several general principles for swarm intelligence [15]:

- **Proximity Principle:** The basic units of a swarm should be capable of simple computation related to its surrounding environment. Here computation is regarded as a direct behavioural response to environmental variance, such as those triggered by interactions among agents. Depending on the complexity of agents involved, responses may vary greatly. However, some fundamental behaviour is shared, such as living-resource searching and nest building.
- **Quality Principle:** Apart from basic computation ability, a swarm should be able to response to quality factors, such as food and safety.
- **Principle of Diverse Response:** Resources should not be concentrated in narrow region. The distribution should be designed so that each agent will be maximally protected facing environmental fluctuations.
- **Principle of Stability and Adaptability:** Swarms are expected to adapt environmental fluctuations without rapidly changing modes since mode changing costs energy.

4.2 Swarm Intelligence Models

Swarm intelligence models are referred to as computational models inspired by natural swarm systems. To date, several swarm intelligence models based on different natural swarm systems have been proposed in the literature, and successfully applied in many real-life applications. Examples of swarm intelligence models are: Ant Colony Optimization [23], Particle Swarm Optimization [24], Artificial Bee Colony [25], Bacterial Foraging [26], Cat Swarm Optimization [27], Artificial Immune System [28], and Glowworm Swarm Optimization [29]. In this section, we will primarily discuss on three of the most popular swarm intelligences models, namely, Ant Colony Optimization and Particle Swarm Optimization.

4.2.1 Ant Colony Optimization (ACO) Model

The first example of a successful swarm intelligence model is Ant Colony Optimization (ACO), which was introduced by M. Dorigo et al. [16, 17, 18], and has been originally used to solve discrete optimization problems in the late 1980s. ACO draws inspiration from the social behaviour of ant colonies. It is a natural observation that a group of *'almost blind'* ants can jointly figure out the shortest route between their food and their nest without any visual information. The following section presents some details about ants in nature, and shows how these relatively unsophisticated insects can cooperatively interact together to perform complex tasks necessary for their survival.

4.2.2 Particle Swarm Optimization (PSO) Model

The second example of a successful swarm intelligence model is Particle Swarm Optimization (PSO), which was introduced by Russell Eberhart, an electrical engineer, and James Kennedy, a social psychologist, in 1995 [30]. PSO was originally used to solve non-linear continuous optimization problems, but more recently it has been used in many practical, real-life application problems. For example, PSO has been successfully applied to track dynamic systems, evolve weights and structure of neural networks, analyze human tremor, register 3D – to – 3D biomedical image, control reactive power and voltage, even learning to play games and music composition. PSO draws inspiration from the sociological behaviour associated with bird flocking. It is a natural observation that birds can fly in large groups with no collision for extended long distances, making use of their effort to maintain an optimum distance between themselves and their neighbours. This section presents some details about birds in nature and overviews their capabilities, as well as their sociological flocking behaviour.

4.2.3 Artificial Bee Colony Optimisation (ABCO) Model

While ACO and PSO are two of the most common examples of optimization techniques inspired by swarm intelligence, there are several other optimization techniques based on SI principles have been proposed in the literature, including Artificial Bee Colony, Bacterial Foraging, Cat Swarm Optimization, Artificial Immune System and Glow-worm Swarm Optimization, among many others. All these SI models intrinsically share the principal inspirational origin of the intelligence of different swarms in nature, such as swarms of *E. coli* bacteria as in Bacterial Foraging, swarms of cells and molecules as in Artificial Immune System, and the amazing swarms of honey bees as in the Artificial Bee Colony System.

What is amazing about honey bee colonies is that they are very efficient in exploiting the best food sources (in terms of distance and quality) based on a group of forager bees. When a forager bee (recruiter) decides to attract more bee mates to a newly discovered good food source, it returns to the hive and starts performing what is known as the – waggle dance to communicate spatial and profitability information about the discovered food source, and recruit more honey bees (dancer followers) to exploit it. The language of waggle dance and its orientation patterns were first deciphered by von Frisch in 1967 [31]. The waggle dance consists of a series of *waggle phases*. A waggle phase starts when the recruiter bee vigorously shakes its body from side to side. The time interval between each waggle phase is called a *return phase,* in which the recruiter bee makes an abrupt turn to the left or right before starting another waggle phase. The waggle dance encodes both (a) spatial and (b) profitability information of the target food source to dance followers.

(a) As for spatial information, the waggle dance encodes two important pieces of information: (i) the direction and (ii) the distance to the target. (i) Direction information is encoded in the *waggle dance orientation*. During the waggle dance, the recruiter bees amazingly align their body with an angle representing the direction of food location relative to current sun direction. This means food sources located directly in line with the current sun direction are represented by a series of waggle phases oriented to the upward/vertical direction. If food sources, however, are located with an angle to the right or left of the sun, their direction is encoded in the waggle dance orientation by a corresponding angle to the right or left of the upward direction. What is more astounding is that recruiter bees have an internal clock that helps them adjust the angles of their dances relative to the sun directional changes throughout the day, even after they have been in their almost dark hive for extended time. (ii) On the other hand, distance information is encoded in the *waggle phase duration*, i.e., dances for close targets have short waggle phases, while dances for remote targets have long waggle phases. Dance followers need both direction and distance information to reach the target food source, which could be several kilometers away from the hive, as they fly in a three-dimensional space, unlike most ants that just normally walk on the ground searching for nearby food sources.

(b) As for profitability information, it is encoded in the overall *waggle dance duration* and the *return phase duration* (or the time interval between waggle phases). The larger the number of waggle phases (or the longer the overall duration of waggle dance), and the shorter time interval between waggle phases, the more profitable the target food source. Even more astoundingly, the nervous system of even beginner recruiter bees has been internally calibrated to assess the profitability of food sources based on different factors: (1) the sugar content of their nectar, (2) their distance from the colony, and (3) the ease with which nectar (or pollen) can be collected. After recruiter bees assess these factors, they decide on two things: firstly, if the food source worth foraging for (by themselves), and secondly if it worth recruiting more honey bees.

The foraging behaviour of a honey bee colony can be summarized as follows: When a forager bee finds a food source, it first returns to the hive and relinquishes its nectar to worker bees to store it in the hive. At that point, the forager bee has three options/decisions to take: (1) it can become a recruiter bee and performs a waggle dance to recruit more bees (the dance followers) to join it in foraging for the food source, if it is worthwhile, (2) it can remain as a forager bee by just going back to the food source and continue foraging there by itself, if it is not really worth advertising for, or (3) it can become an uncommitted follower by abandoning the food source when it is completely exhausted – in this case, the uncommitted-follower bee starts to watch for any waggle dances being performed by other recruiter bees and potentially become a dance-follower bee. The BCO algorithms have interesting applications in numerical optimizations, for example, it can be used to find global optimal solutions of functions. Moreover, recent studies suggest that the BCO algorithms can also be applied to problems in shop scheduling, neural network training and imaging processing.

4.3.1 Swarm Intelligence General Advantages

- **Scalability:** SI systems are highly scalable; their impressive abilities are generally maintained when using groups ranging from just sufficiently few individuals up to millions of individuals. In other words, the control mechanisms used in SI systems are not too dependent on swarm size, as long as it is not too small.
- **Adaptability:** SI Systems respond well to rapidly changing environments, making use of their inherit auto-configuration and self-organization capabilities. This allows them to autonomously adapt their individuals' behaviour to the external environment dynamically on the run-time, with substantial flexibility.
- **Collective Robustness:** SI Systems are robust as they collectively work without central control, and there is no single individual crucial for the swarm to continue to function (due to the redundancy of their individuals). In other words, the fault-tolerance capability of SI systems is remarkably high, since these systems have no single point of failure. A single point of failure is a part of any system that puts the entire system into risk of a complete failure, if it ceased to function.
- **Individual Simplicity:** SI systems consist of a number of simple individuals with fairly limited capabilities on their own, yet the simple behavioural rules at the individual level are practically sufficient to cooperatively emerge sophisticated group behaviour.

4.3.2 Swarm Intelligence General Limitations

The potential of swarm intelligence is indeed fast-growing and far-reaching. It offers an alternative, untraditional way of designing complex systems that neither requires centralized control nor extensive pre-programming. That being said, SI systems still have some limitations, such as:

- **Time-Critical Applications:** Because the pathways to solutions in SI systems are neither pre-defined nor pre-programmed, but rather emergent, SI systems are not suitable for time-critical applications that require (1) on-line control of systems, (2) time critical decisions, and (3) satisfactory solutions within very restrictive time frames, such as the elevator controller and the nuclear reactor temperature controller. It remains to be useful, however, for non-time critical applications that involve numerous repetitions of the same activity.
- **Parameter Tuning:** Tuning the parameters of SI-inspired optimization techniques is one of the general drawbacks of swarm intelligence, like in most stochastic optimization methods, and unlike deterministic optimization methods. In fact, however, since many parameters of SI systems are problem-dependent, they are often either empirically pre-selected according to the problem characteristics in a trial-and-error manner, or even better adaptively adjusted on run time (as in the adaptive ACO and the fuzzy adaptive PSO).
- **Stagnation:** Because of the lack of central coordination, SI systems could suffer from a *stagnation* situation or a premature convergence to a local optimum (e.g., in ACO, stagnation occurs when all the ants eventually follow the same suboptimal path and construct the same tour). This limitation, however, can be controlled by carefully setting algorithm parameters, e.g., the parameter in ACO or the parameter ω of PSO. Different variations of ACO and PSO algorithms could further reduce the probability of that limitation.

5. ALGORITHM PROLOGUE AND OUR ALGORITHM

5.1 Bee Colony Optimization Algorithms

Just like ants, bees have similar food collecting behaviours. Instead of pheromones, bees colony optimization algorithm relies on the foraging behaviour of honey bees. At the first stage, some bees are sent out to look for promising food sources. After a good food source is located, bees return back to colony and perform a waggle dance to spread out information about the source. Three pieces of information are included: 1. distance, 2. direction, 3. quality of food source. The better the quality of food source, the more bees will be attracted. Therefore, the best food source emerges (see Figure 1).

The metaheuristic extracted from the foraging behaviours of bees can also be applied to solve combinatorial problems; especially problems involve global minimum or maximum.

Figure 1. Onlooker bee and dance area: A) employed bee; b) scout bee

Similarly, the BCO metaheuristic undergo several phases:

```
Initialization;
while not terminated do
Employed Bees Phase;
Onlooker Bees Phase;
Scout Bees Phase;
Memorize the best solution;
end
```

5.2 Useful Ideas from Honey Bee Colonies

More recently than ant colonies, also honey bee colonies have attracted a strong interest as a potential source of inspiration for the design of optimization strategies for dynamic, time-varying, and multi-objective problems. Bee colonies show structural characteristics similar to those of ant colonies, such as the presence of a population of minimalist social individuals, and must face analogous problems such as distributed foraging, nest building and maintenance, etc. Bees utilize a sophisticated communication protocol that enables them to communicate directly through bee-to-bee signals and when required, similar to ants, use stigmergic feedback cues for bee-to-group or group-to-bee communication. In these two classes of insects, communication and cooperation is realized according to radically different modalities due to the different nature of these insects (ants mainly walk, while bees mainly fly). In particular, while in the case of ants communication is achieved via a pheromone trail that is laid on the ground while walking, in the case of bees it is a form of visual communication that plays an equivalent role. In the following we briefly point out and discuss the main mechanisms at work in a bee colony which have found their application in the design of routing algorithms.

Adaptive and Age-Related Division of Labour

A honey bee colony consists of morphologically uniform individuals with different temporary specializations. The benefit of the organization is an increased flexibility to adapt to the changing environments. For instance, a nectar forager can become a water forager if the colony is running out on its water supplies. More specifically, in honey bees division of labour is mainly related to age: workers of different ages specialize in different tasks (this phenomenon is called age polytheism or behavioural development). Workers typically perform brood rearing for the first week, engage in other hive maintenance duties (wax secretion, guarding, undertaking, nectar processing) when they are "middle-aged" (2-3 weeks old), and switch to foraging and colony defence when they are about three weeks old. These phases can be adaptively modified in response to the alteration of colony conditions.

Communication Inside the Colony and Worker Recruitment

As in the ant case, also in a bee colony foraging is critical aspect for the survival of the colony and is executed in a fully distributed and competing way. Foraging bees constantly leave the hive searching for new sources of nutrient, bring the nutrient back to the hive, and try to recruit other bees to exploit the food site found by competing with each other during the recruitment process. Foragers announce a food source of interest to their fellow foragers by doing a dance on the dance floor inside the hive. This dance is termed waggle dance. It is a particular figure-eight dance that encodes the direction of the food source in the angle from the sun, and the distance in the duration of each waggle-run. If the distance is very short the waggle dance resembles a round dance. Foragers respond to the waggle dance with a strong preference for choosing nearer food sites over distant ones in order to increase the net energetic efficiency of the colony. The waggle dance is a direct form of agent-to-agents communication. Nectar foragers, upon return to the hive, sometimes also perform across the hive a quite strange dance termed tremble dance. The tremble dance means that the forager has found a rich food source but upon return to the hive, after a certain threshold time, she could not find a food-storer bee to give her nectar. This suggests that the message of the tremble dance is to stimulate the bees inside the hive to increase and/ or to switch to nectar processing activities, and to inhibit the outside foragers from recruiting additional bees. Basically the tremble dance is intended to activate behaviours that keep a colony's nectar processing rate matched with its nectar intake rate.

Stochastic Selection of Food Sites

The unemployed foragers refrain from extensively surveying the dance floor to identify the best food site. On the contrary, they observe maximally two or three dances on the dance floor and then decide to follow the indications of one of them according to a stochastic rule. As a result, a colony distributes its foraging force on multiple food sites such that when one rich food site has been almost fully exploited the colony is already exploiting other sites. In this way an effective balancing between exploitation and exploration is automatically obtained. Sumpter [32] has developed a formal agent-based model using process algebra for the foraging behaviour of honey bee colonies which provides some useful insights about the colony-level strategy for the distribution of the exploitation activities.

5.3 Comparison between Real Bees and Artificial Bees

Table 1. Comparison with real and artificial bees

Criteria	Real Bees	Artificial Bees
Employed Bee Behaviour	Collects food	Computes Quality of Service factor
Onlooker Bee Behaviour	Dancing to represent quality of the food source	Sets a flag to represent the type of the message
Scout Bee Behaviour	Searches for new food	Retransmits message depending on the flag type
Memory Capabilities	Have no memory capabilities	Have memory to store best solutions
Ecological Constraints	Exist, such as predation or competition with other colonies and the colony's level of protection	Ecological constraints do not exist in the artificial / virtual world

5.4 Simulation Model

In the research area of computer and communication networks, simulation is a useful technique since the behaviour of a network can be anticipated by calculating the interaction between different network components using mathematical formulas. As the process of model modification in simulators is relatively cheaper than the complete physical implementation, a wide variety of scenarios can be analysed at low cost (relative to making changes to an actual network).

Next is an illustration to the general framework used to move from a natural phenomenon to a nature inspired algorithm. First, nature inspires humans to develop an observation of a particular natural phenomenon. Then, they create a model and test it using mathematical simulations, which help to refine the original model. Next, the refined model will be used to extract a metaheuristic that can be used as a basis to finally design and tune a nature inspired algorithm (in Figure 2).

5.5 Our Algorithm

The ability of a network to provide a specified quality of service between a set of mobile nodes depends upon the inherent performance properties. Generally, the level of service is based on some parameters or constraints, often known as QoS parameters or QoS constraints. These parameters or QoS constraints are – end to end delay, throughput, jitter, drop packets, latency, loss rate, error rate of stations, the traffic load within the network, reliability, bandwidth etc. Security is one of the most important parameter of QoS. Some other parameters are the control algorithms operating on different network layers and its complexity and energy consumption.

If the requirement is fulfilled then the system is said to be providing some assurance to maintain the quality of service of the network. For example, an application that is delay sensitive may require the QoS in terms of delay guarantees. Some applications may require that the packets should flow at certain minimum bandwidth. In that case, the bandwidth will be an important QoS parameter [33, 34]. Certain application may require a guarantee that the packets are delivered from a given source to destination reliably, then, reliability will be a parameter for QoS.

Figure 2. Mapping with nature to practical simulations

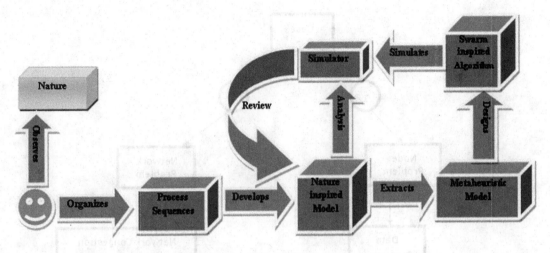

Here we are mainly concerned with two aspects of it:

- **Retransmission Policy:** Where we are mainly concerned with the arrival of the data packet at any cost. We go on retransmitting the packet until it is received at the other end.
- **Time Factor:** Here there is no possibility of delay in receiving data packet at the receiver. So, if the packet does not arrive on time then they cannot be accepted.

We propose to keep a leader node to govern the entry and exit of any external node in the network and to prevent the network from partition. As we know the computational capacity of mobile nodes are not very high so we should apply a less complex scheme with less computational overhead. Our scheme is a light weight one.

To maintain or enhance the QoS of any MANET, we propose an algorithm by applying which any network can improve its quality when it is in degradable cases. Our algorithm is flexible and it can be configured according to the need and application of the network.

Our algorithm is based on the following assumptions:

1. Network is planar.
2. Nodes are connected and each node is aware of the whole network.
3. There is a leader node whose duty is to hold back network from network partition.
4. Weightage of QoS parameters are configurable.
5. Each node is aware of the total number of other nodes in network.
6. Data packets can be send bi-directionally.

In Figure 3 we now show how the node or network problem can be handled by our algorithm to maintain a certain level of QoS.

The algorithmic steps are shown in Algorithm 1 (the algorithm will be set for a certain number of periodic intervals T).

In metaheuristic form this can be depicted as follows:

Figure 3. Algorithm flowchart

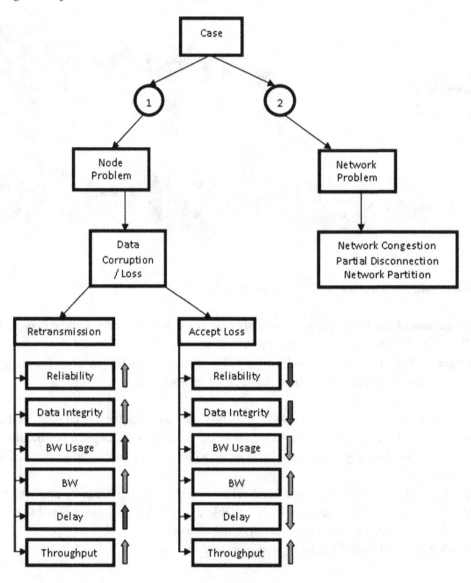

- **Initialization:** All the message types F_m, m = 1, ...,N are initialized. F_m are solutions to the optimization problems and will be tuned by BCO algorithm to minimize or maximize objective function f defined above.
- **QoS Factor Calculating Agent:** are like Employed bees, who will search in the QoS parameters of F_m from memory with a random vector Rm. A fitness will be calculated to determine if R_m leads to a improved quality of service. The usual choice for fitness function T is:

$$T(x_m) = 1 / 1 + f(x_m) \text{ ; if } f(x_m) >= 0; 1 + |f(x_m)| \text{ ; if } f(x_m) < 0 \qquad (1)$$

Algorithm 1.

```
Select the problem mode (node or network)
IF node problem
    Select the message mode
IF message type "imp"
THEN set the QoS parameters in mode 'A'
ELSE (IF message type "unimp")
THEN set the QoS parameters in mode 'B'
ELSE (IF network problem)
THEN set the QoS parameters in mode 'C'
MODE A: Important data content
Need maintain reliability than any other  QoS Metric
Go for Retransmission (mode A)
Reliability will be maintained
Data integrity achieved
Band width usage will be high
Delay will increase
Band width utilization will be low
Throughput will decrease
So efficiency will fall
MODE B: Data content is unimportant
Where time metric is consider  we can accept loss of less important  data
packets
Accept loss (mode B)
Band width usage will be less.
Delay will decrease.
Band width utilization will. increase
Throughput will increase.
So efficiency will improve.
Reliability not maintained
Data integrity not achieved
MODE C:
When Network congestion, Partial disconnection or Network partition occur
Monitor node will control the causing node to come inside the network to stop
network partition (mode C).
```

- **Message Selection Agent:** shares information about type of the messages, like onlooker bees, this agent will probabilistically choose their message type accordingly. Usually, this is calculated depending on the fitness values provided by QoS factor calculating agent. For example, with the above defined fitness value $T(x\sim m)$, the probability value p_m can be calculated:

$$p_m = T(x_m) / \text{Summation } m = 1 \text{ to } N(T(x_m)) \tag{2}$$

- **Message Forwarding Agent:** The third kind of agent is similar to the scout bees. They are usually forwards the message if it is important. However, negative feedback will lower the attractiveness of their previous forwarding information.

6. SIMULATION RESULTS AND ANALYSIS

We have considered a sample network of 13 nodes at the beginning and have applied our QoS algorithm to get the results. Communication range has been taken as 100 Km; hence the neighbourhood distance becomes 50 Km. The beacon interval [35] is computed to be 10 minutes. Initially we have taken 10 consecutive intervals and have compared the QoS of the network with one existing model (DiffServ). The whole example scenario is simulated using QualNet 6.1 network simulator [36].

QualNet is a discrete-event simulator. In discrete-event simulation, a system is modeled as it evolves over time by a representation in which the system state changes instantaneously when an event occurs, where an event is defined as an instantaneous occurrence that causes the system to change its state or to perform a specific action. Examples of events are: arrival of a packet, a periodic alarm informing a routing protocol to send out routing update to neighbours, etc. Examples of actions to take when an event occurs are: sending a packet to an adjacent layer, updating state variables, starting or restarting a timer, etc.

In discrete-event simulation, the simulator maintains an event queue. Associated with each event is its event time, i.e., the time at which the event is set to occur. Events in the event queue are sorted by the event time. The simulator also maintains a simulation clock which is used to simulate time. The simulation clock is advanced in discrete steps, as explained below.

We have used QualNet simulator for all our simulation work, comparisons and results.

QualNet is a discrete-event simulator. In discrete-event simulation, a system is modeled as it evolves over time by a representation in which the system state changes instantaneously when an event occurs, where an event is defined as an instantaneous occurrence that causes the system to change its state or to perform a specific action. Examples of events are: arrival of a packet, a periodic alarm informing a routing protocol to send out routing update to neighbours, etc. Examples of actions to take when an event occurs are: sending a packet to an adjacent layer, updating state variables, starting or restarting a timer, etc.

In discrete-event simulation, the simulator maintains an event queue. Associated with each event is its event time, i.e., the time at which the event is set to occur. Events in the event queue are sorted by the event time. The simulator also maintains a simulation clock which is used to simulate time. The simulation clock is advanced in discrete steps, as explained below.

The simulator operates by continually repeating the following series of steps until the end of simulation:

- The simulator removes the first event from the event queue, i.e., the event scheduled for the earliest time.
- The simulator sets the simulation clock to the event time of the event. This may result in advancing the simulation clock.

The simulator handles the event, i.e., it executes the actions associated with the event. This may result in changing the system state, scheduling other events, or both. If other events are scheduled, they may be scheduled to occur at the current time or in the future.

The advantages of using QualNet are the following:

- Event-driven simulation.
- Built-in measurements on each layer.
- Modular, layered stack design.
- Standard API for composition of protocols across different layers.
- Scalability via support for parallel execution.
- GUI Tools for system/protocol modelling.
- Performance Analyzer for new protocols/scenarios.

Table 2 for the network simulation environment set up for our algorithm.

The initial snap of the network is given in Figure 4.

As we said the initial network starts with 13 nodes and the topology is as shown in the above picture. Node 8 is selected as the leader node with maximum number of neighbours which is 6. In their movement, nodes maintain their topology guided by the leader node. In case of any network splintering possibilities, leader node takes care of the matter by sending proper instruction or control messages to the respective node(s).

The snapshot during running mode is shown in Figure 5.

Above, we have shown one 3D snapshot of the network taken during message communication. The nodes are also mobile in this course of action.

Next we show the packet send and packet received graph for the existing DiffServ QoS algorithm and afterwards we will give the results of our algorithm on the same simulation environmental setup.

Shown in Figure 6 and Figure 7 is the packet send and packet received snaps for all 13 nodes applying the DiffServ algorithm which is default in QualNet 6.1.

Table 2. Simulation environment

Parameters	Value
Number of nodes	13
Communication range	100 Km
Terrain size	1500 Km X 1500 Km
Max velocity	60 Km/hr
Mobility model	Random waypoint
Data rate	2 Mbps
Packet size	512 bytes
MAC Protocol	802.11e
Network protocol	DSR
Radio type	802.11b
Antenna model	Omni directional
IP Output queue scheduler	DiffServ
IP input queue size	150000 bytes
DS Second Scheduler	Weighted Fair
Number of IP Output queues	3
Temperature	290 K

Figure 4. Network topology at start up

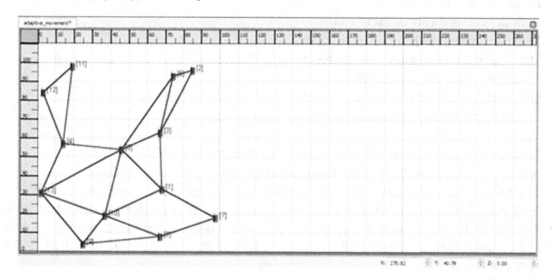

Now we give the data send and received results for all 13 nodes using our algorithm (Figure 8 and Figure 9).

We have taken 10 beacon intervals and have varied the message / packet number from 20 to 1500.

The graph below shows the variation of the QoS with the increase in the number of packets sent through the network. So from the close observations we can conclude that we can tend to the ideal values as we increase the number of packets in the network. The comparison graph is given in Figure 10.

The graph shows that initially though the quality of service factor is more or less equal to that of DiffServ, but later on it increases significantly with the increase in the number of message or packet sent. This proves the convergences of our algorithm.

Figure 5. Network in run mode

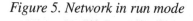

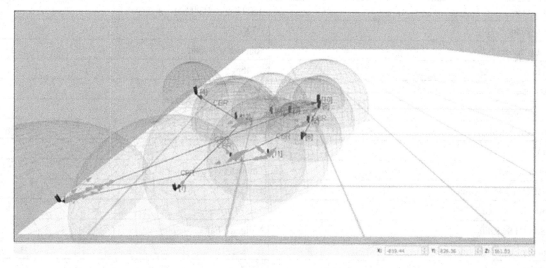

Figure 6. Data send chart for DiffServ algorithm

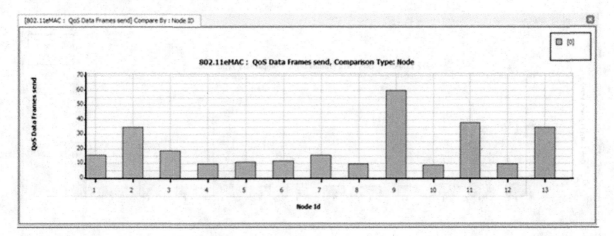

Figure 7. Data received chart for DiffServ algorithm

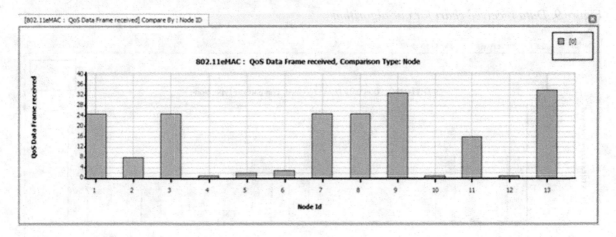

7. CONCLUSION

Wireless devices are getting smaller, cheaper, and more sophisticated. Since these devices become more ubiquitous, organizations are looking for inexpensive ways to keep these devices connected. Due to node mobility and scarcity of resources such as energy of nodes and bandwidth of wireless links, it is much tough to provide QoS guarantee in ad hoc networks. Therefore, while designing such a network we need to look out for several challenging aspects of it and identify optimum and energy aware solutions for each.

Nature is a rich inspirational source and there is still much to learn from. We can take advantage of the social collective behaviour of swarms to solve our real-life problems, by observing how these swarms have survived and solved their own challenges in nature.

Several simple agents interacting locally among themselves can eventually emerge a sophisticated global behaviour. Different swarm intelligence-based computational models are fast-growing, as they are generally computationally inexpensive, robust, and simple. SI-based optimization techniques are far-reaching in many domains, and have a wide range of successful applications on different areas.

Figure 8. Data send chart for our algorithm

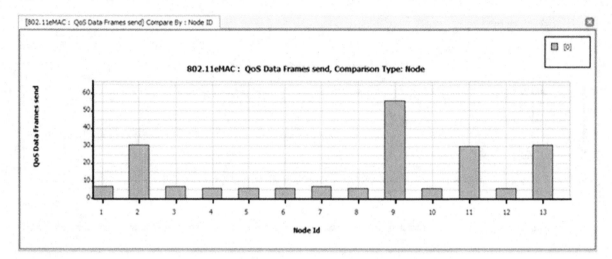

Figure 9. Data received chart for our algorithm

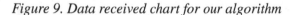
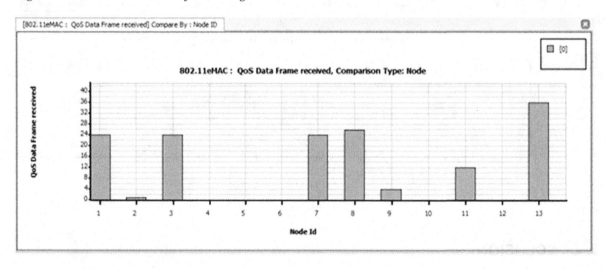

In this chapter we have proposed an energy efficient QoS enhancement scheme for mobile ad hoc network. The algorithm is inspired by artificial bee colony optimisation technique and simulation results show that it can produce better result than the existing schemes.

MANETs are likely to expand their presence in future communication infrastructure. The need of QoS in MANETs thus becomes an important issue. In this chapter we have discussed some of the most important issues that still need further investigation and more research in the area of QoS provisioning in general and in QoS routing in MANETs in particular. Despites of various advantages and unlimited application chances, MANETs are still far from being deployed on large scale commercial basis. This is because of some fundamental adhoc networking problems either remain unsolved or need more optimal solution.

Figure 10. Comparison graph showing the improvement in QoS using our algorithm

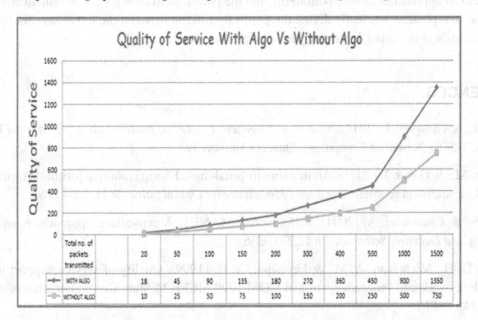

Total no. of packets transmitted	20	50	100	150	200	300	400	500	1000	1500
WITH ALGO	18	45	90	135	180	270	360	450	900	1350
WITHOUT ALGO	10	25	50	75	100	150	200	250	500	750

Several important research issues such as multi class traffic in network, different operational conditions, mobile nodes position identification, packet prioritization, mobility model, layer integration, internet-MANET interaction remain to be addressed to facilitate QoS support in MANETs.

The design of ad-hoc network protocols is significantly more challenging than in the wired domain because of the interference between wireless links. This is especially true if one wishes to guarantee quality of service to flows in an ad-hoc network. A flow on one link can have its quality disrupted by an increase of flow on a neighbouring link. In this chapter we propose an algorithm which can enhance the quality of service in MANET by using intelligent messaging. As per our algorithm, we can implement either the retransmission policy i.e., we want the packet send to be received at the receiver end or we might implement fast transmission where delay cannot be incorporated at any cost. So, QoS can be improved at the cost of one factor, both cannot be implemented together. The key to support QoS in MANETs is QoS routing. QoS routing in MANETs is a growing area of research. Future work can address the above mentioned unexplored challenges.

7.1 Future Research Directions

Here are some more open questions for the readers:

1. Should the individual agents of artificial swarms remain simple? If not, how complex should they be?
2. Should the individual agents remain identical or homogenous? If not, how different should they be?
3. Should the individual agents have the ability to learn by their own?
4. How local should their knowledge of the environment be?
5. How to efficiently tune the parameters of SI systems?

6. Should SI approaches remain bottom-up, and the pathways to their solutions remain emergent?
7. If not, is it possible to clearly define the pathways linking between the lower-level individual interactions and the upper-level emergent group behaviour?

REFERENCES

Ahmed, H., & Glasgow, J. (2012). *Swarm intelligence: Concepts, models and applications* (Technical Report 2012-585). School of Computing, Queen's University.

Bakhouya, M., & Gaber, J. (2007). An immune inspired–based optimization algorithm: Application to the travelling salesman problem. *Advanced Modeling and Optimization*, 9(1), 105–116.

Basu, S. S., & Chaudhuri, A. (2004). Self adaptive MANET: A centralized approach. *Foundation of Computing and Decision Sciences*, 29(4), 271–286.

Cansever, D. H., Michelson, A. M., & Levesque, A. H. (1999). Quality of service support in mobile ad - hoc IP networks. In Proceedings of MILCOM 1999 - IEEE Military Communications Conference (pp. 30 – 34). IEEE.

Chu, S. C., Tsai, P. W., & Pan, J. S. (2006). Cat swarm optimization. In *Proceedings of the 9th Pacific Rim International Conference on Artificial Intelligence* (LNAI), (vol. 4099, pp. 854 – 858). Berlin: Springer. doi:10.1007/11801603_94

Colorni, A., Dorigo, M., Maniezzo, V., & Trubian, M. (1994). Ant system for job–shop scheduling. *Journal of Operations Research, Statistics, and Computer Science*, 34(1), 39–53.

DaSilva, L. A., Reed, J. H., & Newhall, W. (2002). *Ad hoc networks and automotive applications*. Virginia Polytechnic Institute and State University.

Di Caro, G. A. (2004). *Ant colony optimization and its application to adaptive routing in telecommunication networks*. (PhD thesis). Facult'e des Sciences Appliqu'ees, Universit'eLibre de Bruxelles, Brussels, Belgium.

Dorigo, M. (1992). *Optimization, learning and natural algorithms*. (Ph.D. Thesis). DipartimentodiElettronica. Politecnico di Milano, Milan, Italy.

Dorigo, M., Maniezzo, V., & Colorni, A. (1991). *Positive feedback as a search strategy* (Tech. Report 91 – 016). Dipartimento di Elettronica, Politecnico di Milano.

Dorigo, M., & Stützle, T. (2004). *Ant colony optimization*. Cambridge, MA: MIT Press.

Eberhart, R. C., & Kennedy, J. (1995). A new optimizer using particle swarm theory. In *Proceedings of the Sixth International Symposium on Micro Machine and Human Science* (pp. 39 – 43). Academic Press. doi:10.1109/MHS.1995.494215

Frisch, K. V. (1967). *The dance language and orientation of bees*. Cambridge, MA: Harvard University Press.

Gupta, P., & Kumar, P. R. (2000, March). The capacity of wireless network. *IEEE Transactions on Information Theory, 46*(2), 388–404. doi:10.1109/18.825799

Internet Engineering Task Force (IETF) Mobile Ad Hoc Networks. (MANET) Working Group Charter. (n.d.). Retrieved from www.ietf.org/html.charters/manet-charter.html

Jain, R., Kumawat, R., Mandliya, S., & Patidar, M. (2014). Performance evaluation of table driven multipath routing protocols in MANET under varying nodes, traffic load & pause time. *Journal of Innovative Research in Electrical, Electronics. Instrumentation and Control Engineering, 2*(2), 952–956.

Karaboga, D. (2005). *An idea based on honey bee swarm for numerical optimization (Technical Report-TR06).* Erciyes University, Engineering Faculty, Computer Engineering Department.

Karaboga, D., & Basturk, B. (2007). A powerful and efficient algorithm for numerical function optimization: Artificial bee colony (ABC) algorithm. *Journal of Global Optimization, 39*(3), 459–471. doi:10.1007/s10898-007-9149-x

Karimi, H. A., & Krishnamurthy, P. (2001). Real-time routing in mobile networks using GPS and GIS techniques. In *Proceedings of the 34th IEEE Hawaii International Conference on System Sciences.* IEEE. doi:10.1109/HICSS.2001.927201

Kennedy, J., & Eberhart, R. C. (1995). Particle swarm optimization. In *Proceedings of IEEE International Conference on Neural Networks* (pp. 1942 – 1948). IEEE. doi:10.1109/ICNN.1995.488968

Kennedy, J., & Eberhart, R. C. (1997). A discrete binary version of the particle swarm algorithm. In *Proceeding of the 1997 Conference on Systems, Man, and Cybernetics* (pp. 4104 – 4109). Academic Press. doi:10.1109/ICSMC.1997.637339

Krishnanand, K. N., & Ghose, D. (2009). Glow-worm swarm optimization for searching higher dimensional spaces. In *Innovations in swarm intelligence.* Heidelberg, Germany: Springer. doi:10.1007/978-3-642-04225-6_4

Morgan, Y. L., & Kunz, T. (2005). A proposal for an ad-hoc network QoS gateway. In Proceedings of WiMob (vol. 3, pp. 221–228). IEEE. doi:10.1109/WIMOB.2005.1512907

Mounir, B., Pascale, M., Khaldoun, A. A., Cedric, A., & Geraud, A. (2004). Integration of mobile IP and OLSR for universal mobility. In *Wireless networks* (pp. 377–388). Kluwer Publications.

Parsopoulos, K. E., & Vrahatis, M. N. (2010). Particle swarm optimization and intelligence: Advances and applications. Information Science Reference.

Passino, K. M. (2002). Biomimicry of bacteria foraging for distributed optimization and control. *IEEE Control Systems Magazine, 22*(3), 52–67. doi:10.1109/MCS.2002.1004010

Patil, V. P. (2012). Performance evaluation of on demand and table driven protocol for wireless ad hoc network. *Journal of Computer Engineering Science, 2*(9), 1 – 13.

Patil, V. P. (2012). On demand and table driven routing protocol energy efficiency performance evaluation in mobile ad - hoc networks. *Journal of Computer Science and Management Research, 1*(2).

Scalable Network Technologies. (n.d.). *QualNet network simulator 6.1*. Retrieved from www.scalable-networks.com

Sumpter, D. J. T. (2000). *From bee to society: An agent - based investigation of honey bee colonies*. (PhD Thesis). The University of Manchester, Manchester, UK.

Taneja, K., & Patel, R. B. (2007). Mobile ad hoc networks: Challenges and future. In Proceedings of COIT 2007. Academic Press.

Veres, A., Ahn, G., Campbell, A. T., & Sun, L. (2002). SWAN: Service differentiation in stateless wireless adhoc networks. In *Proceedings of IEEE INFOCOM*. IEEE.

Yadav, N. S., & Yadav, R.P. (n.d.). Performance comparison and analysis of table-driven and on-demand routing protocols for mobile ad-hoc networks. *Journal of Information Technology, 4*(2), 101–109.

Zhang, X., Lee, S. B., Gahng-Seop, A., & Campbell, A. T. (2000, April). INSIGNIA: An IP - based quality of service framework for mobile ad hoc networks. *Journal of Parallel and Distributed Computing, 60*(4), 374406.

Zhang, Y., & Gulliver, T. A. (2005). Quality of service for adhoc on-demand distance vector routing. In Proceedings of Wireless and Mobile Computing, Networking and Communications (WiMob'2005) (vol. 3, pp. 192 - 196). Academic Press.

KEY TERMS AND DEFINITIONS

Artificial Bee Colony Optimization: An optimization algorithm in computer science and engineering based on the intelligent foraging behaviour of honey bee swarm.

Mobile Ad Hoc Network (MANET): A wireless, dynamic, autonomous, infrastructure-less network of heterogeneous mobile hosts.

Network Topology: The physical arrangement of the hosts in the network.

QoS Metrics: Used to quantitatively measure the quality of service of a network and the network services that are often considered are error rates, bandwidth, throughput, transmission delay, availability, jitter, etc.

Quality of Service (QoS): Of a computer network is the overall performance of the network, especially in terms of the users' perspective.

QualNet: A paid network simulator by Scalable Network Technologies used to simulate both wired and wireless networks.

Routing: The process of selecting optimum paths in the network.

Swarm Intelligence: The cooperative behaviour of decentralized, self-organized systems, natural or artificial.

Chapter 17
A Uniformly Distributed Mobile Sensor Nodes Deployment Strategy Using Swarm Intelligence

Chinmoy Ghorai
Indian Institute of Engineering Science & Technology, Shibpur

Arpita Debnath
BPC Institute of Technology, India

Abhijit Das
RCC Institute of Information Technology, India

ABSTRACT

WSN consists of spatially dispersed and dedicated sensors for monitoring the physical conditions of the universe and organizing the collected data at a central location. WSN incorporates a gateway that provides wireless connectivity back to the wired world and distributed sensor nodes. Various applications have been proposed for WSN like Ecosystem and Seismic monitoring, where deployment of nodes in a suitable manner is of an immense concern. Currently, sensor nodes are mobile in nature and they are deployed at an accelerated pace. This chapter focuses on developing the mobile nodes in an apt technique to meet the needs of WSNs properly. It considers the swarm intelligence-based movement strategies with the assistance of local communications through which the randomly deployed sensors can arrange themselves to reach the optimal placement to meet the issues like lower cost, lower power consumption, simpler computation, and better sensing of the total area.

1. INTRODUCTION

Wireless sensor networks (WSNs) comprise sensor nodes in which each node is able to supervise the physical area and send collected information to the base station for further analysis as depicted in figure 1. The important key of WSNs is detection and coverage of target. Developments of wireless sensor network enable them to operate with lower cost, lower power consumption, simpler computation, and

DOI: 10.4018/978-1-4666-8291-7.ch017

Figure 1. A typical wireless sensor network

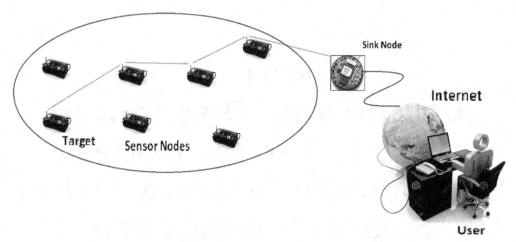

better sensing of the area when sensors move around. Furthermore, sensors also can sense the environment behind the movement, compute the data, and send the collected data to the sink node that can route the data to the other analyzing center through the internet.

Wireless sensor network has prospective in many applications, such as healthcare, environment, industry, and environment monitoring surveillance in military, wildlife monitoring, and battle field. For instance, sensor network can be deployed in the environment for monitoring and controlling of plants and animal behavior or in the ocean for controlling of temperature and seismic activities. However, in many places that are unfriendly, physical deployment is impossible and nodes have to be deployed haphazardly. The main problem in the wireless sensor network is deployment, coverage, and mobility strategy of sensor node; however, the coverage problem depends on a deployment sensor node in the wireless sensor network. Deployment of the sensor nodes can be placed haphazardly in a target area. When network size is large and sensor field is unfriendly, the only choice for deployment of nodes is to scatter with aircraft. However, when sensor nodes are scattered haphazardly, it is difficult to find best strategy for haphazard deployment that could minimize the coverage hole and communication overhead. Minimizing of the coverage hole can improve the quality of service for sensor network. Recently, mobile sensor node has great impact on network coverage. They are equipped with vehicle and move around the area after haphazard deployment to enhance network coverage. However, mobile sensor node is very expensive in comparison to the stationary node. It has maximum utility to increase the network coverage and lifetime and provide fault tolerance and quality service for network. The key objective for mobile node is to cover all area in the network and ensure each position has at least one sensor node for coverage. According to the monitoring area, three types of coverage have been identified: area coverage, target coverage, and barrier coverage. The mobile sensor node moves to exact location and connects to the other sensor node to form path coverage. This paper presents how the deployment of nodes increases the coverage and collects the intended information robustly as mentioned by Mini and Udgata, 2011.

A large number of research activities have been carried out to explore and overcome the constraints of WSNs and solve design and application issues. In this paper swarm based sensor node deployment strategy are discussed and compared with the conventional method. Section 2 of the paper discusses the applications of sensor networks. In Sections 3, the characteristics of sensor networks are described.

In Section 4, various research challenges are discussed. Section 5 describes the performance index of node deployment and principle of swarm intelligence is described in section 6. In Section 7, deployment problems are discussed. In Section 8, the proposal of our method and in Section 9, simulation environment are discussed. Finally, Section 10 describes the result and discussion of our method and in Section 11, conclusion and challenges are described.

2. APPLICATIONS OF WSN

The applications for WSNs are varied, typically involving some kind of monitoring, tracking, or controlling as described by Puccinelli and Haenggi, 2005. Specific applications include habitat monitoring, object tracking, nuclear reactor control, fire detection, and traffic monitoring. In a typical application, a WSN is scattered in a region where it is meant to collect data through its sensor nodes.

- **Area Monitoring:** Area monitoring is a common application of WSNs. In area monitoring, the WSN is deployed over a region where some phenomenon is to be monitored. For example, a large quantity of sensor nodes could be deployed over a battlefield to detect enemy intrusion instead of using landmines. When the sensors detect the event being monitored (heat, pressure, sound, light, electromagnetic field, vibration, etc), the event needs to be reported to one of the base stations, which can take appropriate action (e.g., send a message on the internet or to a satellite). Depending on the exact application, different objective functions will require different data-propagation strategies, depending on things such as need for real-time response, redundancy of the data (which can be tackled via data aggregation and information fusion techniques), need for security, etc.

- **Environmental Monitoring:** A number of WSNs have been deployed for environmental monitoring. Many of these have been short lived, often due to the prototype nature of the projects. Examples of longer-lived deployments are monitoring the state of permafrost in the Swiss Alps: The Perma Sense Project, Perma Sense Online Data Viewer and glacier monitoring.

- **Water/Wastewater Monitoring:** There are many opportunities for using wireless sensor networks within the water/wastewater industries. Facilities not wired for power or data transmission can be monitored using industrial wireless I/O devices and sensors powered using solar panels or battery packs. As part of the American Recovery and Reinvestment Act (ARRA), funding is available for some water and wastewater projects in most states.

- **Landfill Ground Well Level Monitoring and Pump Counter:** Wireless sensor networks can be used to measure and monitor the water levels within all ground wells in the landfill site and monitor leach ate accumulation and removal. A wireless device and submersible pressure transmitter monitors the leach ate level. The sensor information is wirelessly transmitted to a central data logging system to store the level data, perform calculations, or notify personnel when a service vehicle is needed at a specific well. It is typical for leach ate removal pumps to be installed with a totalizing counter mounted at the top of the well to monitor the pump cycles and to calculate the total volume of leach ate removed from the well. For most current installations, this counter is read manually. Instead of manually collecting the pump count data, wireless devices can send data from the pumps back to a central control location to save time and eliminate errors. The control system uses this count information to determine when the pump is in operation, to calculate leach ate extraction volume, and to schedule maintenance on the pump.

- **Flare Stack Monitoring:** Landfill managers need to accurately monitor methane gas production, removal, venting, and burning. Knowledge of both methane flow and temperature at the flare stack can define when methane is released into the environment instead of combusted. To accurately determine methane production levels and flow, a pressure transducer can detect both pressure and vacuum present within the methane production system. Thermocouples connected to wireless I/O devices create the wireless sensor network that detects the heat of an active flame, verifying that methane is burning. Logically, if the meter is indicating a methane flow and the temperature at the flare stack is high, then the methane is burning correctly. If the meter indicates methane flow and the temperature is low, methane is releasing into the environment.

- **Water Tower Level Monitoring:** Water towers are used to add water and create water pressure to small communities or neighborhoods during peak use times to ensure water pressure is available to all users. Maintaining the water levels in these towers is important and requires constant monitoring and control. A wireless sensor network that includes submersible pressure sensors and float switches monitors the water levels in the tower and wirelessly transmits this data back to a control location. When tower water levels fall, pumps to move more water from the reservoir to the tower are turned on.

- **Agriculture:** Using wireless sensor networks within the agricultural industry is increasingly common. Gravity fed water systems can be monitored using pressure transmitters to monitor water tank levels, pumps can be controlled using wireless I/O devices, and water use can be measured and wirelessly transmitted back to a central control center for billing. Irrigation automation enables more efficient water use and reduces waste.

- **Windrow Composting:** Composting is the aerobic decomposition of biodegradable organic matter to produce compost, a nutrient-rich mulch of organic soil produced using food, wood, manure, and/or other organic material. One of the primary methods of composting involves using windrows. To ensure efficient and effective composting, the temperatures of the windrows must be measured and logged constantly. With accurate temperature measurements, facility managers can determine the optimum time to turn the windrows for quicker compost production. Manually collecting data is time consuming, cannot be done continually, and may expose the person collecting the data to harmful pathogens. Automatically collecting the data and wirelessly transmitting the data back to a centralized location allows composting temperatures to be continually recorded and logged, improving efficiency, reducing the time needed to complete a composting cycle, and minimizing human exposure and potential risk. An industrial wireless I/O device mounted on a stake with two thermocouples, each at different depths, can automatically monitor the temperature at two depths within a compost windrow or stack. Temperature sensor readings are wirelessly transmitted back to the gateway or host system for data collection, analysis, and logging. Because the temperatures are measured and recorded continuously, the composting rows can be turned as soon as the temperature reaches the ideal point. Continuously monitoring the temperature may also provide an early warning to potential fire hazards by notifying personnel when temperatures exceed recommended ranges.

- **Greenhouse Monitoring:** Wireless sensor networks are also used to control the temperature and humidity levels inside commercial greenhouses. When the temperature and humidity drops below specific levels, the greenhouse manager must be notified via e-mail or cell phone text message, or host systems can trigger misting systems, open vents, turn on fans, or control a wide variety of system responses. Because some wireless sensor networks are easy to install, they are also easy to move as the needs of the application change.

- **Vehicle Detection:** Wireless sensor networks can use a range of sensors to detect the presence of vehicles ranging from motorcycles to train cars as used by Jeong, 2009.

3. CHARACTERISTICS OF WSN

As wireless sensor network (WSN) is recently considered as one of the most important telecommunication technologies that proves its compatibility and reliability in many applications disciplines. Based on references by Zheng, Jamalipour, 2009 and Romer & Mattern, 2004, WSNs uniquely have the following distinctive characteristics:

- **Dense Self-Deployment:** WSN is a huge spread computational system. Large number of sensors are spread and densely randomly deployed in the network environment. Sensors are configured autonomously as each sensor independently manages its self communication in the network.
- **Limited Processing and Storage:** Sensor nodes are small battery powered autonomous physical devices that highly limited in, computational capabilities and storage capacity.
- **Limited Energy Resources:** Due to the tough nature of WSN applications environment and the fact that sensor nodes are battery powered devices, it is usually hard to change or recharge theses batteries.
- **Sensor Heterogeneity:** Since sensor nodes existence is not guaranteed in the WSN life time, unreliable and inconsistent sensor nodes will prone due to physical damages or failures while harsh deployment.
- **Data Redundancy:** Data can be sent differently by more than one node to central node due to the need of association and communication of sensor nodes as well as the physical nature of the sensor nodes.
- **Application Centric:** As it is always hard to change or modify in the wireless sensor network, the network is usually designed and deployed for a specific application. This mainly affects the design requirements, network size, energy consumption and routing constrains of network.
- **Broadcast Communication:** Sensors in WSN usually depend on exchanging sensed data between multiple sensor nodes and particular sink node using different flooding routing techniques.
- **Topological Inconstancy:** Due to power insufficiency in sensor nodes as well as the harsh environment, Network topology will usually suffer frequent changes such as connection failures, node death, adding new node, energy consumption or channel fading.
- **Limited Transmission Range:** The limited physical characteristic of sensor nodes are usually limited strictly the network capabilities and affect the coverage range and communication quality.

4. RESEARCH CHALLENGES IN WSN

Wei & Fan, 2011 combine the major issues that affect the design and performance of a wireless sensor network are as follows:

4.1 Hardware

Wireless sensor networks are composed of hundreds of thousands of tiny devices which sense the information and pass the same on to a mote. Sensors are used to measure the changes to physical surroundings like pressure, humidity, sound, vibration and changes to the health of person like blood pressure, stress and heartbeat as mentioned by Srivastava, 2010. A Mote consists of processor, memory, battery, A/D converter for connecting to a sensor and a radio transmitter for forming an ad hoc network. A Mote and Sensor together form a Sensor Node. The structure of the sensor node is as shown in Figure 2. There can be different Sensors for different purposes mounted on a Mote. Motes are also sometimes referred to as Smart Dust. A Sensor Node forms a basic unit of the sensor network.

The hardware design issues of sensor nodes are quite different from other applications and they are:

- Radio Range of the sensor nodes should be high i.e., 1-5 kilometers, which ensure the network connectivity and data collection in a network as the surroundings being monitored may not have an installed infrastructure for communication. In many networks the nodes may not establish connection for many days or may go out of range after establishing connection.
- Flash memory chip is used for sensor networks as they are non-volatile and inexpensive.
- Power Consumption of the sensing device should be minimized and sensor nodes should be energy efficient since their limited energy resource determines their lifetime. The node should shut off the radio power supply when not in use to conserve the power. Battery type is another important factor as it can affect the propose of sensor nodes. Battery Protection Circuit to avoid overcharge or discharge problem can be added to the sensor nodes.

4.2 Operating System

An operating system framework for a sensor node should be able to provide memory management and resource management in a constrained surroundings. The various issues in designing an Operating System (OS) for sensor networks are:

- In sensor network a sensor node is mainly answerable for calculation of the extracted data from the local surroundings. It processes the extracted data and manipulates the data as per the requirement

Figure 2. Architecture of a wireless sensor node

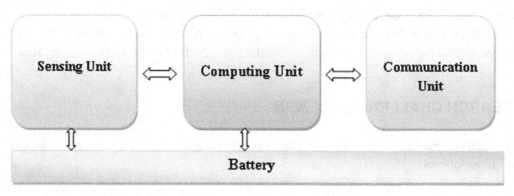

of a particular purpose. For all these activities it requires real time processing and routing the data by which concurrency is managed.

- For sensor nodes the operating system should be hardware independent and application specific. It should support multi-hop routing and simple user level networking abstractions.
- The OS should have inbuilt features to reduce the consumption of battery energy. The OS should be give precedence for higher priority events.
- Various Operating Systems for Sensor nodes like TinyOS, Mantis Operating System and Nano-Qplus have been designed keeping in mind the above design issues.

4.3 Wireless Radio Communication Characteristics

Performance of wireless sensor networks depends on the quality of wireless communication link which is unpredictable in nature. The design issues for communication in WSNs are:

- Low power consumption in sensor networks is needed to enable long operating lifetime by facilitating low duty cycle operation, local signal processing.
- Distributed Sensing effectively acts against various environmental obstacles and care should be taken that the signal strength, consequently the effective radio range is not reduced by various factors like reflection, scattering and dispersions.
- Multi-hop networking may be adapted among sensor nodes to reduce communication link range and also density of sensor nodes should be high.
- We should consider short range transmission to minimize the possibility of being eavesdropped as Long range communication is typically point to point and requires high transmission power.

4.4 Medium Access Schemes

MAC protocols should be premeditated for regulating energy consumption, which in turn influences the lifetime of the network.

The various design issues of the MAC protocols appropriate for sensor network environment are:

- The MAC protocol should have fine-grained control of the transceiver and allows on and off switching of the radio to decide when and how often the on and off mechanism should be done which helps in conserving energy.
- A MAC protocol should avoid collisions from interfering nodes, over emitting, over hearing, control packet overhead and idle listening.
- A MAC protocol should have minimum latency and high throughput when the sensor networks are deployed in critical applications.
- A MAC protocol should include Message Passing.
- MAC Protocols should satisfy the Real-time requirements. Some popular MAC Protocols are S-Mac (Sensor MAC), B-Mac, ZMAC, Time-MAC and WiseMac.

4.5 Deployment

Deployment means setting up an operational sensor network in a real world environment. Sensor nodes can be deployed either by placing one after another in a sensor field or by dropping it from a plane as described by Rani, Devarajan, 2012 and Chandni, Sharma, 2013. Various deployment issues which need to be taken care are:

- When sensor nodes are deployed in real world, Node death due to energy depletion either caused by normal battery discharge or due to short circuits is a common problem which may lead to wrong sensor readings. Also sink nodes acts as gateways and they store and forward the data collected. Hence, problems affecting sink nodes should be detected to minimize data loss.
- Deployment of sensor networks results in network congestion due to many concurrent transmission attempts made by several sensor nodes. Concurrent transmission attempts occur due to inappropriate design of the MAC layer or by repeated network floods.
- Another issue is the physical length of a link. Two nodes may be very close to each other but still they may not be able to communicate due to physical interference in the real world while nodes which are far away may communicate with each other.
- Low data yield is another common problem in real world deployment of sensor nodes. Low data yield means a network delivers insufficient amount of information.
- Self Configuration of sensor networks without human intervention is needed due to random deployment of sensor nodes. A framework is proposed in considering the above deployment issues. POWER is a software environment for planning and deploying wireless sensor network applications into actual environment.

4.6 Localization

Sensor localization is a fundamental and crucial issue for network management and operation. In many of the real world scenarios, the sensors are deployed without knowing their positions in advance and also there is no supporting infrastructure available to locate and manage those once they are deployed as mentioned by Youssef and Sheimy, 2007.

Determining the physical location of the sensors after they have been deployed is known as the problem of localization as mentioned by Kulkarni and Venayagamoorthy, 2011. Location discovery or localization algorithm for a sensor network should satisfy the following requirements:

- The localization algorithm should be distributed since a centralized approach requires high computation at selective nodes to estimate the position of nodes in the whole environment. This increases signaling bandwidth and also puts extra load on nodes close to center node.
- Knowledge of the node location can be used to implement energy efficient message routing protocols in sensor networks.
- Localization algorithms should be robust enough to localize the failures and loss of nodes. It should be tolerant to error in physical measurements.
- Localization algorithm should be accurate, scalable and support mobility of nodes.

4.7 Synchronization

Time Synchronization in a sensor network aims to present a common timescale for local clocks of nodes in the network. A global clock in a sensor system will assist process and evaluate the data correctly and calculate future system behavior. A clock synchronization service for a sensor network has to meet challenges that are significantly different from those in infrastructure based networks.

- Energy utilization in some management schemes is more due to energy hungry equipments like GPS (Global Positioning System) receivers or NTP (Network Time Protocol).
- The lifetime or the duration for the nodes which are spread over a large geographical area needs to be taken into account.
- Sensor nodes need to coordinate and collaborate to achieve a complex sensing task like data fusion.
- Sensor networks span multi hops with higher jitter. So, the algorithm for sensor network clock synchronization needs to achieve multi-hop synchronization even in the presence of high jitter. Various synchronization protocols which can be found in the literature are Reference Broadcast Synchronization (RBS) and Delay Measurement Time Synchronization protocol.

4.8 Calibration

Calibration is the method of adjusting the raw sensor readings obtained from the sensors into corrected values by comparing it with some standard values. Various Calibration issues in sensor networks are:

- A sensor network consists of large number of sensors typically with no calibration interface.
- Access to individual sensors in the field can be limited.
- Reference values might not be readily available.
- Different applications require different calibration.
- Requires calibration in a complex dynamic environment with many observables like aging, decaying, damage etc.

4.9 Network Layer Issues

Routing is vital for sending the data from sensor nodes to Base Station (BS). As discussed in the introduction part, routing in sensor networks is a very demanding issue. Various issues at the network layer are:

- Energy efficiency is a very important criterion. At the network layer, we should to find various methods for discovering energy efficient routes and for relaying the data from the sensor nodes to the BS so that the lifetime of a network can be optimized.
- Routing Protocols should incorporate multi-path design technique. Multi-path is referred to those protocols which set up multiple paths so that a path among them can be used when the primary path fails.
- Path repair is desired in routing protocols whenever a path break is detected.
- As the nodes are scattered randomly resulting in an ad hoc routing infrastructure, a routing protocol should have the property of multiple wireless hops.

- Routing Protocols should take care of heterogeneous nature of the nodes i.e. each node will be different in terms of computation, communication and power. Various type of routing Protocols for WSNs are Sensor Protocols for Information via negotiation (SPIN), Rumor Routing, Direct Diffusion, Low Energy Adaptive Cluster Hierarchy (LEACH), Threshold sensitive Energy Efficient sensor Network protocol (TEEN), Geographic and Energy Aware Routing (GEAR), Sequential Assignment Routing (SAR) and others.

4.10 Transport Layer Issues

End to End reliable communication is provided at Transport layer. The various design issues for Transport layer protocols are:

- In transport layer the messages are fragmented into several segments at the transmitter and reassembled at the receiver. Therefore a transport protocol should ensure orderly transmission of the fragmented segments.
- Limited bandwidth results in congestion which impacts normal data exchange and may also lead to packet loss.
- Bit error rate also results in packet loss and also wastes energy. A transport protocol should be reliable for delivering data to potentially large group of sensors under immense conditions.
- In sensor networks the loss of data, when it flows from source to sink is generally tolerable. But the data that flows from sink to source is sensitive to message loss. (A sensor obtains information from the surrounding environment and passes it on to the sink which in turn queries the sensor node for information) Traditional transport protocols such as UDP and TCP cannot be directly implemented in sensor networks for the following reasons:
  - If a sensor node is far away from the sink then the flow and congestion control mechanism cannot be applied for those nodes.
  - Successful end to end transmissions of packets are guaranteed in TCP but it's not necessary in an event driven applications of sensor networks.
  - Overhead in a TCP connection does not work well for an event driven application of sensor networks.
  - UDP on the other hand has a reputation of not providing reliable data delivery and has no congestion or flow control mechanisms which are needed for sensor networks. Pump Slowly, Fetch Quickly (PSFQ) proposed in one of the popular transport layer protocol.

4.11 Data Aggregation and Data Dissemination

Data gathering is the main intention of sensor nodes. The sensors periodically sense the data from the surrounding environment, process it and transmit it to the base station or sink. The frequency of reporting the data and the number of sensors which report the data depends on the particular application. Data gathering involves scientifically collecting the sensed data from multiple sensors and transmitting the data to the base station for further processing. But the data generated from sensors is often redundant and also the amount of data generated may be very huge for the base station to process it. Hence we need a method for combining the sensed data into high quality information and this is accomplished through Data Aggregation. Some design issues in data aggregation are:

- Sensor networks are naturally unreliable and certain information may be unavailable or expensive to obtain; like the number of nodes present in the network and the number of nodes that are responding and also it is difficult to obtain complete and up-to date information of the neighboring sensor nodes to gather information.
- Making some of the nodes to transmit the data directly to the base station or to have less transmission of data to the base station to reduce energy.
- Eliminate transmission of redundant data using meta- data negotiations as in SPIN protocol.
- Improving clustering techniques for data aggregation to conserve energy of the sensors.

4.12 Database Centric and Querying

Wireless sensor networks have the potential to span and monitor a bulky geographical area producing enormous amount of data. So sensor networks should be able to accept the queries for data and respond with the results. The data flow in a sensor database is very different from the data flow of the traditional database due to the following design issues and requirements of a sensor network:

- The nodes are volatile since the nodes may get depleted and links between various nodes may go down at any point of time but data collection should be interrupted as little as possible.
- Sensor data is exposed more errors than in a traditional database due to interference of signals and device noise.
- Sensor networks produce data continuously in real time and on a large scale from the sensed phenomenon resulting in need of updating the data frequently; whereas a traditional database is mostly of static and centralized in nature.
- Limited storage and scarce of energy is another important constraint that needs to be taken care of in a sensor network database but a traditional database usually consists of plenty of resources and disk space is not an issue.
- The low level communication primitives in the sensor networks are designed in terms of named data rather than the node identifiers which are used in the traditional networks.

4.13 Architecture

Architecture can be considered as a set of rules and guideline for implementing some functionality along with a set of interfaces, functional components, protocols and physical hardware. Software architecture is needed to link the gap between raw hardware capabilities and a complete system. The key issues that must be addressed by the sensor architecture are:

- Numerous operations like continuous monitoring of the channel, encoding of data and transferring of bits to the radio need to be performed in parallel. Also sensor events and data calculations must continue to proceed while communication is in progress.
- A strong and scalable architecture would allow dynamic changes to be made for the topology with minimum update messages being transmitted.
- The system must be flexible to meet the wide range of target application scenarios since the wireless sensor networks to not have a fixed set of communication protocols that they must adhere to.

- The architecture must provide precise control over radio transmission timing. This requirement is driven by the need for ultra-low power communication for data collection application scenarios.
- The architecture must decouple the data path speed and the radio transmission rate because direct coupling between processing speed and communication bit rates can lead to sub-optimal energy performance.

4.14 Programming Models for Sensor Networks

Currently, programmers are too much anxious with low level details like sensing and node to node communication raising a need for programming abstractions. There is considerable research activity investigated by Katiyar, Sinha and Gupta, 2012 for designing programming models for sensor networks due to following issues:

- Since the data collected from the surrounding incident is not for general purpose computing we need a reactive, event driven programming model.
- Resources in a sensor network are very limited, where even a typical embedded OS consuming hundreds of KB of considered too much. So programming models should help programmers in writing energy efficient applications.
- We need to reduce the run time errors and complexity since the applications in a sensor network need to run for a long duration without human intervention.
- Programming models should help programmers to write bandwidth efficient programs and should be accompanied by runtime mechanisms that achieve bandwidth efficiency whenever possible. TinyOS with Nesc and TinyGALS are examples for this category. Improving programming ease in languages such as Nesc and galsC itself provides tremendous opportunities for research.

4.15 Middleware

WSN middleware can be considered as a software infrastructure that glues together the network hardware, operating systems, network stacks and applications. Various issues in designing a middleware for wireless sensor networks are:

- Middleware should provide an interface to the various types of hardware and networks supported by primitive operating system abstractions and also provide new programming paradigm to provide application specific API's rather than dealing with low level specifications.
- Efficient middleware solutions should hide the complexity involved in configuring individual nodes based on their capabilities and hardware architecture.
- Middleware should include mechanisms to provide real time services by dynamically adapting to the changes in the environment and providing consistent data. Middleware should be adaptable to the devices being programmed depending on the hardware capabilities and application needs.
- There should be transparency in the middleware design. Middleware is designed for providing a general framework whereas sensor networks are themselves designed to be application specific. Therefore we need to have some tradeoff between generality and specificity.

- Sensor network middleware should support mobility, scalability and dynamic network organization. Middleware design should incorporate real time priorities. Priority of a message should be assigned at runtime by the middleware and should be based on the context.
- Middleware should support quality of service considering many constraints which are unique to sensor networks like energy, data, mobility and aggregation.
- Security has become of paramount importance with sensor networks being deployed in mission critical areas like military, aviation and in medical field. Several middleware systems have been designed to deal with the aforementioned issues. Mate is a middleware architecture for constructing application specific virtual machines that executes on top of TinyOS.

4.16 Quality of Service

Quality of service is the level of service provided by the sensor networks to its users. The QoS routing algorithms for wired networks cannot be directly applied to wireless sensor networks due to the following reasons:

The performance of the most wired routing algorithms relies on the availability of the precise state information while the dynamic nature of sensor networks make availability of precise state information next to impossible. Nodes in the sensor network may join, leave and rejoin and links may be broken at any time. Hence maintaining and re-establishing the paths dynamically which is a problem in WSN is not a big issue in wired networks as mentioned by Singh, Singh, and Singh, 2010. Various Quality of Service issues in sensor networks are:

- The QoS in WSN is difficult because the network topology may change constantly and the available state information for routing is inherently imprecise.
- Sensor networks need to be supplied with the required amount of bandwidth so that it is able to achieve a minimal required QoS.
- Traffic is unbalanced in sensor network since the data is aggregated from many nodes to a sink node. QoS mechanisms should be designed for an unbalanced QoS constrained traffic.
- Many a time routing in sensor networks need to sacrifice energy efficiency to meet delivery requirements. Even though multi-hops reduce the amount of energy consumed for data collection the overhead associated with it may slow down the packet delivery. Also, redundant data makes routing a complex task for data aggregation affecting thus affecting Quality of Service in WSN.
- Buffering in routing is advantageous as it helps to receive many packets before forwarding them. But multi-hop routing requires buffering of huge amount of data. This limitation in buffer size will increase the delay variation that packets incur while traveling on different routes and even on the same route making it difficult to meet QoS requirements.
- QoS designed for WSN should be able to support scalability. Adding or removing of the nodes should not affect the QoS of the WSN. One of the very first protocols which had QoS support was the Sequential Assignment Routing (SAR).

4.17 Security

Security in sensor networks is as much an important factor as performance and low energy consumption in many applications. Security in a sensor network is very challenging as WSN is not only being deployed in battlefield applications but also for surveillance, building monitoring, and burglar alarms and in critical systems such as airports and hospitals. Since sensor networks are still a developing technology, researchers and developers agree that their efforts should be concentrated in developing and integrating security from the initial phases of sensor applications development; by doing so, they hope to provide a stronger and complete protection against illegal activities and maintain stability of the systems at the same time as proposed by Mahmood, Seah, 2012 and Kumar, 2011.

Following are the basic security requirements to which every WSN application should adhere to:

- Confidentiality is needed to ensure sensitive information is well protected and not revealed to unauthorized third parties. Confidentiality is required in sensor networks to protect information traveling between the sensor nodes of the network or between the sensors and the base station; otherwise it may result in eavesdropping on the communication.

- Authentication techniques verify the identity of the participants in a communication. In sensor networks it is essential for each sensor node and the base station to have the ability to verify that the data received was really sent by a trusted sender and not by an adversary that tricked legitimate nodes into accepting false data. A false data can change the way a network could be predicted.

- Lack of integrity may result in inaccurate information. Many sensor applications such as pollution and healthcare monitoring rely on the integrity of the information to function; for e.g., it is unacceptable to have improper information regarding the magnitude of the pollution that has occurred.

- One of the many attacks launched against sensor networks is the message reply attack where an adversary may capture messages exchanged between nodes and reply them later to cause confusion to the network. So sensor network should be designed for freshness; meaning that the packets are not reused thus preventing potential mix-up.

- In sensor networks secure management is needed at the base station level, since communication in sensor network ends up at the base station. Issues like Key distribution to sensor nodes in order to establish encryption and routing information need secure management. Also, clustering techniques require secure management as well, since each group of nodes may include a large number of nodes that need to be authenticated with each other and exchange data in a secure manner.

- Security and QoS are two opposite poles in sensor networks. Security mechanisms like encryption should be lightweight so that the overhead is minimized and should not affect the performance of the network. Different types of threats in sensor networks are Spoofing and altering the routing information, passive information gathering, node subversion, sinkhole attacks, Sybil attacks, Denial of service attack and jamming as proposed by Vogt, 2009.

5. PERFORMANCE INDEX OF NODE DEPLOYMENT

The main objective of node deployment algorithm are to increase the coverage area, enhance network connectivity, lengthen the network lifetime, make the load balance, improve the correctness of the data transmission and brace the tolerance of nodes. Obviously, it has the certain difficulty if just using random node deployment to completely meet those design objectives. Generally, the optimization of the sensor nodes deployment mainly includes the following performance indexes.

5.1 Coverage Area

Coverage is a central issue in WSN and is related to energy saving, connectivity, and network reconfiguration. It mainly solves how to deploy the sensor nodes to attain effective coverage of the target area so that every point of the target area is observed at least by one sensor node. A good coverage is crucial for the effectiveness of wireless sensor networks as mentioned by Abbasi, Latiff and Chizari, 2014. Assume that the sensor radiation range is the coverage area of disk shape, the radius equal to radiation range, and the ratio of the area covered by node against whole area of deployment is the index of the monitoring area coverage.

Similarly for grid scanning algorithm, in which the obstacle will hinder the detection of sensor node to the target and the accuracy of the target detection probability, is changing with the distance between sensor nodes and detection target. There is a technique of using the minimum quantity of sensor nodes to realize the maximum coverage, and presents the triangle grid computing algorithm which makes any three adjacent nodes form an equilateral triangle. By regulating the distance between nodes to control coverage and proved that the detection area will be completely covered when $d_{th} = \sqrt{3}r$ (r, node perception radius) as mentioned by Liao, Kao and Li, 2011. As shown in Figure 3.

5.2 Network Connectivity

Network connectivity is the communication between the wireless sensor nodes, the node and base station, base station and the client, the client and the server. But in the early days, the network connectivity is not difficult problem. The complete coverage and connectivity of the sensor nodes, which are located in the sensing radius of node and are connected. For this, we only need to build routing between the node and base station to send the data as proposed by Zhang and Liu, 2012.

Figure 3. Maximum coverage areas

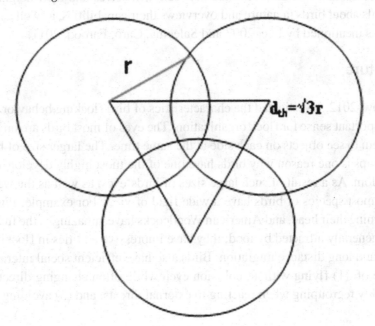

5.3 Network Lifetime

One of the most important requirements of WSN is to reduce the energy consumption. Hence, there is a need for energy efficient communication and routing techniques that will increase the network lifetime as proposed by Gao, Zhang, Song and Wang, 2010. The major cause of energy waste is collision. When a node receives more than one packet at the same time, these packets are termed collided, even when they coincide only partially. All packets that cause the collision have to be discarded and retransmissions of these packets are required, which increases energy consumption. The second reason for energy waste is overhearing, which means that a node receives packets that are destined to other nodes. The third energy waste occurs as a result of control-packet overhead.

6. PRINCIPLE OF SWARM INTELLIGENCE

A swarm is a group of number of simple and identical agents which work together with each other and surroundings to build up collective intelligent behavior to execute task required for their survival as mentioned by Kukunuru, Thella and Davuluri, 2010. Swarm based algorithms recently became known as population based algorithms which are capable to provide solutions to numerous complex problems. Swarm agents are interacting directly or indirectly. Swarm intelligent approach can applied in various problem domains which includes optimization problems, scheduling problems, data analysis and image processing, optimal routing etc. Swarm intelligent models are particle swarm optimization, bacteria foraging etc. Swarm intelligence has number of advantages, which are robustness, self-organization, flexibility and decentralization. This makes swarm intelligence to use in distributed problem solving as investigated by Huang, Zhang, Wang, Qian, 2014 and Valsalan, 2013.

PSO draws inspiration from the sociological behavior associated with bird flocking. It is a natural observation that birds can fly in large groups with no collision for extended long distances, making use of their effort to maintain an optimum distance between themselves and their neighbors. This section presents some details about birds in nature and overviews their capabilities, as well as their sociological flocking behavior as mentioned by Lee, 2007 and Saleema, Caro, Farooq, 2011.

6.1 Birds in Nature

Ahmed and Glasgow, 2012, investigated the characteristics of bird flocking behavior. Vision is considered as the most important sense for flock organization. The eyes of most birds are on both sides of their heads, allowing them to see objects on each side at the same time. The larger size of birds'eyes relative to other animal groups is one reason why birds have one of the most highly developed senses of vision in the animal kingdom. As a result of such large sizes of birds'eyes, as well as the way their heads and eyes are arranged, most species of birds have a wide field of view. For example, Pigeons can see 300 degrees without turning their head, and American Woodcocks have, amazingly, the full 360-degree field of view. Birds are generally attracted by food; they have impressive abilities in flocking synchronously for food searching and long distance migration. Birds also have efficient social interaction that enables them to be capable of: (1) flying without collision even while often changing direction suddenly, (2) scattering and quickly regrouping when reacting to external threats, and (3) avoiding predators.

6.2 Birds Flocking Behavior

The emergence of flocking and schooling in groups of interacting agents (such as birds, fish, penguins, etc.) have long intrigued a wide range of scientists from diverse disciplines including animal behavior, physics, social psychology, social science, and computer science for many decades. Bird flocking can be defined as the social collective motion behavior of a large number of interacting birds with a common group objective. The local interactions among birds (particles) usually emerge the shared motion direction of the swarm, as shown in Figure 4. Such interactions are based on the ――nearest neighbor principle‖ where birds follow certain flocking rules to adjust their motion (i.e., position and velocity) based only on their nearest neighbors, without any central coordination. In 1986, birds flocking behavior was first simulated on a computer by Craig Reynolds. The pioneering work of Reynolds proposed three simple flocking rules to implement a simulated flocking behavior of birds:

Rule 1 - Collision Avoidance: Flock members avoid collisions with nearby flock mates based on their relative position as depicted in Figure 4.

Rule 2 - Flock Centering: Flock members attempt to stay close to nearby flock mates by flying in a direction that keeps them closer to the centroid of the nearby flock mates as depicted in Figure 5.

Rule 3 - Velocity Matching: Flock members attempt to match velocity with nearby flock mates as depicted in Figure 6.

Although the rules of flocking behavior can be considered simple, the flocking is visually complex with an overall motion that looks fluid yet it is made of discrete birds. One should note here that collision avoidance rule serves to – establish the minimum required separation distance, whereas velocity matching rule helps to – maintain such separation distance during flocking; thus, both rules act as a complement to each other. In fact, both rules together ensure that members of a simulated flock are free to fly without running into one another, no matter how many they are. It is worth mentioning that the three aforementioned flocking rules are generally known as separation, cohesion and alignment rules.

Figure 4. Collision avoidance strategy

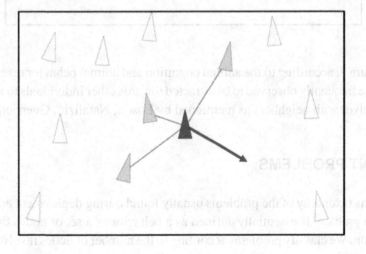

Figure 5. Flock centering strategy

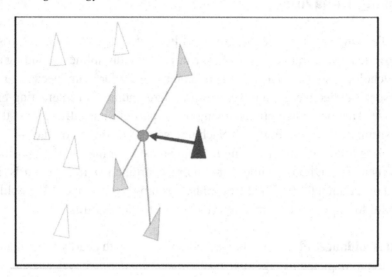

Figure 6. Velocity matching strategy

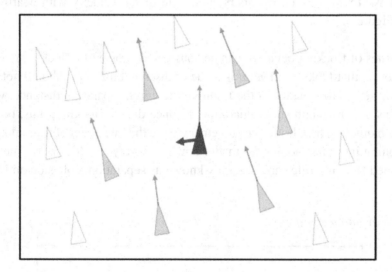

For example, in figure 7, according to the animal cognition and animal behavior research, individuals of animals in nature are frequently observed to be attracted towards other individuals to avoid being isolated and to align themselves with neighbors as mentioned by Loscrí, Natalizio, Guerriero and Aloi, 2012.

7. DEPLOYMENT PROBLEMS

This section contains taxonomy of the problems usually found during deployment according to our own experience. Here, a problem is essentially defined as a behavior of a set of nodes that is not compliant with the specification. We classify problems according to the number of nodes involved into four classes:

Figure 7. The flocking behavior of a group of birds

node problems means that involve only a single node, link problems means that involve two neighboring nodes and the wireless link between them, path problems that involve three or more nodes and a multi-hop path formed by them, and global problems that are properties of the network as a whole.

- **Node Problems:** A common node problem is node death due to energy diminution either caused by "normal" battery expulsion or due to short circuits. Low batteries frequently do not cause a fail-stop behavior of the sensor nodes. Rather, nodes may show Byzantine behavior at certain low battery voltages. For example, wrong sensor readings have been observed at low battery voltage at many cases. Software bugs often result in node reboots, for example, due to failure to restart the watchdog timer of the micro controller. We also observed software bugs resulting in hanging or killed threads, such that only part of the sensor node software continued to operate. Sink nodes act as gateways between a sensor network and the Internet. In many applications they store and forward data collected by the sensor network to a background communications. Hence, problems affecting sink nodes must be promptly detected to limit the impact of data loss.

- **Link Problems:** Field research demonstrated a very high inconsistency of link quality both across time and space resulting in temporary link failures and variable amounts of message loss. Network congestion due to many simultaneous transmission attempts is another source of message loss. Excessive levels of jamming have been caused by accidental synchronization of transmissions by multiple senders, for example, due to inappropriate design of the MAC layer or by repeated network floods. If message loss is remunerated for by retransmissions, a high latency may be observed until a message finally arrives at the destination. Most sensor network protocols require each node in the sensor network to discover and maintain a set of network neighbors. A node with no neighbors presents a problem as it is inaccessible and cannot communicate. Also, neighbor oscillation is problematic, where a node experiences frequent changes of its set of neighbors. A common issue in wireless communication is asymmetric links, where communication between a pair of nodes is only possible in one direction.

- **Path Problems:** Many sensor network applications rely on the ability to relay information across multiple nodes along a multi-hop path. In particular, most sensor applications include one or more sink nodes that broadcast queries or other tasking information to sensor nodes and sensor nodes deliver results back to the sink. Here, it is important that a path exists from a sink to each sensor node, and from each sensor node to a sink. Note that information may be changed as it is traversing such a path, for example due to data aggregation. Two common problems in such applications are hence bad path to sink and bad path to node. For example, selfish nodes have been observed that did not forward receive traffic, but succeeded in sending locally generated messages. Since a path consists of a sequence of links, the former inherits many of the possible problems from the latter such as asymmetric paths, high latency, path oscillations, and high message loss.

- **Global Problems:** In addition to the above problems which can be attributed to a certain subset of nodes, there are also some problems which are global properties of a network. Several of these are failures to meet certain application-defined quality-of-service properties. These include low data yield, high reporting latency, and short network lifetime. Low data yield means that the network delivers an insufficient amount of information.

8. OUR PROPOSAL

Postulation 1: Randomly placed mobile sensor nodes automatically arrange themselves using the swarm intelligence technique (i.e. bird flocking) in the target area for monitoring the surroundings.

Postulation 2: Every sensor node has a unique identity.

Postulation 3: Every sensor node has the basic orientation function and it can calculate the current position and direction.

Postulation 4: All sensor nodes have the same communication ranges. The coverage area of each sensor node is a circular disk. The sensing range is equal to the communication range. Every sensor node can communicate with others without losing data.

Postulation 5: Sensor node cans accurately finish the position migration and node energy is sufficient to support the node deployment process.

Postulation 6: Sensor node can specifically estimate the distance to the sender by the received signal strength of incoming packets.

Postulation 7: Every sensor node installs a precise antenna array, which can identify the angle of every incoming packet. Each sensor also has a precise compass to determine its moving direction.

Various Deployment Strategies

WSN is deployed to measure environment parameters in Region of Interest (ROI) and to send it to a controller node or base station. In WSNs how nodes will deployed is basically application specific and totally dependent on environment. The node deployment option affects the performance of routing protocol basically in terms of energy consumptions. In this paper, the sensors are deployed in three ways in a wireless sensor network environment:

- **Random Deployment:** Sensor nodes are scattered over finite area. When the deployment of nodes is not predefined optimal positioning of cluster head becomes a critical issue to enable energy efficient network operation. Random deployment is generally used in rescue operations. Area of Use: Environmental and Habitual monitoring, etc. In this paper 23 fixed nodes are placed in a random pattern and a PAN coordinator is placed as a root node or sink node which collects the data from the target region.

- **Grid Deployment with Mobility:** A grid-based deployment is considered as a good deployment in WSN, especially for the coverage performance. But when the sensor nodes are mobile the initial position of the nodes are changed which affect the performance of the network as a whole. In this paper 23 mobile nodes are placed in a grid pattern and a PAN coordinator is placed as a root node or sink node which collects the data from the target area. Here we use the random waypoint mobility model for the sensors.

- **Deployment of Sensor Nodes with Mobility using Swarm Intelligence:** Can move to compensate for deployment shortcomings; can be passively moved around by some external force (wind, water, and vehicle); can actively seek out "interesting" areas. Area of Use: Battle field surveillances, Emergency situations (Fire, Volcano, Tsunami), etc.

In this paper 23 mobile nodes are placed in a random pattern and a PAN coordinator is placed as a root node or sink node which collects the data from the target area. Here we use fixed velocity for all the sensors. After the nodes are deployed randomly in the target area, they rearrange themselves using swarm intelligence algorithm. The flowchart of the algorithm is given in the Figure 8.

9. SIMULATION ENVIRONMENT

9.1 Simulator Used

The Qualnet 6.1 network simulator is used for our simulation. QualNet is a fast, scalable and hi-fidelity network modeling software. It enables very efficient and cost-effective development of new network technologies. By building virtual networks in a lab environment, you can test, optimize, and integrate next generation network technologies at a fraction of the cost of deploying physical testbeds. It uses the QualNet Graphical User Interface (GUI) for an integrated network simulation experience for network design, execution and animation, and analysis. QualNet is network modeling software that predicts performance of networking protocols and networks through simulation and emulation. Using emulation and simulation allows you to reproduce the unfavorable conditions of networks in a controllable and repeatable lab setting. QualNet provides thefollowing key benefits:

- **Speed:** QualNet can support real-time and faster than real-time simulation speed, which enables software-in-the-loop, network emulation, hardware-in-the-loop, and human-in-the-loop exercises.
- **Scalability:** QualNet supports thousands of nodes. It can also take advantage of parallel computing architectures to support more network nodes and faster modeling. Speed and scalability are not mutually exclusive with QualNet.
- **Model Fidelity:** QualNet offers highly detailed models for all aspects of networking. This ensures accurate modeling results and enables detailed analysis of protocol and network performance.
- **Portability:** QualNet runs on a vast array of platforms, including Linux, Solaris, Windows XP, and Mac OS X operating systems, distributed and cluster parallel architectures, and both 32- and 64-bit computing.

Figure 8. Flowchart of the proposed method

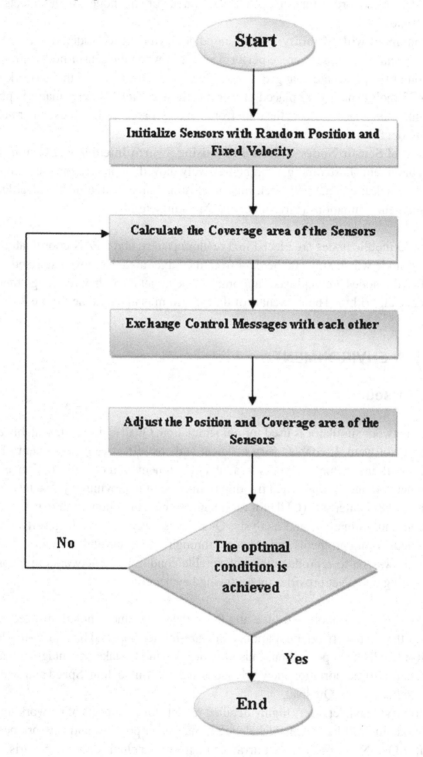

- **Extensibility:** QualNet connects to other hardware & software applications, such as OTB, real networks, and STK, greatly enhancing the value of the network model.

9.2 Simulation Setup

Performance evaluation of wireless ad-hoc sensor networks is done through simulations on a provides scalable simulations of Wireless networks. In our simulation, we consider a mobile ad-hoc sensor network with 23 nodes and a statically placed data sink (root node). Data sink node (24) is a full function device and work as a PAN Coordinator. Considering the parameters proposed by Rana, Kumar and Sharma, 2012, here we used IEEE 802.15.4, wireless standard for PHY and MAC layer, AODV (Ad hoc On-Demand Distance Vector) routing (Scalable Network Technologies).

In the model the components used are:

1. **Wireless Subnet:** The Cloud in the n/w is ZigBee subnet. This subnet is responsible for giving ZigBee properties to all the nodes.
2. **Nodes:** we consider a mobile ad-hoc sensor network with 23 mobile nodes and a statically placed data sink (root node).
3. **Sink Node:** Data sink node (24) is a full function device and work as a PAN Coordinator
4. **CBR Traffic Flow:** We used the application of constant bit rate (CBR).We have taken node 1 to 23 as source and node 24 is taken in Scenario as sink node. We will send 100 packets of each size 64 bytes at start 1s. We have send all packet at 1s interval of time and ending time of simulation is 301s.
5. **Network Layer Parameters:** At network layer IPv4 queue type is FIFO (First in First Out). AODV algorithm is used as routing protocol.
6. **Application Layer Parameters:** Constant bit rate application is run with packet size of 64 bytes and inter packet interval of 1s. Packet transmission starts at 1s and continue till end of simulation.
7. **Scenario:** In the model the components used are Wireless subnet, nodes configured and CBR traffic flow. Simulation parameters as shown in table 1.

We have considered a network topology with 24 sensor nodes. In the application layer we have used Constant Bit Rate (CBR) data traffic applied between source and destination.

The first scenario where 23 nodes are placed randomly and they are communicating with the central PAN coordinator. The data links chosen are Constant Bit Rate (CBR) links where-in the data send is assumed to have constant rate of packet delivery. There are 100 packets of data to be send where-in each packet consists of 64 bytes of data. So 23 nodes are sending the data and the central PAN coordinator is receiving all of it depicted in Figure 9.

The second scenario where 23 nodes are placed in a grid manner with random waypoint mobility and they are communicating with the central PAN coordinator. The data links chosen are Constant Bit Rate (CBR) links where-in the data send is assumed to have constant rate of packet delivery. There are 100 packets of data to be send where-in each packet consists of 64 bytes of data. So 23 nodes are sending the data and the central PAN coordinator is receiving all of it depicted in Figure 10.

The third scenario comprises 23 nodes which are placed using swarm intelligence with random waypoint mobility and they are communicating with the central PAN coordinator. The data links chosen are Constant Bit Rate (CBR) links where-in the data send is assumed to have constant rate of packet

Table 1. Simulation parameters

Parameter	Value
Area	1500m X 1500m
Data Rate	2 Mbps
Items to send	100
Packet Size	64 bytes
Device Type	FFD (for node 24)
FFD Mode	PAN Coordinator
Device Type	RFD (for node 1 to 23)
Mobility Model	Random-Way Point
Physical Layer Radio Type	802.15.4
MAC Protocol	802.15.4
Transmission Power	3 dBm
Packet reception Model	802.15.4
Modulation Scheme	O-QPSK
CCA Mode	Carrier Sense
Energy Model	Mica-Motes
Routing Protocol IPv4	AODV
Mobility Model	Random Waypoint
Antenna Model	Omni directional
Temperature	290 K
SNR Threshold	10 dBm
Simulation Time	300 sec

delivery. There are 100 packets of data to be send where-in each packet consists of 64 bytes of data. So 23 nodes are sending the data and the central PAN coordinator is receiving all of it depicted in Figure 11.

The simulation is made to run for 300 seconds. Each of the 23 nodes on a CBR link to the server (node 24) is made to send an equal number of packets to the PAN coordinator. The size of each packet is 64 bytes. The MAC protocol and the radio Protocols are adjusted to the Zigbee standards of 802.15.4 Radio. The sensor node transmission power is 3dBm.

9.3 Performance Metric

- **Throughput:** Throughput or network throughput is the rate of successful message delivery over a communication channel. This data may be delivered over a physical or logical link, or pass through a node. The throughput is usually measured in bits per second (bit/s or bps), and sometimes in data packets per second or data packets per time slot and is used to measure the performance of the network.
- **End-to-End Delay:** The average end-to-end delay specifies the packet is transmitting from source to destination and calculate the difference between send times and received times. Delays due to route discovery, queuing, propagation and transfer time are included in the delay metric.

Figure 9. Random node placement without mobility

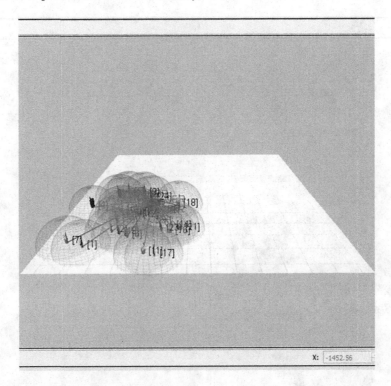

Figure 10. Grid node placement with random waypoint mobility

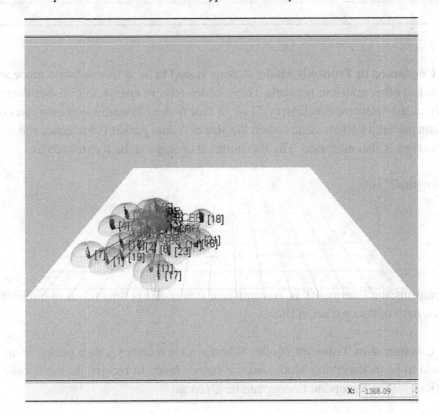

Figure 11. Node placement with swarm intelligence

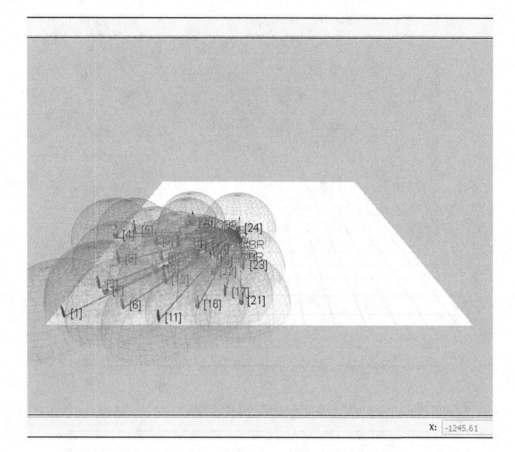

- **Energy Consumed in Transmit Mode:** A node is said to be in transmission mode when it sends data packet to other nodes in network. These nodes require energy to transmit data packet, such energy is called Transmission Energy (Tx), of that nodes. Transmission energy is depended on size of data packet (in Bits), means when the size of a data packet is increased the required transmission energy is also increased. The transmission energy can be formulated as:

Tx = (330*Plength)/2*106

or

PT= Tx / Tt

where Tx is transmission Energy, PT is Transmission Power, T t is time taken to transmit data packet and Plength is length of data packet in Bits

- **Energy Consumed in Transmit Mode:** When a node receives a data packet from other nodes then it said to be in Reception Mode and the energy taken to receive packet is called Reception Energy (Rx), . Then Reception Energy can be given as:

Rx = (230* Plength)/2*10   6

or

PR = R x / Tr

where Rx is a Reception Energy, PR is a Reception Power, Tr is a time taken to receive data packet, and Plength is length of data packet in Bits.

10. RESULT AND DISCUSSION

The Qualnet 6.1 network simulator is used to analyze the performance of random deployment, grid based deployment and Swarm based deployment. The performance of the network is analyzed with respect to the three different node placement strategies. In this analysis twenty three different CBR traffic as described in simulation setup. The results are shown in figures from 12 to 27.

We evaluated:

1.   Average Throughput.

In these graph the Throughput- in random placement model is 1787 bits per second as depicted in Figure 12.

In these graph the Throughput- in grid placement with random waypoint mobility model is 2525 bits per second as depicted in Figure 13.

In these graph the Throughput- in Swarm based placement with fixed mobility model is 12192 bits per second as depicted in Figure 14.

Figure 12. Throughput of random node placement

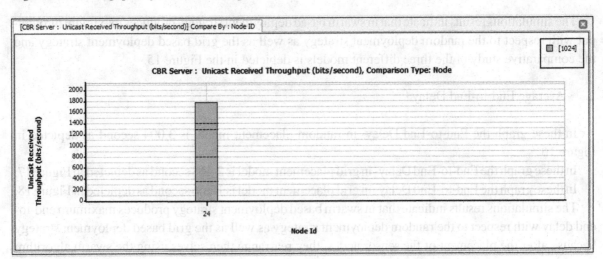

Figure 13. Throughput of grid placement

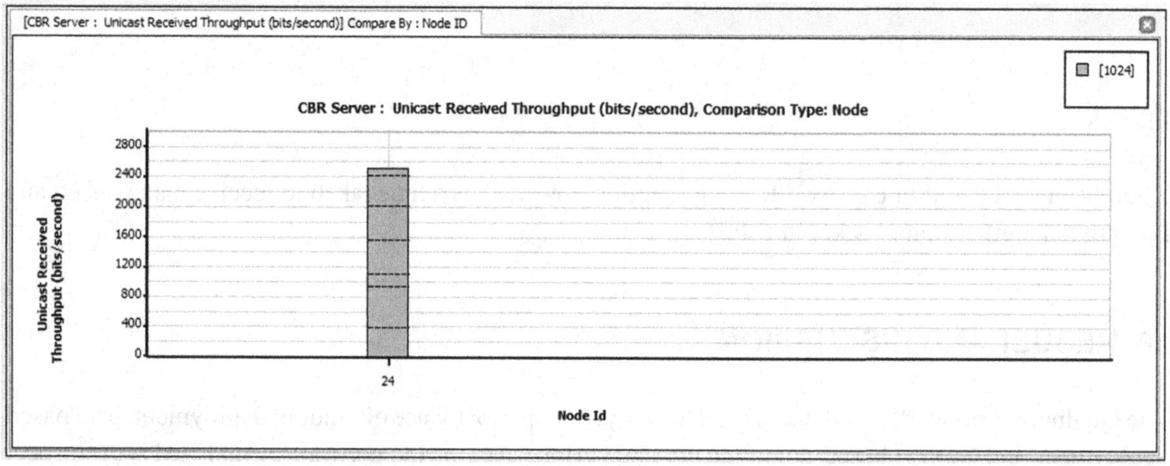

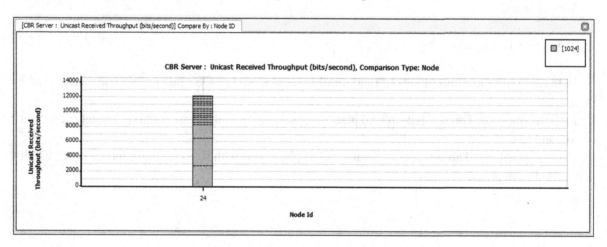

Figure 14. Throughput of node placement using swarm intelligence

The simulations results indicate that in swarm based deployment strategy produces maximum throughput with respect to the random deployment strategy as well as the grid based deployment strategy and the comparative study of the three different models is depicted in the Figure 15.

2.   Average End-to-End Delay.

In these graph the End-to-End Delay- in random placement model is 3.004 second as depicted in Figure 16.

In these graph the End-to-End Delay- in grid placement model is 2.468 second as depicted in Figure 17.

In these graph the End-to-End Delay- in grid placement model is 15.66 second as depicted in Figure 18.

The simulations results indicate that in swarm based deployment strategy produces maximum end-to-end delay with respect to the random deployment strategy as well as the grid based deployment strategy because after the placement of the sensor nodes, they rearrange themselves using the swarm algorithm

Figure 15. Average throughput comparison of random, grid, and swarm based deployment

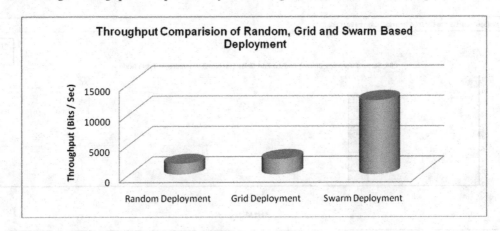

Figure 16. End-to-end delay of random placement

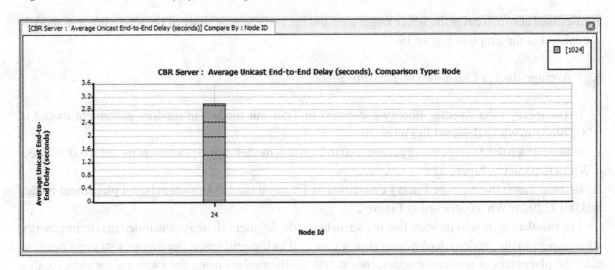

Figure 17. End-to-end delay of grid placement

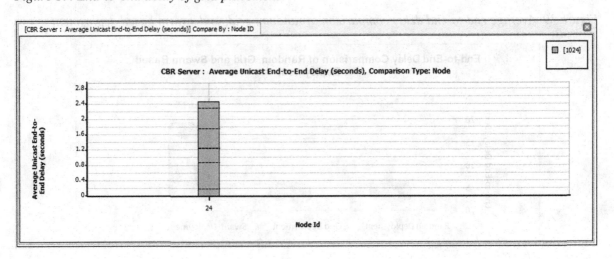

Figure 18. End-to-end delay of grid placement using swarm

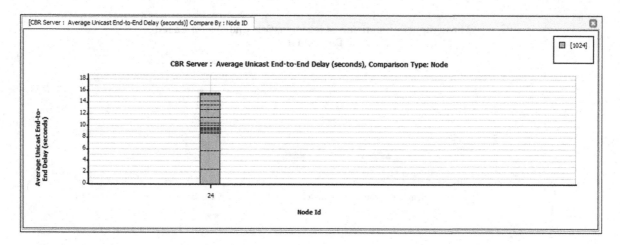

as discussed above to cover the whole target area and the comparative study of the three different models is depicted in the graph in Figure 19.

3.   Average Energy Consumed in Transmit Mode.

In these graph the Average Energy consumed in Transmit mode - in random placement model is 0.00079875 mWh as depicted in Figure 20.

In these graph the Average Energy consumed in Transmit mode - in grid placement model is 0.00078458 mWh as depicted in Figure 21.

In these graph the Average Energy consumed in Transmit mode - in swarm based placement model is 0.00132292 mWh as depicted in Figure 22.

The simulations results indicate that in swarm based deployment strategy consumed maximum energy with respect to the random deployment strategy as well as the grid based deployment strategy because after the placement of the sensor nodes, they rearrange themselves using the swarm algorithm, for this

Figure 19. Average end-to-end delay comparison of random, grid, and swarm based deployment

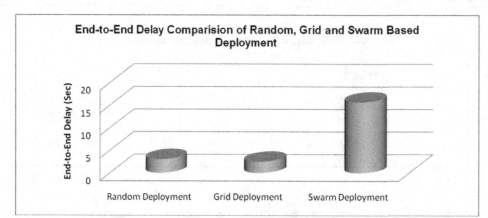

Figure 20. Energy consumed in transmit mode of random placement

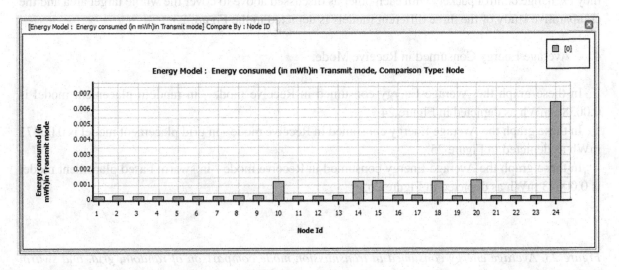

Figure 21. Energy consumed in transmit mode of grid placement

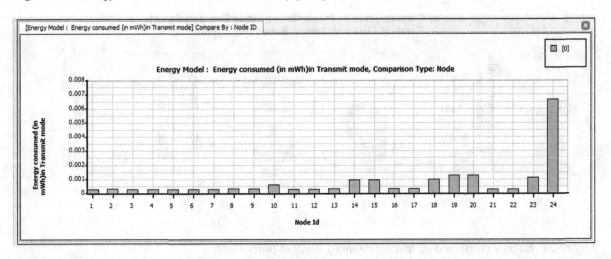

Figure 22. Energy consumed in transmit mode of grid placement using swarm

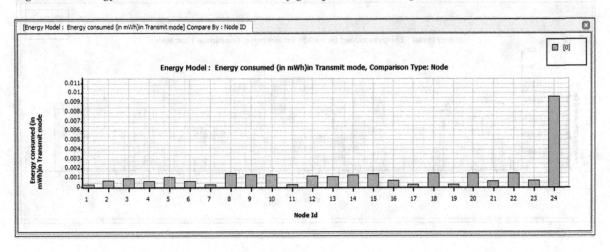

they exchange control packets with each other as discussed above to cover the whole target area and the comparative study of the three different models is depicted in the Figure 23.

4.   Average Energy Consumed in Receive Mode.

In these graph the Average Energy consumed in Receive mode - in random placement model is 0.00385 mWh as depicted in Figure 24.

In these graph the Average Energy consumed in Receive mode - in grid placement model is 0.00371 mWh as depicted in Figure 25.

In these graph the Average Energy consumed in Receive mode - in swarm based placement model is 0.00643 mWh as depicted in Figure 26.

Figure 23. Average energy consumed in transmission mode comparison of random, grid, and swarm based deployment

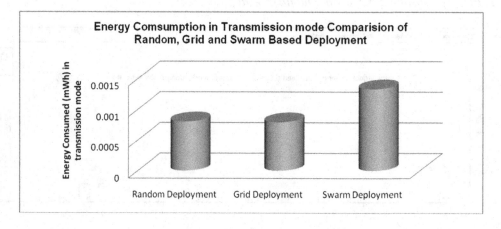

Figure 24. Energy consumed in receive mode of random placement

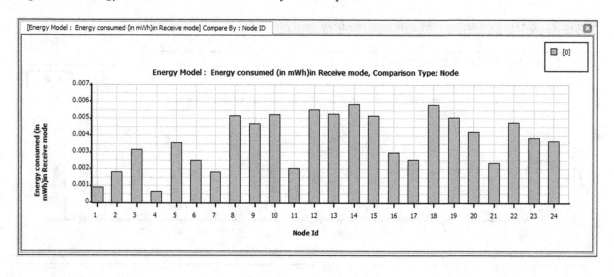

Figure 25. Energy consumed in receive mode of grid placement

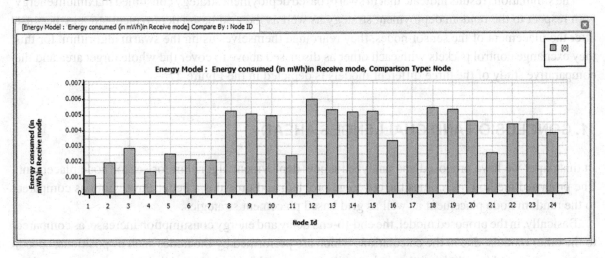

Figure 26. Energy consumed in receive mode of grid placement using swarm

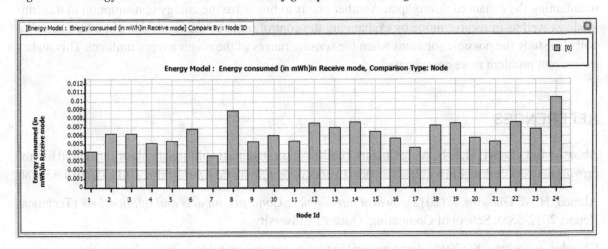

Figure 27. Average energy consumed in receiving mode comparison of random, grid, and swarm based deployment

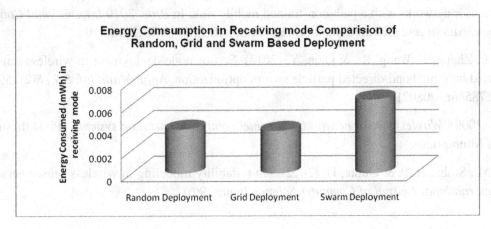

The simulations results indicate that in swarm based deployment strategy consumed maximum energy with respect to the random deployment strategy as well as the grid based deployment strategy because after the placement of the sensor nodes, they rearrange themselves using the swarm algorithm, for this they exchange control packets with each other as discussed above to cover the whole target area and the comparative study of the three different models is depicted in the Figure 27.

11. CONCLUSION AND CHALLENGES AHEAD

In this paper we have proposed and analyzed a new deployment algorithm for sensor node placement. The proposed method overcomes the coverage problem and provides a better throughput as compared to the random node placement as well as grid based placement strategies.

Basically, in the proposed model, the end-to-end delay and energy consumption increase, as compared to the other models, due to the calculations which are performed by the nodes such as positions, speed, coverage area, and for adjusting themselves with respect to the positions and the velocities of each other.

There are two further works for this research. The first one is to decrease the end-to-end delay, maintaining the enhanced throughput. Another one is to minimize the energy consumption in transmit mode as well as in receive mode by exchanging the control packets with each other at a minimal. We will also study the possible solutions when the sensing ranges of the nodes are not uniform. This makes the current problem more complicated.

REFERENCES

Abbasi, M. A., Latiff, M. S. B. A., & Chizari, H. (2014). Bioinspired evolutionary algorithm based for improving network coverage in wireless sensor networks. *Scientific World Journal*. doi: 10.1155/2014/839486

Ahmed, H., & Glasgow, J. (2012). *Swarm intelligence: Concepts, models and applications* (Technical Report 2012-585). School of Computing, Queen's University.

Chandni, & Sharma, K. (2013). Improvement in QoS using sink mobility in WSN. *International Journal of Computer Trends and Technology, 4*(4).

Gao, S., Zhang, H., Song, T., & Wang, Y. (2010). Network lifetime and throughput maximization in wireless sensor networks with a path-constrained mobile sink. In *Proc. 2010 International Conference on Communications and Mobile Computing*. IEEE. doi:10.1109/CMC.2010.219

Huang, H., Zhang, J., Wang, R., & Qian, Y. (2014). Sensor node deployment in wireless sensor networks based on ionic bond-directed particle swarm optimization. *Appl. Math. Inf. Sci., 8*(2), 597–605. doi:10.12785/amis/080217

Jeong, J. (2009). *Wireless sensor networking for intelligent transportation systems*. (Ph.D thesis). University of Minnesota.

Katiyar, M., Sinha, H. P. & Gupta, D. (2012). On reliability modeling in wireless sensor networks-A review. *International Journal of Computer Science Issues, 9*(6).

Kukunuru, N., Thella, B. R., & Davuluri, R. L. (2010). Sensor deployment using particle swarm optimization. *International Journal of Engineering Science and Technology*, 2(10), 5395–5401.

Kulkarni, R. V., & Venayagamoorthy, G. K. (2011). Particle swarm optimization in wireless sensor networks: A brief survey. *IEEE Transactions on Systems, Man and Cybernetics. Part C, Applications and Reviews*. doi:10.1109/TSMCC.2010.2054080

Kumar, A. (2011). A survey on routing protocols for wireless sensor networks. *International Journal of Advances in Engineering Research*, 1(2).

Lee, K. E. (2007). An automated sensor deployment algorithm based on swarm intelligence for ubiquitous environment. *International Journal of Computer Science and Network Security, 7*(12).

Liao, W. H., Kao, Y., & Li, Y. S. (2011). A sensor deployment approach using glowworm swarm optimization algorithm in wireless sensor networks. *Expert Systems with Applications, 38*(10), 12180–12188. doi:10.1016/j.eswa.2011.03.053

Loscrí, V., Natalizio, E., Guerriero, F., & Aloi, G. (2012). Particle swarm optimization schemes based on consensus for wireless sensor networks. In *Proc. MSWiM'12*. ACM. doi:10.1145/2387191.2387203

Mahmood, M. A. & Seah, W. (2012). *Reliability in wireless sensor networks: Survey and challenges ahead*. Elsevier.

Mini, S., & Udgata, S. K. (2011). Coverage and deployment algorithms in wireless sensor networks. *IJCCT, 2*(5).

Puccinelli, D., & Haenggi, D. (2005). Wireless sensor networks: Applications and challenges of ubiquitous sensing. *IEEE Circuits and Systems Magazine*.

Rana, M., Kumar, S., & Sharma, U. (2012). Improvement the performance of mobility pattern in mobile ad-hoc sensor network using qualnet 5.0. *International Journal of Engineering Research and Development, 1*(3).

Rani, K. S. S., & Devarajan, N. (2012). Multiobjective sensor node deployement in wireless sensor networks. *International Journal of Engineering Science and Technology, 4*(4).

Romer, K., & Mattern, F. (2004). The design space of wireless sensor networks. *Wireless Communications, IEEE, 11*(6), 54–61. doi:10.1109/MWC.2004.1368897

Saleema, M., Gianni, A. D. C., & Farooq, M. (2011). Swarm intelligence based routing protocol for wireless sensor networks: Survey and future directions. *Information Sciences, 181*(20), 4597–4624. doi:10.1016/j.ins.2010.07.005

Scalable Network Technologies. (n.d.). *QualNet simulator 6.1*. Retrieved from www.scalable-networks.com

Singh, S. K., Singh, M. P., & Singh, D. K. (2010). *Routing protocols in wireless sensor networks*. Academic Press.

Srivastava, N. (2010). Challenges of next-generation wireless sensor networks and its impact on society. *Journal of Telecommunications, 1*(1).

Valsalan, V. M. (2013). Dynamic deployment of wireless sensor networks using enhanced artificial bee colony algorithm. *International Journal of Science and Research, 2*(4).

Vogt, H. (2009). *Protocols for secure communication in wireless sensor networks*. (Ph.D thesis). Swiss Federal Institute of Technology, Zurich, Switzerland.

Wang, X., Wang, S., & Ma, J. J. (2007). An Improved co-evolutionary particle swarm optimization for wireless sensor networks with dynamic deployment. *Sensors, 7*, 354-370. Retrieved from www.mdpi.org/sensors

Wei, Z., & Zihao, F. (2011). Network coverage optimization strategy in wireless sensor networks based on particle swarm optimization. (Bachelor's Thesis in Electronics). Faculty of Engineering and Sustainable Development, University of Gavle.

Youssef, M., & El-Sheimy, N. (2007). Wireless sensor network: Research vs. reality design and deployment issues. In *Proc. Fifth Annual Conference on Communication Networks and Services Research* (CNSR'07). Academic Press. doi:10.1109/CNSR.2007.71

Zhang, H. & Liu, C. (2012). A review on node deployment of wireless sensor network. *International Journal of Computer Science Issues, 9*(6).

Zheng, J., & Jamalipour, A. (2009). *Wireless sensor networks: A networking perspective*. Wiley.

KEY TERMS AND DEFINITIONS

Delay: The time lag in transmissionof a packet in the network.

Deployment: Basically converting a mechanical, electrical or computer system for a packaged form to an operational state.

Energy Consumption: Consumption of energy or power in case of a device or a system.

QualNet: A commercial simulator of Scalable Network Technologies to simulate wired and wireless network protocols and scenarios.

Swarm Intelligence: An idea generated in AI, which is thecollective behavior of self-organized natural or artificial systems without any central control.

Throughput: The rate of production or the rate at which something can be processed.

WSN: Or Wireless Sensor Network comprises of sensor nodes distributed autonomously in space to monitor various physical or environmental conditions for necessary processing and action.

Chapter 18
Applications of Particle Swarm Optimization in Composite Power System Reliability Evaluation

Mohammed A Benidris
Michigan State University, USA

Salem Elsaiah
Michigan State University, USA

Joydeep Mitra
Michigan State University, USA

ABSTRACT

This chapter introduces a novel technique to evaluate composite power system reliability indices and their sensitivities with respect to the control parameters using a dynamically directed binary Particle Swarm Optimization (PSO) search method. A key point in using PSO in power system reliability evaluation lies in selecting the weighting factors associated with the objective function. In this context, the work presented here proposes a solution method to adjust such weighting factors in a dynamic fashion so that the swarm would always fly on the entire search space rather of being trapped to one corner of the search space. Further, a heuristic technique based on maximum capacity flow of the transmission lines is used in classifying the state space into failure, success, and unclassified subspaces. The failure states in the unclassified subspace can be discovered using binary PSO technique. The effectiveness of the proposed method has been demonstrated on the IEEE RTS.

1. INTRODUCTION

Composite system reliability evaluation aims at determining the reliability of the given power system taking into consideration both transmission and generation systems. In recent years, the task of composite system reliability evaluation has become more complicated. This complexity can be attributed, in

DOI: 10.4018/978-1-4666-8291-7.ch018

part, to the rapid increase in electrical demand and the liberalization of the electricity markets. In fact, the time and computational burden that are spent in evaluating system indices and their sensitivities with respect to the control parameters are of great concern to many researchers and companies all over the globe. Since the inception of reliability evaluation methods, a reasonable amount of work has been presented in the literature to handle the task of reliability evaluation efficiently. Numerous techniques have been proposed in the literature to assess composite system reliability. In this context, analytical and Monte Carlo simulation methods have been used for composite system reliability evaluation (Deng & Singh, 1992; He, Sun, Kirschen, Singh, & Cheng, 2010; Oliveira, Pereira, & Cunha, 1989; Wang, Guo, Wu, & Dong, 2014). It is worthy pointing out here that, composite system reliability evaluation based on analytical approaches are extremely fast; however, they tend to be tedious as the system size increases. On the other hand, Monte Carlo simulation has the ability of handling reliability analysis of complicated systems and has been used for that purpose for a long time. However, the major downside of using Monte Carlo simulation in composite system reliability evaluation is that the time consuming during the course of reliability evaluation increases with system size. These concerns have led to the development of several Population-based Intelligent Search methods, (PIS), such as Genetic Algorithms, Particle Swarm Optimization, Ant colony, and so forth. These population-based techniques along with the some other reliability assessment methods such as importance sampling, state space pruning, and state space decomposition would be helpful in reducing the search space and handling the task of reliability evaluation efficiently.

The use of Binary Particle Swarm Optimization in power system reliability has been found to be an efficient tool in evaluating the reliability indices. However, the task of choosing the weighting factors that are associated with the objective function tends to be tedious and time consuming as trial and error approaches are usually used to prevent the particles from being flying in one direction. In view of these reasons, the development of an automated approach to adjust these weighting factors could save some effort in solving the task of reliability evaluation efficiently.

Composite system reliability indices include, but are not limited to, loss of load probability (LOLP), loss of load frequency (LOLF), loss of load expectation (LOLE), expected energy not supplied (EENS), and expected demand not supplied (EDNS). Even though these indices are of a great importance in both planning and operational power system reliability evaluation, they lack the ability of identifying the influence of each area or equipment on the system reliability. Due to these reasons, significant efforts have been devoted to this area in recent years to evaluate what the system's reliability justifications are and where the best location to invest is which is referred as sensitivity analysis.

Several methodologies for calculating the sensitivity of some reliability indices with respect to the variations in components parameters and system operating limits have been introduced in the literature. One of the advantages of using sensitivity analysis is that it allows planners to enhance the overall system reliability by improving the reliability of each component in a separate manner. The study of the sensitivity of these indices can be viewed as measures of deficiency in both generation and transmission subsystems and, hence, provide sense to the areas that to be reinforced.

In performing sensitivity analysis of the reliability indices as well as the evaluation of the system reliability, the computational time is of concern especially for the online applications. In this chapter, a heuristic technique is used to prune the state space; and thereby reduce the computational effort in evaluating the well-known reliability indices and their sensitivities with respect to component parameters and system operating limits. The heuristic technique differs from the already existed pruning techniques in that it classifies the state space into success, failure and unclassified subspaces instead of pruning the success subspaces. This method is based on calculating the line flow capacity limits of the transmission lines and evaluates the capability of the transmission lines to carry the load. The power carrying capabilities of the transmission lines are calculated at each bus and between buses for every loading scenario. However, some failure states may not be captured by using the line capacity flow model. These states are aggregated in the unclassified subspace. Also, this work proposes a technique to search for failure states in the unclassified subspace, which is developed based on a bounded and directed BPSO. This technique dynamically adjusts the weighting factors associated with the fitness function of the BPSO to force the swarm to fly on the unclassified subspace. Instead of using the dynamically directed BPSO search method to search for failure states in the entire state space, we use this technique to search for failure states in the unclassified subspace. Another intelligence factor is added to the BPSO that reverses the direction of the particles to search in the unclassified subspace if the algorithm discovers that some particles have entered the success and/or failure subspaces. The proposed algorithm tracks the behavior of the particles and then adjusts the objective function coefficients correspondingly. The behavior of the swarm can be evaluated by examining the probabilities of the visited states.

In this chapter, a new technique that is based on the complementary concept is introduced to increase the efficiency and ability of the use of the intelligent search methods in power system reliability evaluation. To show the intelligence property of BPSO technique, a comparison between BPSO and Monte Carlo Simulation methods was presented.

2. BACKGROUND

The BPSO technique has been amply used in power system reliability analysis as a searching tool for success or failure states (Green et al., 2010, Green et al., 2011; Green et al., 2011a, Green, Wang, Alam, & Singh, 2011b; Green et al., 2010; Green et al., 2010a; Zhao & Singh, 2010; Wang & Singh, 2008; Miranda, Carvalho, Rosa, Silva, & Singh, 2009; Yang & Chang, 2009; Suresh & Kumarappan, 2013). PSO has been used in optimal power system reliability planning in (Bakkiyaraj & Kumarappan, 2013).

Also, PSO has been used in selecting the control procedures of FACTS (flexible AC transmission system) to improve composite power system reliability in (Padmavathi, Sahu, & Jayalaxmi, 2014). The BPSO have been used in power system reliability evaluation as searching and scanning tool to search for failure states rather than searching for a single optimum point. An improved particle swarm optimization method has been proposed in (Gholami, Hoseini, & Mohamad Taheri, 2008) to evaluation the annualized indices composite power systems. In searching for failure states, several objective functions have been proposed. The objective function of the BPSO can be single objective or multi-objective. In (Green et al., 2010) (Green et al, 2010a; Green R. C., Wang, Wang, Alam, & Singh, 2010b; Green et al., 2011; Green et al., 2011a; Zhao & Singh, 2010) a single objective function has been used, which is minimum load curtailment to search for success states to be pruned from the state space. The use of multi-objective BPSO as a searching tool for failure states in composite system reliability evaluation has been proposed in (Wang & Singh, 2008; Miranda et al., 2009; Yang & Chang, 2009; Suresh & Kumarappan, 2013; Patra et al., 2006; Mitra & Xu, 2010). One objective is used to maximize load curtailments and the other is used to maximize probabilities of the visited states. These two objective functions were intended to prevent the particles from being trapped to one corner of the state space. Every objective function has a weighting factor by which an algorithm can direct the swarm to fly on the desired search space. The weighting factors associated with the fitness functions have been carefully selected in order to keep the particles to search in the entire state space (Mitra & Xu, 2010; Patra et al., 2006; Benidris, Elsaiah, & Mitra, 2013). Even with two objective functions, if the weighting factors are not chosen carefully, the particles might be trapped to one corner of the search space. To circumvent this difficulty, an effective approach that adjusts these weighting factors is presented in this chapter.

The computational time in evaluating power system reliability, whether using analytical, simulation or intelligent methods, is another difficulty that facing the application of these methods on large systems within the operational time horizon. Several research papers in the power system reliability literature have introduced techniques to reduce the search space and the computational efforts in estimating reliability indices and their sensitivities with respect to system control variables. Singh and Mitra (1997) have introduced the concept of the state space pruning. In their work, arbitrary sets of coherent acceptable subspaces were pruned out from the state space using the concept of partitioning vectors. Then, they perform Monte Carlo simulation for the remaining subspaces. The number of pruned subspaces is system dependent and trade – off between the required time to prune the acceptable subspaces and the required time to perform Monte Carlo simulation for the rest of the subspace. Mitra and Singh (1999) have also used the concept of state space pruning to calculate the frequency and duration indices of composite power systems. Another papers developed the concept of state space pruning using Population-based Intelligent Search (PIS) methods (Green, Wang, & Singh, 2010; Green, L. Wang, Z. Wang, Alam, & Singh, 2010; Green, Z. Wang, L. Wang, Alam, & Singh, 2010a; Green, Wang, Alam, & Singh, 2011; Green, Wang, Alam, & Singh, 2011; Green, Wang, Alam, & Singh, 2011a; Zhao & Singh, 2010). The Genetic Algorithm (GA) and the modified GA were used in (Green et al., 2010; Green et al., 2010a; Zhao & Singh, 2010) to prune the state space and use Monte Carlo simulation for the remaining part of the state space. Binary Particle Swarm Optimization, (BPSO), technique was utilized in (Green et al., 2011; Green et al., 2011a) to prune the state space. Green and et al. (2011) have applied the Artificial Immune Systems (AIS) Optimization technique in pruning the state space. A comparative study of using (PIS) methods specifically Genetic Algorithms (GA), Repulsive Binary Particle Swarm Optimization (RBPSO) and Binary Ant Colony Optimization (BACO) was introduced in (Green et al., 2010). In all of these applications, the PIS methods are utilized as heuristic techniques and therefore selection of the acceleration factors is a crucial part to guarantee the best performance of these methods.

Our approach in pruning the state space works in the other direction of the already existed pruning techniques. In this chapter, instead of pruning the success subspaces, we identify the "definite" failure subspace. We call it definite because all the states inside the boundary of this subspace are definitely failure states. The boundary of this subspace surrounds the origin (all the components are in the down state) of the entire state space.

Different from common applications of BPSO, BPSO is used in this work as a scanning tool to search for a set of system states that significantly contribute to system reliability indices rather than searching for a single optimum or near optimum point in the state space. Also, the applications of the BPSO in power system reliability evaluation have been based on calculating the exact probabilities of the visited states; BPSO is used in chapter to estimate the reliability indices based on a complementary concept.

3. NETWORK MODELLING USING LINEAR PROGRAMMING AND DC POWER FLOW

In performing reliability and sensitivity analysis of composite power systems, a power flow or optimal power flow with objective of minimum load curtailment is usually required to test whether the state under consideration is a failure or success state. Therefore, the task of performing optimal power flow, OPF, is essential in evaluating the reliability indices of power systems. Toward this end, three power flow models have generally been used for composite system reliability assessment. These models are the full AC power flow model, the transportation model or capacity flow model, and the DC power flow model. The task of reliability evaluation using full AC power flow can be inflexible and extremely time consuming. The transportation model, on the other hand, only uses the capacity constraints of the tie-lines and, therefore, it is not applicable for every reliability study. The DC power flow model has been widely utilized in reliability assessment of power systems due to its simplicity of formulation and implementation. Moreover, the DC power flow model has the advantage of being suitable for studies that require extensive computational burden such as composite system reliability and security assessment. Consequently, this model is adopted during the realization of the presented work.

Linear programming with DC power flow model has been used in calculating the reliability indices of composite power systems. If under any scenario the curtailment is unavoidable, the linear programming tries to minimize the amount of load to be shed. Using DC power flow, there are three main constraints which are power balance equation, generation capacity limits and line capacities. The equality constraints are the power balance at each bus and the inequality constraints are the capacity limits of generating units and power carrying capabilities of transmission lines. The load curtailment minimization problem can be posed as (Mitra & Singh, 1996),

$$Loss\ of\ Load = \min\left(\sum_{i=1}^{N_b} C_i\right) \tag{1}$$

subject to

$$\hat{B}\delta + G + C = D$$

$$G \leq G^{\max}$$

$$C \leq D$$

$$b\hat{A}\delta \leq F_f^{\max} \tag{2}$$

$$-b\hat{A}\delta \leq F_r^{\max}$$

$$G, C \geq 0$$

δ unrestricted

where N_b is number of buses in the system, N_t is number of transmission lines, $\hat{B}$ is the augmented node susceptance matrix $(N_b \times N_b)$, b is the transmission line susceptance matrix $(N_t \times N_t)$, $\hat{A}$ is the element-node incidence matrix $(N_t \times N_b)$, δ is the vector of node voltage angles $(N_t \times 1)$, C is the vector of bus load curtailments $(N_b \times 1)$, D is the vector of bus demand $(N_b \times 1)$, $G^{\max}$ is the vector of maximum available generation $(N_b \times 1)$, $F_f^{\max}$ is the vector of forward flow capacities of lines $(N_t \times 1)$, $F_r^{\max}$ is the vector of reverse flow capacities of lines $(N_t \times 1)$, and G is the solution vector of the generation at buses $(N_b \times 1)$.

In the standard minimization problem given by (1) and (2), all generation and network constraints have been taken into consideration. Also, it has been assumed that one of the bus angles is zero in the constraints (2) to work as a reference bus.

4. STATE SPACE REDUCTION TECHNIQUE

In evaluating the reliability indices of composite systems, an optimal power flow with an objective of minimum load curtailment is performed. The DC power flow model in conjunction with the linear programming optimization problem is the most commonly model used in power system reliability evaluation. Performing DC optimal power flow for huge number of scenarios of contingency analyses takes a considerable amount of time and computational efforts. A fast method to perform such screening procedure is of necessity. Further, searching for failure states in the entire state space is time consuming and, hence, a reduction technique is required to reduce the computational time. A heuristic technique is presented and described in this section. This heuristic technique is developed based on calculating the line flow capacity limits of the transmission lines. This technique models power system networks based on network configuration, available generation, loading conditions and transmission line availabilities, and power carrying capabilities.

By examining the above linear programming problem, it can be noted that for any sampled state if one of the following two conditions is satisfied, we can conclude that this state is a failure state: (1) total generation is less than the total load and (2) sum of the capacity of the lines connected to a bus is less than the loading of that bus. Given these conditions, we can construct a heuristic technique that reduces the search space significantly. The procedures can be described as follows (Benidris & Mitra, 2013),

1. Subtract the loads connected to the generation buses from the sampled amount of generation at these buses.
2. Construct a line capacity capability flow matrix (*LCM*) for the given sampled configuration. This matrix can be constructed in the same manner as constructing a "Ybus" from the branch/node incidence matrix (*A*) except that instead of using "-1" for the branch that assumed to enter a node, we use "1". Further, instead of using the diagonal susptance matrix, we use diagonal capacity matrix (*C*) that is, the diagonal entries are the line capacities. The *LCM* matrix can be expressed as follows,

$$LCM = A^T \times C \times A \tag{3}$$

where A^T is the transpose of matrix A.

3.   If at any bus the total generation is larger than the corresponding diagonal element of the *LCM* matrix, adjust the generation at that bus downward to the corresponding diagonal element.
4.   For a state (x), if the value of any of the diagonal elements of the matrix *LCM* is less than the absolute value of the power injection at the corresponding bus or the total generation is less than the total demand, this state is guaranteed to be a failure state.

After reading system data, system states are sampled. For every sampled state, the above search space reduction technique is applied. Failure states are then passed to the linear programming optimization problem and they are solved for the conditions of these states and the reliability indices are updated. These processes are repeated for every sampled system state.

5. REDUCTION IN COMPUTATIONAL TIME

In calculating reliability indices, an optimization problem usually needs to be performed for every system state with different loading scenarios. The process of preparing and modeling power system data to be tested for reliability analysis is performed one time. However, running an optimization problem is required for every system state or any change in system parameters. From a study of wide variety of system sizes and configurations, the optimization problem takes most of the calculation time. For instance, on average, the time required to solve an optimization problem for the systems we have tested took more than 95% of the calculation time for each system state. By performing the reduction technique, not all the states need to be passed to the optimization problem. In other words, if a state is guaranteed to be a success state, no useful results can be shown by solving an optimization problem. On the other hand, failure states should be passed to the analyzer to calculate bus indices. As mentioned above, system indices of the definite failure subspace can be calculated without the need of solving the optimization problem.

The problem of deciding whether we need to perform BPSO for the unclassified subspace can be solved by running the BPSO for a few iterations. If the reliability index under consideration does not change for a few iterations, the algorithm is to be terminated and the indices calculated by the line capacity model are enough to describe the reliability of the system.

5.1 Reduction in Computational Time in Case of Ignoring the Unclassified Subspace

If the transmission lines of the system under consideration are very reliable and have high power limits in comparison with system loading conditions which is the case for most power systems, the proposed line capacity flow model can capture most of the failure states. In this case, performing the search method is not necessary and ignoring this subspace will not cause significant errors.

If we assume the total time required to evaluate system indices by passing every single state to the solver (optimization problem) is T, the total time required to evaluate system indices by passing only the failure states to the solver is T_r, the time required to evaluate every system state is t, the time required by the optimization problem to evaluate every system state is t_r, number of samples is N and the loss of load probability of the system is LOLP, then by ignoring the unclassified subspace the percentage of reduction in the computational time η can be calculated as,

$$\eta = \frac{T - T_r}{T} \times 100\%$$

(4)

where

$$T = N \times t$$

$$T_r \approx N \times \left[LOLP \times t + (1 - LOLP)(t - t_r) \right]$$

here T_r is approximated because the time of performing the heuristic technique to identify the failure states is very small in comparison with the time of preparing system data for every sampled state and the time required by solving the optimization problem.

After some manipulations, Equation (4) can be rewritten as,

$$\eta \approx (1 - LOLP)\frac{t_r}{t} \times 100\%$$

(5)

As an example, if we assume 100,000 states were to be sampled and evaluated in order to reach the desired tolerance and every state takes about 0.01 seconds and if we assume the LOLP of the system is 0.01 and the optimization solver takes 95% of the calculation time of each state, then the time required with solving optimization problem for "every state" is 1000 seconds and the time required by passing only the failure states to the solver is 59.5 seconds. Therefore, the percentage of time reduction of using this technique is 94.05%.

5.2 Reduction in Computational Time in Case of Including the Unclassified Subspace

In case of ignoring the unclassified subspace causes considerable error in evaluating system indices, the proposed directed BPSO should be used. In this case, calculation of the percentage of time reduction is not straight forward and system dependent. Therefore, calculation of this time cannot be determined beforehand.

To calculate the time reduction, another time which is the time spent by performing the BPSO algorithm, T_{BPSO}, is to be added to the time spent to perform the line capacity model, T_r. Now, Equation (4) can be rewritten as,

$$\eta = \frac{T-\left(T_r + T_{BPSO}\right)}{T} \times 100\% \tag{6}$$

The computational efforts required by the algorithm proposed in (Mitra & Xu, 2010) for the entire state space is found to be only 19.31% of performing Monte Carlo Simulation with State Space Pruning (Mitra & Singh, 1999) on the modified IEEE RTS. Since we are applying a dynamically directed BPSO on a subspace of the entire state space, T_{BPSO} in our case should be less than 19.31% of T. Also, the number of states to be visited is very small; hence, the required memory will be small too.

6. THE COMPLEMENTARY CONCEPT

The concept of complementary has been applied in several disciplines to calculate/estimate a parameter from its complementary value. The complementary concept in composite power system reliability evaluation can be defined as: every reliability index that can be evaluated from the failure states, has a complementary value that can be evaluated from the success states as long as the boundaries of an index and its complementary value are known such as probability and energy indices or the index can be equally likely determined from the success or failure states such failure frequency indices. For example, the boundary (minimum and maximum values) of the probability of system failure and the probability of system success is between 0 and 1. Also, the boundaries of expected load curtailment and the expected load supplied are between 0 and the peak load. Frequency indices can be evaluated either from the failure states that transit upwards to success states or from success states that transit downwards to failure states. The complementary concept estimates reliability indices from visited states; rather than the entire state space.

6.1 Theoretical Background

The complementary concept starts with the fact that the sum of the probabilities of the state space is one. Therefore, the sum of the probabilities of the success states and the failure states is also one. The number of states in a state space is 2^n where n is the number of the components. Most power system components (generation and transmission) are highly reliable. Therefore, the state that all system components are in the up state has the highest probability. Not only that, the probability of a state with only one component being in the down state usually less than the probability of the state with all the components are in the up states of order of $1/q_i$ where q_i is the unavailability of component i. This probability order can be generalized for the rest of the states, that is, the probability of a state that has two components in the down state (i and j) is less than the probability of a state with all the components are in the up state of order of $1/q_i q_j$. Therefore, as the number of the components in the down state increases, the probability of a state decreases with reciprocal of the multiplication of the un-availabilities. Therefore, if an intelligent search method discards the states with very small probabilities and captures the states that have most effect on system reliability, the number of states that need to be evaluated can be decreased significantly.

For example, consider a system with ten identical components with availability of 0.95. The probability of all the components are in the up state is 0.59874 and the probability of one component being in the down state is 0.03151. Therefore, the probability order between the two states is 19. The probability of a state with two components are in the down state is 0.00166. The probability order between this state and the state with all components are up state is 361. The probability of the state with all components are in the down state is 9.76563×10^{-14}. Therefore, even with ignoring the states that have small probabilities, we can accurately evaluate the behavior of the system.

For this system, if we consider at most one component being in the down state, we need to evaluate 11 states out of 1024 states and the sum of the probabilities of these states is 0.91386. If we consider at most two components are in the down state, we need to evaluate 56 states out of 1024 states and the sum of the probabilities of these states is 0.98850. This behavior is trivial for small systems with identical components; however, for large systems with non-identical components, it is difficult to trace the behavior of the system analytically. Therefore, if we allow some error tolerance, an intelligent search method can capture the states that have most effect on system reliability. Therefore, the reliability of the system can be approximately evaluated through these states. The indices evaluated from these states, however, will not be equal to the exact indices. Therefore, a method to estimate these indices from the specified states is of necessity. In this work we introduced the concept of complementary to estimate reliability indices.

As the algorithm searches through the state space, the reliability indices and their complementary values become close to each other. For example, the difference between the probability of system failure calculated from the failure states, q, and the probability of system failure calculated from the success states, $p = (1-q)$, goes gradually to zeros as the search progresses. Since, the search method is not intended to visit the entire state space and the reliability indices can approximately evaluated from the relevant states, the reliability indices can be referred to the relevant subspace. Since the sum of probabilities of the entire state space is 1 and the sum of probabilities of the visited states is $q+p$, then a reliability index can estimated over the evaluated subspace as follows,

$$\hat{f}_i(x) = f_i(x) \times \frac{1}{q+p} \tag{7}$$

where $f_i(x)$ is the reliability index under consideration and $\hat{f}_i(x)$ is its estimated value.

6.2 Mathematical Justification

If we evaluate the entire state space and if we denote the loss of load probability q and the probability of load availability p, then the following relationship holds, $q+p=1$.

On the other hand, if we evaluate part of the state space, then $q+p<1$. In this case the estimated value of q is $\hat{q}$, and estimated value of p is $\hat{p}$, will be less than or equal to the exact values, that is $\hat{q} < q$ and $\hat{p} < p$.

If the search tool were able to visit all the failure states without the need to visit the entire state space, then $\hat{q} = q$ and $\hat{p} < p$. On the other hand, if the search tool were able to visit all the success states without the need to visit the entire state space, then $\hat{q} < q$ and $\hat{p} = p$.

Searching for all the failure states or all the success states is computationally expensive and equivalent to state space enumeration. If the search tool intelligently searches uniformly for both success and failure states and if the algorithm does not evaluate the entire state space, then $\hat{q} < q$ and $\hat{p} < p$.

If the algorithm searches for the states that have the most effect on system reliability, then a high cumulative probability of the state space can be evaluated through a small fraction of the state space. Therefore, q and p can be approximated as, $q+p\approx1$.

Through the search process, the q index represents the sum of the probabilities of the failed states visited so far and p index represents the sum of the probabilities of the success states visited so far. The sum of the probabilities of the states visited so far is $q+p$. Therefore, the estimated value of the probabilities of failure over the visited subspace can be expressed as follows,

$$\hat{q} = \frac{q}{q+p} \tag{8}$$

and the estimated value of the probabilities of the success over the visited subspace can be expressed as follows,

$$\hat{p} = \frac{p}{q+p} \tag{9}$$

Same relations can be applied for the other indices that can be calculated from the failure states as well as from the success states.

7. DYNAMICALLY DIRECTED DISCRETE PARTICLE SWARM OPTIMISATION SEARCH METHOD

In performing the proposed heuristic technique, some failure events may not be captured. These events can occur in three scenarios. In the first scenario, an area of the system is isolated from the generation areas (area with loads only) and the transmission lines connecting the loads of this area are sufficient to carry the loads. In the second scenario, an area of only load buses is connected to the rest of the system through a tie line that cannot carry the total load of this area but the transmission lines of this area can carry the load. In the third scenario, line impedances force the power to flow through some capacity limited lines and the power flow will not converge without load curtailment. These scenarios cannot be detected by considering the power carrying capabilities of the transmission lines. Therefore, a search tool should be used to capture these events. However, the search space can be bounded by definite failure subspace and definite success subspace which makes the search method converges to these events with less computational effort.

7.1 State Space Description

Figure 1 shows the state space of a three dimension system. The above reduction technique can detect the definite failure subspace but cannot detect the boundary of the definite success subspace. However, since the reliability indices are evaluated based on the failure states, analysis of the entire success subspace is not important. A large chunk of a success subspace can be truncated by considering all the transmission lines in the up state and determining the vector of minimum generation to satisfy the load. Any state in the state space that has a generation vector larger than or equal to the minimum generation vector is guaranteed to be a success state. Therefore, the boundary of the success subspaces can be used to control the BPSO. Also, most of the unclassified failure states lay around the boundary of the definite failure subspace as shown in Figure 1. Therefore, an intelligent search method, which is bounded between the boundaries of the success and failure subspaces, can efficiently converge to failure states in the unclassified subspace. In this chapter we use "directed" BPSO to search for these states. Nothing sacrosanct about using PSO, any intelligent search algorithm can be used.

7.2 Particle Swarm Optimization

The particle swarm optimization technique (PSO) has been proposed by Kennedy and Eberhart (1995). Later, Kennedy and Eberhart proposed a discrete binary particle swarm optimization (BPSO) to solve combinatorial optimization problems (Kennedy & Eberhart, 1997). The PSO has been proven to be an effective optimization technique and has, therefore, been used in the presented work. In this chapter, we use the BPSO to search for success and failure states rather than looking for optimal solution. In other words, different from common applications of BPSO, BPSO is used in this work as a scanning tool to search for a set of system states that significantly contribute to system reliability indices rather than searching for a single optimum or near optimum point in the state space. Through the scanning and searching process, the algorithm uses probabilities and severities of the visited states to evaluate reliability indices.

Figure 1. Classification of the state space of a three dimension system

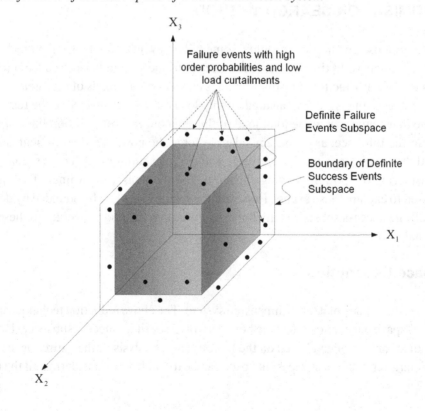

Further, generation and transmission lines states are represented as up or down states; where up states are represented by 1's and down states are represented by 0's. Moreover, we apply bi-objective function that searches through the entire state space for success and failure states. Such objective function is also capable to prevent particles from being trapped to one area of the search space. It is worth noting here that the size of the state space is 2^n where n is the number of system components. Therefore, even for medium systems, the number of states is very large and it is impractical to test the entire state space. Hence, the concept of the estimated indices is adopted in this study so that searching all over the entire state space is reduced (Mitra & Xu, 2010; Patra, Mitra, & Earla, 2006).

BPSO technique searches through the state space and tests the visited states for a possibility of load curtailment. In performing the search process, for every generation, particle velocity v_i or the direction of movement of particle i from position x_i can be governed by the following objective function (Kennedy & Eberhart, 1997; Mitra & Xu, 2010; Patra et al., 2006):

$$v_i^{k+1} = v_i^k + rand() \times c_1 \times \left(P_{pbest_i} - x_i^k\right) + rand() \times c_2 \times \left(P_{gbest_i} - x_i^k\right)$$
$$+ rand() \times c_3 \times \left(C_{pbest_i} - x_i^k\right) + rand() \times c_4 \times \left(C_{gbest_i} - x_i^k\right)$$

$$(10)$$

where k is the iteration number, $rand()$ is a uniformly distributed random number between [0, 1], P_{pbest_i} is the particle best position from the probability of a state prospective particle i has ever encountered, P_{gbest_i} is the group of particles best position from the probability of a state prospective the group has ever encountered, C_{pbest_i} is the particle best position from the load curtailment of a state prospective particle i has ever encountered, C_{gbest_i} is the group of particles best position from load curtailment of a state prospective the group has ever encountered and c_1, c_2, c_3 and c_4 are acceleration factors.

The change in particles positions can be defined by a sigmoid limiting transformation function and a uniformly distributed random number in [0, 1] as following,

$$x_{id} = \begin{cases} 1, & rand() < S\left(v_{id}\right) \\ 0, & \text{otherwise} \end{cases}$$

$$(11)$$

where x_{id} is the dth component of particle i and $S(v_{id})$ is the sigmoid function of dth component of particle i which can be expressed as,

$$S\left(v_{id}\right) = \frac{1}{1 + e^{\left(-v_{id}\right)}}$$

$$(12)$$

Changes of probabilities are limited by V^{max} which limits the ultimate probability of a bit in particle i to have zero or one. Choosing very large or very small values for V^{max} can limit the chance of exploring new vectors. Therefore, a careful selection of V^{max} should be performed. In this work, for a flat start, we have chosen V^{max} to be 2.2 which makes $S(v_{id})$ between 0.9 and 0.1. For next iterations, V^{max} is changed according to particles positions as described in the solution algorithm.

7.3 Use of BPSO in Power System Reliability Evaluation

One of the differences between using BPSO in power system reliability evaluation and Monte Carlo is that the former evaluates the relativity indices by summing up the probabilities of the visited states, while in the latter; the reliability indices are evaluated by dividing the number of encountered failure states to the number of samples. It is well known that Monte Carlo simulation is extremely time consuming in calculating reliability indices for the designated accuracy. However, in performing Monte Carlo simulation, no need to visit all system states since it calculates the weighted values not the exact values. On the other hand, to calculate reliability indices using BPSO, all failure states or success states need to be visited, which is computationally expensive, if not impossible for large systems. Therefore, another technique to overcome this drawback is required. New indices have been introduced in (Mitra & Xu, 2010; Patra et al., 2006) which are normalized LOLP, ($LOLP_{norm}$) and projected LOLP, ($LOLP_{proj}$) to eliminate the necessity of visiting all the failure and success states. The $LOLP_{norm}$ is the ratio between the sum of the probabilities of the failure states (LOLP) to the sum of probabilities of the states encountered so far (1+LOLP-DLOLP); where DLOLP is the dual value of the LOLP which is one minus the sum of probabilities of the success states encountered so far (1-sum of the probabilities of the visited success states). The $LOLP_{proj}$ is the crossings between the tangents of the LOLP and DLOLP. The normalized LOLP can be expressed as follows,

$$LOLP_{norm} = \frac{LOLP}{1 + LOLP - DLOLP}$$
(13)

Again, $LOLP_{norm}$ and $LOLP_{proj}$ are the same as the weighted LOLP index used in Monte Carlo simulation. However, $LOLP_{proj}$ converges to the approximate value of the LOLP faster than $LOLP_{norm}$ (Mitra & Xu, 2010). It can be noted that even though BPSO and Monte Carlo Simulation both evaluate the weighted index, the number of states to be visited using BPSO is significantly less than the number of states to be visited using MCS (Mitra & Xu, 2010).

7.4 Roll of BPSO in Reliability Evaluation

Different from common applications of BPSO, BPSO is used in this work as a scanning tool to search for a set of system states that significantly contribute to system reliability indices rather than searching for a single optimum or near optimum point in the state space. Through the scanning and searching process, the algorithm uses probabilities and severities of the visited states to evaluate reliability indices. However, if the search process is not set properly, BPSO may converge to a single point and no new states would be discovered. If this is the case, reliability indices might be over or under estimated. Several methods have been proposed to spread the search of the PIS methods (Miranda, Keko, & Duque, 2008; Parsopoulos & Vrahatis, 2002; Peram, Veeramachaneni, & Mohan, 2003; Miranda, Carvalho, Rosa, Silva, & Singh, 2009; Wang & Singh, 2008). In (Miranda et al., 2009), it has been found that forgetting the global best and resetting the memory term improves the spreading of the PIS methods. In this work, this method is adapted.

7.5 Directed BPSO

By examining the state space, all possible outcomes of the combination of generation and transmission, the probabilities of the upper part states are larger than the probabilities of the lower part states. Further, load curtailments of the lower part states are larger than load curtailments of the upper part states. If the swarm was to fly on the upper part, it is unlikely to encounter failure states and the opposite is true for the lower part. As mentioned above, using multi-objective function does not guarantee that the particles will fly on the desired search space unless the weighting factors are chosen carefully. Figure 2 and Figure 3 show two situations for badly chosen weighting factors of the objective function. Figure 2-(a) and Figure 3-(a) show the behavior of the particles and Figure 2-(b) and Figure 3-(b) show the expected profile of the reliability indices. In Figure 2, the swarm is trapped to the upper corner of the state space. In this case the normalized LOLP as well as the projected LOLP will be under estimated. As the particles continue to fly on the upper corner, most of the visited states will be success states and more

Figure 2. Reliability indices profile in case the particles are trapped to the upper corner of the state space

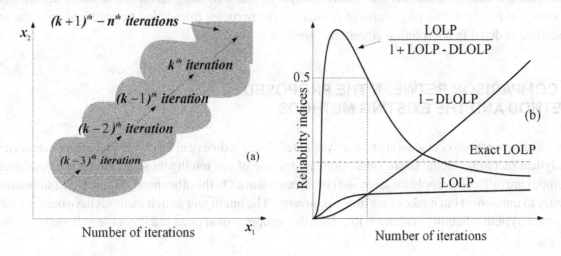

Figure 3. Reliability indices profile in case the particles are trapped to the lower corner of the state space

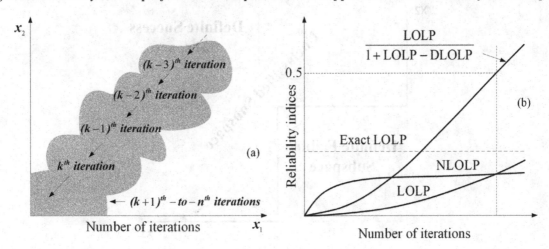

likely no failure states will be captured. Therefore, no much change in the LOLP and the 1-DLOLP is sharply increasing. On the other hand, if the swarm is trapped into the lower corner as shown in Figure 3, most of the visited states will be failure states and unlikely to encounter success states. In this case, LOLP, LOLP_{norm} as well as the LOLP_{proj} will be overestimated. The LOLP index will continue to increase whereas the 1-DLOLP index remains almost constant.

To direct the BPSO to fly on the unclassified subspace and overcome the difficulty of choosing the weighting factors as well as the change in probability limit, we propose a technique that tracks both the normalized LOLP and the number of the new visited states or the mutation rate. This technique was developed based on the normalized loss of load probability index (LOLP_{norm}). The LOLP_{norm} has been introduced in (Mitra & Xu, 2010; Patra et al., 2006) to estimate the LOLP index without the need of searching the entire state space. After performing a few iterations, if LOLP_{norm} continues to increase that means the particles are trapped in the lower corner of the search space. On the other hand, if LOLP_{norm} continues to decrease, that means the particles are trapped in the upper corner of the search space. Also, if no new states are visited and the designated reliability index does not converge to the specified accuracy, then V^{max} is limiting the probability of bit change. Also, if the algorithm discovers that the swarm is entered the classified success and failure subspaces, the weighting factor are adjusted accordingly as shown in Figure 4. The procedures of preventing the particles from being trapped into one area are described in detail in the solution algorithm.

8. COMPARISON BETWEEN THE PROPOSED METHOD AND THE EXISTING METHODS

The existing methods of evaluating power system reliability indices can be divided into three categories: analytical methods, Monte Carlo simulation and the use of the intelligent search methods. Analytical methods are difficult to apply for large and complex systems. On the other hand, Monte Carlo simulation is easy to implement but it takes long time to converge. The intelligent search methods have been utilized in power system reliability evaluation to reduce the computational time. Intelligent search methods have

Figure 4. Redirecting the swarm in case it enters the success or failure subspaces

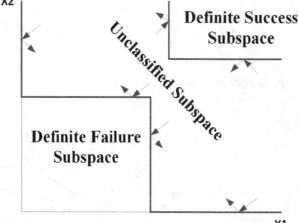

been used in power system reliability to search for failure and success state in the entire state space such as the methods presented in (Mitra & Xu, 2010; Patra et al., 2006). Also, the intelligent search methods have been used in pruning the success subspace and applying Monte Carlo simulation on the remaining part of the state space such as the methods presented in (Green, Wang, & Singh, 2010; Green et al. 2010; Green et al. 2010a; Green et al. 2011; Green et al. 2011a; Green, Wang, Alam, & Singh, 2011a; Zhao & Singh, 2010).

The proposed method prunes both the success and failure subspaces using heuristic techniques and applies a directed BPSO to search for the failure states in the unclassified subspace. The existing methods apply Monte Carlo simulation to search for failure states in the unclassified subspace which requires a significant number of iterations to converge. Also, applying the intelligent search methods on the entire state space can be computationally expensive due to the fact that for each state an optimal power flow it performed. Further, using intelligent search methods for searching for failure and/or success states without the use of a device that directs the swarm can lead to incorrect results (Mitra & Xu, 2010; Patra et al., 2006).

In this chapter, we use a heuristic technique to classify the state space into success, failure and unclassified subspaces. After classifying the state space, a "directed" BPSO is used to search for failure states in the unclassified subspace. From the behavior of the first generations of the BPSO, we use a device to direct the swarm as is explained section 11.

9. CALCULATION OF THE RELIABILITY INDICES

In this work, we have evaluated the well know composite power system reliability indices, namely loss of load probability (LOLP), expected demand not supplied (EDNS), loss of energy expectation LOEE), and loss of load expectation (LOLE). A stopping criterion has been applied to stop the algorithm from sampling if it converges to the desired accuracy.

9.1 Calculation of Probability Indices

The estimated value of the LOLP index can be calculated as follows,

$$LOLP = \sum_{i \in F} P_i(x) \tag{14}$$

where F is the set of states that have load curtailments, $P_i(x)$ is probability of state i and x represents the state of the system. The estimated dual value of the DLOLP index can be expressed as,

$$DLOLP = 1 - \sum_{i \in S} P_i(x) \tag{15}$$

where S is the set of states that do not have load curtailments.

The loss of load probability is approximated by the trajectory of the crossings between the tangents of the LOLP and DLOLP. Both LOLP and DLOLP are monotonically increasing functions and they eventually will reach each other. The loss of load expectation index can be calculated from the loss of load probability index by multiplying by the study period.

9.2 Calculation of Energy Indices

The estimated value of the EDNS index can be calculated as follows,

$$\text{EDNS} = \sum_{i \in F} P_i(x) \times C_i(x) \tag{16}$$

where C_i is the amount of load curtailment of state i. The dual value of the EDNS index is the expected supplied demand. The estimated dual value of the EDNS index (DEDNS) can be expressed as,

$$\text{DEDNS} = \text{Peak Load} - \sum_{i \in S} P_i(x) \times L_i(x) \tag{17}$$

where $L_i(x)$ is the amount of the supplied load of state i.

The expected demand not supplied index is approximated by the trajectory of the crossings between the tangents of the EDNS and DEDNS. Both EDNS and DEDNS are monotonically increasing functions and they eventually will reach each other. The loss of energy expectation index can be calculated from the expected demand not supplied index by multiplying by the study period.

9.3 Calculation of Bus Indices

Calculation of bus indices using linear programming produces multiple solutions and hence bus indices will not be unique (Billinton & Li, 1994). To overcome this difficulty, load curtailment philosophies need to be incorporated in the linear programming problem (Billinton & Li, 1994). Such philosophies can be the priority of each load or part of each load. Also, load can be curtailed according to closeness to the fault location. In this chapter, the loads were divided into three parts with different weighting factors for each part, e.g., w_1, w_2 and w_3 respectively. The first two parts were assumed to represent 25% of the total load and the third part was assumed to represent 50% of the total load. The weighting factor of the first part is assumed to be less than that of the second part and the weighting factor of the second part is assumed to be less than that of the third part or in other words, $w_1 < w_2 < w_3$.

9.4 Modelling of System Components

9.4.1 Modelling of Available Generation

Most buses have several generators which may be similar or different. The unit addition algorithm (Singh & Chen, 1989) is used to construct a discrete probability distribution function for each bus which is known as capacity outage probability and frequency table, COPAFT. This table is constructed based on the capacity states and forced outage rates of units at each bus.

9.4.2 Modelling of System Load

Loads at the buses are modelled based on the cluster load model technique (Singh & Chen, 1989; Singh & Lago-Gonzalez, 1989; Lago-Gonzalez & Singh, 1990; Singh & Deng, 1991). From the chronological loads, clusters are constructed according to the load level and its probability. These clusters are used for each load bus as a percentage of the peak load of the given bus.

9.4.3 Modelling of Transmission Lines

A discrete probability density function is constructed for every transmission line. If a line is tripped for some system state, the line is removed from the bus admittance matrix and its capacity is set to zero.

9.5 Stopping Criteria

A convergence criterion should be applied to stop the algorithm if there is not much change in the reliability indices. In power system reliability analysis using Monte Carlo simulation it was found to be that energy indices are the slowest indices from convergence view point (Billinton & Li, 1994). In this work, we have applied the stopping criterion on the EDNS index.

The stopping criterion considering the EDNS index can be expressed as,

$$\sigma = \frac{\sqrt{Var\left(\mathrm{EDNS}\right)}}{E\left[\mathrm{EDNS}\right]} \qquad (18)$$

where $E\left[\bullet\right]$ is the expectation operator and $Var\left(\bullet\right)$ is the variance function.

After few iterations, the amount of the change in σ is calculated, if this amount is less than or equal to the specified tolerance, the algorithm is to be terminated; otherwise, the simulation will continue.

10. SENSITIVITY ANALYSIS

Sensitivity analyses of reliability indices reported in the literature have been based on calculating the amount of change of these indices with respect to component parameters such as availability, unavailability, capacity, failure rate and repair rate. One of the advantages of the sensitivity analysis is that it allows planners to distribute the available resources in a cost-effect paradigm to enhance system reliability. In the research reported in this chapter, a shadow-price based method is proposed for performing the sensitivity analysis. Shadow prices are used here as indicators of the area or component in which the investment will improve system reliability. The analyses are performed by casting the dispatch operation as an optimization problem, through minimizing load curtailment or maximizing load supplying capability. The optimization is constrained by generator and transmission line capacities.

Shadow price approach was initially proposed by the former Soviet Union economist *Conte Petrovic* in the late 1930s when he was applying linear programming technique to maximize the output of some products (Li, Qu, & Cui, 2009). Several definitions have been reported in the literature for the shadow price (Ramanujan, Li, & Higham, 2009). For instance, from a primal-dual perspective, it can be defined as the primal (x) and dual (y) solutions of the linear programming problem. From the optimization point of view; however, shadow price can be interpreted as the rate of change in the objective function for an infinitesimal change in the right-hand side of the linear programming problem. From a geometric perspective, shadow price can be understood as the sub-gradients of the objective function along the dimension of resource provisioning changes. As it is seen in this section, shadow price approach has numerous applications in different areas due to its multi-facet nature. It has been used in (Li, Liu, & Salazar, 2006) to forecast the short-term transmission congestion. It has also been used in the evaluation of some construction projects and management (Hui, Pei, & Jie, 2009). However, as was mentioned earlier, shadow price has been used here as a decision-making tool for minimum load curtailment.

The most commonly used indices in composite power system are: Loss of Load Probability (LOLP), probability of system failure to meet the demand, Loss of Load Frequency (LOLF), the expected frequency of encountering failure states, and Expected Demand Not Supplied (EDNS), expected demand not supplied due to system deficiency. LOLP and LOLF from their definitions are based on reliability parameters and cannot be directly related to the operating limits. On the other hand, EDNS is based on failure rates, repair rates and units capacities.

10.1 Sensitivity Analysis of LOLP and LOLF with Respect to Component Parameters

Sensitivity studies of LOLP and LOLF to component reliability have been amply described in the literature. Sensitivity analysis can be conducted analytically by enumerating all system states or by simulation. The work in (Melo & Pereira, 1995; Y. Zhao, Zhou, Zhou, & X. Zhao, 2006; Zhu, 2006; Benidris & Mitra, 2014) provides relationships that are suitable for use in state space enumeration.

The sensitivity of LOLP with respect to unavailability u_i of component i can be calculated as follows.

$$\frac{\partial \text{LOLP}}{\partial u_i} = \sum_{x \in X} I_f(x) P(x) \left[\frac{1}{u_i} - \frac{S_i}{(a_i u_i)} \right] \tag{19}$$

where X is the set of all states, x is the state of the system, $P(x)$ is the probability of occurrence of state x, u_i is the probability of failure of component i and a_i is the probability of success of component i. Also, S_i is the state indicator of component i, i.e., $S_i=0$ if component i is in the down state (failure state) and $S_i=1$ if component i is in the up state (success state) and $I_f(x)$ is the system state indicator function which can be expressed as follows.

$$I_f(x) = \begin{cases} 1, & \text{if } x \text{ is a failure state} \\ 0, & \text{if } x \text{ is a success state} \end{cases} \tag{20}$$

Proof:

$$\frac{\partial \text{LOLP}}{\partial u_i} = \sum_{x \in X} \left\{ \left[\partial I_f(x) \big/ \partial u_i \right] P(x) + I_f(x) \left[\partial P(x) \big/ \partial u_i \right] \right\}$$

$$= \sum_{x \in X} I_f(x) \left\{ \left[\partial \left(P(S_1) P(S_2) \cdots P(S_i) \cdots P(S_m) \right) \big/ \partial u_i \right] \right\}$$

$$= \sum_{x \in X} I_f(x) P(x) \left[1 \big/ P(S_i) \right] \left[\partial P(S_i) \big/ \partial u_i \right]$$

If $S_i = 1$,

$$\left[1 / P(S_i) \right] \left[\partial P(S_i) / \partial u_i \right] = \left[1 / P(S_i = 1) \right] \left[\partial P(S_i = 1) / \partial u_i \right] = 1 / a_i \left(\frac{\partial a_i}{\partial u_i} \right) = -1 / a_i = -S_i / a_i$$

where $a_i + u_i = 1$ and

$$\frac{\partial a_i}{\partial u_i} = \frac{\partial (1 - u_i)}{\partial u_i} = -1$$

If $S_i = 0$,

$$\left[1 / P(S_i) \right] \left[\partial P(S_i) / \partial u_i \right] = \left[1 / P(S_i = 0) \right] \left[\partial P(S_i = 0) / \partial u_i \right]$$

$$= 1 / u_i \left(\frac{\partial u_i}{\partial u_i} \right) = 1 / u_i = (1 - S_i) / u_i$$

Therefore, in general,

$$\left[1 / P(S_i) \right] \left[\partial P(S_i) / \partial u_i \right] = (1 - S_i) / u_i - S_i / a_i = 1 / u_i - S_i / (a_i u_i)$$

The sensitivity of LOLP with respect to component failure rate λ_i is given by,

$$\frac{\partial \text{LOLP}}{\partial \lambda_i} = \sum_{x \in X} I_f(x) P(x) \left[\frac{a_i}{\lambda_i} - \frac{S_i}{\lambda_i} \right] \tag{21}$$

Proof:

$$\frac{\partial \text{LOLP}}{\partial \lambda_i} = \sum_{x \in X} \left\{ \left[\partial I_f(x) / \partial \lambda_i \right] P(x) + I_f(x) \left[\partial P(x) / \partial \lambda_i \right] \right\}$$

$$= \sum_{x \in X} I_f(x) \left\{ \left[\partial \left(P(S_1) P(S_2) \cdots P(S_i) \cdots P(S_m) \right) / \partial \lambda_i \right] \right\}$$

$$= \sum_{x \in X} I_f(x) P(x) \left[1 / P(S_i) \right] \left[\partial P(S_i) / \partial \lambda_i \right]$$

If $S_i = 1$,

$$\left[1 / P(S_i) \right] \left[\partial P(S_i) / \partial \lambda_i \right] = \left[1 / P(S_i = 1) \right] \left[\partial P(S_i = 1) / \partial \lambda_i \right]$$

$$= 1 / a_i \left(\frac{\partial a_i}{\partial \lambda_i} \right) = -1 / (\lambda_i + \mu_i) = -S_i / (\lambda_i + \mu_i)$$

where

$$a_i = \mu_i / (\lambda_i + \mu_i)$$

$$u_i = \lambda_i / (\lambda_i + \mu_i).$$

Then,

$$\frac{\partial a_i}{\partial \lambda_i} = \frac{\partial \left(\mu_i / (\lambda_i + \mu_i) \right)}{\partial \lambda_i} = -1 / (\lambda_i + \mu_i)$$

If $S_i = 0$,

$$\left[1 / P(S_i) \right] \left[\partial P(S_i) / \partial \lambda_i \right] = \left[1 / P(S_i = 0) \right] \left[\partial P(S_i = 0) / \partial \lambda_i \right] = 1 / u_i \left(\frac{\partial u_i}{\partial \lambda_i} \right)$$

$$= (1 / u_i) \left(\mu_i / (\lambda_i + \mu_i)^2 \right) = (1 / u_i) a_i \left(1 / (\lambda_i + \mu_i) \right)$$

$$= (a_i / u_i) \left(1 / (\lambda_i + \mu_i) \right) = (a_i / u_i)(1 - S_i) / (\lambda_i + \mu_i)$$

Therefore, in general,

$$\left[1 / P(S_i) \right] \left[\partial P(S_i) / \partial \lambda_i \right] = -S_i / (\lambda_i + \mu_i) + (a_i / u_i)(1 - S_i) / (\lambda_i + \mu_i) = a_i / \lambda_i - S_i / \lambda_i$$

The sensitivity of LOLP with respect to component repair rate μ_i is given by

$$\frac{\partial \text{LOLP}}{\partial \mu_i} = \sum_{x \in X} I_f(x) P(x) \left[-\frac{a_i}{\mu_i} + \frac{S_i}{\mu_i} \right] \tag{22}$$

Proof:

$$\frac{\partial \text{LOLP}}{\partial \mu_i} = \sum_{x \in X} \left\{ \left[\partial I_f(x) / \partial \mu_i \right] P(x) + I_f(x) \left[\partial P(x) / \partial \mu_i \right] \right\}$$

$$= \sum_{x \in X} I_f(x) \left\{ \left[\partial \left(P(S_1) P(S_2) ... P(S_i) ... P(S_m) \right) / \partial \mu_i \right] \right\}$$

$$= \sum_{x \in X} I_f(x) P(x) \left[1 / P(S_i) \right] \left[\partial P(S_i) / \partial \mu_i \right]$$

If $S_i = 1$,

$$\left[1 / P(S_i) \right] \left[\partial P(S_i) / \partial \mu_i \right] = \left[1 / P(S_i = 1) \right] \left[\partial P(S_i = 1) / \partial \mu_i \right] = 1 / a_i \left(\frac{\partial a_i}{\partial \mu_i} \right)$$

$$= (u_i / a_i)(1 / (\lambda_i + \mu_i)) = (u_i / a_i)(S_i / (\lambda_i + \mu_i))$$

where

$$\frac{\partial a_i}{\partial \mu_i} = \frac{\partial \left(\mu_i / (\lambda_i + \mu_i) \right)}{\partial \mu_i} = \lambda_i / (\lambda_i + \mu_i)^2$$

If $S_i = 0$,

$$\left[1 / P(S_i) \right] \left[\partial P(S_i) / \partial \mu_i \right] = \left[1 / P(S_i = 0) \right] \left[\partial P(S_i = 0) / \partial \mu_i \right] = \frac{1}{u_i \left(\dfrac{\partial u_i}{\partial \mu_i} \right)}$$

$$= \left(\frac{1}{u_i} \right) \left(-\frac{\lambda_i}{(\lambda_i + \mu_i)^2} \right) = -\frac{1}{(\lambda_i + \mu_i)} = -(1 - S_i) / (\lambda_i + \mu_i)$$

Therefore, in general,

$$\left[1 / P(S_i) \right] \left[\partial P(S_i) / \partial \mu_i \right] = (u_i / a_i)(S_i / (\lambda_i + \mu_i)) - (1 - S_i) / (\lambda_i + \mu_i) = -a_i / \mu_i + S_i / \mu_i$$

Sensitivity analysis of the LOLF index with respect to the reliability parameters can be derived in the same manner of derivation of the sensitivity analysis of the LOLP index. The sensitivity of LOLF with respect to unavailability u_i of component i can be calculated as follows.

$$\frac{\partial \text{LOLF}}{\partial u_i} = \sum_{x \in X}\left[-I_f(x)P(x)\left(\frac{S_i \mu_i}{a_i^2}\right) + F(x)P(x)\left(\frac{1}{u_i} - \frac{S_i}{a_i u_i}\right)\right] \quad (23)$$

where $F(x)$ is the sum of the repair rates of a failure state x that crosses the boundary and can be expressed as:

$$F(x) = I_f(x)\sum_{i=1}^{m}\lambda_i^{in}(x) \quad (24)$$

where m is the number of components, and

$$\lambda_i^{in}(x) = (1 - S_i)\mu_i - \frac{S_i \mu_i u_i}{a_i} \quad (25)$$

The sensitivity of LOLF with respect to component failure rate λ_i is given by

$$\frac{\partial \text{LOLF}}{\partial \lambda_i} = \sum_{x \in X}\left[-I_f(x)P(x)S_i + F(x)P(x)\left(\frac{a_i}{\lambda_i} - \frac{S_i}{\lambda_i}\right)\right] \quad (26)$$

The sensitivity of LOLF with respect to component repair rate μ_i is given by

$$\frac{\partial \text{LOLF}}{\partial \mu_i} = \sum_{x \in X}\left[I_f(x)(1 - S_i)P(x) + F(x)P(x)\left(-\frac{a_i}{\mu_i} + \frac{S_i}{\mu_i}\right)\right] \quad (27)$$

10.2 Sensitivity Analysis of EDNS

The Expected Demand Not Supplied (EDNS) is an important index because it inherently reflects the severity of reliability events. The sensitivities of this index with respect to u_i, λ_i and μ_i are the same as for the LOLP index except that they are multiplied by the amount of load curtailments. The sensitivity analysis of the EDNS with respect component capacities was derived as follows (Y. Zhao, et al., 2006; Zhu, 2006; Benidris & Mitra, 2014).

$$\frac{\partial EDNS}{\partial C_i} = \sum_{x \in X}I_f(x)P(x)\left(\frac{\partial L_c(x)}{\partial C_i}\right) \quad (28)$$

where C_i is the capacity of component i and $L_c(x)$ is the total load curtailment when the system is at state x. The derivative of the total load curtailment with respect to component capacity can be expressed as

$$\partial L_c\left(x\right)\Big/_{\partial C_i} = \begin{cases} \pi_{g,i}, & \text{if component } i \text{ is a generator} \\ \pi_{t,ij}, & \text{if component } i \text{ is a circuit} \end{cases} \tag{29}$$

where $\pi_{g,i}$ and $\pi_{t,ij}$ are the Lagrange multipliers or shadow prices of generation capacity constraints and transmission lines carrying capability constraints respectively. $\pi_{g,i}$ can be calculated directly from the optimization problem of (1). However, $\pi_{t,ij}$ depends on circuit parameters which are circuit capacity and susceptance. These two parameters are dependent variables and cannot be treated separately. Pereira and Pinto (1985) combined the effect of circuit capacity and susceptance on circuit sensitivity and developed the following expression.

$$\pi_{t,ij} = \left(\pi_{d,i} - \pi_{d,j}\right) \times \left(\theta_j - \theta_i\right) \tag{30}$$

where $\pi_{d,i}$ and $\pi_{d,j}$ are Lagrange multipliers or shadow prices of load constraints of buses i and j respectively and θ_j and θ_i are voltage angles of buses j and i respectively.

11. SOLUTION ALGORITHM

The solution algorithm explains the flow of the procedures of evaluating the reliability indices as well as the technique used to direct and prevent the particles from being trapped in a search subspace. The steps can be explained as follows:

1. Initialize the positions and velocities of the particles, x_i and v_i respectively. Particles positions are initialized by using the forced outage rates of system components; components that are in the up state are represented by 1's and components in the down state are represented in 0's. The length of a particle string equals the number of components. Velocities are initialized to have V^{max} equals 2.2 (probability limits are between 0.9 and 0.1).
2. Check if there are identical particles. If so, discard the identical ones and save the rest of the particles in a temporary array vector by converting the binary numbers to decimal numbers. Check if there are particles already exist in the database, if so set probabilities and load curtailments of the existing particles to zeros to decrease the chance of visiting these states again. Then, save the rest in the database and go to the next step.
3. Compute the exact probability of each particle which represents the probability of a system state. If the probability of a particle is less than a threshold, ε, discard this particle, otherwise go to the next step. In this work, ε was chosen to be 10^{-15}.
4. Set system parameters and update generation and transmission lines status for every particle. Perform the linear programming optimization problem to check if there are load curtailments. Update the reliability indices.

5. Determine and update personal best states' probabilities and best load curtailments. Also, determine and update best global probability and best global load curtailment. Update particles velocities using (4) and update particles positions using (5) and (6).

6. Check the normalized LOLP (LOLP$_{norm}$) whether it is increasing or decreasing and adjust c_1, c_2, c_3 and c_4 accordingly. If it is increasing, increase the values of c_1 and c_2 and decrease the values of c_3 and c_4. Perform the opposite if LOLP$_{norm}$ is decreasing. In this work we adjusted the amount of increasing or decreasing these coefficients according to the amount of change of the LOLP$_{norm}$. Any strategy can be used to adjust these factors. However, the optimum adjustment of these factors is out of the scope of this work. We related the amount of change of these coefficients to the amount of change in LOLP$_{norm}$, (ΔLOLP$_{norm}$), in an exponential form as follows,

$$c_{(1,2)-new} = c_{(1,2)-old} \times e^{(100 \times \Delta LOLP_{norm})}$$

$$c_{(3,4)-new} = c_{(3,4)-old} \times e^{(-100 \times \Delta LOLP_{norm})}$$

7. Check if any of the particles has entered the success and/or failure subspaces. If a particle has entered the success subspace, redirect the particle by using the objective of maximum load curtailment only (ignoring the objective of maximum probability) by setting c_1 and c_2 to zeros. If a particle has entered the failure subspace, redirect the particle by using the objective of maximum probability only (ignoring the objective of maximum load curtailment) by setting c_3 and c_4 to zeros.

8. Check for convergence. If the stopping criterion is met, stop; otherwise go to the next step.

9. Determine the number of newly visited states since the previous iteration. If the number of the new states is less than a threshold, adjust V^{max} and then go to step 2; otherwise go directly to step 2. The threshold is chosen to be 80% of the total number of particles for the first 10 iterations, 50% for the next 10 iterations and 20% thereafter. V^{max} is adjusted according to the direction of the LOLP$_{norm}$ index. If the particles are searching around the success subspace, adjust V^{max} to a large number. On the other hand, if the particles are searching around the failure subspace, adjust V^{max} to a small number. In this work we have chosen 4.0 to be the large number and 2.0 to the small number. Again, the optimum value of V^{max} to better improve the behavior of the search method is out of the scope of this work.

The flowchart of the solution algorithm is shown in Figure 5.

12. APPLICATION

The proposed formulation was applied on two systems, the IEEE RTS (Reliability Test System Task Force of the Application of Probability Methods Subcommittee, 1979) and the modified version of the IEEE RTS. The configuration of the IEEE RTS is shown in Figure 6. The IEEE RTS System has been extensively tested for power system reliability analysis. IEEE RTS consists of 24 buses, 38 transmission lines/transformers (33 transmission lines and 5 transformers) and 32 generating units on 10 buses. The total generation of this system is 3405 MW and total peak load is 2850 MW.

Figure 5. Flowchart of the solution algorithm

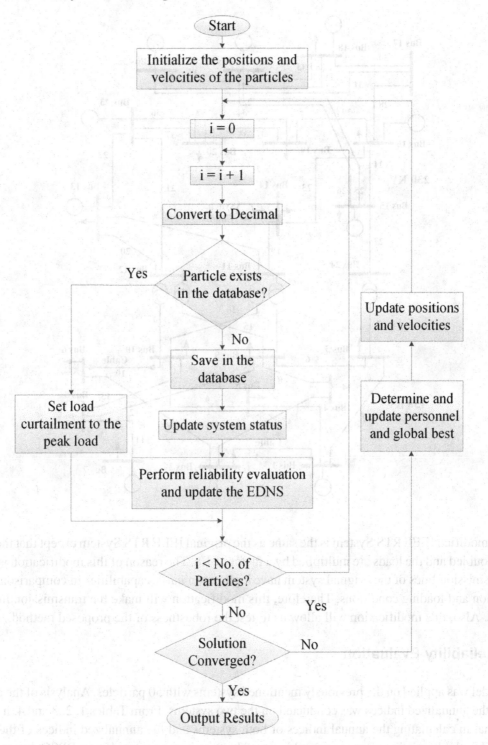

Figure 6. Single line diagram of the IEEE RTS

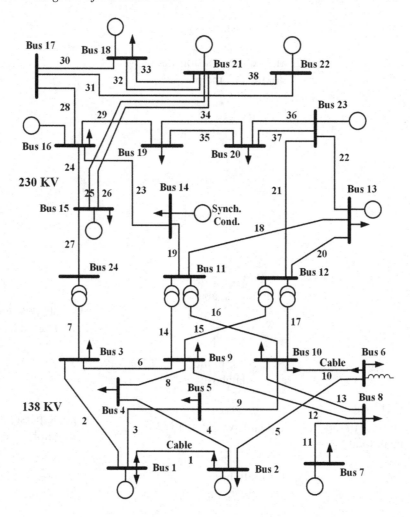

The modified IEEE RTS System is the same as the original IEEE RTS System except that the generation is doubled and the loads are multiplied by a factor of 1.8. The reason of this modification is because the transmission lines of the original system have high power carry capabilities in comparison with the generation and loading conditions. Therefore, this modification will make the transmission lines more stressed. Also, this modification will allow us to test the robustness of the proposed method.

12.1 Reliability Evaluation

The model was applied on the previously mentioned systems with 50 particles. Analysis of the annual as well as the annualized indices was conducted on the two systems. From Tables 1, 2, 3 and 4, it has been found that in calculating the annual indices of both systems and the annualized indices of the original IEEE RTS, the heuristic technique was able to evaluate system indices and no BPSO was performed (terminated after few iterations). On the other hand, in calculating the annualized indices of the modified IEEE RTS, the heuristic technique was not able to evaluate system indices and therefore the proposed BPSO was used to search for the unclassified subspace. Also, from Table 4, the unclassified subspace has a significant effect on the LOLP and LOEE indices and very small effect on the EDNS and LOLE indices. These effects can be interpreted as the unclassified subspace has failure states with relatively high probability but with relatively small load curtailments. This also can be attributed to the fact that failure states that are located far from the origin (all components are in the down state) have high probability and small load curtailments. Therefore, if we were looking for just the EDNS and LOLE indices, the heuristic technique would be enough for this case.

Table 1. Annual indices of the IEEE RTS

Algorithm		LOLP	EDNS MW/yr	LOEE MWh/yr	LOLE h/yr
Proposed	Heuristic	0.00117	0.16374	1430.465	10.22112
	BPSO	---	---	---	---
	Sum	0.00117	0.16374	1430.465	10.22112
Conventional		0.00119	0.16412	1433.752	10.39584

Table 2. Annualized indices of the IEEE RTS

Algorithm		LOLP	EDNS MW/yr	LOEE MWh/yr	LOLE h/yr
Proposed	Heuristic	0.08429	14.67784	128225.60	736.360
	BPSO	---	---	---	---
	Sum	0.08429	14.67784	128225.60	736.360
Conventional		0.08451	14.59761	127524.72	738.279

Table 3. Annual indices of the modified IEEE RTS

Algorithm		LOLP	EDNS MW/yr	LOEE MWh/yr	LOLE h/yr
Proposed	Heuristic	0.00106	0.07395	645.90125	9.26016
	BPSO	---	---	---	---
	Sum	0.00106	0.07395	645.90125	9.26016
Conventional		0.00105	0.07436	649.61330	9.17280

Table 4. Annualized indices of the Modified IEEE RTS

Algorithm		LOLP	EDNS MW/yr	LOEE MWh/yr	LOLE h/yr
Proposed	Heuristic	0.06039	10.31755	90134.083	517.259
	BPSO	0.00976	0.12171	1063.256	85.263
	Sum	0.07015	10.43926	91197.375	612.830
Conventional		0.07017	10.44237	91224.549	613.005

Tables 5 and 6 show the reduction in the computational time by using the proposed algorithm as a percentage of the time of evaluating the same indices using Monte Carlo simulation. These times account for calculating the bus indices for all cases. The average base time using Monte Carlo simulation was found to be 1175 seconds for both systems. Table 7 shows the annual bus indices of the original IEEE RTS.

Table 5. Reduction in the computational time of the IEEE RTS

Category	Time Spent by		Total Time (Seconds)	Time Reduction (%)
	Heuristic Technique (Seconds)	BPSO (Seconds)		
Annual	28.66	0	28.66	97.56
Annualized	144.28	0	144.28	87.72

Table 6. Reduction in the computational time of the Modified IEEE RTS

Category	Time Spent by		Total Time (Seconds)	Time Reduction (%)
	Heuristic Technique (Seconds)	BPSO (Seconds)		
Annual	55.60	0	55.60	95.27
Annualized	336.15	409.75	745.90	36.52

Table 7. Bus annual indices for the IEEE RTS

Bus No.	LOLP	EDNS MW	LOEE MWh/yr	LOLE hr/yr
1	0.00032	0.00555	48.50943	2.75184
2	0.00002	0.00034	2.929904	0.17472
3	0.00006	0.00188	16.41914	0.52416
4	0.00044	0.00530	46.26799	3.80016
5	0.00124	0.01473	128.67821	10.78896
6	0.00042	0.00423	36.93749	3.66912
7	0.00021	0.00398	34.78341	1.79088
8	0.00013	0.00308	26.94283	1.09200
9	0.00005	0.00125	10.90315	0.43680
10	0.00008	0.00238	20.78260	0.69888
13	0.00028	0.01001	87.42760	2.40240
14	0.00096	0.02881	251.65359	8.34288
15	0.00070	0.03126	273.12752	6.11520
16	0.00110	0.01813	158.37621	9.60960
18	0.00018	0.00862	75.30948	1.52880
19	0.00012	0.00329	28.73840	1.04832
20	0.00037	0.00744	64.97050	3.18864

From Tables 1, 2 to 5, the proposed heuristic technique in conjunction with the directed BPSO has accurately evaluated the reliability indices with less computational time than Monte Carlo simulations. For IEEE RTS, the reduction in the computational time is around 97.56% for calculating the annual indices whereas for the annualized indices the reduction in the computational time is around 87.72%. For both cases, evaluating annual and annualized indices, the heuristic technique was able to capture the most relevant failure states. However, for the annualized indices, the computational time was longer than the case of the annual indices due to the fact that for annual indices the system is assumed to operate at the peak load.

From Tables 3, 4 to 6, the proposed heuristic technique in conjunction with the directed BPSO has accurately evaluated the reliability indices with less computational time than Monte Carlo simulations. For Modified IEEE RTS, the reduction in the computational time is around 95.27% for calculating the annual indices whereas for the annualized indices the reduction in the computational time is around 36.52%. For the case of evaluating annual indices, the heuristic technique was able to capture the most relevant failure states. However, for the case of evaluating the annualized indices, some significate failure states were not captured by the heuristic technique. In this case, the BPSO was used to search for the failure states in the unclassified subspace.

The comparison between the proposed method and Monte Carlo simulation was used due the fact that Monte Carlo simulation has been used for long time in composite power system reliability evaluation. A comparison between the proposed method and the existing methods can be easily performed. For instance, applying the intelligent search methods such as PSO, GA, BACO, etc., on the entire state space could evaluate the reliability indices of power systems roughly in about the same computational time. However, as it is clear from the presented results, the heuristic technique has reduced the computational time significantly.

Reliability indices at the buses reflect the curtailment or load shedding at each bus according to the philosophy of the applied load shedding procedure. For example, different load shedding philosophies would produce different bus indices. Some loads can be given high priority so that these loads will not be interrupted unless load shedding is not avoidable. In this chapter, the loads were divided into three parts with different weighting factors as discussed previously.

12.2 Sensitivity Analysis

The proposed formulation was applied on the IEEE RTS (Reliability Test System Task Force of the Application of Probability Methods Subcommittee, 1979) and the results are shown in Tables 8, 9 and 10. In these tables, the sign (#) denotes the bus number and (G) denotes the capacity, i.e., #13G197 means bus 13 generating unit capacity 197 MW. From Table 8, 9 and 10, it is clear that the generating unit (400 MW) at bus 18 has the highest effect on all the studied reliability indices followed by the generating units of buses 21 and 24 for all indices. Consequently, these generating units have the largest impact on system reliability. In other words, these buses are at the highest risk and the most beneficial way to improve the reliability of the system is to increase the availability of these units by adding new units, decreasing repair time and/or using sophisticated methods to decrease units' failure rate.

From Tables 8, 9, and 10, the sensitivity of the LOLP, EDNS and LOLF indices with respect to components' un-availabilities and with respect to the failure rates are positive whereas for the repair rates are negative. This can be attributed to the fact that increasing component failure rate or unavailability would increase the value of the reliability indices (deteriorate system reliability). On the other hand,

Table 8. Sensitivity analysis of the LOLP index for the IEEE RTS

Bus Number Generator Capacity	$\partial LOLP / \partial u_i \times 10^{-2}$	$\partial LOLP / \partial \ddot{e}_i \times {}^{-4}$	$\partial LOLP / \partial \hat{i}_i \times 10^{-4}$
#18G400	33.29905	44.15546	-6.02120
#21G400	33.18920	44.00979	-6.00134
#23G350	26.16603	25.28188	-2.19842
#13G197	20.02105	10.31336	-0.54281
#23G155	11.34010	4.77216	-0.19884
#15G155	11.01719	4.63627	-0.19318
#16G155	10.77760	4.53545	-0.18898
#22G100	4.94948	2.60356	-0.10848
#2G76	4.48367	1.96626	-0.04013
#1G76	4.36122	1.91257	-0.03903

Table 9. Sensitivity analysis of the LOLF index for the IEEE RTS

Bus Number Generator Capacity	$\partial LOLF / \partial u_i$	$\partial LOLF / \partial \ddot{e}_i \times 10^{-2}$	$\partial LOLF / \partial \mu_i \times 10^{-4}$
#18G400	58.64305	77.76229	-660.80623
#21G400	57.52415	76.27860	-641.89222
#23G350	49.01718	47.36089	-202.50560
#13G197	43.04602	22.17411	-16.60056
#23G155	41.51697	17.47125	-27.43647
#15G155	39.63948	16.68116	-25.43609
#16G155	37.98464	15.98477	-23.49279
#22G100	16.69121	8.78003	-16.78555
#2G76	17.06241	7.48253	-6.30312
#1G76	16.41083	7.19679	-5.96487

increasing the repair rate would enhance system reliability. Increasing the repair rate or decreasing the unavailability of a component or decreasing the failure rate can be achieved by different strategies such as hiring more maintenance staff, using more sophisticated methods to reduce the failure rate, installing new equipment, etc.

Table 10. Sensitivity analysis of the EDNS index for the IEEE RTS

Bus Number Generator Capacity	$\partial EDNS / \partial u_i$	$\partial EDNS / \partial \lambda_i \times 10^{-2}$	$\partial EDNS / \partial \mu_i \times 10^{-4}$
#18G400	73.95452	98.06572	-1337.25977
#21G400	73.78475	97.84059	-1334.18991
#23G350	68.91659	66.58790	-579.02520
#13G197	29.80471	15.35317	-80.80615
#23G155	20.02147	8.42547	-35.10614
#15G155	18.68813	7.86438	-32.76824
#16G155	18.83241	7.92509	-33.02120
#22G100	11.23545	5.91016	-24.62565
#2G76	9.13458	4.00587	-8.17524
#1G76	8.76626	3.84434	-7.84560

13. CONCLUSION

A heuristic technique based on line power carrying capabilities and minimum generation vector was applied to reduce the search space. The heuristic technique is conservative in that not all the failure states can be captured and no success state can be classified as failure state. The heuristic technique produces three subspaces, definite failure subspace, definite success subspace and unclassified subspace. This technique is based on evaluating the adequacy of the available power generation and transmission lines capacities to meet the load. Some failure states cannot be captured with considering only generation and line capacities. Most of these states are around the definite failure subspace where the latter is detected by the state space reduction approach. In this chapter, a directed Binary Particle Swarm Optimization technique was utilized to search for the failure states in the unclassified subspace which are closely scattered around the definite failure subspace. Also, this work has introduced a complementary concept that is compatible with intelligent search methods to estimate power system reliability indices.

The proposed algorithm is an extension to the use of the intelligent search methods in composite power system reliability analysis and it is intended to overcome many difficulties that are associated with the use of these techniques. An imperative key in using BPSO in composite system reliability evaluation is the selection of weighting factors of the objective function. Such weighting factors are system dependent and, therefore, their appropriate values should be carefully selected in order to prevent the swarm from being trapped to one corner of the state space. In this work, an effective Particle Swarm Optimization technique has been proposed for reliability assessment of composite systems. The proposed method adjusts the weighting factors associated with the objective function in a dynamic fashion so that the swarm would always fly on the entire search space rather of being trapped to one corner of the search space. The method presented in this chapter is not only easy to implement, but it does not use trial and error process, which have been traditionally adapted in PSO based reliability evaluation studies. The effectiveness of the proposed method has been demonstrated on the IEEE RTS and the modified IEEE

RTS. In these test cases, it has been shown that the results obtained by the proposed method correspond closely to those obtained using Monte-Carlo simulation, while requiring lower computational burden. The proposed method accurately estimates these indices with less computational effort than the conventional Monte Carlo simulation. Also, BPSO showed an intelligence behavior over the Monte Carlo simulation methods.

From the failure states which are captured by the heuristic technique and the binary PSO the sensitivity analyses of power system reliability indices as well as the evaluation of these indices were performed.

REFERENCES

Bakkiyaraj, R., & Kumarappan, N. (2013, May). Optimal reliability planning for a composite electric power system based on Monte Carlo simulation using particle swarm optimization. *International Journal of Electrical Power & Energy Systems*, *47*, 109–116. doi:10.1016/j.ijepes.2012.10.055

Benidris, M., Elsaiah, S., & Mitra, J. (2013). Composite system reliability assessment using dynamically directed particle swarm optimization. In *Proceedings of North American Power Symposium* (pp. 1-6). Champaign, IL: IEEE. doi:10.1109/NAPS.2013.6666953

Benidris, M., & Mitra, J. (2013). Composite power system reliability assessment using maximum capacity flow and directed binary particle swarm optimization. In *Proceedings of North American Power Symposium* (pp. 1-6). Champaign, IL: IEEE. doi:10.1109/NAPS.2013.6666951

Benidris, M., & Mitra, J. (2014). Reliability and sensitivity analysis of composite power systems under emission constraints. *IEEE Transactions on Power Systems*, *29*(1), 404–412. doi:10.1109/TPWRS.2013.2279343

Billinton, R., & Li, W. (1994). *Reliability assessment of electric power systems using Monte Carlo methods*. New York: Plenum Press. doi:10.1007/978-1-4899-1346-3

Deng, Z., & Singh, C. (1992). A new approach to reliability evaluation of interconnected power systems including planned outages and frequency calculations. *IEEE Transactions on Power Systems*, *7*(2), 734–743. doi:10.1109/59.141780

Gholami, M. R., Hoseini, S. H., & Mohamad Taheri, M. (2008). Assessment of power composite system annualized reliability indices based on improved particle swarm optimization and comparative study between the behaviour of GA and PSO. In *Proceedings of IEEE 2nd International Power and Energy Conference* (pp. 1609-1612). Johor Bahru, Malaysia: IEEE.

Green, R. C., Wang, L., Alam, M., & Singh, C. (2011). An examination of artificial immune system optimization in intelligent state space pruning for LOLP estimation. In *Proceedings of North American Power Symposium* (pp. 1-7). Boston: IEEE. doi:10.1109/NAPS.2011.6024868

Green, R. C., Wang, L., Alam, M., & Singh, C. (2011). Intelligent state space pruning using multi – objective PSO for reliability analysis of composite power systems: Observations, analyses, and impacts. In *Proceedings of IEEE Power and Energy Society General Meeting* (pp. 1-8). Detroit, MI: IEEE.

Green, R. C., Wang, L., Alam, M., & Singh, C. (2011). State space pruning for reliability evaluation using binary particle swarm optimization. In *Proceedings of IEEE PES Power Systems Conference and Exposition* (pp. 1–7). Phoenix, AZ: IEEE.

Green, R. C., Wang, L., & Singh, C. (2010). State space pruning for power system reliability evaluation using genetic algorithms. In *Proceedings of IEEE Power and Energy Society General Meeting* (pp. 1-6). Minneapolis, MN: IEEE.

Green, R. C., Wang, L., Wang, Z., Alam, M., & Singh, C. (2010). Power system reliability assessment using intelligent state space pruning techniques: A comparative study. In *Proceedings of IEEE International Conference on Power System Technology* (pp. 1-8). Hangzhou, China: IEEE. doi:10.1109/POWERCON.2010.5666062

Green, R. C., Wang, Z., Wang, L., Alam, M., & Singh, C. (2010). Evaluation of loss of load probability for power systems using intelligent search based state space pruning. In *Proceedings of 11th International Conference on Probabilistic Methods Applied to Power Systems* (pp. 319-324). Singapore: IEEE. doi:10.1109/PMAPS.2010.5528892

He, J., Sun, Y., Kirschen, D. S., Singh, C., & Cheng, L. (2010). *State – space partitioning method for composite power system reliability assessment*. IET.

Hui, Z., Pei, Y., & Jie, L. (2009). Study on the estimating model of shadow prices for national economy evaluation of construction projects. In *Proceedings of International Conference on Management and Service Science* (pp. 1-4). Wuhan, China: IEEE.

Kennedy, J., & Eberhart, R. (1995). Particle swarm optimization. In *Proceedings of IEEE International Conference on Neural Networks* (pp. 942-948). Perth, Australia: IEEE.

Kennedy, J., & Eberhart, R. (1997). A discrete binary version of the particle swarm algorithm. In *Proceedings of IEEE International Conference on Computational Cybernetics and Simulation* (pp. 4104-4108). Orlando, FL: IEEE. doi:10.1109/ICSMC.1997.637339

Lago-Gonzalez, A., & Singh, C. (1990). The extended decomposition – Simulation approach for multi-area reliability calculations. *IEEE Transactions on Power Systems*, *5*(3), 1024–1031. doi:10.1109/59.65934

Li, B., Qu, J., & Cui, Y. (2009). The resources purchase quantity algorithm based on the shadow price and its application in the enterprise management. In *Proceedings of International Conference on Test and Measurement* (pp. 346-349). Hong Kong: IEEE.

Li, G., Liu, C., & Salazar, H. (2006). Forecasting transmission congestion using day-ahead shadow prices. In *Proceedings of IEEE PES Power Systems Conference and Exposition* (pp. 1705–1709). Atlanta, GA: IEEE.

Melo, A. C., & Pereira, M. V. (1995). Sensitivity analysis of reliability indices with respect to equipment failure and repair rates. *IEEE Transactions on Power Systems*, *10*(2), 1014–1021. doi:10.1109/59.387946

Miranda, V., Carvalho, L. M., Rosa, M. A., Silva, A. M., & Singh, C. (2009). Improving power system reliability calculation efficiency with EPSO variants. *IEEE Transactions on Power Systems*, *24*(4), 1772–1779. doi:10.1109/TPWRS.2009.2030397

Miranda, V., Keko, H., & Duque, A. J. (2008). Stochastic star communication topology in evolutionary particle swarms (EPSO). *International Journal of Computational Intelligence Research*, 105-116.

Mitra, J., & Singh, C. (1996). Incorporating the DC load flow model in the decomposition--Simulation method of multi-area reliability evaluation. *IEEE Transactions on Power Systems*, *11*(3), 1245–1254. doi:10.1109/59.535596

Mitra, J., & Singh, C. (1999). Pruning and simulation for determination of frequency and duration indices of composite systems. *IEEE Transactions on Power Systems*, *14*(3), 899–905. doi:10.1109/59.780901

Mitra, J., & Xu, X. (2010). Composite system reliability analysis using particle swarm optimization. In *Proceedings of 11th International Conference on Probabilistic Methods Applied to Power Systems* (pp. 548-552). Singapore: IEEE. doi:10.1109/PMAPS.2010.5528940

Oliveira, G. C., Pereira, M. V., & Cunha, S. H. (1989). A technique for reducing computational effort in Monte Carlo based composite reliability evaluation. *IEEE Transactions on Power Systems*, *4*(4), 1309–1315. doi:10.1109/59.41680

Padmavathi, S. V., Sahu, S. K., & Jayalaxmi, A. (2014). Particle swarm optimization based composite power system reliability analysis using FACTS. *International Journal of Electronics and Electrical Engineering, 3*(2), 105-109.

Parsopoulos, K. E., & Vrahatis, M. N. (2002). Particle swarm optimization method in multiobjective problems. In *Proceedings of ACM Symposium on Applied Computing* (pp. 603-607). Madrid: ACM. doi:10.1145/508791.508907

Patra, S. B., Mitra, J., & Earla, R. (2006). A new intelligent search method for composite system reliability analysis. In *Proceedings of IEEE PES Transmission and Distribution Conference and Exposition* (pp. 803–807). Caracas: IEEE.

Peram, T., Veeramachaneni, K., & Mohan, C. K. (2003). Fitness-distance-ratio based particle swarm optimization. In *Proceedings of IEEE Swarm Intelligence Symposium* (pp. 174-181). Indianapolis, IN: IEEE.

Pereira, M. V., & Pinto, L. M. (1985). Application of sensitivity analysis of load supplying capability to interactive transmission expansion planning. *IEEE Transactions on Power Apparatus and Systems*, *PAS-104*(2), 381–389. doi:10.1109/TPAS.1985.319053

Ramanujan, P., Li, Z., & Higham, L. (2009). Shadow prices versus vickrey prices in multipath routing. In Proceedings of *IEEE Conference on Information and Communication* (pp. 2956–2960). Rio de Janeiro: IEEE.

Reliability Test System Task Force of the Application of Probability Methods Subcommittee. (1979). IEEE reliability test system. *IEEE Transactions on Power Apparatus and Systems*, 2047–2054.

Singh, C., & Chen, Q. (1989). Generation system reliability evaluation using a cluster based load model. *IEEE Transactions on Power Systems*, *4*(1), 102–107. doi:10.1109/59.32466

Singh, C., & Deng, Z. (1991). A new algorithm for multi – area reliability evaluation – Simultaneous decomposition--simulation approach. *Electric Power Systems Research, 21*(2), 129–136. doi:10.1016/0378-7796(91)90027-K

Singh, C., & Lago-Gonzalez, A. (1989). Improved algorithms for multi – area reliability evaluation using the decomposition-simulation approach. *IEEE Transactions on Power Systems, 4*(1), 321–328. doi:10.1109/59.32495

Singh, C., & Mitra, J. (1997). Composite system reliability evaluation using state space pruning. *IEEE Transactions on Power Systems, 12*(1), 471–479. doi:10.1109/59.575787

Suresh, K., & Kumarappan, N. (2013). *Generation maintenance scheduling using improved binary particle swarm optimisation considering aging failures*. IET.

Wang, L., & Singh, C. (2008). Population-based intelligent search in reliability evaluation of generation systems with wind power penetration. *IEEE Transactions on Power Systems, 23*(3), 1336–1345. doi:10.1109/TPWRS.2008.922642

Wang, Y., Guo, C., Wu, Q., & Dong, S. (2014). Adaptive sequential importance sampling technique for short-term composite power system adequacy evaluation. *IET Generation, Transmission and Distribution*, 730-741.

Yang, F., & Chang, C. S. (2009). Optimization of maintenance schedules and extents for composite power systems using multi-objective evolutionary algorithm. *IET Generation, Transmission and Distribution*, 930-940.

Zhao, D., & Singh, C. (2010). Modified genetic algorithm in state space pruning for power system reliability evaluation and its parameter determination. In *Proceedings of North American Power Symposium* (pp. 1-6). Arlington, VA: IEEE.

Zhao, Y., Zhou, N., Zhou, J., & Zhao, X. (2006). Research on sensitivity analysis for composite generation and transmission system reliability evaluation. In *Proceedings of IEEE International Conference on Power System Technology* (pp. 1-5). Chongqing, China: IEEE. doi:10.1109/ICPST.2006.321566

Zhu, T. X. (2006). A new methodology of analytical formula deduction and sensitivity analysis of EENS in bulk power system reliability assessment. In *Proceedings of IEEE PES Power Systems Conference and Exposition* (pp. 825–831). Atlanta, GA: IEEE.

KEY TERMS AND DEFINITIONS

Adequacy Assessment: Estimating the adequacy of the generation to meet the demand without including the constraints of the transmission lines.

Complementary Concept: Every reliability index that can be evaluated from the failure states, has a complementary value that can be evaluated from the success states as long as the boundaries of an index and its complementary value are known or the index can be equally likely determined from the success or failure states.

Composite System: Considering both the generation and transmission in evaluating system reliability.

Pruning: Partitioning the state space into subspaces that can be identified as success and failure subspaces.

Reliability Indices: Indices that are used to assess the reliability of a system.

Sensitivity: Amount of change in the objective function with respect to the constraints.

State Space: All possible outcomes of the combinations of system states.

Weighting Factors: Factors which are used to adjust the direction of the particle swarm.

Chapter 19
Ambiguity Reduction through Optimal Set of Region Selection Using GA and BFO for Handwritten Bangla Character Recognition

Nibaran Das
Jadavpur University, India

Mahantapas Kundu
Jadavpur University, India

Subhadip Basu
Jadavpur University, India

Mita Nasipuri
Jadavpur University, India

ABSTRACT

To recognize different patterns, identification of local regions where the pattern classes differ significantly is an inherent ability of the human cognitive system. This inherent ability of human beings may be imitated in any pattern recognition system by incorporating the ability of locating the regions that contain the maximum discriminating information among the pattern classes. In this chapter, the concept of Genetic Algorithm (GA) and Bacterial Foraging Optimization (BFO) are discussed to identify those regions having maximum discriminating information. The discussion includes the evaluation of the methods on the sample images of handwritten Bangla digit and Basic character, which is a subset of Bangla character set. Different methods of sub-image or local region creation such as random creation or based on the Center of Gravity (CG) of the foreground pixels are also discussed here. Longest run features, extracted from the generated local regions, are used as local feature in the present chapter. Based on these extracted local features, together with global features, the algorithms are applied to search for the optimal set of local regions. The obtained results are higher than that results obtained without optimization on the same data set.

DOI: 10.4018/978-1-4666-8291-7.ch019

INTRODUCTION

For recognizing different patterns identification of local regions where the pattern classes differ significantly is an inherent ability of human cognitive system. This inherent ability of human being may be imitated in any pattern recognition system by incorporating the ability of locating the regions which contain the maximum discriminating information among the pattern classes. The simplest way to do this is to divide the pattern image into a fixed number of equal sized regions. These regions may have some overlap with each other. For each such region, features (often called local features) are extracted. These local regions are then sampled randomly to produce various subsets of them. The recognition performance is evaluated with feature set formed with the local features (for some cases along with some global features)of each of those subsets. The subset, which produces best result, may be considered as an optimal set of local regions where the pattern classes differ significantly. Handwritten character recognition is a typical example of a real world pattern recognition problem which requires huge computation and modelling of perceptual power or cognitive capabilities of human beings, at least to some extent. (Cheriet, El Yacoubi, Fujisawa, Lopresti, & Lorette, 2009). To recognize the handwritten characters, both global and local features jointly or individually are used with a standard classifier. Global features are those features which are extracted from the overall character images. On the other hand, local features are extracted from the sub images of the same.

One of the recent trends for improving the recognition performance of a handwritten character recognition system is to use local features along with global features of the character images. Some works have already been done in the field of handwritten character recognition following the above mentioned principles(Arica & Yarman-Vural, 2001; Basu et al., 2005b, 2009; Cao, Ahmadi, & Shridhar, 1995; Das, Basu, et al., 2009; Due Trier, Jain, & Taxt, 1996; Jaehwa, Govindaraju, & Srihari, 2000; Rajashekararadhya & Ranjan, 2008). In (Rajashekararadhya & Ranjan, 2008), Rajashekararadhya et al. proposed an efficient zone based feature extraction techniques for Handwritten Kanada, Telugu, Tamil, Malayalam numeral recognition. In the paper, they divided the characters into some $M \times N$ zones and average distance features are extracted from the zones. In the paper(Basu et al., 2005b), Basu et al. divided the Bangla digit images into 9 overlapping fixed size sub-images, also termed as windows, interchangeably. From each of these sub-images longest run based features were locally computed. However, a fixed sized window may contain some ambiguous information besides the discriminating one, which may have an adverse effect on the performance of the recognition system. In the paper (Cao et al., 1995) Cao et al. used zone based direction histogram features for recognition of handwritten Roman numerals. The work was primarily motivated by two stage classifier schemes comprising of two different neural networks. To describe different methodologies of offline character recognition systems N. Africa et al (Arica & Yarman-Vural, 2001) cited several feature extraction techniques based on local regions or zones. In the paper (Jaehwa et al., 2000) Jaehwa et al. described a hierarchical feature space based on the zones created by quin tree based zoning scheme. The zones were created dynamically based on the centroids of the contours of the characters. Thus, zones of variable sizes were created for every character of the database. Histogram based gradient and moment based projection features were calculated from those zones in their work. In the approaches(Basu et al., 2009; Das, Basu, et al., 2009), windows of varying sizes were dynamically created on the basis of the centre of gravity (CG) of black pixels of the entire character region and its sub regions (windows) and from each of those regions four longest run features were extracted. Those features along with another set of four longest run features computed globally from the entire character image were used for recognition of Bangla alphabet. The above approach gave better result over the previous one(Basu et al., 2005a) due to dynamic creation of non-empty windows, i.e., each of the windows contains some character shape information. However, none of the above mentioned methods opted to find out the set of local regions where the character shapes differ the most. But, the choice of appropriate local features depend on pinpointing that set of local regions. In literature, few mentions(Basu, Kundu, Nasipuri, & Basu, 2006; Cordella, De Stefano, Fontanella, & Marrocco, 2008; Das et al., 2007; Kudo & Sklansky, 2000; Roy et al., 2012) can be found about formal methods for selection of local features. In the paper (Das et al., 2007) Das et al. described a methodology to identify appropriate group of windows as local regions out of the 16 overlapping fixed sized windows over the whole character image in order to decrease computational cost and achieve high recognition performance. The method used a GA based approach to select the set of windows identifying optimal local regions in the digit images which contain discriminating information among the ten digit classes of Bangla numerals. However, this method is also suffered from the problem of selection of fixed size regions like (Basu et al., 2005a). To overcome the problem of fixed sized windows, variable sized local regions creation and selection strategies can be developed.

A such strategy has been proposed by Das et al. (Das, Sarkar, et al., 2012). In the paper, local regions are created randomly with varying height and width. A certain percentage of overlap among neighbouring regions may be allowed. As the number of such local regions created in this manner is large, an exhaustive search for an optimal set of local regions is a mammoth task. To alleviate this problem, Particle three popular evolutionary algorithms such as Genetic Algorithm, Simulated annealing, Hill climbing have been proposed to select optimal sets of local regions which h will provide better recognition performance. The performances of the methods have been evaluated on Bangla digit samples.

Roy et al. (Roy et al., 2012) described an Artificial Bee Colony based local region selection techniques for the recognition for Arabic, Hindi, Telugu numerals and Bangla Basic character datasets respectively. In this approach eight directional gradient features are extracted from every region of different levels of partitions created using a CG based Quad Tree partitioning approach . The size of the windows which are also not fixed here depend on the CG of the images/sub-images.

From the above discussions, it can be inferred that ambiguity reduction among different local regions for selection of features is very important for handwritten character recognition task. In the present chapter, the potential of Gentic Algorithms(GAs) and Bacterial Foraging Optimization(BFO), a popular swarm intelligence techniques have been discussed for resolving the ambiguities of the character shapes through optimal selection of local regions.

1. GENETIC ALGORITHMS

Genetic algorithm (GA), one of the most popularly used evolutionary tools among soft computing paradigm, is mainly devised to solve real world ill-defined, imprecisely formulated problems requiring huge computation. It is the power of GA to introduce some heuristic methodologies to minimize the search space for optimal solution(s) without sticking at local optima. Due to the inherent power, GA becomes one of the most successful heuristic optimization algorithms. It is widely used to solve problems of diversified fields ranging from engineering to art. After the 28 years of its first introduction(Srinivas & Patnaik, 1994), GA is still remaining one of the most competitive heuristic search technique. A workshop cum conference named Genetic Algorithm Theory and Practice (GPTP) is organized every year to make a system based on Genetic Algorithm as well as to improve the techniques. On the other hand, handwritten character recognition is a typical example of the real world problem which requires huge computation and modelling of perceptual power or cognitive capabilities of human beings, at least to some extent.

In the present chapter, the ambiguities among the character shapes have been resolved to optimally select a group of sub images also termed as local regions from a pool of sub images created randomly covering at least some area (more than a threshold value) of the overall character images. The groups of regions are selected in such a way from the pool, so that it provides highest discriminating attributes. The uniqueness of the present methodology is that the regions which have been selected here have no fixed height and width. It is because, the heights and widths of the regions are generated randomly. From each of the randomly created regions, longest run features (Das, Acharya, et al., 2012), a popular features for character recognition are extracted. Based on these extracted features, the GA is applied to search for the optimal set of local regions which has the best discriminating power. This results in high recognition rate with lesser number of features. The selection is finally validated with a fuzzy template created using the combination of all characters.

1.1 Methodology

Handwritten digit recognition, a subset of handwritten character recognition is a typical example of pattern recognition due to varying shapes and sizes, caused by different handwriting styles of different individuals. Recognition of the characters therefore requires perceptual power or cognitive capabilities of human beings. Due to large varieties of potential applications like extracting data from filled in forms, automatic postal code identification, mail sorting systems, automatic reading of bank cheques etc, handwritten digit recognition is considered as an important problem. Handwritten Bangla digit patterns are used to validate the GA based techniques to achieve high success rate. Figure 1 shows a set of handwritten image samples of the Bangla digit patterns along with its English correspondence.

The process is divided into the following steps:

1. Creation of overlapping/non overlapping set of local regions or sub-images which cover at least certain portion of the overall digit image.
2. Local regions are randomly selected i.e. they have varying sizes covering various portions of the entire digit image. Every local region may be considered as a window also.
3. Some groups of the created local regions are randomly selected as chromosome strings in the first generation for implementing Genetic Algorithm (GA).
4. GA evaluates the fitness function based on extracted local features from the selected local regions along with global feature set extracted from the entire digit image using an MLP classifier with back-propagation algorithm.

Figure 1. Image samples of handwritten Bangla digit patterns

0	২	২	৩	৪	৫	৬	৭	৮	৯
0	1	2	3	4	5	6	7	8	9

5. In different generations, GA produces subsequent generations using the operators, crossover and mutation, and heuristically searches optimized feature set based on their fitness values.
6. The description of the process is shown in details in Algorithm 1.

1.1.1 Random Creation of the Pools of Sub Images

Here local regions are created by generating the coordinates of the sub-images randomly using a program. During the creation of local regions, the following constraints are considered.

1. The region size is greater than a particular threshold value(th1).
2. The maximum size of the region is also restricted by another threshold value(th2).
3. No region can overlap another completely; or overlapping up to a certain degree is allowed.
4. The summation of all the local areas covered by the created local regions should not be less than a certain fraction of the overall area of the image.

1.1.2 Design of Feature Set

Choice of suitable features for pattern classes is a domain specific design issue. Two different feature sets are used for classification of handwritten Bangla digit patterns here. They are denoted by *global feature set* and *local feature set*. The total number of features which are extracted during the experiment is fixed. Throughout the experiment, only the dimensionality of local features varies in accordance with

Algorithm 1.

```
Step 1: Start.
Step 2: Creation of overlapping/non overlapping local regions for different
        sets randomly.
Step 3: Creation of initial population of number of chromosomes(a group of
        local regions, randomly selected from a set, forms each chromosome
        string).
Step 4: Creation of feature vector having and are the number of character
        samples and the number of features representing each chromosome
        respectively.
Step 5: Estimate fitness value of each chromosome with respect to its
        recognition performance using SVM classifier.
Step 6: Evaluate maximum number of generations completed or changes in average
        fitness values between two successive generations.
Step 7: If the fitness value is very small go to Step 12.
Step 8: Selection of chromosomes for next generation using Roulette wheel.
Step 9: Crossover among different chromosomes.
Step 10: Mutation on gene of some of the chromosomes.
Step 11: Go to step 3.
Step 12: Stop.
```

the number of local regions. Both the global and local features are considered to ensure that the selected features should be capable of supplying complementary information about the digit patterns, at least to some extent globally and locally. Before extraction of these features from a digit image, it is binarized and scaled to a size of 32×32 pixels. The different types of features used here are described below:

1.1.2.1 Global Features

- **Shadow Features:** Shadows features are computed by considering the lengths of projections of the digit images on the four sides and eight octants dividing sides of the minimal bounding boxes enclosing the same. Figure 2 shows an illustration of shadow features. Considering the lengths of projections on three sides of each such octant, 24 shadow features are extracted from each digit image, which is divided into eight octants inside the minimal box. Each value of the shadow features so computed is to be normalized by dividing it with the maximum possible length of the projections on the respective side (Das, Basu, et al., 2009).
- **Octant Centroid Features:** Coordinates of centroids of black pixels in all the 8 octants of a digit image are considered to add 16 features in all to the feature set. Figure 3 shows an illustration of the feature (Das, Basu, et al., 2009).
- **Distance Based Features:** To compute the distance-based features the digit images are partitioned in four quadrants. For every quadrant, maximum horizontal and diagonal distances from image boundary to character boundary have been calculated. For four directions $2 \times 4 = 8$ features have been calculated in all (Das, Sarkar, et al., 2012) .
- **Longest Run Features:** 4 longest run features, extracted from the digit images / subimages, are computed row wise, column wise and along two of its major diagonals. The row wise longest-run feature is computed by considering the sum of the lengths of the longest bars that fit consecutive black pixels along each of all the rows of a rectangular subimage region. The three other longest-run features are computed in the same way but along the column wise and two major diagonal wise directions within the rectangle separately. Each of these feature values are normalized by dividing it with a factor $h \times w$, where h and w represent the height and width respectively of the digit image (Das, Basu, et al., 2009).

Figure 2. An illustration for shadow features: (a-d) direction of fictitious light rays as assume for taking the projection of an image segment on each side of all octants; (e) projection of a sample image (Das, Sarkar, et al., 2012).

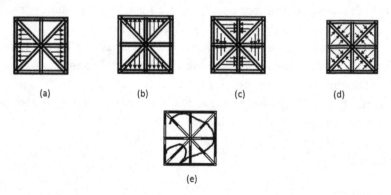

Figure 3. An illustration of the 16 centroid features
(Das, Sarkar, et al., 2012)

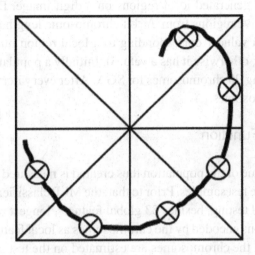

- **Loop Feature:** The region(s) totally enclosed by the digit or a part of the digit is called loop(s). The number of loop(s) varies from one digit to another in Bangla script. The number of loop(s) is treated as a global feature. Very small loops having sizes less than 20 pixels are rejected as noise (Das, Acharya, et al., 2012).

Global feature set consists of 53 features in all. These features are formed with 24 shadow features, 16 octant centroid features, 8 distance based features, 1 feature representing the number of loops, 4 longest run features computed on the overall digit image are considered as global feature set.

1.1.2.2 Local Feature Set

From each of the created regions, 4 longest run features are extracted. Thus, in all, if N numbers of regions is created; $4 \times N$ longest-run features are computed locally from each character image. All these extracted local features are not considered simultaneously for the recognition purpose; a subset of these is selected by GA during experiments, as will be described below.

1.1.3 Encoding the Region Sampling Strategy using GA

Genetic Algorithm (GA) (Srinivas & Patnaik, 1994), an intelligent search and optimization technique based on natural evolution is free from chances of sticking at local minima. Considering the criterion, GA is modelled here to identify the optimal set of local regions having discriminating features of the handwritten Bangla digit patterns. More specifically, a simple Genetic Algorithm (SGA) [4] is used here. To identify the appropriate set of local regions, each local region is numbered uniquely in this work. An optimal combination of these local regions usually does not contain all of them. For implementing the fitness function of the SGA, recognition performances are measured through MLP classifiers trained with features extracted from various combinations of local regions, i.e., the candidate combinations of various local regions, represented with the chromosomes of each population of the GA. It is so that the each local region is treated as a gene of that chromosome.

A N bit binary string is used here to represent a candidate solution or chromosome, in which each bit corresponds to one of the generated local regions on a digit image. During the creation of initial population, the number of active regions from N bit chromosome length are generated randomly. The bit in the chromosome with a value 1 corresponding to a local region number indicates the region is selected for feature extraction; otherwise it has a value 0. Initially a population of candidate solutions is created by randomly generating 20 chromosomes for SGA. After every iteration of SGA, the population size is kept fixed to 20 chromosomes.

1.1.4 Design of Fitness Function

The fitness of each chromosome of the population thus created is measured by obtaining the recognition rate of an MLP classifier on the test samples. Prior to that, the MLP classifier is to be trained with training samples. For both training and testing, besides 53 global features, longest run features, extracted from a combination of different regions encoded by the chromosomes as local features for each digit pattern are used. The fitness values of all the chromosomes are estimated on the test set after training the network with a training set of a population. This process is to be repeated for each chromosome of the population.

1.1.5 Next Generation Creation and Crossover and Mutation Rules

A new population of more promising chromosomes, also called a generation, is to be reproduced from the initial population after evaluation. For this, 20 chromosomes are selected here from the existing population using roulette wheel, weighted proportionally with the fitness values of the chromosomes of the existing population. Once a new population of 20 chromosomes is created in this way, 80% of the chromosomes are selected pairwise randomly for performing the crossover operation over them. The crossover point is selected at the middle of each chromosome.

Once *Crossover* operation is completed, the current population is left with 16 chromosomes undergoing crossover and the 4 remaining chromosomes are carried forward without any change. Half of the chromosomes of this population i.e. 10 number of chromosome are again randomly selected for *Mutation*. The exact bit of a chromosome to be mutated is also selected randomly. In this way, a generation of population is reproduced from the old one, which is to be again evaluated.

1.1.6 The Termination Criteria

After a population is evaluated on the basis of the fitness function, the stopping criterion of SGA is to be tested. In this work, the stopping criterion is reached either after 20 generations have passed or the average fitness value of the current population is greater than or equal to 98% of the maximum fitness value obtained so far.

1.2 Experimental Result

1.2.1 Preparation of Data Set

To conduct experiments with the technique described so far, a database of 6000 samples of handwritten Bangla digits (CMATERdb 3.1.1) are collected from http://code.google.com/p/ cmater db/ is used.

In order to evaluate the proposed method, seven different combinations of variable size local regions are created randomly based on the predefined constraints discussed in Section 2.1.1. Table 1 shows the number of local regions of each set along with the constraints.

SGA is applied on each of the above mentioned window combinations (Set#1 - Set#7) to obtain the optimal window combinations containing maximum discriminatory information for accurate recognition of Bangla digits. The MLP classifiers(Basu et al., 2005a)(Bhowmik, Bhattacharya, & Parui, 2004) are used for evaluating the fitness function of the chromosomes. Each MLP is trained for 5000 iterations of Back Propagation learning algorithm with a learning rate of 0.8 and a momentum of 0.7. Number of hidden neurons used here is 1/3 of the input neurons. The recognition rate of the MLP is taken as fitness value of the chromosome. Table 2 shows the used variables during the experiment. Figure 4 shows a Snapshot of some of the generations of SGA.

Table 3 shows the above mentioned seven different local region combinations (Set#1 – Set#7), along with the produced optimal combinations of windows for each set.

Table 1. The randomly created sets of local regions

Set	Sub-Image Selection Strategy/Pool Design Strategy		
	Image Covered Criteria in Minimum	**Intersection between Two Local Regions in a Chromosome (Percentage of Overall Image)**	**No. of Windows Created**
1	Not followed	0	10 x20 =200
2	Image partitioned into four parts and 2/3 of each part is considered	0	26
3	2/3 area of total image	25	28
4	2/3 area of total image	0	30
5	80% area of total image	0	30
6	80% area of total image	25	28
7	100% of total image	50	16

Table 2. The different constraints used in the present work are shown

	Constraints
Criteria or variable used during region creation	• Maximum size of a region. • Minimum size of a region. • Overlapping criteria between two regions. • Image coverage.
Genetic Algorithm	• Initial population size. • Number of chromosomes selected for crossover. • Crossover point. • Number of mutation points. • Termination criteria.
MLP	• Learning rate. • Momentum. • No of iteration. • Training data set. • Test data set.

Figure 4. A snapshot of some of the generations of SGA

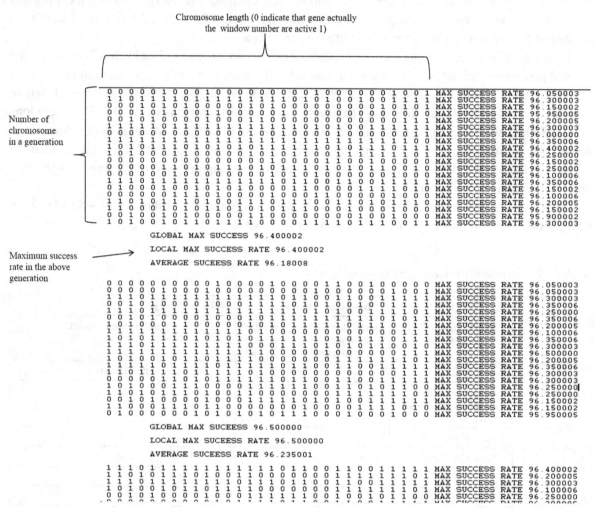

Table 3. Results of experiments with seven different window combinations (Set #1 - Set#7)

Set#	Total No. of Windows	Length of Chromosome String	Number of Optimally Selected Windows	Maximum Success Rate in %
1	200	10	10	96.50
2	26	26	13	96.15
3	28	28	11	96.60
4	24	24	15	96.19
5	30	30	12	97.10
6	28	28	14	96.60
7	16	16	11	95.80

To justify the result of our experiments, a gray level template T have been generated by considering 200 samples each for all the 10 Bangla digits. Figure 5 shows the generated template. Assuming all normalized character patterns of resolution $(M \times N)$, an average pixel value (x, y) have been computed for each pixel position (x, y), $0 \leq x \leq M - 1$ and $0 \leq y \leq N - 1$, for forming the gray level template T for the k number of binary pattern classes, such that

$$\mu(x, y) = \sum_{i=0}^{k} f_i(x, y)$$

where, f_i represents the pixel value at (x, y) position of ith character pattern of the above mentioned digits and $f_i(x, y) \in \{0, 1\}$ (here 0 represents background and 1 represents foreground). If (x, y) is close to zero, it signifies that the pixel position (x, y) may be considered as a background pixel in the digit image.

On the other hand regions having ì value close to 255 i.e. dark regions normally indicate more commonality among the digit patterns. The regions having intermediate ì values are the regions where the digit patterns differ and they generally contain discriminating information about the digit patterns. Table 4 shows the optimized regions selected over the template by the SGA for different sets together with the corresponding initial set of randomly created local regions. It is to be noted, that for Set#1 only 30 local regions of overall regions are shown for simplicity.

From Table 2, it is found that maximum recognition performance of 97.10% is obtained with 12 numbers of optimally selected regions for set#5. The obtained recognition accuracy is better than the recognition accuracy obtained with the other works published previously in (Basu et al., 2005a) (Das et al., 2007).

Figure 5. Grey level template of Bangla digits
(Das, Sarkar, et al., 2012).

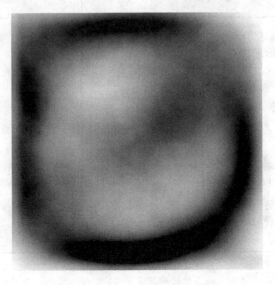

Table 4. Selected regions along with initial set of regions for different set; the selected regions, as shown on the grey level templates indicates that the regions of discriminating/containing discriminating information among the digit patterns are identified properly.

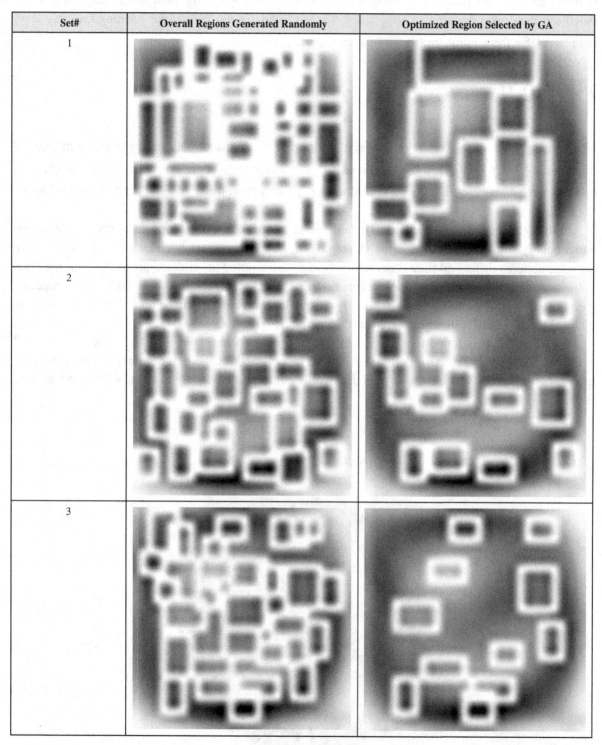

continued on following page

Table 4. Continued

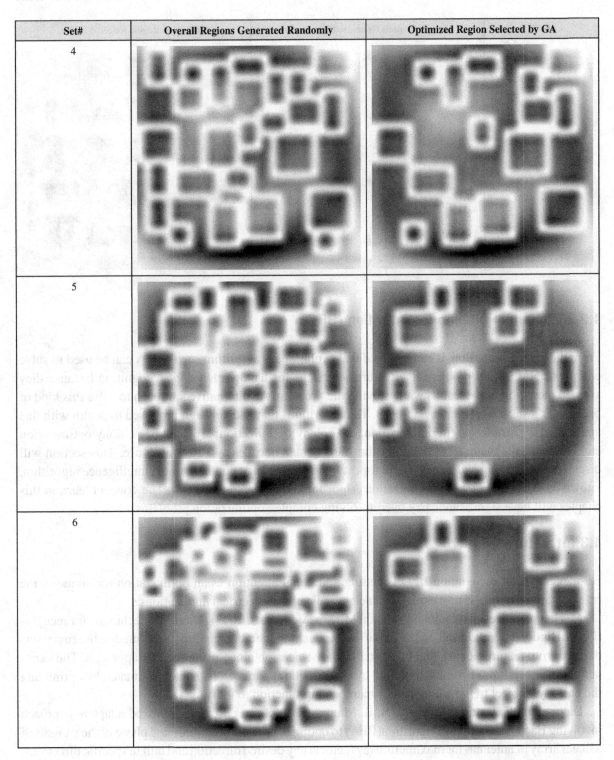

Set#	Overall Regions Generated Randomly	Optimized Region Selected by GA
4		
5		
6		

continued on following page

Table 4. Continued

Set#	Overall Regions Generated Randomly	Optimized Region Selected by GA
7	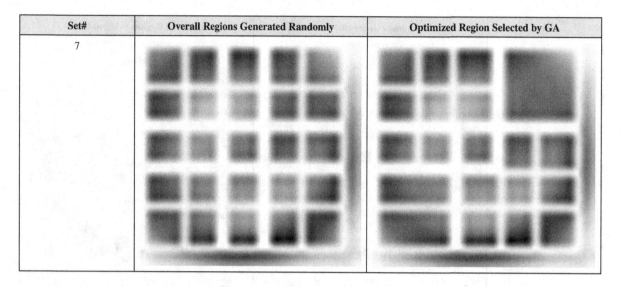	

1.2.2 Bacterial Foraging Optimization (BFO)

From the above discussion, it can be noted that evolutionary algorithm such as GA can be used to solve complex optimization problem like feature selections for handwritten digit recognition because they showed incredibly good results while solving the problem. An alternative approach to solve this kind of problem is swarm intelligence approach. The algorithms that had yet been proposed to dealth with this approach are particle swarm optimization, ant colony optimization, artificial bee colony optimization etc. However, the majority of the algorithms are written decades ago are still in use. This section will discuss an interesting and a very useful aspect of study of a very popular swarm intelligence algorithm, known as Bacteria Foraging optimization Algorithm abbreviated as BFOA. The concept learn in this chapter will have significant carry over in solving complex optimization problems.

1.3 Literature Review

Besides character recognition BFO is getting additional attention as an optimization technique in the research area like image processing, financial applications, electrical applications.

M. Hanmandlu et al. (Hanmandlu, Nath, Mishra, & Madasu, 2007) proposed a technique for recognition of Hindi numerals based on the modified exponential membership function, fitted to the fuzzy sets derived from features, consisting of normalized distances obtained using the box approach. The exponential membership function is modified by two structural parameters that are estimated by optimizing the entropy, subject to the attainment of membership function to unity.

Datta et al. (T. Datta, I. S. Misra, B. B. Mangaraj, 2008) proposed an improved adaptive approach involving Bacterial Foraging Algorithm(BFA) to optimize both the amplitude and phase of the weights of a linear array of antennas for maximum array factor at any desired direction and null in specific directions.

Kim et al. (Kim, Abraham, & Cho, 2007) applied the social foraging behavior of E-coli bacteria to solve optimization problem. They illustrated their proposed method using four test functions and the performance of the algorithm was studied based on crossover, mutation and variation of step sizes, chemotactics steps and the lifetime of the bacteria. The proposed algorithm was used to tune a PID controller of an Automatic Voltage Regulator (AVR).

The static optimization techniques have been used for evolutionary computation since a long time. However there are so many real world problems, which need optimization methodologies suitable for a changing environment. Such an optimization technique suitable for the dynamic environment is proposed by Tang et al. (Tang, Wu, & Saunders, 2006) . In this paper, the Bacterial Foraging Algorithm (BFA) is used as an optimization methodology for dynamically changing environment combining the advantages of both local searches in BFA and new selection scheme for diversity generation. They used the moving peak benchmark (MPB) as the test bed for experiments. Their experiment is evaluated in two ways; the first is concerned with the convergence of the algorithm in random-periodical changes in an environment, which are divided into three ranges from a low probability of changes to a higher one. The second is testing a set of combination of the algorithm parameters which are largely related to accuracy and stability of the algorithm. Then they compared all results with existing BFA(Passino, 2002), and the effectiveness of DBFA for solving dynamic optimization problem. They used the dynamic environment, generated by DFI to evaluate DBFA and compared with BFA with respect to the average best over a period, algorithm accuracy and stability. Their result showed that, on all three ranges of environmental changes, the DBFA was able to produce satisfactory performance, and can react to most of the environmental changes in time.

The BFOA has not only been used in engineering purposes, it has also been used in financial application. Dang et al. (Dang, Brabazon, O'Neill, & Edelman, 2008) proposed bacterial foraging optimization algorithm for financial application. They used BFO with and without swarming effect to estimate the parameters of the EGARCH-M model which is a non-linear problem. Due to the existence of noise in the newly-traded volatility option data, they calibrated the MRLP option pricing model by estimating the corresponding discrete time EGARCH-M model and then taking the limit. The EGARCH-M model is an asymmetric model designed to capture the leverage effect, or negative correlation between asset returns and volatility.

In order to improve the BFO's searching performance, Chen et al. (Chen, Zhu, & Hu, 2008) proposed a new methodology named "Self-adaptive Bacterial Foraging Optimization"(SA-BFO). Instead of the simple description of chemotactic behavior in original BFO, SA-BFO also incorporates the adaptive search strategy, which allows each bacterium strikes a good balance between exploration and exploitation during algorithmic execution by tuning its run-length unit self-adaptively. An extensive studies based on a set of four well-known benchmark functions had been carried out in order to evaluate the performance of SA-BFO. For the comparison purpose they also implemented a real-coded genetic algorithm(GA), the standard Particle Swarm Optimization(PSO), and the original BFO on those function respectively. And the SA-BFO gave markedly superior search performance. They firstly analyzed the foraging behavior of the bacteria in original BFO model. They specially studied the influence of the run length unit parameter on the exploration/exploitation tradeoff for the bacterial foraging behaviors. Then they presented SA-BFO, which cast bacterial foraging optimization into the adaptive fashion by changing the value of the run length unit during the algorithm execution. The four widely used benchmark function they did used to compare the performance of SA-BFO with BFO. They also simulated the self- adaptive foraging process of single bacterium based on the proposed model.

Tripathy and Mishra proposed an improved BFO algorithm for simultaneous optimization of the real power losses and Voltage Stability Limit (VSL) of a mesh power network (Tripathy & Mishra, 2007). In their modified algorithm, instead of the average value, firstly, the minimum value of all the chemotactic cost functions was retained for deciding the bacterium's health. This speeds up the convergence, because on the average scheme described by K. M.Passino(Passino, 2002), it might not retain the fittest bacterium for the subsequent generation. Secondly for swarming, the distances of all the bacteria in a new chemotactic stage were evaluated from the globally optimal bacterium to these points and not the distances of each bacterium from the rest of the others, as suggested by Passino. Simulation results indicated the superiority of the proposed approach over classical BFOA for the multi-objective optimization problem involving the UPFC (Unified Power Flow Controller) location, its series injected voltage, and the transformer tap positions as the variables.

Mishra and Bhende(Mishra & Bhende, 2007) used the modified BFOA to optimize the coefficients of Proportional plus Integral (PI) controllers for active power filters. The proposed algorithm was found to outperform a conventional GA with respect to the convergence speed.

K.M.Bakwad et al.(Bakwad et al., 2008) proposed synchronous bacterial foraging optimization (SBFO) for optimization of multimodal and high dimensional functions. In SBFO, the local search wasperformed through chemotaxis (swimming and tumbling) operation whereas global search was achieved by mutation operator and reproduction event. The said algorithm wasvalidated on a set of seven benchmark functions and its performance was compared with existing algorithms and found to be promising.

However, from all the above research works it can be concluded that the researchers have achieved very satisfactory results by using BFO as an optimization technique. So based on all these previous statistics the same optimization technique have been chosen for our present work.

1.4 Brief Description of Bacterial Foraging Optimization

The general foraging theory of animals is that they search for foods maintaining E / T (where E is the energy obtained and T is the time spent foraging) ratio maximized or maximizes the long-term average rate of energy intake. Generally Evolution optimizes the foraging strategies because animals that have poor foraging performance do not survive. Largely, a foraging strategy involves finding a patch of food (e.g., group of bushes with berries), deciding whether to enter it and search for food, and when to leave the patch. There are predators and risks, energy required for travel, and physiological constraints (sensing, memory, cognitive capabilities). The model of Foraging scenarios and optimal policies can be developed using dynamic programming. Search and optimal foraging decision-making of animals can be broken into three basic types: *cruise* (e.g., tunafish, hawks), *saltatory* (e.g., birds, fish, lizards, and insects), and *ambush* (e.g., snakes, lions). In a cruise search, the animal searches the perimeter of a region. In an ambush, it sits and waits. In salutatory search, an animal typically moves in some directions, stops or slows down, looks around, and then changes direction (it searches throughout a whole region).

Some animals forage as individual and others forage as groups. During social foraging, an animal needs communication capabilities by which it can exploit essentially the sensing capabilities of the group. The group can gang-up on large prey, individuals can obtain protection from predators while in a group, and in a certain sense the group can forage with a type of collective intelligence known as Swarm Intelligence. Social foragers include birds, bees, fish, ants, wild beasts, and primates. Note that, there is a type of cognitive spectrum where some foragers have little cognitive capability and others have higher, but combinely have significant capabilities. Generally, endowing each forager with more capabilities can help them succeed in foraging, both as an individual and as a group. From an engineering perspective, both ends of this type of spectrum are interesting. These foraging strategies of animals are used as optimization technique for engineering purpose. This kind of strategy commonly known as Swarm Intelligence approaches which are also used to solve optimization problems(Kennedy & Eberhart, 2001). However, most of the work is centered on some algorithms such as Particle Swarm Optimization (He, Prempain, & Wu, 2004), Ant Colony Optimization(Leguizamon & Coello Coello, 2007) and Artificial Bee Colony (Karaboga & Basturk, 2008; Roy et al., 2012), Bacterial Foraging Optimization Algorithms(BFOA). Like other swarm intelligence algorithms, BFOA is based on social and cooperative behaviors found in nature. In this scheme, the foraging behavior of *E.coli* bacteria is mimicked. In fact, the way bacteria look for regions of high levels of nutrients can be seen as an optimization process. This idea was explored by Bremermann (Bremermann, 1974) and extended later by Passino (Passino, 2002). Each bacterium tries to maximize its obtained energy for each unit of time expended on the foraging process and avoiding noxious substances. Besides that, swarm search assumes communication among individuals.

The swarm of bacteria behaves as follows:

1. Bacteria are randomly distributed in the map of nutrients.
2. Bacteria move towards high-nutrient regions in the map. Those located in regions with noxious substances or low-nutrient regions will die and disperse, respectively. Bacteria in convenient regions will reproduce (split).
3. Bacteria are located in promising regions of the map of nutrients as they try to attract other bacteria by generating chemical attractants.
4. Bacteria are now located in the highest-nutrient region. Bacteria now disperse as to look for new nutrient regions in the map.

1.4.1 Mechanism of Bacteria Foraging Optimization

The Bacterial Foraging Optimization of *E.Coli* bacteria consists of three important mechanisms namely 1) Chemotaxis 2) Reproduction 3) Elimination & Dispersal.

1.4.1.1 Chemotaxis

The Chemotaxis process is formed with *swimming* and *tumble* activies of a bacterium. A bacterium decides whether it should move in a predefined direction (*swimming*) or an altogether different direction (*tumbling*) depending upon its rotation of flagella. To represent a tumble, a unit length random direction, say $\psi(q)$ is generated. The Bacteria moves towards the directions after tumble.

So particularly,

$$\psi^i\left(q+1,r,s\right) = \psi^i\left(q,r,s\right) + C(i)\psi(q)$$

where $\psi^i\left(q,r,s\right)$ represents the position of the ith bacterium at q^{th} chemotactic step, r^{th} reproductive step, and s^{th} elimination and dispersal step . $C(i)$ -is the size of the step taken in the random direction specified by a tumble, where "C" is termed as "*run length unit*". Chemotaxis is the directed movement of cells towards "attractant" or away from a "repellent". Figure 6 (a-c) shows swimming, tumbling and chemotactic behavior of a bacterium respectively.

Figure 6. Behaviour of a bacterium: (a) swimming (b) tumbling (c) chemotactic behavior

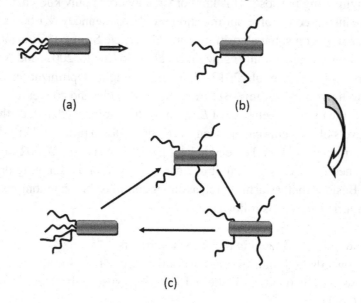

(a)   (b)

(c)

1.4.1.2 Reproduction

After completion of chemotaxis step, the health status of each bacterium is calculated as the sum of step fitness during its whole chemotactic step i.e. $FITVAL^i_{health} = \sum_{q=1}^{N_{Ch_{max}}} FITVAL(i,q,r,s)$ where $N_{Ch_{max}}$ is the maximum step in a chemotaxis process. Then, all the bacteria are sorted in reverse order according to their health status. From this order, only the first half of population survives and a survived bacterium splits into two identical one. It occupies the same position in the environment at 1st step. Thus the population of the bacteria is kept constant in each chemotaxis step.

1.4.1.3 Elimination and Dispersal

From the above two steps, it can be observed that the chemotaxis provides a basis for local search, whereas the reproduction process speeds the convergence process (Passino, 2002). Generally, only chemotaxis and reproduction are not good enough for global optima searching. It is because bacteria may get stuck around the initial positions or local optima. Several methodologies exist in the literature to overcome the local optima either gradually or suddenly. Among which, dispersion after a certain number of reproduction processes is heavily used to overcome the local minima. A bacterium is chosen, according to a preset probability P_{ed} to be dispersed and moved to another position within the environment. These events may prevent the local optima trapping effectively, but incidentally disturb the optimization process.

1.4.2 Pseudo Code of BFO

The following code describes the pseudo code of BFOA

Step 1: Initialize parameters $n, N, N_{Ch}, N_{ch_{max}}, N_{re}, N_{ed}, P_{ed}, C(i)(i = 1, 2, \ ..., N), \psi^i$ and set $q = 0, r = 0, \ s = 0$;

where,

n : Dimension of the search space,

N : The number of bacteria in the search space,

N_{Ch} : Total number of Chemotactic steps taken in a lifetime,

$N_{ch_{max}}$: Maximum number of Chemotactic steps

N_{re} : Total number of Reproduction steps,

N_{ed} : Total number of Elimination–Dispersal events,

P_{ed} : Elimination–Dispersal with probability,

$C(i)$:The size of the step taken in the random direction specified by the tumble.

Step 2: Elimination–dispersal counter: $s = s + 1$.

Step 3: Reproductioncounter: $r = r + 1$

Step 4: Chemotaxis counter: $q = q + 1$

Step 4.1: a chemotactic step for bacterium i is taken For $i = 1, 2, ..., N$ as follows.

Step 4.2: Compute fitness function, $FITVAL(i, q, r, s)$

Step 4.3: Let $FITVAL_{last} = FITVAL(i, q, r, s)$ to save this value to find a better cost via a run.

Step 4.4: Tumble: It generates a random vector $\varpi(i) \in R^n$ with each element $\varpi_j(i)$, where $j = 1, 2, ..., n$ a random number within a range of -1 to +1

Step 4.5: Move: Let

$$\psi^i\left(q + 1, r, s\right) = \psi^i\left(q, r, s\right) + C(i)\frac{\varpi(i)}{\sqrt{(\varpi^T(i)\varpi(i))}}$$

where $\psi^i\left(q, r, s\right)$ represents the position of the ith bacterium at q^{th} chemotactic step, r^{th} reproductive step, and s^{th} elimination and dispersal step . $C(i)$ -is the size of the step taken in the direction specified by a tumble for bacterium i .

Step 4.6: Compute $FITVAL(i, q, r, s)$.

Step 4.7: Swim.

1. Let $k = 0$ (initilization of the swim length).
2. While $k < N_{ch_{max}}$ (if the bacteria have not climbed down too long).
   a. Let k=k+1.
   b. If $(FITVAL(i, q + 1, r, s) < FITVAL_{last})$

$$FITVAL_{last} = FITVAL(i, q+1, r, s),$$

and

$$\psi^i\left(q+1, r, s\right) = \psi^i\left(q, r, s\right) + C(i)\frac{\varpi(i)}{\sqrt{(\varpi^T(i)\varpi(i))}}$$

and $\psi^i\left(q+1, r, s\right)$ is used to compute the new $FITVAL(i, q+1, r, s)$ as in Step 4.6.

    c.   Else $k = N_{ch_{max}}$ End of the while

Step 4.8: Go to next $i+1$ bacterium

If $(i \neq N_{ch_{max}})$ go to Step 4.2 to process the next bacterium.

Step 5: If $(q < N_{ch})$, go to Step 3.

In this case, continue chemotaxis, since the life of the bacteria is not over.

Step 6: Reproduction.
    Step 6.1: For the given r and s, and for each $i = 1, 2, ..., N$,

Let $FITVAL^i_{health} = \sum_{q=1}^{N_{ch_{max}}} FITVAL(i, q, r, s)$ be the health of the bacterium i.

Then, sort the bacteria and chemotactic parameters $C(i)$ in order of ascending cost $FITVAL_{health}$ Here the higher cost means lower health.

    Step 6.2: $N_{rep} = \dfrac{N_s}{2}$ where $N_s = $ total number of selected bacteria after chemotactic steps.

The N_{rep} bacteria with the highest $FITVAL_{health}$ values die and the remaining N_{rep} bacteria with the best values split (this process is performed by the copies that are made are placed at the same locations as their parents).

Step 7: If $(r < N_{re})$ go to Step 3.

In this case the number of specified reproduction have not reached. Therefore It starts the next generation of the chemotactic loop.

Step 8: Elimination–dispersal:

For $i = 1, 2, ..., N$, with probability P_{ed}, eliminate and disperse each bacterium, which results in keeping the number of bacteria in the population constant. To do this, if a bacterium is eliminated, simply disperse one to a random location on the optimization domain.

If $(s < N_{ed})$, then go to Step 2;

Else

end.

Figure 7 shows the flow chart of the discussed steps of the Bacterial Foraging Algorithm.

1.5 Experimental Results

1.5.1 Preparation of Data Set

To conduct experiments with the technique described in the Section 3, a database of 15000 samples of handwritten *Bangla* Basic charcter(CMATERdb 3.1.1) collected from http://code.google.com/p/cmaterdb/ is used. The database is prepared at CMATER Laboratory CSE department, Jadavpur University. The samples of the data were collected on a pre-defined data sheet from people of different age, sex, education groups. Images were optically scanned with the resolution of 300 dpi using a HP F380 flatbed scanner. All the images were first preprocessed using basic operation of skew morphological filtering (Wang, Haese-Coat, & Ronsin, 1995) and then binarized using an adaptive global threshold of (min-Intensity + max-Intensity)/2; finally, the bounding rectangular box of each image was separately normalized to 64x64 pixels. After binarization in the image '0' represents background '1' represents foreground. By dividing the database in 4:1 ratio, training and test sets are formed for evaluation of fitness function for each of the chromosomes created in the present method. Thus, the training set and the test set, used for this work, consist of 12000 samples and 3000 samples respectively

1.5.2 Brief Description of Feature Set

To evaluate the performance of the BFO on the developed database a combination of two different types of features namely, convex hull based features(Das et al., 2014; Das, Pramanik, Basu, Saha, Sarkar, & Kundu, 2009; Das, Pramanik, Basu, Saha, Sarkar, Kundu, et al., 2009) and quad tree based longest run features(Das et al., 2010; Das, Basu, et al., 2009; Das, Reddy, et al., 2012) are used. More specifically, these two features are used here for representation of character images in feature space.

1.5.2.1 Convex Hull Based Feature Set

Is well known that any character shape can be represented by a collection of its topological components or features. Here several such topological features based on the different bays, lakes attributes of a convex hull(Das, Pramanik, Basu, Saha, Sarkar, Kundu, et al., 2009) of handwritten Bangla characters have been used.

For the present work, 28 features are used on the basis of different bays attributes of the convex hull of handwritten Bangla Basic characters. From the top, bottom, right and left boundaries of any image, column and row wise distances of data pixel from convex hull boundary are calculated as d_{cp}. Then the maximum d_{cp}, i.e. total no. of rows having $d_{cp} > 0$, Average d_{cp}, mean x co-ordinate(r_x) having $d_{cp} > 0$, mean y co-ordinate (r_y) having $d_{cp} > 0$, total no. of rows having $d_{cp} = 0$, number of visible bays in this

Figure 7. The flow chart of BFO

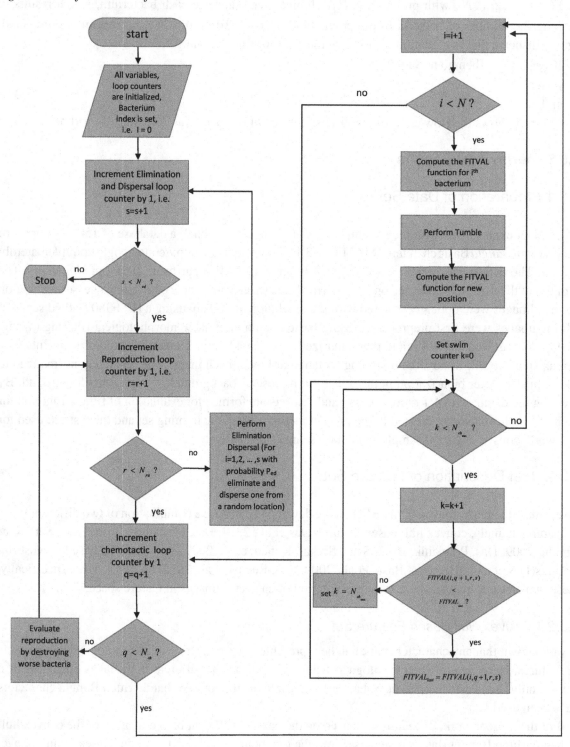

direction are computed as six topological features. From the top, bottom, right and left boundaries of the image (7x4=28) such features are calculated. It is worthy to mention that convex hull shape of a broken character does not differ too much from the shape of an integral character. Though the bays and lakes count might be varied for that case. To avoid the fallacy, a threshold value (4% of the character length) has been used to distinguish a real bays from the bays created due having broken characters. Below the threshold value, bays are not counted for our method. Besides the above twenty eight features derived from four directional segments, three more features are derived from the entire convex hull as: 1)Total number of perimeter pixels having $d_{cp} = 0$, 2) Number of lakes over the convex region, 3) Total number of perimeter pixels having $d_{cp} > 0$. Thus 31 features are extracted from the entire character image based on different bays attributes of the convex hull.

To extract local information, from the character images, each such character pattern is further divided into four sub-images based on the centroid of its convex hull. The convex hulls are then constructed for the character pixels within each such sub-image for computation of different topological features, as described earlier. 124 such features are computed from the 4 sub-images of each digit pattern. This make the total feature count as 155, i.e. 31 features for the overall image and 155 features in all for the four sub-images.

1.5.2.2 Quad-Tree Based Longest Run Features

Before extraction of longest run features from character images, a character image is first organized in to a quad tree of depth 2. To do this, the root node is first created by assigning the entire character image to it. Then all the successors of the root node are created. The character image is then divided into four quadrants along the row and column of the center of gravity of the black pixels therein. The sub-images so created are assigned to the successor nodes from left to right order. The process is repeated for creating all the next level successors and assigning image contents to them in the same way. The character image or sub-images contained by the nodes of the tree are considered here for extraction of features. Four longest run features for this feature set are extracted from each of 21 nodes of the quad tree of depth 2. Thus the number of longest run features 84.

Between the above two feature set, 155 Convexhull based features are used for global feature set along with the 20 Quad-Tree based Longest Run features extracted from the etrire image and the subimges of the depth 1. The other Quad-Tree based Longest Run features extracted from the depth 2 of CG based partitioning are used for optimization purpose based on sub-regions.

1.5.3 Brief Description of Classifier

BFO is applied on the above mentioned data to obtain the optimal set of regions containing maximum discriminatory information for accurate recognition of *Bangla* Basic characters. The Support Vector Machine (Burges, 1998), one of the popularly used classifier, is used for evaluating the fitness values of the Bacteria. For this reason, one of the freely available open source SVM tools named LibSVM(Chang & Lin, 2011) is used . As the optimality of BFOA depends on the starting point of the BFOA, therefore, it is very much difficult to say that the obtained regions for a set are always truly optimum. To overcome these difficulties in the present work, several runs of BFO are used for obtaining different optimal solutions. From these optimal solutions k-quality consensus scheme is adapted to obtain a near true optimal set of regions with maximum success rate.

1.5.4 Results and Discussion

Table 5 shows the top 25 runs of BFOA on Bangla Basic characters with the corresponding windows numbers.

From Table 5, it may be observed that highest success rate of 92.50% could be achieved for different combination of windows (window number 1, 3, 4, 5, 8, 13, 14, 15). As a single BFO does not assure the optimal result. So it is very difficult to find out the optimal set of regions which have highest discriminating power. To overcome these ambiguities 5 quality consensus are used based on the results of above five runs. The corresponding success rates are shown in Table 5.

Table 6 shows that maximum success rate of 93.03% has been achieved for the quality 5. In that quality 13 regions are selected by all the five variations of BFO for the set. On the other hand, 92.23% recognition accuracy have been achieved on test data without using any optimization technique. Therefore, a

Table 5. Results of experiments with for top twenty five runs

Sl#	Optimal Length of Local Regions Selected for the Run	Local Regions Number	Success Rate (In Percentage)
Run#1	8	1, 3, 4, 5, 8, 13, 14, 15	92.5
Run#2	7	2, 3, 4, 5, 10, 12, 13	92.366
Run#3	6	1, 2, 3, 4, 5, 7	92.33
Run#4	6	4, 7, 10, 13, 14, 15	92.33
Run#5	6	1, 2, 3, 4, 9, 10	92.26
Run#6	5	2, 5, 7, 10, 13	92.23
Run#7	6	4, 5, 6, 13, 15, 16	92.23
Run#8	5	2, 3, 5, 7, 10	92.19
Run#9	2	4, 10	92.19
Run#10	5	2, 3, 4, 10, 11	92.19
Run#11	6	1, 2, 3, 4, 9, 12	92.16
Run#12	4	2, 5, 7, 14	92.16
Run#13	5	2, 3, 4, 7, 10	92.16
Run#14	4	2, 4, 10, 13	92.13
Run#15	6	1, 2, 3, 10, 14, 15	92.09
Run#16	3	1, 4, 5	92.09
Run#17	3	1, 4, 5	92.09
Run#18	2	2, 3	92.09
Run#19	3	3, 4, 7	92.033
Run#20	2	2, 5	92
Run#21	4	4, 10, 15, 16	91.93
Run#22	5	8, 13, 14, 15, 16	91.93
Run#23	3	4, 9, 10	91.93
Run#24	3	10, 13, 16	91.93
Run#25	2	5, 7	91.9

Table 6. 5 quality consensus result based on the optimal regions selected by GA

Quality 1		Quality 2		Quality 3		Quality 4		Quality 5	
Length of Local regions	Success Rate(in Percentage)	Length of Local regions	Success Rate(in Percentage)	Length of Local regions	Success Rate(in Percentage)	Length of Local regions	Success Rate(in Percentage)	Length of Local regions	Success Rate(in Percentage)
1	92	2	92.17	7	92.60	10	92.77	13	93.03

gain of 0.80% have been observed with 13 number of subregions instead of 16 sub-regions. Thus BFOA is used for optimal recognition performance on Bangla Basic characters. To compare the utility of local region's features along with global feature set, the recognition performance of SVM classifier on the test data using only the global feature set have been evaluated. Here, the maximum success rate obtained is 91.67%. It may be noted that the accuracy obtained by using the global features is lower than the highest accuracy obtained by inclusion of features from optimal set of regions along with the global features.

CONCLUSION

In the present Chapter, an evolutionary algorithm(GA) and a swarm intelligence technique(BFO) are used to solve ambiguity between different regions during the extraction of the features for handwritten Bangla digit and Bangla character respectively. By following the present techniques, it is being possible to eliminate the regions having no significant effect on the recognition performance. For every case, for both Bangla digit and Basic character, the number of selected local regions are lower than the initially created regions. The obtained results are higher than that results obtained without optimization on the same data set. Thus it is possible to obtain higher recognition accuracy with lesser number of features. The designed techniques may be useful in improving recognition accuracy for patterns belonging to large number of target classes with an optimal tradeoff between the recognition accuracy and computational efficiency. The work can be extended to digits as well as characters of other scripts such as English, Hindi, Arabic etc alongwith pattern recognition task.

REFERENCES

Arica, N., & Yarman-Vural, F. T. (2001). An overview of character recognition focused on off-line handwriting. *IEEE Transactions on Systems, Man and Cybernetics. Part C, Applications and Reviews*, *31*(2), 216–233. doi:10.1109/5326.941845

Bakwad, K. M., Pattnaik, S. S., Sohi, B. S., Devi, S., Gollapudi, S., Sagar, C. V., & Patra, P. K. (2008). Synchronous bacterial foraging optimization for multimodal and high dimensional functions. In *Proceedings of International Conference on Computing, Communication and Networking (ICCCn 2008)* (pp. 1–8). Academic Press. doi:10.1109/ICCCNET.2008.4787680

Basu, S., Das, N., Sarkar, R., Kundu, M., Nasipuri, M., & Basu, D. (2005a). An MLP based approach for recognition of handwritten bangla numerals. In B. Prasad (Ed.), *Proceedings of 2nd Indian International Conference on Artificial Intelligence* (pp. 407–417). Pune, India: Academic Press.

Basu, S., Das, N., Sarkar, R., Kundu, M., Nasipuri, M., & Basu, D. (2009). Recognition of numeric postal codes from multi-script postal address blocks. In S. Chaudhury, S. Mitra, C. Murthy, P. Sastry, & S. Pal (Eds.), Pattern recognition and machine intelligence (Vol. 5909, pp. 381–386). Springer. doi:10.1007/978-3-642-11164-8_62

Basu, S., Das, N., Sarkar, R., Kundu, M., Nasipuri, M., & Basu, D. K. (2005b). Handwritten Bangla alphabet recognition using an MLP based classifier. In *Proceedings of 2nd National Conference on Computer Processing of Bangla* (pp. 285–291). Dhaka, Bagladesh: Academic Press.

Basu, S., Kundu, M., Nasipuri, M., & Basu, D. K. (2006). A two-pass fuzzy-geno approach to pattern classification. In *Proceedings of International Conference on Computer Processing of Bangla* (pp. 130–134). Dhaka. Bangladesh: Academic Press.

Bhowmik, T., Bhattacharya, U., & Parui, S. (2004). Recognition of Bangla handwritten characters using an MLP classifier based on stroke features. In N. Pal, N. Kasabov, R. Mudi, S. Pal, & S. Parui (Eds.), Neural information processing (Vol. 3316, pp. 814–819). Springer. doi:10.1007/978-3-540-30499-9_125

Bremermann, H. (1974). Chemotaxis and optimization. *Journal of the Franklin Institute, 297*(5), 397–404. doi:10.1016/0016-0032(74)90041-6

Burges, C. J. C. (1998). A tutorial on support vector machines for pattern recognition. *Data Mining and Knowledge Discovery, 2*(2), 121–167. doi:10.1023/A:1009715923555

Cao, J., Ahmadi, M., & Shridhar, M. (1995). Recognition of handwritten numerals with multiple feature and multistage classifier. *Pattern Recognition, 28*(2), 153–160. doi:10.1016/0031-3203(94)00094-3

Chang, C.-C., & Lin, C.-J. (2011). LIBSVM: A library for support vector machines. *ACM Transactions on Intelligent Systems and Technology, 2*(3), 1–27. doi:10.1145/1961189.1961199

Chen, H., Zhu, Y., & Hu, K. (2008). Self-adaptation in bacterial foraging optimization algorithm. In *Proceedings of 3rd International Conference on Intelligent System and Knowledge Engineering (ISKE 2008) (Vol. 1*, pp. 1026–1031). Academic Press. doi:10.1109/ISKE.2008.4731080

Cheriet, M., El Yacoubi, M., Fujisawa, H., Lopresti, D., & Lorette, G. (2009). Handwriting recognition research: Twenty years of achievement... and beyond. *Pattern Recognition, 42*(12), 3131–3135. doi:10.1016/j.patcog.2009.03.014

Cordella, L., De Stefano, C., Fontanella, F., & Marrocco, C. (2008). A feature selection algorithm for handwritten character recognition. In *Proceedings of 19th International Conference on Pattern Recognition (ICPR 2008)* (pp. 1–4). Academic Press. doi:10.1109/ICPR.2008.4761834

Dang, J., Brabazon, A., O'Neill, M., & Edelman, D. (2008). Option model calibration using a bacterial foraging optimization algorithm. In M. Giacobini, A. Brabazon, S. Cagnoni, G. Di Caro, R. Drechsler, A. Ekárt, ... S. Yang (Eds.), Applications of evolutionary computing SE - 12 (Vol. 4974, pp. 113–122). Springer Berlin Heidelberg. doi:10.1007/978-3-540-78761-7_12

Das, N., Acharya, K., Sarkar, R., Basu, S., Kundu, M., & Nasipuri, M. (2012). A novel GA-SVM based multistage approach for recognition of handwritten bangla compound characters. In *Proceedings of the International Conference on Information Systems Design and Intelligent Applications 2012* (Vol. 132, pp. 145–152). Academic Press. doi:10.1007/978-3-642-27443-5_17

Das, N., Acharya, K., Sarkar, R., Basu, S., Kundu, M., & Nasipuri, M. (2014). A benchmark image database of isolated Bangla handwritten compound characters. *International Journal on Document Analysis and Recognition*, 1–19.

Das, N., Basu, S., Sarkar, R., Kundu, M., Nasipuri, M., & Basu, D. K. (2007). A soft computing paradigm for handwritten digit recognition with application to Bangla digits. In *Proceedings of International Conference on Modeling and Simulation* (*Vol. 2*, pp. 771–774). Kolkata, India: Academic Press.

Das, N., Basu, S., Sarkar, R., Kundu, M., Nasipuri, M., & Basu, D. K. (2009). An improved feature descriptor for recognition of handwritten Bangla alphabet. In GuruD. S.VasudevT. (Eds.), *International Conference on Signal and Image Processing* (pp. 451–454). Mysore, India: Excel India Publishers.

Das, N., Das, B., Sarkar, R., Basu, S., Kundu, M., & Nasipuri, M. (2010). Handwritten Bangla basic and compound character recognition using MLP and SVM classifier. *Journal of Computing*, 2(2), 109–115.

Das, N., Pramanik, S., Basu, S., Saha, P. K., Sarkar, R., & Kundu, M. (2009). Design of a novel convex hull based feature set for recognition of isolated handwritten Roman numerals. In Proceedings of UB–NE ASEE 2009. University of Bridgeport.

Das, N., Pramanik, S., Basu, S., Saha, P. K., Sarkar, R., Kundu, M., & Nasipuri, M. (2009). Recognition of handwritten Bangla basic characters and digits using convex hull based feature set. In Z. M. Dimitrios A. Karras Etienne E. Kerre, Chunping Li (Ed.), *International Conference on Artificial Intelligence and Pattern Recognition* (pp. 380–386). Orlando, FL: ISRST.

Das, N., Reddy, J. M., Sarkar, R., Basu, S., Kundu, M., Nasipuri, M., & Basu, D. K. (2012). A statistical–topological feature combination for recognition of handwritten numerals. *Applied Soft Computing*, *12*(8), 2486–2495. doi:10.1016/j.asoc.2012.03.039

Das, N., Sarkar, R., Basu, S., Kundu, M., Nasipuri, M., & Basu, D. K. (2012). A genetic algorithm based region sampling for selection of local features in handwritten digit recognition application. *Applied Soft Computing*, *12*(5), 1592–1606. doi:10.1016/j.asoc.2011.11.030

Datta, T., Misra, I. S., Mangaraj, B. B., & Imtiaj, S. (2008). Improved adaptive bacteria foraging algorithm in optimization of antenna array for faster convergence. *Progress In Electromagnetics Research C*, *1*, 143–157. doi:10.2528/PIERC08011705

Due Trier, Ø., Jain, A. K., & Taxt, T. (1996). Feature extraction methods for character recognition-A survey. *Pattern Recognition*, *29*(4), 641–662. doi:10.1016/0031-3203(95)00118-2

Hanmandlu, M., Nath, A. V., Mishra, A. C., & Madasu, V. K. (2007). Fuzzy model based recognition of handwritten Hindi numerals using bacterial foraging. In *Proceedings of 6th IEEE/ACIS International Conference on Computer and Information Science (ICIS 2007)*. (pp. 309–314). IEEE. doi:10.1109/ICIS.2007.103

He, S., Prempain, E., & Wu, Q. H. (2004). An improved particle swarm optimizer for mechanical design optimization problems. *Engineering Optimization*, *36*(5), 585–605. doi:10.1080/03052150410001704854

Jaehwa, P., Govindaraju, V., & Srihari, S. N. (2000). OCR in a hierarchical feature space. *IEEE Transactions on Pattern Analysis and Machine Intelligence*, *22*(4), 400–407. doi:10.1109/34.845383

Karaboga, D., & Basturk, B. (2008). On the performance of artificial bee colony (ABC) algorithm. *Applied Soft Computing*, *8*(1), 687–697. doi:10.1016/j.asoc.2007.05.007

Kennedy, J., & Eberhart, R. C. (2001). *Swarm intelligence*. San Francisco, CA: Morgan Kaufmann Publishers Inc.

Kim, D. H., Abraham, A., & Cho, J. H. (2007). A hybrid genetic algorithm and bacterial foraging approach for global optimization. *Information Sciences*, *177*(18), 3918–3937. doi:10.1016/j.ins.2007.04.002

Kudo, M., & Sklansky, J. (2000). Comparison of algorithms that select features for pattern classifiers. *Pattern Recognition*, *33*(1), 25–41. doi:10.1016/S0031-3203(99)00041-2

Leguizamon, G., & Coello Coello, C. A. (2007). A boundary search based ACO algorithm coupled with stochastic ranking. In *Proceedings of IEEE Congress on Evolutionary Computation, (CEC 2007)* (pp. 165–172). IEEE. doi:10.1109/CEC.2007.4424468

Mishra, S., & Bhende, C. N. (2007). Bacterial foraging technique-based optimized active power filter for load compensation. *IEEE Transactions on Power Delivery*, *22*(1), 457–465. doi:10.1109/TPWRD.2006.876651

Passino, K. M. (2002). Biomimicry of bacterial foraging for distributed optimization and control. *IEEE Control Systems*, *22*(3), 52–67. doi:10.1109/MCS.2002.1004010

Rajashekararadhya, S. V., & Ranjan, P. V. (2008). Efficient zone based feature extration algorithm for handwritten numeral recognition of four popular south Indian scripts. *Journal of Theoretical and Applied Information Technology*, *4*(12), 1171–1181.

Roy, A., Das, N., Sarkar, R., Basu, S., Kundu, M., & Nasipuri, M. (2012). Region selection in handwritten character recognition using artificial bee colony optimization. In *Proceedings of Third International Conference on Emerging Applications of Information Technology (EAIT)* (pp. 183–186). Academic Press. doi:10.1109/EAIT.2012.6407891

Srinivas, M., & Patnaik, L. M. (1994). Genetic algorithms: A survey. *Computer*, *27*(6), 17–26. doi:10.1109/2.294849

Tang, W. J., Wu, Q. H., & Saunders, J. R. (2006). Bacterial Foraging algorithm for dynamic environments. In *Proceedings of IEEE Congress on Evolutionary Computation (CEC 2006)* (pp. 1324–1330). IEEE.

Tripathy, M., & Mishra, S. (2007). Bacteria foraging-based solution to optimize both real power loss and voltage stability limit. *IEEE Transactions on Power Systems*, *22*(1), 240–248. doi:10.1109/TPWRS.2006.887968

Wang, D., Haese-Coat, V., & Ronsin, J. (1995). Shape decomposition and representation using a recursive morphological operation. *Pattern Recognition*, *28*(11), 1783–1792. doi:10.1016/0031-3203(95)00036-Y

KEY TERMS AND DEFINITIONS

Bacteria Foraging Optimization Algorithm: Bacterial Foraging Optimization Algorithm (BFOA), a swarm intelligence algorithm is based on social and cooperative foraging behaviors of *E.coli* bacteria found in nature. The process of looking to the regions of high levels of nutrients by a bacteria can be treated as an optimization process. Bacterial Foraging Optimization Algorithm mimic the process to solve a problem. This idea was explored by Bremermann (Bremermann, 1974) and extended later by Passino (Passino, 2002).

Evolutionary Algorithms: Evolutionary algorithm is used to describe the computational models of evolutionary processes which consists of rules of selection and other operators, such as recombination and mutation as key elements in their design and implementation. After initializing the first population structures, EA evaluates the population and used different selection, recombination, and mutation to generate new population. In this way it reaches towards the goal.

Genetic Algorithm: Genetic algorithm (GA), one of the most popularly used evolutionary tools among soft computing paradigm, is mainly devised to solve real world ill-defined, and imprecisely formulated problems requiring huge computation. It is the power of GA to introduce some heuristic methodologies to minimize the search space for optimal solution(s) without sticking at local optima. Due to the inherent power, GA becomes one of the most successful heuristic optimization algorithms. It is widely used to solve problems of diversified fields ranging from engineering to art.

Global and Local Features: Global features are those features which are extracted from the overall character images. On the other hand, local features are extracted from the sub images of the same.

Handwritten Bangla Basic Character or Numeral Recognition: The Handwritten Bangla Basic character or Numeral recognition is the system by which handwritten Bangla Basic characters or Numerals are scanned into image format and recognize them into machine identifiable format. The process generally includes extraction of features from scanned images, classification of the images by a classifier based on the extracted images. It is worthy to mention here Bangla Basic character consists of 11 vowels and 39 consonants.

Handwritten Character Recognition: The Handwritten character recognition denotes the procedure of recognition of character images in machine editable format such as Unicode or ASCII from the scanned images of handwritten text.

Local Region Selection: The inherent ability of human is to recognize different patterns by focusing on sub-regions or local regions containing maximum discriminatory information. Local region selection procedure denotes identification of those local regions having maximum discriminating properties among inter class patterns and minimum discriminating properties among intra class patterns.

Chapter 20
Particle Swarm Optimization–Based Session Key Generation for Wireless Communication (PSOSKG)

Arindam Sarkar
University of Kalyani, India

Jyotsna Kumar Mandal
University of Kalyani, India

ABSTRACT

In this chapter, a Particle Swarm Optimization-Based Session Key Generation for wireless communication (PSOSKG) is proposed. This cryptographic technique is solely based on the behavior of the particle swarm. Here, particle and velocity vector are formed for generation of keystream by setting up the maximum dimension of each particle and velocity vector. Each particle position and probability value is evaluated. Probability value of each particle can be determined by dividing the position of a particular particle by its length. If probability value of a particle is less than minimum probability value then a velocity is applied to move each particle into a new position. After that, the probability value of the particle at the new position is calculated. A threshold value is selected to evaluate against the velocity level of each particle. The particle having the highest velocity more than predefined threshold value is selected as a keystream for encryption.

1. INTRODUCTION

Cryptography is the practice and study of techniques for secure communication in the existence of third parties (called adversaries). More usually, it is about constructing and analyzing protocols that conquer the way of adversaries and which are associated to a variety of aspects in information security such as data confidentiality, data integrity, authentication, and non-repudiation (Feistel, 1976). Currently new computational environment becomes more distributed, more diverse and more global; the transmission

DOI: 10.4018/978-1-4666-8291-7.ch020

of information is becoming more vulnerable to adversary attacks. Now-a-days appropriate cryptographic technique in light weight devices having very low processing capabilities or limited computing power in wireless communication is the major challenge (Liddell H. G. & Scott R, 1984; Rivest R. L., 1990; Sarkar Arindam & Mandal J. K., 2013). Thus making the design of light weight cryptographic schemes for low processing devices that can counter new cryptanalysis techniques in wireless communication is becoming harder. Therefore, computer network security is a fast moving technology in the field of computer science. Network security using cryptography originally focused on mathematical and algorithmic aspects. As security techniques continue to mature, there is an emerging set of cryptographic techniques always. This advancement of digital communication technology benefitted the field of cryptography. The efficient cryptographic schemes were designed and implemented and also broken subsequently over time (Maurer U., 1993; Delgado-Restituto M., de Ahumada R.L. & Rodriguez-Vazquez A., 1995).

Swarm intelligence (R. C. Eberhart, & J. Kennedy, 1995) is aimed at collective behaviour of intelligent agents in decentralized systems. Most of the basic ideas are derived from the real swarms in the nature, which includes Particle swarm, ant colonies, bird flocking, honeybees, bacteria and microorganisms etc. Swarm models are population-based and the population is initialized with a population of potential solutions. These individuals are then manipulated (optimized) over many several iterations using several heuristics inspired from the social behaviour of insects in an effort to find the optimal solution.

In this chapter a novel particle swarm optimization based session key generation for wireless communication (PSOSKG) has been proposed. The background for Providing broad definitions and discussions of the topic and incorporate views of others presented in the section 2. The section 3 and 4 deals with the objective of the proposed technique and detail analysis of the technique respectively. PSO based Session key generation algorithm, encryption algorithm and decryption algorithm presented in section 5, 6 and 7 respectively. Detail implementation of the proposed technique discussed in the section 8. Section 9 presents the results and analysis of the proposed technique. Conclusions are drawn in section 10 and that of references at end.

2. BACKGROUND

The advances in software technology and systems will give more computational power for cryptanalyst to break the cipher (Mantin and A. Shamir., 2001; Menezes, A.J., Vanstone, S.A. & Van Oorschot, P.C., 2001; Stallings W., 2002). As new computational environment becomes more distributed, more diverse and more global, the transmission of information is becoming more vulnerable to adversary attacks. Thus making the design of cryptographic schemes that can counter new cryptanalysis techniques is becoming harder (Dourlens S., 1995; Stinson D.R., 1995). Recently soft computing approaches provide inspiration in solving problems from various fields. Now-a-days works in the application of soft computing inspired computational paradigm in cryptography become famous. The findings show that the research on applications of soft computing based approaches in cryptography is minimal as compared to other fields. Multiple disciplines have started to work together more closely for last few decades to improve the network security for reliable communication. A number of alternative cryptosystems have gained significant attention during these periods. Soft computing is the most promising one among them. Soft Computing refers to the science of reasoning, thinking and deduction that recognizes and uses the real world phenomena of grouping, memberships, and classification of various quantities under study. As such, it is an extension of natural heuristics and capable of dealing with complex systems because it does not require strict mathematical definitions and distinctions for the system components. Soft computing differs from conventional (hard) computing in that, unlike hard computing, it is tolerant of imprecision, uncertainty, partial truth, and approximation. In effect, the role model for soft computing is the human mind. Soft Computing is a term used in computer science to refer to problems in computer science whose solutions are unpredictable, uncertain and between 0 and 1. Soft Computing became a formal area of study in Computer Science in the early 1990s. Earlier computational approaches could model and precisely analyze only relatively simple systems. More complex systems arising in biology, medicine, the humanities, management sciences, and similar fields often remained intractable to conventional mathematical and analytical methods. That said, it should be pointed out that simplicity and complexity of systems are relative, and many conventional mathematical models have been both challenging and very productive. Soft computing deals with imprecision, uncertainty, partial truth, and approximation to achieve practicability, robustness and low solution cost. As such it forms the basis of a considerable amount of machine learning techniques. Recent trends tend to involve evolutionary and swarm intelligence based algorithms and bio-inspired computation in cryptography. Components of soft computing include:

- **Evolutionary Algorithms:** Evolutionary algorithms (EA) (Julio César Hernández Castro & Pedro Isasi Viñuela, 2005; Sarkar Arindam & Mandal J. K., 2013) are adaptive methods, which may be used to solve search and optimization problems, based on the genetic processes of biological organisms. Over many generations, natural populations evolve according to the principles of natural selection and 'survival of the fittest'. By mimicking this process, evolutionary algorithms are able to 'evolve' solutions to real world problems, if they have been suitably encoded. Usually grouped under the term evolutionary algorithms or evolutionary computation, we find the domains of genetic algorithms, evolution strategies, evolutionary programming, genetic programming and learning classifier systems. They all share a common conceptual base of simulating the evolution of individual structures via processes of selection, mutation, and reproduction. Cultural Algorithms are computational models of cultural evolution (Sarkar Arindam & Mandal J. K., 2012). They consist of two basic components, a population space (using evolutionary algorithms), and a belief space. The two components interact by means of a vote-inherit-promote protocol. Likewise the knowledge acquired by the problem solving activities of the population can be stored in the belief space in the form of production rules etc. Cultural algorithms represent a general framework for producing hybrid evolutionary systems that integrate evolutionary search and domain knowledge.

The application of an evolutionary algorithm to the field of cryptography is rather unique. Few works exist on this topic. Using evolutionary algorithms most of the work has been done in the field of cryptanalysis. This nontraditional application is investigated to determine the benefits of applying an evolutionary algorithm to a cryptanalytic problem, if any. This area is so different from the application areas where evolutionary algorithms are developed. Major works that involves GA focuses on cryptanalysis of cryptographic algorithms and design of cryptographic primitives (Sarkar Arindam & Mandal J. K., 2013). Most cryptanalytic research using GA was done on classical ciphers. An initial attempt was conducted by Spillman et al., whereby GA is exploited to cryptanalysis simple substitution ciphers. Since known cryptanalytic attack for simple substitution ciphers employs frequency distribution of characters in the message, Spillman derived a cost or fitness function based on single-character and diagram frequency distributions in his work. His attempt was fruitful as GA was proven to be highly successful in this cryptanalysis. He suggested the use of trigram frequency distribution and variations on crossover and mutation procedures as future research. Spillman continues his work and illustrated that GA can also be used in the cryptanalysts of public key cryptosystem, the knapsack ciphers. The encryption scheme for knapsack ciphers is based on the NP-complete problem, which is a hard problem. Another initial attempt conducted by Matthews investigated the use of GA in cryptanalysis of transposition ciphers. In this work the fitness function is based on the message length, frequency distribution of diagrams and trigrams tested for, the number of diagrams and trigrams checked for and the likelihood of occurrence in successful deciphered messages.

- **Simulated Annealing:** Simulated annealing is based on the manner in which liquids freeze or metals recrystalize in the process of annealing. In an annealing process, molten metal, initially at high temperature, is slowly cooled so that the system at any time is approximately in thermodynamic equilibrium. If the initial temperature of the system is too low or cooling is done insufficiently slowly the system may become brittle or unstable with forming defects. The initial state of a thermodynamic system is set at energy E and temperature T, holding T constant the initial configuration is perturbed and the change in energy dE is computed. If the change in energy is negative the new configuration is accepted. If the change in energy is positive it is accepted with a probability given by the Boltzmann factor $exp\left(-\dfrac{dE}{T}\right)$. This process is then repeated for few iterations to give good sampling statistics for the current temperature, and then the temperature is decremented and the entire process repeated until a frozen state is achieved at $T=0$. Cryptanalytic attack work covers a variety of classical ciphers that include simple substitution, transposition as well as poly-alphabetic ciphers. Also it gets used in cryptographic technique (Sarkar Arindam & Mandal J. K., 2013). Existing attacks which make use of the genetic algorithm and simulated annealing are compared with the new simulated annealing and tabu search techniques.

- **Artificial Neural Network:** Artificial neural networks have been developed as generalizations of mathematical models of biological nervous systems. In a simplified mathematical model of the neuron, the effects of the synapses are represented by weights that modulate the effect of the associated input signals, and the nonlinear characteristic exhibited by neurons is represented by a transfer function, which is usually the sigmoid, Gaussian function etc. The neuron impulse is then computed as the weighted sum of the input signals, transformed by the transfer function. The learning capability of an artificial neuron is achieved by adjusting the weights in accordance to the chosen learning algorithm (Hassoun M., 1995; J. Kennedy, 1999).

- **Neural Cryptography:** A branch of cryptography dedicated to analyzing the application of stochastic algorithms, especially artificial neural network algorithms, for use in encryption and cryptanalysis. Neural Networks are well known for their ability to selectively explore the solution space of a given problem. This feature finds a natural niche of application in the field of cryptanalysis. At the same time, Neural Networks offer a new approach to attack ciphering algorithms based on the principle that any function could be reproduced by a neural network, which is a powerful proven computational tool that can be used to find the inverse-function of any cryptographic algorithm. The ideas of mutual learning, self learning, and stochastic behavior of neural networks and similar algorithms can be used for different aspects of cryptography, like public-key cryptography, solving the key distribution problem using neural network mutual synchronization, hashing or generation of pseudo-random numbers. Another idea is the ability of a neural network to separate space in non-linear pieces using "bias". It gives different probabilities of activating or not the neural network. This is very useful in the case of Cryptanalysis. Two names are used to design the same domain of researches: Neuro-Cryptography and Neural Cryptography (Dourlens S., 1995). The most used protocol for key exchange between two parties A and B in the practice is Diffie-Hellman protocol (Diffie W. & Hellman M., 1976). Neural key exchange (Hassoun M., 1995), which is based on the synchronization of two tree parity machines, should be a secure replacement for this method. Synchronizing these two machines is similar to synchronizing two chaotic oscillators in chaos communications.

- **Swarm Intelligence:** Swarm intelligence is aimed at collective behaviour of intelligent agents in decentralized systems. Most of the basic ideas are derived from the real swarms in the nature, which includes particle swarm, ant colonies, bird flocking, honeybees, bacteria and microorganisms etc. Swarm models are population-based and the population is initialized with a population of potential solutions. These individuals are then manipulated (optimized) over many several iterations using several heuristics inspired from the social behaviour of insects in an effort to find the optimal solution. Particle Swarm Optimization (PSO) algorithms are inspired by the behavior of natural ant colonies, in the sense that they solve their problems by multi agent cooperation using indirect communication through modifications in the environment. Particle swarm optimizer (PSO) emulates flocking behavior of birds and herding behavior of animals to solve optimization problems. The PSO was introduced by Kennedy and Eberhart in 1995 (J. Kennedy, & R. C. Eberhart, 1995 ; J. Kennedy, 1999). In the PSO domain, there are two main variants: global PSO and local PSO. In the local version of the PSO, each particle's velocity is adjusted according to its personal best position pbest and the best position lbest achieved so far within its neighborhood. The global PSO learns from the personal best position pbest and the best position gbest achieved so far by the whole population.

3. THE OBJECTIVE

The objective of modern cryptographic technique is to provide security for the system where unify computing is an essential component and also for light weight devices having very low processing capabilities or limited computing power in wireless communication.

So it is essential to find some cryptographic techniques where PSO can be used to increase the security of the cryptographic protocol. By keeping in mind the resource constrains criteria of wireless communication the robust and secure encryption/decryption technique which takes less resources for computations and secure session key which is less complex but provides very high degree of security with respect to existing cryptographic techniques along with energy awareness is very much needed in wireless communication.

4. THE TECHNIQUE

The PSO technique begins with an initial population comprises of set of valid and complete set of particles. Then some operators like particles local best and global best positions along with velocity updating rules are used to generate feasible valid particle from the existing one. In this proposed technique a collection of alphanumeric characters is called a keystream and each character in the keystream is known as key. The keystream measurement lengthwise constantly be less than or equal to the plaintext to be encrypt and production of keystream is based on sharing of characters in the plaintext for encryption principle.

In PSO based approach a particle is used to designate a keystream (set of alphanumeric characters). Each particle can have numerous dimensions. Each dimension signifies an individual key inside that keystream. The dimensions in the keystream can be packed or unpacked. For example if the ceiling of dimension of each particle is equal to 256 then it is characterized by Equation 1.

$$Particle_i \, or \, Keystream_i = \left(Key_1, Key_2, ..., Key_{256} \right) \tag{1}$$

which actually indicate a keystream comprises of 256 keys i.e. 256 alphanumeric characters. Keystream length can be attained by counting number of dimensions are packed in the keystream. Usually keystream length is less than or equal to the plaintext. With 256 alphanumeric characters various keystream can be generated of preset rigid length by variation of these prearranged set length characters ordering all viable ways devoid of any recurrence. So, for example if total number of alphanumeric characters = 256 and if key stream length = 192 then among 256 alphanumeric characters 192 alphanumeric characters are nominated such a way so that by ordering all achievable ways with no replication these 192 characters forms multiple keystream having monotonous length i.e. 192. For an example if four characters A, S, M, K are taken to structure keystream of length four among 256 alphanumeric characters. Then there are 24 doable ways of obtaining keystream which are as follows.

ASMK, ASKM, AMSK, AMKS, AKMS, AKSM, SAMK, SAKM, SMAK, SMKA, SKMA, SKAM,

MASK, MAKS, MSAK, MSKA, MKSA, MKAS, KASM, KAMS, KSAM, KSMA, KMSA, KMAS

Using 256 characters total number of generated potential keystream is given in Equation 2.

$$\sum_{c=1}^{256} \frac{256!}{\left(256 - c \right)!} \approx 256! \left(e \right) \approx 256! \times 2.718 \tag{2}$$

According to PSO technique each particle should have an allied velocity. The PSO technique also offers velocity for each and every particle or keystream. This velocity vector also has multiple dimensions. The number of velocity dimension is calculated using following logic.

If (length of (Plaintext)) ≤ maximum keystream dimension then
Set velocity dimension (n) ≤ (length of (Plaintext)) - (length of (keystream))
Else if (length of (Plaintext)) > maximum keystream dimension then
Set velocity dimension (n) ≤ (maximum keystream dimension) - (length of (keystream))

The dimensions in the velocity vector can be filled or unfilled. Total number of engaged dimension in the velocity vector denotes the length of the velocity vector. Velocity vector of *Particle_i* is denoted by *Velocity_i* which is a set of n velocity values one for each character

$Velocity_i = \left(Velocity\_char_1, Velocity\_char_2, \ldots, Velocity\_char_n\right)$. Group of velocity characters form a velocity vector. In this proposed technique maximum keystream dimension is 256. So,

If (length of (Plaintext)) ≤ 256 then
      Set velocity dimension (n) ≤(lengthof(Plaintext)) - (lengthof(keystream))
Else if (lengthof(Plaintext)) > 256 then
      Set velocity dimension (n) ≤ 256 - (lengthof(keystream))

Each particle position is evaluated by counting number of characters in the keystream belonging to a plaintext. Using Equation 3 particle position is evaluated.

$$Particle\_Position\left(Particle_i\right) = count\left(Key_j \in Plaintext\right), \tag{3}$$

where $j = 1, 2, \ldots$, length of ($Particle_i$)
    Likelihood of characters in the keystream appearing in the plaintext is calculated using Equation 4.

$$Prob(Particle_i) = Particle\_Position(Particle_i)/lengthof\ (Particle_i) \tag{4}$$

If (Prob($Particle_i$) ≥ min probability value) then
      return ($Particle_i$ with Prob($Particle_i$) = max probability value)
If (Prob($Particle_i$) < min (probability value)) then
      repeat apply a new velocity to displace the particle potion

Each particle having an old velocity $Velocity_i$ and can be moved to a new location by applying a new velocity $Velocity_k$ on it. The Velocity applied to a particle is a number of characters in the velocity vector occurring in the plaintext and characters are chosen such a way so that these group of characters not occurring in the keystream and velocity vector. Once applying velocity on a particle the velocity characters occupy the dimension which is vacant in the velocity vector given in equation 5.

$$Velocity_k = \left(Velocity_{char_1}, Velocity_{char_2}, \ldots, Velocity_{char_m}\right), \tag{}$$

where $Velocity_k \notin \left(Particle_i, Velocity_i\right)$ and

m (current velocity dimension)=n (previous velocity dimension) - length of ($Velocity_i$)   (5)

The current position of a particle is found by toting up the previous position with the applied velocity given in Equation 6.

$$Current\_position(Particle_i) = previous\_position(Particle_i) + Velocity_k \tag{6}$$

The current likelihood value can be computed by dividing the particle current position with the summation of particle length and velocity vector length.

$$\text{Prob}(Particle_i)=\text{Current\_position}(Particle_i)/(\text{length of }(Particle_i) + \text{length of }(Velocity_i)) \tag{7}$$

$$\text{Compute } Velocity_i = Velocity_i \ \& \ Velocity_k \tag{8}$$

$$\text{Return}(Particle_i \text{ and } Velocity_i \text{ with Prob}(Particle_i)=\max(\text{prob value}) \tag{9}$$

This velocity updating phase continued

until $(\text{Prob}(Particle_i) \geq \max$ probability value)

In this proposed PSO based encryption/decryption keystream generation technique following parameters are used

- Maximum length of PSO based keystream i.e. maximum number of character represents a keystream is $L=256$. N is the number of characters to represents keystream. Maximum value of N is L i.e. 256.
- A predefined threshold value for describing energy factor of Ant agent. This proposed scheme used 0.75 as a threshold value.
- A predetermined value to generate the keys for the characters in the plaintext which is at a position greater than the length of the key stream. The technique uses equation 10 to compute the predetermined value.

$$\text{Predetermined\_value}= \text{length of(plaintext)}/2 \tag{10}$$

PSO based encryption/decryption keystream generation algorithm a threshold value is selected to weigh against velocity level of each Particle. Particle having highest energy level more than predefined threshold value is selected as a keystream.

The Figure 1 shows the flowchart of PSO based keystream generation.

5. PSO BASED SESSION KEY GENERATION ALGORITHM

PSO based keystream generation algorithm a threshold value is selected to weigh against velocity level of each Particle. Particle having highest energy level more than predefined threshold value is selected as a keystream.

Input: Particle with velocity.
Output: PSO based keystream.
Method: A threshold value is selected to weigh against velocity level of each particle. Particle having highest probability more than predefined threshold value is selected as a keystream.

Figure 1. Flowchart of PSO based keystream generation

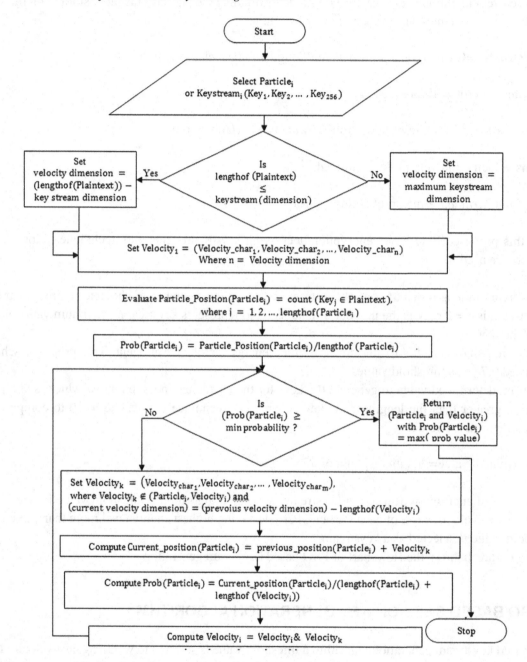

Step 1: Select particle and velocity vector for generation of keystream. Set the maximum dimension of each particle (keystream) equal to 256. Where

$$Particle_i \, or \, Keystream_i = \left(Key_1, Key_2, \ldots, Key_{256} \right) \qquad (11)$$

$$Velocity_i = \left(Velocity\_char_1, Velocity\_char_2, ..., Velocity\_char_n\right) \tag{12}$$

If (length of (Plaintext))$\leq$ 256 the

Set velocity dimension (n)$\leq$(length of (Plaintext))-*(length of (keystream))* $\tag{13}$

Else if (length of (Plaintext)) > 256 then

Set velocity dimension *(n)* $\leq$ 256 - (length of (keystream)) $\tag{14}$

Step 2: Evaluate particle position using following function

$$Particle\_Position\left(Particle_i\right) = count\left(Key_j \in Plaintext\right), \tag{15}$$

where $j = 1, 2, ...,$ length of (*Particle_i*).
Evaluate the probability value using following equation

Prob(*Particle_i*)=Particle_Position(*Particle_i*)/length of (*Particle_i*) $\tag{16}$

If (Prob(*Particle_i*) $\geq$ min probability value) then
return (Particle_i with Prob(Particle_i)=max probability value $\tag{17}$

Step 3: While (Prob (*Particle_i*) < min probability value) *do* repeat apply a *Velocity_k*

$$Velocity_k = \left(Velocity_{char_1}, Velocity_{char_2}, ..., Velocity_{char_m}\right), \tag{18}$$

where $Velocity_k \notin \left(Particle_i, Velocity_i\right)$ and

m (current velocity dimension)= n (prevoius velocity dimension)-*length of (Velocity_i)* $\tag{19}$

Current_position(*Particle_i*) = previous_position(*Particle_i*) + *Velocity_k* $\tag{20}$

Prob(*Particle_i*)= Current_position(*Particle_i*)/(length of (*Particle_i*)+length of (*Velocity_i*)) $\tag{21}$

Compute *Velocity_i* = *Velocity_i* & *Velocity_k* $\tag{22}$

until (Prob(*Particle_i*)$\geq$max(prob value))

Return (*Particle_i* and *Velocity_i* with Prob(*Particle_i*)=max(prob value) $\tag{23}$

Step 4: If the length of the plaintext is grater than the length of the keystream then the values of the keystream are added to a predetermined value to generate the keys for the characters in the plaintext which is at a position grater than the length of the key stream.

The PSO based fittest keystream is used to perform the encryption operation on the plaintext. The detail step of PSO based encryption process is given in section 6.

6. ENCRYPTION ALGORITHM

Input: Source file/source stream i.e. plaintext.
Output: Encrypted file/encrypted stream i.e. cipher text.
Method: The process operates on binary stream and generates encrypted bit stream through Particle Swarm Intelligence (PSO) based encryption.

Step 1: If the length of the plaintext is grater than the length of the PSO based keystream then the values of the keystream are added to a predetermined value to generate the keys for the characters in the plaintext which is at a position grater than the length of the keystream. Predetermined value is calculated using the Equation 24.

Predetermined_value= length of (plaintext)/2 (24)

Step 2: For the very first plaintext block keys are form by the values of the characters in the PSO based keystream.

Step 3: For the successive plaintext blocks PSO based keys are generated by adding predetermined value with the keys of the previous block given in Equation 25 for reducing the key storage load that in turn reduces the space complexity.

Keyforblock(i)= Keyforblock(i-1)+ Predetermined value,

where

$i>=2$ (25)

Step 4: Perform Exclusive-OR operation between plaintext block with key in the PSO based keystream.

Step 5: Consider the outcomes of step 4 as a stream of finite number of bits N, and is divided into a finite number of blocks, each also containing a finite number of bits n, where $1 \leq n \leq N$. Consider the block $C = c_0^j c_1^j c_2^j c_3^j c_4^j \dots c_{n-1}^j$ having size n in the outcomes of step 4.

Step 6: Perform cycle formation techniques on $C = c_0^j c_1^j c_2^j c_3^j c_4^j \dots c_{n-1}^j$ of block of size n. In the following cases $\oplus$ is used to represents the Exclusive-OR operation. Perform the operations given in equation 26 to 29 for generating the first intermediate block $I_1 = c_{n-1}^{j+1}$ from C in the following way:

$$c_{n-1}^{j+1} = c_{n-1}^{j} \tag{26}$$

$$c_{n-2}^{j+1} = c_{n-2}^{j} \oplus c_{n-1}^{j+1} \tag{27}$$

$$c_1^{j+1} = c_1^{j} \oplus c_2^{j+1} \tag{28}$$

$$c_0^{j+1} = c_0^{j} \tag{29}$$

This process continues for a finite number of iterations, which depends on the value of n, the source block C is regenerated. If the number of iterations required regenerating the source block is assumed to be I, then any of the intermediate block is considered as a encrypted block.

In the decryption process the PSO based cipher text is divided into blocks. *Exclusive-OR* guided cycle formation based decryption is performed on each block. After that all blocks are merged together. The PSO generated keystream is use to *Exclusive-OR* with the merged blocks to regenerate the plaintext. The detail step of PSO based decryption process is given in section 7.

7. DECRYPTION ALGORITHM

Input: PSO Encrypted file/ PSO encrypted stream.

Output: Source file/source stream i.e. plaintext.

Method: The process operates on PSO encrypted bit stream and regenerates the plaintext through PSO based decryption.

   Step 1:   Divide the PSO encrypted text into different blocks.

   Step 2:   Perform operation given in equation 6.44 to 6.47 upto (P – i) steps on each block $T = t_0^i t_1^i t_2^i t_3^i t_4^i \ldots t_{n-1}^i$ if the total number of iterations required to complete the cycle is P and the ith step is considered to be the encrypted block.

$$t_{n-1}^{i} = t_{n-1}^{i-1} \tag{30}$$

$$t_{n-2}^{i} = t_{n-2}^{i} \oplus t_{n-1}^{i} \tag{31}$$

$$t_1^{i} = t_1^{i-1} \oplus t_2^{i} \tag{32}$$

$$t_0^{i} = t_0^{i-1} \tag{33}$$

   Step 3:   Merge outcomes of step 2.

   Step 4:   Compute the predetermined value.

   Step 5:   Using predetermined value and keys in the PSO based keystream receiver generates the keys for the portion of the text exceeding the length of the PSO based keystream.

   Step 6:   Generate plaintext by performing Exclusive-OR operation between outcomes of step 3 and PSO based keystream.

8. IMPLEMENTATION

Consider the text to be encrypted is "softcomputing". The minimum probability value is assumed to be 0.75. Each particle comprises of characters representing the particle keystream. The position of the particle is computed by counting the number of characters in the particle keystream occurring in the plaintext. The probability value is found by dividing the particle position by the length of the particle keystream. If the value is less than the minimum probability value a velocity is applied to the particle to move to a new position and the position of the new particle and the probability value is found. The particle having maximum probability value greater than or equal to the minimum probability value in the iteration is the solution. The corresponding particle keystream and velocity keystream are concatenated which forms the keystream for encryption. Table 1 shows the process of obtaining the keystream using PSO based approach. A group of particles denoting the key stream are taken. In this the first particle has a particle keystream "hcv". Since one character in the particle keystream occurs in the plaintext to be encrypted the position of the particle is one. The probability value of the particle is found to be 0.33 which is less than the minimum probability value. Thus a velocity containing one character "gm" is given to the particle to move the particle to a new position. Since the character in the group denoting the velocity occurs in the plaintext, the velocity is found to be two. This is added to the old position of the particle and the new position of the particle is found to have a value of three. The characters in the group denoting the velocity occupy the dimensions in the velocity keystream. The probability value is found to be 0.6 by dividing the new position by the sum of particle keystream length and the velocity keystream length. Since this is also lesser than the minimum probability value a velocity is again given to the particle and the process is repeated and the probability value is found to be 0.75 which is equal than the minimum probability value. This procedure is repeated for other particles in the group. Since the first particle in iteration three has the maximum probability value 0.75 which is greater than the minimum probability value the particle keystream "hcv" and the velocity keystream "gmtof" corresponding to that particle are concatenated to form the keystream "hcvgmtof" chosen for encryption. Each character in the keystream is chosen as the key for encryption. The keys used for encryption looks like a series of random numbers. Using this method the keys cannot be cracked since the keys depends on the characters in the plaintext and a random stream generator is not used for key generation. Table 1 illustrates the PSO based keystream generation process.

Table 1. PSO based keystream generation

Particle Keystream	Position	Probability Value	Velocity	New Position	Velocity Keystream	Probability Value	Velocity	New Position	Velocity Keystream	Probability Value
hcv	1	0.33	gm-2	3	gm	0.6	tof-3	6	gmtof	0.75
rbzlsy	1	0.16	pcu-3	4	pcu	0.44	ma-1	5	pcuma	0.45
csegdx	3	0.5	jb-0	3	jb	0.37	pm-2	5	jbpm	0.50
ecg	2	0.66	uhv-1	3	uhv	0.50	gre-1	4	uhvgre	0.44
Maximum Probability Value		0.66				0.6				0.75

Consider the plaintext to be encrypted is "softcomputing", binary representation of the ASCII value of plaintext is

01110011/01101111/01100110/01110100/01100011/01101111/01101101/01110000/011101
01/01110100/01101001/01101110/01100111

Binary representations of ASCII value of the plaintext are divided into variable size segments. Following are the different segments constructed from S.

S_1 = 0111001101101111 (16 bits)
S_2 = 0110011001110100 (16 bits)
S_3 = 0110001101101111 (16 bits)
S_4 = 0110110101110000 (16 bits)
S_5 = 0111010101110100 (16 bits)
S_6 = 01101001 (8 bits)
S_7 = 0110111001100111 (16 bits)

For each of the segments, an arbitrary intermediate segment, is considered as the encrypted segment. The formation of cycles for segments (0111001101101111) is shown below. After 16 steps cycle is complete and the plaintext is regenerated. An arbitrary intermediate segment (0101001111100011) after iteration-10 considered as an encrypted segment for the segment S_1.

$0111001101101111 \to 0101000100100101^1 \to 0011000011100011^2 \to 0110111110100001^3 \to$ 010
$1101010011111^4 \to 0011011001110101^5 \to 0110110111010011^6 \to 0010010010110001^7 \to$
$0001110001101111^8 \to 0111010000100101^9 \to 0101001111100011^{10} \to 0100111010100001^{11} \to 0100010$
$110011111^{12} \to 0100001101110101^{13} \to 0011111011010011^{14} \to$
$0001010110110001^{15} \to 0111001101101111^{16}$

The formation of cycles for segments S_2 (0110011001110100) is shown below. After 16 steps cycle is complete and the plaintext is regenerated. An arbitrary intermediate segment (0001001001110100) after iteration-8 considered as an encrypted segment for the segment S_2.

$0110011001110100 \to 0010001000101100^1 \to 0110000111100100^2 \to 0101111101011100^3 \to$ 001
$1010100110100^4 \to 0110110011101100^5 \to 0101101110100100^6 \to 0011011010011100^7 \to$
$0001001001110100^8 \to 0000111000101100^9 \to 0000010111100100^{10} \to 0000001101011100^{11} \to 0000000$
$100110100^{12} \to 0000000011101100^{13} \to 0111111110100100^{14} \to$
$0010101010011100^{15} \to 0110011001110100^{16}$

The formation of cycles for segments S_3 (0110001101101111) is shown below. After 16 steps cycle is complete and the plaintext is regenerated. An arbitrary intermediate segment (0101010110011111) after iteration-12 considered as an encrypted segment for the segment S_3.

$0110001101101111 \to 0010000100100101^1 \to 0110000011100011^2 \to 0101111110100001^3 \to$ 010
$0101010011111^4 \to 0100011001110101^5 \to 0011110111010011^6 \to 0001010010110001^7 \to$

$00001100011011111^8 \rightarrow 00000100000100101^9 \rightarrow 0000001111100011^{10} \rightarrow 0111111010100001^{11} \rightarrow 0101010$
$110011111^{12} \rightarrow 0011001101110101^{13} \rightarrow 0110111011010011^{14} \rightarrow$
$0010010110110001^{15} \rightarrow 0110001101101111^{16}$

The formation of cycles for segments S_4 (0110110101110000) is shown below. After 16 steps cycle is complete and the plaintext is regenerated. An arbitrary intermediate segment (0100101001110000) after iteration-4 considered as an encrypted segment for the segment S_4.

$0110110101110000 \rightarrow 0010010011010000^1 \rightarrow 0110001110110000^2 \rightarrow 0101111010010000^3 \rightarrow \quad 010$
$0101001110000^4 \rightarrow 0011100111010000^5 \rightarrow 0110100010110000^6 \rightarrow 0010011110010000^7 \rightarrow$
$0001110101110000^8 \rightarrow 0111010011010000^9 \rightarrow 0101001110110000^{10} \rightarrow 0100111010010000^{11} \rightarrow 0011101$
$001110000^{12} \rightarrow 0110100111010000^{13} \rightarrow 0101100010110000^{14} \rightarrow$
$0011011110010000^{15} \rightarrow 0110110101110000^{16}$

The formation of cycles for segments S_5 (0111010101110100) is shown below. After 16 steps cycle is complete and the plaintext is regenerated. An arbitrary intermediate segment (0110011001011100) after iteration-11 considered as an encrypted segment for the segment S_5.

$0111010101110100 \rightarrow 0101001100101100^1 \rightarrow 0100111011100100^2 \rightarrow 0011101001011100^3 \rightarrow \quad 000$
$1011000110100^4 \rightarrow 0000110111101100^5 \rightarrow 0000010010100100^6 \rightarrow 0000001110011100^7 \rightarrow$
$0000000101110100^8 \rightarrow 0111111100101100^9 \rightarrow 0010101011100100^{10} \rightarrow 0110011001011100^{11} \rightarrow 0010001$
$000110100^{12} \rightarrow 0110000111101100^{13} \rightarrow 0010000010100100^{14} \rightarrow$
$0001111110011100^{15} \rightarrow 0111010101110100^{16}$

The formation of cycles for segments S_6 (01101001) is shown below. After 8 steps cycle is complete and the plaintext is regenerated. An arbitrary intermediate segment (00011101) after iteration-2 considered as an encrypted segment for the segment S_6.

$01101001 \rightarrow 00100111^1 \rightarrow 00011101^2 \rightarrow 00001011^3 \rightarrow 01111001^4 \rightarrow 01010111^5 \rightarrow 01001101^6 \rightarrow$
$00111011^7 \rightarrow 01101001^8$

The formation of cycles for segments S_7 (0110111001100111) is shown below. After 16 steps cycle is complete and the plaintext is regenerated. An arbitrary intermediate segment (0010110011111011) after iteration-6 considered as an encrypted segment for the segment S_7.

$0110111001100111 \rightarrow 0010010111011101^1 \rightarrow 0110001101001011^2 \rightarrow 0010000100111001^3 \rightarrow \quad 000$
$1111000010111^4 \rightarrow 0111010100001101^5 \rightarrow 0010110011111011^6 \rightarrow 0001101110101001^7 \rightarrow$
$0000100101100111^8 \rightarrow 0111100011011101^9 \rightarrow 0010100001001011^{10} \rightarrow 0001100000111001^{11} \rightarrow 0000100$
$00001011^{12} \rightarrow 0111100000001101^{13} \rightarrow 0101011111111011^{14} \rightarrow$
$0011001010101001^{15} \rightarrow 0110111001100111^{16}$

On completion of the cycle formation technique on each segment seven intermediate segments are considered as the encrypted segments. After merging the above seven encrypted segments following PSO based encrypted text is generated.

01010011/11100011/00010010/01110100/01010101/10011111/01001010/01110000/011001
10/01011100/00011101/00101100/11111011

The PSO based keystream "hcvgmtof" has eight characters. Whereas the plaintext "softcomputing" has thirteen characters. So, for the extra five characters PSO based keys are generated by adding predetermined value with the keys of the previous block for reducing the key storage load that in turn reduces the space complexity. Predetermined value is calculated by the equation 34.

$$Predetermined\_value= lengthof(plaintext)/2 \tag{34}$$

So, the predetermined value will be $\left(\dfrac{13}{2} \right) = 6$.

So binary representation of ASCII value of the PSO based keystream is

01101000/01100011/01110110/01100111/01101101/01110100/01101111/01100110/011011
10/01101001/01111100/01101101/01110011

On performing PSO keystream based encryption operation new intermediate encoded text is

00111011/10000000/01100100/00010011/00111000/11101011/00100101/00010110/000010
00/00110101/01100001/01000001/10001000

9. RESULTS AND ANALYSIS

In this section results of proposed technique is computed on different types of files and extensive analysis have been made. The comparative study among proposed and existing RSA, Triple-DES (168 bits), AES (128 bits) (Schneier B., 1995; Stinson D.R., 1995; Stallings W., 2002) has been done based on twenty files by performing different types of experiment. In section 9.1 results of encryption/decryption time is presented. Section 9.2 deals with the comparisons of Avalanche, strict Avalanche and Bit Independence value of proposed and existing techniques. Test for non-homogeneity presented in the section 9.3. Finally, section 9.4 deals with the analysis of character frequencies, entropy, floating frequencies and autocorrelation

9.1 Encryption/Decryption Time

All test programs for the algorithms were equipped to display the total encryption and decryption time. Time taken is the difference between processor clock ticks in starting and end. Times are computed in milliseconds (ms). The lower the time taken, the better is for a typical end user. Since the CPU clock ticks taken as time, there might be a slight variation in actual time. This variation is insignificant and may be ignored.

Section 9.1.1 shows the result on *.dll* files, section 9.1.2 shows the result on *.exe* files, section 9.1.3 shows the result on *.txt* files, section 9.1.4 shows the result on *.doc* files.

9.1.1 .dll Files

Twenty *.dll* files of different sizes varying from 3216 bytes to 5,456,704 bytes have been taken to generate the data containg various attributes for evaluation of the proposed technique. Figures 2 and 3 shows the graphical representation of the relationship between the encryption times against the *.dll* type source files and the decryption times against the *.dll* type source files respectively for proposed, TDES and AES techniques. Enc. and Dec. for proposed and AES are near equal but much lower than that of TDES.

Figure 2. Graphical representation of encryption time against the varying size of input stream of .dll files for proposed and existing techniques

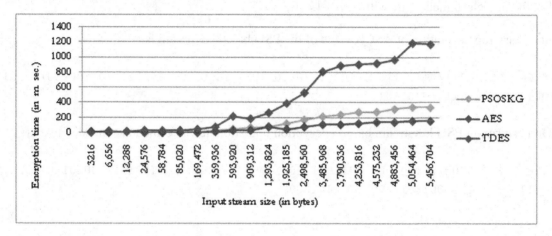

Figure 3. Graphical representation of decryption time against the varying size of input stream of .dll files for proposed and existing techniques

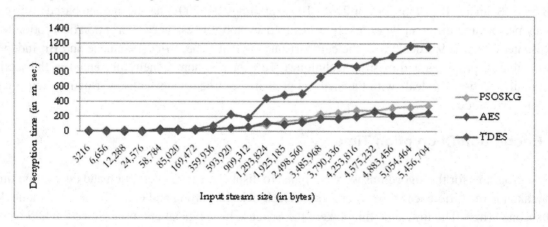

9.1.2 .exe Files

Twenty *.exe* files of sizes varying from 882 bytes to 6542640 bytes have been taken. Table 6.4 shows the encryption and decryption time of *.exe* type files obtained using proposed and existing AES and TDES techniques. Figures 4 and 5 show the pictorial representation of the relationship between the encryption times against the .exe type source files and the decryption times against the .exe type source files respectively for proposed and existing AES and TDES. TDES takes maximum time for both encryption and decryption. In both the figures, the slopes of the curves for TDES are higher for larger source files.

Figure 4. Graphical representation of encryption time against the varying size of input stream of .exe files for proposed and existing techniques

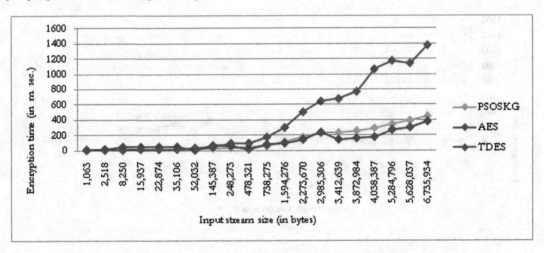

Figure 5. Graphical representation of decryption time against the varying size of input stream of .exe files for proposed and existing techniques

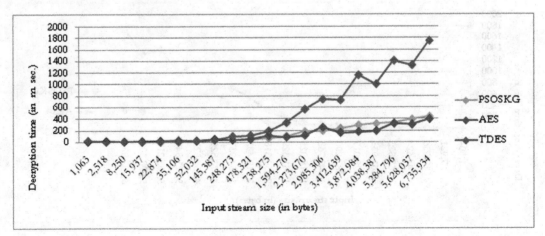

9.1.3 .txt Files

Twenty *.txt* files of sizes varying from 1696 bytes to 6597299 bytes have been taken to generate encryption (Enc.) and decryption times (Dec.). Figures 6 and 7 show the pictorial representation of the relationship between the encryption times against the *.txt* type source files and the decryption times against the *.txt* type source files respectively for proposed and existing AES and TDES. TDES takes maximum time for both encryption and decryption whereas other seven techniques take less times compare to that of TDES. In both the figures, the gradients of the curves for TDES are higher for larger source files.

Figure 6. Graphical representation of encryption time against the varying size of input stream of .txt files for proposed and existing techniques

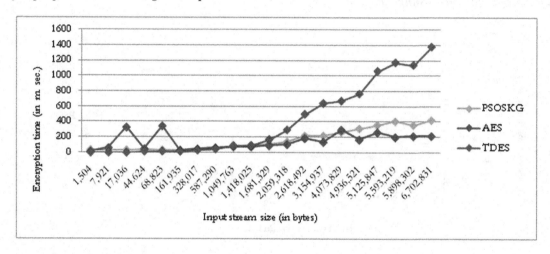

Figure 7. Graphical representation of decryption time against the varying size of input stream of .txt files for proposed and existing techniques

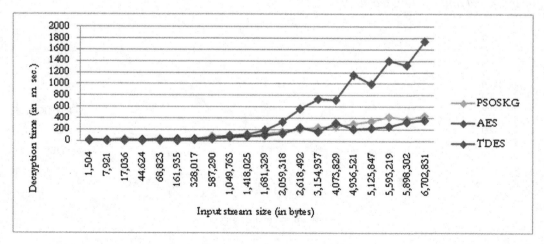

9.1.4 .doc Files

Twenty *.doc* files of sizes varying from 21,052 bytes to 5,472,298 bytes have been taken to generate the data for comparison among proposed and existing AES and TDES. Figures 8 and 9 show the graphical representation of the relationship between the encryption times against the *.doc* type source files and the decryption times against the *.doc* type source files respectively for proposed and existing AES and TDES. TDES takes maximum time for both encryption and decryption whereas other seven techniques take less times compare to that of proposed and existing AES take near same time to encrypt and decrypt the files. In both the figures, the slopes of the curves for TDES are higher for larger source files.

Figure 8. Graphical representation of encryption time against the varying size of input stream of .doc files for proposed and existing techniques

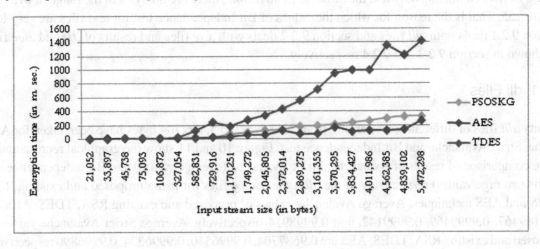

Figure 9. Graphical representation of decryption time against the varying size of input stream of .doc files for proposed and existing techniques

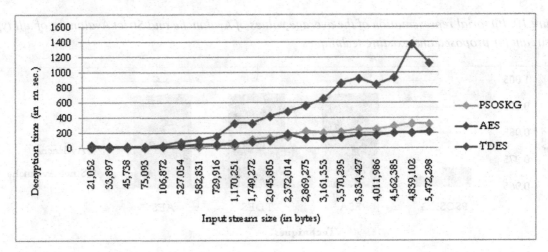

9.2 Avalanche, Strict Avalanche, and Bit Independence

Comparison between the source and encrypted byte has been made and changed of bits in encrypted bytes has been observed for a single bit change in the original message byte for the entire or a relative large number of bytes. The standard deviation from the expected values calculated. Subtract the ratio of the calculated standard deviation with expected value from 1.0 to get the avalanche and Strict Avalanche on a 0.0 –1.0 scale.

A function $f:\{0,1\}^n \to \{0,1\}^n$ satisfies the Bit Independence criteria if $\forall$ i,j,k$\in\{1,2,...,n\}$, with $j{\neq}k$, inverting input bit i cause output bits j and k to change independently. To measure the Bit Independence concept, the correlation coefficient between the jth and k^{th} components of the output difference string is needed, which is called the Avalanche vector A^{e_i}.

The higher and closer value to 1.0, the better Avalanche and Strict Avalanche is said to be satisfied. In case of files contacting only text messages in plain format, there are no bytes in the range of byte 128 to byte 255. That is the reason for which the values of Bit Independence test for text files are very low. Section 9.2.1 deals with *.dll* files and section 9.2.2 deals with *.exe* files and results of *.txt* and *.doc* files are shown in section 9.2.3 and 9.2.4 respectively.

9.2.1 .dll Files

Twenty *.dll* files of different sizes varying from 3216 bytes to 5,456,704 bytes have been taken for Avalanche, Strict Avalanche and Bit Independence test. Figure 10 and 11 show the graphical representation of the comparison of results of Avalanche, Strict Avalanche (average values) and Bit Independence test results (average values) respectively of the *.dll* type source files for using proposed and existing RSA, TDES and AES techniques. Average Avalanche values of proposed and existing RSA, TDES, AES are 0.97189467, 0.9999469, 0.9999142, and 0.9998914 respectively. Average Strict Avalanche values of proposed and existing RSA, TDES, AES are 0.9687704, 0.9996540, 0.9996324, 0.9996890 respectively. Average Bit Independence values of proposed and existing RSA, TDES, AES are 0.7569857, 0.7211989, 0.7147735, and 0.7190952 respectively. Proposed technique has the highest average Bit Independence value which indicates that this technique provides better degree of security.

Figure 10. Pictorial representation of the average values of Avalanche and Strict Avalanche of .dll type bit stream for proposed and existing techniques

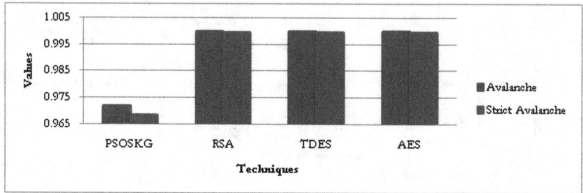

Figure 11. Pictorial representation of the average values of Bit Independence of .dll type bit stream for proposed and existing techniques

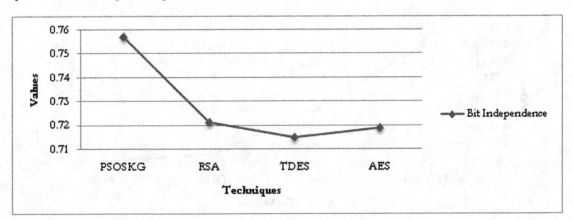

9.2.2 .exe Files

Twenty *.exe* files of different sizes varying from 1,063 bytes to 6,735,934 bytes have been taken for Avalanche, Strict Avalanche and Bit Independence test. Figure 12 and 13 show the graphical representation of the comparison of results of Avalanche, Strict Avalanche (average values) and Bit Independence test results (average values) respectively of the .exe type source files for using proposed and existing RSA, TDES and AES techniques. Average Avalanche values of proposed and existing RSA, TDES, AES are 0.9651026, 0.9997574, 0.9992658, and 0.9996030 respectively. Average Strict Avalanche values of proposed and existing RSA, TDES, AES are 00.9623935, 0.9992551, 0.9983186 and 0.9987340 respectively. Average Bit Independence values of proposed and existing RSA, TDES, AES 0.7709169, 0.7330390, 0.7042388, and 0.7002145 respectively. Proposed technique has the highest average Bit Independence value which indicates that this technique provides better degree of security.

Figure 12. Pictorial representation of the average values of Avalanche and Strict Avalanche of .exe type bit stream for proposed and existing techniques

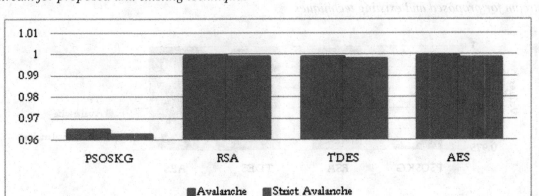

Figure 13. Pictorial representation of the average values of Bit Independence of .exe type bit stream for proposed and existing techniques

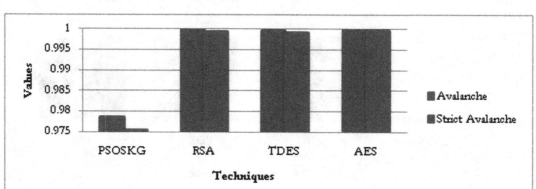

9.2.3 .txt Files

Twenty .txt files of different sizes varying from 1,504 bytes to 6,702,831 bytes have been taken for Avalanche, Strict Avalanche and Bit Independence test. Figure 14 and 15 show the graphical representation of the comparison of results of Avalanche, Strict Avalanche (average values) and Bit Independence test results (average values) respectively of the .txt type source files for and existing RSA, TDES, AES techniques. Average Avalanche values of proposed and existing RSA, TDES, AES are 0.9786178, 0.9998823, 0.9997381, and 0.9998726 respectively. Average Strict Avalanche value of proposed and existing RSA, TDES, AES are 0.9754595, 0.9994315, 0.9992106 and 0.9996183 respectively. Average Bit Independence values of proposed and existing RSA, TDES, AES are 0.4426890, 0.3234268, 0.3016146, and 0.3112921 respectively. Proposed technique has the highest average Bit Independence value which indicates that proposed technique provides better degree of security and comparable to other techniques.

Figure 14. Pictorial representation of the average values of Avalanche and Strict Avalanche of .txt type bit stream for proposed and existing techniques

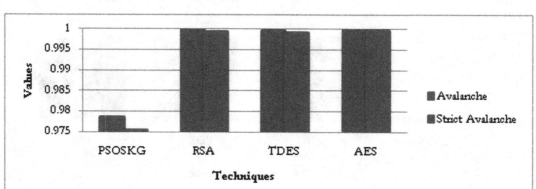

Figure 15. Pictorial representation of the average values of Bit Independence of .txt type bit stream for proposed and existing techniques

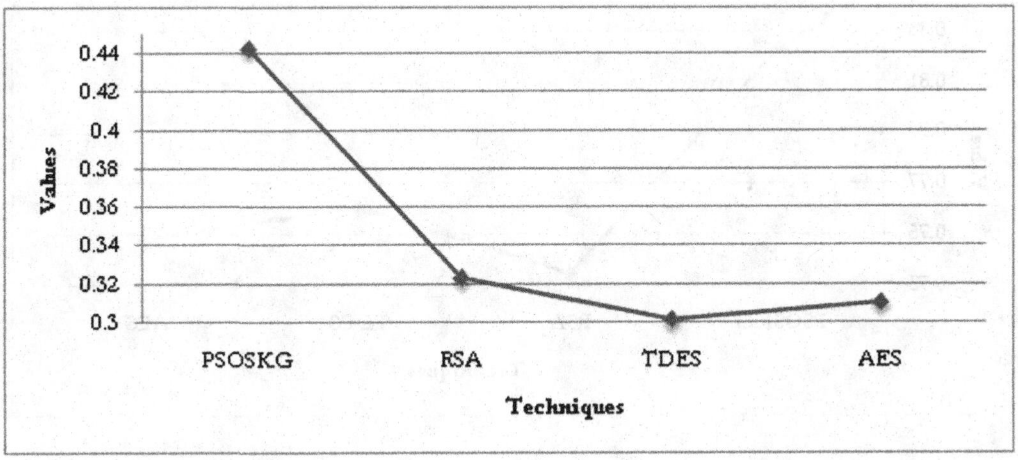

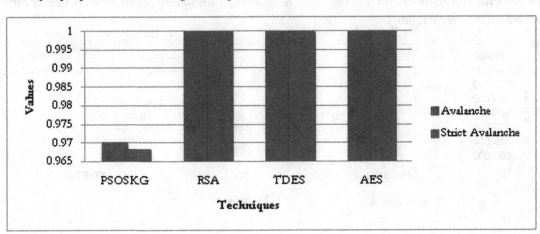

9.2.4 .doc Files

Twenty .doc files of different sizes varying from 21,052 bytes to 5,472,298 bytes have been taken for Avalanche, Strict Avalanche and Bit Independence test. Figure 16 and 17 show the graphical representation of the comparison of results of Avalanche, Strict Avalanche (average values) and Bit Independence test results (average values) respectively of the .doc type source files for proposed and existing RSA, TDES, AES techniques. Average Avalanche values of proposed and existing RSA, TDES, AES are 0.9698779, 0.9999707, 0.9999233, and 0.9999362 respectively. Average Strict Avalanche values of proposed and existing RSA, TDES, AES are 0.9680110, 0.9998032, 0.9997301, and 0.9997919 respectively. Average Bit Independence values of proposed and existing RSA, TDES, AES are 0.8237869, 0.7353065, 0.7611090, and 0.7484538 respectively. Proposed technique has the highest average Bit Independence value which indicates that proposed technique provides better degree of security and comparable to other techniques.

Figure 16. Pictorial representation of the average values of Avalanche and Strict Avalanche of .doc type bit stream for proposed and existing techniques

Figure 17. Pictorial representation of the average values of Bit Independence of .doc type bit stream for proposed and existing techniques

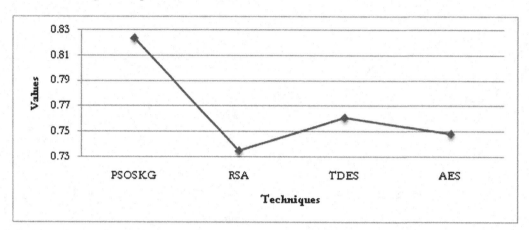

9.3 Test for Non-Homogeneity

Chi-Square value is calculated from the character frequencies using the formula devised by Karl Pearson which is called "Pearsonian Chi-Square". The higher the Chi-Square values the more deviation from the original message. Section 9.3.1 contains the results of *.dll* files and section 9.3.2 deals with *.exe* files. Section 9.3.3 and 9.3.4 deal with the results of *.txt* and *.doc* files respectively.

9.3.1 .dll Files

Twenty *.dll* files of different sizes varying from 3216 bytes to 5,456,704 bytes have been taken to measure the Chi-Square values for different techniques. Figure 18 shows the comparison of the average Chi-Square values of .dll type of source files for proposed and existing TDES, AES. For all proposed techniques, the Chi-Square values of the encrypted files are very high. So, it may obtain better degree of security in proposed which is comparable with that of others.

Figure 18. Pictorial representation of the average values of Chi-Square of .dll type bit stream for proposed and existing techniques

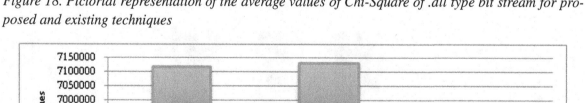

9.3.2 .exe Files

Twenty *.exe* files of different sizes varying from 1063 bytes to 6,735,934 bytes have been taken to measure the Chi-Square values for different techniques. Figure 19 shows the comparison of the average Chi-Square values of .exe type of source files for proposed and existing TDES. For all proposed techniques, the Chi-Square values of the encrypted files are very high. So, it may obtain better degree of security in proposed which is comparable with that of others.

9.3.3 .txt Files

Twenty *.txt* files of different sizes varying from 1504 bytes to 6,702,831 bytes have been taken to measure the Chi-Square values for different techniques. Figure 20 shows the comparison of the average Chi-Square values of .txt type of source files for proposed PSOSKG and AES. For all proposed techniques, the Chi-Square values of the encrypted files are very high. So, it may obtain better degree of security in proposed which is comparable with that of others.

Figure 19. Pictorial representation of the average values of Chi-Square of .exe type bit stream for proposed and existing techniques

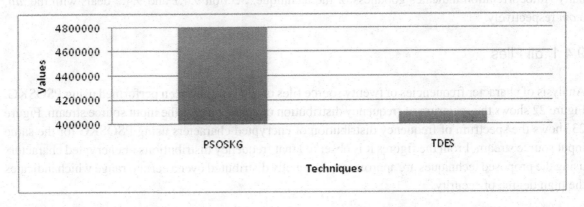

Figure 20. Pictorial representation of the average values of Chi-Square of .txt type bit stream for proposed and existing techniques

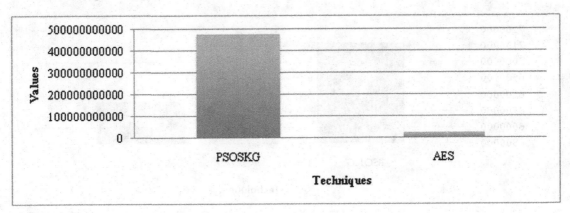

9.3.4 .doc Files

Twenty *.doc* files of different sizes varying from 21,052 bytes to 5,472,298 bytes have been taken to measure the Chi-Square values for different techniques. The average Chi-Square values obtained using proposed PSOSKG and AES are 6713314, and 6763362 respectively. Chi-Square values increase with the increase of source file sizes. Figure 21 shows the comparison of the average Chi-Square values of *.doc* type of source files for proposed PSOSKG and AES. For proposed techniques, the Chi-Square values of the encrypted files are very high. So, it may obtain better degree of security in proposed which is comparable with that of others.

9.4 Analysis of Character Frequencies, Entropy, Floating Frequencies, Autocorrelation

Program access both the original and encrypted files and stores the occurrence of each character in an array. The final output is an excel file to facilitate generation of graph. The smoother or less curves in the spectrum of frequency distribution indicate that it is harder for a cryptanalyst to detect the original text bytes which implies better degree of security. Entropy near to 1 indicates the good encryption technique. Well distributed floating frequencies are indicate the robustness of the encryption and finally Autocorrelation indicates goodness of the technique. Section 9.4.1 and 9.4.2 deals with the *.dll, .com* respectively.

9.4.1 .dll Files

Analysis of character frequencies of twenty source files of *.dll* type has been performed using PSOSKG. Figure 22 shows the spectrum of frequency distribution of characters for the input source stream. Figure 23 shows the spectrum of frequency distribution of encrypted characters using PSOSKG for the same input source stream. From the figures it is observed that frequency distributions of encrypted characters using the proposed techniques are approximately equally distributed over a certain range which indicates the high degree of security.

Figure 21. Pictorial representation of the average values of Chi-Square of .doc type bit stream for proposed and existing techniques

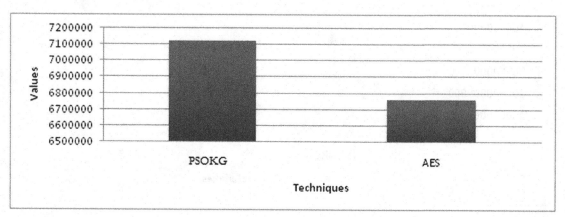

Figure 22. Graphical representation of frequency distribution spectrum of characters for the input source stream

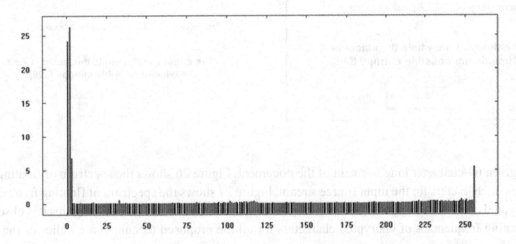

Figure 23. Graphical representation of frequency distribution spectrum of characters for the encrypted stream using PSOSKG

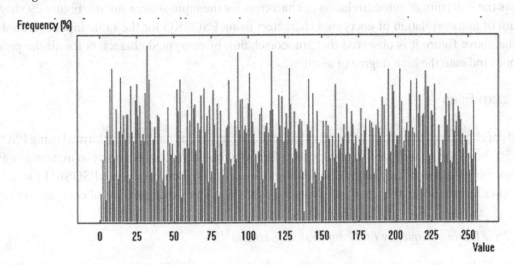

Analysis of entropy of twenty source files of *.dll* type has been performed using PSOSKG. The entropy of a source thus indicates its characteristic distribution. It measures the average amount of information which one can obtain through observation of the source or, conversely, the indeterminacy which prevails over the generated messages when one cannot observe the source. Figure 24 shows the entropy for the input source stream. Figure 25 shows the entropy of encrypted characters using PSOSKG for the same input source stream. From the figures it is observed that entropy of encrypted characters for the proposed techniques is near to eight which indicate the high degree of security.

Analysis of floating frequencies of twenty source files of *.dll* type has been performed using PSOSKG. The floating frequency of a document is a characteristic of its local information content at individual points in the document. The floating frequency specifies how many different characters are to be found

Figure 24. Entropy of the input source stream

Figure 25. Entropy of the encrypted stream using PSOSKG

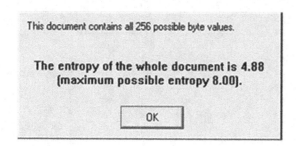

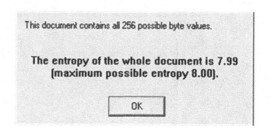

in any given 64-character long segment of the document. Figure 26 shows the spectrum of floating frequencies of characters for the input source stream. Figure 27 shows the spectrum of floating frequencies of encrypted characters using PSOSKG for the same input source stream. From the figures it is observed that floating frequencies of encrypted characters for all the proposed technique are indicates the high degree of security.

Analysis of autocorrelation of twenty source files of *.dll* type has been performed using PSOSKG. The autocorrelation of a document is an index of the similarity of different sections of the document .Figure 28 shows the spectrum of autocorrelation of characters for the input source stream. Figure 29 shows the spectrum of autocorrelation of encrypted characters using PSOSKG for the same input source stream. From the above figure it is observed that autocorrelation of encrypted characters for all the proposed techniques indicate the high degree of security.

9.4.2 .com Files

Analysis of character frequencies of twenty source files of *.com* type has been performed using PSOSKG. Figure 30 shows the spectrum of frequency distribution of characters for the input source stream. Figure 31 shows the spectrum of frequency distribution of encrypted characters using PSOSKG for the same input source stream. From the figures it is observed that frequency distributions of encrypted characters

Figure 26. Floating frequency of the input source stream

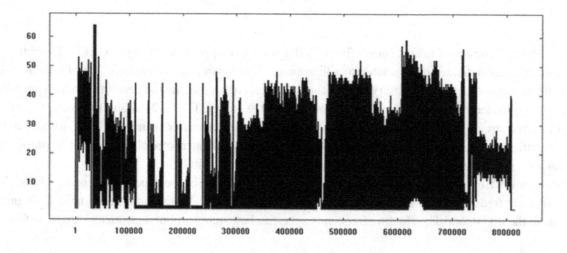

Figure 27. Floating frequency of the encrypted stream using PSOSKG

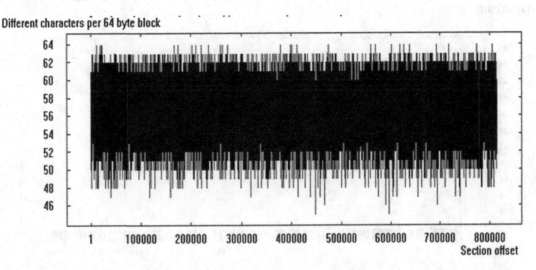

Figure 28. Autocorrelation of the input source stream

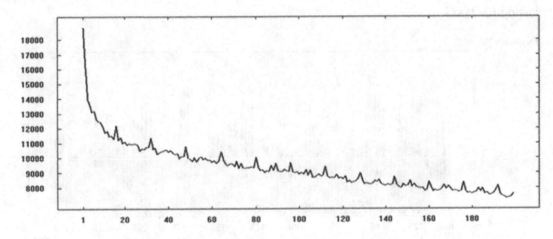

Figure 29. Autocorrelation of the encrypted stream using PSOSKG

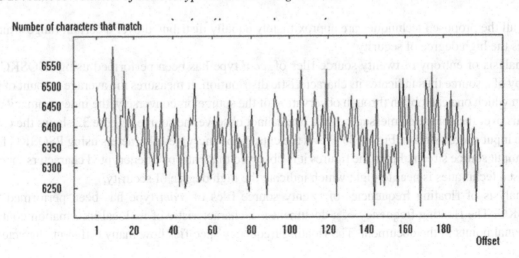

Figure 30. Graphical representation of frequency distribution spectrum of characters for the input source stream

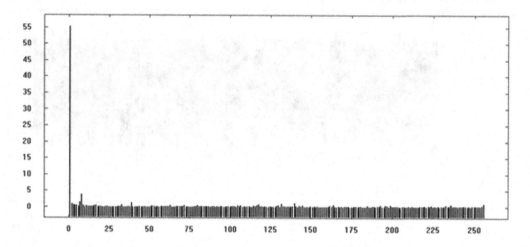

Figure 31. Graphical representation of frequency distribution spectrum of characters for the encrypted stream using PSOSKG

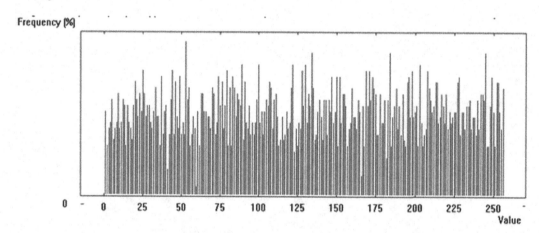

using all the proposed techniques are approximately equally distributed over a certain range which indicates the high degree of security.

Analysis of entropy of twenty source files of *.com* type has been performed using PSOSKG. The entropy of a source thus indicates its characteristic distribution. It measures the average amount of information which one can obtain through observation of the source or, conversely, the indeterminacy which prevails over the generated messages when one cannot observe the source. Figure 32 shows the entropy for the input source stream. Figure 33 shows the entropy of encrypted characters using PSOSKG for the same input source stream. From the figures it is observed that entropy of encrypted characters for all the proposed techniques is near to eight which indicate the high degree of security.

Analysis of floating frequencies of twenty source files of *.com* type has been performed using PSOSKG. The floating frequency of a document is a characteristic of its local information content at individual points in the document. The floating frequency specifies how many different characters are

Figure 32. Entropy of the input source stream

Figure 33. Entropy of the encrypted stream using PSOSKG

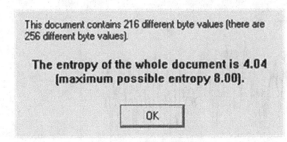

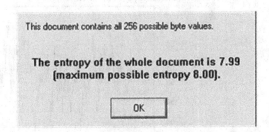

to be found in any given 64-character long segment of the document. Figure 34 shows the spectrum of floating frequencies of characters for the input source stream. Figure 35 shows the spectrum of floating frequencies of encrypted characters using PSOSKG for the same input source stream. From the figures it is observed that floating frequencies of encrypted characters for all the proposed technique are indicates the high degree of security.

Analysis of autocorrelation of twenty source files of *.com* type has been performed using PSOSKG. The autocorrelation of a document is an index of the similarity of different sections of the document .Figure 36 shows the spectrum of autocorrelation of characters for the input source stream. Figure 37 shows the spectrum of autocorrelation of encrypted characters using PSOSKG for the same input source stream. From the above figure it is observed that autocorrelation of encrypted characters for all the proposed techniques indicate the high degree of security.

Table 2 shows the comparisons of length of plan text vs. encryption/decryption key storage among proposed PSOSKG and existing AES, RC4, Vernam Cipher.

In the Particle Swarm Intelligence (PSO) though the keys used for encryption looks like a series of random numbers, the keys cannot be cracked because a random number generator is not used to generate the keys. Also the keystream generation depends on the character distribution in the plain text overcoming the drawback of Vernam cipher. In addition to this the PSO method reduces the number of keys to be stored and distributed compared to that of AES, RC4 (Menezes, A.J., Vanstone, S.A. & Van Oorschot,

Figure 34. Floating frequency of the input source stream

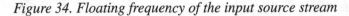

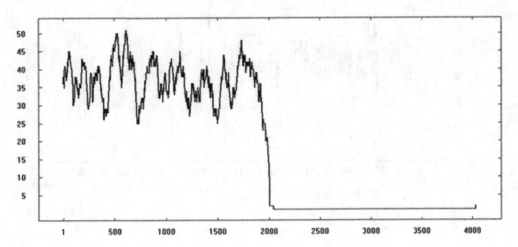

Figure 35. Floating frequency of the encrypted stream using PSOSKG

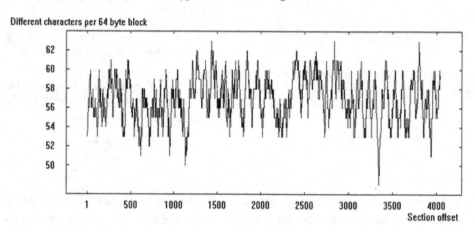

Figure 36. Autocorrelation of the input source stream

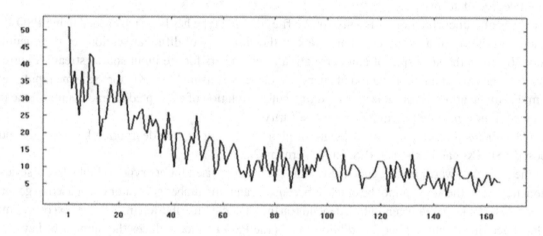

Figure 37. Floating frequency of the encrypted stream using PSOSKG

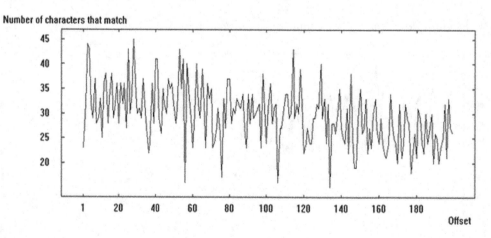

Table 2. Comparisons of length of plan text vs. encryption/decryption key storage among proposed PSOSKG and existing AES, RC4, Vernam Cipher

Length of Plain Text	Key Storage (PSOSKG)	Key Storage (AES)	Key Storage (RC4)	Key Storage (Vernam Cipher)
64	15	128	52	60
120	15	128	106	120
500	15	128	437	500
1000	20	128	913	1000

P.C., 1996), Vernam cipher (Schneier B.,1995) when the length of the plain text is large. The characters used for comparison is stored and each time a velocity is given to the particle only the new characters denoting the velocity are compared with the plain text. Consider the case where the length of the key-stream is nine. Since the characters in the keystream do not change until the solution is obtained it is not necessary that the particle keystream length should be nine initially. Let suppose a particle keystream of length 5 is taken and a velocity whose keystream length is two given to the particle during the first move of the particle. During the second move of the particle a velocity keystream of length two is given and the solution is obtained. Then the minimum number of total comparisons of the characters in the keystream with the plain text is nine to obtain a keystream of length nine. Each time a velocity is given to the particle the characters in the keystream are unique. This would ensure that unlike other method the same characters are not compared with the plain text for their occurrence.

In RC4 the number of keys to be stored is less when compared to Vernam cipher. This stream ci-pher method is vulnerable to analytic attacks. 1 out of every 256 keys is a weak key. These keys can be identified by cryptanalysis which can find whether the generated bytes are strongly correlated with the bytes of the key.

In Vernam cipher the keys are randomly generated using random stream generator. The drawback is that the number of keys to be stored and distributed should be equal to the length of the plain text. Also the keys used to encrypt the plain text can be found if the random number generator is cracked.

Following attacks are considered to test the security and robustness of the proposed technique.

- **Cipher Text Only Attack:** The proposed technique nullifies the success rate of this attack by pro-ducing a robust encrypted cipher text. The strength of resisting exhaustive key search attack relies on a large key space. The cryptanalyst has only the cipher text to work with. In this PSO technique the key is changed for each character of the plaintext to produce a cipher text that is mathematically difficult to break. Since 256 characters are taken and a permutation of these characters is done to get groups of characters of all possible orderings without any repetition forming the key stream, the total number of key streams will be 256!×2.718. Thus the possible number of combinations to be searched is 256!×2.718. Thus a hacker has to try all such key streams to find an appropriate one. This method makes it difficult for the hacker to find out the key stream used for encryption. Thus the size of the key space is 256!×2.718. Proposed technique helps to generate long period of random key streams along with no obvious relationship between the individual bits of the sequence. Also the generated keystreams are of large linear complex. Finally keystream have high degrees of correlation immunity. Thus it is practically difficult to perform a brute-force search in a key-space.

- **Known Plaintext Attack:** The plaintext is encoded using the cycle formation technique. This would increase the security in such a manner that it is difficult to know the values assigned for the characters in the plaintext. This is because there are $2^{lengthofblock}$ possible combination and the hacker has to search those combinations for the values. Also the keys used for encryption has to be found by the cryptanalyst. Proposed technique offers better floating frequency of characters. So, known plaintext attack is difficult in this proposed technique.

- **Chosen Plaintext Attack:** The objective of this attack is to find the secret key. This attack is difficult because there is no obvious relationship between the individual bits of the sequence in plaintext and cipher text. In the proposed technique the cipher text is obtained by performing an Exclusive-OR operation between the encoded plaintext and the characters in the key stream. This proposed technique is not vulnerable to chosen-plaintext attack, since the plaintext is encoded first using cycle generation technique then outcomes of this get Exclusive-OR with PSO based keystream and the outcomes of this is Exclusive-OR with the session key. It is difficult for the hacker to find the key chosen for encryption. So, it is difficult to choose a plaintext of his/her choice and get the corresponding cipher text. Proposed technique passes the frequency (monobit) test, runs test, binary matrix rank test and in each session a fresh CGTHLP based session key is used for encryption which confirms that chosen plaintext attack is very difficult in this technique.

- **Chosen Cipher Text Only Attack:** This technique has a good Chi-Square value this confirms good degree of non-homogeneity and also it passes the discrete Fourier transform test, approximate entropy test, overlapping (periodic) template matching test which confirms that chosen plaintext attack is difficult in this technique. So, it will be difficult get plaintext from the cipher text.

- **Brute Force Attack:** The PSO based key is changed for each character of the plaintext to produce a cipher text that is mathematically impossible to break. Since 256 characters are chosen the total number of keystreams will be 256!×2.718. Thus a hacker has to try all such keystreams to find an appropriate one. This method makes it difficult for the hacker to find out the keystream used for encryption. Encryption is an important issue in wireless communication since it is carried out over the air interface, and is more vulnerable to fraud and eavesdropping. Also the keystream is used to generate the keys for the portion of the plaintext exceeding the length of the keystream. This method of encryption reduces the number of keys to be stored and distributed. Due to high complexity brute force attack will not be feasible. Proposed technique has a good entropy value near to eight which indicates that brute force attack is not be possible in this proposed technique.

10. CONCLUSION

The logic of the proposed PSO based cryptographic techniques in wireless communication is simple to understand and implementation is easy using any high level programming language. Since keys are session based which varies session to session and key size is variable in length, the security of the proposed techniques is good. The strength of the proposed techniques is the adoption of complexity based on energy and resource available in the wireless communication, infrastructure for computing in a node or mesh in wireless communication. For a wireless network having low energy, the number of cascading stages and iteration be less. So, the proposed techniques are very much suitable for the security of the system where energy and resource is one of the main constraints. The proposed techniques can handle any sort of input file of any size. There is no alteration of input file size i.e. after encryption file size remains unchanged. The salient features of all the proposed techniques are summarized as follows:

- Generation of Session key through synchronization,
- No exchange of session key through public channel,
- Very high degree of security,
- Keys are variable in length,
- Encrypt any sort of files,
- Manage to handle files of any size,
- Offers variable block size,
- No space overhead,
- Logics are simple to understand,
- Less complex,
- Easy to implement the algorithms.

REFERENCES

Castro, J. C. H., & Viñuela, P. I. (2005). Evolutionary computation in computer security and cryptography. *New Generation Computing*, 23(3), 193–199. doi:10.1007/BF03037654

Delgado-Restituto, M., de Ahumada, R. L., & Rodriguez-Vazquez, A. (1995). Secure communication through switched-current chaotic circuits. In *Proceedings of the IEEE International Symposium on Circuits and Systems (ISCAS '95)* (Vol. 3, pp. 2237-2240). Seattle, WA: IEEE. doi:10.1109/ISCAS.1995.523873

Diffie, W., & Hellman, M. (1976). New directions in cryptography. *IEEE Transactions on Information Theory*, 22(6), 644–654. doi:10.1109/TIT.1976.1055638

Diffie, W., & Hellman, M. (1976). Multi-user cryptographic techniques. *Proceedings of the AFIPS*, 45, 109–112. doi:10.1145/1499799.1499815

Dourlens, S. (1995). *Neuro-cryptograph*. (MSc Thesis). Dept. of Microcomputers and Microelectronics, University of Paris, Paris, France.

Eberhart, R. C., & Kennedy, J. (1995). A new optimizer using particle swarm theory. In *Proceedings of Sixth Int. Symposium on Micromachine and Human Science* (pp. 39-43). Nagoya, Japan: Academic Press.

Feistel, H. (1973). Cryptography and computer privacy. *Scientific American*, 228(5), 15–23. doi:10.1038/scientificamerican0573-15 PMID:4687783

Hassoun, M. (1995). *Fundamentals of artificial neural networks*. Cambridge, MA: MIT Press.

Kennedy, J. (1999). Small worlds and mega-minds: Effects of neighborhood topology on particle swarm performance. In *Proceedings of the IEEE Congress on Evolutionary Computation (CEC 1999)* (pp. 1931-1938). Piscataway, NJ: IEEE. doi:10.1109/CEC.1999.785509

Kennedy, J., & Eberhart, R. C. (1995). Particle swarm optimization. In *Proceedings of the IEEE International Conference on Neural Networks* (Vol. 4, pp.1942-1948). Piscataway, NJ: IEEE. doi:10.1109/ICNN.1995.488968

Liddell, H. G., & Scott, R. (1984). Greek-English lexicon. Oxford University Press.

Mantin, & Shamir, A. (2001). Weaknesses in the key scheduling algorithm of RC4. In *Selected Areas in Cryptography: Proceedings of the 8th Annual International Workshop* (LNCS), (*Vol. 2259*, pp. 1-24). Berlin, Germany: Springer

Maurer, U. (1993). Secret key agreement by public discussion from common information. *IEEE Transactions on Information Theory, 39*(3), 733–742. doi:10.1109/18.256484

Menezes, A. J., Vanstone, S. A., & Van Oorschot, P. C. (1996). Handbook of applied cryptography. In *Applied cryptography*. Boca Raton, FL: CRC Press. doi:10.1201/9781439821916

Menezes, A. J., Vanstone, S. A., & Van Oorschot, P. C. (2001). *Handbook of applied cryptography* (5th ed.). CRC Press.

RC4 Encryption Algorithm. (n.d.). Retrieved August 4, 2014, from http://www.vocal.com

Rivest, R. L. (1990). Cryptology. In A. Jan Van Leeuwen (Ed.), *Handbook of theoretical computer science* (pp. 717–755). Cambridge, MA: MIT Press.

Sarkar, A., & Mandal, J. K. (2012). Energy efficient wireless communication using genetic algorithm guided faster light weight digital signature algorithm (GADSA). *International Journal of Advanced Smart Sensor Network Systems, 2*(3), 9-25.

Sarkar, A., & Mandal, J. K. (2013a). Computational intelligence based simulated annealing guided key generation in wireless communication (CISAKG). *International Journal on Information Theory, 2*(4), 35-44.

Sarkar, A., & Mandal, J. K. (2013b). Genetic algorithm guided key generation in wireless communication (GAKG). *International Journal on Cybernetics & Informatics, 2*(5), 9-17.

Sarkar, A., & Mandal, J. K. (2013c). Computational intelligence based triple layer perceptron model coordinated PSO guided metamorphosed based application in cryptographic technique for secured communication (TLPPSO). In *Proceedings of the First International Conference on Computational Intelligence: Modeling, Techniques and Applications (CIMTA-2013)* (Vol. 10, pp. 433-442). Kalyani, India: Procedia Technology, Elsevier.

Schneier, B. (1995). *Applied cryptography: Protocols, algorithms, and source code in C* (2nd ed.). Wiley.

Simon, H. (1994). *Neural networks: A comprehensive foundation*. Prentice Hall PTR.

Stallings, W. (2003). *Cryptography and network security: Principles and practices* (3rd ed.). Pearson Education.

Stinson, D. R. (1995). *Cryptography, theory and practice*. Boca Raton, FL: CRC Press.

KEY TERMS AND DEFINITIONS

Encryption: In cryptography, encryption is the process of encoding messages or information in such a way that only authorized parties can read it.

Initial Population: Initial population comprises of set of valid and complete set of particles.

Key Generation: Key generation is the process of generating keys for cryptography. A key is used to encrypt and decrypt whatever data is being encrypted/decrypted.

Key: In cryptography, a key is a piece of information (a parameter) that determines the functional output of a cryptographic algorithm or cipher. Without a key, the algorithm would produce no useful result. In encryption, a key specifies the particular transformation of plaintext into cipher text, or vice versa during decryption.

Keystream: A collection of alphanumeric characters is called a keystream and each character in the keystream is known as key.

Swarm Intelligence: Swarm intelligence is aimed at collective behaviour of intelligent agents in decentralized systems. Most of the basic ideas are derived from the real swarms in the nature, which includes particle swarm, ant colonies, bird flocking, honeybees, bacteria and microorganisms, etc.

Compilation of References

Abbasi, M. A., Latiff, M. S. B. A., & Chizari, H. (2014). Bioinspired evolutionary algorithm based for improving network coverage in wireless sensor networks. *Scientific World Journal*. doi: 10.1155/2014/839486

Abbass, H. A. (2001). MBO: Marriage in honey bees optimization-A haplometrosis polygynous swarming approach. In *Proceedings of IEEE Congress on Evolutionary Computation* (pp. 207-214). IEEE. doi:10.1109/CEC.2001.934391

Abido, M. A. (2007). *Two-level of non-dominated solutions approach to multiobjective particle swarm optimization*. ACM.

Acharjya, D. P., & Geetha Mary, A. (2014). Privacy preservation in information system. In Advances in secure computing, internet services, and applications (pp. 49-72). IGI Global.

Adams, R., & Bischof, L. (1994). Seeded region growing. *IEEE Transactions on Pattern Analysis and Machine Intelligence*, *16*(6), 641–647. doi:10.1109/34.295913

Adhikari, R., & Agrawal, R. K. (2013). Hybridization of artificial neural network and particle swarm optimization methods for time series forecasting. *International Journal of Applied Evolutionary Computation*, *4*(3), 75–90. doi:10.4018/jaec.2013070107

Afify, A. (2013). Intelligent computation for manufacturing. In Z. Li & A. Al-Ahmari (Eds.), *Formal methods in manufacturing systems: Recent advances* (pp. 211–246). Hershey, PA: Engineering Science Reference; doi:10.4018/978-1-4666-4034-4.ch009

Aggeler, D., Canales, F., Coccia, A., Butcher, N., & Apeldoorn, O. (2010). Ultra-fast DC-charge infrastructures for EV-mobility and future smart grids. In Proceedings of Innovative Smart Grid Technologies Conference Europe (ISGT Europe). Gothenburg, Sweden: IEEE. doi:10.1109/ISGTEUROPE.2010.5638899

Agrawal, G., Chameau, J. A., & Bourdeau, P. L. (1997). Assessing the liquefaction susceptibility at a site based on information from penetration testing. In N. Kartam, I. Flood, & J. H. Garrett (Eds.), Artificial neural networks for civil engineers: fundamentals and applications (pp. 185–214). New York: Academic Press.

Ahmed, H., & Glasgow, J. (2012). *Swarm intelligence: Concepts, models and applications* (Technical Report 2012-585). School of Computing, Queen's University.

Ahmed, M. N., Yamany, S. M., Mohamed, N., Farag, A. A., & Moriarty, T. (2002). A modified fuzzy c-means algorithm for bias field estimation and segmentation of MRI data. *IEEE Transactions on Medical Imaging*, *21*(3), 193–199. doi:10.1109/42.996338 PMID:11989844

Ahmed, T. S., Mehdi, G. D., & Adil, S. (2013). Data missing solution using rough set theory & swarm intelligence. *International Journal of Advanced Computer Science & Information Technology*, *2*(3), 1–16.

Ahn, J.-W., Liang, J., & Lee, D.-H. (2010). Classification and analysis of switched reluctance converters. *Journal of Electrical Engineering & Technology*, *5*(4), 571–579. doi:10.5370/JEET.2010.5.4.571

Aickelin, U., Bentley, P., Cayzer, S., Kim, J., & McLeod, J. (2003). Danger theory: The link between AIS and IDS? In *Artificial immune systems* (pp. 147–155). Springer Berlin Heidelberg. doi:10.1007/978-3-540-45192-1_15

Akar, F., Fleming, F., & Edrington, C. S. (2012). *A computationally intelligent maximum torque per ampere control strategy for switched reluctance machines.* Paper presented at the Electric Vehicle Conference (IEVC).

Aleksander, I., & Morton, H. (1995). *An introduction to neural computing.* International Thompson Computer Press.

Alfares, F., & Esat, I. I. (2003). Quantum algorithms; how useful for engineering problems. In *Proc. of the Seventh World Conference on Integrated Design and Process Technology.* Austin, TX: Academic Press.

Ali, H. E., & Najjar, Y. M. (1998). Neuronet-based approach for assessing liquefaction potential of soils. *Transportation Research Record, 1633*(, 1633), 3–8. doi:10.3141/1633-01

Ali, M., Khompatraporn, C., & Zabinsky, Z. (2005). A numerical evaluation of several stochastic algorithm on selected continuous global optimization test problems. *Journal of Global Optimization, 31*(4), 635–672. doi:10.1007/s10898-004-9972-2

Al-Sumait, J., Al-Othman, A., & Sykulski, J. (2007). Application of pattern search method to power system valve-point economic load dispatch. *International Journal of Electrical Power & Energy Systems, 29*(10), 720–730. doi:10.1016/j.ijepes.2007.06.016

Alsumait, J., Sykulski, J., & Al-Othman, A. (2010). A hybrid GA–PS–SQP method to solve power system valve-point economic dispatch problems. *Applied Energy, 87*(5), 1773–1781. doi:10.1016/j.apenergy.2009.10.007

Ambraseys, N. N. (1988). Engineering seismology. *Earthquake Engineering & Structural Dynamics, 17*(1), 1–105. doi:10.1002/eqe.4290170101

Ame, J., Halloy, J., Rivault, C., Detrain, C., & Deneubourg, J. L. (2006). Collegial decision making based on social amplification leads to optimal group formation. *Proceedings of the National Academy of Sciences of the United States of America, 103*(15), 5835–5840. doi:10.1073/pnas.0507877103 PMID:16581903

American Friends of Tel Aviv Univ. (2011, February). Roaches inspire robotics: Researchers use common cockroach to fine-tune robots of the future. *Science Daily,* p. 7.

Anagnostopoulos, C., & Hadjiefthymiades, S. (2012). Swarm intelligence in autonomic computing: The particle swarm optimization case. In P. Cong-Vinh (Ed.), *Formal and practical aspects of autonomic computing and networking: Specification, development, and verification* (pp. 97–117). Hershey, PA: Information Science Reference; doi:10.4018/978-1-60960-845-3.ch004

Andermann, C., & Gloaguen, R. (2009). Estimation of erosion in tectonically active orogenies. Example from the Bhotekoshi catchment, Himalaya (Nepal). *International Journal of Remote Sensing, 30*(12), 3075–3096. doi:10.1080/01431160802558733

Andrus, R. D., & Stokoe, K. H. (1997). Liquefaction resistance based on shear wave velocity. In *Proc., NCEER Workshop on Evaluation of Liquefaction Resistance of Soils.* Nat. Ctr. for Earthquake Engrg. Res., State Univ. of New York.

Andrus, R. D., & Stokoe, K. H. (2000). Liquefaction resistance of soils from shear wave velocity. *Journal of Geotechnial. and Geoenviromental. Engineering, ASCE, 126*(11), 1015–1025.

Andrus, R. D., Stokoe, K. H., & Chung, R. M. (1999). *Draft guidelines for evaluating liquefaction resistance using shear wave velocity measurements and simplified procedure.* Gaithersburg, MD: National Institute of Standards and Technology.

Anegawa, T. (2009). *Desirable characteristics of public quick charger.* Retrieved December, 1, 2011 from www.chademo.com

Angeline, P. J. (1998). Evolutionary optimization versus particle swarm optimization: Philosophy and performance differences. In *Evolutionary programming VII* (pp. 601–610). Springer Berlin Heidelberg. doi:10.1007/BFb0040811

Arango, I. (1996). Magnitude scaling factors for soil liquefaction evaluations. *Journal of Geotechnical Engineering, 122*(11), 929–936. doi:10.1061/(ASCE)0733-9410(1996)122:11(929)

Araujo, T., Nedjah, N., & Mourelle, L. (2008). Quantum-inspired evolutionary state assignment for synchronous finite state machines. *Journal of Universal Computer Science, 14*(15), 2532–2548.

Archibald, R., & Fann, G. (2007). Feature selection and classification of hyperspectral images with support vector machines. *IEEE Geoscience and Remote Sensing Letters*, *4*(4), 674–677. doi:10.1109/LGRS.2007.905116

Arica, N., & Yarman-Vural, F. T. (2001). An overview of character recognition focused on off-line handwriting. *IEEE Transactions on Systems, Man and Cybernetics. Part C, Applications and Reviews*, *31*(2), 216–233. doi:10.1109/5326.941845

Arifin, A., Al-Bahadly, I., & Mukhopadhyay, S. C. (2012). State of the art of switched reluctance generator. *Energy and Power Engineering*, *4*(6), 447–458. doi:10.4236/epe.2012.46059

Arkadan, A. A., ElBsat, M. N., & Mneimneh, M. A. (2009). Particle swarm design optimization of ALA rotor SynRM for traction applications. *IEEE Transactions on Magnetics*, *45*(3), 956–959. doi:10.1109/TMAG.2009.2012482

Arkin, R. (1998). *Behavior-based robotics*. Cambridge, MA: MIT Press.

Arora, V., & Ravi, V. (2013). Data mining using advanced ant colony optimization algorithm and application to bankruptcy prediction. *International Journal of Information Systems and Social Change*, *4*(3), 33–56. doi:10.4018/jissc.2013070103

Asadi, P., Ehsani, M., & Fahimi, B. (2006). *Design and control characterization of switched reluctance generator for maximum output power*. Paper presented at the Applied Power Electronics Conference and Exposition.

Association of Bay Area Governments. (2010). *Bay area electrified vehicle charging infrastructure: Options for accelerating consumer*. Bay Area, CA: Renewable and Appropriate Energy Laboratory.

Attaviriyanupap, P., Kita, H., Tanaka, E., & Hasegawa, J. (2002). A hybrid EP and SQP for dynamic economic dispatch with nonsmooth fuel cost function. *IEEE Transactions on Power Systems*, *17*(2), 411–416. doi:10.1109/TPWRS.2002.1007911

Aytekin, C., Kiranyaz, S., & Gabbouj, M. (2013). Quantum mechanics in computer vision: Automatic object extraction. In *Proc. ICIP 2013* (pp. 2489–2493). Academic Press. doi:10.1109/ICIP.2013.6738513

Babahajyani, P., Habibi, F., & Bevrani, H. (2014). An online PSO-based fuzzy logic tuning approach: Microgrid frequency control case study. In P. Vasant (Ed.), *Handbook of research on novel soft computing intelligent algorithms: Theory and practical applications* (pp. 589–616). Hershey, PA: Information Science Reference; doi:10.4018/978-1-4666-4450-2.ch020

Babu, S. H., Shreyas, H. R., Manikantan, K., & Ramachandran, S. (2014, January). Face recognition using active illumination equalization and mirror image superposition as pre-processing techniques. In *Proceedings of Signal and Image Processing (ICSIP), 2014 Fifth International Conference on* (pp. 96-101). IEEE. doi:10.1109/ICSIP.2014.21

Baig, A. R., Waseem, S., Khan, S., & Fariha, A. (2011). ACO based discovery of comprehensible and accurate rules from medical datasets. *International Journal of Innovative Computing, Information, & Control*, *7*(11), 6147–6159.

Baiming, S., & Emadi, A. (2011). *A digital control for switched reluctance generators*. Paper presented at the Mechatronics (ICM).

Bakhouya, M., & Gaber, J. (2007). An immune inspired–based optimization algorithm: Application to the travelling salesman problem. *Advanced Modeling and Optimization*, *9*(1), 105–116.

Bakkiyaraj, R., & Kumarappan, N. (2013, May). Optimal reliability planning for a composite electric power system based on Monte Carlo simulation using particle swarm optimization. *International Journal of Electrical Power & Energy Systems*, *47*, 109–116. doi:10.1016/j.ijepes.2012.10.055

Bakwad, K. M., Pattnaik, S. S., Sohi, B. S., Devi, S., Gollapudi, S., Sagar, C. V., & Patra, P. K. (2008). Synchronous bacterial foraging optimization for multimodal and high dimensional functions. In *Proceedings of International Conference on Computing, Communication and Networking (ICCCn 2008)* (pp. 1–8). Academic Press. doi:10.1109/ICCCNET.2008.4787680

Balaji, M., & Kamaraj, V. (2011). Particle swarm optimization approach for optimal design of switched reluctance machine. *American Journal of Applied Sciences*, *8*(4), 374–381. doi:10.3844/ajassp.2011.374.381

Balaji, M., & Kamaraj, V. (2012). Evolutionary computation based multi-objective pole shape optimization of switched reluctance machine. *International Journal of Electrical Power & Energy Systems, 43*(1), 63–69. doi:10.1016/j.ijepes.2012.05.011

Bandyopadhyay, S., Maulik, U., & Wang, J. T. L. (2007). Analysis of biological data, a soft computing approach. In engineering and biology informatics (3rd ed.). World Scientific Publishing Co.

Bandyopadhyay, S. (2005). Satellite image classification using genetically guided fuzzy clustering with spatial information. *International Journal of Remote Sensing, 26*(3), 579–593. doi:10.1080/01431160512331316432

Bandyopadhyay, S., Maulik, U., & Mukhopadhyay, A. (2007). Multiobjective genetic clustering for pixel classification in remote sensing imagery. *IEEE Transactions on Geoscience and Remote Sensing, 45*(5), 1506–1511. doi:10.1109/TGRS.2007.892604

Bandyopadhyay, S., Mitra, R., Maulik, U., & Zhang, M. Q. (2010). Development of the human cancer microRNA network. *Silence, 1*(1), 6. doi:10.1186/1758-907X-1-6 PMID:20226080

Bandyopadhyay, S., & Pal, S. K. (2001). Pixel classification using variable string genetic algorithms with chromosome differentiation. *IEEE Transactions on Geoscience and Remote Sensing, 39*(2), 303–308. doi:10.1109/36.905238

Banks, A., Vincent, J., & Anyakoha, C. (2007). A review of particle swarm optimization. Part I: Background and development. *Natural Computing, 6*(4), 467–484. doi:10.1007/s11047-007-9049-5

Banks, A., Vincent, J., & Anyakoha, C. (2008). A review of particle swarm optimization. Part II: Hybridisation, combinatorial, multicriteria and constrained optimization, and indicative applications. *Natural Computing, 7*(1), 109–124. doi:10.1007/s11047-007-9050-z

Bansal, J. C., Singh, P. K., Saraswat, M., Verma, A., Singh, J. S., & Abraham, A. (2011), Inertia weight strategies in particle swarm optimization. In *Proceedings of Third World Congress on Nature and Biologically Inspired Computing*. IEEE. doi:10.1109/NaBIC.2011.6089659

Barakat, N., & Bradley, A. P. (2010). Rule extraction from support vector machines, a review. *Neurocomputing, 74*(1-3), 178–190. doi:10.1016/j.neucom.2010.02.016

Baras, J. S. & Mehta, H. (2003). A probabilistic emergent routing algorithm for mobile ad hoc networks. In *Proc. WiOpt*. Sophia-Antipolis, France: Academic Press.

Bárdossy, A., & Samaniego, L. (2002). Fuzzy rule-based classification of remotely sensed imagery. *IEEE Transactions on Geoscience and Remote Sensing, 40*(2), 362–374. doi:10.1109/36.992798

Barnes, M., & Pollock, C. (1998). Power electronic converters for switched reluctance drives. *Power Electronics. IEEE Transactions on, 13*(6), 1100–1111. doi:10.1109/63.728337

Barr, R. S., Golden, B. L., Kelly, J. P., Resende, M. G., & Stewart, W. R. Jr. (1995). Designing and reporting on computational experiments with heuristic methods. *Journal of Heuristics, 1*(1), 9–32. doi:10.1007/BF02430363

Basu, S., Das, N., Sarkar, R., Kundu, M., Nasipuri, M., & Basu, D. (2005a). An MLP based approach for recognition of handwritten bangla numerals. In B. Prasad (Ed.), *Proceedings of 2nd Indian International Conference on Artificial Intelligence* (pp. 407–417). Pune, India: Academic Press.

Basu, S., Das, N., Sarkar, R., Kundu, M., Nasipuri, M., & Basu, D. (2009). Recognition of numeric postal codes from multi-script postal address blocks. In S. Chaudhury, S. Mitra, C. Murthy, P. Sastry, & S. Pal (Eds.), Pattern recognition and machine intelligence (Vol. 5909, pp. 381–386). Springer. doi:10.1007/978-3-642-11164-8_62

Basu, S., Das, N., Sarkar, R., Kundu, M., Nasipuri, M., & Basu, D. K. (2005b). Handwritten Bangla alphabet recognition using an MLP based classifier. In *Proceedings of 2nd National Conference on Computer Processing of Bangla* (pp. 285–291). Dhaka, Bagladesh: Academic Press.

Basu, S., Kundu, M., Nasipuri, M., & Basu, D. K. (2006). A two-pass fuzzy-geno approach to pattern classification. In *Proceedings of International Conference on Computer Processing of Bangla* (pp. 130–134). Dhaka. Bangladesh: Academic Press.

Basu, S. S., & Chaudhuri, A. (2003). Self-adaptive topology management for mobile ad-hoc network. *Journal of the Institution of Engineers (India)*, *84*, 7–13.

Basu, S. S., & Chaudhuri, A. (2004). Self adaptive MANET: A centralized approach. *Foundation of Computing and Decision Sciences*, *29*(4), 271–286.

Bazi, Y., & Melgani, F. (2006). Toward an optimal SVM classification system for hyperspectral remote sensing images. *IEEE Transactions on Geoscience and Remote Sensing*, *44*(11), 3374–3385. doi:10.1109/TGRS.2006.880628

Bazi, Y., & Melgani, F. (2007). Semisupervised PSO-SVM regression for biophysical parameterestimation. *IEEE Transactions on Geoscience and Remote Sensing*, *45*(6), 1887–1895. doi:10.1109/TGRS.2007.895845

Beer, R. (1990). Intelligence as adaptive behavior: An experiment in computational neuroethology. Academic Press.

Beer, R., Chiel, H., & Sterling, L. (1990). A biological perspective on autonomous agent design. *Robotics and Autonomous Systems*, *6*(1-2), 169–186. doi:10.1016/S0921-8890(05)80034-X

Behrman, E. C., Niemel, J., Steck, J. E., & Skinner, S. R. (1996). A quantum dot neural network. *IEEE Transactions on Neural Networks*.

Beielstein, T., Parsopoulos, K. E., & Vrahatis, M. N. (2002). Tuning PSO parameters through sensitivity analysis. Technical Report, Reihe Computational Intelligence CI124/02. Department of Computer Science, University of Dortmund Universität Dortmund.

Beiranvand, V., Kashani, M. M., & Bakar, A. (2014). Multi objective PSO algorithm for mining numerical association rule without priori discretization. *Expert Systems with Applications*, *41*(9), 4259–4273. doi:10.1016/j.eswa.2013.12.043

Beni, G., & Wang, J. (1989). Swarm intelligence in cellular robotic systems. In *Proceeding of NATO Advanced Workshop on Robots and Biological System*. Academic Press.

Benidris, M., & Mitra, J. (2013). Composite power system reliability assessment using maximum capacity flow and directed binary particle swarm optimization. In *Proceedings of North American Power Symposium* (pp. 1-6). Champaign, IL: IEEE. doi:10.1109/NAPS.2013.6666951

Benidris, M., Elsaiah, S., & Mitra, J. (2013). Composite system reliability assessment using dynamically directed particle swarm optimization. In *Proceedings of North American Power Symposium* (pp. 1-6). Champaign, IL: IEEE. doi:10.1109/NAPS.2013.6666953

Benidris, M., & Mitra, J. (2014). Reliability and sensitivity analysis of composite power systems under emission constraints. *IEEE Transactions on Power Systems*, *29*(1), 404–412. doi:10.1109/TPWRS.2013.2279343

Beni, G., & Wang, J. (1989). Swarm intelligence. In *Proceedings Seventh Annual Meeting of the Robotics Society of Japan* (pp. 425-428). RSJ Press.

Benioff, P. (1982). Quantum mechanical models of turing machines that dissipate no energy. *Physical Review Letters*, *48*(23), 1581–1585. doi:10.1103/PhysRevLett.48.1581

Bentley, J. L. (1990). K-d trees for semi dynamic point sets. In *Proceedings of the 6th Annual 362 Symposium on Computational Geometry* (SCG 90). ACM-SIGACT ACM-SIGGRAPH.

Bezdek, J. C. (1981). *Pattern recognition with fuzzy objective function algorithm*. New York: Plenum. doi:10.1007/978-1-4757-0450-1

Bezdek, J. C., & Pal, N. R. (1988). Some new indexes for cluster validity. *IEEE Transactions on Systems, Man, and Cybernetics. Part B, Cybernetics*, *28*(3), 301–315. doi:10.1109/3477.678624 PMID:18255949

Bhandari, D., Pal, N. R., & Majumder, D. D. (1992). Fuzzy divergence, probability measure of fuzzy events and image thresholding. *Pattern Recognition Letters*, *13*(12), 857–867. doi:10.1016/0167-8655(92)90085-E

Bhandarkar, S. M., & Zhang, H. (1999). Image segmentation using evolutionary computation. *IEEE Transactions on Evolutionary Computation*, *3*(1), 1–21. doi:10.1109/4235.752917

Bhattacharyya, S., & Dey, S. (2011b). An efficient quantum inspired genetic algorithm (QIGA) with a chaotic map model based interference and fuzzy objective function for gray level image thresholding. In *Proceedings of International Conference on Computational Intelligence and Communication Networks (CICN 2011)*. Academic Press. doi:10.1109/CICN.2011.24

Bhattacharyya, S., Dutta, P., & Maulik, U. (2007). Binary object extraction using bi-directional self- organizing neural network (BDSONN) architecture with fuzzy context sensitive thresholding. *Pattern Analysis and Application*, 345-360.

Bhattacharyya, S., Dutta, P., & Maulik, U. (2008). Self organizing neural network (SONN) based gray scale object extractor with a multilevel sigmoidal (MUSIG) activation function. *Foundations of Computing and Decision Sciences, 33*(2), 46–50.

Bhattacharyya, S., Dutta, P., Maulik, U., & Nandi, P. K. (2007). Multilevel activation functions for true color image segmentation using self – organizing neural network (PSONN) architecture: A comparative study. *International Journal on Computer Sciences, 29*(1), 9-21.

Bhattacharyya, S. (2011a). A brief survey of color image preprocessing and segmentation techniques. *Journal of Pattern Recognition Research, 1*(1), 120–129. doi:10.13176/11.191

Bhattacharyya, S., Dutta, P., Chakraborty, S., Chakraborty, R., & Dey, S. (2010). Determination of optimal threshold of a gray-level image using a quantum inspired genetic algorithm with interference based on a random map model. In *Proceedings of 2010 IEEE International Conference on Computational Intelligence and Computing Research (ICCIC 2010)*. IEEE. doi:10.1109/ICCIC.2010.5705806

Bhattacharyya, S., Dutta, P., & Maulik, U. (2006). A self supervised bi-directional neural network (BDSONN) architecture for object extraction guided by beta activation function and adaptive fuzzy context sensitive thresholding. *International Journal of Intelligent Technology, 1*(4), 345–365.

Bhattacharyya, S., Dutta, P., & Maulik, U. (2011). Multilevel image segmentation with adaptive image context based thresholding. *Applied Soft Computing, 11*(1), 946–962. doi:10.1016/j.asoc.2010.01.015

Bhowmik, T., Bhattacharya, U., & Parui, S. (2004). Recognition of Bangla handwritten characters using an MLP classifier based on stroke features. In N. Pal, N. Kasabov, R. Mudi, S. Pal, & S. Parui (Eds.), Neural information processing (Vol. 3316, pp. 814–819). Springer. doi:10.1007/978-3-540-30499-9_125

Bianchi, N., & Bolognani, S. (1998). Design optimisation of electric motors by genetic algorithms. *IEEE Proceedings of Electric Power Applications, 145*(5), 475-483. doi:10.1049/ip-epa:19982166

Billinton, R., & Li, W. (1994). *Reliability assessment of electric power systems using Monte Carlo methods*. New York: Plenum Press. doi:10.1007/978-1-4899-1346-3

Birnie, D. P. III. (2009). Solar-to-vehicle (S2V) systems for powering commuters of the future. *Journal of Power Sources, 186*(2), 539–542. doi:10.1016/j.jpowsour.2008.09.118

Blackwell, T. (2007). Particle swarm optimization in dynamic environments. In *Evolutionary computation in dynamic and uncertain environments* (pp. 29–49). Springer Berlin Heidelberg. doi:10.1007/978-3-540-49774-5_2

Blanzieri, E., & Melgani, F. (2008). Nearest neighbor classification of remote sensing images with the maximal margin principle. *IEEE Transactions on Geoscience and Remote Sensing, 46*(6), 1804–1811. doi:10.1109/TGRS.2008.916090

Bloch, I. (1999). On fuzzy distances and their use in image processing under imprecision. *Pattern Recognition, 32*(11), 1873–1895. doi:10.1016/S0031-3203(99)00011-4

Blum, C. & Roli, A. (n.d.). *Metaheuristic in combinatorial optimization: Overview and conceptual comparison*. IRIDIA: Technical Report, 2001-13.

Boldea, I. (2003). *Control of electric generators: A review.* Paper presented at the Industrial Electronics Society.

Boldea, I. (2010). *Variable speed generators*. Taylor & Francis.

Boldea, I. (2013). *Linear electric machines, drives, and MAGLEVs handbook*. Taylor & Francis. doi:10.1201/b13756

Bonabeau, E., Dorigo, M., & Theraulaz, G. (1999). *Swarm intelligence: From natural to artificial systems*. Oxford Univ. Press.

Bonabeau, E., Henaux, F., Guerin, S., Snyers, D., Kuntz, P., & Theraulaz, G. (1998). Routing in telecommunication networks with 'smart' ant-like agents. In *Proc. 2nd Int. Workshop on Intelligent Agents for Telecommunication Applications*. Paris, France: Academic Press. doi:10.1007/BFb0053944

Botsford, C., & Szczepanek, A. (2009). Fast charging vs. slow charging: Pros and cons for the new age of electric vehicles. In *Proceedings of International Battery Hybrid Fuel Cell Electric Vehicle Symposium*. Stavanger, Norway: World Electric Vehicle Association.

Bouchon-Meunier, B., & Yager, R. R. (1993). Entropy of similarity relations in questionnaires and decision trees. In *Proceedings of Second IEEE International Conference on Fuzzy Systems* (pp. 1225-1230). IEEE. doi:10.1109/FUZZY.1993.327567

Boulanger, R. W., & Idriss, I. M. (2004). Semi-empirical procedures for evaluating liquefaction potential during earthquakes. In *Proceedings of the 11th ICSDEE & 3rd ICEGE*. Academic Press.

Boussaïd, I., Lepagnot, J., & Siarry, P. (2013). A survey on optimization metaheuristics. *Information Sciences*, *237*, 82–117. doi:10.1016/j.ins.2013.02.041

Bovolo, F., Bruzzone, L., & Marconcini, M. (2008). A novel approach to unsupervised change detection based on a semisupervised SVM and a similarity measure. *IEEE Transactions on Geoscience and Remote Sensing*, *46*(7), 2070–2082. doi:10.1109/TGRS.2008.916643

Boyarsky, A., & Gora, P. (2010). A random map model for quantum interference. *Communications in Nonlinear Science and Numerical Simulation*, *15*(8), 1974–1979. doi:10.1016/j.cnsns.2009.08.018

Boyd, D. S., Sanchez-Hernandez, C., & Foody, G. M. (2006). Mapping a specific class for priority habitats monitoring from satellite sensor data. *International Journal of Remote Sensing*, *27*(13), 2631–2644. doi:10.1080/01431160600554348

Boyer, M., Brassard, G., Høyer, P., & Tapp, A. (1998). Tight bounds on quantum searching. *Fortschritte der Physik*, *4*(5), 493–505. doi:10.1002/(SICI)1521-3978(199806)46:4/5<493::AID-PROP493>3.0.CO;2-P

Boyle, G. (Ed.). (2007). *Renewable electricity and the grid: the challenge of variability*. Earthscan.

Brady, G., O'Loughlin, C., Massey, J., Griffiths, D., & Villegas, C. (2012). *Design and test of a linear switched reluctance generator for use in wave-energy applications* Paper presented at the 4th International Conference on Ocean Energy.

Bremermann, H. (1974). Chemotaxis and optimization. *Journal of the Franklin Institute*, *297*(5), 397–404. doi:10.1016/0016-0032(74)90041-6

Brenning, A. (2009). Benchmarking classifiers to optimally integrate terrain analysis and multispectral remote sensing in automatic rock glacier detection. *Remote Sensing of Environment*, *113*(1), 239–247. doi:10.1016/j.rse.2008.09.005

Brink, A. D., & Pendock, N. E. (1996). Minimum cross entropy threshold selection. *Pattern Recognition*, *29*(1), 179–188. doi:10.1016/0031-3203(95)00066-6

Britton, N. F., Franks, N. R., Pratt, S. C., & Seeley, T. D. (2002). Deciding on a new home: How do honeybees agree? *Proceedings. Biological Sciences*, *269*(1498), 1383–1388. doi:10.1098/rspb.2002.2001 PMID:12079662

Brown, M., Gunn, S. R., & Lewis, H. G. (1999). Support vector machines for optimal classification and spectral unmixing. *Ecological Modelling*, *120*(2–3), 167–179. doi:10.1016/S0304-3800(99)00100-3

Brown, M., Lewis, H. G., & Gunn, S. R. (2000). Linear spectral mixture models and support vector machines for remote sensing. *IEEE Transactions on Geoscience and Remote Sensing*, *38*(5), 2346–2360. doi:10.1109/36.868891

Bruzzone, L., Chi, M., & Marconcini, M. (2006). A novel transductive SVM for semisupervised classification of remote-sensing images. *IEEE Transactions on Geoscience and Remote Sensing*, *44*(11), 3363–3373. doi:10.1109/TGRS.2006.877950

Bruzzone, L., & Melgani, F. (2005). Robust multiple estimator systems for the analysis of biophysical parameters from remotely sensed data. *IEEE Transactions on Geoscience and Remote Sensing*, *43*(1), 159–174. doi:10.1109/TGRS.2004.839818

Bruzzone, L., & Persello, C. (2009). A novel context-sensitive semisupervised SVM classifier robust to mislabeled training samples. *IEEE Transactions on Geoscience and Remote Sensing, 47*(7), 2142–2154. doi:10.1109/TGRS.2008.2011983

Burges, C. J. C. (1998). A tutorial on support vector machines for pattern recognition. *Data Mining and Knowledge Discovery, 2*(2), 121–127. doi:10.1023/A:1009715923555

Camara, D., & Loureiro, A. (2001). GPS/ant-like routing algorithm in ad hoc networks. Telecommunication Systems, 18, 85-100.

Cameron, D. E., & Lang, J. H. (1992). *The control of high-speed variable-reluctance generators in electric power systems*. Paper presented at the Applied Power Electronics Conference and Exposition.

Camps-Valls, G., Bruzzone, L., Rojo-Alvarez, J. L., & Melgani, F. (2006b). Robust support vector regression for biophysical variable estimation from remotely sensed images. *IEEE Geoscience and Remote Sensing Letters, 3*(3), 339–343. doi:10.1109/LGRS.2006.871748

Camps-Valls, G., Gomez-Chova, L., Calpe-Maravilla, J., Martin-Guerrero, J. D., Soria-Olivas, E., Alonso-Chorda, L., & Moreno, J. (2004). Robust support vector method for hyperspectral data classification and knowledge discovery. *IEEE Transactions on Geoscience and Remote Sensing, 42*(7), 1530–1542. doi:10.1109/TGRS.2004.827262

Camps-Valls, G., Gomez-Chova, L., Munoz-Mari, J., Rojo-Alvarez, J. L., & Martinez-Ramon, M. (2008). Kernel-based framework for multitemporal and multisource remote sensing data classification and change detection. *IEEE Transactions on Geoscience and Remote Sensing, 46*(6), 1822–1835. doi:10.1109/TGRS.2008.916201

Camps-Valls, G., Gómez-Chova, L., Muñoz-Marí, J., Vila-Francés, J., Amorós-López, J., & Calpe-Maravilla, J. (2006a). Retrieval of oceanic chlorophyll concentration with relevance vector machines. *Remote Sensing of Environment, 105*(1), 23–33. doi:10.1016/j.rse.2006.06.004

Camps-Valls, G., Gomez-Chova, L., Munoz-Mari, J., Vila-Frances, J., & Calpe-Maravilla, J. (2006c). Composite kernels for hyperspectral image classification. *IEEE Geoscience and Remote Sensing Letters, 3*(1), 93–97. doi:10.1109/LGRS.2005.857031

Camps-Valls, G., Mooij, J., & Scholkopf, B. (2010). Remote sensing feature selection by kernel dependence measures. *IEEE Geoscience and Remote Sensing Letters, 7*(3), 587–591. doi:10.1109/LGRS.2010.2041896

Candade, N. (2004) Multispectral classification of Landsat images, a comparison of support vector machine and neural network classifiers. In *ASPRS Annual Conference Proceedings*. Denver, CO: Academic Press.

Cansever, D. H., Michelson, A. M., & Levesque, A. H. (1999). Quality of service support in mobile ad - hoc IP networks. In Proceedings of MILCOM 1999 - IEEE Military Communications Conference (pp. 30 – 34). IEEE.

Cao, J., Ahmadi, M., & Shridhar, M. (1995). Recognition of handwritten numerals with multiple feature and multistage classifier. *Pattern Recognition, 28*(2), 153–160. doi:10.1016/0031-3203(94)00094-3

Cao, X., Chen, J., Imura, H., & Higashi, O. (2009b). A SVM-based method to extract urban areas from DMSP–OLS and SPOT VGT data. *Remote Sensing of Environment, 113*(10), 2205–2209. doi:10.1016/j.rse.2009.06.001

Cao, X., Chen, J., Matsushita, B., Imura, H., & Wang, L. (2009a). An automatic method for burn scar mapping using support vector machines. *International Journal of Remote Sensing, 30*(3), 577–594. doi:10.1080/01431160802220219

Caprari, G., Colot, A., Siegwart, R., Halloy, J., & Deneubourg, J. L. (2005). Animal and robot mixed societies - Building cooperation between microrobots and cockroaches. *IEEE Robotics & Automation Magazine, 12*(2), 58–65. doi:10.1109/MRA.2005.1458325

Caprari, G., Estier, T., & Siegwart, R. (2002). Fascination of down scaling - Alice the sugar cube robot. *Journal of Micro-Mechatronics, 1*(3), 177–189.

Caramanis, M., & Foster, J. M. (2009, December). Management of electric vehicle charging to mitigate renewable generation intermittency and distribution network congestion. In *Proceedings of the 48th IEEE Conference on Decision and Control*. Shanghai: IEEE. doi:10.1109/CDC.2009.5399955

Cardenas, R., Pena, R., Perez, M., Clare, J., Asher, G., & Wheeler, P. (2005). Control of a switched reluctance generator for variable-speed wind energy applications. *IEEE Transactions on Energy Conversion, 20*(4), 781–791. doi:10.1109/TEC.2005.853733

Carrão, H., Gonçalves, P., & Caetano, M. (2008). Contribution of multispectral and multitemporal information from MODIS images to land cover classification. *Remote Sensing of Environment, 112*(3), 986–997. doi:10.1016/j.rse.2007.07.002

Castillo, C., Chollett, I., & Klein, E. (2008). Enhanced duckweed detection using bootstrapped SVM classification on medium resolution RGB MODIS imagery. *International Journal of Remote Sensing, 29*(19), 5595–5604. doi:10.1080/01431160801961375

Castillo, O., & Melin, P. (2012). Optimization of type-2 fuzzy systems based on bio-inspired methods: A concise review. *Information Sciences Elsevier, 205*, 1–19. doi:10.1016/j.ins.2012.04.003

Castro, J. C. H., & Viñuela, P. I. (2005). Evolutionary computation in computer security and cryptography. *New Generation Computing, 23*(3), 193–199. doi:10.1007/BF03037654

Cepeda, J. C., Rueda, J. L., & Erlich, I. (2012). Identification of dynamic equivalents based on heuristic optimization for smart grid applications. In *Proceedings of Evolutionary Computation (CEC),2012 IEEE Congress* (pp. 1-8). IEEE. doi:10.1109/CEC.2012.6256493

Cetin, K. O. (2000). *Reliability-based assessment of seismic soil liquefaction initiation hazard.* (PhD dissertation). University of California, Berkeley, CA.

Cetin, K. O., Seed, R. B., Der Kiureghian, A., Tokimatsu, K., Harder, L. F. Jr, Kayen, R. E., & Moss, R. E. S. (2004). Standard penetration test-based probabilistic and deterministic assessment of seismic soil liquefaction potential. *Journal of Geotechnical and Geoenvironmental Engineering, 130*(12), 1314–1340. doi:10.1061/(ASCE)1090-0241(2004)130:12(1314)

Chakrabarty, K. (2010). Design automation and test solutions for digital microfluidic biochips. *IEEE Transactions on Computer-Aided Design of Integrated Circuits and Systems, 57*, 4–17.

Chakrabarty, K. (2010). Digital microfluidic biochips: A vision for functional diversity and more than Moore. In *Proceedings of 23rd International Conference on VLSI Design* (pp. 452 – 457). Academic Press. doi:10.1109/VLSI.Design.2010.33

Chakrabarty, K., Fair, R., & Zeng, J. (2010). Design tools for digital microfluidic biochips: Towards functional diversification and more than Moore. *IEEE Transactions on Computer-Aided Design of Integrated Circuits and Systems, 29*(7), 1001–1017. doi:10.1109/TCAD.2010.2049153

Chandni, & Sharma, K. (2013). Improvement in QoS using sink mobility in WSN. *International Journal of Computer Trends and Technology, 4*(4).

Chandra Mohan, B., & Baskaran, R. (2012). A survey: Ant colony optimization based recent research & implementation on several engineering domain. *Expert Systems with Applications, 39*(4), 4618–4627. doi:10.1016/j.eswa.2011.09.076

Chandra, S., Bhattacharyya, S., & Chakraborty, S. (2013). A quantum inspired time efficient OptiMUSIG activation function for multilevel image segmentation. In *Proceedings ofIndia Conference (INDICON), 2013 Annual IEEE.* IEEE.

Chang, P. L., & Teng, W. G. (2007). Exploiting the self- organizing map for meical image segmentation. In *Proceedings ofTwentieth IEEE International Symposium on Computer – Based Medical Systems 20.* IEEE.

Chang, W. Y. (2013). The state of charge estimating methods for battery: A review. *ISRN Applied Mathematics, 2013.*

Chang, Y. C., Cheng, C. H., Lu, L. Y., & Liaw, C. M. (2010). *An experimental switched-reluctance generator based distributed power system.* Paper presented at the Electrical Machines (ICEM).

Chang, C.-C., & Lin, C.-J. (2011). LIBSVM: A library for support vector machines. *ACM Transactions on Intelligent Systems and Technology, 2*(3), 1–27. doi:10.1145/1961189.1961199

Changseok, B., Wei, C. Y., Yuk, Y. C., & Sin, L. L. (2010). Feature selection with intelligent dynamic swarm & rough set. *Expert Systems with Applications, 37*(10), 7026–7032. doi:10.1016/j.eswa.2010.03.016

Chang, Y. L., & Li, X. (1994). Adaptive image region-growing. *IEEE Transactions on Image Processing, 3*(6), 868–872. doi:10.1109/83.336259 PMID:18296257

Chatterjee, S., Rahaman, H., & Samanta, T. (2013), Multi-objective optimization algorithm for efficient pin-constrained droplet routing technique in digital microfluidic biochip. In *Proceedings of 14th International Symposium on Quality Electronic Design* (ISQED) (pp. 252–256). Santa Clara, CA: Academic Press. doi:10.1109/ISQED.2013.6523618

Chaturvedi, K. T., Pandit, M., & Srivastava, L. (2008). Self-organizing hierarchical particle swarm optimization for nonconvex economic dispatch. *IEEE Transactions on Power Systems, 23*(3), 1079–1087. doi:10.1109/TPWRS.2008.926455

Chen, G., Guo, W., & Huang, K. (2007). *On line parameter identification of an induction motor using improved particle swarm optimization*. Paper presented at the Control Conference.

Chen, H., Wang, X., Gu, J. J., & Lu, S. (2010). *Design of bilateral switched reluctance linear generator*. Paper presented at the Electric Power and Energy Conference (EPEC). doi:10.1109/EPEC.2010.5697236

Chen, H., Zhu, Y., & Hu, K. (2008). Self-adaptation in bacterial foraging optimization algorithm. In *Proceedings of 3rd International Conference on Intelligent System and Knowledge Engineering (ISKE 2008)* (Vol. 1, pp. 1026–1031). Academic Press. doi:10.1109/ISKE.2008.4731080

Chen, T. W., & Gerla, M. (1998). Global state routing: A New routing scheme for ad-hoc wireless networks. In *Proc. IEEE ICC'98*. IEEE. Retrieved from http://www.ics.uci.edu/~atm/adhoc/paper-collection/gerla-gsr-icc98.pdf

Chen, Z., & Tang, H. (2010). Cockroach swarm optimization. In *Proceedings of IEEE 2nd International Conference on Computer Engineering and Technology* (ICCET) (pp. 652–655). IEEE.

Cheng, L., Yang, Y., Qian, Z. L., Han, R., & Pan, Y. (n.d.). *Continuous cockroach swarm optimization with logistic chaotic map for solving function optimization problems.* Department of Computer Science and Engineering, Huaian College of Information Technology.

Cheng, L., Zhu, D. C., Wang, Z. B., Qian, Z. L., & Pan, Y. (n.d.). *The research in CSO of continuous optimization problem.* Department of Computer Science and Engineering, Huaian College of Information Technology.

Cheng, H. D., & Chen, Y. H. (1999). Fuzzy partition of two-dimensional histogram and its application to thresholding. *Pattern Recognition, 32*(5), 825–843. doi:10.1016/S0031-3203(98)00080-6

Cheng, L., Xu, Y.-H., Zhang, H.-B., Qian, Z.-L., & Feng, G. (2010). New bionics optimization algorithm: Food truck-cockroach swarm optimization algorithm. *Computer Engineering, 36*, 208–209.

Cheng, S., Shi, Y., & Qin, Q. (2013). A study of normalized population diversity in particle swarm optimization. *International Journal of Swarm Intelligence Research, 4*(1), 1–34. doi:10.4018/jsir.2013010101

Chen, H., & Ho, P. (2008). Statistical pattern recognition in remote sensing. *Pattern Recognition, 41*(9), 2731–2741. doi:10.1016/j.patcog.2008.04.013

Chen, J., Wang, C., & Wang, R. (2008a). Combining support vector machines with a pairwise decision tree. *IEEE Geoscience and Remote Sensing Letters, 5*(3), 409–413. doi:10.1109/LGRS.2008.916834

Chen, J., Wang, C., & Wang, R. (2009). Using stacked generalization to combine SVMs in magnitude and shape feature spaces for classification of hyperspectral data. *IEEE Transactions on Geoscience and Remote Sensing, 47*(7), 2193–2205. doi:10.1109/TGRS.2008.2010491

Chen, K. H., Kung, J. W., Min, L. T., Kung, M. W., Angelia, M. A., Wei, C. C., & Ku, S. C. et al. (2014). Gene selection for cancer identification - a decision tree model empowered by particle swarm optimization algorithm. *BMC Bioinformatics, 15*(49), 15–49. PMID:24555567

Chen, S. M., Yeh, M. S., & Hsio, P. Y. (1995). A comparison of similarity measures of fuzzy values. *Fuzzy Sets and Systems, 72*(1), 79–89. doi:10.1016/0165-0114(94)00284-E

Chen, Z. (2011). A modified cockroach swarm optimization. *Advances in Engineering Software, 32*(1), 49–60.

Cheriet, M., El Yacoubi, M., Fujisawa, H., Lopresti, D., & Lorette, G. (2009). Handwriting recognition research: Twenty years of achievement... and beyond. *Pattern Recognition, 42*(12), 3131–3135. doi:10.1016/j.patcog.2009.03.014

Chiang, C. C. (1997). Routing in clustered multihop, mobile wireless networks with fading channel. In *Proc. IEEE SICON'97* (pp. 192-211). IEEE.

Chiang, C.-L. (2005). Improved genetic algorithm for power economic dispatch of units with valve-point effects and multiple fuels. *IEEE Transactions on Power Systems, 20*(4), 1690–1699. doi:10.1109/TPWRS.2005.857924

Chiang, C.-L., & Su, C.-T. (2005). Adaptive-improved genetic algorithm for the economic dispatch of units with multiple fuel options. *Cybernetics and Systems: An Internationl Journal, 36*(7), 687–704. doi:10.1080/01969720591008788

Chiang, J. H., & Hao, P. Y. (2004). Support vector learning mechanism for fuzzy rule based modeling: A new approach. *IEEE Transactions on Fuzzy Systems, 12*(1), 1–12. doi:10.1109/TFUZZ.2003.817839

Chiasson, J., & Vairamohan, B. (2005). Estimating the state of charge of a battery. *IEEE Transactions on Control Systems Technology, 13*(3), 465–470. doi:10.1109/TCST.2004.839571

Chi, M., Feng, R., & Bruzzone, L. (2008). Classification of hyperspectral remote-sensing data with primal SVM for small-sized training dataset problem. *Advances in Space Research, 41*(11), 1793–1799. doi:10.1016/j.asr.2008.02.012

Cho, M., & Pan, D. (2008). A high-performance droplet routing algorithm for digital microfluidic biochips. *IEEE Transactions on Computer-Aided Design of Integrated Circuits and Systems, 27*(10), 1714–1724. doi:10.1109/TCAD.2008.2003282

Chong, E. K. P., & Zak, S. (2001). *An H., introduction to optimization* (2nd ed.). New York: John Wiley & Sons.

Chrisley, R. (1995). Quantum learning. In *Proceedings of the International Symposium, Saariselka*. Lapland, Finland: Finnish Association of Artificial Intelligence.

Chu, S. C., Tsai, P. W., & Pan, J. S. (2006). Cat swarm optimization. In *Proceedings of the 9th Pacific Rim International Conference on Artificial Intelligence* (LNAI), (vol. 4099, pp. 854 – 858). Berlin: Springer. doi:10.1007/11801603_94

Chuang, L. Y., Chang, H. W., Tu, C. J., & Yang, C. H. (2008). Improved binary PSO for feature selection using gene expression data. *Computational Biology and Chemistry, 32*(1), 29–38. doi:10.1016/j.compbiolchem.2007.09.005 PMID:18023261

Chun, D. N., & Yang, H. S. (1996). Robust image segmentation using genetic algorithm with a fuzzy measure. *Pattern Recognition, 29*(7), 1195–1211. doi:10.1016/0031-3203(95)00148-4

Clerc, M. (2006). *Particle swarm optimization*. London, UK: ISTE. doi:10.1002/9780470612163

Clerc, M., & Kennedy, J. (2002). The particle swarm explosion, stability, and convergence in a multidimensional complex space. *IEEE Transactions on Evolutionary Computation, 6*(1), 58–73. doi:10.1109/4235.985692

Clevers, J. G. P. W., van der Heijden, G. W. A. M., Verzakov, S., & Schaepman, M. E. (2007). Estimating grassland biomass using SVM band shaving of hyperspectral. *Data Photogrammetric Engineering & Remote Sensing, 73*(10), 1141–1148. doi:10.14358/PERS.73.10.1141

Cogalton, R. G., & Green, K. (1999). *Assessing the accuracy of remote sensed data, principles and practices*. London: Lewis Publishers.

Colorni, A., Dorigo, M., Maniezzo, V., & Trubian, M. (1994). Ant system for job–shop scheduling. *Journal of Operations Research, Statistics, and Computer Science, 34*(1), 39–53.

Coppia, R., & D'Urso, P. (2005). Fuzzy unsupervised classification of multivariate time trajectories with the Shannon entropy regularization. *Computational Statistics & Data Analysis, 50*(6), 1452–1477. doi:10.1016/j.csda.2005.01.008

Cordasco, G., Scara, V., & Rosenberg, A. L. (2007). Bounded-collision memory-mapping schemes for data structures with applications to parallel memories. *IEEE Transactions on Parallel and Distributed Systems, 18*(7), 973–982. doi:10.1109/TPDS.2007.1024

Cordella, L., De Stefano, C., Fontanella, F., & Marrocco, C. (2008). A feature selection algorithm for handwritten character recognition. In *Proceedings of 19th International Conference on Pattern Recognition (ICPR 2008)* (pp. 1–4). Academic Press. doi:10.1109/ICPR.2008.4761834

Cortes, C., & Vapnik, V. (1995). Support-vector networks. *Machine Learning, 20*(3), 273–297. doi:10.1007/BF00994018

Dalponte, M., Bruzzone, L., & Gianelle, D. (2008). Fusion of hyperspectral and LIDAR remote sensing data for classification of complex forest areas. *IEEE Transactions on Geoscience and Remote Sensing, 46*(5), 1416–1427. doi:10.1109/TGRS.2008.916480

Dalponte, M., Bruzzone, L., Vescovo, L., & Gianelle, D. (2009). The role of spectral resolution and classifier complexity in the analysis of hyperspectral images of forest areas. *Remote Sensing of Environment, 113*(11), 2345–2355. doi:10.1016/j.rse.2009.06.013

Dang, J., Brabazon, A., O'Neill, M., & Edelman, D. (2008). Option model calibration using a bacterial foraging optimization algorithm. In M. Giacobini, A. Brabazon, S. Cagnoni, G. Di Caro, R. Drechsler, A. Ekárt, … S. Yang (Eds.), Applications of evolutionary computing SE - 12 (Vol. 4974, pp. 113–122). Springer Berlin Heidelberg. doi:10.1007/978-3-540-78761-7_12

Das, N., Acharya, K., Sarkar, R., Basu, S., Kundu, M., & Nasipuri, M. (2012). A novel GA-SVM based multistage approach for recognition of handwritten bangla compound characters. In *Proceedings of the International Conference on Information Systems Design and Intelligent Applications 2012* (Vol. 132, pp. 145–152). Academic Press. doi:10.1007/978-3-642-27443-5_17

Das, N., Acharya, K., Sarkar, R., Basu, S., Kundu, M., & Nasipuri, M. (2014). A benchmark image database of isolated Bangla handwritten compound characters. *International Journal on Document Analysis and Recognition*, 1–19.

Das, N., Basu, S., Sarkar, R., Kundu, M., Nasipuri, M., & Basu, D. K. (2007). A soft computing paradigm for handwritten digit recognition with application to Bangla digits. In *Proceedings of International Conference on Modeling and Simulation* (Vol. 2, pp. 771–774). Kolkata, India: Academic Press.

Das, N., Pramanik, S., Basu, S., Saha, P. K., Sarkar, R., & Kundu, M. (2009). Design of a novel convex hull based feature set for recognition of isolated handwritten Roman numerals. In Proceedings of UB–NE ASEE 2009. University of Bridgeport.

Das, N., Pramanik, S., Basu, S., Saha, P. K., Sarkar, R., Kundu, M., & Nasipuri, M. (2009). Recognition of handwritten Bangla basic characters and digits using convex hull based feature set. In Z. M. Dimitrios A. Karras Etienne E. Kerre, Chunping Li (Ed.), *International Conference on Artificial Intelligence and Pattern Recognition* (pp. 380–386). Orlando, FL: ISRST.

Dash, J., Mathur, A., Foody, G. M., Curran, P. J., Chipman, J. W., & Lilles, T. M. (2007). Landcover classification using multi-temporal MERIS vegetation indices. *International Journal of Remote Sensing, 28*(6), 1137–1159. doi:10.1080/01431160600784259

Dash, M., & Liu, H. (1997). Feature selection for classification. *Intelligent Data Analysis, 1*(4), 131–156. doi:10.1016/S1088-467X(97)00008-5

DaSilva, L. A., Reed, J. H., & Newhall, W. (2002). *Ad hoc networks and automotive applications*. Virginia Polytechnic Institute and State University.

Das, N., Basu, S., Sarkar, R., Kundu, M., Nasipuri, M., & Basu, D. K. (2009). An improved feature descriptor for recognition of handwritten Bangla alphabet. In GuruD. S. VasudevT. (Eds.), *International Conference on Signal and Image Processing* (pp. 451–454). Mysore, India: Excel India Publishers.

Das, N., Das, B., Sarkar, R., Basu, S., Kundu, M., & Nasipuri, M. (2010). Handwritten Bangla basic and compound character recognition using MLP and SVM classifier. *Journal of Computing, 2*(2), 109–115.

Das, N., Reddy, J. M., Sarkar, R., Basu, S., Kundu, M., Nasipuri, M., & Basu, D. K. (2012). A statistical–topological feature combination for recognition of handwritten numerals. *Applied Soft Computing, 12*(8), 2486–2495. doi:10.1016/j.asoc.2012.03.039

Das, N., Sarkar, R., Basu, S., Kundu, M., Nasipuri, M., & Basu, D. K. (2012). A genetic algorithm based region sampling for selection of local features in handwritten digit recognition application. *Applied Soft Computing, 12*(5), 1592–1606. doi:10.1016/j.asoc.2011.11.030

Datta, T., Misra, I. S., Mangaraj, B. B., & Imtiaj, S. (2008). Improved adaptive bacteria foraging algorithm in optimization of antenna array for faster convergence. *Progress In Electromagnetics Research C, 1*, 143–157. doi:10.2528/PIERC08011705

Dave, R. N. (1989). Use of the adaptive fuzzy clustering algorithm to detect lines in digital images. *Intell. Robots Comput. Vision VIII, 1192*, 600–611.

Davies, D. L., & Bouldin, D. W. (1979). A cluster separation measure. *IEEE Transactions on Pattern Analysis and Machine Intelligence, 1*(2), 224–227.

Dawei, L., Zhaohui, C., & Binyan, Z. (2005). Particle swarm optimization algorithm with chaos and its performance testing. In *Proceedings of the Second International Conference on Impulsive Dynamical Systems and Applications* (pp. 1330-1335). Academic Press.

De Bao, C., & Chun Xia, Z. (2009). Particle swarm optimization with adaptive population size and its application. *Applied Soft Computing, 9*(1), 39–48. doi:10.1016/j.asoc.2008.03.001

De Garis, H., Gaur, A., & Sriram, R. (2003). Quantum versus evolutionary systems: Total versus sampled search. In *Proceedings of 5th. Int. Conf. on Evolvable Systems (ICES)*. Academic Press.

de Hoon, M. J. L., Imoto, S., Nolan, J., & Miyano, S. (2004). Open source clustering software. *Bioinformatics (Oxford, England), 20*(9), 1453–1454. doi:10.1093/bioinformatics/bth078 PMID:14871861

De Luca, A., & Termini, S. (1972). A definition of non-probabilistic entropy in the setting of fuzzy set theory. *Information and Control, 20*(4), 301–312. doi:10.1016/S0019-9958(72)90199-4

De Micheli, G. (1994). *Synthesis and optimization of digital circuits*. McGraw-Hill.

De Sousa, L., Silvestre, B., & Bouchez, B. (2010). A combined multiphase electric drive and fast battery charger for electric vehicles. In *Proceedings of Vehicle Power and Propulsion Conference (VPPC)*. Lille, France: IEEE. doi:10.1109/VPPC.2010.5729057

de Souto, M. C. P., Soares, R.G.F., de Araujo, D.S.A., Costa, I.G., Ludermir, T.B., & Schliep, A. (2008). Ranking and selecting clustering algorithms using a meta-learning approach. In *Proc. of IEEE International Joint Conference on Neural Networks*. IEEE Computer Society.

de Souto, M. C. P., Costa, I. G., & Araujo, D. S. A., Ludermir, T. B., & Schliep, A. (2008). Clustering cancer gene expression data, a comparative study. *BMC Bioinformatics, 9*(497). PMID:19038021

De, S., Bhattacharyya, S., & Dutta, P. (2010). Efficient grey-level image segmentation using an optimized MUSIG (OptiMUSIG) activation function. *International Journal of Parallel, Emergent and Distributed Systems*, 1-39.

Deb, K., Pratap, A., Agarwal, S., & Meyarivan, T. (2002). A fast and elitist multiobjective genetic algorithm: Nsga-II. *IEEE Transactions on Evolutionary Computation, 6*(2), 182–197. doi:10.1109/4235.996017

Delgado-Restituto, M., de Ahumada, R. L., & Rodriguez-Vazquez, A. (1995). Secure communication through switched-current chaotic circuits. In *Proceedings of the IEEE International Symposium on Circuits and Systems (ISCAS '95)* (Vol. 3, pp. 2237-2240). Seattle, WA: IEEE. doi:10.1109/ISCAS.1995.523873

Dembele, D., & Kastner, P. (2003). Fuzzy c-means method for clustering microarray data. *Bioinformatics (Oxford, England), 19*(8), 973–980. doi:10.1093/bioinformatics/btg119 PMID:12761060

Demir, B., & Ertürk, S. (2007). Hyperspectral image classification using relevance vector machines. *IEEE Geoscience and Remote Sensing Letters, 4*(4), 586–590. doi:10.1109/LGRS.2007.903069

Demir, B., & Erturk, S. (2009). Clustering-based extraction of border training patterns for accurate SVM classification of hyperspectral images. *IEEE Geoscience and Remote Sensing Letters, 6*(4), 840–844. doi:10.1109/LGRS.2009.2026656

Deneubourg, J. L., Aron, S., & Pasteels, J. M. (1990). The self-organizing exploratory pattern of the *Argentine ant. Journal of Insect Behavior, 3*(159). doi:10.1007/BF01417909

Deng, Z., & Singh, C. (1992). A new approach to reliability evaluation of interconnected power systems including planned outages and frequency calculations. *IEEE Transactions on Power Systems, 7*(2), 734–743. doi:10.1109/59.141780

Denholm, P., Kuss, M., & Margolis, R. M. (2013). Co-benefits of large scale plug-in hybrid electric vehicle and solar PV deployment. *Journal of Power Sources, 236,* 350–356. doi:10.1016/j.jpowsour.2012.10.007

De, S., Bhattacharyya, S., & Dutta, P. (2008). OptiMU-SIG: An optimized gray level image segmentor.[IEEE.]. *Proceedings of ADCOM, 2008,* 78–87.

Deutsch, D., & Jozsa, R. (1992). Rapid solution of problems by quantum computation. *Royal Society of London Proceedings Series, 439*(1907), 553–558.

Devi, V. S. (2014). Learning using soft computing techniques. In B. Tripathy & D. Acharjya (Eds.), *Global trends in intelligent computing research and development* (pp. 51–67). Hershey, PA: Information Science Reference; doi:10.4018/978-1-4666-4936-1.ch003

Dey, S., Bhattacharyya, S., & Maulik, U. (2013a). Quantum inspired meta-heuristic algorithms for multi-level thresholding for true colour images. In *Proceedings of IEEE Indicon 2013*. IEEE.

Dey, S., Bhattacharyya, S., & Maulik, U. (2013c). Chaotic map model based interference employed in quantum inspired genetic algorithm to determine the optimum gray level image thresholding. *Global Trends in Intelligent Computing Research and Development,* 68-110.

Dey, S., Bhattacharyya, S., & Maulik, U. (2014a). New quantum inspired tabu search for multi-level colour image thresholding. In *Proceedings of 8th International Conference on Computing for Sustainable Global Development (INDIACom-2014)*. Academic Press.

Dey, S., Bhattacharyya, S., & Maulik, U. (2014d). Quantum inspired automatic clustering for multi-level image thresholding. In *Proceedings of International Conference on Computational Intelligence and Communication Networks (ICCICN 2014)*. Academic Press.

Dey, S., Bhattacharyya, S., & Maulik, U. (2014e). Quantum behaved multi-objective PSO and ACO optimization for multi-level thresholding. In *Proceedings of International Conference on Computational Intelligence and Communication Networks (ICCICN 2014)*. Academic Press.

Dey, S., Saha, I., Maulik, U., & Bhattacharyya, S. (2013b). New quantum inspired meta-heuristic methods for multi-level thresholding. In *Proceedings of 2013 International Conference on Advances in Computing, Communications and Informatics (ICACCI)*. Academic Press.

Dey, S., Bhattacharyya, S., & Maulik, U. (2014c). Quantum inspired genetic algorithm and particle swarm optimization using chaotic map model based interference for gray level image thresholding. *Swarm and Evolutionary Computation, 15,* 38–57. doi:10.1016/j.swevo.2013.11.002

Dey, S., Saha, I., Maulik, U., & Bhattacharyya, S. (2014b). Multi-level thresholding using quantum inspired meta-heuristics. *Knowledge-Based Systems, 67,* 373–400. doi:10.1016/j.knosys.2014.04.006

Di Caro, G. A. (2004). *Ant colony optimization and its application to adaptive routing in telecommunication networks*. (PhD thesis). Facult'e des Sciences Appliqu'ees, Universit'e Libre de Bruxelles, Brussels, Belgium.

DiCaro, G., & Dorigo, M. (1998). AntNet: Distributed stigmergetic control for communication networks. *Journal of Artificial Intelligence Research, 9,* 317–365.

Dieu, V. N., Schegner, P., & Ongsakul, W. (2011). A newly improved particle swarm optimization for economic dispatch with valve point loading effects. In *Proceedings of Power and Energy Society General Meeting, 2011 IEEE* (pp. 1-8). IEEE. doi:10.1109/PES.2011.6039332

Dieu, V. N., Ongsakul, W., & Polprasert, J. (2013). The augmented Lagrange Hopfield network for economic dispatch with multiple fuel options. *Mathematical and Computer Modelling, 57*(1), 30–39. doi:10.1016/j.mcm.2011.03.041

Dieu, V. N., Schegner, P., & Ongsakul, W. (2013). *Pseudo-gradient based particle swarm optimization method for nonconvex economic dispatch*. Springer.

Diffie, W., & Hellman, M. (1976). Multi-user cryptographic techniques. *Proceedings of the AFIPS, 45,* 109–112. doi:10.1145/1499799.1499815

Diffie, W., & Hellman, M. (1976). New directions in cryptography. *IEEE Transactions on Information Theory*, *22*(6), 644–654. doi:10.1109/TIT.1976.1055638

Dinh, T. A., Yamashita, S., & Ho, T. Y. (2014). A logic integrated optimal pin-count design for digital microfluidic biochips. In Proceedings of Design, Automation and Test in Europe Conference and Exhibition (DATE). Academic Press.

Dixon, B., & Canade, M. (2008). Multispectral land use classification using neural networks and support vector machines: One or the other, or both? *International Journal of Remote Sensing*, *29*(4), 1185–1206. doi:10.1080/01431160701294661

Dobry, R., Stokoe, K. H., Ladd, R. S., & Youd, T. L. (1981). Liquefaction susceptibility from S-wave velocity. In *Proc., ASCE Nat. Convention, In Situ Tests to Evaluate Liquefaction Susceptibility*. New York: ASCE.

Dorigo, M. (1992). *Optimization, learning and natural algorithms.* (Doctoral dissertation). Politechnico di Milano, Milano, Italy.

Dorigo, M., & Blum, C. (2004). *Ant colony optimization theory: A survey*. PHI.

Dorigo, M., Maniezzo, V., & Colorni, A. (1991). *Positive feedback as a search strategy* (Tech. Report 91 – 016). Dipartimento di Elettronica, Politecnico di Milano.

Dorigo, M., & Gambardella, L. M. (1997). Ant colony system: A cooperative learning approach to the travelling salesman problem. *IEEE Transactions on Evolutionary Computation*, *1*(1), 53–66. doi:10.1109/4235.585892

Dorigo, M., Maniezzo, V., & Colorni, A. (1996). The ant system: Optimization by a colony of cooperating agents. *IEEE Transactions on Systems, Man, and Cybernetics. Part B, Cybernetics*, *26*(1), 29–41. doi:10.1109/3477.484436 PMID:18263004

Dorigo, M., & Stützle, T. (2004). *Ant colony optimization.* Cambridge, MA: MIT Press.

Dorigo, M., & Thomas, S. (2004). *Ant colony optimization.* The MIT Press. doi:10.1007/b99492

dos Santos Coelho, L., Barbosa, L. Z., & Lebensztajn, L. (2010). Multiobjective particle swarm approach for the design of a brushless DC wheel motor. *IEEE Transactions on Magnetics*, *46*(8), 2994–2997. doi:10.1109/TMAG.2010.2044145

Dourlens, S. (1995). *Neuro-cryptograph.* (MSc Thesis). Dept. of Microcomputers and Microelectronics, University of Paris, Paris, France.

Dubey, H. M., Pandit, M., Panigrahi, B. K., & Udgir, M. (2013). Economic load dispatch by hybrid swarm intelligence based gravitational search algorithm. *International Journal of Intelligent Systems and Applications*, *5*(8), 21–32. doi:10.5815/ijisa.2013.08.03

Dubois, D., & Prade, H. (1990). Rough fuzzy sets and fuzzy rough sets. *International Journal of General Systems*, *17*(2-3), 191–209. doi:10.1080/03081079008935107

Duda, R. O., Hart, P. E., & Stork, D. G. (1981). *Pattern classification and scene analysis*. New York: Wiley.

Due Trier, Ø., Jain, A. K., & Taxt, T. (1996). Feature extraction methods for character recognition-A survey. *Pattern Recognition*, *29*(4), 641–662. doi:10.1016/0031-3203(95)00118-2

Dunn, J. C. (1973). A fuzzy relative of the ISODATA process and its use in detecting compact well-separated clusters. *Journal of Cybernetics*, *3*(3), 32–57. doi:10.1080/01969727308546046

Dunn, J. C. (1974). A fuzzy relative of the ISODATA process and its use in detecting compact, well separated clusters. *Cybernetics*, *3*, 95–104.

Durbha, S. S., King, R. L., & Younan, N. H. (2007). Support vector machines regression for retrieval of leaf are a index from multi angle imaging spectroradiometer. *Remote Sensing of Environment*, *107*(1–2), 348–361. doi:10.1016/j.rse.2006.09.031

Durier, V., & Rivault, C. (1999). Path integration in cockroach larvae. *Blattella germanica* (L.) (Insect: Dictyoptera): direction and distance estimation. *Animal Learning & Behavior*, *27*(1), 108–118. doi:10.3758/BF03199436

Durier, V., & Rivault, C. (2000). Learning and foraging efficiency in German cockroaches. *Blattella germanica* (L.) (Insecta: Dictyoptera). *Animal Cognition*, *3*(3), 139–145. doi:10.1007/s100710000065

Durier, V., & Rivault, C. (2002). Influence of a novel object in the home range of the cockroach. *Blattella germanica. Medical and Veterinary Entomology, 16*(2), 121–125. doi:10.1046/j.1365-2915.2002.00348.x PMID:12109704

Dusmez, S., Cook, A., & Khaligh, A. (2011). Comprehensive analysis of high quality power converters for level 3 off-board chargers. In *Proceedings of Vehicle Power and Propulsion Conference (VPPC)*. Chicago: IEEE doi:10.1109/VPPC.2011.6043096

Eberhart, R. C., & Kennedy, J. (1995, October). A new optimizer using particle swarm theory. In *Proceedings of the Sixth International Symposium on Micro Machine and Human Science* (Vol. 1, pp. 39-43). Academic Press. doi:10.1109/MHS.1995.494215

Eberhart, R. C., & Shi, Y. (2000). Comparing inertia weights and constriction factors in particle swarm optimization. In *Proceedings of the 2000 Congress on Evolutionary Computation* (pp. 84-88). Academic Press. doi:10.1109/CEC.2000.870279

Eberhart, R. C., & Shi, Y. (2001). Particle swarm optimization: developments, applications and resources. In *Evolutionary Computation, 2001:Proceedings of the 2001 Congress on* (Vol. 1, pp. 81-86). IEEE. doi:10.1109/CEC.2001.934374

Eberhart, R., & Shi, Y. (2000). Comparing inertia weights and constriction factors in particle swarm optimization. In *Proceedings of the Congress on Evolutionary Computing* (pp. 84-89). Academic Press.

Eberhart, R. C., & Kennedy, J. (1995). A new optimizer using particle swarm theory. In *Proceedings of Sixth Int. Symposium on Micromachine and Human Science* (pp. 39-43). Nagoya, Japan: Academic Press.

Eberhart, R. C., & Shi, Y. (1998). Comparison between genetic algorithms and particle swarm optimization. In *Evolutionary programming VII* (pp. 611–616). Springer Berlin Heidelberg. doi:10.1007/BFb0040812

Echenique, E., Dixon, J., Cardenas, R., & Pena, R. (2009). Sensorless control for a switched reluctance wind generator, based on current slopes and neural networks. *IEEE Transactions on Industrial Electronics, 56*(3), 817–825. doi:10.1109/TIE.2008.2005940

Eisen, M., Spellman, P., Brown, P., & Botstein, D. (1998). Cluster analysis and display of genome-wide expression patterns. *Proceedings of the National Academy of Sciences of the United States of America, 95*(25), 14863–14868. doi:10.1073/pnas.95.25.14863 PMID:9843981

El Dor, A., Clerc, M., & Siarry, P. (2012). Hybridization of differential evolution and particle swarm optimization in a new algorithm: DEPSO-2S. In *Swarm and evolutionary computation* (pp. 57–65). Springer Berlin Heidelberg. doi:10.1007/978-3-642-29353-5_7

El-Shorbagy. (2013). *Numerical optimization & swarm intelligence for optimization: Trust region algorithm & particle swarm optimization*. Lap Lambert Academic Publishing.

Emmanuel, M., Mario, M. A., & Victor, T. (2010). Compact cancer biomarkers discovery using a swarm intelligence feature selection algorithm. *Computational Biology and Chemistry, 34*(4), 244–250. doi:10.1016/j.compbiolchem.2010.08.003 PMID:20888301

Engelbrecht, A. P. (2005). *Fundamentals of computational swarm intelligence* (Vol. 1). Chichester, UK: Wiley.

Englebrecht, A. P. (2002). *Computational intelligence: An introduction*. New York: John Wiley and sons.

Erickson, D. (2005). Towards numerical prototyping of labs-on-chip: Modeling for integrated microfluidic devices. *Journal of Microfluidics and Nanofluidics, 4*, 159–165.

Erlich, I., Nakawiro, W., & Martinez, M. (2011, July). Optimal dispatch of reactive sources in wind farms. In *Proceedings of Power and Energy Society General Meeting, 2011 IEEE* (pp. 1-7). IEEE. doi:10.1109/PES.2011.6039534

Erlich, I., Venayagamoorthy, G. K., & Worawat, N. (2010, July). A mean-variance optimization algorithm. In *Proceedings of Evolutionary Computation (CEC), 2010 IEEE Congress* (pp. 1-6). IEEE. doi:10.1109/CEC.2010.5586027

Er, M. J., Chen, W., & Wu, S. (2005). High-speed face recognition based on discrete cosine transform and RBF neural networks. *IEEE Transactions on Neural Networks, 16*(3), 679–691. doi:10.1109/TNN.2005.844909 PMID:15940995

Esch, T., Himmler, V., Schorcht, G., Thiel, M., Wehrmann, T., Bachofer, F., & Dech, S. et al. (2009). Large-area assessment to f im pervious surface based on integrated analysis of single-date Landsat-7 images and geospatial vector data. *Remote Sensing of Environment, 113*(8), 1678–1690. doi:10.1016/j.rse.2009.03.012

Everman, W. J., Medline, C. R., Jr, R. D. D., Bauman, T. T., & Biehl, L. (2008). The effect of postmergence herbicides on the spectral reflectance of corn. *Weed Technology, 22*(3), 514–522. doi:10.1614/WT-07-021.1

Ezhov, A. A. (2001). Pattern recognition with quantum neural networks. In Proceedings of Advances in Pattern Recognition ICAPR 2001. Springer Berlin Heidelberg.

Fair, R. B., Khlystov, A., Tailor, T. D., Ivanov, V., Evans, R. D., Srinivasan, V., & Zhou, J. et al. (2007). Chemical and biological applications of digital-microfluidic devices. *IEEE Design & Test of Computers, 24*(1), 10–24. doi:10.1109/MDT.2007.8

Fair, R. B., Su, F., & Chakrabarty, K. (2006). Microfluidics-based biochips: Technology issues, implementation platforms and design automation challenges. *IEEE Transactions on Computer-Aided Design of Integrated Circuits and Systems, 25*(2), 265–277.

Fan, J.-Y., & Zhang, L. (1998). Real-time economic dispatch with line flow and emission constraints using quadratic programming. *IEEE Transactions on Power Systems, 13*(2), 320–325. doi:10.1109/59.667345

Fauvel, M., Benediktsson, J. A., Chanussot, J., & Sveinsson, J. R. (2008). Spectral and spatial classification of hyper spectral data using SVMs and morphological profiles. *IEEE Transactions on Geoscience and Remote Sensing, 46*(11), 3804–3814. doi:10.1109/TGRS.2008.922034

Fauvel, M., Chanussot, J., & Benediktsson, J. A. (2009). Kernel principal component analysis for the classification of hyperspectral remote sensing data over urban areas. *EURASIP Journal on Advances in Signal Processing*.

Feistel, H. (1973). Cryptography and computer privacy. *Scientific American, 228*(5), 15–23. doi:10.1038/scientificamerican0573-15 PMID:4687783

Fernando, W. U. N., Barnes, M., & Marjanovic, O. (2011). *Excitation control and voltage regulation of switched reluctance generators above base speed operation.* Paper presented at the Vehicle Power and Propulsion Conference (VPPC).

Feynman, R. (1982). Simulating physics with computers. *International Journal of Theoretical Physics, 21*(6-7), 467–488. doi:10.1007/BF02650179

Filippi, A. M., & Archibald, R. (2009). Support vector machine-based end member extraction. *IEEE Transactions on Geoscience and Remote Sensing, 47*(3), 771–791. doi:10.1109/TGRS.2008.2004708

Flake, G. (1999). *The computational beauty of nature.* Cambridge, MA: MIT Press.

Fleury, A., Andrade, D., Oliveira, E. S. L., Fleury-Neto, G. A., Oliveira, T. F., Dias, R. J., & Silveira, A. W. F. V. (2008). *Study on an alternative converter performance for switched reluctance generator.* Paper presented at the Industrial Electronics.

Fleury, A., dos Santos e Silva, F., Domingos, J. L., & De Andrade, D. A. (2007). *A switched reluctance generator behavior under different conditions.* Paper presented at the Industrial Electronics.

Floriano, P. N. (2007). *Microchip-based assay systems methods and applications.* Totowa, NJ: Humana Press. doi:10.1007/978-1-59745-426-1

Fogel, D. B. (1997). The advantage of evolutionary computation. World Scientific Press.

Fogel, D. B. (2006). Evolutionary computation: Toward a new philosophy of machine intelligence. Wiley- IEEE Press.

Foody, G. M. (2008). RVM-based multi-class classification of remotely sensed data. *International Journal of Remote Sensing, 29*(6), 1817–1823. doi:10.1080/01431160701822115

Foody, G. M., & Mathur, A. (2004). A relative evaluation of multiclass image classification by support vector machines. *IEEE Transactions on Geoscience and Remote Sensing, 42*(6), 1335–1343. doi:10.1109/TGRS.2004.827257

Foody, G. M., & Mathur, A. (2004b). Toward intelligent training of supervised image classifications, directing training data acquisition for SVM classification. *Remote Sensing of Environment, 93*(1–2), 107–117. doi:10.1016/j.rse.2004.06.017

Foody, G. M., & Mathur, A. (2006). The use of small training sets containing mixed pixels for accurate hard image classification, training on mixed spectral responses for classification by a SVM. *Remote Sensing of Environment, 103*(2), 179–189. doi:10.1016/j.rse.2006.04.001

Foody, G. M., Mathur, A., Sanchez-Hernandez, C., & Boyd, D. S. (2006a). Training set size requirements for the classification of a specific class. *Remote Sensing of Environment, 104*(1), 1–14. doi:10.1016/j.rse.2006.03.004

Fouillet, Y., Jary, D., Chabrol, C., Claustre, P., & Peponnet, C. (2008). Digital microfluidic design and optimization of classic and new fluidic functions for lab on a chip systems. *Journal of Mircofluidics and Nanofluidics, 4*(3), 159–165. doi:10.1007/s10404-007-0164-5

Freixenet, J., Muñoz, X., & Raba, D. (2002). Yet another survey on image segmentation: Region and boundary information integration. In *Proceedings of the 7th European Conference on Computer Vision (ECCV '02)*. Academic Press. doi:10.1007/3-540-47977-5_27

Frisch, K. V. (1967). *The dance language and orientation of bees*. Cambridge, MA: Harvard University Press.

Gaing, Z.-L. (2003). Particle swarm optimization to solving the economic dispatch considering the generator constraints. *IEEE Transactions on Power Systems, 18*(3), 1187–1195. doi:10.1109/TPWRS.2003.814889

Gan, L., Topcu, U., & Low, S. (2011). Optimal decentralized protocol for electric vehicle charging. In *Proceedings of Decision and Control and European Control Conference (CDC-ECC)*. IEEE. doi:10.1109/CDC.2011.6161220

Ganesan, T., Vasant, P., & Elamvazuthy, I. (2012). A hybrid PSO approach for solving non-convex optimization problems. *Archives of Control Sciences, 22*(1), 87–105. doi:10.2478/v10170-011-0014-2

Ganesh, P. K., Aruldoss, A. V. T., Renukadevi, P., & Devaraj, D. (2012). Design of fuzzy expert system for microarray data classification using a novel genetic swarm algorithm. *Expert Systems with Applications, 39*(2), 1811–1821. doi:10.1016/j.eswa.2011.08.069

Gao, S., Zhang, H., Song, T., & Wang, Y. (2010). Network lifetime and throughput maximization in wireless sensor networks with a path-constrained mobile sink. In *Proc. 2010 International Conference on Communications and Mobile Computing*. IEEE. doi:10.1109/CMC.2010.219

Garnier, S., Jost, C., Jeanson, R., Gautrais, J., Asadpour, M., Caprari, G., & Theraulaz, G. (2005a). Collective decision-making by a group of cockroach-like robots. In *Proceedings of Swarm Intelligence Symposium, SIS 2005* (pp. 233–240). Academic Press. doi:10.1109/SIS.2005.1501627

Garnier, S., Jost, C., Jeanson, R., Gautrais, J., Asadpour, M., Caprari, G., & Theraulaz, G. (2005b). Aggregation behaviour as a source of collective decision in a group of cockroach-like-robots. In *Advances in Artificial Life: 8th European Conference, ECAL 2005* (LNAI), (Vol 3630, pp. 169-178). Springer. doi:10.1007/11553090_18

Garnier, S., Gautrais, J., Asadpour, M., Jost, C., & Theraulaz, G. (2009). Self-organized aggregation triggers collective decision making in a group of cockroach-like robots. *Adaptive Behavior, 17*(2), 109–133. doi:10.1177/1059712309103430

Gath, I., & Geva, A. (1989). Unsupervised optimal fuzzy clustering. *IEEE Transactions on Pattern Analysis and Machine Intelligence, 11*(11), 773–781. doi:10.1109/34.192473

Gautam, R. S., Singh, D., Mittal, A., & Sajin, P. (2008). Application of SVM on satellite images to detect hotspots in Jharia coal field region of India. *Advances in Space Research, 41*(11), 1784–1792. doi:10.1016/j.asr.2007.05.011

Gawrys, M., & Sienkiewicz, J. (1994). RSL–The rough set library version 2.0 (ICS Research Report 27/94). Warsaw, Poland: Institute of Computer Science. W. U. of T.

Ge, Q. Z., Ling, Z. C., Qiong, L., Hui, X. X. & Zhang, G. (2008). *High efficient classification on remote sensing images based on SVM*. The International Archives of the Photogrammetry, Remote Sensing and Spatial Information Sciences.

Geman, S., Bienenstock, E., & Doursat, R. (1992). Neural networks and the bias/variance dilemma. *Neural Computation*, *4*(1), 1–58. doi:10.1162/neco.1992.4.1.1

Gerkensmeyer, C., Kintner-Meyer, M. C., & DeSteese, J. G. (2010). *Technical challenges of plug-in hybrid electric vehicles and impacts to the US power system: Distribution system analysis*. United States Department of Energy. doi:10.2172/974954

Gerla, M., Pei, G., & Lee, S. J. (1999). *Wireless, mobile ad-hoc network routing*. Paper presented at IEEE/ACM FOCUS'99, New Brunswick, NJ. Retrieved from www.cs.ucla.edu/NRL/wireless/PAPER/focus99.pdf

Ghoggali, N., & Melgani, F. (2008). Genetic SVM approach to semisupervised multi temporal classification. *IEEE Geoscience and Remote Sensing Letters*, *5*(2), 212–216. doi:10.1109/LGRS.2008.915600

Ghoggali, N., Melgani, F., & Bazi, Y. (2009). A multi-objective genetic SVM approach for classification problems with limited training samples. *IEEE Transactions on Geoscience and Remote Sensing*, *47*(6), 1707–1718. doi:10.1109/TGRS.2008.2007128

Gholami, M. R., Hoseini, S. H., & Mohamad Taheri, M. (2008). Assessment of power composite system annualized reliability indices based on improved particle swarm optimization and comparative study between the behaviour of GA and PSO. In *Proceedings of IEEE 2nd International Power and Energy Conference* (pp. 1609-1612). Johor Bahru, Malaysia: IEEE.

Ghorai, S., Mukherjee, A., Sengupta, S., & Dutta, P. K. (2011). Cancer classification from gene expression data by NPPC ensemble. *IEEE/ACM Transactions on Computational Biology and Bioinformatics*, *8*(3), 659–671. doi:10.1109/TCBB.2010.36 PMID:20479504

Giraldi, G. A., Portugal, R., & Thess, R. N. (2004). *Genetic algorithms and quantum computation*. Available: http://www.arxiv.org/pdf/cs.NE/0403003

Giraud-Carrier, C., Vilalta, R., & Brazdil, P. (2004). Introduction to the special issue on meta-learning. *Machine Learning*, *54*(3), 187–193. doi:10.1023/B:MACH.0000015878.60765.42

Giudici, P. (2003). *Applied data mining: Statistical methods for business and industry*. John Wiley &Sons Inc.

Giudici, P., & Figini, S. (2009). *Applied data mining for business and industry*. Wiley. doi:10.1002/9780470745830

Glaab, E., Garibaldi, J., & Krasnogor, N. (2009). ArrayMining: A modular web-application for microarray analysis combining ensemble and consensus methods with cross-study normalization. *BMC Bioinformatics*, *10*(1), 358. doi:10.1186/1471-2105-10-358 PMID:19863798

Glover, F. & Kochenberger. (2003). *Handbook on metaheuristics*. Kluwer Academic Publishers.

Glover, F. (1989). Tabu search, part I. *ORSA Journal on Computing, 1*, 190–206.

Glover, F. (1990). Tabu search, part II. *ORSA Journal on Computing, 2*(1), 4–32. doi:10.1287/ijoc.2.1.4

Goh, A. T. C. (1994). Seismic liquefaction potential assessed by neural networks. *Journal of Geotechnical Engineering, 120*(9), 1467–1480. doi:10.1061/(ASCE)0733-9410(1994)120:9(1467)

Goh, A. T. C. (1996). Neural-network modeling of CPT seismic liquefaction data. *Journal of Geotechnical Engineering, 122*(1), 70–73. doi:10.1061/(ASCE)0733-9410(1996)122:1(70)

Goh, A. T. C. (2002). Probabilistic neural network for evaluating seismic liquefaction potential. *Canadian Geotechnical Journal, 39*(1), 219–232. doi:10.1139/t01-073

Goh, A. T. C., & Goh, S. H. (2007). Support vector machines: Their use in geotechnical engineering as illustrated using seismic liquefaction data. *Computers and Geotechnics, 34*(5), 410–421. doi:10.1016/j.compgeo.2007.06.001

Gomez-Chova, L., Camps-Valls, G., Bruzzone, L., & Calpe-Maravilla, J. (2010). Meanmap kernel methods for semisupervised cloud classification. *IEEE Transactions on Geoscience and Remote Sensing, 48*(1), 207–220. doi:10.1109/TGRS.2009.2026425

Gómez-Chova, L., Camps-Valls, G., Muñoz-Marí, J., & Calpe, J. (2008). Semisupervised image classification with Laplacian support vector machines. *IEEE Geoscience and Remote Sensing Letters, 5*(3), 336–340. doi:10.1109/LGRS.2008.916070

Gong, T., Xuan, J., Chen, L., Riggins, R. B., Li, H., Hoffman, E. P., & Wang, Y. et al. (2011). Motif-guided sparse decomposition of gene expression data for regulatory module identification. *BMC Bioinformatics*, *12*(82), 16. PMID:21426557

Gonzalez, R. C., & Woods, R. E. (1987). Digital image fundamentals. *Digital Image Processing*, 52-54.

Gonzalez-Longatt, F. M., Rueda, J. L., Erlich, I., Bogdanov, D., & Villa, W. (2012, October). Identification of Gaussian mixture model using mean variance mapping optimization: Venezuelan case. In *Proceedings of Innovative Smart Grid Technologies (ISGT Europe), 2012 3rd IEEE PES International Conference and Exhibition* (pp. 1-6). IEEE.

Gonzalez, R. C., & Woods, R. E. (2002). *Digital image processing*. Prentice Hall.

Gopal, N. N., & Karnan, M. (2010, December). Diagnose brain tumor through MRI using image processing clustering algorithms such as fuzzy C means along with intelligent optimization techniques. In *Proceedings of Computational Intelligence and Computing Research (ICCIC), 2010 IEEE International Conference on* (pp. 1-4). IEEE. doi:10.1109/ICCIC.2010.5705890

Gorai, A., & Ghosh, A. (2009, December). Gray-level image enhancement by particle swarm optimization. In *Proceedings of Nature & Biologically Inspired Computing, 2009: NaBIC 2009. World Congress on* (pp. 72-77). IEEE. doi:10.1109/NABIC.2009.5393603

Gorai, A., & Ghosh, A. (2011, September). Hue-preserving color image enhancement using particle swarm optimization. In Proceedings of Recent Advances in Intelligent Computational Systems (RAICS), 2011 IEEE (pp. 563-568). IEEE. doi:10.1109/RAICS.2011.6069375

Goss, S., Aron, S., Deneubourg, J. L., & Pasteels, J. M. (1989). The self-organized exploratory pattern of the Argentine ant. *Naturwissenschaften*, *76*(12), 579–581. doi:10.1007/BF00462870

Green, R. C., Wang, L., & Singh, C. (2010). State space pruning for power system reliability evaluation using genetic algorithms. In *Proceedings of IEEE Power and Energy Society General Meeting* (pp. 1-6). Minneapolis, MN: IEEE.

Green, R. C., Wang, L., Alam, M., & Singh, C. (2011). An examination of artificial immune system optimization in intelligent state space pruning for LOLP estimation. In *Proceedings of North American Power Symposium* (pp. 1-7). Boston: IEEE. doi:10.1109/NAPS.2011.6024868

Green, R. C., Wang, L., Alam, M., & Singh, C. (2011). Intelligent state space pruning using multi – objective PSO for reliability analysis of composite power systems: Observations, analyses, and impacts. In *Proceedings of IEEE Power and Energy Society General Meeting* (pp. 1-8). Detroit, MI: IEEE.

Green, R. C., Wang, L., Wang, Z., Alam, M., & Singh, C. (2010). Power system reliability assessment using intelligent state space pruning techniques: A comparative study. In *Proceedings of IEEE International Conference on Power System Technology* (pp. 1-8). Hangzhou, China: IEEE. doi:10.1109/POWERCON.2010.5666062

Green, R. C., Wang, Z., Wang, L., Alam, M., & Singh, C. (2010). Evaluation of loss of load probability for power systems using intelligent search based state space pruning. In *Proceedings of 11th International Conference on Probabilistic Methods Applied to Power Systems* (pp. 319-324). Singapore: IEEE. doi:10.1109/PMAPS.2010.5528892

Green, R. C., Wang, L., Alam, M., & Singh, C. (2011). State space pruning for reliability evaluation using binary particle swarm optimization. In *Proceedings of IEEE PES Power Systems Conference and Exposition* (pp. 1–7). Phoenix, AZ: IEEE.

Griffith, E. J., Akella, S., & Goldberg, M. K. (2006). Performance characterization of a reconfigurable planar-array digital microfluidic system. *IEEE Transactions on Computer-Aided Design of Integrated Circuits and Systems*, *25*(2), 345–357. doi:10.1109/TCAD.2005.859515

Grosan, C., & Abraham, A. (2009). A novel global optimization technique for high dimensional functions. *International Journal of Intelligent Systems*, *24*(4), 421–440. doi:10.1002/int.20343

Grosan, C., Abraham, A., & Chis, M. (2006). *Swarm intelligence in data mining*. Springer Berlin Heidelberg. doi:10.1007/978-3-540-34956-3_1

Grover, L. K. (1998). Quantum computers can search rapidly by using almost any transformation. *Physical Review Letters*, *80*(19), 4329–4332. doi:10.1103/PhysRevLett.80.4329

Guerin, S. (1997). *Optimisation multi-agents en environment dynamique: Application au routage dans les reseaux de telecommunications*. (DEA Dissertation). University of Rennes I, France.

Gunes, M., Sorges, U., & Bouazizi, I. (2002). ARA - The ant colony based routing algorithm for manets. In *Proc. ICPP Workshop on Ad Hoc Networks IWAHN* (pp. 79-85). Academic Press. doi:10.1109/ICPPW.2002.1039715

Gupta, P., & Kumar, P. R. (2000, March). The capacity of wireless network. *IEEE Transactions on Information Theory*, *46*(2), 388–404. doi:10.1109/18.825799

Hafed, Z. M., & Levine, M. D. (2001). Face recognition using discrete cosine transform. *International Journal of Computer Vision*, *43*(3), 167–188. doi:10.1023/A:1011183429707

Hammouche, K., Diaf, M., & Siarry, P. (2008). A multilevel automatic thresholding method based on a genetic algorithm for a fast image segmentation. *Computer Vision and Image Understanding*, *109*(2), 163–175. doi:10.1016/j.cviu.2007.09.001

Han, K. H., & Kim, J. H. (2000). Genetic quantum algorithm and its application to combinatorial optimization problem. In *Proceedings of the Congress on Evolutionary Computation* (vol. 2, pp. 1354-1360). Academic Press.

Han, J., & Kamber, M. (2006). *Data mining: Concepts and techniques*. Morgan Kaufmann.

Han, K. H., & Kim, J. H. (2002). Quantum-inspired evolutionary algorithm for a class combinational optimization. *IEEE Transactions on Evolutionary Computation*, *6*(6), 580–593. doi:10.1109/TEVC.2002.804320

Han, K. H., & Kim, J. H. (2004). Quantum-inspired evolutionary algorithms with a new termination criterion, h-epsilon gate, and twophase scheme. *IEEE Transactions on Evolutionary Computation*, *8*(2), 156–169. doi:10.1109/TEVC.2004.823467

Hanmandlu, M., Nath, A. V., Mishra, A. C., & Madasu, V. K. (2007). Fuzzy model based recognition of handwritten Hindi numerals using bacterial foraging. In *Proceedings of 6th IEEE/ACIS International Conference on Computer and Information Science (ICIS 2007)*. (pp. 309–314). IEEE. doi:10.1109/ICIS.2007.103

Hao, C., & Gu, J. J. (2010). Implementation of the three-phase switched reluctance machine system for motors and generators. *IEEE/ASME Transactions on Mechatronics*, *15*(3), 421-432. doi: 10.1109/TMECH.2009.2027901

Hao, C., Xing, W., & Gu, J. J. (2009). *Sliding mode control of switched reluctance linear generator system*. Paper presented at the Networking, Sensing and Control.

Hao, C., Xing, W., & Hui, Z. (2009). *Electromagnetic design of switched reluctance linear machine*. Paper presented at the Power Electronics and Motion Control Conference.

Happ, H. (1977). Optimal power dispatch: A comprehensive survey. *IEEE Transactions on Power Apparatus and Systems*, *96*(3), 841–854. doi:10.1109/T-PAS.1977.32397

Hasanien, H. M. (2011). Particle swarm design optimization of transverse flux linear motor for weight reduction and improvement of thrust force. *IEEE Transactions on Industrial Electronics*, *58*(9), 4048–4056. doi:10.1109/TIE.2010.2100338

Hasanien, H. M., & Muyeen, S. M. (2012). Speed control of grid-connected switched reluctance generator driven by variable speed wind turbine using adaptive neural network controller. *Electric Power Systems Research*, *84*(1), 206–213. doi:10.1016/j.epsr.2011.11.019

Hassoun, M. (1995). *Fundamentals of artificial neural networks*. Cambridge, MA: MIT Press.

Hatamlou, A. (2013). Black hole: A new heuristic optimization approach for data clustering. *Information Sciences*, *222*, 175–184. doi:10.1016/j.ins.2012.08.023

Havens, T., Spain, C., Salmon, N., & Keller, J. (2008). Roach infestation optimization. In *Proceedings of IEEE Swarm Intelligence Symposium*. IEEE.

Hazem, A., & Glasgow, J. (2012). *Swarm intelligence: Concepts, models & applications*. Technical Report. Queen's University.

He, D, Wang, F., & Mao, Z. (2008). Hybrid genetic algorithm for economic dispatch with valve-point effect. *Electric Power Systems Research*, 78(4), 626–633. doi:10.1016/j.epsr.2007.05.008

Heissenbüttel, M., & Braun, T. (2003). Ants-based routing in large scale mobile ad-hoc networks. In *Proceedings of Kommunikation in Verteilten Systemen KiVS03*. Leipzig, Germany: Academic Press.

He, J., Sun, Y., Kirschen, D. S., Singh, C., & Cheng, L. (2010). *State – space partitioning method for composite power system reliability assessment*. IET.

Helterbrand, J. D. (1996). One-pixel-wide closed boundary identification. *IEEE Transactions on Image Processing*, 5(5), 780–783. doi:10.1109/83.499916 PMID:18285168

Hemamalini, S., & Simon, S. (2009). Maclaurin series-based Lagrangian method for economic dispatch with valve-point effect. *Generation, Transmission & Distribution, IET*, 3(9), 859–871. doi:10.1049/iet-gtd.2008.0499

Heppner, F., & Grenander, U. (1990). *A stochastic nonlinear model for coordinated bird flocks. American Association for the Advancement of Science*. AAAS.

Hereford, J. M. (2006). A distributed particle swarm optimization algorithm for swarm robotic applications. In *Proceedings of the IEEE Congress on Evolutionary Computation* (pp. 1678 -1685). IEEE. doi:10.1109/CEC.2006.1688510

He, S., Prempain, E., & Wu, Q. H. (2004). An improved particle swarm optimizer for mechanical design optimization problems. *Engineering Optimization*, 36(5), 585–605. doi:10.1080/03052150410001704854

Hess, A., Malandrino, F., Reinhardt, M. B., Casetti, C., Hummel, K. A., & Barceló-Ordinas, J. M. (2012). Optimal deployment of charging stations for electric vehicular networks. In *Proceedings of the First Workshop on Urban Networking*. Nice, France: ACM. doi:10.1145/2413236.2413238

Hey, T. (1999). Quantum computing: An introduction. Computing & Control Engineering, 10, 105–112.

Hirsh, H. (1999). A quantum leap for AI. *IEEE Intelligent Systems*, 9.

Ho, S. Y., & Lee, K. Z. (2001). An efficient evolutionary image segmentation algorithm. In *Proceedings of IEEE Congress on Evolutionary Computation* (pp. 1327-1334). IEEE.

Hogg, T. (1998). Highly structured searches with quantum computers. *Physical Review Letters*, 80(11), 2473–2476. doi:10.1103/PhysRevLett.80.2473

Hogg, T. (1999). Quantum Search Heuristics. *IEEE Intelligent Systems*, 12–14.

Hogg, T., & Portnov, D. A. (2000). Quantum optimization. *Information Sciences*, 128(3-4), 181–197. doi:10.1016/S0020-0255(00)00052-9

Hojjatoleslami, S. A., & Kittler, J. (1998). Region growing: A new approach. *IEEE Transactions on Image Processing*, 7(7), 1079–1084. doi:10.1109/83.701170 PMID:18276325

Hollander, M., & Wolfe, D. (1999). *Nonparametric statistical methods* (2nd ed.). Wiley.

Holland, J. H. (1975). *Adaptation in natural and artificial systems*. Ann Arbor, MI: Univ. Michigan Press.

Holtz-Eakin, D., & Selden, T. M. (1995). Stoking the fires? CO_2 emissions and economic growth. *Journal of Public Economics*, 57(1), 85–101. doi:10.1016/0047-2727(94)01449-X

Horn, J., Nafpliotis, N., & Nafpliotis, D. E. (1994). A niched pareto genetic algorithm for multiobjective optimization. In *Proc. of the First IEEE Conference on Evolutionary Computation, IEEE World Congress on Computational Intelligence*. IEEE.

Hota, A. R., Juvvanapudi, M., & Bajpai, P. (2014). Issues and solution approaches in PHEV integration to the smart grid. *Renewable & Sustainable Energy Reviews*, 30(0), 217–229. doi:10.1016/j.rser.2013.10.008

Hu, Z. Z. (n.d.). *Quantum computation via neural networks applied to image processing and pattern recognition*. (PhD thesis). University of Western Sydney, Sydney, Australia.

Huang, C. J., & Dun, J. F. (2008). A distributed PSO-SVM hybrid system with feature selection and parameter optimization. *Applied Soft Computing*, 8(4), 1381–1391. doi:10.1016/j.asoc.2007.10.007

Huang, H., Zhang, J., Wang, R., & Qian, Y. (2014). Sensor node deployment in wireless sensor networks based on ionic bond-directed particle swarm optimization. *Appl. Math. Inf. Sci.*, 8(2), 597–605. doi:10.12785/amis/080217

Huang, L., & Wang, G. M. (1995). Image thresholding by minimizing the measures of fuzziness. *Pattern Recognition*, 28(1), 41–51. doi:10.1016/0031-3203(94)E0043-K

Huang, T. W., & Ho, T. Y. (2009). A fast routability and performance driven droplet routing algorithm for digital microfluidic biochips. In *Proceeding of IEEE International Conference on Computer Design* (pp. 445 – 450). IEEE. doi:10.1109/ICCD.2009.5413119

Huang, T. W., & Ho, T. Y. (2011). A two-stage integer linear programming-based droplet routing algorithm for pin-constrained digital microfluidic biochips. *IEEE Transactions on Computer-Aided Design of Integrated Circuits and Systems*, 30(2), 215–228. doi:10.1109/TCAD.2010.2097190

Huang, T. W., Lin, C. H., & Ho, T. Y. (2009). A contamination aware droplet routing for digital microfluidic biochips. In *Proceedings of IEEE/ ACM International Conference on Computer Aided Design* (pp. 151 – 156). IEEE/ACM.

Huang, X., & Zhang, L. (2010). Comparison of vector stacking, multi-SVMs fuzzy output, and multi-SVMs voting methods for multiscale VHR urban mapping. *IEEE Geoscience and Remote Sensing Letters*, 7(2), 261–265. doi:10.1109/LGRS.2009.2032563

Hui, Z., Pei, Y., & Jie, L. (2009). Study on the estimating model of shadow prices for national economy evaluation of construction projects. In *Proceedings of International Conference on Management and Service Science* (pp. 1-4). Wuhan, China: IEEE.

Hung, C. C., Liu, W., & Kuo, B. C. (2008). A new adaptive fuzzy clustering algorithm for remotely sensed images. In *Proceedings of Geoscience and Remote Sensing Symposium*. IEEE.

Hwang, W. L., Su, F., & Chakrabarty, K. (2006). Automated design of pin constrained digital microfluidic arrays for lab-on-a-chip applications. In *Proceedings of Design Automation and Test in Europe (DATE) Conference* (pp. 925 – 930). Academic Press. doi:10.1145/1146909.1147144

Hwang, W. L., Su, F., & Chakrabarty, K. (2006). Droplet routing in the synthesis of digital microfluidic biochips. In *Proceedings of Design Automation and Test in Europe (DATE) Conference* (pp. 323 – 328). Academic Press.

Idoumghar, L., Melkemi, M., Schott, R., & Aouad, M. I. (2011). Hybrid PSO-SA type algorithms for multimodal function optimization and reducing energy consumption in embedded systems. *Applied Computational Intelligence and Soft Computing*, 3.

Imran, M., Hashim, R., & Khalid, N. E. A. (2013). An overview of particle swarm optimization variants. *Procedia Engineering*, 53, 491–496. doi:10.1016/j.proeng.2013.02.063

Ingersoll, J. G., & Perkins, C. A. (1996). The 2.1 kW photovoltaic electric vehicle charging station in the city of Santa Monica, California. In *Proceedings of Twenty Fifth IEEE Photovoltaic Specialists Conference*. Washington, DC: IEEE. doi:10.1109/PVSC.1996.564423

Internet Engineering Task Force (IETF) Mobile Ad Hoc Networks. (MANET) Working Group Charter. (n.d.). Retrieved from www.ietf.org/html.charters/manet-charter.html

Ishii, H., Aoki, T., Nakasuji, M., Miwa, H., & Takanishi, A. (2004). *2004 IEEE international conference on robotics and automation*. IEEE.

Islam, M. T., Thulasiraman, P., & Thulasiram, R. K. (April 2003). A parallel ant colony optimization algorithm for all-pair routing in MANETs. In *Proc. IEEE Int. Parallel and Distributed Processing Symposium IPDPS*. Nice, France: IEEE. doi:10.1109/IPDPS.2003.1213470

Iwata, A., Chiang, C. C., Pei, G., Gerla, M., & Chen, T. W. (1999). Scalable routing strategies for ad hoc wireless networks. IEEE Journal on Selected Areas in Communications. Retrieved from http://www.cs.ucla.edu/nrl/wireless/paper/jsac99.ps.gz

Jacobs, M. A., Barker, P. B., Bluemke, D. A., Maranto, C., Arnold, C., Herskovits, E. H., & Bhujwalla, Z. (2003). Benign and malignant breast lesions, diagnosis with multiparametric mr imaging. *Radiology*, 229(1), 225–232. doi:10.1148/radiol.2291020333 PMID:14519877

Jaehwa, P., Govindaraju, V., & Srihari, S. N. (2000). OCR in a hierarchical feature space. *IEEE Transactions on Pattern Analysis and Machine Intelligence*, 22(4), 400–407. doi:10.1109/34.845383

Jain, A. K., Flynn, P., & Ross, A. A. (2008). Handbook of biometrics. Springer Publication.

Jain, A. K., Pankanti, S., Prabhakar, S., Hong, L., & Ross, A. (2004, August). Biometrics: A grand challenge. In *Proceedings of the 17th IEEE International Conference on Pattern Recognition* (vol. 2, pp. 935-942). IEEE.

Jain, R., Murthy, S. N. J., & Chen, P. L. J. (1995). Similarity measures for image databases. In *Proceedings of IEEE International Conference on Fuzzy Systems* (pp. 1247-1254). IEEE.

Jain, A. K., & Dubes, R. C. (1988). *Algorithms for clustering data*. Englewood Cliffs, NJ: Prentice-Hall.

Jain, K. (1989). *Fundamentals of digital image processing*. Upper Saddle River, NJ: Prentice-Hall.

Jain, R., Kumawat, R., Mandliya, S., & Patidar, M. (2014). Performance evaluation of table driven multipath routing protocols in MANET under varying nodes, traffic load & pause time. *Journal of Innovative Research in Electrical, Electronics. Instrumentation and Control Engineering*, 2(2), 952–956.

Jakhar, R., Kaur, N., & Singh, R. (2011). Face recognition using bacteria foraging optimization-based selected features. *International Journal of Advanced Computer Science and Applications*, 1(3). doi:10.14569/SpecialIssue.2011.010317

James, K., & Russell, E. (1995). Particle swarm optimization. In *Proceedings of IEEE International Conference on Neural Networks* (pp. 1942-1948). IEEE.

Jang-Ho, S., Chang-Hwan, I., Chang-Geun, H., Jae-Kwang, K., Hyun-Kyo, J., & Cheol-Gyun, L. (2006). Multimodal function optimization based on particle swarm optimization. *IEEE Transactions on Magnetics*, 42(4), 1095–1098. doi:10.1109/TMAG.2006.871568

Janson, S., Merkle, D., & Middendorf, M. (2008). Molecular docking with multi-objective particle swarm optimization. *Applied Soft Computing*, 8(1), 666–675. doi:10.1016/j.asoc.2007.05.005

Jantz, R. L. (1987). Anthropological dermatoglyphic research. *Annual Review of Anthropology*, 16(1), 161–177. doi:10.1146/annurev.an.16.100187.001113

Javadi, A. A., Rezania, M., & Mousavi Nezhad, M. (2006). Evaluation of liquefaction induced lateral displacements using genetic programming. *Computers and Geotechnics*, 33(4-5), 222–233. doi:10.1016/j.compgeo.2006.05.001

Jeanson, R., Blanco, S., Fournier, R., Deneubourg, J. L., Fourcassi'e, V., & Theraulaz, G. (2003). A model of animal movements in a bounded space. *Journal of Theoretical Biology*, 225(4), 443–451. doi:10.1016/S0022-5193(03)00277-7 PMID:14615202

Jeong, J. (2009). *Wireless sensor networking for intelligent transportation systems*. (Ph.D thesis). University of Minnesota.

Jiang, M., Li, J., & Tay, Y. C. (1999). Cluster based routing protocol. IETF Draft. Retrieved from http://www.ietf.org/internet-drafts/draft-ietf-manet-cbrp-spec-01.txt

Jiang, Y., & Zhou, Z. (2004). SOM ensemble- based image segmentation. *Neural Processing Letters*, 20(3), 171–178. doi:10.1007/s11063-004-2022-8

Jia-zhao, C., Yu-xiang, Z., & Yin-sheng, L. (2012). A unified frame of swarm intelligence optimization algorithm. *Knowledge Discovery and Data Mining*, 135, 745–751. doi:10.1007/978-3-642-27708-5_103

Jie, G., Hexu, S., Lin, H., Yan, D., & Yi, Z. (2011). *Optimization design of switched reluctance motor based on particle swarm optimization*. Paper presented at the Electrical Machines and Systems (ICEMS).

Johannsen, G., & Bille, J. (1982). A threshold selection method using information measures. *ICPR*, 82, 140–143.

Johnson, D. B., & Maltz, A. (1999). The dynamic source routing protocol for mobile ad hoc networks. IETF Draft. Retrieved from http://www.ietf.org/internet-drafts/draft-ietf-manet-dsr-03.txt

Jolly, L., Jabbar, M. A., & Liu, Q. H. (2005). Design optimization of permanent magnet motors using response surface methodology and genetic algorithms. *IEEE Transactions on Magnetics*, 41(10), 3928–3930. doi:10.1109/TMAG.2005.854966

Juang, C. H., & Chen, C. J. (1999). CPT-based liquefaction evaluation using artificial neural networks. *Computer-Aided Civil and Infrastructure Engineering, 14*(3), 221–229. doi:10.1111/0885-9507.00143

Juang, C. H., Chen, C. J., Rosowsky, D. V., & Tang, W. H. (2000b). CPT-based liquefaction analysis, Part 2: Reliability for design. *Geotechnique, 50*(5), 593–599. doi:10.1680/geot.2000.50.5.593

Juang, C. H., Chen, C. J., Tang, W. H., & Rosowsky, D. V. (2000a). CPT-based liquefaction analysis. Part 1. Determination of limit state function. *Geotechnique, 50*(5), 583–592. doi:10.1680/geot.2000.50.5.583

Juang, C. H., Yuan, H., Lee, D. H., & Ku, C. S. (2002). Assessing CPT-based methods for liquefaction evaluation with emphasis on the cases from the Chi-Chi, Taiwan, earthquake. *Soil Dynamics and Earthquake Engineering, 22*(3), 241–258. doi:10.1016/S0267-7261(02)00013-1

Kak, S. (1995). Quantum neural computing. *Advances in Imaging and Electron Physics, 94*, 259–313. doi:10.1016/S1076-5670(08)70147-2

Kak, S. (1999). Quantum computing and AI. *IEEE Intelligent Systems*, 9–11.

Kannan, S., & Suthapadmanabhan, K. (2010). Closed loop control of excitation parameters for high speed switched reluctance generator using MATLAB/SIMULINK. *International Journal on Electrical Engineering and Informatics, 2*(3), 232-243.

Kapur, J. N., Sahoo, P. K., & Wong, A. K. C. (1985). A new method for gray-level picture thresholding using the entropy of the histogram. *Graphical Models and Image Processing, 29*(3), 273–285. doi:10.1016/0734-189X(85)90125-2

Karaboga, D. (2005). *An idea based on honey bee swarm for numerical optimization (Technical Report-TR06)*. Erciyes University, Engineering Faculty, Computer Engineering Department.

Karaboga, D., & Bahriye Akay, B. (2009). A comparative study of artificial bee colony algorithm. *Applied Mathematics and Computation, 214*(1), 108–132. doi:10.1016/j.amc.2009.03.090

Karaboga, D., & Basturk, B. (2007). A powerful and efficient algorithm for numerical function optimization: Artificial bee colony (ABC) algorithm. *Journal of Global Optimization, 39*(3), 459–471. doi:10.1007/s10898-007-9149-x

Karaboga, D., & Basturk, B. (2008). On the performance of artificial bee colony (ABC) algorithm. *Applied Soft Computing, 8*(1), 687–697. doi:10.1016/j.asoc.2007.05.007

Karaboga, D., & Celal, O. (2011). A novel clustering approach: Artificial Bee Colony (ABC) algorithm. *Applied Soft Computing, 11*(1), 652–657. doi:10.1016/j.asoc.2009.12.025

Karimi, H. A., & Krishnamurthy, P. (2001). Real-time routing in mobile networks using GPS and GIS techniques. In *Proceedings of the 34th IEEE Hawaii International Conference on System Sciences*. IEEE. doi:10.1109/HICSS.2001.927201

Katiyar, M., Sinha, H. P. & Gupta, D. (2012). On reliability modeling in wireless sensor networks-A review. *International Journal of Computer Science Issues, 9*(6).

Kefayati, M., & Caramanis, C. (2010). Efficient energy delivery management for PHEVs. In *Proceedings of First IEEE International Conference on Smart Grid Communications (SmartGridComm)*. Gaithersburg, MD: IEEE. doi:10.1109/SMARTGRID.2010.5621990

Kennedy, J. (2000). Stereotyping, improving particle swarm performance with cluster analysis. In *Proceedings of the 2000 Congress on Evolutionary Computing* (vol. 2, pp. 1507 – 1512). Academic Press. doi:10.1109/CEC.2000.870832

Kennedy, J. (2010). Particle swarm optimization. In Encyclopedia of machine learning (pp. 760-766). Springer US.

Kennedy, J., & Eberhart, R. (1995). Particle swarm optimization. *IEEE International Conference on Neural Networks, 4*, 1942-1948.

Kennedy, J., & Eberhart, R. C. (1997). A discrete binary version of the particle swarm algorithm. In *Proceedings of 1997 IEEE International Conference on Systems, Man, and Cybernetics, Computational Cybernetics and Simulation* (vol. 5, pp. 4104–4108). IEEE. doi:10.1109/ICSMC.1997.637339

Kennedy, J., & Spears, W. (1998). Matching algorithms to problems: an experimental test of the particle swarm and some genetic algorithms on the multimodal problem generator. In *Proceedings of IEEE Congress on Evolutionary Computation* (CEC'98) (pp. 78-83). IEEE. doi:10.1109/ICEC.1998.699326

Kennedy, J. (1999). Small worlds and mega-minds: Effects of neighborhood topology on particle swarm performance. In *Proceedings of the IEEE Congress on Evolutionary Computation (CEC 1999)* (pp. 1931-1938). Piscataway, NJ: IEEE. doi:10.1109/CEC.1999.785509

Kennedy, J., Kennedy, J. F., & Eberhart, R. C. (2001). *Swarm intelligence*. Morgan Kaufmann.

Kennedy, K., & Eberhart, R. (1995). Particle swarm optimization. In *Proc. of IEEE International Conference on Neural Networks (ICNN95)*. IEEE.

Kerckhove, M. (2012). From population dynamics to partial differential equations. *The Mathematica Journal, 14*.

Kim, D. H., Abraham, A., & Cho, J. H. (2007). A hybrid genetic algorithm and bacterial foraging approach for global optimization. *Information Sciences, 177*(18), 3918–3937. doi:10.1016/j.ins.2007.04.002

Kioskeridis, I., & Mademlis, C. (2006). Optimal efficiency control of switched reluctance generators. *IEEE Transactions on Power Electronics, 21*(4), 1062–1072. doi:10.1109/TPEL.2006.876827

Kirby, M., & Sirovich, L. (1990). Application of the Karhunen-Loeve procedure for the characterization of human faces. *IEEE Transactions on Pattern Analysis and Machine Intelligence, 12*(1), 103–108. doi:10.1109/34.41390

Kirkpatrick, S. (1984). Optimization by simulated annealing: Quantitative studies. *Journal of Statistical Physics, 34*(5-6), 975–986. doi:10.1007/BF01009452

Kirkpatrik, S., Gelatt, C. D., & Vecchi, M. P. (1983). Optimization by simulated annealing. *Science, 220*(4598), 671–680. doi:10.1126/science.220.4598.671 PMID:17813860

Klepac, G. (2010). Preparing for new competition in the retail industry. In A. Syvajarvi & J. Stenvall (Eds.), *Data mining in public and private sectors: Organizational and government applications* (pp. 245–266). Hershey, PA: Information Science Reference; doi:10.4018/978-1-60566-906-9.ch013

Klepac, G. (2014). Data mining models as a tool for churn reduction and custom product development in telecommunication industries. In P. Vasant (Ed.), *Handbook of research on novel soft computing intelligent algorithms: Theory and practical applications* (pp. 511–537). Hershey, PA: Information Science Reference; doi:10.4018/978-1-4666-4450-2.ch017

Klepac, G., Kopal, R., & Mršić, L. (2015). *Developing churn models using data mining techniques and social network analysis*. Hershey, PA: IGI Global; doi:10.4018/978-1-4666-6288-9.ch001

Knowles, J. D., & Corne, D. W. (2000). Approximating the non-dominated front using the pareto archived evolution strategy. *Evolutionary Computation, 8*(2), 149-172.

Kohonen, T. (1989). *Self- organization and associative memory*. Berlin, Germany: Springer- Verlag.

Konstantinos, E. P., & Michael, N. V. (2010). Applications in machine learning. In K. Parsopoulos & M. Vrahatis (Eds.), *Particle swarm optimization and intelligence: Advances and applications* (pp. 149–167). Hershey, PA: Information Science Reference; doi:10.4018/978-1-61520-666-7.ch006

Konstantinos, E. P., & Michael, N. V. (2010). Established and recently proposed variants of particle swarm optimization. In K. Parsopoulos & M. Vrahatis (Eds.), *Particle swarm optimization and intelligence: Advances and applications* (pp. 88–132). Hershey, PA: Information Science Reference; doi:10.4018/978-1-61520-666-7.ch004

Kouda, N., Matsui, N., & Nishimura, H. (2004). A multilayered feedforward network based on qubit neuron model. *Systems and Computers in Japan, 35*(13), 43–51. doi:10.1002/scj.10342

Kouda, N., Matsui, N., Nishimura, H., & Peper, F. (2005). An examination of qubit neural network in controlling an inverted pendulum. *Neural Processing Letters, 22*(3), 277–290. doi:10.1007/s11063-005-8337-2

Kress, M., Mostaghim, S., & Seese, D. (2010). Intelligent business process execution using particle swarm optimization. In Information resources management: Concepts, methodologies, tools and applications (pp. 797-815). Hershey, PA: Information Science Reference. doi:10.4018/978-1-60566-705-8.ch003

Krishnanand, K. N., & Ghose, D. (2009). Glow-worm swarm optimization for searching higher dimensional spaces. In *Innovations in swarm intelligence*. Heidelberg, Germany: Springer. doi:10.1007/978-3-642-04225-6_4

Krishnan, R. (2001). *Switched reluctance motor drives: Modeling, simulation, analysis, design, and applications.* Taylor & Francis. doi:10.1201/9781420041644

Kudo, M., & Sklansky, J. (2000). Comparison of algorithms that select features for pattern classifiers. *Pattern Recognition, 33*(1), 25–41. doi:10.1016/S0031-3203(99)00041-2

Kukunuru, N., Thella, B. R., & Davuluri, R. L. (2010). Sensor deployment using particle swarm optimization. *International Journal of Engineering Science and Technology, 2*(10), 5395–5401.

Kulkarni, R. V., & Venayagamoorthy, G. K. (2011). Particle swarm optimization in wireless sensor networks: A brief survey. *IEEE Transactions on Systems, Man and Cybernetics. Part C, Applications and Reviews.* doi:10.1109/TSMCC.2010.2054080

Kulshrestha, P., Wang, L., Chow, M. Y., & Lukic, S. (2009). Intelligent energy management system simulator for PHEVs at municipal parking deck in a smart grid environment. In Proceedings of Power & Energy Society General Meeting. Alberta, Canada: IEEE. doi:10.1109/PES.2009.5275688

Kumar, A. (2011). A survey on routing protocols for wireless sensor networks. *International Journal of Advances in Engineering Research, 1*(2).

Kumar, A. S., Basu, S. K., & Majumdar, K. L. (1997). Robust classification of multispectral data using multiple neural networks and fuzzy integral. *IEEE Transactions on Geoscience and Remote Sensing, 35*(3), 787–790.

Kuo, C.-C. (2008). A novel coding scheme for practical economic dispatch by modified particle swarm approach. *IEEE Transactions on Power Systems, 23*(4), 1825–1835. doi:10.1109/TPWRS.2008.2002297

Kurbatsky, V., Sidorov, D., Tomin, N., & Spiryaev, V. (2014). Optimal training of artificial neural networks to forecast power system state variables. *International Journal of Energy Optimization and Engineering, 3*(1), 65–82. doi:10.4018/ijeoe.2014010104

Kurfurst, J., Duron, J., Skalka, M., Janda, M., & Ondrusek, C. (2011). *Magnet shape optimization of brushless machine by self-organizing migrating algorithm.* Paper presented at the Power Engineering, Energy and Electrical Drives (POWERENG).

Kurup, P. U., & Dudani, N. K. (2001). CPT evaluation of liquefaction potential using neural networks. In *Proceedings of the Fourth International Conference on Recent Advances in Geotechnical Earthquake Engineering and Soil Dynamics.* Academic Press.

Kurup, P. U., & Garg, A. (2005). *Evaluation of liquefaction potential using ART based neural networks.* Paper presented at the Transportation Research Record, 84th Transportation Research Board Annual Meeting, Washington, DC.

Kwang, M. S., & Weng, H. S. (2002). Multiple ant-colony optimization for network routing. In *Proceedings of the First International Symposium on Cyber Worlds* (pp. 277—281). Academic Press.

Kwok, N. M., Ha, Q. P., Liu, D. K., & Fang, G. (2006, October). Intensity-preserving contrast enhancement for gray-level images using multi-objective particle swarm optimization. In *Proceedings of Automation Science and Engineering, 2006: CASE'06. IEEE International Conference on* (pp. 21-26). IEEE. doi:10.1109/COASE.2006.326849

Lagaris, I. E., Likas, A., & Fotiadis, D. I. (1997). Artificial neural network methods in quantum mechanics. *Computer Physics Communications, 104*(1-3), 1–14. doi:10.1016/S0010-4655(97)00054-4

Lago-Gonzalez, A., & Singh, C. (1990). The extended decomposition – Simulation approach for multi-area reliability calculations. *IEEE Transactions on Power Systems, 5*(3), 1024–1031. doi:10.1109/59.65934

Lahti, L., Schäfer, M., Klein, H.-U., Bicciato, S., & Dugas, M. (2012). Cancer gene prioritization by integrative analysis of mRNA expression and DNA copy number data, a comparative review. *Briefings in Bioinformatics.* PMID:22441573

Lanckriet, G., El Ghaoui, L., Bhattacharyya, C., & Jordan, M. (2002). A robust minimax approach to classification. *Journal of Machine Learning Research, 3,* 555–582.

Larose, D. T. (2005). *Discovering knowledge in data: An introduction to data mining.* John Wiley &Sons Inc. doi:10.1002/0471687545

Le Dinh, L., Vo Ngoc, D., & Vasant, P. (2013). Artificial bee colony algorithm for solving optimal power flow problem. *The Scientific World Journal,* 2013. PMID:24470790

Lee, K. E. (2007). An automated sensor deployment algorithm based on swarm intelligence for ubiquitous environment. *International Journal of Computer Science and Network Security, 7*(12).

Lee, K. Y., Sode-Yome, A., & Park, J. H. (1998). Adaptive Hopfield neural networks for economic load dispatch. *IEEE Transactions on Power Systems, 13*(2), 519–526. doi:10.1109/59.667377

Lee, W. P., & Wen, S. T. (2009). Computational methods for discovering gene networks from expression data. *Briefings in Bioinformatics, 10*(4), 408–423. PMID:19505889

Leguizamon, G., & Coello Coello, C. A. (2007). A boundary search based ACO algorithm coupled with stochastic ranking. In *Proceedings ofIEEE Congress on Evolutionary Computation, (CEC 2007)* (pp. 165–172). IEEE. doi:10.1109/CEC.2007.4424468

Letendre, S. (2009). Solar electricity as a fuel for light vehicles. In *Proceedings of the 2006 American Solar Energy Society Annual Conference.* Boulder, CO: ASES.

Li, B., Qu, J., & Cui, Y. (2009). The resources purchase quantity algorithm based on the shadow price and its application in the enterprise management. In *Proceedings ofInternational Conference on Test and Measurement* (pp. 346-349). Hong Kong: IEEE.

Li, Y., & Liu, J. (2009). Remote sensing image classification development in the past decade. In *Proceedings of SPIE* (pp. 338-343). Academic Press.

Li, Y., Gong, H., & Wang, Q. (2010, August). Adaptive enhancement with speckle reduction for SAR images using mirror-extended curvelet and PSO. In *Proceedings of Pattern Recognition (ICPR), 2010 20th International Conference on* (pp. 4520-4523). IEEE. doi:10.1109/ ICPR.2010.1098

Li, Z., Sahinoglu, Z., Tao, Z., & Teo, K. H. (2010, September). Electric vehicles network with nomadic portable charging stations. In Proceedings of Vehicular Technology Conference Fall. Ottawa, Canada: IEEE. doi:10.1109/ VETECF.2010.5594437

Liao, W. H., Kao, Y., & Li, Y. S. (2011). A sensor deployment approach using glowworm swarm optimization algorithm in wireless sensor networks. *Expert Systems with Applications, 38*(10), 12180–12188. doi:10.1016/j. eswa.2011.03.053

Li, B., & Zhuang, Z. Q. (2002). Genetic algorithm based on the quantum probability representation. *Lecture Notes in Computer Science, 2412,* 500–505.

Liddell, H. G., & Scott, R. (1984). Greek-English lexicon. Oxford University Press.

Li, G., Liu, C., & Salazar, H. (2006).Forecasting transmission congestion using day-ahead shadow prices. In *Proceedings of IEEE PES Power Systems Conference and Exposition* (pp. 1705–1709). Atlanta, GA: IEEE.

Lin, C. C. Y., & Chang, Y. W. (2009). ILP based pin-count aware design methodology for microfluidic biochips. In *Proceedings of ACM Design Automation Conference* (pp. 258 – 263). San Francisco, CA: ACM. doi:10.1145/1629911.1629982

Lin, C. H., Huang, T. W., & Ho, T. Y. (2010). A contamination aware droplet routing algorithm for the synthesis of digital microfluidic biochips. *IEEE Transaction on Computer Aided Design of Integrated Circuits and Systems,* 1682 – 1695.

Lin, W. C., Hsu, S. C., & Cheng, A. C. (2014, June). Mass detection in digital mammograms system based on PSO algorithm. In *Proceedings of Computer, Consumer and Control (IS3C), 2014 International Symposium on* (pp. 662-668). IEEE. doi:10.1109/IS3C.2014.178

Lin, C. C. Y., & Chang, Y. W. (2011). Cross-contamination aware design methodology for pin-constrained digital microfluidic biochips. *IEEE Transactions on Computer-Aided Design of Integrated Circuits and Systems*, *30*(6), 817–828. doi:10.1109/TCAD.2011.2108010

Lin, C. F., & Wang, S. D. (2002). Fuzzy support vector machines. *IEEE Transactions on Neural Networks*, *13*(2), 464–471. doi:10.1109/72.991432 PMID:18244447

Lingras, P., & West, C. (2004). Interval set clustering of web users with rough k-means. *Journal of Intelligent Information Systems*, *23*(1), 5–16. doi:10.1023/B:JIIS.0000029668.88665.1a

Liu, G., Chen, J., & Zhong, J. (2012). An integrated SVM and fuzzy AHP approach for selecting third party logistics providers. *Electrotechnical Review*.

Liu, X. P., Li, X., Yeh, A. G. O., He, J. Q., & Tao, J. (2007). Discovery of transition rules for geographical cellular automata by using ant colony optimization. *Science in China Series D-Earth Sciences*, *50*(10), 1578–1588. doi:10.1007/s11430-007-0083-z

Liu, X., & Wang, D. (2006). Image and texture segmentation using local spectra histograms. *IEEE Transactions on Image Processing*, *15*(10), 3066–3077. doi:10.1109/TIP.2006.877511 PMID:17022270

Liu, Z., Yang, H., & Yang, S. (2009). Integration of multilayer SVM classifier and multistage dynamic fuzzy judgment and its application in SCDA measurement. *Journal of Computers*, *4*(11). doi:10.4304/jcp.4.11.1139-1144

Li, Y. C., Cheng, H. Y., Jung, C. L., & Cheng, H. Y. (2012). A hybrid BPSO-CGA approach for gene selection & classification of microarray data. *Journal of Computational Biology*, *19*(1), 68–82. doi:10.1089/cmb.2010.0064 PMID:21210743

Li, Y., Gong, H., Feng, D., & Zhang, Y. (2011). An adaptive method of speckle reduction and feature enhancement for SAR images based on curvelet transform and particle swarm optimization. *IEEE Transactions on Geoscience and Remote Sensing*, *49*(8), 3105–3116.

Lobo, N. S., Hong Sun, L., & Krishnan, R. (2008). Comparison of linear switched reluctance machines for vertical propulsion application: Analysis, design, and experimental correlation. *IEEE Transactions on Industry Applications*, *44*(4), 1134-1142. doi: 10.1109/TIA.2008.926294

Loscrí, V., Natalizio, E., Guerriero, F., & Aloi, G. (2012). Particle swarm optimization schemes based on consensus for wireless sensor networks. In *Proc. MSWiM'12*. ACM. doi:10.1145/2387191.2387203

Lucchese, L., & Mitra, S. K. (2001). Color image segmentation: A state-of-art survey. *Proceedings of the Indian National Science Academy*, *67-A*, 207–221.

Lukac, M., & Perkowski, M. (2002). Evolving quantum circuits using genetic algorithm. In *Proceedings of the NASA/DOD Conference on Evolvable Hardware*. IEEE.

Lukashin, A., & Futchs, R. (1999). Analysis of temporal gene expression profiles, clustering by simulated annealing and determining optimal number of clusters. *Nature Genetics*, *22*(3), 281–285. doi:10.1038/10343 PMID:10391217

Lund, H., & Kempton, W. (2008). Integration of renewable energy into the transport and electricity sectors through V2G. *Energy Policy*, *36*(9), 3578–3587. doi:10.1016/j.enpol.2008.06.007

Luo, Y., & Chakrabarty, K. (2012). Design of pin constrained general – Purpose digital microfluidic biochips. In *Proceeding of 49th Design Automation Conference* (pp. 18 – 25). Academic Press.

Luong, L. D., Vasant, P., Dieu, V. N., Khoa, T. H., & Khanh, D. V. (2013). Self-organizing hierarchical particle swarm optimization for large-scale economic dispatch with multiple fuels considering valve-point effects. In *Proceedings of the 7th Global Conference on Power Control and Optimization (PCO'2013)*. Academic Press.

Luo, Y., & Chakrabarty, K. (2013). Design of pin-constrained general-purpose digital microfluidic biochips. *IEEE Transactions on Computer-Aided Design of Integrated Circuits and Systems*, *32*(9), 1307–1320. doi:10.1109/TCAD.2013.2260192

Ma, Z., Callaway, D., & Hiskens, I. (2010). Decentralized charging control for large populations of plug-in electric vehicles. In *Proceedings of 49th IEEE Conference on Decision and Control (CDC)*. Yokohama: IEEE. doi:10.1109/CDC.2010.5717547

Machado, T. R., & Lopes, H. S. (2005). A hybrid particle swarm optimization model for the traveling salesman problem. In *Proceedings of the International Conference in Coimbra* (pp. 255—258). Academic Press. doi:10.1007/3-211-27389-1_61

Mackay, A., & Weigelt, B. Grigoriadis, A., Kreike, B., Natrajan, R., A'Hern, R., … Reis-Filho, J. S. (2011). Microarray-based class discovery for molecular classification of breast cancer, analysis of interobserver agreement. *JNCI Journal of the National Cancer Institute, 103*(8), 662-673.

MacMinn, S. R., & Sember, J. W. (1989). *Control of a switched-reluctance aircraft engine starter-generator over a very wide speed range*. Paper presented at the Energy Conversion Engineering Conference.

Mademlis, C., & Kioskeridis, I. (2005). Optimizing performance in current-controlled switched reluctance generators. *IEEE Transactions on Energy Conversion, 20*(3), 556–565. doi:10.1109/TEC.2005.852960

Mahmood, M. A. & Seah, W. (2012). *Reliability in wireless sensor networks: Survey and challenges ahead*. Elsevier.

Mahor, A., Prasad, V., & Rangnekar, S. (2009). Economic dispatch using particle swarm optimization: A review. *Renewable & Sustainable Energy Reviews, 13*(8), 2134–2141. doi:10.1016/j.rser.2009.03.007

Mai, C. L. D. A., Nguyen, M. T. T., & Kwok, N. M. (2011, October). A modified unsharp masking method using particle swarm optimization. In *Proceedings of Image and Signal Processing (CISP), 2011 4th International Congress on* (Vol. 2, pp. 646-650). IEEE. doi:10.1109/CISP.2011.6100322

Manoharan, P., Kannan, P., Baskar, S., & Iruthayarajan, M. (2008). Penalty parameter-less constraint handling scheme based evolutionary algorithm solutions to economic dispatch. *IET Generation, Transmission & Distribution, 2*(4), 478–490. doi:10.1049/iet-gtd:20070423

Mantero, P., Gabriele, M., & Serpico, S. B. (2005). Partially supervised classification of remote sensing images through SVM-based probability density estimation. *IEEE Transactions on Geoscience and Remote Sensing, 43*(3), 559–570. doi:10.1109/TGRS.2004.842022

Mantin, & Shamir, A. (2001). Weaknesses in the key scheduling algorithm of RC4. In *Selected Areas in Cryptography: Proceedings of the 8th Annual International Workshop* (LNCS), (*Vol. 2259*, pp. 1-24). Berlin, Germany: Springer

Man, Y., & Gath, I. (1994). Detection and separation of ring-shaped clusters using fuzzy clustering. *IEEE Transactions on Pattern Analysis and Machine Intelligence, 16*(8), 855–861. doi:10.1109/34.308484

Marconcini, M., Camps-Valls, G., & Bruzzone, L. (2009). A composite semisupervised SVM for classification of hyperspectral images. *IEEE Geoscience and Remote Sensing Letters, 6*(2), 234–238. doi:10.1109/LGRS.2008.2009324

Martinez, M., Longpre, L., Kreinovich, V., Starks, S. A., & Nguyen, H. T. (2003). Fast quantum algorithms for handling probabilistic, interval, and fuzzy uncertainty. In *Proceedings of Fuzzy Information Processing Society, 2003. NAFIPS 2003. 22nd International Conference of the North American* (pp. 395–400). Academic Press.

Martinoli, A., & Easton, K. (2003). Modeling swarm robotic systems. In Proc. of the Eight Int. Syrup. on Experimental Robotics ISER-02. Sant'Angelo d'Ischia, Italy: Springer. doi:10.1007/3-540-36268-1_26

Martinoli, A., Easton, K., & Agassounon, W. (2004). Modeling swarm robotic systems: A case study in collaborative distributed manipulation. Int. Journal of Robotics Research, 23(4), 415-436.

Marwaha, S., & Tham, C. K. (2002). A novel routing protocol using mobile agents and reactive route discovery for ad hoc wireless networks. In *Proc. IEEE ICON. IEEE.* doi:10.1109/ICON.2002.1033329

Marwaha, S., Tham, C. K., & Srinivasan, D. (2002). Mobile agent based routing protocol for mobile ad hoc networks. In *Proc. IEEE GLOBECOM. IEEE.* doi:10.1109/GLOCOM.2002.1188062

Masra, S. M. W., Pang, P. K., Muhammad, M. S., & Kipli, K. (2012, December). Application of particle swarm optimization in histogram equalization for image enhancement. In *Proceedings of Humanities, Science and Engineering (CHUSER), 2012 IEEE Colloquium on* (pp. 294-299). IEEE. doi:10.1109/CHUSER.2012.6504327

Matos, F. M., Batista, L. V., & Poel, J. (2008). Face recognition using OCT coefficients selection. In *Proceedings of the ACM Symposium on Applied Computing* (pp. 1753-1757). ACM.

Matsui, N., Takai, M., & Nishimura, H. (2000). A network model based on qubit-like neuron corresponding to quantum circuit. *The Institute of Electronics Information and Communications in Japan (Part III: Fundamental Electronic Science), 83*(10), 67–73.

Matsuo, H., & Mori, K. (2001). Accelerated ants routing in dynamic networks. In *Proceedings of 2nd Int. Conf. Software Engineering, Artificial Intelligence, Networking & Parallel Distributed Computing*. Nagoya, Japan: Academic Press.

Maulik, U., & Bandyopadhyay, S. (2001). Nonparametric genetic clustering, comparison of validity indices. *IEEE Transactions on Systems, Man and Cybernetics. Part C, Applications and Reviews, 31*(1), 120–125. doi:10.1109/5326.923275

Maulik, U., & Bandyopadhyay, S. (2002). Performance evaluation of some clustering algorithms and validity indices. *IEEE Transactions on Pattern Analysis and Machine Intelligence, 24*(12), 1650–1654. doi:10.1109/TPAMI.2002.1114856

Maulik, U., & Bandyopadhyay, S. (2003). Fuzzy partitioning using areal-coded variable-length genetic algorithm for pixel classification. *IEEE Transactions on Geoscience and Remote Sensing, 41*(5), 1075–1081. doi:10.1109/TGRS.2003.810924

Maulik, U., Mukhopadhyay, A., & Bandyopadhyay, S. (2009). Combining pareto-optimal clusters using supervised learning for identifying co-expressed genes. *BMC Bioinformatics, 10*(1), 27. doi:10.1186/1471-2105-10-27 PMID:19154590

Maulik, U., & Sarkar, A. (2010). Evolutionary rough parallel multi-objective optimization algorithm. *Fundamenta Informaticae, 99*(1), 13–27.

Maulik, U., & Sarkar, A. (2012). Efficient parallel algorithm for pixel classification in remote sensing imagery. *GeoInformatica, 16*(2), 391–407. doi:10.1007/s10707-011-0136-5

Maurer, U. (1993). Secret key agreement by public discussion from common information. *IEEE Transactions on Information Theory, 39*(3), 733–742. doi:10.1109/18.256484

Mayfield, D. (2012). *Site design for electric vehicle charging stations, NREL*. US Department of Energy.

McCulloc, W. S., & Pitts, W. (1943). A logical calculus of the ideas immanent in nervous activity. *The Bulletin of Mathematical Biophysics, 5*(4), 115–133. doi:10.1007/BF02478259

McMahon, D. (2008). Quantum computing explained. Hoboken, NJ: John Wiley & Sons, Inc.

Mcmohan, D. (2008). *Quantum computing explained*. Hoboken, NJ: John Wiley & Sons, Inc.

McQueen, J. (1967). Some methods for classification and analysis of multivariate observations. In *Proc. Fifth Berkeley Symp. Math. Statistics and Probability* (pp. 281-297). Academic Press.

Melgani, F., & Bruzzone, L. (2004). Classification of hyper spectral remote sensing images with support vector machines. *IEEE Transactions on Geosciences and Remote Sensing, 42*(8).

Melgani, F., & Bruzzone, L. (2004). Classification of hyperspectral remote sensing images with support vector machines. *IEEE Transactions on Geoscience and Remote Sensing, 42*(8), 1778–1790. doi:10.1109/TGRS.2004.831865

Melo, A. C., & Pereira, M. V. (1995). Sensitivity analysis of reliability indices with respect to equipment failure and repair rates. *IEEE Transactions on Power Systems, 10*(2), 1014–1021. doi:10.1109/59.387946

Mendes, R. P. G., Calado, M. R. A., Mariano, S. J. P. S., & Cabrita, C. M. P. (2011). *Design of a tubular switched reluctance linear generator for wave energy conversion based on ocean wave parameters*. Paper presented at the Electrical Machines and Power Electronics and 2011 Electromotion Joint Conference (ACEMP).

Menezes, A. J., Vanstone, S. A., & Van Oorschot, P. C. (1996). Handbook of applied cryptography. In *Applied cryptography*. Boca Raton, FL: CRC Press. doi:10.1201/9781439821916

Menezes, A. J., Vanstone, S. A., & Van Oorschot, P. C. (2001). *Handbook of applied cryptography* (5th ed.). CRC Press.

Menneer, T. (1998). *Quantum artificial neural networks.* (Ph. D. thesis). The University of Exeter, Exeter, UK.

Menneer, T., & Narayanan, A. (2000). Quantum artificial neural networks vs classical artificial neural networks: Experiments in simulation. In *Proceedings of the IEEE Fourth International Conference on Computational Intelligence and Neuroscience* (pp. 757-759). IEEE.

Menneer, T., & Narayanan, A. (1995). *Quantum-inspired neural networks, technical report R329.* Exeter, UK: Department of Computer Science, University of Exeter.

Mese, E., Sozer, Y., Kokernak, J. M., & Torrey, D. A. (2000). *Optimal excitation of a high speed switched reluctance generator.* Paper presented at the Applied Power Electronics Conference and Exposition.

Michelsen, A., Andersen, B. B., Storm, J., Kirchner, W. H., & Lindauer, M. (1992). How honeybees perceive communication dances, studied by means of a mechanical model. *Behavioral Ecology and Sociobiology*, *30*(3-4), 143–150. doi:10.1007/BF00166696

Miller, D. M., & Koehler, P. G. (2000). Trail-following behavior in the German cockroach (Dictyoptera: Blattellidae). *Journal of Economic Entomology*, *93*(4), 1241–1246. doi:10.1603/0022-0493-93.4.1241 PMID:10985037

Miller, D. M., Koehler, P. G., & Nation, J. L. (2000). Use of fecal extract trails to enhance trap catch in German cockroach (Dictyoptera: Blattellidae) monitoring stations. *Journal of Economic Entomology*, *93*(3), 865–870. doi:10.1603/0022-0493-93.3.865 PMID:10902343

Miller, T. J. E. (1985). Converter volt-ampere requirements of the switched reluctance motor drive. *IEEE Transactions on Industry Applications*, *IA-21*(5), 1136–1144. doi:10.1109/TIA.1985.349516

Miller, T. J. E. (2001). *Electronic control of switched reluctance machines*. Newnes.

Mini, S., & Udgata, S. K. (2011). Coverage and deployment algorithms in wireless sensor networks. *IJCCT, 2*(5).

Miranda, V., Keko, H., & Duque, A. J. (2008). Stochastic star communication topology in evolutionary particle swarms (EPSO). *International Journal of Computational Intelligence Research*, 105-116.

Miranda, V., Carvalho, L. M., Rosa, M. A., Silva, A. M., & Singh, C. (2009). Improving power system reliability calculation efficiency with EPSO variants. *IEEE Transactions on Power Systems*, *24*(4), 1772–1779. doi:10.1109/TPWRS.2009.2030397

Mishra, S., & Bhende, C. N. (2007). Bacterial foraging technique-based optimized active power filter for load compensation. *IEEE Transactions on Power Delivery*, *22*(1), 457–465. doi:10.1109/TPWRD.2006.876651

Mishra, S., Shaw, K., & Mishra, D. (2012). A new meta-heuristic bat inspired classification approach for microarray data. *Procedia Technology*, *4*, 802–806. doi:10.1016/j.protcy.2012.05.131

Mitra, J., & Xu, X. (2010). Composite system reliability analysis using particle swarm optimization. In *Proceedings of 11th International Conference on Probabilistic Methods Applied to Power Systems* (pp. 548-552). Singapore: IEEE. doi:10.1109/PMAPS.2010.5528940

Mitra, P., & Venayagamoorthy, G. K. (2010). Intelligent coordinated control of a wind farm and distributed smart-parks. In *Proceedings of Industry Applications Society Annual Meeting (IAS)*. Houston, TX: IEEE. doi:10.1109/IAS.2010.5615930

Mitra, J., & Singh, C. (1996). Incorporating the DC load flow model in the decomposition--Simulation method of multi-area reliability evaluation. *IEEE Transactions on Power Systems*, *11*(3), 1245–1254. doi:10.1109/59.535596

Mitra, J., & Singh, C. (1999). Pruning and simulation for determination of frequency and duration indices of composite systems. *IEEE Transactions on Power Systems*, *14*(3), 899–905. doi:10.1109/59.780901

Mohamed, J. O. A., & Sivakumar, R. (2010). Ant-based clustering algorithms: A brief survey. *International Journal of Computer Theory & Engineering*, *2*(5), 787–796.

Moon, Y. S. (2004). Recent advances in ear biometrics. In *Proceedings of the 6th IEEE International Conference on Automatic Ear and Gesture Recognition* (pp. 164–169). IEEE.

Moore, M. P., & Narayanan, A. (1995). *Quantum-inspired computing*. Exeter, UK: Department of Computer Science, Old Library, University of Exeter.

Moreau, L., Zaim, M. E., & Machmoum, M. (2012). *Electromagnetic design optimization of a low speed slotted switched reluctance machine using genetic algorithm*. Paper presented at the Electrical Machines (ICEM).

Moreau, L., Machmoum, M., & Zaim, M. E. (2006). Design of low-speed slotted switched reluctance machine for wind energy applications. *Electric Power Components and Systems, 34*(10), 1139–1156. doi:10.1080/15325000600630376

Morgan, Y. L., & Kunz, T. (2005). A proposal for an ad-hoc network QoS gateway. In Proceedings of WiMob (vol. 3, pp. 221–228). IEEE. doi:10.1109/WIMOB.2005.1512907

Morrow, K., Karner, D., & Francfort, J. (2008). *Plug-in hybrid electric vehicle charging infrastructure review*. US Department of Energy-Vehicle Technologies Program.

Moss, R. E. S. (2003). *CPT-based probabilistic assessment of seismic soil liquefaction initiation*. (PhD dissertation). Univ. of California, Berkeley, CA.

Moss, R. E. S., Seed, R. B., Kayen, R. E., Stewart, J. P., Kiureghian, A., & Cetin, K. O. (2006). CPT-based probablistic and deterministic assesment of in situ seismic soil liquefaction potential. *Journal of Geotechnical and Geoenviromental Engineering, ASCE, 132*(8), 1032–1051. doi:10.1061/(ASCE)1090-0241(2006)132:8(1032)

Moss, R. E. S., Seed, R. B., Kayen, R. E., Stewart, J. P., & Tokimatsu, K. (2005). Probabilistic liquefaction triggering based on the cone penetration test. In E. M. Rathje (Ed.), Geotechnical special publication: Vol. 133. *CD Rome ASCE*. Reston, VA.

Motors, T. (2009). Tesla roadster spec sheet 2009. *USA Today*. Retrieved from www.usatoday.com

Mounir, B., Pascale, M., Khaldoun, A. A., Cedric, A., & Geraud, A. (2004). Integration of mobile IP and OLSR for universal mobility. In *Wireless networks* (pp. 377–388). Kluwer Publications.

Mountrakis, G., Im, J., & Ogole, C. (2011). Support vector machines in remote sensing, A Review. *ISPRS Journal of Photogrammetry and Remote Sensing, 66*(3), 247–259. doi:10.1016/j.isprsjprs.2010.11.001

Mueller, M. A. (2005). *Design and performance of a 20 kW, 100 rpm, switched reluctance generator for a direct drive wind energy converter*. Paper presented at the Electric Machines and Drives.

Mukherjee, R., Rahaman, H., Banerjee, I., Samanta, T., & Dasgupta, P. (2012). A heuristic method for co-optimization of pin assignment and droplet routing in digital microfluidic biochip. In *Proceedings of IEEE International Conference on VLSI Design* (pp. 227 -232). IEEE. doi:10.1109/VLSID.2012.75

Murthy, S., & Garcia-Luna-Aceves, J. J. (1996). *An efficient routing protocol for wireless networks. ACM Mobile Networks and Applications Journal*.

Naayagi, R. T., & Kamaraj, V. (2005). *A comparative study of shape optimization of SRM using genetic algorithm and simulated annealing*. Paper presented at the INDICON.

Nakawiro, W., Erlich, I., & Rueda, J. L. (2011, July). A novel optimization algorithm for optimal reactive power dispatch: A comparative study. In *Proceedings of Electric Utility Deregulation and Restructuring and Power Technologies (DRPT), 2011 4th International Conference* (pp. 1555-1561). IEEE. doi:10.1109/DRPT.2011.5994144

Nanda, J., Hari, L., & Kothari, M. (1994). Economic emission load dispatch with line flow constraints using a classical technique. *IEE Proceedings. Generation, Transmission and Distribution, 141*(1), 1–10. doi:10.1049/ip-gtd:19949770

Narayanan, A., & Manneer, T. (2000). Quantum artificial neural network architectures and components. *Information Sciences, 128*(3-4), 231–255. doi:10.1016/S0020-0255(00)00055-4

Narayanan, A., & Moore, M. (1996). Quantum inspired genetic algorithm. In *Proc. of the IEEE Conference on Evolutionary Computation (ICEC'96)* (pp. 61–66). IEEE. doi:10.1109/ICEC.1996.542334

Narla, S., Sozer, Y., & Husain, I. (2012). Switched reluctance generator controls for optimal power generation and battery charging. *IEEE Transactions on Industry Applications*, *48*(5), 1452–1459. doi:10.1109/TIA.2012.2209850

Neumann, H. M., Schär, D., & Baumgartner, F. (2012). The potential of photovoltaic carports to cover the energy demand of road passenger transport. *Progress in Photovoltaics: Research and Applications*, *20*(6), 639–649.

Nguyen, S., & Kachitvichyanukul, V. (2010). Movement strategies for multi-objective particle swarm optimization. *International Journal of Applied Metaheuristic Computing*, *1*(3), 59–79. doi:10.4018/jamc.2010070105

Niblack, W. (1986). *An introduction to image processing*. Englewood Cliffs, NJ: Prentice-Hall.

Nielsen, M. A., & Chuang, I. L. (2000). *Quantum computation and quantum information*. Cambridge, UK: Cambridge Univ. Press.

Niknam, T. (2010). A new fuzzy adaptive hybrid particle swarm optimization algorithm for non-linear, non-smooth and non-convex economic dispatch problem. *Applied Energy*, *87*(1), 327–339. doi:10.1016/j.apenergy.2009.05.016

Niknam, T., & Amiri, B. (2010). An efficient hybrid approach based on PSO, ACO & k-means for cluster analysis. *Applied Soft Computing*, *10*(1), 183–197. doi:10.1016/j.asoc.2009.07.001

Nishida, N., Nagahara, M., Sato, T., Mimori, K., Sudo, T., Tanaka, F., & Mori, M. et al. (2012). Human cancer biology, microarray analysis of colorectal cancer stromal tissue reveals upregulation of two oncogenic microRNA clusters. *Clinical Cancer Research*, 1078.

Niu, Q., Zhou, Z., Zhang, H.-Y., & Deng, J. (2012). An improved quantum-behaved particle swarm optimization method for economic dispatch problems with multiple fuel options and valve-points effects. *Energies*, *5*(9), 3655–3673. doi:10.3390/en5093655

Nocedal, J., & Wright, S. J. (1999). Numerical optimization. Springer.

Noman, N., & Iba, H. (2008). Differential evolution for economic load dispatch problems. *Electric Power Systems Research*, *78*(8), 1322–1331. doi:10.1016/j.epsr.2007.11.007

Noordam, J. C., Van den Broek, W. H. A. M., & Buydens, L. M. C. (2000). Geometrically guided fuzzy *C*-means clustering for multivariate image segmentation. In *Proc. Int. Conf. Pattern Recogn* (vol. 1, pp. 462-465). Academic Press.

Oleszkiewicz, J., Xiao, L., & Liu, Y. (2006). Effectively utilizing global cluster memory for large data-intensive parallel programs. *IEEE Transactions on Parallel and Distributed Systems*, *17*(1), 66–77. doi:10.1109/TPDS.2006.10

Oliveira, G. C., Pereira, M. V., & Cunha, S. H. (1989). A technique for reducing computational effort in Monte Carlo based composite reliability evaluation. *IEEE Transactions on Power Systems*, *4*(4), 1309–1315. doi:10.1109/59.41680

Olsen, R. S. (1997). Cyclic liquefaction based on the cone penetrometer test. In *Proc., NCEER Workshop on Evaluation of Liquefaction Resistance of Soils*. National Center for Earthquake Engineering Research.

Olson, E. A. (2011). *Particle swarm optimization: Theory, techniques and applications*. Nova Science Pub Inc.

Omran, M. (2005). *Particle swarm optimization methods for pattern recognition and image processing*. (Dissertation for the Doctoral Degree). University of Pretoria, Pretoria, South Africa.

Otsu, N. (1979). A threshold selection method from gray level Histograms. *IEEE Transactions Systems. Man and Cybernetics*, *9*(1), 62-66. doi: .1979.431007610.1109/TSMC

Otsu, N. (1979). A threshold selection method from gray level histograms. *IEEE Transactions on Systems, Man, and Cybernetics*, *SMC-9*, 62–66.

Owatchaiphong, S., & Fuengwarodsakul, N. H. (2009). *Multi-objective based optimization for switched reluctance machines using fuzzy and genetic algorithms*. Paper presented at the Power Electronics and Drive Systems.

Ozcan, E., & Mohan, C. K. (1999). Particle swarm optimization: surfing the waves. In *Proceedings of the 1999 IEEE Congress on Evolutionary Computation (CEC 99)*. IEEE. doi:10.1109/CEC.1999.785510

Pacheco, P. (1997). *Parallel programming with MPI*. Morgan Kaufmann.

Pachter, M., & Chandler, P. (1998). Challenges of autonomous control. *IEEE Control Systems Magazine*, *18*(4), 92–97. doi:10.1109/37.710883

Padmanabhan, B., Sivakumar, R., Jasper, J., & Victoire, T. A. A. (2011). Bacterial foraging approach to economic load dispatch problem with non convex cost function. In *Swarm, evolutionary, and memetic computing* (pp. 577–584). Springer.

Padmavathi, S. V., Sahu, S. K., & Jayalaxmi, A. (2014). Particle swarm optimization based composite power system reliability analysis using FACTS. *International Journal of Electronics and Electrical Engineering*, *3*(2), 105-109.

Pal, M. (2006). Support vector machine-based feature selection for land cover classification, a case study with DAIS hyperspectral data. *International Journal of Remote Sensing*, *27*(14), 2877–2894. doi:10.1080/01431160500242515

Pamula, V., Srinivasan, V., & Fair, R. (2004). An integrated digital microfluidic lab-on-a-chip for clinical diagnostics on human physiological fluids. *Journal of Lab Chip*, *4*, 310–315. PMID:15269796

Pan, J. F. Yu., Z., Cheung, N. C., & Guang-zhong, C. (2011). *Design and optimization for the linear switched reluctance generator*. Paper presented at the Power Electronics Systems and Applications (PESA).

Pang, C., Dutta, P., Kim, S., Kezunovic, M., & Damnjanovic, I. (2010). PHEVs as dynamically configurable dispersed energy storage for V2B uses in the smart grid. In *IET Conference Proceedings*. Cyprus: IEEE. doi:10.1049/cp.2010.0903

Panigrahi, B., Yadav, S. R., Agrawal, S., & Tiwari, M. (2007). A clonal algorithm to solve economic load dispatch. *Electric Power Systems Research*, *77*(10), 1381–1389. doi:10.1016/j.epsr.2006.10.007

Pant, M., Thangaraj, R., & Abraham, A. (2009). Particle swarm optimization: Performance tuning and empirical analysis. Foundations of Computational Intelligence, 3, 101-128.

Pappis, C. P., & Karacapilidis, N. I. (1993). A comparative assessment of measures of similarity of fuzzy values. *Fuzzy Sets and Systems*, *56*(2), 171–174. doi:10.1016/0165-0114(93)90141-4

Parikh, J., & Chattopadhyay, D. (1996). A multi-area linear programming approach for analysis of economic operation of the Indian power system. *IEEE Transactions on Power Systems*, *11*(1), 52–58. doi:10.1109/59.485985

Parker, J. T., & Norgard, J. (2008, May). Autofocusing for RF tomography using particle swarm optimization. In *Proceedings of Radar Conference, 2008: RADAR'08* (pp. 1-6). IEEE. doi:10.1109/RADAR.2008.4721018

Park, J.-B., Lee, K.-S., Shin, J.-R., & Lee, K. Y. (2005). A particle swarm optimization for economic dispatch with nonsmooth cost functions. *IEEE Transactions on Power Systems*, *20*(1), 34–42. doi:10.1109/TPWRS.2004.831275

Park, J., Kim, Y., Eom, I., & Lee, K. (1993). Economic load dispatch for piecewise quadratic cost function using Hopfield neural network. *IEEE Transactions on Power Systems*, *8*(3), 1030–1038. doi:10.1109/59.260897

Park, V. D., & Corson, M. S. (1997). *A highly adaptive distributed routing algorithm for mobile wireless networks*. IEEE Infocom. doi:10.1109/INFCOM.1997.631180

Park, Y.-M., Won, J.-R., & Park, J.-B. (1998). A new approach to economic load dispatch based on improved evolutionary programming. *Engineering Intelligent Systems for Electrical Engineering and Communications*, *6*(2), 103–110.

Parsopoulos, K. E., & Vrahatis, M. N. (2002). Particle swarm optimization method in multiobjective problems. In *Proceedings of ACM Symposium on Applied Computing* (pp. 603-607). Madrid: ACM. doi:10.1145/508791.508907

Parsopoulos, K. E., & Vrahatis, M. N. (2010). Particle swarm optimization and intelligence: Advances and applications. Information Science Reference.

Parsopoulos, K. E., & Vrahatis, M. N. (2008). *Multiobjective particles swarm optimization approaches*. IGI Global Publishers.

Passino, K. M. (2002). Biomimicry of bacterial foraging for distributed optimization and control. *IEEE Control Systems Magazine*, 22(3), 52–67. doi:10.1109/MCS.2002.1004010

Patil, V. P. (2012). On demand and table driven routing protocol energy efficiency performance evaluation in mobile ad - hoc networks. *Journal of Computer Science and Management Research, 1*(2).

Patra, S. B., Mitra, J., & Earla, R. (2006). A new intelligent search method for composite system reliability analysis. In *Proceedings of IEEE PES Transmission and Distribution Conference and Exposition* (pp. 803–807). Caracas: IEEE.

Patricelli, G. L., Uy, J. A., Walsh, G., & Borgia, G. (2002). Male displays adjusted to female's response. *Nature, 415*(6869), 279–280. doi:10.1038/415279a PMID:11796996

Paul, P., Elena, M., & Madsen, J. (2009). Tabu search-based synthesis of dynamically reconfigurable digital microfluidic biochips. In *Proceedings of IEEE/ACM Int. Conf. Computer Architecture and Synthesis for Embedded Systems Conference* (pp. 195 – 203). IEEE/ACM.

Pawlak, Z. (1982). Rough set. *International Journal of Information and Computer Science*, 341 - 356.

Pawlak, Z. (1991). Rough Sets, theoretical aspects of reasoning about data. Kluwer Academic Publishers.

Pawlak, Z. (1982). Rough sets. *International Journal of Computer & Information Sciences, 11*(5), 341–356. doi:10.1007/BF01001956

Peng, H. Y., Ling, Z., Deng, W., & Zhu, J. (2011). *Increasing output power of switched reluctance generator with three-level power converter*. Paper presented at the Power and Energy Engineering Conference (APPEEC).

Peram, T., Veeramachaneni, K., & Mohan, C. K. (2003). Fitness-distance-ratio based particle swarm optimization. In *Proceedings of IEEE Swarm Intelligence Symposium* (pp. 174-181). Indianapolis, IN: IEEE.

Pereira, M. V., & Pinto, L. M. (1985). Application of sensitivity analysis of load supplying capability to interactive transmission expansion planning. *IEEE Transactions on Power Apparatus and Systems, PAS-104*(2), 381–389. doi:10.1109/TPAS.1985.319053

Pereira-Neto, A., Unsihuay, C., & Saavedra, O. (2005). Efficient evolutionary strategy optimisation procedure to solve the nonconvex economic dispatch problem with generator constraints. *IEE Proceedings. Generation, Transmission and Distribution, 152*(5), 653–660. doi:10.1049/ip-gtd:20045287

Perkins, C., & Royer, E. M. (1999). Ad hoc on demand distance vector routing. In *Proceedings of the 2ⁿᵈ IEEE Workshop on Mobile Computing Systems and Applications* (pp. 90-100). IEEE. Retrieved from www.beta.ece.ucsb.edu/~eroyer/txt/aodv.ps

Perkins, C. E., & Bhagwat, P. (1994). *Highly dynamic destination-sequenced distance-vector routing (DSDV) for mobile computers*. Comp. Comm. Rev. doi:10.1145/190314.190336

Perus, M. (1997). Mind: Neural computing plus quantum consciousness. In Mind versus computer. IOS Press.

Perus, M. (2000). Neural networks as a basis for quantum associate networks. *Neural Network World, 10*(6), 1001–1013.

Perus, M. (1998). Common mathematical foundations of neural and quantum informatics. *Zeitschrift für Angewandte Mathematik und Mechanik, 78*(1), 23–26.

Perus, M., & Dey, S. K. (2000). Quantum system can realize content addressable associative memory. *Applied Mathematics Letters, 13*(8), 31–36. doi:10.1016/S0893-9659(00)00092-6

Pettinaro, G. C., Kwee, I. W., Gambardella, L. M., Mondada, F., Floreano, D., Nolfi, S., ... (2002). Swarm robotics: A different approach to service robotics. In *Proceedings of the 33rd International Symposium on Robotics 2002*. Academic Press.

Phuangmalai, W., Konghirun, M., & Chayopitak, N. (2012). *A design study of 4/2 switched reluctance motor using particle swarm optimization*. Paper presented at the Electrical Engineering/Electronics, Computer, Telecommunications and Information Technology (ECTI-CON).

Piller, S., Perrin, M., & Jossen, A. (2001). Methods for state-of-charge determination and their applications. *Journal of Power Sources, 96*(1), 113–120. doi:10.1016/S0378-7753(01)00560-2

Podilchuk, C., & Zhang, X. (1996). Face recognition using OCT-based feature vectors. In *Proceedings of IEEE International Conference on Acoustics, Speech and Signal Processing* (vol. 4, pp. 2144-2147). IEEE.

Pothiya, S., Ngamroo, I., & Kongprawechnon, W. (2010). Ant colony optimisation for economic dispatch problem with non-smooth cost functions. *International Journal of Electrical Power & Energy Systems, 32*(5), 478–487. doi:10.1016/j.ijepes.2009.09.016

Prasad, B. D. C. N., Krishna, P. P. E. S. N., & Sagar, Y. (2011). An approach to develop expert systems in medical diagnosis using machine learning algorithms (ASTHMA) and a performance study. *International Journal on Soft Computing, 2*(1), 26–33. doi:10.5121/ijsc.2011.2103

Pratt, S., Mallon, E. B., Sumpter, D. J. T., & Franks, N. R. (2002). Quorum sensing, recruitment, and collective decision-making during colony emigration by the ant leptothorax albipennis. *Behavioral Ecology and Sociobiology, 52*(2), 117–127. doi:10.1007/s00265-002-0487-x

Pringles, R. M., & Rueda, J. L. (2012, September). Optimal transmission expansion planning using mean-variance mapping optimization. In Proceedings of Transmission and Distribution: Latin America Conference and Exposition (T&D-LA), 2012 Sixth IEEE/PES (pp. 1-8). IEEE. doi:10.1109/TDC-LA.2012.6319132

Puccinelli, D., & Haenggi, D. (2005). Wireless sensor networks: Applications and challenges of ubiquitous sensing. *IEEE Circuits and Systems Magazine.*

Pun, T. (1980). A new method for gray-level picture threshold using the entropy of the histogram. *Signal Processing, 2*(3), 223–237. doi:10.1016/0165-1684(80)90020-1

Qianwen, X., Yukun, S., & Ji, X. (2011). *Modeling inductance for bearingless switched reluctance motor based on PSO-LSSVM.* Paper presented at the Control and Decision Conference (CCDC).

Qin, J., Lewis, D., & Noble, W. (2003). Kernel hierarchical gene clustering from microarray gene expression data. *Bioinformatics (Oxford, England), 19*(16), 2097–2104. doi:10.1093/bioinformatics/btg288 PMID:14594715

Qinqing, G., Guangping, Z., Dexin, C., & Ketai, H. (2011, June). Image enhancement technique based on improved PSO algorithm. In *Proceedings of Industrial Electronics and Applications (ICIEA), 2011 6th IEEE Conference on* (pp. 234-238). IEEE. doi:10.1109/ICIEA.2011.5975586

Quraishi, M. I., De, M., Dhal, K. G., Mondal, S., & Das, G. (2013, March). A novel hybrid approach to restore historical degraded documents. In *Proceedings of Intelligent Systems and Signal Processing (ISSP), 2013 International Conference on* (pp. 185-189). IEEE. doi:10.1109/ISSP.2013.6526899

Radun, A. (1994). *Generating with the switched reluctance motor.* Paper presented at the Applied Power Electronics Conference and Exposition.

Rahaman, H., Chakrabarty, K., Bhattacharya, B. B., Mitra, D., & Ghoshal, S. (2011). On residue removal in digital microfluidic biochips. In *ACM Proceedings of 21st Symposium on Great Lakes Symposium on VLSI* (pp. 391 – 394). ACM.

Rahaman, H., Roy, P., & Dasgupta, P. (2010). A novel droplet routing algorithm for digital microfluidic biochips. *ACM Online Proceedings of 20th Symposium on Great Lakes Symposium on VLSI* (pp. 441- 446). ACM.

Rahaman, H., Singha, K., Samanta, T., & Dasgupta, P. (2010). Method of droplet routing in digital microfluidic biochip. In *Proceedings of IEEE/ASME International Conference on Mechatronics and Embedded Systems and Applications* (pp. 251-256). IEEE.

Rajagopalan, S., Jaikaeo, C. & Shen, C.C. (2003). *Unicast routing for mobile ad hoc networks with swarm intelligence* (Technical Report #2003-07). University of Delaware.

Rajashekararadhya, S. V., & Ranjan, P. V. (2008). Efficient zone based feature extration algorithm for handwritten numeral recognition of four popular south Indian scripts. *Journal of Theoretical and Applied Information Technology, 4*(12), 1171–1181.

Rajesh, R., Pugazhendhi, S., & Ganesh, K. (2013). Genetic algorithm and particle swarm optimization for solving balanced allocation problem of third party logistics providers. In J. Wang (Ed.), *Management innovations for intelligent supply chains* (pp. 184–203). Hershey, PA: Business Science Reference; doi:10.4018/978-1-4666-2461-0.ch010

Ramanujan, P., Li, Z., & Higham, L. (2009). Shadow prices versus vickrey prices in multipath routing. In Proceedings of *IEEE Conference on Information and Communication* (pp. 2956–2960). Rio de Janeiro: IEEE.

Ramesh, N., Yoo, J. H., & Sethi, I. K. (1995). Thresholding based on histogram approximation. *IEE Proceedings. Vision Image and Signal Processing, 142*(5), 271–279. doi:10.1049/ip-vis:19952007

Rana, M., Kumar, S., & Sharma, U. (2012). Improvement the performance of mobility pattern in mobile ad-hoc sensor network using qualnet 5.0. *International Journal of Engineering Research and Development, 1*(3).

Rani, K. S. S., & Devarajan, N. (2012). Multiobjective sensor node deployement in wireless sensor networks. *International Journal of Engineering Science and Technology, 4*(4).

Rao, S. S. (1996). *Engineering optimization - Theory and practice*. New York: John Wiley & Sons.

Rashedi, E., Nezamabadi-Pour, H., & Saryazdi, S. (2009). GSA: A gravitational search algorithm. *Information Sciences, 179*(13), 2232–2248. doi:10.1016/j.ins.2009.03.004

Rawson, M., & Kateley, S. (1999). *Electric vehicle charging equipment design and health and safety codes* (No. 1999-01-2941). SAE Technical Paper.

RC4 Encryption Algorithm. (n.d.). Retrieved August 4, 2014, from http://www.vocal.com

Reddick, W. E., Glass, J. O., Cook, E. N., Elkin, T. D., & Deaton, R. J. (1997). Automated segmentation and classification of multispectral magnetic resonance images of brain using artificial neural networks. *IEEE Transactions on Medical Imaging, 16*(6), 911–918. doi:10.1109/42.650887 PMID:9533591

Reddi, S. S., Rudin, S. F., & Keshavan, H. R. (1984). An optimal multiple threshold scheme for image segmentation. *IEEE–SMC, 14*, 611–665.

Reeves, C. R. (1993). Using genetic algorithms with small populations. In *Proc. of the Fifth International Conference on Genetic Algorithms*. Morgan Kaufmann.

Reliability Test System Task Force of the Application of Probability Methods Subcommittee. (1979). IEEE reliability test system. *IEEE Transactions on Power Apparatus and Systems*, 2047–2054.

Rezaee, M. R., Van der Zwet, P. M. J., Lelieveldt, B. P. E., van der Geest, R. J., & Reiber, J. H. C. (2000). A multiresolution image segmentation technique based on pyramidal segmentation and fuzzy clustering. *IEEE Tans. On Image Processing, 9*(7), 1238–1248. doi:10.1109/83.847836 PMID:18262961

Rezazadeh, I., Meybodi, M. R., & Naebi, A. (2011). Adaptive particle swarm optimization algorithm for dynamic environments. In Proceedings of ICSI (LNCS), (vol. 6728, pp. 120 – 129). Berlin: Springer.

Richards, M., & Ventura, D. (2004). Choosing a starting configuration for particle swarm optimization. In *Proceedings of 2004 IEEE International Joint Conference on Neural Networks* (pp. 2309-2312). IEEE.

Rivault, C., & Durier, V. (2004). Homing in German cockroaches, Blattella germanica (L.) (Insecta: Dictyoptera): multi-channelled orientation cues. *Ethology, 110*(10), 761–777. doi:10.1111/j.1439-0310.2004.01018.x

Rivest, R. L. (1990). Cryptology. In A. Jan Van Leeuwen (Ed.), *Handbook of theoretical computer science* (pp. 717–755). Cambridge, MA: MIT Press.

Robertson, P. K., & Campanella, R. G. (1983). Interpretation of cone penetration tests. Part I: Sand. *Canadian Geotechnical Journal, 20*(4), 718–733. doi:10.1139/t83-078

Robertson, P. K., & Campanella, R. G. (1985). Liquefaction potential of sand using the CPT. *Journal of Geotechnical Engineering, 111*(3), 384–403. doi:10.1061/(ASCE)0733-9410(1985)111:3(384)

Robertson, P. K., & Wride, C. E. (1998). Cyclic lique-faction and its evaluation based on the SPT and CPT. In YoudT. L.IdrissI. M., (Eds.), *Proc. of the 1998 NCEER Workshop on Evaluation of liquefaction Resistance of Soils*. NCEER.

Romer, K., & Mattern, F. (2004). The design space of wireless sensor networks. *Wireless Communications, IEEE, 11*(6), 54–61. doi:10.1109/MWC.2004.1368897

Roth, M., & Wicker, S. (2003). Termite: Emergent ad-hoc networking. In *Proceedings of the 2nd Mediterranean Workshop on Ad-Hoc Net- works* (Med-Hoc-Net'2003). Mahdia, Tunisia: Academic Press.

Rousseeuw, P. (1987). Silhouettes, a graphical aid to the interpretation and validation of cluster analysis. *Journal of Computational and Applied Mathematics, 20*, 53–65. doi:10.1016/0377-0427(87)90125-7

Roy, A., Das, N., Sarkar, R., Basu, S., Kundu, M., & Nasipuri, M. (2012). Region selection in handwritten character recognition using artificial bee colony optimization. In *Proceedings ofThird International Conference on Emerging Applications of Information Technology (EAIT)* (pp. 183–186). Academic Press. doi:10.1109/EAIT.2012.6407891

Roy, P., Bhattacharya, S., Bhattacharyay, R., Imam, F. J., Rahaman, H., & Dasgupta, P. (2014). A novel wire planning technique for optimum pin utilization in digital microfluidic biochips. In *Proceedings of13th International Conference on Embedded Systems VLSI Design* (pp. 510 – 515). Mumbai, India: Academic Press. doi:10.1109/VLSID.2014.95

Roy, P., Howladar, P., Bhattacharjee, R., Rahaman, H., & Dasgupta, P. (2013). A new cross contamination aware routing method with intelligent path exploration in digital microfluidic biochips. In *Proceedings of8th International Conference on Design & Technology of Integrated Systems in Nanoscale Era (DTIS)* (pp. 50 – 55). Academic Press. doi:10.1109/DTIS.2013.6527777

Rueda Torres, L. J., & Erlich, I. (2013). Short-term transmission expansion planning by using swarm mean-variance mapping optimization In *Proceedings of the 17th International Conference on Intelligent Systems Application to Power Systems*. Academic Press.

Rueda, J. L., & Erlich, I. (2013, April). Evaluation of the mean-variance mapping optimization for solving multimodal problems. In *Proceedings of Swarm Intelligence (SIS),2013 IEEE Symposium* (pp. 7-14). IEEE. doi:10.1109/SIS.2013.6615153

Ruspini, E. (1970). Numerical methods for fuzzy clustering. *Information Sciences, 2*(3), 319–350. doi:10.1016/S0020-0255(70)80056-1

Rust, M. K., Owens, J. M., & Reierson, D. A. (1995). *Understanding and controlling the German cockroach.* Oxford, UK: Oxford University Press.

Rylander, B., Soule, T., Foster, J., & Alves-Foss, J. (2001). Quantum evolutionary programming. In *Proceedings of the Genetic and Evolutionary Computation Conference (GECCO-2001)*. Morgan Kaufmann.

Saberi, M. M., Sigeru, O., Deris, S., & Yoshioka, M. (2011). Modified binary particle swarm optimization for selecting the small subset of informative genes from gene expression data. *IEEE Transactions on Information Technology in Biomedicine, 15*(6), 813–822. doi:10.1109/TITB.2011.2167756 PMID:21914573

Sabri, N. M., Puteh, M., & Mahmood, M. R. (2013). A review of gravitational search algorithm. *Int. J. Advance. Soft Comput. Appl, 5*(3), 1–39.

Sahoo, B. C., Oommen, T., Misra, D., & Newby, G. (2007). Using the one-dimensional s-transform as a discrimination tool in classification of hyperspectral images. *Canadian Journal of Remote Sensing, 33*(6), 551–560. doi:10.5589/m07-057

Sahoo, P. K., Soltani, S., & Wong, A. K. C. (1988). A survey of thresholding technique. *CVGIP, 41*, 233–260.

Sahoo, P., Wilkins, C., & Yeager, J. (1997). Threshold selection using Renyi's entropy. *Pattern Recognition, 30*(1), 71–84. doi:10.1016/S0031-3203(96)00065-9

Saïd, I., Costagliola, G., Leoncini, I., & Rivault, C. (2005). Cuticular hydrocarbon profiles and aggregation in four Periplaneta species (Insecta: Dictyoptera). *Journal of Insect Physiology, 51*(9), 995–1003. doi:10.1016/j.jinsphys.2005.04.017 PMID:15950236

Saïd, I., Gaertner, C., Renou, M., & Rivault, C. (2005). Perception of cuticular hydrocarbons by the olfactory organs in Periplaneta americana (L.) (Insecta: Dictyoptera). *Journal of Insect Physiology*, *51*(12), 1384–1389. doi:10.1016/j.jinsphys.2005.09.001 PMID:16226272

Salazar, R., Roepman, P., Capella, G., Moreno, V., Simon, I., Dreezen, C., … Tollenaar, R. (2012). Gene expression signature to improve prognosis prediction of stage II and III colorectal cancer. *Journal of Clinical Oncology*, *29*(1), 17-24.

Saleema, M., Gianni, A. D. C., & Farooq, M. (2011). Swarm intelligence based routing protocol for wireless sensor networks: Survey and future directions. *Information Sciences*, *181*(20), 4597–4624. doi:10.1016/j.ins.2010.07.005

Samra, A. S., El Taweel Gad Allah, S., & Ibrahim, R. M. (2003). Face recognition using wavelet transform, fast Fourier transform and discrete cosine transform. In *Proceedings of IEEE 46th Midwest Symposium on Circuits and Systems* (vol. 1, pp. 272-275). IEEE.

Sarkar, A., & Mandal, J. K. (2012). Energy efficient wireless communication using genetic algorithm guided faster light weight digital signature algorithm (GADSA). *International Journal of Advanced Smart Sensor Network Systems*, *2*(3), 9-25.

Sarkar, A., & Mandal, J. K. (2013a). Computational intelligence based simulated annealing guided key generation in wireless communication (CISAKG). *International Journal on Information Theory*, *2*(4), 35-44.

Sarkar, A., & Mandal, J. K. (2013b). Genetic algorithm guided key generation in wireless communication (GAKG). *International Journal on Cybernetics & Informatics*, *2*(5), 9-17.

Sarkar, A., & Mandal, J. K. (2013c). Computational intelligence based triple layer perceptron model coordinated PSO guided metamorphosed based application in cryptographic technique for secured communication (TLPPSO). In *Proceedings of the First International Conference on Computational Intelligence: Modeling, Techniques and Applications (CIMTA-2013)* (Vol. 10, pp. 433-442). Kalyani, India: Procedia Technology, Elsevier.

Sarkar, A., & Maulik, U. (2009a). Parallel point symmetry based clustering for gene microarray data. In *Proceedings of Seventh International Conference on Advances in Pattern Recognition-2009* (ICAPR, 2009). Kolkata, India: IEEE Computer Society.

Sarkar, A., & Maulik, U. (2009b). Parallel clustering technique using modified symmetry based distance. In *Proceedings of 1st International Conference on Computer, Communication, Control and Information Technology (C3IT 2009)*. MacMillan Publishers India Ltd.

Sarkar, A., & Maulik, U. (2013). Cancer gene expression data analysis using rough based symmetrical clustering. In Handbook of research on computational intelligence for engineering, science, and business. Hershey, PA: IGI Global.

Scalable Network Technologies. (n.d.). *QualNet network simulator 6.1*. Retrieved from www.scalable-networks.com

Scalable Network Technologies. (n.d.). *QualNet simulator 6.1*. Retrieved from www.scalable-networks.com

Schneier, B. (1995). *Applied cryptography: Protocols, algorithms, and source code in C* (2nd ed.). Wiley.

Schoonderwoerd, R., Holland, O. E., & Bruten, J. L. (1997). Ant-like agents for load balancing in telecommunication networks. In *Proc. First ACM Int. Conf. on Autonomous Agents* (pp. 209-216). ACM. doi:10.1145/267658.267718

Schutter, G. D., Theraulaz, G., & Deneubourg, J. L. (2001). Article. *Annals of Mathematics and Artificial Intelligence*, *31*, 223. doi:10.1023/A:1016638723526

Seed, H. B., Tokimatsu, K., Harder, L. F., & Chung, R. M. (1984). Influence of SPT procedures in soil liquefaction resistance evaluation, Earthquake Engrg. Res. Ctr., Univ. of California, Berkeley, California. Rep. No. UCB/EERC-84/15.

Seed, H. B., & De Alba, P. (1986). *Use of SPT and CPT tests for evaluating the liquefaction resistance of sands, Use of in situ tests in geotechnical engineering*. ASCE.

Seed, H. B., & Idriss, I. M. (1967). Analysis of soil liquefaction: Niigata earthquake. *J. Soil Mech. and Foun. Div, ASCE*, *93*(3), 83–108.

Seed, H. B., & Idriss, I. M. (1971). Simplified procedure for evaluating soil liquefaction potential. *Journal of the Soil Mechanics and Foundations Division, 97*(9), 1249–1273.

Seed, H. B., & Idriss, I. M. (1982). *Ground motions and soil liquefaction during earthquakes*. Oakland, CA: Earthquake Engineering Research Institute Monograph.

Seed, H. B., Idriss, I. M., & Arango, I. (1983). Evaluation of liquefaction potential using field performance data. *Journal of the Geotechnical Engineering Division, 109*(3), 458–482. doi:10.1061/(ASCE)0733-9410(1983)109:3(458)

Seed, H. B., Tokimatsu, K., Harder, L. F., & Chung, R. (1985). Influence of SPT procedures in soil liquefaction resistance evaluation. *Journal of Geotechnical Engineering, 111*(12), 861–878.

Selvakumar, A. I., & Thanushkodi, K. (2007). A new particle swarm optimization solution to nonconvex economic dispatch problems. *IEEE Transactions on Power Systems, 22*(1), 42–51. doi:10.1109/TPWRS.2006.889132

Sezgin, M., & Sankur, B. (2004). Survey over image thresholding techniques and quantitative performance evaluation. *Journal of Electronic Imaging, 13*(1), 146–165. doi:10.1117/1.1631315

Shafiei, A., & Williamson, S. S. (2010). Plug-in hybrid electric vehicle charging: Current issues and future challenges. In *Proceedings of Vehicle Power and Propulsion Conference (VPPC)*. Lille, France: IEEE. doi:10.1109/VPPC.2010.5729134

Shaw, E. (1962). The schooling of fishes. *Scientific American, 206*(6), 128–138. doi:10.1038/scientificamerican0662-128 PMID:14458553

Shen, C., Wang, P., Paisitkriangkrai, S., & Van Den Hengel, A. (2013). Training effective node classifiers for cascade classification. *International Journal of Computer Vision, 103*(3), 326–347. doi:10.1007/s11263-013-0608-1

Shi Y.Y., Liu Z.F., Zhang, H.C., & Hu, U. D. (2011). Product disassembly sequence planning based on cockroach swarm optimization. *Journal of Hefei University of Technology (Natural Science), 11*.

Shi, Y. (2004). Particle swarm optimization. *IEEE Neural Networks Society*, 8-13.

Shi, Y., & Eberhart, R. C. (2001). Fuzzy adaptive particle swarm optimization. In *Proceedings of the IEEE Congress on Evolutionary Computation*. Seoul, South Korea. IEEE.

Shi, J., & Malik, J. (2000). Normalized cuts and image segmentation. *IEEE Transactions on Pattern Analysis and Machine Intelligence, 22*(8), 888–905. doi:10.1109/34.868688

Shi, Y., & Eberhart, R. C. (1998). A modified particle swarm optimizer. In *Proc. IEEE International Conference on Evolutionary Computation*. IEEE Press.

Shor, P. W. (1997). Polynomial-time algorithms for prime factorization and discrete logarithms on a quantum computer. *SIAM Journal on Computing, 26*(5), 1484–1509. doi:10.1137/S0097539795293172

Silva, J., Lins, R., & Rocha, V., Jr. (2006). Binarizing and filtering historical documents with back-to-front interference. In *Proceedings of SAC ACM Symposium on Applied Computing*. New York: ACM Press.

Simon, H. (1994). *Neural networks: A comprehensive foundation*. Prentice Hall PTR.

Singh, N. K., Fletcher, J. E., Finney, S. J., Grant, D. M., & Williams, B. W. (2005). *Evaluation of sparse PWM converter for switched reluctance generator*. Paper presented at the Power Electronics and Drives Systems.

Singh, C., & Chen, Q. (1989). Generation system reliability evaluation using a cluster based load model. *IEEE Transactions on Power Systems, 4*(1), 102–107. doi:10.1109/59.32466

Singh, C., & Deng, Z. (1991). A new algorithm for multi–area reliability evaluation – Simultaneous decomposition-simulation approach. *Electric Power Systems Research, 21*(2), 129–136. doi:10.1016/0378-7796(91)90027-K

Singh, C., & Lago-Gonzalez, A. (1989). Improved algorithms for multi – area reliability evaluation using the decomposition-simulation approach. *IEEE Transactions on Power Systems, 4*(1), 321–328. doi:10.1109/59.32495

Singh, C., & Mitra, J. (1997). Composite system reliability evaluation using state space pruning. *IEEE Transactions on Power Systems, 12*(1), 471–479. doi:10.1109/59.575787

Singh, S. K., Singh, M. P., & Singh, D. K. (2010). *Routing protocols in wireless sensor networks*. Academic Press.

Singh, S., & Singh, J. N. (2012). *Application of particle swarm optimization: In the field of image processing.* Lap Lambert Academic Publishing.

Sinha, N., Chakrabarti, R., & Chattopadhyay, P. (2003). Evolutionary programming techniques for economic load dispatch. *IEEE Transactions on Evolutionary Computation, 7*(1), 83–94. doi:10.1109/TEVC.2002.806788

Sista, R., Hua, Z., Thwar, P., Sudarsan, A., Srinivasan, V., Eckhardt, A., & Pamula, V. et al. (2008). Development of a digital microfluidic platform for point of care testing. *Lab on a Chip, 8*(12), 2091–2104. doi:10.1039/b814922d PMID:19023472

Skempton, A. W. (1986). Standard penetration test procedures and the effects in sands of overburden pressure, relative density, particle size, aging and overconsolidation. *Geotechnique, 36*(3), 425–447. doi:10.1680/geot.1986.36.3.425

Small, C. (2006). Urban landsat, cities from space. Palisades, NY: NASA Socioeconomic Data and Applications Center (SEDAC).

Smith, A. M. S., Wooster, M. J., Powell, A. K., & Usher, D. (2002). Texture based feature extraction, application to burn scar detection in earth observation satellite sensor imagery. *International Journal of Remote Sensing, 23*(8), 1733–1739. doi:10.1080/01431160110106104

Soares, J., Sousa, T., Morais, H., Vale, Z., Canizes, B., & Silva, A. (2013). Application-specific modified particle swarm optimization for energy resource scheduling considering vehicle-to-grid. *Applied Soft Computing, 13*(11), 4264–4280. doi:10.1016/j.asoc.2013.07.003

Sojoudi, S., & Low, S. H. (2011). Optimal charging of plug-in hybrid electric vehicles in smart grids. In *Proceedings of Power and Energy Society General Meeting.* San Diego, CA: IEEE. doi:10.1109/PES.2011.6039236

Solis, F. J., & Wets, R. J.-B. (1981). Wets, minimization by random search techniques. *Mathematics of Operations Research, 6*(1), 19–30. doi:10.1287/moor.6.1.19

Song, X., Cherian, G., & Fan, G. (2005). Aν-insensitive SVM approach for compliance monitoring of the conservation reserve program. *IEEE Geoscience and Remote Sensing Letters, 2*(2), 99–103. doi:10.1109/LGRS.2005.846007

Sousa, T., Silva, A., & Neves, A. (2004). Particle swarm based data mining algorithms for classification tasks. *Parallel Computing, 30*(5-6), 767–783. doi:10.1016/j.parco.2003.12.015

Spall, J. C. (2003). *Introduction to stochastic search and optimization, estimation, simulation and control.* Wiley. doi:10.1002/0471722138

Spang, R. (2003). Diagnostic signatures from microarrays, a bioinformatics concept for personalized medicine. *BIOSILICO, 1*(2), 64–68. doi:10.1016/S1478-5382(03)02329-1

Srinivas, M., & Patnaik, L. M. (1994). Genetic algorithms: A survey. *Computer, 27*(6), 17–26. doi:10.1109/2.294849

Srinivas, N., & Deb, K. (1994). Multiobjective optimization using nondominated sorting in genetic algorithms. *Evolutionary Computation Journal, 2*(3), 221–248. doi:10.1162/evco.1994.2.3.221

Srivastava, N. (2010). Challenges of next-generation wireless sensor networks and its impact on society. *Journal of Telecommunications, 1*(1).

Stallings, W. (2003). *Cryptography and network security: Principles and practices* (3rd ed.). Pearson Education.

Stark, T. D., & Olson, S. M. (1995). Liquefaction resistance using CPT and field case histories. *Journal of Geotechnical Engineering, 121*(12), 856–869. doi:10.1061/(ASCE)0733-9410(1995)121:12(856)

Stathakis, D., & Vasilakos, A. (2006). Comparison of computational intelligence based classification techniques for remotely sensed optical image classification. *IEEE Transactions on Geoscience and Remote Sensing, 44*(8), 2305–2318. doi:10.1109/TGRS.2006.872903

Stinson, D. R. (1995). *Cryptography, theory and practice.* Boca Raton, FL: CRC Press.

Stojmenovic, M. (2005). Swarm intelligence for routing in ad hoc wireless networks. In Security and routing in wireless networks (pp. 167-188). Nova Science Publishers.

Stokoe, K. H., Nazarian, S., Rix, G. J., Sanchez Salinero, I., Sheu, J. C., & Mok, Y. J. (1988a). In situ seismic testing of hard-to-sample soils by surface wave method: Earthquake engineering and soil dynamics II—Recent advances in ground-motion evaluation. Geotechnical Special Publication, ASCE, 20, 264–289.

Storn, R., & Price, K. (1995). *Differential evolution-a simple and efficient heuristic for global optimization over continuous spaces.* Technical Report TR-95-012. ICSI.

Su, F., & Chakrabarty, K. (2004). Architectural-level synthesis of digital microfluidics-based biochips. In *Proceedings of IEEE International Conference on Computer-Aided Design* (pp. 223 – 228). San Jose, CA: IEEE.

Su, M. H. (2012). *Roach infestation optimization for attribute acceptance sampling plan in construction industry.* Department of Construction Engineering, Master's Thesis.

Su, W., & Chow, M. Y. (2010). An intelligent energy management system for PHEVs considering demand response. In *Proceedings of FREEDM Annual Conference.* NC State University.

Su, W., & Chow, M. Y. (2011). Performance evaluation of a PHEV parking station using particle swarm optimization. In *Proceedings of Power and Energy Society General Meeting.* San Diego, CA: IEEE. doi:10.1109/PES.2011.6038937

Subbaraj, P., Rengaraj, R., Salivahanan, S., & Senthilkumar, T. (2010). Parallel particle swarm optimization with modified stochastic acceleration factors for solving large scale economic dispatch problem. *International Journal of Electrical Power & Energy Systems, 32*(9), 1014–1023. doi:10.1016/j.ijepes.2010.02.003

Subramaniam, D., Druschel, P., & Chen, J. (1997). Ants and reinforcement learning: A case study in routing in dynamic networks. In *Proc. IEEE MILCOM.* Atlantic City, NJ: IEEE.

Subramanian, A., Garcia, M., Dominguez-Garcia, A., Callaway, D., Poolla, K., & Varaiya, P. (2012). Real-time scheduling of deferrable electric loads. In *Proceedings of American Control Conference (ACC).* Montreal, Canada: IEEE. doi:10.1109/ACC.2012.6315670

Su, F., Ozev, S., & Chakrabarty, K. (2004). Test planning and test resource optimization for droplet-based microfluidic systems. In *Proceedings of Europe Test Symposium* (pp. 72 -77). Academic Press.

Suguna, N., & Thanushkodi, K. (2010). A novel rough set reduct algorithm for medical domain based on bee colony optimization. *Journal of Computing, 2*(6), 49–54.

Su, M. C., Chou, C. H., & Hsieh, C. C. (2005). Fuzzy c-means algorithm with a point symmetry distance. *International Journal of Fuzzy Systems, 7*(4), 175–181.

Su, M.-C., & Chou, C.-H. (2001). A modified version of the k-means algorithm with a distance based on cluster symmetry. *IEEE Transactions on Pattern Analysis and Machine Intelligence, 23*(6), 674–680. doi:10.1109/34.927466

Sumpter, D. J. T. (2000). *From bee to society: An agent - based investigation of honey bee colonies.* (PhD Thesis). The University of Manchester, Manchester, UK.

Sun, Z. G., Cheung, N. C., Zhao, S. W., Lu, Y., & Shi, Z. H. (2011). *Design and simulation of a linear switched reluctance generator for wave energy conversion.* Paper presented at the Power Electronics Systems and Applications (PESA).

Supriya, K. D., Ranjit, B., & Roy, A. R. (2001). An application of intuitionistic fuzzy sets in medical diagnosis. *Fuzzy Sets and Systems, 117*(2), 209–213. doi:10.1016/S0165-0114(98)00235-8

Suresh, K., & Kumarappan, N. (2013). *Generation maintenance scheduling using improved binary particle swarm optimisation considering aging failures.* IET.

Su, W., & Chow, M.-Y. (2012a). Performance evaluation of an EDA-based large-scale plug-in hybrid electric vehicle charging algorithm. *IEEE Transactions on Smart Grid, 3*(1), 308–315. doi:10.1109/TSG.2011.2151888

Su, W., & Chow, M.-Y. (2012b). Computational intelligence-based energy management for a large-scale PHEV/PEV enabled municipal parking deck. *Applied Energy, 96*, 171–182. doi:10.1016/j.apenergy.2011.11.088

Takahashi, A., Goto, H., Nakamura, K., Watanabe, T., & Ichinokura, O. (2006). Characteristics of 8/6 switched reluctance generator excited by suppression resistor converter. *IEEE Transactions on Magnetics, 42*(10), 3458–3460. doi:10.1109/TMAG.2006.880388

Talbi, H., Batouche, M., & Draa, A. (2007). A quantum-inspired evolutionary algorithm for multiobjective image segmentation. *International Journal of Mathematics, 1*(2), 109–114.

Taleizadeh, A. A., & Cárdenas-Barrón, L. E. (2013). Metaheuristic algorithms for supply chain management problems. In Supply chain management: Concepts, methodologies, tools, and applications (pp. 1814-1837). Hershey, PA: Business Science Reference. doi:10.4018/978-1-4666-2625-6.ch106

Taneja, K., & Patel, R. B. (2007). Mobile ad hoc networks: Challenges and future. In Proceedings of COIT2007. Academic Press.

Tang, W. J., Wu, Q. H., & Saunders, J. R. (2006). Bacterial Foraging algorithm for dynamic environments. In *Proceedings of IEEE Congress on Evolutionary Computation (CEC 2006)* (pp. 1324–1330). IEEE.

Tan, K. S., & Isa, N. A. M. (2011). Color image segmentation using histogram thresholding fuzzy C- means hybrid approach. *Pattern Recognition, 44*(1), 1–15. doi:10.1016/j.patcog.2010.07.013

Tan, W. S., Hassan, M. Y., Rahman, H. A., Abdullah, M. P., & Hussin, F. (2013). Multi-distributed generation planning using hybrid particle swarm optimisation-gravitational search algorithm including voltage rise issue. *IET Generation, Transmission, & Distribution, 7*(9), 929–942. doi:10.1049/iet-gtd.2013.0050

Tavazoie, S., Hughes, J., Campbell, M., Cho, R., & Church, G. (2001). Systematic determination of genetic network architecture. *Bioinformatics (Oxford, England), 17*, 405–414. PMID:11331234

Techpedia Three Tier Architecture. (n.d.). Retrieved from http://www.techopedia.com/definition/24649/three-tier-architecture

Tiago, S., Silva, A., & Ana, N. (2004). Particle swarm based data mining algorithms for classification tasks. *Parallel Computing, 30*(5/6), 767–783.

Tie, S. F., & Tan, C. W. (2013). A review of energy sources and energy management system in electric vehicles. *Renewable & Sustainable Energy Reviews, 20*, 82–102. doi:10.1016/j.rser.2012.11.077

Ting, T. O., Rao, M. V. C., Loo, C. K., & Ngu, S. S. (2003). Solving unit commitment problem using hybrid particle swarm optimization. *Journal of Heuristics, 9*(6), 507–520. doi:10.1023/B:HEUR.0000012449.84567.1a

Tizhoosh, H. (2005). Image thresholding using type II fuzzy sets. *Pattern Recognition, 38*(12), 2363–2372. doi:10.1016/j.patcog.2005.02.014

Toh, C. K. (1996). A novel distributed routing protocol to support Ad hoc mobile computing. In *Proc. 1996 IEEE 15th Annual Int'l. Phoenix Conf* (pp. 480–486). Comp. and Comm. Retrieved from http://www.ics.uci.edu/~atm/ad-hoc/paper-collection/toh-distributed-routing-ipccc96.pdf

Tokimatsu, K., & Uchida, A. (1990). Correlation between liquefaction resistance and shear wave velocity. *Soil and Foundation, 30*(2), 33–42. doi:10.3208/sandf1972.30.2_33

Torrey, D. A. (2002). Switched reluctance generators and their control. *IEEE Transactions on Industrial Electronics, 49*(1), 3–14. doi:10.1109/41.982243

Tosun, Ö. (2014). Artificial bee colony algorithm. In J. Wang (Ed.), *Encyclopedia of business analytics and optimization* (pp. 179–192). Hershey, PA: Business Science Reference; doi:10.4018/978-1-4666-5202-6.ch018

Tripathy, B. K., Acharjya, D. P., & Cynthya, V. (2011). A framework for intelligent medical diagnosis using rough set with formal concept analysis. *International Journal of Artificial Intelligence & Applications, 2*(2), 45–66. doi:10.5121/ijaia.2011.2204

Tripathy, M., & Mishra, S. (2007). Bacteria foraging-based solution to optimize both real power loss and voltage stability limit. *IEEE Transactions on Power Systems, 22*(1), 240–248. doi:10.1109/TPWRS.2006.887968

Tsai, D. M. (1995). A fast thresholding selection procedure for multimodal and unimodal histograms. *Pattern Recognition Letters, 16*(6), 653–666. doi:10.1016/0167-8655(95)80011-H

Tsujinishi, D., & Abe, S. (2003). Fuzzy least squares support vector machines for multiclass problems. *Neural Networks, 16*(5/6), 785–792. doi:10.1016/S0893-6080(03)00110-2 PMID:12850035

Tsutsui, S. (2004a). Ant colony optimization for continuous domains with aggregation pheromones metaphore. In *Proc. 5th Internat. Conf. on Recent Advances in Soft Computing (RASC'04)* (pp. 207-212). Academic Press.

Tsutsui, S., & Ghosh, A. (2004b). An extension of ant colony optimization for function optimization. In *Proc. 5th Asia Pasific Conference on Simulated evolution and Learning (SEAL04)*. Academic Press.

Tuia, D., & Camps-Valls, G. (2009). Semisupervised remote sensing image classification with cluster kernels. *IEEE Geoscience and Remote Sensing Letters, 6*(2), 224–228. doi:10.1109/LGRS.2008.2010275

Tulpule, P. J., Marano, V., Yurkovich, S., & Rizzoni, G. (2013). Economic and environmental impacts of a PV powered workplace parking garage charging station. *Applied Energy, 108,* 323–332. doi:10.1016/j.apenergy.2013.02.068

Turinici, G., Le Bris, C., & Rabitz, H. (2004). Efficient algorithms for the laboratory discovery of optimal quantum controls. *Physical Review E: Statistical, Nonlinear, and Soft Matter Physics, 40*(016704). PMID:15324201

Turk, M. A., & Pentland, A. P. (1991). Face recognition using eigenfaces. In *Proceedings IEEE Computer Society Conference on Computer Vision and Pattern Recognition (CVPR, 91)* (pp. 586-591). IEEE.

Tusher, V. G., Tibshirani, R., & Chu, G. (1940). Significance analysis of microarrays applied to the ionizing radiation response. *Proceedings of the National Academy of Sciences of the United States of America, 98*(9), 5116–5121. doi:10.1073/pnas.091062498 PMID:11309499

Tyson, J. J., Baumann, W. T., Chen, C., Verdugo, A., Tavassoly, I., Wang, Y., & Clarke, R. et al. (2012). Dynamic models of estrogen signaling and cell fate in breast cancer cells. *Nature Reviews. Cancer, 11*(7), 523–532. doi:10.1038/nrc3081 PMID:21677677

Ul-Haq, A., Buccella, C., Cecati, C., & Khalid, H. A. (2013). Smart charging infrastructure for electric vehicles. In *Proceedings of International Conference on Clean Electrical Power (ICCEP)*. Alghero: IEEE. doi:10.1109/ICCEP.2013.6586984

Uma, S. M., & Kirubakaran, E. (2012). Intelligent heart diseases prediction system using a new hybrid meta-heuristic algorithm. *International Journal of Engineering Research & Technology, 1*(8), 1–7.

Ural, D. N., & Saka, H. (1998). Liquefaction assessment by neural networks. *Electronic Journal of Geotechnical Engineering.* Retrieved from http://geotech.civen.okstate.edu/ejge/ppr9803/index.html

Valle, Y. D., Venayagamoorthy, G. K., Mohagheghi, S., Hernandez, J. C., & Harley, R. G. (2008). Particle swarm optimization: Basic concepts, variants and applications in power systems. *IEEE Transactions on Evolutionary Computation, 12*(2), 171–195. doi:10.1109/TEVC.2007.896686

Valsalan, V. M. (2013). Dynamic deployment of wireless sensor networks using enhanced artificial bee colony algorithm. *International Journal of Science and Research, 2*(4).

Van den Bergh, F. (2002). *An analysis of particle swarm optimizers.* (Doctoral dissertation). Univ. Pretoria, Pretoria, South Africa.

Van den Bergh, F., & Engelbrecht, A. P. (2004). A cooperative approach to participate swam optimization. *IEEE Transactions on Evolutionary Computation, 8*(3), 225–239. doi:10.1109/TEVC.2004.826069

Van der Geest, M., Polinder, H., Ferreira, J. A., & Zeilstra, D. (2012). *Optimization and comparison of electrical machines using particle swarm optimization.* Paper presented at the Electrical Machines (ICEM).

Vandenbroucke, N., Macaire, L., & Postaire, J. G. (2003). Color image segmentation by pixel classification in an adapted hybrid color space: Application to soccer image analysis. *Computer Vision and Image Understanding, 90*(2), 190–216. doi:10.1016/S1077-3142(03)00025-0

Vanneschi, L., Codecasa, D., & Mauri, G. (2011). A comparative study of four parallel and distributed PSO methods. *New Generation Computing, 29*(2), 129–161. doi:10.1007/s00354-010-0102-z

Vapnik, V. (1982). Estimation of dependences based on empirical data (2nd ed.). Springer Verlag.

Vasant, P., Ganesan, T., & Elamvazuthi, I. (2012, January). An improved PSO approach for solving non-convex optimization problems. In *Proceedings of ICT and Knowledge Engineering (ICT & Knowledge Engineering), 2011 9th International Conference* (pp. 80-87). IEEE. doi:10.1109/ICTKE.2012.6152418

Vasant, P., Ganesan, T., Elamvazuthi, I., Barsoum, N., & Faiman, D. (2012, November). Solving deterministic non-linear programming problem using Hopfield artificial neural network and genetic programming techniques. In *AIP Conference Proceedings-American Institute of Physics* (*Vol. 1499*, No. 1, p. 311). Academic Press. doi:10.1063/1.4769007

Vasant, P., & Global, I. (2013). *Meta-heuristics optimization algorithms in engineering, business, economics, and finance.* Information Science Reference. doi:10.4018/978-1-4666-2086-5

Vedral, V., Plenio, M. B., Rippin, M. A., & Knight, P. L. (1997). Quantifying entanglement. *Physical Review Letters*, *78*(12), 2275–2279. doi:10.1103/PhysRevLett.78.2275

Venayagamoorthy, G. K., & Mitra, P. (2011). SmartPark shock absorbers for wind farms. *IEEE Transactions on Energy Conversion*, *26*(3), 990–992. doi:10.1109/TEC.2011.2159549

Venkatalakshmi, K., & Shalinie, S. M. (2010, October). A customized particle swarm optimization algorithm for image enhancement. In *Proceedings of Communication Control and Computing Technologies (ICCCCT), 2010 IEEE International Conference on* (pp. 603-607). IEEE. doi:10.1109/ICCCCT.2010.5670768

Ventura, D., & Martinez, T. (1997). An artificial neuron with quantum mechanical properties. In *Proc. Intl. Conf. Artificial Neural Networks and Genetic Algorithms* (pp. 482–485). Academic Press.

Ventura, D. (1999). Quantum computational intelligence: Answers and questions. *IEEE Intelligent Systems*, 14–16.

Ventura, D., & Martinez, T. (1998). Quantum associative memory. *IEEE Transactions on Neural Networks.*

Veres, A., Ahn, G., Campbell, A. T., & Sun, L. (2002). SWAN: Service differentiation in stateless wireless adhoc networks. In *Proceedings of IEEE INFOCOM.* IEEE.

Victoire, T., & Jeyakumar, A. E. (2004). Hybrid PSO–SQP for economic dispatch with valve-point effect. *Electric Power Systems Research*, *71*(1), 51–59. doi:10.1016/j.epsr.2003.12.017

Vision. (n.d.). Retrieved from http://vision.ucsd.edu/datasetsAll

Vogt, H. (2009). *Protocols for secure communication in wireless sensor networks.* (Ph.D thesis). Swiss Federal Institute of Technology, Zurich, Switzerland.

W3C Specifications. (n.d.). Retrieved from http://www.w3.org/protocols/

Walczak, B., & Massart, D. L. (1999). Rough set theory. *Chemometrics and Intelligent Laboratory Systems*, *47*(1), 1–16. doi:10.1016/S0169-7439(98)00200-7

Wang, X., Wang, S., & Ma, J. J. (2007). An Improved co-evolutionary particle swarm optimization for wireless sensor networks with dynamic deployment. *Sensors*, *7*, 354-370. Retrieved from www.mdpi.org/sensors

Wang, Y., Guo, C., Wu, Q., & Dong, S. (2014). Adaptive sequential importance sampling technique for short-term composite power system adequacy evaluation. *IET Generation, Transmission and Distribution*, 730-741.

Wang, D., Haese-Coat, V., & Ronsin, J. (1995). Shape decomposition and representation using a recursive morphological operation. *Pattern Recognition*, *28*(11), 1783–1792. doi:10.1016/0031-3203(95)00036-Y

Wang, F. (1990). Fuzzy supervised classification of remote sensing images. *IEEE Transactions on Geoscience and Remote Sensing*, *28*(2), 194–201. doi:10.1109/36.46698

Wang, G. H., Chen, J., Cai, T., & Xin, B. (2013). Decomposition-based multi-objective differential evolution particle swarm optimization for the design of a tubular permanent magnet linear synchronous motor. *Engineering Optimization*, *45*(9), 1107–1127. doi:10.1080/0305215X.2012.720682

Wang, H. (2007). A hybrid particle swarm optimization with Cauchy mutation. In *Proceedings of IEEE Swarm Intelligence Symposium* (pp. 356 – 360). IEEE.

Wang, L., & Singh, C. (2008). Population-based intelligent search in reliability evaluation of generation systems with wind power penetration. *IEEE Transactions on Power Systems, 23*(3), 1336–1345. doi:10.1109/TPWRS.2008.922642

Wang, S. (2005). Classification with incomplete survey data: A Hopfield neural network approach. *Computers and Operations Research (Elsevier), 32*(10), 2583–2594. doi:10.1016/j.cor.2004.03.018

Wang, S.-K., Chiou, J.-P., & Liu, C. (2007). Non-smooth/non-convex economic dispatch by a novel hybrid differential evolution algorithm. *Generation, Transmission & Distribution, IET, 1*(5), 793–803. doi:10.1049/iet-gtd:20070183

Wang, W. J. (1997). New similarity measures on fuzzy sets and on elements. *Fuzzy Sets and Systems, 85*(3), 305–309. doi:10.1016/0165-0114(95)00365-7

Wang, X., Yang, J., Teng, X., Xia, W., & Richard, J. (2007). Feature selection based on rough sets & particle swarm optimization. *Pattern Recognition Letters, 28*(4), 459–471. doi:10.1016/j.patrec.2006.09.003

Wang, Z., Sun, X., & Zhang, D. (2007). A PSO – based classification rule mining algorithm. *Advanced Intelligent Computing Theories and Applications, LNCS, 4682*, 377–384.

Wanhui, L. (2012). *A new cockroach swarm optimization for motion planning of mobile robot.* Applied Mechanics and Materials.

Warrender, C., & Forrest, S. (1999). Detecting intrusions using system calls, alternative data models. In *Proceedings of the IEEE Computer Society Symposium on Research in Security and Privacy.* IEEE. doi:10.1109/SECPRI.1999.766910

Wei, T. E., Quinn, R. D., & Ritzmann, R. E. (2004). A CLAWAR that benefits from abstracted cockroach locomotion principles (M. Armada, Ed.). Academic Press.

Wei, Z., & Zihao, F. (2011). Network coverage optimization strategy in wireless sensor networks based on particle swarm optimization. (Bachelor's Thesis in Electronics). Faculty of Engineering and Sustainable Development, University of Gavle.

Weigang, L. (1998). *A study of parallel self-organizing map.* Retrieved from http://xxx.lanl.gov/quant-ph/9808025

Weinacht, T. C., & Bucksbaum, P. H. (2002). Using feedback for coherent control of quantum systems. *Journal of Optics B,* R35–R52.

Wen, O., Zarko, D., & Lipo, T. A. (2006). *Permanent magnet machine design practice and optimization.* Paper presented at the Industry Applications Conference.

White, T., & Pagurek, B. (1998). Towards multi-swarm problem solving in networks. In *Proc. Third Int. Conf. Multi-Agent Systems ICMAS* (pp. 333-340). ICMAS. doi:10.1109/ICMAS.1998.699217

Williams, J. B., Louis, M., Christine, R., & Nalepal, A. (2007). *Cockroaches ecology, behaviour and natural history* Johns Hopkins University Press.

Wollenberg, B., & Wood, A. (1996). Power generation, operation and control. John Wiley & Sons.

Wu, L. U., Songde, M. A., & Hanqing, L. U. (1998). An effective entropic thresholding for ultrasonic imaging. In *Proceedings of ICPR'98: Intl. Conf. Patt. Recog.* (pp. 1522–1524). Academic Press.

Wu, C.-G., Han, H., & Zhi-Feng, H. (2009). A pheromone-rate-based analysis on the convergence time of ACO algorithm. *IEEE Transactions on Systems, Man, and Cybernetics. Part B, Cybernetics, 39*(4), 910–923. doi:10.1109/TSMCB.2009.2012867 PMID:19380276

Wyatt, D. (2003). *Pheromones and animal behaviour.* Cambridge, UK: Cambridge Univ. Press. doi:10.1017/CBO9780511615061

Xiang, Z., & Yan, Z. (2007). Algorithm based on local variance to enhance contrast of fog-degraded image. *Journal of Computer Applications, 2,* 80.

Xianjun, S., Zhifeng, C., Jincai, Y. & CaiXia, C. (2010). *Particle swarm optimization with dynamic adaptive inertia weight.* Paper presented at the Challenges in Environmental Science and Computer Engineering (CESCE).

Xiao, W. P., & Ye, J. W. (2009). *Improved PSO-BPNN algorithm for SRG modeling.* Academic Press.

Xiao, Z., & Young, E. F. Y. (2010). Droplet-routing-aware module placement for cross-referencing biochips. In *Proceedings of International Symposium on Physical Design* (pp. 193 – 199). Academic Press. doi:10.1145/1735023.1735067

Xiao, L. L. (2010). A particle swarm optimization and immune theory based algorithm for structure learning of Bayesian networks. *International Journal of Database Theory and Applications, 3*(2), 61–69.

Xiao, Z., & Young, E. F. Y. (2010). Cross router: A droplet router for cross-referencing digital microfluidic biochips. In *Proceedings of 15th Asia and South Pacific Design Automation Conference (ASP-DAC)* (pp. 269 – 274). Academic Press. doi:10.1109/ASPDAC.2010.5419884

Xia, X., & Elaiw, A. (2010). Optimal dynamic economic dispatch of generation: A review. *Electric Power Systems Research, 80*(8), 975–986. doi:10.1016/j.epsr.2009.12.012

Xie, X. L., & Beni, G. (1991). A validity measure for fuzzy clustering. *IEEE Transactions on Pattern Analysis and Machine Intelligence, 13*(8), 841–847. doi:10.1109/34.85677

Xing, B., & Gao, W. (2014). Post-disassembly part-machine clustering using artificial neural networks and ant colony systems. In *Computational intelligence in remanufacturing* (pp. 135–150). Hershey, PA: Information Science Reference; doi:10.4018/978-1-4666-4908-8.ch008

Xing, B., & Gao, W. (2014a). Overview of computational intelligence. In *Computational intelligence in remanufacturing* (pp. 18–36). Hershey, PA: Information Science Reference; doi:10.4018/978-1-4666-4908-8.ch002

Xu, T., & Chakrabarty, K. (2006). Droplet-trace based array partitioning and a pin assignment algorithm for the automated design of digital microfluidic biochips. In *Proceedings of 4th IEEE Conference on CODES + ISSS 2006* (pp. 112 – 117). IEEE.

Xu, T., & Chakrabarty, K. (2008). Broadcast electrode-addressing for pin-constrained multi-functional digital microfluidic biochips. In *Proceedings of Design Automation Conference* (pp. 173 – 178). Academic Press. doi:10.1145/1391469.1391514

Xu, T., & Chakrabarty, K. (2008). Integrated droplet routing and defect tolerance in the synthesis of digital microfluidic biochips. *ACM Journal on Emerging Technologies in Computing Systems, 4*(3), 11.1 – 11.24

Xue, B., Zhang, M., & Browne, M. N. (2013). Particle swarm optimization for feature selection in classification: A multi-objective approach. *IEEE Transactions on Cybernetics, 43*(6).

Xue, X. D., Cheng, K. W. E., Bao, Y. J., & Leung, J. (2011). *Design consideration of c-core switched reluctance generators for wind energy.* Paper presented at the Power Electronics Systems and Applications (PESA).

Xue, X. D., Cheng, K. W. E., Bao, Y. J., Leung, P. L., & Cheung, N. (2012). Switched reluctance generators with hybrid magnetic paths for wind power generation. *IEEE Transactions on Magnetics, 48*(11), 3863–3866. doi:10.1109/TMAG.2012.2202094

Xu, T., & Chakrabarty, K. (2008). A droplet manipulation method for achieving high throughput in cross referencing based digital microfluidic biochips. *IEEE Transaction on Computer Aided Design of Integrated Circuits and Systems, 27*(11), 1905–1917. doi:10.1109/TCAD.2008.2006086

Xu, Y., Olman, V., & Xu, D. (1999). Clustering gene expression data using a graph theoretic approach, an application of minimum spanning trees. *Bioinformatics (Oxford, England), 17*, 309–318. PMID:12016051

Yadav, N. S., & Yadav, R.P. (n.d.). Performance comparison and analysis of table-driven and on-demand routing protocols for mobile ad-hoc networks. *Journal of Information Technology, 4*(2), 101–109.

Yager, R. Y. (1992). Entropy measures under similarity relations. *International Journal of General Systems, 20*(4), 341–358. doi:10.1080/03081079208945039

Yan, C., Guo, B., & Wu, X. (2012). Empirical study of the inertia weight particle swarm optimization with constrained factor. *International Journal of Soft Computing and Software Engineering, 2*(2).

Yang, F., & Chang, C. S. (2009). Optimization of maintenance schedules and extents for composite power systems using multi-objective evolutionary algorithm. *IET Generation, Transmission and Distribution,* 930-940.

Yang, W., Guo, L., Zhao, T., & Xiao, G. (2007). Improving watersheds image segmentation method with graph theory. In *Proceedings of 2nd IEEE Conference on Industrial electronics and Applications* (pp. 2550-2553). IEEE.

Yang, C. L., Yuh, P. H., & Chang, Y. W. (2007). Bioroute: A network-flow based routing algorithm for digital microfluidic biochips. In *Proceedings of IEEE/ACM Int. Conf. on Computer-Aided Design* (pp. 752 – 757). IEEE/ACM.

Yang, C. L., Yuh, P. H., Sapatnekar, S., & Chang, Y. W. (2008). A progressive ilp based routing algorithm for cross-referencing biochips. In *Proceedings of Design Automation Conference* (pp. 284 – 289). Academic Press.

Yang, L., Wang, L., Sun, Y., & Zhang, R. (2010). Simultaneous feature selection and classification via minimax probability machine. *International Journal of Computational Intelligence Systems, 3*(6), 754–760. doi:10.1080/18756891.2010.9727738

Yang, X. M., Yuan, J. S., Yuan, J. Y., & Mao, H. (2007). A modified particle swarm optimizer with dynamic adaptation. *Applied Mathematics and Computation, 189*(2), 1205–1213. doi:10.1016/j.amc.2006.12.045

Yao, D. & Ionel, D. M. (2011). *A review of recent developments in electrical machine design optimization methods with a permanent magnet synchronous motor benchmark study.* Paper presented at the Energy Conversion Congress and Exposition (ECCE).

Yeh, S., Chang, J., Huang, T., Yu, S., & Ho, T. (2014). Voltage-aware chip-level design for reliability-driven pin-constrained EWOD chips. *IEEE Transactions on Computer-Aided Design of Integrated Circuits and Systems, 33*(9), 1302–1315. doi:10.1109/TCAD.2014.2331340

Yen, J., Chang, F., & Chang, S. (1995). A new criterion for automatic multilevel thresholding. *IEEE Transactions on Image Processing, 4*(3), 370–378. doi:10.1109/83.366472 PMID:18289986

Yeung, J. H. C., & Young, E. F. Y. (2014). General purpose cross-referencing microfluidic biochip with reduced pin-count. In *Proceedings of 19th Asia and South Pacific Design Automation Conference (ASP-DAC)* (pp. 238 – 243). Singapore: Academic Press. doi:10.1109/ASPDAC.2014.6742896

Yeung, J. H. C., Young, E. F. Y., & Choy, C. S. (2014). Reducing pin count on cross-referencing digital microfluidic biochip. In *Proceedings of IEEE International Symposium on Circuits and Systems (ISCAS)* (pp. 790 – 793). Melbourne, Australia: IEEE. doi:10.1109/ISCAS.2014.6865254

Yilmaz, M., & Krein, P. T. (2012). Review of charging power levels and infrastructure for plug-in electric and hybrid vehicles. In *Proceedings of Electric Vehicle Conference (IEVC)*. Greenville, SC: IEEE. doi:10.1109/IEVC.2012.6183208

Yoshiyama, K., & Sakurai, A. (2014). Laplacian minimax probability machine. *Pattern Recognition Letters, 37*(1), 192–200. doi:10.1016/j.patrec.2013.01.004

Yosuf, M. S. (2010). *Nonlinear predictive control using particle swarm optimization: Application to power systems.* Heidelberg, Germany: VDM Verlag Dr. Müller.

Youd, T. L., & Noble, S. K. (1997a). Magnitude scaling factors. In *Proc., NCEER Workshop on Evaluation of Liquefaction Resistance of Soils.* Nat. Ctr. for Earthquake Engrg. Res., State Univ. of Buffalo.

Youd, T. L., Idriss, I. M., Andrus, R. D., Arango, I., Castro, G., Christian, J. T., Dobry, R., ….Stokoe, K. H. (2001). Liquefaction resistance of soils: summary report from the 1996 NCEER and 1998 NCEER/NSF workshops on evaluation of liquefaction resistance of soils. *Journal of Geotechnical and Geoeniromental Engineering, ASCE, 127*(10), 817-833.

Young Su, K., & Byung-Tak, K. (2006). Use of artificial neural networks in the prediction of liquefaction resistance of sands. *Journal of Geotechnical and Geoenvironmental Engineering, 132*(11), 1502–1504. doi:10.1061/(ASCE)1090-0241(2006)132:11(1502)

Young, K. Y. (2001). Validating clustering for gene expression data. *Bioinformatics (Oxford, England), 17*(4), 309–318. doi:10.1093/bioinformatics/17.4.309 PMID:11301299

Youssef, M., & El-Sheimy, N. (2007). Wireless sensor network: Research vs. reality design and deployment issues. In *Proc. Fifth Annual Conference on Communication Networks and Services Research* (CNSR'07). Academic Press. doi:10.1109/CNSR.2007.71

Yuan-Chih, C., & Chang-Ming, L. (2008). On the design of power circuit and control scheme for switched reluctance generator. *IEEE Transactions on Power Electronics, 23*(1), 445–454. doi:10.1109/TPEL.2007.911872

Yu, G., Li, H., Ha, S., Shih, I.-M., Clarke, R., Hoffman, E. P., & Wang, Y. et al. (2011). PUGSVM, a caBIGtm analytical tool for multiclass gene selection and predictive classification. *Bioinformatics (Oxford, England), 27*(5), 736–738. doi:10.1093/bioinformatics/btq721 PMID:21186245

Yuhui, S. (2004). Particle swarm optimization. IEEE Neural Networks Society, 8-14.

Yu, M., Yan, G., & Zhu, Q. W. (2006, August). New face recognition method based on dwt/dct combined feature selection. In *Proceedings of IEEE International Conference on Machine Learning and Cybernetics* (pp. 3233-3236). IEEE. doi:10.1109/ICMLC.2006.258432

Yumin, C., Miao, D., & Wang, R. (2010). A rough set approach to feature selection based on ant colony optimization. *Pattern Recognition Letters, 31*(3), 226–233. doi:10.1016/j.patrec.2009.10.013

Yurong, H., Lixin, D., Xie, D., & Wang, S. (2012). A novel discrete artificial bee colony algorithm for rough set based feature selection. *International Journal of Advancements in Computing Technology, 4*(6), 295–305. doi:10.4156/ijact.vol4.issue6.34

Zadeh, L. A. (1965). Fuzzy sets. *Information and Control, 8*(3), 338–353. doi:10.1016/S0019-9958(65)90241-X

Zhang, G. X., & Rong, H. (2007). Improved quantum-inspired genetic algorithm based time-frequency analysis of radar emitter signals. In *Rough sets and knowledge technology*. Springer.

Zhang, G., Hu, L., & Jin, W. (2004). Resemblance coefficient and a quantum genetic algorithm for feature selection. Lecture Notes in Computer Science, 3245, 155–168.

Zhang, H. & Liu, C. (2012). A review on node deployment of wireless sensor network. *International Journal of Computer Science Issues, 9*(6).

Zhang, H., Shi, W. & Liu, K. (2012). Fuzzy-topology integrated support vector machine for remotely sensed image classification. *IEEE Transactions on Geosciences and Remote Sensing, 50*(3).

Zhang, Y., & Gulliver, T. A. (2005). Quality of service for adhoc on-demand distance vector routing. In *Proceedings of Wireless and Mobile Computing, Networking and Communications (WiMob'2005)* (vol. 3, pp. 192 - 196). Academic Press.

Zhang, Y., Agarwal, P., Bhatnagar, V., Balochian, S., & Yan, J. (2013). Swarm intelligence and its applications. *The Scientific World Journal*. doi:10.1155/2013/528069

Zhang, G. (2011). Quantum inspired evolutionary algorithm: A survey and empirical study. *Journal of Heuristics, 17*(3), 303–351. doi:10.1007/s10732-010-9136-0

Zhang, G. X., Li, N., Jin, W. D., & Hu, L. Z. (2006). Novel quantum genetic algorithm and its application. *Frontiers of Electrical and Electronic Engineering in China, 1*(1), 31–36. doi:10.1007/s11460-005-0014-8

Zhang, G. X., Li, W. D. J. N., & Hu, L. Z. (2004). A novel quantum genetic algorithm and its application. *Tien Tzu Hsueh Pao, 32*(3), 476–479.

Zhang, H., Shi, W., & Liu, K. (2012). Fuzzy-topology integrated support vector machine for remotely sensed image classification. *IEEE Transactions on Geoscience and Remote Sensing, 50*(3), 850–862. doi:10.1109/TGRS.2011.2163518

Zhang, L. M., & Zhou, Z. H. (2007). ML-KNN: A lazy learning approach to multi - label learning. *Pattern Recognition, 40*(7), 2038–2048. doi:10.1016/j.patcog.2006.12.019

Zhang, L., Huang, X., Huang, B., & Li, P. (2006). A pixel shape index coupled with spectral information for classification of high spatial resolution remotely sensed imagery. *IEEE Transactions on Geoscience and Remote Sensing, 44*(10), 2950–2961. doi:10.1109/TGRS.2006.876704

Zhang, Q., Tezuka, T., Ishihara, K. N., & Mclellan, B. C. (2012). Integration of PV power into future low-carbon smart electricity systems with EV and HP in Kansai Area, Japan. *Renewable Energy, 44*, 99–108. doi:10.1016/j.renene.2012.01.003

Zhang, R., & Ma, J. (2009). _ Feature selection for hyperspectral data based on recursive support vector machines. *International Journal of Remote Sensing, 30*(14), 3669–3677. doi:10.1080/01431160802609718

Zhang, W. J. G., & Li, N. (2003). An improved quantum genetic algorithm and its application. *Lecture Notes in Artificial Intelligence, 2639*, 449–452.

Zhang, X., Lee, S. B., Gahng-Seop, A., & Campbell, A. T. (2000, April). INSIGNIA: An IP - based quality of service framework for mobile ad hoc networks. *Journal of Parallel and Distributed Computing, 60*(4), 374406.

Zhang, Y. (1996). A survey on evaluation methods for image segmentation. *Pattern Recognition, 8*(2), 1335–1346. doi:10.1016/0031-3203(95)00169-7

Zhao, D., & Singh, C. (2010). Modified genetic algorithm in state space pruning for power system reliability evaluation and its parameter determination. In *Proceedings of North American Power Symposium* (pp. 1-6). Arlington, VA: IEEE.

Zhao, H., Lingzhi, Y., Hanmei, P., & Kunyan, Z. (2009). *Research and control of SRG for variable-speed wind energy applications.* Paper presented at the Power Electronics and Motion Control Conference.

Zhao, Y., & Chakrabarty, K. (2010). Synchronization of washing operations with droplet routing for cross-contamination avoidance in digital microfluidic biochips. In *Proceedings of IEEE/ACM Design Automation Conference* (pp. 635 – 640). IEEE/ACM. doi:10.1145/1837274.1837437

Zhao, Y., & Chakrabarty, K. (2011). Co-optimization of droplet routing and pin assignment in disposable digital microfluidic biochips. In *Proceedings of ACM/IEEE International Symposium on Physical Design* (pp. 69 – 76). ACM/IEEE. doi:10.1145/1960397.1960413

Zhao, Y., Zhou, N., Zhou, J., & Zhao, X. (2006). Research on sensitivity analysis for composite generation and transmission system reliability evaluation. In *Proceedings of IEEE International Conference on Power System Technology* (pp. 1-5). Chongqing, China: IEEE. doi:10.1109/ICPST.2006.321566

ZhaoHui, C. (2011). A modified cockroach swarm optimization. Elsevier Ltd.

ZhaoHui, C., & Haiyan, T. (2010). Cockroach swarm optimization. In *Proceedings of Computer Engineering and Technology (ICCET)*. IEEE.

Zhaohui, C., & Haiyan, T. (2011). Cockroach swarm optimization for vehicle routing problems. *Energy Procedia, 13*, 30–35.

Zhao, W., Chellappa, R., Phillips, P. J., & Rosenfeld, A. (2003). Face recognition: A literature survey. *ACM Computing Surveys, 35*(4), 399–458. doi:10.1145/954339.954342

Zhao, Y., & Chakrabarty, K. (2012). Cross contamination avoidance for droplet routing in digital microfluidic biochips. *IEEE Transactions on Computer-Aided Design of Integrated Circuits and Systems, 31*(6), 817–830. doi:10.1109/TCAD.2012.2183369

Zhao, Y., Xu, T., & Chakrabarty, K. (2011). Broadcast electrode-addressing and scheduling methods for pin-constrained digital microfluidic biochips. *IEEE Transactions on Computer-Aided Design of Integrated Circuits and Systems, 30*(7), 986–999. doi:10.1109/TCAD.2011.2116250

Zheng, J., & Jamalipour, A. (2009). *Wireless sensor networks: A networking perspective.* Wiley.

Zhijie, L., Xiangdong, L., & Xiaodong, D. (2010). Comparative research on particle swarm optimization & genetic algorithm. *Computer and Information Science, 3*(1), 120–127.

Zhong, T. X. L. (2006). Compare and analysis of enhancement methods of sonar image. *Ship Electronic Engineering, 2*, 045.

Zhou, Z., Wang, Z., & Sun, X. (2013). Face recognition based on optimal kernel minimax probability machine. *Journal of Theoretical and Applied Information Technology, 48*(3), 1645–1651.

Zhu, L., Yu, F. R., Ning, B., & Tang, T. (2012). Optimal charging control for electric vehicles in smart micro grids with renewable energy sources. In *Proceedings of Vehicular Technology Conference (VTC)*. Yokohama: IEEE.

Zhu, G., & Blumberg, D. G. (2002). Classification using ASTER data and SVM algorithms: The case study of Beer Sheva, Israel. *Remote Sensing of Environment, 80*(2), 233–240. doi:10.1016/S0034-4257(01)00305-4

Zhu, T. X. (2006). A new methodology of analytical formula deduction and sensitivity analysis of EENS in bulk power system reliability assessment. In *Proceedings of IEEE PES Power Systems Conference and Exposition* (pp. 825–831). Atlanta, GA: IEEE.

Zielinski, K., & Laur, R. (2007). Stopping criteria for a constrained single-objective particle swarm optimization algorithm. *Informatica, 31*, 51–59.

Ziyan, R., Dianhai, Z., & Chang-Seop, K. (2013). *Multi-objective worst-case scenario robust optimal design of switched reluctance motor incorporated with FEM and Kriging.* Paper presented at the Electrical Machines and Systems (ICEMS).

About the Contributors

Siddhartha Bhattacharyya did his Bachelors in Physics, Bachelors in Optics and Optoelectronics and Masters in Optics and Optoelectronics from University of Calcutta, India in 1995, 1998 and 2000 respectively. He completed PhD in Computer Science and Engineering from Jadavpur University, India in 2008. He is the recepient of the University Gold Medal from the University of Calcutta for his Masters. He is currently an Associate Professor in Information Technology of RCC Institute of Information Technology, Kolkata, India. Prior to this, he was an Assistant Professor in Computer Science and Information Technology of University Institute of Technology, The University of Burdwan, India from 2005-2011. He was a Lecturer in Information Technology of Kalyani Government Engineering College, India during 2001-2005. He is a co-author of a book and about 116 research publications. He was the convener of the AICTE-IEEE National Conference on Computing and Communication Systems (CoCoSys-09) in 2009. He is the co-editor of the Handbook of Research on Computational Intelligence for Engineering, Science and Business; Publisher: IGI Global, Hershey, USA. He was the member of the Young Researchers' Committee of the WSC 2008 Online World Conference on Soft Computing in Industrial Applications. He has been the member of the organizing and technical program committees of several national and international conferences. He was the General Chair of IEEE International Conference on Computational Intelligence and Communication Networks (ICCICN 2014). He is the Associate Editor of International Journal of Pattern Recognition Research since 2010. He is the member of the editorial board of International Journal of Engineering, Science and Technology. His research interests include soft computing, pattern recognition and quantum computing. Dr. Bhattacharyya is a senior member of IEEE and ACM. He is a member of IRSS and IAENG. He is a life member of OSI, CSI and ISTE, India.

Paramartha Dutta (born in 1966) M. Stat, M. Tech (Computer Science) from Indian Statistical Institute Kolkata, Ph. D (Engineering) from presently Indian Institute of Engineering Science and Technology is currently a Professor in the Department of Computer and System Sciences, Visva Bharati University, Santiniketan, India for more eight years. He has about one hundred and sixty papers in Journal and Conference proceedings, six books and three edited books to his credit. He has the experience of successfully handling various projects funded by the Government of India. Moreover, he has supervised three scholars who have earned their Ph. D. Dr. Dutta is member/fellow of different professional bodies including IEEE and ACM.

***

M. Abdullah-Al-Wadud received his B.S. degree in computer science and M.S. in computer science and engineering from the University of Dhaka, Bangladesh in 2003 and 2004, respectively. In 2009, he completed his PhD in Computer Engineering from Kyung Hee University, South Korea. Afterwards, he served as a member of the faculty of the Department of Industrial and Management Engineering in Hankuk University of Foreign Studies, South Korea, from 2009 to 2014. He also served as a lecturer in Faculty of Sciences and Information Technology, Daffodil International University, Bangladesh, and in Faculty of Sciences and Engineering, East West University, Bangladesh, in 2003 and 2004, respectively. Currently, he is working as an associate professor in the Department of Software Engineering, King Saud University, Saudi Arabia. His research interest includes image enhancement, pattern recognition, optimization, sensor and ad hoc networks.

D P Acharjya received his PhD in computer science from Berhampur University, India. He has been awarded with Gold Medal in M. Sc. from NIT, Rourkela. Currently he is working as a Professor in the School of Computing Science and Engineering, VIT University, Vellore, India. He has authored many national and international journal papers, and five books to his credit. In addition to this, he has also edited two books. Also, he has published many chapters in different books published by International publishers. He is reviewer of many international journals such as Fuzzy Sets and Systems, Knowledge Based Systems, and Applied Journal of Soft Computing. Dr. Acharjya is actively associated with many professional bodies like CSI, ISTE, IMS, AMTI, ISIAM, OITS, IACSIT, CSTA, IEEE and IAENG. He was founder secretary of OITS Rourkela chapter. His current research interests include rough sets, formal concept analysis, knowledge representation, data mining, granular computing and business intelligence.

J. Anuradha received her Ph.D. degree in Computer Science and Engineering from VIT University. She has more than 10 years of academic experience and currently working as Associate Professor in School of Computing Science and Engineering, VIT University, Vellore, Tamil Nadu. She has published technical papers in international journals/ proceedings of international conferences/ edited book chapters of reputed publications. She has co-authored a book on soft computing. Her current research interest includes Fuzzy sets and systems, Rough sets and knowledge engineering, Data Mining, Big Data Analytics and Medical Diagnosis.

Soumya Sankar Basu received a Ph.D (Engineering) from Jadavpur University, is an IBM Certified IT Architect and Open group Master Certified Architect. He is a Senior IT Architect in IBM Global Business Services Global Delivery, India. He has over 18 years of experience in various areas of information technology, including solution architecture, architectural governance, application development, application design, and project management. Currently he specializes in Systems Engineering Governance and Application architecture. Dr Basu's research interest lies in Mobile Adhoc Networks, Software Engineering, and Social Network. He has published several papers in international journals and refereed conferences including IEEE, ACM etc. He is a frequent speaker in technology conferences and serves as international program committee member for several conferences. He is passionate about teaching and growing technical community within the organization. He drives and owns the Architectural Thinking Program in IBM India - a part of global ITA education and has enabled architects with basic architectural skills in India and other ASEAN countries He has lived in several ASEAN, European countries and Canada for his professional engagements.

Subhadip Basu received his B.E. degree in Computer Science and Engineering from Kuvempu University, Karnataka, India, in 1999. He received his Ph.D. (Engg.) degree thereafter from Jadavpur University (J.U.) in 2006. He joined J.U. as a senior lecturer in 2006. His areas of current research interest are OCR of handwritten text, gesture recognition, real-time image processing.

Mohammed A. Benidris received his B.Sc. degree in Electrical and Electronic Engineering in 1998 from the University of Benghazi, Libya. Thereafter he joined the Department of Electrical and Electronic Engineering of the same university as an Assistant Lecturer. He subsequently earned his M.Sc. degree in Electrical Engineering with specialization in Power Systems in 2005 from Benghazi University. He received his Ph.D. degree from Michigan State University in 2014. His areas of interest include power system reliability and power system planning (Email: benidris@msu.edu).

Maria do Rosario Alves Calado received the electrical engineering degree from the Instituto Superior Técnico (IST), Lisbon, Portugal, in 1991, the MSc equivalent degree and the PhD degree from University of Beira Interior, Covilhã, Portugal, in 1996 and 2002, respectively. She is currently an Assistant Professor at the University of Beira Interior and a member of the permanent staff of the R&D Unit IT - Instituto de Telecomunicações. Her research interests include electrical machines and actuators, numerical methods applied to electrical engineering and renewable energy. She has about 60 scientific publications.

Subhadip Chandra did his Bachelors and Masters in Information Technology from University of Kalyani and Jadavpur University in 2004 and 2009 respectively. He is currently an Assistant Professor of Information Technology of camellia Institute of Technology, Kolkata, India. Mr. Chandra is a member of ACM.

Atal Chaudhuri, born in 1957, passed Higher Secondary Examination in the year 1975 securing 16th rank in Science Stream in the State of West Bengal. Next he joined Jadavpur University and received the degree of Bachelor of Electronics and Telecommunication in the year 1980 with Distinction Marks. He received his Master of Electronics and Telecommunication Degree with Computer Science specialization in the year 1982 ranking 1st in the said specialization. Next he joined Webel Computers as R&D Engineer and worked for one year and finally came back to Jadavpur University for his research interest. He joined Jadavpur University as lecturer in the year 1985. Shortly he was promoted to the post of Assistantt Professor (then Reader) in the year 1989. He also received his PhD (Engineering) degree in the same year and was promoted to the post of Professor in the Department of Computer Science & Engineering of Jadavpur University in the year 1997. He has also served as Head of the Department of Computer Science & Engineering. He has over 100 publications at both National and International level. Eight scholars have been awarded PhD degree under his guidance and nine more are working with him at present. His current field of interest is Mobile ad-hoc network and Information security. He has served as an Expert for AICTE, NAAC, UGC and NBA team for accreditation of various institutions for last 12 years. He is also an Expert for Public Service Commission. He is a well-known person for delivering technical and popular lectures in his state as well as other states in India and abroad. He is the life member of both Computer Society of India (CSI) and also the Vice chairman of Computer Division of Institute of Engineers India (IEI).

Yildirim Dalkilic (PhD) is a civil engineer by profession and has been working as a research associate in the Civil Eng. Dept. of DEU Faculty of Engineering since 1998. Now he is an Assistant Professor in Erzincan University and he is currently studying for his research on modelling in hydrology, water resources planning and management.

Abhijit Das is a Master of Technology in Information Technology. He did the same from University of Calcutta in 2005 after the completion of Bachelor of Technology in the year 2003 from the Kalyani University. He is presently pursuing PhD on Development of an Autonomous Fault Tolerant Topology Management Scheme for Wireless Ad-hoc Network through Secure Messaging from the department of Computer Science & Engineering, Jadavpur University. Abhijit is on service since 2004 and is presently an Assistant Professor of the department of IT, RCCIIT Kolkata. He has remained the co-author of several international journals and conference proceedings. He was and/or is the programme committee member of several International Conferences as well. Besides serving RCCIIT, he has also remained the guest faculty at West Bengal University of Technology and Techno India Salt Lake. Apart from being a dedicated teacher of the institute, Mr. Das has always remained an integral part of the social and cultural family of the college. Abhijit is exclusively attached with several professional musical projects and is an active singer of the DoorDarshan and All India Radio, Kolkata, India. Mr. Das is the member of Association for Computing Machinery (ACM), USA.

Nibaran Das received his B.Tech degree in Computer Science and Technology from Kalyani Govt. Engineering College under Kalyani University, in 2003. He received his M.C.S.E degree from Jadavpur University, in 2005. He received his PhD (Engg.) degree thereafter from Jadavpur University, in 2012. He joined J.U. as a lecturer in 2006. His areas of current research interest are OCR of handwritten text, Bengali fonts, biometrics and image processing. He has been an editor of Bengali monthly magazine "Computer Jagat" since 2005.

Rajib Das is working as an Assistant Professor in School of Water Resources Engineering, Jadavpur University since 2009. Has experience in experimental works in open channel flow; such as scour downstream of block ramp, scour around bridge piers and presently also working on turbulent flow around bridge piers. He has completed his Master of Engineering from Jadavpur University, Kolkata, India in 2005. Subsequently carried out his research as a Ph.D. Scholar in University of Pisa, Pisa, Italy up to the year 2009, and got his Ph.D. degree in the year 2010 from University of Pisa. He was born on 7th of Jan, 1978.

Deepanwita Datta is currently pursuing a Ph.D. in the Department of Computer Science and Engineering, Indian Institute of Technology (BHU), Varanasi, India. Dr. Datta's broad area of research includes Computer Vision, Machine Learning, Pattern Recognition, Digital Video processing and Bio-informatics.

Arpita Debnath is working as a Lecturer in B.P.C. Institute of Technology, Krishnagar, Nadia, in the department of Computer Science & Technology under Department of Technical Education & Training, W.B. She obtained her B.Tech degree as well as M.Tech degree in CSE Department from Govt. College of Engineering & Ceramic Technology, Kolkata in 2009 and National Institute of Technical Teachers' Training & Research, Kolkata in 2013 respectively. Her academic career was started as an Assistant Teacher of Computer Science (Hons.) in West Bengal School Education Department. She has also served as a Part-Time Faculty of CSE Department in Govt. College of Engineering & Textile Technology, Serampore. Her research interests include Swarm Intelligence and Wireless Networks & E-Learning. She has one International Conference Publication in her credit.

Sandip Dey did his Bachelors in Mathematics in 1999. He completed B-level from DOEACC society and M.Tech in Software Engineering from West Bengal University of Technology in 2005 and 2008 respectively. Currently, he is pusuing Ph.D from Jadavpur University. He is currently an Assistant Professor in the department of Information Technology at Camellia Institute of Technology, Kolkata, India since 2009. Prior to this, he was a Lecturer in the department of Computer Application at Narula Institute of Technology, Kolkata, India. He has 10 publications in international journals and conference proceedings. His research interests include soft computing, quantum computing and image analysis. He is a member of ACM. He has been the member of the technical program committee of 2014 IEEE International Conference on Computational Intelligence and Communication Networks (ICCICN 2014) to be held at Kolkata.

Vo Ngoc Dieu received his B.Eng. and M.Eng. degrees in electrical engineering from Ho Chi Minh City University of Technology, Ho Chi Minh city, Vietnam, in 1995 and 2000, respectively and his D.Eng. degree in energy from Asian Institute of Technology (AIT), Pathumthani, Thailand in 2007. He is Research Associate at Energy Field of Study, AIT and lecturer at Department of Power Systems, Faculty of Electrical and Electronic Engineering, Ho Chi Minh City University of Technology, Ho Chi Minh city, Vietnam. His interests are applications of AI in power system optimization, power system operation and control, power system analysis, and power systems under deregulation.

Salem Elsaiah received his B.Sc. and M.Sc. degrees from University of Benghazi, Benghazi, Libya. He is currently pursuing a Ph.D. program in Electrical Engineering at Michigan State University. His doctoral research focuses on optimal design and assessment of distribution systems. His research interests include power system planning, Micro-grids, and reliability. (email: elsaiahs@msu.edu).

Chinmoy Ghorai did his B.Tech in Computer Science and Engineering from Govt. College of Engineering and Ceramic Technology and M.Tech in Information Technology from University of Calcutta (A.K.C. School of Information Technology). He started his academic career as a Lecturer in the Department of Information Technology, Govt. College of Engineering & Textile Technology, Serampore. He is also attached with University of Calcutta as well as RCCIIT as a Guest Faculty. His research interests include Mobile Ad-hoc Networks & Sensor Networks. He has two years of research experience in this domain and his works got published in international journals and conferences.

Hariharan Rajadurai received the B.E degree in cse from Anna University, Tamil nadu, India, in 2010, the M.Tech degree in information technology from Vellore Institute of Technology, Tamil nadu, India, in 2013. From July 2013 to July 2014 he was an assistant professor in Annai mira engineering college and technology in Vellore, Tamil nadu, India. Since 2014, he is currently working towards the Ph.D. degree in the field of soil and data mining at the Vellore Institute of Technology, Tamil nadu, India. His area of interest in the field of research includes artificial neural network, pile foundation, meta models.

Jagan J. is currently working as the Junior Research Fellow (JRF) for the Sponsored Research project by BRNS in the Centre for Disaster Mitigation and Management (CDMM), VIT University, Vellore. He is also pursuing the M.S. (By Research) in Geotechnical Engineering in the same department. He is specifically working on the effective stress parameter of unsaturated soil. He also published his research papers in journals in that field and also in other geotechnical related problems. He had completed his Bachelor of Engineering (B.E.) in Civil Engineering in Adhiyamaan College of Engineering, Hosur.

Mitra Joydeep is an Associate Professor of Electrical Engineering at Michigan State University, East Lansing. Prior to this, he was Associate Professor at New Mexico State University, Las Cruces, Assistant Professor at North Dakota State University, Fargo, and Senior Consulting Engineer at LCG Consulting, Los Altos, CA. He received a Ph.D. in Electrical Engineering from Texas A&M University, College Station, and a B.Tech. (Hons.), also in Electrical Engineering, from Indian Institute of Technology, Kharagpur. His research interests include power system reliability, distributed energy resources, and power system planning (Email: mitraj@msu.edu).

Truong Hoang Khoa received B.Eng. degree in electrical engineering from Ho Chi Minh City University of Technology, Vietnam, in 2012. He is currently a master student in Universiti Teknologi PETRONAS, Malaysia. His interest is applications of AI in power system optimization.

Goran Klepac, Ph.D., works as a head of Stretegic unit in Sector of credit risk in Raiffeisenbank Austria d.d., Croatia. In several universities in Croatia, he lectures subjects in domain of data mining, predictive analytics, decision support system, banking risk, risk evaluation models, expert system, database marketing and business intelligence. As a team leader, he successfully finished many data mining projects in different domains like retail, finance, insurance, hospitality, telecommunications, and productions. He is an author/coauthor of several books published in Croatian and English in domain of data mining.

Santosh Kumar is currently pursuing a Ph.D. in the Department of Computer Science and Engineering, Indian Institute of Technology (BHU), Varanasi, India. His broad area of research includes Biometrics, Machine Learning, Computer Vision, Pattern Recognition, Digital Image Processing, Digital Video processing, and Bio-informatics.

Mahantapas Kundu received his B.E.E, M.E.Tel.E and Ph.D. (Engg.) degrees from Jadavpur University, in 1983, 1985 and 1995, respectively. Prof. Kundu has been a faculty member of J.U since 1988. His areas of current research interest include pattern recognition, image processing, multimedia database, and artificial intelligence.

Jyotsna Kumar Mandal, M. Tech. (Computer Science, University of Calcutta), Ph.D. (Engg., Jadavpur University) in the field of Data Compression and Error Correction Techniques, Professor in Computer Science and Engineering, University of Kalyani, India. He is a Life Member of CSI, CRSI, ACM, IEEE, Fellow member of IETE. He is the former Dean of Faculty of Engineering, Technology & Management, working in the field of Network Security, Steganography, Remote Sensing & GIS Application, and Image Processing. He has 26 years of teaching and research experience. Nine Scholars awarded Ph.D., one submitted and eight are pursuing. Total number of publications is more than three hundred in addition to publication of five books from LAP Lambert, Germany.

Silvio Jose Mariano received the electrical engineering degree and the M.Sc. degree from the Technical University of Lisbon, Instituto Superior Técnico, Lisbon, Portugal, respectively, in 1990 and 1994 and the Ph.D. degree from the University of Beira Interior, Covilhã, Portugal, in 2002. He is currently an Associate Professor at the University of Beira Interior and a member of the permanent staff of the R&D Unit IT - Instituto de Telecomunicações. His research interests include hydrothermal scheduling, power industry restructuring, and optimal control. He is the author or coauthor of more than 80 scientific papers presented at international conferences or published in reviewed journals.

Ujjwal Maulik is a Professor in the Department of Computer Science and Engineering, Jadavpur University, Kolkata, India since 2004. He did his Bachelors in Physics and Computer Science in 1986 and 1989 respectively. Subsequently, he did his Masters and Ph.D. in Computer Science in 1992 and 1997 respectively. He chaired the Department of Computer Science and Technology Kalyani Govt. Engg. College, Kalyani, India during 1996-1999. Dr. Maulik has worked in several leading universities and laboratories across the world. Dr. Maulik is a co-author of 7 books and more than 250 research publications. He is the recipient of Govt. of India BOYSCAST fellowship in 2001, Alexander Von Humboldt Fellowship for Experienced Researchers in 2010, 2011 and 2012 and Senior Associate of ICTP, Italy in 2012. He coordinators five Erasmus Mundus Mobility with Asia (EMMA) programs (European-Asian mobility program). Dr. Maulik has been the Program Chair, Tutorial Chair and Member of the program committee of many international conferences and workshops. He is the Associate Editors of "IEEE Transaction on Fuzzy Systems" and "Information Sciences" and also in the editorial board of many journals including "Protein & Peptide Letters". Moreover, he has also served as guest co-editors of special issues of journals including "IEEE Transaction on Evolutionary Computation". He is the founder Member of IEEE Computational Intelligence Society (CIS) Chapter, Kolkata section and has worked as Secretary and Treasurer in 2011, as Vice Chair in 2012 and as the Chair in 2013 as well as 2014. He is a Fellow of Indian National Academy of Engineering, West Bengal Association of Science and Technology, Institution of Engineering and Telecommunication Engineers, Institution of Engineers and Senior Member of IEEE. His research interests include Computational Intelligence, Bioinformatics, Combinatorial Optimization, Pattern Recognition, and Data Mining.

Rui P. G. Mendes received the electromechanical degree and the M.Sc. degree from University of Beira Interior, Covilhã, Portugal, in 2009 and 2011, respectively. He is currently a PhD Student at University of Beira Interior and a collaborator of the R&D Unit IT - Instituto de Telecomunicações. His research areas include electrical machines and renewable energy conversion systems.

Mita Nasipuri received her B.E.Tel.E., M.E.Tel.E., and Ph.D. (Engg.) degrees from Jadavpur University, in 1979, 1981 and 1990, respectively. Prof. Nasipuri has been a faculty member of J.U since 1987. Her current research interest includes image processing, pattern recognition, and multimedia systems. She is a senior member of the IEEE, U.S.A., Fellow of I.E (India) and W.B.A.S.T, Kolkata, India.

Amartya Neogi is serving Dr. B.C. Roy Engineering College, (affiliated to West Bengal University of Technology), Durgapur, West Bengal, India as a full time Assistant Professor in Computer Science discipline. He has 13 years teaching experience and 8 years research experience. He obtained his Ph.D degree from department of Computer Science, The University of Burdwan, India in 2013. He has published 24 research papers in Journals/Conference proceedings. His area of specialization is soft computing and Bio inspired intelligent algorithms. He is a life member of Indian Statistical Institute, Library & Documentation Science Division, Kolkata. Additionally, he has reviewed few papers of national/ international journals.

Kauser Ahmed P received his M.Tech. degree in information technology with specialization in networking from VIT University, India; M. Sc. Degree in computer science from VIT University, India and is currently pursuing his Ph. D. in computer science and engineering from VIT University, Vellore, India. Presently he is working as Assistant Professor in school of computing science and engineering, VIT University, India. He has several peer-reviewed national and international conferences and journals publications. He is associated with many professional bodies like CSI, ISTE, IACSIT, CSTA, IEEE, IRSS and IAENG. He is a reviewer of many international conferences sponsored by IACSIT and IAENG. His current research interests include soft computing, big data analytics, bio-inspired computing and bio informatics.

Indrajit Pan has obtained B.E. in Computer Science and Engineering with Honors from The University of Burdwan in 2005 and M. Tech. in Information Technology from Bengal Engineering and Science University, Shibpur. He was awarded with University Medal for his performance during M. Tech.. Indrajit received is Ph. D. in Engineering from Department of IT of Indian Institute of Engineering Science and Technology, Shibpur in 2015. He is presently working as a faculty in Department of Information Technology at RCCIIT, Kolkata. His major research interest involves Algorithm design and analysis, Intelligent Systems, and Computational methods for CAD.

Imran Rahman received his Bachelor of Science in Engineering from Department of Electrical and Electronic Engineering, Islamic University of Technology (IUT), Gazipur, Bangladesh in the year of 2011. He is currently pursuing his Master of Science (by research) in the Department of Fundamental and Applied Sciences, Universiti Teknologi PETRONAS, Tronoh, Perak, Malaysia. His current research interests are smart grid optimization, optimization of plug-in hybrid electric vehicles (PHEVs), and computational intelligence techniques.

Tuhina Samanta is presently an assistant professor in Indian Institute of Engineering Science and Technology, Shibpur. She completed her B.Tech and M.Tech from the Institute of Radiophysics and Electronics, Calcutta University in 2003 and 2005 respectively. She received her Ph.D (Engineering) from Bengal Engineering and Science University, Shibpur, in January, 2010. She was awarded Canodia Research Scholarship during her M.Tech. She co-authored some IEEE/ACM/Springer international conferences that received best paper awards. Her present research area is design of algorithms, and complexity analysis for VLSI physical design, and physical design for digital microfluidic biochip, and Wireless sensor network. She has pursued Post Doctoral research from UCF, Florida in 2014 - 2015 under the aegis of Prof. C. V. Raman Fellowship from Government of India. She has also managed couple of research projects from AICTE and UGC as Principal Investigator and Co Principal Investigator.

Pijush Samui is a professor at Centre for Disaster Mitigation and Management in VIT University, Vellore, India. He obtained his B.E. at Bengal Engineering and Science University; M.Sc. at Indian Institute of Science; Ph.D. at Indian Institute of Science. He worked as a postdoctoral fellow at University of Pittsburgh (USA) and Tampere University of Technology (Finland). His research interests cover a wide range of subjects in geotechnical engineering, including application of soft computing in geotechnical engineering, numerical modeling, landslide, risk and reliability analysis, geostatistics, slope stability, pile foundation, site characterization, rock mechanics, development of different experimental devices and modeling of different seismic hazards. Dr. Samui is the member of several national and international professional societies like Indian Geotechnical Society, Institution of Engineers, Indian Science Congress, World federation of Soft Computing, and Geotechnical Engineering for Disaster Mitigation and Rehabilitation (JWG-DMR).

V. Santhi is working as Associate professor in VIT University, Vellore, India. She has more than 20 years of experience in both academic and Industry. She has pursued her B.E. in Computer Science and Engineering from Bharathidasan University. She obtained her M.Tech. in Computer Science and Engineering from Pondicherry University, Puducherry. She has received her Ph.D. Degrees in Computer Science and Engineering from VIT University, Vellore, India. She has carried out her research in Image Processing. She is senior member of IEEE and she is holding membership in many professional bodies. Her areas of research include Image Processing, Digital Signal Processing, Digital Watermarking, Data Compression and Computational Intelligence. She has published many papers in reputed journals and International conferences. She is a reviewer for many refereed Journals.

Anasua Sarkar is currently pursuing her PhD work on Bioinformatics in Jadavpur University, Kolkata, India. She was also awarded EMMA-EPU fellowship, 2011 to pursue her research work at LaBRI, University Bordeaux1, France. She is presently an Assistant Professor in IT Department, Government College of Engineering and Leather Technology, Kolkata since 2007. She has published 12 original research papers in peer-reviewed journals. She is also a co-author in 10 book chapters and 15 conference papers and is a reviewer in journals of Parallel and Distributed Computing (JPDC), Elsevier and IEEE SMCC-C. She is also a Student member, ISCB, 2010-2011, SMIEEE since 2014, member CSTA, ACM Chapter, ACM IGUCCS and IAENG. She has worked with INRIA MAGNOME group for 18 months in France for the expansion of Genolevures database for inclusion of PISO and ARAD species. Her research interests include Proteomics, Phylogenetics, Computational Biology, Pattern Recognition, Data Mining, Bioinformatics, Embedded, and Parallel Systems.

Arindam Sarkar works in the Department of Science & Technology (DST). He is a Govt. of INDIA INSPIRE Fellow (Senior Research Fellow (SRF-Professional) in Computer Science & Engineering stream in the Department of Computer Science & Engineering, University of Kalyani, MCA (VISVA BHARATI, Santiniketan, University First Class First Rank Holder), M.Tech (CSE, K.U, University First Class First Rank Holder), and he is working in the field of cryptography and soft computing. Mr. Sarkar's total number of publications is 38.

V.Shanti is an associate professor in the school of computing science and engineering, VIT University, Vellore. She has published several papers in international journals and conferences. Her current research interest includes Data Mining, soft computing and Image processing.

Balbir Singh Mahinder Singh is from Malaysia, born in September 1967. He graduated with B.Sc. (Ed) Hons (Physics) in 1991, obtained his MSc (Physics) in 1996 and PhD in 2004 from Universiti Sains Malaysia. He joined Universiti Teknologi PETRONAS as a lecturer in 1999. Currently he is an Associate Professor and Head of the Fundamental and Applied Sciences Department. His research interest is in the area of solar energy utilization for electricity generation, solar hydrogen production and hybrid renewable energy based electricity generating systems.

Sanjay Kumar Singh received the M. Tech. and Ph.D. degrees in computer science. Dr. Singh's broad area of research includes Biometrics, Machine Learning, Computer Vision, and Pattern Recognition. He is currently an Associate Professor at the Indian Institute of Technology (BHU), Varanasi, India. He has more than 60 publications in refereed journals, book chapters, and conferences.

B.K. Tripathy is a senior professor in the school of computing sciences and engineering, VIT University, Vellore since 2007. He has produced 20 PhDs, 13 M.Phils and 01 M.S student so far. He has published more than 250 papers in different international journals, conference proceedings and edited research volumes. He has edited two research volumes for IGI publications. He is in the editorial board or review panel of over 50 journals including Springer, Science Direct, IEEE and World Scientific publications. He is a life member/ senior member/member of 21 international forums including ACM, IEEE, ACEEE and CSI. His current interest includes Fuzzy sets and systems, Rough sets and knowledge engineering, Multiset theory, List theory, Data clustering and database anonymisation, content based learning, remote laboratories, Soft set analysis, Image processing, cloud computing and Social Network Analysis.

Pandian Vasant is an Executive Editor of Global Journal of Technology and Optimization and Co-Editor-in-Chief of International Journal of Energy Optimization and Engineering. His main research interests are in the areas of Optimization Methods and Applications to Decision Making and Industrial Engineering, Fuzzy Optimization, Computational Intelligence, and Hybrid Soft Computing. Pandian Vasant has co-authored 200 research papers and articles in national journals, international journals, conference proceedings, conference paper presentation, and special issues lead guest editor, lead guest editor for book chapters' project, conference abstracts, edited books and book chapters. In the year 2009, Pandian Vasant was awarded top reviewer for the journal Applied Soft Computing (Elsevier). He has been Co-editor for AIP Conference Proceedings of PCO (Power Control and Optimization) conferences from 2008 until 2013 and editorial board member of international journals in the area of Soft Computing, Hybrid Optimization and Computer Applications. Currently he's an Editor-in-Chief of International Journal of Computing and Optimization. Google Scholar Citations: h-index is 17; i10-index is 30 (Citation Indices).

Index

E

Ear Recognition 189
Earthquake 110, 190-193, 206-218, 527
Economic Dispatch 219-222, 245-254, 387, 412
Electrode Activation Constraints 261
Electrowetting 263, 264, 291-293
Encryption 567, 663-671, 674-677, 680-684, 690, 696, 700-704
Energy Consumption 187, 387, 415, 540, 554, 558, 560, 567, 568, 585, 591
Energy Security 406, 416
Entropy 4, 7, 8, 31, 34-36, 39, 340, 343-349, 355, 357, 450, 469-472, 479, 643, 680, 690-694, 697, 698, 701
Evolutionary Algorithms 23, 33, 55, 101, 297, 331, 334, 337, 405, 412, 421, 634, 661, 665

F

Filtering 36, 39, 41, 142, 161, 164, 337-339, 350, 355, 357, 417, 654
Finite Element Method 484, 495, 511
Firefly 101, 156, 253
Fuzzy Method 448
Fuzzy Set 40, 62, 75, 77, 97, 110, 299, 448-450, 453, 455, 467, 472, 482

G

gbest 15, 40-44, 47-53, 60-64, 155, 177, 230, 304, 311, 315, 396, 418, 433, 491, 492, 512, 667
Gene Expression 73, 76, 77, 86, 94-100, 472-482
Genetic Algorithm 3, 14, 21-23, 31-43, 75, 94, 97, 100, 109, 155, 220, 221, 245-247, 251, 252, 330, 333, 344, 345, 348, 351, 443, 457, 476, 484, 519, 520, 596, 630-635, 638, 648, 660, 661, 666, 703
Genetic Algorithms (GA) 14, 15, 22-25, 41, 43, 51, 52, 55, 56, 155, 220, 236, 244, 246, 337, 346, 351, 352, 407, 457, 484, 596, 624, 628-635, 638, 639, 643, 648, 656, 658, 661, 662, 665, 666
Geometry Optimization 522
Global and Local Features 633, 636, 662
Global Optimization 36, 87, 101, 118, 144, 146, 155, 173, 221, 413, 416, 484, 533, 551, 660
Gravitational Search Algorithm 250, 251, 385-388, 396, 399-403, 407-418

H

Handwritten Bangla character recognition 632
Handwritten Character Recognition 633-635, 659-662
Histogram Equalization 164, 337, 338, 344-348, 356, 357, 461
Hunger Behavior 115-118, 149
Hybrid Cockroach System 102, 149

I

Identification Process 162, 186, 189
Image 1-11, 21-23, 28-39, 59, 61, 86, 87, 142, 154, 158, 161-166, 169, 170, 174, 182, 184, 189, 214, 217, 296-305, 308-357, 443, 445, 448-450, 453-458, 461-482, 533, 535, 569, 633-639, 643, 655-659, 662
Image Enhancement 336-348, 355-357
Image Restoration 161, 336, 350, 357
Image Segmentation 1, 2, 11, 33, 34, 39, 86, 161, 296-299, 308-312, 321-337, 341, 351, 448, 453, 454, 478
Image Thresholding 2, 22, 23, 31-39, 217, 469
Indiscernibility Relation 76-80
Information Systems 74, 101, 292, 441, 659
Initial Population 116, 119, 121, 136, 156, 348, 394, 491, 500, 511-514, 637-640, 667, 703
Intensity Transformation 337, 339, 346, 357

K

Key 39, 75, 101, 110, 112, 148, 161, 164, 189, 218, 222, 225, 254, 264, 266, 293, 335, 357-360, 367, 369, 384-387, 406, 415, 422, 423, 439, 440, 447, 448, 482, 521-525, 531, 550, 552, 555, 564, 567, 575, 591, 593, 627, 631, 661-668, 671, 674-679, 696-704
Key Generation 663, 664, 671, 677, 703
Keystream 663, 668-680, 696-701, 704
K-Means Algorithm 454, 461, 463, 479, 482, 493, 495

L

lbest 40-42, 177, 667
Linear Electric Machine 483, 522
Linear Switched Reluctance Generator 483, 485, 498, 509, 511, 517, 520
Liquefaction 190-195, 203, 206-218
Local Region Selection 634, 662

Printed in the United States
By Bookmasters